Touring France

Also available:

© The Caravan Club Limited 2020
Published by The Caravan and Motorhome
Club Limited
East Grinstead House, East Grinstead
West Sussex RH19 1UA

General Enquiries: 01342 326944
Travel Service Reservations: 01342 316101
Red Pennant Overseas Holiday Insurance:
01342 336633
Website: camc.com

Editor: Kate Walters
Publishing service provided by Fyooz Ltd
Printed by Stephens & George Ltd
Merthyr Tydfil
ISBN: 978-1-9993236-2-2

Maps and distance charts generated from Collins
Bartholomew Digital Database
Maps ©Collins Bartholomew Ltd 2020, reproduced
by permission of HarperCollins Publishers.

Cover
from

£60*

Red Pennant Overseas Holiday, Breakdown and Emergency Insurance

- Roadside assistance & Recovery including repatriation.

- Travel Insurance including cancellation and medical emergencies.

- Cover is available for multiple trips in a year, or for single trips up to 365 days**

- Friendly emergency services team
  Based at our Head Office, our multi-lingual team are ready to help when you need us.

For full details of cover offered, including limitations and exclusions that apply, a sample of the policy wording is available upon request.

Call 01342 336 633 or visit camc.com/redpennant

Terms and conditions:
Price is based on two travellers under the age of 50 on a 5 day single trip policy with motoring and personal cover. Additional premiums may apply on larger and/or vehicles over 15 years old.
*** Age limits apply*

Welcome...

...to another year of touring across Europe!

Wherever and however you travel, people who camp (whether in a caravan, motorhome, campervan or tent) share a sense of adventure and freedom that you don't get from other types of holidays.

However as we enter 2020 we are still in a period of uncertainty regarding the UK's position in the European Union and what will happen when we leave. While it is unlikely that Brexit will stop us from touring the EU, you might need to plan further ahead and do more research before you travel.

At the time of this book going to press much of what will change once the UK leaves the EU is unknown, and therefore it is very difficult to advise on issues such as border controls, customs, visa requirements and pet passports. Therefore you're strongly advised to check this information before you travel, especially if the UK has already left or will leave the EU while you're travelling. Check camc.com/overseas for our most up-to-date advice.

So as you start another year of touring adventures, I would like to thank you for continuing to buy and contribute to these guides. If you can, please spare five minutes to fill in one of the site report forms at the back of this book or visit camc.com/europereport to let us know what you think about the sites you've stayed on this year. Happy touring!

Kate Walters

Kate Walters, Editor

Contents

How to use this guide

The Handbook

This includes general information about touring in France, such as legal requirements, advice and regulations.

Country Introductions

Following on from the Handbook chapters you will find the Country Introductions containing information, regulations and advice specific to each country. You should read the Country Introduction in conjunction with the Handbook chapters before you set off on your holiday.

Campsite Entries

After the country introduction you will find the campsite entries listed alphabetically under their nearest town or village. Where there are several campsites shown in and around the same town they will be listed in clockwise order from the north.

To find a campsite all you need to do is look for the town or village of where you would like to stay, or use the maps at the back of the book to find a town where sites are listed.

For an explanation of the site entries and a guide to symbols please see the following pages. You'll also find a guide to site entries on the fold out on the rear cover.

Campsite Fees

Campsite entries show high season fees per night for an outfit plus two adults. Prices given may not include electricity or showers, unless indicated. Outside of the main holiday season many sites offer discounts on the prices shown and some sites may also offer a reduction for longer stays.

Campsite fees may vary to the prices stated in the site entries, especially if the site has not been reported on for a few years. You are advised to always check fees when booking, or at least before pitching, as those shown in site entries should be used as a guide only.

Site Maps

Each town and village listed alphabetically in the site entry pages has a map grid reference number, e.g. 3B4. The map grid reference number is shown on each site entry.

The maps can be found at the end of each country section. The reference number will show you where each town or village is located, and the site entry will tell you how far the site is from that town. Place names are shown on the maps in two colours:

Red where we list a site which is open all year (or for at least eleven months of the year)

Black where we only list seasonal sites which close in winter.

These maps are intended for general campsite location purposes only; a detailed road map or atlas is essential for route planning and touring.

The scale of the map means that it isn't possible to show every town or village where a campsite is listed, so some sites in small villages may be listed under a nearby larger town instead.

Satellite Navigation

Most campsite entries now show a GPS (sat nav) reference. There are several different formats of writing co-ordinates, and in this guide we use decimal degrees, for example 48.85661 (latitude north) and 2.35222 (longitude east).

Minus readings, shown as -1.23456, indicate that the longitude is west of the Greenwich meridian. Most of Spain, the western extreme of France and all of Portugal will have minus figures, while the majority of Europe are east of the Greenwich meridian.

Manufacturers of sat navs all use different formats of co-ordinates so you may need to convert the co-ordinates before using them with your device. There are plenty of online conversion tools which enable you to do this quickly and easily - just type 'co-ordinate converter' into your search engine.

Please be aware if you are using a sat nav device some routes may take you on roads that are narrow and/or are not suitable for caravans or large outfits.

The GPS co-ordinates given in this guide are provided by members and checked wherever possible, however we cannot guarantee their accuracy due to the rural nature of most sites. The Caravan and Motorhome Club cannot accept responsibility for any inaccuracies, errors or omissions or for their effects.

Site Report Forms

With the exception of campsites in The Club's Overseas Site Booking Service (SBS) network, The Caravan and Motorhome Club does not inspect sites listed in this guide. Virtually all of the sites listed in Touring France are from site reports submitted by users of these guides.

Sites which are not reported on for five years are deleted from the guide, so even if you visit a site and find nothing has changed we'd still appreciate an update to make sure that the site isn't archived.

You will find site report forms towards the back of the book, or you can submit them at camc.com/europereport - use the abbreviated site report form if you are reporting no changes, or only minor changes, to a site entry. The full report form should be used for new sites or if sites have changed a lot.

Please submit reports as soon as possible. Information received by mid August will be used in the next edition of Touring Spain & Portugal. Reports received after that date are still very welcome and will appear in the following edition. The editor is unable to respond individually to site reports submitted due to the large quantity that we receive.

Tips for Completing Site Reports

- If possible fill in a site report form while at the campsite. Once back at home it can be difficult to remember details of individual sites, especially if you visited several during your trip.

- When giving directions to a site, remember to include the direction of travel, e.g. 'from north on D137, turn left onto D794 signposted Combourg' or 'on N83 from Poligny turn right at petrol station in village'. Wherever possible give road numbers, junction numbers and/or kilometre post numbers, where you exit from motorways or main roads. It is also helpful to mention useful landmarks such as bridges, roundabouts, traffic lights or prominent buildings.

We very much appreciate the time and trouble you take submitting reports on campsites that you have visited; without your valuable contributions it would be impossible to update this guide.

Acknowledgements

Thanks go to the AIT/FIA Information Centre (OTA), the Alliance Internationale de Tourisme (AIT), the Fédération International de Camping et de Caravanning (FICC) and to the national clubs and tourist offices of those countries who have assisted with this publication.

Every effort is made to ensure that information provided in this publication is accurate. The Caravan and Motorhome Club Ltd has not checked these details by inspection or other investigation and cannot accept responsibility for the accuracy of these reports as provided by members and non-members, or for errors, omissions or their effects. In addition The Caravan and Motorhome Club Ltd cannot be held accountable for the quality, safety or operation of the sites concerned, or for the fact that conditions, facilities, management or prices may have changed since the last recorded visit. Any recommendations, additional comments or opinions have been contributed by people staying on the site and are not those of The Caravan and Motorhome Club.

The inclusion of advertisements or other inserted material does not imply any form of approval or recognition, nor can The Caravan and Motorhome Club Ltd undertake any responsibility for checking the accuracy of advertising material.

Explanation of a Campsite Entry

Site map grid reference

Distance and direction of the site from the centre of the listing town in kilometres (or metres), together with the aspect of the site (urban, rural or coastal).

GPS co-ordinates – latitude and longitude in decimal degrees. Minus figures indicate that the site is west of the Greenwich meridian

The town under which the campsite is listed, as shown on the relevant Sites Location Map at the end of each country's site entry pages

Campsite name

Campsite address.

Site information shown by symbols, a guide to which can be found on the next page or inside the rear cover. Where further information is available (e.g. a price for dogs or if a toilet block is heated) is shown after the symbol.

Site contact details, including telephone number, email address and website address where available.

Directions to the site are shown in bold text.

Additional site information, including pitch information and electric information. For details of the abbreviations used please see the following pages.

Comments and opinions of tourers who have visited the site shown in italic text

AIRVAULT *4H1* (1km N Rural) *46.83200, -0.14690*
Camping de Courte Vallée, 8 Rue de Courte Vallée,
79600 Airvault **05 49 64 70 65; info@caravanning
france.com; www.caravanningfrance.com**

🐕 €1.50 ♀♂ ⊞ ♨ ⑤ ⟋ ≋ 🦋 ♔ ⟁ ⑪ ⇲ 🏕 ≋ (htd)

Fr N, S or W leave D938 sp Parthenay to Thouars rd at La Maucarrière twd Airvault & foll lge sp to site. Site on D121 twd Availles-Thouarsais. NB If app fr NE or E c'vans not permitted thro Airvault - watch carefully for sp R at Gendarmerie. Well sp fr all dirs. 3*, Sm, mkd, hdstg, hdg, pt shd, pt sl, EHU (13A) inc (poss long lead req); gas; bbq; red long stay; twin axles; TV; 8% statics; adv bkg acc; ccard acc; games rm; bike hire; fishing; CKE. *"Peaceful, popular; pleasant, helpful British owners; excel, clean & vg facs, poss stretched high ssn; conv Futuroscope & Puy du Fou theme park; mkt Sat; not as well kept & expensive compared to similar sites; c'van storage; town dissapointing, empty shops; new rest & bar(2018)."* **€33.00, 1 Mar-15 Nov, L14.**

2018

Guide price for 2 adults, an outfit and a pitch in high season.

The year in which the site was last reported on by a visitor. Sites are archived if we don't receive a report for 5 years so please consider sending in a report if you visit a site with an older date shown.

Opening dates for the site, may give specific dates or the general months of opening. If no dates are present the site will be open all year, as shown by the ⊞ in the symbols section.

Booking reference for a site the Club's Overseas Travel Service work with, i.e. bookable via the Club.

Guide to symbols

Symbol	Explanation
12	The site is open all year. Some sites may decide to close if they are not busy so call ahead out of season.
	Dogs are allowed on site, usually at an extra cost (shown if known). Please see the description or member comments for any restrictions.
	Toilets available. If followed by (cont) they will be continental style toilets.
WD	Chemical toilet disposal.
	Showers available.
	Family bathroom or baby and toddler room on site. Facilities may vary.
	Toilet and/or shower facilities available for disabled guests on site. Facilities may vary.
	Laundry facilities available. Facilities and costs may vary.
	Electric hook ups are available. See the description for details of the amperage, costs and any further information.
MSP	Motorhome service point. Low level waste discharge point for motor caravans; fresh water tap and rinse facilities should also be available
	Quiet site - set in a peaceful location although at busy times you may still experience noise from other site users.

Symbol	Explanation
	Wi-Fi available, usually at an extra cost.
	Bar on site or nearby if followed by nr.
	Restaurant on site or nearby if followed by nr.
	Snack bar, cafe or takeaway on site.
	Shop on site or nearby if followed by nr.
	Playground or play area on site. Age restrictions may apply.
	Entertainment on site - this may either be evening entertainment or organised daytime activities or excursions.
	Pool on site. Where known the listing will specify if heated (htd), covered (covrd).
	Paddling pool for younger children on site
	Beach nearby, followed by the distance and information about the type of beach where known.

Site Description Abbreviations

Each site entry assumes the following unless stated otherwise:

Level ground, open grass pitches, drinking water on site, clean wc unless otherwise stated (own sanitation required if wc not listed), site is suitable for any length of stay within the dates shown.

aspect
> urban – within a city or town, or on its outskirts
> rural – within or on edge of a village or in open countryside
> coastal – within one kilometre of the coast

size of site
> sm – max 50 pitches
> med – 51 to 150 pitches
> lge – 151 to 500 pitches
> v lge – 501+ pitches

pitches
> hdg pitch – hedged pitches
> mkd pitch – marked or numbered pitches
> hdstg – some hard standing or gravel

levels
> sl – sloping site
> pt sl – sloping in parts
> terr – terraced site

shade
> shd – plenty of shade
> pt shd – part shaded
> unshd – no shade

Site Facilities

adv bkg -
> acc – advance booking accepted
> rec – advance booking recommended
> req - advance booking required

beach - symbol followed by:
> 1km – distance to beach
> sand beach – sandy beach
> shgl beach – shingle beach

bus/metro/tram
> Public transport within 5km

chem disp
> Dedicated chemical toilet disposal facilities;
> chem disp (wc) – no dedicated point; disposal via wc only

CKE
> Camping Key Europe accepted

CL-type
> Very small, privately-owned, informal and usually basic, farm or country site similar to those in the Caravan and Motorhome Club's network of Certificated Locations

el pnts - symbol followed by
> Mains electric hook-ups available for a fee;
> inc – cost included in site fee quoted
> 10A – amperage provided
> conn fee – one-off charge for connection to metered electricity supply
> rev pol – reversed polarity may be present (see Electricity and Gas section

Eng spkn
> English spoken by campsite reception staff

gas
> Supplies of bottled gas available on site or nearby

Mairie
> Town hall (France); will usually make municipal campsite reservations

NH
> Suitable as a night halt

open 1 Apr-15 Oct
> Where no specific dates are given, opening dates are assumed to be inclusive, ie Apr-Oct – beginning April to end October (NB: opening dates may vary from those shown; check before travelling, particularly when travelling out of the main holiday season)

phone
> Public payphone on or adjacent to site

pool - symbol followed by:
> Indoor – indoor pool
> htd – heated pool
> covrd – indoor pool or one with retractable cover

red CCI/CCS
> Reduction in fees on production of a Camping Card International or Camping Card Scandinavia

BBQ
barbecues allowed (may be restricted to a separate, designated area)

serviced pitch
Electric hook-ups and mains water inlet and grey water waste outlet to pitch;
all – to all pitches
50% – percentage of pitches

shwrs - symbol followed by:
inc – cost included in site fee quoted

ssn
Season;
high ssn – peak holiday season
low ssn – out of peak season

50% statics
Percentage of static caravans/mobile homes/ chalets/fixed tents/cabins or long term seasonal pitches on site, including those run by tour operators

sw
Swimming nearby;
1km – nearest swimming
lake – in lake
rv – in river

TV
TV rm – separate TV room (often also a games room)
TV (pitch) – cable or satellite connections to pitches

Other Abbreviations

AIT	Alliance Internationale de Tourisme
a'bahn	Autobahn
a'pista	Autopista
a'route	Autoroute
a'strada	Autostrada
adj	Adjacent, nearby
alt	Alternative
app	Approach, on approaching
arr	Arrival, arriving
avail	Available
Ave	Avenue
bdge	Bridge
bef	Before
bet	Between
Blvd	Boulevard
C	Century, eg 16thC
c'van	Caravan
CC	Caravan and Motorhome Club
ccard acc	Credit and/or debit cards accepted (check with site for specific details)
cent	Centre or central
clsd	Closed
conn	Connection
cont	Continue or continental (wc)
conv	Convenient
covrd	Covered
dep	Departure
diff	Difficult, with difficulty
dir	Direction
dist	Distance
dual c'way	Dual carriageway
E	East
ent	Entrance/entry to
espec	Especially
ess	Essential
excel	Excellent
facs	Facilities
FIA	Fédération Internationale de l'Automobile
FICC	Fédération Internationale de Camping & de Caravaning
FFCC	Fédération Française de Camping et de Caravaning
FKK/FNF	Naturist federation, ie naturist site
foll	Follow

fr	From
g'ge	Garage
gd	Good
grnd(s)	Ground(s)
hr(s)	Hour(s)
immac	Immaculate
immed	Immediate(ly)
inc	Included/inclusive
indus est	Industrial estate
INF	Naturist federation, ie naturist site
int'l	International
irreg	Irregular
junc	Junction
km	Kilometre
L	Left
LH	Left-hand
LS	Low season
ltd	Limited
mkd	Marked
mkt	Market
mob	Mobile (phone)
m'van	Motor caravan
m'way	Motorway
N	North
narr	Narrow
nr, nrby	Near, nearby
opp	Opposite
o'fits	Outfits
o'look(ing)	Overlook(ing)
o'night	Overnight
o'skts	Outskirts
PO	Post office
poss	Possible, possibly
pt	Part
R	Right
rd	Road or street
rec	Recommend/ed
recep	Reception
red	Reduced, reduction (for)
reg	Regular
req	Required
RH	Right-hand
rlwy	Railway line
rm	Room
rndabt	Roundabout
rte	Route
RV	Recreational vehicle, ie large motor caravan
rv/rvside	River/riverside

S	South
san facs	Sanitary facilities ie wc, showers, etc
snr citizens	Senior citizens
sep	Separate
sh	Short
sp	Sign post, signposted
sq	Square
ssn	Season
stn	Station
strt	Straight, straight ahead
sw	Swimming
thro	Through
TO	Tourist Office
tour ops	Tour operators
traff lts	Traffic lights
twd	Toward(s)
unrel	Unreliable
vg	Very good
vill	Village
W	West
w/end	Weekend
x-ing	Crossing
x-rds	Cross roads

Documents

Camping Key Europe

Camping Key Europe (CKE) is a useful touring companion. Not only does it serve as ID at campsites, meaning that you don't have to leave your passport at reception, it also entitles you to discounts at over 2200 sites.

CKE also offers third-party liability insurance for families including up to three children, which provides cover for loss or damage that occurs while on site. For more information on the scheme and all its benefits visit www.campingkey.com.

You can purchase the CKE from the Club by calling 01342 336633, or it is provided free for Red Pennant Overseas Holiday Insurance customers taking out 'Motoring' cover.

If you are using a CKE or CCI card as ID at a site, make sure that you collect your card when checking out. Also check that you have been given your own card instead of someone else's.

Driving Licence

A full (not provisional), valid driving licence should be carried at all times when driving abroad. You must produce it when asked to do so by the police and other authorities, or you may be liable for an immediate fine and confiscation of your vehicle(s).

If your driving licence is due to expire while you are away it can be renewed up to three months before expiry - contact the DVLA if you need to renew more than three months ahead.

Rules regarding driving with a provisional licences vary across Europe, so you may not be entitled to drive in some EU countries unless you have a full licence.

All EU countries recognise the photocard driving licence introduced in the UK in 1990, subject to the minimum age requirements (normally 18 years for a vehicle with a maximum weight of 3,500 kg carrying no more than 8 people).

Old-style green paper licences or Northern Irish licences issued before 1991 should be updated before travelling as they may not be recognised by local authorities.

Passport

In many EU countries everyone is required to carry photographic ID at all times. Enter next-of-kin details in the back of your passport and keep a separate photocopy. It's also a good idea to leave a photocopy of it with a relative or friend at home.

You can also scan or take a photo of your passport to keep saved on your smart phone or in a cloud storage service so you are able to access it while you're away.

The following information applies to British passport holders only. For information on passports issued by other countries you should contact the local embassy.

Applying for a Passport

Each person travelling out of the UK (including babies) must hold a valid passport - it is no longer possible to include children on a parent's passport. A standard British passport is valid for ten years, or 5 years for under 16s.

All newly issued UK passports are now biometric, also known as e-passports, which contain a microchip with information which can be used to authenticate the holder's identity.

Full information and application forms are available from main post offices or from the Identity & Passport Service's website, www.gov.uk where you can complete an online application. Allow at least six weeks for first-time passport applications, for which you may need to attend an interview at your nearest Identity and Passport Service (IPS) regional office. Allow three weeks for a renewal application or replacement of a lost, stolen or damaged passport.

Passport Validity

Most countries in the EU only require your passport to be valid for the duration of your stay. However, in case your return home is delayed it is a good idea make sure you have six month's validity remaining. Any time left on a passport (up to a maximum of nine months) will be added to the validity of your new passport on renewal.

Schengen Agreement

The Schengen Agreement allows people and vehicles to pass freely without border checks from country to country within the Schengen area (26 countries). Where there are no longer any border checks you should still not attempt to cross land borders without a full, valid passport. It is likely that random identity checks will be made for the foreseeable future in areas surrounding borders. The United Kingdom and Republic of Ireland do not fully participate in the Schengen Agreement.

Due to the current migrant crisis in Europe some countries have temporarily restored their borders. A current list of countries affected is available on the EU website: **ec.europa.eu/home-affairs/what-we-do/policies/borders-and-visas/schengen/reintroduction-border-control_en**.

Pets resident anywhere in the British Isles (excluding the Republic of Ireland) are able to travel freely within the British Isles and are not subject to PETS rules.

For details of how to obtain a Pet Passport visit www.defra.gov.uk or call 0370 241 1710.

Returning to the UK

On your return to the UK with your pet you will need to visit a vet between 24 and 120 hours prior to your return journey in order for your pet to be treated for tapeworm. The vet will need to sign your pet passport - ensure that they put the correct date against their signature or you may not fall within the correct time range for travel. Ask your campsite to recommend a local vet, or research vets near to the port you will be returning from before you travel.

Regulations for Pets

Some campsites do not accept dogs at all and some have restrictions on the number and breed of dogs allowed. Visit camc.com/overseasadvice for more information and country specific advice.

In popular tourist areas local regulations may ban dogs from beaches in the summer months.

Pet Travel Scheme (PETS)

The Pet Travel Scheme (PETS) allows owners of dogs, cats and ferrets from qualifying European countries, to bring their pets into the UK (up to a limit of five per person) without quarantine. The animal must have an EU pet passport, be microchipped and be vaccinated against rabies. Dogs must also have been treated for tapeworm. It also allows pets to travel from the UK to other EU qualifying countries.

There are country specific regulations regarding certain breeds of dogs. You can't import breeds classed as dangerous dogs to many countries, and other breeds will require additional documentation. For more information or to find out which breeds are banned or restricted visit camc.com/pets or call us on 01342 336766.

Travelling with Children

Some countries require evidence of parental responsibility for people travelling alone with children, especially those who have a different surname to them (including lone parents and grandparent). The authorities may want to see a birth certificate, a letter of consent from the child's parent (or other parent if you are travelling alone with your own child) and some evidence as to your responsibility for the child.

For further information on exactly what will be required at immigration contact the Embassy or Consulate of the countries you intend to visit.

Vehicle documents

Caravan Proof of Ownership (CRIS)

In Britain and Ireland, unlike most other European countries, caravans are not formally registered in the same way as cars. This may not be fully understood by police and other authorities on the Continent. You are strongly advised, therefore, to carry a copy of your Caravan Registration Identification Scheme (CRIS) document.

MOT Certificate

Carry your vehicle's MOT certificate (if applicable) as you may need to show it to the authorities if your vehicle is involved in an accident, or in the event of random vehicle checks. If your MOT certificate is due to expire while you are away you should have the vehicle tested before you leave home.

Tax

While driving abroad you still need to have current UK vehicle tax. If your vehicle's tax is due to expire while you are abroad you may apply to re-license the vehicle at a post office, by post, or in person at a DVLA local office, up to two months in advance.

Since October 2014 the DVLA have no longer issued paper tax discs - EU Authorities are aware of this change.

Vehicle Registration Certificate (V5C)

You must always carry your Vehicle Registration Certificate (V5C) and MOT Certificate (if applicable) when taking your vehicle abroad. If yours has been lost, stolen or destroyed you should apply to a DVLA local office on form V62. Call DVLA Customer Enquiries on 0300 790 6802 for more information.

Hired or Borrowed Vehicles

If using a borrowed vehicle you must obtain a letter of authority to use the vehicle from the registered owner. You should also carry the Vehicle Registration Certificate (V5C).

In the case of hired or leased vehicles, including company cars, when the user does not normally possess the V5C, ask the company which owns the vehicle to supply a Vehicle On Hire Certificate, form VE103, which is the only legal substitute for a V5C. The BVRLA, the trade body for the vehicle rental and leasing sector, provide advice on hired or leased vehicles - see www.bvrla.co.uk or call them on 01494 434747 for more information.

If you are caught driving a hired vehicle abroad without this certificate you may be fined and/or the vehicle impounded.

Visas

British citizens holding a full UK passport do not require a visa for entry into any EU countries, although you may require a permit for stays of more than three months. Contact the relevant country's UK embassy before you travel for information.

British subjects, British overseas citizens, British dependent territories citizens and citizens of other countries may need visas that are not required by British citizens. Again check with the authorities of the country you are due to visit at their UK embassy or consulate. Citizens of other countries should apply to their own embassy, consulate or High Commission.

Insurance

Car, Motorhome and Caravan Insurance

It is important to make sure your outfit is covered whilst you are travelling abroad. Your car or motorhome insurance should cover you for driving in the EU, but check what you are covered for before you travel. If you are travelling outside the EU or associated countries you'll need to inform your insurer and may have to pay an additional premium.

Make sure your caravan insurance includes travel outside of the UK, speak to your provider to check this. You may need to notify them of your dates of travel and may be charged an extra premium dependent on your level of cover.

The Caravan and Motorhome Club's Car, Caravan Cover and Motorhome Insurance schemes extend to provide policy cover for travel within the EU free of charge, provided the total period of foreign travel in any one year does not exceed 270 days for Car and Motorhome Insurance and 182 for Caravan Insurance. It may be possible to extend this period, although a charge may apply.

Should you be delayed beyond these limits notify your broker or insurer immediately in order to maintain your cover until you can return to the UK.

If your outfit is damaged during ferry travel (including while loading or unloading) it must be reported to the carrier at the time of the incident. Most insurance policies will cover short sea crossings (up to 65 hours) but check with your insurer before travelling.

Visit camc.com/insurance or call 01342 336610 for full details of our Caravan Cover or for Car or Motorhome Insurance call 0345 504 0334.

European Accident Statement

Your car or motorhome insurer may provide you with a European Accident Statement form (EAS), or you may be given one if you are involved in an accident abroad. The EAS is a standard form, available in different languages, which gives all parties involved in an accident the opportunity to agree on the facts. Signing the form doesn't mean that you are accepting liability, just that you agree with what has been stated on the form. Only sign an EAS if you are completely sure that you understand what has been written and always make sure that you take a copy of the completed EAS.

Vehicles Left Behind Abroad

If you are involved in an accident or breakdown abroad which prevents you taking your vehicle home, you must ensure that your normal insurance will cover your vehicle if left overseas while you return home. Also check if you're covered for the cost of recovering it to your home address.

In this event you should remove all items of baggage and personal belongings from your vehicles before leaving them unattended. If this isn't possible you should check with your insurer if extended cover can be provided. In all circumstances, you must remove any valuables and items liable for customs duty, including wine, beer, spirits and cigarettes.

Legal Costs Abroad

If an accident abroad leads to you being taken to court you may find yourself liable for legal costs – even if you are not found to be at fault. Most UK vehicle insurance policies include cover for legal costs or have the option to add cover for a small additional cost – check if you are covered before you travel.

Holiday Travel Insurance

A standard motor insurance policy won't cover you for all eventualities, for example vehicle breakdown, medical expenses or accommodation so it's important to also take out adequate travel insurance. Make sure that the travel insurance you take out is suitable for a caravan or motorhome holiday.

Remember to check exemptions and exclusions, especially those relating to pre-existing medical conditions or the use of alcohol. Be sure to declare any pre-existing medical conditions to your insurer.

The Club's Red Pennant Overseas Holiday Insurance is designed specifically for touring holidays and can cover both motoring and personal use. Depending on the level of cover chosen the policy will cover you for vehicle recovery and repair, holiday continuation, medical expenses and accommodation.

Visit camc.com/redpennant for full details or call us on 01342 336633.

Holiday Insurance for Pets

Taking your pet with you? Make sure they're covered too. Some holiday insurance policies, including The Club's Red Pennant, can be extended to cover pet expenses relating to an incident normally covered under the policy – such as pet repatriation in the event that your vehicle is written off.

However in order to provide cover for pet injury or illness you will need a separate pet insurance policy which covers your pet while out of the UK. For details of The Club's Pet Insurance scheme visit camc.com/petins or call 0345 504 0336.

Home Insurance

Your home insurer may require advance notification if you are leaving your home unoccupied for 30 days or more. There may be specific requirements, such as turning off mains services (except electricity), draining water down and having somebody check your home periodically. Read your policy documents or speak to your provider.

The Club's Home Insurance policy provides full cover for up to 90 days when you are away from home (for instance when touring) and requires only common sense precautions for longer periods of unoccupancy. See camc.com/homeins or call 0345 504 0335 for details.

Personal Belongings

The majority of travellers are able to cover their valuables such as jewellery, watches, cameras, laptops, and bikes under a home insurance policy. This includes the Club's Home Insurance scheme.

Specialist gadget insurance is now commonly available and can provide valuable benefits if you are taking smart phones, tablets, laptops or other gadgets on holiday with you. The Club offers a Gadget Insurance policy - visit camc.com/gadget or call 01342 779413 to find out more.

Customs

Caravans and Vehicles

A caravan, motorhome or trailer tent imported into France from an EU country can stay there indefinitely, although you must have a purchase invoice showing that tax (VAT) has been paid in the country of purchase.

Although a permit is not required for vehicles being imported on a permanent basis, they must be covered by an EU certificate of conformity. This can be issued by the manufacturer, their representative in France or by the "Direction Régionale de l'Environnement, de l'Aménagement et du Logement" (DREAL). Vehicles that do not conform to EU standards, and vehicles over 4 years old, must be presented to the DREAL for an inspection.

Borrowed Vehicles

If you are borrowing a vehicle from a friend or relative, or loaning yours to someone, you should be aware of the following:

- The total time the vehicle spends abroad must not exceed six months.
- The owner of the caravan must provide the other person with a letter of authority.
- The owner cannot accept a hire fee or reward.
- The number plate on the caravan must match the number plate on the tow car.
- Both drivers' insurers must be informed if a caravan is being towed and any additional premium must be paid.

Currency

You must declare cash of €10,000 (or equivalent in other currencies) or more when travelling between the UK and a non-EU country. The term 'cash' includes cheques, travellers' cheques, bankers' drafts, notes and coins. You don't need to declare cash when travelling within the EU.

For further information contact HMRC Excise & Customs Helpline on 0300 200 3700.

Customs Allowances

Travelling within the European Union

If you are travelling to the UK from within the EU you can bring an unlimited amount of most goods without being liable for any duty or tax, but certain rules apply. The goods must be for your own personal use, which can include use as a gift (if the person you are gifting the goods to reimburses you in any way this is not classed as a gift), and you must have paid duty and tax in the country where you purchased the goods. If a customs official suspects that any goods are not for your own personal use they can question you, make further checks and ultimately seize both the goods and the vehicle used to transport them. Although no limits are in place, customs officials are less likely to question you regarding your goods if they are under the following limits:

- 800 cigarettes
- 400 cigarillos
- 200 cigars
- 1kg tobacco
- 10 litres of spirits
- 20 litres of fortified wine (e.g. port or sherry)
- 90 litres of wine
- 110 litres of beer

The same rules and recommended limits apply for travel between other EU countries.

Travelling outside the EU

There are limits to the amount of goods you can bring back into the UK from countries outside the EU. All goods must be for your own personal use. Each person aged 17 and over is entitled to the following allowance:

- 200 cigarettes, or 100 cigarillos, or 50 cigars, or 250gms tobacco
- 1 litre of spirits or strong liqueurs over 22% volume, or 2 litres of fortified wine, sparkling wine or any other alcoholic drink that's less than 22% volume
- 4 litres of still wine
- 16 litres of beer
- £390 worth of all other goods including perfume, gifts and souvenirs without having to pay tax and/or duty

For further information contact HMRC National Advice Service on 0300 200 3700.

Duty-Free Imports from Andorra

Duty-free shopping is permitted in Andorra, which is not a member of the EU, but there are limits on the amount of goods which can be exported:

- 1.5 litre of spirits over 22 % vol or 3 litres spirits under 22 % vol or sparkling wine
- 5 litres of still wine
- 300 cigarettes or 150 cigarillos or 75 cigars or 400g of tobacco
- 75g perfume + 375 ml eau de cologne

There are also limits on other items such as coffee, tea and other food products, so if in any doubt check before you travel.

Medicines

There is no limit to the amount of medicines you can take abroad if they are obtained without prescription (i.e. over the counter medicines). Medicines prescribed by your doctor may contain controlled drugs (e.g. morphine), for which you will need a licence if you're leaving the UK for 3 months or more.

Visit www.gov.uk/travelling-controlled-drugs or call 020 7035 0771 for a list of controlled drugs and to apply for a licence.

You don't need a licence if you carry less than 3 months' supply or your medication doesn't contain controlled drugs, but you should carry a letter from your doctor stating your name, a list of your prescribed drugs and dosages for each drug. You may have to show this letter when going through customs.

Personal Possessions

Visitors to countries within the EU are free to carry reasonable quantities of any personal possessions such as jewellery, cameras, and electrical equipment required for the duration of their stay. It is sensible to carry sales receipts for new items in case you need to prove that tax has already been paid.

Prohibited and Restricted Goods

Regardless of where you are travelling from the importation of some goods into the UK is restricted or banned, mainly to protect health and the environment. These include:

- Endangered animals or plants including live animals, birds and plants, ivory, skins, coral, hides, shells and goods made from them such as jewellery, shoes, bags and belts.

- Controlled, unlicensed or dangerous drugs.
- Counterfeit or pirated goods such as watches, CDs and clothes; goods bearing a false indication of their place of manufacture or in breach of UK copyright.
- Offensive weapons such as firearms, flick knives, knuckledusters, push daggers, self-defence sprays and stun guns.
- Pornographic material depicting extreme violence or featuring children

This list is not exhaustive; if in doubt contact HMRC on 0300 200 3700 (+44 2920 501 261 from outside the UK) or go through the red Customs channel and ask a Customs officer when returning to the UK.

Plants and Food

Travellers from within the EU may bring into the UK any fruit, vegetable or plant products without restriction as long as they are grown in the EU, are free from pests or disease and are for your own consumption. For food products Andorra, the Channel Islands, the Isle of Man, San Marino and Switzerland are treated as part of the EU. From most countries outside the EU you are not allowed to bring into the UK any meat or dairy products. Other animal products may be severely restricted or banned and it is important that you declare any such products on entering the UK. For up to date information contact the Department for Environment, Food and Rural Affairs (Defra) on 0345 33 55 77 or +44 20 7238 6951 from outside the UK. You can also visit www.defra.gov.uk to find out more.

Money

Being able to safely access your money while you're away is a necessity for you to enjoy your break. It isn't a good idea to rely on one method of payment, so always have a backup plan. A mixture of a small amount of cash plus one or two electronic means of payment are a good idea.

Traveller's cheques have become less popular in recent years as fewer banks and hotels are willing or able to cash them. There are alternative options which offer the same level of security but are easier to use, such as prepaid credit cards.

Local Currency

It is a good idea to take enough foreign currency for your journey and immediate needs on arrival, don't forget you may need change for tolls or parking on your journey. Currency exchange facilities will be available at ports and on ferries but rates offered may not be as good as you would find elsewhere.

The Post Office, banks, exchange offices and travel agents offer foreign exchange. All should stock Euros but during peak holiday times or if you need a large amount it may be sensible to pre-order your currency. You should also pre-order less common currencies. Shop around and compare commission and exchange rates, together with minimum charges.

Banks and money exchanges in central and eastern Europe won't usually accept Scottish and Northern Irish bank notes and may be reluctant to change any sterling which has been written on or is creased or worn.

Foreign Currency Bank Accounts

Frequent travellers or those who spend long periods abroad may find a Euro bank account useful. Most such accounts impose no currency conversion charges for debit or credit card use and allow fee-free cash withdrawals at ATMs. Some banks may also allow you to spread your account across different currencies, depending on your circumstances. Speak to your bank about the services they offer.

Prepaid Travel Cards

Prepaid travel money cards are issued by various providers including the Post Office, Travelex, Lloyds Bank and American Express.

They are increasingly popular as the PIN protected travel money card offers the security of Traveller's Cheques, with the convenience of paying by card. You load the card with the amount you need before leaving home, and then use cash machines to make withdrawals or use the card to pay for goods and services as you would a credit or debit card. You can top the card up over the telephone or online while you are abroad. However there can be issues with using them with some automated payment systems, such as pay-at-pump petrol stations and toll booths, so you should always have an alternative payment method available.

These cards can be cheaper to use than credit or debit cards for both cash withdrawals and purchases as there are usually no loading or transaction fees to pay. In addition, because they are separate from your bank account, if the card is lost or stolen you bank account will still be secure.

Credit and Debit Cards

Credit and debit cards offer a convenient way of spending abroad. For the use of cards abroad most banks impose a foreign currency conversion charge of up to 3% per transaction. If you use your card to withdraw cash there will be a further commission charge of up to 3% and you will be charged interest (possibly at a higher rate than normal) as soon as you withdraw the money.

There are credit cards available which are specifically designed for spending overseas and will give you the best available rates. However they often have high interest rates so are only economical if you're able to pay them off in full each month.

If you have several cards, take at least two in case you encounter problems. Credit and debit 'Chip and PIN' cards issued by UK banks may not be universally accepted abroad so check that your card will be accepted if using it in restaurants or other situations where you pay after you have received goods or services

Contact your credit or debit card issuer before you leave home to let them know that you will be travelling abroad. In the battle against card fraud, card issuers frequently query transactions which they regard as unusual or suspicious, causing your card to be declined or temporarily stopped. You should always carry your card issuer's helpline number with you so that you can contact them if this happens. You will also need this number should you need to report the loss or theft of your card.

Dynamic Currency Conversion

When you pay with a credit or debit card, retailers may offer you the choice of currency for payment, e.g. a euro amount will be converted into sterling and then charged to your card account. This is known as a 'Dynamic Currency Conversion' but the exchange rate used is likely to be worse than the rate offered by your card issuer, so will work out more expensive than paying in the local currency.

Emergency Cash

If an emergency or theft means that you need cash in a hurry, then friends or relatives at home can send you emergency cash via money transfer services. The Post Office, MoneyGram and Western Union all offer services which, allows the transfer of money to over 233,000 money transfer agents around the world. Transfers take approximately ten minutes and charges are levied on a sliding scale.

Crossing the Channel

Booking Your Ferry

If travelling at peak times, such as Easter or school holidays, make reservations as early as possible. Each ferry will have limited room for caravans and large vehicles so spaces can fill up quickly, especially on cheaper crossings. If you need any special assistance request this at the time of booking.

When booking any ferry crossing, make sure you give the correct measurements for your outfit including bikes, roof boxes or anything which may add to the length or height of your vehicle - if you underestimate your vehicle's size you may be turned away or charged an additional fee.

The Caravan and Motorhome Club is an agent for most major ferry companies operating services. Call The Club's Travel Service on 01342 316 101 or see camc.com/ferries to book.

The table at the end of this section shows ferry routes from the UK to the Continent and Ireland. Some ferry routes may not be operational all year, and during peak periods there may be a limit to the number of caravans or motorhomes accepted. For the most up-to-date information visit camc.com/ferries or call the Club's Travel Services team.

On the Ferry

Arrive at the port with plenty of time before your boarding time. Motorhomes and car/caravan outfits will usually either be the first or last vehicles boarded onto the ferry. Almost all ferries are now 'drive on – drive off' so you won't be required to do any complicated manoeuvres. You may be required to show ferry staff that your gas is switched off before boarding the ferry.

Be careful using the ferry access ramps, as they are often very steep which can mean there is a risk of grounding the tow bar or caravan hitch. Drive slowly and, if your ground clearance is low, consider whether removing your jockey wheel and any stabilising devices would help.

Vehicles are often parked close together on ferries, meaning that if you have towing extension mirrors they could get knocked or damaged by people trying to get past your vehicle. If you leave them attached during the ferry crossing then make sure you check their position on returning to your vehicle.

Channel Tunnel

The Channel Tunnel operator, Eurotunnel, accepts cars, caravans and motorhomes (except those running on LPG) on their service between Folkestone and Calais. You can just turn up and see if there is availability on the day, however prices increase as it gets closer to the departure time so if you know your plans in advance it is best to book as early as possible.

On the Journey

You will be asked to open your roof vents prior to travel and you will also need to apply the caravan brake once you have parked your vehicle on the train. You will not be able to use your caravan until arrival.

Pets

It is possible to transport your pet on a number of ferry routes to the Continent and Ireland, as well as on Eurotunnel services from Folkestone to Calais. Advance booking is essential as restrictions apply to the number of animals allowed on any one crossing. Make sure you understand the carrier's terms and conditions for transporting pets. Brittany Ferries ask for all dogs to be muzzled when out of the vehicle but this varies for other operators so please check at the time of booking.

Once on board pets are normally required to remain in their owner's vehicle or in kennels on the car deck and you won't be able to access your vehicle to check on your pet while the ferry is at sea. On longer crossings you should make arrangements at the on-board information desk for permission to visit your pet in order to check its well-being. You should always make sure that ferry staff know your vehicle has a pet on board.

Information and advice on the welfare of animals before and during a journey is available on the website of the Department for Environment, Food and Rural Affairs (Defra), www.defra.gov.uk.

Gas

UK based ferry companies usually allow up to three gas cylinders per caravan, including the cylinder currently in use, however some may restrict this to a maximum of two cylinders. Some operators may ask you to hand over your gas cylinders to a member of the crew so that they can be safely stored during the crossing. Check that you know the rules of your ferry operator before you travel.

Cylinder valves should be fully closed and covered with a cap, if provided, and should remain closed during the crossing. Cylinders should be fixed securely in or on the caravan in the position specified by the manufacturer.

Gas cylinders must be declared at check-in and the crew may ask to inspect each cylinder for leakage before travel.

The carriage of spare petrol cans, whether full or empty, is not permitted on ferries or through the Channel Tunnel.

LPG Vehicles

Vehicles fully or partially powered by LPG can't be carried through the Channel Tunnel. Gas for domestic use (e.g. heating, lighting or cooking) can be carried, but the maximum limit is 47kg for a single bottle or 50kg in multiple bottles. Tanks must be switched off before boarding and must be less than 80% full; you will be asked to demonstrate this before you travel.

Most ferry companies will accept LPG-powered vehicles but you must let them know at the time of booking. During the crossing the tank must be no more than 75% full and it must be turned off. In the case of vehicles converted to use LPG, some ferry companies also require a certificate showing that the conversion has been carried out by a professional - before you book speak to the ferry company to see what their requirements are.

Club Sites Near Ports

If you've got a long drive to the ferry port, or want to catch an early ferry then an overnight stop near to the port gives you a relaxing start to your holiday. The following table lists Club sites which are close to ports.

Club Members can book online at camc.com or call 01342 327490. Non-members can book by calling the sites directly on the telephone numbers below when the sites are open.

Please note that Commons Wood, Fairlight Wood, Hunter's Moon and Old Hartley are open to Club members only. Non-members are welcome at all other sites listed below.

Port	Nearest Club Site	Tel No.
Cairnryan	New England Bay	01776 860275
Dover, Folkestone, Channel Tunnel	Bearsted	01622 730018
	Black Horse Farm*	01303 892665
	Daleacres	01303 267679
	Fairlight Wood	01424 812333
Fishguard, Pembroke	Freshwater East	01646 672341
Harwich	Cambridge Cherry Hinton*	01223 244088
	Commons Wood*	01707 260786
Holyhead	Penrhos	01248 852617
Hull	York Beechwood Grange*	01904 424637
	York Rowntree Park*	01904 658997
Newcastle upon Tyne	Old Hartley	0191 237 0256
Newhaven	Brighton*	01273 626546
Plymouth	Plymouth Sound	01752 862325
Poole	Hunter's Moon*	01929 556605
Portsmouth	Rookesbury Park	01329 834085
Rosslare	River Valley	00353 (0)404 41647
Weymouth	Crossways	01305 852032

* Site open all year

Ferry Routes and Operators

Route	Operator	Approximate Crossing Time	Maximum Frequency
Belgium			
Hull – Zeebrugge	P & O Ferries	12-14 hrs	1 daily
France			
Dover – Calais	P & O Ferries	1½ hrs	22 daily
Dover – Calais	DFDS Seaways	1½ hrs	10 daily
Dover – Dunkerque	DFDS Seaways	2 hrs	12 daily
Folkestone – Calais	Eurotunnel	35 mins	3 per hour
Newhaven – Dieppe	DFDS Seaways	4 hrs	2 daily
Plymouth – Roscoff	Brittany Ferries	6 hrs	2 daily
Poole – St Malo (via Channel Islands)*	Condor Ferries	5 hrs	1 daily (May to Sep)
Portsmouth – Caen	Brittany Ferries	6 / 7 hrs	3 daily (maximum)
Portsmouth – Cherbourg	Brittany Ferries	3 hrs	2 daily (maximum)
Portsmouth – Le Havre	Brittany Ferries	3¼ / 8 hrs	1 daily (minimum)
Portsmouth – St Malo	Brittany Ferries	9 hrs	1 daily
Ireland – Northern			
Cairnryan – Larne	P & O Irish Sea	1 / 2 hrs	7 daily
Liverpool (Birkenhead) – Belfast	Stena Line	8 hrs	2 daily
Cairnryan – Belfast	Stena Line	2 / 3 hrs	7 daily
Ireland – Republic			
Cork – Roscoff*	Brittany Ferries	14 hrs	1 per week
Dublin - Cherbourg	Irish Ferries	19 hrs	1 per week
Fishguard – Rosslare	Stena Line	3½ hrs	2 daily
Holyhead – Dublin	Irish Ferries	2-4 hrs	Max 4 daily
Holyhead – Dublin	Stena Line	2-4 hrs	Max 4 daily
Liverpool – Dublin	P & O Irish Sea	8 hrs	2 daily
Pembroke – Rosslare	Irish Ferries	4 hrs	2 daily
Rosslare – Cherbourg*	Irish Ferries	19½ hrs	3 per week
Rosslare – Cherbourg	Stena Line	19 hrs	3 per week
Rosslare – Roscoff*	Irish Ferries	19½ hrs	4 per week
Netherlands			
Harwich – Hook of Holland	Stena Line	7 hrs	2 daily
Hull – Rotterdam	P & O Ferries	11-12 hrs	1 daily
Newcastle – Ijmuiden (Amsterdam)	DFDS Seaways	15½ hrs	1 daily
Spain			
Portsmouth – Bilbao	Brittany Ferries	24 / 32 hrs	1 - 3 per week
Portsmouth or Plymouth – Santander	Brittany Ferries	20 / 32 hrs	4 per week

*Not bookable through The Club's Travel Service.
Note: Services and routes correct at time of publication but subject to change.

Motoring advice

Preparing for Your Journey

The first priority in preparing your outfit for your journey should be to make sure it has a full service. Make sure that you have a fully equipped spares kit, and a spare wheel and tyre for your caravan – it is easier to get hold of them from your local dealer than to have to spend time searching for spares where you don't know the local area.

Club members should carry their UK Sites Directory & Handbook with them, as it contains a section of technical advice which may be useful when travelling. The Club also has a free advice service covering a wide range of technical topics – download free information leaflets at camc.com/advice or contact the team - call 01342 336611 or email technical@camc.com.

For advice on issues specific to countries other than the UK, Club members can contact the Travel Service Information Officer; email travelserviceinfo@camc.com or call 01342 336766.

Weight Limits

From both a legal and a safety point of view, it is essential not to exceed vehicle weight limits. It is advisable to carry documentation confirming your vehicle's maximum permitted laden weight - if your Vehicle Registration Certificate (V5C) does not state this, you will need to produce alternative certification, e.g. from a weighbridge.

If you are pulled over by the police and don't have certification you will be taken to a weighbridge. If your vehicle(s) are then found to be overweight you will be liable to a fine and may have to discard items to lower the weight before you can continue on your journey.

Some Final Checks

Before you start any journey make sure you complete the following checks:

- All car and caravan or motorhome lights are working and sets of spare bulbs are packed.
- The coupling is correctly seated on the towball and the breakaway cable is attached.
- Windows, vents and hatches are shut.
- On-board water systems are drained.
- Mirrors are adjusted for maximum visibility.
- Corner steadies are fully wound up and the brace is handy for your arrival on site.

- Any fires or flames are extinguished and the gas cylinder tap is turned off. Fire extinguishers are fully charged and close at hand.
- The over-run brake is working correctly.
- The jockey wheel is raised and secured, the handbrake is released.

Driving in France

Driving abroad for the first time can be a daunting prospect, especially when towing a caravan. Here are a few tips to make the transition easier:

- Remember that sat navs may take you on unsuitable roads, so have a map or atlas to hand to help you find an alternative route.
- It can be tempting to try and get to your destination as quickly as possible but we recommend travelling a maximum of 250 miles a day when towing.
- Share the driving if possible, and on long journeys plan an overnight stop.
- Remember that if you need to overtake or pull out around an obstruction you will not be able to see clearly from the driver's seat. If possible, always have a responsible adult in the passenger seat who can advise you when it is clear to pull out. If that is not possible then stay well back to get a better view and pull out slowly.
- If traffic builds up behind you, pull over safely and let it pass.
- Driving on the right should become second nature after a while, but pay particular attention when turning left, after leaving a rest area, petrol station or site or after a one-way system.
- Stop at least every two hours to stretch your legs and take a break.

Accidents

Drivers involved in an accident or those who commit a traffic offence may be required to take a saliva or urine drugs test as well as a breathalyser test. In the event of an accident where people are injured or if emergency assistance is required, dial 17 (police) or 112 from any phone.

Alcohol

In both France and Andorra the maximum legal level of alcohol is 50 milligrams in 100 millilitres of blood, i.e. less than permitted in the UK (80 milligrams). To ensure you stay under the limit it is best to avoid drinking at all if you plan to drive. For novice drivers who have less than 3 years' experience the limit has been reduced to 20 milligrams, which effectively means you cannot drink any alcohol at all. The police carry out random breath tests and penalties are severe.

There is a legal requirement to carry a breathalyser, however there is currently no punishment for non-compliance. Check camc.com/overseasadvice for the most up-to-date advice before you travel.

Breakdown Service

If you break down on a motorway or in a motorway service area you must call the police directly. They can be called from one of the orange emergency telephones placed every 2km along motorways. If you are in a service area, ask service station staff to contact the police for you, or dial 112 from a public phone and the police will be able to pinpoint your exact whereabouts. The police will arrange breakdown and towing assistance. No breakdown vehicle will enter a motorway without police authority.

Charges for motorway assistance are fixed by the government. The basic cost (2015) of repairing a vehicle up to 1,800 kg in weight, on the spot from Monday Friday, from 8am to 6pm is €122.84 or €151.90 for vehicles over 1800kg. After 6pm and over weekends and public holidays a 50% supplement applies.

If you have taken out breakdown insurance you should contact your insurance provider once the breakdown service has arrived in order to establish a means of payment. Your insurance provider cannot summon the police on your behalf if you breakdown on a motorway.

Headphones

From June 2015 it is illegal to drive any vehicle or cycle while wearing headphones or headsets. This includes listening to music or using headphones to make phone calls.

Fuel

Unleaded petrol pumps are marked 'Essence Sans Plomb'. Diesel pumps are marked Gas Oil or Gazole.

Petrol stations may close on Sundays and those at supermarkets, where petrol is generally cheaper, may close for lunch. At supermarkets it is advisable to check the height and width clearance before towing past the pumps. Credit cards are generally accepted. Some automatic pumps at unmanned petrol stations are operated by credit cards and some may not accept credit or debit cards issued outside France. Away from major roads and towns try not to let your fuel tank run too low as you may have difficulty finding an open petrol station, especially at night or on Sundays.

Fuel containing 10% bioethanol is on sale at many petrol stations in France alongside the regular Euro 95 unleaded fuel, which it will eventually replace. Pumps are labelled SP95-E10. This fuel can be used in most modern vehicles manufactured since 2000 but if you are in any doubt about using it then regular Euro 95 or 98 Super Plus unleaded fuel is still available at most petrol stations. Check your vehicle handbook or visit www.acea.be and search for 'E10' to find the publication 'Vehicle compatibility with new fuel standards'.

To find the cheapest fuel in any area log on to www.zagaz.com and simply click on the map of France to find the locations of petrol stations, together with prices charged. Alternatively view the French government website, www.prix-carburants.gouv.fr which gives fuel prices all over the country.

Members of the Caravan and Motorhome Club can check current average fuel prices by country at camc.com/overseasadvice.

Automotive Liquefied Petroleum Gas (LPG)

LPG (also called Gepel or GPL) is available in petrol stations across France, especially on motorways. However LPG may not be available in more rural areas so you are advised to fill up at the first opportunity. Maps showing their company's outlets are issued free by most LPG suppliers, e.g. Shell, Elf, etc. A list of locations is available at the website stations.gpl.online.fr. LPG is not available in Andorra.

Low Emission Zones

A low emission zone was introduced in Paris from July 2015, initially only affecting vehicles over 3500kg. From 1st July 2016 vehicles under 3500kg which are rated Euro 1 for emissions standards will also be included, and then Euro 2-4 will also be regulated at different stages. You are advised to check the most up-to-date information at www.lowemissionzones.eu before you travel.

Motorhomes Towing Cars

If you are towing a car behind a motorhome, our advice would be to use a trailer with all four wheels of the car off the ground. Although

France doesn't have a specific law banning A-frames, they do have a law which prohibits a motor vehicle towing another motor vehicle.

Overtaking and Passing

Crossing a solid single or double centre line is heavily penalised. Outside built-up areas, outfits weighing more than 3,500 kg, or more than 7m in length, are required by law to leave at least 50m between themselves and the vehicle in front. They are only permitted to use the two right-hand lanes on roads with three or more lanes and, where overtaking is difficult, should slow down or stop to allow other smaller vehicles to pass.

Parking

As a general rule, all prohibitions are indicated by road signs or by yellow road markings. Stopping or parking on the left-hand side of the road is prohibited except in one-way streets.

In most French cities parking meters have largely been replaced by 'pay and display' machines which take coins and credit or debit cards. Where parking signs show 'Horodateur' or 'Stationnement Payant' you must obtain a ticket from a nearby machine.

In Paris two red routes ('axe rouge') have been created on which stopping and parking are prohibited. Elsewhere, drivers must observe parking restrictions indicated by signs. Car parks are expensive and the best advice is to use public transport, which is cheap and efficient.

In many cities and towns there are blue zones (indicated by blue street markings) where you can sometimes park for free, usually for one hour between 9am and 12pm and between 2pm and 7pm from Monday to Saturday. You must display a parking disc ('disque de contrôle/stationnement') in your windscreen; these are available free, or for a small fee, from garages, travel agencies, motoring organisations, tourist offices, police stations, tobacconists and some shops.

Priority

In built up areas, give way to traffic coming from the right, unless otherwise indicated. Outside built-up areas traffic on all main roads of any importance has right of way, indicated by the following signs:

Priority road

Priority road

On entering towns, the same sign will often have a line through it, warning that vehicles may pull out from a side road on the right and will have priority.

End of priority road

On steep gradients, vehicles travelling downhill must give way to vehicles travelling uphill.

Public Transport

In built-up areas you must stop to allow a bus to pull out from a bus stop. Take particular care when school buses have stopped and passengers are getting on and off.

Overtaking trams in motion is normally only allowed on the right, unless on a one way street where you can overtake on the left if there is not enough space on the right. Do not overtake a tram near a tram stop, which can be in the centre of the road. When a tram or bus stops to allow passengers on and off, you should stop to allow them to cross to the pavement. Give way to trams which are turning across your carriageway.

Pedestrian Crossings

Stopping to allow pedestrians to cross at zebra crossings is not always common practice on the Continent. Pedestrians expect to wait until the road is clear before crossing, while motorists behind may be taken by surprise by your stopping. The result may be a rear-end shunt or vehicles overtaking you at the crossing and putting pedestrians at risk.

Roads

French roads fall into three categories: autoroutes (A) i.e. motorways; national (N) roads; and departmental (D) roads. There are over 10,500 kilometres of motorways, on most of which tolls are levied. British motorists will find French roads relatively uncongested.

Andorra

Travellers to Andorra from France should be aware that conditions on the road from Toulouse to Andorra, the N20/E9, can quickly become difficult in severe winter weather and you should be prepared for delays. Stick to main roads in Andorra when towing and don't attempt the many unsurfaced roads.

Road Signs and Markings

Directional signposting on major roads is generally good. Signs may be placed on walls pointing across the road they indicate and this may be confusing at first. Generally a sign on the right pointing left means that you go straight ahead. The same sign on the right pointing right means 'turn right' at the first opportunity. The words 'tout droit' mean 'go straight ahead' or 'straight on'.

Road signs on approach to roundabouts and at junctions usually do not show road numbers, just the destination, with numbers being displayed once you are on the road itself. Make sure you know the names of places along your proposed route, and not just the road numbers. Once you have seen your destination town signposted continue along the road until directed otherwise. Intermediate junctions or roundabouts where you do not have to turn usually omit the destination name if the route to it is straight on.

Lines on the carriageway are generally white. A yellow zigzag line indicates a bus stop, blue markings indicate that parking is restricted and yellow lines on the edge of the roadway also indicate that stopping and/or parking is prohibited. A solid single or double white line in the centre of the road indicates that overtaking is not permitted. STOP signs mean stop - you must come to a complete halt otherwise you may be liable to a fine if caught.

Whilst road signs conform to international standards, some other commonly used signs you may see include:

French	English translation
Allumez vos feux	Switch on lights
Attention	Caution
Bouchon	Traffic jam
Chausée deformée	Uneven road
Chemin sans issue	No through road
Col	Mountain pass
Créneau de dépassement	2-lane passing zone, dual carriageway
Déviation	Diversion
Fin d'interdiction de stationner	End of parking restrictions
Gravillons	Loose chippings
Interdit aux piétons	No pedestrians
Itineraire bis	Alternative route
Péage	Toll
Ralentissez	Slow down
Rappel	Continued restriction
Rétrécissement	Narrow lane
Route barrée	Road closed
Sens interdit	No entry
Sens unique	One-way street
Serrez à gauche/droite	Keep left/right
Stationnement interdit	No parking
Tout droit	Straight on
Toutes directions	All directions
Travaux	Road works
Virages	Bends

Andorra

Main roads are prefixed 'CG' (Carretera General) and side roads are prefixed 'CS' (Carretera Secundaria). CG road signs are white on red and CS signs are white on green.

Recently-Qualified Drivers

The minimum age to drive in France is 18 years and this also applies to foreign drivers. Driving without professionally qualified supervision/instruction on a provisional licence is not allowed.

Roundabouts

At roundabouts drivers must give way to traffic already on the roundabout, i.e. on the left, if indicated by a red-bordered triangular sign showing a roundabout symbol with the words 'Vous n'avez pas la priorité' or 'Cédez le passage' underneath.

Traffic on the roundabout has priority

In the absence of these signs traffic entering the roundabout has priority, however it is always very important to be watchful and to take extra care at roundabouts and junctions to avoid accidents.

Traffic Jams

The A6/A7 (the Autoroute du Soleil) from Paris via Lyon to the south are busy motorways prone to traffic jams. Travelling from the north, bottlenecks are often encountered at Auxerre, Chalon-sur-Saône, Lyon, Valence and Orange. An alternative route to the south is the A20, which is largely toll-free, or the toll-free A75 via Clermont-Ferrand.

During periods of severe congestion on the A6, A7 and A10 Paris-Bordeaux motorways, traffic police close off junctions and divert holiday traffic onto alternative routes or 'Itinéraires Bis' which run parallel to main roads.

The signs above indicate these routes. For a traffic calendar, indicating when certain areas are most prone to traffic jams, together with a real-time congestion map and regional phone numbers to call for traffic/travel information, see www.bison-fute.equipement.gouv.fr.

Realtime traffic information on traffic conditions on motorways can be found on www.autoroutes.fr.

In general, Friday afternoons and Saturday mornings are busiest on roads leading south, and on Saturday and Sunday afternoons roads leading north may well be congested. Many French people drop everything for lunch and, therefore, between noon and 2pm roads are quieter.

At the start of the school holidays in early July, at the end of July and during the first and last few days of August, roads are particularly busy. Avoid the changover weekend at the end of July/beginning of August when traffic both north and south bound can be virtually at a standstill. Traffic can also be very heavy around the Christmas/New Year period and on the weekend of any public holiday.

Andorra

There is heavy traffic in Andorra-la-Vella town centre on most days of the year. During the peak summer holiday period you are likely to encounter queues of traffic on the Envalira pass from France on the N22. Traffic is at its worst in the morning from France and in the afternoon and evening from Andorra and you are recommended to use the Envalira Tunnel to avoid some of the congestion and reduce travel time.

Traffic Lights

There is no amber light after the red light in the traffic light sequence.

A flashing amber light indicates caution, slow down, proceed but give way to vehicles coming from the right. A flashing red light indicates no entry; it may also be used to mark level crossings, obstacles, etc.

A yellow arrow at the same time as a red light indicates that drivers may turn in the direction of the arrow, traffic permitting, and providing they give way to pedestrians.

Watch out for traffic lights which may be mounted high above the road and hard to spot.

Violation of Traffic Regulations

Severe fines and penalties are in force for motoring offences and the police are authorised to impose and collect fines on the spot. Violations include minor infringements such as not wearing a seat belt, not carrying a set of spare bulbs or not respecting a STOP sign. More serious infringements such as dangerous overtaking, crossing a continuous central white line and driving at very high speeds, can result in confiscation of your driving licence.

If the offence committed is serious and likely to entail a heavy fine and the suspension of your driving licence or a prison sentence, a motorist who is not resident in France and has no employment there must deposit a guarantee. The police may hold a vehicle until payment is made.

Drivers who are deemed to have deliberately put the lives of others in danger face a maximum fine of €15,000 and a jail sentence. Failure to pay may result in your car being impounded. Your driving licence may also be suspended for up to five years.

By paying fines on the spot (request a receipt) or within three days, motorists can avoid court action and even reduce the fine. Standard fines can now be paid electronically in post offices and newsagents equipped with a dedicated terminal or by visiting www.amendes.gouv.fr.

Motorways

France has 11,500 kilometres of excellent motorways. Tolls are payable on most routes according to distance travelled and category of vehicle(s) and, because motorways are privately financed, prices per km vary in different parts of the country. Emergency telephones connected to the police are located every 2km.

Motorway Service Areas

Stopping is allowed for a few hours at the service areas of motorways, called 'aires', and some have sections specially laid out for caravans. Most have toilet facilities and a water supply but at 'aires' with only basic facilities, water may not be suitable for drinking, indicated by a sign 'eau non potable'. In addition there are 'aires de repos' which have picnic and play areas, whereas 'aires de services' resemble UK motorway service areas with fuel, shop, restaurant and parking facilities for all types of vehicle.

Motorway Tolls

Motorways tolls are common throughout France by a number of different operating companies, although there are numerous stretches, particularly around large cities, where no tolls are levied. Vehicles are classified as follows:

Category 1: (Light Vehicles) Vehicle with overall height under 2m and gross vehicle weight not exceeding 3,500kg. Train with overall height under 2m and gross vehicle weight of towing vehicle not exceeding 3,500kg.

Category 2: (Intermediate Vehicles) Vehicle with overall height from 2m to 3m and gross vehicle weight up to 3,500kg. Train with overall height from 2m to 3m and gross vehicle weight up to 3,500kg.

Category 3: (HGV or bus with two axles) Vehicle with overall height of 3m or more. Vehicle with gross vehicle weight of more than 3,500kg. On the A14 all twin-axle buses are in category 4.

Category 4: (HGV or bus with three or more axles) Vehicle with more than two axles and height of 3m or more, or gross vehicle weight of more than 3,500kg. Train with overall height of 3m or more. Train with towing vehicle having gross vehicle weight of more than 3,500kg.

Motorists driving Category 2 vehicles adapted for the transport of disabled persons pay the toll specified for Category 1 vehicles. Holding a disabled person's Blue Badge does not automatically entitle foreign motorists to pay Category 1 charges, and the decision whether to downgrade from Category 2 to 1 will be made by the person at the toll booth, based on experience of similar vehicles registered in France.

To calculate the tolls payable on your planned route see www.viamichelin.com and tick the box marked 'Caravan' (ticking this box

will also give the toll for a motorhome) and select the 'Michelin recommended' route. For more detailed information, consult the websites of the individual motorway operating companies, a list of which can be found on www.autoroutes.fr/en/asfa/french-motorway-companies (English option). Alternatively calculate tolls payable on your chosen route on www.autoroutes.fr.

Toll payments may be made in cash or by credit card, but be aware that when paying with a credit card you may not be asked for a signature or required to key in a PIN. Pre-paid credit cards, Maestro and Electron are not accepted.

On less frequently-used motorways, toll collection is increasingly by automatic machines equipped with height detectors. It is simplest to pay with a credit card but there should be a cash/change machine adjacent. There are lanes at nearly all toll plazas specifically for drivers who have a Liber-t toll tag which allows them to pay for tolls directly from their bank account. Club members can benefit from a free Liber-t tag application (normally €10) - visit camc.com/sanef for details.

Speed Limits

Police are strict about speeding - motorists caught driving more than 40 km/h (25mph) over the speed limit face immediate confiscation of their driving licence. Speed limits on motorways (in dry weather) are higher than in the UK – although they are lower on ordinary roads.

Fixed speed cameras are common on both motorways and major roads. The use of mobile speed cameras and radar traps is frequent, even on remote country roads, and may be operated from parked vans or motor bikes, or they may be hand-held. They may also be in use on exit slip roads from motorways or major roads where there is a posted speed limit. Motorway toll booths will also calculate your speed from the distance you have travelled and the time it has taken.

Radar Detectors

Radar detectors, laser detectors or speed camera jammers are illegal in France. If caught carrying one – even if it is not in use – you are liable to both a fine of up to €1,500 and confiscation of the device, and possibly confiscation of your vehicle if you're unable to pay the fine. GPS or sat nav devices which pinpoint the position of fixed speed cameras are also illegal in France. You can still use the device, but you must disable the function which pinpoints speed cameras.

Inside Built-up Areas

The general speed limit is 50 km/h (31 mph) which may be raised to 70 km/h (44 mph) on important through roads, indicated by signs. The beginning of a built-up area is marked by a road sign giving the name of the town or village in blue or black letters on a light background with a red border. The end of the built-up area is indicated by the same sign with a red diagonal line through it. See examples below:

Therefore, when you enter a town or village, even if there is no actual speed limit warning sign, the place name sign itself indicates that you are entering a 50 km/h zone. The end of the 50 km/h zone is indicated by the place name sign crossed out. The word 'rappel' on a speed limit sign is a reminder of that limit.

The speed limit on stretches of motorway in built-up areas is 110 km/h (68 mph), except on the Paris ring road where the limit is 80 km/h (50 mph).

Outside Built-up Areas

General speed limits are as follows:

- On single carriageway roads 90 km/h (56 mph)

- On dual-carriageways separated by a central reservation 110 km/h (68 mph)

- On motorways 130 km/h (81 mph)

These general speed limits also apply to private cars towing a trailer tent or caravan, provided the gross train mass (fully laden weight of the car, plus the cars towing limit) of the vehicle does not exceed 3,500 kg. If the gross train mass of the towing vehicle is over 3,500 kg the speed limits are 90 km/h (56 mph) on motorways, 80-90 km/h (50 mph) on dual carriageways and 80 km/h (50 mph) on single carriageways.

Large motorhomes over 3,500 kg have a speed limit of 110 km/h (68 mph) on motorways, 100 km/h (62 mph) on dual carriageways and 80 km/h (50 mph) on single carriageway roads.

For full details of speed regulations see camc.com/overseasadvice.

Adverse Weather Conditions

In case of rain or adverse weather conditions, general speed limits are lowered as follows:

- On motorways 110 km/h (68 mph)

- On urban motorways and dual carriageways 100 km/h (62 mph)

- Outside built-up areas 80 km/h (50 mph)

A speed limit of 50 km/h (31 mph) applies on all roads (including motorways) in foggy conditions when visibility is less than 50 metres.

Discover more of Europe

Price Match Guarantee*

La Masseria, Italy

We offer over 340 top quality overseas sites, all handpicked and inspected by us.

If you book an overseas site, ferry or Eurotunnel crossing you will get the best price with our Price Match Guarantee.*

We have something for everyone!

Visit: camc.com/overseas

Or call: 01342 488 378

CARAVAN AND MOTORHOME CLUB
SINCE 1907

Motoring Equipment

Essential Equipment

The equipment that you legally have to carry differs by country. For a full list see the Essential Equipment table at the end of this chapter. Please note equipment requirements and regulations can change frequently. To keep up to date with the latest equipment information visit camc.com/overseasadvice.

Child Restraint Systems

Children under 10 years of age are not permitted to travel in front seats of vehicles, unless there are no rear seats in the vehicle, the rear seats are already occupied with other children, or there are no seat belts in the rear. In these situations a child must not be placed in the front seats in a rear-facing child seat, unless any airbag is deactivated. Children up to 10 must travel in an approved child seat or restraint system, adapted to their size. A baby up to 13kg in weight must be carried in a rear facing baby seat. A child between 9kg and 18kg in weight must be seated in a child seat. A child from 15kg in weight up to the age of 10 can use a booster seat with a seat belt.

Children must not travel in the front of a vehicle if there are rear seats available. If they travel in the front the airbag must be deactivated and again they must use an EU approved restraint system for their size.

Fire Extinguisher

As a safety precaution, an approved fire extinguisher should be carried in all vehicles. This is a legal requirement in several countries in Europe.

Lights

When driving in on the right headlights should be adjusted if they are likely to dazzle other road users. You can do this by applying beam deflectors, or some newer vehicles have a built-in adjustment system. Some high-density discharge (HID), xenon or halogen lights, may need to be taken to a dealer to make the necessary adjustment.

Remember also to adjust headlights according to the load being carried and to compensate for the weight of the caravan on the back of your car. Even if you do not intend to drive at night, it is important to ensure that your headlights are correctly adjusted as you may need to use them in heavy rain, fog or in tunnels. If using tape or a pre-cut adhesive mask remember to remove it on your return home.

All vehicle lights must be in working condition. If your lights are not in working order you may be liable for a fine of up to €450 and confiscation of your vehicle is a possibility in some European countries.

Headlight-Flashing

On the Continent headlight-flashing is used as a warning of approach or as an overtaking signal at night, and not, as is commonly the case in the UK, an indication that you are giving way. Be more cautious with both flashing your headlights and when another driver flashes you. If a driver flashes his headlights they are generally indicating that he has priority and you should give way, contrary to standard practice in the UK.

Hazard Warning Lights

Hazard warning lights should not be used in place of a warning triangle, but should be used in addition to it.

Nationality Plate

A nationality plate must be fixed to the rear of both your car or motorhome and caravan. Checks are made and a fine may be imposed for failure to display a nationality plate correctly. If your number plates have the Euro-Symbol on them there is no requirement to display an additional GB sticker within the EU and Switzerland. If your number plate doesn't have the EU symbol or you are planning to travel outside of the EU you will need a GB sticker.

GB is the only national identification code allowed for cars registered in the UK.

Reflective Jackets / Waistcoats

If you break down outside of a built-up area it is normally a legal requirement that anyone leaving the vehicle must be wearing a reflective jacket or waistcoat. Make sure that your jacket is accessible from inside the car as you will need to put it on before exiting the vehicle. Carry one for each passenger as well as the driver.

Route Planning

It is always a good idea to carry a road atlas or map of the countries you plan to visit, even if you have Satellite Navigation. You can find information on UK roads from Keep Moving – www.keepmoving.co.uk or call 09003 401100. Websites offering a European route mapping service include www.google.co.uk/maps, www.mappy.com or www.viamichelin.com.

Satellite Navigation/GPS

European postcodes don't cover just one street or part of a street in the same way as UK postcodes, they can cover a very large area. GPS co-ordinates and full addresses are given for site entries in this guide wherever possible, so that you can programme your device as accurately as possible.

It is important to remember that sat nav devices don't usually allow for towing or driving a large motorhome and may try to send you down unsuitable roads. Always use your common sense, and if a road looks unsuitable find an alternative route.

Use your sat nav in conjunction with the directions given in the site entries, which have been provided by members who have actually visited. Please note that directions given in site entries have not been checked by the Caravan and Motorhome Club.

In nearly all European countries it is illegal to use car navigation systems which actively search for mobile speed cameras or interfere with police equipment (laser or radar detection).

Car navigation systems which give a warning of fixed speed camera locations are legal in most countries with the exception of France, Germany, and Switzerland where this function must be de-activated.

Seat Belts

The wearing of seat belts is compulsory throughout Europe. On-the-spot fines will be incurred for failure to wear them and, in the event of an accident failure to wear a seat belt may reduce any claim for injury. See the country introductions for specific regulations on both seat belts and car seats.

Spares

Caravan Spares

It will generally be much harder to get hold of spare parts for caravans on the continent, especially for UK manufactured caravans.

It is therefore advisable to carry any commonly required spares (such as light bulbs) with you.

Take contact details of your UK dealer or manufacturer with you, as they may be able to assist in getting spares delivered to you in an emergency.

Car Spares

Some car manufacturers produce spares kits; contact your dealer for details. The choice of spares will depend on the vehicle and how long you are away, but the following is a list of basic items which should cover the most common causes of breakdown:

- Radiator top hose
- Fan belt
- Fuses and bulbs
- Windscreen wiper blade
- Length of 12V electrical cable
- Tools, torch and WD40 or equivalent water repellent/ dispersant spray

Spare Wheel

Your local caravan dealer should be able to supply an appropriate spare wheel. If you have any difficulty in obtaining one, the Club's Technical Department can provide Club members with a list of suppliers on request.

Tyre legislation across Europe is more or less consistent and, while the Club has no specific knowledge of laws on the Continent regarding the use of space-saver spare wheels, there should be no problems in using such a wheel provided its use is in accordance with the manufacturer's instructions. Space-saver spare wheels are designed for short journeys to get to a place where it can be repaired and there will usually be restrictions on the distance and speed at which the vehicle should be driven.

Towbar

The vast majority of cars registered after 1 August 1998 are legally required to have a European Type approved towbar (complying with European Directive 94/20) carrying a plate giving its approval number and various technical details, including the maximum noseweight. Your car dealer or specialist towbar fitter will be able to give further advice.

All new motorhomes will need some form of type approval before they can be registered in the UK and as such can only be fitted with a type approved towbar. Older vehicles can continue to be fitted with non-approved towing brackets.

Tyres

Tyre condition has a major effect on the safe handling of your outfit. Caravan tyres must be suitable for the highest speed at which you can legally tow, even if you choose to drive slower.

Most countries require a minimum tread depth of 1.6mm but motoring organisations recommend at least 3mm. If you are planning a long journey, consider if they will still be above the legal minimum by the end of your journey.

Tyre Pressure

Tyre pressure should be checked and adjusted when the tyres are cold; checking warm tyres will result in a higher pressure reading. The correct pressures will be found in your car handbook, but unless it states otherwise to add an extra 4 - 6 pounds per square inch to the rear tyres of a car when towing to improve handling. Make sure you know what pressure your caravan tyres should be. Some require a pressure much higher than that normally used for cars. Check your caravan handbook for details.

Tyre Sizes

It is worth noting that some sizes of radial tyre to fit the 13" wheels commonly used on older UK caravans are virtually impossible to find in stock at retailers abroad, e.g. 175R13C.

After a Puncture

A lot of cars now have a liquid sealant puncture repair kit instead of a spare wheel. These should not be considered a permanent repair, and in some cases have been known to make repair of the tyre impossible. If you need to use a liquid sealant you should get the tyre repaired or replaced as soon as possible.

Following a caravan tyre puncture, especially on a single-axle caravan, it is advisable to have the non-punctured tyre removed from its wheel and checked inside and out for signs of damage resulting from overloading during the deflation of the punctured tyre.

Winter Driving

Snow chains must be fitted to vehicles using snow-covered roads in compliance with the relevant road signs. Fines may be imposed for non-compliance. Vehicles fitted with chains must not exceed 50 km/h (31mph).

They are not difficult to fit but it's a good idea to carry sturdy gloves to protect your hands when handling the chains in freezing conditions. Polar Automotive Ltd sells and hires out snow chains, contact them on 01892 519933, www.snowchains.com, or email: polar@snowchains.com.

In Andorra winter tyres are recommended. Snow chains must be used when road conditions necessitate their use and/or when road signs indicate.

Warning Triangles

In almost all European countries it is compulsory to carry a warning triangle which, in the event of vehicle breakdown or accident, must be placed (providing it is safe to do so) on the carriageway at least 30 metres from the vehicle. In some instances it is not compulsory to use the triangle but only when this action would endanger the driver.

A warning triangle should be placed on the road approximately 30 metres (100 metres on motorways) behind the broken down vehicle on the same side of the road. Always assemble the triangle before leaving your vehicle and walk with it so that the red, reflective surface is facing oncoming traffic. If a breakdown occurs round a blind corner, place the triangle in advance of the corner. Hazard warning lights may be used in conjunction with the triangle but they do not replace it.

Essential Equipment Table

The table below shows the essential equipment required for each country. Please note that this information was correct at the time of going to print but is subject to change.

For up to date information on equipment requirements for countries in Europe visit camc.com/overseasadvice.

Country	Warning Triangle	Spare Bulbs	First Aid Kit	Reflective Jacket	Additional Equipment to be Carried/Used
Andorra	Yes (2)	Yes	Rec	Yes	Dipped headlights in poor daytime visibility. Winter tyres recommended; snow chains when road conditions or signs dictate.
Austria	Yes	Rec	Yes	Yes	Winter tyres from 1 Nov to 15 April.*
Belgium	Yes	Rec	Rec	Yes	Dipped headlights in poor daytime visibility.
Croatia	Yes (2 for vehicle with trailer)	Yes	Yes	Yes	Dipped headlights at all times from last Sunday in Oct - last Sunday in Mar. Spare bulbs compulsory if lights are xenon, neon or LED. Snow chains compulsory in winter in certain regions.*
Czech Rep	Yes	Yes	Yes	Yes	Dipped headlights at all times. Replacement fuses. Winter tyres or snow chains from 1 Nov - 31st March.*
Denmark	Yes	Rec	Rec	Rec	Dipped headlights at all times. On motorways use hazard warning lights when queues or danger ahead.
Finland	Yes	Rec	Rec	Yes	Dipped headlights at all times. Winter tyres Dec - Feb.*
France	Yes	Rec	Rec	Yes	Dipped headlights recommended at all times. Legal requirement to carry a breathalyser, but no penalty for non-compliance.

Country	Warning Triangle	Spare Bulbs	First Aid Kit	Reflective Jacket	Additional Equipment to be Carried/Used
Germany	Rec	Rec	Rec	Rec	Dipped headlights recommended at all times. Winter tyres to be used in winter weather conditions.*
Greece	Yes	Rec	Yes	Rec	Fire extinguisher compulsory. Dipped headlights in towns at night and in poor daytime visibility.
Hungary	Yes	Rec	Yes	Yes	Dipped headlights at all times outside built-up areas and in built-up areas at night. Snow chains compulsory on some roads in winter conditions.*
Italy	Yes	Rec	Rec	Yes	Dipped headlights at all times outside built-up areas and in poor visibility. Snow chains from 15 Oct - 15 April.*
Luxembourg	Yes	Rec	Rec	Yes	Dipped headlights at night and daytime in bad weather.
Netherlands	Yes	Rec	Rec	Rec	Dipped headlights at night and in bad weather and recommended during the day.
Norway	Yes	Rec	Rec	Rec	Dipped headlights at all times. Winter tyres compulsory when snow or ice on the roads.*
Poland	Yes	Rec	Rec	Rec	Dipped headlights at all times. Fire extinguisher compulsory.
Portugal	Yes	Rec	Rec	Rec	Dipped headlights in poor daytime visibility, in tunnels and in lanes where traffic flow is reversible.
Slovakia	Yes	Rec	Yes	Yes	Dipped headlights at all times. Winter tyres compulsory when compact snow or ice on the road.*
Slovenia	Yes (2 for vehicle with trailer)	Yes	Rec	Yes	Dipped headlights at all times. Hazard warning lights when reversing. Use winter tyres or carry snow chains 15 Nov - 15 Mar.
Spain	Yes (2 Rec)	Rec	Rec	Yes	Dipped headlights at night, in tunnels and on 'special' roads (roadworks).
Sweden	Yes	Rec	Rec	Rec	Dipped headlights at all times. Winter tyres 1 Dec to 31 March.
Switzerland (inc Liechtenstein)	Yes	Rec	Rec	Rec	Dipped headlights recommended at all times, compulsory in tunnels. Snow chains where indicated by signs.

NOTES:
1) All countries: seat belts (if fitted) must be worn by all passengers.
2) Rec: not compulsory for foreign-registered vehicles, but strongly recommended
3) Headlamp converters, spare bulbs, fire extinguisher, first aid kit and reflective waistcoat are strongly recommended for all countries.
4) In some countries drivers who wear prescription glasses must carry a spare pair.
5) Please check information for any country before you travel. This information is to be used as a guide only and it is your responsibility to make sure you have the correct equipment.

* For more information and regulations on winter driving please see the Country Introduction.

Route Planning

Sea

Leeuwarden
Bremerhaven
Groningen
Assen
Bremen
Hamburg
Schwerin
Szczecin
Bydgoszcz

ANDS
rlem
g,
AMSTERDAM
Utrecht
Apeldoorn
Arnhem
Bocholt
Osnabrück
Hannover
Potsdam
Berlin
Gorzów Wielkopolski
Poznań
POLAND
Łódź
Magdeburg

Essen
Dortmund
Düsseldorf
Leipzig
Erfurt
Dresden
Wrocław
Opole

Troisdorf
Liège
GERMANY
Liberec
Katowice

BELGIUM
Hradec
Králové
Ostrava

Wiesbaden
Frankfurt
am Main
Karlovy Vary
PRAHA
CZECHIA
(CZECH REPUBLIC)
Olomouc
Zlín
Zilina

LUXEMBOURG
Mainz
Plzeň

LUXEMBOURG
Saarbrücken
Nürnberg
České
Budějovice
Brno
Trenčín
SLOVAKI

Metz
Karlsruhe
Trnava
Nitra

Châlons-en-
Champagne
Sindelfingen
Stuttgart

Strasbourg
München
Linz
WIEN
BRATISLAVA
BUDAPEST

Salzburg
Sopron
Győr
Szombathely
Veszprém

Dijon
Basel
Zürich
LIECHTENSTEIN
Innsbruck
AUSTRIA
Graz
HUNGAR
Nagykanizsa

BERN
Luzern
SWITZERLAND
Klagenfurt
Maribor
Pécs

Lausanne
Bolzano
SLOVENIA
LJUBLJANA
ZAGREB
Osijek

Genève
Trento
Trieste
Karlovac
Slavonski
Brod

Milano
Verona
Venezia
Rijeka
CROATIA
Banja Luka
Tuzla

Grenoble
Torino
Pula
BOSNIA AND
HERZEGOVIN
Zenica
SARAJEVO

Genova
Bologna
Zadar

Nice
MONACO
Firenze
SAN MARINO
Ancona
Split
Mosta

eille
Livorno
Perugia
Dubrovnik

Bastia
ITALY
L'Aquila
Pescara

Corse
(Corsica)
(France)
Ajaccio
ROMA
Campobasso
Bari

Sea
Sardegne
(Sardinia)
(Italy)
Olbia
Sassari
Tyrrhenian
Sea
Napoli
Potenza

Adriatic Sea

© Collins Bartholomew Ltd 202

Mountain roads

Mountain Passes

Mountain passes can create difficult driving conditions, especially when towing or driving a large vehicle. You should only use them if you have a good power to weight ratio and in good driving conditions. If in any doubt as to your outfit's suitability or the weather then stick to motorway routes across mountain ranges if possible.

The tables on the following pages show which passes are not suitable for caravans, and those where caravans are not permitted. Motorhomes aren't usually included in these restrictions, but relatively low powered or very large vehicles should find an alternative route. Road signs at the foot of a pass may restrict access or offer advice, especially for heavy vehicles. Warning notices are usually posted at the foot of a pass if it is closed, or if chains or winter tyres must be used.

Caravanners are particularly sensitive to gradients and traffic/road conditions on passes. The maximum gradient is usually on the inside of bends but exercise caution if it is necessary to pull out. Always engage a lower gear before taking a hairpin bend and give priority to vehicles ascending. On mountain roads it is not the gradient which puts strain on

your car but the duration of the climb and the loss of power at high altitudes: approximately 10% at 915 metres (3,000 feet) and even more as you get higher. To minimise the risk of the engine overheating, take high passes in the cool part of the day, don't climb any faster than necessary and keep the engine pulling steadily. To prevent a radiator boiling, pull off the road safely, turn the heater and blower full on and switch off air conditioning. Keep an eye on water and oil levels. Never put cold water into a boiling radiator or it may crack. Check that the radiator is not obstructed by debris sucked up during the journey.

A long descent may result in overheating brakes; select the correct gear for the gradient and avoid excessive use of brakes. Even if you are using engine braking to control speed, caravan brakes may activate due to the overrun mechanism, which may cause them to overheat.

Travelling at altitude can cause a pressure build up in tanks and water pipes. You can prevent this by slightly opening the blade valve of your portable toilet and opening a tap a fraction.

Mountain Pass Information

The dates of opening and closing given in the following tables are approximate. Before attempting late afternoon or early morning journeys across borders, check their opening times as some borders close at night.

Gradients listed are the maximum which may be encountered on the pass and may be steeper at the inside of curves, particularly on older roads.

Gravel surfaces (such as dirt and stone chips) vary considerably; they can be dusty when dry and slippery when wet. Where known to exist, this type of surface has been noted.

In fine weather winter tyres or snow chains will only be required on very high passes, or for short periods in early or late summer. In winter conditions you will probably need to use them at altitudes exceeding 600 metres (approximately 2,000 feet).

Tunnels

Long tunnels are a much more commonly seen feature in Europe than in the UK, especially in mountainous regions. Tolls are usually charged for the use of major tunnels.

Dipped headlights are usually required by law even in well-lit tunnels, so switch them on before you enter. Snow chains, if used, must be removed before entering a tunnel in lay-bys provided for this purpose.

'No overtaking' signs must be strictly observed. Never cross central single or double lines. If overtaking is permitted in twin-tube tunnels, bear in mind that it is very easy to underestimate distances and speed once inside. In order to minimise the effects of exhaust fumes close all car windows and set the ventilator to circulate air, or operate the air conditioning system coupled with the recycled air option.

If you break down, try to reach the next lay-by and call for help from an emergency phone. If you cannot reach a lay-by, place your warning triangle at least 100 metres behind your vehicle. Modern tunnels have video surveillance systems to ensure prompt assistance in an emergency. Some tunnels can extend for miles and a high number of breakdowns are due to running out of fuel so make sure you have enough before entering the tunnel.

Tables and Maps

Much of the information contained in the following tables was originally supplied by The Automobile Association and other motoring and tourist organisations. The Caravan and Motorhome Club haven't checked this information and cannot accept responsibility for the accuracy or for errors or omissions to these tables.

The mountain passes, rail and road tunnels listed in the tables are shown on the following maps. Numbers and letters against each pass or tunnel in the tables correspond with the numbers and letters on the maps.

Converting Gradients

20% = 1 in 5	11% = 1 in 9
16% = 1 in 6	10% = 1 in 8
14% = 1 in 7	8% = 1 in 12
12% = 1 in 8	6% = 1 in 16

Abbreviations

MHV	Maximum height of vehicle
MLV	Maximum length of vehicle
MWV	Maximum width of vehicle
MWR	Minimum width of road
OC	Occasionally closed between dates
UC	Usually closed between dates
UO	Usually open between dates, although a fall of snow may obstruct the road for 24-48 hours.

Major Alpine Mountain Passes

Before using any of these passes, please read the advice at the beginning of this chapter.

Pass / Height In Metres (Feet)	From / To	Max gradient	Conditions and Comments
❶ Allos (France) 2250 (7382)	Colmars / *Barcelonnette*	10%	UC early Nov-early Jun. MWR 4m (13'1") Very winding, single track, mostly unguarded pass on D908; passing bays on southern slope; poor surface, MWV 1.8m (5'11"). Not recommended for caravans.
② Aravis (France) 1498 (4915)	La Clusaz / *Flumet*	9%	OC Dec-Mar. MWR 4m (13'1"). Fine scenery; D909, fairly easy road. Poor surface in parts on Chamonix side. Some single-line traffic.
③ Ballon d'Alsace (France) 1178 (3865)	Giromagny / *St Maurice-sur-Moselle*	11%	OC Dec-Mar. MWR 4m (13'1") Fairly straightforward ascent/descent; narrow in places; numerous bends. On road D465.
④ Bayard (France) 1248 (4094)	Chauffayer / *Gap*	14%	UO. MWR 6m (19'8") Part of the Route Napoléon N85. Fairly easy, steepest on the S side with several hairpin bends. Negotiable by caravans from N-to-S via D1075 (N75) and Col-de-la-Croix Haute, avoiding Gap.
❺ Brouis (France) 1279 (4196)	Nice / *Col-de-Tende*	12.50%	UO. MWR 6m (19'8") Good surface but many hairpins on D6204 (N204)/S20. Steep gradients on approaches. Height of tunnel at Col-de-Tende at the Italian border is 3.8m (12'4) Not recommended for caravans.
⑥ Bussang (France) 721 (2365)	Thann / *St Maurice-sur-Moselle*	7%	UO. MWR 4m (13'1") A very easy road (N66) over the Vosges; beautiful scenery.
⑦ Cabre (France) 1180 (3871)	Luc-en-Diois / *Aspres-sur-Buëch*	9%	UO. MWR 5.5m (18') An easy pleasant road (D93/D993), winding at Col-de-Cabre.
❽ Cayolle (France) 2326 (7631)	Barcelonnette / *Guillaumes*	10%	UC early Nov-early Jun. MWR 4m (13'1") Narrow, winding road (D902) with hairpin bends; poor surface, broken edges with steep drops. Long stretches of single-track road with passing places. Caravans prohibited.
⑨ Croix Haute (France) 1179 (3868)	Monestier-de-Clermont / *Aspres-sur-Buëch*	7%	UO on N75. MWR 5.5m (18') Well-engineered road (D1075/N75); several hairpin bends on N side.
⑩ Faucille (France) 1323 (4341)	Gex / *Morez*	10%	UO. MWR 5m (16'5") Fairly wide, winding road (N5) across the Jura mountains; negotiable by caravans but probably better route via La Cure-St Cergue-Nyon.

Before using any of these passes, please read the advice at the beginning of this chapter.

Pass Height in Metres (Feet)	From To	Max gradient	Conditions and Comments
⑪ **Forclaz** (Switzerland – France) 1527 (5010)	Martigny *Argentière*	8.50%	UO Forclaz; OC Montets Dec-early Apr. MWR 5m (16'5") MWV 2.5m (8'2") Good road over the pass and to the French border; long, hard climb out of Martigny; narrow and rough over Col-des-Montets on D1506 (N506).
⑫ **Galibier** (France) 2645 (8678)	La Grave *St Michel-de-Maurienne*	12.50%	UC Oct-Jun. MWR 3m (9'10") Mainly wide, well-surfaced road (D902) but unprotected and narrow over summit. From Col-du-Lautaret it rises over the Col-du-Telegraphe then 11 more hairpin bends. Ten hairpin bends on descent then 5km (3.1 miles) narrow and rough; easier in N to S direction. Limited parking at summit. Not recommended for caravans. (There is a single-track tunnel under the Galibier summit, controlled by traffic lights; caravans are not permitted).
⑬ **Gorges-du-Verdon** (France) 1032 (3386)	Castellane *Moustiers-Ste Marie*	9%	UO. MWR probably 5m (16'5") On road D952 over Col-d'Ayen and Col-d'Olivier. Moderate gradients but slow, narrow and winding. Poss heavy traffic.
⑭ **Iseran** (France) 2770 (9088)	Bourg-St Maurice *Lanslebourg*	11%	UC mid Oct-late Jun. MWR 4m (13'1") Second highest pass in the Alps on road D902. Well-graded with reasonable bends, average surface. Several unlit tunnels on N approach. Not recommended for caravans.
⑮ **Izoard** (France) 2360 (7743)	Guillestre *Briançon*	12.50%	UC late Oct-mid Jun. MWR 5m (16'5") Fine scenery. Winding, sometimes narrow road (D902) with many hairpin bends; care required at several unlit tunnels near Guillestre. Not recommended for caravans.
⑯ **Larche (della Maddalena)** (France – Italy) 1994 (6542)	La Condamine-Châtelard *Vinadio*	8.50%	OC Dec-Mar. MWR 3.5m (11'6") An easy, well-graded road (D900); long, steady ascent on French side, many hairpins on Italian side (S21). Fine scenery; ample parking at summit.
⑰ **Lautaret** (France) 2058 (6752)	Le Bourg-d'Oisans *Briançon*	12.50%	OC Dec-Mar. MWR 4m (13'1") Modern, evenly graded but winding road (D1091), and unguarded in places; very fine scenery; suitable for caravans but with care through narrow tunnels.
⑱ **Leques** (France) 1146 (3760)	Barrême *Castellane*	8%	UO. MWR 4m (13'1") On Route Napoléon (D4085). Light traffic; excellent surface; narrow in places on N ascent. S ascent has many hairpins.
⑲ **Mont Cenis** (France – Italy) 2083 (6834)	Lanslebourg *Susa*	12.50%	UC Nov-May. MWR 5m (16'5") Approach by industrial valley. An easy highway (D1006/S25) with mostly good surface; spectacular scenery; long descent into Italy with few stopping places. Alternative Fréjus road tunnel available.

Before using any of these passes, please read the advice at the beginning of this chapter.

Pass Height In Metres (Feet)	From To	Max gradient	Conditions and Comments
(20) **Montgenèvre** (France – Italy) 1850 (6070)	Briançon *Cesana-Torinese*	9%	UO. MWR 5m (16'5") An easy, modern road (N94/S24) with some tight hairpin bends on French side; road widened & tunnels improved on Italian side. Much used by lorries; may be necessary to travel at their speed and give way to oncoming large vehicles on hairpins.
Montets (See Forclaz)			
(21) **Morgins** (France – Switzerland) 1369 (4491)	Abondance *Monthey*	14%	UO. MWR 4m (13'1") A lesser used route (D22) through pleasant, forested countryside crossing French/Swiss border. Not recommended for caravans.
(22) **Petit St Bernard** (France – Italy) 2188 (7178)	Bourg-St Maurice *Pré-St Didier*	8.50%	UC mid Oct–Jun. MWR 5m (16'5") Outstanding scenery, but poor surface and unguarded broken edges near summit. Easiest from France (D1090); sharp hairpins on climb from Italy (S26). Vehicles towing another vehicle prohibited.
(23) **Restefond (La Bonette)** (France) 2802 (9193)	Barcelonnette *St Etienne-de-Tinée*	16%	UC Oct–Jun. MWR 3m (9'10") The highest pass in the Alps. Rebuilt, resurfaced road (D64) with rest area at summit – top loop narrow and unguarded. Winding with hairpin bends. Not recommended for caravans.
(24) **Schlucht** (France) 1139 (3737)	Gérardmer *Munster*	7%	UO. MWR 5m (16'5") An extremely picturesque route (D417) crossing the Vosges mountains, with easy, wide bends on the descent. Good surface.
(25) **Tenda (Tende)** Italy – France 1321 (4334)	Borgo-San Dalmazzo *Tende*	9%	UO. MWR 6m (19'8") Well-guarded, modern road (S20/ND6204) with several hairpin bends; road tunnel (height 3.8m) at summit narrow with poor road surface. Less steep on Italian side. Caravans prohibited during winter.
(26) **Vars** (France) 2109 (6919)	St Paul-sur-Ubaye *Guillestre*	9%	OC Dec–Mar. MWR 5m (16'5") Easy winding ascent and descent on D902 with 14 hairpin bends; good surface.

Technical information by courtesy of the Automobile Association. Additional update and amendments supplied by caravanners and tourers who have themselves used the passes and tunnels. The Caravan and Motorhome Club has not checked the information contained in these tables and cannot accept responsibility for their accuracy, or for any errors, omissions, or their effects.

The Alpine maps only show the major Alpine mountain passes for France. For other countries please refer to the Touring Europe guide.

Major Alpine Road Tunnels

Before using any of these tunnels, please read the advice at the beginning of this chapter.

	Tunnel	Route and Height above Sea Level	General Information and Comments
Ⓐ	Frejus (France – Italy) 12.8 km (8 miles)	**Modane to Bardonecchia** 1220m (4000')	MWR 9m (29'6"), tunnel height 4.3m (14'). Min/max speed 60/70 km/h (37/44 mph). Return tickets valid until midnight on 7th day after day of issue. Season tickets are available. Approach via A43 and D1006; heavy use by freight vehicles. Good surface on approach roads. Tolls charged. www.sftrf.fr
Ⓑ	Mont Blanc (France – Italy) 11.6 km (7.2 miles)	**Chamonix to Courmayeur** 1381m (4530')	MHV 4.7m (15'5"), MWV 6m (19'6") On N205 France, S26 (Italy). Max speed in tunnel 70 km/h (44 mph) – lower limits when exiting; min speed 50 km/h. Leave 150m between vehicles; ensure enough fuel for 30km. Return tickets valid until midnight on 7th day after issue. Season tickets are available. Tolls charged. www.tunnelmb.net
-	Ste Marie-aux-Mines (France) 6.8 km (4.25 miles)	**St Dié to Ste-Marie-aux Mines** 772m (2533')	At 7km, this is the longest road tunnel situated entirely in France. Also known as Maurice Lemaire Tunnel, through the Vosges in north-east France from Lusse on N159 to N59. Tolls charged. Alternate route via Col-de-Ste Marie on D459.

NOTES: *Dipped headlights should be used (unless stated otherwise) when travelling through road tunnels, even when the road appears to be well lit. In some countries police make spot checks and impose on-the-spot fines.*

During the winter wheel chains may be required on the approaches to some tunnels. These must not be used in tunnels and lay-bys are available for the removal and refitting of wheel chains.

Major Pyrenees Mountain Passes

Before using any of these passes, please read the advice at the beginning of this chapter.

	Pass Height In Metres (Feet)	From To	Max Gradient	Conditions and Comments
27	**Aubisque** (France) 1710 (5610)	Eaux Bonnes *Argelés-Gazost*	10%	UC mid Oct–Jun. MWR 3.5m (11'6") Very winding; continuous on D918 but easy ascent; descent including Col-d'Aubisque 1709m (5607 feet) and Col-du-Soulor 1450m (4757 feet); 8km (5 miles) of very narrow, rough, unguarded road with steep drop. Not recommended for caravans.
28	**Col-d'Haltza and Col-de-Burdincurutcheta** (France) 782 (2565) and 1135 (3724)	St Jean-Pied-de-Port *Larrau*	11%	UO. A narrow road (D18/D19) leading to Iraty skiing area. Narrow with some tight hairpin bends; rarely has central white line and stretches are unguarded. Not for the faint-hearted. Not recommended for caravans.
29	**Envalira** (France – Andorra) 2407 (7897)	Pas-de-la-Casa *Andorra*	12.5%	OC Nov–Apr. MWR 6m (19'8") Good road (N22/CG2) with wide bends on ascent and descent; fine views. MHV 3.5m (11'6") on N approach near l'Hospitalet. Early start rec in summer to avoid border delays. Envalira Tunnel (toll) reduces congestion and avoids highest part of pass. See *Pyrenean Road Tunnels* in this section.
30	**Ibañeta (Roncevalles)** (France – Spain) 1057 (3468)	St Jean-Pied-de-Port *Pamplona*	10%	UO. MWR 4m (13'1") Slow and winding, scenic route on N135.
31	**Peyresourde** (France) 1563 (5128)	Arreau *Bagnères-de-Luchon*	10%	UO. MWR 4m (13'1") D618 somewhat narrow with several hairpin bends, though not difficult. Not recommended for caravans.
32	**Port** (France) 1249 (4098)	Tarascon-sur-Ariege *Massat*	10%	OC Nov–Mar. MWR 4m (13'1") A fairly easy, scenic road (D618), but narrow on some bends.
33	**Portet-d'Aspet** (France) 1069 (3507)	Audressein *Fronsac*	14%	UO. MWR 3.5m (11'6") Approached from W by the easy Col-des-Ares and Col-de-Buret; well-engineered but narrow road (D618); care needed on hairpin bends. Not recommended for caravans.
34	**Pourtalet** (France – Spain) 1792 (5879)	Laruns *Biescas*	10%	UC late Oct–early Jun. MWR 3.5m (11'6") A fairly easy, unguarded road, but narrow in places. Easier from Spain (A136), steeper in France (D934). Not recommended for caravans.
35	**Puymorens** (France) 1915 (6283)	Ax-les-Thermes *Bourg-Madame*	10%	OC Nov–Apr. MWR 5.5m (18') MHV 3.5m (11'6") A generally easy, modern tarmac road (N20). Parallel toll road tunnel available. See *Pyrenean Road Tunnels* in this section.
36	**Quillane** (France) 1714 (5623)	Axat *Mont-Louis*	8.5%	OC Nov–Mar. MWR 5m (16'5") An easy, straightforward ascent and descent on D118.

Pass Height In Metres (Feet)	From To	Max Gradient	Conditions and Comments
(37) **Somport** (France – Spain) 1632 (5354)	Accous Jaca	10%	UO. MWR 3.5m (11'6") A favoured, old-established route; not particularly easy and narrow in places with many unguarded bends on French side (N134); excellent road on Spanish side (N330). Use of road tunnel advised – see *Pyrenean Road Tunnels* in this section. NB Visitors advise re-fuelling no later than Sabiñánigo when travelling south to north.
(38) **Tourmalet** (France) 2114 (6936)	Ste Marie-de-Campan *Luz-St Sauveur*	12.5%	UC Oct-mid Jun. MWR 4m (13'1") The highest French Pyrenean route (D918); approaches good, though winding, narrow in places and exacting over summit; sufficiently guarded. Rough surface & uneven edges on west side. Not recommended for caravans.

Major Pyrenees Road Tunnels

Tunnel	Route and Height Above Sea Level	General Information and Comments
(AA) **Bielsa** (France – Spain) 3.2 km (2 miles)	**Aragnouet to Bielsa** 1830m (6000')	Open 24 hours but possibly closed October-Easter. On French side (D173) generally good road surface but narrow with steep hairpin bends and steep gradients near summit. Often no middle white line. Spanish side (A138) has good width and is less steep and winding. Used by heavy vehicles. No tolls. Please note the tunnel may be undergoing repair works and as a result may be closed at certain times and on certain days.
(BB) **Envalira** (France – Spain via Andorra) 2.8 km (1.75 miles)	**Pas de la Casa to El Grau Roig** 2000m (6562')	Tunnel width 8.25m. On N22/CG2 France to Andorra. Tolls charged.
(CC) **Puymorens** (France –Spain) 4.8 km (2.9 miles)	**Ax-les-Thermes to Puigcerda** 1515m (4970')	MHV 3.5m (11'6"). Part of Puymorens pass on N20/E9. Tolls charged.
(DD) **Somport** (France – Spain) 8.6 km (5.3 miles)	**Urdos to Canfranc** 1116m (3661')	Tunnel height 4.55m (14'9"), width 10.5m (34'). Max speed 90 km/h (56 mph); leave 100m between vehicles. On N134 (France), N330 (Spain). No tolls.

Motorway
Motorway (Proposed)
Motorway Road Tunnel
Major/Main Roads
Minor Mountain Passes (suitability for caravans not checked)
Major Mountain Passes Suitable for Caravans
Major Mountain Passes Unsuitable for Caravans
Major Road Tunnels

0   10   20   30   40   50 km

These maps should be used in conjunction with the information in the Mountain Passes and Tunnels tables in this chapter.

2000m – +3000m
1000m – 2000m
100m – 1000m
0 – 100m

Keeping in Touch

Telephones

You might need to use a telephone at some point while you're away, whether to keep in touch with family and friends or call ahead to sites. Even if you don't plan to use one, it's best to make sure you have access to a phone in an emergency.

International Direct Dial Calls

Each country has a unique dialing code you must use if phoning from outside that country. You can find the international dialing code for any country by visiting www.thephonebook. bt.com. First dial the code then the local number. If the area code starts with a zero this should be omitted.

The international access code to dial the UK from anywhere in the world is 0044.

Ringing Tones

Ringing tones vary from country to country, so may sound very different to UK tones. Some ringing tones sound similar to error or engaged tones that you would hear on a UK line.

Using Mobile Phones

Mobile phones have an international calling option called 'roaming' which will automatically search for a local network when you switch your phone on. The EU abolished roaming charges in 2017, but you should contact your service provider to check if there are any charges for your tariff.

Storing telephone numbers in your phone's contact list in international format (i.e. use the prefix of +44 and omit the initial '0') will mean that your contacts will automatically work abroad as well as in the UK.

Global SIM Cards

If you're planning on travelling to more than one country consider buying a global SIM card. This will mean your mobile phone can operate on foreign mobile networks, which will be more cost effective than your service provider's roaming charges. For details of SIM cards available, speak to your service provider or visit www.0044.co.uk or www.globalsimcard.co.uk.

You may find it simpler to buy a SIM card or cheap 'pay-as-you-go' phone abroad if you plan to make a lot for local calls, e.g. to book campsites or restaurants. This may mean that you still have higher call charges for international calls (such as calling the UK).

Before buying a different SIM card, check with you provider whether your phone is locked against use on other networks.

Hands-Free

Legislation in Europe forbids the use of mobile or car phones while driving except when using hands-free equipment. In some European countries it is now also illegal to drive while wearing headphones or a headset - including hands-free kits.

If you are involved in an accident whilst driving and using a hand-held mobile phone, your insurance company may refuse to honour the claim.

Accessing the internet

If you have a phone plan that includes mobile data then you should be able to use this as normal within the European Union. Check with you network provider, and please note that this is likely to change if the UK leaves the EU.

Internet Access

Wi-Fi is available on lots of campsites in Europe, the cost may be an additional charge or included in your pitch fee. Most larger towns may have internet cafés or libraries where you can access the internet, however lots of fast food restaurants and coffee chains now offer free Wi-Fi for customers so you can get access for the price of a coffee or bite to eat.

Many people now use their smartphones for internet access. Another option is a dongle – a device which connects to your laptop to give internet access using a mobile phone network. While these methods are economical in the UK, overseas you will be charged data roaming charges which can run into hundreds or thousands of pounds depending on how much data you use. If you plan on using your smartphone or a dongle abroad speak to your service provider before you leave the UK to make sure you understand the costs or add an overseas data roaming package to your phone contract.

Making Calls from your Laptop

If you download Skype to your laptop you can make free calls to other Skype users anywhere in the world using a Wi-Fi connection. Rates for calls to non-Skype users (landline or mobile phone) are also very competitively-priced. You will need a computer with a microphone and speakers, and a webcam is handy too. It is also possible to download Skype to an internet-enabled mobile phone to take advantage of the same low-cost calls – see www.skype.com.

Club Together

If you want to chat to other members either at home or while you're away, you can do so on The Club's online community Club Together. You can ask questions and gather opinions on the forums at camc.com/together.

Radio and Television

The BBC World Service broadcasts radio programmes 24 hours a day worldwide and you can listen on a number of platforms: online, via satellite or cable, DRM digital radio, internet radio or mobile phone. You can find detailed information and programme schedules at www.bbc.co.uk/worldservice.

Whereas analogue television signals were switched off in the UK during 2012, no date has yet been fixed for the switch off of analogue radio signals.

Digital Terrestrial Television

As in the UK, television transmissions in most of Europe have been converted to digital. The UK's high definition transmission technology may be more advanced than any currently implemented or planned in Europe. This means that digital televisions intended for use in the UK might not be able to receive HD terrestrial signals in some countries.

Satellite Television

For English-language TV programmes the only realistic option is satellite, and satellite dishes are a common sight on campsites all over Europe. A satellite dish mounted on the caravan roof or clamped to a pole fixed to the drawbar, or one mounted on a foldable free-standing tripod, will provide good reception and minimal interference. Remember however that obstructions to the south east (such as

tall trees or even mountains) or heavy rain, can interrupt the signals. A specialist dealer will be able to advise you on the best way of mounting your dish. You will also need a satellite receiver and ideally a satellite-finding meter.

The main entertainment channels such as BBC1, ITV1 and Channel 4 can be difficult to pick up in mainland Europe as they are now being transmitted by new narrow-beam satellites. A 60cm dish should pick up these channels in most of France, Belgium and the Netherlands but as you travel further afield, you'll need a progressively larger dish. See www.satelliteforcaravans.co.uk (created and operated by a Club member) for the latest changes and developments, and for information on how to set up your equipment.

Medical Matters

Before You Travel

You can find country specific medical advice, including any vaccinations you may need, from www.nhs.uk/healthcareabroad, or speak to your GP surgery. For general enquiries about medical care abroad contact NHS England on 0300 311 22 33 or email england.contactus@nhs.uk.

If you have any pre-existing medical conditions you should check with your GP that you are fit to travel. Ask your doctor for a written summary of any medical problems and a list of medications , which is especially important for those who use controlled drugs or hypodermic syringes.

Always make sure that you have enough medication for the duration of your holiday and some extra in case your return is delayed. Take details of the generic name of any drugs you use, as brand names may be different abroad, your blood group and details of any allergies (translations may be useful for restaurants).

An emergency dental kit is available from High Street chemists which will allow you temporarily to restore a crown, bridge or filling or to dress a broken tooth until you can get to a dentist.

A good website to check before you travel is www.nathnac.org/travel which gives general health and safety advice, as well as highlighting potential health risks by country.

European Health Insurance Card

Before leaving home apply for a European Health Insurance Card (EHIC). British residents temporarily visiting another EU country are entitled to receive state-provided emergency treatment during their stay on the same terms as residents of those countries, but you must have a valid EHIC to claim these services.

To apply for your EHIC visit www.ehic.org.uk, call 0300 330 1350 or pick up an application form from a post office. An EHIC is required by each family member, with children under 16 included in a parent or guardian's application. The EHIC is free of charge, is valid for up to five years and can be renewed up to six months before its expiry date. Before you travel remember to check that your EHIC is still valid.

An EHIC is not a substitute for travel insurance and it is strongly recommended that you arrange full travel insurance before leaving home regardless of the cover provided by your EHIC. Some insurance companies require you to have an EHIC and some will waive the policy excess if an EHIC has been used.

If your EHIC is stolen or lost while you are abroad contact 0044 191 2127500 for help. If you experience difficulties in getting your EHIC accepted, telephone the Department for Work & Pensions for assistance on the overseas healthcare team line 0044 (0)191 218 1999 between 8am to 5pm Monday to Friday. Residents of the Republic of Ireland, the Isle of Man and Channel Islands, should check with their own health authorities about reciprocal arrangements with other countries.

Travel Insurance

Despite having an EHIC you may incur high medical costs if you fall ill or have an accident. The cost of bringing a person back to the UK in the event of illness or death is never covered by the EHIC.

Separate additional travel insurance adequate for your destination is essential, such as the Club's Red Pennant Overseas Holiday Insurance – see camc.com/redpennant.

First Aid

A first aid kit containing at least the basic requirements is an essential item, and in some countries it is compulsory to carry one in your vehicle (see the Essential Equipment Table in the chapter Motoring – Equipment). Kits should contain items such as sterile pads, assorted dressings, bandages and plasters, antiseptic wipes or cream, cotton wool, scissors, eye bath and tweezers. Also make sure you carry something for upset stomachs, painkillers and an antihistamine in case of hay fever or mild allergic reactions.

If you're travelling to remote areas then you may find it useful to carry a good first aid manual. The British Red Cross publishes a comprehensive First Aid Manual in conjunction with St John Ambulance and St Andrew's Ambulance Association.

Accidents and Emergencies

If you are involved in or witness a road accident the police may want to question you about it. If possible take photographs or make sketches of the scene, and write a few notes about what happened as it may be more difficult to remember the details at a later date.

For sports activities such as skiing and mountaineering, travel insurance must include provision for covering the cost of mountain and helicopter rescue. Visitors to the Savoie and Haute-Savoie areas should be aware that an accident or illness may result in a transfer to Switzerland for hospital treatment. There is a reciprocal healthcare agreement for British citizens visiting Switzerland but you will be required to pay the full costs of treatment and afterwards apply for a refund.

Sun Protection

Never under-estimate how ill exposure to the sun can make you. If you are not used to the heat it is very easy to fall victim to heat exhaustion or heat stroke. Avoid sitting in the sun between 11am and 3pm and cover your head if sitting or walking in the sun. Use a high sun protection factor (SPF) and re-apply frequently. Make sure you drink plenty of fluids.

Tick-Borne Encephalitis (TBE) and Lyme Disease

Hikers and outdoor sports enthusiasts planning trips to forested, rural areas should be aware of tick-borne encephalitis, which is transmitted by the bite of an infected tick. If you think you may be at risk, seek medical advice on prevention and immunisation before you leave the UK.

There is no vaccine against Lyme disease, an equally serious tick-borne infection, which, if left untreated, can attack the nervous system and joints. You can minimise the risk by using an insect repellent containing DEET, wearing long sleeves and long trousers, and checking for ticks after outdoor activity.

Avoid unpasteurised dairy products in risk areas. See www.tickalert.org or telephone 01943 468010 for more information.

Water and food

Water from mains supplies throughout Europe is generally safe, but may be treated with chemicals which make it taste different to tap water in the UK. If in any doubt, always drink bottled water or boil it before drinking.

Food poisoning is potential anywhere, and a complete change of diet may upset your stomach as well. In hot conditions avoid any food that hasn't been refrigerated or hot food that has been left to cool. Be sensible about the food that you eat – don't eat unpasteurised or undercooked food and if you aren't sure about the freshness of meat or seafood then it is best avoided.

Returning Home

If you become ill on your return home tell your doctor that you have been abroad and which countries you have visited. Even if you have received medical treatment in another country, always consult your doctor if you have been bitten or scratched by an animal while on holiday. If you were given any medicines in another country, it may be illegal to bring them back into the UK. If in doubt, declare them at Customs when you return.

Electricity and Gas

Electricity

General Advice

The voltage for mains electricity is 230V across the EU, but varying degrees of 'acceptable tolerance' mean you may find variations in the actual voltage. Most appliances sold in the UK are 220-240V so should work correctly. However, some high-powered equipment, such as microwave ovens, may not function well – check your instruction manual for any specific instructions. Appliances marked with 'CE' have been designed to meet the requirements of relevant European directives.

The table below gives an approximate idea of which appliances can be used based on the amperage which is being supplied (although not all appliances should be used at the same time). You can work it out more accurately by making a note of the wattage of each appliance in your caravan. The wattages given are based on appliances designed for use in caravans and motorhomes. Household kettles, for example, have at least a 2000W element. Each caravan circuit will also have a maximum amp rating which should not be exceeded.

Electrical Connections – EN60309-2 (CEE17)

EN60309-2 (formerly known as CEE17) is the European Standard for all newly fitted connectors. Most sites should now have these connectors, however there is no requirement to replace connectors which were installed before this was standardised so you may still find some sites where your UK 3 pin connector doesn't fit. For this reason it is a good idea

Amps	Wattage (Approx)	Fridge	Battery Charger	Air Conditioning	LCD TV	Water Heater	Kettle (750W)	Heater (1kW)
2	400	✓	✓					
4	900	✓	✓		✓	✓		
6	1300	✓	✓	*	✓	✓	✓	
8	1800	✓	✓	✓**	✓	✓	✓	✓**
10	2300	✓	✓	✓**	✓	✓	✓	✓**
16	3600	✓	✓	✓	✓	✓	✓	✓**

*	Usage possible, depending on wattage of appliance in question
**	Not to be used at the same time as other high-wattage equipment

to carry a 2-pin adapter. If you are already on site and find your connector doesn't fit, ask campsite staff to borrow or hire an adaptor. You may still encounter a poor electrical supply on site even with an EN60309-2 connection.

If the campsite does not have a modern EN60309-2 (CEE17) supply, ask to see the electrical protection for the socket outlet. If there is a device marked with IDn = 30mA, then the risk is minimised.

Hooking Up to the Mains

Connection should always be made in the following order:

- Check your outfit isolating switch is at 'off'.
- Uncoil the connecting cable from the drum. A coiled cable with current flowing through it may overheat. Take your cable and insert the connector (female end) into your outfit inlet.
- Insert the plug (male end) into the site outlet socket.
- Switch outfit isolating switch to 'on'.
- Use a polarity tester in one of the 13A sockets in the outfit to check all connections are correctly wired. Never leave it in the socket. Some caravans have these devices built in as standard.

It is recommended that the supply is not used if the polarity is incorrect (see Reversed Polarity).

Warnings:

If you are in any doubt of the safety of the system, if you don't receive electricity once connected or if the supply stops then contact the site staff.

If the fault is found to be with your outfit then call a qualified electrician rather than trying to fix the problem yourself.

To ensure your safety you should never use an electrical system which you can't confirm to be safe. Use a mains tester such as the one shown on the right to test the electrical supply.

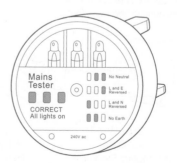

Always check that a proper earth connection exists before using the electrics. Please note that these testers may not pick up all earth faults so if there is any doubt as to the integrity of the earth system do not use the electrical supply.

Disconnection

- Switch your outfit isolating switch to 'off'.
- At the site supply socket withdraw the plug.
- Disconnect the cable from your outfit.

Motorhomes – if leaving your pitch during the day, don't leave your mains cable plugged into the site supply, as this creates a hazard if the exposed live connections in the plug are touched or if the cable is not seen during grass-cutting.

Reversed Polarity

Even if the site connector meets European Standard EN60309-2 (CEE17), British caravanners are still likely to encounter the problem known as reversed polarity. This is where the site supply 'live' line connects to the outfit's 'neutral' and vice versa. You should always check the polarity immediately on connection, using a polarity tester available from caravan accessory shops. If polarity is reversed the caravan mains electricity should not be used. Try using another nearby socket instead. Frequent travellers to the Continent can make up an adaptor themselves, or ask an electrician to make one for you, with the live

and neutral wires reversed. Using a reversed polarity socket will probably not affect how an electrical appliance works, however your protection is greatly reduced. For example, a lamp socket may still be live as you touch it while replacing a blown bulb, even if the light switch is turned off.

Shaver Sockets

Most campsites provide shaver sockets with a voltage of 220V or 110V. Using an incorrect voltage may cause the shaver to become hot or break. The 2-pin adaptor available in the UK may not fit Continental sockets so it is advisable to buy 2-pin adaptors on the Continent. Many modern shavers will work on a range of voltages which make them suitable for travelling abroad. Check you instruction manual to see if this is the case.

Gas

General Advice

Gas usage can be difficult to predict as so many factors, such as temperature and how often you eat out, can affect the amount you need. As a rough guide allow 0.45kg of gas a day for normal summer usage.

With the exception of Campingaz, LPG cylinders normally available in the UK cannot be exchanged abroad. If possible, take enough gas with you and bring back the empty

Site hooking up adaptor

Adaptateur de prise au site (secteur)
Campingplatz-anschluss (netz)

Extension lead to outfit

Câble de rallonge à la caravane
Verlâengerungskabel zum wohnwagen

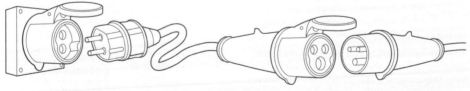

Site outlet
Prise du site
Campingplatz-Steckdose

Mains adaptor
Adaptateur Secteur
Netzanschlußstacker

16A 230V AC

cylinders. Always check how many you can take with you as ferry and tunnel operators may restrict the number of cylinders you are permitted to carry for safety reasons.

The full range of Campingaz cylinders is widely available from large supermarkets and hypermarkets, although at the end of the holiday season stocks may be low. Other popular brands of gas are Primagaz, Butagaz, Totalgaz and Le Cube. A loan deposit is required and if you are buying a cylinder for the first time you may also need to buy the appropriate regulator or adaptor hose.

If you are touring in cold weather conditions use propane gas instead of butane. Many other brands of gas are available in different countries and, as long as you have the correct regulator, adaptor and hose and the cylinders fit in your gas locker these local brands can also be used.

Gas cylinders are now standardised with a pressure of 30mbar for both butane and propane within the EU. On UK-specification caravans and motorhomes (2004 models and later) a 30mbar regulator suited to both propane and butane use is fitted to the bulkhead of the gas locker. This is connected to the cylinder with a connecting hose (and

sometimes an adaptor) to suit different brands or types of gas. Older outfits and some foreign-built ones may use a cylinder-mounted regulator, which may need to be changed to suit different brands or types of gas.

Warnings:

- Refilling gas cylinders intended to be exchanged is against the law in most countries, however you may still find that some sites and dealers will offer to refill cylinders for you. Never take them up on this service as it can be dangerous; the cylinders haven't been designed for user-refilling and it is possible to overfill them with catastrophic consequences.

- Regular servicing of gas appliances is important as a faulty appliance can emit carbon monoxide, which could prove fatal. Check your vehicle or appliance handbook for service recommendations.

- Never use a hob or oven as a space heater.

The Caravan and Motorhome Club publishes a range of technical leaflets for its members including detailed advice on the use of electricity and gas – you can request copies or see camc.com/advice-and-training.

Safety and security

EU countries have good legislation in place to protect your safety wherever possible. However accidents and crime will still occur and taking sensible precautions can help to minimise your risk of being involved.

Beaches, Lakes and Rivers

Check for any warning signs or flags before you swim and ensure that you know what they mean. Check the depth of water before diving and avoid diving or jumping into murky water as submerged objects may not be visible. Familiarise yourself with the location of safety apparatus and/or lifeguards.

Use only the designated areas for swimming, watersports and boating and always use life jackets where appropriate. Watch out for tides, undertows, currents and wind strength and direction before swimming in the sea. This applies in particular when using inflatables, windsurfing equipment, body boards, kayaks or sailing boats. Sudden changes of wave and weather conditions combined with fast tides and currents are particularly dangerous.

Campsite Safety

Once you've settled in, take a walk around the site to familiarise yourself with its layout and locate the nearest safety equipment. Ensure that children know their way around and where your pitch is.

Natural disasters are rare, but always think about what could happen. A combination of heavy rain and a riverside pitch could lead to flash flooding, for example, so make yourself aware of site evacuation procedures.

Be aware of sources of electricity and cabling on and around your pitch – electrical safety might not be up to the same standards as in the UK.

Poison for rodent control is sometimes used on sites or surrounding farmland. Warning notices are not always posted and you are strongly advised to check if staying on a rural site with dogs or children.

Incidents of theft on campsites are rare but when leaving your caravan unattended make sure you lock all doors and shut windows. Conceal valuables from sight and lock up any bicycles.

Children

Watch out for children as you drive around the site and don't exceed walking pace.

Children's play areas are generally unsupervised, so check which are suitable for your children's ages and abilities. Read and respect the displayed rules. Remember it is your responsibility to supervise your children at all times.

Be aware of any campsite rules concerning ball games or use of play equipment, such as roller blades and skateboards. When your children attend organised activities, arrange when and where to meet afterwards. You should never leave children alone inside a caravan.

Fire

Fire prevention is important on sites, as fire can spread quickly between outfits. Certain areas of southern Europe experience severe water shortages in summer months leading to an increased fire risk. This may result in some local authorities imposing restrictions at short notice on the use of barbecues and open flames.

Fires can be a regular occurrence in forested areas, especially along the Mediterranean coast during summer months. They are generally extinguished quickly and efficiently but short term evacuations are sometimes necessary. If visiting forested areas familiarise yourself with local emergency procedures in the event of fire. Never use paraffin or gas heaters inside your caravan. Gas heaters should only be fitted when air is taken from outside

the caravan. Don't change your gas cylinder inside the caravan. If you smell gas turn off the cylinder immediately, extinguish all naked flames and seek professional help.

Make sure you know where the fire points and telephones are on site and know the site fire drill. Make sure everyone in your party knows how to call the emergency services.

Where site rules permit the use of barbecues, take the following precautions to prevent fire:

- Never locate a barbecue near trees or hedges.
- Have a bucket of water to hand in case of sparks.
- Only use recommended fire-lighting materials.
- Don't leave a barbecue unattended when lit and dispose of hot ash safely.
- Never take a barbecue into an enclosed area or awning – even when cooling they continue to release carbon monoxide which can lead to fatal poisoning.

Swimming Pools

Familiarize yourself with the pool area before you venture in for a swim - check the pool layout and identify shallow and deep ends and the location of safety equipment. Check the

gradient of the pool bottom as pools which shelve off sharply can catch weak or non-swimmers unawares.

Never dive or jump into a pool without knowing the depth – if there is a no diving rule it usually means the pool isn't deep enough for safe diving.

For pools with a supervisor or lifeguard, note any times or dates when the pool is not supervised. Read safety notices and rules posted around the pool.

On the Road

Don't leave valuables on view in cars or caravans, even if they are locked. Make sure items on roof racks or cycle carriers are locked securely.

Near to ports British owned cars have been targeted by thieves, both while parked and on the move, e.g. by flagging drivers down or indicating that a vehicle has a flat tyre. If you stop in such circumstances be wary of anyone offering help, ensure that car keys are not left in the ignition and that vehicle doors are locked while you investigate.

Always keep car doors locked and windows closed when driving in populated areas. Beware of a 'snatch' through open car windows at traffic lights, filling stations or in traffic jams. When driving through towns and cities keep your doors locked. Keep handbags, valuables and documents out of sight at all times.

If flagged down by another motorist for whatever reason, take care that your own car is locked and windows closed while you check outside, even if someone is left inside.

Be particularly careful on long, empty stretches of motorway and when you stop for fuel. Even if the people flagging you down appear to be officials (e.g. wearing yellow reflective jackets or dark, 'uniform-type' clothing) lock your vehicle doors. They may appear to be friendly and helpful, but could be opportunistic thieves. Have a mobile phone to hand and, if necessary, be seen to use it.

Road accidents are a increased risk in some countries where traffic laws may be inadequately enforced, roads may be poorly maintained, road signs and lighting inadequate, and driving standards poor. It's a good idea to keep a fully-charged mobile phone with you in your car with the number of your breakdown organisation saved into it. On your return to the UK there are increasing issues with migrants attempting to stowaway in vehicles, especially if you're travelling through Calais.

The UK government have issued the following instructions to prevent people entering the UK illegally:

- Where possible all vehicle doors and storage compartments should be fitted with locks.

- All locks must be engaged when the vehicle is stationary or unattended.

- Immediately before boarding your ferry or train check that the locks on your vehicle haven't been compromised.

- If you have any reason to suspect someone may have accessed your outfit speak to border control staff or call the police. Do not board the ferry or train or you may be liable for a fine of up to £2000.

Overnight Stops

Overnight stops should always be at campsites and not at motorway service areas, ferry terminal car parks, petrol station forecourts or isolated 'aires de services' on motorways where robberies are occasionally reported. If you decide to use these areas for a rest then take appropriate precautions, for example, shutting all windows, securing locks and making a thorough external check of your vehicle(s) before departing. Safeguard your property, e.g. handbags, while out of the caravan and beware of approaches by strangers.

For a safer place to take a break, there is a wide network of 'Aires de Services' in cities, towns and villages across Europe, many specifically for motorhomes with good security and overnight facilities. They are often less isolated and therefore safer than the motorway aires. It is rare that you will be the only vehicle staying on such areas, but take sensible precautions and trust your instincts.

Personal Security

Petty crime happens all over the world, including in the UK; however as a tourist you are more vulnerable to it. This shouldn't stop you from exploring new horizons, but there are a few sensible precautions you can take to minimise the risk.

- Leave valuables and jewellery at home. If you do take them, fit a small safe in your caravan or lock them in the boot of your car. Don't leave money or valuables in a car glovebox or on view. Don't leave bags in full view when sitting outside at cafés or restaurants, or leave valuables unattended on the beach.

- When walking be security-conscious. Avoid unlit streets at night, walk away from the kerb edge and carry handbags or shoulder bags on the side away from the kerb. The less of a tourist you appear, the less of a target you are.

- Keep a note of your holiday insurance details and emergency telephone numbers in more than one place, in case the bag or vehicle containing them is stolen.

- Beware of pickpockets in crowded areas, at tourist attractions and in cities. Be especially aware when using public transport in cities.

- Be cautious of bogus plain-clothes policemen who may ask to see your foreign currency or credit cards and passport. If approached, decline to show your money or to hand over your passport but ask for credentials and offer instead to go to the nearest police station.

- Laws and punishment vary from country to country so make yourself aware of anything which may affect you before you travel. Be especially careful on laws involving alcohol consumption (such as drinking in public areas), and never buy or use illegal drugs abroad.

- Respect customs regulations - smuggling is a serious offence and can carry heavy penalties. Do not carry parcels or luggage through customs for other people and never cross borders with people you do not know in your vehicle, such as hitchhikers.

The Foreign & Commonwealth Office produces a range of material to advise and inform British citizens travelling abroad about issues affecting their safety - www.gov.uk/foreign-travel-advice has country specific guides.

Money Security

We would rarely walk around at home carrying large amounts of cash, but as you may not have the usual access to bank accounts and credit cards you are more likely to do so on holiday. You are also less likely to have the same degree of security when online banking as you would in your own home. Take the following precautions to keep your money safe:

- Carry only the minimum amount of cash and don't rely on one person to carry everything. Never carry a wallet in your back pocket. Concealed money belts are the most secure way to carry cash and passports.

- Keep a separate note of bank account and credit/debit card numbers. Carry your credit card issuer/bank's 24-hour UK contact number with you.

- Be careful when using cash machines (ATMs) – try to use a machine in an area with high footfall and don't allow yourself to be distracted. Put your cash away before moving away from the cash machine.

- Always guard your PIN number, both at cash machines and when using your card to pay in shops and restaurants. Never let your card out of your sight while paying.

- If using internet banking do not leave the PC or mobile device unattended and make sure you log out fully at the end of the session.

Winter Sports

If you are planning a skiing or snowboarding holiday you should research the safety advice for your destination before you travel. A good starting point may be the relevant embassy for the country you're visiting. All safety instructions should be followed meticulously given the dangers of avalanches in some areas.

The Ski Club of Great Britain offer a lot of advice for anyone taking to the mountains, visit their website www.skiclub.co.uk to pick up some useful safety tips and advice on which resorts are suitable for different skill levels.

British Consular Services Abroad

British Embassy and Consular staff offer practical advice, assistance and support to British travellers abroad. They can, for example, issue replacement passports, help Britons who have been the victims of crime, contact relatives and friends in the event of an accident, illness or death, provide information about transferring funds and provide details of local lawyers, doctors and interpreters. But there are limits to their powers and a British Consul cannot, for example, give legal advice, intervene in court proceedings, put up bail, pay for legal or medical bills, or for funerals or the repatriation of bodies, or undertake work more properly done by banks, motoring organisations and travel insurers.

If you are charged with a serious offence, insist on the British Consul being informed. You will be contacted as soon as possible by a Consular Officer who can advise on local procedures, provide access to lawyers and insist that you are treated as well as nationals of the country which is holding you. However, they cannot get you released as a matter of course.

British and Irish embassy contact details can be found in the Country Introduction chapters.

British Embassy in France

35 RUE DU FAUBOURG ST HONORE
75363 PARIS CEDEX 08 PARIS
Tel: 01 44 51 31 00
www.ukinfrance.fco.gov.uk

There are also Consulates in Bordeaux, Lille, Lyon and Marseilles.

Irish Embassy in France

12 AVENUE FOCH, 75116 PARIS
Tel: 01 44 17 67 00
www.embassyofireland.fr

There are also Irish Consulates-General/Consulates in Cannes, Cherbourg, Lyon and Monaco.

For Consular help while in Andorra contact the British Consulate-General in Barcelona:

AVDA DIAGNOL 477-13, 08036 BARCELONA

Tel: 00 34 902 109 356

www.ukinspain.fco.gov.uk

Campsites

The quantity and variety of sites across France means you're sure to find one that suits your needs – from full facilities and entertainment to quiet rural retreats. If you haven't previously toured outside of the UK you may notice some differences, such as pitches being smaller or closer together.

Camping in France

There are approximately 10,400 campsites throughout France classified from 1 to 5 stars, including many small farm sites. Higher rated sites often have a wider range of facilities available. All classified sites must display their classification, current charges, capacity and site regulations at the site entrance.

Casual/wild camping is prohibited in many state forests, national parks and nature reserves, and in all public or private forests in the départements of Landes and Gironde, along the Mediterranean coast including the Camargue, parts of the Atlantic and Brittany coasts, Versailles and Paris, and along areas of coast that are covered by spring tides.

Booking a Campsite

To save the hassle of arriving to find a site full it is best to book in advance, especially in high season. If you don't book ahead arrive no later than 4pm (earlier at popular resorts) to secure a pitch, after this time sites fill up quickly. You also need to allow time to find another campsite if your first choice is fully booked.

You can often book directly via a campsite's website using a credit or debit card to pay a deposit if required. Please be aware that some sites regard the deposit as a booking or admin fee and will not deduct the amount from your final bill.

Overseas Travel Service

The Club's Overseas Travel Service offers members an site booking service on over 250 campsites in Europe. Full details of these sites plus information on ferry special offers and Red Pennant Overseas Holiday Insurance can be found in the Club's Venture Abroad brochure – call 01342 327410 to request a copy or visit camc.com/overseas.

Overseas Site Booking Service sites show heir booking code (e.g. G04) at the end of their listing. We can't make reservations for any other campsites in this guide.

Overseas Site Night Vouchers

The Club offers Overseas Site Night Vouchers which can be used at over 300 Club inspected sites in Europe. The vouchers cost £21.95 each (2019 cost) and you'll need one voucher per night to stay on a site in low season and two per night in high season. You'll also be eligible for the Club's special packaged ferry rates when you're buying vouchers. For more information and the view the voucher terms and conditions visit www.camc.com/overseasoffers or call 01342 327 410.

Caravan Storage

Storing your caravan on a site in Europe can be a great way to avoid a long tow and to save on ferry and fuel costs. Before you leave your caravan in storage always check whether your insurance covers this, as many policies don't.

If you aren't covered then look for a specialist policy - Towergate Insurance (tel: 01242 538431 or www.towergateinsurance.co.uk) or Look Insurance (tel: 0333 777 3035 or www.lookinsuranceservices.co.uk) both offer insurance policies for caravans stored abroad.

Facilities and Site Description

All of the site facilities shown in the site listings of this guide have been taken from member reports, as have the comments at the end of each site entry. Please remember that opinions and expectations can differ significantly from one person to the next.

The year of report is shown at the end of each site listing – sites which haven't been reported on for a few years may have had significant changes to their prices, facilities, and opening dates. It is always best to check any specific details you need to know before travelling by contacting the site or looking at their website.

Sanitary Facilities

Facilities normally include toilet and shower blocks with shower cubicles, wash basins and razor sockets. In site listings the abbreviation 'wc' indicates that the site has the kind of toilets we are used to in the UK (pedestal style). Some sites have footplate style toilets and, where this is known, you will see the abbreviation 'cont', i.e. continental. European sites do not always provide sink plugs, toilet paper or soap so take them with you.

Waste Disposal

Site entries show (when known) where a campsite has a chemical disposal and/or a motorhome service point, which is assumed to include a waste (grey) water dump station and toilet cassette-emptying point. You may find fewer waste water disposal facilities as on the continent more people use the site sanitary blocks rather than their own facilities.

Chemical disposal points may be fixed at a high level requiring you to lift cassettes in order to empty them. Disposal may simply be down a toilet. Wastemaster-style emptying points are not very common in Europe. Formaldehyde chemical cleaning products are banned in many countries. In Germany the 'Blue Angel' (Blaue Engel) Standard, and in the Netherlands the 'Milieukeur' Standard, indicates that the product has good environmental credentials.

Finding a Campsite

Directions are given for all campsites listed in this guide and most listings also include GPS co-ordinates. Full street addresses are also given where available. The directions have been supplied by member reports and haven't been checked in detail by the Club. For information about using satellite navigation to find a site see the Motoring Equipment section.

Overnight Stops

Many towns and villages in France provide dedicated overnight or short stay areas specifically for motorhomes, usually with security, electricity, water and waste facilities. These are known as 'Aires de Services' and are usually well signposted with a motorhome icon. Aires vary from region to region. Some are free of charge while others charge a small fee. Facilities also vary - some will have electrics available as well as other facilities, whilst others will just provide a basic parking area.

There are guidebooks available which list just these overnight stops, Vicarious Books publish an English guide to Aires including directions and GPS co-ordinates. Contact 0131 208 3333 or visit their website www.vicarious-shop.com.

Many campsites in popular tourist resorts have separate overnight areas of hardstanding with appropriate facilities, often adjacent to, or just outside, the main campsite area. Look for the 'Stop Accueil Camping-Car' sign.

Motorhomes are also welcome to park overnight free of charge at approximately 1,500 vineyards and farms throughout France through an organisation called France Passion. Membership is open to motorhomes only - write to France Passion, BP 57, 84202 Carpentras. Alternatively join online at www.france-passion.com. It is illegal to spend the night at the roadside.

For security reasons you shouldn't spend the night on petrol station service areas, ferry terminal car parks or isolated 'Aires de Repos' or 'Aires de Services' along motorways.

Municipal Campsites

Municipal sites are found in towns and villages all over France. Once very basic, many have been improved in recent years and now offer a wider range of facilities. They can usually be booked in advance through the local town hall or tourism office. When approaching a town you may find that municipal sites are not always named and signposts may simply state 'Camping' or show a tent or caravan symbol. Most municipal sites are clean, well-run and reasonably priced but security may be basic.

These sites may be used by seasonal workers, market traders and travellers in low season and as a result there may be restrictions or very high charges for some types of outfits (such as twin axles) in order to discourage this. If you may be affected check for any restrictions when you book.

Naturist Campsites

Some naturist sites are included in this guide and are shown with the word 'naturist' after their site name. Those marked 'part naturist' have separate areas for naturists. Visitors to naturist sites aged 16 and over usually require an INF card or Naturist Licence - covered by membership of British Naturism (tel 01604 620361, visit www.british-naturism.org.uk or email headoffice@british-naturism.org.uk) or you can apply for a licence on arrival at any recognised naturist site (a passport-size photograph is required).

Opening Dates and times

Opening dates should always be taken with a pinch of salt - including those given in this guide. Sites may close without notice due to refurbishment work, a lack of visitors or bad weather. Outside the high season it is always best to contact campsites in advance, even if the site advertises itself as open all year.

Following incidents in recent years some authorities in southern France have introduced tighter regulations for sites liable to flooding, including limiting opening dates from April/May until August/September in some areas.

Most sites will close their gates or barriers overnight – if you are planning to arrive late or are delayed on your journey you should call ahead to make sure you will be able to gain access to the site. There may be a late arrivals area outside of the barriers where you can pitch overnight. Motorhomers should also consider barrier closing times if leaving site in your vehicle for the evening.

Check out time is usually between 10am and 12 noon – speak to the site staff if you need to leave very early to make sure you can check out on departure. Sites may also close for an extended lunch break, so if you're planning to arrive or check out around lunchtime check that the office will be open.

Pets on Campsites

Dogs are welcome on many sites, although you may have to prove that all of their vaccinations are up to date before they are allowed onto the site. Certain breeds of dogs are banned in some countries and other breeds will need to be muzzled and kept on a lead at all times. A list of breeds with restrictions by country can be found at camc.com/pets.

Sites usually charge for dogs and may limit the number allowed per pitch. On arrival make yourself aware of site rules regarding dogs, such as keeping them on a lead, muzzling them or not leaving them unattended in your outfit. In popular tourist areas local regulations may ban dogs from beaches during the summer. Some dogs may find it difficult to cope with changes in climate. Also watch out for diseases transmitted by ticks, caterpillars, mosquitoes or sandflies - dogs from the UK will have no natural resistance. Consult your vet about preventative treatment before you travel.

Visitors to parts of central France should be aware of the danger of Pine Processionary Caterpillars from mid-winter to late spring. Dogs should be kept away from pine trees if possible or fitted with a muzzle that prevents the nose and mouth from touching the ground. This will also protect against poisoned bait sometimes used by farmers and hunters.

In the event that your pet is taken ill abroad a campsite should have information about local vets.

Dogs are required to wear a collar identifying their owners at all times. If your dog goes missing, report the matter to the local police and the local animal welfare organisation.

See the Documents section of this book for more information about the Pet Travel Scheme.

Prices and Payment

Prices per night (for an outfit and two adults) are shown in the site entries. If you stay on site after midday you may be charged for an extra day. Many campsites have a minimum amount for credit card transactions, meaning they can't be used to pay for overnight or short stays. Check which payment methods are accepted when you check in.

Sites with automatic barriers may ask for a deposit for a swipe card or fob to operate it.

Extra charges may apply for the use of facilities such as swimming pools, showers or laundry rooms. You may also be charged extra for dogs, Wi-Fi, tents and extra cars.

A tourist tax, eco tax and/or rubbish tax may be imposed by local authorities in some European countries. VAT may also be added to your campsite fees.

Registering on Arrival

Local authority requirements mean you will usually have to produce an identity document on arrival, which will be held by the site until you check out. If you don't want to leave your passport with reception most sites accept a document such as the Camping Key Europe (CKE) or Camping Card International (CCI).

CKE are available for Club members to purchase by calling 01342 336633 or are free to members if you take out the 'motoring' level of cover from the Club's Red Pennant Overseas Holiday Insurance.

General Advice

If you've visiting a new site ask to take a look around the site and facilities before booking in. Riverside pitches can be very scenic but keep an eye on the water level; in periods of heavy rain this may rise rapidly.

Speed limits on campsites are usually restricted to 10 km/h (6 mph). You may be asked to park your car in a separate area away from your caravan, particularly in the high season.

The use of the term 'statics' in the campsite reports in this guide may to any long-term accommodation on site, such as seasonal pitches, chalets, cottages, fixed tents and cabins, as well as static caravans.

Complaints

If you want to make a complaint about a site issue, take it up with site staff or owners at the time in order to give them the opportunity to rectify the problem during your stay.

The Caravan and Motorhome Club has no control or influence over day to day campsite operations or administration of the sites listed in this guide. Therefore we aren't able to intervene in any dispute you should have with a campsite, unless the booking has been made through our Advanced Booking Service - see listings that have a booking code at the end of the entry (e.g. G04).

Campsite Groups

Across Europe there are many campsite groups or chains with sites in various locations.

You will generally find that group sites will be consistent in their format and the quality and variety of facilities they offer. If you liked one site you can be fairly confident that you will like other sites within the same group.

If you're looking for a full facility site, with swimming pools, play areas, bars and restaurants on site you're likely to find these on sites which are part of a group. You might even find organised excursions and activities such as archery on site.

France

📍 Chateau de Sully-sur-Loire

Population (approx): 67 million

Capital: Paris

Area: 549,970 sq km

Bordered by: Andorra, Belgium, Germany, Italy, Luxembourg, Monaco, Spain, Switzerland

Terrain: Mostly flat plains or gently rolling hills in north and west; mountain ranges in south and east

Climate: Temperate climate with regional variations; generally warm summers and cool winters; harsh winters in mountainous areas; hot summers in central and Mediterranean areas

Coastline: 3,427km

Highest Point: Mont Blanc 4,807m

Language: French

Local Time: GMT or BST + 1, i.e. 1 hour ahead of the UK all year

Currency: Euros divided into 100 cents; £1 = €1.16, €1 = £0.87 (October 2019)

Telephoning: From the UK dial 0033 for France and omit the initial 0 of the 10-digit number you are calling. Mobile phone numbers start 06. For Monaco the code is 00377.

Emergency Numbers: Police 112; Fire brigade 112; Ambulance 112.

Public Holidays 2020

Jan 1; Apr 13; May 1, 8 (VE Day), 21; Jun 1; Jul 14 (Bastille Day); Aug 15; Nov 1, 11 (Armistice Day); Dec 25.

Find out more

French Government Tourist Board
Maison de la France
Lincoln House
300 High Holborn
London
WC1V 7JH
Tel: 09068 244123
Website: www.franceguide.com
Email: info.uk@atout-france.fr

Opening Hours

Banks – Mon-Fri 9am-noon & 2pm-4pm/5pm/6pm; in Paris Mon-Fri 10am-5pm; some open Sat & close on Mon. Early closing the day before a public holiday.

Museums – 10am-5pm; closed Mon or Tues. In Paris many open late once a week.

Post Offices – Mon-Fri 8am/9am-6pm/7pm; Sat 8am/9am-noon.

Shops: Food shops - Tues-Sat 7am/9am-6.30pm/7.30pm; some food shops i.e. bakers, grocers, etc, are open sun morning. Other shops - Tues-Sat 9am/10am-7.30pm. Shops generally close all or half day on Mon; in small towns shops close for lunch from noon to 2pm. Major Shops - Mon-Sat 9am/10am-7pm. Supermarkets may stay open until 9pm/10pm. Shops in tourist areas may open on Sunday.

Touring in France

France is divided administratively into 'régions', each of which consists of several 'départements'. There are 96 départements in total including Corsica, and these are approximately equivalent to our counties.

Paris, the capital and hub of the region known as the Ile-de-France, remains the political, economic, artistic, cultural and tourist centre of France. Visit www.parisinfo.com for a wealth of information on what to see and do in the city. A Paris Pass, valid for 2 to 6 days, entitles you to free entrance (ahead of the queues) to over 60 Paris attractions and free unlimited public transport plus discounts and free offers – see www.parispass.com.

Visitors under the age of 26 are admitted free to permanent collections in national museums; show your passport as proof of age. National museums, including the Louvre, are closed on Tuesday, with the exception of Versailles and the Musée d'Orsay which are closed on Monday. Entrance to national museums is free on the first Sunday of every month. Municipal museums are usually closed on Monday and public holidays.

Restaurants must display priced menus outside and most offer a set menu 'plat du jour' or 'table d'hôte' which usually represents good value. A service charge of 15% is included in restaurant bills but it is also expected to leave a small tip if you have received good service. Smoking is not allowed in bars and restaurants.

France has a large network of well-marked, long-distance footpaths and hiking trails – Les Sentiers de Grande Randonnée – which generally follow ancient tracks formerly used by pilgrims, merchants and soldiers. In addition to these 'GR'

paths there are also 'PR' paths (Chemins de Petite Randonnée) which are most suited for local hiking. For a list of GR routes see www.gr-infos.com or contact the French Tourist Board or local tourist offices in France for more information.

Cycling

A number of French towns are actively promoting the use of bicycles. Initiatives include increasing the number of cycle paths, providing parking space for bicycles and constructing shelters and cycle hire points in car parks. You may hire bicycles at many local tourist offices and from some railway stations.

Recent initiatives have included the improvement of cycle tracks along rivers and canals and many former gravel tracks have been replaced with tarmac along the Rivers Rhône, Loire and Yonne/Canal de Nivernais. It is understood that similar improvements will take place along the Canal de Bourgogne.

In and around Paris there are 370 kilometres of cycle lanes, and bicycles, known as 'Les Vélibs', are available for hire at very reasonable rates at more than 1,600 self-service stations – roughly one every 300 metres.

The French Tourist Board has information on cycle routes and tours throughout France.

Place names used in the Site Entry listings which follow can be found in Michelin's France Atlas, scale 1:200,000 (1 cm = 2 km).

Local Travel

Several large cities have metro or tram systems and all have a comprehensive bus network. The Paris metro network comprises 16 lines and around 300 stations, and has many connections to the RER (regional suburban rail network) and the SNCF national railway system. Tickets for the metro, also valid on RATP buses, can be bought singly from vending machines at the turnstiles or from ticket offices, but a 'carnet' of 10 tickets is a more economical option. Your ticket is valid for an hour and a half from the time it is validated at the machines, on buses or at metro stations.

For tourists Paris Visite travel passes are available allowing unlimited travel for one to five days across some or all of the travel zones and a range of discounts at attractions.

For further information see www.ratp.fr.

Senior citizens aged 60 and over are entitled to a discount of up to 25% when using French railways. Show your passport as proof of age.

Ferries

Car ferry services operate all year across the Gironde estuary between Royan and Le Verdon eliminating a 155km detour. 2015 prices are €41.30 single journey for car, caravan under 3m and 2 adults or €54.10 for car, caravan over 3m and 2 adults. A motorhome and 2 adults costs €47.90. Between Blaye and Lamarque north of Bordeaux approximate 2015 prices are €28.20 single journey for car, caravan under 3m and 2 adults or for a motorhome and 2 adults, and €33.60 for car, caravan over 3m.

See www.bernezac.com for more details.

Ferry services operate from Marseille, Nice and Toulon to Corsica. For information contact:

Southern Ferries
30 Churton Street
London
SW1V 2LP
www.southernferries.co.uk
mail@southernferries.com

Channel Islands

Ferry services operate for cars and passengers between Poole and Portsmouth and St Malo via Jersey and Guernsey. Caravans and motorhomes are permitted to enter Jersey, subject to certain conditions, including pre-booking direct with a registered campsite and the acquisition of a permit. For further information and details of the campsites on Jersey where caravans are permitted, see www.jersey.com or contact The Club's Travel Service Information Officer, email: travelserviceinfo@camc.com.

There are three campsites on Guernsey but, for the moment, the authorities in Guernsey do not permit entry to trailer caravans. Motorhomes can only be taken onto the island if they are stored under cover and not used for human habitation. Trailer tents can be taken onto the island without restrictions.

Medical advice

In France an EHIC will allow you to claim reimbursement of around 70% of standard doctors' and dentists' fees, and between 35% and 65% of the cost of most prescribed medicines.

For the address of a doctor 'conventionné', i.e. working within the French state healthcare system, ask at a pharmacy. After treatment make sure you are given a signed statement of treatment ('feuille de soins') showing the amount paid as you will need this for a refund.

Pharmacies dispense prescriptions and first aid. Your prescription will be returned to you and you should attach this, together with the stickers (vignettes) attached to the packaging of any medication or drugs, to the 'feuille de soins' in order to obtain a refund.

If you are admitted to hospital make sure you present your EHIC on admission. This will save you from paying any refundable costs up front and ensure that you only pay the patient contribution. You may have to pay a co-payment towards your treatment and if you are an inpatient you will have to pay a daily hospital charge. These charges are not refundable in France but you may be able to seek reimbursement when back in the UK. Applications for refunds should be sent to a local sickness insurance office (Caisse Primaire d'Assurance-Maladie) and you should receive payment at your home address within about two months.

Andorra is not a member of the EU and there are no reciprocal emergency healthcare arrangements with Britain. You will be required to pay the full cost of medical treatment so make sure that you have comprehensive travel insurance which includes cover for travel to non-EU countries.

ABBEVILLE *3B3* (14km SE Rural) *50.03416, 1.98383*
Camp Municipal La Peupleraie, 80510 Long
03 22 31 84 27 or 03 22 31 80 21; bacquet.lionel
@free.fr; www.long.fr

🐏 ♦♦ ⬛ 🚻 ⬛ ⌁ 🍴 ✕ nr ⊕ nr 🔌 nr ⚠

Exit A16 at junc 21 for D1001 N then turn L at
Ailly-le-Haut Clocher onto D32 for Long & foll sp.
2*, Med, mkd, pt shd, EHU (6A) inc (caution - poss
rev pol & poss other elec concerns) (long lead req);
bbq; red long stay; 90% statics; adv bkg acc; fishing
adj; CKE. *"Pretty, busy site beside Rv Somme; gd san
facs; gd walking/cycling by rv; site busy 1st week
Sep - flea mkt in town; interesting area; old power
stn museum; warden lives on site; conv en rte Calais;
san facs v clean; quiet peaceful site; highly rec."*
€9.00, 15 Mar-15 Nov. **2018**

ABBEVILLE *3B3* (10km SW Rural) *50.08586, 1.71519*
Camping Le Clos Cacheleux, Rue des Sources, Route
de Bouillancourt, 80132 Miannay 03 22 19 17 47;
raphael@camping-lecloscacheleux.fr; www.camping-
lecloscacheleux.fr

🐏 €2.10 ♦♦ ⬛ ⬛ ⌁ 🍴 🦋 ♟ ✕ ⊕ 🔌 ⚠ ✎
🏊 (covrd, htd, indoor) ⛱

Fr A28 exit junc 2 onto D925 sp Cambron. In 5km at
Miannay turn S onto D86 sp Bouillancourt. Site thro
vill of R opp sister site Camping Le Val de Trie which is
sp fr A28. 3*, Med, mkd, hdg, pt shd, pt sl, EHU (10A) inc
(poss long lead req); gas; bbq (charcoal, gas); cooking facs;
TV; Eng spkn; adv bkg acc; ccard acc; tennis 3km; games
area; games rm; sauna; spa; treatment rooms; library; kids'
club; bike rental; CKE. *"Pleasant, peaceful, wooded site;
lge pitches; charming, helpful owner; farm animals; fishing
pond; all services (inc shop, rest & pool) are on sister site 'Le
Val de Trie' on opp side of rd, accessed via steep track 500m
fr site ent; no o'fits over18m; htd covrd pool, paddling pool
adj; jacuzzi; gd walking, cycling; gd for dogs; san facs in a bad
state (2019)."* **€28.60, 1 Mar-15 Oct, P12.** **2019**

ABBEVILLE *3B3* (10km SW Rural) *50.08570, 1.71480*
Camping Le Val de Trie, 1 Rue des Sources,
Bouillancourt-sous-Miannay, 80870 Moyenneville
03 22 31 48 88; raphael@camping-levaldetrie.fr;
www.camping-levaldetrie.fr

🐏 €2.10 ♦♦ (htd) ⬛ ⬛ ⌁ 🍴 🦋 ♟ ✕ ⊕ 🔌 ⚠ ✎
🏊 (covrd, htd) ⛱

Fr A28 exit junc 2 onto D925 sp Cambron. In 5km
at Miannay turn S onto D86 sp Bouillancourt. Site
thro vill on L. Site sp fr A28. NB Last pt of app narr
with bends. 4*, Med, hdstg, mkd, hdg, shd, pt sl, EHU
(6-10A) inc; gas; bbq; red long stay; TV; 1% statics;
phone; Eng spkn; adv bkg acc; ccard acc; lake fishing;
games rm; CKE. *"Beautiful, well-run site; well- shd;
welcoming, helpful, conscientious owner; excel, clean,
modern, san facs, ltd LS; gd family site; woodland
walks; interesting area; conv Calais; great location for
visiting the Somme area."* **€28.00, 1 Apr-29 Sep.**
2019

ABBEVILLE *3B3* (7km NW Rural) *50.14166, 1.76237*
Camping Le Château des Tilleuls, Rue de la Baie,
80132 Port-le-Grand 03 22 24 07 75; contact@
chateaudestilleuls.com; www.chateaudes
tilleuls.com

🐏 ♦♦ (htd) ⬛ ⬛ ♦ ⌁ 🍴 🦋 🦋 ♟ ✕ ⊕ 🔌 ⚠ 🏊 (htd)

Fr N on A16 join A28 dir Rouen. At junc 1 take D40
dir St Valery-sur-Somme, site on R in approx 3km.
3*, Med, hdstg, hdg, mkd, pt shd, sl, terr, EHU (10-16A)
€4; bbq; red long stay; TV; Eng spkn; adv bkg acc;
ccard acc; games rm; bike hire; tennis; CKE. *"Pleasant
site; improvements in progress (2011); lge, v sl pitches;
find suitable pitch bef booking in; long uphill walk fr
recep; unisex san facs; new pitches far fr ent; site being
updated; new san facs (2015); well run; v clean; excel."*
€26.50, 1 Mar-30 Dec. **2015**

"There aren't many sites open at this time of year"

If you're travelling outside peak season
remember to call ahead to check site opening
dates – even if the entry says 'open all year'.

ABRETS, LES *9B3* (2km E Rural) *45.54065, 5.60834*
Kawan Village Le Coin Tranquille, 6 Chemin des
Vignes, 38490 Les Abrets 04 76 32 13 48; contact@
coin-tranquille.com; www.coin-tranquille.com

🐏 €2 ♦♦ ⬛ ⬛ ♦ ⌁ 🍴 ♟ ✕ ⊕ 🔌 ⚠ ✎
🏊 (covrd, htd) ⛱

Fr N exit A43 at junc 10 Les Abrets & foll D592 to
town cent. At rndbt at monument take D1006 twd
Chambéry/Campings; cont for 500m then turn L
sp Le Coin Tranquille; cross level x-ing & cont for
500m to site. Fr S on A48 exit junc 10 at Voiron onto
D1075 to Les Abrets; turn R at rndabt onto D1006
twd Le Pont-de-Beauvoisin, then as above. 4*, Lge,
mkd, hdg, pt shd, EHU (10A) €5; gas; bbq; TV; Eng
spkn; adv bkg req; ccard acc; bike hire; archery; games
area; games rm; CKE. *"Well-kept, well-run site in gd
location; no o'fits over 8m unless bkd in adv; lge narr
pitches; busy/noisy site, but some quiet pitches avail;
helpful & friendly staff; horseriding 7km; fishing 7km;
golf 15km; well-kept, clean san facs, ltd LS; lovely pool;
vg activities for children; poss flooding in wet weather;
excel."* **€34.00, 1 Apr-31 Oct, M05.** **2019**

ABRETS, LES 9B3 (3km S Rural) 45.47079, 5.54688
Camping Le Calatrin (formerly Municipal), 799 Rue
de la Morgerie, 38850 Paladru 04 76 32 37 48;
camping.le.calatrin@gmail.com; www.camping-
paladru.fr

🏕 €3.50 ♦♦♦ 🚻 🛁 ♿ 🗑 ⊘ ✉ ♙ 🍽 🛒 ⚠ ♨

S fr Les Abrets on D1075; turn R onto D50 to
Paladru; site 1km beyond vill on L, on brow of hill.
Or exit A48 junc 9 & foll sp 'Lac de Paladru'; 3km
after rndabt junc of D50 & D17, site on R (by another
rndabt). 3*, Med, mkd, hdg, shd, terr, EHU (10A) €4
(long lead poss req); gas; bbq; sw nr; red long stay; TV;
30% statics; bus 200m; Eng spkn; adv bkg acc; fishing;
games area; watersports; games rm; tennis 500m;
bike hire; CKE. "Attractive site; direct access to lake; lge
pitches; welcoming & helpful owners; gd recreational facs;
nice walks; excel." €17.00, 1 Apr-30 Sep.   2017

"That's changed – Should I let the Club know?"

If you find something on site that's different
from the site entry, fill in a report and let us
know. See camc.com/europereport.

ACCOUS 8G2 (0.5km NW Rural) 42.97717, -0.60592
Camping Despourrins, Route du Somport, D'Arrechau,
64490 Accous 06 76 45 42 61 or 05 59 34 53 50;
info@maison-despourrins.com; www.maison-des
pourrins.com

🏕 ♦♦♦ 🚻 🛁 ⊘ ✉ 🍽 nr ⊕ nr 🛒 nr

On N134 rte to & fr Spain via Somport Pass. Site
sp on main rd. 2*, Sm, pt shd, EHU (6A) €2.70; bbq;
10% statics; fishing. "Clean, tidy NH; conv Col de
Somport." €10.50, 1 Mar-31 Oct.   2019

AGAY 10F4 (0.7km E Coastal) 43.4328, 6.86868
Camping Agay Soleil, 1152, Boulevard de la plage
RD559, 83530 Agay 04 94 82 00 79; contact@agay-
soleil.com; www.agay-soleil.com

🏕 €2 ♦♦♦(htd) 🚻 🛁 🛒 ♿ 🗑 ⊘ 🍽 ♙ ⊕ 🛒 ⚠ ♨ sand adj

E fr St Raphaël on D559 site on R after passing Agay
dir Cannes. Or (to avoid busy St Raphaël) fr A8 exit
junc 38 on D37 & foll sp St Raphaël, then Agay/
Valescure on D100 for approx 8 km; L at rndabt
by beach in Agay; site far side of bay immed after
watersports club. 3*, Med, mkd, hdstg, pt shd, pt sl,
terr, EHU (10A) €5; gas; bbq (elec); train & bus 500m;
Eng spkn; adv bkg rec; games area; watersports;
CKE. "Superb location on sea front; excel modern
facs; many pitches too sm for awning; extra for beach
pitches; dogs not acc high ssn;excel; sm pleasant site;
direct access to beach; lge o'fits phone ahead; vg."
€31.00, 1 Mar-1 Nov.   2019

AGAY 10F4 (1.5km S Coastal) 43.41995, 6.85696
Royal Camping, Plage de Camp-Long, 83530 Agay
04 94 82 00 20; contact@royalcamping.net;
www.royalcamping.net

🏕 ♦♦♦ 🚻 🛁 ♿ 🗑 ⊘ ♙ 🍽 nr ⊕ nr 🛒 ♨ sand adj

On D559 twd St Raphaël. Turn at sp Tiki Plage &
site. Stop in ent rd at recep bef ent site.
3*, Sm, mkd, hdstg, pt shd, EHU (6A) €3.50; gas;
10% statics; phone; bus 200m; Eng spkn; adv bkg acc;
CKE. "Gd walks; lovely site; some pitches adj to beach
in sep area; vg." €25.00, 10 Feb-4 Nov.   2018

AGAY 10F4 (1km W Coastal) 43.43376, 6.85245
Camping des Rives de l'Agay, Ave de Gratadis, 83530
Agay 04 94 82 02 74; reception@lesrivesdelagay.fr;
www.lesrivesdelagay.fr

🏕 €3 ♦♦♦(htd) 🚻 🛁 🛒 ♿ 🗑 ⊘ 🍽 ⊕ 🛒 ♨ (htd) 🛶 (htd) 🎣
♨ sand 500m

Fr Agay take D100 dir Valescure, site in 400m on L.
NB Dangerous bend & steep ent. 4*, Med, hdg, mkd,
shd, EHU (6A) €3.60; gas; 10% statics; Eng spkn;
bkg acc; CKE. "San facs & pool v clean; gd pool with
shd; excel site." €28.00, 9 Mar-7 Nov.   2016

AGAY 10F4 (4km NW Rural/Coastal) 43.45408,
6.83254 Esterel Caravaning, Ave des Golfs, 83530
Agay/St Raphaël 04 94 82 03 28; contact@esterel-
caravaning.fr; www.esterel-caravaning.fr

🏕 €4 ♦♦♦(htd) 🚻 🛁 🛒 ♿ 🗑 ⊘ 🍽 ♙ ⊕ 🛒 ⚠ ♨
♨ (covrd, htd) 🎣 ♨ sand 3km

Fr A8 foll sps for St Raphaël & immed foll sp 'Agay
(par l'interieur)/Valescure' into D100/Ave des Golfs,
approx 6km long. Pass golf courses & at end of rd
turn L at rndabt twds Agay. Site ent immed after a L
hand bend. 5*, Lge, hdstg, mkd, hdg, pt shd, pt sl, terr,
serviced pitches; EHU (10A) inc (poss rev pol); gas;
bbq (charcoal, elec, gas); red long stay; twin axles; TV;
50% statics; Eng spkn; adv bkg acc; ccard acc; squash;
waterslide; tennis; golf nr; archery; bike hire; games
rm; games area; CKE. "Superbly situated, busy site
adj Esterel forest; undergrnd disco; 8 local golf clubs;
friendly, helpful staff; gd san facs; gd for families -
excel leisure activities; excel rest & shop; now classified
as a 5 star site; conv Gorges du Verdon, Massif de
l'Estérel, Monaco, Cannes & St Tropez; individual san
facs to some pitches (extra charge); min stay 1 week
high ssn (Sun to Sun); various pitch prices; ltd lge
pitches avail; some pitches v sl & poss diff; ltd facs LS;
mkt Wed; excel." 6 Apr-28 Sep, C21.   2019

"I like to fill in the reports as I travel from site to site"

You'll find report forms at the back of this
guide, or you can fill them in online at
camc.com/europereport.

FRANCE

AGDE *10F1* (7km SE Coastal) *43.29645, 3.52255*
Centre Hélio-Marin René Oltra (Naturist), 1 Rue des Néréïdes, 34307 Le Cap-d'Agde **04 67 01 06 36 or 04 67 01 06 37; contact@centrenaturiste-oltra.fr; www.centrenaturiste-oltra.fr**

🐕 €3.40 ‖‖ [wc] ♨ ♿ 🚿 ⊙ / [MP] ✉ ⍦ ⊕ ▣ ⚓ 🏊 ⏛ sand adj

S fr m'way A9 Agde-Pézenas junc on N312/D612 for 14km to Cap d'Agde turn-off; foll Camping Naturist sp to site on E side of Le Cap-d'Agde.
4*, V lge, mkd, hdg, pt shd, serviced pitches; EHU (6A) inc; 50% statics; bus adj; Eng spkn; adv bkg rec; ccard acc; INF card. *"Naturist area in Cap-d'Agde has all facs; lovely beach; gd size pitches; friendly atmosphere; modern san facs; gd family facs; excel; great location; gd public transport & walking; facs upgraded (2015); v busy but mostly quiet."* **€42.00, 15 Mar-14 Oct.**
2018

"We must tell the Club about that great site we found"

Get your site reports in by mid-August and we'll do our best to get your updates into the next edition.

AGDE *10F1* (2km SW Rural) *43.29806, 3.45639*
Camping Le Neptune, 46 Boulevard du St Christ, 34300 Agde **04 67 94 23 94; info@camping neptune.com; www.campingleneptune.com**

🐕 €3 ‖‖ [wc] ♨ ♦ ♿ 🚿 ⊙ / ✉ ⍦ ⍦ ⊕ nr ⚓ ⏛ 🏊 (htd)
⌂ ⏛ sand 2km

Fr A9 exit junc 34 onto N312, then E on D612. Foll sp Grau d'Agde after x-ing bdge. Site on D32E on E bank of Rv Hérault on 1-way system.
4*, Lge, mkd, hdg, pt shd, EHU (6-10A) inc; gas; bbq; TV; 40% statics; phone; Eng spkn; adv bkg rec; ccard acc; games area; tennis; CKE. *"Peaceful, pleasant, clean site; helpful owners; dog breed restrictions - check bef travel; modern facs, ltd LS; liable to flood after heavy rain; easy rvside walk/cycle to vill; gd cycleways; rv cruises; boat launch/slipway 500m; v popular site; gd facs; excel."* **€41.00, 1 Apr-30 Sep.**
2018

AGDE *10F1* (3km SW Coastal) *43.29440, 3.45010*
Camping Les Romarins, Le Grau d'Agde, 34300 Agde **04 67 94 18 59; contact@romarins.com; www.romarins.com**

🐕 €3.30 ‖‖ [wc] ♨ ♦ ♿ 🚿 ⊙ / ✉ ⍦ ⍦ ⊕ nr ⚓ ⏛ ♦
🏊 (htd) ⏛ sand 1km

Fr Agde take rd to Grau d'Agde, site at ent to Grau d'Agde adj Rv Hérault. 4*, Med, hdstg, mkd, pt shd, EHU (10A) inc; bbq; twin axles; 25% statics; bus; Eng spkn; adv bkg acc; bike hire; games area; CKE. *"Pleasant town with many bars, rests; shop; helpful owner; excel site; v.busy; small pitches; crowded; gd location; nr rv & cycling to beach."*
€40.00, 30 May-12 Oct.
2019

AGEN *8E3* (8km NW Rural) *44.24368, 0.54290*
Camping Le Moulin de Mellet, Route de Prayssas, 47450 St Hilaire-de-Lusignan **05 53 87 50 89; moulin. mellet@wanadoo.fr; www.camping-moulin-mellet.com**

🐕 €3.80 ‖‖ [wc] ♨ ♦ ♿ ▣ / ✉ ⊕ ♨ ⚓ nr ⏛ 🏊

NW fr Agen on N113 twd Bordeaux for 5km. At traff lts just bef Colayrac-St Cirq take D107 N twd Prayssas for 3km. Site on R. 3*, Sm, mkd, shd, EHU (10A) €3.80 (poss rev pol); gas; bbq; phone; Eng spkn; adv bkg acc; games rm; CKE. *"Delightful, well-run site; helpful, friendly new owners; sm children's farm; RVs & twin axles phone ahead; excel; spotless facs; rest & bar open in LS; pretty location; gd for long stay."*
€30.00, 1 Apr-10 Oct.
2019

AGON COUTAINVILLE *1D4* (0.3km NE Urban/Coastal) *49.05105, -1.59112* **Camp Municipal Le Martinet,** Blvd Lebel-Jéhenne, 50230 Agon-Coutainville **02 33 47 05 20; martinetmarais@wanadoo.fr; www.agoncoutainville.fr or www.coutainville.com**

🐕 €3.20 ‖‖ ♨ ♿ ⊙ / [MP] ⚓ nr ⏛ ⏛ sand 600m

Fr Coutances take D44 to Agon-Coutainville; site sp nr Hippodrome. 2*, Med, hdg, mkd, pt shd, EHU (6A); bbq; 55% statics; bus; Eng spkn; adv bkg acc; ccard acc; CKE. *"V pleasant site; ltd facs LS; horse racecourse adj; vg."* **€18.00, 1 Apr-30 Oct.**
2018

AIGLE, L' *4E2* (14km W Rural) *48.78841, 0.46533*
Camp Municipal des Saints-Pères, 61550 St Evroult-Notre-Dame-du-Bois **06 78 33 04 94 (mob) or 02 33 34 93 12 (Mairie); mairiestevroultnddubois @wanadoo.fr**

🐕 €0.20 ‖‖ [wc] ♨ ♿ / [MP] ⍦ nr ⊕ nr ⚓ nr ⏛

Fr L'Aigle on D13, on ent vill site on L by lake.
2*, Sm, hdstg, pt shd, terr, EHU (4-10A) €1.50-2.50; sw nr; watersports; fishing; CKE. *"Pleasant lakeside vill; facs gd & clean with hot water, ltd LS; quiet; walks; on edge of sm vill opp ruins of ancient abbey; friendly, helpful staff, but no Eng spkn."*
€14.00, 1 Apr-30 Sep.
2016

AIGNAN *8E2* (0.6km S Rural) *43.69290, 0.07528*
Camping Le Domaine du Castex, 32290 Aignan **05 62 09 25 13; info@domaine-castex.com; www.gers-vacances.com**

[12] 🐕 €4 ‖‖ ♨ ♿ ▣ / [MP] ✉ ⍦ ⊕ ♨ ⚓ nr ⏛ 🏊

Fr N on D924/N124 turn S on D20 thro Aignan onto D48; in 500m g'ge on R, immed after turn L; site sp. Fr S on D935 turn E at Monplaisir onto D3/D48 to Aignan; site on R bef vill. 3*, Sm, hdg, mkd, hdstg, pt shd, EHU (10A) €3; bbq; sw nr; TV; 4% statics; phone; Eng spkn; adv bkg acc; ccard acc; tennis adj; games area; CKE. *"Lovely site in grnds of medieval farmhouse; helpful Dutch owners; modern san facs; excel pool & rest; squash adj; gd touring cent for Bastide vills; mkt Mon; phone ahead LS; vg."* **€20.00**
2016

FRANCE

AIGUES MORTES *10F2* (3.5km W Rural) *43.56300, 4.15910* **Yelloh! Village La Petite Camargue,** 30220 Aigues-Mortes 04 66 53 98 98; info@yellohvillage-petite-camargue.fr; www.yellohvillage-petite-camargue.com or www.yellohvillage.co.uk

🐕 €4 � ⬛ ⚓ 🔥 ♿ 🚿 ∥ ⬛ ♈ 🍴 ⊕ 🍴 🅱 /Ⅲ ∥ 🛶 ⛵
🏊 sand 3km

Heading S on N979 turn L onto D62 bef Aigues-Mortes & go over canal bdge twd Montpellier; site on R in 3km; sp. 4*, V lge, mkd, pt shd, EHU (10A) inc; bbq (charcoal, gas); TV; 50% statics; Eng spkn; adv bkg acc; ccard acc; games rm; serviced; horseriding; bike hire; tennis; games area; jacuzzi; CKE. *"Lively, busy, well-run, youth-oriented commercial site with many sports facs; no o'fits over 7m; clean san facs, poss stretched high ssn; excel pool complex; bus to beach high ssn; some sm pitches; take care o'head branches; gd cycling; mkt Wed & Sun."* **€44.00, 26 Apr-15 Sep, C04.** 2017

AIGUILLON *7D2* (0.9km NE Rural) *44.30467, 0.34491* **Camp Municipal du Vieux Moulin,** Route de Villeneuve, 47190 Aiguillon 05 53 79 60 12; www.ville-aiguillon.eu

♦11 ⬛ ⚓ ∥ 🍴 nr ⊕ nr 🅱 nr /Ⅲ

On ent town on D813, turn E onto D666 to site on bank of Rv Lot. Clearly sp. Or exit A62 junc 6 at Damazan onto D8 to Aiguillon. 2*, Med, mkd, shd, EHU (10A) inc. *"Gd site adj old mill house by rv; gd san facs; conv A62; NH only."*
€10.00, 1 Jul-31 Aug. 2019

"I need an on-site restaurant"

We do our best to make sure site information is correct, but it is always best to check any must-have facilities are still available or will be open during your visit.

AIGUILLON SUR MER, L' *7A1* (1km W Coastal) *46.34349, -1.32006* **Camp'Atlantique Bel Air,** 2 Route de Bel Air, 85460 L'Aiguillon-sur-Mer 02 51 20 41 94; belair.camp-atlantique.co.uk

🐕 €3.50 ♦11 ⚓ 🔥 ⬛ ∥ 🍴 ⊕ 🍴 🅱 /Ⅲ ∥ 🛶 🏊 sand 800m

Fr La Roche-sur-Yon take D747 to La Tranche-sur-Mer via coast rd D46 to La Faute-sur-Mer. Cross bdge to L'Aiguillon-sur-Mer. Site 1km W of town on D44. Sp fr all dir. 4*, Lge, pt shd, EHU (3A) €3.50; bbq; 10% statics; adv bkg acc; waterslide; archery; bike hire. *"Excel, clean, friendly site; pony trekking."*
€42.00, 1 Apr-30 Sep. 2015

AINHOA *8F1* (2.5km SW Rural) *43.29143, -1.50394* **Camping Xokoan,** Quartier Dancharia, 64250 Ainhoa 05 59 29 90 26; etchartenea@orange.fr; www.camping-xokoan.com

12 🐕 ♦11 ⬛ ⚓ 🔥 ♿ ⬛ ∥ ⬛ ♈ 🍴 ⊕ 🅱 nr /Ⅲ

S fr Ainhoa on D20, site on L in 2km. Narr ent & app. Fr Spain on N121B, pass Frontier site 250m on R. 3*, Sm, mkd, hdstg, pt shd, pt sl, EHU (6A) €3.50; bbq; adv bkg acc; games rm; CKE. *"Conv for N Spain & Pyrenees; gd walks; v interesting & scenic site in grnds of sm hotel; gd."* **€17.50** 2017

AINHOA *8F1* (0.4km NW Urban) *43.30913, -1.50178* **Aire Naturelle Harazpy (Zaldua),** 64250 Ainhoa 05 59 29 89 38 or 05 59 29 90 26 (LS); etchartenea@orange.fr; www.camping-harazpy.com

🐕 🐕 ♦11 ⬛ ⚓ ♿ ⬛ ∥ ⬛ ♈ 🅱

Take D918 E fr St Jean-de-Luz sp Espelette: in approx 20km turn R on D20 sp Ainhoa. App church in Ainhoa turn R thro open car park to rd at rear; site on R in 250m. Site sp. Sm, mkd, pt shd, pt sl, terr, EHU (10A) inc; phone; adv bkg acc; CKE. *"Beautiful location; conv Spanish border; helpful staff; excel walking area."* **€17.50, 1 Apr-30 Sep.** 2016

AIRE SUR LA LYS *3A3* (2km NE Urban) *50.64390, 2.40630* **Camp Municipal de la Lys,** Bassin des Quatre Faces, Rue de Fort Gassion, 62120 Aire-sur-la-Lys 03 21 95 40 40; camping@ville-airesurlalys.fr; www.ville-airesurlalys.fr

♦11 (htd) ⬛ ⚓ ∥ ♈

Fr town cent, find main sq & exit to R of town hall. Thro traff lts turn R into narr lane just bef rv bdge dir of Hazebrouck. Site poorly sp. High vehicles beware low bdge at site ent. 2*, Sm, hdstg, mkd, hdg, pt shd, EHU (6A) €2.10; 95% statics. *"Ltd touring pitches; ltd but clean san facs; not suitable lge o'fits; rec for NH only; v welcoming; waterside pitches; vg NH; easy walk to town."* **€12.00, 1 Apr-31 Oct.** 2016

AIRE SUR L'ADOUR *8E2* (0.7km NE Urban) *43.70259, -0.25792* **Camping Les Ombrages de l'Adour,** Rue des Graviers, 40800 Aire-sur-l'Adour 05 58 71 75 10; hetapsarl@yahoo.fr; www.camping-adour-landes.com

🐕 €1.80 ♦11 ⬛ ⚓ 🔥 ⬛ ∥ ⬛ 🍴 🅱 /Ⅲ

Turn E on S side of bdge over Rv Adour in town. Site close to bdge & sp, past La Arena off rd to Bourdeaux. 2*, Med, pt shd, EHU (10A) inc; bbq; adv bkg acc; ccard acc; fishing 500m; tennis 500m; games area. *"Vg; htd pool 500m; canoeing 500m; v clean facs but dated."* **€19.00, 16 Apr-15 Oct.** 2016

AIRVAULT *4H1* (1km N Rural) *46.83200, -0.14690*
Camping de Courte Vallée, 8 Rue de Courte Vallée,
79600 Airvault **05 49 64 70 65; info@caravanning
france.com; www.caravanningfrance.com**

🐕 €1.50 ♙♟(htd) [wo] 🛇 ⚲ 🖵 ✏ [MSP] 🍴 ⛱ 𝕿 ⑪ ⛽ 🏊 /Ⅲ 🛥(htd)

**Fr N, S or W leave D938 sp Parthenay to Thouars rd
at La Maucarrière twd Airvault & foll lge sp to site.
Site on D121 twd Availles-Thouarsais. NB If app fr
NE or E c'vans not permitted thro Airvault - watch
carefully for sp R at Gendarmerie. Well sp fr all dirs.**
3*, Sm, mkd, hdstg, hdg, pt shd, pt sl, EHU (13A) inc
(poss long lead req); gas; bbq; red long stay; twin axles;
TV; 8% statics; adv bkg acc; ccard acc; games rm; bike
hire; fishing; CKE. *"Peaceful, popular; pleasant, helpful
British owners; excel, clean & vg facs, poss stretched high
ssn; conv Futuroscope & Puy du Fou theme park; mkt
Sat; not as well kept & expensive compared to similar
sites; c'van storage; town dissapointing, empty shops;
new rest & bar(2018)."* **€33.00, 1 Mar-15 Nov, L14.**
2018

AIX EN PROVENCE *10F3* (9km E Rural) *43.51771,
5.54128* **FFCC Camping Ste Victoire,** Quartier La
Paradou,. 13100 Beaurecueil **04 42 66 91 31; camping
victoire@orange.fr; www.campingsaintevictoire.com**

🐕 €1.10 ♙♟(htd) [wo] 🛇 ⚲ 🖵 ✏ [MSP] 🍴 ⛱ 🐕nr /Ⅲ

**Exit A8/E80 junc 32 onto D7n dir Aix, then R onto
D58 & foll sp for 3km.** 2*, Sm, hdg, mkd, hdstg, shd,
EHU (6A)(some rev pol & poss no neutral); red long
stay; TV; phone; bus; adv bkg acc; archery; bike hire;
CKE. *"Well-run site in attractive hilly, wooded area;
friendly, helpful owners; clean, basic, dated & small san
facs, ltd LS, but clean; various pitch sizes; lge o'fits poss
diff manoeuvring; pool 9km; some pitches too soft for
lge o'fits when wet; no twin axles; no lighting at night;
gd walking & climbing; lovely location; shady; frequent
cheap bus to Aix; narr rds; site can be diff to find."*
€21.50, 5 Mar-30 Nov. 2018

AIX EN PROVENCE *10F3* (3km SE Urban) *43.51556,
5.47431* **Airotel Camping Chantecler,** Val-St André,
13100 Aix-en-Provence **04 42 26 12 98; info@camping
chantecler.com; www.campingchantecler.com**

[12] 🐕 €3.60 ♙♟(htd) [wo] 🛇 ⚲ 🖵 ✏ 🐕 𝕿 ⑪ ⛽ 🐕 /Ⅲ ✏ 🛥

**Fr town inner ring rd foll sps Nice-Toulon, after 1km
look for sp Chantecler to L of dual c'way. Foll camp
sp past blocks of flats. Well sp in Val-St André. If on
A8 exit at junc 31 sp Val-St André; R at rndabt; R at
Rndabt; L at 2nd traff lts onto Ave Andre Magnan;
R ar rndabt; site sp. If app fr SE on D7n turn R
immed after passing under A8.** 4*, Lge, hdstg, hdg,
pt shd, sl, terr, EHU (5A) €4.10 (long lead poss req);
gas; bbq (elec, gas); red long stay; TV; bus; adv bkg
acc; ccard acc; site clsd 1 & 2 Jan; CKE. *"Lovely, well-
kept, wooded site; facs ltd LS; some site rds steep - gd
power/weight ratio rec; access poss diff some pitches;
rec request low level pitch & walk to pitch bef driving to
it; ent narr; recep clsd 12.30-13.30; gd pool; conv city;
vg touring base; access diff to some pitches, refurb san
facs now htd & excel (2014)."* **€28.70** 2019

AIX LES BAINS *9B3* (3km W Rural) *45.70005, 5.88666*
Camp Municipal International du Sierroz, Blvd
Robert Barrier, Route du Lac, 73100 Aix-les-Bains
**04 79 61 89 89; info@camping-sierroz.com;
www.camping-sierroz.com**

🐕 €1.60 ♙♟(htd) [wo] 🛇 ⚲ 🖵 ✏ [MSP] 🍴 𝕿 ⑪ ⛽ ⛱ /Ⅲ

**Fr Annecy S on D1201, thro Aix-les-Bains, turn R at site
sp. Keep to lakeside rd, site on R. Nr Grand Port.**
3*, Lge, hdg, mkd, shd, EHU (6A) inc; gas; TV;
5% statics; bus (ask at recep for free pass); adv bkg
acc; ccard acc; golf 4km; games area; CKE. *"Pleasant
location; lake adj for watersports; lge pitches;
poss travellers & v unclean facs LS (June 2010)."*
€23.60, 15 Mar-15 Nov. 2019

AIZELLES *3C4* (0.4km NW Rural) *49.49076, 3.80817*
Camping du Moulin (Merlo), 16 Rue du Moulin,
02820 Aizelles **03 23 22 41 18 or 06 14 20 47 43
(mob); magali.merlo@orange.fr; www.camping-
du-moulin.fr**

♙♟ [wo] 🛇 ✏ 🍴 ⛱ 🐕nr /Ⅲ

**Fr Laon take D1044 dir Reims; in 13km turn L on
D88 to Aizelles; site sp in vill 'Camping à la Ferme'.
Fr Reims on A26 exit junc 14 onto D925 then D1044
N. Turn R to Aizelles on D889 past Corbeny. Turn
onto Rue du Moulin & site on R in 250m. Camping
sp at church says 100m but allow 300m to see
ent. NB Lge o'fits take care sharp R turn at ent
to site.** Sm, pt shd, pt sl, EHU (10A) inc (poss rev
pol, poss long lead req); Eng spkn; ccard acc; fishing
800m; CKE. *"Attractive, well-kept CL-type farm site;
v friendly, helpful owners; basic san facs need update;
gates clsd 2200-0700; wonderful well maintained site
in a sm pretty vil; conv Calais 3 hrs; vg site; conv for
Zeebrugge; few statics."*
€16.00, 1 Apr-15 Oct. 2018

"Satellite navigation makes touring much easier"

Remember most sat navs don't know if you're
towing or in a larger vehicle – always use yours
alongside maps and site directions.

AIZENAY *2H4* (1.7km SE Rural) *46.73410, -1.58950*
FFCC Camping La Forêt, 1 Rue de la Clairière, 85190
Aizenay **02 51 34 78 12; info@camping-laforet.com;
www.camping-laforet.com**

🐕 €1.30 ♙♟ [wo] 🛇 ⚲ 🖵 ✏ [MSP] 🍴 ⛱ 𝕿 ⑪nr ⛽ ⛱ /Ⅲ 🛥(htd)

**Exit Aizenay on D948 twd La Roche-sur-Yon. Site
1.5km on L.** 3*, Med, hdg, mkd, pt shd, EHU (6A)
€2.70; gas; bbq; sw nr; 10% statics; phone; adv bkg
acc; ccard acc; tennis; bike hire; CKE. *"Undergoing
refurbishment 2013; new bar & ent; v pleasant site; gd
size pitches."* **€18.00, Easter-30 Sep.** 2015

AIZENAY 2H4 (8km NW Rural) 46.75282, -1.68645
Camping Val de Vie, Rue du Stade, 85190 Maché
02 51 60 21 02; campingvaldevie@bbox.fr;
www.campingvaldevie.fr

🏕 €3 ⛟ ⬥ wc 🛁 ⬥ ♿ ⏚ ⁄ 🐾 ⟁ nr ⛰ ⚓ (htd)

Fr Aizenay on D948 dir Challans. After 5km turn L
onto D40 to Maché. Fr vill cent cont twd Apremont.
Sm, blue site sp 100m on L. 3*, Med, hdg, mkd, pt
shd, pt sl, serviced pitches; EHU (6-10A) €3.50-4; gas;
bbq; twin axles; red long stay; 20% statics; Eng spkn;
adv bkg acc; fishing; bike hire; tennis excl; boat hire.
*"Lovely, peaceful, well-run site in pretty vill; new young
owners upgrading facs & rds (2011); warm welcome;
clean san facs, steel pegs useful; gd touring base; gd
cycling; excel."* **€25.60, 1 Apr-1 Oct.** 2016

AJACCIO 10H2 (26km N Coastal) 42.04791, 8.74919
Camping A Marina, Golfe de la Liscia, 20111
Calcatoggio 95 52 21 84 or 72 83 62 34; fabiani.
famille@wanadoo.fr; www.camping-amarina.com

🏕 ⛟ (htd) wc 🛁 ⬥ ♿ ⏚ ⁄ MP 🦋 ⟡ 🍽 🖻 ⚓ ⟁ ⛰ sandy adj

Take D81 N fr Ajaccio for 20km; site ent on L 3km
fr turn off to Calcatoggio. Foll sp to end of lane.
Sm, hdg, pt shd, EHU (16A) €4; bbq; 50% statics; Eng
spkn; ccard acc; games area. *"Sm garden site adj to
beautiful sandy bay; excell san facs, bar; friendly, family
run; an oasis; excel."* **€35.00, 1 Apr-31 Oct.** 2015

ALBAN 8E4 (1km NW Rural) 43.89386, 2.45416
Camp Municipal La Franquèze, 81250 Alban 05 63 55
91 87 or 05 63 55 82 09 (Mairie); mairie.alban@
wanadoo.fr; www.campingtarn.com/fr/camping-
municipal-la-franqueze

⛟ ⏚ 🛁 ⏚ ⁄ 🦋 ⛰

W of Albi on D999 turn L at ent to Alban. Site 300m
on R, sp. 2*, Sm, hdg, pt shd, pt sl, terr, EHU (6A)
€2.10; adv bkg acc; rv fishing; CKE. *"Beautiful area,
conv Tarn Valley; vg; water taps scarce; gd hilltop site
with views."* **€14.00, 1 Jun-30 Sep.** 2019

ALBERT 3B3 (1.5km N Urban) 50.01136, 2.65556
Camp Municipal du Vélodrome, Ave Henri Dunant,
80300 Albert 03 64 62 22 53 or 06 42 58 71 64;
campingalbert@laposte.net; www.camping-
albert.com

🏕 ⛟ wc 🛁 ♿ ⁄ MP ⟡ 🖻 nr

Fr town cent take Rue Godin E adj to Basilica &
foll sp for site. Easiest access fr Bapaume (N) twds
Albert; turn R at camping sp on edge of town.
2*, Med, mkd, pt shd, EHU (4-10A) €2.20-4.40 (rev
pol); red long stay; 40% statics; Eng spkn; adv bkg acc;
fishing adj; CKE. *"Pleasant, well-run, well maintained,
clean site; nr lake; friendly, helpful warden; poss
security prob; conv for Lille, Arras & Amien by train &
for WW1 battlefields etc; poss rlwy noise; facs basic
but rates reasonable; if office close find pitch and
inform warden later; gates clsd fairly early, will need
ent code if late; easy walk into Albert; semi sep aire;
unisex shwrs & wc."* **€19.50, 1 Apr-11 Oct.** 2019

ALBERT 3B3 (5km NE Rural) 50.04141, 2.66868
International Camping Bellevue, 25 Rue d'Albert,
80300 Authuille 03 22 74 59 29 or 06 71 96 88 78
(mob); camping.bellevue0767@orange.fr; camping
bellevue.pagesperso-orange.fr

🏕 €1 ⛟ wc 🛁 ⁄ 🐾 ♿ ⟁

Take D929 Albert to Bapaume rd; in 3km turn L at
La Boiselle, foll sp to Aveluy cont to Authuille. Site
on R in vill cent. 2*, Med, hdg, pt shd, pt sl, EHU (6A)
inc (rev pol); 80% statics; adv bkg acc; rv fishing 500m;
CKE. *"Helpful owner; basic site, well maintained; useful
touring Somme WW1 battlefields; walking dist of
Thiepval Ridge; gd NH; lovely site; excel rest in vill; san
facs old fashioned but clean; church clock chiming thro
night."* **€17.00, 15 Mar-31 Oct.** 2017

ALBERT 3B3 (14km SW Rural) 49.91930, 2.57985
FFCC Camping Les Puits Tournants, 6 Rue du Marais,
80800 Sailly-le-Sec 03 22 76 65 56; camping.puits
tournants@wanadoo.fr; www.camping-les-puits-
tournants.com

🏕 ⛟ (htd) wc 🛁 ♿ ⏚ ⁄ MP 🦋 ⟡ 🍽 🖻 ⚓ ⛰ (htd) 🏊

Fr N exit A1 junc 14 onto D929 dir Amiens, at Albert
take D42 S to Sailly-Laurette then turn R onto D233
to Sailly-le-Sec & foll sp. Or fr S exit junc 13 twd
Albert onto D1029. At Lamotte-Warfusée R onto
D42 to Sailly-Laurette, turn L to Sailley-le-Sec.
3*, Med, hdstg, mkd, pt shd, EHU (4A) €3; gas; bbq;
sw; TV; 60% statics; Eng spkn; adv bkg acc; ccard acc;
games area; bike hire; canoe hire; fishing; horseriding
5km; tennis 2km. *"Lovely, pleasant family-run site;
amiable staff; gd clean san facs, need updating; grass
pitches muddy when wet; tight ent, lge o'fits poss
diff; gd pool; walks by rv; excel; picturesque site nr
rv Somme; nice dog walks by rv; facs poss stretched
in HS; new pools & rest under construction (2017)."*
€25.00, 1 Apr-31 Oct. 2017

"There aren't many sites open at this time of year"

If you're travelling outside peak season
remember to call ahead to check site opening
dates – even if the entry says 'open all year'.

ALBERTVILLE 9B3 (0.7km NNE Urban) 45.67922,
6.39636 **Camp Municipal Les Adoubes,** Ave du
Camping, 73200 Albertville 04 79 32 06 62 or 06 85
84 02 56; hello@camping-albertville.fr;
www.camping-albertville.fr

🏕 ⛟ (htd) wc 🛁 ♿ ⁄ ⟡ 🍽 nr ♿ nr 🖻 nr

Site is 200m fr town cent; over bdge on banks of
Rv Arly. Med, mkd, pt shd, pt sl, EHU (10A) €3.50; gas;
bbq; twin axles; TV; 5% statics; Eng spkn; adv bkg acc;
ccard acc; CKE. *"Excel site in excel location; plenty of
rm, even high ssn; v helpful staff; site yourself if recep
clsd; well kept; 10% red for CC memb; under new
management; site being upgraded for 2015; rallies acc."*
€20.50, 1 Jan-30 Oct & 1 Dec-31 Dec. 2015

FRANCE

ALBI *8E4* (2km NE Urban) *43.93485, 2.16213*
Albirondack Park, Camping Lodge & Spa (formerly Camping Caussels), 31 Allée de la Piscine, 81000 Albi 05 63 60 37 06 or 06 84 04 23 13 (mob); albirondack @orange.fr; www.albirondack.fr

🏕 €5 ♦♦(htd) 🅆 🏔 ♨ 🕭 🖥 ✦ 🄼 🐾 ⑪ 🍴 🛒nr 🛆 ⚓(htd)

Fr Albi ring rd/bypass exit sp Lacause/St Juéry (do not turn twd Millau). Strt over & foll sp Géant-Casino hypmkt & 'Centre Ville', then foll camping/piscine sp. 3*, Med, mkd, pt shd, pt sl, EHU (10A) €5.70; bbq; 10% statics; bus; adv bkg acc; CKE. *"Vg, popular site in conv position; pitches unlevelled - soft in wet & some poss diff lge o'fits due trees; gd walk (40 min) by rv to town cent; Albi Cathedral; spa; Toulouse Lautrec exhibitions; spa & pool inc; excel rest; excel clean modern san facs; beware of low lying wooden & concrete posts; v cramped site; rec arr early."* €36.50, 20 Jan-10 Nov & 2 Dec-31 Dec.   2018

"That's changed – Should I let the Club know?"

If you find something on site that's different from the site entry, fill in a report and let us know. See camc.com/europereport.

ALENCON *4E1* (3km SW Rural) *48.42566, 0.07321*
Camp Municipal de Guéramé, 65 Rue de Guéramé, 61000 Alençon 02 33 26 34 95; camping.guerame@ orange.fr; www.ville-alencon.fr

🏕 €1.90 ♦♦(htd) 🅆 🏔 ♨ 🕭 🖥 ✦ 🄼 🍴 🛒nr 🛆 ⚓

Located nr town cent. Fr N on D38 take N12 W (Carrefour sp). In 5km take D1 L sp Condé-sur-Sarthe. At rndabt turn L sp Alençon then R immed after Carrefour supmkt, foll site sp. Site is sp fr D112 inner ring rd. 2*, Med, hdg, hdstg, pt shd, EHU (5A) €3.10 (check EHU carefully) (poss long lead req); bbq; TV; Eng spkn; adv bkg acc; bike hire; horseriding; rv fishing; tennis; canoeing; CKE. *"Helpful warden; clean san facs; o'night m'vans area; pool complex 700m; barrier/recep clsd 1800 LS; LS phone ahead to check site open; some pitches poss flood in heavy rain; rvside walk to town thro arboretum; peaceful site."* €15.00, 1 Apr-30 Sep.   2015

ALERIA *10H2* (7km N Coastal) *42.16155, 9.55265*
Camping-Village Riva-Bella (Part Naturist), 20270 Aléria 04 95 38 81 10; riva-bella@orange.fr; www.naturisme-rivabella.com

12 🏕 €3.50 ♦♦♦ 🏔 🕭 ✦ 🄼 🐾 🍴 ⑪ 🍴 🛒 🛆 ⚓ 🏖sand adj

Fr Bastia S on N198 for 60km, site sp to L. Poor rd access (2011). 3*, Med, pt shd, EHU €4.30; red long stay; TV; 10% statics; adv bkg acc; fishing; games area; watersports; bike hire; tennis; INF card. *"Site untidy early ssn (2011); fitness rm; steam rm; sauna; spa treatments; poss insect problem; naturist site 15 May-20 Sep, non-naturist rest of year - but always sm end beach avail for naturists."* €36.00   2016

ALET LES BAINS *8G4* (0.3km W Rural) *42.99490, 2.25525* Camping Val d'Aleth, Ave Nicolas Pavillon, 11580 Alet-les-Bains 04 68 69 90 40; info@valdaleth .com; www.valdaleth.com

12 🏕 €1.55 ♦♦(htd) 🅆 🏔 ♨ 🕭 🖥 ✦ 🄼 🍴 ⑪nr 🛒 🛆

Fr Limoux S on D118 twd Quillan; in approx 8km ignore 1st L turn over Aude bdge into vill but take alt rte for heavy vehicles. Immed after x-ing rv, turn L in front of casino & ent town fr S; site sp on L. 2*, Sm, hdg, mkd, hdstg, shd, pt sl, EHU (10A) €2.75-4; gas; bbq (gas); red long stay; 25% statics; phone; Eng spkn; adv bkg acc; ccard acc; bike hire; CKE. *"Rvside (no sw) site in attractive, medieval vill; sm pitches (lge o'fits need to book); friendly, helpful British owner; gd clean san facs; v few facs in vill; poss unkempt early ssn; conv Carcassonne & Cathar country - scenic; ACSI acc."* €20.00   2016

ALLEGRE LES FUMADES *10E2* (2km NE Rural) *44.2089, 4.25665* Camping Le Château de Boisson, 30500 Allègre-les-Fumades 04 66 24 85 61 or 04 66 24 82 21; reception@chateaudeboisson.com; www. chateaudeboisson.com or www.les-castels.com

🏕 €5 ♦♦ 🅆 🏔 ♨ 🕭 🖥 ✦ 🄼 🐾 🍴 ⑪ 🍴 🛒 🛆 ✦ ⚓(covrd, htd) 📶

Fr Alès NE on D904, turn R after Les Mages onto D132, then L onto D16 for Boisson. Fr A7 take exit 19 Pont l'Esprit, turn S on N86 to Bagnols-sur-Cèze & then D6 W. Bef Vallérargues turn R onto D979 Lussan, then D37 & D16 to Boisson. 4*, Lge, mkd, hdg, shd, pt sl, EHU (6A) inc; gas; bbq (elec, gas); red long stay; 80% statics; phone; Eng spkn; adv bkg acc; ccard acc; games rm; tennis; bike hire. *"Vg, well-run, peaceful site; no o'fits over 7m high ssn; no dogs 9 Jul-20 Aug; gd sized pitches, poss some v sm; helpful staff; excel san facs; excel rest & facs; superb pool complex."* €39.00, 12 Apr-27 Sep, C34.   2016

AMBAZAC *7B3* (3km NE Rural) *45.97158, 1.41315* Camping L'Ecrin Nature, 87240 Ambazac 06 52 92 71 65 or 05 55 56 60 25; contact@campinglecrinature. com; www.campinglecrinature.com

🏕 ♦♦♦ 🅆 🏔 ♨ 🕭 🖥 ✦ 🄼 🐾 🍴 🛒 🛆 ⚓(htd)

Fr A20 foll sp to Ambazac; site on D914. 3*, Med, hdg, mkd, pt shd, pt sl, terr, EHU (6A) €3.50; bbq; 15% statics; Eng spkn; adv bkg acc; ccard acc; lake fishing. *"Excel waterside site with lovely views, o'looking lake; v friendly new owners, who cont to improve this eco site; san facs clean; ctr for mountain biking & walking; much improved site; gd pool; hg rec; use barrier intercom to contact bureau on arr (bureau clsd midday-3pm); shgl beach adj (sw not allowed); excel site; peaceful; use intercom to gain access."* €21.00, 8 Apr-2 Oct.   2017

AMBERT *9B1* (1km S Urban) *45.53951, 3.72867*
Camping Les Trois Chênes, Rue de la Chaise-Dieu,
63600 Ambert 04 73 82 34 68; tourisme@ville-
ambert.fr; www.camping-ambert.com

On main rd D906 S twd Le Puy on L bet Leisure Park
& Aquacentre. 3*, Med, hdg, mkd, pt shd, serviced
pitches; EHU (10A) €3.25; 80% statics; adv bkg acc;
waterslide; CKE. "Excel, well-kept site; gd, clean san
facs; rvside walk to town; htd pool adj; rec arrive bef
noon peak ssn; recep & barrier clsd 1900 LS; steam
museum & working paper mill nr; steam train 1.5km;
vg." €21.60, 26 Apr-29 Sep. 2019

AMBIALET *8E4* (0.8km ESE Rural) *43.94181, 2.38686*
Camping La Mise à l'Eau, Fédusse, 81430 Ambialet
05 63 79 58 29; contact@camping-ambialet.com;
www.camping-ambialet.fr

Fr Albi E on D999; in 15km, after Villefranche-
d'Albigeois, turn L onto D74 to Ambialet; turn R at
junc; in 100m bear L; site on L. Sharp turn, turning
pnt avail down rd. NB App via D74 as v narr tunnels
on D172/D700 to E & W of Ambialet. Sm, mkd, pt
shd, EHU (6-10A) €2.15; adv bkg acc; kayaking; CKE.
"Easy walk to pretty vil; bar 500ml; clean facs; excel;
pretty rvside site; no chem disp facs on site, use public
toilet in vill." €17.00, 1 May-31 Oct. 2016

AMBOISE *4G2* (1km N Rural) *47.41763, 0.98717*
Camp Municipal L'Ile d'Or, 37400 Amboise 02 47 57
23 37 or 02 47 23 47 38 (Mairie); camping@ville-
amboise.fr; www.camping-amboise.com

Fr N exit A10 exit junc 18 onto D31/D431 to
Amboise; at turn R onto D751 dir Blois & get in L
lane to cross bdge on D431; site a turning L off
bdge, on lge wooded island in Rv Loire. Fr S exit
A85 junc 11 onto D31 dir Amboise; foll Centre Ville
sp to rv on D431; get in L/H lane to cross bdge (dir
Nazelles); turn R off bdge to site on island.
2*, Lge, mkd, pt shd, EHU (6A) inc (poss rev pol); red
long stay; TV; phone; Eng spkn; adv bkg acc; ccard acc;
fishing; games area; tennis; CKE. "Lovely, spacious,
secure site in gd location adj Rv Loire & park; well-kept;
lge pitches; htd pool & waterslide 500m (high ssn); nice
rest & bar; easy walk to interesting old town; vg dog
walking; conv Parc Léonardo Da Vinci (last place he
lived) & Château d'Amboise; midsummer week music
festival in adj park - check date; no twin axles; m'van
o'night area open all year, excel stop out of ssn; gd
value; vg; excel san facs, stretched in high ssn; v busy."
€16.00, 31 Mar-9 Oct. 2017

AMBOISE *4G2* (7km NE Rural) *47.44580, 1.04669*
Camping Le Jardin Botanique, 9 bis, Rue de la Rivière,
37530 Limeray 02 47 30 13 50; campingjardin
botanique@wanadoo.fr; www.camping-jardin
botanique.com

NE fr Amboise on D952 on N side of Rv Loire dir
Blois; in approx 6km turn L for Limeray & then
immed turn L onto Rue de la Rivière; site on L in
500m. NB Rec not to app fr Limeray, narr rds & diff
for lge o'fits. 3*, Med, hdg, mkd, hdstg, pt shd, EHU
(10A) €5 (poss rev pol); gas; bbq; red long stay; TV;
20% statics; Eng spkn; adv bkg acc; bike hire; tennis;
games area; CKE. "Gd for Loire chateaux; 500m fr rv;
friendly & helpful owner; gd for children; gd gourmet
rest adj; poss muddy when wet; gd cycle rtes; poorly
maintained facs (2014)." €20.50 2015

AMBRIERES LES VALLEES *4E1* (2km SW Rural)
48.39121, -0.61680 Camping Le Parc de Vaux,
35 Rue des Colverts, 53300 Ambrières-les-Vallées
02 43 04 90 25; parcdevaux@camp-in-ouest.com;
www.parcdevaux.com

Fr S on D23 turn R at sp 'Parc de Loisirs de Vaux'.
Site in approx 100m on bank Rv Varenne. Check in
at Office de Tourisme bef site recep.
3*, Med, hdg, mkd, hdstg, pt shd, terr, EHU (10A)
€3.20 (poss long lead req) (poss rev pol); bbq; red long
stay; TV; 40% statics; Eng spkn; adv bkg acc; tennis;
canoe hire; fishing; games area; bike hire; waterslide;
CKE. "Excel site in beautiful surroundings; lake adj;
helpful recep; nice rvside site adj to leisure pool; vill 20
mins along rv." €19.00, 6 Apr-4 Nov. 2019

"I like to fill in the reports as I travel from site to site"

You'll find report forms at the back of this
guide, or you can fill them in online at
camc.com/europereport.

AMIENS *3C3* (10km N Rural) *49.97240, 2.30150*
FFCC Camping du Château, Rue du Château, 80260
Bertangles 09 51 66 32 60; camping@chateau
bertangles.com; www.chateaubertangles.com

Foll N25 N of Amiens; after 8km turn W on D97
to Bertangles. Well sp in vill. 2*, Sm, hdg, pt shd,
EHU (5A) €3.70 (poss rev pol); red long stay; bus;
CKE. "Pleasant, peaceful, well-kept site by chateau
wall; busy high ssn, early arr rec (bef 1600); pleasant
welcome; clean, old san facs; ltd recep hrs, pitch
yourself; grnd soft when wet; Amiens attractive city;
gd walks; conv a'routes & NH; excel; gd value; basic
site, needs updating; lovely location; gd dogs walk adj."
€21.00, 21 Apr-11 Sep. 2017

FRANCE

AMIENS *3C3* (5km NW Urban) *49.92091, 2.25883*
Camping Parc des Cygnes, 111 Ave des Cygnes,
80080 Amiens-Longpré **03 22 43 29 28;** alban@
parcdescygnes.com; www.parcdescygnes.com

🐕 €2.40 👪(htd) ⬛ ♨ ♿ ⬛ ∥ ᴹˢᶠ 🦋 ♏ 🍽 ⓘ♨🛒nr ⚱

**Exit A16 junc 20 twds Amiens onto ring rd Rocade
Nord exit junc 40. At 1st rndabt foll sp Amiens,
Longpré D412; foll sp Parc de Loisirs & site.**
4*, Med, mkd, pt shd, EHU (10A) inc on most pitches
(poss long lead req); gas; bbq; twin axles; TV; phone;
bus to city adj; adv bkg rec; ccard acc; fishing nr; bike
hire; games rm; kayaking; CKE. *"Peaceful, well-kept,
secure site in parkland; leisure park adj; lge pitches;
helpful, welcoming staff; gd, clean san facs, ltd LS; ring
bell by recep if office clsd; no o'fits over 11m high ssn;
access to grass pitches off hard areas - m'vans can keep
driving wheels on in wet weather; gd canal-side cycling/
walk to city; Amiens cathedral worth visit; longer leads
req for some pitches; conv Somme battlefields; gd; rec;
50% of pitches have EHU; san facs adequate but need
updating (2018)."* **€29.00, 1 Apr-14 Oct, P11.** 2018

"I need an on-site restaurant"

We do our best to make sure site information
is correct, but it is always best to check any
must-have facilities are still available or will
be open during your visit.

ANCENIS *2G4* (5km SW Rural) *47.34400, -1.20693*
Camp Municipal Beauregret, 49530 Drain **02 40 98
20 30** or 02 40 98 20 16 (Mairie); mairie-sg.drain@
wanadoo.fr

👪 ⬛ ♨ ♿ ⬛ ∥ ᴹˢᶠ 🦋 🛒nr ⚱ ✎

**Fr Ancenis take D763 S for 2km, turn R onto D751 &
cont for 3km. Site on R bef vill of Drain on L.**
2*, Sm, hdg, pt shd, EHU (10A) inc (poss rev pol); bbq;
TV; adv bkg acc; games area. *"Secluded, tranquil site;
immac san facs up steps - ltd number; poss not suitable
lge o'fits; warden calls am & pm; gd fishing; lake nrby;
nice quiet site."* **€13.00, 1 May-30 Sep.** 2019

ANCENIS *2G4* (1.5km W Rural) *47.36201, -1.18721*
FFCC Camping de l'Ile Mouchet, 44156 Ancenis Cedex
02 40 83 08 43 or 06 62 54 24 73 (mob); camping-ile-
mouchet@orange.fr; www.camping-estivance.com

🐕 👪(htd) ⬛ ♨ ⬛ ∥ ᴹˢᶠ 🦋 🍽 🍽 ⓘ♨🛒nr ⚱ ✎

**Fr S, exit N249 at Vallet onto D763 to Ancenis; turn
L immed after x-ing Rv Loire & foll sp; site on banks
of rv. Or fr N, exit A11 junc 20 onto D923 to Ancenis;
cont on D923 over rndabt; foll D923 along rv; in
400m, at next rndabt, do not cross rv but cont strt
on onto D23; site sp to L in 700m.** 3*, Med, mkd, pt
shd, EHU (6-10A) €4 (rev pol); gas; TV; 12% statics;
Eng spkn; adv bkg acc; ccard acc; waterslide; tennis
50m; games rm; CKE. *"Excel touring base; ltd facs
LS; some steps; rvside walks; gd site with modern
facs; worth a couple of nights; recep clsd 1200-1430."*
€11.00, 2 Apr-23 Oct. 2016

ANDELYS, LES *3D2* (2.5km SW Rural) *49.23582,
1.40016* **Camping de L'Ile des Trois Rois,** 1 rue
Gilles Nicolle, 27700 Les Andelys **02 32 54 23 79;**
campingtroisrois@aol.com; www.camping-trois-
rois.com

🐕 €4 👪(htd) ⬛ ♨ ♿ ⬛ ∥ ᴹˢᶠ 🦋 ♏ 🍽 ⓘ♨ ⚱ ✎
🛒(htd) 📖

**Fr Rouen S on A13, exit junc 18 onto D135 & foll
sp Les Andelys. Cross bdge over Rv Seine & turn
immed R at rndabt, site on R on rvside. Site sp
fr town cent.** 3*, Med, hdstg, mkd, hdg, pt shd, EHU
(10A) inc; gas; bbq; red long stay; TV; 20% statics;
phone; Eng spkn; adv bkg acc; ccard acc; fishing;
bike hire; games rm; CKE. *"Well-kept site on Rv
Seine; extra lge pitches avail; friendly, helpful staff;
gd security; conv Rouen, Evreux, Giverny; bowling
alley; view ruins of Château Gaillard; nice place, nice
people; excel; refurbished, clean, modern san facs, sw
pool, vg bar & rest; easy walk to old town; hugh site;
gd dog walk adj."* **€29.00, 15 Mar-15 Nov.** 2019

See advertisement

ANDERNOS LES BAINS *7D1* (5km NW Coastal) 44.77287, -1.14144 **Camping La Cigale,** Route de Lège, 33740 Arès 05 56 60 22 59; contact@camping-lacigale-ares.com; www.camping-lacigale-ares.com
€1 (htd) 900m

Fr Andernos proceed NW on D3 to Arès. Take Cap-Ferret rd D106. Site on L in 1km. 4*, Sm, mkd, pt shd, EHU (6-10A); gas; bbq; twin axles; 50% statics; bus 1km; Eng spkn; adv bkg rec; games rm. "*Excel family-run site; v clean; gd sized pitches; bike hire adj; cycle rtes; supmkt 2km.*" **€42.00, 27 Apr-25 Sep.**   **2017**

ANDUZE *10E1* (1.4km NW Rural) 44.06430, 3.97694 **Camping Castel Rose,** 30140 Anduze 04 66 61 80 15; castelrose@wanadoo.fr; www.castelrose.com
€2

Fr Alès S on D6110 & W on N910A to Anduze. **Foll sp Camping L'Arche.** 3*, Lge, shd, EHU (6-10A) €3.20-4; gas; TV; Eng spkn; adv bkg rec; fishing; boating. "*Excel site by rv; friendly, helpful owners; attractive countryside; gd cent touring Cévennes.*" **€50.00, 12 Apr-22 Sep.**   **2019**

ANGERS *4G1* (15km SE Rural) 47.44332, -0.40881 **Camping du Port Caroline,** Rue du Pont Caroline, 49800 Brain-sur-l'Authion 02 41 80 42 18; info@campingduportcaroline.fr; www.campingduportcaroline.fr
€3 (htd) nr (htd)

E fr Angers on D347 turn onto D113, site sp at ent to vill. 3*, Med, hdg, mkd, hdstg, pt shd, EHU (10A) inc; bbq; TV; 5% statics; adv bkg acc; ccard acc; games rm; tennis nr; fishing nr. "*Gd touring base; games area adj; skateboarding; site clsd Feb; lge pitches.*" **€15.00, 1 Apr-31 Oct.**   **2017**

ANDUZE *10E1* (2km NW Rural) 44.06785, 3.97336 **Camping L'Arche,** Route de Saint Jean du Gard, 30140 Anduze 04 66 61 74 08; contact@camping-arche.fr; www.camping-arche.fr
€3.80 (htd) (covrd, htd)

Fr Alès S on D6110/D910A to Anduze. On D907, sp on R. Access poss dff lge o'fits/m'vans. 3*, Lge, mkd, shd, EHU (10A) €2; gas; bbq; red long stay; TV; 10% statics; Eng spkn; adv bkg acc; waterslide; CKE. "*Well-run site; gd san facs; beautiful area; bamboo gardens worth visit; 24hr security patrols; excel rest; outstanding site; vg value.*" **€48.00, 1 Apr-30 Sep.**   **2019**

See advertisement

ANGERS *4G1* (6km SW Urban) 47.45387, -0.59463 **Camping du Lac de Maine,** Ave du Lac de Maine, 49000 Angers 02 41 73 05 03; camping@lacdemaine.fr; www.camping-angers.fr
€2.30 (htd) nr (htd)

W fr Angers on D723, exit at 'Quartier du Lac de Maine' then foll sp to site & Bouchemaine. After 4 rndabts site on L; sp W of Rv Maine. Fr S on D160 or A87, turn onto D4 at Les Ponts-de-Cé. In 6km, cross Rv Maine to Bouchemaine & turn R to Pruniers dir Angers. Site on R at Pruniers town exit sp. 4*, Med, hdstg, mkd, hdg, pt shd, serviced pitches; EHU (10A) €4.20 (rev pol); gas; bbq; sw nr; red long stay; twin axles; TV; 10% statics; phone; bus adj; Eng spkn; adv bkg rec; ccard acc; boating; fishing; tennis 800m; games area; windsurfing 500m; jacuzzi; bike hire; CKE. "*Excel, lge, well-run site in leisure park; pitches narr, some suitable v l'ge o'fits; height barrier at ent 3.2m; conv Loire chateaux; pay 6 nights, stay 7; hypmkt 2km; facs ltd in LS; solar shwrs; few lights on site; gd cycling & walking rte; canoeing; gd bus svrs; excel san facs; v helpful recep; bread avail.*" **€30.00, 23 Mar-28 Oct.**   **2018**

FRANCE

ANGOULEME *7B2* (6.7km N Rural) *45.68573, 0.14994* **Camping du Plan d'Eau,** 1 rue du Camping, 16710 St Yrieix-sur-Charante **05 45 92 14 64; camping@grandangouleme.fr; www.camping-angouleme.fr**

🐕 ♦♦♦ (htd) [wc] ♨ ♿ ▣ ⚊ ✖ 🦋 ⛺ ♟ ▽ ⊕ ♨ ▦ ⌂ ⚓

Fr N or S on N10/E606 turn NW & foll sp St Yrieix-sur-Charante, 'Plan d'Eau' & 'Nautilis - Centre Nautique'. Site sp. 3*, Med, hdg, mkd, pt shd, EHU (10A) €3.50; gas; bbq; sw nr; TV; 10% statics; Eng spkn; adv bkg acc; ccard acc; games area; watersports. *"Superb location; gd; rather bare site; notices warn of poss flooding."* **€16.50, 1 Apr-31 Oct.**   **2015**

ANGOULEME *7B2* (23km NW Rural) *45.79769, 000.63639* **Camping Marco de Bignac (formerly Les Sablons),** Chemin de la Résistance, 16170 Bignac **05 45 21 78 41; info@marcodebignac.com; www.marcodebignac.com**

🐕 ♦♦♦ (htd) [wc] ♨ ♿ ▣ ⚊ ✖ 🦋 ⛺ ♟ ▽ ⊕ ▦ ⌂ ✂ ⚓

Fr N10 approx 14km N Angoulême take exit La Touche & foll D11 W thro Vars; at Basse turn R onto D117 & foll sp in Bignac. (Foll sp not Sat Nav due to new rd layout at Basse). 3*, Med, mkd, pt shd, EHU (3-6A) €3-4; bbq (charcoal, elec, gas); twin axles; red long stay; 3% statics; bus adj; Eng spkn; adv bkg acc; ccard acc; games area; tennis; fishing; watersports; bike hire; pets corner; CKE. *"Attractive, peaceful, tidy, lakeside site; worth long drive; scenic area; lge pitches; welcoming, helpful British owners; clean refurb san facs; gd rest; pleasant walk round lake; lake adj; ideal for Angoulême Circuit des Remparts; excel; pets corner; excel."* **€29.00, 1 Feb-30 Nov.   2019**

ANNECY *9B3* (10km SE Rural) *45.84070, 6.16450* **Camping Le Solitaire du Lac,** 615 Route de Sales, 74410 St Jorioz **04 50 68 59 30 or 06 88 58 94 24 (mob); contact@campinglesolitaire.com or campinglesolitaire@wanadoo.fr; www.campinglesolitaire.com**

🐕 €2.60 ♦♦♦ [wc] ♨ ▣ ⚊ ✖ 🦋 ⛺ ♟ ▽ ⊕ ♨ ⚓ nr ⌂

Exit Annecy on D1508 twd Albertville. Site sp on N o'skts of St Jorioz. 3*, Med, mkd, pt shd, EHU (5A) €3.50; gas; bbq; sw; red long stay; TV; 10% statics; Eng spkn; adv bkg acc; ccard acc; boat launch; games area; bike hire; CKE. *"Nice, well-run site in excel location; water to MH's charge €0.20 per 60l; popular but quiet; cycle track; sm pitches; clean, modern san facs; direct access to Lake Annecy; sh walk to public beach & water bus; cycle path nr; gd touring base; excel; perfect for boating & cycling; v helpful staff."* **€29.00, 8 Apr-23 Sep.   2017**

ANNECY *9B3* (11km SE Rural) *45.82423, 6.18523* **Camping Le Familial,** 400 Route de Magnonnet, 74410 Duingt **04 50 68 69 91; contact@annecy-camping-familial.com; www.annecy-camping-familial.com**

🐕 €1.70 ♦♦♦ [wc] ♨ ▣ ⚊ ✖ 🦋 ⛺ ♟ ⌂

Fr Annecy on D1508 twd Albertville. 5km after St Jorioz turn R at site sp Entrevernes onto D8, foll sp past Camping Champs Fleuris. 2*, Sm, mkd, hdstg, pt shd, pt sl, EHU (6A) €4.30; bbq; twin axles; TV; Eng spkn; adv bkg rec; ccard acc; games area; CKE. *"Gd site in scenic area; gd atmosphere; generous pitches; friendly, helpful owner; communal meals & fondu evenings; conv lakeside cycle track; mobile homes for rent, sleeps 6; excel."* **€22.50, 1 Apr-30 Sep.   2018**

ANNECY *9B3* (12km SE Rural) *45.88990, 6.22367* **Camping La Ferme de Ferrières,** 74290 Alex **04 50 02 87 09; campingfermedesferrieres@voila.fr; www.camping-des-ferrieres.com**

🐕 €1 ♦♦♦ (cont) [wc] ♨ ♿ ▣ ⚊ ✖ 🦋 ⛺ ♟ ⌂

Take D909 on E side of lake out of Annecy twds Thônes; look out for sp on L after turn off to Château de Menthon. Site off D909 approx 1km W of Alex. 2*, Med, pt shd, pt sl, terr, EHU (5A) €2.80; bbq; phone; Eng spkn; adv bkg acc; ccard acc; games rm; CKE. *"Spectacular views; peaceful, clean site away fr crowds; friendly & accommodating owner; high standard san facs; pitches muddy when wet; gd NH; basic facs; fair."* **€16.50, 1 Jun-30 Sep.   2015**

"Satellite navigation makes touring much easier"

Remember most sat navs don't know if you're towing or in a larger vehicle – always use yours alongside maps and site directions.

ANNECY *9B3* (1.7km S Rural) *45.89100, 6.13236* **Camp Municipal Le Belvédère,** 8 Route du Semnoz, 74000 Annecy **04 50 45 48 30; camping@ville-annecy.fr; www.annecy.fr**

🐕 ♦♦♦ (htd) [wc] ♨ ♿ ▣ ⚊ ✖ ♟ ⊕ ♨ ⚓ ⌂

Exit A41 junc 16; initially foll sp 'Albertville' into town; then foll sp 'Le Lac' and 'Le Semnoz'; site is on R off Route du Semnoz (Route du Semnoz is A41). 'Le Semnoz is a mountain running S fr Annecy. 3*, Lge, mkd, pt shd, pt sl, terr, EHU (16A) €3.20 (poss rev pol); gas; TV; phone; Eng spkn; adv bkg rec; ccard acc; fishing; bike hire; excursions; sailing; CKE. *"Lovely, tidy site in beautiful setting; well lit at night; sm pitches; staff helpful; san facs OK; steep footpath to old town; sep statics area; excel; dogs free; v friendly helpful staff; forest walks."* **€27.00, 25 Mar-16 Oct.   2016**

FRANCE

ANNECY *9B3* (10km S Rural) *45.82995, 6.18215*
Village Camping Europa, 1444 Route d'Albertville, 74410 St Jorioz **04 50 68 51 01; info@camping-europa.com; www.camping-europa.com**

🐕 €3 👫 wc ♨ 🚿 👤 ⚙ ⁄ MSP 🦋 ♀ ☂ 🍴 ⊕ 🛒 🏊 nr ⚠ ✒
🏊 (htd)

Fr Annecy take D1508 sp Albertville. Site on R 800m S of St Jorioz dir Albertville. Look for lge yellow sp on o'skirts of St Jorioz. 4*, Med, hdg, pt shd, serviced pitches; EHU (6A) €3.80; bbq (elec, gas); red long stay; twin axles; TV; 20% statics; Eng spkn; adv bkg acc; ccard acc; bike hire; jacuzzi; boat hire; fishing; waterslide; games rm; tennis 700m; windsurfing; CKE. *"Peaceful site; friendly staff; facs stretched high ssn; vg rest; excel for m'vans; conv Chamonix & Mont Blanc; variable pitch prices; cycle track adj; some pitches tight lge o'fits; gd tourist base; excel; no water points around site, collect fr toilet block; brilliant pool complex; no hot water in sinks; gd cycling area."* **€40.00, 30 Apr-17 Sep.** **2016**

ANNECY *9B3* (6km S Urban) *45.85482, 6.14395*
Camping au Coeur du Lac, Les Choseaux, 74320 Sévrier **04 50 52 46 45; info@aucoeurdulac.com; www.campingaucoeurdulac.com**

🐕 👫 wc ♨ 🚿 👤 ⚙ ⁄ MSP 🦋 ♀ 🍴 ⚠ ✒ ☂

S fr Annecy on D1508 sp Albertville. Pass thro Sévrier cent. Site on L at lakeside 1km S of Sévrier. 300m after McDonald's. 3*, Med, mkd, hdstg, pt shd, pt sl, terr, EHU (4A) €3.60, long cable rec; sw; bus nrby; Eng spkn; adv bkg req; ccard acc; boat hire; bike hire; CKE. *"Busy, nice site in lovely location; gd views of lake fr upper terr; tight for lge o'fits - sm, sl pitches; dogs not acc high ssn; ok san facs; gd access to lake beach & cycle path; excel, espec LS; v popular site."* **€28.00, 1 Apr-30 Sep.** **2016**

ANNECY *9B3* (6km S Rural) *45.84333, 6.14175*
Camping Le Panoramic, 22 Chemin des Bernets, Route de Cessenaz, 74320 Sévrier **04 50 52 43 09; info@camping-le-panoramic.com; www.camping-le-panoramic.com**

🐕 €1.60 👫 (htd) wc ♨ 🚿 👤 ⚙ 🦋 ♀ 🍴 ⊕ 🛒 ⚠ 🏊 ☂ 2km

Exit A41 junc 16 Annecy Sud onto D1508 sp Albertville. Thro Sévrier to rndabt at Cessenaz (ignore all prior sp to site) & take 1st R onto D10. In 200m turn R up hill to site in 2km. 3*, Lge, mkd, pt shd, pt sl, terr, EHU (4-6A) €3.20-4.20 (some rev pol); sw; TV; Eng spkn; ccard acc; games rm; CKE. *"Fantastic views fr many pitches; blocks/wedges ess for sl pitches; excel pool/bar area; rec for families; new san facs (2012); excel views of lake; v friendly staff; high rec."* **€31.00, 19 Apr-29 Sep.** **2019**

ANNECY *9B3* (6.5km S Urban) *45.84412, 6.15354*
Camping de l'Aloua, 492 Route de Piron, 74320 Sévrier **04 50 52 60 06; camping.aloua@wanadoo.fr; www.camping-aloua-lac-annecy.com**

🐕 €2 👫 wc ♨ 🚿 👤 ⚙ ⁄ MSP 🍴 ⊕ 🛒 ⚠ ✒ ☂ shgl 300m

Foll sp for Albertville D1508 S fr Annecy. Site on E side, approx 1.4km S of Sevrier vill. Turn L at Champion supmkt rndabt & foll sp twd lake. 2*, Lge, hdg, mkd, shd, EHU (2-10A) €2.50-4.80; sw nr; TV; phone; Eng spkn; adv bkg acc; fishing adj; watersports adj; archery; boating adj; CKE. *"Gd base for lake (no dir access fr site); cycle track around lake; night security; poss noisy at night with youths & some rd noise; basic san facs; pleasant owners; well run & maintained site; nr lac Annecy, Carrefour & g'ge; bike track or bus to Annecy; vg."* **€23.00, 18 Apr-19 Sep.** **2015**

"There aren't many sites open at this time of year"

If you're travelling outside peak season remember to call ahead to check site opening dates – even if the entry says 'open all year'.

ANNECY *9B3* (6.5km S Rural) *45.84806, 6.15129*
FFCC Camping Les Rives du Lac, 331 Chemin du Communaux, 74320 Sévrier **04 50 52 40 14; lesrivesdulac-annecy@ffcc.fr; www.lesrivesdulac-annecy.com**

🐕 €1.20 👫 wc ♨ 🚿 👤 ⚙ ⁄ MSP 🦋 ♀ ☂ nr ⚠ ✒ shgl

Take D1508 S fr Annecy sp Albertville, thro Sévrier sp FFCC. Turn L 100m past (S) Lidl supmkt, cross cycle path & turn R & foll sp FFCC keeping parallel with cycle path. Site on L in 400m. 3*, Med, mkd, pt shd, EHU (10A) €4; bbq; sw; bus nr; Eng spkn; adv bkg acc; sailing; fishing; CKE. *"Beautiful situation; generous pitches; helpful staff; excel new toilet block; water bus to Annecy nr; gd touring base; walking; red CC members (check first); walking, sailing & cycling; cycle rte adj."* **€32.00, 30 Mar-29 Sep.** **2019**

ANNONAY *9C2* (4km N Urban) *45.25799, 4.67426*
Camp Municipal de Vaure, Rue Mathieu Duret, 07100 Annonay **04 75 33 73 73 or 04 75 33 46 54; www.mairie-annonay.fr**

🐕 €1.50 👫 ♨ 🚿 ⚙ ⁄ 🦋 ♀ 🍴 ☂ nr 🏊 (covrd, htd) 🏛

Sp fr o'skts of town & foll sp St Etienne. Fr St Etienne & NW on D1082 & D820 twd Annonay. For R onto D206 S & foll camping/piscine sp to site. Sm, hdg, mkd, pt shd, EHU (6-10A) €2.50-3.50; 10% statics; tennis; games area. *"Helpful staff; gd; basic facs; site not v secure."* **€10.00, 1 Apr-31 Oct.** **2016**

ANTIBES *10E4* (2km N Urban/Coastal) *43.60536, 7.11255* **Camping Caravaning Le Rossignol,** Ave Jean Michard-Pelissier, Juan-les-Pins, 06600 Antibes **04 93 33 56 98; campinglerossignol@wanadoo.fr; www.campingrossignol.com**

€2.50 nr (htd) shgl 1.2km

Turn W off N7 Antibes-Nice at sp to Hospitalier de la Fontonne then bear L along Chemin des Quatres past hospital & traff lts junc. In 400m turn R at rndabt into Ave Jean Michard Pelissier, site 200m on R. NB Narr ent off busy rd. 3*, Med, hdstg, mkd, hdg, shd, terr, EHU (10A) €5; gas; bbq (elec, gas); red long stay; TV; Eng spkn; adv bkg acc; ccard acc; games area; games rm; tennis 2km; CKE. *"Conv Antibes & surrounding area; peaceful site; sm pitches."* **€32.60, 13 Apr-28 Sep.** **2019**

APT *10E3* (8km N Rural) *43.92050, 5.34120* **Domaine des Chenes Blancs,** Route de Gargas, 84490 St Saturnin-lès-Apt **04 90 74 09 20 or 06 63 90 37 66; contact@leschenesblancs.com; www.vaucluse-camping.com**

€4 (htd)

Fr W on D900 twd Apt, at NW o'skts of Apt turn N on D101, cont approx 2km turn R on D83 into Gargas; thro Gargas & in 4km turn L at camp sp; site on R in 300m. Narr rd. 3*, Lge, hdg, shd, EHU (6A) inc; bbq; TV; Eng spkn; adv bkg rec; ccard acc; lake fishing 5km; games area. *"Well-run, popular site in gd location; pitches amongst oaks poss diff lge o'fits; steel pegs req due stony grnd; friendly staff; vg, modern san facs; nice pool; excel touring base; lots of facs; dated san facs (2015); dusty."* **€32.60, 28 Mar-17 Oct.** **2015**

"That's changed – Should I let the Club know?"

If you find something on site that's different from the site entry, fill in a report and let us know. See camc.com/europereport.

APT *10E3* (0.5km NE Urban) *43.87753, 5.40302* **Camp Municipal Les Cèdres,** 63 Impasse de la Fantaisie, 84400 Apt **04 90 74 14 61 or 04 90 74 14 61 (mob); lucie.bouillet@yahoo.fr; www.camping-les-cedres.fr**

€1 (htd)

In town turn N off D900 onto D22 twd Rustrel, site sp. Site on R in 200m immed after going under old rlwy bdge. 2*, Med, mkd, pt shd, EHU (6-10A) €3.50; gas; cooking facs; adv bkg acc; ccard acc; CKE. *"Excel site in lovely location; sm pitches; pitching poss haphazard LS; friendly staff; clean san facs; some pitches muddy when wet; cycle tracks; conv Luberon vills & ochre mines; phone ahead to check open LS; v lge mkt Sat; gd NH; site in 2 parts; popular; gd touring cent."* **€16.00, 1 Mar-31 Oct.** **2019**

ARAMITS *8F1* (0.3km W Rural) *43.12135, -0.73215* **Camping Barétous-Pyrénées,** Quartier Ripaude, 64570 Aramits **05 59 34 12 21; contact@camping-pyrenees.com; www.camping-pyrenees.com**

€2.80 nr nr (htd)

SW fr Oloron-Ste Marie take D919 sp Aramits, Arette. Fr Aramits cont on D919 sp Lanne; site on R; well sp. 4*, Sm, mkd, pt shd, serviced pitches; EHU (10A) €4.90; twin axles; TV; 50% statics; Eng spkn; adv bkg acc; games rm; bike hire; CKE. *"Friendly, helpful owner; well-kept, clean, lovely site but muddy when wet; ltd facs LS; dated but v clean; gd base for Pyrenees; poss unrel opening dates - phone ahead LS; excel bistro 400m; vg."* **€28.00, 1 Apr-17 Oct.** **2015**

"I like to fill in the reports as I travel from site to site"

You'll find report forms at the back of this guide, or you can fill them in online at camc.com/europereport.

ARBOIS *6H2* (1.5km E Urban) *46.90331, 5.78691* **Camp Municipal Les Vignes,** 5 Rue de la Piscine, 39600 Arbois **03 84 66 14 12 or 03 84 25 26 19; campinglesvignes@hotmail.fr; http://alexandrachti.wix.com/camping-les-vignes**

€2.50

Fr N or S, ent town & at rndabt in cent foll camp sp on D107 dir Mesnay. Site adj stadium & pool. NB Steep slopes to terr & narr ent unsuitable lge o'fits. 3*, Med, hdg, mkd, hdstg, pt shd, pt sl, terr, EHU (10A) inc; gas; twin axles; TV; Eng spkn; adv bkg acc; ccard acc; tennis; fishing 1km; CKE. *"Beautiful setting; clean san facs but poss stretched high ssn; site clsd 2200-0800 LS; ltd facs LS; pitches on lower tier mostly sl; pleasant sm town, home of Louis Pasteur a must see; htd pool adj; Roman salt works, grottoes nr; lge fair 1st w/end in Sep; excel; linear site; shd pitches at W end furthest fr main facs; poss rallies."* **€25.00, 16 Apr-2 Oct.** **2019**

ARC EN BARROIS *6F1* (0.5km W Urban) *47.95052, 5.00523* **Camp Municipal Le Vieux Moulin,** 52210 Arc-en-Barrois **03 25 02 51 33 (Mairie); mairie.arc.en.barrois@wanadoo.fr**

€2.18 (htd) nr

Exit A5 junc 24 onto D10 S to Arc-en-Barrois; turn R onto D3 thro vill; site on L on o'skirts. Or fr D65 turn L onto D6 about 4km S of Châteauvillain; site on R on D3 at ent to vill, adj rv. 4*, Med, pt shd, EHU (6A) inc; bbq; TV; tennis adj; CKE. *"Attractive, peaceful, lovely, well-kept site by sm rv; adj vill sports field; basic, clean san facs but need update - excel hot shwrs; warden calls early eve, poss not on Sundays; gd wildlife; beautiful vill; conv NH fr A5 or longer."* **€17.00, 1 May-30 Sep.** **2017**

FRANCE

ARCACHON *7D1* (0.5km E Coastal) *44.65089, -1.17381*
Camping Club d'Arcachon, 5 Allée de la Galaxie,
33312 Arcachon 05 56 83 24 15; info@camping-
arcachon.com; www.camping-arcachon.com

🐕 €4 ♨(htd) �‖ ﹦♨♿🖂 ⌿ ᴹˢᴾ 👙 ⍦ 🍴 🄣 ♨ 🍺 ⟋⟍ ⚓ ⚊
⚲ sand 1.5km

Exit A63 ont A660 dir Arcachon. Foll sp 'Hôpital
Jean Hameau' & site sp. 4*, Lge, hdstg, mkd, hdg, pt
shd, terr, EHU (10A) €4; gas; bbq; TV; 40% statics;
Eng spkn; adv bkg acc; ccard acc; bike hire; site clsd
mid-Nov to mid-Dec; CKE. "*Vg site in pine trees;*
excel touring base; gd facs; access rds narr - poss
diff manoeuvring into pitches; gd network cycle
tracks; private san facs avail; easy walk to town."
€44.00, 1 Jan-14 Nov, 15 Dec-31 Dec. 2017

ARCACHON *7D1* (9km E Coastal) *44.64400, -1.11167*
Camping de Verdalle, 2 Allée de l'Infante, La Hume,
33470 Gujan-Mestras 05 56 66 12 62; camping.
verdalle@wanadoo.fr; www.campingdeverdalle.com

🐕 €1.50 ♨♿ �‖ ﹦♿ 🖂 ⌿ 👙 ⍦ 🍺 nr ⚲ sand adj

Fr A63 take A660 twd Arcachon. Turn R at rndabt
junc with D652 sp La Hume. In vill at junc with
D650 turn L, then R at rndabt; then 3rd turning
on R after rlwy line. 2*, Med, hdg, pt shd, EHU
(10A) inc; bbq (sep area); phone; bus adj; Eng spkn;
adv bkg acc; ccard acc; CKE. "*Lovely, well-kept site*
in excel position in Arcachon bay; friendly, helpful
owner; cycling/walking; conv local attractions; vg."
€28.00, 1 Apr-3 Oct. 2019

ARCIS SUR AUBE *4E4* (0.5km N Urban) *48.53907,*
4.14270 Camping de l'Ile Cherlieu, Rue de Châlons,
10700 Arcis-sur-Aube 03 25 37 98 79; camping-arcis@
hermans.cx

🐕 €1.60 ♨♿ �‖ ﹦♿ 🖂 ⌿ 👙 ⍦ 🍴 nr ⍦ nr 🍺 nr ⟋⟍

Fr A26 junc 21 foll sp to Arcis. Fr town cent take
D677/N77 dir Châlons-en-Champagne. Turn R after
rv bdge, site sp. 3*, Med, mkd, shd, EHU (10-16A)
inc (poss rev pol); bbq; Eng spkn; rv fishing adj; CKE.
"*Pleasant, well-kept site on island surrounded by rv;*
friendly, helpful Dutch owners; gd, clean san facs;
popular NH, rec arr early; bar 500m; vg site; quiet by
10pm; muddy in wet weather; gd site, improves each
year; excel facs." **€22.00, 10 Apr-1 Oct.** 2018

ARCIS SUR AUBE *4E4* (8km S Rural) *48.46696,*
4.12633 FFCC Camping La Barbuise, 10700 St Remy-
sous-Barbuise 03 25 37 50 95 or 03 25 37 41 11;
www.camping-ffcc.com

12 🐕 ♨♿ �‖ ﹦♿ 🖂 ᴹˢᴾ ⍦

Fr Arcis-sur-Aube, take D677 twd Voué; site on L bef
vill of Voué, sp. Fr S exit A26 junc 21 onto D441 W;
then onto D677 S twd Voué & as bef. 1*, Sm, pt shd,
pt sl, EHU (4A) inc (poss rev pol); bbq; phone; adv bkg
acc; CKE. "*Lovely, peaceful, spacious CL-type site; early*
arr rec; site yourself, owner calls eves (cash only); easy
access & pitching for lge o'fits; charming owners; san
facs basic but clean; elec heaters not allowed; dogs on
leads only; pool 8km; conv NH off A26 or sh stay; 2 pin
adapter ess; bar high ssn only." **€9.00** 2019

ARDRES *3A3* (0.5km N Urban) *50.85726, 1.97551*
Camping Ardresien, 64 Rue Basse, 62610 Ardres
03 21 82 82 32

🐕 ♨♿ ⓦ ﹦⌿

Fr St Omer on D943 to Ardres, strt on at lights in
town onto D231; site 500m on R - easy to o'shoot;
v narr ent, not suitable twin-axles. 1*, Sm, hdg,
pt shd, EHU (16A) inc; 95% statics; CKE. "*Basic*
site; friendly staff; walk to lakes at rear of site; ltd
touring pitches; conv Calais & local vet; NH only."
€15.00, 1 May-30 Sep. 2018

ARDRES *3A3* (10km SE Rural) *50.83865, 1.97612*
Camping St Louis, 223 Rue Leulène, 62610 Autingues
03 21 35 46 83; camping-saint-louis@sfr.fr;
www.campingstlouis.com

🐕 ♨♿ ⓦ ﹦♨♿ 🖂 ⌿ 👙 ⍦ ⍦ 🄣 ♨ 🍺 ⟋⟍ ⌿

Fr Calais S on D943 to Ardres; fr Ardres take D224 S
twd Licques, after 2km turn L on D227; site well sp
in 100m. Or fr junc 2 off A26 onto D943 dir Ardres.
Turn L just after Total g'ge on R on app to Ardres.
Well sp. If app fr S via Boulogne avoid Nabringhen &
Licques as narr, steep hill with bends. NB Mkt Thurs
am - avoid R turn when leaving site. 3*, Med, hdg,
mkd, pt shd, EHU (10A) inc (long lead poss req, poss
rev pol); gas; bbq; 70% statics; phone; Eng spkn; adv
bkg req; ccard acc; games rm; CKE. "*Peaceful, well-*
kept, well-run, busy site; conv Dunkerque, Calais ferries;
some gd sized pitches; gd welcome & friendly; clean
san facs poss stretched high ssn; ltd touring pitches;
phone ahead to check avail high ssn; early dep/late arr
area; automatic exit barrier; barrier opens 0600 high
ssn; gd rest; vg vet in Ardres; vg, conv NH; lovely clean,
improved site; newly refurb san facs, excel (2015);
well maintained; can be booked thro Pitchup.com."
€25.00, 1 Apr-18 Oct. 2018

ARDRES *3A3* (10km SE Rural) *50.80867, 2.05569*
Hôtel Bal Caravaning, 500 Rue du Vieux Château,
62890 Tournehem-sur-la-Hem 03 21 35 65 90;
contact@hotel-bal.com; www.hotel-bal.com

ⓦ ﹦♿ ⌿ 👙 ⍦ 🍴 nr ⍦ nr ⟋⟍ ⌿

Fr S on A26 leave at exit 2; turn R onto D217 then R
onto D943 dir St Omer. Turn R in Nordausques onto
D218 (approx 1km), pass under A26, site is 1km on
L - ent thro Bal Parc Hotel gates. Fr N or S on D943,
turn R or L in Nordausques, then as above.
3*, Med, mkd, hdg, hdstg, pt shd, pt sl, EHU (10A)
inc (poss rev pol); gas; 80% statics; Eng spkn;
adv bkg acc; ccard acc; tennis; CKE. "*Tidy area*
for tourers, but few touring pitches; sports grnd &
leisure cent adj; htd wc (in hotel in winter); gd rest &
bar; 25km Cité Europe mall; gd NH; ltd facs in LS."
€20.00, 1 Apr-31 Oct. 2016

ARDRES *3A3* (9km SE Rural) *50.82193, 2.07577*
Camping Le Relax, 318 Route de Gravelines, 62890
Nordausques **03 21 35 63 77; camping.le.relax@
cegetel.net**

ᵻᵻᵻ 🅦 ⚐ 🖭 🖉 ♿ ⅀ nr ⌂

Fr N on D943 in vill 25km S of Calais at beginning
of vill, turn L at sp. Site 200m on R. Or fr S on
A26, leave at junc 2 & take D943 S for 1km into
Nordausques, then as above. NB Ent diff, beware
low o'hanging roof on recep. 2*, Med, hdg, pt shd,
EHU (6A) €2.20 (poss rev pol); 90% statics; adv
bkg req; CKE. *"Obliging owner; sm pitches & sharp
access, not suitable lge o'fits; basic san facs, poss
tired high ssn; conv A26, Calais & war sites; NH only."*
€13.00, 1 Apr-30 Sep. 2016

ARGELES GAZOST *8G2* (1km N Rural) *43.01218,
-0.09709* **Camping Sunêlia Les Trois Vallées,** Ave des
Pyrénées, 65400 Argelès-Gazost **05 62 90 35 47;
3-vallees@wanadoo.fr; www.l3v.fr**

🛉 ⅀ €2 **ᵻᵻᵻ**(htd) 🅦 ⚐ 🖭 ♿ 🖉 ⍾ 🍽 Ⓨ ⅀ nr ⌂ 🏊 (htd)

S fr Lourdes on D821, turn R at rndabt sp Argelès-
Gazost on D821A. Site off next rndabt on R.
4*, Lge, mkd, pt shd, EHU (6A) inc (poss rev pol); TV;
30% statics; adv bkg req; ccard acc; sauna; games
area; bike hire; waterslide; games rm; golf 11km.
*"Excel touring base; views of Pyrenees; conv Lourdes;
interesting area; red facs LS; excel san facs; v helpful
staff."* **€46.00, 11 Apr-18 Oct.** 2015

ARGELES GAZOST *8G2* (4km NE Rural) *43.01124,
-0.07748* **Camping Deth Potz,** 40 route de Silhen,
65400 Boô-Silhen **05 62 90 37 23; contact@deth-
potz.fr; www.deth-potz.fr**

🛉 ⅀ €1 **ᵻᵻᵻ** 🅦 ⚐ 🖭 ♿ 🖭 🖉 Mℙ 🦋 ⍾ 🏊

Fr Lourdes on D821 to Argeles Gazost. At 2nd
rndabt foll Luz-St-Sauveur sp for 100m over rv and
turn L sp Boo-Silhen. Site on L in 1km.
2*, Med, mkd, pt shd, pt sl, terr, EHU (3-10A) €3-6; bbq;
twin axles; TV; 20% statics; Eng spkn; adv bkg acc;
games rm; games area; CKE. *"Family run site, o'looking
woodland; site has upper (terr) and lower (flat) area;
gd for walking, climbing, stunning scenery; vg site."*
€17.00, 1 Jan-10 Oct & 10 Dec-31 Dec. 2015

ARGELES GAZOST *8G2* (7km SE Rural) *42.98120,
-0.06535* **Camping Le Viscos,** 16 Route de Préchac,
65400 Beaucens **05 62 97 05 45; domaineviscos@
orange.fr**

🛉 ⅀ €1 **ᵻᵻᵻ** 🅦 ⚐ 🖭 🖉 🦋 ⍾ ⅀ nr ⌂

Fr Lourdes S twd Argelès-Gasost on D821. Cont twd
Luz & Gavarnie to L of Argelès town, & turn L within
500m, sp Beaucens. Turn R to D13, site 2.5km on L.
2*, Med, shd, pt sl, EHU (2-10A) €2-4.50 (rev pol); gas;
bbq; red long stay; adv bkg req; lake fishing 500m; CKE.
*"Delightful site; landscaped grnds; excel, clean san facs;
pool 4km; gd rests in area."*
€17.50, 1 May-15 Oct. 2015

ARGELES GAZOST *8G2* (1km S Rural) *42.98670,
-0.08854* **Camping Les Frênes,** 46 Route des Vallées,
65400 Lau-Balagnas **05 62 97 25 12; campinglesfrenes.fr**

ᵻᵻᵻ(htd) 🅦 ⚐ 🖭 ♿ 🖉 🦋 ⅀ nr ⌂ 🖉 🏊

Site on R of D821 twd S. 3*, Med, hdg, shd, EHU
(10A)€4.40; gas; bbq; red long stay; TV; 10% statics;
adv bkg rec; games rm; rv fishing 1km. *"Gd site."*
€18.40, 15 Dec-15 Oct. 2017

ARGELES GAZOST *8G2* (2km S Rural) *42.98826,
-0.08923* **Kawan Village Le Lavedan,** 44 Route des
Vallées, 65400 Lau-Balagnas **05 62 97 18 84; contact@
lavedan.com; www.lavedan.com**

🛉 ⅀ €2.50 **ᵻᵻᵻ**(htd) 🅦 ⚐ 🖭 ♿ 🖭 🖉 ⍾ 🍽 Ⓨ ⊛ ⍾ ⅀ nr ⌂ 🖉
🏊 (covrd, htd) 🖱

Fr Lourdes S on D821 dir Argelès-Gazost/Cauterets;
2km after Argelès on D921 site on R after vill of Lau-
Balagnas. 4*, Med, mkd, shd, EHU (3A) €3 (poss rev
pol; extra for 10A); gas; bbq; TV; 80% statics; phone;
Eng spkn; adv bkg acc; ccard acc; games rm; CKE. *"In
beautiful valley; friendly, relaxed staff; clean modern
san facs; rd noise if pitched adj to rd & poss noise fr
entmnt in café; excel cycle rte to Lourdes; vg; quiet
pleasant site."* **€37.00, 15 Mar-30 Oct.** 2017

> ## "We must tell the Club about that great site we found"
>
> Get your site reports in by mid-August and we'll
> do our best to get your updates into the next
> edition.

ARGELES GAZOST *8G2* (3km S Rural) *42.9871, -0.1061*
Camping du Lac, 29 Chemin d'Azun, 65400 Arcizans-
Avant **05 62 97 01 88; campinglac@campinglac65.fr;
www.campinglac65.fr**

🛉 ⅀ €2.50 **ᵻᵻᵻ** ⚐ 🖭 ♿ 🖭 🖉 🦋 ⍾ ⊛ nr ♿ ⌂ 🏊 (htd)

Fr Lourdes S thro Argelès-Gazost on D821 & D921.
At 3rd rndabt take exit for St Savin/Arcizans-Avant.
Cont thro St Savin vill & foll camp sp; site on L just
thro Arcizans-Avant vill. NB: Dir rte to Arcizans-
Avant prohibited to c'vans. 4*, Med, hdg, mkd, pt
shd, pt sl, EHU (5-10A) €4.30-5; gas; TV; Eng spkn; adv
bkg acc; bike hire; games rm; CKE. *"Excel, beautiful,
peaceful, scenic & attractive site; mountain views; gd
size pitches; clean san facs; gd for touring; excel rest."*
€34.00, 20 May-20 Sep. 2015

FRANCE

ARGELES GAZOST *8G2* (11km SW Rural) *42.94139, -0.17714* **Camping Pyrénées Natura,** Route du Lac, 65400 Estaing 05 62 97 45 44; info@camping-pyrenees-natura.com; www.camping-pyrenees-natura.com

🏕 €3 ♨(htd) ⬚ ♨ ⚲ ⛄ ▣ ✉ ⟋ ᴹᴾ 🦋 ♒ 🍴 ♨ 🛒

Fr Lourdes take D821 to Argelès Gazost; fr Argelès foll sp Col d'Aubisque & Val d'Azun onto D918; after approx 7.5km turn L onto D13 to Bun; after Bun cross rv & turn R onto D103 twd Estaing; site in 3km - rd narr. NB Rd fr Col d'Aubisque steep, narr & not suitable c'vans or lge m'vans. 4*, Med, hdg, mkd, pt shd, terr, EHU (3-10A) €2-5 (poss rev pol); gas; bbq; TV; 20% statics; Eng spkn; adv bkg acc; ccard acc; sauna; games area; solarium; games rm; CKE. *"Superb, peaceful, well-kept, scenic site; friendly, helpful owners; clean unisex san facs; vg takeaway; gd for young families; no plastic grnd-sheets allowed; adj National Park; birdwatching area; excel; home cooked food at bar; no o'fits over 7.5m high ssn; pool 4km; vg site, one of the best ever visited."* €30.00, 18 Apr-10 Oct, D22.   2015

ARGELES SUR MER *10G1* (1km N Coastal) *42.56320, 3.03498* **Camping Les Marsouins,** Ave de la Retirada, 66702 Argelès-sur-Mer 04 68 81 14 81; lesmarsouins@cielavillage.com; www.campsud.com

🏕 €3 ♨ ⬚ ♿ ⛄ ▣ ✉ ⟋ ᴹᴾ ♒ 🍴 ① ♨ 🛒 ⛰ ♨ ♨(htd)

♨ sand 800m

Fr Perpignan take exit 10 fr D914 & foll sp for Argelès until Shell petrol stn on R. Take next L just bef rv into Allée Ferdinand Buisson to T-junc, turn L at next rndabt dir Plage-Nord. Take 2nd R at next rndabt, site on L opp Spanish war memorial. 3*, V lge, mkd, hdg, shd, EHU (5A) inc; gas; bbq (elec, gas); 20% statics; Eng spkn; adv bkg acc; ccard acc; games area; windsurfing 1km; games rm; bike hire; sailing 1km. *"Lovely, well-kept, well-run site; clean san facs; busy rd to beach, but worth it; many sm coves; gd area for cycling; TO on site; excel; gd pool/slides; v conv for town/beach."* €47.00, 14 Apr-8 Oct.   2017

ARGELES SUR MER *10G1* (3km NE Coastal) *42.55583, 3.04222* **Camping Les Pins,** Ave du Tech, Zone des Pins, 66700 Argelès-sur-Mer 04 68 81 10 46; camping@les-pins.com; www.les-pins.com

🏕 €4 ♨ ⬚ ♨ ⚲ ⛄ ▣ ✉ ⟋ 🦋 ♒ ♨ 🛒 ⛰ ♨ sand 200m

Exit D914 junc 10, foll sp Pujols & Plage-Nord, site sp. 3*, Lge, mkd, hdg, pt shd, EHU (6A) inc; gas; Eng spkn; adv bkg rec; ccard acc; games area; CCI. *"Cent for beach & town; pleasant, helpful staff; clean, modern san facs; quiet peaceful site; supmkt nrby."* €48.00, 4 Apr-4 Oct.   2019

ARGELES SUR MER *10G1* (3.5km NE Coastal) *42.57543, 3.0431* **Camping Le Soleil,** Route du Littoral, Plage-Nord, 66700 Argelès-sur-Mer 04 68 81 14 48; camping.lesoleil@wanadoo.fr; www.camping-le-soleil.fr

♨♨ ⬚ ♨ ⚲ ⛄ ▣ ✉ ⟋ ᴹᴾ ♒ 🍴 ① ♨ 🛒 ⛰ ♨ ♨ ♨ ♨ sand adj

Exit D914 junc 10 & foll sp Argelès Plage-Nord. Turn L onto D81 to site. Site sp among others. 4*, V lge, mkd, pt shd, EHU (6A) €3.70; gas; TV; 50% statics; phone; Eng spkn; adv bkg req; ccard acc; bike hire; rv fishing adj; horseriding; tennis; games area. *"Lovely views; excel site for partially-sighted & handicapped; rec visit to Collioure; vg."* €32.50, 16 May-30 Sep.   2016

"I need an on-site restaurant"

We do our best to make sure site information is correct, but it is always best to check any must-have facilities are still available or will be open during your visit.

ARGELES SUR MER *10G1* (4km NE Coastal) *42.57245, 3.04115* **Camping La Marende,** Avenue du Littoral, 66702 Argelès-sur-Mer 04 68 81 03 88; info@marende.com; www.marende.com

🏕 €2.50 ♨♨ ⬚ ♨ ⚲ ⛄ ▣ ✉ ⟋ ᴹᴾ 🦋 ♒ 🍴 ① ♨ 🛒 ⛰ ♨ ♨

♨ sand adj

Fr Perpignan S on D914 exit junc 10 Argelès-sur-Mer; foll sp Plage Nord; after 2km at rndabt turn L sp St Cyprian; at next rndabt turn R sp Plages Nord & Sud; site on L in 800m. L onto unmade rd. 4*, V lge, mkd, hdg, shd, serviced pitches; EHU (6-10A) inc; gas; bbq (elec, gas); TV; 12% statics; phone; Eng spkn; adv bkg acc; ccard acc; jacuzzi; games area; CKE. *"Beautiful site; lge pitches; friendly, helpful family owners; 1st class facs; excel pool; many static tents high ssn; gd area for cycling & walking; aquarobics, scuba diving lessons Jul & Aug; v quiet Sept; shared facs."* €38.00, 29 Apr-24 Sep.   2016

ARGELES SUR MER *10G1* (2km E Urban/Coastal) *42.55317, 3.04375* **Camping La Chapelle,** Ave du Tech, 66702 Argelès-sur-Mer 04 68 81 28 14; contactlc@camping-la-chapelle.com; www.camping-la-chapelle.com

🏕 €4 ♨♨ ⬚ ♨ ⚲ ⛄ ▣ ✉ ⟋ 🦋 ♒ 🍴 nr ① nr ♨ ⛰ ♨ ♨ 200m

Fr A9 exit junc 42 onto D900/D914 to Argelès-sur-Mer. At junc 10 cont thro Argelès vill & foll sp Argelès-Plage. In 2.5km turn L at rndabt, bear L at Office de Tourisme, site immed L. 3*, Lge, mkd, hdg, shd, EHU (6A) €6.50; 30% statics; Eng spkn; adv bkg acc; tennis 200m; CKE. *"Narr site rds poss diff lge o'fits; ltd facs LS; gd."* €30.00, 20 Apr-28 Sep, C25.   2019

ARGELES SUR MER *10G1* (5km SE Coastal) *42.53413, 3.06826* **Camping Les Criques de Porteils,** Corniche de Collioure, 66701 Argelès-sur-Mer **04 68 81 12 73;** contactcdp@lescriques.com; www.lescriques.com

🐕 €4 ♦♦↑ (htd) 🆆 🏊 ♨ ♿ ➡ ∥ 📶 ♈ 🍴 🗇 🎣 🛒 ⚠ 🏖 (htd)

🐾 shgl adj

Fr N on A9/E15 take exit junc 42 onto D914 Argelès-sur-Mer. Fr S exit junc 43 onto D618. In abt 16km R onto D914. At exit 13 leave D914 sp Collioure & foll site sp. Site by Hôtel du Golfe 1.5km fr Collioure. 5*, Lge, mkd, hdg, pt shd, pt sl, terr, EHU (5A) €6; gas; TV; 15% statics; phone; Eng spkn; adv bkg acc; fishing; tennis; games area; games rm; watersports; CKE. *"Excel, well-run site; variable size pitches, some uneven - not all suitable for lge o'fits; splendid views fr many terr pitches; steps to beach; scuba diving; clean, modern, well kept san facs; exposed, poss v windy; gd walks; v challenging (30 min) walk to Collioure but stunning; some narr site rds; gd rest; site shop fully stocked."* **€58.50, 24 Mar-27 Oct, C16.** **2018**

ARGELES SUR MER *10G1* (8km W Urban) *42.52667, 2.93515* **Camp Municipal Le Vivier,** 31 Rue du Stade, 66740 Laroque-des-Albères **04 68 89 00 93 or 04 68 95 49 97;** tourisme@laroque-des-albères.fr; www.laroque-des-alberes.fr

🐕 €4 ♦♦↑ 🆆 🏊 ♿ ➡ ∥ 🦋 🐾 nr ⚠

D2 fr Argelès-sur-Mer to Laroque-des-Albères; foll sp in cent of vill. Site on rvside. 2*, Lge, mkd, pt shd, pt sl, EHU (6A) €3; bbq; 5% statics; bus 300m; adv bkg acc; CKE. *"Peaceful, simple site on edge Pyrenees, pleasant vill; vg."* **€24.00, 15 Jun-15 Sep.** **2016**

"Satellite navigation makes touring much easier"

Remember most sat navs don't know if you're towing or in a larger vehicle – always use yours alongside maps and site directions.

ARGELES SUR MER *10G1* (8km W Rural) *42.52366, 2.94446* **Camping Les Albères,** 66740 Laroque-des-Albères **04 68 89 23 64;** contact@camping-des-alberes.com; www.camping-des-alberes.com

♦♦↑ 🆆 🏊 ♨ ♿ ➡ ∥ 📶 ♈ 🍴 🗇 🎣 🐾 nr ⚠ ♫ 🏖 (covrd, htd)

Fr A9 exit junc 43 onto D618 dir Argelès-sur-Mer/Port Vendres. Turn R onto D50 to Laroque-des-Albères. In vill at T-junc turn L, then turn R at rndabt & foll sp to site on D11. 3*, Med, mkd, pt shd, terr, EHU (6A) €5; bbq (gas); TV; 5% statics; phone; Eng spkn; tennis; games area; CKE. *"Attractive, peaceful site under slopes of Pyrenees; friendly owners; gd san facs; gd walking area; excel."* **€36.00, 6 Apr-28 Sep.** **2019**

ARGENTAN *4E1* (0.5km SE Urban) *48.73991, -0.01668* **Camp Municipal du Parc de la Noé,** 34 Rue de la Noé, 61200 Argentan **02 33 36 05 69;** camping@argentan.info; www.argentan.fr

♦♦↑ (htd) 🆆 🏊 ♨ ➡ ∥ 🦋 ♈ 🐾 nr ⚠

S fr Caen on D958 foll camping sp fr by-pass. At rndabt in town cent foll sp to Alencon (Blvd Carnot). In 300m turn L and foll camping signs. NB. Site ent immed on R on entering Rue de la Noe. 2*, Sm, shd, EHU (12A) inc; TV; 10% statics; adv bkg req; games area; rv. *"Superb, clean, tidy site adj town park; excel, clean san facs; gd touring base; lovely town; park adj; lake adj; immac site run by efficient, helpful warden; busy even mid Sept, rec arr early; gates close at 8pm, use adj aire."* **€12.00, 2 Apr-1 Oct.** **2018**

ARGENTAN *4E1* (3.6km S Rural) *48.71841, -0.01077* **FFCC Aire Naturelle du Val de Baize (Huet des Aunay),** 18 Rue de Mauvaisville, 61200 Argentan **02 33 67 27 11;** mhuetdesaunay@orange.fr; www.normandiealaferme.com

🐕 ♦♦↑ 🆆 ♿ ∥ 📶 🦋 🐾 nr ⚠

Take D958 fr Argentan twd Sées & Alençon; site clearly sp on D958 - turn R just bef leaving Argentan boundary. Site adj T-junc N of farm buildings. Sm, hdstg, pt shd, EHU (6A); 10% statics; Eng spkn; adv bkg acc; CKE. *"Charming, well-kept site; pool 2.5km; B&B; lge pitches in orchard; clean but dated facs, ltd LS; friendly welcome; NH only; ring in advance to check opening dates."* **€13.00, Unknown-30 Sep.** **2016**

ARGENTAT *7C4* (4km SW Rural) *45.07531, 1.91689* **Camping Sunélia au Soleil d'Oc,** 19400 Monceaux-sur-Dordogne **05 55 28 84 84;** info@campingsoleildoc.com; www.campingsoleildoc.com

🐕 €3 ♦♦↑ 🆆 🏊 ♨ ♿ ➡ ∥ 📶 ♈ 🍴 🗇 🎣 🛒 ⚠ ♫ 🏖 🛶

Fr N exit A20 junc 46a dir Tulle, then D1120 to Argentat. Fr Argentat take D12 sp Beaulieu. In 4km in Laygues turn L over bdge x-ing Rv Dordogne, site in 300m. 4*, Med, mkd, hdg, pt shd, terr, EHU (6A) €4.10; gas; bbq; red long stay; TV; 10% statics; phone; Eng spkn; adv bkg acc; ccard acc; canoeing; games area; games rm; bike hire; rv; archery; CKE. *"Ideal family site high ssn & peaceful LS; some pitches on rv bank; ltd water points; gd walking & other activities; many beautiful vills in area; tours arranged."* **€20.70, 16 Apr-30 Oct.** **2016**

ARGENTIERE LA BESSEE, L' *9C3* (5km S Rural) *44.75765, 6.57995* **FFCC Camping Le Verger,** 05310 La Roche-de-Rame **04 92 20 92 23;** info@campingleverger.com; www.campingleverger.com

12 🐕 ♦♦↑ 🆆 🏊 ♨ ∥ 📶 🦋 🍴 🗇 ♈ 🐾 nr ⚠

S fr Briançon on N94; site 500m L of rd bef vill; sp. 3*, Sm, hdg, shd, terr, EHU (3-10A) €3.50; sw nr; TV; 25% statics; phone; Eng spkn; adv bkg acc. *"Grass pitches in orchard; excel, well-maintained facs; beautiful; ideal loc for visiting Ecrins area; fantastic value; hg rec."* **€16.00** **2018**

FRANCE

ARGENTIERE LA BESSEE, L' *9C3* (8km NW Rural)
44.84354, 6.48989 **Camping Indigo Vallouise** (formerly Les Chambonnettes), 05290 Vallouise 04 92 23 30 26 or 06 82 23 65 09 (mob); vallouise@ camping-indigo.com; www.camping-indigo.com

🐾 €1.80 (htd) 🏕 ⚁ 🛒 👶 🚻 ♿ 🅿 ⚓ 🏊 ♈ 📶 nr ⓦ nr ⛟ 🚲 nr 🏔

Take N94 Briançon-Gap, on N o'skts of L'Argentière-la-Bessée take D994 W dir Vallouise. In cent of Vallouise turn L over bdge & immed L, site in 200m on rvside. 2*, Med, mkd, pt shd, pt sl, EHU (10A) €5.30; bbq; twin axles; TV; 25% statics; phone; Eng spkn; adv bkg acc; ccard acc; games area; games rm; tennis; CKE. *"Mountain scenery; gd facs; bar 500m; gd cent for walking, skiing, canoeing; pool 3km; white-water rafting at nrby rv; interesting vill; gd."* €32.00, 25 May-29 Sep, M17. **2019**

"There aren't many sites open at this time of year"

If you're travelling outside peak season remember to call ahead to check site opening dates – even if the entry says 'open all year'.

ARGENTON LES VALLEES *4H1* (0.9km N Rural)
46.9877, -0.4504 **Camp Municipal du Lac d'Hautibus**, Rue de la Sablière, 79150 Argenton-les-Vallées 05 49 65 95 08 or 05 49 65 70 22 (Mairie); mairie-argenton-chateau@cegetel.net; www.campings-poitou-charentes.com

🏕 ⚁ 🛒 👶 🚻 🅿 ⚓ 📶 ♈ ⛟ nr 🏔

Fr E or W on D759, site well sp in town, on lakeside. 2*, Med, hdg, pt sl, EHU (6A) €2.50; sw nr; 10% statics; Eng spkn; games rm; tennis 100m; CKE. *"Beautifully-situated, well-kept site; pool 100m; interesting, quiet town; excel."* €14.00, 1 Apr-30 Sep. **2016**

ARGENTON SUR CREUSE *7A3* (13km SW Rural)
46.54192, 1.40328 **Camping La Petite Brenne** (Naturist), La Grande Metairie, 36800 Luzeret 02 54 25 05 78; info@lapetitebrenne.com; www.lapetitebrenne.com

🏕 ⚁ 🛒 ⛺ 👶 🚻 ♿ 🅿 ⚓ 📶 ♈ 🏊 ♈ ⓦ ⚓ 🏔 ✂ 🚣 (covrd, htd) ⛸

Fr A20 exit junc 18 sp Luzeret/Prissac; foll D55 to Luzeret vill. After bdge in vill turn L, then next L to site. Med, pt shd, pt sl, EHU (10A) €5 (long leads poss req); bbq; red long stay; twin axles; 10% statics; phone; Eng spkn; adv bkg rec; ccard acc; games rm; sauna; horseriding; games area; CKE. *"Excel family site; friendly Dutch owners; lge pitches; excel san facs; ideal for children; pools excel; gd rest; gd walking in National Park; great facs."* €32.00, 22 Apr-1 Oct. **2017**

ARGENTON SUR CREUSE *7A3* (2km NW Rural)
46.59636, 1.50619 **Camp Municipal Les Chambons**, 37 Rue des Chambons, 36200 Argenton-sur-Creuse 06 47 81 59 35 & 09 66 84 06 01; campingles chambons@gmail.com; www.campingleschambons.fr

12 🏕 ⓦ ⚁ ⛺ 👶 🚻 ♈ 📶 ♈ ⓦ nr ⛟ nr 🏔

Fr A20 exit junc 17 onto D937 dir Argenton; turn R at rndabt, then L at mini rndabt nr supmkt sp St Marcel; foll rd downhill over rlwy bdge; then 1st R in 100m. But best app fr N on D927 to avoid traff calming rd humps; at town sp cross rlwy bdge & turn R immed past LH turn for Roman archaeological museum; foll camping sp on narr, busy app rd. 3*, Med, hdstg, mkd, shd, pt sl, EHU (5A) €3.60 (poss long lead req); gas. *"Beautiful, peaceful, well-kept site by rv; helpful warden; v muddy after heavy rain & poss uneven pitches by rv; rvside walk into interesting old town; no need to unhitch so useful for early start; quiet in day, busy in evening as popular NH high ssn; excel."* €20.00 **2019**

ARGENTON SUR CREUSE *7A3* (6km NW Rural)
46.62965, 1.47882 **Camp Municipal Les Rives de la Bouzanne**, 36800 Le Pont Chrétien-Chabenet 02 54 25 80 53 or 02 54 25 81 40 (Mairie); commune. pontchretien@wanadoo.fr

🐾 €0.50 🏕 ⓦ ⚁ 🛒 ⛺ 👶 🚻 ♈ ⛟ nr ⛟ nr 🏔

Exit A20 junc 17 onto D927; site well sp over rv bdge. Or fr St Gaultier on D927 dir Argenton-sur-Creuse; turn R in Le Pont Chrétien-Chabenet, bef rv bdge, site 50m on L. 2*, Med, pt shd, EHU (6A) inc; bbq; phone; Eng spkn; adv bkg rec; CKE. *"Picturesque, quiet, rvside site; site yourself, warden calls; gd, drained pitches; immac san facs; conv A20; excel NH."* €13.00, 15 Jun-10 Sep. **2016**

"That's changed – Should I let the Club know?"

If you find something on site that's different from the site entry, fill in a report and let us know. See camc.com/europereport.

ARLES *10E2* (8km NE Rural) *43.72336, 4.71861*
Huttopia Fontvieille (foremerly Municipal des Pins), Rue Michelet, 13990 Fontvieille 04 90 54 78 69; fontvieille@huttopia.com; www.huttopia.com

🐾 €1.50 🏕 ⓦ ⚁ 🛒 👶 🚻 ♈ ⛟ nr 🏔

Take D570 fr Arles to Avignon, in 2km turn R on D17 to Fontvieille, at far end of vill turn R at rndabt, foll sp. 3*, Med, mkd, hdg, pt shd, pt sl, EHU (6A) €3; red long stay; TV; bus; Eng spkn; adv bkg acc; games area; games rm; CKE. *"Delightful, pleasant quiet site in pines; friendly staff; vg san facs; 15-20 mins walk to lively vill with rests & 2 supmkts; quiet forest walks; tennis in vill; nr Arles; lots of attractions locally; vg."* €35.00, 30 Mar-14 Oct. **2018**

For a guide to symbols see the fold out on the rear cover

ARLES *10E2* (7km E Rural) *43.64799, 4.70625*
Camping La Bienheureuse, 13280 Raphèle-les-Arles
04 90 98 48 06; contact@labienheureuse.com;
www.labienheureuse.com

🐕 €2.50 ♨♨ ⓦ🅳 ⚓ ♿ ⬛ ╱ 🅼 ♈ ⓨ ㅒ ♨ ⛰ ⚓ 🏊 ⛴

Fr Arles E on D453, site on L 5km after Pont-de-
Crau. W fr Salon-de-Provence on A54/N113; exit
N113 junc 12 onto N1435 to St Martin-de-Crau;
cont past St Martin-de-Crau on N1435; in 2km
rd becomes D435 to Raphèle-les-Arles; site on R
900m after Raphèle-les-Arles. 3*, Med, hdg, pt shd,
EHU (16A); twin axles; 50% statics; phone; bus adj;
Eng spkn; adv bkg acc; horseriding nr; CKE. *"Pleasant
site; obliging British owners; 700m to shops/bar in
vill; gd facs; gd dog walk along nrby lanes and canal."*
€21.00, 1 Mar-31 Oct.   **2019**

"I like to fill in the reports as I travel from site to site"

You'll find report forms at the back of this
guide, or you can fill them in online at
camc.com/europereport.

ARLES *10E2* (5km SE Urban) *43.65942, 4.65416*
Camping L'arlesienne, 149 Draille Marseillaise, Pont
de Crau, 13631, Arles 04 90 96 02 12; contact@
larlesienne.com; www.larlesienne.com

🐕 €1.50 ♨♨ (htd) ⓦ🅳 ⚓ ⬛ ╱ 🅼🅿 ㅒ ⓘ 🏊 nr ⛰ ⚓ 🏊

Exit Arles E by D453 sp Pont-de-Crau or junc 7
fr N113 dir Raphèle-les-Arles; 200m after exit vill
take 1st exit at rndabt then R at Flor Hotel sp on
D83E. Site in 50m on R adj hotel. 3*, Med, pt shd,
EHU (6A) €4; TV; 80% statics; bus fr rndabt; Eng spkn;
games area. *"Many mosquitoes; red facs LS; v muddy
after rain; visit Les Baux citadel early morning bef
coach parties arr; no o'fits over 5.5m allowed (but poss
not enforced); gd birdwatching; poss no site lighting LS;
conv Arles."* **€27.00, 1 Apr-1 Nov.**   **2016**

ARMENTIERES *3A3* (3km E Rural) *50.68774,
2.93279* **Camping L'Image,** 140 Rue Brune, 59116
Houplines 03 20 35 69 42 or 06 81 61 56 82 (mob);
campimage@wanadoo.fr; www.campingimage.com

🔟 ♨♨ (htd) ⓦ🅳 ⚓ ⬛ ╱ 🅼 ⓨ ㅒ ⛰ ⚓ 🏊

Exit A25 junc 8 sp Armentières, onto D945 N twd
Houplines; pass on R Chemin du Pilori in 1.8km;
then pass on R Hameau de L'Hépinette in 2.2km;
turn R into Rue Brune in 3km; site in 1km on R. Ent
not v clearly sp. 3*, Med, hdg, shd, serviced pitches;
EHU (6-10A) inc (take care electrics, poss prob 2011);
90% statics; Eng spkn; adv bkg acc; tennis; games
area; CKE. *"Mainly statics, adv bkg rec; friendly, helpful
staff; dated san facs, poss unclean & unkempt (2011);
pitches exposed & poss v windy; gd NH prior to ferry."*
€28.00   **2017**

ARNAY LE DUC *6H1* (1km E Rural) *47.13388, 4.49835*
Camping L'Etang de Fouché, Rue du 8 Mai 1945,
21230 Arnay-le-Duc 03 80 90 02 23; info@camping
fouche.com; www.campingfouche.com

🐕 €2 ♨♨ (htd) ⓦ🅳 ⚓ ♿ ♨ ⬛ ╱ 🅼 ♈ ⓨ ㅒ ⓘ ⚓ 🏊 ⛰ ⚓
🏊 (htd) ⛴

App by D906 to Arnay (site sp); turn E onto D17,
site on R in 2km. 4*, Lge, hdstg, mkd, hdg, pt shd,
EHU (6A) €4; bbq; sw nr; TV (pitch); TV; Eng spkn; adv
bkg acc; ccard acc; bike hire; waterslide; fishing; tennis;
games rm; CKE. *"Excel lakeside site with pleasant
views; lge pitches; friendly staff; gd san facs; attractive
sm town; gd touring base S Burgundy; gd for young
families."* **€32.00, 19 Apr-13 Oct.**   **2019**

ARRAS *3B3* (14km E Rural) *50.27347, 2.94852*
Camping La Paille Haute, 145 Rue de Seilly, 62156
Boiry-Notre-Dame 03 21 48 15 40; lapaillehaute@
wanadoo.fr; www.la-paille-haute.com

🐕 ♨♨ ⓦ🅳 ⚓ ♿ ♨ ⬛ ╱ 🅼 ♈ 🦋 ⓨ ㅒ ⓘ ⚓ 🏊 ⛰ ⚓ 🏊 (htd) ⛴

Fr Calais take A26/A1 twd Paris, exit junc 15 onto
D939 twd Cambrai; in 3km take D34 NE to Boiry-
Notre-Dame & foll camp sp. Fr D950 Douai-Arras
rd, at Fresnes turn S onto D43, foll sp to Boiry in
7km, site well sp in vill. 2*, Med, hdstg, hdg, pt shd,
terr, EHU (6A) €4 (poss rev pol); bbq; red long stay;
60% statics; Eng spkn; ccard acc; tennis; games rm;
site open w/ends in winter; lake fishing; CKE. *"Popular
NH; useful & reliable; pretty site with views; rec arr
early; lge pitches; friendly, helpful owner; gd for
children; Calais over 1hr; conv WW1 sites & A26; gd reg
used site; gd for long stay; peaceful vill; pitches muddy
in wet weather; san facs updated and excel; gd dogs
walk adj."* **€30.00, 1 Apr-31 Oct.**   **2018**

ARRENS-MARSOUS *8G2* (0.9km NE Rural) *42.95991,
-0.20645* **Camping Mialanne,** 63 route du Val d'Azun,
65400 Arrens-Marous 05 62 92 67 14 or 05 62 37 96
08; mialanne@orange.fr; www.campingmialanne.fr

🐕 (€0.50) ♨♨ ⓦ🅳 ⚓ ⬛ ╱ 🅼 ♈ ⓨ ㅒ nr ⓘ nr ⚓ nr ⛰

Sp on D918 bet Arrens-Marsous, 10km WSW of
Argeles-Gazost. (Opp ent of Camping La Heche).
3*, Med, mkd, pt shd, terr, EHU (10A) €3.10; bbq
(charcoal, gas); twin axles; phone; bus 300m; Eng
spkn; adv bkg acc; ccard acc; games rm; CKE. *"Friendly
fam site; htd pool 300m; 300m to vill, conv Arrens &
Estaing; san facs extended (2015); vg."*
€17.00, 1 Jun-30 Sep.   **2016**

ARROMANCHES LES BAINS *3D1* (3km E Coastal)
49.33963, -0.58188 **Camp Municipal Quintefeuille,**
Ave Maurice Schumann, 14960 Asnelles 02 31 22 35
50; campingquintefeuille@wanadoo.fr;
www.camping-asnelles.com

♨♨ ⓦ🅳 ⚓ ♿ ⬛ ╱ 🦋 ㅒ nr ⓘ nr ⚓ nr ⛰ 🏖 sand 300m

Site sp on D514, but visible fr vill sq in Asnelles.
2*, Med, mkd, unshd, EHU; fishing; tennis; games area.
€14.50, 1 Apr-2 Nov.   **2019**

ARROU *4F2 (0.9km NW Rural) 48.10189, 1.11556*
Camp Municipal du Pont de Pierre, 28290 Arrou
02 37 97 02 13 (Mairie); mairie.arrou@wanadoo.fr;
www.loirevalleytourism.com

🏠 wc ♨ ઙ 🖪 🗸 MP 🦋 Ⴤ nr ⊕nr 🎣nr 🏧 🌲 sand adj

Take D15 fr Cloyes. Site sp in vill of Arrou.
2*, Med, hdg, mkd, unshd, pt sl, EHU (6-10A) €2-3;
bbq; 10% statics; phone; adv bkg acc; horseriding;
lake fishing; bike hire; tennis; CKE. *"Lovely, peaceful,
well-kept site in park-like setting; lge pitches; excel,
clean san facs; gd security; htd pool, paddling pool
adj; phone warden (or call at hse) if off & barrier
clsd; gd rvside walks/cycle rides; excel value; rec."*
€8.00, 1 May-30 Sep. 2017

"We must tell the Club about that great site we found"

Get your site reports in by mid-August and we'll
do our best to get your updates into the next
edition.

ARZON *2G3 (0.8km NE Coastal) 47.55303, -28.8294*
Camp Municipal Le Tindio, Kerners, 56640 Arzon
02 97 41 25 59; www.camping-arzon.fr

🏠 €1.20 🏠 wc ♨ ઙ 🖪 🗸 MP 🏧 🌲 sand 1km

Fr Vannes or Muzillac on D780 turn R at rndabt on
o'skts of Arzon. Site clearly sp. 3*, Lge, pt shd, pt sl,
EHU (6-10A) €2.50; 3% statics; adv bkg acc; golf nr.
*"Site o'looks Gulf of Morbihan; direct access to sea;
excel san facs; gd value; sm boat launching fr site."*
€13.00, 1 Apr-3 Nov. 2016

ARZON *2G3 (2km NE Coastal) 47.56031, -2.87854*
Camping de Bilouris, Route de Kerners, 56640 Arzon
02 97 53 70 55; campingbilouris@gmail.com;
www.campingdebilouris.com

🏠 €2.50 🏠 wc ♨ ઙ 🗸 ⍩ Ⴤ 🌲

Fr Vannes foll D780 for abt 23km. On app Arzon
foll sp for site. Sm, hdg, pt shd, pt sl, EHU (6A) €3;
bbq; 60% statics; Eng spkn; adv bkg rec. *"Coastal
walks, boating & kayaking; miles of off-rd cycling; vg."*
€23.00, 1 Apr-1 Nov. 2017

ARZON *2G3 (2km W Coastal) 47.54403, -2.90945*
Camp Municipal de Port-Sable, Port Navalo, 56640
Arzon 02 97 53 71 98; portsable@arzon.fr;
www.camping-arzon.fr

🏠 €1.40 🏠 wc ♨ ઙ 🖪 🗸 MP 🦋 ⍩ Ⴤnr 🏧 🌲 sand adj

Fr N165/E60 take D780 to Sarzeau, cont to Arzon.
Site sp fr last rndabt bef fort. 3*, Med, pt shd, pt sl,
EHU (6A) €2.30; gas; Eng spkn; ccard acc; fishing;
sailing school. *"Vg, spacious site; beautiful position
nr beach with views; gd beach for children; walk into
marina; boat excursions; gd facs; gd for m'vans - rests
nrby."* **€18.50, 1 Apr-15 Oct.** 2016

ASPET *8G3 (1km SW Rural) 43.00969, 0.79665*
Camp Municipal Le Cagire, 31160 Aspet 05 61 88 51 55;
camping.aspet@wanadoo.fr; www.mairie-aspet.fr/
rubrique/afficher/21

🏠 €0.50 🏠 wc ♨ ઙ 🗸 🦋 Ⴤnr ⊕nr 🎣nr

Exit A64 at junc 18 St Gaudens & take D5 S. In
14km, site sp on R in vill of Aspet. Sp 'Camping,
Stade.' 2*, Sm, mkd, shd, EHU (6A) €2.50;
30% statics; adv bkg acc; games area; tennis 300m;
CKE. *"Pleasant, gd, clean, well kept site nr lively, sm
town; rec arr bef 1800 hrs high ssn; pool 300m; basic
facs; some pitches muddy when wet; some hdstg."*
€11.00, 1 Apr-30 Sep. 2015

ASPRES SUR BUECH *9D3 (6.5km W Rural)
44.53048, 5.68371* FFCC Aire Naturelle La Source
(Pardoe), 05140 St Pierre-d'Argençon 04 92 58
67 81 or 06 78 32 30 40 (mob); info@lasource-
hautesalpes.com; www.lasource-hautesalpes.com

🏠 €1.50 🏠 wc ♨ ઙ 🖪 🗸 MP 🦋 ⍩ Ⴤ ⊕ ॐ 🏧

Fr S on D1075 at Aspres-sur-Buëch turn onto D993
dir Valence to St Pierre-d'Argençon; after 6km site
sp. Fr N on D93, cont onto D993 over Col de Cabre;
site sp on L bef St Pierre-d'Argençon.
Sm, mkd, pt shd, pt sl; EHU (6/10A) €4; bbq; twin axles;
red long stay; phone; Eng spkn; adv bkg acc; ccard acc;
CKE. *"Peaceful, well-kept CL-type site in woodland/open
field; friendly, helpful British owners; clean san facs;
takeaway; chambre d'hôte on site; htd pool (4km); highly
rec; ideally located for all mountain sports, walking,
climbing, watersports, gliding, flying & cycling; 3 luxury
Teepees for hire; major improvements planned(2014);
excel."* **€18.00, 15 Apr-15 Oct.** 2017

ASSERAC *2G3 (5km NW Coastal) 47.44533, -2.44766*
Camping Le Moulin de l'Eclis, Pont Mahé, 44410
Assérac 02 40 01 76 69; info@camping-leclis.com;
www.camping-leclis.com

🏠 €3 🏠 wc ♨ ઙ 🖪 🗸 MP 🦋 ⍩ Ⴤ ⊕nr ॐ 🎣 🏧 ✎
🏊 (covrd, htd) ⛴ 🌲 sand adj

Fr D774 turn N onto D83 to Assérac. Take D82 two
coast to Pont Mahé, site sp. 4*, Lge, mkd, hdg, pt shd,
EHU (6-10A) €3.60-4; bbq (elec, gas); TV; 60% statics;
phone; Eng spkn; adv bkg acc; ccard acc; games area;
bike hire; waterslide; sailing school; watersports. *"Excel
family site; conv Guérande; vg touring base; superb new
(2013) san facs."* **€41.60, 1 Apr-20 Oct.** 2019

"I need an on-site restaurant"

We do our best to make sure site information
is correct, but it is always best to check any
must-have facilities are still available or will
be open during your visit.

Make sure you check any essential information with the site before you travel

ATTICHY *3C4* (1km SSE Rural) *49.40664, 3.05295* **Camping De l'Aigrette (Formaly Camp municipal Fleury),** 22 Rue Fontaine-Aubier, 60350 Attichy **03 44 42 15 97** or **06 62 83 79 35 (mob);** contact@ campingdelaigrette.com; www.campingde laigrette.com

🐕 €0.50 ⋔ (htd) 🆆 🛁 ⅃ ∥ ᴹˢᴾ 🦋 ♈ ⑭ nr ⅃ nr ⚠ ⚓

Fr Compiègne E on N31. After 16km turn L at traff lts sp Attichy & site. Over iron bdge & turn R to site on lakeside. 3*, Sm, hdg, pt shd, EHU (10A) €2; bbq; 30% statics; fishing; site clsd 25 Dec - 31 Jan; CKE. "*Attractive, clean site in pleasant vill; many w/end statics, few touring pitches; helpful wardens live on site; modern san facs, stretched high ssn; gd security; excel NH LS; excel site.*" **€16.00, 1 Mar-30 Nov.** **2015**

"Satellite navigation makes touring much easier"

Remember most sat navs don't know if you're towing or in a larger vehicle – always use yours alongside maps and site directions.

AUBENAS *9D2* (10km S Rural) *44.53693, 4.41039* **Camping Les Peupliers,** 07200 Vogüé **04 75 37 71 47;** girard.jean-jacques@club-internet.fr; www.camping peupliers.com

🐕 €2.30 ⋔ (htd) 🆆 🛁 ⚲ ⅃ ∥ ᴹˢᴾ 🦋 ♈ Ⓨ ⑭ ⅃ ⚠ ⚓

Fr Aubenas take D104 S twd Alès. In 2km, turn L onto D579 dir Vogüé/Vallon Pont d'Arc. In 9km, pass L turn to Vogüé. Immed after x-ing rv, turn R at rndabt. Site on R in 300m, (2nd site of 3 on rd). 3*, Lge, mkd, pt shd, EHU (6A) €4.10; gas; bbq; 10% statics; phone; adv bkg acc; ccard acc; CKE. "*Gd touring base; access to rv for canoeing & fishing; sm shop on site with ltd stock.*" **€24.00, 5 Apr-30 Sep.** **2015**

AUBERIVES SUR VAREZE *9B2* (8km E Rural) *45.42830, 4.92823* **Kawan Village Camping Le Bontemps,** 5 Impasse du Bontemps, 38150 Vernioz **04 66 60 07 00;** contact@camping-lebontemps.fr; www.camping-lebontemps.com

🐕 €3 ⋔ 🛁 ⚲ ⅃ ∥ ᴹˢᴾ Ⓨ Y ⑭ ⅃ ⚠ ⚓ ⚲

Take N7 S fr Vienne. At Le Clos turn L onto D37 thro Cheyssieu & Vernioz, site approx 9km E of Vernioz. Fr S, on N7 N of vill of Auberives R onto D37, site on R in 8km. Tight ent - rec swing wide. NB Also sp Hotel de Plein Air. 4*, Lge, mkd, pt shd, terr, EHU (6A) inc (poss long lead req); bbq; TV; 30% statics; adv bkg acc; ccard acc; games rm; tennis; lake fishing; games area; CKE. "*Attractive, well-kept site; popular NH high ssn; wildlife sanctuary; helpful staff; no o'fits over 10m high ssn; excel sports facs; vg NH/long stay; new san facs (2014).*" **€30.00, 13 Apr-29 Sep, M10.** **2019**

AUBERIVES SUR VAREZE *9B2* (1.6km S Rural) *45.41284, 4.81358* **Camping des Nations,** 38550 Clonas-sur-Varèze **04 74 84 95 13** or **04 14 42 42 84;** contact@campingdesnations.com; www.camping desnations.com

🐕 €1 ⋔ (htd) 🆆 🛁 ⅃ ∥ 🦋 ⑭ nr ⚓

Fr Vienne S on N7; site sp on R in 12km. Or fr S exit A7 junc 12 onto N7 dir Vienne; do not go into Clonas vill; site on L adj Hotel des Nations. 3*, Med, mkd, hdg, shd, EHU (9A) inc; bbq; adv bkg req; CKE. "*Pleasant, well-kept, well-laid out site; gd sized pitches; gd, v clean san facs; site muddy when wet; poss under-used; ltd facs LS; poss irreg cleaning end of ssn; useful NH/touring base for Spain & the Med; vg site; friendly, helpful staff.*" **€22.00, 1 Mar-31 Oct.** **2016**

AUBETERRE SUR DRONNE *7C2* (1km SE Rural) *45.26786, 0.17474* **Camping Base de Loisirs d'Aubeterre Sur Dronne (formerly Municipal),** Route de Ribérac, 16390 Aubeterre-sur-dronne **05 45 98 50 33;** mairie.aubeterre-sur-dronne@wanadoo.fr; www. aubeterresurdronne.com/hebergement/camping

🐕 €1 ⋔ (cont) 🆆 🛁 ∥ 🦋 ♈ Y ⑭ ⅃ ⅃ nr ⚠

On D2 fr Chalais, take D17 around S end of town. Turn R over rv & site on R adj sports grnd. 3*, Med, pt shd, EHU (10A) €2.50; 10% statics; Eng spkn; rv fishing adj; bike hire; tennis adj; boating adj. "*Excel site; gd for children; friendly staff; picturesque town; conv touring Périgord.*" **€20.00, 1 May-30 Sep.** **2019**

"There aren't many sites open at this time of year"

If you're travelling outside peak season remember to call ahead to check site opening dates – even if the entry says 'open all year'.

AUBIGNY SUR NERE *4G3* (1.5km E Rural) *47.48435, 2.45703* **FLOWER Camping des Etangs,** Route de Sancerre, 18700 Aubigny-sur-Nère **02 48 58 02 37;** camping.aubigny@orange.fr; www.camping-aubigny.com or www.flowercampings.com

🐕 €2 ⋔ (htd) 🆆 🛁 ⅃ ∥ 🦋 ♈ ⑭ nr ⅃ ⚠ ⚓ (covrd, htd) ⅃

D940 fr Gien, turn E in vill of Aubigny onto D923, foll sp fr vill; site 1km on R by lake, after Camp des Sports & just bef end of vill sp. Avoid town cent due congestion. 4*, Med, mkd, hdstg, pt shd, EHU (6-10A) inc; bbq; TV; 10% statics; phone; Eng spkn; adv bkg acc; bike hire; fishing; games rm; CKE. "*Vg site with lake views; pretty medieval vill with historical links to Scotland; mkt Sat; 2nd w/e July Scottish Son & Lumière event adj site!*" **€26.00, 1 Apr-30 Sep.** **2019**

FRANCE

AUDIERNE *2F1 (3km SE Coastal) 48.00723, -4.50799*
Camping de Kersiny-Plage, 1 Rue Nominoé, 29780
Plouhinec **02 98 70 82 44; info@kersinyplage.com;**
www.kersinyplage.com

🎪 €2 � ⓌⒹ ♨ ⚲ 🖥 ⫽ 🦋 ⛺ 🏧 ♒ sand

Fr Audierne on D784 turn R at 2nd traff lts in
Plouhinec, cont for 1km; turn L into Rue Nominoé
(sp diff to see) for 100m. Or fr Quimper on D784 to
Plouhinec, turn L at 1st traff lts & as bef.
2*, Med, hdg, pt shd, terr, EHU (8A) €3; bbq (gas); Eng
spkn; CKE. *"Quiet, peaceful site; beautiful location
& beach; most pitches superb sea views; welcoming,
friendly owner; clean san facs; barrier clsd 2300-0730;
not much in area for children except beach; gd coastal
walks; vg, rec."* **€15.00, 14 May-17 Sep.**   **2016**

AULUS LES BAINS *8G3 (0.5km NW Rural) 42.79402,
1.33197* **Camp Municipal Le Coulédous,** 09140 Aulus-
les-Bains **05 61 66 43 56; campinglecouledous@
orange.fr; www.camping-aulus-couledous.com**

12 🎪 €1 � (htd) ⓌⒹ ♨ ⚲ 🖥 ⫽ 🦋 ⛺ 🏧 nr /🏔\

Take D618 fr St Girons. After 13km cross rv; turn R
onto D3 sp Aulus-les-Bains. On app to Oust turn L
onto D32, site approx 17km on R at ent to vill on
rvside. 2*, Med, hdstg, mkd, pt shd, sl, EHU (10A)
€4.50-6.50; 10% statics; Eng spkn; adv bkg acc; site clsd
mid-Nov to mid-Dec; CKE. *"Gd walking & skiing (16km);
sm spa in vill; bar 300m; excel; san facs clean but tired;
church clock chimes thro night."* **€19.00**   **2017**

AUMALE *3C3 (0.5km W Rural) 49.76618, 1.74618*
Camp Municipal Le Grand Mail, Chemin du Grand
Mail, 76390 Aumale **02 35 93 40 50 (Mairie);
communeaumale@wanadoo.fr; www.aumale.com**

🎪 €2 � ♨ ⚲ 🖥 ⫽ 🖼 🏧 nr /🏔\

Clearly sp in town; long steep climb to ent.
2*, Med, pt shd, EHU (6A) €2.40; bike hire; fishing 1km.
*"Gd site; clean, modern san facs; conv Channel ports;
steep slope fr town to site; gd NH."*
€18.00, 1 Apr-30 Sep.   **2019**

AUNAY SUR ODON *3D1 (0.5km NE Urban) 49.02530,
-0.62515* **Camp Municipal La Closerie,** Rue de Caen,
14260 Aunay-sur-Odon **02 31 77 32 46 or 07850
511893; mairieaunaysurodon@orange.fr;
www.aunaysurodon.fr**

🎪 €1.55 � ⓌⒹ ♨ ⚲ 🖥 ⫽ 🖼 🦋 🏧 nr

Exit A84 junc 43 sp Villers-Bocage/Aunay & take D6
twd Aunay. In approx 3km bef Aunay town sp, turn
L sp 'Zone Industrielle', in 200m turn R at rndabt.
Site on R in 100m nr sports stadium. 2*, Sm, mkd,
pt shd, pt sl, EHU €2.80; Eng spkn; games area; CKE.
*"Delightful, attractive vill; Sat mkt; vet avail; conv NH
for Caen ferry & gd touring base; helpful, welcoming
warden."* **€7.50, 6 Jul-31 Aug.**   **2017**

AUPS *10E3 (0.9km SE Rural) 43.62378, 6.22903*
Camping Les Prés, 181 Route de Tourtour, 83630
Aups **04 94 70 00 93; lespres.camping@wanadoo.fr;
www.campinglespres.com**

� (htd) ♨ ⚲ 🖥 ⫽ 🦋 Ⓣ ⑪ ♨ 🏧 nr /🏔\ ♒ 🏊

Fr cent of Aups on rd to Tourtour, site on R. Rough
rd. 3*, Med, hdg, mkd, pt shd, EHU (10A); gas; TV;
10% statics; adv bkg acc. *"Peaceful, friendly site;
recep clsd 1200 to 1500; ent not rec for lge o'fits."*
€27.00, 1 Mar-31 Oct.   **2015**

AUPS *10E3 (0.5km W Rural) 43.62455, 6.21760*
International Camping, Route de Fox-Amphoux,
83630 Aups **04 94 70 06 80; camping-aups@
internationalcamping-aups.com; www.international
camping-aups.com**

🎪 €1 � ⓌⒹ ♨ ⚲ 🖥 ⫽ 🦋 Ⓣ ⑪ ♨ 🏧 ♒ 🏊

Site on L on D60 nr vill cent. 3*, Lge, mkd, hdg, pt shd,
EHU (16A) €5.30; 80% statics; Eng spkn; adv bkg rec;
ccard acc; tennis; games rm. *"Vg site in beautiful area;
lge pitches; gd rest."* **€19.00, 1 Apr-30 Sep.**   **2016**

AURAY *2F3 (7km S Rural) 47.64402, -2.93774*
FFCC Camping du Parc-Lann, 52 Rue Thiers, Le
Varquez, 56400 Le Bono **02 97 57 93 93 or 07 88 00
79 47; campingduparclann@wanadoo.fr;
www.campingduparclann.fr**

🎪 €0.70 � ⓌⒹ ♨ ⚲ 🖥 ⫽ 🖼 🏧 nr /🏔\

S fr Auray on D101 sp Le Bono. Site well sp in Le Bono.
2*, Med, hdg, mkd, pt shd, EHU (6A) €2.30 (long lead
req); bbq; phone; bus; games area; ice; CKE. *"Lovely quiet
site in pretty area; gd, clean san facs poss stretched high
ssn & ltd LS; pool 5km; warden on site 1800-1900 only LS;
gd walking."* **€14.00, 1 May-30 Sep.**   **2016**

AURAY *2F3 (8km SW Rural) 47.64256, -3.05406*
FFCC Camping de Kergo, Route de Carnac, 56400
Ploemel **02 97 56 80 66; contact@campingkergo.com;
www.campingkergo.com**

🎪 €0.70 � ⓌⒹ ♨ ⚲ 🖥 ⫽ 🏧 nr /🏔\ ♒ sand 5km

Fr Auray take D768 SW sp Carnac. After 4km turn
NW on D186 twd Ploemel & foll sp. 3*, Med, mkd, pt
shd, EHU (6-10A) inc; 10% statics; adv bkg rec; CKE.
*"Lovely, peaceful site, lots of trees; gd, clean san facs
but dated (2015); ltd LS; welcoming, friendly, helpful
owners; gd size pitches; ideal for cycling into Carnac."*
€16.00, 1 May-30 Sep.   **2017**

AURAY *2F3 (8km W Rural) 47.66406, -3.09985*
FFCC Camp Municipal Le St Laurent, Kergonvo,
56400 Ploemel **02 97 56 85 90; contact@camping-
saint-laurent.fr; www.camping-saint-laurent.fr**

12 🎪 €1.40 � (htd) ⓌⒹ ♨ ⚲ 🖥 ⫽ 🖼 🦋 Ⓣ ⑪ ♨ /🏔\
♒ (htd) 🏊

Fr Auray on D22 twd Belz/Etel; after 8km turn L on
D186 to Ploemel & site on L in 200m. 3*, Med, hdstg,
shd, EHU (10A) €4; bbq; 10% statics; adv bkg acc;
games area. *"Peaceful site; friendly staff; red facs LS."*
€23.50   **2019**

AURILLAC 7C4 (1.4km NE Urban) 44.93551, 2.45596
Camp Municipal de l'Ombrade, Chemin du Gué
Bouliaga, 15000 Aurillac **04 71 48 28 87**

🐕 ⭐ ♨ 🚿 ⚅ 🚐 🍴 🐾 nr ⚓

**Take D17 N fr Aurillac twd Puy-Mary; site on banks
of Rv Jordanne. Well sp fr town.** 3*, Lge, mkd, shd,
pt sl, EHU (10A) €2.10; bbq; TV; games rm. "Well-
managed, spacious site; lge pitches; interesting, lge mkt
town; vg; excel new san fac (2014)."
€16.00, 15 Jun-15 Sep.   2015

AUTRANS 9C3 (0.5km E Rural) 45.17520, 5.54770
Kawan Village au Joyeux Réveil, Le Château, 38880
Autrans **04 76 95 33 44; camping-au-joyeux-reveil@
wanadoo.fr; www.camping-au-joyeux-reveil.fr**

🐕 ⭐(htd) 🆓 ♨ ♿ ⚅ 🚿 🗑 🦋 ♈ 🍴 ⊕ nr 🐾 nr ⚓
🏊(htd) 🎣

**Fr Villard-de-Lans take D531 to Lans-en-Vercors &
turn L onto D106 to Autrans. On E side of vill site
sp at 1st rndabt. NB App on D531 fr W fr Pont-en-
Royans not rec - v narr rd & low tunnels.**
4*, Med, mkd, pt shd, pt sl, EHU (2-10A) €2-8; gas;
bbq; TV (pitch); TV; 60% statics; phone; bus 300m; Eng
spkn; adv bkg acc; ccard acc; golf 20km; games area;
tennis 300m; bike hire; rv fishing; waterslide; CKE. "Site
in Vercors National Park with excel views; winter sport
facs, 1050m altitude; modern san facs; excel; well run
site; friendly staff." **€44.00, 1 May-30 Sep.**   2019

AUTUN 6H1 (2km N Rural) 46.96478, 4.29381
Camp de la Porte d'Arroux (formerly Municipal),
Les Chaumottes, 71400 Autun **03 85 52 10 82;
www.aquadis-loisirs.com**

🐕 €1.35 ⭐ 🆓 ♨ ♿ ⚅ 🚿 🗑 🍴 ⊕ 🐾 ⚓

**Fr Autun foll dir for Saulieu on D980; site on L 500m
after passing thro Roman Arch; only site in Autun.**
3*, Sm, hdg, hdstg, pt shd, EHU (10A) €3.30 (poss
rev pol); bbq; sw; twin axles; TV; phone; Eng spkn;
adv bkg acc; ccard acc; bike hire; fishing; canoeing;
games area; CKE. "Lovely, quiet, clean site; busy NH
high ssn; sm pitches; views fr some pitches; friendly,
helpful staff; gd san facs, poss stretched high ssn; no
twin axles; v muddy when wet (tow avail); vg, lively
rest & bar; medieval architecture & Roman walls
around town; m'van Aire de Service nr lake in town;
mkt Wed/Fri; poss overpriced for nature of site."
€21.00, 6 Mar-5 Nov.   2016

AUTUN 6H1 (12km NW Rural) 47.01227, 4.19150
Camping Les Deux Rivières, Le Pré Bouché, 71400
La Celle-en-Morvan **03 45 74 01 38; info@les2
rivieres.com; www.les2rivieres.com**

🐕 ⭐(wc) ♨ ♿ ⚅ 🚿 🗑 🦋 ♈ 🍴 ⚓ 🏊(htd)

**Fr Autun take D978 sp to Chateau-Chinon for
approx 12km. Site on R as entering vill. 300m
fr main rd.** 3*, Med, mkd, hdg, pt shd, bbq; twin axles;
Eng spkn; adv bkg acc; games area; CKE. "V friendly
Dutch owners; well kept clean site; supmkt in Autun;
excel." **€26.00, 1 May-20 Sep.**   2015

AUXERRE 4F4 (2km SE Urban) 47.78678, 3.58721
Camp Municipal, 8 Rue de Vaux, 89000 Auxerre
**03 86 52 11 15 or 03 86 72 43 00 (Mairie); camping.
mairie@auxerre.com; www.auxerre.com**

🐕 ⭐(wc) ♨ ♿ ⚅ 🚿 🍴 🐾 ⚓

**Exit A6 at Auxerre; at junc N6 ring rd foll sp Vaux &
'Stade'; site sp by Rv Yonne. Or fr N6 (N) take ring
rd, site/stadium sp. Site also well sp fr town cent
as 'L'Arbre Sec'.** 3*, Lge, mkd, pt shd, EHU (6A) inc
(long lead poss req); TV; adv bkg acc; fishing 300m;
CKE. "Lovely, peaceful, well-kept site; lge pitches;
friendly staff; gd clean san facs, tight access to sinks;
pool 250m; poss cr & noisy during football ssn; site
poss flooded stormy weather; ltd EHU for site size,
pnts locked & unlocked by warden; no vehicles 2200-
0700; pretty town; popular NH; few water taps."
€13.00, 15 Apr-15 Sep.   2015

AUXERRE 4F4 (10km S Rural) 47.70704, 3.63563
FFCC Camping Les Ceriselles, Route de Vincelottes,
89290 Vincelles **03 86 42 50 47; www.camping
ceriselles.com**

🐕 ⭐(htd) 🆓 ♨ ♿ ⚅ 🚿 🗑 🦋 ♈ 🍴 ⊕ nr 🐾 nr ⚓ 🏊

**Leave A6 at Auxerre Sud. Fr Auxerre, take D606 S
twd Avallon. 10km fr Auxerre turn L into Vincelles.
In 400m immed after 'Atac Marche', turn L into
site access rd, sp as Camping Les Ceriselles. Site is
approx 16km fr a'route exit.** 4*, Med, hdstg, mkd, pt
shd, EHU (10A) inc (poss rev pol); bbq; red long stay;
TV; 10% statics; phone; Eng spkn; adv bkg acc; ccard
acc; bike hire; CKE. "Excel, busy site by canal, poss full
late Jun; friendly, helpful owner; 1st dog free, max 2; gd
san facs, poss insufficient high ssn & ltd LS; lovely walks
to vill & along canal; cycle track to Auxerre & Clamecy;
highly rec; high ssn overflow area; secure o'night area;
gas adj; v popular." **€21.00, 1 Apr-1 Oct.**   2018

AUXI LE CHATEAU 3B3 (0.5km NW Rural) 50.2341,
2.1058 **Camp Municipal des Peupliers,** 22 Rue du
Cheval, 62390 Auxi-le-Château **03 21 41 10 79**

⭐(wc) ♨ ⚅ 🚿 🗑 🍴 nr ⊕ 🐾 nr ⚓

**Fr S on D925, turn N onto D933 at Bernaville to
Auxi-le-Château; turn W onto D941; then turn R in
300m into Rue du Cheval; site sp in 500m by
football stadium. Or take D928 S fr Hesdin; in 11km
take D119 to Auxi-le-Château.** 3*, Med, hdg, unshd,
EHU (3-6A) €1.85; 5% statics; adv bkg acc; fishing;
sailing. "Easy walk into town; dir access to rv; supmkt
300m; excel NH or short stay."
€14.00, 1 Apr-30 Sep.   2018

AUXONNE 6G1 (1km NW Rural) 47.19838, 5.38120
Camping L'Arquebuse, Route d'Athée, 21130 Auxonne
03 80 31 06 89; camping.arquebuse@wanadoo.fr;
www.campingarquebuse.com

🏕 €1.80 � (htd) 🚾 ♨ 🖳 ⊘ 🗤 🍴 🍸 ⊕ 🕏 🐾 nr 🄰 ♨

On D905 Dijon-Geneva, site sp on L bef bdge at ent
to Auxonne. 3*, Med, pt shd, EHU (10A) €3.70 (poss
rev pol); gas; bbq; twin axles; TV; 40% statics; Eng
spkn; adv bkg acc; ccard acc; waterskiing; fishing; clsd
2200-0700; windsurfing; sailing; CKE. "Pleasant rvside
site; friendly staff; san facs tatty & dated; htd pool
adj; poss busy w/ends as NH; interesting town; child
friendly site." **€21.00, 4 Mar-16 Dec.** 2017

AVAILLES LIMOUZINE 7A3 (7km E Rural) 46.12342,
0.65975 FFCC Camp Municipal Le Parc, 86460
Availles-Limouzine 05 49 48 51 22; camping.leparc@
wanadoo.fr; www.campingleparc.monsite-orange.fr

🏕 €2.65 � 🚾 ♨ 🕏 ⊘ 🗤 🦋 🍴 🐾 nr 🄰 🖳

Fr Confolens N on D948 & turn R on D34 to Availles-
Limouzine. Site on Rv Vienne by town bdge.
2*, Med, pt shd, EHU (10A) inc; gas; Eng spkn; adv
bkg acc; CKE. "Attractive, well-run site in beautiful
position; rv views; vg playgrnd; barrier clsd 2200-
0800; poss scruffy LS; vg value; permanent warden."
€16.50, 1 Apr-30 Sep. 2017

AVALLON 4G4 (2km SE Rural) 47.48030, 3.91246
Camp Municipal Sous Roches, Rue Sous Roche;
89200 Avallon 03 86 34 10 39; campingsousroche@
ville-avallon.fr; www.campingsousroche.com

🏕 � ♨ 🕏 ⊘ 🗤 🖳 ⊕ nr 🐾 🄰

App town fr a'route or fr SE on N6. Turn sharp L at
2nd traff lts in town cent, L in 2km at sp Vallée du
Cousin (bef bdge), site 250m on L. If app fr S care
needed when turning R after bdge. 3*, Med, hdstg,
pt shd, terr, EHU (6A) €3.80; bbq; rv fishing adj; CKE.
"Popular, well-kept site in lovely location nr rv; friendly,
helpful staff; excel immac san facs; conv Morvan
National Park; poss flood warning after heavy rain; no
twin axles or o'fits over 2,500kg; attractive town; steep
walk to town; excel." **€18.00, 1 Apr-15 Oct.** 2016

AVESNES-SUR-HELPE 3B4 (9km ENE Rural) 50.143096,
4.028659 Camping Municipal de La Boissellerie,
rue de la Place 59740, Felleries 06 83 80 87 29 or
03 27 59 03 46; campingdaboisselleriefelleries@
orange.fr; www.felleries.fr

🏕 � 🚾 ♨ 🕏 ⊘ 🗤 🦋 🍴 nr 🐾 🄰

Fr N2 19km S of Maubeuge. Turn E on D962. At
Sars-Poteries turn S on D80 or D104. Site sp in vill.
Med, pt shd, EHU (6A) €4; bbq (charcoal, elec, gas);
Eng spkn; adv bkg acc. "Conv N2 N/S or D1043 W/E;
lovely area of wooded hills; Rock Fest 1 w/e per year;
excel." **€15.40, 15 Apr-30 Sep.** 2019

AVIGNON 10E2 (4km N Rural) 43.97063, 4.79928
Viva Camp la Laune (formerly Municipal), Chemin
St Honoré, 30400 Villeneuve-lès-Avignon 04 90 25 76
06 or 04 90 25 61 33; campingdelalaune@wanadoo.
fr; www.camping-villeneuvelezavignon.com

🏕 €1.50 � 🚾 ♨ 🕏 🗤 🗤 🍴 🍸 🐾 🄰 ♨

Fr Avignon, take N100 twd Nîmes over rv bdge.
At W end of 2nd pt of rv bdge, turn R onto N980 sp
Villeneuve-lès-Avignon. Site is 3km on R just past
town battlements on L. Adj sports complex. NB
Do not foll sat nav rote thro Pujaut. 3*, Med, mkd,
hdstg, hdg, shd, EHU €3.10 (poss rev pol); bbq;
twin axles; TV; 10% statics; phone; bus; Eng spkn; adv
bkg acc; ccard acc; games area; CKE. "Lovely, peaceful;
helpful staff; excel security; sports facs adj; gd walks/
cycle rides; htd pool adj; in walking dist of Villeneuve-
lès-Avignon with fort & abbey; gd bus to Avignon;
sports complex adj (free to campers, but ltd acc); vg
local mkt; poss rlwy noise at night; floods in heavy
rain; new owners, site deteriorated; scruffy out of ssn."
€26.00, 1 Apr-15 Oct. 2016

AVIGNON 10E2 (9km NE Rural) 43.99057, 4.91340
Camping Avignon Parc (formerly Camping Flory),
385 Route d'Entraigues, 84270 Vedène 04 90 31 00 51

🏕 €2.50 � 🚾 ♨ 🕏 🖳 ⊘ 🗤 🦋 🍴 🍸 ⊕ 🕏 🐾 🄰 ♨ (htd)

Fr A7 exit 23 dir Carpentras for 3km then Vedene.
3*, Lge, mkd, pt shd, pt sl, EHU (10A) €4 (poss rev
pol); gas; bbq; twin axles; 15% statics; phone; bus;
Eng spkn; adv bkg acc; games area; games rm; CKE.
"Conv touring base Vaucluse; uneven pitches & paths;
facs poss stretched high ssn & ltd LS; lovely pool; vg."
€29.00, 24 May-24 Sep. 2017

"I like to fill in the reports as I travel from site to site"

You'll find report forms at the back of this guide, or you can fill them in online at camc.com/europereport.

AVIGNON 10E2 (8km S Urban) 43.88361, 4.87010
Camping de la Roquette, 746 Ave Jean Mermoz,
13160 Châteaurenard 04 90 94 46 81; contact@
camping-la-roquette.com; www.camping-la-
roquette.com

🏕 €2 � 🚾 ♨ 🕏 🖳 ⊘ 🗤 🦋 🍴 🍸 ⊕ 🕏 🐾 nr 🄰 ♨ 🖳

Exit A7/D907 Avignon S to Noves; take D28 to
Châteaurenard 4km; foll sp to site & Piscine
Olympic/Complex Sportiv. 3*, Med, hdg, mkd, pt shd,
serviced pitches; EHU (10A) €4; TV; phone; Eng spkn;
adv bkg rec; ccard acc; tennis; CKE. "Gd touring cent;
sm pitches; owners friendly, helpful; clean facs; gd
walks." **€22.00, 1 Apr-31 Oct.** 2019

AVIGNON *10E2* (12km W Rural) *43.95155, 4.66451*
Camping Le Bois des Ecureuils, 947 Chemin De La Beaume, 30390 Domazan **04 66 57 10 03; infos@ boisdesecureuils.com; www.boisdesecureuils.com**

12 🅃 €1.70 ♨ wo ♨ ♨ ♨ ∥ 🐾 ⛱ ⊙nr ♨ 🎿 ♨ 🚵 ⛷(htd)

Exit A9/E15 at Remoulins junc 23 twd Avignon on N100. Site on R in 6km. Fr S on N7 foll sp for Nîmes onto N100. Go over 2 lge rndabts, site about 6km on L at rndabt. 2*, Sm, mkd, hdstg, shd, EHU (6A) inc; gas; bbq; TV; 5% statics; phone; Eng spkn; adv bkg rec; CKE. *"Ideal for touring Avignon & Pont du Gard; friendly owners; clean facs; steel awning pegs ess; many long-stay residents LS; v shd; tired site; mostly residential in LS."* **€20.00**   **2018**

AVIGNON *10E2* (1km NW Urban) *43.95670, 4.80222*
Camping du Pont d'Avignon, 10 Chemin de la Barthelasse, 84000 Avignon **04 90 80 63 50; contact@ aquadis-loisirs.com; www.aquadis-loisirs.com**

🅃 €2.70 ♨ wo ♨ ♨ ♨ ∥ /mp ♈ ⛉ ① ♨ 🎿 ⚠ 🚵 ⛷⛱

Exit A7 junc 23 Avignon Nord dir Avignon Centre (D225) then Villeneuve-les-Avignon. Go round wall & under Pont d'Avignon; then cross rv dir Villeneuve, Ile de la Barthelasse. Turn R onto Ile de la Barthelasse. 4*, Lge, mkd, hdg, shd, EHU (6-10A); gas; bbq; cooking facs; red long stay; TV; phone; Eng spkn; adv bkg req; ccard acc; games rm; car wash; games area; tennis; CKE. *"Superb, well-run, busy site; welcoming, helpful staff; lovely pool; gd sized pitches but most with high kerbs; poss flooded LS; extra for c'vans over 5.5m; Avignon festival Jul/Aug; best site for Avignon - 20 mins walk or free ferry; rec arr early even LS; san facs ltd but recently refurbished (2014)."* **€39.00, 1 Mar-17 Nov.**   **2019**

AVIGNON *10E2* (1km NW Urban) *43.95216, 4.79946*
FFCC Camping Bagatelle, 25 allée Antoine Pinay - Ile de la Barthelasse, 84000 Avignon **04 90 86 30 39; camping.bagatelle@wanadoo.fr; www.camping bagatelle.com**

12 🅃 €2.40 ♨(htd) ♨ ♨ ♨ ♨ ∥ /mp ① 🎿 ⚠ 🚵

Exit D907 at Avignon Nord. After passing end of old bdge bear L, then onto new Daladier bdge & take immed R turn over bdge foll sp to Barthelasse & Villeneuve-lès-Avignon. Caution - do not foll Nîmes sp at more southerly bdge (Pont d'Europe). 3*, Lge, mkd, pt shd, EHU (6-10A) €3.50-4.50; gas; ccard acc; fishing; games area; boating; tennis 2km; CKE. *"Busy site on rv bank; sm pitches; helpful staff; facs dated but clean, ltd LS & poss stretched high ssn; narr site rds; suggest find pitch bef driving in; pool 100m; if recep unmanned, go to bar or supmkt to check in; free ferry to town; site low lying & poss damp; highly rec; ideal location, sh walk into Avignon Cent."* **€30.00**   **2016**

AVRANCHES *2E4* (10km W Rural) *48.69663, -1.47434*
FFCC Camping La Pérame, 50530 Genêts **02 33 70 82 49**

🅃 €0.90 ♨ ♨ ∥ ∥ ⚠

Fr Avranches on N175; in 1km turn L on D911 thro Genêts. Turn R onto D35 immed after passing thro Genêts, site on R in 1km. 2*, Sm, pt shd, EHU (10A) €3 (rev pol); 60% statics; phone; CKE. *"CL-type site in apple orchard nr sm vill; pleasant owner; gd views of Mont-St Michel fr vill; poss ltd & unkempt LS; poss boggy after heavy rain; guided walks to Mont St Michel; rec; farm produce; excel, quiet, simple site; all grass; pricey but special."* **€15.00, 1 May-30 Sep.**   **2017**

AXAT *8G4* (2km E Rural) *42.80775, 2.25408*
Camping de la Crémade, 11140 Axat **06 70 07 43 21 or 04 68 74 06 12; campinglacremade@orange.fr; www.campinglacremade.com**

🅃 €1 ♨ wo ♨ ♨ ♨ ∥ 🐾 ⛷ ⚠

S fr Quillan on D117, cont 1km beyond junc with D118 twd Perpignan. Turn R into site, sp, narr access. Med, hdg, pt shd, pt sl, EHU (6A) €2.50; bbq; 5% statics; Eng spkn; adv bkg acc; games rm; CKE. *"Pleasant, well-maintained site in beautiful location; few level pitches; gd san facs; conv for gorges in Aude Valley."* **€22.00, 1 May-24 Sep.**   **2019**

AYDAT *9B1* (3km W Rural) *45.66195, 2.94857*
Camping Les Volcans, La Garandie, 63970 Aydat **04 73 79 33 90; campinglesvolcans@akeonet.com; www.campinglesvolcans.com**

🅃 €2 ♨ wo ♨ ♨ ∥ /mp 🐾 ♈ ♈ ① nr ♨ 🎿 ⚠ ⛷(htd)

⛺ sand 3km

Fr N exit A75 junc 2 onto D2089 dir Bourboule; in 18km turn S onto D213 to Verneuge; in 1km fork R onto D5 dir Murol; in 1.5km turn R onto D788 sp La Grandie; turn R into vill; turn R again & site on L in 100m. Fr S exit A73 junc 5 onto D213 W; in 16km turn S in Verneuge onto D5; after 1.5km turn W onto D788 sp La Garandie; in vill turn R just after phone box, site on L in 100m. 3*, Sm, mkd, pt shd, pt sl, EHU (6A) €5; sw nr; 2% statics; Eng spkn; adv bkg acc; games area; horseriding 3km; watersports 3km. *"Relaxing site; friendly, helpful new owners improving (2011); lge pitches; no twin axles; excel walking & cycle rtes nr; beautiful area; gd touring base; excel clean & well stocked facs; loads of hot water always on supply."* **€18.00, 6 Apr-2 Nov.**   **2019**

FRANCE

AZAY LE FERRON *4H2* (8km N Rural) *46.91949, 1.03679* **Camping Le Cormier,** Route de St Flovier, 36290 Obterre **02 54 39 27 95 or 0844 232 7271 (UK); mike@loireholidays.biz; www.loireholidays.biz**

🔢 🐕 👫(htd) 🆆 🍴 ⚡ 🚲 🦋 📶 ⓦ nr 🛥

Fr Azay-le-Ferron N on D14, site on R just N of Obterre. Or fr Loches S on D943 for 3.5km, turn onto D41 to St Flovier then turn L onto D21 sp Obterre. In 1km turn R onto D14, site on L in 4km. Sm, mkd, hdstg, hdg, pt shd, EHU (10A) €4; bbq; twin axles; TV; Eng spkn; adv bkg acc; ice; games area; games rm. *"Friendly, helpful British owners (CC members); dogs free; spacious pitches; excel touring/walking base; nr Brenne National Park; excel birdwatching; vg."* **€20.00** **2019**

AZAY LE RIDEAU *4G1* (0.6km SE Urban) *47.25919, 0.46992* **FFCC Camp Municipal Le Sabot,** Rue du Stade, 37190 Azay-le-Rideau **02 47 45 42 72 or 02 47 45 42 11 (Mairie); camping.lesabot@wanadoo.fr; www.azaylerideau.fr**

🐕 👫(wd) 🍴 ⚡ & 🚲 🦋 📶 ⓦ nr 🛥 nr 🏔

Best app is fr D751 by-pass to avoid narr town - ignore Azay-le-Rideau sps until Carrefour rndabt. Strt ahead for 1km, site visible at 2nd rndabt. 3*, V lge, mkd, pt shd, EHU (10A) €4.50 (poss rev pol); bbq; red long stay; TV; Eng spkn; adv bkg rec; ccard acc; games area; fishing; CKE. *"Pleasant, spacious, scenic site by rv & chateau; friendly, helpful recep; poss long dist to san facs fr some pitches - cent facs have steps; san facs stretched high ssn, ltd LS; htd pool adj; site prone to flooding; recep open 0800-1200 & 1400-1700; when site clsd m'vans can stay on car park by rv o'night - no facs but well lit (enq at TO); gd loc nr to town and rests; excel."* **€19.00, 1 Apr-31 Oct.** **2017**

BADEN *2F3* (0.9km SW Rural) *47.61410, -2.92540* **Camping Mané Guernehué,** 52 Rue Mané er Groëz, 56870 Baden **02 97 57 02 06; info@camping-baden.com; www.camping-baden.com or www.yelloh village.co.uk**

🐕 €6 👫(htd) 🆆 🍴 ⚡ & 🚲 🦋 📶 🍴 Y ⓦ 🛥 🏔 ✎ 🛥(covrd, htd) 🏊 🏖 sand 5km

Exit N165 sp Arradon/L'Ile aux Moines onto D101 to Baden (10km); in Baden vill turn R at camp sp immed after sharp L-hand bend; in 200m bear R at junc; site on R. Sp at both ends of vill. 4*, Lge, mkd, hdg, pt shd, terr, serviced pitches; EHU (10A) €4.70; bbq; red long stay; TV; 35% statics; phone; Eng spkn; ccard acc; sauna; jacuzzi; games rm; golf 1.5km; waterslide; lazy river; spa treatments; fishing; bike hire; games area; tennis 600m; horse riding school; kids' clubs; gym; mini golf; watersports 3km. *"Mature, pleasant site; fitness rm; gd views; excel san facs; some narr site rds; excel."* **€55.00, 5 Apr-30 Sep, B26.** **2019**

BAERENTHAL *5D3* (2km N Rural) *48.98170, 7.51230* **Camp Municipal Ramstein-Plage,** Rue de Ramstein, 57230 Baerenthal **03 87 06 50 73; camping.ramstein@wanadoo.fr; www.baerenthal.eu**

🐕 €1.90 👫(htd) 🆆 🍴 ⚡ & 🚲 🦋 📶 Y ⓦ 🛥 🏔 ✎ 🛥(htd)

Fr N62 turn onto D36 sp Baerenthal, site sp on lakeside. 3*, Lge, hdg, mkd, pt shd, pt sl, EHU (12A) €3.50; sw nr; 80% statics; Eng spkn; adv bkg acc; tennis; games area. *"Attractive location in important ecological area; generous pitches; modern san facs; m'van o'night area; gd walks; birdwatching; conv Maginot Line; excel."* **€22.60, 1 Apr-30 Sep.** **2015**

BAGNERES DE BIGORRE *8F2* (2km SE Rural) *43.05566, 0.16510* **Camping La Pommeraie,** 2 Ave Philadelphe, 65200 Gerde **05 62 91 32 24; campinglapommeraie@gmail.com; www.campinglapommeraie.com**

🔢 🐕 (€1.30) 👫(htd) 🆆 🍴 ⚡ 🚲 🦋 📶 ⓦ nr 🛥 nr 🏔

App fr E, exit A64 junc 14 (Tournay) onto D20/D938 to Bagnères-de-Bigorre; on ent town turn L at traff lts & foll sp to site. App fr W, exit A64 junc 12 (Tarbes); leave ring rd at junc with D935 & cont to Bagnères-de-Bigorre; foll site sps fr town. 2*, Sm, mkd, hdstg, shd, pt sl, EHU (6A) €1.50; bbq; 10% statics; phone; Eng spkn; adv bkg acc; games rm; CKE. *"Mountain views; htd covrd pool 2km; friendly owners; bike hire in Bagnères; excel walking, mountain biking & touring base; gd, clean, well maintained site; ideal tourist area."* **€9.00** **2017**

BAGNERES DE BIGORRE *8F2* (2km SE Urban) *43.07485, 0.16869* **Camping Les Palomieres,** 20 Route Palomieres, 65200 Bagnères-de-Bigorre **05 62 95 59 79; camping-les-palomieres@wanadoo.fr; www.camping-les-palomieres.com**

🔢 🐕 👫(wd) 🍴 ⚡ 🚲 🦋 🛥 🏔

Take D938 fr Bagnères dir Toulouse, after 2km turn R at Haut de la Côte. Site sp. Sm, pt shd, pt sl, EHU (A-6A) €1.50-4.25; sw nr; 50% statics; adv bkg rec. *"Gd views of Pyrenees; simple site; local specialities."* **€8.50** **2018**

BAGNERES DE BIGORRE *8F2* (13km NW Rural) *43.11196, 0.04931* **Aire Naturelle Le Cerf Volant (Dhom),** 7 Cami de la Géline, 65380 Orincles **05 62 42 99 32; lecerfvolant1@yahoo.fr**

🐕 👫(wd) 🆆 🍴 ⚡ & 🚲 🦋 🏔

Fr Bagnères-de-Bigorre on D935; turn L onto D937 dir Lourdes; site on L opp D407. Single track app rd for 150m. Sm, pt shd, EHU (15A) €2.30; CKE. *"Farm site - produce sold Jul-Aug; conv Lourdes & touring Pyrenees; gd, clean site; lovely site; quiet."* **€11.00, 15 May-15 Oct.** **2015**

FRANCE

Located between Paris and Brittany, at about 55 miles from the Mont Saint Michel and the landing beaches, in the heart of the Normandy, in green surroundings, with casino, golf, swimming pool, tennis and horseback riding. Come and discover the charm of the countryside and the untouched magic of a 19th century touristic and thermal region.

CAMPING DE LA VÉE ***
250 pitches on offer
F-61140 Bagnoles de l'Orne Normandie
Tel : 0033(0) 233 378 745
camping@bagnolesdelorne.com - www.campingbagnolesdelorne.com

BAGNOLES DE L'ORNE *4E1* (1.6km SW Urban) *48.54783, -0.41995* **Camp Municipal de la Vée,** Avenue du President Coty, 61140 Bagnoles-de-l'Orne **02 33 37 87 45; info@campingbagnolesdelorne. com; www.campingbagnolesdelorne.com**

🐾 €1.70 ⛺(htd) 🅦 ♨ ⚲ 🚿 ⚥ 🛒 🦋 ⛱ 🍽 🍴 ⊕ ♨ 🅿nr ⛰

Access fr D335 in vill of Bagnoles-Château. Or fr La Ferté-Macé on D916 for 6km sp Couterne. Well sp fr all dirs. 3*, Lge, hdg, mkd, pt shd, pt sl, EHU (10A) €3.50 (poss rev pol); gas; bbq; TV; phone; bus adj; Eng spkn; ccard acc; golf nr; tennis nr; CKE. *"Excel, well-kept, well-run site in vg location; vg, spotless facs; htd pool 1.5km; mini golf nr; easy walk to beautiful thermal spa town & lake; free bus to town cent at site ent; forest walks; archery nrby; gd for dogs; gd value; town bus €1 per day."* **€18.00, 3 Mar-11 Nov.** 2018

See advertisement

"I need an on-site restaurant"

We do our best to make sure site information is correct, but it is always best to check any must-have facilities are still available or will be open during your visit.

BAGNOLS SUR CEZE *10E2* (3km NE Rural) *44.17358, 4.63694* **Camping Les Genêts d'Or,** Chemin de Carmigan, 30200 Bagnols-sur-Cèze **04 66 89 58 67; info@camping.genets-dor.com; www.camping-genets-dor.com**

🐾 ⛺(htd) 🅦 ♨ ⚲ 🚿 🛒 🦋 ⛱ 🍴 ⊕ ♨ 🅿 ⛰ 🏊 🛶(htd) 🚣

N fr Bagnols on N86 over rv bdge, turn R into D360 immed after Total stn. Foll sp to site on rv. 4*, Med, mkd, hdstg, pt shd, pt sl, EHU (6A) €5.50 (poss rev pol); gas; 10% statics; Eng spkn; adv bkg req; ccard acc; games rm; fishing 2km; games area. *"Excel, clean site; welcoming Dutch owners; gd pool; canoeing 2km; no dogs Jul/Aug; wildlife in rv; gd rest; highly rec."* **€33.00, 20 Apr-20 Sep.** 2016

BAIGNES STE RADEGONDE *7B2* (0.5km SW Rural) *45.38187, -0.23862* **FFCC Camp Municipal,** Le Plein, 16360 Baignes-Ste-Radegonde **05 45 78 79 95 or 05 45 78 40 04 (Mairie); point.i@live.fr; www.baignes-sainte-radegonde.fr**

🛡 ♨ ⚲ 🚿 ⚥ 🦋 🅿nr

Fr N10 turn W onto D2 to Baignes; site well sp on rvside. 2*, Sm, pt shd, EHU (6A) €3; adv bkg acc; ccard acc; tennis nr; CKE. *"Warden calls pm; excel new san facs (2018); chem disp in vill; attractive sm town nr cycle track; excel."* **€27.00, 1 Apr-31 Oct.** 2018

BAILLEUL *3A3* (3.5km N Rural) *50.76160, 2.74956* **Camping Les Saules (Notteau),** 453 Route du Mont Noir, 59270 Bailleul **03 28 49 13 75; www.ferme-des-saules.com**

🐾 🛡 🅦 ♨ 🚿 🦋 🅿 ⛰

N fr Lille on A25 exit junc 10 & head N into Bailleul cent; in town cent at traff lts turn R onto D23/N375; after 400m turn L on D23; in 2km just bef Belgian border turn L onto D223. Site on L in 300m. Sm, hdstg, pt shd, EHU (6A) €3.35; bbq; 90% statics; Eng spkn; CKE. *"Farm site; friendly owner; conv Calais, Dunkerque & WW1 sites; lovely, excel site, highly rec well kept and comfortable site; 1st class farm shop; unkempt in LS; 2 pin adapter ess; new san facs (2017)."* **€11.50, 1 Apr-31 Oct.** 2017

BAIN DE BRETAGNE *2F4* (13km W Rural) *47.8200, -1.8299* **Camp Municipal Le Port,** Rue de Camping, 35480 Guipry **02 99 34 72 90 (Mairie) or 02 99 34 28 26**

🛡 ♨ ⚲ 🚿 🦋 🅿nr ⛰

W fr Bain-de-Bretagne on D772, cross rv at Messac; cont on D772 sharp L at Leader supmkt into Ave du Port; site sp bef ent Guipry. NB Do not app after dark as rv is at end of app rd. V sharp turn at Leader supmkt into Ave du Camping. 2*, Med, mkd, hdg, pt shd, EHU (10A) €3 (poss long lead req); rv fishing; CKE. *"Excel, pretty site; friendly; warden on duty am & late pm; barrier 1.9m locked at times but phone for help or go to pitch 30; delightful rv walks & cycle paths; cruising & hire boats avail; nr classic cars museum; phone Mairie for warden's number, who calls early PM."* **€10.00, Easter-15 Oct.** 2018

BALAZUC *9D2* (2km E Rural) *44.50778, 4.40333*
Camping Le Chamadou, Mas de Chaussy, 07120
Balazuc 08 20 36 61 97 or 07 87 64 34 77 (mob);
infos@camping-le-chamadou.com; www.camping-
le-chamadou.com

🐕 €2.60 🚻 (htd) 🚱 ♨ ⚓ ⊟ ✗ 🏊 ♈ ⌶ ♨ 🗲 🄰 🛶 🛝 🛶

Fr Ruoms foll D579 dir Aubenas. After approx 9km
turn R under viaduct, site sp. Keep R up narr rd
to site. App recep on foot fr car pk. 3*, Med, hdg,
hdstg, pt shd, pt sl, EHU (10A) €4.20 (some rev pol);
bbq (elec); TV; 10% statics; phone; Eng spkn; adv bkg
rec; ccard acc; canoe hire; kayak hire; waterslide; CKE.
*"Excel, well-run, family site; panoramic views; most
pitches spacious."* **€24.00, 1 Apr-31 Oct.** **2017**

BALBIGNY *9B1* (2.7km NW Rural) *45.82558, 4.16196*
Camping La Route Bleue, Route D56 du Lac de
Villerest, Pralery, 42510 Balbigny 04 77 27 24 97
or 06 85 52 98 66 (mob); camping.balbigny@
wanadoo.fr; camping-de-la-route-bleue.fr

🚻 🚱 ♨ ♿ ⊟ ✗ ⫿ 🏊 ⌶ 🖭 ☕ 🗲 🄰 🛶 🛝

Fr N on D1082, take 1st R after a'route (A89/72)
junc N of Balbigny onto D56. Fr S on D1082, turn L
at RH bend on N o'skirts of Balbigny, D56, sp Lac de
Villerest & St Georges-de-Baroille. Well sp.
3*, Med, hdg, mkd, pt shd, pt sl, EHU (10A) (poss long
lead req); bbq; red long stay; adv bkg acc; ccard acc;
fishing; games rm; CKE. *"Nice site on rv bank; views
over rv some pitches; helpful, friendly & welcoming
staff; san facs updated (2017); sports complex
adj; ltd EHU; extra for twin axles; conv A72; excel;
lovely area; lge pitches; gd NH; ok long stay; fishing."*
€22.00, 15 Mar-31 Oct. **2017**

BALLEROY *1D4* (1km NE Rural) *49.18680, -0.82463*
Camping Le Clos De Balleroy, Route de Castillon,
14490 Balleroy 02 31 21 41 48; info@camping-leclos
deballeroy.fr; www.camping-leclosdeballeroy.fr

🚻 🚱 ♨ ⊟ ✗ 🖭 ⌶ 🗲 🛶

Fr N13 junc 37 turn S onto D572. After 6.8km in Le
Tronquay turn L onto D73, sp Castillon. Site on R in
5km bef Balleroy. 3*, Sm, pt shd, EHU (16A); games
area. *"Conv for Normandy coast and Bayeux; gd."*
€24.00, 15 Mar-15 Nov. **2016**

BANON *10E3* (2km S Rural) *44.02607, 5.63088*
Camping L'Epi Bleu, Les Gravières, 04150 Banon
04 92 73 30 30 or 06 15 61 68 63 (mob); camping
epibleu@aol.com; www.campingepibleu.com

🐕 €4 🚻 🚱 ♨ ♿ ⊟ ✗ 🏊 ⌶ 🖭 ☕ 🗲 🄰 🛶 (htd) 🛝

Fr D4100 8km S of Forcalquier turn R onto D5 N
thro St Michel-L'Observatoire & Revest twd Banon
(approx 25km). Turn L on D51 twds Simiane-la-
Rotunde. Site on R in 500m immed bef town,
sp at junc. 3*, Med, shd, EHU (10A) €5; bbq; TV;
70% statics; Eng spkn; adv bkg acc; games area; CKE.
*"Vg, wooded site; pleasant owners; gd walking & cycling
tours; access to some pitches diff for lge o'fits; san fac
tired but clean (2015); uphill 30m walk to vill with sm
supmkt."* **€30.00, 4 Apr-30 Sep.** **2015**

BANYULS SUR MER *10H1* (1.5km SW Rural)
42.47665, 3.11904 **Camp Municipal La Pinède,** Ave
Guy Malé, 66650 Banyuls-sur-Mer 04 68 88 32 13;
camp.banyuls@banyuls-sur-mer.com;
www.banyuls-sur-mer.com

🐕 🚻 🚱 ♨ ⊟ ✗ 🖭 🦋 ☕ 🗲 nr 🄰 🌴 shgl 1km

On D914 foll sp to Banyuls-sur-Mer; turn R at
camping sp at cent of sea-front by town hall; foll
sp to site. 2*, Lge, hdg, mkd, pt shd, pt sl, terr, EHU
(4-13A) €2-3; Eng spkn; ccard acc; CKE. *"Busy, friendly
site; spacious pitches, some with sea view; narr site rds;
vg, clean facs."* **€17.50, 23 Feb-12 Nov.** **2018**

BAR LE DUC *6E1* (2km E Urban) *48.77433, 5.17415*
FFCC Camp Municipal du Château de Marbeaumont,
Rue du Stade, off Rue de St Mihiel, 55000 Bar-le-Duc
03 29 79 17 33 (TO) or 03 29 79 11 13 (LS);
barleduc.tourisme@wanadoo.fr; www.tourisme-
barleduc.com

🚻 🚱 ♨ ⊟ ✗ 🗲 nr

Fr town cent foll Camping sps. Rue de St Mihiel is
pt of D1916 dir Verdun. Fr NW on D994/D694 or
fr SE on N1135, at rndabt turn E onto D1916 sp
Metz, Verdun & St Mihiel. In 200m turn L into Rue du
Stade sp Camping. Site on L in 100m.
1*, Sm, pt shd, EHU (16A) €3 (poss long lead req).
*"Barrier clsd 1100-1500; delightful site in grnds of
chateau; friendly & helpful warden; clean, modern san
facs; no twin axles; check gate opening times; lovely
walk into historic town; gd NH; vg site; nice open plan
site."* **€13.00, 1 May-15 Oct.** **2018**

BARCARES, LE *10G1* (1km SW Coastal) *42.77462,
3.02207* **Camping L'Europe,** Route de St Laurent,
66420 Le Barcarès 04 68 86 15 36; reception@
europe-camping.com; www.europe-camping.com

🔢 🐕 ♨ €8 🚻 ♨ ♿ ⊟ ✗ ⌶ ☕ 🗲 🄰 🛝 🛶

Exit A9 at Perpignan N & take D83 sp Le Barcarès.
After 9km turn R on D81 sp Canet Plage, L on D90
sp Le Barcarès. Site on R. 3*, Lge, mkd, hdg, shd, EHU
(16A) inc; gas; red long stay; 50% statics; Eng spkn;
adv bkg acc; tennis; archery; waterslide; CKE. *"Gd
location; tidy pitches, all have individual san facs (tired
early ssn 2010); ltd facs LS; gd cycle rte to beach &
shops; disco; gd winter NH."* **€21.00** **2017**

BARCELONNETTE *9D4* (9km W Rural) *44.39686,
6.54605* **Domaine Loisirs de l'Ubaye,** Vallée de l'Ubaye,
04340 Barcelonnette 04 92 81 01 96; info@
loisirsubaye.com; www.loisirsubaye.com

🐕 €3.50 🚻 ♨ ♿ ⊟ ✗ ⌶ ☕ 🗲 🄰 🛶 (htd)

Site on S side of D900. 4*, Lge, mkd, shd, terr, EHU
(6A) €3.50; gas; red long stay; TV; phone; watersports;
bike hire; CKE. *"Magnificent scenery; gd site; friendly."*
€29.50, 15 May-15 Oct. **2016**

BARFLEUR *1C4* (0.7km NW Urban/Coastal) *49.67564, -1.26645* **Camp Municipal La Blanche Nef,** 12 Chemin de la Masse, 50760 Gatteville-le-Phare **02 33 23 15 40; www.camping-barfleur.fr**

🐕 €2.04 👫(htd) WD ♨ ᗡ 🖨 / MP 🦋 ۩ 🍴 ᵷ 🛒nr 🏧 🌲sand adj

Foll main rd to harbour; half-way on L side of harbour & turn L at mkd gap in car pk; cross sm side-rd & foll site sp on sea wall; site visible on L in 300m. Site accessible only fr S (Barfleur).
3*, Med, unshd, pt sl, EHU (6-10A); 45% statics; Eng spkn; adv bkg acc; ccard acc; CKE. *"Gd sized pitches; vg facs; lovely site; sea views; gd beach; gd birdwatching, walking, cycling; m'vans all year; walking dist to fishing vill; clean washing facs; bread van at 9am."*
€21.40, 15 Feb-15 Nov.   2018

BARFLEUR *1C4* (1km NW Coastal) *49.67971, -1.27364* **Camping La Ferme du Bord de Mer,** 43 Route du Val de Saire, 50760 Gatteville-Phare **060 895 2434; camping.gatteville@gmail.com; www.camping-gatteville.fr**

12 🐕 €1.45 👫 WD ♨ ᗡ / 🦋 🍴 ᵷ 🛒nr 🏧 🦎 🌲sand adj

On D901 fr Cherbourg; on o'skts of Barfleur turn L onto D116 for Gatteville-Phare. Site on R in 1km.
2*, Sm, mkd, hdg, pt shd, pt sl, serviced pitches; EHU (3-10A) €3.40-5.30; gas; 25% statics; phone; games rm. *"CL-type site; sheltered beach; coastal path to vill & lighthouse; conv ferries (30 mins); Sep 2002 member reported high-strength poison against rodents in field adj site - no warning notices displayed, beware children or dogs; gd."* €15.00   2016

BARNEVILLE CARTERET *1C4* (3.5km SE Coastal) *49.35952, -1.74879* **Camping du Golf,** Saint Jean de la Rivière, 50270 Barneville-Cartere **02 33 04 78 90; contact@camping-du-golf.fr; www.camping-du-golf.co.uk**

🐕 €4 👫 WD ♨ ᗡ 🖨 / 🦋 ۩ 🍴 🏧nr ᵷ 🛒 🏧 🦎
🏊(covrd, htd) 🌲sandy 1km

Fr Barneville-Carteret, turn W on D130, after 1.5km turn L. Site on R after 1.5km. Site well sp fr Barneville-Carteret. 4*, Lge, hdg, mkd, unshd, EHU (6A) inc; gas; twin axles; Eng spkn; adv bkg req; ccard acc; games rm; CKE. *"Gd quiet site with clean facs; 18 hole course; horse ridding nrby."*
€37.00, 1 Apr-1 Nov.   2017

BASTIA *10G2* (11km S Coastal) *42.62922, 9.46835* **Camping San Damiano,** Lido de la Marana, 20620 Biguglia **04 95 33 68 02; san.damiano@wanadoo.fr; www.campingsandamiano.com**

🐕 €0.90 👫 WD ♨ ᗡ 🖨 / ۩ 🛒 🏧 🏊 🌲sandy adj

S fr Bastia on N193 for 4km. Turn SE onto Lagoon Rd (sp Lido de Marana). Site on L in 7km.
3*, Lge, pt shd, unshd, EHU (6A) €3.40; red long stay; 60% statics; Eng spkn; ccard acc; games area; games rm; CKE. *"San facs basic but clean; cycle path; big site, spread out; no water points; rd and aircraft noise."*
€34.00, 1 Apr-31 Oct.   2019

BAUD *2F3* (7km W Rural) *47.88239, 3.10818* **Camp Municipal de Pont Augan,** Pont Augan, 56150 Baud **02 97 51 04 74; camping.p.augan@live.fr; camping-pontaugan.com**

🐕 Fr 👫(htd) WD ♨ ᗡ 🖨 / MP 🦋 ۩ 🍴nr 🏧nr 🛒 🏧

Fr Baud, W on D6. Site on R on ent vill.
3*, Sm, mkd, hdg, pt shd, EHU (10A) €3; bbq; Eng spkn; adv bkg acc; canoeing adj; fishing adj; games area; bike hire; CKE. *"Peaceful site; barrier & office ltd opening hrs but parking area avail; warden calls morning & teatime; ltd groceries; 4 gites on site; vg."*
€15.00, 1 Apr-30 Sep.   2018

BAUGE *4G1* (1km E Rural) *47.53889, -0.09637* **Camp Municipal du Pont des Fées,** Chemin du Pont des Fées, 49150 Baugé **02 41 89 14 79 or 02 41 89 18 07 (Mairie); camping@ville-bauge.fr; www.ville-bauge.fr**

👫 WD ♨ ᗡ / MP 🦋 🛒nr

Fr Saumur traveling N D347/D938 turn 1st R in Baugé onto D766. Foll camping sp to site by sm rv; ent bef rv bdge. 2*, Sm, mkd, hdg, pt shd, EHU (4A) €2.70; bbq; phone; adv bkg acc; ccard acc; fishing; tennis 150m. *"Excel countryside; pleasant, well-kept site; pools 150m; obliging wardens; Aldi within walking dist; camping car site adj; excel municipal well kept site."* €13.50, 15 May-15 Sep.   2015

BAUME LES DAMES *6G2* (6km S Rural) *47.32506, 6.36127* **Camping L'Ile,** 1 Rue de Pontarlier, 25110 Pont-les-Moulins **03 81 84 15 23; info@campingdelile.fr; www.campingdelile.fr**

🐕 👫 WD ♨ ᗡ / 🍴nr 🏧nr 🛒nr 🏧

S fr Baume-les-Dames on D50, site on L on ent Pont-les-Moulins. 1*, Sm, pt shd, EHU (6A) €2.50; gas; red long stay; 10% statics; Eng spkn; adv bkg acc; CKE. *"Tidy, basic site in pleasant setting by Rv Cusancin; helpful, friendly owner; bread 100m; bar 500m; pool 6km; clean, basic facs; gd."* €11.50, 1 May-7 Sep.   2016

BAYEUX *3D1* (0.5km N Urban) *49.28392, -0.69760* **Camp Municipal des Bords de L'Aure,** Blvd d'Eindhoven, 14400 Bayeux **02 31 92 08 43; campingmunicipal@mairie-bayeux.fr; www.mairie-bayeux.fr**

🐕 👫 WD ♨ ᗡ 🖨 / MP ۩ 🛒 🏧

Site sp off Périphérique d'Eindhoven (Bayeux by-pass, D613). Fr W (Cherbourg) exit N13 junc 38, turn L over N13, then R onto D613 thro Vaucelles. At rndabt cont on D613 (3rd exit) Blvd d'Eindhoven. Site on R immed after traff lts, almost opp Briconaute DIY store. Fr E (Caen) on N13 exit junc 36 onto D613 N; foll ring rd across 2 rndabts, 4 traff lts, site on L opp Bayeux town sp. 3*, Lge, hdg, hdstg, pt shd, EHU (6A) €3.66 (poss rev pol); gas; red long stay; phone; Eng spkn; adv bkg req; CKE. *"Excel, well-kept site; indoor pool adj; avoid perimeter pitches (narr hdstgs & rd noise); no twin axles; office open LS; gd footpath to town along stream; Bayeux festival 1st w/ end July; conv ferries; lge mkt Sat; new, clean san facs & lndry facs (2018)."* €22.00, 30 Mar-3 Nov.   2019

BAYEUX *3D1* (18km SE Rural) *49.15722, -0.76018*
Camping Caravaning Escapade, Rue de l'église, 14490
CAHAGNOLLES **02 31 21 63 59;** escapadecamping@
orange.fr; www.campinglescapade.net

🏕 €2.70 ♨ [wc] ♨ 🔒 🗑 ✏ ♒ 🍴 🏊 (htd)

**Fr Saint Paul du Varnay take D99 Cahagnolles on
the L; foll rd for aprrox 2.5km; turn L & aft church
campsite on R.** 4*, Med, mkd, pt shd, EHU (10A)
€3.90; bbq; adv bkg acc; ccard acc. *"Lovely site; well
looked after & cared for; clean san facs; friendly owners
& staff; recep rm for events; pt of Flower Campings
chain."* **€28.00, 1 Apr-30 Sep.** 2019

BAYEUX *3D1* (7km SE Rural) *49.24840, -0.60245*
Camping Le Château de Martragny, 52 Hameau
Saint-Léger, 14740 Martragny **02 31 80 21 40;**
chateau.martragny@wanadoo.fr; www.chateau-
martragny.com or www.chateau-martragny.fr

🏕 €1 ♨ [wc] ♨ 🔒 🗑 ✏ [MSP] ♒ 🍴 ⊕ 🗑 🏊 🏚 ✏
🏊 (htd) 🚿

**Fr Caen going NW on N13 dir Bayeux/Cherbourg,
leave at Martragny/Carcagny exit. Strt on & take
2nd R (past turn for Martragny/Creully) into site
& chateau grnds. Fr Bayeux after leaving N13
(Martragny/Carcagny), go L over bdge to end of rd,
turn L then take 2nd R into Chateau grnds.**
4*, Lge, mkd, pt shd, pt sl, EHU (15A) €5.50 (long lead
poss req, poss rev pol); gas; bbq; TV; Eng spkn; adv bkg
acc; ccard acc; games rm; tennis; fishing; horseriding
500m; CKE. *"Popular, attractive, 1st class site on
lawns of chateau; attractive area; relaxed atmosphere;
friendly, helpful staff; new superb, modern san facs
(2013); gd rest; no o'fits over 8m; poss muddy when
wet; conv cemetaries; D-Day beaches 15km; Sat mkt in
Bayeux; conv Caen ferry; excel."*
€36.00, 2 May-12 Sep, N06. 2019

BAYEUX *3D1* (8km SE Rural) *49.25041, -0.59251*
Camping Le Manoir de l'Abbaye (Godfroy), 15 Rue
de Creully, 14740 Martragny **02 31 80 25 95;**
yvette.godfroy@libertysurf.fr; http://godfroy.
pagesperso-orange.fr

🏕 €2.30 ♨ [wc] ♨ 🔒 🗑 ✏

**Take N13 Bayeux, Caen dual c'way for 7km,
fork R sp Martagny. Over dual c'way L at T-junc,
then 1st R sp D82 Martragny & Creully site on R
500m. Sharp L steep turn into site.** Sm, pt shd,
EHU (15A) €4.(poss rev pol); Eng spkn; adv bkg acc;
CKE. *"Peaceful, relaxing, well-kept site; lovely grnds;
helpful, welcoming owners; steps to ltd san facs;
meals & wine avail on request; winter storage; conv
Ouistreham ferries; highly rec; wc, shwr, kitchen fac's
in same rm; v restful; some elec hookups rev polarity."*
€23.00, 15 Mar-15 Oct. 2019

BAYEUX *3D1* (9km NW Rural) *49.33120, -0.80240*
Camping Reine Mathilde, 14400 Etréham **02 31
21 76 55;** campingreinemathilde@gmail.com;
www.camping-normandie-reinemathilde.com

🏕 €2.50 ♨ (htd) [wc] ♨ 🔒 🗑 ✏ ♒ 🦋 ♒ 🍴 ⊕ 🗑 🏊 🏚 ✏
🏊 (htd) 🚿 🌳 sand 5km

**NW fr Bayeux on D6 turn L to Etréham (D100); site
3km (sp). Or W fr Bayeux on N13 for 8km, exist junc
38. At x-rds 1.5km after vill of Tour-en-Bessin turn R
on D206 to Etréham & bear L at church.**
3*, Med, mkd, hdg, pt shd, EHU (6A) €4.70; TV;
15% statics; phone; Eng spkn; adv bkg acc; fishing
1km; bike hire; CKE. *"Well-kept, attractive site; lge, well
spaced hdg pitches; mv service pnt nr; app rds quite narr;
friendly, helpful warden; gd, clean san facs; conv D-Day
beaches etc; excel."* **€26.70, 30 Mar-30 Sep.** 2019

BAYONNE *8F1* (11km NE Rural) *43.52820, -1.39157*
Camping Lou P'tit Poun, 110 Ave du Quartier Neuf,
40390 St Martin-de-Seignanx **05 59 56 55 79;**
contact@louptitpoun.com; www.louptitpoun.com

🏕 €5.90 ♨ [wc] ♨ 🔒 🗑 ✏ [MSP] 🍴 ⊕ 🗑 🏊 nr 🏚 ✏ 🏊 🚿

**Fr Bordeaux exit A63 junc 6 dir Bayonne Nord;
then take D817 dir Pau & St Martin-de-Seignanx;
site sp on R in 7km.** 3*, Lge, mkd, hdg, pt shd, terr,
serviced pitches; EHU (10A) inc; gas; bbq (elec, gas);
red long stay; TV; 17% statics; phone; Eng spkn; adv
bkg acc; ccard acc; games area; games rm; tennis;
CKE. *"Charming, spacious, family-run site; gd sized
pitches; friendly staff; gd clean san facs; ltd facs
LS; conv Biarritz, St Jean-de-Luz & a'route; excel."*
€40.00, 9 Jun-15 Sep, A39. 2017

BAZAS *7D2* (2km SE Rural) *44.43139, -0.20167*
Campsite Le Paradis de Bazas, Route de Casteljaloux,
33430 Bazas **05 56 65 13 17;** paradis@franceloc.fr;
www.camping-paradis-bazas.fr

🏕 €3 ♨ [wc] ♨ 🔒 🗑 ✏ ♒ 🦋 ♒ 🍴 🏊 nr 🏚 🏊 (htd)

**Exit A62 junc 3 onto N524 twd Bazas, then D655.
Cont thro town cent & foll sp Casteljaloux/
Grignols. Site sp on R.** 4*, Sm, hdg, mkd, pt shd, pt
sl, EHU (6-16A) €3.25-4.90; gas; red long stay; TV;
6% statics; Eng spkn; adv bkg acc; CKE. *"Pleasant,
relaxed, well-kept site in picturesque location; views
of chateau & town; friendly, helpful staff; san facs
v smart but poss stretched high ssn; pleasant walk/
cycle track to interesting, walled town; vineyards nr."*
€25.00, 1 Apr-29 Sep. 2017

BEAUGENCY *4F2* (0.8km E Rural) *47.77628, 1.64294* **Camp Municipal du Val de Flux,** Route de Lailly-en-Val, 45190 Beaugency **02 38 44 50 39 or 02 38 44 83 12;** camping@ville-beaugency.fr; www.camping-beaugency.fr

🐾 €2 ♦♦ (htd) ⬚ ⚓ ♿ ▭ ⬚ / MSP 🦋 ▼ ⑪ nr ⬚ ▓ nr ⚠ ⚓ 🏖 sand

Exit A10 junc 15 onto D2152. In Beaugency turn L at traff lts nr water tower onto D925 & again over rd bdge. Site sp on S bank of Rv Loire. 2*, Lge, mkd, pt shd, EHU (10A) inc (rev pol); red long stay; 10% statics; Eng spkn; ccard acc; fishing; watersports; CKE. *"Beautiful, welcoming, well-kept site; views over Loire; helpful, friendly staff; free 1 night site for m'vans over rv on other side of town; poss unrel opening dates LS, rec phone ahead; vg location close to town; coded ent barrier; next to rv and bdge to town; some rd noise at busy times; facs gd but far away fr pitches; scruffy & unkempt; town dilapidated; free WiFi around shop; gd cycling."* **€20.40, 1 Apr-11 Sep.** **2018**

BEAULIEU SUR DORDOGNE *7C4* (5km N Rural) *45.02167, 1.83960* **Camping la Champagne,** La Champagne, 19120 Brivezac **06 48 47 23 51;** info@campinglachampagne.com; www.campingla champagne.com

🐾 €2.50 ♦♦ ⬚ ⚓ ♿ ▭ / MSP 🦋 🛶 ⚓

Fr Beaulieu-sur-Dordogne take D940, sp Tulle. R onto D12, sp Argentat. R onto D136. R again after bdge. Site 600m on R. 2*, Sm, mkd, pt shd, terr, EHU (6A) €3; bbq; sw nr; twin axles; phone; Eng spkn; adv bkg acc; CCI. *"Aire Naturella (max 25 vans); fishing; canoeing; horseriding nr; peaceful, spacious rvside location; Dutch owners."* **€22.00, 1 May-15 Sep.** **2019**

BEAULIEU SUR DORDOGNE *7C4* (0.3km E Urban) *44.97950, 1.84040* **Huttopia Beaulieu Sur Dordogne (formerly Camping des Iles),** Blvd Rodolphe-de-Turenne, 19120 Beaulieu-sur-Dordogne **05 55 91 02 65;** www.huttopia.com

🐾 €2 ♦♦ (htd) ⬚ ⚓ ♿ ▭ / 🦋 ⚓ ▼ ⑪ ⚓ ▓ nr ⚠ ⚓ 🏖

Exit A20 junc 52 ont D158/D38 dir Collonges-la-Rouge; cont on D38 & turn R onto D940 to Beaulieu-sur-Dordogne; site sp fr o'skts of town. Or on D940 N fr Bretenoux, turn R in Beaulieu town sq, site about 200m on island in Rv Dordogne. NB 3m height limit at ent. 3*, Med, mkd, shd, EHU (10A) inc (poss long lead req); red long stay; 15% statics; Eng spkn; adv bkg rec; games rm; rv; fishing; bike hire; games area; canoeing. *"Delightful, wooded site; pitches by rv excel (extra charge); plenty shd; friendly staff; gd clean san facs, ltd LS; attractive medieval town; gd value; highly rec."* **€30.70, 20 Apr-30 Sep, A21.** **2018**

BEAULIEU SUR LOIRE *4G3* (0.3km E Rural) *47.54407, 2.82167* **FFCC Camp Municipal du Canal,** Route de Bonny, 45630 Beaulieu-sur-Loire **02 38 35 89 56 or 02 38 35 32 16 (LS);** renault.campingbeaulieu@ orange.fr; www.beaulieu-sur-loire.fr

♦♦ ⬚ ⚓ ♿ / ▭ ▼ nr ⑪ nr ▓ nr

Exit A77 junc 21 Bonny-sur-Loire, cross rv to Beaulieu-sur-Loire on D296. On E o'skirts of vill on D926, nr canal. 2*, Sm, mkd, hdstg, hdg, pt shd, EHU (10A) €4; Eng spkn; adv bkg acc; CKE. *"Well-kept site in pleasant area; direct access to canal; some sm pitches diff lge o'fits; site yourself, warden calls 0800-0900 & 1830-1930; no security; clean modern san facs; gd walking along canal & Rv Loire; boat trips; poss workers' statics LS; mkt Wed; lovely hdg pitches; conv Aqueduct at Briare."* **€10.40, 4 Apr-1 Nov.** **2017**

BEAUMONT DE LOMAGNE *8E3* (1km E Urban) *43.88406, 0.99800* **Village de Loisirs Le Lomagnol,** Ave du Lac, 82500 Beaumont-de-Lomagne **05 63 26 12 00;** villagedeloisirslelomagnol@wanadoo.fr; www.villagelelomagnol.fr

🐾 €2 ♦♦ ⬚ ⚓ ♿ / ▼ ⑪ ⚓ ▓ ⚠ 🏊

On SE of D928 at E end of vill. Sp 'Centre de Loisirs, Plan d'Eau'. 3*, Med, mkd, pt shd, EHU (10A) inc (poss long lead req); sw; 25% statics; canoe hire; golf; tennis; jacuzzi; sauna; waterslide; bike hire; fishing. *"Gd quality, modern site; interesting old town; mkt Sat; facs tired LS."* **€18.00, 1 Apr-30 Oct.** **2016**

BEAUMONT DU PERIGORD *7D3* (7km SW Rural) *44.75603, 0.70216* **Centre Naturiste de Vacances Le Couderc (Naturist),** 24440 Naussannes **05 53 22 40 40;** info@lecouderc.com; www.lecouderc.com

🐾 €4.65 ♦♦ ⬚ ⚓ ♿ / 🦋 ⚓ ▼ ⑪ ⚓ ▓ ⚠ ⚓ (htd) 🏖

Fr D660 at D25 W thro Naussannes & hamlet of Leydou. Just beyond Leydou turn R into site, well sp. 1*, Lge, mkd, pt shd, pt sl, EHU (5A) €4.50; red long stay; 10% statics; adv bkg req; ccard acc; jacuzzi; sauna; bike hire. *"Beautiful site with relaxed atmosphere; friendly, helpful Dutch owners; gd san facs; superb pond; naturist walks on site; gd walking/cycling area; Bastide towns nrby; new sauna,steam rm/spa (2015); new camping field; pond cleaned & enlarged; vg entmnt & activity prog for kids & adults."* **€41.00, 1 Apr-15 Oct.** **2017**

BEAUMONT SUR OISE *3D3* (8km SW Rural) *49.12805, 2.18318* **Parc de Séjour de l'Etang,** 10 Chemin des Belles Vues, 95690 Nesles-la-Vallée **01 34 70 62 89;** campinparis@gmail.com; www.campinparis.com

🐾 €2 ♦♦ (htd) ⬚ ▭ ⬚ / 🦋 ▓ nr ⚠

Fr D927 Méru-Pontoise rd, turn L onto D64 at sp L'Isle Adam. After passing thro Nesles-la-Vallée camp sp on L. 4*, Med, hdg, pt shd, serviced pitches; EHU (3A) inc (rev pol); Eng spkn; lake fishing adj; CKE. *"Lovely, peaceful, out-of-the-way setting; spacious pitches; friendly, helpful staff; gd facs; conv day trips to Paris & Versailles; excel."* **€22.00, 1 Apr-30 Sep.** **2016**

BEAUMONT SUR SARTHE *4F1* (1km E Rural) *48.22382, 0.13651* **FFCC Camp Municipal du Val de Sarthe,** Rue de l'Abreuvoir, 72170 Beaumont-sur-Sarthe **02 43 97 01 93; camping-beaumontssarthe@orange.fr; www.beaumontsursarthe.com**

🏕 €0.50 ♦♦♦ 🚮 🔳 ♨ ᵴ ⚕ / ᴹᴾ 📶 ⓗ nr 🛁 nr /▥

Fr D338 Alençon-Le Mans, turn sharp L at 2nd set of traff lts in cent of Beaumont & foll sp twd E of town. Fr Le Mans on A28 exit 21 onto D6, R onto D338 & R at traff lts & foll sp. NB Narr, sloping app thro town rds with blind corners. Narr site access. 3*, Med, hdg, mkd, pt shd, EHU (10A) inc (long cable poss req & poss rev pol); TV; Eng spkn; adv bkg rec; ccard acc; fishing adj; rv boating adj; CKE. "Beautiful, peaceful, well-run rvside site; lge pitches, some by rv; no twin axles & poss no c'vans over 2,000 kg; barrier clsd 2200; easy walk to interesting, pretty town; mkt Tues; rec; nice clean site; pleasant & friendly; well maintained site; recep open 1000-1200, 1600-1900 (May, Jun & Sep), 900-1200, 1500-2000 (Jul & Aug); barrier unattended bet 1200-1400; pool 500m; admission only aft 4pm; popular NH." €15.50, 1 May-30 Sep. 2018

"There aren't many sites open at this time of year"

If you're travelling outside peak season remember to call ahead to check site opening dates – even if the entry says 'open all year'.

BEAUNE *6H1* (1km N Urban) *47.03304, 4.83911* **Camp Municipal Les Cent Vignes,** 10 Rue Auguste Dubois, 21200 Beaune **03 80 22 03 91; campingles centvignes@mairie-beaune.fr; www.beaune.fr**

🏕 ♦♦♦ (htd) 🔳 ♨ ᵴ ⚕ 🔳 / ᴹᴾ 📶 🍴 ⓗ 🍴 🛁 /▥

Fr N on A31 & fr S on A6 at junc with m'ways A6/A31 take A6 sp Auxerre-Paris; after 1km leave at junc 24 to join D974 twd Beaune; after approx 1.5km, turn R at 2nd traff lts fr a'route to site (sp) in 200m. If app fr S on D974 site well sp fr inner ring rd & foll sp to Dijon (not a'route sps). Also sp fr Mersault/L'Hôpital x-rds. 4*, Med, hdstg, hdg, mkd, pt shd, EHU (16A) €3.80 (some rev pol); gas; bbq; TV; phone; Eng spkn; ccard acc; bike hire; games area; tennis; CKE. "Popular, well-run site; rec arr early even LS; gd modern san facs; vg rest; most pitches gd size but narr site rds makes access some pitches diff, a mover useful; tight turns & low trees poss diff lge o'fits; twin axles; in walking dist of Beaune; v conv site; hypmkt 2km; superb new san facs 2013; excel site; adv bkg in writing only bef 30 May; pool 800m; many pitches with own service pnts." €25.00, 15 Mar-31 Oct. 2017

BEAUNE *6H1* (3.5km NE Rural) *47.02668, 4.88294* **Camping Les Bouleaux,** 11 Rue Jaune, 21200 Vignoles **03 80 22 26 88**

12 🏕 ♦♦♦ (htd) 🔳 ♨ ᵴ ⚕ / 🐾 🛁

Exit A6 at junc 24.1; 500m after toll turn R at rndabt, in 1.5km turn R sp Dole rndabt. Immed after x-ing m'way turn L sp Vignoles. L again at next junc then R & foll camping sp. Site in approx 1.5km in cent Chevignerot; fr town cent take D973 (E) sp Dole. In 2km cross a'route & 1st L (N) sp Vignoles. Well sp. 3*, Sm, hdg, mkd, pt shd, EHU (6A) inc (rev pol altered on request); adv bkg rec; CKE. "Attractive, well-kept, busy site, even in LS; rec arr early high ssn; some gd sized pitches, most sm; superb clean new san facs; poss stretched high ssn & ltd LS; poss muddy after rain - park on rdways; conv NH fr a'route; basic site; long lead may be req'd; excel site; excel walking in area; helpful owner." €19.00 2018

BEAUNE *6H1* (8km SW Rural) *46.98573, 4.76855* **La Grappe d'Or (formally Kawan Village),** 2 Route de Volnay, 21190 Meursault **03 80 21 22 48; info@camping-meursault.com; www.camping-meursault.com**

🏕 €1.40 ♦♦♦ (htd) 🔳 ♨ ᵴ ⚕ 🔳 / ᴹᴾ 📶 🍴 🍴 ⓗ ᴊ 🛁 /▥ 🎣

Fr N-S, Exit A6 Junc 24.1 SP Beaune Centre Hospices, at rndabt foll sp to Chalon sur Saône RN 74, after 7km foll sp to Meursault, turn r, foll sp for site. 3*, Med, mkd, pt shd, terr, EHU (10A) inc; gas; sw; phone; Eng spkn; adv bkg req; waterslide; bike hire; tennis; games area; CKE. "Lovely family site; busy high ssn - arr early; all pitches views over vineyards; friendly, helpful owners; basic facs stretched; ltd water pnts & poss steep climb fr lower pitches; some pitches uneven, sm or obstructed by trees - poss diff access lge o'fits; poss muddy when wet; barrier clsd 2200-0730; rambling; sh walk to lovely vill; gd cycle paths; vg; popular site; well run; if full use site at Santenay." €26.60, 5 Apr-13 Oct. 2019

BEAUNE *6H1* (7km NW Rural) *47.06861, 4.8029* **Camping de Savigny-les-Beaune,** Route de Bouilland, 21420 Savigny-lès-Beaune **03 80 26 15 06 or 06 83 23 93 37 (mob); contact@camping-savigny-les-beaune.fr; www.camping-savigny-les-beaune.fr**

🏕 €1.20 ♦♦♦ 🔳 ♨ ᵴ / ᴹᴾ 🐾 📶 ᴊ 🛁 nr /▥

Fr Beaune ring rd turn N on D974 sp Dijon; in 200m turn L sp Savigny; in 100m ignore camping sp & bear R to Savigny (3km); site 1km thro vill on L. 2*, Med, mkd, pt shd, pt sl, EHU (6A) €3.50 (some rev pol); bbq; adv bkg acc; bike hire; CKE. "Pleasant, busy NH in beautiful area; pleasant staff; modern basic san facs; no twin axles; gd touring base; conv A6, A31, A36 & Beaune; easy walk to vill; excel quiet site." €14.00, 15 Mar-15 Oct. 2016

BEAUVAIS *3C3* (16km E Rural) *49.40506, 2.25803*
Camping de la Trye, Rue de Trye, 60510 Bresles
03 44 07 80 95 or 06 10 40 30 29 (mob);
www.camping-de-la-trye.com

12 🐕 👫 wc ♨ ⚲ ♿ 🛁 ⁄ ☀ MP 🏕 🅿 🛝 🏊 ⚓

Exit N31 (Beauvais to Clermont) at Bresles; foll
site sp. Med, hdg, mkd, pt shd, sl, EHU (6A) inc; bbq;
75% statics; adv bkg acc; ccard acc; bike hire; CKE.
*"Helpful Dutch owners; cycle & walking rtes; theme
parks nrby; trampoline; largely a holiday chalet/static
site with ltd no of touring pitches; pony rides; fair NH/
sh stay."* **€20.00** **2016**

BEAUVILLE *7D3* (0.5km SE Rural) *44.27210, 0.88850*
Camping Les Deux Lacs, 47470 Beauville 05 53 95
45 41; camping-les-2-lacs@wanadoo.fr;
www.les2lacs.info

🐕 €2.15 👫 wc ♨ ⚲ ♿ 🛁 ⁄ MP 🦋 🍴 🍽 🛝 ⛱ 🌲nr 🅿

Fr D656 S to Beauville, site sp on D122. NB Steep
descent to site - owners help when leaving if
necessary. 3*, Med, hdg, mkd, shd, terr, EHU (6A)
€2.45; sw nr; red long stay; 10% statics; Eng spkn; adv
bkg acc; ccard acc; fishing; games area; watersports;
CKE. *"Peaceful; gd fishing; pleasant walk to vill;
vg; Dutch owners; facs inadequate when site full."*
€28.00, 1 Apr-31 Oct. **2017**

BEAUVOIR SUR MER *2H3* (5km E Rural) *46.92298,
-1.99036* **Camping Le Fief d'Angibaud,** 85230 St
Gervais 02 51 68 43 08; camping.fief.angibaud@
orange.fr; www.campinglefiefangibaud.com

🐕 €1.50 👫 wc ♨ ⚲ 🛁 ⁄ MP 🦋 🍴 🛝nr 🌲 sand 5km

Fr Beauvoir-sur-Mer E on D948 to St Gervais turn
L after PO/Mairie onto D59 twd Bouin (narr ent
easy to miss); in 2km pass sm chapel; take 2nd rd
on L; site on R after 500m. Sm, mkd, pt shd, EHU
(6-13A) €3.50; bbq; twin axles; red long stay; Eng spkn;
adv bkg rec; golf nr; fishing nr; CKE. *"Excel, simple
site adj farm; lge pitches; pleasant, helpful British
owners; clean san facs but need update (2010); conv
Ile de Noirmoutier; ferry to Ile d'Yeu, coastal resorts;
free parking close to beach (blue flag); gd cycling
area; vg value; gd for rallies; gite on site; bike hire."*
€19.50, 16 Apr-24 Sep. **2016**

BEDOIN *10E2* (0.5km W Rural) *44.12468, 5.17249*
Camp Municipal de la Pinède, Chemin des Sablières,
84410 Bédoin 04 90 65 61 03; campingmunicipal@
bedoin.fr; www.bedoin.fr

🐕 €1.50 👫 (htd) wc ♨ ⚲ ♿ 🛁 ⁄ MP 🛝 🌲nr 🅿 🌲 🏊 (htd)

Take D938 S fr Malaucène for 3km, L onto D19 for
9km to Bédoin. Site adj to vill & sp. 2*, Med, hdstg,
mkd, shd, sl, terr, EHU (16A) inc; bus; Eng spkn; adv
bkg acc; ccard acc; CKE. *"Pool clsd Mon; 5 min walk
to vill; mkt Mon; steep terr site; vans towed to pitch if
req; steep climb to some san facs; v clean; v friendly;
excel pool; v popular; MH site adj; easy walk to town."*
€18.50, 15 Mar-31 Oct. **2017**

BELCAIRE *8G4* (4km SW Rural) *42.79207, 1.92477*
Camping Les Sapins, Ternairols, 11340 Camurac
04 68 20 38 11; info@lessapins-camurac.com;
www.lessapins-camurac.com

🐕 €2 👫 (htd) wc ♨ ⚲ ♿ 🛁 ⁄ 🦋 🍴 🍽 🍽 ① ♨ 🌲nr 🅿 🛝 🏊 ⛱

Easiest app fr N - at Bélesta on D117 turn S onto
D16/D29/D613 to Belcaire then cont to Camurac,
site 1km SE of vill. Or take D613 fr Ax-les-Thermes
(1st 10km over Col de Chioula diff climb - gd power/
weight ratio). Site sp in vill of Camurac & visible fr rd.
App rd fairly steep for sh dist. 2*, Med, mkd, pt shd,
pt sl, EHU (10A) €3; bbq (elec, gas); TV; 33% statics;
Eng spkn; adv bkg acc; ccard acc; horseriding; games
area; site clsd 1 Nov-15 Dec; CKE. *"Lovely, peaceful site
in beautiful surroundings; welcoming, friendly, helpful
Dutch owners; excel walking; in Cathar region; vg;
highly rec; winter sports; mountain biking; ltd facs LS."*
€24.50, 1 Jan-1 Nov, 15 Dec-31 Dec. **2017**

"That's changed – Should I let the Club know?"

If you find something on site that's different
from the site entry, fill in a report and let us
know. See camc.com/europereport.

BELCAIRE *8G4* (0.3km W Rural) *42.81598, 1.95098*
Les Chalets Du Lac (formerly Municipal), 4 Chemin
Lac, 11340 Belcaire 04 68 20 39 47; chaletsdulac@
gmail.com; www.camping-pyrenees-cathare.fr

🐕 👫 wc ♨ ⚲ 🛁 ⁄ 🦋

Site on D613 bet Ax-les-Thermes & Quillan.
2*, Sm, mkd, shd, pt sl, EHU (10A) €2; sw nr; phone;
tennis nr; horseriding nr; CKE. *"Site by lake; site
yourself, warden dels; gd cent for walking; historic vill
of Montaillou nr; excel; conv for Georges de la Frau."*
€20.30, 1 Jun-15 Sep. **2019**

BELFORT *6G3* (1.8km N Urban) *47.65335, 6.86445*
FFCC Camping de l'Etang des Forges, 11 Rue du
Général Béthouart, 90000 Belfort 03 84 22 54 92;
contact@camping-belfort.com; www.camping-
belfort.com

🐕 €2 👫 (htd) wc ♨ ⚲ ♿ 🛁 ⁄ MP 🦋 🍴 🍽 🍽 ① nr 🌲 🌲nr 🅿 ⁄ 🏊

Exit A36 junc 13; go thro cent of Belfort; then foll sp
Offemont on D13, then site sp. Or fr W on N19 site
well sp. 3*, Med, hdg, mkd, pt shd, EHU (6A) €3.50;
bbq; red long stay; twin axles; TV; 5% statics; bus; Eng
spkn; adv bkg acc; ccard acc; fishing adj; watersports
adj; archery; CKE. *"Pleasant, well-kept, basic site; some
lovely pitches; friendly; modern, unisex san facs with
third cont wc, but needs updating (2014); lovely walk
around lake fr site ent; cycle paths; conv for Corbusier's
chapel at Ronchamp."* **€21.00, 7 Apr-30 Sep.** **2016**

BELLAC *7A3* (11km SW Rural) *46.05718, 0.97766*
Fonclaire Holidays, 87300 Blond **05 55 60 88 26;**
fontclair@neuf.fr; www.fonclaireholidays.com

🔟 🐕 ♂♀ wo ▲ ᴸ ᴳ ∥ 🦋 ⵏ T nr ⊕nr 🝙 ⚏ /ⵏ 🏊(htd)

**Fr Bellac take D675 S dir St Junien. Site on L in
approx 7km, 2km bef Mortemart.** Sm, hdstg, pt shd,
EHU (6A) €4 (poss long lead req); sw; Eng spkn; adv
bkg acc; Badminton; CKE. *"Lovely & peaceful, spacious
CL-type site in lovely location; welcoming, helpful British
owners; Glamping units on site; gd facs; gd hdstg in wet;
nr Oradour-sur-Glane martyr vill; conv Futuroscope; gd
cycling; gd; v quiet rural location; no night lighting; gd
NH/longer; excel.* **€18.00**   **2019**

BELLEME *4E2* (1km SW Urban) *48.37420, 0.55370*
Camp Municipal Le Val, Route de Mamers, 61130
Bellême **02 33 25 30 77 or 06 24 70 55 17;**
www.campingduperchebellemois.com

🐕 €0.50 ♂♀ wo ▲ ∥ ⚏ nr /ⵏ

**Fr Mortagne, take D938 S to Bellême; turn R ent
town on D955 Alençon rd; site sp on L half-way
down hill.** 2*, Sm, hdg, pt shd, pt sl, EHU (8A) €2.65
(poss long lead req); adv bkg rec; tennis adj; fishing.
*"Pretty, well-kept site; some pitches v sl; warden
visits twice daily; gd san facs; poss long water hoses
req; pitches poss soft when wet; steep walk to town."*
€14.50, 15 Apr-15 Oct.   **2019**

BELLENTRE *9B4* (2km E Rural) *45.57576, 6.73553*
Camping L'Eden, 73210 Landry **04 79 07 61 81;**
info@camping-eden.net; www.camping-eden.net

🐕 €1.50 ♂♀(htd) wo ▲ 🝙 ∥ 🦋 ⵏ T ⓘ 🝙 ⚏ /ⵏ 🏊(htd)

**Fr N90 Moûtiers to Bourg-St Maurice at 20km
turn R sp Landry; site on L after 500m adj Rv
Isère.** 4*, Med, mkd, hdstg, hdg, pt shd, EHU (10A)
€4-6; gas; TV; phone; Eng spkn; adv bkg acc; ccard
acc; games rm. *"Gd cent mountain sports; helpful,
friendly owner; red facs LS; ltd site lighting; ski bus;
poss unkempt end of ssn; gd cycle track to town."*
€26.00, 15 Dec-5 May & 25 May-15 Sep.   **2016**

BELLEY *9B3* (8km E Rural) *45.76860, 5.76985*
Camping Du Lac du Lit du Roi, La Tuilière, 01300
Massignieu-de-Rives **04 79 42 12 03; info@
camping-savoie.com; www.camping-savoie.com**

🐕 €4 ♂♀(htd) wo ▲ ᴸ ᴳ ∥ ᴹˢᴾ ⵏ T ⓘ 🝙 🏊 ⚏

**Fr D1504 turn E onto D992 to Massignieu-de-Rives,
site sp. Site on NE of lake nr Les Mures.**
4*, Med, hdg, mkd, pt shd, terr, EHU (10A) inc (long
lead req); gas; bbq; sw; red long stay; TV; 20% statics;
phone; Eng spkn; adv bkg req; ccard acc; boating;
tennis; bike hire; CKE. *"Superb location; many pitches
on lake with lovely views; some lge pitches, others v
sm; lack of site maintenance (2010); few water pnts
(2009); bkg fee; v friendly site, idyllic location; recep
clsd 1200-1330."* **€28.60, 16 Apr-17 Sep.**   **2016**

BELMONT SUR RANCE *8E4* (0.5km W Rural)
43.81777, 2.75108 **Camping Val Fleuri du Rance,**
Route de Lacaune, 12370 Belmont-sur-Rance **05 65
99 04 76 or 06 88 42 28 78 (mob); marjandejong@
wanadoo.fr; www.campinglevalfleuri.com**

🐕 €1.50 ♂♀ wo ▲ ᴸ 🝙 ∥ ⚏ ⓘ ⚏ nr

**On D32 on ent vill fr SW; on L side of rd on sh
unmade service rd. NB diff ent/exit to/fr S.**
3*, Sm, hdg, mkd, pt shd, EHU (6A) €3.50; gas;
10% statics; Eng spkn; adv bkg acc; rv fishing; tennis;
CKE. *"Attractive valley setting; helpful Dutch owners;
attractive sm town; pool 500m; v welcoming."*
€20.00, 1 Apr-15 Oct.   **2019**

BELVES *7D3* (12km SW Rural) *44.75813, 0.90222*
Camping Terme d'Astor (Naturist), 24540, St Avit-
Rivière **05 53 63 24 52; camping@termedastor.com;
www.termedastor.com**

🐕 ♂♀ wo ▲ ᴸ ᴳ 🝙 ∥ 🦋 ⵏ T ⓘ 🝙 ⚏ /ⵏ 🏊 🎣

**Leave D710 at Belvès onto D53; in 4km turn R onto
D26 to Bouillac; pass thro vill; then turn 2nd L. Well
sp.** 3*, Med, mkd, shd, pt sl, EHU (6A) €5.20; gas; bbq;
TV; 10% statics; phone; Eng spkn; adv bkg acc; ccard
acc; INF; naturist; games rm; jacuzzi; archery; canoeing
nr; tennis nr; excursions. *"Gd cent for Dordogne rv &
chateaux; vg; horseriding nrby; poss low ampage & rev
pol on some pitches."* **€37.00, 1 May-30 Sep.**   **2016**

BELVES *7D3* (5km SW Rural) *44.75258, 0.98330*
FLOWER Caming Les Nauves, Le Bos-Rouge,
24170 Belvès **05 53 29 12 64; campinglesnauves@
hotmail.com; www.lesnauves.com or www.flower
campings.com**

🐕 €4 ♂♀ wo ▲ ᴸ ᴳ 🝙 ∥ ᴹˢᴾ ⵏ T ⓘ 🝙 ⚏ nr /ⵏ 🏊 ⚏

**On D53 fr Belvès. Site on L just after junc to Larzac.
Avoid Belves cent - use lorry rte dir Monpazier.**
3*, Med, hdg, pt shd, pt sl, EHU (6A) inc; bbq; twin axles;
TV; 10% statics; Eng spkn; adv bkg acc; ccard acc; bike
hire; games area; games rm; horseriding; CCI. *"Excel
site; gd views fr some pitches; sl site; interesting towns
nrby; sm pool."* **€28.00, 11 Apr-26 Sep.**   **2015**

BENODET *2F2* (1.5km E Coastal) *47.86670, -4.09080*
Camping Du Letty, Rue du Canvez, 29950 Bénodet
**02 98 57 04 69; reception@campingduletty.com;
www.campingduletty.com**

🐕 €2.30 ♂♀ wo ▲ ᴸ ᴳ ∥ ᴹˢᴾ 🦋 ⵏ T ⓘ 🝙 ⚏ /ⵏ 🝙
🏊(covrd, htd) 🝙 🏖 sand adj

**Fr N ent town on D34, foll sp Fouesnant D44. Le
Letty sp R at rndabt. Fr E on N165 take D44 sp
Fouesnant & foll rd to o'skirts Bénodet. After town
sp, site is sp.** 4*, Lge, mkd, hdstg, hdg, pt shd, pt sl,
EHU (10A) €4; gas; bbq (gas); TV; phone; Eng spkn; adv
bkg acc; ccard acc; golf nr; tennis; games area; kayak
hire; sauna; games rm; gym; squash; horseriding nr;
waterslide; CKE. *"Excel, well-run, beautifully laid-out
site; clean & well-equipped; lovely beach adj; excel
playgrnd; many activities; aqua park; library; friendly,
helpful staff; highly rec."* **€33.00, 11 Jun-5 Sep.**   **2017**

For a guide to symbols see the fold out on the rear cover

FRANCE

BENODET *2F2* (0.5km SE Coastal) *47.86780, -4.09750*
Camping du Poulquer, 23 rue du Poulquer,
29950 Bénodet **02 98 57 04 19; contact@campingdu poulquer.com; www.campingdupoulquer.com**

🚐 €2 🏕 ⓦⒹ ♨ ⚲ ♿ 🖃 ⊘ 🦋 ♈ 🍽 Ⓓnr 🅿 🛒 🏍 ⚓

🏊 (covrd, htd) 🎣 🌳 sand adj

Fr N ent town on D34. At rndabt after junc with D44 strt onto Rue Penfoul. At next rndabt (tourist info office on R after rndabt) go strt dir La Plage until reach seafront; turn L at seafront then L at end of prom at camping sp; site in 100m on R. Fr E on N165 take D44 sp Fouesnant & foll rd to o'skirts Bénodet. After town sp, site is sp. 4*, Lge, mkd, hdg, pt shd, pt sl, EHU (6-10A) inc (long lead poss req, poss rev pol); bbq; TV; 5% statics; Eng spkn; adv bkg acc; jacuzzi; games rm; waterslide; golf nr; tennis; CKE. "*Lovely, well-kept, family-run site; bike hire 1km; boat trips nrby; friendly, helpful owner; aqua park; no o'fits over 7.5m high ssn; gd, clean san facs, poss tired end of ssn; quiet site LS; mkt Mon; rec; vg; gd cafe/bar & shop; indoor pool open LS.*" **€30.80, 1 May-30 Sep. B16.** 2018

BENODET *2F2* (5km W Coastal) *47.86903, -4.12848*
Camping Le Helles, 55 Rue du Petit-Bourg, 29120 Combrit-Ste Marine **02 98 56 31 46; contact@le-helles.com; www.le-helles.com**

🚐 €2.60 🏕 (htd) ⓦⒹ ♨ ⚲ ♿ 🖃 ⊘ 🦋 ♈ ⚲ 🅿 🛒 🏊 (htd)
🎣 🌳 sand 300m

Exit D44 S dir Ste Marine, site sp. 3*, Med, mkd, pt shd, pt sl, EHU (6-10A); bbq; 10% statics; Eng spkn; adv bkg acc; ccard acc; CKE. "*Vg site with lge pitches, some shd; gd, clean modern san facs; friendly, helpful owners; excel beach within 5 min walk; vg long stay; 2 pools indoor and out.*" **€14.00, 1 Apr-23 Oct.** 2016

BERGERAC *7C3* (2km S Urban) *44.84902, 0.47635*
Camping La Pelouse (formerly Municipal), 8 bis Rue Jean-Jacques Rousseau, 24100 Bergerac
05 53 57 06 67; campinglapelouse@orange.fr; www.entreprisefrery.com

🚐 €1.25 🏕 (htd) ⓦⒹ ♨ ♿ 🖃 ⊘ 🅼🄿 🦋 🛒nr 🏍

On S bank of Rv Dordogne 300m W of old bdge opp town cent. Do not ent town, foll camping sp fr bdge, ent on R after L turn opp block of flats. Well sp, on Rv Dordogne. 3*, Med, mkd, pt shd, pt sl, EHU (6A); gas; Eng spkn; adv bkg acc; rv fishing adj; CKE. "*Peaceful, spacious site on rv bank; friendly warden; san facs ltd LS; easy walk by rv into attractive old town; no twin axles & c'vans over 6m; site poss clsd earlier if weather bad; pitches poss muddy when wet; rec arr bef 1400 high ssn site has lots of trees so not all pitches in sun; facs updated 2012.*" **€20.00, 1 Apr-31 Oct.** 2017

BERGERAC *7C3* (14km W Rural) *44.83849, 0.33052*
FFCC Camping Parc Servois, 11 Rue du Bac, 24680 Gardonne **06 84 38 24 33; mfounaud24@orange.fr; www.parcservois.com**

🚐 €0.70 🏕 ⓦⒹ ♨ ⚲ ♿ 🖃 ⊘ 🅼🄿 🦋 Ⓓnr 🛒nr

Fr D936 Bergerac to Bordeaux, in vill of Gardonne turn R into sm rd 100m after traff lts; site at end of rd by rv. Well sp in vill. 1*, Sm, pt shd, EHU (10A) poss rev pol; Eng spkn; CKE. "*Pretty, CL-type site on bank of Rv Dordogne; lge pitches; helpful warden; facs immac but dated & poss stretched when site full; gates clsd 2200-0800 with pedestrian access; sm mkt Wed & Sun; excel, well run site.*" **€14.00, 30 Apr-30 Sep.** 2019

BERGUES *3A3* (0.6km N Urban) *50.97248, 2.43420*
Camping Le Vauban, Blvd Vauban, 59380 Bergues **03 28 68 65 25; cassiopee.tourisme@wanadoo.fr**

🚐 €1.05 🏕 (cont) ⓦⒹ ♨ ⚲ ♿ 🖃 ⊘ 🦋 🛒 ♈nr Ⓓnr 🛒nr 🏍

Exit A16 junc 60 twd Bergues on D916. In 2km turn L onto D2 dir Coudekerque vill. In 2km turn R at rndabt onto D72 to Bergues thro Couderkerque vill, then turn R immed after canal. Site on R as rd bends to L. 3*, Med, hdg, mkd, pt shd, terr, EHU (6A) inc (poss rev pol); 60% statics; adv bkg acc; CKE. "*Pleasant site; sm pitches poss diff lge o'fits; ltd manoeuvring in site rds; friendly & helpful; gates clsd 2130-0700 & poss clsd 1230-1730; lovely fortified town; conv Dunkerque & Calais; NH only; san facs updated (2015).*" **€16.00, 1 Apr-31 Oct.** 2015

"I like to fill in the reports as I travel from site to site"

You'll find report forms at the back of this guide, or you can fill them in online at camc.com/europereport.

BERNAY *3D2* (2km S Urban) *49.08020, 0.58703*
Camp Municipal, Rue des Canadiens, 27300 Bernay **02 32 43 30 47; camping@bernay27.fr; www.ville-bernay27.fr**

🚐 🏕 ⓦⒹ ♨ ♿ 🖃 ⊘ 🅼🄿 🦋 ♈ 🍽nr Ⓓnr 🛒nr 🏍

Site sp fr S'most (Alençon) rndabt off Bernay by-pass D438; twd France Parc Exposition then 1st L & on R. Well sp. 3*, Sm, mkd, hdg, pt shd, EHU (10A) €3.65 (poss rev pol); TV; phone; adv bkg acc; CKE. "*Well-kept site; well set-out pitches, diff sizes; helpful & friendly staff; gd clean facs, but dated; barrier clsd 2200-0700; excel, conv NH A28; excel, lovely site; pool 300m; debit card acc; Bernay worth a visit.*" **€16.00, 1 May-30 Sep.** 2016

BERNY RIVIERE *3C4* (1.5km S Rural) *49.40603, 3.12860*
Camping La Croix du Vieux Pont, Rue de la Fabrique,
02290 Berny-Rivière **03 23 55 50 02; info@la-croix-du-vieux-pont.com; www.la-croix-du-vieux-pont.com**
12 🐕 ♀♀(htd) ⟨WD⟩ ⚲ 🛁 ☕ 🖭 ⫽ ⟨MSP⟩ 🦋 🎵 ☂ ⊕ ⅆ 🛒 ⚠ 🚴
🏊(covrd, htd)

On N31 bet Soissons & Compiègne. At site sp turn
onto D13, then at Vic-sur-Aisne take next R, R again
then L onto D91. Foll sp to site on o'skts of Berny.
5*, V lge, hdg, hdstg, pt shd, serviced pitches; EHU
(6A) €2.50 (poss rev pol, no earth & ltd supply); gas;
sw; TV; Eng spkn; adv bkg rec; ccard acc; games rm;
waterslide; gym; tennis; bike hire; horseriding; boating;
archery; fishing; golf; CKE. *"Pleasant, v lge, well-run,
clean site; busy LS; lge pitches, some rvside; excel for
families or older couples; friendly, helpful staff; vg san
facs, ltd LS; some sh stay pitches up steep bank; beauty
cent; some pitches worn/uneven end of ssn (2010);
some pitches liable to flood; many tour op statics high
ssn; site open all yr but no services Nov-Mar; excel;
tourers pitch on open area."* **€37.00, P15.** 2015

BERNY RIVIERE *3C4* (6km S Rural) *49.39280, 3.15161*
Camping La Halte de Mainville, 18 Chemin du Routy,
02290 Ressons-le-Long **03 23 74 26 69; lahaltede
mainville@wanadoo.fr; www.lahaltede
mainville.com.planete-moto.com**
🐕 ♀♀(htd) ⟨WD⟩ ⚲ 🛁 ☕ ⫽ ⟨MSP⟩ 🦋 🛒 nr ⚠ 🏊(htd) 🍴

Fr Soissons W on N31 dir Compiègne, in approx 8km
look for site sp on L. Clearly sp. 3*, Lge, mkd, hdg,
pt shd, EHU (10A) €3 (poss rev pol); bbq; 60% statics;
phone; Eng spkn; adv bkg rec; games area; tennis;
fishing; CKE. *"Pleasant, clean, conv NH; friendly,
helpful staff; 1 hr fr Disneyland; vg; lovely area."*
€21.50, 8 Jan-8 Dec. 2015

BESANCON *6G2* (6km NE Rural) *47.26472, 6.07255*
Camping de Besancon - La Plage, 12 Route de Belfort,
25220 Chalezeule **03 81 88 04 26; contact@
campingdebesancon.com; www.campingde
besancon.com**
🐕 €1.35 ♀♀(htd) ⟨WD⟩ ⚲ 🛁 ☕ 🖭 ⫽ ⟨MSP⟩ ⊕ nr ⅆ 🛒 nr ⚠

Exit A36 junc 4 S; foll sp Montbéliard & Roulons
onto D683; site in 1.5km on R, 200m after rlwy
bdge; well sp fr D683. Fr Belfort 2.65m height
restriction; foll sp to Chalezeule & 300m after
supmkt turn L to rejoin D683, site in 200m on
rvside. 3*, Med, mkd, pt shd, terr, EHU (16A) (poss
rev pol); bbq; twin axles; 50% statics; bus to city;
Eng spkn; ccard acc; kayaking; CKE. *"Helpful staff;
htd pool adj; excel modern san facs; access to opp
side of dual c'way under sm tunnel, suggest going to
rndabt to make the turn; tram to city 1.5km uphill."*
€25.00, 15 Mar-31 Oct. 2018

BEZIERS *10F1* (7km SE Urban) *43.3169, 3.2842*
Camping Les Berges du Canal, Promenade des
Vernets, 34420 Villeneuve-les-Béziers **04 67 39 36 09;
contact@lesbergesducanal.com; www.lesbergesdu
canal.fr**
🐕 €3 ♀♀(htd) ⟨WD⟩ ⚲ 🛁 ☕ 🖭 ⫽ ⟨MSP⟩ 🎵 ⊕ ⅆ 🛒 ⚠ 🏊(htd)

Fr A9 exit junc 35 & foll sp for Agde. Exit 1st
rndabt for D612 dir Béziers then 1st L onto D37
sp Villneuve-les-Béziers. Foll site sp to site adj
canal. 3*, Med, hdg, mkd, shd, EHU (16a) €2.50
(poss rev pol); 45% statics; Eng spkn; adv bkg acc;
bike hire; CKE. *"Pleasant site; facs clean & modern
but poss stretched in ssn; noisy, fr rlwy yard; some
pitches tight lge o'fits; pleasant stroll along canal."*
€28.50, 12 Mar-15 Oct. 2016

BEZIERS *10F1* (12km SW Rural) *43.31864, 3.14276*
Camping Les Peupliers, 7 Promenade de l'Ancien Stade,
34440 Colombiers **04 67 37 05 26; contact@camping-
colombiers.com; www.camping-colombiers.com**
12 🐕 €3 ♀♀(htd) ⟨WD⟩ ⚲ 🛁 ☕ 🖭 ⫽ ⟨MSP⟩ 🎵 ☂ ⊕ nr ⅆ 🛒 nr ⚠ 🏊

SW fr Béziers on D609 (N9) turn R on D162E &
foll sp to site using heavy vehicle rte. Cross canal
bdge & fork R; turn R & site on L. Easier ent fr D11
(Béziers-Capestang) avoiding narr vill rds, turn L at
rndabt at end of dual c'way sp Colombiers; in 1km
at rlwy bdge, go strt on; in 100m turn L (bef canal
bdge) where rd turns sharp R. 3*, Med, mkd, pt shd,
EHU (10A) €3.50 (inc in high ssn) (poss rev pol); gas;
bbq; red long stay; 25% statics; adv bkg acc; CKE. *"Nr
Canal du Midi away fr busy beach sites; modern san
facs; no twin axles; excel walking & cycling; pleasant
sm vill, conv NH; gd rest in vill; diff for lge o'fits; touring
pitches among statics; 45km to stn for Carcassonne."*
€28.50 2019

"We must tell the Club about that great site we found"

Get your site reports in by mid-August and we'll
do our best to get your updates into the next
edition.

BIARRITZ *8F1* (4.6km S Coastal) *43.45305, -1.57277*
Yelloh! Village Ilbarritz, Ave de Biarritz, 64210 Bidart
**05 59 23 00 29; contact@camping-ilbarritz.com;
www.camping-ilbarritz.com**
🐕 €4 ♀♀(htd) ⟨WD⟩ ⚲ 🛁 ☕ 🖭 ⫽ 🎵 🍴 ⊕ ⅆ 🛒 ⚠ 🏊(htd) 🏖sand 600m

S fr Bayonne on D810, by-pass Biarritz. 1km after
A63 junc turn R at rndabt immed after Intermarché
on R; sp to Pavillon Royal. Site 1km on R sp.
4*, Lge, mkd, shd, pt sl, terr, EHU (10A) inc; gas; TV;
80% statics; phone; Eng spkn; adv bkg req; ccard acc;
games area; horseriding; bike hire; tennis; golf nr; CKE.
*"Attractive, mature site; lge pitches, need blocks as v
sl; narr access rds poss diff long o'fits; excel pool; gd
beaches nrby; gd."* **€50.00, 27 Mar-5 Oct.** 2015

FRANCE

BIARRITZ *8F1* (5km S Coastal) *43.43371, -1.59040*
Camping Ur-Onéa, Rue de la Chapelle, 64210
Bidart 05 59 26 53 61; contact@uronea.com;
www.uronea.com

🐕 €2.50 ♦♦ wo ⚲ ♨ ♿ 🗑 ✗ 💀 ♈ Ⴭ 🍴 Ⓗ ♨ 🏊 ⚠ ✗
🏊 (htd) 🛁 🏖 sand 600m

Exit A63 junc 4 dir Bidart, fr Bidart on D810 sp
St Jean de Luz, L at traff lts in town where site sp,
then 2nd R, L at motel, site is 300m on L. Access
fr main rd a bit tricky, 2nd access further S is easier
for lge o'fits. 3*, Lge, hdstg, mkd, pt shd, terr, serviced
pitches; EHU (10A) inc; gas; bbq; TV; 20% statics;
phone; Eng spkn; adv bkg acc; ccard acc; CKE. "*Well-*
kept site 600m fr Bidart; various pitch sizes, most not
terr; suitable for o'fits up to 8m; staff friendly & helpful;
excel, clean san facs; conv Pays Basque vills; new covrd/
open pool (2014)." **€46.70, 6 Apr-22 Sep.** **2019**

See advertisement above

BIARRITZ *8F1* (8.7km S Coastal) *43.43838, -1.58184*
Village Camping Sunêla Berrua, Rue Berrua, 64210
Bidart 05 59 54 96 66; contact@berrua.com;
www.berrua.com

🐕 €4.20 ♦♦ wo ♨ ♨ ♿ 🗑 ✗ msp ♈ Ⴭ Ⓗ ♨ 🏊 ⚠ 🏊 (htd)
🛁 🏖 1km

Exit A63 junc 4 dir Bidart, fr Bidart on D810 sp St Jean
de Luz, L at 1st traff lts, site sp. 4*, Lge, pt shd, pt
sl, EHU (6A) €6.20 (poss long lead req); gas; bbq; TV;
50% statics; phone; bus 1km; Eng spkn; adv bkg acc;
ccard acc; tennis; bike hire; waterslide; golf 2km; archery;
CKE. "*Busy, well-kept site in attractive location; steam rm;*
excel, clean facs; pitches tight lge o'fits; site rds narr, low
trees, some high kerbs; muddy after rain; gd rest; sh walk
to vill; gd; pleasant staff." **€46.00, 1 Apr-27 Sep.** **2015**

BIARRITZ *8F1* (2km SW Coastal) *43.4625, -1.5672*
Camping Biarritz, 28 Rue Harcet, 64200 Biarritz
05 59 23 00 12; info@biarritz-camping.fr;
www.biarritz-camping.fr

♦♦ wo ♨ ♿ 🗑 ✗ ♈ Ⓗ ♨ 🏊 ⚠ ✗ 🏊 (htd) 🛁 🏖 sand 1km

S fr Bayonne on D810, by-pass Biarritz & cont to junc
of D810 coast rd sp Bidart & Biarritz; double back on
this rd, take 1st exit at next rndabt, 1st L dir Biarritz
Cent, foll sp to site in 2km. Lge, mkd, pt shd, pt sl, terr,
EHU (10A) €4; gas; 10% statics; bus at gate; adv bkg
acc; ccard acc; tennis 4km; CKE. "*One of better sites in*
area, espec LS." **€24.00, 12 May-14 Sep.** **2016**

See advertisement below

BIARRITZ 8F1 (3.5km SW Coastal) 43.45525, -1.58119 **Camping Pavillon Royal,** Ave du Prince de Galles, 64210 Bidart 05 59 23 00 54; info@pavillon-royal.com; www.pavillon-royal.com

🏕🍴 wc ♨ ⚓ ♿ 🚿 ✉ MsP 🌳 📶 🛒 🍴 ⚡ 🚗 🏊 (htd) 🛝

🏖 sand adj

Exit A63/E4 junc 4; then take D810 S dir Bidart. At rndabt after Intermarché supmkt turn R (sp Biarritz). After 600m turn L at site sp. 4*, Lge, hdg, mkd, pt shd, pt sl, serviced pitches; EHU (10A) inc (long lead poss req); gas; bbq; TV; Eng spkn; adv bkg rec; ccard acc; tennis nr; golf 500m; games rm; horseriding 2km; bike rental; spa treatments; massages; gym. "*Lovely, well-kept, busy site in beautiful location beside beach; various pitch sizes, some with sea views, some sm & diff lge o'fits; direct access via steps to excel beach; fitness rm; san facs poss irreg cleaning LS; mkt Sat; excel; adv bkg rec as ess; no o'fits over 8m; avoid pitches on perimeter fence as damage to vehicles fr stray golf balls; vg, helpful, friendly staff; excel shwrs, wc, shop, bar & rest.*" **€64.00,** 13 May-29 Sep, A06.   2019

See advertisement above

BIARRITZ 8F1 (4km SW Coastal) 43.44431, -1.58166 **Camping Erreka,** Ave de Cumba, 64210 Bidart 05 59 54 93 64; erreka@seagreen.fr; www.seagreen-campingerreka.com

🏕🍴 wc ♨ ⚓ 🚿 ✉ MsP 🦋 🍴 🛒 📶 ⚡ 🚗 🏊 🛝 sand 800m

Site at junc of D810 Biarritz by-pass & main rd into town cent; well sp. 3*, Lge, pt shd, pt sl, terr, EHU (6A) €4; gas; TV; 75% statics; adv bkg acc; ccard acc; CKE. "*Some pitches sl & poss v diff to get into, rec adv bkg to ensure suitable pitch; access rds v steep.*" **€22.00,** 16 Jun-16 Sep.   2016

BINIC 2E3 (1km S Coastal) 48.59216, -2.8238 **Camping Le Panoramic,** Rue Gasselin, 22520 Binic 02 96 73 60 43; lepanoramic22@gmail.com; www.lepanoramic.net

🐕 €2.50 🏕🍴 (htd) wc ♨ ⚓ 🚿 ✉ 🦋 🍴 🛒 📶 ⚡ 🚗 🏊 (htd) 🛝

🏖 sand 500m

D786 St Brieuc-Paimpol. 1st slip rd for Binic & 1st R up hill 100m, site sp. 3*, Med, mkd, pt shd, pt sl, terr, EHU (10A) €5 (poss rev pol); gas; bbq; 75% statics; golf adj. "*Pleasant site; coastal path nr; clean, excel facs, easy walk to beach & town.*" **€30.00,** 2 Apr-30 Sep.   2016

See advertisement below

LA RIVE

RESORT & SPA
★★★★★

At the heart of the forest of Landes
and with direct access to the
Biscarrosse lake, the Domaine de
La Rive will have the pleasure of
welcoming you in its new modern
and bright reception.

You will also discover an aquatic park of
more than 6500 m² including 3370 m²
covered and heated with a wave pool,
a hot tub, a Jacuzzi and outside a new swim lane
of 30m long in addition to the 200 m of slides
and the wild river, our great success.

In 2020, new sanitaires worthy of the largest
Resorts, are being build, to reflect even more the
spirit of a 5 stars! Always in an eco-responsible spirit,
these new facilities reflect our desire to integrate our
facilities into the environment around us: new functional
spaces in an innovative setting!

40600 BISCARROSSE (France) | +33 (0)5 58 78 12 33 | info@larive.fr   www.larive.fr

BINIC *2E3* (4km S Coastal) *48.57875, -2.78498*
Camping Le Roc de l'Hervieu, 19 Rue d'Estienne d'Orves, 22590 Pordic **02 96 79 30 12; le.roc.de.lhervieu@ wanadoo.fr; www.campinglerocdelhervieu.fr**

🏕️ wo ♨ ♿ 🚿 / ⇌ 🦋 ⊥ 🎿 ⚠ �🟤 sand 600m

Site on E side of vill off N786, Binic-St Brieuc rd. Turn E in cent of vill, sp to Les Madières then sp Le Roc de l'Hervieu. 3*, Med, hdg, pt shd, EHU (10A) €3.60; bbq; 10% statics; fishing. *"Gd walking; pleasant, gd site."* **€21.00, 1 May-30 Sep.** 2017

BISCARROSSE *7D1* (4.5km N Rural) *44.42715, -1.16078*
Camping Bimbo, 176 Chemin de Bimbo, 40600 Biscarrosse **05 58 09 82 33; info@campingbimbo.fr; www.campingbimbo.fr**

🏕️ wo ♨ ⛳ / ⛺ 🟡 ⊥ ⊕ ⊥ (htd) 🛶

Fr Biscarrosse take D652 N. At rndabt take 2nd exit (D305) sp Biscarrosse Lac. After 1.5km turn R twds Chemin de Bimbo, site on R in 500m. 4*, Med, shd, EHU (3-10A) inc (poss rev pol); 80% statics; adv bkg acc; games area; watersports 1km. *"Excel full facs site; beach 10km excel for surfing; bakery, pizzeria & creperie on site."* **€54.00, 1 Apr-30 Sep.** 2019

BISCARROSSE *7D1* (5km N Rural) *44.43535, -1.15496*
Camping Village Mayotte Vacances, 368 Chemin des Roseaux, 40600 Biscarrosse **05 58 78 00 00; camping@mayottevacances.com; www.mayotte vacances.com**

🐕 €5 🏕️ wo ♨ ♿ 🚿 / ⇌ 🦋 ⊥ ⊕ ⚠ 🟤 ⊥ 🎿

Twd NE fr Biscarrosse on D652 L sp Navarrosse & at 1st fork R to Mayotte, foll camping sp. 4*, V lge, mkd, pt shd, EHU (10A) inc (poss rev pol); gas; bbq; sw nr; TV; 95% statics; Eng spkn; adv bkg rec; ccard acc; tennis; waterslide; games rm; sailing school; bike hire; jacuzzi; CKE. *"Excel leisure facs; vg for families; suitable o'fits up to 8m; rec."* **€43.00, 3 Apr-3 Oct.** 2016

BISCARROSSE *7D1* (8km NE Rural) *44.46230, -1.12900* **Camping de la Rive,** Route de Bordeaux, 40600 Biscarrosse **05 58 78 12 33; info@larive.fr; www.campinglarive.co.uk**

🐕 €13 🏕️ (htd) wo ♨ ⛳ ♿ / ⛺ 🟡 ⊕ ⊥ ⚠ / 🎿 (covrd, htd) 🛶

Fr Bordeaux on A63 dir Bayonne/San Sebastian; at junc 22 turn off onto A660; cont until 1st junc where turn L onto D216; cont for 17km to Sanguinet; cont on A652 for 3km; site sp on R nr Lake Cazaux. 4*, V lge, mkd, hdg, EHU (6A) inc; gas; bbq (gas); sw nr; TV; 30% statics; phone; Eng spkn; adv bkg acc; ccard acc; games rm; jacuzzi; tennis; waterslide; bike hire; watersports; games area; CKE. *"On banks of Lake Cazaux-Sanguinet in delightful area; bustling site high ssn; many acitivies for all ages; no c'van/m'van over 9m; some pitches diff lge o'fits due trees; gd beaches; gd cycling; lovely rest, pleasant staff."* **€76.00, 12 Apr-30 Aug.** 2019

See advertisement on previous page

BISCARROSSE *7D1* (8km NW Coastal) *44.45804, -1.23968* **Campéole Camping Le Vivier,** 681 Rue du Tit, 40600 Biscarrosse-Plage **05 58 78 25 76; contact@andretriganogroupe.com; www.campeole.co.uk**

🐕 €2.50 🏕️ wo ♨ ⛳ / ⛺ 🦋 ⊕ ⊥ ⊕ ⛵ ⊥ ⚠ / 🎿 (htd) 🖐 🟤 sand 800m

Fr Arcachon & Pyla-sur-Mer, take D218, D83 to Biscarrosse Plage. Town o'skts site sp to R. Foll sps. 3*, Lge, pt shd, EHU (10A) inc (poss rev pol); 25% statics; ccard acc; fishing; bike hire; games rm; boating; tennis; horseriding nr. *"Sandy site in pine forest; access to beach via path thro dunes."* **€41.40, 28 Apr-17 Sep.** 2017

BIZE MINERVOIS *8F4* (0.2km SW Urban) *43.31584, 2.87070* **Camping De La Cesse,** Esplanade Champs de Foire, 11120 Bize-Minervois **04 68 46 14 40; marieange.lurqui@gmail.com; www.audetourisme.com**

🐕 €1.20 🏕️ wo ♨ ⛳ / ⛺ ⊕ nr ⊥ nr

Exit N fr D5/D11 Béziers-Carcassonne rd onto D26 to Bize-Minervois (D26 is 800m to E of D607); site in 1.8km on L, just bef rv bdge in S of vill. 1*, Sm, mkd, pt shd, EHU (5A) €2.30; bbq; phone; adv bkg acc; CKE. *"Peaceful, relaxing site; in need of TLC (2015)."* **€12.00, 1 May-30 Sep.** 2015

"Satellite navigation makes touring much easier"

Remember most sat navs don't know if you're towing or in a larger vehicle – always use yours alongside maps and site directions.

BLANGY LE CHATEAU *3D1* (0.5km N Rural) *49.24670, 0.27370* **Camping Le Domaine du Lac,** 14130 Blangy-le-Château **02 31 64 62 00; info@ domaine-du-lac.fr; www.domaine-du-lac.fr**

🐕 🏕️ wo ♨ ⛳ / ⛺ ⊕ ⊥ ⊕ 🛶 ⊥

Fr Pont-l'Evêque & A13 S on D579 twd Lisieux. In 5km turn L onto D51 to Blangy where at fountain (rndabt) turn L, taking care. In 200m at end of vill turn L onto D140 Rte de Mesnil & site 200m on R. Site is 5km SE of Pont-l'Evêque. 3*, Med, mkd, pt shd, pt sl, EHU (6A) inc (long lead poss req); gas; bbq; 70% statics; adv bkg acc; ccard acc; games rm; tennis; lake fishing; CKE. *"Peaceful NH in lovely area; friendly British owner; poss uneven pitches; tired, access to pitches diff when wet; pretty vill; gd walks; conv Honfleur; 1hr to Le Havre ferry; NH only; mainly statics; facs poorly maintained."* **€24.00, 1 Apr-31 Oct.** 2019

Make sure you check any essential information with the site before you travel

BLANGY LE CHATEAU *3D1* (3km SE Rural) *49.22525, 0.30438* **Camping Le Brévedent,** 14130 Le Brévedent **02 31 64 72 88 or 02 31 64 21 50 (LS); contact@ campinglebrevedent.com; www.campingle brevedent.com**

🏕 (htd) 🅆 🏊 ♿ 🚻 ⊘ 🅿 💆 ☕ 🍴 Ⓟ Ⓣ 🚲 🎣 🛶 (htd) ⛵

Fr Pont l'Evêque & A13 go S on D579 twd Lisieux; after 5km turn L onto D51 twd Blangy-le-Château. In Blangy bear R at rndabt to stay on D51 & foll sp to Le Brévedent & Moyaux; site on L in just after le Breveden vill. 4*, Med, mkd, pt shd, pt sl, EHU (10A) (poss long leads req, poss rev pol); bbq; TV; 10% statics; phone; Eng spkn; adv bkg acc; ccard acc; horseriding 2km; games area; bike hire; tennis; games rm; golf 11km; lake fishing; kids' club; playground; CKE. *"Pleasant, busy site with all amenities, around lake in grnds of chateau; welcoming, helpful staff; no o'fits over 8m; some modern san facs, ltd LS; gd pool; rallies welcome; excel."* **€44.00, 13 Apr-15 Sep, N01.** 2019

> ## "There aren't many sites open at this time of year"
>
> If you're travelling outside peak season remember to call ahead to check site opening dates – even if the entry says 'open all year'.

BLANGY SUR BRESLE *3C2* (2km SE Rural) *49.92378, 1.65693* **Camping Aux Cygnes d'Opale (formerly Municipal),** Zone de Loisirs, 76340 Blangy-sur-Bresle **02 35 94 55 65 or 09 72 32 88 40; contact@ auxcygnesdopale.fr; www.auxcygnesdopale.fr**

🏕 €2 🏕 🅆 🏊 ♿ 🚻 ⊘ 🅿 💆 Ⓟ Ⓣ nr Ⓗnr 🛒nr 🎪

Leave A28 at junc 5, R at T-junc onto D49, site on L in 800m. 3*, Med, mkd, unshd, EHU (5-16A) €3 (poss rev pol); bbq; 20% statics; phone; adv bkg rec; tennis nr; CKE. *"Attractive, well-kept site adj lakes; conv Calais, A28 & D928; gd san facs; adv bkg rec lge o'fits high ssn; no twin axles; pleasant & helpful warden; rec wait for warden for pitching; mini golf nr; poss waterlogged in wet (& ent refused); avoid during Int'l Petanque Competition 3rd w/end June on adj leisure cent; excel NH; new owners (2013), many improvements; new pool."* **€21.00, 1 Apr-31 Oct.** 2016

BLANGY SUR BRESLE *3C2* (8km W Rural) *49.95430, 1.55098* **Camp Municipal La Forêt,** 76340 Bazinval **02 32 97 04 01; bazinval2@wanadoo.fr**

🏕 🅆 🏊 🅿 🦋 🛒nr 🎪

NW fr Blangy on D49 for 6km, then D149 to Bazinval. Site sp. 1*, Sm, hdg, pt shd, pt sl, EHU (10A) €4 (poss rev pol); twin axles; Eng spkn; games area; games rm; CKE. *"Gd san facs, poss inadequate; site yourself, warden calls early eve; poss travellers on site; NH only; lovely, peaceful site; conv Dieppe; vg."* **€10.40, 1 Apr-30 Oct.** 2018

BLENEAU *4G3* (12km NE Rural) *47.75833, 3.09960* **Camping Le Bois Guillaume,** 89350 Villeneuve-les-Genêts **03 86 45 45 41; camping@bois-guillaume.com; www.bois-guillaume.com**

12 🏕 €1.40 🏕 (htd) 🅆 🏊 💆 🅿 Ⓟ Ⓣ Ⓗ 🎪 🛶 (htd)

Fr W on D965 dir St Fargeau. At Mézilles take D7 thro Tannerre-en-Puisaye; stay on D7 & after 3.5km foll sp for site. Or fr A6 exit junc 18 onto D16 thro Charny, then turn L onto D119 to Champignelles; take D7 dir Tannere for approx 2km; turn R & foll sp to site. 4*, Med, hdstg, mkd, hdg, shd, EHU (5-10A) €3.10-4.60; gas; Eng spkn; tennis; bike hire; games area; CKE. *"Friendly staff; clean, tidy site; facs ltd LS; vg rest."* **€14.00** 2016

BLERE *4G2* (0.6km E Urban) *47.32791, 0.99685* **Camping La Gâtine (Formaly Municipal),** Rue de Cdt Le Maître, 37150 Bléré **02 47 57 92 60; info@campingblereplage.com**

🏕 €1.20 🏕 🅆 🏊 ♿ 🚻 🅿 💆 🦋 Ⓟ Ⓣ nr ♨ 🛒nr 🎪

Exit A10 S of Tours onto A85 E. Exit A85 junc 11 dir Bléré. Site in 5km adj sports cent on S side of Rv Cher. 3*, Lge, mkd, pt shd, EHU (10A) €4 (poss rev pol & long lead poss req); bbq; twin axles; adv bkg acc; ccard acc; rv fishing adj; CKE. *"Excel, well-kept, peaceful, pleasant site; clean san facs, some dated & stretched when site full, some modernised; some dated EHU poss unrel in wet; gd cent for wine rtes & chateaux; htd pool adj high ssn; unrel opening dates LS; new management; looking a bit neglected (2017); excel cycle routes adj."* **€18.00, 1 Apr-10 Oct.** 2017

BLOIS *4G2* (5km NE Rural) *47.605289, 1.374560* **Camping Le Val de Blois,** RD951 Lac de Loire 41350, Blois/Vineuil **02 54 79 93 57; contact@camping-loisir-blois.com; www.camping-loisir-blois.com**

🏕 €1.20 🏕 (htd) 🅆 🏊 💆 🦋 Ⓟ 💆 🎪

Fr N exit 17 from A10 onto D200 thro Blois. Over bdge, turn off to D951. Site sp 3km to E. Fr S on d174, turn off D951 before bdge. Site sp 3km to E. 3*, Med, hdg, pt shd, pt sl, EHU 6A; gas; bbq (charcoal, elec, gas); sw nr; 10% statics; Eng spkn; ccard acc; bike hire; CKE. *"Situated on Loire rv; vast cycling area; facs stretched in high ssn; vg."* **€23.60, 30 Mar-12 Oct.** 2019

BLOIS *4G2* (18km W Rural) *47.54427, 1.15712* **Ferme de Prunay,** 41150 SEILLAC **09 53 86 02 01 or 06 98 99 09 86; contact@prunay.com; www.prunay.fr**

🏕 🏕 🅆 🏊 🏊 🅿 💆 Ⓟ Ⓣ 🚲 🛒 🎪 🎣 🛶 ⛵

Take exit Blois on the A10; foll dir for Angers Chateau Renault until Molineuf, then Chambon sur Cisse and Seillac, rd D131. 4*, Med, mkd, pt shd, EHU (12A); bbq; TV; Eng spkn; ccard acc; bike hire; games area; fishing. *"In the heart of the Loire Valley; spacious pitches; v nice site; san facs tired."* **€37.00, 31 Mar-3 Nov.** 2018

BOEN SUR LIGNON *9B1* (1km S Urban) *45.73688, 4.00777* **Camping Municipal Domaine De Giraud,** Rue de Camping, 42130 Boen Sur Lignon **04 77 97 39 96; contact@camping-orangerie.com; www.camping-orangerie.com**

🐕 ♻ ♿ ⅰ ♨ ⛟ ⚠ ⚿

Fr Clermont Ferrand head E on D2089. Cont onto D1089. Site well sp immed on exiting Boen sur Lignon. Med, mkd, pt shd, pt sl, EHU (10A); bbq; twin axles; TV; 4% statics; Eng spkn; games area; games rm; CCI. *"Peaceful, well run site, 10 mins stroll fr town cent with rest, bars, shops, supmkt & lndry; sports facs nrby; vg."* **€18.60, 20 Mar-20 Oct.** **2019**

BOIS DE CENE *2H4* (0.9km S Rural) *46.93395, -1.88728* **Camping Le Bois Joli,** 2 Rue de Châteauneuf, 85710 Bois-de-Céné **02 51 68 20 05; contact@camping-leboisjoli.com; www.camping-leboisjoli.com**

🐕 €3.50 ♻ ♿ ⅰ ♨ ⛟ ⚿ ⚹ ⚊ nr ⚠ ⚿ ⚊ (covrd, htd) ⚓

Fr D21 turn R at church in cent of vill, site on R in 500m on rd D28. 3*, Med, hdg, pt shd, EHU (10A); gas; bbq; 10% statics; phone; bus in vill; Eng spkn; adv bkg acc; fishing; bike hire; games area; tennis; CKE. *"Friendly, helpful owner; clean san facs; gd walks; lovely pool; great site; ltd facs LS; rec; excel."* **€28.50, 1 Apr-10 Oct, A35.** **2019**

BOLLENE *9D2* (5.5km E Rural) *44.29811, 4.78645* **FFCC Camping et Centre Equestre La Simioune,** Quartier Guffiage, 84500 Bollène **04 90 30 44 62; la-simioune@wanadoo.fr; www.la-simioune.fr**

🐕 €2 ♻ ♿ ⅰ ♨ ⛟ ⚿ ⚹ ⚊ nr ⚠ ⚿ ⚊ ⚓

Exit A7 junc 19 onto D994/D8 dir Carpentras (Ave Salvatore Allende D8). At 3rd x-rd turn L into Ave Alphonse Daudet dir Lambique & foll rd 3km to sp for camping on L, then site 1km. 3*, Sm, shd, pt sl, EHU (6A) €3; bbq; 10% statics; adv bkg rec; horseriding; CKE. *"In pine forest; facs ltd in winter; pony club for children & adults; NH only; lovely site."* **€24.00, 1 Mar-31 Oct.** **2017**

BOLLENE *9D2* (7km E Rural) *44.29124, 4.83837* **FFCC Camping Le Pont du Lez,** Ave es Côtes du Rhône, 26790 Suze-la-Rousse **04 75 98 82 83; camping-lepontdulez@wanadoo.fr**

🐕 €1.40 ♻ ♨ ⛟ ⚿ ⚹ ⚊ nr ⚠

E fr Bollène on D94 to Suze-la-Rousse; L in vill sq; R immed bef rv bdge. 2*, Sm, pt shd, EHU (6-10A) €3.40 (long lead poss req); TV; fishing; games area; CKE. *"Lovely but decrepit (2009); basic, clean facs - hot water to shwrs only; lovely area."* **€13.00, 1 Apr-30 Sep.** **2017**

BONIFACIO *10H2* (15km N Coastal) *41.47326, 9.26318* **Camping Rondinara,** Suartone, 20169 Bonifacio **04 95 70 43 15; reception@rondinara.fr; www.rondinara.fr**

🐕 €2.60 ♻ ♿ ⅰ ♨ ⛟ ⚿ ⚹ ⚊ ⚹ ⚿ ⚊ ⚠ ⚊ ⚓ sand 400m

Fr Bonifacio take N198 dir Porte-Vecchio for 10km, then turn R onto D158 dir Suartone (lge camp sp at turning). Site in 5km. NB D158 single track, many bends & hills. 4*, Med, pt shd, pt sl, EHU (6A) €3.60; bbq; 10% statics; Eng spkn; ccard acc; games area; watersports; games rm; CKE. *"Excel rest; idyllic location by bay; excel new san facs 2013; rd to campsite steep and narr in places; adv bkg for mkd pitches fr May."* **€35.70, 15 May-30 Sep.** **2019**

BONNAC LA COTE *7B3* (1.4km S Rural) *45.93238, 1.28977* **Camping Le Château de Leychoisier,** 1 Route de Leychoisier, 87270 Bonnac-la-Côte **05 55 39 93 43; contact@leychoisier.com; chateau-de-leychoisier.pagesperso-orange.fr**

🐕 €3 ♻ ♿ ⅰ ♨ ⛟ ⚿ ⚹ ⚊ ⚹ ⚿ ⚊ ⚠ ⚊

Fr S on A20 exit junc 27 & L at T-junc onto D220. At rndabt take 3rd exit then 1st L onto D97. At mini-rndabt in Bonnac take 2nd exit, site on L in 1km. Fr N exit A20 junc 27, turn R at T-junc onto D97, then as above. 5*, Med, mkd, hdg, pt shd, sl, EHU (10A) inc; bbq (charcoal, gas); twin axles; TV; phone; Eng spkn; adv bkg acc; ccard acc; games rm; fishing; tennis; CKE. *"Peaceful site in grnds of chateau; lge pitches; welcoming, friendly & helpful staff; no o'fits over 20m; clean san facs but dated, unisex; excel rest; extra for m'vans; blocks req some pitches; rallies welcome; conv NH nr m'way; excel; ccard not acc for 1 night stay; access for lge o'fits diff; gd rest/pool area; less commercial then other Les Castels sites."* **€34.00, 15 Apr-20 Sep, L11.** **2017**

BONNAL *6G2* (3.5km N Rural) *47.50777, 6.35583* **Camping Le Val de Bonnal,** 1 Chemin du Moulin, 25680 Bonnal **03 81 86 90 87; www.camping-valdebonnal.com et www.les-castels.com**

🐕 €2 ♻ ♿ ⅰ ♨ ⛟ ⚿ ⚹ ⚊ ⚹ ⚿ ⚊ ⚠ ⚊ ⚓

Fr N on D9 fr Vesoul or Villersexel to Esprels, turn S onto D49 sp 'Val de Bonnal'. Fr S exit A36 junc 5 & turn N onto D50 sp Rougemont, site sp to N of Rougemont. 4*, Lge, mkd, pt shd, EHU (5-10A) inc (poss rev pol); gas; bbq; sw nr; twin axles; TV; 40% statics; Eng spkn; adv bkg acc; ccard acc; fishing; golf 6km; games rm; gym; bike hire; waterslide; canoe hire; watersports; CKE. *"Attractive, busy site; lge accessible pitches; excel welcome; modern, clean san facs; gd child activities; ltd facs LS; tour ops."* **€48.40, 7 May-6 Sep, J01.** **2016**

BONNEVAL *4F2* (1km SE Rural) *48.17080, 1.38640*
Camping Le Bois Chièvre, Route de Vouvray,
St Maurice, 28800 Bonneval **02 37 47 54 01**

🐕 €1.20 ♦♦(htd) ⊞ ᕒ ᕒ ⊠ ⁄ ᗦ ❈ Ⴤ ⓘ ♨ ᕒ nr ⽊

**Rec app fr N (Chartres), or SE (D27 fr Patay/Orléans)
as app fr S thro town is narr & diff. Fr Chartres take
N10 into Bonneval & foll camp sp (mainly to L).**
3*, Med, hdg, hdstg, mkd, shd, pt sl, EHU (6A) inc (rev
pol); bbq; 10% statics; Eng spkn; adv bkg acc; CKE.
*"Well-run, well-kept site in woodland; gd, lge pitches;
htd pool adj inc; friendly, helpful staff; vg facs but
poss stretched in ssn; vg NH for Le Havre or Dieppe."*
€17.00, 1 Apr-20 Oct. **2018**

BONNIERES SUR SEINE *3D2* (7km E Rural) *49.04646,
1.66256* **Camping Loisirs des Groux,** 1 Chemin de L'ile,
78270 Mousseaux-sur-Seine **01 34 79 33 86;**
www.campingdesgroux.com

🐕 ♦♦ ᕒ ᕒ ⊠ ⁄ ᗦ ❈ ⁽ᵖ⁾

**Fr W exit A13 junc 15 onto D113 dir Bonnières. Cont
thro Bonnières, turn L onto D37 Mousseaux/Base
de Loisirs. Cont strt on D37/D124/D125 & then turn
R & foll site sp. Fr E exit A13 junc 14 sp Bonnières
& foll sp Zone Industrielle. At rndabt take D113
Bonnières, then as above.** 3*, Med, mkd, hdg, pt shd,
EHU (6A) €3.18; bbq; sw nr; 90% statics; Eng spkn;
adv bkg rec; ccard acc; games area; CKE. *"Conv Paris
(65km), Versailles, Rouen, Giverny; lge pitches; friendly,
helpful staff; basic, dated san facs; leisure cent inc pool
2km; poss clsd earlier than published dates - phone
ahead to check in LS; long winding track fr main rd;
poor quality."* **€20.00, 15 Mar-30 Nov.** **2016**

BONNIEUX *10E2* (1.6km W Rural) *43.81893, 5.31170*
Camp Municipal du Vallon, Route de Ménerbes, 84480
Bonnieux **04 90 75 86 14 or 06 48 08 46 79 (mob);**
contact@campinglevallon.com; www.camping
levallon.com

🐕 €2 ♦♦ ᕒ ᕒ ⊠ ⁄ ᗦ ⁽ᵖ⁾ Ⴤ ♨ ᕒ ⽊

**Fr Bonnieux take D3 twd Ménerbes, site sp on L
on leaving vill.** 1*, Med, mkd, pt shd, terr, EHU (6-
10A) €3.80; Eng spkn; CKE. *"Beautiful, quaint, 'olde
worlde' site in wooded area; friendly warden; basic facs
but clean; gd walking & mountain biking; attractive
hilltop vill; gd touring base; gd rest in walking dist."*
€19.50, 15 Mar-15 Oct. **2015**

BONZEE *5D1* (1.6km E Rural) *49.09539, 5.61173*
Base de Loisirs du Colvert Les Eglantines, 55160
Bonzée **03 29 87 31 98;** campingscolvert@free.fr;
http://base-de-loisirs-du-colvert.fr

🐕 €1.26 ♦♦ ⊞ ᕒ ᕒ ⊠ ⁄ ᗦ Ⴤ ⓘ ♨ ᕒ ⽊

**Fr Verdun take D903 twd Metz for 18km; in
Manheulles, turn R to Bonzée in 1km; at Bonzée
turn L for Fresnes; site on R, adj Camping
Marguerites. Or fr A4 exit junc 32 to Fresnes; then
foll sp Bonzée.** 3*, Med, hdg, mkd, pt shd, EHU (4-6A)
€3.71-5.30; gas; bbq; sw nr; twin axles; 80% statics;
phone; Eng spkn; adv bkg acc; ccard acc; boating
adj; waterslide; fishing; tennis 1.5km; CKE. *"Spacious
pitches in well-planned sites (2 sites together); facs ltd
LS; v friendly staff."* **€15.50, 1 Apr-27 Sep.** **2016**

BORDEAUX *7C2* (7km N Rural) *44.89701, -0.58317*
Camping Le Village du Lac Bordeaux, Blvd Jacques
Chaban Delmas, 33520 Bordeaux-Bruges **05 57 87 70
60;** contact@village-du-lac.com; www.camping-
bordeaux.com

12 🐕 €5 ♦♦(htd) ᕒ ᕒ ᕒ ⊠ ⁄ ᗦ ❈ ⁽ᵖ⁾ Ⴤ ⓘ ♨ ᕒ ⽊ ⊠ ᕒ

**On ring rd A630 take exit 5 twd lake; site sp on N
side of lake, 500m N of Parc des Expositions.**
4*, Lge, hdstg, mkd, pt shd, EHU (10A) inc; bbq; sw;
TV; 50% statics; bus/tram to city; Eng spkn; adv bkg
acc; ccard acc; fishing adj; games rm; bike hire; CKE.
*"Busy, poorly laid out, modern site; friendly staff;
san facs poss streched high ssn; plenty elec & water
pnts; excel rest; conv Bordeaux; easy access fr ring rd;
pitches poss soft and muddy after rain; bus/tram conn
to city; vg rest; gd unisex facs."* **€34.00** **2017**

BORDEAUX *7C2* (4km S Urban) *44.75529, -0.62772*
Camping Beausoleil, 371 Cours du Général de Gaulle,
33170 Gradignan **05 56 89 17 66;** camping
beausoleil@wanadoo.fr; www.camping-
beausoleil-gradignan.fr

12 🐕 €1 ♦♦(htd) ⊞ ᕒ ᕒ ᕒ ⊠ ⁄ ❈ ⁽ᵖ⁾ Ⴤ nr ⓘ nr ᕒ nr

**Fr N take exit 16 fr Bordeaux ring rd onto D1010 sp
Gradignan. Fr S exit A63 junc 24 onto D211 to Jauge
then D1010 to Gradignan. Site S of Gradignan on
R after Beau Soleil complex, sp.** 2*, Sm, mkd, hdstg,
hdg, pt shd, pt sl, EHU (6-10A) €1.50 -3 (poss rev pol);
bbq (elec, gas); sw nr; 70% statics; bus/tram 250m;
Eng spkn; adv bkg rec; CKE. *"Pleasant, family-run site;
helpful owners; vg, modern, clean san facs; ltd touring
pitches; sm pitches not suitable lge o'fits; adv bkg
rec; excel; gd sm site; booking necessary; htd pool &
waterslides 5km; highly rec; excel & cheap park & ride
tram sys 6km away; lovely quiet gdn site; easy bus rte
to city."* **€20.00** **2017**

BOULOGNE SUR MER 3A2 (17km E Rural) 50.73337, 1.82440 **Camping à la Ferme Le Bois Groult (Leclercq)**, 120 impasse du Bois Groult, 62142 Henneveux Le Plouy 03 21 33 32 16; leclercq.gilbert0643@orange.fr; www.leboisgroult.fr

12 🛒 €1 ♨ 🛁 ♿ 🍽 🐶 ♟ ☕ nr

Take N42 fr Boulogne twd St Omer, take exit S dir Desvres (D127). Immed at rndabt foll sp Colembert. On ent Le Plouy turn R at the calvary & foll sp to site in 1km. Sm, hdstg, pt shd, pt sl, EHU (6-10A) €5; adv bkg acc. "*Charming, well-kept, peaceful CL-type site; pleasant & helpful owner; no barrier; WWI places of interest; easy access fr N42; ideal NH to/fr ferry/tunnel; excel; v clean & tidy site; vg; shwrs €2.*" **€15.00** 2018

> ## "I like to fill in the reports as I travel from site to site"
>
> You'll find report forms at the back of this guide, or you can fill them in online at camc.com/europereport.

BOULOGNE SUR MER 3A2 (8km SSW Coastal) 50.67128, 1.57079 **FFCC Camp Municipal La Falaise**, Rue Charles Cazin, 62224 Equihen-Plage 03 21 31 22 61; camping.equihen.plage@orange.fr; www.camping-equihen-plage.fr

🛒 €2.40 ♨ 🅆 ♨ 🖳 ♿ 🍽 🛆 🏖 sand 200m

Exit A16 junc 28 onto D901 dir Boulogne, then D940 S. Turn R to Condette then foll sp Equihen-Plage, site sp in vill. Access fr D901 via narr rds. 3*, Med, hdg, pt shd, sl, terr, EHU (10-16A) €4.90-5.40 (poss rev pol); 85% statics; phone; adv bkg acc; ccard acc; games rm; watersports; CKE. "*Pleasant, well-run site in excel location, but poss windy; excel clean facs; sl pitches poss diff long o'fits; steep rd to beach.*" **€24.00, 28 Mar-12 Nov.** 2015

BOULOU, LE 8G4 (3.5km N Rural) 42.54157, 2.83431 **Camping Le Mas Llinas**, 66165 Le Boulou 04 68 83 25 46; info@camping-mas-llinas.com; www.camping-mas-llinas.com

🛒 €2.20 ♨ (htd) 🅆 ♨ ♿ 🖳 ♦ 🛆 🏖 🔥

Fr Perpignan, take D900 S; 1km N of Le Boulou turn R at Intermarché supmkt 100m to mini rndabt, turn L & foll sp to Mas-Llinas to site in 2km. Or fr A9 exit 43 & foll sp Perpignan thro Le Boulou. L at rndabt adj Leclerc supmkt, site well sp. 3*, Med, pt shd, terr, EHU (5-10A) €4.10-5.20; gas; bbq; TV; 10% statics; phone; Eng spkn; adv bkg acc; bike hire; games area; games rm; CKE. "*Friendly, welcoming owners; peaceful, scenic site, mountain views; v peaceful; beware poss high winds on high pitches; ltd water points at top levels; ltd facs LS; facs clean; gd sized pitches; golden orioles on site.*" **€27.00, 1 Feb-30 Nov.** 2017

BOULOU, LE 8G4 (4km SW Rural) 42.50664, 2.79502 **Camping de la Vallée**, Route de Maureillas, 66490 St Jean-Pla-de-Corts 04 68 83 23 20; campingde lavallee@yahoo.fr; www.campingdelavallee.com

🛒 €2.50 ♨ (htd) 🅆 ♨ ♨ ♿ 🖳 ♦ 🍽 🐶 🍽 🍴 ⓗ ♦ ☕ nr

🛆 ♦ 🏖

Exit A9 at Le Boulou. Turn W on D115. Turn L after 3km at rndabt, into St Jean-Pla-de-Corts, thro vill, over bdge, site on L. 3*, Med, mkd, pt shd, EHU (5A) €4; sw nr; red long stay; TV; 50% statics; phone; bus adj; Eng spkn; adv bkg acc; ccard acc; fishing 1km; archery; CKE. "*Lovely well-kept site; easy access lge, well mkd pitches; friendly, helpful owners with gd local info; excel san facs; conv NH fr A9 or longer; highly rec.*" **€24.60, 1 Apr-31 Oct.** 2018

BOULOU, LE 8G4 (4km W Rural) 42.50908, 2.78429 **FFCC Camping Les Casteillets**, 66490 St Jean Pla-de-Corts 04 68 83 26 83; jc@campinglescasteillets.com; www.campinglescasteillets.com

12 ♨♨ 🅆 ♨ ♿ 🖳 ♦ 🍽 🐶 🍴 ⓗ ♦ ☕ 🛆 ♦ 🏖

Exit A9 at Le Boulou; turn W on D115; after 3km turn L immed after St Jean-Pla-de-Corts; site sp on R in 400m. NB Narr app last 200m. 3*, Med, mkd, pt shd, serviced pitches; EHU (6A) €3.30 (poss rev pol); gas; red long stay; TV; 10% statics; Eng spkn; adv bkg rec; tennis; games area. "*Lovely, friendly, scenic, well run site; lge pitches; conv for touring & en rte NE Spain; low lying; gd food in rest; gd.*" **€28.00** 2018

BOURBON LANCY 9A1 (1km S Rural) 46.61949, 3.75506 **Camping Le Plan d'Eau du Breuil**, 71140 Bourbon Lancy 03 86 37 95 83 or 03 85 89 20 98; contact@aquadis-loisirs.com; www.aquadis-loisirs.com

🛒 €1.50 ♨ 🅆 ♨ 🖳 ♦ 🍽 🐶 🍴 ♦ 🏖 🖺

Site sp fr town, on lakeside. 3*, Sm, pt shd, pt sl, EHU (6A); bbq; TV; adv bkg acc; CKE. "*Excel; 2km to town; lake adj; bike rec.*" **€16.00, 1 Jun-15 Sep.** 2017

BOURBON L'ARCHAMBAULT 9A1 (1km W Rural) 46.58058, 3.04804 **Camp Municipal de Bourbon l'Archambault**, 03160 Bourbon-l'Archambault 04 70 67 08 83 or 06 82 82 62 50; https://camping-municipal-de-bourbon-larchambault.business.site/

♨♨ ♨ ♿ ♦ 🍽 🐶 🍴 ☕ nr

Exit D953 at Bourbon-l'Archambault onto D1 northwards; in 400m turn L into Blvd Jean Bignon. Site sp. 2*, Lge, pt shd, sl, EHU (6-10A) €2-2.20; 75% statics; tennis nr. "*Beautifully laid-out in park surroundings; htd pool 300m; waterslide 300m; gd pitches; excel updated san facs (2013); charming town; excel.*" **€6.40, 1 Mar-12 Nov.** 2019

BOURBOULE, LA 7B4 (3km NE Rural) 45.59680, 2.75130 **FFCC Camping Le Panoramique,** Le Pessy, 63150 Murat-le-Quaire **04 73 81 18 79; info@camping panoramique.fr; www.campingpanoramique.fr**

🐾 €1.70 ♦♦(htd) ⓦ ♨ ⚡ 🛒 ⋀ MSP 🦋 ☂ ⓗ nr 🔌 nr ⚠ ⛱

Exit A89 junc 25; cont strt until junc with D922; turn R; in 3km turn R onto D219 dir Mont-Dore; in 5km pass thro Murat-le-Quaire; in 1km turn L in Le Pessy; site on L in 300m. Site well sp fr D922. 3*, Med, mkd, pt shd, terr, EHU (6-10A) €4.30-5.60; gas; 50% statics; phone; adv bkg acc; games rm; CKE. "Site well set-out; mountain views; friendly, helpful recep; clean but dated facs; vg." **€24.00, 15 Feb-15 Mar & 12 Apr-30 Sep.** 2016

BOURDEAUX 9D2 (1km SE Rural) 44.57854, 5.12791 **Camping Les Bois du Châtelas,** Route de Dieulefit, 26460 Bourdeaux **04 75 00 60 80; contact@ chatelas.com; www.chatelas.com**

🐾 €5 ♦♦(htd) ⓦ ♨ ⚡ ♿ 🛒 ⋀ MSP ⓦ ☂ 🍴 🔌 ⚠ 🍽 ⛱(covrd, htd) 🚣

Fr N exit A7 m'way junc 16 onto D104, head twd Crest. Shortly bef Crest turn R onto D538 S thro Bourdeaux & cont dir Dienlefit (still on D538), site in 1km on L, well sp. 5*, Med, mkd, pt shd, terr, EHU (10A) inc; gas; bbq (elec, gas); cooking facs; TV; 30% statics; phone; Eng spkn; adv bkg req; ccard acc; games area; horseriding 5km; bike hire; games rm; waterslide; sauna; fitness rm; CKE. "In lovely, scenic area; site on steep slope; no o'fits over 8m high ssn; gd walking." **€34.70, 11 Apr-13 Sep, M11.** 2016

BOURG ACHARD 3D2 (1km W Rural) 49.35330, 0.80814 **Camping Le Clos Normand,** 235 Route de Pont Audemer, 27310 Bourg-Achard **02 32 56 34 84 or 06 40 25 53 14 (mob); contact@leclosnormand-camping.com; leclosnormand-camping.fr**

🐾 ♦♦ ♨ ♿ 🔌 ⚠ ⛱ 🚣

1km W of vill of Bourg-Achard, D675 Rouen-Pont Audemer or exit A13 at Bourg-Achard junc. 3*, Med, mkd, hdg, pt shd, pt sl, EHU (6A) €3.40 (poss rev pol & poss long lead req); gas; 10% statics; adv bkg acc; ccard acc; CKE. "Vg, clean san facs; plenty hot water; many pitches uneven; gd; muddy when wet." **€21.00, 15 Apr-30 Sep.** 2016

BOURG ARGENTAL 9C2 (2km E Rural) 45.29910, 4.58183 **Camping Domaine de l'Astrée,** L'Allier, 42220 Bourg-Argental **04 77 39 72 97 or 04 77 39 63 49 (TO); prl@bourgargental.fr**

12 🐾 €1.60 ♦♦ ⓦ ♿ 🛒 🔌 ⚠ ⛱

S fr St Etienne on D1082 to Bourg-Argental, thro town, site well sp on R soon after rndabt & opp filling stn. Fr Annonay or Andance site on L of D1082 at start of Bourg-Argental, adj rv. 3*, Sm, mkd, hdstg, pt shd, EHU (4-6A) inc (long cable poss req); gas; bbq; 60% statics; phone; ccard acc; waterslide; games rm; tennis; fishing; bike hire; CKE. "Pleasant site with modern facs; htd pool 600m; vg." **€19.50** 2017

BOURG D'OISANS, LE 9C3 (2km NE Rural) 45.06401, 6.03895 **Camping La Cascade,** Route de l'Alpe d'Huez, 38520 Le Bourg-d'Oisans **04 76 80 02 42; lacascade@ wanadoo.fr; www.lacascadesarenne.com**

🐾 ♦♦(htd) ⓦ ♨ ⚡ ♿ 🛒 ⋀ MSP 🦋 ☂ 🔌 nr ⚠ ⛱(htd)

Fr W drive thro Le Bourg-d'Oisans & cross bdge over Rv Romanche. Approx 800m E of town turn onto D211, sp Alpe-d'Huez. Site on R in 600m. 4*, Med, mkd, pt shd, EHU (16A) €4.30; 10% statics; Eng spkn; adv bkg acc; ccard acc; CKE. "V friendly, helpful staff; discounts for ski passes fr recep; modern san block; superb high pressure shwrs." **€37.00, 1 Jan-30 Sep & 15 Dec-31 Dec.** 2015

BOURG D'OISANS, LE 9C3 (13km SE Rural) 44.98611, 6.12027 **Camping Le Champ du Moulin,** Bourg d'Arud, 38520 Vénosc **04 76 80 07 38; info@ champ-du-moulin.com; www.champ-du-moulin.com**

🐾 €2 ♦♦ ⓦ ♨ ♿ 🛒 ⋀ MSP 🦋 🍴 ☂ ⓗ 🔌 ⚠

On D1091 SE fr Le Bourg-d'Oisans sp Briançon for about 6km; turn R onto D530 twd La Bérarde & after 8km site sp. Turn R to site 350m after cable car stn beside Rv Vénéon. NB Site sp bef vill; do not cross rv on D530. 3*, Med, hdg, mkd, pt shd, EHU (6-10A) €7.20-9.80 (extra charge in winter, poss rev pol); gas; bbq; red long stay; TV; 20% statics; Eng spkn; adv bkg req; ccard acc; fishing nr; rafting nr; horseriding nr; sauna; games rm; tennis nr; CKE. "Lovely, well-run site by alpine torrent (unguarded); friendly, helpful owners; ltd facs LS; htd pool adj; access to pitches poss diff lge o'fits; ideal for walking, climbing & relaxing; no o'fits over 10m; lots of outdoor activities to enjoy; cable car to Les Deux Alpes adj (closes end Aug); mkt Tue Vénosc (high ssn); highly rec." **€29.00, 1 Jan-28 Apr, 1 Jun-15 Sep, 15 Dec-31 Dec, M03.** 2019

BOURG D'OISANS, LE 9C3 (4km NW Rural) 45.09000, 6.00750 **Camping Ferme Noémie,** Chemin Pierre Polycarpe, Les Sables, 38520 Le Bourg-d'Oisans **04 76 11 06 14 or 06 87 45 08 75 (mob); ferme. noemie@orange.fr; www.fermenoemie.com**

🐾 ♦♦(htd) ⓦ ♨ ♿ 🛒 ⋀ MSP 🦋 ⓗ nr 🔌 nr ⚠

On D1091 Grenoble to Briançon; Les Sables is 4km bef Le Bourg-d'Oisans; turn L next to church, site in 400m. 2*, Sm, mkd, unshd, EHU (16A) €3.50; bbq (gas); red long stay; 25% statics; phone; bus 500m; adv bkg acc; ccard acc; cycling; fishing; games area; CKE. "Simple site in superb location with excel facs; helpful British owners; lots of sports; skiing; walking; gd touring base lakes & Ecrins National Park; pool 3km; excel site." **€29.00, 1 May-30 Oct.** 2017

FRANCE

FRANCE

BOURG D'OISANS, LE 9C3 (7km NW Rural) 45.11388, 6.00785 **RCN Camping Belledonne,** Rochetaillée, 38520 Le Bourg-d'Oisans **04 76 80 07 18; belledonne@rcn.fr; www.rcn-campings.fr**

🐕€7 ⋔⋔ 🅆 ♨ ⚲ ♿ ⛟ ⌨ ☒ 🦋 ↑ 🍴 ⊕ ⓐ 🍺 ⚠ ♨ 🚣 (htd) ⛵

Fr S of Grenoble take N85 to Vizille then D1091 twd Le Bourg-d'Oisans; in approx 25km in Rochetaillée turn L onto D526 sp Allemont. Site 100m on R. 4*, Med, hdg, shd, EHU (10A) inc; bbq; TV; Eng spkn; ccard acc; sauna; games area; tennis; games rm; fishing 500m; horseriding; windsurfing; CKE. "Beautiful, well-run site in lovely location; no o'fits over 7.5m high ssn; friendly Dutch owners; access to many pitches tight; no twin axles; gd for teenagers; excel pool with views; many walks; gd touring base; La Marmotte cycle race (early Jun) & Tour de France usually pass thro area & access poss restricted; mkt Sat; excel new san facs (2018), gd rest; v helpful staff." **€41.60, 11 May-2 Oct, M02.** 2018

"We must tell the Club about that great site we found"

Get your site reports in by mid-August and we'll do our best to get your updates into the next edition.

BOURG EN BRESSE 9A2 (11km NE Rural) 46.29078, 5.29078 **Camp Municipal du Sevron,** Chemin du Moulin, 01370 St Etienne-du-Bois **04 74 24 05 47** or 06 47 97 50 73 (mob); campingdusevron@gmail.com; www.campingdusevron.fr

🐕€1.06 ⋔⋔ 🅆 ♨ ⚲ 🍺nr

On D1083 at S end of vill of St Etienne-du-Bois on E side of rd. 3*, Sm, hdg, pt shd, EHU (10A) €2.05; 50% statics; Eng spkn; ccard acc; rv fishing; tennis. "Gd NH; dated but clean facs; friendly; sm pitches; late arr get v sm pitches; poss rd & rlwy noise; gd shwrs & plenty hot water; gd facs." **€17.00, 1 Mar-25 Oct.** 2018

BOURG ET COMIN 3D4 (0.5km NE Rural) 49.39871, 3.66072 **Camping de la Pointe,** 5 Rue de Moulins, 02160 Bourg-et-Comin **03 23 25 87 52;** michel.pennec@9online.fr; www.tourisme-paysdelaon.com

12 🐕€2 ⋔⋔(htd) 🅆 ♨ ⚲ 🦋 🍴nr ⊕ ♨ ⛵(covrd, htd)

Leave A26/E17 at junc 14 & turn W along D925 dir Soissons for 15km. Site on R on ent vill. 2*, Sm, hdg, pt shd, EHU (6A) €3.20; bbq; phone; bus 500m; Eng spkn; adv bkg acc; CKE. "CL-type site in orchard; narr ent & access to pitches poss diff lge o'fits; most pitches sm & not suitable lge o'fits; EHU is only 2 pin; gd rest; gd walking area; 10 mins fr Parc Nautique de l'Ailette with watersports; conv Aisne Valley; bar 500m; v accommodating owner; htd pool OAY; wifi not reliable." **€20.80** 2018

BOURG MADAME 8H4 (6km NW Rural) 42.45979, 1.91075 **Camping Le Robinson,** 25 Ave Gare Internationale, 66760 Enveitg **04 68 04 80 38 or 06 11 81 25 46 (mob);** lerobinson-cerdagne@wanadoo.fr; www.robinson-cerdagne.com

12 🐕€1.50 ⋔⋔ 🅆 ♨ ⚲ ♿ ⛟ 🦋 ⊕nr ⓐ 🍺nr ⚠ ♨ 🚣

Fr Bourg-Madame, take N20 N twd Foix. Thro vill of Enveitg & turn L down Chemin de la Gare & L at camping sp. 2*, Lge, mkd, shd, pt sl, EHU (4-13A) €3-9; gas; bbq; TV; 10% statics; phone; adv bkg acc; games rm. "Beautiful setting; winter sports cent; conv Barcelona, Andorra; conv scenic rte train (Train Jaune); new management; new shwr block (excel)." **€20.00** 2015

BOURG ST ANDEOL 9D2 (1.8km N Rural) 44.38131, 4.64840 **Camping du Lion,** Quartier Ile Chenevrier, 07700 Bourg-St Andéol **04 75 54 53 20;** contact@campingdulion.com; www.campingdulion.com

🐕€3 ⋔⋔ ♨ ⚲ 🦋 🍴 🍺 ♨ 🚣

Exit A7 at junc 18 or 19 onto N7. At Pierrelatte turn W on D59 to Bourg-St Andéol. Site sp fr cent town dir Viviers. 3*, Med, mkd, shd, EHU (6A) €3; 10% statics; adv bkg acc; games rm; games area. "Peaceful site in woodland setting; muddy when wet; dir access to rv; highly rec; new san facs (2015)." **€35.00, 1 Apr-30 Sep.** 2016

BOURGES 4H3 (2km S Urban) 47.07228, 2.39497 **Camp Municipal Robinson,** 26 Blvd de l'Industrie, 18000 Bourges **02 48 20 16 85;** camping@ville-bourges.fr; www.ville-bourges.fr

🐕€2.15 ⋔⋔(htd) 🅆 ♨ ⚲ 🦋 ↑nr ⊕nr ⚠

Exit A71/E11 at junc 7, foll sp Bourges Centre & bear R at 'Autres Directions' sp; foll site sp; site at traff lts on N side of S section of inner ring rd half-way bet junc with D2144 & D2076. NB: site access is via a loop - no L turn at traff lts, but rndabt just past site if turning missed. If on outer ring rd D400, app city on D2144 & then as above. Sp on app rds to site gd. 3*, Med, mkd, hdg, hdstg, pt shd, serviced pitches; EHU (10-16A) €3.40-8 (poss rev pol); bbq (elec, gas); red long stay; twin axles; bus adj; Eng spkn; ccard acc; CKE. "Attractive, well-kept, well-organised, busy, rvside site in gd location; helpful, friendly staff; pool 300m inc; excel, immac san facs; some v lge pitches, some sm & poss diff ent; most pitches hdstg; excel NH or longer; 20 min walk to historic town." **€24.00, 30 Mar-28 Oct.** 2018

"I need an on-site restaurant"

We do our best to make sure site information is correct, but it is always best to check any must-have facilities are still available or will be open during your visit.

For a guide to symbols see the fold out on the rear cover

BOURGUEIL *4G1* (0.8km S Rural) *47.26991, 0.16873*
Camp Municipal Parc Capitaine, 37140 Bourgueil
02 47 97 85 62 or 02 47 97 25 00 LS; camping@
bourgueil.fr; www.bourgueil.fr

🐕 €1.38 ♿ 🅿 ♨ ⚓ 🚻 ⚡ 🔤 ✉ 🛒 nr ⛰

N on D749 fr junc 5 of A85, site 1km on R. Fr W
(Longue) via D10 & by-pass, S at rndabt on D749 to
site on L in 200m. Do not app fr N via D749 thro
town cent. 3*, Med, hdg, mkd, pt shd, EHU (10A)
€2.50 (poss long lead req); gas; sw; ccard acc; CKE.
*"Ideal cent Loire châteaux; 2 sites - one on R for
tourers; excel; barrier ent & exit by code; office clsd
1230-1500 but warden lives upstairs; conv fr A85 &
Loire valley; vg; san facs need refurb."*
€15.00, 15 May-15 Sep.   **2017**

"Satellite navigation makes touring much easier"

Remember most sat navs don't know if you're
towing or in a larger vehicle – always use yours
alongside maps and site directions.

BOUSSAC *7A4* (2km NE Rural) *46.37192, 2.20036*
Camping du Château de Poinsouze, Route de la
Châtre, 23600 Boussac-Bourg 05 55 65 02 21;
camping-de-poinsouze@gmail.com; www.camping-
de-poinsouze.com

🐕 €3 ♿ 🅿 ♨ ⚓ 🚻 ⚡ 🔤 ✉ 🎣 Ⓣ ♨ 🛒 ⛰ 🚲 ⛵ 🛶

Fr junc 10 on A71/E11 by-pass Montluçon via N145
dir Guéret; in 22km turn L onto D917 to Boussac;
cont on D917 dir La Châtre; site 3km on L. Or
fr Guéret on N145, exit Gouzon, at rndabt take D997
to Boussac, then as above. 4*, Med, mkd, unshd, pt
sl, serviced pitches; EHU (6-20A) inc (poss rev pol);
bbq; TV; 10% statics; Eng spkn; adv bkg req; ccard acc;
horseriding 5km; games area; games rm; waterslide;
lake fishing; golf 20km; bike hire; CKE. *"Peaceful,
relaxed site by lake in chateau grnds; well-kept &
well-run; lge pitches, some sl; no o'fits over 15m; dogs
not acc Jul/Aug welcoming, helpful owners; superb
san facs; excel rest & snacks; gd for young children; gd
walking."* **€39.00, 11 May-13 Sep, L16.**   **2019**

BOUSSAC *7A4* (2km W Rural) *46.34938, 2.18662*
Camping Creuse-Nature (Naturist), Route de
Bétête, 23600 Boussac 05 55 65 18 01; creuse-
nature@wanadoo.fr; www.creuse-nature.com

🐕 €5.50 ♿ ♨ ⚓ 🚻 ⚡ 🔤 ✉ Ⓣ ♨ 🛒 ⛰ 🚲 ⛵(covrd, htd) 🛶

Fr Boussac take D917 N twd La Châtre. In 500m turn
L (W) on D15 sp Bétête. Site on R in 2.5km, clearly sp.
4*, Med, hdg, mkd, pt shd, pt sl, EHU (10A) €4.50 (poss
long lead req); 10% statics; Eng spkn; adv bkg acc;
ccard acc; fishing; games area. *"Excel site in lovely area;
great pitches; charming & helpful owners; clean facs;
easy walk to town & interesting château; great location."*
€35.70, 1 Apr-15 Oct.   **2019**

BRACIEUX *4G2* (0.5km N Urban) *47.55060, 1.53743*
Camping Indigo les Châteaux, 11 Rue Roger
Brun, 41250 Bracieux 02 54 46 41 84; chateaux@
camping-indigo.com; www.camping-indigo.com

🐕 €2.80 ♿ 🅿 ♨ ⚓ 🚻 ⚡ 🔤 ✉ Ⓗ nr 🛒 nr ⛰ ⛵(covrd) 🛶

Fr S take D102 to Bracieux fr Cour-Cheverny. Fr N
exit Blois on D765 dir Romorantin; after 5km take
D923 to Bracieux & site on R on N o'skts of town
opp church, sp. 3*, Lge, hdg, mkd, hdstg, pt shd, EHU
(10A) €2.75 (poss long lead req); red long stay; TV;
10% statics; Eng spkn; adv bkg acc; ccard acc; tennis;
games rm; bike hire; CKE. *"Peaceful spot; attractive
forest area; busy high ssn; gd security; gd touring
base; gas 300m; bike tracks; well run site; all san
blocks replaced (2013); superb; excel, well run site."*
€32.00, 30 Mar-4 Nov.   **2018**

BRANTOME *7C3* (1km E Rural) *45.36074, 0.66035*
Camping Brantôme Peyrelevade, Ave André Maurois,
24310 Brantôme 05 53 05 75 24; info@camping-
dordogne.net; www.camping-dordogne.net

🐕 €2 ♿(htd) 🅿 ♨ ⚓ 🚻 ⚡ 🔤 ✉ � Ⓣ 🎣 🛒 nr ⛰ 🚲
⛵ 🛶 🌊 sand adj

Fr N on D675 foll sp Centre Ville; ent vill & turn L
onto D78 Thiviers rd, site sp at turn; in 1km on R
past stadium opp g'ge. Fr S D939 foll sp 'Centre
Ville' fr rndabt N of town. Then L onto D78 Thiviers
rd & foll sp. Do not foll 'Centre Ville' sp fr rndabt
S of town, use by-pass. Football stadium best ref
point for ent. 3*, Lge, mkd, hdg, pt shd, EHU (10A)
inc; bbq; sw nr; TV; Eng spkn; adv bkg acc;
ccard acc; tennis nr; CKE. *"Spacious, well-kept rvside
site; attractive courtyard layout; friendly, helpful
owners; excel, modern, gd san facs; facs stretched in
high ssn; grnd poss soft after heavy rain; 10 min walk to
lovely town (the Venice of Périgord); mkt Wed; games
area adj; beautiful countryside; gd walking & cycling;
excel; some pitches heavily shd; excel family camping."*
€26.00, 1 May-30 Sep.   **2017**

BRASSAC *8F4* (11km SE Rural) *43.59700, 2.60732*
Camping Le Rouquié, Lac de la Ravière, 81260
Lamontélarie 05 63 70 98 06; camping.rouquie@
wanadoo.fr; www.campingrouquie.fr

🐕 ♿ 🅿 ♨ ⚓ 🚻 ⚡ ✉ Ⓣ 🎣 🛒 ⛰ 🚲

Fr Brassac take D62 to N side of Lac de la Ravière;
site on lakeside. 2*, Med, mkd, pt shd, terr, EHU (3-
6A) €4; bbq; sw; TV; 50% statics; adv bkg acc; ccard
acc; bike hire; watersports adj; games area; fishing;
sailing; CKE. *"Ltd facs LS; gd lake views; site needs
TLC."* **€28.00, 1 May-31 Oct.**   **2019**

BRASSAC *8F4* (5km S Rural) *43.60835, 2.47148*
FFCC Camping Le Plô, Le Bourg, 81260 Le Bez
05 63 74 00 82; info@leplo.com; www.leplo.com

🐕 €1.50 � ⚊ ♨ ⚍ ⚌ ⧄ ⫽ 🦋 ⵢ ⅾ ☎ nr ⚓ ⛵

Fr Castres on D622 to Brassac; then D53 S to Le Bez, site sp W of Le Bez. 3*, Med, mkd, pt shd, terr, EHU (6A) €3; bbq; Eng spkn; adv bkg acc; games area; games rm; bike hire; CKE. *"Lovely location; well-equipped site; excel, clean san facs; friendly, helpful Dutch owners; beautiful, historical area with National Park; much wildlife; cafés & gd rest nrby; vg."* €31.50, 1 May-30 Sep.   **2019**

BRAUCOURT *6E1* (5km SW Rural) *48.55425, 4.79235*
FLOWER Camping Presqu'île de Champaubert, Lac du Der, 52290 Braucourt 03 25 04 13 20; camping-de-braucourt@wanadoo.fr; www.lescampingsduder.com or www.flowercampings.com

🐕 €1 ♦♦ ⚊ ♨ ⚍ ⫽ ⧄ 🦋 ⵢ ⅾ ⚓ ⚓

Fr St Dizier take D384 SW twd Montier-en-Der & Troyes. In Braucourt R onto D153 sp Presq'île de Champaubert, site on L in 2km. Site situated on Lac du Der-Chantecoq. 4*, Lge, mkd, hdg, shd, serviced pitches; EHU (10A) €4 (rev pol); gas; sw nr; TV; 60% statics; phone; ccard acc; boating; fishing; watersports; CKE. *"Beautiful lge beach; birdwatching; lge pitches; improved san facs; gates clsd 2230; ltd spaces."* €26.00, 15 Apr-25 Nov.   **2016**

BRENGUES *7D4* (0.5km S Rural) *44.57509, 1.83261*
Camp Municipal de Brengues, 46320 Brengues
05 81 48 06 99

♦♦ ⚊ ⚍ ⫽ ⵢ ⅾ ☎ nr ⧄

W fr Figeac on D13. After 6km turn L onto D41. After 17km, turn L at x-rds with D38, site ent 100m on R bef bdge over Rv Célé. 3*, Sm, mkd, pt shd, EHU (10A) inc (rev pol); sw; tennis; CKE. *"Warden now onsite."* €15.00, 1 Jun-30 Sep.   **2018**

> ## "There aren't many sites open at this time of year"
>
> If you're travelling outside peak season remember to call ahead to check site opening dates – even if the entry says 'open all year'.

BRESSE, LA *6F3* (3.2km E Rural) *47.99893, 6.91801*
FFCC Camp Municipal Le Haut des Bluches,
5 Route des Planches, 88250 La Bresse
03 29 25 64 80; www.hautdesbluches.com

⏱ 🐕 ♦♦ (htd) ⚊ ♨ ⚍ ⫽ ⵢ ⅾ ☎ ⧄

Leave La Bresse on D34 Rte de la Schlucht. Site on R in 3km. 3*, Med, mkd, pt shd, terr, EHU (4-13A) €2-4.80; bbq; TV; 10% statics; Eng spkn; adv bkg acc; ccard acc; games rm; site clsd early Nov-mid Dec; games area; CKE. *"Excel site in attractive setting; NH area for m'vans; excel san facs; pool in vill; gd walks fr site; conv winter sports."* €20.00   **2017**

BRESSUIRE *4H1* (2.6km S Rural) *46.82923, -0.50223*
Camping Le Puy Rond, Allee du Puy Rond, Cornet, 79300 Bressuire 05 49 72 43 22 or 06 85 60 37 26 (mob); puyrondcamping@gmail.com; www.puyrondcamping.com

🐕 €1.50 ♦♦ (htd) ⚊ ♨ ⚍ ⫽ 🦋 ⵢ ⅾ ☎ nr ⧄ ⚓

Fr N149 foll site sp on rte 'Poids Lourds' to site on D38. Fr 'Centre Ville' foll sp for Fontenay-Le-Comte; turn R 100m after overhead bdge & go across junc to site. Well sp. 3*, Sm, mkd, pt shd, pt sl, terr, EHU (6-10A) €3.50; bbq; twin axles; red long stay; 15% statics; Eng spkn; adv bkg acc; ccard acc; fishing 1km; CKE. *"Gd touring base, poss tired early ssn; friendly British owners; san facs updated & v gd (2016); adv bkg ess for twin axles; winter storage avail; vg."* €25.00, 15 Mar-30 Sep.   **2017**

BREST *2E2* (6.6km SW Coastal) *48.36544, -4.54163*
Camping du Goulet, Ste Anne-du-Porzic, 29200 Brest
02 98 45 86 84; campingdugoulet@wanadoo.fr; www.campingdugoulet.com

⏱ 🐕 €1.50 ♦♦ (htd) ⚊ ♨ ⚍ ⫽ 🦋 ⅾ ☎ ⧄ ⚓ sand 1km

On D789 turn L at site sp. Approx 4km fr Brest after R bend at T junc, turn L & L again at site sp; down hill to site. 4*, Med, unshd, pt sl, terr, EHU (6-10A) €3-3.50; 15% statics; adv bkg acc; games area; games rm; waterslide; CKE. *"Excel site; great location; but to Centerville; P&R to city."* €26.00   **2015**

BRETENOUX *7C4* (0.2km N Urban) *44.91650, 1.83816*
Camping La Bourgnatelle, 46130 Bretenoux
05 65 10 89 04; contact@dordogne_vacances.fr; www.dordogne-vacances.fr

🐕 €1.50 ♦♦ ⚊ ⚍ ⫽ 🦋 ☎ nr ⧄ ⚓

In town 100m fr D940. 4*, Lge, pt shd, EHU (5-10A) €3; adv bkg acc; canoe hire; rv; fishing. *"Lovely site along banks of Rv Cère; clean site; gd fishing; lovely town MD Tues."* €25.00, 1 Apr-31 Oct.   **2019**

BRETEUIL SUR L'ITON *4E2* (0.3km SSE Urban) *48.83175, 0.91258* Camping Les Berges de l'Iton, 53 rue du Fourneau, 27160 Breteuil-sur-Iton 02 32 62 70 35 or 06 84 75 70 32 (mob); campinglesberges-de-liton@orange.fr; www.campinglesbergesdeliton.com

🐕 ♦♦ (htd) ⚊ ⚍ ⫽ ⵢ ⅾ ⧄

Fr Evreux take D830 twd Conches-en-Ouche. L onto D840 to Breteuil, then foll sp for site. 3*, Med, hdg, mkd, hdstg, pt shd, pt sl, EHU (6A) inc; gas; bbq; 66% statics; adv bkg acc; INF; CCI. *"Well kept, landscaped site; gd NH; mkt on Wednesdays; helpful staff; vg."* €23.70, 1 Apr-30 Sep.   **2019**

BRETIGNOLLES SUR MER *2H3* (1km E Urban)
46.63583, -1.85861 **Camping La Trévillière**, Route de Bellevue, 85470 Bretignolles-sur-Mer **02 51 90 09 65 or 02 51 33 05 05; info@chadotel.com; La Trévillière**
🐕 €3.90 ♟ wo ⚓ ♨ ♿ ☕ ∥ msp ♛ ⍾ ♬ ♖ ⚓ ⚲
⚓ (covrd, htd) 🏖 ⚓ sand 1.5km

S along D38 fr St Gilles Croix-de-Vie twd Olonne-sur-Mer, site is sp to L in Bretignolles-sur-Mer. Site 1km fr town cent nr football stadium. Sp fr town cent.
4*, Lge, mkd, hdg, pt shd, serviced pitches; EHU (6A) inc; gas; bbq (gas); red long stay; TV; 70% statics; phone; Eng spkn; adv bkg acc; ccard acc; bike hire; waterslide; fishing; horseriding 5km; watersports 3km; games rm; CKE. "Friendly, family site; lge pitches; no c'van/m'van over 8m high ssn; quiet; gd cycling area; salt marshes worth a visit; mkt Thu & Sun."
€48.00, 5 Apr-20 Sep, A26.   **2018**

BRETIGNOLLES SUR MER *2H3* (3.4km S Coastal)
46.603957, -1.840665 **Camping L'Ocean**, 17 rue du Brandais, 85470 Brem-sur-Mer **02 51 90 59 16; contact@cybelevacances.com; www.campingde locean.fr**
🐕 €6 ⚓ ♨ ♬ ⍾ ♖ ⚓ (covrd, htd) ⚓ sand

Fr La Roche-sur-Yon and Les Sables d'Olonne foll A87. Then D160. Take dir of Bretignolles-sur-Mer.
5*, Med, pt shd, bbq (gas); bus/train; adv bkg acc.
"Biggest indoor waterpark in Vendée; cycling rte fr site." **NP 46, 6 Apr-3 Nov.**   **2019**

BRETIGNOLLES SUR MER *2H3* (4km S Coastal)
46.60413, -1.83231 **Camping Le Chaponnet**, 16 Rue du Chaponnet, 85470 Brem-sur-Mer **02 51 90 55 56; campingchaponnet@wanadoo.fr; www.le-chaponnet.com**
🐕 €6 ♟ wo ⚓ ♨ ♿ ☕ ∥ ♬ ⍾ ⍾ ♖ ⚓ ⚲
⚓ (covrd, htd) ⚓ sand 1km

Fr La Roche-sur-Yon on N160 dir Les Sables-d'Olonne. Turn R onto D87 thro St Mathurin vill & take 1st R (just after church) D38 dir L'Ile d'Olonne. Foll sp Brem-sur-Mer, go thro vill & foll sp 'Océan' (nr bakery & bar); turn L opp hairdresser, site in 50m along 1-way rd. 4*, Lge, hdg, pt shd, EHU (10A) inc; gas; bbq; TV; 75% statics; phone; adv bkg acc; ccard acc; gym; games area; sauna; bike hire; waterslide; games rm; jacuzzi; tennis; CKE. "Gd beaches adj; vg."
€34.00, 14 Apr-15 Sep, A05.   **2019**

BRIANCON *9C4* (3.8km SW Rural) *44.87737, 6.61634*
Camping Les Cinq Vallées, St Blaise, 05100 Briançon **04 92 21 06 27; infos@camping5vallees.com; www.camping5vallees.com**
♟ wo ⚓ ♨ ♿ ☕ ∥ msp ♛ ⍾ ♖ ⚓ ⚲ (htd)

S of Briançon by N94 to vill St Blaise. Ent on L. Med, pt shd, pt sl, EHU (10A) inc; TV; 80% statics; games rm. "Vg site; traffic noise barely noticeable; gd shop on site with takeaway food; lge supmkt 2km."
€23.60, 1 Jun-30 Sep.   **2015**

BRIARE *4G3* (6km S Rural) *47.60018, 2.76101*
Camping Municipal L'ecluse des Combles, Chemin de Loire, 45360 Châtillon-sur-Loire **02 38 36 34 39 or 06 32 07 83 45; camping.chatillonsurloire@ orange.fr; www.camping.chatillon-sur-loire.com**
🐕 €1.20 ♟ (htd) ⚓ ♨ ♿ ☕ ∥ msp ♛ ⍾ nr ⍾ nr ⍾ nr ⚓

SE fr Briare on N7, in 4km turn SW onto D50. Site immed bef rv bdge on R. Care needed over bdge after ent. 2*, Med, pt shd, terr, EHU (6A) inc; gas; bbq; Eng spkn; fishing; games rm; CKE. "Basic site with some nice pitches by Rv Loire & historic canal; pleasant staff; right of way along rv bank passes thro site; mkt 2nd Thurs of month; vg; canal viaduct at Briare worth visit; site neglected; pitch yourself; warden in off late afternoon." **€16.50, 1 Apr-31 Oct.**   **2017**

BRIARE *4G3* (0.5km W Rural) *47.64137, 2.72560*
Camping Le Martinet, Quai Tchékof, 45250 Briare **02 38 31 24 50 or 02 38 31 24 51; campingbriare@ recrea.fr; www.campinglemartinet.fr**
🐕 €1 ♟ ♿ ☕ ♬ ⍾ ♛ ⍾ nr ⍾ nr ⍾ nr

Exit N7 into Briare. Fr N immed R after canal bdge; fr S L bef 2nd canal bdge; sp. 3*, Lge, mkd, unshd, EHU (10A) €3.60; adv bkg acc; fishing adj. "Gd views some pitches; pretty bars & rests along canal; gd walking & cycling; interesting town; gates close 2200; slightly neglected (2009); OK sh stay; san facs old style but clean." **€22.00, 30 Mar-30 Sep.**   **2018**

BRIENNE LE CHATEAU *6E1* (6km S Rural) *48.34876, 4.52726* **Camping Le Tertre**, Route de Radonvilliers, 10500 Dienville **03 25 92 26 50; campingdutertre@ wanadoo.fr; www.campingdutertre.fr**
🐕 €1 ♟ wo ⚓ ♨ ♿ ☕ ∥ msp ♬ ⍾ ♛ ⍾ ♖ ⚓ ⚲
⚓ (htd) 🏖

On D443 S fr Brienne-le-Château; at Dienville turn R at rndabt onto D11; site on R in 200m, sp. NB Site opp Lake Amance harbour, foll sp 'Le Port'.
3*, Med, hdstg, hdg, mkd, pt shd, serviced pitches; EHU (6-10A) €4 (poss long lead req); gas; bbq; TV; 10% statics; phone; bus 500m; Eng spkn; adv bkg acc; ccard acc; gym; games area; fishing; games area; gym; CKE. "Pleasant site 2 mins fr vill; man-made lake with sailing; excel site for all watersports & other activities; cycle tracks; vg; excel rest."
€25.00, 20 Mar-12 Oct.   **2016**

BRIGNOGAN PLAGES *1D2* (1km NW Coastal) *48.67278, -4.32916* **Camping de la Côte des Légendes**, Keravezan, 29890 Brignogan-Plages **02 98 83 41 65; contact@campingcotedeslegendes.com; www.campingcotedeslegendes.com**
🐕 €1.40 ♟ wo ⚓ ♨ ♿ ☕ ∥ msp ♬ ⍾ ♛ ⍾ ♖ ⚓ ⚲ ⚓ sand adj

Fr Roscoff on D10, fr Brest on D788/770 or fr N12 exit dir Lesneven. In Brignogan foll sp Brignogan-Plages & 'Centre Nautique'. 3*, Lge, hdg, hdstg, mkd, pt shd, EHU (5-10A) €3.15-4.05 (poss rev pol); bbq; red long stay; TV; 30% statics; phone; Eng spkn; adv bkg acc; ccard acc; sailing; watersports; CKE. "On beautiful sandy cove; friendly, helpful staff; site guarded 24 hrs; ltd facs LS; vg touring base in interesting area; vg."
€20.00, 29 Mar-12 Nov.   **2015**

FRANCE

BRIGNOLES *10F3* (9km SE Rural) *43.33919, 6.12579* **Camping La Vidaresse,** 83136 Ste Anastasie-sur-Issole **04 94 72 21 75; info@campinglavidaresse.com; www.campinglavidaresse.com**

€3 nr (covrd, htd)

On DN7 2km W of Brignoles at rndabt take D43 dir Toulon. In about 10km turn L at rndabt to D15. Do not ent vill, go strt & site is approx 250m on R. 3*, Med, mkd, hdg, pt shd, terr, EHU (10A) €5 (poss rev pol); gas; bbq (elec, gas); 40% statics; adv bkg acc; ccard acc; tennis; fishing 200m; games area; CKE. *"Well-managed, family site in lovely area; peaceful; friendly & helpful; facs adequate; excel pool; gd touring base Haute Provence, Gorges du Verdon & Riviera; vineyard adj; gd."* **€25.00, 20 Mar-30 Sep.** **2019**

BRILLANE, LA *10E3* (5km E Rural) *43.92282, 5.92369* **Camping les Oliviers,** Chemin St Sauveur, 04700 Oraison **04 92 78 20 00; camping-oraison@wanadoo.fr; www.camping-oraison.com**

12 €2.50

Exit A51 junc 19; take rd E to Oraison in 2km; site sp in vill. 4*, Med, mkd, pt shd, pt sl, terr, EHU (16A) €4.50; gas; TV; 10% statics; Eng spkn; adv bkg acc; ccard acc; games area; bike hire; games rm; CKE. *"Pleasant, family-run site among olive trees; friendly, helpful owners; walks fr site; conv Verdon gorge; adj elec sub-stn, elec cables run over small pt of site, not obtrusive; gd."* **€25.50** **2015**

BRILLANE, LA *10E3* (2.6km W Rural) *43.93305, 5.86777* **Camping Le Moulin de Ventre,** 04300 Niozelles **04 92 78 63 31 or 06 63 51 53 55 (mob); moulindeventre@gmail.com; www.moulin-de-ventre.com**

€3 (htd)

Exit A51 junc 19 at La Brillane; turn R onto D4096, then L onto D4100 sp Niozelles & Forcalquier. Site in 3km on L just after bdge, adj Rv Lauzon. 4*, Med, mkd, hdg, pt shd, pt sl, serviced pitches; EHU (10A) inc; gas; bbq (gas); twin axles; red long stay; TV; 10% statics; phone; Eng spkn; adv bkg acc; ccard acc; rv fishing adj; games rm; CKE. *"Pleasant, peaceful, wooded site by lake & rv; rvside pitches have drop to rv; excel touring base; boat hire adj; lavendar fields in flower Jun/Jul; site neglected; poor san facs."* **€38.50, 9 Apr-30 Sep.** **2016**

BRIONNE *3D2* (0.5km N Urban) *49.20256, 0.71554* **Camp Municipal La Vallée,** Rue Marcel Nogrette, 27800 Brionne **02 32 44 80 35; www.ville-brionne.fr**

nr nr

Fr D438 N or S on by-pass, turn N at D46 junc, pass Carrefour supmkt on L & take 1st R, site on L. 2*, Sm, hdg, pt shd, EHU (8A) €3.45; gas; bbq; 10% statics; CKE. *"Excel, well maintained site in lovely vill; gd san facs, poss ltd LS; sh walk to supmkt; clean facs but ltd."* **€15.00, 30 Apr-30 Sep.** **2017**

BRIONNE *3D2* (6km N Rural) *49.24174, 0.70339* **Camp Municipal Les Marronniers,** Rue Louise Givon, 27290 Pont-Authou **02 32 42 75 06 or 06 27 25 21 45 (mob); lesmarroniers27@orange.fr or camping municipaldesmarronniers@orange.fr; www.normandie-accueil.fr**

12 €1.35 (htd) nr nr

Heading S on D438 take D130 just bef Brionne sp Pont-Audemer (care req at bdge & rndabts). Site on L in approx 5km, well sp on o'skts of Pont-Authou; foll sp in vill. 2*, Med, mkd, hdstg, pt shd, EHU (10A) €3.40 (poss rev pol); bbq; 50% statics; adv bkg acc; fishing; bike hire; CKE. *"Useful, clean stop nr Rouen & m'way; friendly recep; clean san facs; best pitches far side of lake; few hdstg; adv bkg rec; some statics unsightly; stream runs thro site; beautiful valley with many historic towns & vills; excel walking; gd NH; pretty but basic site; recep & security gate cls 1800 in LS."* **€13.00** **2018**

BRIONNE *3D2* (9km N Rural) *49.23648, 0.72265* **FFCC Camping Saint Nicolas (formerly Municipal),** 15 Rue St Nicolas, 27800 Le Bec-Hellouin **02 32 44 83 55 or 06 84 75 70 32 (Mob); campingstnicolas@orange.fr; www.campingsaintnicolas.fr**

€1.50 (htd) nr nr (htd, indoor)

Exit A28 junc 13 onto D438 then take D581 to Malleville-sur-le-Bec; site on R 1km after Malleville. Well sp. 3*, Med, pt shd, EHU (10A) €3.50; bbq; 10% statics; tennis nr; horseriding nr; CKE. *"Attractive, peaceful, well-kept site in pleasant location; spacious pitches; friendly, helpful warden; vg, clean san facs; gate clsd 2200-0700; gd dog walks; vg cycling; attractive countryside; conv NH nr Calais; rec; delightful vill; rec dir in book; vist to Abbey at Bec Hellouin a must."* **€20.40, 15 Mar-15 Oct.** **2017**

BRISSAC QUINCE *4G1* (2km NE Rural) *47.35944, -0.43388* **Le Domaine de L'Etang,** Route de St Mathurin, 49320 Brissac-Quincé **02 41 91 70 61; info@campingetang.com; www.campingetang.com**

€2.10-9.10 (htd) (covrd, htd)

Fr N on A11, exit junc 14 onto N260 passing E of Angers, following sp for Cholet/Poitiers. After x-ing Rv Loire, foll sp to Brissac-Quincé on D748. Foll sp for St Mathurin/Domaine de l'Etang on D55 to site. 4*, Med, hdstg, mkd, hdg, pt shd, serviced pitches; EHU (10A) inc; gas; bbq (charcoal, gas); red long stay; twin axles; TV; Eng spkn; adv bkg acc; ccard acc; bike hire; waterslide; games rm; lake fishing; golf 8km; CKE. *"Excel, well-cared for site amongst vineyards; lge pitches; staff pleasant & helpful; clean, modern facs; leisure facs gd for children; pleasant 15 min rvside walk to Brissac-Quincé; wine tasting; gd touring base Loire valley; mkt Thu; rec Apocalypse Tapestry at Chateau d'Angers; gd for walks & sightseeing."* **€35.00, 21 Apr-16 Sep, L15.** **2018**

BRISSAC QUINCE *4G1* (4km S Rural) *47.33317, -0.43664* **Camping à la Ferme Domaine de la Belle Etoile,** La Belle Etoile, 49320 Brissac-Quincé 06 62 32 99 40 (mob); vincent_esnou74@hotmail.com; www.domaine-belle-etoile.fr

Take D748 S fr Angers dir Poitiers. At D761 rndabt cont on D748 sp N-D-d'Allençon. Site sp at 2nd turn on L in 500m. Sm, pt shd, EHU (5A) €3; bbq; Eng spkn. *"Excel CL-type site in vineyard with wine-tasting & farm produce; clean, modern facs; troglodyte caves, mushroom farms & château nrby; v friendly owners."* **€10.50, 1 Apr-1 Nov.** 2015

BRIVE LA GAILLARDE *7C3* (19km SW Rural) *45.06942, 1.43060* **Camping La Magaudie,** La Magaudie Ouest, 19600 Chartrier-Ferrière 05 55 85 26 06 or 06 85 22 54 78; camping@lamagaudie.com; www.lamagaudie.com

Exit A20 junc 53 onto D920/D19 dir Chasteaux. After rlwy bdge take 2nd L to Chartrier & foll blue sps to site. NB Diff app climbing up narr lane with no passing spaces for 1km. 1*, Sm, mkd, pt shd, sl, EHU (10A) €3.50; bbq (gas); sw nr; 5% statics; Eng spkn; adv bkg acc; CKE. *"Helpful Dutch owners; vg site & facs but v ltd LS; rec arr early high ssn; excel; superb rest; tranquil & relaxing."* **€23.00, 15 Apr-15 Apr.** 2016

BROMMAT *7D4* (0.3km E Rural) *44.83083, 2.68638* **Camping Municipale,** Le Bourg, 12600 Brommat 05 65 66 00 96; mairie-de.brommat@wanadoo.fr; www.brommat.fr

Fr D98, cross rv bdge, cont uphill to Mairie. Turn R in front of Mairie and cont strt on. Campsite on R. Sm, hdg, pt shd, EHU (6A); sw nr; TV; bus 50m; adv bkg acc; tennis 2km; fishing; CCI. *" Beautiful adj walk; vg."* **€13.00, 15 May-15 Sep.** 2019

BROUSSES ET VILLARET *8F4* (0.5km S Rural) *43.33932, 2.25201* **Camping Le Martinet Rouge,** 11390 Brousses-et-Villaret 04 68 26 51 98 or 06 91 34 41 60 (mob); camping.lemartinetrouge@orange.fr; www.camping-martinet.co.uk

Fr D118 Mazamet-Carcassonne, turn R 3km after Cuxac-Carbades onto D103; turn L in Brousses & foll sp. 3*, Med, hdg, pt shd, pt sl, EHU (6-10A); TV; 20% statics; phone; bus; Eng spkn; adv bkg acc; horseriding; waterslide; trout fishing; games area; canoeing; CKE. *"Helpful owners, great for walking or mountain biking; cather castles, abbeys & churchs, Canal du Midi; forest, lakes, rv & caverns; excel site."* **€25.00, 9 Apr-19 Oct.** 2019

BUGUE, LE *7C3* (1km SE Urban) *44.90980, 0.93160* **FFCC Camping Les Trois Caupain,** Le Port, 24260 Le Bugue Dordogne 05 53 07 24 60 or 06 85 48 44 25 (mob); info@camping-bugue.com; www.camping-des-trois-caupain.com

Exit Le Bugue town cent on D703 twd Campagne. Turn R at sp after 400m to site in 600m on rvside. 3*, Med, mkd, pt shd, EHU (6-16A) €4-4.30 (rev pol); gas; 25% statics; adv bkg acc. *"Beautiful, lovely, well run site; pleasant, helpful owners; cycle along rv to pretty town; excel; new pool; mkt in Le Bugue well worth a visit; rv adj; games area adj; ideal cent for touring the Dordogne region; lots of attractions; gd rest."* **€21.00, 1 Apr-30 Oct.** 2017

BUGUE, LE *7C3* (3km SE Rural) *44.90663, 0.97412* **Camping Le Val de la Marquise,** Le Petit Moulin, 24260 Campagne 05 53 54 74 10; contact@levaldelamarquise.com; www.camping-dordogne-marquise.com

Fr D703 bet Le Bugue & Les Eyzies take D35 at Campagne dir St Cyprien, site sp. 4*, Med, mkd, pt shd, terr, EHU (10-15A); bbq; 5% statics; phone; Eng spkn; adv bkg acc; lake fishing; games area; CKE. *"Peaceful, attractive site; poss diff access to pitches for lge c'vans due narr site rds & low terrs; clean san facs; beautiful pool; Michelin starred rest nrby; brilliant site; great loc; excel fam facs; warm welcome fr new owner; pleasant town, great mkt; high rec."* **€30.00, 28 Apr-30 Sep.** 2018

"That's changed – Should I let the Club know?"

If you find something on site that's different from the site entry, fill in a report and let us know. See camc.com/europereport.

BUGUE, LE *7C3* (6km SW Rural) *44.87990, 0.88576* **Camping du Port de Limeuil,** 24480 Alles-sur-Dordogne 05 53 63 29 76; didierbonvallet@aol.com; www.leportdelimeuil.com

Exit Le Bugue on D31 sp Le Buisson; in 4km turn R on D51 sp Limeuil; at 2km turn L over rv bdge; site on R after bdge. 3*, Med, hdg, mkd, pt shd, pt sl, serviced pitches; EHU (5A) €3.50; gas; bbq; 40% statics; Eng spkn; adv bkg acc; bike hire; canoe hire; games rm; CKE. *"Superb location & site for all ages; rv adj; lge pitches; clean san facs, ltd LS; tour ops."* **€32.00, 26 Apr-23 Sep, A16.** 2019

BUGUE, LE 7C3 (9km NW Rural) 44.95130, 0.85070
Camping St Avit Loisirs, 24260 St Avit-de-Vialard
05 53 02 64 00; contact@saint-avit-loisirs.com;
www.saint-avit-loisirs.com or www.les-castels.com

€2-5.10 ⭐ [WO] ⚓ ♿ ♨ ☐ ✎ [MP] 🦋 🍴 ⛄ 🍺 ⚠ ✗

☒ (covrd, htd) 🚮

Leave N89/E70 SE of Périgueux & turn S onto D710
for approx 32km; about 3km N of Le Bugue turn R
sp St Avit-de-Vialard. Turn R in vill & cont for approx
1.5km, site on R. NB Narr, twisting app rd.
5*, Lge, hdg, pt shd, pt sl, EHU (6A) inc; gas; bbq;
TV; adv bkg acc; ccard acc; games area; golf nr; bike
hire; games rm; waterslide; horseriding nr; tennis;
watersports nr; CKE. "Excel, well-kept, well-run, busy
site; gd sized pitches; friendly welcome; no o'fits over
7m; gd, clean san facs; archery nrby; gd touring base;
conv for Lascaux; many static tents; amazing array of
watersport facs." €49.00, 26 Mar-24 Sep, D10.   2016

BUIS LES BARONNIES 9D2 (0.6km N Urban) 44.27558,
5.27830 **Camp Municipal,** Quartier du Jalinier, 26170
Buis-les-Baronnies 04 75 28 04 96 or 06 60 80
40 53 (mob)

🐾 €1.20 ⭐ [WO] ⚓ ☐ ✎ 🦋 🍴

Fr Vaison-la-Romaine S on D938; turn L onto D54/
D13/D5 to Buis-les-Baronnies; cont N onto D546;
at bend turn R over rv bdge; turn L along rv, then
1st R. Site split into 2 either side of sw pool; recep
in upper site. Med, hdg, mkd, pt shd, pt sl, EHU (6A)
€3; 5% statics; phone; bus 300m; CKE. "Lovely views;
san facs dated but clean; not suitable lge o'fits but lger,
more accessible pitches on lower level; attractive town;
gd mkt Wed & Sat; fair; warden in off 1900-2000 only."
€11.50, 1 Mar-11 Nov.   2015

"There aren't many sites open at this time of year"

If you're travelling outside peak season
remember to call ahead to check site opening
dates – even if the entry says 'open all year'.

BUIS LES BARONNIES 9D2 (5km SW Rural) 44.25190,
5.24370 **Camping La Gautière,** La Penne-sur-l'Ouvèze,
26170 Buis-les-Baronnies 04 75 28 02 68;
accueil@camping-lagautiere.com; www.camping-
lagautiere.com

🐾 €2.50 ⭐ (htd) ⚓ ☐ ✎ 🦋 🍴 ⛄ 🍺 ⚠ ✗

On D5 Vaison-la-Romaine to Buis-les-Baronnies rd,
on L. 3*, Sm, mkd, pt shd, EHU (3-10A) €3-4.60; gas;
bbq; 5% statics; phone; bus adj; Eng spkn; adv bkg
acc; ccard acc; games rm; fishing nr; horseriding nr;
games area; CKE. "Beautiful situation; haphazard pitch
size; diff for o'fits over 6m; climbing at Rocher St Julien
& Gorges d'Ubrieux; helpful owners; ACSI acc; excel
cycling." €24.50, 26 Mar-31 Oct.   2016

BURTONCOURT 5D2 (1km W Rural) 49.22485, .
6.39929 **FFCC Camping La Croix du Bois Sacker,**
57220 Burtoncourt 03 87 35 74 08; camping.croix
sacker@wanadoo.fr; www.campingcroixsacker.com

🐾 €1.70 ⭐ ⚓ ♿ ☐ ✎ [MP] 🦋 🍴 🍴 ⛄ nr 🍺 ⚠ ✗

Exit A4 junc 37 sp Argancy; at rndabt foll sp Malroy;
at 2nd rndabt foll sp Chieuilles & cont to Vany;
then take D3 for 12km dir Bouzonville; turn R onto
D53A to Burtoncourt. 2*, Lge, hdstg, mkd, hdg, pt
shd, terr, EHU (6A) inc; gas; TV; 10% statics; phone;
bus 300m; Eng spkn; adv bkg acc; fishing; tennis;
games area; CKE. "Lovely, wooded site in beautiful
location; lge pitches; pleasant, friendly owners;
clean san facs; forest walks; gd security; gd NH or
sh stay en rte Alsace/Germany; conv Maginot Line;
excel; Hachenberg Ouvrage tour highly rec (30km)."
€20.00, 1 Apr-20 Oct.   2016

"That's changed – Should I let the Club know?"

If you find something on site that's different
from the site entry, fill in a report and let us
know. See camc.com/europereport.

BUXIERES-SOUS-MONTAIGUT 7A4 (3.8km SW Rural)
46.19271, 2.81994 **Camping Les Suchères,** Les
Sucheres, 63700 Buxierères-sous-Montaigut
33 04 73 85 92 66; sucheres@gmail.com;
www.campinglessucheres.com

🐾 €1.50 ⭐ [WO] ⚓ ♿ ☐ ✎ 🦋 🍴 🍴 ⚠ ☒

Head SE on D92, cont on Buxières. Take Les Gouttes
to Les Sucheres; 1st R onto Buxières; cont onto Les
Gouttes after 7m turn R twd Les Sucheres, L twd Les
Sucheres, 1st R onto Les Sucheres, turn L to stay on
Les Sucheres, take the 1st L to stay on Les Sucheres;
site on R. Sm, pt sl, EHU (6A) €3; bbq; TV; Eng spkn;
CCI. "Helpful Dutch owners; lovely peaceful site; gd
walking area; Montaigut within walking dist; shop;
access to the site could be diff for lge o'fits as rd narr
for last km; quiet." €27.80, 1 Apr-30 Sep.   2019

BUZANCAIS 4H2 (0.5km N Urban) 46.89309, 1.41801
Camp Municipal La Tête Noire, Allée des Sports,
36500 Buzançais 06 59 88 78 32; buzancais@
wanadoo.fr

🐾 €1.50 ⭐ ⚓ ♿ ☐ ✎ [MP] 🦋 🍴 nr ⛄ nr 🍺 nr ⚠ ✗

D943 fr Châteauroux thro town cent, cross rv,
immed turn R into sports complex. 3*, Lge, hdstg,
pt shd, EHU (16A) inc; red long stay; 10% statics;
adv bkg acc; CKE. "Pleasant, peaceful, well-kept
site on rv; clean facs; no access when office clsd but
ample parking; no twin axles; pool 500m; gd fishing."
€16.00, 15 Apr-15 Oct.   2019

BUZANCY *5C1* (1.5km SW Rural) *49.42647, 4.93891*
Camping La Samaritaine, 08240 **03 24 30 08 88;**
contact@camping-lasamaritaine.fr; www.camping-
lasamaritaine.fr

🐾 €2.20 ⚏ wD ♨ ♿ 🍴 ✎ msp 🦋 ⛱ 🍽 ⊕nr ♨ ⚒ ⛺

Fr Sedan take D977 dir Vouziers for 23km. Turn
L onto D12, cont to end & turn L onto D947 for
Buzancy. On ent Buzancy in 100m turn 2nd R immed
after g'ge on R sp Camping Stade. Foll sp to site on
L past football pitches. 3*, Med, hdstg, mkd, hdg,
pt shd, serviced pitches; EHU (10A) inc; bbq (charcoal,
gas); sw nr; TV; 10% statics; phone; Eng spkn; adv bkg
acc; tennis; games rm; horseriding nr; fishing; CKE.
*"Beautiful area for walking/cycling; library; helpful,
pleasant staff; excel facs, ltd LS."*
€21.00, 19 Apr-13 Sep, L30.   **2019**

CABOURG *3D1* (6km W Coastal) *49.28319, -0.19098*
Camping Le Point du Jour, Route de Cabourg, 14810
Merville-Franceville-Plage **02 31 24 23 34;** contact@
camping-lepointdujour.com; www.camping-
lepointdujour.com

🐾 €3 ⚏(htd) wD ♨ ♿ 🍴 ✎ msp 🦋 ⚑ 🍽 ⊕ ♨ ⚒ ⛺ ✦
⛷(covrd, htd) 🏖 sand adj

Fr Ouistreham on D514 turn E at Bénouville onto
D224, cross bdge onto D514, site on L dir Cabourg,
8km beyond Pegasus Bdge at far end of Merville.
Or fr A13/D675 exit Dozulé dir Cabourg, then D514
to site. 4*, Med, hdg, pt shd, EHU (10A) €5 (poss rev
pol); gas; bbq; red long stay; TV; 40% statics; bus;
adv bkg acc; ccard acc; games rm; CKE. *"Site with sea
views; direct access to Sword Beach (D-Day) & sand
dunes; conv Pegasus Bdge; some pitches might be diff
for lge o'fits; open till 2300 for late ferry arr, v obliging;
ent & exit diff; sm-med pitches, many sl; facs tired."*
€37.00, 31 Mar-30 Oct, N03.   **2017**

"I like to fill in the reports as I travel from site to site"

You'll find report forms at the back of this
guide, or you can fill them in online at
camc.com/europereport.

CABOURG *3D1* (6km W Coastal) *49.28296, -0.19072*
Camping Village Ariane, 100 Route de Cabourg,
14810 Merville-Franceville-Plage **02 31 24 52 52;**
info@loisirs-ariane.com; www.camping-ariane.com

🐾 €3 ⚏(htd) wD ♨ ♿ 🍴 ✎ 🦋 ⚑ 🍽 ⊕nr ⛺ ✦ 🏊 sand 300m

Fr Ouistreham on D514 turn E at Bénouville onto
D224, cross bdge onto D514 to site dir Cabourg. Or
fr A13/D675 exit Dozulé dir Cabourg, then D514 to
site. 3*, Lge, mkd, pt shd, EHU (6-10A) €4; gas; red
long stay; TV; 10% statics; Eng spkn; adv bkg acc;
games area; tennis nr; games rm; watersports nr; CKE.
€12.00, 1 Apr-5 Nov.   **2018**

CABRERETS *7D3* (1km NE Rural) *44.50771, 1.66234*
Camping Cantal, 46330 Cabrerets **05 65 31 26 61**

⚏ wD ♨ ✎ 🐾

Fr Cahors take D653 E for approx 15km bef turning
R onto D662 E thro Vers & St Géry. Turn L onto D41
to Cabrerets. Site 1km after vill on R.
2*, Sm, pt shd, pt sl, serviced pitches; EHU €2.50; rv
canoeing nr; CKE. *"Superb situation; v interesting vill;
peaceful site; warden calls; grnd slightly bumpy; excel
san facs; not suitable lge o'fits; conv Pech Merle; gd
cycling rte; quiet; friendly; overhanging trees, care
when pitching; unisex san facs; vg."*
€12.00, 1 Apr-15 Oct.   **2017**

"We must tell the Club about that great site we found"

Get your site reports in by mid-August and we'll
do our best to get your updates into the next
edition.

CADENET *10E3* (5km N Rural) *43.767986, 5.372672*
Les Hautes Prairies, 28 route de Vaugines 84160,
Lourmarin **04 90 68 02 89;** leshautesprairies@
campasun.eu; www.campasun-lourmarin.eu

🐾 €5 ⚏ wD ♨ ✎ 🦋 ⚑ 🍽 ⊕ ♨ ⚒ nr ⛺ 🏊

Fr D973 take exit to Cadenet. Fork L (eastbnd)
at rd junc twrds Lourmarin. In Lourmarin turn R
at 2nd rndabt. Site on R in 0.5km. 3*, Med, hdstg,
mkd, hdg, pt shd, pt sl, EHU (10A) inc; bbq (sep area);
twin axles; bus adj; Eng spkn; adv bkg acc; ccard
acc; jacuzzi; sm shop in recep; games area; CKE. *"Gd
gateway for Luberon area; lovely spacious site; v clean,
well maintained facs (new 2016); v helpful staff; gd
security (barrier); excel & enjoyable experience; excel."*
€45.00, 6 Apr-29 Sep.   **2019**

CADENET *10E3* (10km NE Rural) *43.76871, 5.44970*
Camping Lou Badareu, La Rasparine, 84160
Cucuron **04 90 77 21 46;** contact@loubadareu.com;
www.loubadareu.com

🐾 €1.80 ⚏ wD ♨ ♿ 🍴 ✎ 🦋 ⚒ ⛺ 🏊

In Cadenet foll sp for church (église) onto D45 dir
Cucuron; S of Cucuron turn onto D27 (do not go
into town); site is E 1km. Well sp fr D27.
2*, Sm, mkd, pt shd, pt sl, EHU (10A) €4.50 (long lead
poss req); own san rec; 10% statics; phone; CKE.
*"Pretty farm site in cherry orchard, vineyard and olive
grove adj; basic but adequate san facs; natural spring-
fed pool; friendly, helpful owner; sep access for high
vans; lge shd camping field."*
€16.70, 1 Apr-15 Oct.   **2017**

CAEN *3D1* (20km N Coastal) *49.32551, -0.39010* **Sandaya La Côte de Nacre,** 17 Rue du Général Moulton, 14750 St Aubin-sur-Mer **02 31 97 14 45; cdn@sandaya.fr; www.sandaya.fr/cdn**

€5 (htd) (covrd, htd) sand 500m

Fr Caen on D7 dir Douvres-la-Délivrande, Langrune-sur-Mer & St Aubin. Site in St Aubin-sur-Mer on S side of D514; clearly sp on o'skts. 5*, Lge, hdstg, mkd, hdg, pt shd, EHU (10A); bbq (charcoal); TV; 70% statics; phone; Eng spkn; adv bkg rec; ccard acc; sauna; waterslide; bike hire; games rm; tennis 200m; CKE. *"Ideal for families; lge pitches; conv Caen ferry, Normandy beaches, WW2 sites; helpful staff; excel modern san facs; poss waterlogging; gd cycle tracks along sea front LS; easy walk into quiet vill; vg; payment on arr, no refund for early dep; vg site."*
€25.50, 3 Apr-20 Sep, N11. **2019**

CAGNES SUR MER *10E4* (4km N Rural) *43.68717, 7.15589* **Camping Le Val Fleuri,** 139 Vallon-des-Vaux, 06800 Cagnes-sur-Mer **04 93 31 21 74; valfleur2@wanadoo.fr; www.campingvalfleuri.fr**

€1.50 nr (htd) shgl 4km

Fr Nice take D6007 W twd Cannes. On app Cagnes turn R & foll sp Camping; site on R after 3km, well sp. NB 3.3m height restriction on this rte.
3*, Sm, pt shd, terr, EHU (3-10A); Eng spkn; adv bkg acc. *"Gd, clean, improving site, efficient NH; divided by rd (not busy); some sm pitches; helpful, friendly owners; bus to Nice; dated facs (2014); diff access lge o'fits; no offsite parking."* **€31.00, 6 Apr-28 Sep.** **2019**

CAGNES SUR MER *10E4* (5km S Coastal) *43.63128, 7.12993* **Camping Parc des Maurettes,** 730 Ave du Docteur Lefebvre, 06270 Villeneuve-Loubet **04 93 20 91 91; info@parcdesmaurettes.com; www.parcdesmaurettes.com**

€4 (htd) nr nr nr (htd, indoor) shgl 1km

Fr Nice exit A8 junc 47, turn L onto D6007 dir Antibes; foll sp Intermarché, then R into Rue des Maurettes; site in 250m. N fr Cannes on A8 exit Villeneuve-Loubet-Plage junc 46; foll D241 over D6007 & rwly line, U-turn back over rwly line, then R onto D6007 dir Antibes as above. NB Site on steep cliff with narr winding rds packed with trees; diff ent.
3*, Med, mkd, pt shd, terr, serviced pitches; EHU (3-10A) €5.30; gas; bbq (charcoal, sep area); twin axles; red long stay; TV (pitch); train Nice 400m; Eng spkn; adv bkg rec; ccard acc; jacuzzi; CKE. *"Well-kept site; variable pitch size/price; excel base for Nice, Cannes, Antibes & Monaco; trains & bus fare gd value."*
€35.80, 10 Jan-15 Nov. **2019**

CAGNES SUR MER *10E4* (7km S Rural) *43.62027, 7.12583* **Camping La Vieille Ferme,** 296 Blvd des Groules, 06270 Villeneuve-Loubet-Plage **04 93 33 41 44; info@vieilleferme.com; www.vieilleferme.com**

12 €2.50 (htd) nr (covrd, htd) shgl 1km

Fr W (Cannes) take Antibes exit 44 fr A8, foll D35 dir Antibes 'Centre Ville'. At lge junc turn onto D6007, Ave de Nice, twd Biot & Villeneuve-Loubet sp Nice (rlwy line on R). Just after Marineland turn L onto Blvd des Groules. Fr E (Nice) leave A8 at junc 47 to join D6007 twd Antibes, take 3rd turning after Intermarché supmkt; site well sp fr D6007.
4*, Med, mkd, hdg, pt shd, pt sl, terr, serviced pitches; EHU (2A-10A) €3 - €7; gas; bbq (elec, gas); red long stay; TV; 40% statics; bus, train nr; Eng spkn; adv bkg acc; ccard acc; games rm. *"Peaceful, well-kept family-run site; well-drained pitches, some lge; san facs need refurb (2010); beach not suitable children & non-swimmers; no o'fits over 8m; excel pool; gd walking, cycling & dog walking as lge park adj; some aircraft & rd noise; vg value LS; excel; be wary of bike thieves; nice bar/rest; friendly staff; v quiet at night; bus & train nrby."* **€41.00, C22.** **2018**

CAGNES SUR MER *10E4* (1km NW Urban) *43.67159, 7.13845* **Camping Le Colombier,** 35 Chemin de Ste Colombe, 06800 Cagnes-sur-Mer **04 93 73 12 77; campinglecolombier06@gmail.com; www.campinglecolombier.com**

€2.50 (htd) nr nr 2.5km

N fr Cagnes cent foll 1-way system dir Vence. Half way up hill turn R at rndabt dir Cagnes-sur-Mer & R at next island. Site on L 300m, sp fr town cent.
3*, Sm, hdg, mkd, pt shd, EHU (2-16A) (poss rev pol) €2-8; red long stay; TV; 10% statics; phone; Eng spkn; bike hire; CKE. *"Friendly, family-run site; dogs not acc Jul/Aug; sm pool adj."* **€30.00, 1 Apr-1 Oct.** **2019**

CAGNES SUR MER *10E4* (4km NW Rural) *43.68272, 7.08391* **Camping Les Pinèdes,** Route de Pont de Pierre, 06480 La Colle-sur-Loup **04 93 32 98 94; info@lespinedes.com; www.lespinedes.com**

€3.60 (htd)

Exit A8 junc 47; take D6007 dir Nice, then D2 sp Villeneuve-Loubet; turn R at rndabt sp Villeneuve-Loubet & cross rv bdge; go thro sh tunnel, other side is Cagnes-sur-Mer & rndabt; turn L onto D6 to Colle-sur-Loup; site on R sh dist after Colle-sur-Loup. NB Take 2nd turning into site (1st leads to rest).
4*, Lge, hdstg, mkd, hdg, pt shd, pt sl, terr, serviced pitches; EHU (6-10A) €4.60-5.90 (poss rev pol); bbq (elec, gas); sw nr; red long stay; TV; 20% statics; Eng spkn; adv bkg acc; ccard acc; rv fishing adj; games rm; archery; tennis adj; horseriding adj; games area; solarium; CKE. *"Excel, family-run site set in pine & oak trees; no c'vans over 6m (excluding towbar) & m'vans over 8m high ssn; helpful & friendly; spacious pitches; steep access to pitches - poss diff lge o'fits, help avail; adequate san facs; gd rest at site ent; highly rec; vg site has everything you need; spacious pitches; excel pool."*
€43.00, 1 Apr-30 Sep, C30. **2019**

CAHORS *7D3* (2km N Urban) *44.46318, 1.44226*
Camping Rivière de Cabessut, Rue de la Rivière,
46000 Cahors 05 65 30 06 30; contact@cabessut.com;
www.cabessut.com

🐕 €2 👪 ⓌⒸ ▲ ♿ ⑤ 🐾 / ᴹᴾ 🦋 ⑨ ☂ 🛒 ⚠ 🏊

Fr N or S on D820, at S end Cahors by-pass take L
onto D620 sp Rodez. At traff lts by bdge do not cross
rv but bear R on D911. In 1km at site sp turn L. Site
on E bank of Rv Lot, well sp fr town. Site at end of
long lane. 1.8km to site fr bdge (Pont Cabessut). (NB:
Fr N if leaving A20 at J57 - Do not foll Sat Nav.)
3*, Med, hdg, mkd, pt shd, serviced pitches; EHU
(10A) inc (poss rev pol); gas; bbq (gas); 5% statics;
phone; bus to Cahors 600m; adv bkg req; CKE. *"Lovely,
well-run site by rv; beautiful area; pleasant, mostly lge
pitches, sm pitches diff access when site full; gd for
children; walk to town by rv 1.8km; food mkt Wed, full
mkt Sat; hypmkt 1.5km; excel san facs; well maintained
site, helpful, commited owners; rv adj; great site with
lge sunny or shd pitches; pre-ordered bread delivered
daily; lge o'fits turned away if grnd is damp; adv bkg
req Jul/Aug; free shuttle bus to Cahors 600m at park &
ride."* **€26.00, 1 Apr-30 Sep.** 2019

CAHORS *7D3* (8km N Rural) *44.52585, 1.46048*
Camping Les Graves, 46090 St Pierre-Lafeuille 05 65
36 83 12; infos@camping-lesgraves.com;
www.camping-lesgraves.com

🐕 €1.50 👪 ⓌⒸ ▲ ♿ ⑤ 🐾 / ᴹᴾ 🍴 ⑨ ☂ ⚠ 🏊

Leave A20 at junc 57 Cahors Nord onto D820. Foll
sp St Pierre-Lafeuille; at N end of vill, site is opp
L'Atrium wine cave. 3*, Med, hdg, pt shd, sl, EHU (6-
10A) €2.50-3.50 (poss rev pol); 5% statics; Eng spkn;
adv bkg rec; ccard acc; bike hire; CKE. *"Scenic site; lge
pitches; poss clsd during/after wet weather due boggy
grnd; disabled facs over stony rd & grass; ltd facs LS;
conv A20; nice, quiet, clean site."*
€20.00, 1 Apr-31 Oct. 2018

CAHORS *7D3* (8km N Rural) *44.53136, 1.45926*
Camping Quercy-Vacances, Mas de la Combe, 46090
St Pierre-Lafeuille 05 65 36 87 15; quercyvacances@
wanadoo.fr; www.quercy-vacances.com

🐕 €1.50 👪 ⓌⒸ ▲ ♿ ⑤ 🐾 / ᴹᴾ 🦋 ⑨ 🍴 ⑨ ☂ 🛒 ⚠ 🏊 🍴

Heading N on D820, turn L at N end of St Pierre-
Lafeuille turn W at site sp N of vill, site in 700m
down lane. Site sp fr main rd. Fr A20 exit junc 57
& foll sp N20. 4*, Med, mkd, pt shd, pt sl, EHU (10A)
€3.30-5.30; gas; twin axles; TV; 50% statics; phone;
Eng spkn; adv bkg acc; ccard acc; games area; CKE.
*"Pretty site; most pitches slightly sl; clean, modern
san facs; poss unkempt LS; helpful owner; vg; tennis
& horse riding nrby; gd for Cahors & Lot Valley."*
€23.00, 1 Apr-30 Sep. 2017

CAJARC *7D4* (6.4km NE Rural) *44.50612, 1.89667*
Camping Les Cournoulises, 46160 Montbrun 06 15
53 00 58 (mob); lescournoulises@sfr.fr;
http://lescournoulises.perso.sfr.fr

🐕 €0.50 👪 ⓌⒸ ♿ ⑤ 🐾 / 🦋 ⑨ ☂ 🛒 ⚠

Fr Cahors foll D662 or fr Figeac D19. Foll D622
along N bank of R Lot for 6km. Site well sp on app.
2*, Sm, mkd, pt shd, EHU (6A) €3; bbq (charcoal,
sep area); twin axles; red long stay; bus adj; Eng
spkn; adv bkg acc; games area; canoe hire; tennis nr;
fishing; CKE. *"Lge pitches; teepee & trapper tents on
site (for hire); many attractions within 30km radius;
dir access to rv; fishing rods avail; friendly, helpful
owner; excel; paragliding; trekking; htd pool 6km;
beautiful site; spotless facs; wonderful; highly rec."*
€14.00, 1 Apr-10 Oct. 2017

CAJARC *7D4* (0.3km SW Urban) *44.48374, 1.83928*
Camp Municipal Le Terriol, Rue Le Terriol, 46160
Cajarc 05 65 40 72 74 or 05 65 40 65 20 (Mairie);
mairie.cajarc@wanadoo.fr; www.cajarc.fr

🐕 👪 (cont) ⓌⒸ ▲ ♿ ⑤ 🐾 / 🍴 nr ⑨ nr 🛒 / ⚠

Fr Cahors dir Cajarc on D662 on L foll sp to site.
2*, Sm, hdstg, hdg, mkd, pt shd, EHU (10A) inc
(poss rev pol); bbq; phone; Eng spkn; adv bkg acc;
tennis 500m; CKE. *"Gd sized pitches; clean, basic
facs; lovely sm town on Rv Lot; pool 500m; vg."*
€15.50, 1 May-30 Sep. 2017

CAJARC *7D4* (6km W Rural) *44.4735, 1.7835*
Camping Ruisseau du Treil, 46160 Larnagol
05 65 31 23 39; contact@lotcamping.com;
www.lotcamping.com

🐕 €3.90 👪 ⓌⒸ ▲ ♿ ⑤ 🐾 / 🦋 🍴 ☂ ⚠ 🏊

Exit A20 junc 57 onto D49 sp St Michel; in 4km turn
R onto D653; after 5.5km in Vers at mini-rndabt turn
L onto D662; site on L immed after leaving Larnagol.
Or fr Figeac foll D19 thro Cajarc. At top of hill leaving
Cajarc turn R onto D662 sp Cahors & Larnagol. Site sp
on R 300m bef Larnagol on blind bend. 3*, Sm, mkd,
pt shd, pt sl, EHU (6A) €4; bbq; sw nr; TV; 4% statics;
adv bkg acc; canoeing adj; fishing adj; games rm;
bike hire; horseriding; CKE. *"Beautiful, spacious,
peaceful site in lovely area; well-run; friendly, helpful
British owners; clean san facs but ltd when site full;
lge pitches poss uneven; many long-stay/returning
campers; library; guided walks; vg touring base; excel."*
€28.00, 8 May-8 Sep. 2019

CALAIS *3A3* (12km NE Coastal) *50.98907, 1.98545*
Les Argousiers, 766 rue des hemmes, 62215 Oye-Plage
03 21 35 32 78; lesargousiers@wanadoo.fr;
www.lesargousiers.com

🐕 €2 👪 ⓌⒸ ▲ ⑤ 🐾 / ᴹᴾ 🦋 🐾 sand 2km

Take D940 fr A16 (exit 49) or Calais. In Oye-Plage,
turn L & foll sp for Les Argousiers Camping. Sm, hdg,
unshd, EHU; bbq; twin axles; 95% statics; bus 100m;
CKE. *"Few touring pitches; gd NH; friendly & helpful
owners."* **€13.70, 1 Mar-31 Jan.** 2015

FRANCE

CALAIS 3A3 (13km SW Rural) 50.91160, 1.75127 **Camping Les Epinettes,** Impasse de Mont Pinet, 62231 Peuplingues 03 21 85 21 39; lesepinettes@aol.com; www.lesepinettes.fr

🛖 €1.50 ⑪ ⅢⅢ ⌂ ♨ ✗ 🐕 🍽 ⑪ nr 🛒 ∧ 🌳 sand 3km

A16 fr Calais to Boulogne, exit junc 40 W on D243 sp **Peuplingues,** go thro vill & foll sp; site on L in 3km. 2*, Lge, hdg, pt shd, pt sl, EHU (4-10A) €1.60-3.80; 80% statics; phone; adv bkg acc; ccard acc; CKE. "Pleasant, easy-going, quiet site; conv NH for m'way, ferries & tunnel; some pitches sm; san facs clean; when bureau clsd, site yourself - warden calls eve or call at cottage to pay; library; if arr late, park on grass verge outside main gate - use facs excel elec, pay half price; few touring pitches." **€15.50, 1 Apr-31 Oct.** 2017

CALAIS 3A3 (4km SW Coastal) 50.95677, 1.81101 **Camp du Fort Lapin,** Route Provincial 940, 62231 Sangatte-Blériot Plage 03 21 97 67 77; campingdufortlapin@orange.fr; www.campingdu fortlapin.fr

🛖 ⅢⅢ ⑪ ⌂ ♨ ♿ 🔲 ✗ 🐕 🍽 Ⓨ ⑪ ♨ 🛒 nr ∧ 🌳 sand adj

Fr E exit junc 43 fr A16 Calais cent, dir beach (Blériot-Plage). Turn L along coast onto D940 dir Sangatte; site on R in dunes shortly after water tower, opp sports cent; site sp fr D940. Fr S exit A16 junc 41 to Sangatte; at T-junc turn R onto D940; site on L just bef water tower. 3*, Med, mkd, unshd, pt sl, EHU (10A) inc (poss rev pol); bbq; 50% statics; phone; bus; adv bkg acc; CKE. "Conv ferry; warden lives on site; rec arr bef 1700 high ssn; gates clsd 2300-0700; recep 0900-1200 & 1600-2000, barrier clsd when recep clsd; ltd parking outside espec w/end - phone ahead for access code; gd bus service; basic, clean, adequate san facs (shwrs and lndry clsd after 2100); conv Auchan & Cité Europe shops; poss youth groups high ssn; conv NH; close to beach; clean tidy site; adequate facs; grnd v well drained; easy cycle into Calais or walk along the promenade to the harbour ent." **€18.40, 1 Apr-31 Oct.** 2018

CALAIS 3A3 (5km W Coastal) 50.94610, 1.75798 **Camping des Noires Mottes,** Rue Pierre Dupuy, 62231 Sangatte; www.ville-sangatte.fr

🛖 €1.30 ⅢⅢ ⑪ ⌂ ♨ 🔲 ✗ 🍽 🛒 nr ∧ 🌳 sand 500m

Fr A16 exit junc 41 sp Sangatte onto D243, at T-junc in vill turn R then R again bef monument. 3*, Lge, hdg, mkd, pt shd, pt sl, EHU (10A) €4.10; 90% statics; bus 500m; Eng spkn; adv bkg rec; CKE. "Conv ferries & Eurotunnel; lge pitches; san facs clean; barrier - no arr bef office opens 1500 (1600 LS); san facs clsd o'night & poss 1200-1600; some pitches boggy when wet; windy spot; OK NH; well maintained site." **€23.60, 1 Apr-31 Oct.** 2018

CALAIS 3A3 (3km NW Coastal) 50.96603, 1.84370 **Aire Communale,** Plage de Calais, Ave Raymond Poincaré, 62100 Calais 03 21 97 89 79, 03 21 46 66 41 or 06 79 62 93 22 (mob); camping@marie-calais.fr

🔢12 ⅢⅢ ⑪ nr 🛒 nr

A16 exit junc 43 dir Blériot-Plage/Calais cent & foll sp for beach (plage). Site nr harbour wall & Fort Risban. Well sp fr town cent. Med,. "M'vans only; well-kept, busy site; gd NH to/fr ferries; obtain token/pass fr Camp Municipal adj; warden calls to collect fee pm or pay at Camp Municipal." **€8.00** 2016

CALAIS 3A3 (3km NW Coastal) 50.959323, 1.831833 **Camping Municipal Le Grande Gravelot,** 62100 Calais 03 91 91 52 34; camping@mairie-calais.fr

🛖 🐕 ⅢⅢ ⑪ ⌂ ♨ ♿ 🔲 ✗ 🅼🅿 🍽 🍽 🐕 🌳 250m

Head for Calais beach. Site at end of Port de Plaisance dock on rd behind hses & flats o'look beach. Med, mkd, hdg, unshd, EHU (16A) inc; twin axles; TV; phone; bus; Eng spkn; adv bkg acc; sauna; games rm; bike hire; CCI. "Excel; aire de svr adj to site all year round; site patrolled at night; local cafes nrby; short walk to town." **€17.00, 1 Apr-31 Oct.** 2018

CAMARET SUR MER 2E1 (3km NE Coastal) 48.28070, -4.56490 **Camping Le Grand Large,** Lambézen, 29570 Camaret-sur-Mer 02 98 27 91 41; contact@ campinglegrandlarge.com; www.campinglegrand large.com

🛖 €3 ⅢⅢ ⑪ ⌂ ♨ ♿ 🔲 ✗ 🅼🅿 🍽 🍽 Ⓨ ♨ 🛒 ∧
🏊 (htd) 🏄 🌳 shgl 500m

On D8 bet Crozen & Camaret, turn R at ent to Camaret onto D355, sp Roscanvel. Foll sps to site in 3km. 4*, Med, hdg, mkd, pt shd, pt sl, EHU (10A) inc; gas; bbq; TV; adv bkg acc; ccard acc; tennis; boating. "Coastal views fr some pitches, lovely beach; pleasant, helpful owners; 45 min cliff top walk to town; excel; excel location; do not arr bef 2pm if not prebooked." **€28.00, 30 Mar-30 Sep.** 2018

CAMARET SUR MER 2E1 (4km NE Coastal) 48.28788, -4.56540 **Camping Plage de Trez-Rouz,** Route de Camaret à Roscanvel, 29160 Crozon 02 98 27 93 96; contact@trezrouz.com; www.trezrouz.com

🛖 €1.50 ⅢⅢ ⑪ ⌂ ♨ ♿ 🔲 ✗ 🍽 🍽 Ⓨ ⑪ ♨ 🛒 ∧
🏊 (htd) 🌳 sand

Foll D8 to Camaret-sur-Mer & at rndabt turn N sp Roscanvel/D355. Site on R in 3km. 3*, Med, mkd, hdg, pt shd, pt sl, EHU (16A) €3.50; 10% statics; adv bkg acc; horseriding 2km; tennis 500m; CKE. "Great position opp beach; conv for Presqu'île de Crozon; gd facs but stretched high ssn; site scruffy LS; friendly helpful owner; gd hot shwrs." **€19.00, 15 Mar-15 Oct.** 2016

CAMBRAI *3B4* (2.5km W Urban) *50.17533, 3.21534*
FFCC Camp Municipal Les Trois Clochers, 77 Rue
Jean Goudé, 59400 Cambrai 03 27 70 91 64

🏕👭 (htd) **ⓦ 🔥 ♨ ♿ ⊘ ⬛** ⓘ nr **🔋** nr

Exit A2 junc 14; at rndabt after slip rd (with 6 exits)
take D630 dir Cambrai; in 1km (by Buffalo Grill)
turn L onto D630; in 200m turn L onto D939; in
100m turn L into Rue Jean Goudé. Or fr Cambrai
W on D939; after x-ing rv bdge cont on D939 until
traff lts in 300m; go strt over traff lts, then in 100m
turn L into Rue Jean Goudé. Site sp fr all dirs on
ent town. 3*, Sm, hdg, unshd, EHU (5-8A) €2.50; Eng
spkn. *"Beautiful, well-kept site; gd, spacious pitches;
v conv Calais; early arr rec high ssn; v helpful, friendly
manager; gd san facs, ltd & stretched when site full;
interesting town; excel; 5 min walk to Aldi supmkt; hg
rec."* **€14.50, 15 Apr-15 Oct.** **2017**

CANCALE *2E4* (10km S Coastal) *48.61592, -1.85151*
Camping de l'Ile Verte, 42 Rue de l'Ile Verte, 35114
St Benoît-des-Ondes 02 99 58 62 55; camping-ile-
verte@sfr.fr; www.campingdelileverte.com

🏕 €2.50 **👭** (htd) **ⓦ 🔥 ⬛ ⊘** MSP **🦋 ⓣ** nr ⓘ nr **🔋 ⚫ 🏖** sand adj

Site on S side of vill. Fr Cancale, take D76 SW for
approx 4km, then turn L onto D155 into St Benoît.
Foll site sp. 3*, Sm, hdg, pt shd, EHU (6A) €4
(poss rev pol); gas; 3% statics; phone; adv bkg acc;
CKE. *"Well-kept, tidy site on edge of vill; facs poss
stretched high ssn; big pitches but narr access rds."*
€28.00, 30 Mar-31 Oct. **2018**

CANCON *7D3* (12km W Rural) *44.53461, 0.50555*
Camping Le Moulin, Lassalle, 47290 Monbahus 05 53
01 68 87; info@lemoulin-monbahus.com;
www.lemoulin-monbahus.com

12 🏕 👭 (wo) **🔥 ♨ ♿ ⊘** ⓘ **🔋** nr **⚫ ⬛ ✏ 🏖** (htd)

Fr N21 turn W at Cancon on D124 sp Miramont. In
7.5km at Monbahus pass thro vill cent take L turn,
still on D124 sp Tombeboeuf. In 3km lge grain silos
on L, site next on R. Sm, mkd, hdstg, pt shd, EHU
(5-10A) €3 (most pitches 5A only avail); bbq; Eng spkn;
adv bkg acc; bike hire; CKE. *"CL-type site in garden;
friendly British owners; bistro; clean, basic san facs; vg
pool; B & B avail; extra for twin axles over 5m; excel."*
€17.00 **2016**

CANDE SUR BEUVRON *4G2* (0.9km S Rural)
47.48952, 1.25834 **La Grande Tortue,** 3 Route de
Pontlevoy, 41120 Candé-sur-Beuvron 02 54 44 15 20;
camping@grandetortue.com; www.grande
tortue.com

🏕 €4.50 **👭** (htd) **ⓦ 🔥 ♨ ♿ ⊘** MSP **🦋 ⓣ ⓨ** ⓘ **⚫ 🔋 ⚠**

✏ 🏊 (covrd, htd) **⛵**

Exit A10 junc 17 (Blois) & foll 'Autres/Toutes
Directions' or 'Vierzon' to cross Rv Loire; immed
after bdge R onto D951/D971 dir Chaumont;
ignore D173 R fork & foll D751 thro Chailles &
Villelouet; R at rndabt to go thro Cande; fork L
after Cande; site on L in abt 100m.
5*, Lge, hdstg, mkd, hdg, pt shd, pt sl, EHU (10A)
€3.50; gas; bbq; TV; 50% statics; Eng spkn; adv
bkg acc; ccard acc; bike hire; games area; CKE.
*"Excel, rustic site amongst trees; poss diff access
due trees; helpful staff; vg, clean san facs; gd
pool; gd for children; gd cycling; gourmet rest
by rv bdge in vill; conv Loire chateaux; gd rest."*
€47.00, 4 Apr-13 Sep. **2019**

See advertisement

CANET PLAGE *10G1* (3km N Coastal) *42.70808,
3.03332* **Camping Le Brasilia,** 2 Ave des Anneux du
Roussillon, 66140 Canet-en-Roussillon 04 68 80 23 82;
info@lebrasilia.fr; www.brasilia.fr

🏕 €4 **👭** (wo) **🔥 ♨ ♿ ⊘** MSP **🦋 ⓨ ⓣ** ⓘ **⚫ 🔋 ⚠ ✏**

🏊 (htd) **⛵ 🏖** sand 150m

Exit A9 junc 41 sp Perpignan Nord & Rivesaltes
onto D83 dir Le Barcarès & Canet for 10km; then
take D81 dir Canet for 10km until lge rndabt which
goes under D617 (do not foll sp to Canet to R) -
cont round rndabt & foll sp Ste Marie-le-Mer (to
go back the way you came). Then take 1st R sp Le
Brasilia. 5*, V lge, mkd, hdg, pt shd, serviced pitches;
EHU (10A) inc; gas; bbq (elec, gas); twin axles; TV;
35% statics; bus to Canet; Eng spkn; ccard acc; bike
hire; tennis; fishing; archery; games rm; CKE. *"Excel,
well-run, well laid-out site; gd sized pitches; friendly
staff; immac san facs; excel facs, espec for families/
children/teenagers; rvside walk adj; conv day trips to
Barcelona,Carcassonne etc; daily mkt in Canet except
Mon."* **€54.00, 12 Apr-4 Oct, C01.** **2017**

FRANCE

CANET PLAGE *10G1* (3.5km N Coastal) *42.70905, 3.03285* **Camping Le Bosquet,** Ave des Anneaux du Roussillon, 66140 Canet-Plage **04 68 80 23 80;** campinglebosquet@club-internet.fr; www.campinglebosquet.com

🛒 ℰ3 � ⓦ ♨ ♿ 🅿 ∥ 🐕 ▼ ⑪ ⛵ 🔋 ⚠ ⚓ 🏊 ♇ sand 400m

Exit A9 junc 41 onto D83 dir Le Barcarès; then turn R onto D81 dir Canet; in Canet at lge rndabt go R round until exit dir Torreilles & Ste Marie; then immed after rndabt take sm rd on R; site sp. Or E on D617 fr Perpignan, turn L on D11 in Canet & foll sp. 3*, Med, hdg, mkd, pt shd, EHU (5A) €3.50; gas; bbq; TV; phone; bus adj; Eng spkn; adv bkg acc; ccard acc; games rm; games area; CKE. *"Family-run site nr excel sand beach; shops 2km - plenty of choice; gd touring base; vg."* **€49.00, 6 Apr-5 Oct.** 2019

CANET PLAGE *10G1* (4km NE Coastal) *42.72724, 3.03377* **Camping La Pergola,** 66470 Ste Marie la Mer 02 51 20 41 94; contact@camp-atlantique.com; www.campinglapergola.com

託 (cont) ♨ ∥ 🐕 🔋 ♇ sand 500m

S fr Narbonne, exit N9 at Salses & foll D11 to St Marie-sur-Mer. St Marie-Plage beach for St Marie-sur-Mer. Site not sp but on D12 to coast. 3*, Lge, pt shd, EHU; gas; adv bkg acc. *"No lge o'fits; v tricky maneuvering as too many trees."* **€39.00, 3 Apr-20 Sep.** 2015

CANET PLAGE *10G1* (4km W Urban) *42.70114, 2.99850* **Kawan Village Ma Prairie,** 1 Ave des Coteaux, 66140 Canet-en-Roussillon **04 68 73 26 17;** ma.prairie@wanadoo.fr; www.maprairie.com

🛒 ℰ5 託 ⓦ ♨ ♿ 🅿 ∥ 🐕 ⑪ ▼ ⛵ 🔋nr ⚠ ♇ 🏊 ♇ 🏊 sand 3km

Leave A9/E15 at junc 41, sp Perpignan Centre/Canet-en-Roussillon. Take D83, then D81 until Canet-en-Roussillon. At rndabt, take D617 dir Perpignan & in about 500m leave at exit 5. Take D11 dir St Nazaire, pass under bdge & at rndabt turn R. Site on L. 4*, Lge, hdg, shd, serviced pitches; EHU (10A) inc; gas; bbq (elec, gas); TV; 20% statics; bus to town nr; Eng spkn; adv bkg req; ccard acc; waterslide; games rm; sailing; waterskiing; canoeing; CKE. *"Peaceful, popular site; friendly, helpful owners; o'fits 7.5m & over by request; reg bus to beach (Jul/Aug); daily mkt Perpignan; gd."* **€51.00, 4 May-21 Sep, C05.** 2019

CANNET DES MAURES, LE *10F3* (4km N Rural) *43.42140, 6.33655* **FFCC Camping Domaine de la Cigalière,** Route du Thoronet, 83340 Le Cannet-des-Maures **04 94 73 81 06;** www.domaine-lacigaliere.com

🛒 ℰ2 託 ⓦ ♨ ♿ 🅿 ∥ 🐕 ▼ 🍴 ⚠ 🏊 (htd)

Exit A8 at Le Cannet-des-Maures onto D17 N dir Le Thoronet; site in 4km on R, sp. 3*, Med, hdg, mkd, hdstg, pt shd, pt sl, EHU (6A) €4; bbq (elec, gas); 20% statics; CKE. *"Peaceful site; lge pitches; St Tropez 44km; vg site."* **€32.00, 1 Apr-1 Nov.** 2019

CANOURGUE, LA *9D1* (7.4km W Rural) *44.43638, 3.1475* **Municipal la Vallèe,** Miége Rivière 48500 Canilhac **04 66 32 91 14 or 04 66 32 80 05;** commune.canilhac@wanadoo.fr

🛒 ℰ1 託 ⓦ ♨ ♿ 🅿 ∥ 🐕 ▼ ⑪ 🍴 ♨ 🔋 ⚠ 🏊 (htd) 🚣

Leave A75 at junc 40. Take D988 W, sp St Laurent d'Olt. Site on L at level x-ing after 10 mins. 2*, Sm, hdg, pt shd, EHU (16A) €3; bbq; TV; 10% statics; phone; adv bkg acc; games rm; fishing; CCI. *"Sm shop; supmkt 5km; next to rv (sw not allowed); horseriding nr; golf nr; canoeing nr; paintballing & quad biking nrby; conv for Gorges du Tarn & Aubrac; St Laurent d'Olt worth a visit."* **€17.00, 13 Jun-15 Sep.** 2019

CANY BARVILLE *3C2* (3km N Rural) *49.80375, 0.64960* **Camping Maupassant,** 12 Route de la Folie, 76450 Vittefleur **02 35 97 97 14;** campingmaupassant@orange.fr; www.camping-maupassant.com

🛒 託 (htd) ⓦ ♨ ♿ 🅿 ∥ 🐕

S fr St Valery-en-Caux on D925 dir Cany-Barville; site sp turning to R 700m bef Cany-Barville. 2*, Med, hdg, mkd, hdstg, pt shd, EHU (6A) €3.30; gas; bbq (charcoal); 10% statics; phone; adv bkg acc; CKE. *"Friendly staff; gd NH; gd, clean site; 10 touring pitches."* **€20.00, 9 Mar-14 Dec.** 2016

CAPESTANG *10F1* (0.5km W Urban) *43.32759, 3.03865* **Camp Municipal de Tounel,** 1 Rue Georges Brassens, Ave de la République, 34310 Capestang **04 67 49 85 95;** mairie@ville-capestang.fr; www.capestang.fr

🛒 託 (cont) ⓦ ♨ ♿ 🅿 ∥ 🐕 ⑪nr 🔋nr ⚠

Fr Béziers on D11, turn R twd vill of Capestang, approx 1km after passing supmkt. Site on L in leisure park opp Gendamarie. 1*, Med, hdg, pt shd, EHU (6A) €3; tennis; bike hire; fishing. *"300m fr Canal de Midi; excel walks or bike rides; lovely rest in vill; LS site yourself, fees collected; facs poss tired LS; poss diff access to pitches for long o'fits; ltd EHU; poss resident workers; NH only."* **€15.00, 1 May-30 Sep.** 2019

CARCASSONNE *8F4* (8.6km N Rural) *43.25999, 2.36509* **FFCC Camping Das Pinhiers,** Chemin du Pont Neuf, 11620 Villemoustaussou **04 68 47 81 90;** camping daspinhiers@wanadoo.fr; www.camping-carcassonne.net

🛒 ℰ3 託 ⓦ ♨ ∥ 🐕 ▼ 🍴 ♨ 🔋 ⚠ 🏊

Exit A6 junc 23 Carcassonne Ouest & foll sp Mazamet on D118; R at rndabt with filling stn; turn R & foll camping sp. 3*, Med, hdg, shd, pt sl, EHU (10A) inc; 10% statics; bus 1 km; Eng spkn; adv bkg acc; ccard acc; CKE. *"Diff to pitch lge vans due hdg pitches & sl; san facs basic & stretched high ssn; general area rather run down (2009); office clsd noon-2pm."* **€18.00, 1 Apr-31 Oct.** 2015

FRANCE

CARCASSONNE *8F4* (10km NE Rural) *43.28305,*
2.44166 **Camping Le Moulin de Ste Anne,** Chemin de
Ste Anne, 11600 Villegly-en-Minervois **04 68 72 20 80;**
contact@moulindesainteanne.com; www.moulinde
sainteanne.com

🐕€3.50 ♿(htd) 🚿 ⚓ 🚻 ♿ 🗑 ∥ 🅿 💷 ⛟ ♔ 🍽 ₳ ⛱nr ⚠
⚓(htd)

Leave A61 junc 23 Carcassone Ouest dir Mazamet;
after approx 14km onto D620 to Villegly, site sp at
ent to vill. NB Turning R off D620 hidden by trees,
then over narr bdge; long o'fits need wide swing in.
4*, Med, mkd, hdg, unshd, pt sl, terr, EHU (10A) inc;
bbq; red long stay; 25% statics; adv bkg acc;
ccard acc; games area; CKE. "Pretty, clean site; lge
pitches; friendly, helpful owner; ltd san facs; pitches poss
diff/muddy in wet; gd touring base; poss local youths
congregate on motorbikes nrby in eve; min 3 nights high
ssn; vg." **€25.00**, 29 Mar-15 Oct, C28.   **2019**

CARCASSONNE *8F4* (10km E Rural) *43.21498, 2.47031*
Camping La Commanderie, 6 Chemin Eglise,11800
Rustiques **04 68 78 67 63 or 06 25 28 35 80 (mob);**
contact@campinglacommanderie.com;
www.campinglacommanderie.com

🐕€2 ♿(htd) 🚿 ⚓ 🗑 ∥ 💷 ⛟ ♔ ₳ 🅗 🚮 ⛱nr ⚠ ⚓

Fr Carcassonne take D6113/D610 E to Trèbes
(approx 8km); at Trèbes take D610 & after 2km L
onto D906, then L onto D206; site on R; foll sp
'Rustiques'. Or fr A61 ext junc 24 onto D6113 to
Trèbes & then as bef. 3*, Sm, mkd, pt shd, pt sl, EHU
(6A) inc; 10% statics; phone; Eng spkn; adv bkg acc;
ccard acc; CKE. "Pleasant, helpful owner & staff;
modern san facs; patron sells own wines; gd cycling
along canal fr Trèbes; conv A61; gd NH en rte Spain;
superb refurbished pool; excel; quiet relaxing site;
excel site improving year on year, running track and
12 fitness machines added this year."
€25.00, 1 Apr-15 Oct.   **2018**

CARCASSONNE *8F4* (7.6km E Rural) *43.20700, 2.44258*
FFCC Camping à l'Ombre des Micocouliers, Chemin
de la Lande, 11800 Trèbes **04 68 78 61 75; infos@**
campingmicocouliers.com; www.audecamping.com

🐕€1.50 ♿(htd) 🚿 ⚓ 🗑 ∥ 🅿 📨 💷 ⛟ ♔ ₳ 🛒 ∅

Fr Carcassonne, take D6113 E for 6km to Trèbes;
go under rlway bdge; fork L onto D610; turn R
immed bef rv bdge; site on L in 200m. Fr W foll
D6113 thro Trebes; at rndabt at E of town take last
exit to L sp Sports Centre, site on R. 4*, Med, mkd,
shd, EHU (6A); bbq; TV; phone; Eng spkn; rv fishing;
CKE. "Pleasant, sandy site by rv; well shd; friendly &
helpful staff; gd, clean but dated san facs, 1 block up
15 steps; ltd EHU; Trèbes in walking dist; vg cycling,
13 km cycle to Carcassonne along cana, bus for €1;
gd base Canal du Midi; can be noisy fr local youths on
mbikes; walk into town needs care with busy rd; lovely
site; adv to arr early as popular site; site improved,
new tiling & paint in toilet block (2015); v.busy."
€26.00, 1 Apr-30 Sep.   **2015**

CARCASSONNE *8F4* (6km S Rural) *43.17938, 2.37024*
Camping à l'Ombre des Oliviers, Ave du Stade, 11570
Cazilhac **04 68 79 65 08 or 06 81 54 96 00 (mob);**
florian.romo@wanadoo.fr; www.alombredes
oliviers.com

📶 🐕€2 ♿ 🚿 ⚓ 🗑 ∥ 💷 ♔ ₳ ⛱nr ⚠ ⚓

Fr N & W exit Carcassonne by D6113 dir Narbonne.
Cross rv & turn S onto D104, then D142/D56 to
Cazilhac, site sp. 3*, Sm, pt shd, EHU (6-10A) €3 (poss
rev pol); bbq; TV; 10% statics; adv bkg acc; games
area; tennis; site clsd 1st week Jan. "Site in pleasant
position; if office clsd phone owner on mob, or site
yourself; helpful owners; v ltd facs LS; insufficient san
facs when site full & ltd other facs; few water pnts;
pitches poss muddy/soft when wet; bus to old city nrby;
site very shabby (2014); san facs need maintenance
(2015)." **€23.00**   **2015**

CARCASSONNE *8F4* (15km NW Rural) *43.29861,*
2.22277 **Camping de Montolieu,** L'Olivier, 11170
Montolieu **04 68 76 95 01 or 06 31 90 31 92 (mob);**
nicole@camping-de-montolieu.com; www.camping-
de-montolieu.com

🐕€2.50 ♿(htd) 🚿 ⚓ 🗑 ∥ ♔ ₳ ⛱nr 🅗nr ⛱nr

Fr D6113 4km W Carcassonne, take D629 twd
Montolieu; site on R in 2.5km after Moussoulens. Sp
fr D6113, approx 5km dist. App thro Montolieu not
rec. 3*, Sm, hdg, mkd, pt shd, EHU (5A) inc; gas; bbq;
10% statics; phone; adv bkg acc; games area; games
rm; CKE. "Well-run site in lovely countryside; pool 100m;
manoeuvring tight; excel facs; conv Carcassonne; highly
rec." **€19.60**, 25 Mar-31 Oct.   **2019**

"I need an on-site restaurant"

We do our best to make sure site information
is correct, but it is always best to check any
must-have facilities are still available or will
be open during your visit.

CARCES *10F3* (0.5km SE Urban) *43.47350, 6.18826*
Camping Les Fouguières, 165 chemin des Fouguières,
83570 Carcès **34 94 59 96 28 or 06 74 29 69 02
(mob); info@camping-les-fouguieres.com;**
www.camping-les-fouguieres.com

🐕€2 ♿ 🚿 ⚓ 🗑 ∥ 📨 💷 ♔ ₳ ⚠ ⚓(htd)

Exit A8 junc 35 at Brignoles onto D554 to Le Val;
then take D562 to Carcès. Site sp off D13. Narr app
rd, diff entry & exit for long o'fits. Med, pt shd, EHU
(14A) €3; gas; sw nr; TV; 80% statics; phone; bus;
Eng spkn; canoeing nr; fishing nr. "Pleasant, clean,
well-shd site; friendly, helpful owner; Rv Caramy runs
thro site; interesting, medieval town; Lake Carcès 2km;
don't miss Entrecasteaux chateau; mkt Sat; excel."
€32.00, 10 Mar-30 Nov.   **2019**

CARNAC *2G3* (1km N Rural) *47.59683, -3.06035*
Camping La Grande Métairie, Route des Alignements de Kermario, 56342 Carnac **02 97 52 24 01; info@lagrandemetairie.com; www.lagrandemetairie.com**

🏕 €4 ⚑(htd) 🔲 ♨ 🚿 ♿ 🖃 ⁄ 🆗 🦋 ♈ 🍴 ⑪ 🏊 ⚒ ⏏ 🖊 🍽(covrd, htd) 🏖 ⊥ sand 2.5km

Fr Auray take N768 twd Quiberon. In 8km turn L onto D119 twd Carnac. La Métairie site sp 1km bef Carnac (at traff lts) turn L onto D196 to site on R in 1km. 4*, V lge, mkd, hdg, pt shd, EHU (6A) €3; gas; bbq; TV; 80% statics; Eng spkn; adv bkg acc; ccard acc; games rm; watersports 2.5km; sailing 2.5km; tennis; waterslide. *"Excel facs; vg pool complex; friendly, helpful staff; rec."* **€42.00, 2 Apr-10 Sep.** 2017

"Satellite navigation makes touring much easier"

Remember most sat navs don't know if you're towing or in a larger vehicle – always use yours alongside maps and site directions.

CARNAC *2G3* (3km N Rural) *47.60801, -3.09049*
Camping Les Bruyères, Kerogile, 56340 Plouharnel **02 97 52 30 57; contact@camping-lesbruyeres.com; www.camping-lesbruyeres.com**

🏕 €2 ⚑(htd) 🔲 ♨ 🚿 ♿ 🖃 ⁄ 🆗 🦋 ♈ 🍴 ⑪ 🏊 ⚒ ⏏ 🖊 ⊥ sand 3km

Fr Vannes W on E60/N165, at Auray take D768 dir Quiberon. At rndabt approx 2km fr Plouharnel turn L into Rte du Hahon, site in 500m, sp. 3*, Med, hdstg, mkd, hdg, pt shd, EHU (6A) €3.70; bbq; TV; 30% statics; Eng spkn; adv bkg acc; ccard acc; tennis; games area; CKE. *"V pleasant, well-run, peaceful site; library; bicycles; pony rides; vg."* **€30.00, 6 Apr-29 Sep.** 2019

CARNAC *2G3* (2km NE Rural) *47.60820, -3.06605*
Camping Le Moustoir, 71 Route du Moustoir, 56340 Carnac **02 97 52 16 18; info@lemoustoir.com; www.lemoustoir.com**

🏕 €1 ⚑ 🔲 ♨ 🚿 ♿ 🖃 ⁄ 🆗 ⑪ 🍴 ⑪ 🏊 ⚒ ⏏ 🖊 🍽(covrd, htd) 🏖 ⊥ sand 4km

Fr N165 take D768 at Auray dir Carnac & Quiberon. In 5km take D119 dir Carnac, site on L at ent to Carnac. 3*, Lge, mkd, hdg, pt shd, pt sl, EHU (10A) inc; bbq; TV; 60% statics; Eng spkn; adv bkg acc; ccard acc; games area; waterslide; bike hire; tennis; CKE. *"Attractive, friendly, well-run site; facs clean but stretched; megaliths nrby; Sun mkt."* **€43.00, 14 Apr-9 Sep, B19.** 2017

CARNAC *2G3* (2.4km NE Rural) *47.5964, -3.0617*
Camping Le Moulin de Kermaux, Route de Kerlescan, 56340 Carnac **02 97 52 15 90; moulin-de-kermaux@wanadoo.fr; www.camping-moulinkermaux.com**

🏕 €2.50 ⚑(htd) 🔲 ♨ 🚿 ♿ 🖃 ⁄ 🆗 🦋 ♈ 🍴 ⑪ 🏊 ⏏ 🖊 🍽(covrd, htd) 🏖 ⊥ sand 3km

Fr Auray take D768 S sp Carnac, Quiberon. In 8km turn L onto D119 twds Carnac. 1km bef Carnac take D196 (Rte de Kerlescan) L to site in approx 500m opp round, stone observation tower for alignments. Fr St Trinite Sur Mer, take D781, cont to rndabt nr St Michel Tumulus on o'skirts of Carnac. Exit R onto D119. In 1km fork R onto D196, site on R in 1km. 3*, Med, hdg, mkd, pt shd, EHU (6A) €4 (poss rev pol); gas; bbq; TV; 50% statics; phone; bus adj; Eng spkn; adv bkg acc; ccard acc; sauna; waterslide; games area; jacuzzi; CKE. *"Well-kept, friendly, attractive site nr standing stones; many repeat visitors; excel."* **€38.00, 19 Apr-13 Sep.** 2015

CARNAC *2G3* (3.5km NE Rural) *47.60198, -3.03672*
Camping de Kervilor, Route du Latz, 56470 La Trinité-sur-Mer **02 97 55 76 75; infos@camping-kervilor.com; www.camping-kervilor.com**

🏕 €2.90 ⚑ 🔲 ♨ 🚿 ♿ 🖃 ⁄ 🆗 ♈ 🍴 ⑪ 🏊 ⏏ 🖊 🍽(covrd, htd) 🏖 ⊥ sand 4km

Sp fr island in cent of Trinité-sur-Mer. 4*, Lge, hdstg, mkd, hdg, pt shd, EHU (6-10A) €3.85-4.35; gas; bbq; 5% statics; Eng spkn; adv bkg acc; ccard acc; waterslide; solarium; bike hire; games area; tennis; CKE. *"Busy, well-kept family site; lge pitches; clean dated unisex san facs; 20 min walk into La Trinité-sur-Mer (1.5km); gd cycling to Carnac & megaliths; great site; excel loc; easy walk to lovely town."* **€29.00, 1 Apr-18 Sep.** 2018

"There aren't many sites open at this time of year"

If you're travelling outside peak season remember to call ahead to check site opening dates – even if the entry says 'open all year'.

CARNAC *2G3* (2km E Rural/Coastal) *47.5810, -3.0576*
Camping Les Druides, 55 Chemin de Beaumer, 56340 Carnac **02 97 52 08 18; contact@camping-les-druides.com; www.camping-les-druides.com**

🏕 €2.50 ⚑ 🔲 ♨ 🚿 ♿ 🖃 ⁄ 🆗 🦋 ⑪ nr ⚒ nr 🖊 🍽(htd) ⊥ sand 500m

Go E on seafront Carnac Plage to end; turn N onto Ave d'Orient; at junc with Rte de la Trinité-sur-Mer, turn L, then 1st R; site 1st on L in 300m. 3*, Med, hdg, pt shd, pt sl, EHU (6A) €3.70; TV; 5% statics; Eng spkn; adv bkg acc; ccard acc; games rm; CKE. *"Friendly welcome."* **€41.50, 13 Apr-3 Sep.** 2019

CARNAC *2G3* (3km E Rural) *47.61122, -3.02908*
Camping du Lac, 56340 Carnac 02 97 55 78 78;
info@lelac-carnac.com; www.lelac-carnac.com
🅃 €2 ♨ 🏕 🚿 ⚇ ♿ ⛲ 📶 🦋 🐾 ⚑ 🚴 (htd) ⚓sand 3km

Fr Auray (by-pass) take D768 sp Carnac; in 4km turn
L on D186; after 4km look for C105 on L & foll sp to
site. Fr E end of quay-side in La Trinité-sur-Mer take
main Carnac rd & in 100m turn R onto D186; in 2km
R on C105, R on C131; sp. 3*, Med, hdg, pt shd, pt sl,
serviced pitches; EHU (6A) €3.60; gas; bbq; TV;
50% statics; phone; Eng spkn; adv bkg acc; ccard acc;
bike hire; CKE. *"Excel, beautiful, woodland site
o'looking tidal lake; helpful owner; clean, well-cared for;
multi-sport court; fitness rm; superb pool; gd cycling &
walking; vg; lovely sunsets & sunrises."*
€36.00, 1 Apr-30 Sep. 2017

CARNAC *2G3* (2km SE Coastal) *47.58116, -3.05804*
Camping Le Dolmen, Chemin de Beaumer, 56340
Carnac 02 97 52 12 35; contact@campingledolmen.
com; www.campingledolmen.com
🅃 €3 ♨ (htd) ⚇ 🏕 🚿 ♿ ⛲ 📶 🦋 💧 ⚇ 🐾 nr ⚑ 🚴
🚴 (htd) ⚓ ⚓sand 500m

Fr N on D768 twd Quiberon; turn L onto D781 twd
La Trinité-sur-Mer. At Montauban turn R at rndabt
dir Kerfraval & Beaumer, site in 700m, sp. 3*, Med,
hdstg, mkd, hdg, pt shd, pt sl, EHU (10A) €4.70; bbq;
2% statics; adv bkg acc; ccard acc; games area; games
rm; CKE. *"Excel, v friendly, clean, pleasant site; v well
maintained; generous size pitches; modern, clean san
facs; highly rec."* **€38.00, 2 Apr-23 Sep.** 2018

CARNAC *2G3* (1km S Coastal) *47.57667, -3.06817*
Camping Les Menhirs, Allé saint michel, 56343 Carnac
02 97 52 94 67; contact@lesmenhirs.com;
www.lesmenhirs.com
♨ ⚇ 🏕 🚿 ♿ ⚇ 🦋 🐾 🚴 (htd) ⚓sand 350m

Fr Auray foll sps to Carnac, Carnac Plage. Site past
shopping cent rd on L, sp by camping sps. 4*, Lge, pt
shd, pt sl, EHU (6A) €4.80; gas; 50% statics; adv bkg
acc; sauna; jacuzzi; games rm. *"Extra charge for larger
pitches; excel san facs; excel location, nr rest, shops &
beach."* **€56.00, 1 Apr-30 Sep.** 2017

CARNAC *2G3* (3.5km NW Rural) *47.59468, -3.09659*
Camping Les Goélands, Kerbachic, 56340 Plouharnel
02 97 52 31 92; contact@camping-lesgoelands.com;
www.camping-lesgoelands.com
🅃 €1 ♨ ⚇ 🏕 🚿 ⚇ 🐾 nr ⚑ ⚓sand 3km

Take D768 fr Auray twd Quiberon. In Plouharnel
turn L at rndabt by supmkt onto D781 to Carnac.
Site sp to L in 500m. 2*, Med, pt shd, EHU (3-6A)
€3.50; gas; adv bkg rec. *"Good facs; gd-sized pitches;
gate clsd at 2200; nr beaches with bathing & gd
yachting; bells fr adj abbey not too intrusive; conv
for megalithic sites; high standard, pleasant, quiet
site; facs basic; clean and tidy; new owners (2015)."*
€20.00, 1 Apr-31 Oct. 2016

CARNAC *2G3* (7.5km NW Rural) *47.62882, -3.14511*
Camping Les Mégalithes, Kerfélicité, 56410 Erdeven
02 97 55 68 76 or 02 97 55 68 09; campingdes
megalithes@orange.fr; www.campingdesmegalithes.fr
🅃 €1 ♨ (htd) ⚇ 🏕 ♿ ⚇ 🦋 💧 🍴 nr ⚇ nr 🐾
🚴 ⚓shgl 2km

Fr Carnac take D781 thro Plouharnel after further
4km; site on L in 500m. 3*, Med, hdg, mkd, pt shd, pt
sl, EHU (10A); twin axles; 40% statics; Eng spkn; adv
bkg acc; games area. *"Excel, peaceful, well maintained
site with lge pitches but poorly lit; poss diff to
manoeuvre lge c'vans; conv for megalithic alignments;
v clean facs; helpful & welcoming staff; family run
site; pool area beautiful but busy."*
€30.00, 1 May-21 Sep. 2015

CARPENTRAS *10E2* (7km N Rural) *44.09723, 5.03682*
Camping Le Brégoux, Chemin du Vas, 84810
Aubignan 04 90 62 62 50 or 04 90 67 10 13 (LS);
camping-lebregoux@wanadoo.fr; www.camping-
lebregoux.fr
🅃 €1.90 ♨ ⚇ 🏕 🚿 ♿ ⚇ 🦋 🍴 nr ⚇ nr 🐾 ⚑ 🚴

Exit Carpentras on D7 sp Bollène. In Aubignan turn
R immed after x-ing bdge, 1st R again in approx
250m at Club de Badminton & foll site sp at fork.
2*, Lge, hdstg, mkd, hdg, pt shd, EHU (10A) €3.80
(poss long lead req); bbq; TV; 2% statics; phone;
Eng spkn; adv bkg acc; ccard acc; games rm; golf
nr; tennis; CKE. *"Popular site in beautiful area; lge
pitches & gd access; helpful, friendly staff; gates clsd
2200-0700; poss flooding in heavy
rain; pool 5km in ssn; excel walking & cycling nrby; gd
value; gd; san facs upgraded, modern & clean (2015)."*
€11.40, 1 Mar-31 Oct. 2015

CARPENTRAS *10E2* (6km S Urban) *43.99917, 5.06591*
Camp Municipal Coucourelle, Ave René Char,
84210 Pernes-les-Fontaines 04 90 66 45 55 or
04 90 61 31 67 (Mairie); camping@pernesles
fontaines.fr; www.tourisme-pernes.fr
🅃 €0.50 ♨ ⚇ 🏕 ♿ ⚇ 🦋 🐾 nr ⚇ nr ⚑

Take D938 fr Carpentras to Pernes-les-Fontaines;
then take D28 dir St Didier (Ave René Char pt of
D28). Site sp (some sps easily missed). Foll sp sports
complex, site at rear of sw pool. 2*, Sm, hdg, mkd,
shd, EHU (10A) €3.50; bbq; adv bkg acc; ccard acc;
tennis adj; fishing 2.5km; CKE. *"Pleasant, well-run site;
views of Mont Ventoux; most pitches lge but some sm
& narr; excel clean facs; m'vans can park adj to mv point
free when site clsd; pool 2.5km; gates close 1930; no
twin axles; free use of adj pool; attractive old town,
easy parking; adv bkg rec LS; vg."*
€15.50, 1 Apr-30 Sep. 2016

FRANCE

CARPENTRAS 10E2 (4km SW Rural) 44.0398, 5.0009
Camp Municipal de Bellerive, 54 Chemin de la Ribière,
84170 Monteux **04 90 66 81 88 or 04 90 66 97 52 (TO);**
camping.bellerive@orange.fr; www.provence
guide.com

🛉 ℰ1 � wo ♨ ♿ ⚫ ⁄ ♥ ⚐ Ⴔ nr ℗ nr ☒ nr ⚌

Site on N edge of Monteux cent, sp off ring rd
Monteux N, immed after rlwy x-ing. 2*, Sm, hdg,
mkd, hdstg, pt shd, serviced pitches; EHU (6-10A)
€2.50; red long stay; 10% statics; phone; bus; CKE.
"Gd, busy, lovely site; rec arr early high ssn; helpful,
friendly, v helpful warden lives adj; gd security; vg,
clean, modern san facs; trees a problem for sat TV -
choose pitch carefully; park adj gd for children; 5 min
walk to vill; poss muddy when wet; poss some workers'
statics LS; Mistral blows early & late ssn; pool 4km;
gd touring base; free WiFi; no grey water drainage."
€14.40, 1 Apr-15 Oct.   **2018**

CASSIS 10F3 (1.5km N Coastal) 43.22417, 5.54126
Camping Les Cigales, 43 Ave de la Marne, 13260
Cassis **04 42 01 07 34; www.campingcassis.com**

🛉 ℰ1.10 ♦♦♦ wo ♨ ♿ ⁄ ☒ ⚐ Ⴔ ℗ ⚌ ⚌ 🏊 shgl 1.5km

App Cassis on D41E, then at 2nd rndabt exit D559
sp Cassis, then turn 1st R sp Les Calanques into Ave
de la Marne, site immed on R. Avoid town cent as
rds narr. 4*, Lge, hdg, mkd, hdstg, pt shd, pt sl, EHU
(3A) €2.60 (poss rev pol & poss long lead req); gas;
30% statics; phone; Eng spkn; ccard acc; CKE. "Gd base
for Calanques; v busy w/ends; popular attractive resort,
but steep walk to camp site; poss tired san facs end
ssn; poss diff lge o'fits due trees; v strong pegs req to
penetrate hardcore; bus to Marseille cent fr campsite."
€25.00, 15 Mar-15 Nov.   **2019**

CASTELJALOUX 7D2 (10km SE Rural) 44.27262, 0.18969
Camping Moulin de Campech, 47160 Villefranche-du-
Queyran **05 53 88 72 43; camping@moulinde
campech.co.uk; www.moulindecampech.co.uk**

🛉 ℰ2.40 ♦♦♦ wo ♨ ♿ ⚫ ⁄ ♥ ⚐ Ⴔ ℗ ⚌ ☒ ⚐ 🏊 (htd)

Fr A62 exit junc 6 (sp Damazan & Aiguillon). Fr toll
booth take D8 SW sp Mont-de-Marsan. In 3km turn
R in Cap-du-Bosc onto D11 twd Casteljaloux. Site on
R in 4km. Or fr Casteljaloux S on D655 then SW on
D11 after 1.5km. Site on L after 9.5km.
3*, Sm, mkd, hdg, pt shd, EHU (6A) €4; bbq; phone;
adv bkg acc; ccard acc; lake fishing; games rm; golf
nr; CKE. "Superb, peaceful rvside site in wooded valley;
well-run; lge pitches; friendly, helpful & welcoming
British owners; clean, dated san facs, needs refurb
(2014); gd pool; excel, gd value rest; BBQ suppers;
gd cycling; no o'fits over 8.2m; interesting area ideal
for nature lovers; excel site; many social events."
€32.00, 1 Apr-7 Oct, D16.   **2017**

CASTELLANE 10E3 (2.7km SE Rural) 43.83833, 6.54194
Camping La Ferme de Castellane, Quartier La Lagne,
04120 Castellane **04 92 83 67 77; accueil@camping-
la-ferme.com; www.camping-la-ferme.com**

🛉 ℰ1 ♦♦♦ wo ♨ ♿ ⚫ ⁄ ♥ ⚐ Ⴔ nr ℗ nr ☒ nr ⚌

Fr Castellane take D6085 dir Grasse. In 1km turn
R (at Rest L'Escapade) then site in 1km, sp. Narr
app rd with passing places. 3*, Sm, mkd, pt shd, terr,
EHU €3.50; TV; 25% statics; Eng spkn; adv bkg acc;
ccard acc; games rm; CKE. "Vg, clean, friendly site;
gd touring base; breakfast and BBQ evenings at rest."
€17.00, 27 Mar-20 Sep.   **2016**

CASTELLANE 10E3 (0.3km SW Urban) 43.84623,
6.50995 **Camping Frédéric Mistral,** 12 Ave Frédéric
Mistral, 04120 Castellane **04 92 83 62 27; www.camping-
frederic-mistral.fr**

♦♦♦ (htd) wo ♨ ♿ ⁄ ♥ ⚐ Ⴔ ℗ ⚌ ☒ nr

In town turn onto D952 sp Gorges-du-Verdon, site
on L in 100m. 2*, Med, mkd, pt shd, serviced pitches;
EHU (6A) €3 (poss rev pol); 2% statics; adv bkg acc;
CKE. "Friendly owners; pool 200m; gd san facs but
poss stretched in ssn; gd base for gorges etc; gd."
€21.00, 1 Mar-11 Nov.   **2017**

CASTELLANE 10E3 (0.5km SW Rural) 43.84570,
6.50447 **Camping Notre Dame,** Route des Gorges du
Verdon, 04120 Castellane **04 92 83 63 02;
camping-notredame@wanadoo.fr; www.camping-
notredame.com**

🛉 ♦♦♦ wo ♨ ♿ ⚫ ⁄ ♥ ⚐ ℗ nr ☒ ⚌

N fr Grasse on D6085, turn L in Castellane at sq
onto D952 to site on R in 500m. 3*, Sm, pt shd, EHU
(6A) €3.50; gas; 20% statics; phone; Eng spkn; adv bkg
acc; CKE. "Ideal touring base; helpful owners; poss a bit
unkempt early ssn; excel." **€26.50, 1 Apr-8 Oct.**
                                          2019

CASTELLANE 10E3 (1.5km SW Rural) 43.83921,
6.49370 **Sandaya Domaine du Verdon,** D952, 04120
Castellane **04 92 83 61 29; ver@sandaya.fr;
www.sandaya.co.uk**

🛉 ℰ5 ♦♦♦ wo ♨ ♿ ⚫ ⁄ ♥ ⚐ Ⴔ ℗ ⚌ ☒ ⚌ ⚐ 🏊 (htd) 🚲

Fr Castellane take D952 SW twd Grand Canyon du
Verdon & Moustiers-Ste Marie. After 1.5km turn L into
site. NB To avoid Col de Lèques with hairpins use N202
& D955 fr Barrême instead of D6085.
4*, V lge, mkd, hdg, pt shd, serviced pitches; EHU (6A)
inc; gas; bbq (elec, gas); sw; TV; 60% statics; Eng spkn;
ccard acc; games rm; rv fishing adj; waterslide; canoeing;
archery; games area; horseriding nr; CKE. "Excel site by
rv; no o'fits over 8m; gd sized pitches; gd, clean san facs,
modern & dated blocks; quiet, rural walk to town; mkt
Wed & Sat." **€25.00, 12 Jun-14 Sep.**   **2019**

CASTELNAUDARY 8F4 (7km E Rural) 43.31723, 2.01582 **FFCC Camping à la Ferme Domaine de la Capelle (Sabatte),** St Papoul, 11400 St Martin-Lalande 04 68 94 91 90; www.domaine-la-capelle.fr/en

🐕 €1 ♦♦♦ (htd) [wc] 🏔 🖪 ⚊ 🐾 🌀 ⒵ nr

Fr D6113 Castelnaudary/Carcassonne, take D103 E & foll sp to St Papoul & site in 2km. Well sp. NB Ent poss awkward lge o'fits. Sm, hdg, mkd, pt shd, pt sl, EHU (4A) €2.50; bbq; phone; Eng spkn; CKE. *"Delightful, peaceful, spacious CL-type site; friendly, helpful owner; vg san facs, poss stretched when site full; ltd EHU; gd walking; nr St Papoul Cathar vill with abbey; ideal NH for Spain; excel; close to ind site, gd cycling."* €14.50, 1 Apr-30 Sep. **2016**

CASTIES LABRANDE 8F3 (1.5km W Rural) 43.32502, 0.99046 **Camping Le Casties,** Le Bas de Lebrande, 31430 Casties-Labrande 05 61 90 81 11; contact@ camping-lecasties.fr; www.camping-lecasties.fr

🐕 €1 ♦♦♦ [wc] 🏔 🖪 ⚊ 🐾 🌀 Ⅰ ⚊ Ⓐ ⚊ ⚊

S fr Toulouse, exit A64 junc 26 onto D626; after Pouy-de-Touges turn L onto & foll camping sp. 1*, Med, hdg, pt shd, EHU (5A) €1; bbq; 10% statics; phone; Eng spkn; adv bkg acc; ccard acc; tennis; fishing; CKE. *"Remote; lge hdg pitches; staff friendly & helpful; value for money; lovely pool; excel; new vg san facs (2013); v peaceful; sm farm for children."* €12.50, 1 May-30 Sep. **2019**

CASTILLON LA BATAILLE 7C2 (0.6km E Urban) 44.85350, -0.03550 **Camp Municipal La Pelouse,** Chemin de Halage, 33350 Castillon-la-Bataille 05 57 40 04 22 or 05 56 40 00 06 (Mairie)

♦♦♦ 🏔 🌀 🐾 ⒵

Site in town on N bank of Rv Dordogne. After x-ing rv on D17 fr S to N, take 1st avail rd on R to rv. 2*, Sm, shd, EHU (15A) inc; adv bkg acc; CKE. *"Peaceful, lovely site by rv; busy high ssn; pitches poss rough & muddy when wet; helpful warden; facs dated but clean; conv town; trans, St Emillion & wine area; gd NH."* €17.00, 1 May-15 Oct. **2018**

CASTRES 8F4 (2km NE Urban) 43.62054, 2.25401 **Camping de Gourjade,** Ave de Roquecourbe, 81100 Castres 05 63 59 33 51; contact@campingde gourjade.net; www.campingdegourjade.net

🐕 €2 ♦♦♦ [wc] 🏔 ⚊ 🖪 🐾 🌀 🦋 Ⅰ ⒵ ⒶⒸ ⚊

Leave Castres NE on D89 sp Rocquecourbe; site on R in 2km. Well sp. Ave de Roquecourbe is pt of D89. 3*, Med, hdg, pt shd, terr, EHU (6-16A) inc (poss rev pol); gas; bbq; 5% statics; bus; ccard acc; cycling; golf adj; CKE. *"Lovely site in beautiful park on Rv Agout; lge pitches; helpful staff; gd, tired clean san facs; 9 hole golf course adj; some lower pitches sl & poss soft; boat fr site to town; extra charge twin axles; gd security; poss groups workers LS; leisure cent & golf adj; vg cycling; highly rec; rest open evenings only; well run; excel for long or sh stay."* €22.80, 1 Apr-30 Sep. **2017**

CASTRIES 10E1 (2.6km NE Rural) 43.69406, 3.99585 **Camping Domaine de Fondespierre,** 277 Route de Fontmarie, 34160 Castries 04 67 91 20 03; accueil@campingfondespierre.com; www.camping fondespierre.com

🐕 €3 ♦♦♦ (htd) [wc] 🏔 ⚊ 🖪 🐾 🌀 [mp] 🦋 Ⅰ Ⓨ ⒯ 🏔 ⚊ Ⓐ ⚊

Fr A9 exit junc 28 sp Vendargues, foll sp for Castries on D610. Cont thro Castries in dir of Sommieres. Aprox 1.5km past Castries turn L and foll camp sp. 3*, Med, hdstg, mkd, hdg, pt shd, terr, EHU (10A) inc (poss long lead req); bbq (sep area); sw nr; 40% statics; phone; Eng spkn; adv bkg acc; ccard acc; games area; tennis adj; bike hire; golf 2.5km; CKE. *"Gd walking area; poss travellers & site poss unkempt LS; site rds narr with sharp, tree-lined bends - poss diff access to pitches for lge o'fits; NH; superb vill."* €34.00, 4 Jan-19 Dec. **2016**

CAUDEBEC EN CAUX 3C2 (10km SE Urban) 49.48373, 0.77247 **Camp Municipal du Parc,** Rue Victor Hugo, 76940 La Mailleraye-sur-Seine 02 35 37 12 04; mairie-sg.lamailleyrayesurseine@wanadoo.fr

♦♦♦ [wc] 🏔 🌀 🦋 Ⅰ nr ⒯ nr ⒵ nr 🏔

Fr N on D131/D490 turn E onto D65. Or fr S on D913. Site sp in cent of town close to rv bank. 1*, Sm, hdg, pt shd, pt sl, EHU (6A) inc. *"Pleasant, tidy site; site yourself, warden calls; adequate, clean san facs; gd walking area; vg NH."* €12.50, 1 Apr-30 Sep. **2015**

CAUNES MINERVOIS 8F4 (1km S Rural) 43.32380, 2.52592 **Camp Municipal Les Courtals,** Ave du Stade, 11160 Caunes-Minervois 04 68 24 04 77 or 06 38 70 86 25; mairie.de.caunes@wanadoo.fr; www.odeeanaude.eu/catalogaude2/campsite-municipal-les-courtals-p-449.html

♦♦♦ 🏔 🌀 [wc] 🦋 ⒵ nr 🏔

Sp fr D620 at stadium & adj rv. 1*, Sm, pt shd, EHU (4A) inc; phone; games area. *"Pleasantly situated site; office opens 1800; gate locked 2100; site self, warden calls; pool 6km; rv adj; interesting town."* €12.00, 15 Jan-15 Dec. **2019**

CAUSSADE 8E3 (1.8km N Urban) 44.16582, 1.54446 **Camp Municipal de la Piboulette,** Rue de la Piboulette, 82300 Caussade 05 63 93 09 07; secretariat@mairie-caussade.com; www.mairie-caussade.fr

🐕 €1.25 ♦♦♦ [wc] 🏔 ⚊ 🖪 🐾 🌀 🦋 Ⓨ ⒵ nr 🏔

S on D820 fr Cahors (40km), turn L off D820 on ent Caussade onto D17 (Rte de Puylaroque). About 750m turn L (sp), site on R in 100m; lge grass stadium. 2*, Med, mkd, pt shd, serviced pitches; EHU (3A/8A) €1.90; adv bkg acc; CKE. *"Pleasant site adj lake; spacious, mostly shd pitches; pleasant warden; excel, clean san facs, poss tired LS; sports cent adj; gates locked 2100 LS; easy 15 min walk to town; gd walks; pool on far side of stadium; gd cycling round lake; conv A20 & Gorges de l'Aveyron; vg mkt Mon; excel value; vg."* €10.00, 1 May-30 Sep. **2015**

CAUSSADE *8E3* (9km NE Rural) *44.18273, 1.60305*
Camping de Bois Redon, 10 Chemin de Bonnet, 82240
Septfonds **05 63 64 92 49 or 06 78 35 79 97 (Mob);**
info@campingdeboisredon.com; www.campingde
boisredon.com

Exit A20 junc 59 to Caussade, then onto D926 to
Septfonds (narr rds); after rndabt turn 3rd L; site sp.
Site in 2km. One-way system when leaving site.
3*, Sm, mkd, pt shd, pt sl, EHU (10A) €3.50;
10% statics; Eng spkn; adv bkg req; bike hire; CKE.
"Well-shd, spacious site in ancient oak forest with
walks; charming Dutch owners; Septfonds nr with
all facs; new shwrs (2013/14); enthusiastic owners
continually making improvements; excel site; immac
new san fac block." **€24.50**   2016

CAUSSADE *8E3* (10km NW Rural) *44.24323, 1.47735*
Camping Le Faillal, 46 Blvd Pasteur, 82270 Montpezat-
de-Quercy **05 63 02 07 08 or 07 68 59 25 32;**
contact@parcdufaillal.com; www.parcdufaillal.com

N on D820, turn L onto D20, site clearly sp on R in
2km. (Do not take D38 bef D20 fr S). 2*, Med, hdg,
pt shd, pt sl, terr, EHU (10A) €3.70; bbq; TV; phone;
Eng spkn; adv bkg acc; games rm; tennis adj; games
area; CKE. "Pretty, well-kept site; friendly, helpful staff;
gd, clean san facs, poss ltd; super pool; many pitches
unavail after heavy rain; access to some pitches diff;
old town a 'must'; rec pay night bef dep; excel; horse
drawn carriage rides, pony rides, kayaking, rafting,
paintball." **€22.00**   2017

CAUTERETS *8G2* (2.5km NE Rural) *42.91092, -0.09934*
Camping GR10, Route de Pierrefitte, 65110 Cauterets
06 20 30 25 85; contact@gr10camping.com;
www.gr10camping.com

N fr Cauterets on D920; site in 2.5km on R. Med, mkd,
shd, terr, EHU €4; TV; 25% statics; Eng spkn; games
rm; tennis; games area. "Pretty site; canyoning (guide
on site); excel." **€20.00, 25 Jun-1 Sep.**   2019

CAVAILLON *10E2* (8km E Rural) *43.84220, 5.13284*
Camp Municipal Les Royères du Prieuré, La Combe-
St Pierre, 84660 Maubec **04 90 76 50 34;**
camping.maubec@c-lmv.fr; www.campingmaubec-
luberon.com

Heading E fr Cavaillon on D2, thro vill of Robion, in
400m at end vill sp turn R to Maubec. Site on R in
1km bef old vill. (Avoid any other rte with c'van).
Diff access at ent, steep slope. Sm, pt shd, terr, EHU
(6-10A) €5; 10% statics; CKE. "Awkward site for lge
o'fits, otherwise vg; san facs stretched high ssn; conv
A7; san facs refurbed; restful site; wine tasting on Tue
eve." **€13.00, 1 Apr-15 Oct.**   2018

CAVAILLON *10E2* (1km S Rural) *43.82107, 5.03723*
Camp Municipal de la Durance, 495 Ave Boscodomini,
84300 Cavaillon **04 90 71 11 78;** contact@camping-
durance.com; www.camping-durance.com

S of Cavaillon, nr Rv Durance. Fr A7 junc 25 foll
sp to town cent. In 200m R immed after x-ing rv.
Site sp (Municipal Camping) on L. 3*, Lge, pt shd,
EHU (4A-10A) €2.50- 6.50; TV; 30% statics; adv bkg
acc; tennis; fishing; games area. "Site OK; gd NH
only; close to town; decent facs; reasonably priced."
€18.60, 1 Apr-30 Sep.   2018

CAVAILLON *10E2* (9km S Rural) *43.78182, 5.04040*
Camping de la Vallée Heureuse, Quartier Lavau, 13660
Orgon **04 84 80 01 71;** camping.valleeheureuse@
gmail.com; www.valleeheureuse.com

Sp in Organ town cent. 3*, Lge, mkd, shd, terr, EHU
(16A); bbq; sw nr; TV; Eng spkn; adv bkg acc; CKE.
"Site adj to old quarry in beautiful position; friendly,
helpful staff; superb san facs; gd pool; gd walking; café;
interesting area; conv m'way; isolated site; vill 1.5km."
€25.00, 25 Mar-31 Oct.   2016

CAVAILLON *10E2* (12km SW Rural) *43.76058, 4.95154*
FFCC Camping Les Oliviers, Ave Jean Jaurès, 13810
Eygalières **04 90 95 91 86;** campinglesoliviers13@
gmail.com; www.camping-les-oliviers.com

Exit A7 junc 25; D99 dir St Rémy-de-Provence;
in 8km camping sp on L; in vill well sp. Sm, hdg,
pt shd, EHU (6A) inc; bbq (elec, gas); adv bkg acc.
"Lovely, friendly site in olive grove nr scenic vill; quiet
site; facs rustic but v clean; pitches cramped for lge
o'fits; simple site; diff acc for lge o'fits; free WiFi."
€19.00, 30 Mar-30 Sep.   2018

CAVALAIRE SUR MER *10F4* (2km NE Rural) *43.18220,
6.51610* **Kawan Village Cros de Mouton,** Chemin de
Cros de Mouton, 83240 Cavalaire-sur-Mer **04 94 64
10 87 or 04 94 05 46 38;** campingcrosdemouton@
wanadoo.fr; www.crosdemouton.com

Exit A8 junc 36 dir Ste Maxime on D125/D25, foll sp
on D559 to Cavalaire-sur-Mer. Site sp on coast app
fr Grimaud/St Tropez & Le Lavandou; diff access.
3*, Lge, mkd, shd, terr, serviced pitches; EHU (10A); gas;
TV; 10% statics; phone; Eng spkn; adv bkg rec; ccard
acc; bike hire; CKE. "Attractive, well-run, popular site in
hills behind town - rec adv bkg even LS; lge pitches avail;
poss diff access to pitches due steep site rds - help avail;
pleasant, welcoming & efficient staff; gd san facs; gd
pool; vg rest & bar; buses to St Tropez; excel; lovely views;
steep walk fr town." **€36.00, 21 Mar-31 Oct.**   2015

CAVALAIRE SUR MER *10F4* (3km NE Coastal) *43.19450, 6.55495* **Sélection Camping,** 12 Blvd de la Mer, 83420 La Croix-Valmer 04 94 55 10 30; camping-selection@wanadoo.fr; www.selection-camping.com

🐕€4 ♦♦♦(htd) wo ♨ ♣ ♿ ⬛ ⌁ msp ♥ ⚲ 𝖸 ⊕ ♨ 🛒 ⚞ ✈
🏊(htd) ⛴ ⛱ sand 400m

Off N559 bet Cavalaire & La Croix-Valmer, 2km past La Croix at rndabt turn R sp Barbigoua, site in 200m. 4*, Lge, mkd, hdg, shd, terr, EHU (10A) €5; gas; TV; 20% statics; phone; bus; Eng spkn; adv bkg req; games area. *"Excel location; sm pitches; private bthrms avail; dogs not acc Jul/Aug; vg san facs; excel pool; excel site."* **€35.00, 15 Mar-15 Oct.** 2018

See advertisement

CAVALAIRE SUR MER *10F4* (0.9km S Urban) *43.16956, 6.53005* **Camping de La Baie,** Blvd Pasteur, 83240 Cavalaire-sur-Mer 04 94 64 08 15 or 04 94 64 08 10; contact@camping-baie.com; www.camping-baie.com

🐕€4 ♦♦♦(htd) ♨ ♣ ♿ ⬛ ⌁ ♥ ⚲ 𝖸 ⊕ ♨ 🛒 ⚞ ✈(htd)
⛴ ⛱ sand 400m

Exit A8 sp Ste Maxime/St Tropez & foll D25 & D559 to Cavalaire. Site sp fr seafront. 4*, Lge, mkd, pt shd, pt sl, EHU (10A) €6; bbq; 10% statics; Eng spkn; adv bkg acc; ccard acc; sailing; games area; jacuzzi; watersports; games rm. *"Well-run, busy site; pleasant staff; excel pool & facs; nr shops, beach, marina & cafes; cycle paths; gd location; diving 500m; sm pitches; narr rd."* **€55.00, 15 Mar-15 Nov.** 2019

CAYEUX SUR MER *3B2* (4km NE Coastal) *50.20291, 1.52641* **Camping Les Galets de la Mollière,** Rue Faidherbe, 80410 La Mollière-d'Aval 03 22 26 61 85; info@campinglesgaletsdelamolliere.com; www.campinglesgaletsdelamolliere.com

🐕€3 ♦♦♦ wo ♨ ♣ ♿ ⬛ ⌁ msp ♥ ⚲ 𝖸 🛒 🚲 ⚞(htd) ⛴
⛱ sand 500m

Fr Cayeux-sur-Mer take D102 N along coast for 3km. Site on R. 3*, Lge, mkd, pt shd, EHU (6A) inc; gas; bbq; 25% statics; games area; games rm; CKE. *"Spacious, much improved, wooded site with lge pitches; barrier clsd 2300-0700; pleasant staff; dirty pitches; unhelpful staff; poor."* **€33.00, 3 Apr-1 Nov.** 2015

CAYLAR, LE *10E1* (4km SW Rural) *43.83629, 3.29045* **Camping Mas de Messier,** St Félix-de-l'Héras, 34520 Le Caylar 04 67 44 52 63; info@masdemessier.com; www.masdemessier.com

🐕 ♦♦♦ wo ♨ ♣ ⬛ ⌁ ♥ ⚲ 🛒nr ⚞ ✈

Fr N exit A75 junc 49 onto D9 thro Le Caylar. Turn R sp St Félix & foll sp St Félix-de-l'Héras; at x-rds in St Félix turn R, site in 1km on L. Fr S exit A75 junc 50; foll sp to St Félix-de-l'Héras; at x-rds turn R & as bef. Sm, hdg, pt shd, pt sl, EHU (10A) €3; Eng spkn; adv bkg req; CKE. *"Excel views fr some pitches; friendly, helpful Dutch owner; facs excel; access unsuitable lge o'fits; meals avail some eves; gd walking; excel long or sh stay; dogs free; low rates in LS."* **€23.00, 15 Apr-1 Oct.** 2018

CAYLUS *8E4* (0.5km E Rural) *44.23368, 1.77636* **FFCC Camping de la Bonnette,** 672 route de la Bonnette, 82160 Caylus 05 63 65 70 20 or 06 07 34 61 99; info@campingbonnette.com; www.camping bonnette.com

🐕€1.50 ♦♦♦ wo ♨ ♣ ♿ ⬛ ⌁ msp ♥ ⚲ 𝖸 ⊕ 🛒nr ⚞ ✈ ✈

Fr A20 exit junc 59 dir Caylus; thro Caylus to g'ge on L. Turn R in 1km over next crossrds & foll site sps to site on R in 1km. 3*, Med, mkd, hdg, pt shd, EHU (10A) €3.50; bbq; red long stay; 10% statics; Eng spkn; adv bkg rec; games area. *"Nice, tidy, scenic site on edge of medieval vill - worth a visit; friendly owner; pitches in groups of 4, not v private."* **€19.00, 29 Mar-4 Oct.** 2019

CEAUCE *4E1* (1km N Rural) *48.49812, -0.62481*
Camp Municipal de la Veillotière, Chemin de la
Veillotière, 61330 Ceaucé **02 33 38 31 19; mairie-
ceauce@wanadoo.fr**
🏕🛂 wc ⚓ ♿ ⚑ ∿ 🐾 ⌬ ℗ 🦽 ⚠

S fr Domfront on D962 dir Mayenne, at rndabt in
Ceaucé turn L. Site in 200m on R adj sm lake.
Sm, hdg, pt shd, pt sl, EHU (6A) inc; fishing adj. *"Well-
kept site on edge vill; gd; nice as always; bar 200m;
quiet cycle rte to Ambrieves Les Vallees; warden calls
eves."* **€11.00, 1 May-30 Sep.**   **2018**

CERCY LA TOUR *4H4* (0.9km S Urban) *46.86680,
3.64328* **Camp Municipal Le Port,** 58360 Cercy-la-
Tour 03 86 50 55 27 or 03 86 50 07 11 (Mairie)**
🐕 🏕🛂 wc ∿ 🐾

At Decize take D981 E; in 12 km L onto D37, then
L onto D10 to Cercy-la-Tour; site sp in vill. Adj
municipal pool, Rv Aron & canal. Med, hdstg, pt shd,
EHU inc; phone; Eng spkn; CKE. *"Clean & tidy site;
immac san facs; gd cycling/walking along canal; excel
value; excel."* **€9.00, 25 Apr-25 Oct.**   **2017**

CERESTE *10E3* (9km W Rural) *43.84361, 5.49666*
Camping à la Ferme (Bouscarle), Les Monguets,
84400 Castellet-en-Luberon 04 90 75 28 62
🐕 €1 ⚓ wc ⚓ ∿

Fr W on D900 (Apt) ignore Camping à la Ferme sp
to R nr St Martin-de-Castillon (v narr rd). Cont 2km
to La Bègude & turn R onto D223 dir Le Boisset.
Site 3km on R, well sp. Sm, shd, pt sl, EHU (4A) €3
(long lead req); Eng spkn; adv bkg acc; CKE. *"Excel,
scenic CL-type site on fruit farm; friendly owners; excel
walking, cycling."* **€13.00, Easter-1 Nov.**   **2015**

CERET *8H4* (1km E Rural) *42.48981, 2.76305*
Camping Les Cerisiers, Mas de la Toure, 66400 Céret
09 70 35 00 30; www.campingcerisiers.fr
12 🐕 🏕🛂 ⚓ ♿ ⚓ ∿ 🐾 ⊺ nr ⚐ nr ⚠ 🦐

Exit A9 junc 43 onto D115, turn off for cent of
Céret. Site is on D618 approx 800m E of Céret twd
Maureillas, sp. Tight ascent for lge o'fits.
2*, Med, mkd, shd, EHU (4A); gas; sw nr; TV;
60% statics; phone; site clsd Jan; CKE. *"Site in cherry
orchard; gd size pitches; facs dated & ltd LS; footpath to
attractive vill with modern art gallery; pool 600m; conv
Andorra, Perpignan, Collioure."* **€18.00**   **2019**

CERILLY *4H3* (10km N Rural) *46.68210, 2.78630*
Camping des Ecossais, La Salle, 03360 Isle-et-
Bardais 04 70 66 62 57 or 04 70 67 50 96; ecossais@
campingstroncais.com; www.campingstroncais.com
🐕 €1.50 🏕🛂 wc ⚓ ♿ 🖥 ∿ 🐾 ⚑ ℗ nr ⚔ 🦽 ⚠

Fr Lurcy-Lévis take D978A SW, turn R onto D111 N
twd Isle-et-Bardais & foll camp sp. Ent tight.
2*, Med, hdg, pt shd, pt sl, EHU (10A) inc; bbq; sw; twin
axles; 10% statics; adv bkg acc; games area; games
rm; fishing; CKE. *"Excel; v busy high ssn; ltd facs LS;
gd cycling; site in oak forest; rec; mountain bike nec on
forest tracks."* **€12.00, 1 Apr-30 Sep.**   **2016**

CERNAY *6F3* (0.9km SW Urban) *47.80448, 7.16999*
**Camping Les Cigognes (formerly Camping Les
Acacias),** 16 Rue René Guibert, 68700 Cernay 03 89
75 56 97; campinglescigognes@orange.fr;
www.camping-les-cigognes.com
🐕 €1.20 🏕🛂 wc ⚓ ♿ 🖥 ∿ 🐾 🐕 ℗ ⊺ ⌬ 🦽 🦐 🏊

Fr N on D83 by-pass, exit Cernay Est. Turn R into
town at traff lts, immed L bef rv bdge, site sp on L;
well sp. 3*, Lge, mkd, pt shd, EHU (5A) €3.50 (poss rev
pol); red long stay; 25% statics; CKE. *"Friendly staff;
clean, tidy site; storks nesting over some pitches; sh
walk to town."* **€18.00, 1 Apr-30 Sep.**   **2015**

CERNAY LA VILLE *4E3* (0.8km NW Rural) *48.67630,
1.97208* **Cernay Vacances,** 37 Rue de la Ferme, 78720
Cernay-la-Ville 33 13 48 52 123; albert.koning@free.fr;
www.cernayvacances.com
12 🐕 🏕🛂 wc ⚓ ∿ 🐾 🐕

Fr Rouen take A13 twrds Paris, then A12 twrds
Rambouillet. Aft Leon de Bruxelles rest & metro
take exit Mesnil - St. Denis. At rndabt pass by D58
twrds le-Mesnil, dir Dampierre. In Dampierre turn R
onto D91 then L onto D149 twrds Senlisse. At top of
this rd turn onto D906, aft 500mtrs at Peugeot g'ge
turn R on Rue des Moulins strt to fm. Sm, pt shd,
EHU €4; cooking facs; Eng spkn; adv bkg acc; games
area. *"Vg."* **€16.00**   **2017**

CHABLIS *4F4* (0.6km SE Rural) *47.81376, 3.80563*
Camp Municipal Le Serein, Quai Paul Louis Courier,
89800 Chablis 03 86 42 44 39 or 03 86 42 80 80 (Mairie);
mairie-chablis@chablis.net; www.chablis.net
🐕 €1.50 🏕 ⚓ ♿ ∿ 🐾 ℗ nr 🦽 nr ⚠

W fr Tonnere on D965; in approx 16km exit D965
for Chabilis; in 300m, just bef x-ing Rv Serein, turn
L at camping sp onto Quai Paul Louis Courier; site
in 300m on R. 2*, Med, hdg, mkd, shd, EHU (5A)
€2; Eng spkn; adv bkg acc; CKE. *"Attractive, tidy
site; facs poss stretched high ssn; friendly & helpful
warden, calls 0800-1200 & 1600-2000; easy walk to
attractive town; vineyards & wine cellars nrby; excel
Sun mkt; warden attaches elec supply to locked post."*
€12.00, 2 Jun-15 Sep.   **2016**

CHAGNY *6H1* (0.7km W Urban) *46.91187, 4.74567*
Camping du Pâquier Fané, 20 Rue du Pâquier Fané,
71150 Chagny 03 85 87 21 42; camping-chagny
@orange.fr; www.campingchagny.com
🐕 €1 🏕🛂 wc ⚓ ♿ 🖥 ∿ 🐾 🐕 ⊺ nr ℗ ⚠

Clearly sp in town. 3*, Med, hdg, mkd, pt shd, EHU
(16A) inc; gas; Eng spkn; fishing; tennis adj; CKE.
*"Well laid-out, well-lit vg site; friendly, helpful resident
wardens; clean san facs; htd pool adj; many pitches sm
& diff med/lge o'fits; on wine rte; gd cycling nrby (voie
verte)."* **€24.60, 29 Mar-31 Oct.**   **2019**

FRANCE

CHAILLAC *7A3* (0.6km SW Rural) *46.43260, 1.29602*
Camp Municipal Les Vieux Chênes, 36310 Chaillac
02 54 25 61 39 or 02 54 25 74 26 (Mairie); chaillac-mairie@wanadoo.fr

12 🚐 ♦♦ (htd) WD ▲ ᶜ 🖪 ∥ 🦋 ☂ nr ⑪ nr 🅿 nr 🕭

Exit N20 S of Argenton-sur-Creuse at junc 20 onto
D36 to Chaillac. Thro vill, site 1st L after sq by
'Mairie', adj Lac du Rochegaudon. Fr S exit J21, take
D10 sp St Benoit du Sault. Fr there turn L onto D36
and foll instructions above. 3*, Sm, hdg, mkd, pt shd,
pt sl, EHU (16A) inc (poss rev pol); bbq; sw nr; Eng
spkn; adv bkg acc; waterslide; fishing adj; tennis adj;
CKE. *"Excel site, beautiful location, friendly wardens,
well kept san facs, gd local supmkt 2 mins walk (clsd
Mon); lake nrby."* **€11.40**   **2018**

CHALAIS *7C2* (10km NW Rural) *45.32758, -0.02385*
Chez Sarrazin, 16480 Brossac 05 45 78 21 57 or
07 80 52 27 32; chezsarrazin@yahoo.co.uk;
www.chezsarrazin.net

🚐 ☂2 ♦♦ WD ▲ ᶜ 🖪 ∥ 🦋 ⑪ 🛶

N10 S fr Angouleme, leave exit for Barbezieux to
Brossac & Chalais on D731, 700m after rndabt at
Brossac Gare, L twd Brie Sous Chalais. After 1.4km R
at 4 wheelie bins sp Chez Sarrazin Camping.
Sm, shd, pt sl, EHU (10A); bbq; Eng spkn; adv bkg acc;
games area. *"Natural site in beautiful setting; many
historical vills; walks; san facs & pool excel; charming
& peaceful; excel; steep path to shwrs; helpful owners;
well equipped."* **€28.00, Easter-31 Oct.**   **2017**

"I like to fill in the reports as I travel from site to site"

You'll find report forms at the back of this guide, or you can fill them in online at camc.com/europereport.

CHALANDRAY *4H1* (0.8km N Rural) *46.66728, -0.00214*
Camping du Bois de St Hilaire, Rue de la Gare, 86190
Chalandray 05 49 60 20 84 or 01246 852823 (UK);
acceuil@camping-st-hilaire.com; www.camping-st-hilaire.com

🚐 ☂1 ♦♦ (htd) WD ▲ ᶜ 🖪 ∥ MSP 🦋 ⑪ ☂ 🛒 nr 🅿 🦮 🛶 (htd)

Foll N149 bet Parthenay & Vouille; at xrds in vill,
turn N into Rue de la Gare (D24); site 750m on R
over rlwy line. 3*, Sm, mkd, hdg, shd, EHU (10A)
€3.95; bbq (charcoal, elec, gas); twin axles; TV; phone;
bus 750m; Eng spkn; adv bkg acc; ccard acc; tennis;
games rm; games area; mini golf; boules pitch; fire
pit; CCI. *"Friendly, helpful British owners; situated
in mature forest area, sh walk fr vill; 20 mins fr
Futuroscope; lge pitches; excel, clean site & pool; c'van
storage; poss muddy in wet weather; woodland walks;
excel bakery in vill."* **€25.00, 1 May-30 Sep.**   **2019**

CHALLANS *2H4* (10km SE Rural) *46.81522, -1.77472*
Camping Domaine de Bellevue, Bellevue Du Ligneron,
85670 Saint Christophe du Ligneron 02 51 93 30 66
or 06 21 55 54 29 (mob); contact@vendee-camping-bellevue.com; www.vendee-camping-bellevue.com

12 🚐 ☂3 ♦♦ ▲ ᶜ 🖪 ∥ ⑪ 🦋 ☂ (htd)

Fr S: On Route National D948 exit Saint Christophe
du Lingeron; turn W in dir Saint Gilles Croix de Vie/
Commequirers; at rndbt cont strt on; take 2nd R at
Bellevue du Ligneron. 3*, Med, hdg, EHU (16) €4;
bbq; 50% statics; Eng spkn; adv bkg acc; ccard acc;
fishing; games rm; bike hire; CKE. *"Gd value for
money; in lovely Vendee region; gd fishing on site; new
site with friendly owners; takeaway; v lge pitches."*
€14.00   **2016**

CHALLANS *2H4* (4km S Rural) *46.81869, -1.88874*
FFCC Camping Le Ragis, Chemin de la Fradinière,
85300 Challans 02 51 68 08 49; info@camping-leragis.com; www.camping-leragis.com

🚐 ☂4 ♦♦ (htd) WD ▲ ᶜ 🖪 ∥ MSP 🦋 ⑪ ☂ 🍴 ⑪ nr 🦮 🅿 🦮 🛶 🕭
🛶 (htd)

Fr Challans go S on D32 Rte Les Sables, turn R onto
Chemin de la Fradinière & foll sp. 3*, Lge, mkd, hdg,
pt shd, EHU (10A) €4; gas; bbq; twin axles; TV;
50% statics; bus 1km; Eng spkn; adv bkg acc; ccard
acc; waterslide; games area. *"Vg; homegrown veg;
tickets for Puy Du Fou; night car park; conv Vendee
coast; lake fishing; petanque; traditional French site;
kids club 4-10; v friendly staff."*
€25.00, 1 Apr-31 Oct.   **2016**

CHALON SUR SAONE *6H1* (3km E Rural) *46.78411,
4.87136* Camping du Pont de Bourgogne, Rue Julien
Leneveu, 71380 St Marcel 03 85 48 26 86 or 03 85 94
16 90 (LS); campingchalon71@wanadoo.fr;
www.camping-chalon.com

🚐 ☂2.60 ♦♦ (htd) WD ▲ ᶜ 🖪 ∥ MSP 🍴 ⑪ 🦮 🅿 🕭

Fr A6 exit junc 26 (sp Chalon Sud) onto N80 E; foll
sp Chalon-sur-Saône; at 1st rndabt go strt over (sp
Louhans & St Marcel) & over flyover; take 4th exit
on 2nd rndbt; immed after this rndabt fork R thro
Les Chavannes (still on N80). Turn R at traff lts bef
bdge. (DO NOT CROSS BDGE). Site in 500m.
3*, Med, hdg, mkd, hdstg, pt shd, terr, EHU (6-10A)
inc (rev pol); gas; bbq; TV; 2% statics; Eng spkn; adv
bkg acc; ccard acc; games rm; bike hire; canoeing nr;
rv fishing; CKE. *"Peaceful, well-run rvside site in gd
location; lge pitches, some by rv; helpful, friendly staff;
excel clean san facs, poss stretched high ssn; vg rest/bar;
pool 500m; no o'fits over 12m; rvside walks; lovely town,
20 min walk; conv NH fr A6; vg; gd cycling; shopping ctr
nrby."* **€30.70, 1 Apr-30 Sep, L17.**   **2019**

CHALONNES SUR LOIRE *2G4* (1.5km E Rural) *47.35164, -0.74679* **Camping Les Portes de la Loire,** Le Candais, 49290 Chalonnes-sur-Loire **41 78 02 27; contact@ lesportesdelaloire.fr**

🏕 🎇 ⛱ ♨ ⚊ / MP ⚋ /⚠

Fr D723 cross bdge to Challones. In town turn L sp Rochefort-Sur-Loire. Site on L of this rd in abt 1km. 3*, Lge, mkd, pt shd, EHU (10A) €3; bbq; twin axles; adv bkg acc. *"Close to rv & town; peaceful setting; lge pitches; gd touring base; vg; excel san facs."* **€20.00, 1 May-30 Sep.** 2016

CHALONNES SUR LOIRE *2G4* (10km NW Urban) *47.39211, -0.87082* **Camping La Promenade,** Quai des Mariniers, 49570 Montjean-sur-Loire **02 41 39 02 68 or 06 26 32 60 28 (mob); contact@ campinglapromenade.com; www.campingla promenade.com**

🏕 €2 🎇 WD ⛱ ♨ ⚊ / 🦋 ⚋ 🍽 ⚋ Y ⑨ 🅿 🚂 nr /⚠ ⚘ 🛶 (htd) 🛁 🎣 sand 600m

Exit Angers on N23 twd Nantes. Exit 1km beyond St Germain-des-Prés dir Montjean-sur-Loire. Cross rv then R on D210 to site in 500m. 3*, Lge, hdg, mkd, pt shd, EHU (10A) €4; gas; bbq; twin axles; TV; 30% statics; Eng spkn; adv bkg acc; ccard acc; games area; CKE. *"Friendly, young owners; interesting sculptures in vill & at Ecomusée; gd for Loire cycling; new san facs (2014) diff exit to R for lge vehicles; fishing nr; vg."* **€20.00, 1 Apr-30 Sep.** 2015

CHALONS EN CHAMPAGNE *5D1* (3km S Urban) *48.93579, 4.38299* **Camping de Châlons en Champagne,** 11-15 Rue de Plaisance, 51000 Châlons-en-Champagne **03 26 68 38 00; camping. chalons@orange.fr; www.aquadis-loisirs.com**

🏕 €1.50 🎇 (htd) WD ⛱ ♨ ⚊ / MP 🦋 ⚋ Y ⚊ 🚂 nr /⚠

Fr N on A26 exit junc 17, on D3 foll sp to Chalons en Champagne, then to Fagnières. Strt on at traff lts, then L at 1s rndabt. Turn R, sp Vitry le François, site sp. Fr S exit junc 18 onto D977, then D5 over rv & canal nr town cent; then foll site sp to R. Fr N44 S of Châlons sp St Memmie; foll site sp. D977 fr N into Châlons, cont on main rd to traff lts at 6 x-rds & turn R, site well sp. Or exit A4 junc 27 onto N44; turn R at St Memmie; site sp. NB some sps in area still show old town name 'Châlons-sur-Marne'. Do not use SatNav. 4*, Med, hdg, mkd, hdstg, pt shd, EHU (6-10A) (poss long lead req & rev pol, 2 pin adapter req); bbq; red long stay; twin axles; TV; bus; Eng spkn; adv bkg acc; ccard acc; tennis; games area; CKE. *"Popular site adj park; generous pitches, inc hdstg; rec arr early or phone ahead; check barrier arrangements if need early dep; gates shut 2130 LS & 2300 high ssn; ltd bus service; poss noisy high ssn - pop concerts in adj area; hypmkt 1km; flat walk to lovely, interesting town; conv touring base & NH; friendly helpful recep; seasonal workers in Sep; san facs neglected but clean."* **€35.00, 5 Mar-24 Aug.** 2019

CHALUS *7B3* (10km NW Rural) *45.71540, 0.91956* **Camping Parc Verger,** Le Halte, 87150 Champagnac-la-Rivière, Limousin **0844 232 8500 (Fr UK) or 05 55 01 22 83 or 06 04 09 05 20 (mob); pvbureau@ parcverger.com; www.parcverger.com**

12 🏕 🎇 (htd) WD ⛱ ♨ 🎣 ⚊ / MP 🦋 ⚋ Y nr ⑨ nr 🚂 🛶

N fr Châlus on D901; in 9km turn L onto D75 sp Champagnac-la-Rivière; site on L in 150m. Sm, mkd, hdstg, unshd, EHU (16A) inc; bbq; sw; twin axles; red long stay; bus 150m; Eng spkn; adv bkg acc; ccard acc; CKE. *"Lovely site; welcoming, friendly, helpful British owners; lge pitches suitable for RVs; gd clean san facs, poss stretched high ssn; gd mkd walks nrby; 15km-long walk/cycle path adj (old rwly track); red grass pitch; excel local vet; excel area for walking; bike hire."* **€18.00** 2016

CHAMBERY *9B3* (5km E Rural) *45.55151, 5.98416* **Camp Municipal Le Savoy,** Parc des Loisirs, Chemin des Fleurs, 73190 Challes-les-Eaux **04 79 72 97 31; www.camping-challesleseaux.com**

🏕 €1.40 🎇 WD ⛱ ♨ 🎣 ⚊ / ⚋ 🦋 ⑨ nr 🚂 nr

On o'skts of town app fr Chambéry on D1006. Pass airfield, lake & tennis courts on L, L at traff lts just bef cent of Challes-les Eaux sp Parc de Loisirs, at Hôtel Les Neiges de France foll camp sp to site in 100m. Fr A41 exit junc 20, foll sp Challes-les-Eaux, then 'Centre Ville', then D1006 N. 3*, Med, hdstg, mkd, shd, serviced pitches; EHU (6-10A) €2.90; gas; sw nr; red long stay; bus; adv bkg acc; ccard acc; fishing adj; tennis adj. *"Well-designed, well-run, clean site in beautiful setting; diff sized pitches; level (suitable wheelchairs); friendly, helpful staff; excel modern san facs; excel walking; well run site, rec hotel school rest in term time."* **€18.00, 1 Apr-8 Oct.** 2017

"We must tell the Club about that great site we found"

Get your site reports in by mid-August and we'll do our best to get your updates into the next edition.

CHAMBERY *9B3* (25km SW Rural) *45.53804, 5.79973* **Camping Les Peupliers,** Lac d'Aiguebelette, 73610 Lépin-le-Lac **04 79 36 00 48 or 06 66 10 09 99 (mob); info@camping-lespeupliers.net; www.camping-lespeupliers.net**

🏕 €1.20 🎇 WD ⛱ ♨ / 🦋 ⚋ Y ⑨ nr 🚂 nr /⚠

Exit A43 junc 12 & foll sp Lac d'Aiguebelette (D921). Turn L at rndabt & foll rd on L of lake. Site on R after sm vill. 2*, Lge, hdg, mkd, pt shd, EHU (6A) €3.50; sw nr; ccard acc; fishing; CKE. *"Pleasant site in beautiful setting, espec lakeside pitches; friendly, helpful owner; busy w/ends."* **€19.00, 1 Apr-31 Oct.** 2015

FRANCE

CHAMBON SUR LAC 7B4 (2km W Rural) 45.57127, 2.89067 **Camping de Serrette,** Serrette, 63790 Chambon-sur-La 04 73 88 67 67; camping.de. serrette@wanadoo.fr; campingdeserrette.com

🐕 €2.50 ⭑⭑ 🅆🅒 ♨ ⬦ ⬧ ➗ ∥ 🅜🅢🅟 ☂ 🍴 ⊕ ♨ ⚡ ⛁ 🅰 ⚓ 🎣

Fr A75, exit 6, foll D996 dir Mont Dore. Foll site sp after Lac Chambo. After 1.5km turn L onto D636. Site on R. Sharp turn at ent. 3*, Sm, hdg, mkd, pt shd, pt sl, terr, EHU (10A) €4.80; bbq; sw nr; twin axles; TV; 50% statics; phone; Eng spkn; adv bkg acc; table tennis; games rm; CKE. *"Excel walking area; watersports on Lac Chambon; gd site."* **€26.70, 28 Apr-17 Sep.**
2016

"I need an on-site restaurant"

We do our best to make sure site information is correct, but it is always best to check any must-have facilities are still available or will be open during your visit.

CHAMONIX MONT BLANC 9B4 (3km NE Rural) 45.9378, 6.8925 **Camping La Mer de Glace,** 200 Chemin de la Bagna, Praz de Chamonix, 74400 Chamonix 04 50 53 44 03; info@chamonix-camp.com; www.chamonix-camping.com

🐕 ⭑⭑(htd) 🅆🅒 ♨ ⬦ ⬧ ➗ ∥ 🅜🅢🅟 🦋 ☂ 🍴 nr ⊕ nr ⬧ ⛁ nr 🅰

Foll sp on D1506 thro Chamonix dir Argentière & Swiss Frontier; site well sp on R in 3km but ent under bdge 2.4m. Rec, to avoid low bdge cont to 1st rndabt in Praz-de-Chamonix & foll sp to site (R at rndabt). 3*, Med, mkd, hdg, hdstg, pt shd, pt sl, EHU (10A) €3; bbq; bus & train 500m; Eng spkn; CKE. *"Well-run, wooded site with superb views; sm pitches; helpful staff; vg facs; bar 500m; v conv trains/buses; close to Flégère lift; sports cent nr; htd pool 2km; path to town via woods & rv; excel."* **€25.00, 4 May-9 Oct.**
2016

CHAMONIX MONT BLANC 9B4 (7km NE Rural) 45.97552, 6.92224 **Camping Le Glacier d'Argentière,** 161 Chemin des Chosalets, 74400 Argentière 04 50 54 17 36; info@campingchamonix.com; www.camping chamonix.com

🐕 €0.50 ⭑⭑ 🅆🅒 ♨ ⬦ ⬧ ➗ ∥ 🦋 ☂ ⛁ nr

On Chamonix-Argentière D1506 rd bef Argentière take R fork twd Argentière cable car stn. Site immed on R. 2*, Med, pt shd, pt sl, EHU (2-10A); bbq; Eng spkn; adv bkg acc; games area; CKE. *"Alpine excursions; cable cars adj; mountain views; friendly, helpful owners; gd friendly site; Alpine views; quiet relaxed site; bus stop 1 min; 10 min walk to Argentiere Vill', train stn & cable car; mkd paths fr site; free travel on local buses & trains inc."* **€24.00, 15 May-30 Sep.**
2019

CHAMONIX MONT BLANC 9B4 (1.6km SW Rural) 45.91466, 6.86138 **Camping Iles des Barrats,** 185 Chemin de l'Ile des Barrats, 74400 Chamonix 04 50 53 51 44; campingiledesbarrats74@orange.fr; www.campingdesbarrats.com

🐕 €1 ⭑⭑ 🅆🅒 ♨ ➗ ∥ 🅜🅢🅟 🦋 ⛁ nr

Fr Mont Blanc tunnel take 1st L on app Chamonix, foll sp to hospital, site opp hospital. Do not go into town. 3*, Sm, mkd, unshd, pt sl, EHU (5-10A) €3.30-4.30; gas; sw nr; Eng spkn; adv bkg acc; CKE. *"Great little site; superb mountain views; friendly family owners; immac facs; 10 mins level walk to town; 10 mins cable car Mont Blanc; excel; bus & train pass fr recep."* **€31.00, 1 Jun-23 Sep.**
2017

CHAMONIX MONT BLANC 9B4 (3.5km SW Rural) 45.90203, 6.83716 **Camping Les Deux Glaciers,** 80 Route des Tissières, Les Bossons, 74400 Chamonix 04 50 53 15 84; info@les2glaciers.com; www.les2glaciers.com

🐕 ⭑⭑(htd) 🅆🅒 ♨ ⬦ ⬧ ➗ ∥ ☂ 🍴 ⊕ ⬧ ⛁ 🅰

Exit Mont Blanc tunnel foll sps Geneva turn L on D1506 (Chamonix-Geneva rd), in 2km turn R for Les Bossons & L under bdge. Fr W foll sps Chamonix & Mont Blanc tunnel. On dual c/way turn R at sp `Les Bossons' & site after Mercure Hotel; adj Les Cimes site; site clearly sp fr D1205. 3*, Med, pt shd, sl, EHU (6-10A) €2.50-7; bus; Eng spkn; games rm; table tennis; CKE. *"Pleasant, well-kept site in wonderful location just under Mont Blanc; roomy pitches; clean facs; poss diff site for lge o'fits over 6m; if recep clsd pitch & wait until 1730; ideal for walking; skating rink 4km; funicular adj to Glacier des Bossons; rec arr early high ssn; pool 4km; highly rec; vg."* **€22.50, 1 Jan-15 Nov & 15 Dec-31 Dec.**
2017

"Satellite navigation makes touring much easier"

Remember most sat navs don't know if you're towing or in a larger vehicle – always use yours alongside maps and site directions.

CHANAC 9D1 (0.5km S Urban) 44.46519, 3.34670 **Camp Municipal La Vignogue,** Rue de Plaisance, 48230 Chanac 04 66 48 24 09 or 06 82 93 60 68 (mob); gites-camping-chanac@orange.fr; www.chanac.fr

🐕 €1 ⭑⭑(htd) 🅆🅒 ♨ ⬦ ⬧ ➗ ∥ 🦋 ☂ 🍴 nr ⊕ nr ⛁ nr

Exit A75 junc 39.1 onto N88 to Chanac; site well sp in vill. Sm, mkd, pt shd, pt sl, EHU (6A) inc; bbq; 10% statics; Eng spkn; adv bkg acc. *"Excel; bar 500m; pool adj; rec arr early (bef 1800)."* **€15.50, 15 Apr-30 Sep.**
2017

CHANTILLY *3D3* (5km NW Rural) *49.22571, 2.42862* **Camping Campix,** 60340 St Leu d'Esserent **03 44 56 08 48;** campix@orange.fr; www.campingcampix.com

🏕 €2 🏕(htd) 🆆 🚿 🔥 ♿ 🍴 ∥ 🅿 🦋 🍴 ⓦ 🚿 🚲 ⛵

Exit A1 junc 8 to Senlis; cont W fr Senlis on D924 thro Chantilly, x-ing Rv Oise to St Leu-d'Esserent; leave town on D12 NW twd Cramoisy thro housing est; foll site sp for 1km, winding app.
3*, Med, hdstg, mkd, shd, terr, EHU (6-10A) €3.50 (min 25m cable poss req); gas; bbq; sw nr; red long stay; phone; Eng spkn; adv bkg acc; ccard acc; fishing; games rm; CKE. *"Beautiful, peaceful site in former quarry - poss unguarded, vertical drops; helpful owner & friendly staff; wide variety of pitches - narr, steep access & o'hanging trees on some; conv Paris Parc Astérix & Disneyland (Astérix tickets fr recep); sh walk to vill; rec; gd facs; long elec leads maybe needed."*
€27.00, 7 Mar-30 Nov. **2018**

CHANTILLY *3D3* (7km NW Rural) *49.21225, 2.40270* **Camping L'Abbatiale,** 39 Rue Salvador Allendé, 60340 St Leu-d'Esserent **03 44 56 38 76;** contact@camping-abbatiale.fr; http://campingabbatiale.wix.com/campingabbatiale

12 🏕 🏕(htd) 🆆 🚿 ∥ 🅿 🦋 🍴 ⓦ 🚿 🔥 ⚠ 🅿 🏖sandy 1km

S twds Paris on A1 exit Senlis; cont W fr Senlis on D924/D44 thro Chantilly x-ing Rv Oise to St Leu-d'Esserent; cont on D44, x-ing D603 which becomes Rue Salvador Allendé in 700m; foll site sps; avoid rv x-ing on D17 fr SW; v narr bdge. 3*, Sm, mkd, hdg, hdstg, pt shd, EHU (3A) €2.50 (some rev pol); bbq (sep area); twin axles; red long stay; phone; bus adj; Eng spkn; adv bkg acc; ccard acc; games rm; games area. *"Chantilly & chateau interesting; conv for Chantilly, Paris & L'oise Valley; gd walks nrby (woodland & rvside); v friendly family owned & managed; lge nbr of statics on site but does not detract fr touring pitches nor impact on facs; best site in area."* **€18.00** **2015**

CHANTONNAY *2H4* (12km NE Rural) *46.75168, -0.94568* **Camping La Baudonnière,** Route des Salinières, 85110 Monsireigne **02 51 66 43 79;** tombann1962@gmail.com; www.labaudonniere.com

12 🏕 🏕 🆆 🚿 🔥 ♿ ∥ 🦋 ⓦ 🔥 🅿 ⚠

Fr Chantonnay take D960B NE dir St Prouant & Pouzauges. In St Prouant take D23 to Monsireigne. Foll rd downhill, cross sm rv & as rd starts to climb take 2nd L sp Reaumur; in 400m L onto Rue des Salinières. Site on L in 800m. Sm, pt shd, pt sl, EHU (10A) €4; bbq; Eng spkn; adv bkg acc; games rm; tennis 2km. *"V relaxing, peaceful, pretty CL-type site; welcoming, friendly, helpful Irish owners; excel san facs; conv Puy de Fou theme park; vg; v well kept site."*
€22.00 **2019**

CHAPELLE D'ANGILLON, LA *4G3* (1km SE Rural) *47.36044, 2.44261* **Camping Paradis Nature (formerly Municipal Les Murailles),** Route d'Henrichemont, 18380 La Chapelle-d'Angillon **06 70 29 52 00;** christelle@camping-paradis-nature.com; www.camping-paradis-nature.com

🏕 🏕 🆆 🚿 🔥 ♿ ∥ 🍴 nr ⓦ nr 🅿 nr ⚠

Fr Bourges or Aubigny-sur-Nère on D940, turn E onto D926; turn onto D12 in vill, site on R, sp.
2*, Sm, pt shd, pt sl, EHU (6A) €3.20; bbq; 10% statics; ccard acc; lake fishing adj; CKE. *"Lake adj with castle o'looking; quiet; vg; red for 3 nights or more."*
€17.00, 1 Apr-24 Oct. **2015**

CHAPELLE EN VERCORS, LA *9C3* (0.2km S Urban) *44.9695, 5.4156* **Camp Municipal Les Bruyères,** Ave des Bruyères, 26420 La Chapelle-en-Vercors **04 75 48 21 46**

🏕 €1 🏕(htd) 🆆 🚿 🔥 ♿ ∥ 🅿 🦋 🍴 nr ⓦ nr 🅿 nr ⚠

Take D518 N fr Die over Col de Rousset. Fr N on A49 exit 8 to N532 St Nazaire-en-Royans, then D76 thro St Thomas-en-Royans, then D216 to St Laurent-en-Royans. Take D2 round E flank of Combe Laval (2 sh 2-lane tunnels). Fr Col de la Machine foll D76 S 1km, then D199 E over Col de Carri to La Chapelle. (D531 fr Villard de Lons, D76 over Combe Laval & D518 Grandes Goulet not suitable for c'vans & diff lge m'vans due narr rds & tunnels & 5km of o'hanging ledges.) 2*, Med, hdstg, pt shd, pt sl, EHU (6A); TV; 10% statics; adv bkg acc; cycling; fishing; horseriding; CKE. *"Excel base for beautiful Vercors plateau; friendly welcome; climbing; pool 300m; excel value; choose own pitch; clean & immac san facs; excel cycling; vg."*
€13.50, 1 May-1 Oct. **2016**

CHAPELLE HERMIER, LA *2H4* (4km SW Rural) *46.66652, -1.75543* **Camping Le Pin Parasol,** Châteaulong, 85220 La Chapelle-Hermier **02 51 34 64 72;** contact@campingpinparasol.fr; www.campingpinparasol.fr

🏕 €6 🏕 🆆 🚿 🔥 ♿ ∥ 🅿 🦋 🍴 🍴 ⓦ 🅿 🚿 ⚠ 🏊 🚿(htd) ⛳

Exit A83 junc 4 onto D763/D937 dir La Roche-sur-Yon; turn R onto D948; at Aizenay turn R onto D6 twd St Gilles Croix-de-Vie; after 10km at x-rds turn L onto D21; in La Chapelle-Hermier foll D42 twds L'Aiguillon-sur-Vie; site sp in 4km. 5*, Lge, mkd, hdg, unshd, pt sl, terr, EHU (16A) inc; gas; bbq; sw nr; TV; 45% statics; Eng spkn; adv bkg acc; ccard acc; games rm; fishing 200m; excursions; fitness rm; archery; bike hire; games area; waterslide; tennis; CKE. *"On banks of Lake Jaunay; access to lake down sm path; lge pitches; friendly staff; no o'fits over 11m; boating 200m; canoeing 200m; excel facs; adventure zone; lovely pools; away fr crowds but close to beaches; pleasant walks & cycle tracks around lake; beautiful site; v well kept."* **€42.00, May - September, A36.** **2019**

FRANCE

CHARITE SUR LOIRE, LA *4G4* (0.5km W Urban)
47.17683, 3.01058 **FFCC Camp Municipal La Saulaie,**
Quai de la Saulaie, 58400 La Charité-sur-Loire
03 86 70 00 83 or 03 86 70 15 06 (LS); camping@
lacharitesurloire.fr; www.campinglacharitesurloire.fr

🐕 €2 ♀♀ ⓌⓄ 🏖 🔥 ♿ 🗑 ╱ 🐾 ⛵ 🏋 nr

Exit A77 junc 30 & foll sp 'Centre Ville'. Turn L over
Rv Loire sp Bourges; take 2nd R bef next bdge.
Fr Bourges on N151, turn L immed after x-ing 1st
bdge over Rv Loire. Foll sp. NB Take care when
turn R over narr rv bdge when leaving site - v high
kerb. 3*, Med, mkd, pt shd, EHU (10A); sw nr; red long
stay; CKE. "Lovely, well-kept site on rv island; warm
welcome, helpful staff; gd security; poss school groups
high ssn; LS phone to check open; beautiful town;
playgrnd & htd pool, paddling pool adj inc (pool opens
1 Jul); welcoming staff; new san facs (2016); site v well
maintained." **€21.00, 1 Apr-28 Sep.**   **2017**

CHARLEVILLE MEZIERES *5C1* (3.5km N Urban)
49.77813, 4.72245 **Camp Municipal Mont Olympe,**
Rue des Pâquis, 08000 Charleville-Mézières **03 24 33
23 60 or 03 24 32 44 80; camping-charleville
mezieres@wandadoo.fr**

🐕 €1.60 ♀♀ (htd) ⓌⓄ 🏖 🔥 🍴 ╱ 🅼🅿 🛒 ♈ 🏋 ⓝⓇ 🏋 nr 🅰

Fr N43/E44 head for Hôtel de Ville, with Hôtel de
Ville on R, cont N along Ave des Arches, turn R
at 'Gare' sp & cross rv bdge. At 'Gare' turn sharp
L immed along Rue des Pâquis, site on L in 500m,
visible fr rd. Well sp fr town cent. 3*, Med, hdg, mkd,
hdstg, pt shd, serviced pitches; EHU (10A) €3.95; gas;
bbq; TV; 10% statics; Eng spkn; ccard acc; fishing;
boating; games rm; CKE. "Lovely, spacious, well-kept
site on Rv Meuse; v lge pitches extra; helpful staff;
htd covrd pool adj; san facs clean, new (2018); useful
snack bar; easy walk to charming town; excel; NH for
m'van's." **€20.00, 1 Apr-30 Sep.**   **2018**

CHARLIEU *9A1* (1km E Urban) *46.15851, 4.18088*
FFCC Camp Municipal de la Douze, chemin du Camping,
42190 Charlieu **04 77 72 86 01; camp-charlieu@
voila.fr**

🐕 ♀♀ (htd) ⓌⓄ 🏖 ♿ 🗑 ╱ 🅼🅿 🍴 🛒 🏋 nr 🅰 ⚓

N fr Roanne on D482 to Pouilly-sous-Charlieu, then E
on D487 to Charlieu town cent, site sp in town, by sw
pool. NB Do not confuse with Camp Municipal Pouilly-
sous-Charlieu which is sp fr main rd. 3*, Med, hdg, pt
shd, EHU (6A) inc; sw nr; twin axles; 5% statics; Eng spkn;
adv bkg acc; boating adj; fishing adj; games area; CKE.
"Gd clean new san facs (2018); vg value; quiet; new cycle
rte to Loire; canal cycle paths; sw & tennis adj; historical
town." **€16.00, 1 Apr-30 Sep.**   **2018**

CHARMES *6E2* (1km N Rural) *48.37706, 6.28974*
Camp Municipal Les Iles, 20 Rue de l'Ecluse, 88130
Charmes **03 29 38 87 71 or 03 29 38 85 85; andre.
michel63@wanadoo.fr; www.ville-charmes.fr**

🐕 ♀♀ ⓌⓄ 🏖 🔥 🗑 ╱ 🐾 ⓌⓄ ♈ 🍴 🛒 🏋 nr 🅰

Exit N57 for Charmes, site well sp on Rv Moselle.
Do not confuse with sp for 'Camping Cars'. 3*, Med,
mkd, pt shd, EHU (10A) €3.55; gas; bbq; red long stay;
phone; Eng spkn; adv bkg acc; kayak hire; fishing; CKE.
"Lovely site bet rv & canal; lge pitches; friendly staff;
footpath to town; m'van o'night area in town; vg value;
gd; v lge pitches." **€16.50, 1 Apr-30 Sep.**   **2017**

CHARNY *4F3* (0.9km N Rural) *47.89078, 3.09419*
FFCC Camping des Platanes, 41 Route de la Mothe,
89120 Charny **03 86 91 83 60; info@campingles
platanes.fr; www.campinglesplatanes.fr**

🐕 €3 ♀♀ (htd) ⓌⓄ 🏖 🔥 ♿ 🗑 ╱ 🐾 ⓌⓄ ♈ 🍴 🛒 🏋 nr 🅰 ⚓

Exit A6 junc 18 onto D943 to Montargis. Turn S onto
D950 to Charny, site on R as ent vill; sp. 3*, Med, hdg,
mkd, pt shd, serviced pitches; EHU (10A) inc; gas; bbq;
red long stay; TV; 60% statics; Eng spkn; adv bkg acc;
bike hire; tennis 500m; rv fishing 150m; CKE. "Pleasant,
peaceful site; gd sized pitches; friendly, helpful owners;
excel, clean san facs; sh walk to vill; gd walking; gd touring
base." **€22.50, 1 Apr-30 Oct.**   **2016**

CHAROLLES *9A2* (0.5km E Rural) *46.43972, 4.28208*
FFCC Camp Municipal, Route de Viry, 71120
Charolles **03 85 24 04 90 or 32 17 10 10 62; camping.
charolles@orange.fr**

🐕 €1.50 ♀♀ (htd) ⓌⓄ 🏖 🔥 ♿ 🗑 ╱ 🐾 ⓌⓄ ♈ 🍴 🛒 🏋 nr 🅰
⚓ (htd) 🅱

Exit N79 at E end of by-pass sp Vendenesse-lès-
Charolles; at rndabt foll camping sp; then sharp R
bottom hill bef town; site on L, next to Municipal
pool. 3*, Med, hdstg, hdg, mkd, pt shd, pt sl, EHU (6A)
€2; bbq; twin axles; 2% statics; adv bkg rec; ccard acc;
games rm; CKE. "Well-kept site; sm pitches; friendly,
helpful warden; gd, modern san facs; pool adj high ssn
(proper sw trunks req); m'van area outside site;
negligible security; canoe's avail, launching stn to rv on
site; excel." **€14.00, 1 Apr-5 Oct.**   **2018**

CHARTRE SUR LE LOIR, LA *4F2* (0.5km W Rural)
47.73220, 0.57451 **Camping Le Vieux Moulin,**
Chemin des Bergivaux, 72340 La Chartre-sur-le Loir
02 43 44 41 18; bordduloir@orange.fr

🐕 €1.50 ♀♀ (htd) ⓌⓄ 🏖 🔥 ♿ 🗑 ╱ 🐾 ⓌⓄ ♈ 🍴 🛒 🏋 nr 🅰 ⚓ (htd)

Sp fr D305 in town. Fr S exit A28 junc 27 onto
D766 dir Beaumont-la-Ronce; then take D29 to
La Chartre-sur-le Loir; go over rv, turn L immed
after bdge. Fr N leave A20 at junc 24 & foll D304 to
Chartre, site well sp on R bef bdge. 3*, Med, hdg,
mkd, pt shd, EHU (5-10A) €4-5 (poss rev pol); bbq;
TV; 20% statics; Eng spkn; adv bkg rec; 15% red
CC members; rv fishing; bike hire; CKE. "Beautiful,
well-kept rvside site; helpful, friendly staff; excel pool;
gd for dogs; v lge MH's acc; gd base for chateaux,
forest & Loir Valley; excel; pleasant walk to town."
€24.00, 1 Mar-30 Nov.   **2018**

CHARTRES *4E2* (3km SE Urban) *48.43433, 1.49914* **Camping Les Bords de l'Eure,** 9 Rue de Launay, 28000 Chartres **02 37 28 79 43; ets-ya-roussel-montigny@orange.fr; www.camping-de-chartres.fr**

🅃 €1.08 �♦♦ (htd) ♨ ♣ ♿ ⊡ ∥ ☒ 🦋 ♈ ∥ ⚠

Exit N123 ring rd at D935, R at T-junc dir Chartres; then R at 2nd traff lts dir Chartres immed after rlwy bdge; site on L in 400m; inside of ring rd. Also sp fr town cent on N154 fr N, foll sp town cent under 2 rlwy bdges, L at traff lts sp Orléans, after 1km site sp. Fr SE on N154 cross ring rd, foll site sp & turn L at 2nd traff lts; site on R. 3*, Med, hdg, mkd, shd, EHU (6A) €4 (poss rev pol); bbq; 10% statics; Eng spkn; adv bkg acc; ccard acc; fishing; CKE. *"Popular, spacious, pleasant, well laid-out, dir access to rv; unisex san facs clean but tired, stretched when busy; some pitches diff lge o'fits; gates clsd 2200-0700; poss ssn workers; poss unkempt early ssn; when wet grnd soft & muddy in places; easy walk or cycle along rv to Chartres, well lit at night; rec Son et Lumière; ideal NH & longer; vg; attractive site, bottom of hill, some awkward pitches; friendly helpful staff; excel situation."* **€23.00, 1 Mar-31 Oct.** **2017**

CHASSENEUIL SUR BONNIEURE *7B3* (10km E Rural) *45.83283, 0.55811* **Camping Le Paradis,** Mareuil, 16270 Mazières **05 45 84 92 06 or 078 66 49 67 41 (mob); info@le-paradis-camping.com; www.le-paradis-camping.com**

�12 🐕 ♦♦♦ ⊡ ♨ ♣ ♿ ⊡ ∥ ☒ 🦋 ☂ nr ⚙ nr ☎ ⚠

Fr Limoges W on N141 twd Angoulême, turn L at 1st traff lts in Roumazières-Loubert D161. Site sp in 2km at t-junc. 4*, Sm, hdstg, mkd, hdg, pt shd, EHU (10-16A) €5.50-8.50; bbq; sw nr; 20% statics; Eng spkn; bus 1km; adv bkg rec; fishing nr; tennis nr; games area; watersports 5km; CKE. *"Clean, tranquil site; gd sized pitches; vg; immac san facs; welcoming, helpful British owners; helpful & friendly; gd touring base; adv bkg rec lge o'fits; excel; min €30 for 1 night stays; storage avail; highly rec."* **€19.50** **2016**

CHATAIGNERAIE, LA *2H4* (6km E Rural) *46.64854, -0.66580* **Camping La Viollière,** 85120 Breuil-Barret **02 51 87 44 82; vendeevacances@gmail.com; http://vendeevacances.googlepages.com/**

🅃 €1 ♦♦♦ ⊡ ♨ ∥ 🦋 ♈ ☂ nr ⚙ nr ☎ nr

Take D949B E thro La Châtaigneraie for 5km. Cont thro Breuil-Barret & site 2nd R after passing under rlwy bdge. Sm, pt shd, pt sl, EHU (6A) inc (poss long lead req); bbq; Eng spkn; adv bkg acc. *"Peaceful, relaxing CL-type site; v lge pitches with views; helpful British owners; excel."* **€18.00, Apr-Oct.** **2019**

CHATEAU ARNOUX *10E3* (3km NE Rural) *44.10476, 6.01680* **Camping Sunêlia L'Hippocampe,** Route Napoléon, 04290 Volonne **04 92 33 50 00; camping@l-hippocampe.com; www.l-hippocampe.com**

🅃 €2 ♦♦♦ ⊡ ♨ ♣ ♿ ⊡ ∥ ☒ 🦋 ♈ ☂ ⚙ ☎ ⚠ ♣ ☒ (htd) ⛵

Exit A51 junc 21 onto D4085 12km S of Sisteron twd Volonne vill over rv. Turn R on D4 on ent vill & foll camp sp 1km. 4*, Lge, hdstg, mkd, hdg, pt shd, serviced pitches; EHU (10A) inc (poss rev pol); bbq (elec, gas); red long stay; TV; 10% statics; Eng spkn; adv bkg acc; ccard acc; canoeing; fishing; games area; waterslide; bike hire; rafting; tennis; games rm; CKE. *"Pleasant, busy, well-run site; spacious, well-screened pitches; various pitch sizes/prices, some by lake; some pitches poss diff due trees; scruffy."* **€42.00, 25 Apr-30 Sep, C09.** **2015**

> ## "There aren't many sites open at this time of year"
>
> If you're travelling outside peak season remember to call ahead to check site opening dates – even if the entry says 'open all year'.

CHATEAU CHINON *4H4* (6km S Rural) *47.00587, 3.90548* **FFCC Camping L'Etang de la Fougeraie,** Hameau de Champs, 58120 St Léger-de-Fougeret **03 86 85 11 85; info@campingfougeraie.fr; www.campingfougeraie.com**

🅃 €1.70 ♦♦♦ ⊡ ♨ ♣ ⊡ ∥ ☒ 🦋 ♈ ⚙ ☎ ⚠

Fr Château-Chinon S on D27; in approx 3km turn R onto D157 to St Léger-de-Fougeret; in vill foll sps S dir Onlay to site in 2.5km. 3*, Med, hdg, mkd, pt shd, terr, EHU (6A) €3.20; bbq; sw; TV; Eng spkn; games area; bike hire; games rm; fishing; CKE. *"Beautiful, tranquil situation; most pitches & face lake; donkey rides; welcoming, efficient owners; facs at top of terr - poss stretched high ssn & ltd LS; gd rest; poss diff lge o'fits; pitches muddy when wet; excel."* **€29.00, 1 Apr-30 Sep, L24.** **2019**

CHATEAU DU LOIR *4G1* (8km E Rural) *47.71250, 0.49930* **Camping du Lac des Varennes,** Route de Port Gauthier, 72340 Marçon **02 43 44 13 72; contact@lacdesvarennes; www.lacdesvarennes.com**

🅃 €1.80 ♦♦♦ (htd) ⊡ ♨ ♣ ♿ ⊡ ∥ ☒ 🦋 ♈ ☂ ⚙ ♣ ☎ ⚠ ∥

Fr N on D338 fr Château-du-Loir dir Vendôme for 3km. Turn L onto D305 sp Marçon. In vill turn L onto D61 over bdge. Site on R by lake. 3*, Lge, hdg, hdstg, mkd, pt shd, EHU (10A) €3.40 (poss rev pol, poss long lead req); bbq; sw nr; red long stay; 11% statics; Eng spkn; adv bkg rec; ccard acc; boat hire; watersports; horseriding; tennis; bike hire; CKE. *"Pretty site in lovely situation bet lake & rv; friendly, helpful staff; gd security; gd walks & cycling; san facs basic & unisex; LS off clsd 1200-1600; new owners (2016)."* **€20.00, 1 Apr-30 Oct.** **2016**

FRANCE

CHATEAU GONTIER *4F1* (2km N Urban) *47.83851, -0.69965* **Camping Le Parc,** 15 Route de Laval, 53200 Château-Gontier 02 43 07 35 60; camping.parc@cc-chateau-gontier.fr; www.sudmayenne.com

12 🐕 ♀♀(htd) ⬜ ♨ ⅙ 🖭 ∥ 🅿 😈 ▼ 🛒nr 🅰 ⚘

App Château-Gontier fr N on N162, at 1st rndabt on bypass take 1st exit. Site on R in 250m. 3*, Sm, mkd, pt shd, sl, EHU (6-10A) inc (rev pol); TV; 20% statics; ccard acc; tennis; fishing; games rm; CKE. *"V pleasant, beautiful site; most pitches sl, some o'look rv; superb clean unisex san facs; rvside path to attractive town; mkt Thurs; excel site, gd pitches; superb clean san facs; helpful staff; pool 800m; lots of activity on rv to watch."* **€18.00**   **2018**

CHATEAU GONTIER *4F1* (12km SE Rural) *47.74985, -0.64258* **Camping des Rivières,** Rue du Port, 53200 Daon 02 43 06 94 78; www.campingdaon.fr

♀♀ ⬜ ♨ ⅙ 🖭 ∥ 😈 🛒nr

On town side of rv bdge, turn down lane & site ent on R at bottom of hill. 2*, Med, pt shd, EHU (10A) €3; sw nr; adv bkg acc; tennis nr; CKE. *"Vg clean & well-cared for site; some pitches diff to access; mini golf nr; boating on adj Rv Mayenne; great san facs."* **€13.00, 1 Apr-30 Sep.**   **2016**

CHATEAU RENAULT *4G2* (7km S Urban) *47.54471, 0.88786* **Camp Municipal du Moulin,** Rue du Lavoir, 37110 Villedômer 02 47 55 05 50 or 02 47 55 00 04 (Mairie); mairie.villedomer@wanadoo.fr

🐕 €1 ♀♀ ⬜ ♨ ∥ ▼nr ⊕nr 🛒nr

Fr A10 exit junc 18 onto D31 dir Château-Renault. Turn W onto D73 sp to Auzouer & Villedômer. Fr Château-Renault S on D910, site sp dir Villedômer. 1*, Sm, hdg, shd, EHU (10A) €3; adv bkg rec; rv fishing; fishing 2km. *"Gd, clean facs but old-fashioned; pitch yourself if warden not present; does not accept twin axles."* **€14.00, 15 Jun-15 Sep.**   **2016**

CHATEAU RENAULT *4G2* (0.5km W Urban) *47.59283, 0.90687* **Camp Municipal du Parc de Vauchevrier,** Rue Paul-Louis-Courier, 37110 Château-Renault 02 47 29 54 43 or 02 47 29 85 50 (LS); camping. vauchevrier@orange.fr; www.ville-chateau-renault.fr

♀♀ ⬜ ♨ ⅙ 🖭 ∥ 🅿 ▼nr ⊕nr 🛒nr 🅰 🛶(htd)

At Château-Renault foll sp to site 800m fr D910. If app fr a'route turn L on ent town & site on R of main rd adj Rv Brenne. 2*, Med, mkd, hdg, pt shd, EHU (6A) €2.20 (long lead poss req); tennis; fishing; CKE. *"Pleasant site by rv in park; lge pitches; friendly, helpful warden; clean, modern san facs, ltd LS; bar 300m; gd NH nr D910; no twin axles."* **€14.00, 1 May-15 Sep.**   **2016**

CHATEAUBRIANT *2F4* (1.5km S Urban) *47.70305, -1.37789* **Camp Municipal Les Briotais,** Rue de Tugny, 44110 Chateaubriant 02 40 81 14 38 or 02 40 81 02 32; h.menet@ville-chateaubriant.fr; www.tourisme-chateaubriant.fr/camping-municipal-des-briotais

🐕 €0.35 ♀♀ ♨ ⅙ ∥ 🅿 😈 ▼nr ⊕nr 🛒nr

App fr Nantes (D178) site sp on S end of town. Or fr Angers on D963/D163 foll sp at 1st rndabt; fr town cent, foll sps thro town. 2*, Sm, hdg, pt shd, EHU €2.70; games area. *"11thC chateau in town; site locked o'night; site on municipal playing field; gd NH; pool in town."* **€6.00, 1 May-30 Sep.**   **2016**

CHATEAUDUN *4F2* (2km N Urban) *48.08008, 1.33141* **Camp Municipal Le Moulin à Tan,** Rue de Chollet, 28200 Chateaudun 02 37 45 05 34 or 02 37 45 22 46 (LS); tourisme-chateaudun@wanadoo.fr

♀♀ ⬜ ♨ ⅙ 🖭 ∥ 🅿 ⊕nr 🛒nr 🅰

App Châteaudun fr N on N10; turn R onto D3955 at 2nd rndabt (supmkt & Buffalo Grill on L); L at next rndabt onto D955; in 800m turn L into Rue de Chollet. App Châateaudun fr S on N10, turn L onto D3955 & then as bef. Site adj Rv Loir & well sp fr D955. 2*, Med, mkd, pt shd, EHU (6A) inc; TV; 5% statics; fishing; games area; canoeing; CKE. *"Gd touring base; quiet/under-used LS; helpful warden; some night flying fr nrby military airfield; htd covrd pool 2km; security gate 2.1m height; no twin axles; gd; rec open fr 0700 - 2200; walks fr site; OK NH."* **€13.00, 1 Apr-30 Sep.**   **2017**

"That's changed – Should I let the Club know?"

If you find something on site that's different from the site entry, fill in a report and let us know. See camc.com/europereport.

CHATEAULIN *2E2* (2km S Rural) *48.18754, -4.08515* **Camping La Pointe,** Route de St Coulitz, 29150 Châteaulin 02 98 86 51 53; lapointecamping@aol.com; www.lapointesuperbecamping.com

🐕 €1 ♀♀ ⬜ ♨ ♨ ⅙ 🖭 ∥ 🅿 😈 ♈ ▼nr ⊕nr 🛒 🅰

Exit N165 onto D887 to Châteaulin; in town cent, cross bdge & turn L along rv on D770; after approx 750m, turn L at sp for St Coulitz; in 100m turn R into site. NB if app fr S to Châteaulin on D770, do not attempt to turn R at sp for St Coulitz (tight turn); go into town & turn round. 3*, Med, hdstg, mkd, hdg, pt shd, pt sl, EHU (10A) €3 (poss rev pol); bbq; phone; Eng spkn; adv bkg acc; rv fishing nrby; games rm; bike hire; CKE. *"Charming, peaceful, spacious site in wooded setting; well-run; helpful & friendly British owners; immac san facs; rvside path to town; gd cycling, walking & fishing; gd touring base; gd."* **€21.00, 15 Mar-15 Oct.**   **2015**

FRANCE

CHATEAUNEUF DU FAOU *2E2* (1km S Urban)
48.18306, -3.80986 **Gites & Camping de Penn ar Pont,** Rue de la Liberation, 29520 Chateauneuf du Faou **02 98 81 81 25 or 06 60 24 75 42;**
gites.pennarpont@orange.fr; www.pennarpont.com

🐕 €2 ⅋ᵢ 👖 (wᴅ) ♨ / ᴍᴘ 🦋 ⵙ nr ♨ nr

Take D36 S, go over bdge, site at 1st R turn.
Sm, hdg, mkd, pt shd, terr, EHU (16A) €3.50; bbq; Eng spkn; adv bkg acc. *"Steep rd on site, diff for lge o'fits; jazz fest last w/end of July; gd; san facs clean but needs upgrade; typical sm municipal site in beautiful setting."*
€15.00, 1 Apr-31 Oct. **2018**

CHATEAUNEUF SUR LOIRE *4F3* (1km S Rural)
47.85643, 2.22426 **FFCC Camping de la Maltournée,** Route de Châteauneuf, 45110 Châteauneuf-sur-Loire **02 38 58 42 46 or 06 32 11 41 13 (mob);**
contact@camping-chateauneufsurloire.fr;
www.camping-chateauneufsurloire.com

🐕 €1.35 ⅋ᵢ (htd) (wᴅ) ♨ ♿ 🗑 / ᴍᴘ 🦋 ⵙ ♨ nr ♨

S fr Chateauneuf cent, cross rv on D11; take 1st L, site in 300m on S bank of Rv Loire. 2*, Lge, pt shd, EHU (10A) €4.20; 75% statics; adv bkg acc; canoeing; CKE. *"Well-kept, busy site; helpful, pleasant staff; clean, modern san facs; chem disp v basic via narr pipe; some m'van pitches beside rv; conv Orléans; security barrier; poss ssn workers; gd cycling base for Evro Velo."* **€18.00, 15 Apr-31 Oct.** **2018**

"I like to fill in the reports as I travel from site to site"

You'll find report forms at the back of this guide, or you can fill them in online at camc.com/europereport.

CHATEAUNEUF SUR LOIRE *4F3* (8.6km W Urban)
47.86884, 2.11597 **Camping de l'Isle aux Moulins,** Rue du 44ème Régiment d'Infanterie, 45150 Jargeau **02 38 59 70 04 or 02 54 22 26 61 (LS);**
camping.jargeau@orange.fr; www.jargeau.fr

🐕 €1.20 ⅋ᵢ (htd) (wᴅ) ♨ ♿ 🗑 / ᴍᴘ 🦋 ⵙ nr ♨ nr ♨ 🎣

Exit Châteauneuf W on D960 dir Orléans; at St Denis-de l'Hôtel turn sharp L onto D921 to Jargeau over Loire bdge; immed after x-ing bdge turn R into Blvd Jeanne d'Arc sp Camping; in 200m cont strt on into Rue du 44ème Régiment d'Infanterie; site on R in 300m. Site clearly visible on R of bdge on W bank of rv. NB App rd & turning to site is v narr; do not arr 1200-1330 (lunch time) as parking diff. 2*, Lge, mkd, pt shd, pt sl, EHU (5A) €3.50; dbq; twin axles; red long stay; 2% statics; bus 500m; Eng spkn; adv bkg acc; ccard acc; bike hire; games area; rv fishing adj; CKE. *"V pleasant rvside site; lge pitches amongst trees; friendly farming family; modern san facs; poss muddy when wet; pool adj; sh walk to sm town; conv for Orleans."*
€19.00, 1 Apr-31 Oct. **2015**

CHATEAUPONSAC *7A3* (0.2km SW Rural) *46.13163, 1.27083* **Camping De La Gartempe,** Ave de Ventenat, 87290 Chateauponsac **05 55 76 55 33; campingdela** gartempe@gmail.com; www.campingdelagartempe.fr

12 🐕 €1 ⅋ᵢ 👖 (htd) (wᴅ) ♨ ♿ / ⵙ 🦋 nr ♨ ♨

Fr N exit A20 junc 23.1 sp Châteauponsac; go thro vill, well sp on L on rvside. Fr S exit A20 junc 24 sp Châteauponsac & then as above. 3*, Sm, hdg, mkd, pt shd, terr, EHU (6A) €3 (poss rev pol); Eng spkn; adv bkg acc; kayaking; archery; CKE. *"Pleasant site; gd san facs; pitches muddy in wet; not suitable lge m'vans; activities down steep hill by rv; poss noise fr parties in rest; children's activites; adj to holiday bungalows/gites; helpful owners; nice vill."* **€16.00** **2018**

CHATEAUROUX *4H2* (2km N Rural) *46.82368, 1.69496* **Camp Municipal Le Rochat-Belle Isle,** Rue du Rochat, 36000 Châteauroux **06 02 71 14 55 or 02 54 08 96 29; campinglerochat@gmail.com;** www.camping-lerochat.fr

🐕 €1.50 ⅋ᵢ 👖 (wᴅ) ♨ ♿ 🗑 / ᴍᴘ 🦋 ⵙ nr ♨ nr ♨

Exit A20 junc 13 onto D943/N143 S; foll sp Châteauroux; site sp bef town. Site on banks of Rv Indre, just S of Lac de Belle-Isle. Sp in town. 3*, Med, pt shd, EHU (5-10A) inc; gas; Eng spkn. *"Leisure park adj with pool & windsurfing on lake; friendly welcome & helpful; gd, modern, clean san facs; poss music till late w/end high ssn; poss travellers; pleasant walk into town along rv; lge brocante mkt 1st Sun of month Oct-Jul; vg; nice site; excel family site."* **€20.00, 25 Mar-23 Oct.** **2017**

CHATEL DE NEUVRE *9A1* (1.3km NE Rural) *46.4131, 3.31884* **Camping Deneuvre,** Route De Moulins, 03500 Châtel-de-Neuvre **04 70 42 04 51; campingdeneuvre@** wanadoo.fr; www.camping-deneuvre.fr

🐕 €1 ⅋ᵢ 👖 (wᴅ) ♨ ♿ 🗑 / ᴍᴘ 🦋 ⵙ ⵙ 👖 (wᴅ) ♨ ♨

S fr Moulins on D2009; sp N of vill on E side of D2009. 3*, Med, mkd, hdstg, pt shd, EHU (4A) inc; gas; Eng spkn; adv bkg acc; canoe hire; CKE. *"Site by Rv Allier in nature reserve; clean but not smart; useful NH without unhitching; friendly welcome; excel clean san facs; ltd facs LS; meals avail; splendid place for walking, fishing, cycling & birdwatching; diff ent/exit for lge o'fits; no twin axles."* **€20.00, 1 Apr-30 Sep.** **2016**

CHATEL DE NEUVRE *9A1* (0.4km W Rural) *46.40320, 3.31350* **Canoe Camping la Courtine,** 7 Rue de St Laurant, 03500 Châtel-de-Neuvre **04 70 42 06 21; mail@** camping-lacourtine.com; www.camping-lacourtine.com

12 🐕 ⅋ᵢ 👖 (htd) (wᴅ) ♨ ♿ 🗑 / ᴍᴘ 🦋 ⵙ 👖 (wᴅ) ♨ nr ♨ ♨

Fr N on D2009 to cent of vill, turn L at x-rds onto D32; site in 500m. 2*, Sm, mkd, hdstg, pt shd, EHU (6-10A) €3-5 (poss rev pol); TV; Eng spkn; adv bkg acc; CKE. *"Friendly welcome; untidy ent masks v nice site; German family-owned site; access to Rv Allier for canoeing, fishing; walking in nature reserve; liable to flood & poss clsd LS, phone ahead to check; conv LS NH; lovely woodland setting."* **€17.00** **2018**

CHATEL MONTAGNE *9A1* (0.5km W Rural) *46.11526, 3.67700* **Camping Retro Passion,** La Croix Cognat, 03250 Chatel Montagne 04 70 59 31 38; camping retropassion@gmail.com; www.camping-retro-passion.fr

🐕 � �ⓦ⒟ ▲ ♨ ⅙ 🍴 ⁄ MꜱP 🐾 ♕ ⟱ ♨ ₴ 🏖

SW fr Lapalisse on D7, in 15km L on D25 to Chatel Montagne. Site on L bef vill. Sm, mkd, pt shd, pt sl, terr, EHU (6A); bbq; twin axles; TV; 5% statics; Eng spkn; adv bkg acc; games area; games rm; tennis 100m; bike hire; CKE. *"Vg."* **€18.00, 15 Apr-31 Oct.**   **2015**

CHATELAILLON PLAGE *7A1* (2km N Urban) *46.08632, -1.09489* **Camping L'Océan,** Ave d'Angoulins, 17340 Châtelaillon-Plage 05 46 56 87 97; reception@ oceancamping.fr; www.oceancamping.fr

🐕 ₠2 ♔virtual ▲ ♨ ⅙ 🍴 ⁄ ⟱ nr ⓦ nr ₴ 🏖 sand 500m

Fr La Rochelle take D602 to Châtelaillon-Plage, site sp on L in 300m (after passing g'ge & L'Abbaye camp site). 3*, Med, mkd, hdg, EHU (10A) €5; bbq; phone; bus; Eng spkn; ccard acc; waterslide; ice. *"Very nice, excel site; gd cycle rtes; top class facs; occasional noise fr rlwy & clay pigeon range; park & ride 400m; beautiful man made lake/beach; new owner (2017)."* **€33.00, 20 May-23 Sep.**   **2017**

CHATELAILLON PLAGE *7A1* (2.5km SE Coastal) *46.05491, -1.08331* **Camping Au Port Punay,** Les Boucholeurs, Allée Bernard Moreau, 17340 Châtelaillon-Plage 05 17 81 00 00; contact@camping-port-punay.com; www.camping-port-punay.com

🐕 ₠2.50 ♔virtual ▲ ♨ 🍴 ⁄ 🐾 ♕ ⟱ ⓘ ♨ ⓦ nr ⼭ ₴ 🏖

🏖 sand 500m

Fr N exit D137 La Rochell-Rochefort rd onto D109; strt on at 1st rndabt, L at 2nd rndabt; then cont for 2.8km to end (harbour); turn L, keep R along narr one-way st; at next junc to L, site sp. Fr S exit D137 onto D203 sp Les Boucholeurs; at rndabt in 1km foll site sp to edge of Châtelaillon & turn R, foll sp. Site in 500m. 3*, Lge, pt shd, EHU (10A) €5; gas; TV; 25% statics; Eng spkn; adv bkg acc; bike hire; games area. *"Busy but quiet site; immac san facs; friendly, energetic, helpful owners; steel pegs req; sm pitches; excel; lovely area & location."* **€37.00, 28 Apr-24 Sep.**   **2017**

See advertisement

CHATILLON EN DIOIS *9D3* (0.6km E Urban) *44.69450, 5.48817* **Camp Municipal Les Chaussières,** 26410 Châtillon-en-Diois 04 75 21 10 30 or 04 75 21 14 44 (Mairie); camping.chatillonendiois@ wanadoo.fr; www.camping-chatillonendiois.com

🐕 ₠2.10 ♔virtual ⓦ⒟ ▲ ⁄ MꜱP 🐾 ⟱ nr ⓦ nr ⼭ ♨

Fr Die take D93 S for 6km then L on D539 to Châtillon (8km) site sp on R on ent to town. 2*, Med, mkd, pt shd, EHU (10A) €3.60; bbq; 30% statics; phone; Eng spkn; adv bkg acc; ccard acc; ice; canoeing; fishing; cycling; horseriding; tennis; CKE. *"Wardens off site 1130- 1630; pool adj; pleasant sweet site, wardens friendly and helpful."* **€21.00, 1 Apr-13 Oct.**   **2019**

CHATILLON SUR CHALARONNE *9A2* (0.5km SE Urban) *46.11622, 4.96172* **FFCC Camp Municipal du Vieux Moulin,** Ave Jean Jaurès, 01400 Châtillon-sur-Chalaronne 04 74 55 04 79; camping@chatillon-sur-chalaronne.org; www.camping-vieuxmoulin.com

🛨 €2 ♦¶♦ wo ♨ ♿ 🗑 ⋰ � Ⅰ nr ⊕ nr ⫨ 🗑 nr /◻\

Exit A6 junc 30 to Châtillon-sur-Chalaronne; pick up D7 on S side of vill; site on R in 400m. Ave Jean Jaurès is pt of D7. Site sp in town. 4*, Med, hdg, hdstg, shd, EHU (10A) €4 (long lead req on some pitches); 50% statics; phone; adv bkg acc; ccard acc; fishing; CKE. *"Lovely site in picturesque area; helpful warden; immac facs, ltd LS; check office opening hrs for early dep; leisure cent adj; if office clsd ring bell, warden will open barrier; lovely medieval town cent; pool adj inc; excel model rlwy; bar adj; mkt Sat; site remains excel, new municipal pool under construction next door."* **€25.80, 15 Apr-30 Sep.** **2019**

CHATILLON SUR INDRE *4H2* (0.8km N Rural) *46.99116, 1.17382* **Les Rives de L'Indre (formerly municipal),** Rue de Moulin de la Grange, 36700 Châtillon-sur-indre 07 61 39 81 62 or 02 54 38 17 86; camping-chatillon-sur-indre@orange.fr; www.chatillon-sur-indre.fr

🛨 ♦¶♦ ♨ ♿ ⋰ 🌀 👑 ⊕ nr 🗑 nr /◻\

Site well sp in vill. N twd Loches then foll sp. 3*, Med, mkd, hdg, pt shd, EHU (6A) €3; bbq; CKE. *"Lovely, relaxed, well-kept site; friendly, helpful warden; 4 chalets; gd, clean san facs; conv Loire chateaux; gd birdwatching area; interesting old town; htd pool 400m (proper sw trunks only); lge mkt Fri; excel value; call warden if barrier clsd; warden onsite 0800-1100/1630-2000."* **€12.00, 1 Apr-31 Oct.** **2017**

CHATILLON SUR SEINE *6F1* (1km E Urban) *47.85955, 4.57975* **Camp Municipal Louis Rigoly,** Esplanade Saint Vorles, 21400 Châtillon-sur-Seine 03 80 91 03 05 or 03 80 91 13 19 (LS); contact@camping-chatillon surseine.com; camping-chatillonsurseine.com

🛨 ♦¶♦ wo ♨ ♿ 🗑 ⋰ MP 🌀 👑 🗑 nr /◻\ 🛶

Fr N, cross rv bdge (Seine); cont approx 400m twd town cent; at lge metal fountain forming rndabt turn L, foll sp to site. Fr S turn R & foll camping sp. Rec lge o'fits proceed thro town to metal fountain. Turn R & foll sp to site. 2*, Med, mkd, hdg, pt shd, pt sl, EHU (6A) €2.30-4.65; gas; Eng spkn; adv bkg acc; jacuzzi; tennis; fishing; CKE. *"Pretty site adj park; clean, tidy, well-spaced pitches; helpful, welcoming warden; htd pool adj; excel, clean new san facs; easy walk to old town & famous museum housing Celtic Vix treasures; vg; excel disabled san facs."* **€17.30, 1 Apr-30 Sep.** **2017**

CHATRE, LA *7A4* (3km N Rural) *46.60131, 1.97808* **Camp Municipal Solange-Sand,** Rue du Pont, 36400 Montgivray 02 54 06 10 34 or 02 54 06 10 36; mairie.montgivray@wanadoo.fr

🛨 ♦¶♦ wo ♨ ♿ 🗑 ⋰ 🌀

Fr La Châtre take rd to Montgivray, foll camping sp. Fr Châteauroux on D943 SE twd La Châtre turn R 2km S of Nohant on D72. Site behind church. 2*, Med, mkd, pt shd, EHU (10A) inc (poss rev pol); bbq; CKE. *"Pleasant site in chateau grnds; new san facs (2016); gd access; warden calls am & pm; gd rest adj; gd walks; quiet but occ noise fr nrby hall; excel; v gd for stop over or sh stay; welcoming staff."* **€12.40, 15 Mar-15 Oct.** **2017**

CHAUMONT *6F1* (1km NW Urban) *48.11790, 5.13334* **Camp Municipal Parc Ste Marie,** Rue des Tanneries, 52000 Chaumont 03 25 32 11 98 or 03 25 30 60 27 (Mairie); sports@ville-chaumont.fr

🛨 €1.50 ♦¶♦ (cont) wo ♨ ⋰ ⫨ 🗑 nr /◻\

Site on Chaumont W by-pass joining N19 Troyes rd to N67 St Dizier rd. Do not try to app fr town cent. Exit A5 at exit 24, foll sp to town cent, bef town foll sp to site. 2*, Sm, hdg, mkd, pt shd, pt sl, EHU (10A) inc (poss long lead req); 20% statics; CKE. *"Rec arr early; care needed with steep access to some sl pitches; friendly warden; ent barrier under warden control at all times; gd NH; doesn't acc m'vans."* **€14.00, 2 May-30 Sep.** **2015**

CHAUMONT SUR LOIRE *4G2* (1km NE Rural) *47.48444, 1.19417* **Camp Municipal Grosse Grève,** Ave des Trouillas, 41150 Chaumont-sur-Loire 02 54 20 95 22 or 02 54 20 98 41 (Mairie); mairie.chaumontsloire@wanadoo.fr; www.camping-chaumont-sur-loire.com

♦¶♦ (htd) wo ♨ ♿ 🗑 ⋰ Ⅰ nr ⊕ nr /◻\

Fr N side of rv on D952 cross bdge to Chaumont on D1, turn R immed & R under bdge. Site sp in vill on D751. 2*, Med, pt shd, EHU (6-16A) €2-3.50 (poss long lead req); bbq; canoeing; tennis; fishing; bike hire; horseriding; CKE. *"Pleasant site by rv; gd, clean san facs; no twin axles; interesting chateau; cycle track along Loire; gd value; excel."* **€12.00, 29 Apr-30 Sep.** **2016**

CHAUVIGNY *7A3* (1km E Urban) *46.57072, 0.65326* **Camp Municipal de la Fontaine,** Rue de la Fontaine, 86300 Chauvigny 05 49 45 99 10; camping-chauvigny@cg86.fr; www.chauvigny.fr

🛨 €1.80 ♦¶♦ (htd) wo ♨ ♿ 🗑 ⋰ ⫨ 🗑 nr /◻\

N151 fr Poitiers to Chauvigny. Turn L in cent Chauvigny just bef gate. Site well sp fr Chauvigny. 3*, Med, pt shd, EHU (15A) inc; bbq; adv bkg acc; tennis 1km; bike hire; CKE. *"Popular; well-kept; well-run site adj park & lake; views of castle; lge pitches; helpful, friendly staff; excel immac san facs; o'night m'vans area; delightful walk to cent; mkts Tue, Thur & Sat; a real find; gd value; rec; vg; interesting town; gd touring base; €20 for barrier key; new ehu pnts & new barrier(2018)."* **€16.40, 1 Apr-30 Sep.** **2018**

FRANCE

CHEF BOUTONNE 7A2 (2km W Rural) 46.10767, -0.09342 **Camping Le Moulin,** 1 Route de Niort, 79110 Chef-Boutonne 05 49 29 73 46 or 06 89 60 00 49 (mob); info@campingchef.com; www.campingchef.com

🏠 12 🐕 €1.50 ♦♦♦(htd) 🆆🅳 ▲ ♨ ♿ ▣ ∥ 🐾 🍴 ❞ 🍽 ⊕ 🖥 🛒 nr ⋒ ✎ 🏊(htd)

Fr D950 to or fr Poitiers, turn E onto D740 to Chef-Boutonne, site on R. Fr N10 turn onto D948 to Sauzé-Vaussais then L onto D1 to Chef-Boutonne; then take D740 dir Brioux-sur-Boutonne; site on L.
3*, Sm, hdstg, mkd, hdg, pt shd, EHU (10A); bbq (charcoal, elec, gas); twin axles; red long stay; 10% statics; Eng spkn; adv bkg acc; ccard acc; ice; CKE. "Well-kept site; lge pitches; friendly, helpful British owners; v gd rest; much bird life; conv Futuroscope & La Rochelle; vg; clean san facs refurbed with disabled facs (2018); peaceful; mv service pnt 1km; rest & bar refurb (2018); site acc rallies; excel; chge for wifi." **€21.60** **2019**

CHEMILLE 2G4 (1.5km SW Rural) 47.20182, -0.73486 FFCC **Camping Coulvée,** Route de Cholet, 49120 Chemillé 02 41 30 42 42 or 02 41 30 39 97 (Mairie); camping-chemille-49@wanadoo.fr; www.camping-coulvee-chemille.com

🐕 €1.70 ♦♦♦ 🆆🅳 ▲ ♿ ▣ ∥ 🅼🆂🅿 🐾 🍴 ⋒ 🏊 sand

Fr Chemillé dir Cholet on D160, turn R in 1km.
3*, Sm, hdg, pt shd, terr, EHU (10A) €3.60; bbq; sw; red long stay; Eng spkn; adv bkg acc; CKE. "Clean facs; helpful staff; gd pitches, soft when wet; poss unrel opening dates; pedalos; mkt Thurs; mkd cycling and walking rtes fr site." **€23.60, 1 May-15 Sep.** **2016**

CHENONCEAUX 4G2 (1.5km E Rural) 47.32905, 1.08816 **Camping de l'Ecluse,** Route de la Plage, 37150 Chisseaux 02 47 23 87 10 or 06 15 83 21 20 (mob); sandrine@campingdelecluse-37.fr; www.camping delecluse-37.fr

🐕 €1.50 ♦♦♦ 🆆🅳 ▲ ♿ ▣ ∥ 🅼🆂🅿 🍴 🖥 🛒 nr ⋒

E fr Chenonceaux on D176; cross bdge; immed hard R & foll rv bank; site in 300m. 2*, Med, mkd, pt shd, EHU (16A) €3.90 (rev pol); phone; Eng spkn; adv bkg acc; ccard acc; canoeing; watersports; fishing; CKE. "Rv trips; fishing; gd walking; some rd/rlwy noise; gd." **€12.50, 1 Mar-31 Oct.** **2019**

CHERBOURG 1C4 (18km NE Coastal) 49.6928, -1.4387 **Camping De La Plage,** 2 Village de Fréval, 50840 Fermanville 02 33 54 38 84; campingdelaplage. fermanville@wanadoo.fr; www.campingdelaplage-fermanville.com

🐕 €2.50 ♦♦♦ 🆆🅳 ▲ ∥ 🐾 🍴 🛒 ⋒ 🏊 300m, sand

Fr Cherbourg on D116 dir Barfleur, site in 12km on L. 3*, Med, hdg, unshd, EHU (10A); 70% statics; Eng spkn; adv bkg req. "Friendly owner; conv for ferry & D-Day landing beaches; poss unrel opening dates; vg." **€20.50, 1 Apr-15 Oct.** **2018**

CHERBOURG 1C4 (10km E Coastal) 49.66720, -1.48772 **Camping L'Anse du Brick,** 18 L'Anse du Brick, 50330 Maupertus-sur-Mer 02 33 54 33 57; contact@adbcamping.com; www.anse-du-brick.com or www.les-castels.com

🐕 €4.50 ♦♦♦ 🆆🅳 ▲ ♨ ♿ ▣ ∥ 🅼🆂🅿 🐾 🍴 ❞ 🍽 ⊕ 🖥 🛒 ⋒ ✎ 🏊(htd, indoor) 🛁 🌲 sand adj

At rndabt at port take 2nd exit sp Caen, Rennes & Mont St Michel; at 2nd rndabt take 3rd exit sp Caen & Mont St Michel (N13); at 3rd rndabt take 2nd exit onto dual c'way sp St Lô, Caen (N13), Bretteville-sur-Mer; exit on D116 & foll sp thro Bretteville-en-Saire (take care lge speed hump in Le Becquet); turn R for site just after R-hand blind bend & turning for Maupertus; up v steep incline. 5*, Med, mkd, hdg, shd, sl, terr, serviced pitches; EHU (10A) inc (poss rev pol); gas; bbq; TV; adv bkg acc; ccard acc; archery; waterslide; bike hire; tennis; games rm; kayak rental; CKE. "Attractive, well-kept site in beautiful setting; conv ferry; gd clean san facs; max 2 dogs per pitch; some pitches for lge o'fits; no o'fits over 8m; conv Landing Beaches, Barfleur, coastal nature reserve." **€53.00, 3 Apr-14 Sep, N14.** **2019**

CHERBOURG 1C4 (3.6km NW Urban/Coastal) 49.65576, -1.65257 **Camp Municipal de la Saline,** Rue Jean Bart, 50120 Equeurdreville-Hainneville 02 33 93 88 33 or 02 33 53 96 00 (Mairie); mairie-equeurdreville@ dialoleane.com; www.equeurdreville.com

🏠 12 🐕 €0.50 ♦♦♦(htd) 🆆🅳 ▲ ♿ ▣ ∥ 🍴 ⊕ nr 🛒 nr 🏊 sand adj

Fr ferry terminal foll D901 & sp Beaumont-Hague. On dual c'way beside sea look out for site sp to L at traff lts. 2*, Med, mkd, hdg, hdstg, pt shd, pt sl, terr, EHU (10A) €4.56; 50% statics; phone; adv bkg acc; fishing; CKE. "Sea views; boules & skateboard park adj; aquatic cent 500m; mv service pnt nr; cycle path to town; secured at night; excel NH for ferry." **€17.50** **2016**

CHEVERNY 4G2 (3km S Rural) 47.47798, 1.45070 **Camping Les Saules,** 102 Route de Contres, 41700 Cheverny 02 54 79 90 01; contact@camping-cheverny.com; www.camping-cheverny.com

🐕 €2 ♦♦♦(htd) 🆆🅳 ▲ ♨ ♿ ▣ ∥ 🅼🆂🅿 🐾 🍴 ❞ 🍽 ⊕ 🖥 🛒 ⋒ 🏊(htd) 🛁

Exit A10 junc 17 dir Blois Sud onto D765 to Romorantin. At Cour-Cheverny foll sp Cheverny & chateau. Fr S on D956 turn R onto D102 just N of Contres, site on L just bef Cheverny. Well sp fr all dirs. 4*, Lge, mkd, shd, EHU (10A) €3.50 (poss long lead req); gas; bbq; red long stay; TV; 2% statics; phone; Eng spkn; adv bkg rec; ccard acc; fishing; golf nr; games rm; tennis nr; excursions; bike hire; CKE. "Beautiful, well-run site; friendly, welcoming, helpful owners; excel san facs; castle adj; excel pool; all pitches under trees; muddy after heavy rain; many excel cycle & walking rtes nr; Cheverny chateau worth visit; little train & boat rides; excel; gd rest." **€36.00, 1 Apr-17 Sep, L01.** **2016**

CHINON *4G1* (0.5km SW Rural) *47.16397, 0.23377*
Camping de L'Ile Auger, Quai Danton, 37500 Chinon
02 47 93 08 35; camping-chinon@cc-cvl.fr;
www.camping-chinon.com

🏕🐕 €1.20 ♟ 🆗 ♨ ♿ 🚿 🚮 MSP 🦋 ♙ 🍴 nr ⚠

On S side of rv at bdge. Fr S foll sp Chinon
St Jacques; when app 2nd bdge on 1-way 'loop',
avoid R lane indicated for x-ing bdge & cont strt
past S end of main bdge to site on R. Fr N foll sp
'Centre Ville' round castle, cross bdge, site on R.
Well sp in town & opp castle. 2*, Lge, hdg, mkd, pt
shd, EHU (12A) inc (poss rev pol); red long stay; TV
(pitch); phone; ccard acc; canoe hire; CKE. *"Excel,
well-kept site in gd location; twin axles discretionary;
poss midge prob; poss travellers; gd cycle rtes; gd
views of chateau; rec; automatic ent barrier; htd pool
300m; well laid out; new san facs (2017); 5min walk
to town; exc value; hg rec boat trip on Rv Vienne."*
€18.50, 1 Apr-3 Oct.   2018

CHINON *4G1* (14km NW Rural) *47.20693, 0.08127*
Camping Belle Rive, 2 Route de Chinon, 37500
Candes-St Martin 02 47 97 46 03; contact@
camping-candes.fr; www.camping-candes.fr

🏕🐕 €1.30 ♟ ♨ 🆗 🚿 🚮 🦋 🍴 ♙ 🛒 🛢 nr ⚠

Fr Chinon take D751. Site on R bef junc with D7, on
S bank of Rv Vienne. 2*, Med, mkd, pt shd, EHU (16A)
€3.10; sw nr; adv bkg acc; fishing adj; CKE. *"Pleasant
rvside site; san facs on 2 floors, need update & poss
stretched if site busy; conv Saumur & chateaux; excel
location; scruffy & ill kempt site."*
€16.00, 15 Apr-30 Sep.   2016

CIOTAT, LA *10F3* (4km NE Coastal) *43.18733,
5.65810* Campsite La Baie des Anges (formerly
Les Oliviers), Chemin des Plaines Baronnes, 13600
La Ciotat 04 42 83 15 04; info@homair.com;
www.camping-laciotat.fr or www.homair.com

🏕 ♟ 🆗 ♨ ♿ 🚿 🚮 🍴 ♙ 🄳nr 🛢nr ⚠ 🛶 🏊 shgl 800m

Fr La Ciotat, foll D559 coast rd sp Bandol & Toulon.
Site in 4km, look for lge sp on L. Caution x-ing
dual c'way. 4*, V lge, shd, pt sl, terr, EHU (6A) (poss
rev pol); gas; 80% statics; bus 300m; Eng spkn; adv
bkg acc; ccard acc; tennis; CKE. *"Sea views many
pitches; friendly staff; gd touring base; v nice."*
€35.00, 12 Apr-1 Oct.   2019

CIVRAY *7A2* (1km NE Urban) *46.15835, 0.30169*
Camping de Civray, Route de Roche, 86400 Civray
05 17 34 50 02 or 06 08 51 88 80; campingdecivray@
gmail.com; www.camping-de-civray.com

🏕🐕 ♟ 🆗 ♨ 🚿 🚮 MSP 🦋 ♙ 🍴 🄳 🛢 nr ⚠ 🏊 (htd)

Civray 9km E of N10 halfway bet Poitiers &
Angoulême. Site outside town SE of junc of D1 &
D148. Sp on D148 & on S by-pass. Avoid town cent
narr rds. 2*, Med, pt shd, pt sl, EHU (6-10A) €3 (poss
long lead req); bbq; sw nr; 50% statics; Eng spkn; ccard
acc; golf; bike hire; fishing adj; CKE. *"Pleasant rvside
site, walk to town; pitches soft when wet; vg rest; conv
town cent; mkt Wed; vg; new owners; ltd san facs."*
€15.00, 10 Apr-2 Nov.   2017

CLAIRVAUX LES LACS *6H2* (1.2km SE Rural) *46.56431,
5.7562* Yelloh! Village Le Fayolan, Chemin de Langard,
39130 Clairvaux-les-Lacs 03 84 25 88 52; fayolan@
odesia.eu; www.campinglefayolan.fr or
www.yellohvillage.co.uk

🏕🐕 €4 ♟ 🆗 ♨ ♿ 🚿 🚮 🦋 🍴 ⊕ 🛢 🛒 ⚠ 🏊 (covrd, htd)

Fr town foll campsite sp, last site along lane adj
to lake. 4*, V lge, mkd, hdg, pt shd, terr, serviced
pitches; EHU (6A) inc (poss rev pol); gas; twin axles;
TV; 16% statics; Eng spkn; adv bkg rec; ccard acc;
waterslide; games rm; tennis 1km; bike hire; sauna;
CKE. *"Excel, clean site; extra for lakeside pitches high
ssn; pleasant sm town in easy walking dist; lovely area."*
€48.00, 3 May-8 Sep, J11.   2019

CLAIRVAUX LES LACS *6H2* (1km S Rural) *46.56761,
5.75480* Camping La Grisière et Europe Vacances,
Chemin Langard, 39130 Clairvaux-les-Lacs 03 84 25
80 48; bailly@la-grisiere.com; www.la-grisiere.com

🏕🐕 €1 ♟ (htd) 🆗 ♨ ♿ 🚿 🚮 MSP 🦋 🍴 🛒 🛢 ⚠

Turn S off D678 in Clairvaux opp church onto D118;
fork R in 500m & foll site sps to lake. Sp in vill.
Camping La Grisière ent after Camping Les Lacs.
3*, V lge, mkd, pt shd, pt sl, EHU (6-10A) €2.60; bbq;
sw nr; TV; 5% statics; phone; bus 700m; Eng spkn;
ccard acc; bike hire; watersports; tennis 1km; fishing;
canoe hire; CKE. *"Lovely views in beautiful area; lge
pitches; excel site; quiet; few facs."*
€25.00, 1 May-30 Sep.   2016

CLAIRVAUX LES LACS *6H2* (10km SW Rural)
46.52311, 5.67350 Camping de Surchauffant, Pont
de la Pyle, 39270 La Tour-du-Meix 03 84 25 41 08;
info@camping-surchauffant.fr; www.camping-
surchauffant.fr

🏕🐕 €1.60 ♟ ♨ ♿ 🚿 🚮 MSP 🦋 🍴 ⊕ 🛢 🛒 nr ⚠ 🛶 🏊 🛶

Fr Clairvaux S on D27 or D49 to D470. Foll sp Lac
de Vouglans, site sp. 3*, Med, mkd, pt shd, pt sl,
EHU (6A) €3; bbq; TV; 10% statics; Eng spkn; adv
bkg acc; ccard acc; watersports; sailing. *"Vg facs;
lovely location; dir access to lake; hiiking trails."*
€19.00, 22 Apr-19 Sep.   2016

CLAIRVAUX LES LACS *6H2* (7km W Rural) *46.59976,
5.68824* Camping Beauregard, 2 Grande Rue, 39130
Mesnois 03 84 48 32 51; reception@juracamping
beauregard.com; www.juracampingbeauregard.com

🏕🐕 €2.20 ♟ (htd) 🆗 ♨ ♿ 🚿 🚮 🦋 🍴 nr ⊕ nr 🛢 nr ⚠
🏊 (htd) 🛶 sand 800m

S fr Lons-le-Saunier on D52/D678, about 1km bef
Pont-de-Poitte turn L on D151. Site 1km on L opp rd
junc to Pont-de-Poitte. 3*, Lge, hdg, mkd, hdstg, pt
shd, pt sl, terr, EHU (6A) €4 (poss long lead req); gas;
10% statics; Eng spkn; adv bkg acc; tennis; bike hire;
games rm. *"Super site, clean & well-run; different sized
pitches; excel san facs, ltd LS; excel rest; kayaking nr;
poss muddy when wet; new indoor pool with jacuzzi
and sauna (2012), extremely gd quality."*
€31.00, 28 Mar-30 Sep, J13.   2019

CLAMECY *4G4* (1.3km SE Urban) *47.45133, 3.52770*
Camp Municipal du Pont-Picot, Rue de Chevroches, 58500 Clamecy **07 86 86 14 31; clamecycamping@ orange.fr; www.clamecy.fr**

♦♦ WD ♨ ♣ ⊟ ✔ ₩ ♣nr ⚠

On N151 fr S, exit N151 at rndabt 3km SW of town cent, cross level x-ing then R at rndabt on D23, take 1st L, site sp in 2.4km. Narr app rd. App fr N or E thro town not rec. Do not use sat nav thro town. 2*, Med, pt shd, pt sl, EHU (6A) inc; sw; CKE. *"Pleasant, peaceful site bet rv & canal in beautiful location; friendly, helpful staff; facs poss inadequate when busy; town 10 min walk on towpath; gd cycling; gd NH; narr bdge just bef ent."* **€17.00, 1 Apr-30 Sep.** 2019

CLAYETTE, LA *9A2* (0.5km E Urban) *46.29159, 4.32020*
Camping des Bruyères, 9 Route de Gibles, 71800 La Clayette **09 72 77 61 85 or 03 85 28 09 15; contact@ campingbruyeres.com; http://campingbruyeres.com**

♠ €1.60 ♦♦(htd) WD ♨ ♿ ⊟ ✔ ₩ ♀ ☂nr ♣nr ⚠ ♪

Site on D79, 100m fr D987 & lake. 3*, Med, hdg, mkd, hdstg, shd, sl, EHU (6A) inc; gas; bbq; 10% statics; phone; adv bkg acc; boating; games area; tennis; CKE. *"Pleasant, well-kept site o'looking lake & chateau; friendly, helpful staff; gd-sized pitches; htd pool adj Jun-Aug inc; excel; 20 min walk to town; supmkt 10 min walk."* **€25.00, 18 Apr-30 Sep.** 2019

CLECY *3D1* (1.4km E Rural) *48.91491, -0.47374*
FFCC Camping Les Rochers des Parcs, La Cour, 14570 Clécy **02 31 69 70 36; camping.normandie@ gmail.com; www.camping-normandie-clecy.fr**

♠ €1.60 ♦♦(htd) ♨ ♣ ♿ ⊟ ✔ MP ₩ ♀ ☂ ⊕nr ♣ ♣nr ⚠

Fr Condé take D562 dir Caen; turn R onto D133a sp Clécy & Le Vey; do not take turning to Clécy cent but cont downhill, past museum on L & then over bdge; turn R in 150m at campsite sp; site on R. 3*, Med, hdstg, mkd, pt shd, pt sl, EHU (6A) €3.50; bbq; red long stay; 10% statics; phone; Eng spkn; games area; bike hire; rv fishing. *"Lovely rvside situation; friendly, helpful owner; facs poss stretched high ssn & ltd LS; excel cent for walking."* **€23.00, 1 Apr-30 Sep.** 2018

CLERMONT FERRAND *9B1* (16km SE Rural) *45.70027, 3.16953* **Camping Le Clos Auroy,** Rue de la Narse, 63670 Orcet **04 73 84 26 97; www.camping-le-clos-auroy.com**

12 ♠ €2.25 ♦♦(htd) WD ♨ ♿ ⊟ ✔ ₩ ♀ ☂ ♣nr ⚠ ♪
♨(htd) 🛁

S on A75 take exit 5 sp Orcet; foll D213 to Orcet for 2km, at rndabt onto D52, take 1st L, site on R. Do not foll SatNav to site. 4*, Med, mkd, hdstg, hdg, pt shd, terr, EHU (10A) €5 (poss rev pol); gas; red long stay; 10% statics; phone; Eng spkn; adv bkg acc; ccard acc; tennis; rv fishing 500m; CKE. *"Excel, well-kept; site poss open all year; easy access; lge pitches, poss v high hedges; superb htd san facs; pitches by rv poss liable to flood; extra charge for sh stay m'vans; ltd fresh water points & diff to use for refill; vg winter site; interesting town; gd dog walks adj; snack & bar only open high ssn; vg value; helpful staff; gd site."* **€33.80** 2017

CLERMONT FERRAND *9B1* (5km W Rural) *45.75845, 3.05453* **Huttopia Royat (was Camping Indigo Royat),** Route de Gravenoire, 63130 Royat **04 73 35 97 05; royat@camping-indigo.com; www.europe. huttopia.com**

♠ €4 ♦♦(htd) WD ♨ ♿ ♣ ⊟ ✔ MP ₩ ♀ ☂ ⊕ ♣ ♣ ⚠ ♪
♨(htd) 🛁

Site diff to find fr Clermont-Ferrand cent. Fr N, leave A71 at Clermont-Ferrand. Foll sp Chamalières /Royat, then sp Royat. Go under rlwy bdge & pass thermal park on L. At mini-rndabt go L & up hill. At statue, turn L & go up long hill. Look for site sp & turn R. Site on R. NB Do not go down steep rd with traff calming. NB sat nav directs up v narr rds & steep hills. 4*, Lge, hdstg, mkd, pt shd, terr, serviced pitches; EHU (10A) €5.20; gas; bbq; TV; 10% statics; phone; Eng spkn; adv bkg acc; ccard acc; bike hire; tennis; CKE. *"Excel, clean, spacious, lovely site; set on hillside in trees; gd size earth pitches; views at top levels over Clermont; clean san facs; facs ltd in LS; conv touring base; new recep; vg."* **€40.00, 22 Mar-3 Nov, L18.** 2019

CLISSON *2H4* (1.3km N Urban) *47.09582, -1.28216*
Camp Municipal du Vieux Moulin, Rue de la Fontaine Câlin, Route de Nantes, 44190 Clisson **02 40 54 44 48 or 06 20 29 08 42 (mob);.camping.clissonsevremaine.fr**

♠ €1.12 ♦♦ WD ♨ ♣ ⊟ ✔ ₩ ⊕nr ♣nr

1km NW of Clisson cent on main rd to Nantes, at rndabt. Look for old windmill nr ent on L of rd. Leclerc hypmkt on opp side of rd; site sp fr town cent. Narr ent. 3*, Sm, hdg, pt shd, pt sl, EHU 10A inc; TV; Eng spkn; adv bkg acc; fishing adj; boating; horseriding adj; tennis adj; game rm. *"Gd municipal site; lge pitches; gd clean san facs; if office clsd pitch self, book in later; picturesque town 15 min walk; bar 500m; hypmkt 500m; mkd walks; interesting old town with castle ruins; next to retail park; excel rest in town."* **€24.50, 1 Mar-30 Nov.** 2018

CLOYES SUR LE LOIR *4F2* (1km N Rural) *48.00240, 1.23304* **Parc de Loisirs Le Val Fleuri,** Route de Montigny, 28220 Cloyes-sur-le-Loir **02 37 98 50 53; info@val-fleuri.fr; www.val-fleuri.fr**

♠ €2 ♦♦(htd) WD ♨ ♣ ⊟ ✔ ₩ ♀ ☂ ⊕ ♣ ⚠ ♨

Located on L bank of Rv Loir off N10; site sp. 4*, Lge, hdg, pt shd, EHU (5A) inc; bbq; twin axles; 50% statics; phone; Eng spkn; adv bkg acc; ccard acc; waterslide; bike hire; €3; CKE. *"Facs gd for children but ltd LS; well-run, pleasant site in wooded valley; site fees inc use of sm leisure park, pedalos & rowing boats on Rv Loir; vg san facs."* **€38.00, 15 Mar-15 Nov.** 2017

CLUNY *9A2* (0.5km E Urban) *46.43086, 4.66756*
Camp Municipal St Vital, 30 Rue de Griottons, 71250
Cluny 03 85 59 08 34; camping.st.vital@orange.fr;
www.camping-cluny.blogspot.com

🐕 👭(htd) 🅦 🚿 ᷭ 🞋 🗑 ⁄ ♈ 🚲 ⚏

E fr Cluny on D15 (sp Azé & Camping) across narr rv
bdge; in 200m turn R into Rue de Griottonste; site
on L in 100m. Site adj sw pool. To avoid bdge app
fr S on D15. 3*, Lge, mkd, hdstg, pt shd, sl, EHU (6A)
€4.50 (poss rev pol); gas; bbq; twin axles; adv bkg rec;
ccard acc; fishing; horseriding nr; bike hire; games rm;
tennis. "*Well-run, tidy site; helpful staff; gd clean san
facs; cycle & walking rte adj (Voie Verte); frequent rlwy
noise daytime; interesting town; htd pool adj inc; excel,
reliable site; well organised and pleasant; busy site.*"
€19.00, 26 Apr-5 Oct.   **2017**

CLUNY *9A2* (12km S Rural) *46.33744, 4.61123*
Camping du Lac, 8 Rue du Port, 71520 St Point
03 85 50 52 31; reservation@campingsaintpoint.
com; www.campingsaintpoint.com

🐕 €2 👭(htd) 🅦 🚿 ᷭ ⁄ 🗑 ♈ 🍽 🏊 Ⓘ 🚲 🔋nr ⚏

Turn S off N79, Mâcon/Paray-le-Monial rd, turn L
bef Ste Cécile on D22; site sp at junc; site 100m on
R after St Point vill. 3*, Med, hdg, mkd, pt shd, pt
sl, terr, EHU (16A) inc; bbq; sw nr; TV; 30% statics;
phone; adv bkg acc; fishing; boat hire; tennis 4km;
CKE. "*Cluny attractive town & abbey; lge pitches;
clean & basic san facs & ltd LS; lovely scenery &
pleasant lake; on edge of Beaujolais; sp walks fr
site; peaceful area with wooded hills & valleys.*"
€17.60, 15 Apr-15 Oct.   **2018**

CLUSAZ, LA *9B3* (6km N Rural) *45.93972, 6.42777*
Camping L'Escale, Route de la Patinoire, 74450
Le Grand-Bornand 04 50 02 20 69; contact@
campinglescale.com; www.campinglescale.com

🐕 €2.30 👭(htd) 🅦 🚿 ♨ ᷭ 🞋 🗑 ⁄ 🗑 ♈ 🍽 Ⓘ 🚲 🔋nr ⚏
🏊 (covrd, htd) 🎿

Exit A41 junc 17 onto D16/D909 E dir La Clusaz.
At St Jean-de-Sixt turn L at rndabt sp Le Grand
Bornand. After 1.5km foll camping sp on main rd
& at junc turn R sp for site & 'Vallée du Bouchet'.
Site is 1st exit R at rndabt at end of this rd. D4 S
fr Cluses not rec while towing as v steep & winding.
3*, Med, mkd, pt shd, pt sl, terr, EHU (10A) inc poss
rev pol); gas; bbq; TV; 20% statics; adv bkg req; ccard
acc; archery; tennis; fishing; games rm; CKE. "*Family-
run site in scenic area; bike hire 250m; gd san facs; no
c'vans over 8.5m or m'vans over 8m high ssn, Feb & wk
of New Year; serviced pitch in summer; vg rest; sh walk
to attractive vill; winter sports; free use htd ski/boot
rm in winter; boggy in wet weather; vg mkt Wed; excel
site; ski bus; gd sports facs.*" **€32.00, 1 Jan-12 Apr,
22 May-27 Sep & 19 Dec-31 Dec, M07.**   **2015**

COEX *2H4* (2.5km W Rural) *46.67679, -1.76899*
RCN Camping La Ferme du Latois, 85220 Coëx
03 43 74 50 90; www.rcn.nl/fermedulatois

🐕 €5 👭(htd) 🅦 🚿 ᷭ 🞋 🗑 ⁄ ♈ ♈ 🍽 Ⓘ 🚲 🔋 ⚏ 🏊

Exit D948 at Aizenay onto D6 dir St Gilles-Croix-
de-Vie; at Coëx take D40 SW sp Brétignolles; site
in 1.5km on L. 4*, Lge, pt shd, EHU inc (poss rev pol);
bbq (gas); 20% statics; phone; Eng spkn; adv bkg acc;
games rm; games area; lake fishing; bike hire. "*Spacious
pitches; cycle rtes adj; conv Lac du Jaunay & Lac du Gué-
Gorand; excel.*" **€41.00, 19 Apr-27 Sep.**   **2019**

COGNAC *7B2* (2.5km NE Rural) *45.70920, -0.31284*
Camping de Cognac, Blvd de Châtenay, 16100 Cognac
05 45 32 13 32; contact@campingdecognac.com;
www.campingdecognac.com

🐕 €1.50 👭 🅦 🚿 ᷭ 🞋 🗑 ⁄ 🗑 🍽 Ⓘ 🚲 🔋 ⚏ 🚣 🏊

Fr N141 foll 'Camping' sp to town cent. Turn R at
'Speedy' g'ge, site immed on R in 2km after x-ing rv;
foll sp 'Base de Plein Air'. Take care ent barrier.
3*, Med, hdg, mkd, hdstg, pt shd, EHU (6A) inc (poss
long leads req & poss rev pol); bbq; red long stay;
5% statics; phone; bus; Eng spkn; adv bkg acc; ccard
acc; games area; rv boating; rv fishing; CKE. "*Excel lge
park with many facs; helpful staff; clean modern san
facs but dated; gates clsd 2200-0700 (1800 LS); night
watchman high ssn; no twin axles; footpath to town;
conv Cognac distilleries (vouchers fr site recep); cycle
rte to town cent.*" **€22.40, 1 May-27 Sep.**   **2018**

COGNAC *7B2* (10km E Rural) *45.67160, -0.22718*
Camping De Bourg (formerly Camping du Port),
16200 Bourg-Charente 06 15 16 67 82 or 06 03 06
85 07 (mob)

🐕 👭 🅦 🚿 ⁄ Ⓘ 🔋nr 🔋nr

Exit N141 onto D158 dir Bourg-Charente; turn L in
800m & site on R. Site sp fr D158. Chicane-type ent
gates. 1*, Sm, pt shd, pt sl, EHU (6A) €3; red long
stay; fishing; tennis. "*Delightful site on banks of Rv
Charente; friendly staff; facs v basic & ltd but clean,
poss stretched high ssn; site on 2 levels, lower one
sl; gd walks & cycle path to Jarnac & Cognac; gd; find
placement, owner will call; vg value; v quiet site.*"
€10.00, 1 May-15 Sep.   **2017**

COGNAC *7B2* (16km E Urban) *45.67606, -0.17349*
FFCC Camping de l'Ile Madame, 16200 Gondeville
06 26 91 40 92; campingilemadame@orange.fr;
camping-jarnac.jimdo.com

🏕 €2.50 🚻 ♨ 🛁 🚐 🍴 ⓗ nr ▓ nr ⚠ ♿ 🏊

Turn E at S end of rv bdge at S end of town.
Fr Angoulême on N141, exit junc sp 'Jarnac Est'; foll
sp Jarnac thro 1 rndabt into Jarnac; at traff lts (LH
lane) turn L sp Tourist Info/Camping; cross rv bdge
& immed turn L to site. 3*, Lge, pt shd, EHU (6-10A)
€3.20 (rev pol); red long stay; TV; adv bkg acc; golf
nr; games area; CKE. *"Pleasant, well-run site; gd sized
pitches; easy walk into Jarnac with shops & rests; gd
walks along rv; nr Courvoisier bottling plant; excel; boat
trips along rv; canoe hire nr; poss noise fr adj sports
grnd & disco; site redesigned & new san facs (2015)."*
€14.00, 15 Apr-30 Sep. **2017**

COGNAC LA FORET *7B3* (1.5km SW Rural) *45.82494,
0.99674* **Camping des Alouettes,** Les Alouettes,
87310 Cognac-la-Forêt 05 55 03 26 93; info@camping-
des-alouttes.com; www.camping-des-alouettes.com

🏕 €1 🚻 ♨ 🛁 ♿ 🍴 ⓦ 🦋 ⓨ Ⓣ ⓗ 🛒 ▓ nr ⚠ ♿ 🎣

Fr Aixe-sur-Vienne on D10, site W of Cognac-la-Forêt
on D10, sp to L. 3*, Med, hdg, pt shd, pt sl, EHU (10A)
€3; bbq; sw nr; 10% statics; Eng spkn; adv bkg acc;
tennis 700m; CKE. *"Beautiful location; friendly Dutch
owners; conv war vill Oradour-sur-Glane & Richard Lion
Heart sites; excel facs, peaceful, relaxing, vg site; lge
pitches; well run site."* **€23.00, 1 Apr-30 Sep.** **2017**

COLMAR *6F3* (2km E Urban) *48.07942, 7.38665*
Camping de l'Ill, 1 Allée du Camping, 68180 Horbourg-
Wihr 03 89 41 15 94; colmar@camping-indigo.com;
www.campingdelill.com

🏕 €4 🚻 (htd) ⓦ ♨ 🛁 🚐 🍴 ⓜ ⓨ Ⓣ ⓗ 🛒 ⚠ ♿

Exit A35 junc 25 onto D415, foll Freibourg sp. At
2nd rndabt turn L to Colmar cent, site on rvside on
L bef bdge. 3*, Lge, hdg, mkd, hdstg, shd, pt sl, terr,
EHU (10A) €4.80 (poss rev pol); TV; 10% statics; bus/
train to city cent; Eng spkn; adv bkg acc; ccard acc;
bike hire; CKE. *"Lovely, clean, rvside site; excel san facs;
gd rest; some pitches req steel pegs; much noise fr
a'route; gd for town; sep area for NH, bus only to town,
san facs tired, supmkt 900m."*
€22.50, 21 Mar-31 Dec, J12. **2015**

COLMAR *6F3* (7km SW Rural) *48.04272, 7.29970*
Camping des Trois Châteaux, 10 Rue du Bassin,
68420 Eguisheim 03 89 23 19 39; camping.
eguisheim@orange.fr; www.camping-eguisheim.fr

🏕 €3 🚻 ⓦ ♨ 🛁 ♿ 🍴 ⓜ Ⓣ nr ⓗ nr ▓ nr ⚠

Foll D83 S (Colmar by-pass) R at sp Eguisheim.
R into vill to site at top of vill, foll camp sp.
3*, Med, mkd, pt shd, pt sl, terr, EHU (8-10A) €3-5 (poss
rev pol); gas; adv bkg req; ccard acc; CKE. *"Popular,
well-run, clean, busy site; no c'vans over 7m (inc draw
bar); mv pitches flat but some c'van pitches sl & poss
diff; gd touring base; weekly wine-tasting events; stork
park adj; rec arr early; excel; cycle rte to cent of Colmar;
gd."* **€19.00, 26 Mar-5 Nov & 30 Nov-24 Dec.** **2018**

COLMAR *6F3* (7km W Urban) *48.08517, 7.27253*
**Camping Le Medieval (formerly Municipal Les
Cigognes),** Quai de la Gare, 68230 Turckheim 03 89 27
02 00; reception@camping-turckheim.fr;
en.camping-turckheim.fr

🏕 €2.50 🚻 (htd) ⓦ ♨ 🛁 🚐 🍴 ⓜ 🦋 ⓨ ▓ nr ⚠ ♿ 🏊

Fr D83 twd Turchkeim turn W onto D11 to
Turckheim. On ent vill, turn immed L down 1-way rd
after x-ing rlwy lines. Do not cross rv bdge. Site on L
bef bdge, adj stadium. 3*, Med, hdg, pt shd, EHU
(16A) €4; bbq; twin axles; TV; bus adj, train 250m; Eng
spkn; ccard acc; games rm; CKE. *"Lovely site with med
pitches; cycle rtes nr; resident storks; sh walk to
interesting, beautiful old vill with rests; gd touring base;
gd, excel san facs; poss cr in June, high ssn & w/ends;
new management (2016); friendly helpful staff; open
26 Dec-28 Dec for Christmas mkt; vg; close to historic
sites and medieval castles; wine tasting & sales; great
site; new shwr block (2017); cycle rte to Colmar &
vineyards."* **€19.00, 7 Apr-23 Oct & 30 Nov-24 Dec.**
2018

COLMARS *9D4* (2km SW Rural) *44.19148, 6.59690*
Camping Le Haut Verdon, 04370 Villars-Colmars
04 92 83 40 09; info@lehautverdon.com;
www.lehautverdon.com

🏕 €4 🚻 (htd) ⓦ ♨ 🛁 ♿ 🍴 ⓜ 🦋 ⓨ Ⓣ ⓗ 🛒 ⚠ ♿ 🎣 (htd) 🛶

Only app fr S on D955 & D908 fr St André-les-Alps
thro Beauvezer. Clearly sp on ent Villars-Colmars
on R. Do not take D908 via Annot/Le Fugeret with a
caravan(Do not confuse with Municipal site approx
5km bef this site). 4*, Sm, mkd, hdstg, pt shd, EHU (6-
10A) €3-4; gas; bbq; sw nr; twin axles; TV; 50% statics;
50m; adv bkg acc; rv fishing; games area; games rm;
bike hire; CKE. *"Superb setting on Rv Verdon; gd, clean
san facs; helpful staff; conv Colmars, flower meadows,
Allos Lake; site nr Mercantour National Pk; scenic rte to
Barcelonnette via Col d'Allos, not suitable for c'vans; ski
area at Allos; gd."* **€28.00, 28 Apr-14 Oct.** **2018**

COMBOURG *2E4* (6km SW Rural) *48.38090, -1.83290*
Camping Domaine du Logis, 35190 La Chapelle-aux-
Filtzméens,Ille-et-Vilaine 02 99 45 25 45 or
06 85 78 69 71 (mob); domainedulogis@wanadoo.fr;
www.domainedulogis.com

🏕 €2 🚻 ⓦ ♨ 🛁 ♿ 🍴 ⓜ 🦋 ⓨ Ⓣ ⓗ 🛒 ▓ nr ⚠ ♿
🎣 (htd) 🛶

Fr N176 at junc for Dol-de-Bretagne branch R onto
D155 sp Dol & take D795 S to Combourg. Then take
D13 twd St Domineuc, go thro La Chapelle-aux-
Filtzméens & site on R in 1km. 4*, Lge, mkd, hdg, pt shd,
EHU (10A) inc; gas; bbq; red long stay; TV; 10% statics;
phone; Eng spkn; adv bkg acc; ccard acc; gym; games
area; games rm; fishing nr; bike hire; fitness rm; CKE. *"Set
in chateau grnds; lge flat grassy pitches; helpful, pleasant
staff; gd, clean san facs; gd touring base, conv St Malo,
Mont St Michel, Dinan & Channel Islands; mkt Mon; excel;
no o'fits over 12m; beautiful; v child oriented; canoe
800m; superb pool."* **€33.00, 1 Apr-2 Oct, B02.** **2017**

COMPS SUR ARTUBY *10E3* (1km NW Rural) *43.71543, 6.49862* **Camp Municipal du Pontet,** 83840 Comps-sur-Artuby 04 94 76 91 40; mairie.compsurartuby@wanadoo.fr

🏕 🚶 wc 🚻 ⚲ 🦋 🍽 ℮ 🏊

Fr Comps-sur-Artuby take D71 sp Grand Canyon du Verdon. Site sp on R in 1km. 2*, Med, mkd, pt shd, terr, EHU (6A) €3; phone; CKE. *"Vg, well-laid out, wooded site; conv Gorges du Verdon; easy access; ltd san facs at top of site."* **€8.00, 1 May-31 Oct.** **2019**

CONCARNEAU *2F2* (6km S Coastal) *47.85628, -3.89999* **Camping Le Cabellou Plage,** Ave de Cabellou, Kersaux, 29185 Concarneau 02 98 97 37 41; info@le-cabellou-plage.com; www.le-cabellou-plage.com

🏕 ℮4 🚻 (cont) wc ⚲ ♿ 🔥 ⚲ 🦋 🍽 🛒 🏊 (htd) 🏖 🏝 sand adj

Fr N165 turn onto D70 dir Concarneau. At 5th rndabt (Leclerc supmkt) foll dir Tregunc. After Moros bdge take 2nd exit at next rndabt dir Le Cabellou-Plage. Site sp on L. 4*, Lge, mkd, hdg, hdstg, pt shd, EHU (10A) inc; TV; 20% statics; bus at site ent; Eng spkn; adv bkg acc; ccard acc; games area; bike hire; games rm; watersports. *"Pleasant seaside site; vg san facs; gd walking fr site; gd for town via ferry."* **€36.00, 28 Apr-15 Sep, B34.** **2017**

"I need an on-site restaurant"

We do our best to make sure site information is correct, but it is always best to check any must-have facilities are still available or will be open during your visit.

CONCARNEAU *2F2* (1.5km NW Urban/Coastal) *47.8807, -3.9311* **Camping Les Sables Blancs,** Ave du Dorlett, 29900 Concarneau 02 98 97 16 44; contact@camping-lessablesblancs.com; www.camping-les-sablesblancs.com

🏕 ℮2 🚻 (htd) wc ⚲ ♿ 🔥 🎱 ⚲ 🦋 🍽 🍴 ℮ 🏊 nr 🏖 🏝 (htd) 🏖 🏝 sand 400m

Exit N165 to Concarneau dir 'Centre Ville'. Then foll sp 'La Côte' 300m after traff lts. Site on R, sp. 4*, Med, hdstg, mkd, hdg, pt shd, pt sl, terr, EHU (10A) €4; bbq; red long stay; TV; 3% statics; phone; bus 300m; Eng spkn; adv bkg acc; ccard acc; jacuzzi; games rm; games area; CKE. *"Nice, clean, family site in woodland; many sm pitches; friendly staff; excel san facs; superb pool; gd rest; pleasant walk to town, 1.5km; mkt Mon & Thurs; vg; well run; some pitches uneven; steep walk to san facs."* **€34.00, 1 Apr-31 Oct.** **2017**

CONCARNEAU *2F2* (3km NW Coastal) *47.89054, 3.93847* **Camping Les Prés Verts aux 4 Sardines,** Kernous-Plage, 29900 Concarneau 02 98 97 09 74 or 07 87 90 90 01 (mob); info@presverts.com; www.presverts-campingconcarneau.com

🏕 ℮2 🚻 wc ⚲ 🔥 ⚲ 🛒 🦋 🍴 ℮ nr 🏖 🏊 (htd) 🏖

Exit N165 onto D70 dir Concarneau. At rndabt by Leclerc supmkt foll sp 'Centre Ville' (Town Centre) with Leclerc on L. Strt over at 2nd rndabt then bear R at the next rndabt onto Rue de Kerneach & down slope. Bear L at 1st rndabt & R at next. Keep R to join coast rd & foll sp La Forêt-Fouesnant; pass Hôtel Océans; site 3rd rd on L in 1.5km. 3*, Med, hdg, mkd, pt shd, pt sl, serviced pitches; EHU (6A-10A) inc (poss rev pol & long lead req); bbq (charcoal, gas); TV; 10% statics; adv bkg acc; ccard acc; games rm; horseriding 1km; sailing 1km. *"Peaceful, scenic, busy site; path to sandy cove below; gd sized pitches, lge pitches extra; family-run, friendly helpful staff; basic san facs, run down, ltd LS; poss unkempt LS; dir access to beach; no o'fits over 8m; gd touring base; walk along coastal path to Concarneau; mkt Mon & Fri; cycle track (old rlwy track) 300m fr site; gd location."* **€28.00, 1 May-30 Sep, B24.** **2017**

CONDOM *8E2* (10km N Rural) *44.03324, 0.36614* **Camping Le Mouliat,** RD 219, 47600 Moncrabeau 05 53 65 43 28; contact@camping-le-mouliat.fr; www.camping-mouliat.fr

🏕 🚶 wc ⚲ ♿ 🔥 ⚲ 🛒 🍴 🍽 🏊 🏖

N fr Condom on D930 for 9.5km, then R on D219. Site on L in 0.5km, just bef rv bdge. 3*, Sm, hdg, mkd, pt shd, EHU €4.50; bbq; twin axles; 10% statics; games area; CKE. *"Quiet LS; conv for Condom/Nerac; takeaway; helpful, cheery owners; vg."* **€24.00, 1 May-1 Oct.** **2015**

CONDOM *8E2* (4km NE Rural) *43.97491, 0.42038* **Camping à la Ferme (Rogalle),** Guinland, 32100 Condom 05 62 28 17 85; rogalle.guinland@wanadoo.fr; http://campingdeguinland.monsite-orange.fr

🏕 🚶 wc ⚲ ⚲ 🦋 ℮ nr 🛒 nr 🏖

NE fr Condom on D931, turn R onto D41. Pass water tower on R, site ent on L at bottom of hill just bef sm lake on R. Sm, shd, EHU (6-10A) €3; bbq; 10% statics; tennis nr. *"Vg CL-type site in pine grove; canoe hire nr; gd views; friendly owner; clean facs."* **€9.00, 1 Apr-30 Oct.** **2017**

CONDRIEU *9B2* (5.7km SE Rural) *45.42413, 4.78251* **Camping Le Daxia,** Route du Péage, 38370 St Clair-du-Rhône 04 74 56 39 20; info@campingledaxia.com; www.campingledaxia.com

🏕 ℮1.85 🚻 wc ⚲ ♿ 🔥 ⚲ 🛒 🦋 🍽 🍴 ℮ 🏊 nr 🏖 🏊 🏖

S fr Vienne on D386; turn L in Condieu sp D28 Les Roches-de-Condrieu & Le Péage-de-Roussillon; foll sp A7 Valance & 'Camping' onto D4. Site on L well sp fr Condrieu. 4*, Med, hdg, mkd, pt shd, EHU (5-10A) €2.40-2.85; bbq; adv bkg acc; games rm; CKE. *"Vg site; on edge of sm rv with beach."* **€23.00, 1 Apr-30 Sep.** **2017**

CONFOLENS 7A3 (0.5km N Rural) 46.01905, 0.67531
Camp Municipal des Ribières, Ave de St Germain, 16500 Confolens 05 45 85 35 27 or 05 45 84 01 97 (Mairie); contact@mairieconfolens.com; http://www.campingdesribieres.fr/

🐕 ♥¶ [WD] 🛁 ♨ ♿ 🚽 ⚟ [MSP] 🎱 ☂ nr ⚏

Fr N foll D951 dir Confolens turn L sp St Germain-de-Confolens, site on R in 7km at edge of town bet rd & rv. NB Diff app fr S thro vill. 3*, Med, mkd, pt shd, EHU (16A); gas; bbq; sw nr; 3% statics; phone; Eng spkn; adv bkg req; bike hire; boating; fishing; games area. *"Interesting, pretty town; facs neglected & ltd LS; m'van o'night area outside site; pool 200m; warden calls am & pm; great site; lovely location; excel."* **€21.00, 1 Apr-1 Oct.** 2018

CONQUES 7D4 (8km E Rural) 44.55948, 2.46184
Camping L'Etang du Camp, 12320 Sénergues 05 65 46 01 95; info@etangducamp.fr; www.etangducamp.fr

🐕 €1.50 ♥¶ [WD] 🛁 ♨ ♿ 🚽 ⚟ [MSP] 🦋 🎱 ⚏

Fr S on D901 dir Conques; at St Cyprien turn R onto D46 sp Sénergues; foll sp Sénergues up hill for 6km; 2nd L at the top; foll Camping sp. 4*, Med, mkd, hdg, pt shd, EHU (6A) €3.70; bbq (charcoal); 10% statics; Eng spkn; adv bkg acc; fishing in private lake; ice; bike hire; games area; canoeing nr; games rm; CKE. *"Well-situated, well-kept site; quiet & relaxing; warm welcome, British owners; modern, clean san facs; gd base for touring, walking & cycling; htd pool 6km; conv Conques; highly rec; excel; gd security."* **€22.00, 1 Apr-30 Sep.** 2018

CONQUET, LE 2E1 (2km N Coastal) 48.36748, -4.75990
Camping Les Blancs Sablons, 29217 Le Conquet 02 98 36 07 91; www.les-blancs-sablons.com

♥¶ [WD] 🛁 ♿ 🚽 ⚟ 🎱 ☂ nr ⚑ nr ⚏ ⚏ (htd) 🏖 sand 100m

Exit Brest on D789 to Le Conquet. Turn R after 22km (1.8km bef Le Conquet) on D67 twd St Renan, turn L after 700m on D28 twd Ploumoguer. After 2km, turn L at x-rds twd Plage des Blancs Sablons, site on L in 1km. 2*, Lge, mkd, unshd, pt sl, EHU (16A) €3 (long lead poss req); adv bkg acc; ccard acc; CKE. *"Gd views fr some pitches; some soft pitches; ltd facs LS & dated but clean with gd hot water; bar 500m; lovely old fishing town."* **€21.00, 1 Apr-31 Oct.** 2017

CORCIEUX 6F3 (1km ESE Rural) 48.16826, 6.89006
Camping Le Clos de la Chaume, 671 Rue d'Alsace, 88430 Corcieux 03 29 50 76 76 or 06 85 19 62 55 (mob); info@camping-closdelachaume.com; www.camping-closdelachaume.com

🐕 €1.90 ♥¶ [WD] 🛁 ♨ ♿ 🚽 ⚟ [MSP] 🦋 🎱 ☂ nr ⚑ nr ⚏ nr ⚏ 🏊

Take D145 fr St Dié, then D8 thro Anould & bear R onto D60. Site in 3km on R at ent to vill. 3*, Med, hdstg, mkd, hdg, pt shd, serviced pitches; EHU (8-10A) €5; gas; bbq; red long stay; twin axles; TV; 15% statics; phone; Eng spkn; adv bkg acc; ccard acc; fishing; games area; games rm; CKE. *"Lovely, peaceful site in beautiful area; stream runs thro; friendly & helpful owners; bike hire 800m; san facs poss stetched & busy high ssn; conv Gérardmer & Alsace wine rte; excel; acess rd vg; highly rec; family owned; v well run; excel covrd pool."* **€23.00, 27 Apr-20 Sep, J08.** 2019

See advertisement

CORDES SUR CIEL 8E4 (5km SE Rural) 44.04158, 2.01722 **Camping Redon,** Livers-Cazelles, 81170 Cordes-sur-Ciel 09 80 50 42 72 or 06 47 46 13 62 (mob); info@campredon.com; www.campredon.com

🐕 €2.25 ♥¶ [WD] 🛁 ♨ ♿ 🚽 ⚟ [MSP] 🎱 ☂ ⚑ nr ⚏ nr ⚏ 🏖

Off D600 Albi to Cordes rd. Exit on D107 to E. Site sp. 3*, Sm, hdg, pt shd, pt sl, EHU (6-16A) €4.25; gas; red long stay; TV; phone; bus 1km; Eng spkn; adv bkg acc; CKE. *"Well-kept, well-run site; views fr some pitches; friendly, helpful Dutch owner; excel facs, poss stretched high ssn; ecological septic tank - environmentally friendly liquid sold on site; conv Bastides in area; highly rec; lovely."* **€30.00, 22 Apr-22 Oct.** 2017

FRANCE

CORDES SUR CIEL *8E4* (3km W Rural) *44.06681, 1.92408* **Camping Le Garissou,** Les Cabannes, 81170 Cordes-sur-Ciel **05 63 56 27 14; contact@legarissou.fr; www.legarissou.fr**

€1.50

Take D600 fr Cordes thro Les Cabanes; site sp on L at bottom of hill, 1.5km after Les Cabanes. 3*, Med, mkd, pt shd, terr, EHU (6A) inc. *"Hilltop site; pool complex adj; excel views; clean facs."*
€16.50, 15 Mar-10 Nov. **2015**

CORMATIN *9A2* (0.5km N Rural) *46.54841, 4.68351* **Camping Le Hameau des Champs,** Route de Chalon, 71460 Cormatin **03 85 50 76 71; camping.cormatin@wanadoo.fr; www.le-hameau-des-champs.com**

€1 (htd) nr

Fr Cluny N on D981 dir Cormatin for approx 14km, site N of town sp on L, 300m after chateau. Look for line of European flags. 3*, Sm, mkd, hdg, unshd, pt sl, EHU (13A) €3.70 (long lead poss req); bbq (elec, gas); cooking facs; sw nr; TV; 10% statics; phone; Eng spkn; adv bkg acc; ccard acc; bike hire; CKE. *"Well-kept, secure site in lovely countryside; welcoming, friendly owner; lge pitches; ltd EHU, adv bkg rec; gd facs, poss stretched high ssn; rest open LS; Voie Verte cycling rte adj; excel municipal site; sm town but gd local store; Chateau closeby."* **€18.00, 1 Apr-30 Sep.** **2019**

COSNE COURS SUR LOIRE *4G3* (5km SW Rural) *47.40923, 2.91792* **Camping de l'Ile,** Ile de Cosne, 18300 Bannay **09 72 25 89 83; info@camping-ile-cosne.com; www.camping-ile-cosne.com**

€0.90 (htd)

Fr Cosne take Bourges rd, D955, over 1st half of bdge, ent immed on L, 500m strt. On rv island. 3*, Lge, shd, EHU (10A) €4; bbq; TV; 10% statics; ccard acc; bike hire; CKE. *"Helpful staff; views of Rv Loire; gd san facs; gd NH; supmkt Carrefour closeby; gd rest opp; town within walking dist."*
€18.00, 1 Apr-30 Oct. **2016**

COULANGES SUR YONNE *4G4* (9km E Rural) *47.53610, 3.63326* **Camp Municipal Le Petit Port,** 89660 Châtel-Censoir **03 86 81 01 98 (Mairie) or 06 80 32 59 50 (mob); campinglepetitport@orange.fr or mairie-de-chatel-censoir@wanadoo.fr; www.chatel-censoir.com**

€0.50 nr

Fr Auxerre or Clamecy on N151 at Coulanges turn E onto D21, S side of rv & canal to Châtel-Censoir; site sp. 1*, Med, pt shd, EHU (6A) €3 (poss rev pol); bbq; sw nr; twin axles; 10% statics; phone; Eng spkn; fishing adj; CKE. *"Attractive, peaceful site bet rv & canal; friendly, busy resident warden; OK san facs; some pitches muddy when wet; beautiful area with gd cycling; concerts at w/ends; excel."*
€8.50, 27 Apr-30 Sep. **2018**

COULON *7A2* (0.8km N Rural) *46.32739, -0.58437* **Camp Municipal La Niquière,** Route de Benet, 79510 Coulon **05 49 35 81 19 or 05 49 35 90 26 (Mairie); tourisme.coulon79@orange.fr; www.ville-coulon.fr**

€0.50 nr

Fr N148 at Benet take D1 to Coulon to site on L at ent to Coulon. 2*, Sm, pt shd, EHU (10A) €3.10; gas; boat hire. *"Well-kept site; dated but clean san facs; sports facs adj; ent only with barrier card - collect fr Mairie when site office clsd; 10 min walk to vill; gd NH; gd ctr for Marais Poitevin; Coulon is a v attractive town."* **€16.00, 1 Apr-30 Sep.** **2016**

COULON *7A2* (2km W Rural) *46.31444, -0.60888* **Camping La Venise Verte,** 178 Route des Bords de Sèvre, 79510 Coulon **05 49 35 90 36; accueil@camping-laveniseverte.fr; www.camping-lavenise verte.fr**

€2

Exit A83 junc 9 onto D148 to Benet. Turn R at rndabt onto D25E sp Benet cent & foll sp for Coulon thro Benet. In Coulon turn R at traff lts onto D123 sp Le Vanneau-Irleau & Arcais. Cont for approx 3km with canal on L to site R bef canal bdge. Site sp. 4*, Med, mkd, pt shd, EHU (10A) inc (poss rev pol); bbq (charcoal, gas); twin axles; 20% statics; phone; Eng spkn; adv bkg acc; ccard acc; canoe hire; fishing; bike hire; games rm; boating; CKE. *"Superb, peaceful eco site in park-like setting; v friendly helpful owner; excel facs; gd rest; gd sized pitches (some with reinforced plastic grid), but some sm & diff due trees & posts; ACSI; excel touring base for nature lovers; gd walking & cycle paths beside waterways; pretty town; lovely area; much revisited site; well placed pitches; gd facs; beautiful, tranquil location; highly rec; excel family run site; charming vill walkable."*
€30.50, 1 Apr-15 Oct, A37. **2019**

> **"There aren't many sites open at this time of year"**
>
> If you're travelling outside peak season remember to call ahead to check site opening dates – even if the entry says 'open all year'.

COULON *7A2* (6km W Rural) *46.33020, -0.67524* **Camping Le Relais du Pêcheur,** 85420 Le Mazeau **02 51 52 93 23; campinglerelaisdupecheur@orange.fr; www.lerelaisdupecheur.fr**

nr

Fr Fontenay-le-Comte take N148 SE. At Benet turn R onto D25 thro vill to Le Mazeau. Turn L in vill then R over canal bdge. Site on L in 500m. 2*, Med, hdg, pt shd, EHU (16A) €3.50; Eng spkn; adv bkg acc; CKE. *"Pleasant, clean site in delightful location; gd cyling & walks; new owners, resident warden; facs being updated (2016)."* **€13.00, 1 Apr-15 Oct.** **2017**

COURBIAC 7D3 (1.7km W Rural) 44.37818, 1.01807
FFCC Le Pouchou, 47370 Courbiac 05 53 40 72 68
or 06 42 83 37 62 (mob); lepouchou@gmail.com;
www.camping-le-pouchou.com

🐾 €1.80 ♟♟ ⬛ 🏊 ⬆ ⬇ ➕ ⧉ ∥ ⬛ ❦ ⑨ 🍴 ⬛ 🛒 ⯃ ⬛ 🛶 ⬛

S fr Fumel on D102 thro Tournon-d'Agenais;
Courbiac sp to L on S side of town; site on R in
2.5km (1.5km bef Courbiac). 3*, Sm, pt shd, pt sl,
EHU (10A) €4 (poss rev pol); TV (pitch); 10% statics;
Eng spkn; adv bkg req; fishing; horseriding; bike hire;
site clsd 21 Dec-9 Jan; archery; CKE. *"Vg site in lovely
setting; lge pitches each with picnic table; many sl
pitches poss diff; gd, clean facs; gd views; friendly,
hospitable owners; gd cycling; peaceful location."*
€16.00, 1 Mar-30 Jun, 1 Jul-31 Aug,
1 Sep-30 Nov.   2019

COURPIERE 9B1 (5km NE Rural) 45.79199, 3.60583
Camping Le Grün du Chignore, Les Plaines, 63120
Vollore-Ville 04 73 53 73 37; camping-du-chignore@
hotmail.fr; www.campingauvergne.fr

🐾 €1.50 ♟♟ ⬛ 🏊 ⬆ ⬇ ∥ ⬛ ❦ ⑨ 🍴 ⬛ ⑨ 🛒 ⬛ ⯃

D906 S fr Thiers; at Courpière turn L onto D7 to
Vollore-Ville; cont on D7 past vill; site on R in 500m.
2*, Sm, mkd, hdg, pt shd, EHU (10A) €4; bbq (sep
area); 10% statics; Eng spkn; adv bkg acc; ccard acc;
games area. *"Situated above fishing lake; rolling hills;
helpful & welcoming owners; facs pitches stretched high
ssn; poss clsd on Weds in April; gd walks; chateau in
Vollore-Ville; bar pt of vill life; highly rec; excel; vg, new
deep pool; gd size level pitches; gd value pizza rest;
hiking guide maps at recep; excel value; some rd noise
on upper terrace."* €15.40, 1 Apr-31 Oct.   2018

COURSEULLES SUR MER 3D1 (1.2km NE Coastal)
49.33417, -0.44433 **Camp Municipal Le Champ de
Course,** Ave de la Libération, 14470 Courseulles-sur-
Mer 02 31 37 99 26 (Mairie); camping.courseulles@
wanadoo.fr; www.courseulles-sur-mer.com

🐾 €1.90 ♟♟ ⬛ 🏊 ⬆ ⬇ ∥ ⬛ ❦ ⑨ 🍴 ⬛ ⑨ 🛒 ⯃ ⬛ ⬛ sand

Fr N814 by-pass thro Caen, take exit 5 onto D7 &
D404 dir Courseulles-sur-Mer. On ent to town, foll
sp 'Campings' at 1st rndabt Site on D514 on R. Gd
sp's for site. 4*, Lge, mkd, hdg, unshd, EHU (10A)
€4.50; bbq; TV; 15% statics; phone; Eng spkn; adv
bkg acc; ccard acc; games area; horseriding nr; tennis
nr; CKE. *"Nice site adj beach; friendly staff; facs clean;
boat hire nrby; early dep for ferry catered for; conv
D-Day landing beach; gd dog walks; mini golf nr; oyster
beds & daily fish mkt; vg; excel modern & clean san
facs; pool adj; exit barriers open at 7am; supmkt 0.5
km."* €23.50, 1 Apr-30 Sep.   2015

COURSEULLES SUR MER 3D1 (8km SW Rural)
49.28949, -0.52970 **Camp Municipal des Trois
Rivières,** Route de Tierceville, 14480 Creully 02 31 80
90 17; contact@camping-les-3-rivieres.com;
www.camping-les-3-rivieres.com

🐾 €1.20 ♟♟ (htd) ⬛ 🏊 ⬆ ⬇ ⧉ ∥ ❦ ⑨ 🍴 ⬛ nr ⑨ nr 🛒 nr ⬛

⬛ sand 5km

Fr Caen ring rd, exit junc 8 onto N13 dir Bayeux; in
15km turn R onto D82 to Creully; site on R 500m
past cent of Creully. 3*, Med, hdg, mkd, pt shd, pt sl,
EHU (10A) €4.10 (long leads req, poss rev pol); bbq
(charcoal, gas); twin axles; 9% statics; Eng spkn; adv
bkg acc; ccard acc; games area; games rm; table
tennis; tennis; CKE. *"Friendly, helpful warden; facs not
v clean, stretched high ssn; pool 5km; conv D-Day
beaches, Bayeux; barrier clsd 1500-1700; gd cycling;
standard of maintenance is poor; run down site and
unkept (2019); many ssn vans."*
€20.40, 6 Apr-13 Oct.   2019

COURVILLE SUR EURE 4E2 (0.5km S Urban) 48.44629,
1.24157 **Camp Municipal Les Bords de l'Eure,** Ave
Thiers, 28190 Courville-sur-Eure 02 37 23 76 38
or 02 37 18 07 90 (Mairie); secretaria-mairie@
courville-sur-eure.fr; www.courville-sur-eure.fr

🐾 ♟♟ (htd) ⬛ 🏊 ⬆ ∥ ❦ ⑨ nr 🛒 nr

Turn N off D923 19km W of Chartres. Site on bank
of rv. Foll sp. 2*, Med, hdg, pt shd, EHU (16A) €3.30.
*"Lovely, peaceful rvside site; spacious pitches; friendly
warden; no twin axles; Eng spkn; conv Chartres;
mkt Thurs; easy walk into town; gd security, oniste
warden; mv service pnt adj; pool 200m; site basic but
lge pitches and v well kept; facs gd and spotless."*
€7.80, 30 Apr-18 Sep.   2016

"That's changed – Should I let the Club know?"

If you find something on site that's different
from the site entry, fill in a report and let us
know. See camc.com/europereport.

COUTRAS 7C2 (7.5km NW Rural) 45.07929, -0.20839
Camping Le Chêne du Lac, 3 Lieu-dit Chateauneuf,
33230 Bayas 05 57 69 13 78 or 06 07 98 92 65 (mob);
lechenedulac@orange.fr; www.camping-lechene
dulac.com

🐾 €2 ♟♟ ⬛ 🏊 ⬆ ⬇ ∥ ❦ ⑨ 🍴 ⬛ 🛒 ⬛

Fr Coutras W on D10 to Guitres; N fr Guitres on
D247 to Bayas; site 2km N of Bayas, sp. 3*, Sm, mkd,
pt shd, EHU (10A) €4.30-5; gas; bbq (sep area);
25% statics; Eng spkn; adv bkg acc; CKE. *"Helpful
owner; pedalos & canoes adj; vg; red facs in winter;
great site; friendly, helpful new owners; v relaxed
atmosphere; excel."* €24.00, 1 Mar-30 Nov.   2017

COUTURES 4G1 (1km NE Rural) 47.37440, -0.34690
Camping Parc de Montsabert, 49320 Coutures **02 41 57 91 63**; camping@parcdemontsabert.com; www.parcdemontsabert.com

🐾 €4 ♥♥(htd) 🆆 ♨ ᚖ ⅄ 🖥 ⁄ 🦋 ⟂ ⅄ ⊕ ䷀ 🥘nr 🗚 ✐ ♒(covrd, htd) 🎣

Easy access on R side of Rv Loire bet Angers & Saumur. Take D751 to Coutures & fr town cent foll sp for site. 1st R after 'Tabac' & foll rd to site (1st on R bef chateau). 4*, Med, hdg, hdstg, mkd, pt shd, pt sl, serviced pitches; EHU (5-10A) inc; TV; 15% statics; phone; bus 1km; Eng spkn; adv bkg acc; ccard acc; bike hire; tennis; gym; games area; games rm; CKE. *"Ideal for chateaux & wine cellars; lge pitches."*
€29.00, 12 Apr-8 Sep. 2016

COZES 7B1 (0.7km NW Urban) 45.58650, -0.83568
Camping Le Sorlut (formerly Municipal), Rue de Stade, 17120 Cozes **06 45 46 07 90 or 05 46 90 75 99**; contact@camping-charente-maritime-cozes.com; www.camping-charente-maritime-cozes.com/

♥♥ 🆆 ♨ 🖥 ⁄ 🦋 🥘nr 🗚 ♒

Fr bypass D730 turn into Cozes at Royan end. Foll sp for camping. Turn L at supmkt, site 400m on L. 2*, Med, mkd, pt shd, EHU (6A) €2.50; tennis; CKE. *"Pleasant site close to Royan; friendly, helpful warden; no twin axles; popular with long stay British; excel new san facs (2016); number plate recognition barrier."*
€16.00, 15 Apr-14 Oct. 2018

CRAON 2F4 (1.7km E Urban) 47.84819, -0.94409
Camp Municipal du Mûrier, Rue Alain Gerbault, 53400 Craon **02 43 06 96 33 or 02 43 06 13 09 (Mairie)**; www.campingdecraon53.fr

♥♥ ♨ 🖥 ⁄ 🦋 ♒ ䷀ 🗚 ✐

Fr Laval take D771 S to Craon. Site sp fr town cent. 3*, Sm, hdg, pt shd, EHU (6-10A) €2.90; red long stay; adv bkg acc; tennis. *"Lge pitches; easy walk to town; pool 200m; office clsd Tues & Sun LS, when barrier key req (2010); local chateau gardens; excel; new modern san block (2018)."* **€12.00, 1 May-21 Sep.** 2018

CREMIEU 9B2 (4km NW Rural) 45.74829, 5.22486
Camping à la Ferme des Epinettes, 11 Rue de l'Eglise, 38460 St Romain-de-Jalionas **04 74 90 94 90**; info@camping-cremieu.com; www.camping-cremieu.com

12 🐾 €1 ♥♥(htd) 🆆 ♨ 🖥 ⁄ 🦋 🥘nr

N fr Crémieu on D517; in 3km site sp on R, immed bef rndabt on edge of St Romain-de-Jalionas. 200m after turning R off D517 (into Rue de l'Eglise), turn L into Rue des Epinettes & site ent. Site on R in 100m. 1*, Sm, mkd, EHU (16A); 20% statics; jacuzzi. *"Gd NH for interesting & historic town of Lyon and Crémieu; helpful owners; ltd facs LS; gd touring base; Pérouges worth visit; trams/metro fr Meyzieu to Lyon; rec; lovely, peaceful site; run down (2014); narr rds; statics mainly for workers; movers needed for lge o'fits; no resident warden."* **€17.00** 2019

CREON 7D2 (3km NW Rural) 44.78372, -0.37108
FFCC Camping Caravaning Bel Air, 33670 Créon **05 56 23 01 90**; info@camping-bel-air.com; www.camping-bel-air.com

🐾 €2.50 ♥♥(htd) 🆆 ♨ ᚖ ⅄ 🖥 ⁄ MSP 🦋 ♒ ⅄ ⊕ ䷀ 🥘 🗚 ♒

Fr A10/E70 at junc 24 take D936 E fr Bordeaux sp Bergerac. Approx 15km E turn SE onto D671 sp Créon & cont for 5km. Site on L, 1.5km after Lorient. 3*, Med, hdg, mkd, hdstg, pt shd, EHU (10A) €3.60; gas; red long stay; 50% statics; Eng spkn; adv bkg acc; ccard acc; CKE. *"Helpful owners; immac, modern san facs; rest sm & ltd; facs v ltd LS; no twin axles; some pitches v restricted and tight; phone ahead to check open LS; gd NH; poss music festival in next field; clsd to vehicles 2200-0800; poss rd noise; nr cycle path to Bordeaux and Sauverne."* **€25.00, 15 Jan-15 Dec.** 2019

CRESPIAN 10E1 (0.5km S Rural) 43.87850, 4.09590
Kawan Village Le Mas de Reilhe, 30260 Crespian **04 66 77 82 12**; info@camping-mas-de-reilhe.fr; www.camping-mas-de-reilhe.fr

🐾 €3 ♥♥(htd) 🆆 ♨ ᚖ ⅄ 🖥 ⁄ MSP 🦋 ♒ ⅄ ⊕ ䷀ 🥘 🗚 ✐ ♒(htd) 🎣

Exit A9 at Nîmes Ouest N onto N106 dir Alès for 5km. Fork R, then L over bdge onto D999 dir Le Vigan. Foll rd for 24km, R at x-rds onto D6110 to site on R just on ent Crespian. Take care - ent on a bend on busy rd. 4*, Med, mkd, pt shd, pt sl, terr, EHU (10A) inc; bbq (elec, gas); red long stay; TV; Eng spkn; ccard acc; games area; table tennis; games rm; CKE. *"Quiet, relaxing & lovely site; friendly staff; no o'fits over 7.5m; clean, modern excel san facs; wine-tasting adj; conv Nîmes, Uzès & Cévennes National Park; excel."* **€33.60, 23 Apr-29 Sep, C10.** 2019

CREST 9D2 (1km SE Urban) 44.72410, 5.02755
Camping Les Clorinthes, Quai Soubeyran, 26400 Crest **04 75 25 05 28**; clorinthes@wanadoo.fr; www.lesclorinthes.com

🐾 €3-3.50 ♥♥(htd) 🆆 ♨ ᚖ ⅄ 🖥 ⁄ 🦋 ♒ ⅄ ䷀ 🥘 ✐ ♒ 🎣 🚣

S fr Crest twd Nyons on D538, cross bdge cont to rndabt,take last exit foll sp to site. 3*, Lge, hdg, hdstg, mkd, pt shd, EHU (6A) €4.20; gas; sw nr; TV; 10% statics; phone; adv bkg acc; CKE. *"Well-maintained site in beautiful situation; friendly, family run; dir access rv; gd, modern san facs; easy walk or cycle to vill; sports complex 500m; mkt Tue & Sat, snacks and bar high ssn only."*
€27.00, 28 Apr-14 Sep. 2015

For a guide to symbols see the fold out on the rear cover

FRANCE

CREVECOEUR LE GRAND *3C3* (13km SW Rural)
49.57569, 1.93899 **Camping du Vieux Moulin,**
2 Rue des Larris, 60690 Roy-Boissy **03 44 46 29 46**

🚶 wc 🏕 🕹 ∥ 🦋 ⚲

**Fr Marseille-en-Beauvasis SW onto D930 dir
Gournay-en-Bray; in 1.5km site sp to R at Roy-
Boissy.** 1*, Sm, pt shd, EHU inc (poss rev pol);
10% statics; phone. *"Farm site in area with few sites;
beautiful countryside; pitch yourself, owner calls eves;
excel."* **€10.00, 1 Apr-31 Oct.**   **2017**

CRIEL SUR MER *3B2* (1.5km N Coastal) *50.02568,
1.30855* **FFCC Camp Municipal Le Mont Joli Bois,**
29 Rue de la Plage, 76910 Criel-sur-Mer **02 35 50 81
19 or 06 08 80 67 35 (mob); camping.criel@
wanadoo.fr; www.montjolibois.mobi**

12 🐕 €1.60 🚶(htd) wc 🏕 🕹 🖥 ∥ MP 🦋 ⚲ nr ⊕ nr 🦆 nr ⚲

⚲ shgl 500m

**Fr D925 take D222 into Criel cent. Turn R opp
church into D126 for 1.6km to beach. Turn L then
immed R & foll beach rd to site in 1.5km.**
3*, Med, hdg, mkd, pt shd, pt sl, terr, EHU (4-6A) €3-
4.60; TV; 50% statics; bus; CKE. *"Lovely site, facs need
refurb."* **€14.50**   **2015**

CROTOY, LE *3B2* (1.5km N Rural) *50.22968, 1.64140*
Camping La Ferme de Tarteron, Route de Rue, 80550
Le Crotoy **03 22 27 06 75; contact@letarteron.fr;
www.letarteron.fr**

🚶 wc 🏕 ∥ 🦋 ⚲ 🍴 🦆 ⚲ ⚲(htd) ⚲ sand 1.5km

**Fr A16 exit junc 24 onto D32, then D940 around Rue
twd Le Crotoy. Pass D4 dir St Firmin site on L.** 3*, Med,
hdg, mkd, pt shd, EHU (4-10A) €3.50-8; gas; 80% statics.
*"Conv Marquenterre bird park & steam train fr Le Crotoy;
v clean, basic san facs; 2km walk to town, off rd; barrier
ent."* **€30.00, 1 Apr-31 Oct.**   **2018**

CROTOY, LE *3B2* (4km N Coastal) *50.24941, 1.61145*
Camping Les Aubépines, 800 Rue de la Maye, St
Firmin, 80550 Le Crotoy **03 22 27 01 34; lesaubepines
@baiedesommepleinair.com; www.baiedesomme
pleinair.com**

🐕 €2 🚶(htd) wc 🏕 🕹 🕹 🖥 ∥ 🦋 ⚲ 🦆 🗄 ∥ ⚲(htd) 🍴

⚲ sand 1km

**Exit A16 junc 23 to Le Crotoy via D40 & D940; then
foll sp St Firmin; site sp. Or exit A16 junc 24 onto D32
dir Rue; by-pass Rue but take D4 to St Firmin; sp 1 km
after church. Site on rd to beach on W of D4.**
4*, Med, hdg, mkd, pt shd, EHU (3-10A) €3-8 (poss long
lead req); gas; bbq; 40% statics; phone; Eng spkn; adv
bkg acc; ccard acc; horseriding; bike hire; games rm; CKE.
*"Peaceful, popular, well-run site; tourers sited with statics;
lovely pool; gd cycling & walking; check office opening
hrs for early dep; Marquenterre ornithological park 3km;
steam train 3km; excel."* **€29.00, 25 Mar-1 Nov.**   **2016**

CROZON *2E2* (6.5km E Coastal) *48.24204, -4.42932*
Camping L'Aber, Tal-ar-Groas,50 Route de la Plage de
l'Aber, 29160 Crozon **02 98 27 02 96 or 06 75
62 39 07 (mob); contact@camping-aber.com;
www.camping-aber.com**

🐕 €1.50 🚶 🏕 🕹 ∥ 🦋 🍴 🦆 ⚲(htd) ⚲ sand 1km

**On D887 turn S in Tal-ar-Groas foll camp sp to site
in 1km on R.** 3*, Med, mkd, pt shd, pt sl, terr, EHU (5A)
€3.40; gas; 50% statics; adv bkg acc; fishing; sailing;
windsurfing. *"Great views."*
€20.60, 1 Apr-31 Oct.   **2017**

CUISEAUX *9A2* (5km W Rural) *46.49570, 5.32662*
Camping Le Domaine de Louvarel, 71480
Champagnat **03 85 76 62 71; info@louvarel.com;
www.louvarel.com**

🐕 €2 🚶(htd) wc 🏕 🕹 🖥 ∥ MP 🦋 🕹 🍴 ⊕ 🗄 ⚲ ⚲(htd)
🗄 ⚲ sand

**Exit A39 junc 9 dir Cuiseaux; foll sp 'Base de Loisirs
de Louvarel'. Or fr D1083 exit Champagnat & foll sp
to site on lakeside.** 3*, Med, mkd, hdg, pt shd, terr,
EHU (10A) incl; bbq; sw nr; 7% statics; phone; Eng
spkn; adv bkg acc; bike hire; games area; boating;
fishing; CKE. *"Excel, clean site; helpful manager; o'night
m'vans area; excel, immac san facs; nice rest & bar; gd
walking; free use of canoes; busy."*
€34.00, 15 Apr-16 Sep.   **2019**

"We must tell the Club about
that great site we found"

Get your site reports in by mid-August and we'll
do our best to get your updates into the next
edition.

CUVILLY *3C3* (1.5km N Rural) *49.56750, 2.70790*
Camping de Sorel, 24 Rue St Claude, 60490 Orvillers-
Sorel **03 44 85 02 74; contact@aestiva.fr;
www.camping-sorel.com**

🚶(htd) wc 🏕 🕹 🕹 🖥 ∥ ⚲ 🦋 🕹 🍴 ⊕ 🗄 🦆 /M

**Exit A1/E15 at junc 12 (Roye) S'bound or 11
(Ressons) N'bound. Site on E of D1017.** 3*, Med, mkd,
pt shd, EHU (10A) €3; bbq; TV; 50% statics; games
area. *"Pleasant situation; conv NH A1 & Calais; friendly
staff; facs need updating (2014); rec early arr in ssn;
rv fishing 10km; busy at w/end; 30 mins Parc Astérix;
plenty to visit."* **€21.00, 1 Feb-15 Dec.**   **2019**

DAGLAN 7D3 (4km N Rural) 44.76762, 1.17590
Camping Le Moulin de Paulhiac, 24250 Daglan
05 53 28 20 88; francis.armagnac@wanadoo.fr;
www.moulin-de-paulhiac.com

🐕 €1.90 ♨ 🚾 ♨ 🌡 🔥 🍴 ⛱ 🐾 🍽 🛒 🌳 🛝 🏧 ⚡ 🛶 (htd)
🏊 shgl

D57 SW fr Sarlat, across rv into St Cybranet &
site in 2km. Fr Souillac W on D703 alongside Rv
Dordogne; x-ing rv onto D46 (nr Domme) & D50,
to site. Med, hdg, mkd, shd, EHU (6-10A) €3.70-4.40;
gas; TV; 20% statics; Eng spkn; adv bkg acc; ccard
acc; canoeing; waterslide; rv fishing adj; CKE. "*Pretty
site; friendly, helpful staff; vg fruit/veg mkt Sun in vill;
highly rec.*" **€25.00, 15 May-16 Sep.**   2017

See advertisement

"I need an on-site restaurant"

We do our best to make sure site information
is correct, but it is always best to check any
must-have facilities are still available or will
be open during your visit.

DAMAZAN 7D2 (1.5km S Rural) 44.27966, 0.27739
Camping Du Lac (formerly Municipal), Lac du
Moulineau, 47160 Saint Pierre de Buzet 05 53 89 74 36
or 06 27 11 03 57; contact@campingdulac47.com;
www.campingdulac47.com

🐕 ♨ 🚾 🌡 🔥 🍴 🌳 🍽 🛒 🏧 🐾 ⚡

Fr A62 take junc 6, turn R at rndabt onto D8; almost
immed take slip rd sp Damazan/Buzet-dur-Baïse; at
top take 2nd R sp Buzet (1st turning goes to lake
only). Site 1km on R, sp fr rd. 2*, Sm, mkd, hdstg, hdg,
pt shd, pt sl, EHU (10A) €3; bbq; sw nr; 2% statics; adv
bkg acc; CKE. "*Pretty site by lake; helpful staff; next
to cricket club; clean basic san facs; attractive Bastide
town; conv NH; needs updating; fair; easy access fr
a'route.*" **€24.50, 1 Jul-31 Aug.**   2015

DANGE ST ROMAIN 4H2 (3km N Rural) 46.96944,
0.60399 Camp Municipal, 8 Rue des Buxières, 86220
Les Ormes 05 49 21 23 43; les-ormes@cg86.fr;
www.tourisme-vienne.com

🐕 €1.20 ♨ 🚾 🌡 🔥 🍴 🌳 🍽 🛒 🏧 🐾 ⚡

Turn W off D910 in cent Les Ormes onto D1a sp
Vellèches & Marigny-Marmande, foll site sp to
site on rv. 2*, Med, mkd, pt shd, pt sl, EHU (10A)
inc; bbq; 10% statics; Eng spkn; adv bkg acc; tennis
100m; canoe launching area; CKE. "*Lovely, quiet,
peaceful setting on rv bank; helpful warden; clean
basic modern san facs; poss travellers; quiet vill in
walking dist; chateau in walking dist; gd NH; vg.*"
€11.00, 1 Apr-30 Sep.   2018

DAX 8E1 (1.5km W Rural) 43.71189, -1.07304
Camping Les Chênes, Allée du Bois de Boulogne,
40100 Dax 05 58 90 05 53; campingleschenes@
bala-dax.fr; www.camping-leschenes-dax.com

🐕 €1.50 ♨ (htd) 🚾 🌡 🔥 🍴 🌳 🛒 🍽 🏧 ⚡ 🐾 🛝 ⚡ 🛶

Fr D824 to Dax, foll sp Bois de Boulogne, cross rlwy
bdge & rv bdge & foll camp sp on rv bank. Well sp.
4*, Lge, mkd, shd, serviced pitches; EHU (10A) inc; gas;
bbq; TV; 80% statics; Eng spkn; adv bkg acc; ccard acc;
games rm; bike hire; CKE. "*Excel position; easy walk
along rv into town; poss noise fr school adj; conv thermal
baths at Dax; modernised site with uptodate htd, clean
san facs; lovely pool and child area; interesting spa
town.*" **€19.50, 15 Mar-31 Oct.**   2018

DAX 8E1 (11km W Rural) 43.68706, -1.14687
FFCC Camping à la Ferme Bertranborde (Lafitte),
975 Route des Clarions, 40180 Rivière-Saas-et-
Gourby 05 58 97 58 39; bertranborde@orange.fr

12 🐕 €0.50 ♨ 🚾 🌡 🔥 🍴 🐾 🛒 🍽 🐾 ⚡

Turn S off D824 5km W of Dax onto D113, sp
Angoumé; at x-rd in 2km turn R (by water tower);
then immed L; site on R in 100m, well sp. Or fr N10/
A63, exit junc 9 onto D824 dir Dax; in 5km turn R
onto D113, then as bef. Sm, pt shd, pt sl, EHU (4-10A)
€2.50-4.50; own san rec; bbq; Eng spkn; adv bkg acc;
ice; CKE. "*Peaceful CL-type site; beautiful garden;
friendly, helpful owners; meals on request; min 2 nights
high ssn; poss travellers festival time; excel; lovely site.*"
€16.40   2016

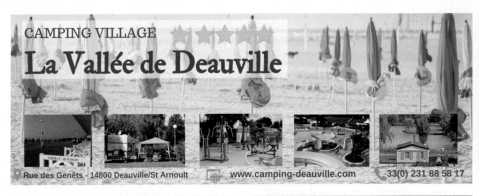

CAMPING VILLAGE
La Vallée de Deauville

Rue des Genêts - 14800 Deauville/St Arnoult · www.camping-deauville.com · 33(0) 231 88 58 17

DAX *8E1* (3km NW Rural) *43.72020, -1.09365*
FFCC Camping Les Pins du Soleil, Route des Minières,
La Pince, 40990 St Paul-les-Dax **05 58 91 37 91;**
info@pinsoleil.com; www.pinsoleil.com

🐕 €2 ⅋⅋(htd) 🚐 ♨ ⚷ ♿ 🖭 ⦿ 🍴 ⅋⅋nr ♨ 🔧 ⚐ ⚓ ♨ ⛱

**Exit N10 junc 11 sp Dax onto D16. Cross D824 & turn
R onto D459 S. Cross rndabt & cont on D459, Route
des Minières. Site sp in pine forest.**
4*, Med, mkd, hdg, pt shd, pt sl, serviced pitches;
EHU (5A) €2; gas; bbq; red long stay; TV; 25% statics;
phone; Eng spkn; ccard acc; tennis 2km; games area;
bike hire. *"Nice, quiet site (LS); various pitch sizes,
some spacious; soft, sandy soil poss problem when
wet; helpful, friendly staff; excel pool; spa 2km; conv
Pyrenees & Biarritz; vg; not well maintained (2018); NH
only."* **€26.00, 1 Apr-31 Oct.** **2018**

"Satellite navigation makes touring much easier"

Remember most sat navs don't know if you're
towing or in a larger vehicle – always use yours
alongside maps and site directions.

DEAUVILLE *3D1* (3km S Urban) *49.32903, 0.08593*
Camping La Vallée de Deauville, Ave de la Vallée,
14800 St Arnoult **02 31 88 58 17; www.camping-
deauville.com**

🐕 €4.20 ⅋⅋(htd) 🚐 ♨ ⚷ ♿ 🖭 ⅋ ⦿ 🍴 ⚐ 🔧 ⚓ ⚐ ♨

⛱(covrd, htd) 🏖 sand 4km

**Fr Deauville take D27 dir Caen, turn R onto
D278 to St Arnoult, foll site sp.** 4*, Lge, hdg, mkd,
hdstg, pt shd, EHU (10A) inc; gas; 80% statics;
phone; Eng spkn; ccard acc; waterslide; games
rm; lake fishing; CKE. *"Easy access to beaches &
resorts; conv Le Havre using Pont de Normandie;
lake walks & activities on site; excel san facs."*
€36.60, 1 Apr-1 Nov. **2019**

See advertisement

DECAZEVILLE *7D4* (9km NE Rural) *44.62920, 2.32030*
Camping La Plaine, Le Bourg, 12300 St Parthem
**05 65 64 05 24 or 05 65 43 03 99; infos@camping-
laplaine.fr; www.camping-laplaine.fr**

🐕 €1.50 ⅋⅋ 🖭 🚐 ♨ ⚷ ⦿ 🍴 🔧 ♨ ⚐ ⛱

**N fr Decazeville on D963; in 6km over narr bdge
take 1st turn R onto D42 to St Parthem. Site 1km
past vill on R.** 2*, Med, hdg, mkd, pt shd, EHU (6A) inc;
bbq; 5% statics; phone; Eng spkn; adv bkg acc; tennis;
CKE. *"Idyllic setting on banks of Rv Lot; friendly Dutch
owners; excel walking; vg."*
€24.50, 1 Apr-31 Oct. **2017**

DECAZEVILLE *7D4* (3km NW Rural) *44.58819, 2.22145*
FFCC Camping Le Roquelongue, 12300 Boisse-
Penchot **05 65 63 39 67; info@camping-roquelongue.
com; www.camping-roquelongue.com**

12 🐕 ⅋⅋ 🖭 🚐 ♨ 🔧 ⦿ 🍴 🔧 ⚓ ♨ ⛱(htd)

**Fr D963 N fr Decazeville turn W onto D140 & D42
to Boisse-Penchot. Rte via D21 not rec (steep hill
& acute turn). Site mid-way bet Boisse-Penchot &
Livinhac-le-Haut on D42.** 2*, Med, mkd, hdg, pt shd,
EHU (6-10A) €4.20-4.80; gas; 10% statics; phone; adv
bkg acc; canoeing; tennis; fishing; bike hire; CKE. *"Direct
access Rv Lot; pitches gd size; san facs clean; no twin
axles; excel base for Lot Valley."* **€18.30** **2016**

DEYME *8F3* (0.4km NE Rural) *43.48672, 1.5322*
Camping Les Violettes, Porte de Toulouse, 31450
Deyme **05 61 81 72 07; campinglesviolettes@
wanadoo.fr; www.campinglesviolettes.com**

12 🐕 €0.70 ⅋⅋(htd) 🚐 ♨ ⦿ 🖭 ⅋ 🍴 ⦿ 🔧 ⚓ ♨

**SE fr Toulouse to Carcassonne on N113, sp on L,
12km fr Toulouse (after passing Deyme sp).**
2*, Med, mkd, hdstg, pt shd, EHU (6A) €4; bbq; TV;
60% statics; CKE. *"Helpful, friendly staff; facs run
down (Jun 2009); poss muddy when wet; 800m fr
Canal du Midi & 10km fr Space City; Park & Ride 2.5km
& metro to Toulouse; san facs updated (2018); sw pool
nrby."* **€25.00** **2018**

DIE *9D2* (1km NE Rural) 44.75444, 5.37778
FFCC Camping La Riou-Merle, Route de Romeyer, 26150 Die **04 75 22 21 31; lerioumerle@gmail.com; www.camping-lerioumerle.com**

Fr Gap on D93 heading twd Valence. Cont on D93 twd town cent; R on D742 to Romeyer. Site on L in 200m. On D93 fr Crest foll sp round town cent onto D742. 3*, Med, pt shd, pt sl, EHU (10A) €4.20; 30% statics; Eng spkn; fishing. *"Clean, well laid out site; friendly, helpful staff; gd san facs; 15 min walk to attractive town; rec."* **€27.00, 1 Apr-15 Oct.** 2016

DIEPPE *3C2* (3km S Urban) 49.90040, 1.07472
Camping Vitamin, 865 Chemin des Vertus, 76550 St Aubin-sur-Scie **02 35 82 11 11; camping-vitamin@ wanadoo.fr; www.camping-vitamin.com**

Fr E or W leave Peripherique (D925) S at D927 (sp Rouen). At rndabt take exit onto Canadiens Ave/ N27. About 850m take exit twrds Belvedere. Then R onto Rue de la Briqueterie. Site on the R. 4*, Med, hdg, mkd, unshd, EHU (10A) inc; 80% statics; adv bkg acc; ccard acc; games area; CKE. *"Lovely, well-kept site; san facs immac; poss boggy in wet; conv ferries; excel; auto barrier for early dep; v useful & gd value; on bus rte to Dieppe; off clsd 1200-1430; lots of statics & ssn workers; lge retail pk nrby; Aldi at ent; fully equipped site; fair."* **€29.50, 31 Mar-1 Oct.** 2018

DIEPPE *3C2* (5km S Rural) 49.87063, 1.14426
Camping des 2 Rivières, 76880 Martigny **02 35 85 60 82; www.camping-2-rivieres.com**

Martigny vill on D154 S fr Dieppe. If appr fr Dieppe, ent is on L bef vill sp. Med, pt shd, EHU (6A) €3.05; adv bkg rec; horseriding nr; watersports nr. *"Attractive, pleasant, spacious site by lge lake; access poss diff long o'fits due parked vehicles; mountain biking nrby; Arques forest nrby; cycle paths; highly rec."* **€20.60, 31 Mar-08 Oct.** 2017

DIEPPE *3C2* (4km SW Rural) 49.89820, 1.05705
Camping La Source, 63 Rue des Tisserands, Petit-Appeville, 76550 Hautot-sur-Mer **02 35 84 27 04; info@camping-la-source.fr; www.camping-la-source.fr**
sand 3km

Fr Dieppe ferry terminal foll sp Paris, take D925 W dir Fécamp. In 2km at Petit Appeville turn L, site in 800m on rvside. NB 4m bdge bef ent & narr rd to site - not suitable v lge o'fits. 3*, Med, mkd, pt shd, EHU (10A) €4.20; sw nr; TV; 10% statics; adv bkg acc; ccard acc; golf 4km; bike hire; games area; boating adj; games rm; fishing adj; CKE. *"Lovely, well-kept site in attractive setting; pleasant, vg, clean san facs; footpath to Le Plessis vill; gd cycling; excel NH for ferry; MH pitches sm, but backs onto delightful stream and fmland."* **€30.00, 15 Mar-15 Oct.** 2019

DIEPPE *3C2* (6km SW Rural) 49.90886, 1.04069
Camping Marqueval, 1210 Rue de la Mer, 76550 Pourville-sur-Mer **02 35 82 66 46; contact@camping lemarqueval.com; www.campinglemarqueval.com**
sand 1.2km

Site well sp fr D75. 2*, Lge, mkd, hdg, pt shd, EHU (6A) €2.50; bbq; TV; 70% statics; Eng spkn; adv bkg acc; ccard acc; games rm; lake fishing; CKE. *"Attractive, well-kept site; san facs clean but tired; delightful coastal area close by; Bois Du Moutiers gdns highly rec; spa; dog walk on site."* **€28.00, 20 Mar-15 Oct.** 2017

DIEPPE *3C2* (9km SW Urban) 49.87297, 1.04497
Camp Municipal du Colombier, 453 Rue Loucheur, 76550 Offranville **02 35 85 21 14**
shgl 5km

W fr Dieppe on D925, take L turn on D55 to Offranville, site clearly sp in vill to Parc du Colombier. NB Pt of site cul-de-sac, explore on foot bef towing in. 3*, Med, mkd, hdg, pt shd, EHU (10A) €2.20 (poss rev pol); ga s; 80% statics; Eng spkn; CKE. *"Pleasant setting in ornamental gardens; vg clean site & facs; helpful staff; gates clsd 2200-0700; ask warden how to operate in his absence; conv ferries; easy walk to town; rec; gd site; michelin star rest adj."* **€21.00, 1 Apr-15 Oct.** 2017

DIEULEFIT *9D2* (1km SW Urban) 44.52129, 5.06126
Le Domaine des Grands Prés, Chemin de la Bicoque, 26220 Dieulefit **04 75 49 94 36 or 06 30 57 08 43 (mob); info@lesgrandspres-dromeprovencale.com; www.lesgrandspres-dromeprovencale.com**

Fr N of A7 take exit 17 twd Dieulefit/Montelimar. At rndabt, take 2nd exit onto N7. Turn L onto D74. Drive thro the vill of Souzet, La Batie-Rolland & la Begude de Mazenc. Campsite located bef town on S side of the rd on the R. 3*, Med, hdstg, mkd, pt shd, EHU (10A) €3.90; bbq; TV; bus 0.2km; Eng spkn; adv bkg acc; ccard acc; CCI. *"Site on o'skirts of vill (10 min walk) with all facs with unusual accomodations; attractive, well run site."* **€24.00, 20 Mar-1 Nov.** 2016

DIGOIN *9A1* (1km W Urban) 46.47985, 3.96780
Camping de la Chevrette, 41 Rue de la Chevrette, 71160 Digoin **03 85 53 11 49; info@lachevrette.com; www.lachevrette.com**

Fr S exit N79/E62 at junc 24 sp Digoin-la-Grève D994, then on D979 cross bdge over Rv Loire. Take 1st L, sp campng/piscine. 3*, Med, hdstg, hdg, pt shd, pt sl, terr, EHU inc (10A) rev pol; 5% statics; Eng spkn; adv bkg acc; fishing; CKE. *"Pleasant, well-run site by rv; diff sized pitches, some lge; friendly, helpful owner; ltd facs LS; barrier clsd 2200-0700; htd pool adj; pleasant walk & dog walking by rv to town; lovely cycle rides along canals; gd NH; canoe hire avail."* **€22.00, 1 Apr-30 Sep.** 2018

DIJON 6G1 (3km W Urban) 47.32127, 5.01108
Camping du Lac Kir, 3 Blvd du Chanoine Kir, 21000 Dijon 03 80 30 54 01; reservation@camping-du-lac-dijon.com; www.camping-du-lac-dijon.com

🐕 €2 👫 [wc] 🏠 ♨ ⚥ 🛒nr

Site situated nr N5, Lac Kir. Fr Dijon ring rd take N5 exit (W) sp A38 twd Paris. At traff lts L sp A31, site immed on R under 3m high bdge. Do not tow thro town cent. 3*, Med, mkd, hdstg, pt shd, EHU (10-16A) inc (poss rev pol & long lead req); gas; sw; bus adj; Eng spkn; ccard acc; fishing; boating; CKE. *"Rvside path to town; wonderful surrounding area; proof of dog vaccination req, dogs must be on leads; easy bus to town; gd security; poss flooding; Aire for MH at ent (€10 per night); one point for chem disp."* **€20.00, 1 Apr-31 Oct.** **2017**

DINAN 2E3 (3km N Rural) 48.48903, -2.00855
Camping Beauséjour, La Hisse, 22100 St Samson-sur-Rance 02 96 39 53 27; beausejour-stsamson@orange.fr; www.beausejour-camping.com

🐕 €2.05 👫 🏠 ♨ ♿ 🔥 ⚥ 🛒 🦋 🍴 ⊕ 🏊 🛒 ⛰ 🏄 (htd)

Fr Dinan take N176/D766 N twd Dinard. In 3km turn R onto D12 dir Taden then foll sp thro Plouer-sur-Rance to La Hisse; site sp. Fr N exit N176/E401 dir Plouer-sur-Rance, then foll sp La Hisse. 3*, Med, hdg, mkd, pt shd, pt sl, EHU (10A) €3.45 (poss rev pol); red long stay; 40% statics; phone; Eng spkn; adv bkg acc; ccard acc; tennis; games area; sailing; CKE. *"Pleasant, well-kept site; gd pool; quiet & spacious Jun & Sep; no twin axles; excel rv walks; excel well maintained site; footpath down to Rance and rvside walks; gd facs; off open 1000-1230 & 1600-1930; new plots may be diff for lge o'fits."* **€20.00, 1 May-30 Oct.** **2019**

DINAN 2E3 (4km NE Rural) 48.47138, -2.02277
Camping la Hallerais, 4 rue de la Robardais, 22100 Taden 02 96 39 15 93 or 02 96 87 63 50 (Mairie); contact@camping-lahallerais.com; www.camping-lahallerais.com

🐕 👫 (htd) [wc] 🏠 ♿ 🔥 ⚥ 🛒 🦋 🍴 ⊕nr ⊕ 🏊nr 🛒nr ⛰
🏄 (htd) 🚿 ⛵shgl 10km

Fr Dinan take N176/D766 N twd Dinard. In 3km turn R onto D12 to Taden. Foll La Hallerais & Taden sp to site. Fr N176 take exit onto D166 dir Taden; turn onto D766 dir Taden, then L onto D12A sp Taden & Camping. At rndabt on ent Taden take 1st exit onto D12 sp Dinan; site rd is 500m on L. Do not ent Dinan. Site adj Rv Rance. 4*, Lge, mkd, pt shd, terr, serviced pitches; EHU (6A) inc (rev pol); gas; bbq; TV; 80% statics; Eng spkn; adv bkg acc; ccard acc; tennis; fishing; horseriding 500m; games rm. *"Lovely site, well maintained; clean san facs; vg pool; phone ahead if arr late at night LS; ltd office hrs LS - report to bar; sh walk to Taden; rvside walk to Dinan medieval town; rv trips; no o'fits over 9m (check in adv rec); storage facs; gd walking, cycling; mkt Thur am & Fri eve; rec; excel; san facs refurb (2017); v helpful owner."* **€22.00, 11 Mar-12 Nov, B01.** **2018**

DINAN 2E3 (0.9km S Urban) 48.44743, -2.04631
Camp Municipal Châteaubriand, 103 Rue Châteaubriand, 22100 Dinan 02 96 39 11 96 or 02 96 39 22 43 (LS); campingmunicipaldinan@wanadoo.fr; www.brittanytourism.com

🐕 €1.50 👫 [wc] 🏠 🔥 ⚥ [MSP] 🍴 nr ⊕nr 🛒nr

Fr N176 (E or W) take slip rd for Dinan cent; at lge rndbt in cent take 2nd R; down hill to site on L (500m) after 2nd set of traff lts. 2*, Sm, mkd, pt shd, pt sl, EHU (6A) €2.70; bbq; phone; Eng spkn; adv bkg acc; ccard acc; games area; CKE. *"Pleasant, helpful staff; high kerb onto pitches; poss mkt traders; opening dates vary each year; check time when barrier locked, espec LS; gd cent for Rance valley, St Malo & coast; gd location; bar adj; san facs old but clean; 20 min walk to chateau & town; excel position nr park; more level pitches in lower area of site beyond san block."* **€15.00, 1 Jun-30 Sep.** **2017**

DINARD 2E3 (0km W Coastal) 48.6309, -2.08413
Camping La Touesse, 171 Rue de la Ville Gehan, La Fourberie, 35800 St Lunaire 02 99 46 61 13; camping.la.touesse@wanadoo.fr; www.campinglatouesse.com

🐕 €1.50 👫 🔥 ♿ 🔥 ⚥ 🍴 🛒 ⛰ 🏄 ⛵sand 300m

Exit Dinard on St Lunaire coast rd D786, site sp. 3*, Med, mkd, pt shd, EHU (5-10A) €3.30-3.70; TV; adv bkg req; golf 2km; tennis 1.5km; CKE. *"Vg well-kept site; gd beach & rocks nr; friendly recep."* **€30.00, 1 Apr-30 Sep.** **2017**

DIVONNE LES BAINS 9A3 (3km N Rural) 46.37487, 6.12143 **Camping Huttopia Divonne-les-Bains,** Quartier Villard, 01220 Divonne-les-Bains 04 50 20 01 95; www.huttopia.com

🐕 €5 👫 (htd) [wc] 🏠 🔥 ⚥ 🦋 🍴 ⊕ 🏊 🛒 🏄 🏄 (htd) 🚿

Exit E62 dir Divonne-les-Bains approx 12km N of Geneva. Fr town on D984, foll sp to site. 3*, Lge, hdg, mkd, shd, sl, terr, EHU (4A) €5; gas; sw nr; TV; 50% statics; Eng spkn; adv bkg acc; ccard acc; tennis; games area; CKE. *"Helpful owner; levellers req; Lake Geneva 8km; new recep & san facs renovated (2015)."* **€32.00, 19 Apr-29 Sep.** **2019**

DOL DE BRETAGNE 2E4 (7km NE Coastal) 48.60052, -1.71182 **Camping de l'Aumône,** 35120 Cherrueix 02 99 48 84 82 or 06 48 64 60 16 (mob); laumone@orange.fr; www.camping-de-laumone.fr

🐕 👫 [wc] 🏠 🔥 ⚥ [MSP] 🍴 🛒nr ⛰ 🏄1km

Exit D797 Pontorson-Cancale rd S onto D82, opp rd leading into vill of Cherrueix. Site in 100m. 3*, Med, unshd, EHU (10A) €3.50; gas; bbq; 20% statics; Eng spkn; adv bkg rec; bike hire; CKE. *"Sm chateau; gd sized pitches; modern san facs; noise fr adj rd daytime; sand yachting nrby; beach not suitable for sw; vg; pleasant, friendly owners."* **€22.70, 15 Apr-6 Nov.** **2017**

FRANCE

DOL DE BRETAGNE 2E4 (6km E Rural) 48.54941, -1.68386 **FFCC Camping du Vieux Chêne,** Le Motais, 35120 Baguer-Pican **02 99 48 09 55; vieux.chene@ wanadoo.fr; www.camping-vieuxchene.fr**

🅿️ ⛺₃ 🍴 💻 ♨ 🚿 🚮 ∥ MsP 🦋 🍴 ☂ ⊕ 🐕 🛒 ◪ ⚠ 🏊 (htd) 🔵

Leave N176 E of Dol on slip rd sp Baguer-Pican. At traff lts turn L thro vill, site on R of D576 at far end vill adj lake. 4*, Lge, mkd, hdg, pt shd, pt sl, EHU (10A) inc (poss rev pol & poss long cable req); gas; bbq (charcoal, gas); red long stay; TV; phone; Eng spkn; adv bkg acc; ccard acc; tennis; games rm; lake fishing; games area; horseriding; CKE. "Well-kept site in grnds of former farm; 3 sm unfenced lakes; plenty rm for pitch access; no o'fits over 7.5m high ssn; various pitch sizes, some sm & some with fruit trees; friendly & helpful staff; gd san facs; shop & rest ltd LS; mkt in Dol Sat; boggy when wet." **€30.00, 1 May-20 Sep.** 2016

DOL DE BRETAGNE 2E4 (7km SE Rural) 48.49150, -1.72990 **Les Ormes, Domaine & Resort,** 35120 Epiniac **02 99 73 53 60 or 02 99 73 53 01; info@ lesormes.com; www.lesormes.com**

🅿️ ⛺₃ 🍴 💻 ♨ 🚿 🚮 ∥ 🍴 ☂ ⊕ 🐕 🛒 ◪ ⚠ ∥ 🏊 (htd) 🔵

Exit N176/E401 at W end of Dol-de-Bretagne; then S fr Dol on D795 twd Combourg & Rennes, in 7km site on L of rd, clearly sp. 5*, V lge, mkd, hdg, pt shd, pt sl, serviced pitches; EHU (6-16A) inc (poss long lead req); gas; bbq (charcoal, gas); TV; 80% statics; Eng spkn; adv bkg acc; ccard acc; lake fishing; bike hire; tennis; archery; golf; waterslide; canoeing; games rm; horseriding; CKE. "Busy site set in well-kept chateau grnds; cricket; o'fits 8m & over by request only; helpful staff; clean san facs; covrd aquacentre; conv Mont St Michel, St Malo & Dinan; pedalos; disco at night; mkt Sat; golfing discount for campers; poss noisy (disco); excel all round." **€64.00, 14 Apr-16 Sep, B08.** 2019

DOLE 6H2 (1.6km E Rural) 47.08937, 5.50339 **FFCC Camping Le Pasquier,** 18 Chemin Victor et Georges Thévenot, 39100 Dole **03 84 72 02 61; camping-pasquier@wanadoo.fr or lola@camping-le-pasquier.com; www.camping-le-pasquier.com**

🅿️ ⛺₁.₅₀ 🍴 (htd) 💻 ♨ 🚿 🚮 ∥ MsP 🦋 🍴 ☂ 🛒 ◪ ⚠ ∥ 🏊

Fr A39 foll sp dir Dole & Le Pasquier. Fr all dir foll sp 'Centre ville' then foll site name sp & 'Stade Camping' in town; well sp. Site on rvside private rd. Narr app. 3*, Lge, hdg, mkd, pt shd, EHU (10A) inc (rev pol); twin axles; red long stay; 10% statics; Eng spkn; ccard acc; fishing; rv; CKE. "Generous pitches; aqua park 2km; friendly recep; gd clean san facs; pleasant pool; walk along rv (otters!) into Dole; dir access rv 500m; mkt Tues, Thur, Sat; poss cr; lovely site." **€23.00, 15 Mar-25 Oct.** 2019

DOMFRONT 4E1 (0.5km S Urban) 48.58808, -0.65045 **Camp Municipal Champ Passais,** 4 Rue du Champ Passais, 61700 Domfront **02 33 37 37 66 or 02 33 38 92 24 (LS); mairie-de-domfront@wanadoo.fr; http://camping-municipal-domfront.jimdo.com**

🅿️ ⛺€0.80 🍴 💻 ♨ 🚿 🚮 ∥ 🍴 ☂ nr ⊕ nr 🛒 nr ◪

Fr N on D962 foll Laval sps into Domfront; then take D976 W dir Mont-St Michel; site turning in 400m on L; well sp bet old quarter & town cent. Fr S on D962 well sp fr edge of town. 2*, Sm, hdg, mkd, hdstg, pt shd, terr, EHU (10A) €3; TV; phone; Eng spkn; rv fishing nrby; CKE. "Pleasant, well-kept terr site; helpful, charming staff; gd security; sh, steep walk to medieval town; no twin axles; vg; site still excel value; shade improving with growing trees." **€7.30, 1 Apr-30 Sep.** 2018

DOMPIERRE LES ORMES 9A2 (0.5km NW Rural) 46.36369, 4.47460 **Camp Municipal Le Village des Meuniers,** 71520 Dompierre-les-Ormes **03 85 50 36 60; villagedesmeuniers@yahoo.fr; www.villagedesmeuniers.com**

🅿️ ⛺₂ 🍴 💻 ♨ 🚿 🚮 ∥ 🍴 ☂ 🛒 nr ◪ ⚠ ∥ 🏊 (htd)

Fr A6 exit Mâcon Sud onto N79 dir Charolles. After approx 35km take slip rd onto D41 for Dompierre-les-Ormes. Well sp nr stadium. 4*, Med, hdg, mkd, pt shd, terr, serviced pitches; EHU (16A) €4.50; gas; adv bkg req; ccard acc; tennis; bike hire; waterslide; CKE. "Excel, clean site with views; v lge pitches; o'flow field with full facs high ssn; facs stretched high ssn; excel for children; gd sp walks in area; pools, rest, bar etc used by public; free m'van hdstg outside site ent." **€33.00, 12 Apr-20 Oct, L25.** 2019

DOMPIERRE SUR BESBRE 9A1 (1.5km S Urban) 46.51378, 3.68276 **Camp Municipal,** La Madeleine, Parc des Sports, 03290 Dompierre-sur-Besbre **04 70 34 55 57 or 04 70 48 11 39 (Mairie); camping@ mairie-dsb.fr; www.dompierre-sur-besbre.fr**

🅿️ ⛺₁ 🍴 (htd) 💻 ♨ 🚿 🚮 ∥ MsP 🦋 🍴 🛒 nr

At E end of town nr rv behind stadium; sp. 2*, Med, hdg, shd, pt sl, EHU (10A) inc; bbq; phone; Eng spkn; adv bkg acc; CKE. "Smart, well-run, busy site; v well kept gd san facs, but poss stretched high ssn; excel sports complex; gd for Loire Valley, vineyards & chateaux; highly rec LS; excel; large easy acc pitches; gd adj park for dog walking; rv walks; cycling & running tracks; town v close; full sports facs adj; v friendly recep; rec." **€12.00, 15 May-15 Sep.** 2016

DONJON, LE 9A1 (0.5km N Urban) 46.35317, 3.79188 **Camp Municipal,** 4 Chemin Denys Bournatot, 03130 Le Donjon **04 70 99 56 35 or 04 70 99 50 25 (Mairie); mairie-le-donjon@wanadoo.fr; www.allier-tourisme.com**

🅿️ 🍴 ♨ 🚿 ∥ MsP 🦋 🍴 ☂ nr ⊕ nr 🛒 nr

Fr Lapalisse N on D994. Site sp fr town cent on D166 dir Monétay-sur-Loire. 2*, Sm, pt shd, pt sl, EHU (10A) €2.50; fishing 900m; windsurfing 900m; sailing 900m; CKE. **€8.00, 1 May-31 Oct.** 2016

DONZENAC *7C3* (1.5km S Rural) *45.21978, 1.51784*
FFCC Camping La Rivière, Route d'Ussac, 19270
Donzenac 05 55 85 63 95; info@campingdonzenac.
com; www.campinglariviere.jimdo.com

🐕 €1.10 ♨ 🆆 🏛 ⚓ 🚿 🔥 ✉ ⚑ 🍴 ⛱ 🏊 ⚒ 🛝 🏄 (htd)

Fr N exit A20 at junc 47 (do not use junc 48); take
exit at rndabt dir Donzenac D920. In 3km on ent
Donzenac keep on D920 & go down hill to rndabt.
Take 2nd exit D170 sp Uzzac, site on R in 500m. NB
Avoid app thro Donzenac as narr & diff for lge o'fits.
Fr S exit junc 49 to Ussac. 3*, Med, mkd, pt shd, EHU
(10A) €3.10; gas; TV; adv bkg rec; bike hire; games
rm; fishing 5km; tennis; games area. "Excel facs."
€22.50, 2 May-30 Sep. 2019

DORMANS *3D4* (9km NE Rural) *49.10638, 3.73380*
Camping Rural (Nowack), 10 Rue de Bailly, 51700
Vandières 03 26 58 02 69 or 03 26 58 08 79;
champagne@nowack.fr; www.champagne-
nowack.com

♨ 🏛 ✉ 🚿 🛝

Fr N3, turn N at Port Binson, over Rv Marne, then
turn W onto D1 for 3km, then N into Vandières.
Site on R about 50m fr start of Rue Bailly, sp
'Champagne Nowack' or 'Camping Nowack.'
Sm, pt shd, pt sl, EHU (6-10A) inc; bbq; TV; adv bkg
acc; ccard acc; tennis 2km; fishing 1km; CKE.
"Charming, peaceful, CL-type site in orchard; friendly
owners; lovely, well-kept modern san facs; fresh water
tap beside chem disp (2011); boating 6km; site poss
muddy when wet; site pt of vineyard, poss grape
pickers in Sep, champagne can be bought; pool 8km;
excel value." **€17.00, 1 Apr-1 Nov.** 2017

DOUAI *3B4* (11km S Rural) *50.29004, 3.04945* **FFCC**
Camp Municipal de la Sablière, Rue du 8 Mai 1945,
62490 Tortequesne 03 21 24 14 94; camping@
tortequesne.fr; www.tortequesne.fr

🐕 €0.50 ♨ 🏛 🚿 ✉ 🍴 nr 🛝

Fr D643 Douai-Cambrai rd; turn S onto D956 to
Tortequesne where site sp. 2*, Sm, mkd, hdstg, hdg,
pt shd, EHU (6A) €3; 80% statics; tennis; games area;
CKE. "Gd site; park & fishing adj; late night arr area;
new & clean san facs (2014); recep open 10:00-12:00
and 16:30-20:00; walking in La Valée de la Sensée;
family friendly site; barrier locked when warden leaves
(am & pm)." **€15.00, 1 Apr-30 Sep.** 2017

DOUAI *3B4* (12km S Rural) *50.27374, 3.10565*
Camp Municipal Les Biselles, Chemin des Bisselles,
59151 Arleux 03 27 89 52 36 or 03 27 93 10 00;
office.tourisme@arleux.com

🐕 ♨ 🏛 ⚓ 🚿 ✉ 🍴 🛝 🏄

Exit A2 junc 14 at Cambrai & take D643 twd Douai,
after 5km turn W at Bugnicourt to Arleux. Site sp in
vill adj canal La Sensée. 3*, Lge, hdg, mkd, shd, EHU
€6.85; 96% statics; phone; adv bkg acc; rv fishing;
tennis 200m; games area. "Very few touring pitches;
basic san facs; gd cycling along canal."
€17.50, 1 Apr-31 Oct. 2015

DOUARNENEZ *2E2* (14km W Coastal) *48.08416,*
-4.48194 **Camping Pors Péron,** 29790 Beuzec-Cap-
Sizun 02 98 70 40 24; info@campingporsperon.com;
www.campingporsperon.com

🐕 €1.60 ♨ 🆆 🏛 ⚓ 🚿 ✉ 🍴 🍴 ⚑ 🍴 ⛱ 🏊 ⚒ 🏄 sand 200m

W fr Douarnenez take D7 sp Poullan-sur-Mer. Thro
Poullan & in approx 4km turn R sp Pors-Piron, foll
site & beach sp. Site bef Beuzec-Cap-Sizun vill.
2*, Med, hdg, mkd, pt shd, pt sl, EHU (10A) inc (long
lead req); gas; bbq; 5% statics; adv bkg acc; bike hire;
games area; CKE. "Pleasant, quiet site nr beautiful
sandy cove; friendly, helpful British owners; immac san
facs, poss insufficient high ssn & long way fr some
pitches; poss ltd privacy in ladies' facs; gd; excel site
leaflet; gd pitches; excel well maintained site; highly
rec; best pitches now taken up by cabins."
€25.40, 30 Mar-30 Sep. 2019

DOUARNENEZ *2E2* (4km W Urban) *48.09895,*
-4.36189 **Camping de Kerleyou,** 29100 Douarnenez-
Tréboul 02 98 74 13 03; info@camping-kerleyou.com;
www.camping-kerleyou.com

🐕 €2.50 ♨ 🏛 ⚓ 🚿 ✉ 🍴 ⚑ 🍴 ⛱ 🏊 ⚒ 🏄 🛝 (htd) 🍴
🌲 1km

Ent Douarnenez fr E on D7, soll sp 'Cent Ville', L at
traff lts past Treboul. Cross over bdge into Ave la
Gare, at PO turn L then 1st L, up hill, at rndabt take
3rd exit. Foll sp to site. 3*, Med, hdg, mkd, unshd,
pt sl, EHU (10A); bbq; TV; 70% statics; phone; Eng
spkn; adv bkg acc; games rm; games area. "Excel."
€23.00, 9 Apr-20 Sep. 2015

DOUARNENEZ *2E2* (6km W Rural) *48.08166,*
-4.40722 **Camping de la Baie de Douarnenez,** Route
de Douarnenez, 29100 Poullan-sur-Mer 02 98 74 26
39; info@camping-douarnenez.com; www.camping-
douarnenez.com or www.flowercampings.com

🐕 €5 ♨ (htd) 🆆 🏛 ⚓ 🚿 ✉ 🍴 ⚑ 🍴 🍴 ⚒ 🛝 🏄
🏄 (covrd, htd, indoor) 🍴 🌲 sand 5km

Fr E take circular rd around Douarnenez on D7/
D765 dir Audierne & Poullan-sur-Mer, Tréboul &
Pointe-du-Van. Site on L off D7 1km fr Poullan-sur-
Mer vill, shortly after church spire becomes visible.
4*, Med, hdg, mkd, pt shd, EHU (10A) inc; gas; bbq
(charcoal, gas); TV; Eng spkn; adv bkg acc; ccard acc;
bike hire; watersports 4km; games area; tennis; games
rm; lake fishing; pools; mini golf; CKE. "Tranquil site
in woodland; gd sized pitches; staff friendly; ltd facs
LS; entmnt well away fr most pitches; gd for families;
mkd walks, guided high ssn; no o'fits over 10m high ssn;
statics (tour ops); mkt Mon & Fri; pools & water slides
great fun." **€36.00, 5 Apr-15 Sep, B37.** 2019

FRANCE

FRANCE

DOUE LA FONTAINE 4G1 (2km SW Rural) 47.17390, -0.34750 **Camping La Vallée des Vignes,** 49700 Concourson-sur-Layon 02 41 59 86 35; info@campingvdv.com; www.campingvdv.com

🎪 €3 🏕(htd) 🆔 ♨ ⚓ ♿ 🍴 ✉ ✎ 🦋 ⛱ ☂ 🍽 ⊕ 🛒 ⚡ ⚠ ✦ 🏊(htd) 🎣

D960 fr Doué-la-Fontaine (dir Cholet) to Concourson-sur-Layon; site 1st R 250m after bdge on leaving Concourson-sur-Layon. Or fr Angers foll sp dir Cholet & Poitiers; then foll sp Doué-la-Fontaine. 4*, Med, mkd, pt shd, serviced pitches; EHU (10A) €4; gas; bbq; red long stay; TV; 5% statics; bus; Eng spkn; adv bkg acc; ccard acc; bike hire; CKE. "Peaceful site poss open all yr weather permitting - phone to check; vg, clean, well-maintained facs; pool open & htd early ssn; some pitches diff lge o'fits due o'hanging trees; conv for Loire chateaux & Futuroscope; new French owners (2016), v helpful." **€28.00, 1 Apr-30 Sep.** 2017

DOUE LA FONTAINE 4G1 (18km W Rural) 47.18032, -0.43574 **Camping KathyDave,** Les Beauliers, 49540 La Fosse de Tigné 02 41 67 92 10 or 06 14 60 81 63 (mob); bookings@camping-kathydave.co.uk; www.camping-kathydave.co.uk

🎪 🏕(htd) 🆔 ♨ ♿ 🍴 ✎ 🦋 ⛱ ☂ nr ⊕ nr

Fr Doué-la-Fontaine on D84 to Tigne, turn S thro La Fosse-de-Tigné. Pass chateau, site sp on R. NB Tight turn in, access poss diff lge o'fits. Sm, mkd, pt shd, pt sl, EHU (8A) €3.50 (poss rev pol); bbq (gas); twin axles; Eng spkn; adv bkg acc; CKE. "Tranquil, rural orchard site in picturesque area; welcoming, helpful, v friendly British owners; many regular visitors; gd san facs; some pitches restricted by trees; gd touring base; adults only preferred; phone ahead rec; excel; dogs free; sm CL type site in an old orchard; vg." **€13.00, 1 Jun-30 Sep.** 2015

"There aren't many sites open at this time of year"

If you're travelling outside peak season remember to call ahead to check site opening dates – even if the entry says 'open all year'.

DOUE LA FONTAINE 4G1 (8km W Rural) 47.19355, -0.37075 **Camping Les Grésillons,** Chemin des Grésillons, 49700 St Georges-sur-Layon 02 41 50 02 32; camping.gresillon@wanadoo.fr; www.camping-gresillons.com

🎪 🏕(htd) 🆔 ♨ ⚓ ♿ 🍴 ✎ 🦋 ⛱ ☂ nr ⊕ 🛒 ⚠ ✦ 🏊(htd)

Fr Doué-la-Fontaine on D84, site sp. In St Georges-sur-Layon turn L opp church. 3*, Sm, hdg, hdstg, pt shd, terr, EHU (6-10A) €2.90-3.50; red long stay; 28% statics; Eng spkn; adv bkg acc; ccard acc; rv fishing 200m; games area; CKE. "Delightful site in area of vineyards; friendly, helpful owner; gem of a site." **€20.00, 1 Apr-30 Sep.** 2017

DOUSSARD 9B3 (3km N Rural) 45.80302, 6.20608 **Camping Le Taillefer,** 1530 Route de Chaparon, 74210 Doussard 04 50 44 30 30; info@campingletaillefer.com; www.campingletaillefer.com

🎪 €2.50 🏕 🆔 ♨ ♿ 🍴 ✎ 🗺 🦋 ☂ 🛒 🍽 ⚠ ✦ shgl 3km

Fr Annecy take D1508 twd Faverges & Albertville. At traff lts in Bredannaz turn R, then immed L for 1.5km; site immed on L by vill sp 'Chaparon'. Do NOT turn into ent by Bureau but stop on rd & ask for instructions as no access to pitches fr Bureau ent. Or, to avoid Annecy, fr Faverges, along D1508, turn L (sp Lathuile) after Complex Sportif at Bout-du-Lac. Turn R at rndabt (sp Chaparon), site is on R after 2.5km. 2*, Sm, mkd, pt shd, pt sl, terr, EHU (6A) €4.50 (check rev pol); bbq (charcoal, gas); sw nr; red long stay; TV; Eng spkn; adv bkg acc; games rm; bike hire; watersports 2km; sailing; tennis 100m; rafting. "Peaceful, simple, family-run site nr Lake Annecy; fantastic mountain views; access some pitches poss diff due steep terraces; friendly, helpful owners; dated, clean san facs; no o'fits over 8m high ssn; canyoning; climbing; vg rest in easy walking dist; mkt Mon; worth another visit." **€34.00, 1 Apr-04 Nov, M06.** 2019

DOUVILLE 7C3 (2km S Rural) 44.99271, 0.59853 **Camping Lestaubière,** Pont-St Mamet, 24140 Douville 05 53 82 98 15 or 06 82 28 23 97; lestaubiere@gmail.com; camping-lestaubiere.fr

🎪 €3.50 🏕 ♨ ⚓ ♿ 🍴 ✎ 🗺 🦋 ⛱ ☂ 🍽 ⊕ ✦ ⚠ ✦ 🏊(htd) 🎣

Well sp fr N & S on N21. Approx 21km N of Bergerac. Exit fr N21 sp Pont St. Mamet. 3*, Med, mkd, pt shd, EHU (6-10A) €4-5; gas; bbq; sw; twin axles; TV; 10% statics; phone; Eng spkn; adv bkg acc; ccard acc; tennis 5km; games area; lake fishing; games rm; CKE. "Spacious, park-like site with beautiful views; v lge pitches; owned by friendly, helpful Dutch couple; twin axles (high ssn only); vg modern san facs; superb out of ssn; site in 2 sep sections; a few v lge drive thro pitches; excel." **€35.00, 15 Apr-30 Sep.** 2018

DRAGUIGNAN 10F3 (4km S Rural) 43.51796, 6.47836 **Camping La Foux,** Quartier La Foux, 83300 Draguignan 04 94 68 18 27; www.camping-lafoux.com

🎪 €3.90 🏕 ♨ 🍴 ✎ 🦋 ☂ 🍽 ⊕ 🛒 ⚠ ✦

Fr A8, take Le Muy intersection onto N555 N to Draguignan. Site ent on R at ent to town sp Sport Centre Foux. Fr Draguignan, take N555 S; just after 'End of Draguignan' sp, double back at rndabt & turn R. 2*, Lge, unshd, pt sl, EHU (4-10A) €3.50-5; TV; fishing. "Friendly staff; v poor san facs; care needed long vehicles on ent site; unshd, but many trees planted (2011); poss flooding when wet; easy access to Riviera coast." **€16.00, 20 Jun-30 Sep.** 2016

For a guide to symbols see the fold out on the rear cover

DREUX *4E2* (9.5km NW Rural) *48.76149, 1.29041*
Camping Etangs de Marsalin, 3 Place du Général de Gaulle, 28500 Vert-en-Drouais **02 37 82 92 23;** contact@campingdemarsalin.fr; www.camping demarsalin.fr

🔟 🛏 ♿(htd) 🅦 ♨ ♿ 🖃 ∥ 🦋 ♟ 🍴 nr Ⓗnr 👜 🏊

Fr W on N12 dir Dreux, cross dual c'way bef petrol stn onto D152 to Vert-en-Drouais; on ent turn R to church, site on L. Well sp. 2*, Med, hdg, mkd, hdstg, pt shd, pt sl, EHU (6-10A), €4.60 (poss rev pol, long leads poss req, avail at recep); 80% statics; Eng spkn; lake fishing 2km; CKE. *"Peaceful location; working families on site; friendly, helpful staff; basic, clean san facs; touring pitches at far end far fr facs; muddy when wet; lovely vill; conv Versailles; NH only; site tidy and clean; bar 100m; facs refurb (2016)."* **€18.00**   **2018**

DUNKERQUE *3A3* (4.6km NE Coastal) *51.05171, 2.42025* **Camp Municipal La Licorne,** 1005 Blvd de l'Europe, 59240 Dunkerque **03 28 69 26 68; contact@campingdelalicorne.com; www.campingdela licorne.com**

🛏 €0.90 ♿(htd) 🅦 ♨ ♿ 🖃 ∥ 🅼🅿 🦋 ♟ Ⓗ 👜 nr 🏊 🏖
🏖 sand adj

Exit A16 junc 62 sp 'Malo'; at end of slip rd traff lts turn L sp Malo-les-Bains; in 2km (at 5th traff lts) turn R at camping sp; at 2nd traff lts past BP g'ge turn L. Site on L (cont strt to rndabt & return on opp side of dual c'way to ent). 3*, Lge, mkd, unshd, pt sl, EHU (10A) (poss long lead); gas; 50% statics; bus fr site ent; Eng spkn; adv bkg acc; ccard acc; clsd 2200-0700; CKE. *"V gd, secure NH for ferries - obtain gate code for early depart; pitches uneven; many site rd humps; promenade along sea front to town cent; site backs onto sand dunes & beach (used for Dunkirk evacuation of Allied Forces in 1940); poss windy; m'van o'night area; gd san facs; bus stop nr site ent; very attractive site; site tired, clean san facs."* **€25.00, 1 Apr-11 Nov.**   **2019**

DURBAN CORBIERES *8G4* (0.5km N Rural) *43.00017, 2.81977* **Camping Municipal De Durban-Corbieres,** Lespazo, 11360 Durhan-Corbieres **04 68 45 06 81 or 06 42 48 69 05; mairiededurham@orange.fr; www.audetourisme.com**

🛏 ♿ ♨ ∥ 🦋 🦋

Fr A61 take exit 25, foll D611 S across to Durban Corbieres. Site sp on R on entering Vill. Sm, hdg, pt shd, pt sl, EHU (10A); bbq; twin axles; 10% statics; bus 0.5km; adv bkg acc; CCI. *"Tranquil site surrounded by rugged hills; pool 0.5km; Cathar castle in vill; vg."* **€11.00, 15 Jun-15 Sep.**   **2019**

EAUX PUISEAUX *4F4* (1km SW Rural) *48.11696, 3.88317* **Camping à la Ferme des Haut Frênes (Lambert),** 6 Voie de Puiseaux, 10130 Eaux-Puiseaux **03 25 42 15 04; les.hauts.frenes@wanadoo.fr; www.les-hauts-frenes.com**

🔟 🛏 €2 ♿(htd) 🅦 ♨ ♿ 🖃 ∥ 🦋 ♟ Ⓗnr 👜 nr 🏔

N fr St Florentin or S fr Troyes on N77. Ignore D374 but take next turning D111 in NW dir. Site in 2km; well sp. Long o'fits take care at ent gate. 3*, Med, hdstg, hdg, mkd, pt shd, EHU (6-15A) €2-3 (poss some rev pol); gas; bbq; red long stay; TV; Eng spkn; adv bkg acc; games rm; tennis 3km; CKE. *"Well-kept, tidy farm site in beautiful setting; lge, level pitches; helpful, friendly owners; gd san facs; meals on request; own facs adv high ssn; loyalty card; cider museum in vill; conv m'way; excel NH en rte S; super; v quiet site; gd."* **€18.00**   **2018**

ECHELLES, LES *9B3* (6km NE Rural) *45.45679, 5.81327* **Camping La Bruyère,** Hameau Côte Barrier, 73160 St Jean-de-Couz Chartreuse **04 79 65 79 11 or 04 79 65 74 27 (LS) or 06 29 47 27 43 (mob); camping-labruyere@orange.fr; www.campingsavoie.com**

🛏 €1 ♿ 🅦 ♨ 🖃 ∥ 🦋 ♟ Ⓗ👜 nr 🏔

Heading S on D1006 Chambéry-Lyon rd, after x-ing Col de Coux 15km S of Chambéry take D45 to St Jean-de-Couz; site sp. 2*, Med, hdg, pt shd, pt sl, EHU (4-10A) €2.90-5.90; gas; bbq; TV; 3% statics; adv bkg acc. *"Peaceful site; magnificent scenery; friendly, helpful owner; vg, clean facs; gd walking area; football; volleyball; Chartreuse caves open to public adj; vg base for touring Chartreuse mountains; video games; waymkd walks fr site; site well looked after; lovely."* **€15.00, 15 May-30 Sep.**   **2017**

ECHELLES, LES *9B3* (0.2km SE Urban) *45.43462, 5.75615* **Camping L'Arc-en-Ciel,** Chemin des Berges, 38380 Entre-Deux-Guiers **04 76 66 06 97; info@camping-arc-en-ciel.com; www.camping-arc-en-ciel.com**

🛏 €1.10 ♿ ♨ ♿ 🖃 ∥ 🍴 Ⓗnr 👜 nr

Fr D520 turn W sp Entre-Deux-Guiers. On ent vill turn R into Ave de Montcelet dir Les Echelles & R again in 100m. Site sp fr D520. 3*, Med, hdg, mkd, pt shd, pt sl, EHU (2-4A) €2.50-4.30; gas; 40% statics; CKE. *"Conv La Chartreuse area with spectacular limestone gorges; gd."* **€20.00, 1 Apr-15 Oct.**   **2019**

ECHELLES, LES *9B3* (6km S Rural) *45.39107, 5.73656* **Camp Municipal Les Berges du Guiers,** Le Revol, 38380 St Laurent-du-Pont **04 76 55 20 63 or 04 76 06 22 55 (LS); camping.st-laurent-du-pont@wanadoo.fr; www.camping-chartreuse.com**

🛏 €1 ♿ 🅦 ♨ ♿ 🖃 ∥ 🅼🅿 🦋 ♟ 🍴 nr Ⓗnr 👜 nr 🏔

On D520 Chambéry-Voiron S fr Les Echelles. On ent St Laurent-du-Pont turn R just bef petrol stn on L. 2*, Sm, mkd, pt shd, EHU (5A) €3.50; bbq; Eng spkn; tennis 100m; CKE. *"Clean & well-kept; pool 300m; pleasant area; gates clsd 1100-1530; vg."* **€17.50, 15 Jun-15 Sep.**   **2017**

FRANCE

ECOMMOY *4F1* (0.4km NE Urban) *47.83367, 0.27985* **Camp Municipal Les Vaugeons,** 19 Rue de la Charité, 72220 Ecommoy 06 49 55 03 70; lau66san@aol.fr; www.camping-ecommoy.com

♦♦♦ [wc] ♨ ♨ ♿ 🗑 ✉ ❄ ☕ 🔔 nr /🏔\

Heading S on D338 foll sp. Turn E at 2nd traff lts in vill; sp Stade & Camping. Also just off A28. 2*, Med, pt shd, pt sl, EHU (6A) €2.35; Eng spkn; adv bkg acc; tennis; CKE. *"Site full during Le Mans week (nr circuit); gd san facs; new arr no access when recep clsd, hrs 0900-1130 & 1500-2030; coarse sand/grass surface."* **€10.00, 1 May-30 Sep.** **2019**

EGLETONS *7C4* (2km NE Rural) *45.41852, 2.06431* **Camping du Lac,** 10 Le Pont, 19300 Egletons 05 55 93 14 75; campingegletons@orange.fr; www.camping-egletons.com

[12] ❄ €1.30 ♦♦♦ [wc] ♨ ♨ ♿ 🗑 ✉ ❄ ☕ Ⓣ ⊕ ☕ 🔔 nr /🏔\ ⚓ 🚴 🛶

Fr Egletons on D1089 for approx 2km, site 300m past Hôtel Ibis on opp site of rd. 3*, Med, mkd, pt shd, terr, EHU (10A) inc; gas; sw nr; TV; 30% statics; phone; Eng spkn; fishing 300m; watersports 300m; CKE. *"Lovely, wooded site in attractive area; lge pitches; friendly owners; vg; san facs dated but clean."* **€13.00** **2015**

EGUZON CHANTOME *7A3* (1.5km NE Urban) *46.44556, 1.58314* **Camping Eguzon La Garenne,** 1 Rue Yves Choplin, 36270 Eguzon-Chantôme 02 54 47 44 85; info@campinglagarenne.eu; www.campinglagarenne.eu

❄ €1.50 ♦♦♦ [wc] ♨ ♨ ♿ 🗑 ✉ ❄ ☕ ✉ ❄ Ⓣ ⊕ ☕ 🔔 nr /🏔\ 🚴 ⚓ (htd)

Exit A20 junc 20 onto D36 to Eguzon; on ent vill sq cont strt on, foll sp; site on L in 300m. 4*, Med, hdg, pt shd, pt sl, EHU (6-10A) inc; bbq; sw nr; TV; 3% statics; phone; Eng spkn; adv bkg acc; watersports 4km; cycling; CKE. *"All you need on site or in vill; excel; well run, attractive site; poss OAY, phone ahead; only 2 hdstg; gas 300m; site is improving; gd; clean, tidy; v friendly Dutch owners; ACSI acc."* **€26.00, 10 Mar-15 Oct.** **2018**

ELNE *10G1* (3km E Coastal) *42.60695, 2.99098* **Camping Le Florida,** Route Latour-Bas-Elne, 66200 Elne 04 68 37 80 88; info@campingleflorida.com; www.campingleflorida.com

[12] ❄ ♦♦♦ [wc] ♨ ♨ ♿ 🗑 ✉ ❄ [MSP] ❄ ☕ Ⓣ ⊕ nr ☕ 🔔 nr /🏔\ ⚓ 🚴 🛶 🏖 🏊 sand 4km

Exit A9 junc 42 Perpignan-Sud onto D914 dir Argelès-sur-Mer. Exit D914 junc 7 onto D11 dir Elne Centre, then D40 sp St Cyprien to Latour-Bas-Elne, site sp. 4*, Lge, mkd, pt shd, EHU (6A) €4; bbq; TV; 70% statics; phone; Eng spkn; adv bkg acc; ccard acc; games area; games rm; tennis; CKE. *"Excel site; bus to beach high ssn."* **€43.00** **2016**

ELNE *10G1* (4km S Rural) *42.57570, 2.96514* **Kawan Village Le Haras,** Domaine St Galdric, 66900 Palau-del-Vidre 04 68 22 14 50; contact@camping-le-haras.com; www.camping-le-haras.com

❄ €4 ♦♦♦ [wc] ♨ ♨ ♿ 🗑 ✉ ❄ [MSP] ☕ Ⓣ ⊕ ☕ /🏔\ 🚴 ⚓ 🛶

Exit A9 junc 42 sp Perpignan S dir Argelès-sur-Mer on D900 (N9) & then D914; then exit D914 junc 9 onto D11 to Palau-del-Vidre. Site on L at ent to vill immed after low & narr rlwy bdge. 3*, Med, shd, EHU (10A) €5; bbq (elec, gas); TV; 10% statics; Eng spkn; adv bkg acc; ccard acc; tennis 1km; fishing 50m; archery; games rm; CKE. *"Peaceful, well-kept, family-owned site in wooded parkland; helpful, friendly warden; san facs poss red LS; gd rest & pool; 5 mins walk to delightful vill; no o'fits over 7m high ssn; rds around site poss liable to flood in winter; many walks in area; Collioure worth visit; conv Spanish border; excel."* **€35.00, 1 Apr-30 Sep, C26.** **2019**

EMBRUN *9D3* (3.5km S Urban) *44.54725, 6.48852* **Camping le Petit Liou,** Ancienne route de Baratier, 05200 Baratier 04 92 43 19 10; info@camping-lepetitliou.fr; www.camping-lepetitliou.com

❄ €1.50 ♦♦♦ [wc] ♨ ♨ ♿ 🗑 ✉ ❄ [MSP] ☕ Ⓣ ❄ 🔔 /🏔\ 🚴 (htd) 🛶

On N94 fr Gap to Briancon turn R at rndabt just bef Embrun. First L after 150m then 1st R. Site on L in 250m, sp. 2*, Lge, mkd, hdg, pt shd, pt sl, EHU (3-10A) €3.60-€4.20; bbq; 5% statics; Eng spkn; adv bkg acc; games rm; bike hire; CKE. *"Lovely mountain views; vg."* **€22.00, 1 May-21 Sep.** **2016**

EMBRUN *9D3* (2.4km SW Urban) *44.55440, 6.48610* **Camping La Vieille Ferme,** La Clapière, 05200 Embrun 04 92 43 04 08; info@campingembrun.com; www.campingembrun.com

❄ €3 ♦♦♦ [wc] ♨ ♨ ♿ 🗑 ✉ ❄ [MSP] ☕ Ⓣ ⊕ ☕ 🔔 nr /🏔\ 🚴

On N94 fr Gap, at rndabt 3rd exit sp Embrun cross Rv Durance then take 1st R, sp La Vielle Ferme, keep L down narr lane, site ent on R. Access poss diff for lge o'fits. 4*, Med, mkd, pt shd, EHU (6-10A) €5-6 (pos rev pol); red long stay; Eng spkn; adv bkg acc; rafting; watersports. *"Friendly, Dutch family-run site; canyoning; gd facs; pretty town."* **€33.00, 26 Apr-1 Oct.** **2015**

EMBRY *3B3* (0.7km NW Rural) *50.49365, 1.96463* **Aire de Service Camping-Cars d'Embryère,** 62990 Embry 03 21 86 77 61

[12] ♦♦♦ ♨ ♿ 🗑 ✉ ❄ [MSP]

N fr Embry site is just off D108 dir Hucqueliers & Desvres. Sm, hdstg, EHU £2; bbq. *"M'vans only; modern, well-kept site; jetons fr ccard-operated dispenser for services; conv Boulogne & Calais; simple but well equipped; picnic area & gardens; lovely area."* **€6.00** **2015**

ENTRAIGUES *9C3* (0.4km SW Rural) *44.90064, 5.94606* **Camp Municipal Les Vigneaux,** 38740 Entraigues 04 76 30 17 05 or 06 43 76 22 66 (mob); camping.muriebillard@orange.fr

🛖 €1 ⊞ 🏕 ዿ 🖫 ⁄ ᴹˢᴾ 🦋 🍴nr

S on D1085 (N85) fr La Mure, turn L on D114, fork R on D26 to Valbonnais. This rd becomes D526. Site on L on ent Entraigues, 4km beyond Lake Valbonnais. Ent on bend in rd, more diff if ent fr Bourg-d'Oisans. 2*, Sm, mkd, pt shd, EHU (6A) €2 (poss rev pol); red long stay; 15% statics; adv bkg acc; fishing; CKE. "Clean facs; National Park adj; warden visits am & pm." **€14.00, 1 May-30 Sep.** 2015

ENTRAYGUES SUR TRUYERE *7D4* (1.6km S Rural) *44.64218, 2.56406* **Camping Le Val de Saures (formerly Municipal),** 12140 Entraygues-sur-Truyère 05 65 44 56 92; info@camping-valdesaures.com; www.camping-valdesaures.com

🛖 €1.50 ⊞ 🏕 ዿ 🖫 ⁄ 🦋 🍴nr ⁄Ⅲ 🏊

Fr town cent take D920 (twds Espalion) & in 200m turn R over narr rv bdge and then R onto D904. In 200m fork R onto new rd and thro sports complex to site. 3*, Med, mkd, pt shd, EHU (6A) €3.50; 10% statics; Eng spkn; ccard acc. "Pleasant, friendly, gd site; in great situation; footbdge to town over rv; vg, well-kept san facs; recep clsd Sun & pm Mon LS; pool adj; gd touring base." **€25.00, 3 June-22 Sep.** 2019

"That's changed – Should I let the Club know?"

If you find something on site that's different from the site entry, fill in a report and let us know. See camc.com/europereport.

EPERNAY *3D4* (1km NW Urban) *49.05734, 3.95042* **Camp Municipal d'Epernay,** Allées de Cumières, 51200 Epernay 03 26 55 32 14; camping.epernay@free.fr; www.epernay.fr

🛖 €1.80 ⊞ (htd) ᵂᴰ 🏕 ዿ 🖫 ⁄ ᴹˢᴾ 🍴 ⅄ ☕ 🍴 ⁄Ⅲ

Fr Reims take D951 twd Epernay, cross rv & turn R at rndabt onto D301 sp Cumières (look for sp 'Stade Paul Chandon'), site sp. Site adj Stadium. Avoid town at early eve rush hr. 2*, Med, hdg, mkd, pt shd, EHU (10A) inc (poss long lead req); bbq; red long stay; phone; Eng spkn; adv bkg acc; ccard acc; fishing; tennis; bike hire; games area; canoeing; CKE. "Attractive, well-run site on Rv Marne in lovely location; generous pitches; friendly, helpful staff; gd spacious san facs; barrier open 0800-2100 & 0700-2200 high ssn; parking outside; rec arr early; footpaths along rv into town; htd covrd pool 2km; waterslide 2km; Mercier train tour with wine-tasting; site used by grape pickers; no twin axles or c'vans over 6m acc; gd value; boulangerie and cafe nrby." **€22.00, 28 Apr-1 Oct.** 2017

EPINAL *6F2* (2km E Urban) *48.17930, 6.46780* **Camping Parc du Château,** 37 Rue du Petit Chaperon Rouge, 88000 Epinal 03 29 34 43 65 or 03 29 82 49 41 (LS); parcduchateau@orange.fr

⊞ 🛖 €3 ⊞ (htd) 🏕 ዿ 🖫 ⁄ ᴹˢᴾ ⅄ ☕ ⁄Ⅲ 🏊

Sp fr town cent. Or fr N57 by-pass take exit sp Razimont, site sp in 1km. 2*, Med, mkd, hdg, hdstg, pt shd, terr, EHU (6-10A) €5-6; gas; bbq; red long stay; TV; 20% statics; Eng spkn; adv bkg acc; ccard acc; tennis; CKE. "Lge pitches; ltd facs LS; walk thro park to town; helpful new owners who have improved site; sep m'van park adj, fr €12; exceptionally clean." **€20.00** 2016

EPINAL *6F2* (8km W Rural) *48.16701, 6.35975* **Kawan Village Club Lac de Bouzey,** 19 Rue du Lac, 88390 Sanchey 03 29 82 49 41; lacdebouzey@orange.fr; www.lacdebouzey.com

⊞ 🛖 €4 ⊞ (htd) ᵂᴰ 🏕 ዿ 🖫 ⁄ ᴹˢᴾ 🦋 🍴 ⅄ ☕ ☕ 🍴 ⁄Ⅲ ⁄ 🏊 (htd) 🏖

Fr Epinal take D460 sp Darney. In vill of Bouzey turn L at camp sp. Site in few metres, by reservoir. 4*, Lge, mkd, hdg, hdstg, pt shd, pt sl, terr, EHU (10A) €7; gas; bbq; red long stay; TV; 15% statics; phone; Eng spkn; adv bkg acc; ccard acc; bike hire; fishing; horseriding; games area; CKE. "Excel site; lake adj; sl slightly but pitches fairly level; ACSI discount in LS; gd cycling area; nice cycle ride to Epinal; pleasant position opp lake." **€22.00** 2016

ERQUY *2E3* (3.6km NE Coastal) *48.64201, -2.42456* **Camping Les Hautes Grées,** Rue St Michel, Les Hôpitaux, 22430 Erquy 02 96 72 34 78; hautesgrees@wanadoo.fr; www.camping-hautes-grees.com

🛖 €1.70 ⊞ (htd) ᵂᴰ 🏕 ዿ 🖫 ⁄ ᴹˢᴾ ⅄ ☕ 🍴 ⁄Ⅲ ⁄ 🏊 (htd) 🏖 sand 400m

Fr Erquy NE D786 dir Cap Fréhel & Les Hôpitaux sp to site. 3*, Med, mkd, hdstg, hdg, pt shd, EHU (10A) €4.70 (rec long lead); gas; bbq; TV; 10% statics; adv bkg acc; ccard acc; gym; sauna; fishing; horseriding; tennis; CKE. "Lovely, well-run site; well-kept pitches, extra charge lge ones; helpful staff; modern facs; excel site." **€26.00, 6 Apr-3 Oct.** 2015

ERQUY *2E3* (5km SSW Coastal) *48.604565, -2.489502* **Camping La Vallée,** St Pabu, 22430 Erquy 02 96 72 06 22; contact@campinglavallee.fr; www.campinglavallee.fr

🛖 €2 ⊞ ᵂᴰ ዿ 🖫 ⁄ ᴹˢᴾ 🦋 🍴 🏊 ⁄Ⅲ 🏖 500m

Foll d786 fr Val Andre twrds Erquy. As dual c'way ends, becoming 2 way, turn L immed. Foll sp for 750m. 3*, Sm, mkd, pt shd, terr, EHU (10A) €4.50; bbq; 20% statics; Eng spkn; adv bkg acc; sauna; games area; bike hire; CKE. "Vg site." **€26.60, 28 Apr-18 Sep.** 2018

ERVY LE CHATEL *4F4* (1km E Rural) *48.04018, 3.91900* **Camp Municipal Les Mottes,** 10130 Ervy-le-Châtel **03 25 70 07 96 or 03 25 70 50 36 (Mairie);** mairie-ervy-le-chatel@wanadoo.fr; www.ervy-le-chatel.fr

🐕 €1.50 ♦♦ ♨ ᕓ ▣ ⁄ 🦋 ▤nr ⌂

Exit N77 sp Auxon (int'l camping sp Ervy-le-Châtel) onto D374, then D92; site clearly sp. 2*, Med, pt shd, EHU (5A) €2.50; adv bkg acc; tennis; rv fishing 300m; CKE. *"Pleasant, well-kept, grassy site; lge pitches; vg facs; v friendly, helpful staff; no twin axles; rests in vill; rec; excel sm site; v clean."* **€16.00, 15 May-4 Oct.** **2017**

ESPALION *7D4* (0.3km E Urban) *44.52176, 2.77098* **Camping Roc de l'Arche,** 12500 Espalion **05 65 44 06 79;** info@rocdelarche.com; www.rocdelarche.com

🐕 €0.50 ♦♦ ♨ ᕓ ▣ ⁄ MSP 🦋 ▤nr ⌂

Sp in town off D920 & D921. Site on S banks of Rv Lot 300m fr bdge in town. 2*, Med, hdg, mkd, pt shd, EHU (6-10A); bbq; adv bkg acc; canoeing; fishing; tennis. *"Well-kept site; gd sized pitches, water pnts to each; service rds narr; pool adj inc; friendly, helpful warden; clean, modern san facs; excel."* **€26.30, 6 May-13 Sep.** **2019**

ESPALION *7D4* (5km E Rural) *44.51376, 2.81849* **Camping Belle Rive,** 40 rue du Terral Saint Come, 12500 Aveyron **06 98 22 91 59;** bellerive12@orange.fr; www.camping-bellerive-aveyron.com

🐕 €0.70 ♦♦ ▣ ⁄ MSP 🦋 ⁺ ⓗnr ▤nr

Fr Espalion take D987 to St Côme-d'Olt; cont thro vill to x-rds at far side; turn R by cemetery (small sp to site) down narr rd. Med, pt shd, EHU (6-10A) inc (poss rev pol & long lead may be req); 10% statics; Eng spkn. *"Pleasant rvside site; friendly, helpful owner; conv acc to delightful medieval vill; excel; gd walking/driving."* **€14.00, 1 May-30 Sep.** **2015**

ESSAY *4E1* (0.6km S Rural) *48.53799, 0.24649* **FFCC Camp Municipal Les Charmilles,** Route de Neuilly, 61500 Essay **02 33 29 15 46;** lescharmillescamping@gmail.com; www.camping-lescharmilles.com

♦♦ ▣ ⁄ MSP 🦋 ⁺ ⌂

Exit A28 junc 18 (Alençon Nord) onto D31 to Essay (sp L'Aigle); turn R in vill dir Neuilly-le-Bisson; site on R in 400m. 2*, Sm, hdg, pt shd, EHU (6A) €3 (reverse pol); 50% statics; adv bkg acc. *"Lge pitches, some diff to access; site yourself, warden calls in eve to pay; historical vill; fair NH; no hot water; old style European EHU."* **€10.00, 1 Apr-30 Sep.** **2019**

> **"I like to fill in the reports as I travel from site to site"**
>
> You'll find report forms at the back of this guide, or you can fill them in online at camc.com/europereport.

ESTAGEL *8G4* (3km W Rural) *42.76566, 2.66583* **Camping La Tour de France (formerly La Tourèze),** Route d'Estagel, 66720 Latour-de-France **06 15 14 23 46;** camping.latoureze@wanadoo.fr; www.camping-latourdefrance.fr

🐕 €3 ♦♦ ᵂᴰ ♨ ᕓ ▣ ⁄ MSP 🦋 ▤nr ⓗnr ▤nr ⌂

Fr D117 at Estagel turn S onto D612 then R onto D17 to Latour. Site on R on ent to vill. 2*, Med, mkd, shd, EHU (10A) €3.50; sw nr; red long stay; 13% statics; phone; Eng spkn; adv bkg acc; ccard acc. *"Pretty vill & wine 'cave' in walking dist; rec visit Rv Agly barrage nrby; htd pool 3km; helpful staff; excel; peaceful; welcoming, helpful, young owners; many ptiches with trees, diff for lge o'fits."* **€22.50, 1 Apr-14 Oct.** **2018**

ESTANG *8E2* (0.5km E Rural) *43.86493, -0.10321* **Camping Les Lacs de Courtès,** Courtès, 32240 Estang **05 62 09 61 98;** contact@lacsdecourtes.com; www.lacsdecourtes.com

🐕 €3 ♦♦ ᵂᴰ ♨ ᕓ ▣ ⁄ MSP 🦋 ⁺ Ⓣ ⓗnr ⌂ ▤nr ⌂ ✎
🏊 (htd) 🛥

W fr Eauze site sp fr D30. Fr Mont-de-Marsan D932 take D1 to Villeneuve-de-Marsan, then D1/D30 to Estang. 3*, Sm, hdg, mkd, pt shd, terr, EHU (6A) €3; TV; 50% statics; Eng spkn; adv bkg acc; lake fishing; tennis; games area. *"Gd family site; no bar/rest end of Aug; excel walking area; area for m'vans open all yr; gd rest in vill; vg."* **€28.00, 25 Apr-20 Oct.** **2017**

ETRETAT *3C1* (5km E Rural) *49.69880, 0.27580* **Camping de l'Aiguille Creuse,** 24 Rue de l'Aiguille, 76790 Les Loges **02 35 29 52 10;** camping@aiguillecreuse.com; www.campingaiguillecreuse.com

🐕 €3 ♦♦ ♨ ᕓ ▣ ⁄ MSP 🦋 ⁺ Ⓣ ⓗnr ⌂ ▤nr ⌂ ✎
🏕 3km

On S side of D940 in Les Loges; sp. 4*, Med, mkd, unshd, EHU (10A) inc; bbq; TV; adv bkg acc; tennis; games rm. *"Facs ltd LS; conv Etretat; gd; gd ctr for cliff top walks and inland villages."* **€29.50, 1 Apr-16 Sep, N08.** **2018**

ETRETAT *3C1* (1km SE Urban/Coastal) *49.70053, 0.21428* **Camp Municipal,** 69 Rue Guy de Maupassant, 76790 Éetretat **02 35 27 07 67**

♦♦ (htd) ᵂᴰ ♨ ᕓ ▣ ⁄ MSP 🦋 ▤nr ⌂ 🏕shgl 1km

Fr Fécamp SW on D940 thro town cent of Etretat & site on L. Or fr Le Havre R at 2nd traff lts; site on L in 1km on D39. 2*, Med, mkd, hdstg, pt shd, pt sl, EHU (6A) €6 (poss rev pol); gas; bbq; phone; ccard acc; CKE. *"Busy, well-kept site; lge pitches; conv Le Havre ferry; friendly & helpful staff; clean san facs but dated; level walk to pleasant seaside resort, attractive beach nr; gd cliff top walks nr; m'van o'night area adj (no EHU) open all yr €8; early arr high ssn rec; excel; lovely site; clsd 1200-1500."* **€19.00, 1 Apr-15 Oct.** **2018**

For a guide to symbols see the fold out on the rear cover

EU *3B2* (0.3km W Rural) *50.05065, 1.40996*
Camp Municipal du Parc du Chateau, Le Parc du
Château, 76260 Eu **02 35 86 20 04;**
camping-du-chateau@ville-eu.fr; www.ville-eu.fr

🏕️ ⬛ ♨ 🛒 ⅃ 🐕nr 🏊 shgl 3km

App fr Blangy on D1015 turn L at junc with D925
& foll camp sp to site in grnds of Hôtel de Ville
(chateau). Fr Abbeville on D925 fork R at 1st rndabt
in town S of rlwy then immed strt on over cobbled
rd to chateau walls. Turn R at chateau walls into
long, narr app rd thro trees. Med, hdstg, hdg, pt shd,
terr, EHU (16A) (poss rev pol); gas; 10% statics; Eng
spkn. *"Louis-Philippe museum in chateau; poor san facs;
easy uphill walk to town thro forest behind chateau;
Eu worth visit, an alt to seaside towns nrby; vg Fri mkt;
gd local dog walks; recep 0900-1200/1400-2100; rec."*
€10.00, 1 Apr-31 Oct. 2017

"We must tell the Club about that great site we found"

Get your site reports in by mid-August and we'll
do our best to get your updates into the next
edition.

EVIAN LES BAINS *9A3* (6km W Rural) *46.39388,
6.52805* **FFCC Camping Les Huttins,** 350 Rue de la
Plaine, Amphion-les-Bains, 74500 Publier **04 50 70
03 09;** campingleshuttins@gmail.com;
www.camping-leshuttins.com

🐕 €1 🏕️ ⬛ ♨ 🛒 ⅃ 🗺 🦋 ☂ nr ⓦ nr 🏊 ⛰

Fr Thonon on D1005 twds Evian, at start of
Amphion turn L onto Rte du Plaine sp; ent 200m on
R after rndabt. Fr Evian on D1005 twds Thonon, at
end of Amphion turn R & foll sp. 2*, Med, mkd, shd,
EHU €3; gas; bbq; sw nr; TV; 5% statics; Eng spkn;
adv bkg acc; tennis adj. *"Spacious, simple, relaxed site
in beautiful area; hypmkt 300m; enthusiastic, helpful
owners; pool 200m; sports complex 200m; basic, clean
san facs; gd base for Lake Léman; poss unrel opening
dates - phone ahead; excel; site run by siblings."*
€22.40, 1 May-30 Sep. 2019

EVRON *4F1* (9km SE Rural) *48.09423, -0.35642*
Glamping Sainte-Suzanne (formerly Municipal),
10 Rue de la Croix Couverte, 53270 Ste Suzanne
02 43 10 49 60; contact@glamping-saintesuzanne.fr;
www.glamping-saintesuzanne.fr

🏕️ ⬛ ♨ 🛒 ⅃ ☂ nr ⓦ nr 🏊

Take D7 SW fr Evron sp Ste Suzanne. Site 800m S
(downhill) after this sm fortified town. 2*, Sm, mkd,
hdg, pt shd, pt sl, EHU (10A) inc; bbq; 25% statics; Eng
spkn; adv bkg acc; horseriding adj; CKE. *"Remodelled
site with new facs (2017); llovely area; unspoilt town &
castle with historic Eng conns; walking adj; 8 EHU pnts;
excel; rec."* **€10.00, 1 May-30 Sep.** 2017

EVRON *4F1* (1.6km SW Urban) *48.15077, -0.41223*
Camp Municipal de la Zone Verte, Blvd du Maréchal
Juin, 53600 Evron **02 43 01 65 36;** camping@evron.fr;
www.camping.evron.fr

12 🐕 €0.80 🏕️(htd) ⬛ ♨ & 🛒 ⅃ 🗺 🦋 ☂ nr ⛰

Site on ring rd 200 yards fr Super-U supmkt; clearly
sp fr all rds into town. 3*, Med, hdg, pt shd, EHU
(6-10A) €1.60-2.45; red long stay; 50% statics; adv bkg
acc. *"Attractive, peaceful, comfortable, well-kept site
with many flowers; gd, clean san facs; restricted recep
hrs in winter - warden on site lunchtime & early eve only;
poss maintenance issues early ssn (2011); no twin axles;
some worker's c'vans; sports complex adj; htd pool adj;
highly rec for sh or long stay; excel; gd value; san facs
dated (2015); gd dog walk."* **€10.00** 2015

EYMET *7D2* (5km SW Rural) *44.63211, 0.39977*
Camping Le Moulin Brûlé, 47800 Agnac **05 53 83 07
56;** thebeales@wanadoo.fr; www.campingsw
france.co.uk

🏕️ ⬛ ♨ 🛒 ⅃ ⛰ 🏊

Fr S on D933 at Miramont-de-Guyenne (6km S of
Eymet) turn E onto D1; in 4km turn L onto C501 dir
Eymet; site on L in 2km. Or fr N approx 1km after
Eymet turn L onto C1 sp Chateau Pèchalbet. In
1.5km at x-rds turn L sp Bourgougnague, site on R in
2km. NB Narr lanes & bends on app. Sm, hdstg, mkd,
pt shd, sl, EHU (10-16A) €4; bbq (charcoal); 1% statics;
adv bkg rec; games area. *"Lovely, peaceful, well-kept
site in pleasant surroundings; friendly British owners;
gd clean san facs; gd cycling & walking; excel; animals
not permitted."* **€19.00, 1 May-15 Sep.** 2015

"I need an on-site restaurant"

We do our best to make sure site information
is correct, but it is always best to check any
must-have facilities are still available or will
be open during your visit.

EYMET *7D2* (0.2km W Urban) *44.66923, 0.39615*
Camping du Château (formerly Municipal), Rue de la
Sole, 24500 Eymet **05 53 23 80 28 or 06 98 16 97 93
(mob);** eymetcamping@aol.com; www.eymet
camping.fr

🐕 🏕️ ⬛ ♨ & 🛒 ⅃ 🗺 🦋 ⅌ ☂ nr ⓦ nr 🏊 nr ⛰

Thro Miramont onto D933 to Eymet. Turn opp
Casino supmkt & foll sp to site. Sp on ent to Eymet
fr all dirs. 2*, Sm, mkd, hdg, pt shd, EHU (10A) €3
(poss rev pol); sw nr; red long stay; Eng spkn; adv
bkg acc; bike hire; boat hire; CKE. *"Lovely site by rv
behind medieval chateau; friendly, helpful owner;
clean but tired san facs; pool 1.5km; gas 300m; wine
tasting on site; lake nrby; Thur mkt; excel; peaceful
site nr lovely Bastide town; no arr bet 1200-1500."*
€11.50, 1 Apr-30 Sep. 2016

EYMOUTIERS *7B4* (8km N Rural) *45.80560, 1.84342*
Camping Les 2 Iles (formerly Municipal Les Peyrades), Auphelle, Lac de Vassivière, 87470 Peyrat-le-Château **05 55 35 60 81; les2iles.camping@orange.fr; www.campingslelacdevassiviere.jimdo.com**

🛒 👫 [wc] ♨ 🖥 ⊘ ⁄ [MP] 🦋 ⍨ ⅋ nr ⊕ nr 🎣 nr 🏔 ⛵ *sand adj*

Fr Peyrat E on D13, at 5km sharp R onto D222 & foll sp for Lac de Vassivière. At wide junc turn L, site on R. Med, pt shd, pt sl, EHU (5A) €2.50; bbq; sw nr; twin axles; 25% statics; Eng spkn; adv bkg acc; games area; games rm. *"Helpful warden; some pitches o'look lake; new fac block (2015); v gd."*
€20.70, 2 Apr-31 Oct. 2016

FALAISE *3D1* (0.5km W Urban) *48.89545, -0.20476*
FFCC Camp Municipal du Château, 3 Rue du Val d'Ante, 14700 Falaise **02 31 90 16 55 or 02 31 90 30 90 (Mairie); camping@falaise.fr; www.falaise.fr/tourisme/le-camping**

🛒 €2.20 👫 [wc] ♨ ☔ 🖥 ⊘ ⁄ [MP] 🦋 ⍨ ⅋ nr ⊕ nr 🎣 nr 🏔

Fr N on N158, at rndabt on o'skirts of town, turn L into vill; at next rndabt by Super U go strt on; at 2nd mini-rndabt turn R; then sp on L after housing estate. Or fr S on D958, at 1st rndabt foll sp town cent & site. Cont down hill thro town then up hill to 1st rndabt, site sp, then sp on L after housing est. 2*, Med, hdg, mkd, pt shd, pt sl, terr, EHU (6-10A) €4.20; bbq; red long stay; TV; TV (pitch); Eng spkn; adv bkg acc; ccard acc; tennis; CKE. *"Lovely, peaceful, well-kept site in pleasant surroundings; pitches poss diff lge o'fits; htd pool in town; clean, well kept san facs (lots of hot water) poss ltd LS & stretched high ssn & clsd 2200-0800; pitch self & pay later; uphill walk to town, birthplace of William the Conqueror; vet in Falaise; mkt Sat am; excel; useful for ferry port."*
€19.00, 1 May-30 Sep. 2015

FANJEAUX *8F4* (2.5km S Rural) *43.16558, 2.02702*
FFCC Camping à la Ferme Les Brugues (Vialaret), 11270 Fanjeaux **04 68 24 77 37; lesbrugues@free.fr; http://lesbrugues.free.fr**

🛒 👫 [wc] ♨ ☔ 🖥 ⁄ 🦋 ⍨ ⅋ nr ⊕ nr 🎣 🏔

Exit A61 junc 22 onto D4/D119 (dir Mirepoix) to Fanjeaux; cont on D119 dir Mirepoix; at top of hill turn L onto D102 sp La Courtète (past rest La Table Cathare & fuel stn) & in 100m turn R to site in 2.5km. Site well sp fr Fanjeaux. Sm, hdg, mkd, shd, pt sl, terr, EHU (10-16A) inc (rev pol); 10% statics; Eng spkn; adv bkg acc; games rm; CKE. *"Delightful, peaceful, 'off the beaten track' site adj sm lake; care req sm children; well-kept; v lge pitches, some o'looking lake; friendly, helpful owners; gd clean san facs; many walks; beautful countryside; excel touring base; rec."*
€19.50, 1 Jun-30 Sep. 2018

FAVERGES *9B3* (7.3km NW Urban) *45.77510, 6.22585*
Camping La Serraz, Rue de la Poste, 74210 Doussard **04 50 44 30 68; info@campinglaserraz.com; www.campinglaserraz.com**

🛒 €2.50 👫 [wc] ♨ ☔ 🖥 ⊘ ⁄ [MP] 🦋 ⍨ ⅋ ⊕ 🏔 🎣 ⛵ *(htd)* 🏊

Exit Annecy on D1508 twd Albertville. At foot of lake ignore sp on R for Doussard Vill & take next turn R. Site on L in 1km, bef PO, sp. 5*, Med, pt shd, EHU (16A) inc; bbq; sw nr; twin axles; 50% statics; Eng spkn; adv bkg acc; games area; bike hire; games rm; sauna; CCI. *"Excel site; diving course for 8-14 year olds in Jul & Aug; spa opening 2014."*
€47.00, 1 May-15 Sep. 2019

FAYENCE *10E4* (6km W Rural) *43.3500, 6.39590*
Camping La Tuquette (Naturist), The High Suanes 83440 Fayence **04 94 76 19 40; robert@tuquette.com; www.tuquette.com**

🛒 €2 👫 [wc] ♨ ☔ 🖥 ⊘ ⁄ 🦋 ⍨ ⅋ ⊕ ♨ 🏔 🏊 *(htd)*

Fr Fayence take N562. At km 64.2 sp turn R, site ent 100m. 2*, Sm, mkd, pt shd, terr, EHU (6A) €4.60; bbq; 10% statics; Eng spkn; adv bkg acc; INF card. *"Vg, lovely, clean site; friendly owners, family run."*
€36.40, 10 Apr-26 Sep. 2018

FECAMP *3C1* (6km SE Rural) *49.74041, 0.41660*
Camping Les Falaises de Toussaint (formerly Municipal Le Canada), D926 76400 Toussaint **02 35 29 78 34; info-lesfalaises@ka-vacances.com; ka-vacances.com**

🛒 👫 *(htd)* [wc] ♨ ☔ 🖥 ⊘ ⁄ 🦋 ⍨ ⅋ nr ⊕ nr 🎣 nr 🏔 🏊 *4km*

On D926 N of Toussaint. Sp fr main rd. 2*, Med, mkd, hdg, pt shd, pt sl, EHU (4-10A) inc; bbq (gas); twin axles; 70% statics; Eng spkn; adv bkg acc; games area; CKE. *"Lovely quiet site; helpful warden; clean san facs; gd; excel."*
€20.00, 15 Mar-15 Nov. 2019

FERE, LA *3C4* (1.7km N Urban) *49.66554, 3.36205*
Camp Municipal du Marais de la Fontaine, Rue Vauban, 02800 La Fère **03 23 56 82 94**

🛒 €1.20 👫 [wc] ♨ ☔ 🖥 ⁄ 🦋 ⍨ ⅋ nr ⊕ nr 🎣

S on D1044 (St Quentin to Laon); R onto D338; turn E at rndabt; ignore sp 1st camping sp; turn N at next rndabt; site sp. Or Exit A26 junc 12 onto D1032 SW; in 2km turn R onto D35; in 4km pass under D1044; in 400m turn R; in 800m turn R at traff lts; foll over bdge to sports complex. 2*, Sm, hdg, mkd, pt sl, EHU (15A) €3.50; bbq; red long stay; rec; CKE. *"Well-kept site adj leisure cent; conv Calais, 2hrs 30mins; clean san facs; pitching awkward due sm pitches & narr site rds; warden lives adj site - on arr open double gates & ring doorbell to register; htd covrd pool adj; gates shut 2200-0700 - no vehicle/person access; avoid 1st w/end June as Wine & Food Festival held on site; conv A26; gd NH; generous sized pitches."*
€14.00, 1 Apr-30 Sep. 2015

Make sure you check any essential information with the site before you travel

FRANCE

FERRIERES EN GATINAIS *4F3* (0.3km N Rural) *48.09198, 2.78482* **Camp Municipal Le Perray/Les Ferrières,** Rue du Perray, 45210 Ferrières-en-Gâtinais 06 71 43 25 95 (mob) or 02 38 87 15 44 (Mairie); camping@ferrieresengatinais.fr; www.ferrieresen gatinais.fr

⛺ 🚿 WD ♨ ⊟ ∥ MP 🦋 ⑨ Ⓗnr ⚡nr 🏔 ♪

N fr Mantargis on N7; R onto D96/D32 sp Ferrières & foll camp sp. 2*, Med, mkd, pt shd, EHU (10A) inc; 50% statics; tennis; rv fishing adj. *"Vg site; direct access to sm rv; sports facs adj; gd facs & security; old pretty town with lovely church; supmkt clsd Sun-Mon; pool adj; call to check if open; free WiFi; off clsd 1200-1500, no access to site at this time."*
€12.00, 1 Apr-30 Oct.   2018

FERTE ST AUBIN, LA *4F3* (1km N Urban) *47.72553, 1.93565* **Camp Municipal Le Cosson,** Ave Löwendal, 45240 La Ferté-St Aubin 02 38 76 55 90; camping ducosson45@outlook.fr

⛺ €2 🚿 WD ∥ ♪ Ⓗnr ⚡nr ⛵(htd)

S fr Orléans on D2020; ent on R on N o'skts twd Municipal pool. Turning onto Rue Lowendal. 2*, Sm, pt shd, EHU (6A) inc (poss rev pol); phone; Eng spkn; fishing adj; CKE. *"Agreeable, spacious site; friendly, helpful recep; clean, ltd facs; easy walk to delightful town & gd rests; nr park & chateau; poss travellers LS; conv A71; gd NH."*
€16.00, 26 Apr-29 Sep.   2019

FERTE VIDAME, LA *4E2* (1.2km SW Rural) *48.60760, 0.89005* **Camping Les Abrias du Perche,** Route de la Lande, 28340 La Ferte Vidame 02 37 37 64 00; info@campingperchenormandie.fr; www.camping perchenormandie.fr

⛺ €2.50 🚿 WD ♨ ♨ ∥ MP 🦋 ⑨ Ⓣ 🏔 ♪ ⛵(covrd, htd)

Fr N12 take D45 (D24) twds Moussenvilliers and la Ferte Vidame. Site on R (D15.1). Sm, mkd, hdstg, pt shd, EHU (6A) €2.50; bbq; twin axles; 50% statics; bus 1km; adv bkg acc; games rm; bike hire; CKE. *"Close to sports ctr, forest walks and fishing; vg; max 2 dogs; fishing nr; long cable poss req; poss rev pol."*
€17.50, 1 Feb-31 Dec.   2017

FEUILLERES *3C3* (0.4km W Rural) *49.94851, 2.84364* **Camping du Château et de l'Oseraie,** 12 Rue du Château, 80200 Feuillères 03 22 83 17 59 or 06 16 97 93 42 (mob-LS); jsg-bred@wanadoo.fr; www.camping-chateau-oseraie.com

⛺ €1.20 🚿 WD ♨ ⊟ ∥ MP ⑨ Ⓣ 🏔 ♪ ⛵(htd)

Fr A1/E15 exit 13.1 Maurepas onto D938 dir Albert & then L onto D146; R at staggered x-rds in Feuillères (by church) & site on R in 500m. 3*, Med, hdg, mkd, hdstg, pt shd, EHU (10A) inc (poss rev pol); gas; bbq; red long stay; 10% statics; Eng spkn; adv bkg rec; ccard acc; games rm; fishing; tennis; games area; CKE. *"Excel, well-kept, well-run site; gd sized pitches; friendly staff; clean san facs; conv A1 a'route, WW1 battlefields & Disneyland Paris."* **€24.00, 15 Mar-31 Oct.   2018**

FEURS *9B2* (1km N Urban) *45.75457, 4.22595* **Camp Municipal Le Palais,** Route de Civens, 42110 Feurs 06 63 37 24 57; www.camping-rhonealpes.com

⛺ €0.61 🚿(htd) WD ♨ ⊟ ∥ MP 🦋 ♪ ⚡ 🏔

Site sp fr D107 on N o'skts of town. Site in corner of sports campus next to Boulodrome. 3*, Lge, pt shd, EHU (6A) €3.05; gas; 80% statics; phone; CKE. *"Pleasant, spacious, beautifully-kept site; busy, espec w/ends; pool adj; clean san facs."*
€17.40, 1 Apr-31 Oct.   2017

FIGEAC *7D4* (2km E Rural) *44.60989, 2.05015* **Camping Caravanning Domaine Du Surgie,** Domaine du Surgié, 46100 Figeac 05 61 64 88 54; contact@ marc-montmija.com; www.domainedusurgie.com

⛺ €2.50 🚿 WD ♨ ⊟ ∥ MP 🦋 ⑨ Ⓣ ⑨ ⚡ 🏔 ♪

Fr Figeac foll sp Rodez (on D840 S) to site by Rv Célé adj leisure complex. Foll sps 'Base Loisirs de Surgie'. Narr ent, light controlled. Or appr fr E on D840, immed after passing under rlwy arch a v sharp R turn into narr rd (keep R thro traff lts); site on L in 700m. NB Recep at beginning of rd to leisure cent & camping. 4*, Med, hdg, mkd, pt shd, EHU (10A) inc; red long stay; 30% statics; Eng spkn; adv bkg acc; boating; bike hire; tennis. *"Excel pool complex adj (free to campers); peaceful LS; pleasant 2km walk or car park just outside town; ent clsd 1200-1600 LS; adj rv unfenced; htd pool & waterslide adj; mkt Sat; vg."*
€27.00, 1 Apr-30 Sept.   2015

FIGEAC *7D4* (7km SE Urban) *44.57328, 2.07296* **Camp Municipal Les Rives d'Olt,** Blvd Paul-Ramadier, 12700 Capdenac-Gare 05 65 80 88 87 or 05 65 80 22 22 (Mairie); camping.capdenac@wanadoo.fr

⛺ 🚿 WD ♨ ⊟ ∥ MP 🦋 Ⓣnr ⚡ Ⓗnr ⚡nr

Fr Figeac on D840 dir Rodez; at Capdenac turn R onto D994 over rv bdge; immed after x-ing rv bdge turn R onto D86. Site in 200m on R by rv. 3*, Med, hdg, mkd, shd, EHU (9A) €2.90; TV; 5% statics; tennis adj; CKE. *"Site beside Rv Lot; ent clsd 1200-1600 LS; gd fishing, walking & cycling; gas adj; new security barrier."*
€11.00, 10 Apr-30 Sep.   2017

FISMES *3D4* (0.8km W Urban) *49.30944, 3.67138* **Camp Municipal de Fismes,** Allée des Missions, 51170 Fismes 03 26 48 10 26; contact@fismes.fr; www.fismes.fr

⛺ 🚿 WD ♨ ♨ ∥ ⚡nr

Fr Reims NW on N31. At Fismes do not ent town, but stay on N31 dir Soissons. Site on L down little lane at end of sports stadium wall. Or exit A4 junc 22 sp Soissons & Fismes & as bef. 2*, Sm, hdstg, unshd, EHU (12A) €3.50 (poss rev pol); bbq (elec, gas); train; adv bkg acc; games area; horseriding 5km; CKE. *"Vg site; gd, clean san facs; warden on site ltd hrs; gates locked 2200-0700; train to Reims nr; conv Laon, Epernay, Reims; mkt Sat am; vg NH; site clean and tidy; excel; site nr rd junc."* **€13.00, 1 May-15 Sep.   2017**

FRANCE

FLECHE, LA *4G1* (10km E Rural) *47.70230, 0.07330*
Camp Municipal La Chabotière, Place des Tilleuls, 72800 Luché-Pringé **02 43 45 10 00**; contact@lachabotiere.com; www.lachabotiere.com or www.loir-valley.com

€1.50

SW fr Le Mans on D323 twd La Flèche. At Clermont-Créans turn L on D13 to Luché-Pringé. Site sp. 3*, Med, mkd, hdg, pt shd, pt sl, EHU (10A) inc (poss rev pol); TV; 10% statics; phone; Eng spkn; adv bkg acc; bike hire; CKE. "*Lovely, well-kept site by Rv Loir; helpful, friendly warden; pool adj high ssn; clean, modern facs; gd site for children; many cycle rtes; conv chateaux; nice vill nrby; avoid Le Mans motor bike week - poss many bikers on site; excel.*"
€16.00, 1 Apr-15 Oct.   2018

FLECHE, LA *4G1* (0.9km W Urban) *47.69514, -0.07936* Camping Municipal de la Route d'Or, Allée du Camping, 72200 La Flèche **02 43 94 55 90**; info@camping-laroutedor.com; camping-lafleche.com

€1 (htd)

Fr NW dir Laval D306, keep to W of town, leave S on D306 twd Bauge; site on L after x-ing rv; sp. Fr S take dir for A11 & Laval, site clearly sp on R on rvside. 4*, Lge, hdg, mkd, hdstg, pt shd, EHU (10A) €3.80 (poss long lead req); gas; bbq; phone; Eng spkn; ccard acc; fishing nr; canoeing nr; games area; tennis; CKE. "*Lovely, busy site in beautiful location by rv; well kept, run & maintained site; lge pitches; v friendly, welcoming, helpful staff; facs ltd LS; ring for ent code if office clsd; no twin axles; attractive, easy, sh walk across rv to attractive town; mkt Wed; rec; mkt Sun & Wed; defibrillator on site; new excel san facs (2016); recep clsd 1200-1400; gd value.*"
€18.00, 1 Mar-31 Oct.   2018

FLERS *4E1* (3km E Urban) *48.75451, -0.54341* Camping de la Fouquerie (formerly du Pays de Flers), 145 La Fouquerie 61100 Flers **02 33 65 35 00**; campingflers@flers-agglo.fr; https://notre.guide/campingdelafouquerie/en

Fr E on D924 thro town cent, site on L in 2 km. Fr W on D924 dir Centre Ville, site on R. 1*, Sm, pt shd, EHU (6A); bbq; 15% statics; Eng spkn; bike hire; games area; CCI. "*Easy walk to interesting town; excel.*"
€12.00, 1 Apr-31 Oct.   2019

FLEURAT *7A4* (1km E Rural) *46.24027, 1.68666* Camping Les Boueix, Les Boueix, 23320 Fleurat 09 63 61 23 80; info@campinglesboueix.com; www.campinglesboueix.com

12   €1.50

Fr N145 N onto D5 take slipway or D6 into Fleurat. Turn E at x-rds to Les Boueix then 2nd L. Site in middle of fork in rd. Sm, hdg, mkd, pt shd, sl, EHU (16A) €3.50 (€5 winter); bbq; Eng spkn; adv bkg acc; fishing; CKE. "*Beautiful, quiet & relaxing CL-type site; lge pitches with views; welcoming, helpful British owners; vg san facs; sl poss diff m'vans; well-stocked fishing lake nrby; lovely walks; ideal for beautiful Creuse Valley; rallies welcome; conv A20; highly rec.*"
€16.00   2016

FLEURIE *9A2* (0.7km S Rural) *46.18758, 4.69895* Vivacamp La Grappe Fleurie, La Verne, 69820 Fleurie 04 74 69 80 07; info@beaujolais-camping.com; www.beaujolais-camping.fr

€3.10

S dir Lyon on D906 turn R (W) at S end of Romanèche onto D32; 4km to vill of Fleurie (beware sharp turn in vill & narr rds) & foll site sp. 4*, Med, hdg, mkd, pt shd, terr, serviced pitches; EHU (10A) inc; gas; 10% statics; Eng spkn; adv bkg rec; ccard acc; tennis; CKE. "*Clean, well-run, busy site; friendly staff; excel san facs; lovely pool; gates & wash rms clsd 2200-0700; clean, spacious san facs; path to town thro vineyards (uphill); wine tasting; sm mkt Sat; excel.*" €27.00, 8 Apr-8 Oct.   2017

See advertisement

FRANCE

FLORAC *9D1* (1km N Rural) *44.33569, 3.59002*
FFCC Camping Le Pont du Tarn, Route de Pont de
Montvert, 48400 Florac **04 66 45 18 26 or 04 66 45
17 96 (LS); contact@camping-florac.com;
www.camping-florac.com**

🛞 €2 ⵌ(htd) ⱳ ♨ 🛁 ⵘ 🏍 🦋 ⵠ nr ⓝ nr 🛒 nr 🅿️ 🛶

**Exit Florac N on N106 & turn R in 500m by by-pass
on D998; site on L in 300m.** 3*, Lge, hdg, mkd, pt
shd, EHU (10A) €4.20; bbq (charcoal, elec); sw nr;
60% statics; phone; Eng spkn; adv bkg rec; rv fishing
adj; CKE. *"Nice, well-kept, well-run site in beautiful
area; clean san facs, needs updating (2016); no twin
axles; 20 min walk to town; gd touring base; lge
pitches; lge mkt Thurs; vg value; excel site on rv; well
situated."* **€28.50, 1 Apr-1 Nov.** **2017**

FLORAC *9D1* (2.5km NE Rural) *44.34528, 3.61008*
FFCC Camping Chantemerle, La Pontèze, 48400
Bédouès **04 66 45 19 66 or 06 73 86 53 16 (mob);
chante-merle@wanadoo.fr; www.camping-
chantemerle.com**

🛞 €1.50 ⵌ ⱳ ♨ 🛁 🏍 🦋 ⵠ 🛒 🅿️

**Exit Florac N on N106; in 500m turn R onto D998; in
2.5km site on L, past Bédouès vill cent.** 2*, Med, mkd,
pt shd, pt sl, EHU (6A) €2.80; sw nr; 10% statics; Eng
spkn; games rm; CKE. *"Lovely location; helpful owner;
gd walking; conv Gorges du Tarn, Cévennes National
Park; vg; water and EHU now avail on lower pitches;
sm rest, home cooked food; excel site."*
€22.40, 14 Apr-16 Oct. **2017**

FOIX *8G3* (2km N Rural) *42.98911, 1.61565*
Camping du Lac, Quartier Labarre, 09000 Foix
**05 61 65 11 58; camping-du-lac@wanadoo.fr;
www.campingdulac.com**

⑫ 🛞 €1.50 ⵌ ⱳ ♨ ♨ 🛁 🏍 ⵠ ⵠ ⓣ 🅿️ 🛒 nr 🔟 🦯
🛶 🛁

Fr N on N20 foll sp for 'Centre Ville', site on R in
2km. Fr S onto on N20 thro tunnel & take 1st exit
N of Foix & foll sp 'Centre Ville', then as above. Site
opp Chausson building materials store. 3*, Lge, mkd,
pt shd, EHU (6A) inc; bbq; TV; 75% statics; bus to Foix
adj (not Sun); Eng spkn; adv bkg rec; ccard acc;
windsurfing; boating; tennis; CKE. *"Busy site w/end;
quiet, spacious pitches on L of camp; modern san facs,
poss stretched high ssn; site & facs poss uncared for
early ssn (2011); gates clsd 2300-0700; pleasant town;
NH only LS."* **€27.40** **2017**

FOIX *8G3* (3km NW Rural) *42.97151, 1.57243*
Camp Municipal de Rieutort, 09000 Cos **05 61 65
39 79 or 06 71 18 10 38 (mob); bernard.blazy09@
orange.fr; http://camping-municipal-cos09.fr**

⑫ 🐕 ⵌ(htd) ♨ ♨ 🛁 🏍 ⵠ ⓝ nr 🛒 nr 🅿️ 🛶

Fr Foix take D117 dir Tarbes. Turn R onto D17 then
at rndabt onto D617, site on L in 3km. NB Narr
app rds. 2*, Sm, pt shd, pt sl, serviced pitches; EHU
(5A) €1.80; tennis; CKE. *"Pleasant site amongst trees
with gd views; friendly, helpful warden; gd san facs,
ltd LS; sm step into disabled facs; no c'vans over 6m."*
€11.00 **2015**

FONTAINEBLEAU *4E3* (5km NE Rural) *48.42215,
2.74872* **Camp Municipal Grange aux Dîmes,**
Rue de l'Abreuvoir/Rue de l'Eglise, 77210 Samoreau
**01 64 23 72 25; mairie-de-samoreau@wanadoo.fr;
www.samoreau.fr**

ⵌ(htd) ⱳ ♨ 🛁 🏍 ⵠ ⓣ nr ⓝ nr 🅿️ 🛒 nr

Fr cent of Fontainebleau take D210 (dir Provins);
in approx 4km at rndabt cross bdge over Rv Seine;
take R at rndabt; site sp at end of rd thro Samoreau
vill; site twd rv. 1*, Med, hdg, mkd, pt shd, pt sl, EHU
(10A) inc (poss rev pol); phone; bus; adv bkg acc; CKE.
*"Peaceful site in attractive location by Rv Seine; gd
sized pitches; helpful staff; gd, immac san facs; adj
vill hall poss noisy w/end; jazz festival late Jun; conv
palace, Paris (by train) & Disneyland; clsd 2200-0700;
excel; waterpoints around site could do with upgrade."*
€22.00, 1 Mar-31 Oct. **2018**

FONTAINEBLEAU *4E3* (10km S Rural) *48.31740,
2.69650* **Camping Les Prés,** Chemin des Prés, 77880
Grez-sur-Loing **01 64 45 72 75; camping-grez@
wanadoo.fr; www.camping-grez-fontainebleau.info**

🐕 ⵌ ⱳ ♨ ♨ 🛁 🏍 🦯 ⵠ ⵠ ⓣ nr ⓝ nr 🛒 🅿️

Fr Fontainebleau on D607 twd Nemours (S) for 8km;
look for camping sps. At traff island turn L onto
D40D, in 1km immed after x-ing bdge turn R; site on
L. Do not tow into Grez-sur-Loing. 2*, Med, mkd, hdg,
pt shd, EHU (5A) €3; gas; red long stay; 80% statics;
phone; Eng spkn; adv bkg acc; ccard acc; fishing; canoe
hire; bike hire; CKE. *"In attractive area; helpful British
owner; 80% statics; site poss unkempt/scruffy end of
ssn; vg."* **€17.00, 20 Mar-11 Nov.** **2017**

FONTAINEBLEAU *4E3* (14km S Rural) *48.33362,
2.75386* **Camping Le Parc du Gué,** Route de Montigny,
La Genevraye, 77690 Montigny-sur-Loing **01 64 45 87
79; contact@camping-parcdugue.com;
www.camping-parcdugue.com**

🐕 €3.70 ⵌ(htd) ⱳ ♨ ♨ 🛁 🏍 ⵠ 🦋 ⵠ ⓣ 🅿️ 🛒 🔟 🛶(htd)
🛁

Do not tow thro Montigny-sur-Loing, v narr tight
turns. Site is E of Montigny, N of La Genevraye off
D104. App fr S Nemours on D40, slow rd but safe,
or fr NE, Moret-sur-Loing D606/D104. 2*, Lge, hdg,
mkd, pt shd, EHU (10A) €3.60; bbq; sw nr; 70% statics;
Eng spkn; adv bkg acc; ccard acc; fishing; games area;
watersports; CKE. *"Beautiful, wooded country; kayaks;
mkt Sat 2km; excel walking & cycling; new pool (2015);
vg."* **€21.00, 15 Mar-30 Nov.** **2016**

FONTENAY TRESIGNY *4E3* (7km NE Rural) *48.75050, 2.89728* **Camping des Quatre Vents,** 77610 Crèvecoeur-en-Brie **01 64 07 41 11; contact@ caravaning-4vents.fr; www.caravaning-4vents.fr**

🏕 €3 ♟(htd) � ♨ ♿ ⚲ 🗑 ∥ 🌂 ☕ 🍴 🐕 ⚱nr 🎡 ⛵

At Calais take A26/E15 dir Arras; at Arras take A1/ E15 dir Paris; next take A104 dir A4 Metz/Nancy/ Marne-la-Vallée, then A4 dir Metz/Nancy, exit junc 13 onto D231 dir Provins; after rndabt with lge monument turn R dir Crèvecoeur-en-Brie & foll site sp. **Site in 13km.** 3*, Lge, hdg, mkd, pt shd, serviced pitches; EHU (6A) inc; bbq; TV; 50% statics; phone; Eng spkn; adv bkg req; ccard acc; games rm; horseriding; games area; CKE. *"Friendly, well-run, beautiful site; lge, well-kept pitches; welcoming, helpful staff; san facs spacious & v clean; pleasant pool; conv Disneyland & Paris; poss muddy when wet; vg; beautiful countryside ideal for cycling; no o'fits over 10m high ssn; restfull even in high ssn."* **€30.00, 20 Mar-1 Nov, P09.** 2016

FONTES *10F1* (0.9km N Rural) *43.54734, 3.37999* **FFCC Camping L'Evasion,** Route de Cabrières, 34320 Fontès **04 67 25 32 00; www.campingevasion.com**

🏕 €2.80 ♟ owd ♨ ♿ ⚲ 🗑 ∥ MsP 🌂 ☕ 🍴 Ⓨ ⊕ ♨ 🎡 ⛵

Fr A75 exit junc 59 (Pézenas). At rndabt take D124 to Lézignan-la-Cèbe then fork L, cont on D124 to Fontès. In vill foll sp to site. 3*, Sm, mkd, hdg, pt shd, pt sl, EHU (10A) €3.50; gas; bbq; 75% statics; phone; adv bkg acc; CKE. *"Excel san facs; touring pitches amongst statics (long-term residents); helpful owners."* **€22.50, 14 Mar-2 Nov.** 2016

FORCALQUIER *10E3* (0.7km E Urban) *43.96206, 5.78718* **Camping Indigo Forcalquier,** Route de Sigonce, 04300 Forcalquier **04 92 75 27 94; forcalquier@camping-indigo.com; www.camping-indigo.com**

🏕 €4 ♟ owd ♨ ♿ ⚲ 🗑 ∥ MsP 🌂 ☕ 🍴 ⊕ ♨ ⚱nr 🎡 ⛵(htd) 🛗

Fr A51 exit junc 19 La Brillane onto D4100 to Forcalquier. Site sp. 3*, Med, mkd, pt shd, pt sl, serviced pitches; EHU (10A) €5.30 (long read poss req); TV; 10% statics; phone; Eng spkn; adv bkg acc; games area; CKE. *"Pleasant site in lovely location; excel m'van facs; access for lge o'fits & m'vans poss diff due v narr site rds & awkward corners; walking dist fr town cent; v friendly & helpful staff; famous lge mkt on Mon."* **€29.60, 3 Apr-28 Sep.** 2015

FORCALQUIER *10E3* (6.5km S Urban) *43.91096, 5.78210* **FFCC Camping l'Eau Vive,** 04300 Dauphin **04 92 79 51 91; info@leauvive.fr; www.leauvive.fr**

🏕 €3.50 ♟(htd) owd ♨ ⚲ 🗑 ∥ 🌂 🐕 ⚱ 🎡 🍴 ⛵

S fr Forcalquier on D4100 dir Apt; in 2.5km turn L onto D13 (at Mane); site on R in 3km. Or fr D4096, turn onto D13 at Volx; site on L in 6km (800m past Dauphin). 3*, Med, mkd, shd, EHU (3-6A) €3.50-4.50; bbq (gas, sep area); TV; bus 800m; Eng spkn; adv bkg acc; games area; tennis; games rm; bike hire. *"Well-run, super site; helpful owners; vg pools; vg for children; excel."* **€23.50, 1 Apr-31 Sep.** 2016

FORCALQUIER *10E3* (4km NW Rural) *43.97235, 5.73800* **Camping Le Domaine des Lauzons (Naturist),** 04300 Limans **04 92 73 00 60; leslauzons@ wanadoo.fr; www.camping-lauzons.com**

🏕 €4 ♟ owd ♨ ♿ ⚲ 🗑 ∥ 🌂 ☕ 🍴 Ⓨ ⊕ ♨ 🐕 ⚱ 🎡 ⛵ ⛵(htd)

Exit A51 junc 19 onto N100 dir Avignon; in Forcalquier at rndabt turn L onto D950/D313 sp Banon; site on R in approx 6km. Lge site sp. Diff app. 4*, Med, mkd, pt shd, pt sl, terr, EHU (6A) €4.50; gas; bbq (charcoal, gas); TV; 25% statics; phone; Eng spkn; adv bkg acc; ccard acc; waterslide; games area; ice; sauna; games rm; INF card req; archery. *"Pleasant site in wooded valley; wonderful scenery; excel family site; helpful, friendly staff; most san facs modern, ltd LS; excel pool area; walks fr site; Forcalquier lovely town; excel touring base; pony rides; many activities; access diff lge o'fits, tractor help avail; INF not compulsory."* **€37.60, 14 Apr-13 Oct.** 2018

FORET FOUESNANT, LA *2F2* (2km SE Coastal) *47.89904, -3.96138* **Camping Les Saules,** 54 Route de la Plage, 29940 La Forêt-Fouesnant **02 98 56 98 57; info@camping-les-saules.com; www.camping-les-saules.com**

🏕 €2.50 ♟(htd) owd ♨ ♿ ⚲ 🗑 ∥ MsP 🌂 ☕ 🍴 Ⓨ nr ⊕ nr ⚱nr 🎡 ⛵ 🏖 sand 150m

Take N783 Concarneau-Quimper (by-pass) thro Le Poteau Vert, turn L at sp Kerleven. On ent vill, site on R opp Stereden Vor site. 3*, Lge, hdg, shd, pt sl, EHU (6A) €3; bbq; twin axles; TV; 60% statics; phone; bus adj; Eng spkn; adv bkg acc; ccard acc; games rm; sailing 150m; windsurfing 150m; fishing 150m; CKE. *"Well run family site; many touring pitches with direct access to beach; yacht marina nrby-boat trips; gd walking on coastal path; excel."* **€27.00, 1 May-28 Sep.** 2015

FORGES LES EAUX *3C2* (1km S Urban) *49.60603, 1.54302* **Camp Municipal La Minière,** 3 Blvd Nicolas Thiese, 76440 Forges-Les-Eaux **02 35 90 53 91; campingforges@gmail.com; www.campingforges.com/en**

♟ ♨ ⚲ 🗑 ∥ 🌂 ⚱nr

Fr Forges-les-Eaux cent, take D921 S sp Lyons-la-Forêt. In 750m turn R foll sp, camp on R in 150m. **NB 3,500kg limit in town all dirs.** 2*, Med, hdg, mkd, pt shd, pt sl, EHU (6A) inc (rev pol); CKE. *"Well-presented site; mv service pnt adj; lge pitches; friendly warden, warm welcome; v basic, clean san facs; poss diff access some pitches; m'van o'night area opp; htd pool in town; pleasant town with excel WWII Resistance Museum; gd local vet; useful NH; gd access to town; dog walk on site."* **€17.00, 15 Mar-15 Oct.** 2017

FOUGERES *2E4* (2.5km E Urban) *48.3544, -1.1795*
Camp Municipal de Paron, Route de la Chapelle-Janson, 35300 Fougères **02 99 99 40 81;**
campingmunicipal35@orange.fr; www.ot-fougeres.fr

🐾 ♦¶ ⓦ ♨ 🖥 ∥ 🦋 ⑪ nr ♨ nr 🏕

Fr A84/E3 take junc 30 then ring rd E twd N12. Turn L at N12 & foll sp. Site on D17 sp R after Carrefour. Well sp on ring rd. 2*, Med, hdg, hdstg, pt shd, pt sl, serviced pitches; EHU (5-10A) €3.60-4.10 (poss rev pol); adv bkg acc; ccard acc; tennis; horseriding adj; CKE. *"Well-kept site in pleasant parkland setting; lge pitches, poss soggy when wet; popular NH; helpful warden; gd clean facs; gates clsd 2200-0900 & 1230-1730 card pass avail, parking avail in adj car park; tours of 12thC castle; old town worth visit; Sat mkt; excel; excel san facs."* **€14.00, 27 Apr-16 Sep.** **2018**

FOURAS *7A1* (0.5km NE Coastal) *45.99264, -1.08680*
Camp Municipal du Cadoret, Blvd de Chaterny, 17450 Fouras **05 46 82 19 19;** www.campings-fouras.com

12 🐾 €2.90 ♦¶ ⓦ 🛁 ♨ 🖥 ∥ ♨ 🍴 ⓟ ⑪ ♨ nr ⚓ 🏊 (htd) 🚲
🏖 sand adj

Fr Rochefort take N137, L onto D937 at Fouras, fork R at sp to site in 1km. At next rndabt take 3rd exit into Ave du Cadoret, then 1st R at next rndabt. 3*, Lge, mkd, hdg, pt shd, pt sl, EHU (6-10A) €3.50-5.40 (poss long lead req); gas; 50% statics; bus to La Rochelle, Rochefort, ferry to Ile d'Aix; Eng spkn; adv bkg acc; golf 5km; fishing; games area; tennis 1km; boating; CKE. *"Popular, well-kept site; vg location; well shd; lge pitches; clean san facs, unisex LS; coastal footpath; pleasant town; a favourite; highly rec; gd conv site."* **€24.00** **2015**

FREJUS *10F4* (5km SW Rural) *43.39890, 6.67531*
Camping Domaine de la Bergerie, Vallée-du-Fournel, Route du Col-du-Bougnon, 83520 Roquebrune-sur-Argens **04 98 11 45 45;** info@domainelabergerie.com; www.domainelabergerie.com

🐾 €6 ♦¶ ⓦ ♨ ♨ 🛁 🖥 ∥ 🦋 ♨ ⓨ ⑪ ♨ ♨ 🏕 ✎
🏊 (covrd, htd) 🚲

On DN7 twd Fréjus, turn R onto D7 sp St Aygulf & Roquebrune-sur-Argens; after passing Roquebrune, site sp in approx 6km on R. 4*, V lge, mkd, hdg, pt shd, terr, serviced pitches; EHU (6A) inc (extra for 10A); gas; red long stay; 70% statics; Eng spkn; adv bkg acc; ccard acc; tennis; jacuzzi; sauna; archery; games area; lake fishing; waterslide. *"Well-organised site; entmnt/activities for all ages; mini farm; early bkg ess for summer; excel."* **€47.00, 28 Apr-30 Sep.** **2019**

See advertisement

FREJUS *10F4* (11.6km W Rural) *43.44535, 6.65790*
Camping Le Moulin des Iscles, Chemin du Moulin des Iscles, 83520 Roquebrune-sur-Argens **04 94 45 70 74;** moulin.iscles@wanadoo.fr; www.campingdesiscles.com

🐾 €2.50 ♦¶ (htd) ⓦ ♨ ♨ 🛁 🖥 ∥ 🦋 ♨ ⓨ ⑪ ♨ ♨ 🏕 ✎

Twd Fréjus on DN7, turn R onto D7 to St Aygulf sp Roquebrune. Site on L after passing thro Roquebrune vill. 3*, Med, mkd, shd, EHU (6A) €3.90; bbq; TV; 10% statics; adv bkg acc; ccard acc; games rm; rv fishing; canoeing. *"Excel well-kept, well-run site by rv; water skiing nrby; helpful owners; gd security."* **€28.00, 1 Apr-30 Sep.** **2015**

FRANCE

FREJUS *10F4* (6km NW Rural) *43.46944, 6.67805*
Camping La Bastiane, 1056 Chemin des Suvières,
83480 Puget-sur-Argens 04 94 55 55 94; info@
labastiane.com; www.labastiane.com

🐕 €4 ♨♨ 🏠 ♨ ♂ ♿ 🗑 ∥ WC ▓ ✖ ♖ ‼ ∀ 🗋 ⅆ 🅱 /∏ ✗ ♨ (htd) 📶

Exit A8 at junc 37 Puget/Fréjus. At DN7 turn R dir
Le Muy & in 1km turn R immed after 2nd bdge. Foll
sp to site. Fr DN7 turn L at traff lts in Puget, site is
2km N of Puget. 5*, Lge, mkd, hdg, shd, pt sl, EHU
(10A) inc; bbq (elec); red long stay; TV; 40% statics;
phone; Eng spkn; adv bkg acc; ccard acc; bike hire;
tennis; games area; games rm; watersports; CKE.
*"Excel, family-run, friendly site; cinema; car wash area;
conv m'way (no m'way noise); clean san facs; gd rest."*
€50.20, 21 Apr-9 Oct. 2017

FRONTIGNAN *10F1* (6km S Coastal) *43.44970, 3.80540*
Sandaya Les Tamaris, 140 Ave d'Ingril, 34110
Frontignan- Plage 04 67 43 44 77; tam@sandaya.fr;
www.sandaya.co.uk

🐕 €3 ♨♨ (htd) WC ▓ 🏠 ♨ ♿ 🗑 ∥ MP ✖ ♖ ‼ ∀ 🗋 ⅆ 🅱 /∏ ✗
♨ (htd) 📶 🏖 sand adj

Fr A9/E15 exit junc 32 St Jean-de-Védas & foll
sp Sète. At next rndbt foll sp Sète N112. After
approx 8km turn L sp Vic-la-Gardiole onto D114.
Cross rlwy & Canal du Rhône. Pass Les Aresquiers-
Plages & turn L in 500m, site sp on L in 500m.
Fr N on D613, take N300 to Sète; then N112 to
Frontignan-Plage. 5*, Lge, hdstg, mkd, hdg, pt shd,
serviced pitches; EHU (10A) inc; bbq; red long stay;
TV; 50% statics; phone; adv bkg rec; ccard acc; lake
fishing; bike hire; watersports; horseriding nr; games
rm. *"Popular, family-run site; direct access to beach;
sm pitches; archery; weights rm; friendly, helpful staff;
gd clean san facs; vg for families; excel pool; late arr
area; gd rest; lovely town; mkt Thu & Sat am; excel."*
€25.00, 03 Apr-27 Sep. 2019

FUMEL *7D3* (8km E Rural) *44.49810, 1.06670*
Camping Le Ch'Timi, La Roque, 46700 Touzac
05 65 36 52 36; info@campinglechtimi.com;
www.campinglechtimi.com

🐕 €1.90 ♨♨ WC ▓ 🏠 ♨ ♿ 🗑 ∥ ✖ ♖ ‼ ∀ 🗋 ⅆ 🅱 /∏ ✗ ♨ 📶

Exit N20-E9 junc 57 onto D820 dir Cahors; turn R at
rndabt onto D811 sp Villeneuve-sur-Lot; in Duravel
take 3rd exit at rndabt onto D58, sp Vire-sur-Lot;
in 2.5km cross bdge & turn R at rndabt onto D8, sp
Touzac; site on R on rvside, on hill, in about 1.5km.
Well sp. NB D8 not suitable lge c'vans or m'vans.
3*, Med, hdg, mkd, pt shd, pt sl, EHU (6A) €4.20; gas;
bbq; twin axles; TV; 13% statics; phone; Eng spkn;
adv bkg acc; ccard acc; tennis; games area; games
rm; archery; bike hire; fishing 100m; CKE. *"Site in gd
position; friendly, helpful Dutch owners; immac facs,
ltd LS; rv nr site, down steep steps; access some pitches
poss diff lge o'fits; gd local rests; no o'fits over 7m
high ssn; canoeing 100m; wine-tasting tours; mkt Puy
l'Evêque Tue; wonderful stay, rec; v well kept; rv view fr
some pitches; ACSI acc."*
€28.00, 1 Apr-30 Sep, D05. 2015

GAILLAC *8E4* (5km E Urban) *43.90929, 1.98311*
Camping Les Pommiers, Aigueleze, 81600 Rivières
05 63 33 02 49; info@camping-lespommiers.com;
www.camping-lespommiers.com

🐕 €2 ♨♨ WC ▓ 🏠 ♨ ♿ 🗑 ∥ MP ✖ ♖ ‼ ∀ 🗋 ⅆ 🅱 /∏ ✗ ♨ (htd) 📶

Fr A68, Albi - Toulouse take exit 10, foll sp Espace
Loisirs d'Aigueleze. 3*, Med, hdstg, mkd, hdg, pt shd,
EHU (10-13A) €4.50; bbq; sw; twin axles; red long
stay; TV; 25% statics; phone; Eng spkn; adv bkg acc;
games area; bike hire; CCI. *"Visit Albi by sightseeing
boat on Rv Tarn or by train; canoe hire 150m; bike
hire 150m; vg; conv Albi, Cordes, P&R Toulose; excel;
well kept clean site; friendly, welcoming owners;
conv for bastide vill; sm eve mkt Mon in hg ssn nr."*
€27.00, 1 Apr-30 Sep. 2018

GAILLAC *8E4* (2km W Urban) *43.89674, 1.88522*
FFCC Camping des Sources, 9 Ave Guynemer,
81600 Gaillac 05 63 57 18 30; camping-gaillac@
orange.fr; www.camping-gaillac.fr

🐕 €2 ♨♨ (htd) WC ▓ 🏠 ♨ ♿ 🗑 ∥ MP ✖ ♖ ‼ ∀ 🗋 nr /∏ ✗

Exit A68 junc 9 onto D999 then in 3.5km at rndabt
turn onto D968 dir Gaillac. In 100m turn R immed
past Leclerc petrol stn, then L by Aldi. Site 200m on
R, well sp fr town cent. Sharp turn into ent.
3*, Med, hdg, hdstg, mkd, pt shd, terr, EHU (10A) €3;
TV; 10% statics; ccard acc; CKE. *"Peaceful, clean & tidy
site; friendly, helpful staff; gd, modern san facs; steep
walk to recep & bar but san facs at pitch level; purpose-
made dog-walk area; gd touring base Tarn & Albi region
& circular tour Bastides; cent of wine area; not suitable
lge o'fits; gd; call recep fr Aldi carpk to operate barrier."*
€14.50, 1 Apr-31 Oct. 2017

GANGES *10E1* (7km E Rural) *43.92630, 3.78951*
Camp Municipal Le Grillon, Place de l'Eglise, 34190
Montoulieu 04 67 73 79 31 or 06 61 75 35 11;
camping.montoulieu@sfr.fr; http://camping.
montoulieu.fr

12 🐕 ♨♨ 🏠 ♨ ♿ 🗑 ∥ MP ✖ ♖ ∀ ⅆ /∏ ✗

Fr Ganges take D999 E. At La Cadière-et-Cambo turn
R onto D195 (site sp). Site on R in 3km.
3*, Sm, hdstg, hdg, pt shd, pt sl, EHU (6A) inc;
40% statics. *"Gd cent for outdoor activities; gd, modern
facs; useful winter NH; fairly isolated."* €17.60 2019

For a guide to symbols see the fold out on the rear cover

GANNAT *9A1* (10km W Rural) *46.10838, 3.07347*
Camping La Filature de la Sioule, Route de Chouvigny, 03450 Ebreuil **04 70 90 72 01; camping.filature@gmail.com; www.campingfilature.com**

🏕 👫 🚐 wc ♨ ⚲ ᗰ ⚕ 🔌 ♀ 👗 🍴 🏊 ⚂ 🚙

Fr A71 exit 12 (not 12.1); foll sp to Ebreuil, after rv bdge in vill turn L onto D998 then cont onto D915. Site on L in abt 1 km. 4*, Med, mkd, hdg, pt shd, EHU (6A) €3.50; gas; bbq; red long stay; TV; 10% statics; Eng spkn; adv bkg acc; ccard acc; canoeing; horseriding; tennis 800m; bike hire; trout fishing; CKE. *"Peaceful, pleasant rvside site in orchard; lge pitches; helpful British owners; clean facs but tired, ltd LS; vg value food high ssn (gd home cooking); vg walking area; mv service pnt 800m; conv A71; no hdstg, v soft grnd; poor water pressure in shwrs; site unkept (2015)."* **€26.00, 15 Apr-1 Oct.** **2016**

GAP *9D3* (1.5km N Rural) *44.58030, 6.08270*
Camping Alpes-Dauphiné, Route Napoléon, 05000 Gap **04 92 51 29 95; info@alpesdauphine.com; www.alpesdauphine.com**

🏕 €2.10 👫(htd) wc ♨ ⚲ ᗰ ⚕ MSP 👗 ♀ 🍴 ⊕ ⚂ 🏊 ᗰ 🎿(htd) 🚤

On N85, sp. 4*, Med, hdstg, mkd, pt shd, pt sl, terr, EHU (6A) €3; gas; TV; 20% statics; phone; Eng spkn; adv bkg rec; ccard acc; games area; CKE. *"Pleasant site with views; modern, well maintained san facs; m'vans need levellers; gd touring base; lack of maintenance early ssn (2011); conv NH; gd site; excel rest."* **€27.00, 15 Apr-20 Oct.** **2017**

GAP *9D3* (10km S Rural) *44.45708, 6.04785*
Camping Le Chêne, Route de Marseille, 05130 Tallard **04 92 54 13 31; contact@camping-lechene.com; www.camping-lechene.com**

🏕 👫 ♨ ᗰ ⚕ 🍴 🏊 ⚂ nr ᗰ 🚤 (htd)

Fr S take N85 twds Gap; turn R at traff lts onto D942; site on R after 3km. Fr Gap take N85 S; turn L at traff lts, D942; site on R 3km. 3*, Sm, mkd, hdstg, pt shd, sl, terr, EHU (6A) €3.5; bbq (sep area); phone; adv bkg acc; tennis; CKE. *"Poss unsuitable for lgs o'fits, sm pitches; lovely setting; new san facs (2018), but ltd for site size; site needs tlc."* **€13.00, 6 Apr-13 Oct.** **2018**

GAVARNIE *8G2* (4km N Rural) *42.75896, 0.00069*
Camping Le Pain de Sucre, quartier Couret, 65120 Gavarnie **05 62 92 47 55 or 06 75 30 64 22 (mob); camping-gavarnie@wanadoo.fr or info@camping-gavarnie.com; www.camping-gavarnie.com**

🏕 €2.15 👫 wc ♨ ⚲ ᗰ ⚕ MSP 👗 ⊕ nr ⚂ nr ᗰ

N of Gavarnie, across rv by sm bdge; clearly visible & sp fr rd. 2*, Med, pt shd, EHU (2-10A) €2.30-6.50 (long lead poss req); bbq; ccard acc. *"Gd base for walking; gd facs; access to national park; vg; gd clean san facs; fantastic view of Cirque."* **€20.00, 1 Jan-15 Apr, 1 Jun-30 Sep & 15 Dec-31 Dec.** **2016**

GENNES *4G1* (0.7km NE Rural) *47.34205, -0.22985*
Camping Au Bord de Loire, Ave des Cadets-de-Saumur, 49350 Gennes **02 41 38 04 67 or 06 95 00 24 87; contact@camping-auborddeloire.com; www.camping-auborddeloire.com**

🏕 €1.60 👫 wc ♨ ᗰ ⚕ 👗 ♀ 🍴 🏊 nr ᗰ ⚕ 🚤

At Rv Loire bdge cross S to Gennes on D751B. Site 200m on L. Ent to site thro bus terminus/car park on ent to Gennes. 2*, Med, pt shd, pt sl, EHU (10A) €3.40; bbq; red long stay; 2% statics; CKE. *"Delightful, relaxing, well-kept site by Rv Loire, spacious pitches, main san facs block up 18 steps, vg; htd pool in vill; Loire cycle rte passes gate; new san facs block (2015); v easy walk to vill."* **€16.80, 13 Apr-30 Sep.** **2018**

"We must tell the Club about that great site we found"

Get your site reports in by mid-August and we'll do our best to get your updates into the next edition.

GERARDMER *6F3* (7km E Rural) *48.06755, 6.94830*
FFCC Camping Les Jonquilles, Route du Lac, 88400 Xonrupt-Longemer **03 29 63 34 01; info@camping-jonquilles.com; www.camping-jonquilles.com**

🏕 €1.50 👫 wc ♨ ⚲ ᗰ ⚕ MSP 👗 ♀ 🍴 ⊕ ⚂ 🏊 ᗰ

Sp off D417 SE of Xonrupt-Longemer. Fr W thro Gérardmer on D417 (sp Colmar) in approx 1km over bdge & turn R at T-junc (still on D417). After 3km turn R opp hotel Auberge du Lac & almost immed R round W end of lake for 500m to T-junc, turn L, site on S bank 1km. 2*, Lge, mkd, unshd, pt sl, EHU (6-10A) €3.50-5.20; gas; sw nr; TV; 10% statics; phone; bus 1km; Eng spkn; adv bkg acc; ccard acc; sailing; fishing; CKE. *"Friendly, well-maintained, family-run site; gd views; poss uneven pitches; some noise fr entmnt at night; excel for Haute Vosges region; great lakeside site; busy rd."* **€18.00, 17 Apr-4 Oct.** **2015**

GEX *9A3* (1.4km E Urban) *46.33430, 6.06744*
Camping Les Genêts, 400 Ave des Alpes, 01170 Gex **04 50 42 84 57 or 06 79 17 13 69 (mob); les.2b@hotmail.fr; www.gex.fr/decouvrir-gex/camping**

🏕 €1 👫 wc ♨ ⚲ ᗰ ⚕ 👗 🍴 ⚂ nr ᗰ

Fr all dir head for 'Centre Ville'; at rndabt take D984 twd Divonne/Lausanne. Site sp to R (tight turn) after rlwy sheds (poor sp in town) & Musée Sapeurs Pompiers. 3*, Med, hdg, hdstg, pt shd, pt sl, EHU (16A) €2.90; TV; phone; Eng spkn; adv bkg acc; games area; CKE. *"Excel, attractive, well-kept site; excel games facs/playgrnd; friendly, helpful staff; clean san facs; quiet with lots of privacy; conv Geneva; wifi in recep; gates clsd 2200-0800; 20 mins fr Geneva airport."* **€17.50, 1 May-31 Oct.** **2017**

FRANCE

GIEN *4G3* (3km S Rural) *47.68233, 2.62289*
Camping Touristique de Gien, Rue des Iris, 45500
Poilly-lez-Gien **02 38 67 12 50; info@camping-gien.com;
www.camping-gien.com**

Off D952 Orléans-Nevers rd; turn R over old rv
bdge in Gien & then R again onto D951; site on R
on Rv Loire. Alt dir fr D940 (Argent-sur-Sauldre -
Gien) at rndbt take rd sp Gien. Take L at traff lts
bef old bdge; site on R, 1km S of rv. 3*, Lge, hdstg,
mkd, hdg, pt shd, pt sl, EHU (10A) €5; bbq; sw nr;
red long stay; TV; 20% statics; phone; Eng spkn; adv
bkg acc; ccard acc; tennis; canoeing; games rm; bike
hire; CKE. *"Lovely rvside site; views of old bdge &
town some pitches; excel staff; gd san facs; vg facs;
no sw allowed in rv; easy walk to town across bdge;
porcelain factory 'seconds'; vg value; gd rest; san facs
unisex; excel site, highly rec; nice situation; bar adj;
gas adj; flock of sheep/goats traverse the site daily."*
€27.00, 3 Mar-4 Nov.   2018

GIEN *4G3* (8km S Rural) *47.64152, 2.61528*
Les Bois du Bardelet, Route de Bourges, Poilly
45500 Gien **02 38 67 47 39; contact@bardelet.com;
www.bardelet.com**

Fr Gien take D940 dir Bourges; turn R onto D53,
then R again onto unclassified rd to go back
across D940; foll sp to site on L side of this rd. Site
well sp fr D940. 5*, Lge, hdstg, mkd, hdg, pt shd, pt
sl, EHU (10-16A) inc (some rev pol); gas; bbq; red
long stay; twin axles; TV; 17% statics; phone; adv
bkg acc; ccard acc; archery; bike hire; fitness rm;
jacuzzi; canoeing; games area; tennis; lake fishing;
horseriding 5km; games rm; CKE. *"Pleasant, well-
kept, well-run site; friendly welcome; modern, immac
san facs, poss stretched high ssn; some pitches
poss diff access; beautiful o'door pool; gd for young
children; guided walks; remote site in countryside."*
€28.00, 3 Apr-30 Sep, L05.   2019

See advertisement

GISORS *3D3* (7km SW Rural) *49.25639, 1.70174*
Camp Municipal de l'Aulnaie, Rue du Fond-de-l'Aulnaie,
27720 Dangu **02 32 55 43 42; etangcampingdangu@
orange.fr; http://euredangu.e-monsite.com/**

On ent Gisors fr all dirs, take ring rd & exit dir Vernon
D10, then L onto D181 dir Dangu. Site on L bef
Dangu. Site sp fr D10. NB speed humps. 3*, Lge, mkd,
pt shd, EHU (10A) €2.80; gas; sw; 90% statics; adv bkg
acc; fishing; CKE. *"Lakeside site; Gisors attractive town;
conv Giverny & Gisors local attractions; beautiful site."*
€14.00, 1 Apr-31 Oct.   2019

GIVET *5B1* (0.5km N Urban) *50.14345, 4.82614*
Caravaning Municipal La Ballastière, 16 Rue Berthelot,
08600 Givet **03 24 42 30 20; sa.mairiegivet@
wanadoo.fr; www.tourisme-champagne-
ardenne.com**

Site at N end of town on lake. Foll 'Caravaning' sp
fr W end of rv bdge or Dinant rd. 2*, Med, hdstg,
hdg, mkd, pt shd, EHU (10A) inc; bbq; 60% statics;
CKE. *"Nr Rv Meuse; adj sports & watersports complex;
picturesque town; walking dist to shops & rest;
vg; pool adj; conv for Rv Meuse cycleway; fair NH;
scruffy & unkept san facs, rundown but clean (2018)."*
€9.00   2018

GIVET *5B1* (2km SW Rural) *50.12993, 4.80721*
Camping Le Sanglier, 63 Rue des Grands Jardins,
08600 Rancennes **03 24 42 72 61 or 06 47 98
62 41 (mob); gilbert.gachet0455@orange.fr**

Off D949 Givet to Beauraing. Immed after x-ing
rv bdge turn R. Turn R again foll sp to site at end
narr access rd on rvside. 1*, Sm, pt shd, pt sl, terr,
EHU (4A); 60% statics; phone; Eng spkn; adv bkg acc;
watersports; fishing; CKE. *"Gd touring base; clean,
basic facs; gd NH."* **€9.00, 1 May-30 Sep.**   2015

GIVORS *9B2* (10km NW Urban) *45.61498, 4.67068*
Camping La Trillonnière, Boulevard du General de
Gaulle, 69440 Mornant **04 82 29 21 89 or 04 78 44 16
47; contact@la-trillonniere.fr; www.la-trillonniere.fr**

🛉 €1 ♦♦ wc ▲ ♨ ⚲ ⌷ ╱ ⌂ ⁑ 🅦 nr �.nr ⚑

**Exit A7 at Givors & foll sp for St Etienne via D488,
thro Givors onto D2 till sp seen for Mornant via D34,
cont on D34 up hill for 7km, cross D342 & cont 1km
to o'skts of Mornant, L at junc island & site on L.**
2*, Med, pt shd, pt sl, EHU (10A) inc; twin axles;
20% statics; Eng spkn; adv bkg acc; CKE. *"Well
managed, quiet site on edge of lovely vill in Monts du
Lyonnais; walks in hills; Lyon accessible by bus (outsite
gate) & metro; excell new san facs; 6 chalets."*
€25.00, 15 May-30 Sep.   **2018**

GIVRE, LE *7A1* (1.5km S Rural) *46.44472, -1.39832*
Camping La Grisse, 85540 Le Givre **02 51 30 83 03;
info@campinglagrisse.com; www.campinglagrisse.com**

12 🛉 €2 ♦♦ wc ▲ ♨ ⌷ ╱ ⁑ ⚑

**Fr Luçon take D949 & turn L at junc with D747 (La
Tranche rd). Turn L in 3km & foll sps.** 3*, Sm, pt shd,
EHU (16A) €4; 50% statics; Eng spkn; adv bkg acc;
ccard acc; games area; CKE. *"Peaceful, friendly, farm
site; lge pitches; clean, modern facs; beautiful area/
beach; gd for dogs; knowledgeable owner of local
area."* **€29.00**   **2017**

GONDRIN *8E2* (3km SE Rural) *43.86936, 0.25844*
Camping La Brouquère, Betbézé, 32330 Gondrin
**05 62 29 19 44; camping@brouquere.com;
www.brouquere.com**

🛉 €1 ♦♦ wc ▲ ♨ ⚲ ⌷ ╱ 🦋 ⁑ 𝚼 ⚑

**Fr Condom S on D931; pass thro Gondrin & turn S
onto D113 dir Courrensan; site sp in 2km.**
Sm, mkd, shd, pt sl, EHU (10A) €2.50; bbq; TV; Eng
spkn; adv bkg acc; bike hire. *"V quiet, CL-type site;
friendly Dutch owners; immac san facs; wine-tasting;
local produce, inc Armagnac; excel; adults only."*
€17.00, 30 Apr-1 Oct.   **2016**

GORDES *10E2* (2km N Rural) *43.92689, 5.20207*
Camping Les Sources, Route de Murs, 84220 Gordes
**04 90 71 12 48; contact@campingdessources.com;
www.campingdessources.com**

🛉 €5 ♦♦ wc ▲ ♨ ⌷ ╱ 🦋 𝚼 ⊕ ♨ 🚿 ⚑ ╱ 🏊

**Fr A7 junc 24, E on D973; then D22; then D900
twds Apt. After 18km at Coustellet turn N onto D2
then L on D15 twds Murs; site on L in 2km beyond
Gordes.** 2*, Med, mkd, hdstg, pt shd, terr, EHU (6A)
€4.40 (long lead poss req); red long stay; 25% statics;
Eng spkn; adv bkg acc; ccard acc; games rm; bike hire;
games area; CKE. *"Lovely location & views; friendly
staff; modern, clean san facs; gd pool; access rds
narr; sm pitches v diff lge o'fits; ask for easy pitch &
inspect on foot; some steep rds to pitches as site on
hillside; 24 hr security barriers; gd walking; mkt Tues."*
€37.70, 6 Apr-28 Sep.   **2019**

GOUAREC *2E3* (0.6km SW Rural) *48.22555, -3.18307*
Camping Tost Aven, Au Bout du Pont, 22570 Gouarec
**02 96 24 87 86; bertrand.cocherel@orange.fr;
www.brittanycamping.com**

🛉 €3 ♦♦ wc ▲ ♨ ⌷ ╱ 🦋 𝚼 nr ⊕ nr 🚿.nr ⚑ ╱

Sp fr town cent bet rv & canal. 2*, Med, pt shd, EHU
(10A) €2.40; bbq; sw nr; bus 200m; Eng spkn; adv bkg
acc; bike hire; canoe hire. *"Clean, relaxed, tidy site bet
Nantes-Brest canal & rv on edge of vill; gas adj;
towpath for cycling; great!"*
€12.00, 1 May-15 Sep.   **2018**

GOUDARGUES *10E2* (1km NE Rural) *44.22056,
4.47884* **Camping Les Amarines,** La Vérune Cornillon,
30630 Goudargues **04 66 82 24 92; les.amarines@
wanadoo.fr; www.campinglesamarines.com**

🛉 €3 ♦♦ (htd) ▲ ♨ ⚲ ⌷ ╱ 🦋 𝚼 ♨ ⚑ ╱ 🏊 (htd)

**Fr D980 foll sp onto D23 & site bet Cornillon &
Goudargues.** 3*, Med, hdg, mkd, shd, EHU (6A) €3.50;
adv bkg acc; rv fishing. *"Lge pitches; site liable to flood
after heavy rain; excel."* **€32.00, 1 Apr-1 Oct.**   **2019**

GOURDON *7D3* (10km W Rural) *44.75491, 1.23999*
Camping Le Convivial, La Gréze, 24250 St Martial de
Nabirat **05 53 28 43 15; contact@campingleconvivial.
com; www.campingleconvivial.com**

🛉 €1.60 ♦♦ (htd) wc ▲ ♨ ⚲ ⌷ ╱ 🦋 ⁑ 𝚼 ⊕ 🚿 🚿.nr ⚑ 🏊

**SW fr Gourdon, take D673 twd Salviac. Bef Pont
Carral turn R onto D6 which becomes D46. Site
1.5km N St Martial on L.** Sm, hdg, pt shd, pt sl,
EHU (8A); bbq; twin axles; 25% statics; Eng spkn;
ccard acc; games area; fishing 1km; CCI. *"Beautiful,
spacious site off tourist track; friendly & welcoming
owners; cycle trail in pretty valley of Céon nrby; vg."*
€19.70, 1 Apr-31 Oct.   **2019**

"I need an on-site restaurant"

We do our best to make sure site information
is correct, but it is always best to check any
must-have facilities are still available or will
be open during your visit.

GOUZON *7A4* (0.6km S Urban) *46.18785, 2.23913*
Camp Municipal de la Voueize, 1 Ave de la Marche,
23230 Gouzon **05 55 81 73 22; camping-gouzon@
orange.fr; www.camping-lavoueize.fr**

🛉 €0.50 ♦♦ wc ▲ ♨ ╱ 🦋 𝚼 nr ⊕ nr 🚿.nr ⚑

**On E62/N145 Guéret/Montluçon exit at sp for
Gouzon. In cent of vill bear R past church & site is
sp on edge of Rv Voueize.** 2*, Sm, pt shd, EHU (10A)
inc (poss rev pol); adv bkg acc; golf 2km; bike hire;
fishing. *"Lovely aspect; friendly recep; clean site; facs
poss tired high ssn; gd walking & cycling rtes; gd NH;
birdwatching on lake 8km; snacks/bar Jul & Aug only;
gas adj; big trees; adj rv; san facs tired."*
€15.50, 1 May-16 Oct.   **2015**

GRAMAT 7D4 (7km SE Rural) 44.74767, 1.79954
Camping Le Teulière, L'Hôpital Beaulieu, 46500
Issendolus 05 65 40 86 71; laparro.mcv@free.fr;
http://laparro.mcv.free.fr

Site on R on D840 at L'Hôpital, clearly sp. Access
fr ent narr & tight corners, not for underpowered.
2*, Sm, pt shd, pt sl, EHU (20A) €2.65 (poss rev pol);
bbq; TV; 10% statics; adv bkg acc; tennis; fishing.
"Conv Rocamadour; basic san facs; ltd facs LS; site rds
unmade, steep & narr - gd traction req; pitches muddy
when wet." **€9.35** 2016

GRANDCAMP MAISY 1C4 (0.5km W Coastal)
49.38814, -1.05204 **Camping Le Joncal,** Le Petit Nice,
14450 Grandcamp-Maisy 04 92 28 38 48; camping
dujoncal@hotmail.fr; www.campingdujoncal.com

Ent on Grandcamp port dock area; visible fr vill.
Fr N13 take D199 sp Grandcamp-Maisy & foll Le Port
& Camping sps. 3*, Lge, hdg, mkd, pt shd, EHU (6-
10A) €5.40-7.50; gas; bbq; 80% statics; bus. "Conv
for D Day beaches; some pitches at water's edge; excel
morning fish mkt close by; gd NH."
€23.50, 1 Apr-30 Sep. 2019

GRANDE MOTTE, LA 10F1 (2km NW Coastal) 43.56440,
4.07528 **FFCC Camping La Petite Motte à La Grande-
Motte,** 195 Allée des Peupliers, 34280 La Grande-Motte
04 67 56 54 75; camping.lagrandemotte@ffcc.fr;
www.camping-lapetitemotte.com

Exit A9 for Lunel or Montpellier Est to La Grande
Motte, site sp on D59 & D62 coast rd.
2*, Lge, shd, EHU (6A) €4.30; red long stay; twin axles;
10% statics; adv bkg acc; horseriding nr; watersports
nr; games area; tennis nr; golf nr; CKE. "Walk to
beach thro ave of trees & footbdge over rds; helpful
staff; clean modern san facs; cycle rtes nrby; m'van
o'night area; vg; 2nd san fac modernised (2015)."
€20.50, 29 Mar-30 Sep. 2015

GRANVILLE 1D4 (6km NE Coastal) 48.86976, -1.56380
Kawan Village La Route Blanche, 6 La Route Blanche,
50290 Bréville-sur-Mer 02 33 50 23 31; larouteblanche@
camping-breville.com; www.campinglaroute
blanche.com

Exit A84 junc 37 onto D924 dir Granville. Bef
Granville turn L onto D971, then L onto D114 which
joins D971e. Site on R bef golf club. Nr Bréville sm
airfield. 5*, Lge, hdstg, mkd, hdg, pt shd, serviced
pitches; EHU (6-10A) €4-5; gas; bbq; red long stay;
TV; 40% statics; phone; Eng spkn; adv bkg acc; ccard
acc; tennis nr; waterslide; sailing school; golf nr; games
area; CKE. "Pleasant, busy site with vg clean facs; staff
friendly & helpful; disabled seatlift in pool; gd walking,
cycling & beach; pleasant old walled town & harbour;
vg." **€39.50, 6 Apr-23 Sep.** 2018

GRANVILLE 1D4 (8km SE Rural) 48.79790, -1.5244
Camping Le Château de Lez-Eaux, 50380 St Pair-
sur-Mer 02 33 51 66 09; bonjour@lez-eaux.com;
www.lez-eaux.com

App site on D973 Granville to Avranches rd (not
via St Pair). Cont strt thro 1st rndabt at Geant and
next rndabt for 2km, site sp on R.
5*, Lge, mkd, pt shd, pt sl, serviced pitches; EHU
(10-16A) inc; bbq; twin axles; TV; 80% statics;
ccard acc; games rm; lake fishing; bike hire; tennis;
horseriding 4km; waterslide; games area; CKE.
"Superb, beautiful site in grnds of chateau; children's
indoor aqua park; easy access; spacious pitches,
various prices; helpful & friendly staff; clean, modern
san facs; excel pool complex; gd for children; boat
hire 7km; great for dogs; gd cycling & gd cycle rte to
beach; gd touring base; conv Mont St Michel, Dol &
landing beaches; mkt Thu St Pair; highly rec."
€46.00, 1 Apr-13 Sep, N02. 2019

See advertisement

For a guide to symbols see the fold out on the rear cover

GRASSE *10E4* (5.5km SE Urban) *43.63507, 6.94859*
Camping Caravaning La Paoute, 160 Route de
Cannes, 06130 Grasse **04 93 09 11 42; camppaoute@
hotmail.com; www.campinglapaoute.com**

12 ⛺ ♚♛ wc ♨ ⬛ ∅ MsP ♟ 🍴 ♨ ⚓ nr ⚠ (htd)

**Sp fr Grasse town cent on Route de Cannes (secondary
rd to Cannes, NOT D6185), a 10 min drive.** 3*, Med,
hdg, mkd, pt shd, sl, terr, EHU (10A) €4; 15% statics; bus
500m; games rm; CKE. *"Gd, quiet site; m'vans acc out of
ssn but adv bkg req."* **€31.00**   **2019**

GRAVELINES *3A3* (4km NW Coastal) *51.00250,
2.09694* **Camping de la Plage,** 115 Rue du Maréchal-
Foch, 59153 Grand-Fort-Philippe **03 28 65 31 95;
campingdelaplage@campingvpa.fr; www.camping-
de-la-plage.info**

🐾 €2 ♚♛(htd) wc ♨ ♨ ∅ MsP 🦋 ♟ ⚓ nr ⚠ ♣ 🏖 sand 500m

**Exit A16 junc 51 dir Grand-Fort-Philippe; at o'skts of
town turn R sp Camping ***; cont into town cent;
foll rd along quayside; foll rd to L past lge crucifix;
turn R at next x-rds; site on R.**
3*, Med, hdg, hdstg, pt shd, terr, EHU (10A) €3.70
(poss long lead req); 20% statics; adv bkg acc; ccard
acc; CKE. *"Various pitch sizes; ltd EHU; pleasant walk
to sea front; night security guard; conv ferries; rec adv
bkg; san facs excel; pool 3km; friendly, attractive site."*
€15.00, 1 Apr-31 Oct.   **2016**

GRAVESON *10E2* (2km SE Rural) *43.84408, 4.78080*
Camping Les Micocouliers, 445 Route de Cassoulen,
13690 Graveson **04 90 95 81 49; micocou@free.fr;
www.camping-les-micocouliers-provence.fr**

🐾 €2 ♚♛ wc ♨ ♨ ∅ MsP ♟ 🍴 nr ⊕ nr ⚓ ♣

**Leave A7 junc 25 onto D99 St Rémy-de-Provence
then D5 N past Maillane, site on R.** 3*, Med, hdg,
mkd, unshd, EHU (4-13A) €4.40-7; bbq; 8% statics;
phone; Eng spkn; adv bkg rec; bike hire; games area;
tennis 1km; CKE. *"Peaceful but busy site; pretty &
well-kept; friendly, helpful, welcoming owners; excel,
immac san facs; lovely sm pool; vg cycling; attractive,
interesting area; excel; additional san facs built (2014)."*
€31.00, 15 Mar-15 Oct.   **2016**

GRAY *6G2* (1km E Rural) *47.45207, 5.59999*
Camp Municipal Longue Rive, Rue de la Plage, 70100
Gray **03 84 64 90 44; tourisme-gray@wanadoo.fr;
www.ville-gray.fr**

🐾 €0.85 ♚♛ ♨ ♨ ∅ MsP 🍴 nr ⊕ nr ⚓ nr ⚠

**S on D67 to Gray. cross rv bdge, L at rndabt, after
300m sp La Plage. Well sp fr all rtes.** 3*, Med, mkd,
hdg, pt shd, EHU (10A) €2.45; gas; Eng spkn; tennis;
boating; fishing; CKE. *"Lovely setting on Rv Saône;
friendly recep; new high quality facs; poss stretched high
ssn; twin axles; pool opp; many pitches waterlogged
early ssn; several Bastide vills within cycling dist; NH
only."* **€14.50, 15 Apr-30 Sep.**   **2015**

GRENOBLE *9C3* (19km S Rural) *45.08553, 5.69872*
Camping à la Ferme Le Moulin de Tulette (Gaudin),
Route du Moulin de Tulette, 38760 Varces-Allières-
et-Risset **06 37 74 61 70; campingdetulette@
gmail.com; www.camping-moulindetulette.fr**

🐾 €1 ♚♛ wc ♨ ♨ ♨ ∅ 🦋 ♟ ⚓ nr ♣

**Fr A51, exit junc 12 to join D1075 N, Varces in approx
2km. Turn R at traff lts & foll sp to site, (approx 2km
fr D1075). If driving thro Grenoble look for sp Gap -
D1075 diff to find; on ent Varce foll site sp.**
Sm, mkd, pt shd, pt sl, EHU (5-10A) inc; Eng spkn; adv
bkg acc; CKE. *"Peaceful, picturesque, well-kept site
with views; friendly, helpful owners; facs ltd but clean -
stretched high ssn; gd base for touring/x-ing Alps; new
lge pool."* **€19.00, 1 May-30 Sep.**   **2015**

GRENOBLE *9C3* (4.5km SW Urban) *45.16687, 5.69897*
Camping Caravaning Les 3 Pucelles, 58 Rue des
Allobroges, 38180 Seyssins **04 76 96 45 73;
amico.francoise@gmail.com; www.camping-trois-
pucelles.com**

12 ♚♛(htd) wc ♨ ♨ ∅ 🍴 ⊕ ♨ ⚓ ⚠ ♣

**On A480 in dir of rocade (by-pass) S exit 5B, on R
after supmkt then foll sp to R then L. Clearly sp.
Well sp fr m'way.** Sm, hdg, hdstg, pt shd, EHU (16A)
meter; 70% statics; phone; bus nr; CKE. *"Site pt of
hotel campus run by friendly family; sm pitches; san
facs need refurb; conv Grenoble by bus/tram; NH
only; poorly maintained; tram to city 300m fr site."*
€21.00   **2015**

GREOUX LES BAINS *10E3* (1.2km S Rural) *43.75158,
5.88185* **Camping Le Verseau,** Route de St Pierre,
04800 Gréoux-les-Bains **04 92 77 67 10 or 06 22 72 93
25 (mob); info@camping-le-verseau.com;
www.camping-le-verseau.com**

🐾 €2.50 ♚♛ wc ♨ ♨ ∅ ∅ 🦋 ♟ 🍴 ⊕ ♨ ⚓ nr ⚠ ♣ 🏊

**Fr W on D952 to Gréoux. Go under bdge then bear
L just bef petrol stn. Cross rv (narr bdge), site on R
in 500m.** 3*, Med, hdg, pt shd, pt sl, EHU (10A) €3.90;
bbq (elec, gas); phone; adv bkg acc; tennis 1km; CKE.
"Friendly owners; interesting spa town; great views."
€23.00, 1 Mar-31 Oct.   **2016**

GREZILLE *4G1* (1km E Rural) *47.32751, -0.33512*
Ferme du Bois Madame, Frédéric Gauthier, 49320
Grézillé **02 41 54 20 97 or 06 87 23 32 55 (mob);
ferme.boismadame@wanadoo.fr; www.fermedu
boismadame.com**

12 🐾 €0.50 ♚♛ wc ♨ ♨ ∅ MsP

**Turn L off D761 (Angers-Poitiers) in Les Alleuds sp
Grézillé (D90); in 3.5km turn R sp Grézillé (D276);
after 1.4km in Grézillé turn L and immed R sp
Gennes (D176). Site on R in 1km.** Sm, hdg, pt shd,
EHU (10-12A); adv bkg acc; bike hire. *"Friendly
welcome; CL feel to site but lge & more facs; working
farm & stables; horse-drawn carrige trip avail in ssn;
gd."* **€13.00**   **2015**

GRIGNAN *9D2* (0.5km S Urban) *44.41731, 4.90950*
Camping de Grignan, 2 Avenue de Grillon, 26230
Grignan **04 75 01 92 23; contact@campingde
grignan.fr; www.campingdegrignan.fr**

🐕 ⭐ 👫 wc ♨ ⚓ 🚿 ⊘ ✉ 🐾 ♻ Ⴤ ⊻ ⚓(htd) 🛶

N7 S fr Montelimar on N7 N fr Orange, then D133
onto D541, dir Nyons for 17km. Grignan sp Camping
Municipal in vill. Sm, lge, hdg, mkd, pt shd, EHU (6A);
bbq; twin axles; bus; Eng spkn; adv bkg rec; CKE. *"10
min walk to town & Chateau and Saint Sauveur Church;
excel."* **€16.00, 20 Apr-17 Sep.** **2017**

GRILLON *9D2* (1.5km S Rural) *44.38307, 4.93046*
Camping Le Garrigon, Chemin de Visan, 84600 Grillon
**04 90 28 72 94; contact@camping-garrigon.com;
www.camping-garrigon.com**

🐕 ⭐ 👫 wc ♨ ⚓ 🚿 ⊘ ✉ ♻ Ⴤ ⊻ ⚓ Ⴤ ⊻ nr 🏔 ⚓(htd)

A7, exit Montelmar-Sud, twds Gap. Take D541 then
Grillon cent & foll sp to site. 4*, Med, mkd, pt shd,
EHU (10A); bbq (elec, gas); 10% statics; Eng spkn;
adv bkg acc; ccard acc; games rm; CKE. *"Pleasant
site in attractive area; nice pool; updated san facs
(2015); level but some rough or uneven grnd; vg."*
€28.50, 14 Mar-13 Nov. **2016**

GRIMAUD *10F4* (6.8km E Coastal) *43.28205, 6.58614*
Camping de la Plage, 98 Route National, St Pons-les-
Mûres, 83310 Grimaud **04 94 56 31 15; campingplage
grimaud@wanadoo.fr; www.camping-de-la-plage.fr**

🐕 €2.20 ⭐ 👫 wc ♨ ⚓ 🚿 ⊘ ✉ ♻ MSP 🐾 ♻ Ⴤ ⚓ 🏔 ⚓ 🏖 sand

Fr St Maxine turn onto D559 sp to St Tropez; site
3km on L on both sides of rd (subway links both
parts). 3*, Lge, pt shd, EHU (4-16A) €4.70-14; gas; adv
bkg req; ccard acc; tennis; CKE. *"Pitches adj beach or in
shd woodland - some sm; site tired but lovely situation
& views compensate; clean facs, refurb 2015; cycle
tracks; site poss flooded after heavy rain; used every
yr for 44 yrs by one CC member (2011); conv for ferry
to St Tropez, rec as beautiful, helpful friendly efficient
staff."* **€40.00, 11 Apr-13 Oct.** **2019**

GRIMAUD *10F4* (7.3km E Coastal) *43.283754, 6.591659*
Camping Les Mures, 2721 route du Littoral 83310,
Grimaud **04 94 56 16 97 or 04 94 56 16 17 (mob);
info@camping-des-mures.com; www.camping-des-
mures.com**

🐕 €3 👫(htd) ♨ ⚓ 🚿 ⊘ ✉ MSP 🐾 Ⴤ ⚓ 🏔 ♻ ⚓ adj

Fr St Maxine take coast rd D559 twrds St Tropez.
Site on R after 5km. 4*, Lge, mkd, pt shd, pt sl, terr,
EHU 6-10A; bbq; twin axles; TV; 10% statics; phone;
bus adj; Eng spkn; adv bkg acc; games area; CCI.
*"Excel; gd access rds; site split both sides of rd; beach
pitches avail for extra cost; v friendly staff; gd rest;
ACSI acc."* **€59.00, 6 Apr-13 Oct.** **2019**

GUDAS *8G3* (2km S Rural) *42.99269, 1.67830*
Camping Mille Fleurs (Naturist), Le Tuillier, 09120
Gudas **05 61 60 77 56; info@camping-millefleurs.com;
www.camping-millefleurs.com**

🐕 €2.25 👫 wc ♨ ⚓ 🚿 ⊘ ✉ ♻ 🐾 Ⴤ ⊻ ⊕ ⚓

Do not use SatNav thro Dalou. App Foix on the N20
fr Toulouse foll sp Foix-Tarbes. Pass Camping du lac
on R, cont approx 2.2km, at traff lghts turn L sp D1
Laroque d'Olmes, Lieurac, l'Herm). Foll D1 for 6.5km
until junc D13 (Care req, sharp bend). Turn L sp Col
de Py, Mirepoix, cont past quarry, L fork (sp Gudas,
Varhilles). After 2km sp Millefleurs, le Tuilier, turn L
over bdge. Site in approx 2km bef Gudas.
1*, Sm, hdg, mkd, pt shd, pt sl, terr, EHU (6-10A)
€3.75; bbq; twin axles; phone; Eng spkn; adv bkg rec;
sauna; INF card req. *"Excel, scenic, beautiful, peaceful
site; lovely owners; gd pitches; 2 c'vans for hire; clean
facs; gd base Andorra, Toulouse & Carcassonne; great
touring base."* **€29.00, 1 Apr-1 Nov.** **2017**

GUEMENE PENFAO *2G4* (1km SE Rural) *47.62575,
-1.81857* **Flower Camping L'Hermitage,** 46 Ave du
Paradis, 44290 Guémené-Penfao **02 40 79 23 48;
camping.hermitage@wanadoo.fr; www.camping
lhermitage.com**

🐕 €2 👫 wc ♨ ⚓ 🚿 ⊘ ✉ MSP 🐾 Ⴤ ⊕ ⚓ Ⴤ nr 🏔 ♻ ⚓

On D775 fr cent of Guémené-Penfao, dir
Châteaubriant for 500m, turn R, site sp.
3*, Med, hdstg, mkd, pt shd, EHU (6A) €3.50; gas;
bbq; sw nr; TV; 20% statics; phone; Eng spkn; adv bkg
acc; jacuzzi; games rm; waterslide; bike hire; fishing
300m; tennis; canoeing; games area; CKE. *"Gd walking
in area; htd covrd pool adj; site not ready early ssn."*
€22.50, 1 Apr-15 Oct. **2017**

"Satellite navigation makes touring much easier"

Remember most sat navs don't know if you're
towing or in a larger vehicle – always use yours
alongside maps and site directions.

GUERANDE *2G3* (3km N Rural) *47.34954, -2.43170*
Camping La Fontaine, Kersavary, Route de St-Molf,
44350 Guérande **02 40 24 96 19 or 06 08 12 80 96
(mob); lafontaine.guerande@orange.fr;
www.camping-lafontaine.com**

🐕 €2 👫 wc ♨ ⚓ 🚿 ⊘ ✉ ♻ 🐾 Ⴤ ⊕ nr Ⴤ nr 🏔 ♻ ⚓(htd) 🛶

Fr Guérande take N774 N sp La Roche-Bernard; in 1
km, opp windmill, fork L onto D233 sp St-Molf; site
on L in 500m. 3*, Med, hdg, hdstg, mkd, pt shd, EHU
(6A) €4; bbq; twin axles; 10% statics; Eng spkn; adv
bkg rec; games area; CKE. *"Pleasant, peaceful site; lge
pitches; helpful staff; san facs clean & new (2015); gd."*
€24.00, 3 Apr-18 Oct. **2016**

GUERANDE 2G3 (7km W Coastal) 47.32856, -2.49907
Camping Les Chardons Bleus, Blvd de la Grande
Falaise, 44420 La Turballe **02 40 62 80 60; camping
leschardonsbleus@mairielaturballe.fr; www.camping-
laturballe.fr**

🛉 €2.55 ♦♦♦ ⊞ ▲ ♿ ⬛ ∥ 🍴 Ⳛ ⊕ ⅀ ⵣ Ⳓ ⊿ ♦ ⵣ(htd)
⬛ ⵣ sand adj

**Foll D99 to La Turballe. Site well sp fr town cent
along D92.** 3*, Lge, mkd, hdg, unshd, EHU (10A) inc
(poss rev pol, long lead poss req); gas; phone; Eng
spkn; ccard acc; CKE. *"Well-run, well-kept site in great
location; mv service pnt adj; warm welcome; gd, clean
san facs, poss stretched high ssn; ltd EHU when full;
variable opening dates, phone ahead to check early
ssn; nature reserve adj with bird life; superb beach adj,
pt naturist; walk along beach to pretty fishing port of
La Turballe with rests; vg modern facs & pool area;
pinewoods; gd kids club for younger children; on cycle
rte, excel."* **€23.00, 1 Mar-29 Sep, A46.** **2019**

"There aren't many sites open at this time of year"

If you're travelling outside peak season
remember to call ahead to check site opening
dates – even if the entry says 'open all year'.

GUERET 7A4 (10km S Rural) 46.10257, 1.83528
Camp Municipal Le Gué Levard, 5 Rue Gué Levard,
23000 La Chapelle-Taillefert **05 55 51 09 20 or
05 55 52 36 17 (Mairie); www.ot-gueret.fr**

🛉 ♦♦♦ ⊞ ▲ ♿ ⬛ ∥ ⅀ 🦋 Ⳓ

**Take junc 48 fr N145 sp Tulle/Bourganeuf (D33 thro
Guéret); S on D940 fr Guéret, turn off at site sp. Foll
sp thro vill, well sp.** 1*, Sm, hdstg, pt shd, sl, terr, EHU
(16A) €2.50; bbq (sep area); 20% statics; adv bkg acc;
fishing in Rv Gartempe; CKE. *"Attractive, peaceful,
well-kept site hidden away; vg san facs; site yourself,
warden calls 1900; all pitches sl so m'van levelling diff;
gd auberge in vill (clsd most of Jul & Aug); gd walking;
sports facs nr; phone ahead to check open LS; excel
little site."* **€11.00, 1 Apr-1 Nov.** **2016**

GUERET 7A4 (1.4km W Rural) 46.16387, 1.85882
Camp du Plan d'Eau de Courtille (formerly Municipal),
Rue Georges Aullon, 23000 Guéret **05 55 81 92 24**

🛉 ♦♦♦ ▲ ♿ ⬛ ∥ ⅀ 🍴 nr ⊕ nr ⵣ nr Ⳓ

**Fr W on N145 take D942 to town cent; then take
D914 W; take L turn bef lake sp; site in 1.5km along
lakeside rd with speed humps. Site sp.** 3*, Med, hdg,
mkd, pt shd, pt sl, EHU (10A) inc; bbq; sw; phone;
watersports; CKE. *"Pleasant scenery; well-managed
site; beach sand; narr ent to pitches; mkd walks nrby;
pool 1.5km; ramps needed for m'vans; bread delivered;
busy NH."* **€20.00, 1 Apr-30 Sep.** **2018**

GUIGNICOURT 3C4 (0.5km SE Urban) 49.43209,
3.97035 **Camping au Bord de l'Aisne (Formaly
Municipal),** 14b Rue des Godins, 02190 Guignicourt
**03 23 79 74 58; campingguignicourt@orange.fr;
www.camping-aisne-picardie.fr**

🛉 €1.70 ♦♦♦(htd) ⬛ ▲ ♿ ∥ ⅀ 🦋 Ⳛ 🍴 ⊕ nr ⵣ ⵣnr Ⳓ
ⵣ(covrd, htd)

**Exit A26 junc 14 onto D925 to Guignicourt; after
passing under rlway bdge cont on D925 for 800m;
then turn R at Peugeot g'ge down narr rd to site
(12% descent at ent & ramp). Site sp in vill on rv
bank.** 2*, Med, mkd, hdg, pt shd, EHU (6-10A) inc
(poss rev pol, poss long cable req); bbq; red long stay;
20% statics; phone; train 500m; Eng spkn; adv bkg
acc; ccard acc; fishing; CKE. *"Pretty, well-kept/run,
excel site in beautiful setting on banks of rv; v pretty &
quiet; popular gd NH, conv A26; well-guarded; friendly,
v helpful staff; poss muddy when wet; pleasant town;
excel touring base Reims, Epernay; easy access despite
gradient; excel; v clean, refurbished & modern facs; facs
stretched in high ssn; fair."* **€31.00, 1 Apr-31 Oct, P02.** **2019**

GUILLESTRE 9D4 (1.8km SW Rural) 44.65854, 6.63836
Camping La Rochette (formerly Municipal), 05600
Guillestre **04 92 45 02 15 or 06 62 17 02 15 (mob);
guillestre@aol.com; www.campingguillestre.com**

🛉 ♦♦♦ ▲ ♿ ⬛ ∥ 🦋 Ⳛ ⵣ Ⳓ ♦

**Exot N94 onto D902A to Guillestre. In 1km fork R on
side rd at camp sps. Site on L in 1km.** 3*, Lge, mkd, pt
shd, EHU (6-10A) €2.80-3.70; gas; bbq; phone; adv bkg
acc; tennis adj; fishing; games area. *"Spectacular views;
lge pitches; Dutch-owned site; helpful staff; superb
san facs; dir access to rv; public pool adj; conv Queyras
National Park."* **€19.50, 15 May-30 Sep.** **2015**

GUILVINEC 2F2 (2.5km W Coastal) 47.80388,
-4.31222 **Camping la Plage,** Chemin des Allemands,
Penmarc'h, 29760 Guilvinec **02 98 58 61 90; info@
yellohvillage-la-plage.com; www.villagelaplage.com**

🛉 €6 ♦♦♦ ⬛ ▲ ♿ ⬛ ∥ 🦋 Ⳛ 🍴 ⊕ ⅀ ⵣ Ⳓ ♦
ⵣ(covrd, htd) ⬛ ⵣ sand adj

**Fr Quimper, Pont l'Abbé on D785 SW to Plomeur;
turn S onto D57 sp Guilvinec. Bear R on app to town
& v soon after turn R sp Chapelle de Tremor. Foll
site to site in 1.5km.** 4*, Lge, pt shd, EHU (5A) inc;
gas; bbq; 60% statics; adv bkg acc; ccard acc; sauna;
fitness rm; archery; tennis; games rm; waterslide; bike
hire. *"Ideal for families; spacious pitches; no o'fits over
8m high ssn; site rds poss diff lge o'fits; excel touring
base; mkt Tue & Sun."*
€50.00, 12 Apr-14 Sep, B15. **2019**

GUINES *3A3* (1km SW Rural) *50.86611, 1.85694*
Camping De La Bien Assise, Route D231 62340
Guînes 03 21 35 20 77; castels@bien-assise.com;
www.camping-la-bien-assise.com

🐕 €3 ♿(htd) 🅆 ♨ ♿ 🚿 🌐 🍴 ⛺ 🍹 Ⓗ 🚲 🎱 🎢 ⚓
⛴(covrd, htd) 🛝

Fr Calais or Boulogne, leave A16 at junc 43; foll
D305 then D127 to Guines; cont to junc with D231;
turn R (across S of vill and cont to rndabt) site ent
on L. Fr S (A26 or D943), take D231 to Guines.
5*, Lge, mkd, hdg, pt shd, pt sl, EHU (10A) inc (poss
rev pol); gas; bbq (charcoal, gas); red long stay; twin
axles; TV; 20% statics; Eng spkn; adv bkg req; ccard
acc; bike hire; games rm; horseriding 3km; waterslide;
golf nr; tennis; CKE. *"Pleasant, busy, excel site in grnds
of chateau; well-kept & well-run; gd sized pitches
with easy access; conv ferries - late arr area; pleasant,
cheerful, helpful staff; clean san facs, stretched when
site full; excel rest, clsd in Jan; vg pool complex;
grass pitches, some soft LS & boggy when wet; vet
in Ardres (9km), site will book for you; even if notice
says 'Complete' check for sh stay; mkt Fri; ACSI acc;
v popular NH stop; one san fac block newly refurb
(2016)."* **€36.20, 31 Mar-29 Sep, P05.** **2018**

GUISE *3C4* (0.5km SE Urban) *49.89488, 3.63372*
FFCC Camping de la Vallée de l'Oise, 33 Rue du
Camping, 02120 Guise 03 23 61 14 86

🐕 ♿♿ ♨ 🌐 🦋 🐾 nr 🎢 ⚓

Foll Vervin sp in town & camp clearly sp fr all dirs
in town. 3*, Lge, pt shd, EHU (6-10A) €5.50 (rev pol);
TV; 50% statics; Eng spkn; adv bkg acc; rv fishing adj;
bike hire; games rm; CKE. *"Spacious, beautifully kept,
friendly site; busy w/ends; gd san facs; barrier always
open, warden not always on site; canoe hire adj; if arr
late, pitch & pay next morning; interesting old town; gd
value."* **€19.00, 15 Apr-15 Oct.** **2018**

HAGUENAU *5D3* (2.6km SW Urban) *48.80233,
7.76439* **Camp Municipal Les Pins,** 20 Rue de la
Piscine, 67500 Haguenau 03 88 73 91 43 or
03 88 93 70 00; tourisme@ville-haguenau.fr;
www.ville-haguenau.fr

🐕 €1 ♿♿(htd) 🅆 ♨ ♿ 🌐 🦋 🍴 nr Ⓗ nr 🐾 nr 🎢

Fr S on D263, after passing Haguenau town sp turn
L at 2nd set of traff lts (opp Peugeot g'ge). Site sp
fr D263. 1*, Med, mkd, pt shd, tent, EHU (6A) inc; gas;
bbq; phone; bus 500m; Eng spkn; adv bkg acc; CKE. *"Lge
pitches; helpful staff; clean, modern san facs; meals avail
fr warden; grnd firm even after heavy rain; excel; pleasant
town."* **€13.00, 1 May-30 Sep.** **2016**

**"That's changed – Should I let
the Club know?"**

If you find something on site that's different
from the site entry, fill in a report and let us
know. See camc.com/europereport.

HAMBYE *1D4* (1.6km N Rural) *48.9600, -1.2600*
Camping aux Champs, 1 Rue de la Ripaudière, 50450
Hambye 02 33 90 06 98; michael.coles@wanadoo.fr;
www.campingauxchamps.com

🐕 ♿♿(htd) 🅆 ♨ 🌐 🦋 🐾 🍴 nr Ⓗ nr 🐾 nr

Exit A84 junc 38 onto D999 to Percy; then turn L
at town cent rndabt onto D58 to Hambye; at mkt
sq proceed to junc, strt sp Le Guislain, past Mairie;
site on R in 1.5 km on D51. Sm, hdstg, unshd, EHU
(10A) €3; red long stay; Eng spkn; adv bkg req; CKE.
*"Peaceful, well kept CL-type site; friendly, helpful
British owners; adults only; excel, clean san facs;
Hambye Abbey nrby; bell foundry at Villedieu-les-Poêls
worth visit; 1 dog only; conv ferry ports; a must if in
Normandy."* **€20.00, 1 Apr-30 Oct.** **2019**

**"I like to fill in the reports as I
travel from site to site"**

You'll find report forms at the back of this
guide, or you can fill them in online at
camc.com/europereport.

HARDELOT PLAGE *3A2* (3km NE Urban) *50.64661,
1.62539* **Caravaning du Château d'Hardelot,**
21 Rue Nouvelle, 62360 Condette 03 21 87 59 59;
contact@camping-caravaning-du-chateau.com;
www.camping-caravaning-du-chateau.com

🐕 ♿♿ ♨ ♿ 🌐 🅿 🦋 🍴 nr 🎢 ⚓ 🏖 sand 3km

Take D901 S fr Boulogne, R turn onto D940 dir Le
Touquet; then R at rndabt on D113 to Condette;
take 2nd turning to Château Camping, R at next
rndabt & site 400m on R. Fr S leave A16 at exit 27
to Neufchâtel-Hardelot, take D940 twd Condette &
turn L at 1st rndabt onto D113, then as above. Not
well sp last 3km. Tight turn into site ent.
3*, Med, hdg, mkd, pt shd, pt sl, EHU (10A) €4.70 (poss
rev pol); 30% statics; Eng spkn; adv bkg rec; horseriding;
games rm; tennis 500m; golf; CKE. *"Lovely, well-run,
wooded site; busy high ssn; vg LS; sm pitches; helpful,
friendly owners; sm multi-gym; clean, modern san facs;
tight access some pitches; conv Calais (site barrier opens
0800)."* **€28.60, 1 Apr-31 Oct.** **2016**

HARDINGHEN *3A3* (0.5km SE Rural) *50.79462,
1.81369* **Camping à la Ferme Les Piloteries,**
Rue de l'Eglise, 62132 Hardinghen 03 21 85 01 85;
lespiloteries@free.fr; http://lespiloteries.free.fr

♿♿ 🅆 ♨ 🌐 🦋 🎢

Fr N exit A16 junc 36 at Marquise onto D191 to
Hardinghen; turn R onto D127 (where D191 turns
sharp L); site in 1km (concealed ent). Sm, pt shd, pt
sl, EHU (6A) €2; bbq. *"Vg CL-type site; friendly owner;
lovely site; well looked after; rec; narr ent; gd NH."*
€11.00, 16 Apr-2 Oct. **2017**

HAUTEFORT 7C3 (3km NE Rural) 45.27248, 1.16861
Camping Belle Vue, La Contie 24390 Boisseuilh **05 53 51 62 71** or 0117 230 2320 (fr UK); cbv@dordogne-camping.org; www.dordogne-camping.org

🐕 €2 ♨ 🅦 ♨ ♿ ∅ ✉ 💆 ♈ Ⴤ ① 🎱 ⛵

Fr Limoges take D704 and cont until St Agnan. Take turning for Hautefort and pass supmkt on L and the Chateau on R. At next x-rds turn L onto D72 and cont over 3 bdges until La Contie. Site is last hse on R. Sm, shd, EHU (6A); bbq; twin axles; 25% statics; Eng spkn; adv bkg acc; CKE. *"Beautiful views of chateau Hautefort, illuminated at night; excel customer svrs; breakfast delivered to pitch each morning; excel."* €23.00, 1 May-30 Sep. **2017**

HAUTEFORT 7C3 (4km NE Rural) 45.28081, 1.15917
Camping La Grenouille, Brégérac, 24390 Hautefort **05 53 50 11 71**; info@lagrenouillevacances.com; www.lagrenouillevacances.com

🐕 ♈ ♨ 🅦 ♨ ∅ 💆 ① 🎱 ⛰ ⛵

Fr N on D704 at Cherveil-Cubas take D77 dir Boisseuilh/Teillots. In 4km turn R & in 800m turn L to site. Fr S on D704 at St Agnan take D62 sp Hautefort/Badefols d'Ans. Pass 'Vival' (sm shop on L) in Hautefort & turn L dir Boisseuilh. After 1st bdge turn L to La Besse & site in 2km. Sm, pt shd, pt sl, EHU (8A) €3.50; bbq; Eng spkn; adv bkg acc; ice; CKE. *"Tranquil, scenic, well-kept CL type site; friendly, helpful, Dutch owners; vg san facs; meals avail; goats, guinea pigs, chickens in pens on site; gd walking; dogs free; highly rec."* €21.50, 22 Apr-15 Oct. **2016**

"We must tell the Club about that great site we found"

Get your site reports in by mid-August and we'll do our best to get your updates into the next edition.

HAYE DU PUITS, LA 1D4 (6km N Urban) 49.38725, -1.52755 **FFCC Camp Municipal du Vieux Château,** Ave de la Division-Leclerc, 50390 St Sauveur-le-Vicomte **02 33 41 79 06**; basedeloisirs@sslv.fr; www.ville-saint-sauveur-le-vicomte.fr

🐕 €1.50 ♈ ♨ ♿ ∅ 💆 ① Ⴤ ⛰

Fr Cherbourg on N13/D2 site on R after x-ing bdge at St Sauveur-le-Vicomte, sp. 2*, Med, mkd, pt shd, pt sl, EHU (10A) €2.40 (poss rev pol); bbq; TV; phone; adv bkg acc; ccard acc; games area; games rm; tennis 1km; CKE. *"Excel site in chateau grnds; friendly warden; gd clean facs; ideal 1st stop fr Cherbourg; office open until 2200 for late arr; barrier clsd 2200-0800; vg auberge opp; helpful warden; Eng not spkn; sh walk to friendly, nice town."* €14.00, 15 May-17 Sep. **2017**

HAYE DU PUITS, LA 1D4 (3km SW Rural) 49.27292, -1.55896 **Camping La Bucaille,** 50250 Montgardon **02 33 07 46 38**; info@labucaille.com; www.labucaille.com

🐕 ♈ 🅦 ♨ ♿ ∅ 💆 ♈ Ⴤ nr ① nr Ⴤ nr 🏖 sand 4km

Fr Cherbourg S on N13 & D2 twd St Sauveur-le-Vicomte, then D900 to La Haye-du-Puits. Fr cent of La Haye turn onto D136 Rte de Bretteville-sur-Ay for approx 2km, site sp at L turn, site on L. Sm, pt shd, pt sl, EHU (10A) €5; bbq; adv bkg acc. *"Pleasant quiet, 'hide-way' CL-type site; lge grassy pitches; width restriction 3m; friendly British owners; ideal for walking; dogs free; excel; peaceful, well kept with super hosts."* €17.00, 1 Apr-30 Sep. **2016**

HERBIGNAC 2G3 (0.3km E Rural) 47.44802, -2.31073 **Camp Le Ranrouet,** 7 Allee des Pres Blancs, 44410 Herbignac **02 40 15 57 56**; campingleranrouet@orange.fr; www.camping-parc-de-la-briere.com

♈ 🅦 ♨ ∅ 💆 Ⴤ nr ① nr Ⴤ nr ✿ ⛵ (htd)

Site at intersection D774 & D33 on E edge of vill. 3*, Med, mkd, pt shd, EHU (6A); TV; CKE. *"Immac san facs; gd cent for Guérande."* €18.00, Easter-30 Oct. **2019**

HERIC 2G4 (2km W Rural) 47.41329, -1.67050 **Camping La Pindière,** La Denais, Route de la Fay-de-Bretagne, 44810 Héric **06 63 78 57 44**; contact@camping-la-pindiere.com; www.camping-la-pindiere.com

12 🐕 €1.40 ♈ 🅦 ♨ ♂ ♿ ∅ 💆 ♈ Ⴤ ① 🎱 Ⴤ ⛰ ⛵ (htd) 🛝

Exit N137 twd Héric at traff lts in town, leave town & turn W onto D16 (sp Camping). Site on L after rndabt supmkt, turn at sp Notre Dames-des-Landes. 3*, Med, hdg, mkd, hdstg, pt shd, EHU (6-10A) €3.20-4.80; gas; bbq (charcoal); twin axles; TV; 80% statics; phone; Eng spkn; adv bkg rec; ccard acc; sports facs; horseriding 200m; tennis; CKE. *"Pleasant site; lge, grass pitches, soft in wet weather; warm welcome; helpful owners; gd clean san facs; gd NH before St Malo; gd walks."* €22.50 **2019**

HERISSON 7A4 (0.8km WNW Rural) 46.51055, 2.70576 **Camp Municipal de l'Aumance,** Rue de Crochepot, 03190 Hérisson **04 70 06 88 22, 04 70 06 80 45** or 06 63 46 21 49 (mob); www.allier-tourisme.com

♈ ♨ ∅ ⛰

Exit A71 junc 9 onto D2144 N; turn R onto D11 dir Hérisson; immed bef T-junc with D3 turn L at blue sp (high on L) into Rue de Crochepot; site on R down hill. NB-Avoid towing thro town. 2*, Med, mkd, pt shd, EHU (6A) €2.80; phone; games area. *"Delightful rvside site; idyllic setting; old san facs but gd & clean; warden calls eves; rec; peaceful and picturesque; easy walk to vil; lovely site; sm gd supmkt & fuel at Vallons; rv fishing reserved for campers - permit necessary; remarkable value; site on 2 levels, higher level better in wet weather."* €8.00, 1 Apr-31 Oct. **2016**

HESDIN *3B3* (4km SE Rural) *50.35950, 2.07650*
Camping Rural St Ladre, 66 Rue Principale, 62770 St Georges **03 21 04 83 34; bd-martin@wanadoo.fr;** http://martinbernard.monsite-orange.fr

👪 wc 🚿 ⚲ 🦋 🚐

Fr Hesdin SE on D340 for 5.5km. Site on L after St Georges, ent narr lane next cottage on bend. Fr W on D939 or D349 foll sp Frévent, then St Georges. Sp to site poor. Sm, mkd, hdg, pt shd, EHU (5A) €2.40; adv bkg acc; CKE. *"Pleasant, peaceful, CL-type site in orchard; basic facs but clean; welcoming, pleasant owner; conv Channel ports, Agincourt & Crécy; usual agricultural noises; gd rests in Hesdin."*
€9.00, 1 May-30 Sep. 2017

HIRSON *3C4* (10km N Rural) *50.00585, 4.06195*
FFCC Camping Les Etangs des Moines, 100 rue des Etangs, 59610 Fourmies **03 27 63 05 26; contact@etangs-des-moines.fr**

🏠 €1 👪 wc 🚿 ⚲ 🔧 🍽 🍴 🚲 🛒 nr 🏔 🏊 (htd)

Fr D1043 Hirson by-pass head N on D963 to Anor. Turn L onto D156 dir Fourmies, site sp on R on ent town. Site also well sp off D42 & thro Fourmies. 3*, Med, hdg, hdstg, pt shd, EHU (10A) €3.30; bbq; 80% statics; Eng spkn; CKE. *"Textile & eco museum in town; shwrs run down, other facs gd; vg."*
€15.00, 1 Apr-31 Oct. 2019

HONFLEUR *3C1* (6km S Rural) *49.40083, 0.30638*
Camping Domaine Catinière, 910 Route de la Morelle, 27210 Fiquefleur-Equainville **02 32 57 63 51; info@camping-catiniere.com; www.camping-catiniere.com**

🏠 €2 👪 🚿 ⚲ 🔧 🛁 🍴 🍽 🚲 🏊 (htd)

Fr A29/Pont de Normandie (toll) bdge exit junc 3 sp Le Mans, pass under m'way onto D580/D180. In 3km go strt on at rndabt & in 100m bear R onto D22 dir Beuzeville; site sp on R in 500m. Do not app fr Beuzeville, c'vans not allowed in vill. 3*, Sm, hdg, mkd, pt shd, EHU (4A) inc or (8-13A) €1-1.50 (long lead poss req, poss rev pol); bbq; TV; 15% statics; Eng spkn; adv bkg rec; ccard acc; rv fishing; waterslide; games rm; CKE. *"Attractive, well-kept, busy site; pleasant, helpful, friendly owners; clean but dated unisex san facs, stretched high ssn & ltd LS; some pitches quite sm; unfenced stream on far boundary; gd touring base & NH; gd walks; easy parking for m'vans nr town; 20 mins to Le Havre ferry via Normandy bdge; no o'fits over 8.50m; conv A13; highly rec; lovely pool; ACSI acc."* **€32.00, 1 Apr-15 Oct, N16.** 2019

HONFLEUR *3C1 (3.5km SW Rural) 49.39777, 0.20861*
Camping La Briquerie, 14600 Equemauville **02 31 89 28 32; info@campinglabriquerie.com; www.camping labriquerie.com**

🐕 €3 🏕 ⓦ 🚿 ♿ 🔥 🛒 ⁄ 🏧 ♡ 🍽 🕀 🚮 ⓩnr ⚠ ✎

🏊 (htd) 🏖 sand 2.5km

Fr Honfleur head S on D579A. At rndabt cont strt onto D62, site on R. Fr S take D579 dir Honfleur Cent. Pass water tower n turn L at Intermarché rndabt, site on R in 300m. 5*, Lge, hdg, pt shd, EHU (5-10A) €4-5 (poss rev pol); gas; bbq; TV; 50% statics; bus nr; Eng spkn; adv bkg req; games rm; tennis 500m; horseriding 500m; fitness rm; waterslide; CKE. *"Lge pitches; staff helpful; gd clean san facs; late/early ferry arr; local vets geared up for dog inspections, etc; gd; cash only."* **€34.70, 1 Apr-30 Sep.** **2016**

HONFLEUR *3C1 (1km NW Coastal) 49.42445, 0.22753*
Camping du Phare, Blvd Charles V, 14600 Honfleur 02 98 83 45 06; camping.du.phare@orange.fr; www.camping-du-phare.com

🐕 €3 🏕 ⓦ 🚿 ♿ ⁄ 🏧 🍽 🕀 nr 🚮 ⓩnr ⚠ 🏖 sand 100m

Fr N fr Pont de Normandie on D929 take D144; at ent to Honfleur keep harbour in R; turn R onto D513 sp Trouville-sur-Mer & Deauville (avoid town cent); fork L past old lighthouse to site entry thro parking area. Or fr E on D180; foll sp 'Cent Ville' then Vieux Bassin dir Trouville; at rectangular rndabt with fountain turn R sp Deauville & Trouville, then as above. 2*, Med, hdg, pt shd, EHU (16A) inc; gas; bbq; 10% statics; phone; Eng spkn; fishing; CKE. *"Gd clean site in excel location; conv NH Le Havre ferry; busy high ssn, rec arr early; friendly owners; san facs basic & tired but clean, ltd LS; barrier clsd 2200-0700; m'van pitches narr & adj busy rd; some soft, sandy pitches; easy walk to town/harbour; sep m'van Aire de Service nr harbour; new disabled san facs (2015); conv Honfleur by foot; nice site; own san facs rec."* **€23.00, 1 Apr-30 Sep.** **2017**

HOULGATE *3D1 (1km E Coastal) 49.29390, -0.06820* **Camping La Vallée,** 88 Rue de la Vallée, 14510 Houlgate **02 31 24 40 69; camping.lavallee@ wanadoo.fr; www.campinglavallee.com**

🐕 €5 🏕 (htd) ⓦ 🚿 ♿ ⁄ 🏧 🍽 🕀 🚮 ⚠ ✎

🏊 (covrd, htd) 🚣 🏖 sand 900m

Exit junc 29 or 29a fr A13 onto D45 to Houlgate. Or fr Deauville take D513 W. Bef Houlgate sp, turn L & foll sp to site. 5*, Lge, mkd, hdg, pt shd, pt sl, terr, serviced pitches; EHU (6A) inc; gas; TV; 85% statics; Eng spkn; adv bkg req; ccard acc; games rm; bike hire; waterslide; lake fishing 2km; tennis; golf 1km; CKE. *"Superb, busy site; friendly recep; clean san facs; some pitches poss sm for lge o'fits; sep area m'vans; 1,5km walk to sandy beach and town; bkg fee; ACSI acc; fam/child orientated site."* **€47.00, 1 Apr-1 Nov.** **2019**

See advertisement opposite

HOURTIN *7C1 (10km W Coastal) 45.22296, -1.16472*
Camping La Côte d'Argent, Rue de la Côte d'Argent, 33990 Hourtin-Plage 05 56 09 10 25; info@cca33.com; www.cca33.com

🐕 €5.50 🏕 ⓦ 🚿 ♿ 🔥 🛒 ⁄ 🏧 🦋 ♡ 🍽 🕀 🚮 ⓩnr ⚠ ✎

🏊 (covrd, htd) 🏖 sand 300m

On D1215 at Lesparre-Médoc take D3 Hourtin, D101 to Hourtin-Plage, site sp. 4*, V lge, mkd, shd, pt sl, terr, EHU (10A) inc; bbq; sw nr; red long stay; 30% statics; phone; Eng spkn; adv bkg acc; ccard acc; bike hire; watersports; horseriding; fishing 4km; games area; ice; waterslide; games rm; jacuzzi; CKE. *"Pleasant, peaceful site in pine trees & dunes; poss steel pegs req; conv Médoc region chateaux & vineyards; ideal for surfers & beach lovers."* **€53.00, 14 May-18 Sep.** **2017**

See advertisement on next page

HUELGOAT *2E2 (3km E Rural) 48.36275, -3.71532*
FFCC Camping La Rivière d'Argent, La Coudraie, 29690 Huelgoat 02 98 99 72 50; campriviere@ orange.fr; www.larivieredargent.com

🐕 €1.60 🏕 ⓦ 🚿 ⁄ 🏧 🦋 🕀 🚮 ⓩnr ⚠ 🏊 (htd, indoor)

Sp fr town cent on D769A sp Poullaouen & Carhaix. 2*, Med, mkd, hdg, shd, EHU (6-10A) €3.60-4.30; red long stay; adv bkg acc; tennis. *"Lovely wooded site on rv bank; some rvside pitches; gd walks with maps provided; san facs updated (2017) well maintained, v clean; site self; poss rev pol; excel dog walks fr site; v friendly & helpful new owners (2018); excel."* **€26.00, 1 Apr-30 Sep.** **2018**

HYERES *10F3 (9km S Coastal) 43.02980, 6.15490*
Camping La Tour Fondue, Ave des Arbanais, 83400 Giens 04 94 58 22 86; info@camping-latourfondue.com; www.camping-latourfondue.com

🐕 €3 🏕 ⓦ 🚿 ⁄ 🏧 🍽 🕀 🚮 ✎ 🏊 adj

D97 fr Hyères, site sp. Med, hdg, pt shd, pt sl, terr, EHU (6A) €4.70; 10% statics; Eng spkn; adv bkg acc; ccard acc; games area. *"Pleasant, sister site of Camping Presqu'île de Giens with easier access; sm pitches; no dogs on beach; only water point at 'Sanitaires' (by recep); superb new san facs (2014)."* **€36.00, 23 Mar-3 Nov.** **2019**

ILE BOUCHARD, L' *4H1 (0.5km N Urban) 47.12166, 0.42857* **Camping Les Bords de Vienne,** 4 Allée du Camping, 37220 L'Ile-Bouchard **02 47 95 23 59; info@campingbordsdevienne.com; www.camping bordsdevienne.com**

🐕 €1.50 🏕 ⓦ 🚿 ⁄ 🦋 🕀 🚮 ⓩnr ⚠ 🏊

On N bank of Rv Vienne 100m E of rd bdge nr junc of D757 & D760. Fr E, turn L bet supmkt & pharmacy. 3*, Med, mkd, pt shd, pt sl, EHU (6-16A) €3.50; gas; sw nr; red long stay; 10% statics; Eng spkn; adv bkg acc; ccard acc; tennis 500m; CKE. *"Lovely, clean rvside site; attractive location; poss travellers; conv Loire chateaux."* **€28.00, 15 Mar-25 Oct.** **2019**

FRANCE

Camping Caravaning La Côte d'Argent ★★★★★

- Situated 300 m from the beach and 4 km from the largest natural lake in France.
- 5000m² of water park, fully heated.
- Over 100km of bike paths from the campsite.

33990 HOURTIN-PLAGE - **Tél : +33 (0)5 56 09 10 25** - info@cca33.com
www.camping-cote-dargent.com

Airotel

ILLIERS COMBRAY *4E2* (2km SW Rural) *48.28667, 1.22697* **FLOWER Camping Le Bois Fleuri,** Route de Brou, 28120 Illiers-Combray **02 37 24 03 04; infos@ camping-chartres.com; www.camping-chartres.com or www.flowercampings.com**

🛖 €4 ♦♦ (htd) 🆆🅆 🏊 🕭 ⚽ 🌊 🦋 ⴹ ⑪ nr ⴰ 🛒 nr 🏔 🚿 🎣

S on D921 fr Illiers for 2km twd Brou. Site on L. 3*, Med, hdg, hdstg, pt shd, serviced pitches; EHU (6A) €3.50; gas; 30% statics; adv bkg acc; fishing adj; games area; CKE. *"Many pitches wooded & with flowers; popular NH; excel san facs; ltd water/EHU; htd pool 200m; uneven grnd makes access diff; gd security; excel cycle path to vill."* €23.00, 1 Apr-31 Oct.   2018

"I need an on-site restaurant"

We do our best to make sure site information is correct, but it is always best to check any must-have facilities are still available or will be open during your visit.

INGRANDES *4H2* (1km N Rural) *46.88700, 0.58800* **Camping Le Petit Trianon de St Ustre,** 1 Rue du Moulin de St Ustre, 86220 Ingrandes-sur-Vienne **05 49 02 61 47; contact@domaine-petit-trianon.com; www.petit-trianon.com**

🛖 €3 ♦♦ 🆆🅆 🏊 🕭 🕭 🕭 🌊 🦋 ⑪ 🛒 🏔 🚿 🎣 (htd) 🎣

Leave A10/E5 at Châtellerault Nord exit 26 & foll sp Tours. Cross rv heading N on D910 twd Tours & Dangé-St Romain. At 2nd traff lts in Ingrandes (by church), turn R. Cross rlwy line & turn L at site sp in 300m. After 1.5km turn R at site sp, site at top of hill. NB Site ent narr, poss diff lge o'fits. 4*, Med, mkd, pt shd, pt sl, EHU (10A) inc; gas; bbq; TV; Eng spkn; adv bkg acc; ccard acc; horseriding 1km; rv fishing 3km; games rm; tennis 1.5km; bike hire; games area; CKE. *"Lovely site in chateau grnds; charming old buildings; gd sized pitches; friendly, helpful staff; excel facs."* €38.85, 6 Apr-24 Sep, L07.   2019

ISLE JOURDAIN, L' *8F3* (0.5km NW Urban) *43.61569, 1.07839* **Camping Municipal du Pont Tourné,** 32600 L'Isle Jourdain **05 62 07 25 44**

🛖 🐕 ♦♦ 🆆🅆 🏊 🌊 🦋

Exit N124 to town cent. Site well sp. Med, mkd, shd, EHU (10A); bbq; adv bkg acc; CCI. *"Sports ctr adj to site; shop nr; vg; security barrier; excel Sat mkt; wifi avail at TO; vg walking & cycling; lakes next to site; v relaxing; hg rec."* €12.80, 6 Jul-1 Sep.   2017

FRANCE

ISLE SUR LA SORGUE, L' *10E2* (6.5km E Rural)
43.91087, 5.10665 **Camping La Coutelière,** Route de
Fontaine-de-Vaucluse, 84800 Lagnes **04 90 20 33 97;**
info@camping-lacouteliere.com; www.camping-la
couteliere.com

🏕 €4.50 ⊞ ♨ & 🖳 🗐 🛒 ⊤ ⑭ ♨ 🗚 🖋 🛶

Leave L'Isle-sur-la-Sorgue by D900 dir Apt, fork L
after 2km sp Fontaine-de-Vaucluse. Site on L on D24
bef ent Fontaine. 3*, Med, hdg, shd, EHU (10A) €4.40;
40% statics; phone; Eng spkn; adv bkg acc; canoeing
nr; tennis; CKE. *"Attractive, busy site by rv; walking/
cycling on canal towpath; 2km easy cycle ride to
Fontaine; ltd san facs LS; poss unkept LS; lovely area;
gd."* **€32.00, 1 Apr-10 Oct.** **2015**

ISLE SUR LE DOUBS, L' *6G2* (0.4km N Rural)
47.45288, 6.58338 **Camping Les Lûmes,** 10 Rue des
Lûmes, 25250 L'Isle-sur-le-Doubs **03 81 92 73 05 or
06 85 42 97 81;** contact@les-lumes.com; www.les-
lumes.com

🏕 €1.20 ⊞ ♨ 🖳 🗗 🗚

Well sp fr town edge on D683 bef rv bdge.
3*, Med, pt shd, EHU (10A) €4 (long lead req & poss
rev pol; sw; 20% statics; Eng spkn; adv bkg acc; CKE.
"Busy site; san facs need upgrade & up steps; gd."
€13.50, 1 May-30 Sep. **2018**

ISPAGNAC *9D1* (1km W Rural) *44.37232, 3.53035*
FFCC Camp Municipal Le Pré Morjal, 48320 Ispagnac
04 66 45 43 57; lepremorjal@gmail.com;
www.campingdupremorjal.com

🏕 €1.20 ⊞ (htd) ⊞ ♨ ↨ & 🖳 🗗 🛒 ⑭ ♨ 🗚 nr 🗚 🖳

On D907B 500m W of town, turn L off D907B
& then 200m on R, sp. 3*, Med, hdg, pt shd, EHU
(10-16A) €3; bbq; sw nr; TV; games area; games rm.
*"Lovely family site; gd sized pitches on rocky base,
poss muddy when wet; pool 50m inc; friendly staff; gd
rvside walks; vg base for Tarn & Joute Gorges; early
ssn poss unkempt & irreg cleaning of san facs (2010)."*
€23.50, 1 Apr-31 Oct. **2019**

ISSOIRE *9B1* (3km E Rural) *45.55113, 3.27423*
FFCC Camp Municipal du Mas, Ave du Dr Bienfait,
63500 Issoire **04 73 89 03 59 or 04 73 89 03 54 (LS);**
camping-mas@wanadoo.fr; www.camping-
issoire.com

🏕 €0.50 ⊞ (htd) ⊞ ♨ ↨ & 🖳 🗗 🛒 ⑭ ♨ nr 🗚

Fr Clermont-Ferrand S on A75/E11 take exit 12 sp
Issoire; turn L over a'route sp Orbeil; at rndabt, take
1st exit & foll site sp. 3*, Med, unshd, EHU (10-13A)
€3.35 (long lead poss req); gas; red long stay; TV;
5% statics; phone; Eng spkn; adv bkg rec; ccard acc;
fishing adj; tennis 500m; CKE. *"Lovely, well-kept, basic
site in park-like location; lge pitches; helpful warden;
new, modern san facs; site poss boggy after rain;
conv A75; excel touring base or NH; easy cycle rte to
Issoire."* **€21.00, 1 Apr-5 Nov.** **2016**

ISSOUDUN *4H3* (3km N Rural) *46.96361, 1.99011*
Camp Municipal Les Taupeaux, 37 Route de Reuilly,
36100 Issoudun **02 54 03 13 46 or 02 54 21 74 02;**
tourisme@issoudun.fr; www.issoudun.fr

🏕 ⊞ ♨ 🖋 🛒 🗚

Fr Bourges SW on N151, site sp fr Issoudun on D16
nr Carrefour supmkt. Sm, hdg, mkd, pt shd, EHU
€3.70. *"Pleasant site off RR; mv service pnt adj; conv
A71 & N151."* **€11.00, 15 May-15 Sep.** **2016**

JARD SUR MER *7A1* (2km NE Rural) *46.42624,
-1.56564* **Camping La Mouette Cendrée,** Les Malécots,
85520 St Vincent-sur-Jard **02 51 33 59 04;**
camping.mc@orange.fr; www.mouettecendree.com

🏕 €3 ⊞ ⊞ & 🖳 🗗 🛒 ♨ nr 🗚 🖋 🛶 🖳 🏖 sand 2km

Fr Les Sables-d'Olonne take D949 SE to Talmont-
St-Hilaire; then take D21 to Jard-sur-Mer; at rndabt
stay on D21 (taking 2nd exit dir La Tranche-sur-Mer
& Maison de- Clemanceau); in 500m turn L onto
D19 sp St Hilaire-la-Forêt & foll site sps. Site on L in
700m. 3*, Med, hdg, mkd, pt shd, EHU (10A) inc; bbq
(elec, gas); 30% statics; Eng spkn; adv bkg acc; ccard
acc; golf 10km; waterslide; windsurfing 2km; fishing;
horseriding 500m; bike hire; games rm; CKE. *"Busy site
high ssn; gd pitches; welcoming, helpful owners; san
facs poss stretched when site full; no o'fits over 7.5m
high ssn; vg pool; gd woodland walks & cycle rtes nr;
mkt Mon."* **€27.50, 1 Apr-30 Sept, A20.** **2018**

JARD SUR MER *7A1* (2km SE Coastal) *46.41980,
-1.52580* **Camping La Bolée d'Air,** Route du Bouil,
Route de Longeville, 85520 St Vincent-sur-Jard
02 51 90 36 05 or 02 51 33 05 05; info@chadotel.com;
www.chadotel.com

🏕 €3.90 ⊞ (htd) ⊞ ♨ ↨ & 🖳 🗗 🛒 ⑭ ⊤ ♨ 🗚 🗚 🖋
🏖 (covrd, htd) 🖳 🏖 sand 900m

Fr A11 junc 14 dir Angers. Take N160 to La Roche-
sur-Yon & then D747 dir La Tranche-sur-Mer to
Moutier-les-Mauxfaits. At Moutiers take D19 to
St Hilaire-la-Forêt & then L to St Vincent-sur-Jard. In
St Vincent turn L by church sp Longeville-sur-Mer,
site on R in 1km. 4*, Lge, mkd, hdg, pt shd, serviced
pitches; EHU (10A) inc; gas; bbq (charcoal, gas); red
long stay; TV; 25% statics; Eng spkn; adv bkg acc;
ccard acc; sauna; bike hire; games rm; waterslide;
jacuzzi; tennis; CKE. *"Popular, v busy site high ssn; mkt
Sun; no o'fits over 8m; whirlpool; access some pitches
poss diff lge o'fits; excel."*
€39.00, 1 Apr-24 Sep, A31. **2018**

JAUNAY CLAN *4H1* (7km NE Rural) *46.72015, 0.45982* **Camping Lac de St Cyr,** 86130 St Cyr **05 49 62 57 22; contact@campinglacdesaintcyr.com; www.campinglacdesaintcyr.com**

🛖 €3 ♦♦♦ 🆆🅳 ⚓ 🖐 🗑 ∥ ᴹˢᴾ 🦋 🍴 ⑭ 🚲 🆉 🛝 ✎

Fr A10 take Châtellerault Sud exit & take D910 dir Poitiers; at Beaumont turn L at traff lts for St Cyr; foll camp sp in leisure complex (Parc Loisirs) by lakeside - R turn for camping. Or fr S take Futuroscope exit to D910. 4*, Lge, mkd, hdg, pt shd, pt sl, serviced pitches; EHU (10A) inc (poss rev pol); gas; bbq; sw; red long stay; TV; 15% statics; Eng spkn; adv bkg acc; ccard acc; games area; boat hire; golf adj; watersports; games rm; fishing; sailing; canoeing; tennis; fitness rm; bike hire; CKE. "*Excel, well-kept site in leisure complex; lovely setting by lake; gd sized pitches; helpful recep; no o'fits over 8m; gd, clean san facs, poss stretched high ssn; gd rest; some pitches poss diff lge o'fits; rec long o'fits unhitch at barrier due R-angle turn at barrier - poss diff long o'fits; Futuroscope approx 13km; highly rec; excel site; gd size pitches; friendly helpful staff.*"
€33.00, 30 Mar-30 Sep, L09. 2017

JAUNAY CLAN *4H1* (2km SE Urban) *46.66401, 0.39466* **Kawan Village Le Futuriste,** Rue du Château, 86130 St Georges-les-Baillargeaux **05 49 52 47 52; camping-le-futuriste@wanadoo.fr; www.camping-le-futuriste.fr**

12 🛖 €2.50 ♦♦♦ (htd) 🆆🅳 ⚓ 🖐 🗑 ∥ ᴹˢᴾ 🦋 🍴 ⑭ 🚲 🆉 🛝 ✎ 🏊 (covrd, htd)

On A10 fr N or S, take Futuroscope exit 28; fr toll booth at 1st rndabt take 2nd exit. Thro tech park twd St Georges. At rndabt under D910 take slip rd N onto D910. After 150m exit D910 onto D20, foll sp. At 1st rndabt bear R, over rlwy, cross sm rv & up hill, site on R. 4*, Med, mkd, hdg, pt shd, serviced pitches; EHU (6A) inc (check earth & poss rev pol); gas; bbq; TV; 10% statics; Eng spkn; adv bkg acc; ccard acc; games area; games rm; lake fishing; waterslide; CKE. "*Lovely, busy, secure site; well-kept; friendly, helpful family owners; vg clean facs, ltd LS - facs block clsd 2200-0700; vg pool; vg for families; hypmkt 2km; ideal touring base for Poitiers & Futuroscope (tickets fr recep); vg value, espec in winter; conv a'route; excel.*"
€33.00 2017

JAUNAY CLAN *4H1* (5km SE Rural) *46.65464, 0.37786* **Camp Municipal Parc des Ecluzelles,** Rue Leclanché, 86360 Chasseneuil-du-Poitou **05 49 62 58 85 or 05 49 52 77 19 (LS); maire@mairie-chasseneuildupoitou.fr; www.ville-chasseneuil-du-poitou.fr**

🛖 ♦♦♦ 🆆🅳 ⚓ 🖐 ∥ ᴹˢᴾ 🦋 🆉 nr 🛝

Fr A10 or D910 N or Poitiers take Futuroscope exit 28/18. Take Chasseneuil rd, sp in town to site. 2*, Sm, mkd, hdstg, pt shd, EHU (8A) inc; bbq. "*Vg, clean site; lge pitches; conv Futuroscope; immac; htd pool adj inc; v simple site with the vg san facs, helpful staff; gd bus service into the city.*"
€19.50, 11 Apr-27 Sep. 2015

JOIGNY *4F4* (2km W Rural) *47.98143, 3.37439* **FFCC Camp Municipal,** 68 Quai d'Epizy, 89300 Joigny **03 86 62 07 55; camping.joigny@orange.fr; www.ville-joigny.fr/index.php**

♦♦♦ 🆆🅳 ∥ ᴹˢᴾ 🦋 🍴 ⑭ nr 🆉 nr

Fr A6 exit junc 18 or 19 to Joigny cent. Fr cent, over brdg, turn L onto D959; turn L in filter lane at traff lts. Foll sp to site. 2*, Sm, hdg, hdstg, pt shd, EHU (10A) inc; sw nr; fishing adj; tennis; horseriding; CKE. "*V busy site; liable to flood in wet weather; v helpful warden; pool 4km; interesting town; v modern clean san facs; quiet in May; some sm pitches; v helpful warden; local wine avail to buy.*"
€13.40, 1 May-30 Sep. 2018

JONZAC *7B2* (4km SW Rural) *45.42916, -0.44833* **FFCC Camping Les Castors,** 8 Rue Clavelaud, St Simon de Bordes, 17500 Jonzac **05 46 48 25 65; camping-les-castors@wanadoo.fr; www.camping castors.com**

🛖 €1.60 ♦♦♦ 🆆🅳 ⚓ 🖐 🗑 ∥ ᴹˢᴾ 🦋 🍴 🍴 🛝 ✎ 🏊 (covrd)

Fr Jonzac take D19 S twds Montendre, after approx 2km, immed after ring rd rndabt, turn R into minor rd. Site ent adj. 4*, Med, hdg, hdstg, pt shd, EHU (6-10A) €4.20-4.90; sw nr; TV; 50% statics; CKE. "*Peaceful, friendly, well-maintained site; gd facs; excel pool; gd; ent & exit gate can be diff for c'vans.*"
€17.60, 15 Mar-30 Oct. 2015

"There aren't many sites open at this time of year"

If you're travelling outside peak season remember to call ahead to check site opening dates – even if the entry says 'open all year'.

JOSSELIN *2F3* (1.5km W Rural) *47.95230, -2.57338* **Domaine de Kerelly,** Le bas de la lande, 56120 Guégon **02 97 22 22 20 or 06 27 57 22 79 (mob); domainede kerelly@orange.fr; www.camping-josselin.com**

🛖 ♦♦♦ 🆆🅳 ⚓ 🖐 🗑 ∥ ᴹˢᴾ 🦋 🍴 ⑭ 🆉 nr 🛝 🏊

Exit N24 by-pass W of town sp Guégon; foll sp 1km; do not attempt to cross Josselin cent fr E to W. Site on D724 just S of Rv Oust (canal). 3*, Med, hdg, pt shd, terr, EHU (6-10A) €3.80-4.50; bbq; TV; phone; Eng spkn; adv bkg acc; ccard acc; bike hire; CKE. "*Vg, clean san facs; site rds steep; pleasant walks; poss diff if wet; walk to Josselin, chateau & old houses; gd cycling; family run; gd food; mini golf.*"
€20.00, 1 Apr-31 Oct. 2018

JUMIEGES *3C2* (1km E Rural) *49.43490, 0.82970*
Camping de la Forêt, Rue Mainberte, 76480 Jumièges
02 35 37 93 43; info@campinglaforet.com;
www.campinglaforet.com

🐕 🏕️(htd) 🔛 ♨ ⚲ ♿ 🅿 ✗ 🦋 ⛺ 🎣 ⑭nr ♨ 🥤 ⚠ 🛝(htd) 🚤

Exit A13 junc 25 onto D313/D490 N to Pont de
Brotonne. Cross Pont de Brotonne & immed turn R
onto D982 sp Le Trait. Cont thro town & in 1km turn
R onto D143 sp Yainville & Jumièges. In Jumièges
turn L at x-rds after cemetary & church, site on R
in 1km. NB M'vans under 3.5t & 3m height can take
ferry fr Port Jumièges - if towing do not use sat nav
dirs. 4*, Med, mkd, hdg, pt shd, EHU (10A) €5 (poss rev
pol); gas; bbq; TV; 30% statics; phone; bus to Rouen;
adv bkg acc; ccard acc; watersports; bike hire; games
rm; fishing; tennis; games area. *"Nice site, well-situated
in National Park; busy; some sm pitches; gd, clean san
facs but poss stretched high ssn; interesting vill; conv
Paris & Giverny; no o'fits over 7m high ssn; gd walking,
cycling; ferries across Rv Seine; gd for dogs; children
loved it."* **€29.00, 1 Apr-31 Oct, N15.**   **2017**

KAYSERSBERG *6F3* (7km NW Rural) *48.18148,
7.18449* **Camping Les Verts Bois,** 3 Rue de la Fonderie,
68240 Fréland 03 89 47 57 25 or 06 81 71 89 38 (mob);
gildas.douault@sfr.fr; www.camping-lesvertsbois.com

🐕 €0.70 🏕️(htd) 🔛 ♨ 🔥 ✗ 🦋 🍽 ⑭ ♨ 🥤nr

Sp off N415 Colmar/St Dié rd bet Lapoutroie &
Kaysersberg. Site approx 5km after turn fr main rd
on D11 at far end of vill. Turn L into rd to site when
D11 doubles back on itself. 2*, Sm, pt shd, pt sl, terr,
EHU (6-10A) €2.70-3.20; gas; bbq; Eng spkn; adv bkg
acc; ccard acc; CKE. *"Lovely site in beautiful, peaceful
setting adj rv; friendly welcome; excel; fishing & bird
watching; cheese farms 2 miles away; a must for
cheese lovers; v helpful owners; excel rest."*
€19.00, 1 Apr-31 Oct.   **2019**

KRUTH *6F3* (2km N Rural) *47.94355, 6.95418*
Camping du Schlossberg, 19 rue du Bourbach, 68820
Kruth 03 89 82 26 76; camping@schlossberg.fr;
www.schlossberg.fr

🐕 🏕️ 🔛 ♨ 🔥 ♿ ✗ 🅿 ♨ 🍽 🥤 ⚠

Fr N66 turn N on D13 for Fellering and Kruth.
Leaving Kruth twd Wildenstein, turn L at camping
sp. Foll rd round and turn R bef no entry sp.
3*, Lge, mkd, pt shd, pt sl, EHU (6A) €3; 20% statics;
phone; Eng spkn; adv bkg acc; games area; games
rm; CKE. *"Boules & quoytes on site; Go Ape 2km;
lake with peddleoes; walking; castle ruins; excel."*
€17.00, 1 Apr-7 Oct.   **2015**

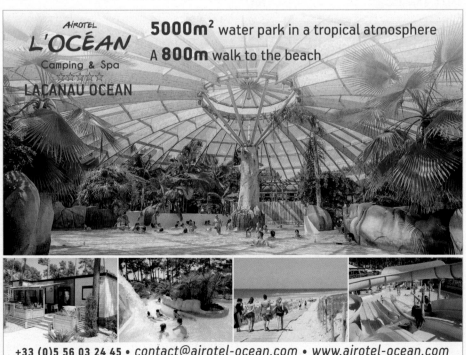

LABENNE *8E1* (4km S Rural) *43.56470, -1.45240*
Camping du Lac, 518 Rue de Janin, 40440 Ondres
05 59 45 28 45 or 06 80 26 91 51 (mob); contact@
camping-du-lac.fr; www.camping-du-lac.fr

🏕 €5 ⛺ (htd) ⬜ ♨ ♿ 🚿 ⊡ ∥ ⛐ 🍴 ⊕ 🎿 ♨ nr ⅏ 🏊 🏄

sand 4km

Fr N exit A63 junc 8 onto N10 S. Turn R just N of
Ondres sp Ondres-Plage, at rndabt turn L & foll site
sp. Fr S exit A63 junc 7 onto N10 to Ondres. Cont
thro town cent & turn L at town boundary, then as
above; tight turns thro housing est.
3*, Med, hdg, mkd, pt shd, terr, EHU (10A) €4; gas; red
long stay; 60% statics; phone; Eng spkn; adv bkg req;
bike hire; fishing; boating; games area; CKE. *"Peaceful,
charming lakeside site by lake; twin axles LS only; gd
welcome; helpful staff; ltd facs LS; vg pool; excel."*
€45.00, 21 Mar-2 Oct. **2017**

LABENNE *8E1* (3km SW Coastal) *43.59533, -1.45651*
Camping Le Sylvamar, Ave de l'Océan, 40440
Labenne 05 59 45 75 16; camping@sylvamar.fr;
www.sylvamar.fr or www.yellohvillage.co.uk

⛺ ⬜ ♨ ♿ 🚿 ⊡ ∥ ⛐ ♨ 🍴 ⊕ 🎿 ♨ nr ⅏ 🏄 ♨

sand 800m

Exit A63 junc 7 onto D85; then take N10 N to
Labenne; turn L onto D126; site sp. Lge, hdg, mkd, pt
shd, serviced pitches; EHU (10A) inc; bbq; 50% statics;
Eng spkn; adv bkg acc; ccard acc; waterslide; CKE.
*"Site amongst pine trees; sauna; spa; creche; sandy
pitches; fitness rm; beauty cent; gd location; vg facs."*
€43.00, 9 Apr-25 Sep. **2017**

"That's changed – Should I let the Club know?"

If you find something on site that's different
from the site entry, fill in a report and let us
know. See camc.com/europereport.

LACANAU OCEAN *7C1* (1km N Coastal) *45.00823,
-1.19322* **Airotel Camping de l'Océan,** 24 Rue du
Repos, 33680 Lacanau-Océan 05 56 03 24 45;
airotel.lacanau@wanadoo.fr; www.airotel-ocean.com

🏕 €4 ⛺ ⬜ ⊡ ∥ ⛐ 🍴 ⊕ 🎿 🏄 ♨ *sand 600m*

On ent town at end of sq in front of bus stn turn
R, fork R & foll sp to site (next to Camping Grand
Pins). 4*, Lge, pt shd, pt sl, EHU (15A) inc; gas; TV;
adv bkg acc; fishing; watersports; bike hire; tennis.
*"Attractive site/holiday vill in pine woods behind sand
dunes; surfing school nrby; care in choosing pitch due
soft sand; gd, modern san facs; some pitches tight
access."* **€33.00, Easter-27 Sep.** **2017**

See advertisement on previous page

LACANAU OCEAN *7C1* (5km SE Rural) *44.98620,
-1.13410* **Camping Le Tedey,** Par Le Moutchic, Route
de Longarisse, 33680 Lacanau-Océan 05 56 03 00 15;
camping@le-tedey.com; www.le-tedey.com

⛺ ⬜ ♨ ♿ 🚿 ⊡ ∥ ⛐ ♨ 🍴 ♨ ⅏ ♨

Fr Bordeaux take D6 to Lacanau & on twd
Lacanau-Océan. On exit Moutchic take L fork twd
Longarisse. Ent in 2km well sp on L. 3*, V lge, mkd,
shd, EHU (10A) €4.30; gas; sw nr; TV; 10% statics;
Eng spkn; adv bkg rec; ccard acc; bike hire; boating;
golf 5km; CKE. *"Peaceful, friendly, family-run site in
pine woods - avoid tree sap; golf nr; gd cycle tracks; no
EHU for pitches adj beach; access diff some pitches;
excel site."* **€35.60, 25 Apr-19 Sep.** **2019**

See advertisement opposite

LACAPELLE VIESCAMP *7C4* (1.6km SW Rural)
44.91272, 2.24853 **Camping La Presqu'île du Puech
des Ouilhes,** 15150 Lacapelle-Viescamp 04 71 46 42 38
or 06 80 37 15 61 (mob); contact@cantal-camping.fr;
www.camping-lac-auvergne.com

🏕 €2 ⛺ ⬜ ♨ ♿ 🚿 ⊡ ∥ ⛐ 🍴 ⊕ 🎿 ♨ nr ⅏ 🏄 ♨ *sand adj*

W fr Aurillac on D120; at St Paul-des-Landes turn
S onto D53 then D18 to Lacapelle-Viescamp. Foll
sp Base de Loisirs, Plage-du-Puech des Ouilhes &
Camping. Site beside Lake St Etienne-Cantalès.
3*, Med, hdstg, hdg, mkd, pt shd, EHU (16A) €3; sw nr;
10% statics; Eng spkn; fishing; canoeing; tennis; games
rm; watersports. *"Friendly, helpful young owners;
excel."* **€19.00, 15 Jun-15 Sep.** **2019**

LACAUNE *8E4* (6km E Rural) *43.69280, 2.73790*
Camping Domaine Le Clôt, Les Vidals, 81230 Lacaune
05 63 37 03 59; campingleclot@orange.fr;
www.pageloisirs.com/le-clot

🏕 €1.50 ⛺ (htd) ⬜ ♨ ♿ ⊡ ∥ ⛐ ⊕ 🎿 ♨ nr ⅏

Fr Castres to Lacaune on D622. Cont on D622 past
Lacaune then turn R onto unclassified rd to Les
Vidals. Site sp 500m on L after Les Vidals. 2*, Sm, pt
shd, terr, EHU (6-10A) €3.25-4; Eng spkn; CKE. *"Excel
site; modern, immac san facs; gd views; gd walking in
Monts de Lacaune; lake sw 12km; fishing 12km; sailing
12km; windsurfing 12km; friendly Dutch owner; site rd
steep & narr; vg rest."* **€22.00, 15 Apr-15 Oct.** **2016**

LAGRASSE *8F4* (0.7km N Rural) *43.09516, 2.61893*
Camp Municipal de Boucocers, Route de Ribaute,
11220 Lagrasse 04 68 43 10 05 or 04 68 43 15 18;
mairielagrasse@wanadoo.fr; www.audetourisme.com

🏕 €2.10 ⛺ ⬜ ♨ ♿ ∥ ⛐ ⊕ nr ♨ nr

1km on D212 fr Lagrasse to Fabrezan (N).
1*, Sm, hdstg, pt shd, pt sl, EHU (15A) €2.80; sw nr;
phone; adv bkg acc; CKE. *"At cent of 'off-the-beaten-
track' beautiful touring area; helpful warden; simple but
gd san facs; gd walking; path down to lagrasse cent;
o'looks superb medieval town; rec arr early; hillside
walk into vill needs care; site run down at then of ssn;
no entry barrier, site self, pay when warden calls; excel,
well kept site; Lagrasse Abbey & town worth a visit."*
€15.00, 15 Mar-15 Oct. **2018**

For a guide to symbols see the fold out on the rear cover

LAGUEPIE *8E4* (1km E Rural) *44.14780, 1.97892*
Camp Municipal Les Tilleuls, 82250 Laguépie
05 63 30 22 32 or 05 63 30 20 81 (Mairie); camping.
lestilleuls0837@orange.fr; www.camping-les-
tilleuls.com

🐕 🏕 ⚓ ⚐ 🚿 ♿ / ⚑ 🦋 ∀ nr ♨ nr ⚠

**Exit Cordes on D922 N to Laguépie; turn R at bdge,
still on D922 sp Villefranche; site sp to R in 500m;
tight turn into narr lane. NB App thro Laguépie poss
diff lge o'fits.** Med, pt shd, terr, EHU (10A) €2.70; sw;
TV; 44% statics; phone; adv bkg acc; canoe hire; fishing;
tennis; games area. *"Attractive setting on Rv Viaur;
friendly welcome; excel playgrnd; gd touring base; conv
Aveyron gorges."* **€14.00, May-Oct.** **2018**

LAGUIOLE *7D4* (0.5km NE Rural) *44.68158, 2.85440*
Camp Municipal Les Monts D'Aubrac, 12210 Laguiole
05 65 44 39 72 or 05 65 51 26 30 (LS);
http://campinglesmontsdaubraclaguiole.jimdo.com

🐕 🏕 WD ⚓ ⚐ / MSF 🦋 ∀ nr ♨ nr ⚐ nr

**E of Laguiole on D15 at top of hill. Fr S on D921 turn
R at rndabt bef ent to town. Site sp.**
Med, hdg, mkd, pt shd, pt sl, EHU (16A) inc; phone;
CKE. *"Clean & well cared for site; pleasant vill."*
€19.00, 15 May-15 Sep. **2019**

LAISSAC *7D4* (3km SE Rural) *44.36525, 2.85090*
FLOWER Camping La Grange de Monteillac,
Chemin de Monteillac, 12310 Sévérac-l'Eglise
05 65 70 21 00 or 06 87 46 90 83 (mob); info@
le-grange-de-monteillac.com; www.la-grange-de-
monteillac.com or www.flowercampings.com

🐕 €1.50 🏕 WD ⚓ ⚐ 🚿 ♿ / ⚑ 🦋 ∀ ♨ ⚠ ⚐ 🏊 🛶

**Fr A75, at junc 42, go W on N88 twds Rodez; after
approx 22km; bef Laissac; turn L twds Sévérac-
l'Eglise; site sp.** 4*, Med, hdg, mkd, unshd, pt sl, terr,
EHU (6A) inc (long lead poss req); TV; 10% statics;
phone; Eng spkn; adv bkg rec; bike hire; tennis;
horseriding; CKE. *"Beautiful, excel site; bar & shops
high ssn."* **€41.00, 24 May-15 Sep.** **2019**

LALLEY *9D3* (0.3km S Rural) *44.75490, 5.67940*
Camping Belle Roche, Chemin de Combe Morée,
38930 Lalley 04 76 34 75 33; contact@campingbelle
roche.com; www.campingbelleroche.com

🐕 €1.50 🏕 WD ⚓ ⚐ 🚿 ♿ / MSF 🦋 ∀ ∀ nr ♨ ⚠ ⚐ 🏊 (htd)

**Off D1075 at D66 for Mens; down long hill into
Lalley. Site on R thro vill.** 3*, Med, hdstg, hdg, pt
shd, pt sl, EHU (10A) €4 (poss rev pol, poss long lead
req); gas; bbq; TV; 10% statics; adv bkg acc; ccard
acc; games area; tennis 500m; CKE. *"Well-kept, scenic
site; spacious pitches but little shd; friendly, welcoming
owners; clean, vg modern san facs, poss stretched high
ssn; pleasant pool area; nr Vercors National Park; vg
walking/cycling; don't miss The Little Train of La Mure;
conv NH; v nice site; highly rec superb in every way."*
€29.50, 31 Mar-14 Oct. **2019**

> ## "I like to fill in the reports as I travel from site to site"
>
> You'll find report forms at the back of this guide, or you can fill them in online at camc.com/europereport.

LAMALOU LES BAINS *10F1* (2km SE Rural) *43.57631,
3.06842* **Camping Domaine de Gatinié,** Route de
Gatinié, 34600 Les Aires 04 67 95 71 95 or 04 67 28
41 69 (LS); gatinie@wanadoo.fr; www.domaine
gatinie.com

🐕 €2 🏕 WD ⚓ ⚐ 🚿 ♿ / 🦋 ∀ ♨ ⚠ ⚐ 🏊 🛶

**Fr D908 fr Lamalou-les-Bains or Hérépian dir Poujol-
sur-Orb, site sp. Fr D160 cross rv to D908 then as
above.** 3*, Med, hdg, mkd, pt shd, pt sl, EHU (6A) inc;
bbq; sw nr; red long stay; 10% statics; Eng spkn; adv
bkg acc; fishing; horseriding 2km; tennis 2km;
canoeing; games area; golf 2km; CKE. *"Beautiful,
peaceful situation; many leisure activities; vg; helpful
staff, leafy pleasant site in a lovely area."*
€19.00, 1 Apr-31 Oct. **2019**

LAMASTRE *9C2* (5km NE Rural) *45.01173, 4.62410*
Camping Les Roches, 07270 Le Crestet **04 75 06 20 20;**
camproches@nordnet.fr; www.campinglesroches.com
🛒 €4.50 ♨ ⓦ ♨ 🚻 🚿 ♿ 🛒 ⧄ ♨ ⓜ 🛒 🍴 Ⓗ 🚲 ♨ 🚗 🏍 ⛱ (htd)
Take D534 fr Tournon-sur-Rhône dir Lamastre. 3km
fr vill. Do not use Sat Nav. Sm, hdstg, mkd, pt shd, terr,
EHU (6A) €4.50; bbq; sw nr; TV; 30% statics; bus 1km;
Eng spkn; adv bkg acc; ccard acc; games area; tennis
3km; fishing 500m; CKE. *"Friendly family-run site; clean
facs; lovely views; gd base for touring medieval vills; gd
walking; site rd steep; on hillside abv rv valley; diff for lge
o'fits; excel rest."* **€23.50, 1 May-30 Sep.** **2019**

LANDEDA *2E1* (2km NW Coastal) *48.59333, -4.60333*
Camping des Abers, 51 Toull Tréaz, Plage de Ste
Marguerite, 29870 Landéda **02 98 04 93 35;** info@
camping-des-abers.com; www.camping-des-abers.com
🛒 €2.50 ♨ ⓦ ♨ 🚻 🚿 ♿ 🛒 ⧄ ♨ ⓜ 🛒 🍴 Ⓗ nr 🚲 ♨ 🏍 ♨
🏕 sand adj
Exit N12/E50 at junc with D788 & take D13 to
Lannilis. Then take D128A to Landéda & foll green
site sp. 4*, Lge, mkd, hdg, pt shd, terr, EHU (10A)
€3 (long lead poss req); gas; bbq; red long stay; TV;
10% statics; Eng spkn; adv bkg rec; ccard acc; bike
hire; fishing; games rm; classes; CKE. *"Attractive,
landscaped site on wild coast; views fr high pitches;
friendly, helpful manager; san facs clean, some new,
others old; some pitches muddy when wet; no o'fits
over 8m high ssn; access to many pitches by grass
tracks, some sl; gd walks, cycling; excel; some problems
with voltage."* **€22.50, 1 May-30 Sep, B30.** **2019**

LANDIVISIAU *2E2* (9.3km NE Urban) *48.57724,
-4.03006* **Camp Municipal Lanorgant,** 29420 Plouvorn
02 98 61 32 40 (Mairie); www.plouvorn.com/aire-de-
camping-cars
♨ ♨ 🛒 ♨ ⓜ 🛒 🍴 nr Ⓗ nr 🚲 nr 🏍 🏕 sand
Fr Landivisiau, take D69 N twd Roscoff. In 8km turn
R onto D19 twd Morlaix. Site sp, in 700m turn R.
NB Care req entry/exit, poss diff lge o'fits. 2*, Sm,
hdg, mkd, pt shd, terr, EHU (10A) inc; bbq; sw; adv bkg
acc; tennis; fishing; canoe hire. *"Ideal NH for ferries;
lge pitches; sailboards hire; nr lake."*
€5.20, 26 Jun-15 Sep. **2016**

LANGEAC *9C1* (0.8km NE Rural) *45.10251, 3.49980*
Camp Municipal du Pradeau/Des Gorges de l'Allier,
43300 Langeac **04 71 77 05 01;** infos@campingla
ngeac.com; www.campinglangeac.com
🛒 €1.05 ♨ ⓦ ♨ 🚻 🚿 ♿ 🛒 ⧄ ♨ ⓜ 🛒 Ⓗ nr 🚲 🏍 ♨ ⛱
Exit N102 onto D56 sp Langeac; in 7km join D585
into Langeac; pass under rlwy; at 2nd rndabt in 1km
turn L to site, just bef junc with D590. Fr S on D950
to Langeac, take 1st R after rv bdge; then 1st exit
at rndabt in 100m. 3*, Lge, pt shd, EHU (10A) €2.60
(poss long lead req); sw nr; TV; 10% statics; phone;
bus 1km; Eng spkn; bike hire; fishing adj; canoeing adj;
CKE. *"Beautiful location on Rv Allier; tourist train thro
Gorges d'Allier fr Langeac; walking rtes adj; barrier to
site poss clsd after sept 11am-5pm; gd san facs; gd
local mkt; excel NH."* **€13.00, 1 Apr-31 Oct.** **2015**

LANGOGNE *9D1* (2km W Rural) *44.73180, 3.83995*
Camping Les Terrasses du Lac, 48300 Naussac **04 66
69 29 62;** info@naussac.com; www.naussac.com
🛒 €3.30 ♨ ⓦ ♨ 🚻 🚿 ♿ 🛒 ⧄ ♨ ⓜ 🛒 🍴 Ⓗ 🚲 ♨ 🚗 nr 🏍 ♨
⛱
S fr Le Puy-en-Velay on N88. At Langogne take D26
to lakeside, site sp. 3*, Lge, pt shd, terr, EHU (6A)
€2.50; bbq; sw nr; TV; 10% statics; phone; Eng spkn;
adv bkg acc; horseriding 3km; games area; sailing
school; bike hire; golf 1km; watersports adj; CKE.
*"Vg views; steep hill bet recep & pitches; vg cycling &
walking."* **€23.30, 15 Apr-1 Oct.** **2018**

LANGRES *6F1* (6km E Rural) *47.87190, 5.38120*
Kawan Village Le Lac de la Liez, Rue des Voiliers, 52200
Peigney **03 25 90 27 79;** contact@camping-liez.fr;
www.campingliez.com
🛒 €3 ♨ (htd) ⓦ ♨ 🚻 🚿 ♿ 🛒 ⧄ ♨ ⓜ 🛒 🍴 Ⓗ 🚲 ♨ 🏍 ♨
⛱ (covrd, htd) 🏊
Exit A31 at junc 7 (Langres Nord) onto DN19; at
Langres turn L at traff lts onto D74 sp Vesoul,
Mulhouse, Le Lac de la Liez; at rndabt go strt on
sp Epinal, Nancy; after Champigny-lès-Langres
cross over rlwy bdge & canal turning R onto D52
sp Peigney, Lac de la Liez; in 3km bear R onto D284
sp Langres Sud & Lac de la Liez; site on R in 800m.
Well sp fr N & S. 5*, Lge, mkd, hdg, hdstg, pt shd,
terr, EHU (10A) €5.50; bbq; sw nr; TV; 15% statics;
phone; Eng spkn; ccard acc; bike hire; sauna; golf
10km; boat hire; watersports; fishing; horseriding
10km; tennis; games rm; CKE. *"Popular, well-run,
secure site; lake views fr some pitches; various sized
pitches; helpful, friendly staff; san facs ltd LS; blocks
poss req some pitches; some sm pitches & narr access
rds diff manoeuvre lge o'fits; no o'fits over 10m; spa;
vg rest; rec arr bef 1600 high ssn; gd walks & cycle rte
by picturesque lake; interesting & historic town; poor."*
€37.00, 1 Apr-25 Sep, J05. **2016**

LANGRES *6F1* (15km S Rural) *47.74036, 5.30727*
Camping du Lac, 14 rue Cototte, 52190 Villegusien le
Lac **25 88 45 24;** richard-emmanuel@hotmail.fr;
www.tourisme-langres.com
🛒 ♨ (htd) ⓦ ♨ 🚻 🚿 ♿ 🛒 ⧄ ♨ ⓜ 🍴 Ⓗ 🚲 ♨ 🚗 nr 🏍 ♨ ⛱ 🏕
Take N19, foll N19 to Ave du Capitaine Baudoin,
then foll Ave du Général de Gaulle, foll D974 to D26
in Villegusien-le-Lac, cont on D26, turn L onto D26,
turn L, turn R, site on L. 1*, Med, mkd, shd, pt sl, EHU;
bbq (gas); sw; twin axles; adv bkg acc; windsurfing;
trekking; games rm; tennis; fishing; sailing. *"V pleasant
site in lovely setting, some slight rd noise; beach
lifeguard."* **€22.00, 15 Mar-30 Oct.** **2019**

LANGRES *6F1* (7.5km S Rural) *47.81210, 5.32080*
Camping de la Croix d'Arles, 52200 Bourg **03 25 88
24 02;** croix.arles@yahoo.fr; www.campingdelacroix
darles.com

🐕 ♿ 🗓 wc ♨ ♿ 🖫 🖭 🎵 ⚲ 🍴 ⊕ 🍴 ♨ △ ⚓

Site is 4km S of Langres on W side of D974 (1km S of
junc of D974 with D428). Site opp junc of D51 with
D974. Fr Dijon poss no L turn off D974 - can pull
into indust est N of site & return to site, but memb
reported that L turn now poss (2011).
3*, Med, hdg, mkd, hdstg, pt shd, pt sl, EHU (10A) €4
(poss rev pol) (long cable req); phone; Eng spkn; ccard
acc; CKE. *"Popular site, fills up quickly after 1600;
friendly staff; some lovely secluded pitches in woodland;
gd san facs; access poss diff lge o'fits; muddy after rain;
unkempt LS; poss haphazard pitching when full; conv
NH Langres historic town; nice, sm rest on site; easy to
reach."* **€22.00, 15 Mar-31 Oct.** **2018**

LANGRES *6F1* (1km SW Urban) *47.86038, 5.32894*
Camp Municipal Navarre, 9 Blvd Maréchal de Lattre
de Tassigny, 52200 Langres **03 25 87 37 92 or
06 10 74 10 16;** contact@campingnavarre.fr;
www.camping-navarre-langres.fr

🐕 ♿ (htd) wc ♨ ♿ 🖫 🍴 ♨ 🖭 nr

App fr N or S on D619/D674, cont on main rd until
lge rndabt at top of hill & go thro town arched
gateway; site well sp fr there. NB Diff access for
lge o'fits thro walled town but easy access fr D619.
Med, pt shd, pt sl, EHU (10A) €3.10 (long lead req
& poss rev pol); bbq; phone; Eng spkn; CKE. *"Well-
situated, busy NH, gd views fr some pitches; on arr
site self & see warden; rec arr bef 1630; helpful staff;
excel, modern unisex san facs; lovely walk round citadel
ramparts; delightful town; vg site, views and location;
warden mulit-lingual and helpful; conv for shops, rest,
Friday mkt, cathedral."* **€18.30, 10 Mar-5 Nov.** **2017**

LANGRES *6F1* (13km SW Rural) *47.79528, 5.23278*
Camping de la Croisée, 3 Route De Auberive, 52250
Flagey **03 25 88 01 26;** yannick.durenne52@orange.fr;
www.campingdelacroisee.com

12 🐕 ♿ (htd) wc ♨ 🖭 🦋 🖭 🍴 ♨ △

Exit A31 at J6 direction Langres D428. Campsite
1km on L (opp junc to Flagey). Med, hdstg, hdg, mkd,
pt shd, bbq (charcoal, gas); ccard acc; red low ssn...
"Conv NH stop as 2km fr A31 m'way; farm animals; gd."
€17.00 **2018**

LANILDUT *2E1* (1km N Coastal) *48.48012, -4.75184*
Camping du Tromeur, 11 Route du Camping, 29840
Lanildut **02 98 04 31 13;** contact@tromeur.fr;
www.tromeur.fr

🐕 €1 ♿ wc ♨ 🖫 🦋 🖭 🍴 nr ⊕ nr 🖭 nr

Site well sp on app rds to vill. 2*, Med, EHU €3 (poss
long lead req & poss rev pol); bbq; phone. *"Clean,
sheltered site; san facs gd; harbour & sm beach; LS
warden am & pm only - site yourself; wooded walk into
vil."* **€15.00, 1 May-30 Sep.** **2019**

LANLOUP *2E3* (0.4km W Rural) *48.71369, -2.96711*
FFCC Camping Le Neptune, 22580 Lanloup
02 96 22 33 35; contact@leneptune.com;
www.leneptune.com

🐕 €3 wc ♨ ♿ 🖫 🍴 🖭 🍴 ♨ 🖭 nr 🖭 △ ⚓ (covrd, htd)
🏕 sand 2km

Take D786 fr St Brieuc or Paimpol to Lanloup, site sp.
NB Take care sat nav dirs (2011). 3*, Med, mkd, hdg,
pt shd, EHU inc; gas; bbq; TV; 15% statics; phone; Eng
spkn; adv bkg acc; horseriding 4km; bike hire; tennis
300m; CKE. *"Excel, well-maintained site nr beautiful
coast; various pitch sizes; clean san facs; friendly,
helpful owner; highly rec."* **€30.00, 31 Mar-9 Oct.**
2017

LANNE *8F2* (1km NW Rural) *43.17067, 0.00186*
Camping La Bergerie, 79 Rue des Chênes, 65380
Lanne **05 62 45 40 05;** camping-la-bergerie@
orange.com; www.camping-la-bergerie.com

🐕 €2 ♿ (htd) ♨ ♿ 🍴 🦋 🖭 🍴 🖭 △ ⚓

Fr Lourdes take N21 N dir Tarbes; turn R onto D16
(Rue des Chênes) dir Lanne; site on R in 200m.
3*, Med, mkd, shd, EHU (10A) €3.8 (poss rev pol); gas;
bus 200m; Eng spkn; adv bkg acc; tennis; CKE. *"Well-
run site; friendly owners; some rd noise & aircraft noise
at night; gd san facs; poss unkempt LS; poss flooding
wet weather."* **€19.00, 15 Mar-15 Oct.** **2017**

LANNION *1D2* (9km NNW Coastal) *48.73833, -3.54500*
FFCC Camping Les Plages de Beg-Léguer,
Route de la Côte, 22300 Lannion **02 96 47 25 00;**
info@campingdesplages.com; www.campingdes
plages.com

🐕 €1 ♿ wc ♨ ♿ 🖫 🍴 🖭 🦋 🍴 ♨ ⊕ 🖭 △
⚓ (covrd, htd) 🛁 🏕 sand 500m

Fr Lannion take rd out of town twd Trébeurden
then twd Servel on D65, then head SW off that
rd twd Beg Léguer (sp). 3*, Lge, mkd, hdg, pt shd,
EHU (6A) €3.50 (poss long lead req); gas; red long
stay; TV; 20% statics; phone; bus 400m; Eng spkn;
adv bkg acc; ccard acc; windsurfing; fishing; sailing;
tennis; CKE. *"Pleasant, peaceful, well-run family site;
charming French owner who speaks excel Eng; superb
pool complex & vg children's play area; lge grass
pitches; immac, modern san facs; one of the best sites
in France; many superb rest in nrby seaside resorts;
stunning beaches; cliftop location; adj to GR34 coastal
path; phone LS; excel, fam oriented facs; conv for
beach."* **€31.70, 29 May-22 Sep.** **2019**

LANSLEBOURG MONT CENIS *9C4* (0.3km SW Rural)
45.28417, 6.87380 **Camp Municipal Les Balmasses,**
Chemin du Pavon, 73480 Lanslebourg-Mont-Cenis
06 38 28 92 84; info@camping-les-balmasses.com;
www.camping-les-balmasses.com

🐕 ♿ ♨ ♿ 🖫 🍴 🖭 nr △

Fr Modane, site on R on rv on ent to town.
2*, Med, mkd, pt shd, EHU (6-10A) €4.50-5.40; bbq;
phone; Eng spkn; CKE. *"Pleasant, quiet site by rv;
mountain views; clean facs; conv NH bef/after Col du
Mont-Cenis."* **€14.00, 1 Jun-20 Sep.** **2019**

LAON *3C4* (3km W Rural) *49.56190, 3.59583*
Camp La Chênaie (formerly Municipal), Allée de la Chênaie, 02000 Laon 03 23 23 38 63 or 03 23 20 25 56; contact.camping.laon@gmail.com; www.camping-laon.com

🐕 €2 ♦♦(htd) ⬜ ♨ ♂ ♿ ⬛ ⁄ 🅼🅿 🦋 ⁎ 🖳 ⋔

Exit A26 junc 13 onto N2 sp Laon; in 10km at junc with D1044 (4th rndabt) turn sp Semilly/Laon, then L at next rndabt into site rd. Site well sp. 3*, Sm, hdstg, hdg, mkd, pt shd, sl, terr, EHU (10A) €3.40 (poss rev pol); bbq; red long stay; twin axles; 10% statics; phone; Eng spkn; adv bkg acc; fishing 50m; CKE. *"Peaceful, pleasant site in gd location; popular NH; well-mkd pitches - lgest at end of site rd; pool (2.5km); extremely helpful staff; no twin axles; if travelling Sept phone to check site open; m'van parking nr cathedral; vg; woodland glades; gd NH; site now privately owned, pool under construction (2016)."*
€21.00, 1 Apr-30 Sep. 2016

LAPALISSE *9A1* (0.3km S Urban) *46.24322, 3.63950*
Camping de la Route Bleue, Rue des Vignes, 03120 Lapalisse 04 70 99 26 31, 04 70 99 76 29 or 04 70 99 08 39 (LS); contact@lapalissetourisme.com; www.lapalisse-tourisme.com

🐕 €1 ♦♦(htd) ♨ ♿ ⬛ ⁄ 🅼🅿 🦋 🖳 nr ⋔

S fr Moulins on N7; at rndabt junc with D907 just bef Lapalisse, take 3rd exit onto Ave due Huit Mai 1945 (to town cent), foll rd for 1.5km, over rv bdg, round RH bend onto Rue des Vignes, site on R in 500m. 3*, Med, mkd, pt shd, EHU (6-9A) €2.40; Eng spkn; CKE. *"Popular, excel NH off N7 in pleasant parkland setting; gd clean san facs; pleasant 10 min walk thro adj park to town; no twin axles; poss flooding after heavy rain; adequate sans but need upgrade."*
€11.90, 28 Apr-15 Oct. 2019

LARGENTIERE *9D2* (5km SE Rural) *44.50347, 4.29430*
Camping Les Châtaigniers, Le Mas-de-Peyrot, 07110 Laurac-en-Vivarais 04 75 36 86 26; chataigniers@hotmail.com; www.chataigniers-laurac.com

🐕 €2 ♦♦(htd) ⬜ ♨ ♂ ♿ ⬛ ⁄ 🦋 ⋔ ♒

Fr Aubenas S on D104 dir Alès; site sp fr D104. Site on one of minor rds leading to Laurac-en-Vivarais. 3*, Med, mkd, pt shd, pt sl, EHU (10A) €3; bbq (gas); 15% statics; adv bkg acc. *"Attractive, great, clean site; some pitches deep shd; sun area; gd pool; sh uphill walk to vill shops & auberge; vg."*
€25.00, 1 Apr-30 Sep. 2016

LARGENTIERE *9D2* (1.6km NW Rural) *44.56120, 4.28615* **Domaine Les Ranchisses,** Route de Rocher, Chassiers, 07110 Largentière **04 75 88 31 97;** reception@lesranchisses.fr; www.lesranchisses.fr

🏕 €6 ⊪ 🄦 🛆 ᷂ & 🄰 ⚊ 🄼⚡ 🖤 🍴 ⊕🍴 🗑 /🄰 ✦
🗝 (covrd, htd) 🖽

Exit A7/E15 junct 17/18 (Montelimar N or S) on to N7 dir Montelimar to take N102. Fr Aubenas S on D104 sp Alès. 1km after vill of Uzer turn R onto D5 to Largentière. Go thro Largentière on D5 in dir Rocher/Valgorge; site on L in 1.5km. DO NOT use D103 bet Lachapelle-Aubenas & Largentière - too steep & narr for lge vehicles & c'vans. NB Not rec to use sat nav dirs to this site. 4*, Lge, mkd, pt shd, EHU (10A) inc; gas; bbq (elec, gas); sw; TV; 30% statics; adv bkg req; ccard acc; games rm; fishing; bike hire; games area; canoeing. *"Lovely, well-run, busy site adj vineyard; gd sized pitches; friendly, helpful staff; gd, immac san facs; o'fits over 7m by request; excel rest & takeaway; lovely pools; gd choice of sporting activities; wellness cent; poss muddy when wet; noisy rd adj to S end of site; mkt Tues am; first class; 5 star site in lovely location."* **€56.00, 13 Apr-21 Sep, C32.** 2019

LARUNS *8G2* (0.8km S Rural) *42.98241, -0.41591* **Camping Les Gaves,** Quartier Pon, 64440 Laruns **05 59 05 32 37;** campingdesgaves@wanadoo.fr; www.campingdesgaves.com

🗓 🏕 €3 ⊪ (htd) 🄦 🛆 ⚊/ 🖤 🍴 🗑 nr /🄰

Site on S edge of town, N of Hôtel Le Lorry & bdge. Fr town sq cont on Rte d'Espagne (narr exit fr sq) to end of 1-way system. After Elf & Total stns turn L at site sp immed bef bdge (high fir tree each side of bdge ent). Ignore 1st site on L. At v constricted T-junc at ent to quartier 'Pon', turn R & foll rd into site. App no suitable lge o'fits. 3*, Med, mkd, pt shd, serviced pitches; EHU (3-10A) €2.60-4.50; TV; 75% statics; fishing; games area; games rm; rv fishing adj; CKE. *"Beautiful, lovely site; nr vill; htd covrd pool 800m; facs tired (2015); level walk to vill."* **€24.00** 2015

LAURENS *10F1* (1km S Rural) *43.53620, 3.18583* **Camping L'Oliveraie,** Chemin de Bédarieux, 34480 Laurens **04 67 90 24 36;** oliveraie@free.fr; www.oliveraie.com

🗓 🏕 €2 ⊪ (htd) 🄦 🛆 ᷂ & 🄰 ⚊/ 🖤 🍴 ⊕🍴 🗑 /🄰 ⚓

Clearly sp on D909 Béziers to Bédarieux rd. Sp reads Loisirs de L'Oliveraie. 3*, Med, mkd, hdstg, pt shd, terr, EHU (10A) €3.20-4.60 (poss rev pol); TV; 30% statics; phone; adv bkg acc; ccard acc; site clsd 15 Dec-15 Jan; games rm; CKE. *"Helpful staff; gd, clean san facs; sauna high ssn; site becoming tatty (2011); in wine-producing area; gd winter NH."* **€35.00** 2019

LAVAL *2F4* (17km N Rural) *48.17467, -0.78785* **Camp Municipal Le Pont,** 53240 Andouillé **02 43 69 72 72 (Mairie)**

⊪ 🄦 🛆 🄰 ⚊/ 🖤 🍴 🗑 nr /🄰

Fr Laval N on D31 dir Ernée. In 8km turn R onto D115 to Andouillé. Site on L bef hill to vill cent. 2*, Sm, hdg, pt shd, EHU (3A) inc. *"Pretty, busy, basic site; vg, clean san facs; warden on site am & pm; site liable to flood."* **€6.00, 1 Apr-31 Oct.** 2015

LAVANDOU, LE *10F3* (2km S Coastal) *43.11800, 6.35210* **Camping du Domaine,** La Favière, 2581 Route de Bénat, 83230 Bormes-les-Mimosas **04 94 71 03 12;** mail@campdudomaine.com; www.campdudomaine.com

🏕 (not acc Jul/Aug) ⊪ 🄦 🛆 ᷂ & 🄰 ⚊/ 🄼 🖤 🍴 ⊕🍴 🗑 /🄰 ✦ 🏖 sand adj

App Le Lavandou fr Hyères on D98 & turn R on o'skts of town clearly sp La Favière. Site on L in 2.3km about 200m after ent to Domaine La Favière (wine sales) - ignore 1st lge winery. If app fr E do not go thro Le Lavandou, but stay on D559 until sp to La Favière. 4*, V lge, mkd, pt shd, terr, EHU (10A) inc (long lead poss req); gas; bbq (gas); TV; 10% statics; phone; Eng spkn; adv bkg req; ccard acc; tennis; games rm; CKE. *"Lge pitches, some with many trees & some adj beach (direct access); well-organised site with excel facs; gd walking & attractions in area."* **€55.00, 4 Apr-31 Oct.** 2019

See advertisement opposite

LAVANDOU, LE *10F3* (2.7km W Urban) *43.13630, 6.35439* **Camping St Pons,** Ave Maréchal Juin, 83960 Le Lavandou **04 94 71 03 93;** campingstpons@ netcourrier.com; www.campingstpons.com

🏕 €3.90 ⊪ 🄦 🛆 🄰 ⚊/ 🍴 ⊕🍴 🗑 nr /🄰 ✦ 🏖 sand 800m

App fr W on D98 via La Londe. At Bormes keep R onto D559. At 1st rndabt turn R sp La Favière, at 2nd rndabt turn R, then 1st L. Site on L in 200m. 2*, Med, mkd, shd, EHU (6A) inc; 10% statics; phone; Eng spkn; CKE. *"Much improved site; helpful owner."* **€26.00, 29 Apr-1 Oct.** 2017

LAVANDOU, LE *10F3* (8km NW Rural) *43.16262, 6.32152* **Camping Manjastre,** 150 Chemin des Girolles, 83230 Bormes-les-Mimosas **04 94 71 03 28;** manjastre@infonie.fr; www.campingmanjastre.com

🗓 🏕 €1.50 ⊪ (htd) 🄦 🛆 ᷂ & 🄰 ⚊/ 🄼 🖤 ⊕🍴 🗑 /🄰 ⚓ 🖽

App fr W on D98 about 3km NE of where N559 branches off SE to Le Lavandou. Fr E site is 2km beyond Bormes/Collobrières x-rds; sp. 3*, Lge, mkd, hdg, pt shd, sl, terr, EHU (10A) €4.70; bbq; TV; 10% statics; Eng spkn; adv bkg acc; CKE. *"Lovely site in vineyard on steep hillside with 3 san facs blocks; dohs not acc Jul/Aug; c'vans taken in & out by tractor; facs poss stretched in ssn; winter storage avail."* **€30.00** 2015

LAVELANET *8G4* (1km SW Urban) *42.92340, 1.84477*
Camping Le Pré Cathare, Rue Jacquard, 09300
Lavelanet **05 61 01 55 54; leprecathare@orange.fr;**
www.leprecathare.fr

🐕 €1 ‖‖(htd) �📶 ♨ 🔥 🚻 ⚊ / 🦋 ⛱ 🍴 ⛷ nr ⚠ ⚓

Fr Lavelanet, take D117 twd Foix & foll sp (foll sp
for sports complex). Adj 'piscine'. 3*, Med, mkd, pt
shd, EHU (15A) €3; bbq; TV; 80% statics; adv bkg
acc; games area; tennis 800m; CKE. *"Gd sized pitches,
some with mountain views; excel san facs; poss open in
winter with adv bkg; pool adj; gates locked 2200; quiet
town; vg."* **€20.00, 15 Mar-31 Oct.** **2017**

LE BUISSON *9D1* (10km NNE Rural) *44.705795,
3.282804* **Camping Municipal Aumont Aubrac,**
D809 48130 Peyre en Aubrac **04 66 42 80 02;**
www.ot-aumont-aubrac.fr

🐕 ⚊ ♨ 🔥 / 🦋

Travelling on A75 between Millau and St Flour
South. Leave at J35. Med, pt shd, EHU 6A; twin axles;
CKE. *"V pleasant quiet campsite; perfect for NH; gd
walk in area; vg."* **€12.00, 1 Jun-30 Sep.** **2019**

"I need an on-site restaurant"

We do our best to make sure site information
is correct, but it is always best to check any
must-have facilities are still available or will
be open during your visit.

LEGE *2H4* (10km SW Rural) *46.82121, -1.64844*
Camp Municipal Les Blés d'Or, 10 rue de la Piscine,
85670 Grand'Landes **02 51 98 51 86; mairiegrand
landes@wanadoo.fr; www.vendee-tourisme.com**

12 ‖‖ ⚊ ⚊ / 🦋 🍴 nr ⏦ nr ⚠

Take D753 fr Legé twd St Jean-de-Monts. In 4km
turn S on D81 & foll sp. Fr S on D978, turn W sp
Grand-Landes. 3km N of Palluau. 2*, Sm, pt shd,
pt sl, EHU (16A) €2.30; gas; 30% statics; Eng spkn;
adv bkg acc. *"V pleasant site; height barrier only, cars
24hr access; immac but dated facs; pay at Mairie adj; v
useful."* **€10.50** **2017**

LEGE-CAP-FERRET *7D1* (6km W Coastal) *44.73443,
-1.1960* **Camping Les Viviers,** Ave Léon Lesca,
Claouey, 33950 Lège-Cap-Ferret **05 56 60 70 04;
reception@lesviviers.com; www.lesviviers.com**

🐕 €5 ‖‖(htd) �📶 ♨ 🔥 🚻 ⚊ / 🅼 🦋 ⛱ 🍴 ⏦ ⚓ ⚠ ⚓
🏊 (covrd, htd) ⚊ ⚱ ⛱ sand adj

Fr N exit A10/A630 W of Bordeaux onto D106 sp
Cap-Ferret. Foll D106 thro Arès & vill of Claouey
on W side of Bassin d'Arcachon, site on L after LH
bend (approx 1.5km after Claouey).
4*, V lge, mkd, hdg, pt shd, EHU (10A) inc; gas; bbq
(elec, gas); red long stay; TV; 27% statics; bus; Eng
spkn; adv bkg req; ccard acc; games rm; sauna;
windsurfing; fishing; tennis; waterslide; games area;
bike hire; sailing; CKE. *"Sand pitches, various positions
& prices; clean san facs; sea water lagoon with private
sand beach adj; cinema; vg leisure facs and waterpark
on site; free night bus along peninsular; vg site."*
€50.00, 28 Mar-13 Sep. **2016**

See advertisement

LEMPDES SUR ALLAGNON *9C1* (1.2km N Rural)
45.38699, 3.26598 **Camping Le Pont d'Allagnon
(formerly CM au Delà de l'Eau),** Rue René Filiol, off
Route de Chambezon, 43410 Lempdes-sur-Allagnon
**04 71 76 53 69; centre.auvergne.camping@orange.fr;
www.campingenauvergne.com**

‖‖ ⚊ ♨ 🔥 🚻 ⚊ / 🅼 🦋 🍴 ⛷ nr ⚠

Going S on A75 exit junc 19 (ltd access) onto D909;
turn R on D654 bef vill, site sp at junc. Or fr junc 20
going N; foll sp. Site just outside vill. 3*, Med, hdg, pt
shd, EHU (16A) €3.40; phone; adv bkg acc; ccard acc;
games rm; tennis; rv fishing; games area. *"Pleasant
site in beautiful area; pool 100m; conv NH A75; gd."*
€25.00, 28 Mar-19 Oct. **2019**

LEON *8E1* (4km N Rural) *43.90260, -1.31030*
Camping Sandaya Le Col Vert, Lac de Léon, 40560
Vielle-St Girons **05 58 42 94 06; www.sandaya.co.uk/
our-campsites/le-col-vert**

🐾 €4.70 ♂♀ [wc] ♨ ⚲ ⚳ ▣ ⚌ / [MP] ♈ 🍴 ⑪ ⚗ ❄ ⚑ ✦
≋ (covrd, htd) ⛵

Exit N10 junc 12; at Castets-des-Landes turn R onto
D42 to Vielle-St Girons. In vill turn L onto D652
twd Léon sp Soustons. In 4km, bef Vielle, take 2nd
of 2 RH turns twd Lac de Léon. Site on R at end
of rd in 1.5km. 4*, V lge, shd, serviced pitches; EHU
(3A) inc; gas; bbq (elec, gas); sw nr; red long stay;
TV; 60% statics; adv bkg acc; ccard acc; canoeing nr;
games rm; windsurfing nr; archery; tennis; sailing nr;
bike hire; fishing nr; horseriding; CKE. *"Lakeside site in
pine forest; fitness rm; some pitches 800m fr facs; ideal
for children & teenagers; wellness cent; no c'van/m'van
over 6.5m; daily mkt in Léon in ssn; excel location."*
€64.00, 12 Apr-7 Sep, A08. 2019

LEON *8E1* (9km NW Coastal) *43.90830, -1.36380*
Domaine Naturiste Arna (Naturist), Arnaoutchot,
5006 Route de Pichelèbe, 40560 Vielle-St Girons
05 58 49 11 11; contact@arna.com; www.arna.com

🐾 €3.50 ♂♀ [wc] ♨ ⚲ ⚳ ▣ ⚌ / [MP] 🦋 ♈ 🍴 ⑪ ⚗ ❄ ⚑ ✦
≋ (covrd, htd) ⛵ 🌴 sand adj

Fr St Girons turn R onto D328 at Vielle sp Pichelèbe.
Site in 5km on R. 3*, Lge, hdstg, shd, pt sl, EHU
(3-10A) €4.50-6.10 inc; gas; bbq (elec, gas); red long
stay; TV; 80% statics; Eng spkn; adv bkg acc; ccard
acc; games area; golf nr; bike hire; waterslide; games
rm; tennis; watersports 5km; archery. *"Excel site in
pine forest; Arna Forme Spa; some pitches soft sand;
clean san facs, ltd LS; no o'fits over 6.5m; lake adj;
spa cent; excel LS site; access lge o'fits poss diff due
trees; superb beach; daily mkt in Léon in ssn; new
hdstg pitches with elec/water for MH's; great facs."*
€40.00, 9 Apr-25 Sep. 2018

LERAN *8G4* (2km E Rural) *42.98368, 1.93516*
Camping La Régate, Route du Lac, 09600 Léran
**05 61 03 09 17 or 06 08 48 08 63 (mob); contact@
campinglaregate.com; www.campinglaregate.com**

🐾 €1 ♂♀ [wc] ♨ ⚲ ▣ / ♈ 🍴 ⑪ nr ❄ nr ⚑ ✦

Fr Lavelanet go N on D625, turn R onto D28 & cont
to Léran. Site sp fr vill. Ent easily missed - rd past
it is dead end. 3*, Med, hdg, mkd, shd, terr, EHU (8A)
€3.70; bbq; 10% statics; phone; adv bkg acc; ccard acc;
watersports. *"Conv Montségur chateau; leisure cent
nr; pony trekking; clean san facs; lake adj; gd location;
pool adj; mkd walking & cycle rtes around adj lake."*
€33.60, 30 Mar-26 Oct. 2019

LES MOUTIERS EN RETZ *2H3* (4km SSE Coastal)
47.036544, -1.984846 **Domaine du Collet,** Route Verte
44760 Les Moutiers-en-Retz **00 33 2 40 21 40 92;
contact@domaine-du-collet.com; www.domaine-du-
collet.com**

🐾 €5 ♂♀ [wc] ♨ ⚲ ⚳ ▣ / [MP] 🦋 ♈ 🍴 ⑪ ⚑ ✦ ≋ (covrd, htd) ⛵

🌴 100m

SW fr Nantes on D723, after 9km turn L D751 sp
Noirmoutier; in abt 8km at Port-Saint-Père turn L
sp D758/Noirmoutier; in abt 18km foll D758 thro
Bourgneuf-en-Retz (beware narr sharp turn); at
mini-rndabt go L onto D758; at rndabt take 2nd exit
sp Port du Collet; in abt 2km turn R over bdge; aft
1km fork R and site on R aft 1km. 4*, Lge, pt shd, TV;
70% statics; games rm. *"Very quiet; gd for families."*
€40.00, 1 Apr - 31 Oct, B36. 2019

LESCHERAINES *9B3* (2.5km SE Rural) *45.70279,
6.11158* **Camp Municipal de l'Ile,** Base de Loisirs,
Les Iles du Chéran, 73340 Lescheraines **04 79 63 80 00;
contact@savoie-camping.com; www.iles-du-cheran.
com**

🐾 €1.50 ♂♀ [wc] ♨ ⚲ ⚳ ▣ / [MP] 🦋 ♈ 🍴 ⑪ nr ⚗ ❄ ⚑ ✦

Fr Lescheraines foll sp for Base de Loisirs.
3*, Lge, mkd, pt shd, EHU (6-10A) €2.40-3.50; bbq; sw;
5% statics; phone; Eng spkn; boat hire; fishing; canoe
hire; CKE. *"Beautiful, scenic, lakeside setting; v helpful
staff; gd walks."* **€16.50, 19 Apr-28 Sep.** 2019

LESPERON *8E1* (4km SW Rural) *43.96657, -1.12940*
Le Laha Camping (formerly Parc de Couchoy),
3000 Route de Linxe, 40260 Lesperon **05 58 89 60 15;
www.lelaha.com**

🐾 €1 ♂♀ [wc] ♨ ⚲ ⚳ ▣ / 🦋 ♈ 🍴 ⚗ ❄ nr ⚑ ⛵

Exit N10 junc 13 to D41 sp Lesperon; in 1km turn L,
thro vill of Lesperon; L at junc onto D331; bottom
of hill turn R & immed L; site on R in 3km dir Linxe.
3*, Sm, mkd, pt shd, EHU (6A); gas; bbq (elec, gas); sw
nr; red long stay; twin axles; 10% statics; phone; Eng
spkn; adv bkg acc; ccard acc; CKE. *"Lovely but isolated
site on edge of wine country; gd facs on lakes for
sailing, windsurfing; British owners; clean san facs; vg;
new owners."* **€27.50, Apr-Oct.** 2019

LEZIGNAN CORBIERES *8F4* (1km NW Urban)
43.20475, 2.75255 **Camp Municipal de la Pinède,**
Ave Gaston Bonheur, 11200 Lézignan-Corbières
**04 68 27 05 08; reception@campinglapinede.fr;
www.campinglapinede.fr**

🐾 €2.10 ♂♀ [wc] ♨ ⚲ ⚳ ▣ / [MP] 🦋 ♈ 🍴 ⑪ ⚗ ❄ nr

On D6113 fr Carcassonne to Narbonne on N of rd;
foll 'Piscine' & 'Restaurant Le Patio' sp.
3*, Med, hdstg, hdg, pt shd, pt sl, terr, EHU (6A) inc;
gas; bbq (gas); 5% statics; adv bkg acc; tennis; CKE.
*"Well-run, clean, popular site; helpful, friendly staff; gd
san facs; gd m'van facs; htd pool adj; some pitches diff
due high kerb; no o'fits over 5m; superb pool; mkt Wed;
gd touring base or NH."* **€19.00, 1 Apr-30 Oct.** 2015

FRANCE

LICQUES 3A3 (1.8km SE Rural) 50.77974, 1.94766
Camping Les Pommiers des Trois Pays, 273 Rue
du Breuil, 62850 Licques **03 21 35 02 02; contact@
pommiers-3pays.com; www.pommiers-3pays.com**

🛞 €1 👬 ⭘⭕ ♨ ⛟ ♿ 🚮 🗑 MP ❦ 🛈 🍴 ⛺ nr ⚟ ⚡
🏊 (covrd, htd)

Fr Calais to Guînes on D127 then on D215 to
Licques; take D191 fr vill & foll sp; site on L in 1km.
Or exit A26 junc 2 onto D217 to Licques; turn L
onto D215; cont strt on & site on L on far side of
vill. NB sloping ent, long o'fits beware grounding.
4*, Med, mkd, hdg, pt shd, sl, EHU (16A) €4.80; bbq;
red long stay; TV; 65% statics; Eng spkn; adv bkg acc;
ccard acc; games rm; golf 25km; fishing 2km; sailing
25km; games area. "Site v full early Jun, adv bkg rec;
lge pitches; friendly, helpful owners; gd quality facs, ltd
LS, rest clsd; gd beaches nr; gd walking; conv Calais/
Dunkerque ferries; gd; excel san facs; busy, well-run
site; sm pool for children; clean facs; only 0.75h fr
Calais ferry." €29.00, 15 Mar-31 Oct.   2019

LIGNY LE CHATEL 4F4 (0.5km SW Rural) 47.89542,
3.75288 **Camp Municipal La Noue Marrou,** 89144
Ligny-le-Châtel **03 86 47 56 99 or 03 86 47 41 20
(Mairie); camping.lignylechatel@orange.fr;
www.mairie-ligny-le-chatel-89.fr**

🐕 👬 ⭘⭕ ♨ ♿ 🚮 MP ❦ 🍴 🛈 ⛺ ⚟

Exit A6 at junc 20 Auxerre S onto D965 to Chablis. In
Chablis cross rv & turn L onto D91 dir Ligny. On ent
Ligny turn L onto D8 at junc after Maximart. Cross
sm rv, foll sp to site on L in 200m. 2*, Sm, mkd, pt
shd, EHU (16A) inc; bbq (charcoal, elec, gas); sw nr;
phone; bus 200m; Eng spkn; ccard acc; tennis; games
area; CKE. "Well-run site; lge pitches; no twin axles;
v welcoming, friendly warden lives on site; san facs
dated but clean; pleasant vill with gd rests; popular NH;
excel." €12.00, 15 Apr-1 Oct.   2019

LIGUEIL 4H2 (2km N Rural) 47.05469, 0.84615
Camping de la Touche, Ferme de la Touche, 37240
Ligueil **02 47 59 54 94; booklatouche@hotmail.co.uk;
www.theloirevalley.com**

12 👬 ⭘⭕ ♨ 🚮 ❦ 🍴 ⛺ nr ⚟ 🏊

Fr Loches SW on D31; turn L at x-rds with white
cross on R 2km after Ciran; in 500m turn R, site on R
bef hotel. Fr A10 exit junc 25 Ste Maure-de-Touraine
& foll sp to Ligueil; then take D31 dir Loches; turn
L at white cross. Sm, mkd, hdstg, pt shd, EHU (10A)
€5; adv bkg acc; ccard acc; bike hire; fishing; CKE.
"Well-maintained, relaxed CL-type site; lge pitches;
welcoming, helpful British owners; c'van storage; excel
san facs; gd walking & touring base; dogs free; much
wild life; conv m'way; gd; cycling dist fr pleasant vill."
€15.50   2015

LILLEBONNE 3C2 (4km W Rural) 49.53024, 0.49763
Camping Hameau des Forges, 76170 St Antoine-la-
Forêt **02 35 39 80 28 or 02 35 91 48 30**

12 🐕 👬 ⭘⭕ ♨ 🚮 ❦ 🗑

Fr Le Havre take rd twds Tancarville bdge, D982
into Lillebonne, D81 W to site on R in 4km (pt
winding rd). Fr S over Tancarville bdge onto D910 sp
Bolbec. At 2nd rndabt turn R onto D81, site 5km on
L. NB Concealed ent by notice board and post-box.
1*, Med, pt shd, EHU (5A) inc; 90% statics; adv bkg
acc; CKE. "Basic, clean, open site; staff welcoming &
helpful; poss statics only LS & facs ltd; site muddy when
wet; conv NH for Le Havre ferries late arr & early dep;
Roman amphitheatre in town worth visit; site & facs
tired (2019); fair." €16.40   2019

LIMOGES 7B3 (5km N Rural) 45.86949, 1.27625
Camping d'Uzurat, 40 Ave d'Uzurat, 87280 Limoges
**05 55 38 49 43; contact@campinglimoges.fr;
www.campinglimoges.fr**

🐕 €1.50 👬 (htd) ⭘⭕ ♨ ⛟ ♿ 🚮 MP ❦ 🍴 ⛺ nr ⚟

Fr N twd Limoges on A20 take exit 30 sp Limoges
Nord Zone Industrielle, Lac d'Uzurat; foll sp to Lac
d'Uzarat & site. Fr S twd Limoges on A20 exit junc
31 & foll sp as above. Well sp fr A20. 3*, Lge, hdstg,
pt shd, serviced pitches; EHU (10A) €3.60; red long
stay; 10% statics; phone; bus; Eng spkn; ccard acc;
lake fishing; CKE. "Lovely site by lake; gd sized pitches;
friendly & helpful staff; clean modern san facs; pitch on
chippings - awnings diff; hypmkt 500m; poss red opening
dates - phone ahead LS; poss mkt traders;m'van o'night
area; conv martyr vill Oradour-sur-Glane; gd touring
base; conv m'way; popular NH; frequent bus into city."
€19.00, 15 Mar-31 Oct.   2017

LIMOGNE EN QUERCY 7D4 (0.6km W Rural)
44.39571, 1.76396 **Camp Municipal Bel-Air,** 46260
Limogne-en-Quercy **05 65 24 32 75 or 06 84 27 22 95;
camping.lebelair@free.fr; www.camping-le-bel-air.fr**

👬 ♨ 🚮 ❦ 🍴 nr ⚟ nr 🏊

E fr Cahors on D911 just bef Limogne vill. W
fr Villefranche on D911 just past vill; 3 ents about
50m apart. 3*, Sm, mkd, shd, sl, EHU (6A) inc; adv bkg
rec. "Friendly welcome; if warden absent, site yourself;
pleasant vill." €18.00, 1 Apr-1 Oct.   2019

LISIEUX 3D1 (2km N Rural) 49.16515, 0.22054 **Camp
Municipal de La Vallée,** 9 Rue de la Vallée,
14100 Lisieux **02 31 62 00 40 or 02 31 48 18 10 (LS);
tourisme@cclisieuxpaysdauge.fr; www.lisieux-
tourisme.fr**

👬 ⭘⭕ ♨ ❦ 🍴 nr 🛈 ⚡ nr

N on D579 fr Lisieux twd Pont l'Evêque. Approx
500m N of Lisieux take L to Coquainvilliers onto D48
& foll sp for Camping (turn L back in Lisieux dir). Site
on D48 parallel to main rd. On app to site look for
Volvo dealer & Super U supmkt.
3*, Med, hdstg, pt shd, EHU (6A) €2.50-4.50; gas;
20% statics; bus fr ent; CKE. "Interesting town,
childhood home of St Thérèse; helpful warden; v clean
san facs; gd." €14.30, 1 May-30 Sep.   2017

LISLE *7C3* (6km SW Rural) *45.25731, 0.49573*
Camp Municipal Le Pré Sec, 24350 Tocane-St Apre 05 53 90 40 60 or 05 53 90 70 29; commune-de-tocane-st-apre@orange.fr; www.campingdupresec.com

🐕 ♟ WD ♨ ᴖ ᴑ ∥ MSP ♈ ☂nr ⚠

Fr Ribérac E on D710 sp Brantôme. Fr E or W at Tocane St Apre, take bypass rd at rndabt. Site sp at both rndabts - dist 500m. Site is on N side of D710 (fr Riberac dir, there is a gab bet cent reservation to turn L.) Ent thro lge car park for Tocan Sports, barrier to site 100m back. 3*, Med, hdg, shd, EHU (6-10A) €1.80; bbq; twin axles; 10% statics; phone; bus 200m; Eng spkn; adv bkg acc; CKE. *"Gd; canoeing nrby on Rv Dronne."* **€10.00, 2 May-30 Sep.** 2019

"Satellite navigation makes touring much easier"

Remember most sat navs don't know if you're towing or in a larger vehicle – always use yours alongside maps and site directions.

LOCHES *4H2* (1km S Urban) *47.12255, 1.00175*
Kawan Village La Citadelle, Ave Aristide Briand, 37600 Loches 02 47 59 05 91 or 06 21 37 93 06 (mob); camping@lacitadelle.com; www.lacitadelle.com

🐕 €3 ♟(htd) WD ♨ ᴖ ᴑ ∥ MSP ♈ ☂ ① ⓐ ☂ ⚠ ∥ ⚓(htd)

Fr any dir take by-pass to S end of town & leave at Leclerc rndabt for city cent; site well sp on R in 800m. 4*, Lge, hdg, mkd, pt shd, EHU (10A) €4.70 (poss rev pol) (poss long lead req); gas; bbq; red long stay; TV; 30% statics; Eng spkn; adv bkg rec; ccard acc; golf 9km; tennis nr; boating; games area; bike hire; fishing; CKE. *"Attractive, well-kept, busy site nr beautiful old town; views of citadel; gd sized pitches, poss uneven; helpful staff; facs poss stretched; barrier clsd 2200-0800; poss no night security (2010); rvside walk into town; poss mosquitoes; site muddy after heavy rain; mkt Wed & Sat am; excel site; lge serviced pitches; sh walk to a beautiful medieval town."* **€31.70, 26 Mar-7 Oct.** 2016

LOCMARIAQUER *2G3* (2km NW Coastal) *47.57982, - 2.97394* **Camping Lann Brick,** Lieu Dit Lann-Brick, 56740 Locmariaquer 02 97 57 32 79 or 06 42 22 29 69 (mob); camping.lanbrick@wanadoo.fr; www.camping-lannbrick.com

🐕 €2.60 ♟(cont) WD ♨ ᴖ ᴑ ∥ MSP 🦋 ♈ ☂ ☂nr ⚠ ∥ ⚓(htd) 🏊 ☂0.5km

N165/E60, exit Crach via D28 dir Locmariaquer. L Onto D781. Sp on R 2km bef Locmariaquer. 3*, Med, mkd, hdg, shd, EHU (6/10A); bbq; twin axles; TV; 40% statics; phone; bus adj; Eng spkn; adv bkg acc; ccard acc; bike hire; CKE. *"Gd; quiet well managed site; helpful & friendly owners; facs well maintained & spotless; easy walk to beach; delightful site; gd location for Gulf of Morbihan; easy cycle rte; hg hdg."* **€27.60, 16 Mar-31 Oct.** 2019

LOCQUIREC *2E2* (2km SW Coastal) *48.67940, -3.65320* **Camping Municipal Du fond de la Baie,** Route de Plestin, 29241 Locquirec 02 98 67 40 85; campingdufonddelabaie@gmail.com; www.camping locquirec.com

⑫ 🐕 €1 ♟ WD ♨ ᴖ ᴑ ☂ MSP 🦋 ♈ ☂ ① ⓐ ☂ ∥ ☂ sand adj

Fr D786 Morlaix-Lannion, turn L (traff lts) at Plestin-Les-Graves onto D42. At T junc on reaching Bay turn L onto D64. Site on R on app Locquirec. 2*, Lge, mkd, pt shd, gas; bbq; twin axles; 6% statics; phone; bus adj; Eng spkn; adv bkg acc; ccard acc. *"Beautifully situated beachside site; vill 1.5km; flat site; fishing, boating & shellfishing; gd."* **€19.00** 2016

LODEVE *10E1* (3km S Urban) *43.71247, 3.32179* **Camping Les Vals,** 2000 route de Puech, 34700 Lodève 04 30 40 17 80 or 06 04 01 18 78; campinglesvals@ yahoo.fr; www.camping-les-vals.org

🐕 ♟ WD ♨ ᴖ ᴑ ∥ MSP 🦋 ♈ ☂ ① ⓐ ☂ ⚠ ∥ ⚓ 🏊

Fr N: A75 exit 52 dir Lodéve. Foll av. Fumel, not the cent. R over Vinas bdge dir Puech. Fr S: A75 exit 53 dir Lodéve cent dir Puech on Vinas bdge. 2km on the D148. 3*, Med, hdg, mkd, pt shd, pt sl, terr, EHU (6A); sw nr; TV; 30% statics; phone; Eng spkn; adv bkg acc; games area; watersports adj; games rm; bike hire; tennis; rv fishing adj; CKE. *"Gd site; v ltd facs LS."* **€26.00, 15 Apr-30 Oct.** 2015

LODEVE *10E1* (9km S Rural) *43.67182, 3.35429* **Camp Municipal Les Vailhés,** Baie des Vailhes, Lac du Salagou, 34700 Lodève 04 11 95 01 82; camping@ lodevoisetlarzac.fr; www.campinglesvailhes.com

🐕 ♟ WD ♨ ᴖ ᴑ ∥ 🦋 ⚠

Fr N exit A75 junc 54 onto D148 dir Octon & Lac du Salagou. Foll site sp. Fr S exit A75 junc 55. 3*, Lge, hdg, mkd, pt shd, terr, EHU (16A) inc; bbq; sw; 20% statics; Eng spkn; fishing; watersports; CKE. *"Peaceful, remote site by lake; pleasant staff; no facs nrby; excel walks; gd."* **€8.00, 1 Apr-30 Sep.** 2018

LONGEVILLE SUR MER *7A1* (3km SW Coastal) *46.41310, -1.52280* **Camping Les Brunelles,** Rue de la Parée, Le Bouil, 85560 Longeville-sur-Mer 02 51 33 50 75; camping@les-brunelles.com; www.les-brunelles.com

🐕 €5.50 ♟ ᴖ ᴑ ᴑ ☂ ∥ MSP ♈ ☂nr ⓐ ☂ ⚠ ∥ ⚓(covrd, htd) 🏊 ☂ sand 800m

Site bet Longeville-sur-Mer & Jard-sur-Mer; foll D21. 4*, Lge, mkd, pt shd, pt sl, serviced pitches; EHU (10A) inc; TV; 75% statics; Eng spkn; adv bkg acc; ccard acc; gym; sauna; bike hire; horseriding 2km; games area; waterslide; watersports; tennis; golf 15km. *"Gd san facs."* **€25.00, 7 Apr-22 Sep, A02.** 2017

FRANCE

LONS LE SAUNIER 6H2 (2.7km NE Rural) 46.68437, 5.56843 **Camping La Marjorie,** 640 Blvd de l'Europe, 39000 Lons-le-Saunier 03 84 24 26 94; info@ camping-marjorie.com; www.camping-marjorie.com

🐕 €2.60 ♨ 📶 🛁 🚰 ♿ 🔥 ⊘ 🍴 🛒 ⛽ /🏔 ♨ 🏊 (covrd, htd)

Site clearly sp in town on D1083 twd Besançon. Fr N bear R dir 'Piscine', cross under D1083 to site. 4*, Lge, hdg, hdstg, pt shd, terr, EHU (10A) inc (poss rev pol); gas; twin axles; phone; Eng spkn; ccard acc; golf 8km; games area; CKE. "Lovely site in beautiful area; conv location; lge pitches; welcoming, friendly, helpful owners; excel, spotless san facs; 20 mins walk to interesting old town & Laughing Cow Museum; ideal touring base; rec; excel; by busy main rd; well run; aquatic cent adj; red facs in LS; upper terr nr to superior facs; long lead poss needed." **€25.00, 1 Apr-15 Oct.** **2019**

LORIENT 2F2 (6km N Rural) 47.82041, -3.40689 **Camping Ty Nénez,** Route de Lorient, 56620 Pont-Scorff 02 97 32 51 16; contact@camping-tynenez.com; www.lorient-camping.com

12 🐕 €1 ♨(htd) 📶 🛁 🚰 ♿ 🔥 ⊘ 🅿 🍴 ⊕ 🛒 nr 🏊(htd)

N fr N165 on D6, look for sp Quéven in approx 5km on R. If missed, cont for 1km & turn around at rndabt. Site sp fr Pont-Scorff. 3*, Med, hdg, pt shd, EHU (16A) €3; bbq; 10% statics; Eng spkn; adv bkg acc; games area. "Site barrier locked 2200-0800; excel LS; peaceful NH; tidy, organised site; excel htd facs; gd base for S Brittany." **€29.00** **2017**

LORIENT 2F2 (10km NE Rural) 47.80582, -3.28347 **Camping d'Hennebont (formerly Municipal St Caradec),** Quai St Caradec, 56700 Hennebont 07 88 41 06 41 or 02 97 36 21 73; campinghennebont@gmail.com; campinghennebont.wixsite.com/bretagne

🐕 ♨ 📶 🛁 ♿ 🔥 🅿 🛒 🦋 ⊕ 🍴 nr /🏔

Fr S on D781 to Hennebont. In town cent turn L & cross bdge, then sharp R along Rv Blavet for 1km. On R on rv bank. 2*, Med, mkd, pt shd, EHU inc; 10% statics; Eng spkn; adv bkg acc; bike hire; CKE. "Pretty site; excel fishing; peaceful; pleasant sh walk into sm town; site barrier locked 2200-0700; tel on arri; excel customer care." **€13.00, 1 Apr-15 Sep.** **2019**

LOUDEAC 2E3 (2km E Urban) 48.17764, -2.72834 **Campsite Seasonova Aquarev,** Les Ponts es Bigots, 22600 Loudéac 02 96 26 21 92; contact@camping-aquarev.com; www.vacances-seasonova.com

🐕 ♨ 📶 🛁 🚰 ♿ 🔥 ⊘ 🅿 ⊕ /🏔

Fr Loudeac take N164 twrds Rennes. Site on L by lake. 2*, Med, mkd, pt shd, EHU (10A) inc; 10% statics; adv bkg acc; games area; CKE. "Walks; tennis; fishing; archery; vg." **€19.00, 31 Mar-15 Oct.** **2017**

LOUDUN 4H1 (1km W Rural) 47.00379, 0.06337 **Camp Municipal de Beausoleil,** Chemin de l'Etang, 86200 Loudun 05 49 98 14 22 or 05 49 98 15 38; mairie@ville-loudun.fr; www.ville-loudun.fr

♨ 🛁 ♿ 🅿 🦋 nr /🏔

On main rte fr Poitiers to Saumur/Le Mans; N on D347 around Loudun, foll sp; turn L just N of level x-ing, then on R approx 250m. 3*, Sm, hdg, mkd, pt shd, terr, EHU (10A) inc; bus adj; Eng spkn; lake fishing adj; CKE. "Beautiful, well-kept site; lge pitches; site yourself, warden calls am & pm; friendly & helpful; excel; long way fr the town." **€22.00, 15 May-31 Aug.** **2019**

LOURDES 8F2 (1km N Urban) 43.09697, -0.04336 **Camping de la Poste,** 26 Rue de Langelle, 65100 Lourdes 05 62 94 40 35

♨ 🛁 ♿ 🅿 📶

Fr NW take D940/D914 sp Centre Ville. At traff lts turn R. Go under rlwy bdge, at rndabt take 2nd exit sp Centre Ville. In 400m at La Poste turn L into Rue de Langelle. Site on R in 400m sp "Camping". Entry thro archway. Fr NE take N21/D914 sp Cent Ville. Sm, pt shd, EHU (3-10A); train 500m, bus 1km; adv bkg acc; CKE. "Well supervised by friendly, helpful owners; excel food mkt; basic facs; gd NH." **€12.50, 1 Apr-30 Sep.** **2016**

> **"There aren't many sites open at this time of year"**
>
> If you're travelling outside peak season remember to call ahead to check site opening dates – even if the entry says 'open all year'.

LOUVIE JUZON 8F2 (1km E Rural) 43.08940, -0.41019 **FFCC Camping Le Rey,** Quartier Listo, Route de Lourdes, 64260 Louvie-Juzon 05 59 05 78 52; nadia@camping-pyrenees-ossau.com; www.camping-pyrenees-ossau.com

🐕 €2 ♨(htd) 📶 🛁 ♿ 🔥 🅿 🦋 ⊕ 🍴 ⊕ nr 🛒 nr /🏔 ♨ 🏊

Site on L at top of hill E fr Louvie; v steep app. 3*, Sm, mkd, pt shd, pt sl, EHU (6A) €3.30; 50% statics; phone; adv bkg acc; site clsd last 2 weeks Nov & last 2 weeks Jan; watersports nr; fishing nr; games area; CKE. "Fascinating area; chateau nr; lovely, friendly site; not all facs open in LS; nice town." **€22.00, 1 Jan-15 Jan, 1 Feb-15 Nov & 1 Dec-31 Dec.** **2015**

FRANCE

LOUVIERS *3D2* (3.5km W Rural) *49.21490, 1.13279*
Camping Le Bel Air, Route de la Haye-Malherbe, Hameau de St-Lubin, 27400 Louviers **02 32 40 10 77;** contact@camping-lebelair.fr; www.camping-lebelair.fr

🐕 €2.50 [icons] (htd)

Site well sp in Louviers. Fr cent foll D81 W for 2.5km dir La Haye-Malherbe; twisting rd uphill; site on R. Or if travelling S leave A13 at junc 19 to Louviers & as bef. NB In town cent look for sm green sp after Ecole Communale (on L) & bef Jardin Public - a narr rd (1-way) & easy to miss. 3*, Med, mkd, hdg, hdstg, shd, EHU (6A) €4.90; gas; 30% statics; Eng spkn; adv bkg acc; ccard acc; CKE. "Access to pitches diff long o'fits, poss mover req; check barrier opening times; bowling; poss NH only (2013); gd site and dog walks on site; handy for Newhaven Dieppe rte." **€24.00, 15 Mar-15 Oct.** **2016**

LUCHON *8G3* (2km N Rural) *42.80806, 0.59667*
Camping Pradelongue, 31110 Moustajon **05 61 79 86 44;** contact@camping-pradelongue.com; www.camping-pradelongue.com

🐕 €2 [icons] (htd)

Site is on D125c on W of D125 main rd fr Luchon. Ent at Moustajon/Antignac going S. Site adj Intermarché; sp. 4*, Lge, mkd, hdg, pt shd, EHU (2-10A) €2-4; bbq; 10% statics; Eng spkn; adv bkg acc; ccard acc; games area; CKE. "Excel, well-run, tidy, big site; mountain views; gd sized pitches; friendly, helpful owners; rec; excel clean san facs; big supmkt adj; 20mins walk to lovely town; excel for walking, mountain & rd cycling." **€26.00, 1 Apr-30 Sep.** **2015**

LUCON *7A1* (11km E Rural) *46.46745, -1.02792*
Camp Municipal Le Vieux Chêne, Rue du Port, 85370 Nalliers **02 51 30 91 98 or 02 51 30 90 71;** nalliers. mairie@wanadoo.fr

[icons]

Fr Luçon E on D949 dir Fontenay-le-Comte; 500m after ent Nalliers turn R onto D10 (Rue de Brantome); after level x-ing cont strt on for 50m (leaving D10); then Rue du Port on L. Site sp on D949 but easy to miss. 2*, Sm, hdg, mkd, pt shd, EHU (4-13A) €3.90; adv bkg acc; CKE. "Excel, clean site; site yourself on lge pitch; in LS contact Mairie for ent to site; vg NH; conv for rd to Bordeaux." **€14.50, 15 May-15 Sep.** **2015**

LUCON *7A1* (17km SE Rural) *46.39174, -01.01952*
Camping l'île Cariot, Rue Du 8 Mai, 85450 Chaillé-les-Marais **02 5156 7527;** camping.ilecariot@gmail.com; camping-chaille-les-marais.com

🐕 €1.65 [icons] (htd)

In Chaille take D25, sp in town. 3*, Sm, mkd, pt shd, EHU (10A) €3.90; bbq; TV; bus adj; Eng spkn; adv bkg acc; games area; games rm; CKE. "Cycle & walking rtes fr site; nr 'Green Venice'; free canoeing on canal; excel." **€19.00, 1 Apr-30 Sep.** **2016**

LUDE, LE *4G1* (1km NE Rural) *47.65094, 0.16221*
Camp Municipal au Bord du Loir, Route du Mans, 72800 Le Lude **02 43 94 67 70;** camping@ville-lelude.fr; www.camping-lelude.com

[icons]

Fr town cent take D305 (E); in 1km take D307 (N) sp 'Le Mans'; site immed on L. Well sp. Fr E on D305, avoid cent of Vaas, use HGV route. 3*, Med, mkd, hdg, pt shd, EHU (10A) inc; bbq (gas); TV; 10% statics; phone; Eng spkn; adv bkg acc; ccard acc; fishing; cycling; tennis; canoeing; CKE. "Well-kept, well-run site; warm welcome, helpful staff; modern san facs; vg walk to town; Château du Lude & excel rest nrby; highly rec; gd." **€13.00, 1 Apr-4 Oct.** **2016**

LUNEL *10E2* (3km S Rural) *43.65666, 4.14111*
Camping Le Bon Port, 383 Chemin de Mas St Angé, 34400 Lunel **04 67 71 15 65;** contact@camping bonport.com; www.campingbonport.com

🐕 €3.50 [icons]

Exit A9 junc 27 S dir La Grande Motte, D61. Site sp on L. 4*, Lge, mkd, hdg, pt shd, EHU (5A) €4; bbq (gas); TV; 50% statics; adv bkg acc; games area; waterslide. "Site scruffy; ltd facs out of ssn; narr site rds; new leisure pools being completed (2015)." **€37.00, 4 Apr-30 Sep.** **2015**

LUSIGNAN *7A2* (0.5km N Rural) *46.43712, 0.12369*
Camp Municipal de Vauchiron, Chemin de la Plage, 86600 Lusignan **05 49 43 30 08 or 05 49 43 31 48** (Mairie); lusignan@cg86.fr; www.lusignan.fr

[icons]

Site sp fr D611, 22km SW of Poitiers; foll camp sp in Lusignan to rvside. 2*, Med, pt shd, EHU (15A) €2.40 (poss rev pol); bbq; sw nr; phone; adv bkg acc; ccard acc; fishing; boat hire; CKE. "Beautiful, peaceful site in spacious park; lge pitches; forest & rv walks adj; friendly, helpful resident warden; excel clean san facs; steep walk to historic town; highly rec; rv fishing." **€13.50, 15 Apr-30 Sep.** **2017**

LUSSAC LES CHATEAUX *7A3* (13km SW Rural) *46.32231, 0.67384* **Camp Municipal du Renard,** 8 route de la Mairie, 86150 Queaux **05 49 48 48 32 or 05 49 48 48 08** (Mairie); contact@queaux.fr; www.queaux.fr

[icons]

Fr Lussac cross rv bdge sp Poitiers & immed turn L. Foll sp to Gouex & Queaux. Site on D25 S of vill. 2*, Med, mkd, pt shd, pt sl, EHU (6A) €2.50; 10% statics; Eng spkn. "Lovely rvside site nr pleasant vill; manned high ssn or apply to Mairie." **€9.00, 15 Jun-15 Sep.** **2017**

FRANCE

LUXEUIL LES BAINS *6F2* (0.5km N Rural) *47.82315, 6.38200* **FFCC Camping du Domaine de Chatigny, 14 Rue Grammont, 70300 Luxeuil-les-Bains 03 84 93 97 97; camping.lechatigny@chainethermale.fr; www.domaine-du-chatigny.com**

★ €1.70 ♦♦♦(htd) ⬚ ⬚ ⛆ 🐾 ∅ / MSP 🦋 ♈ 🍽 ⊕ ⚲ 🅿 nr ⤢ ⛵

N fr Vesoul on N57; turn L at rndabt into Luxeuil-les-Bains; foll Camping sp. Vehicular access fr Rue Ste Anne. 3*, Med, hdstg, mkd, hdg, pt shd, terr, EHU (16A) €3.50-4.50; gas; bbq; TV; 20% statics; bus 300m; Eng spkn; adv bkg acc; ccard acc; CKE. *"New (2009), high standard site; indoor tennis court; gd."* **€8.00, 1 Mar-31 Oct.** 2019

LUZ ST SAUVEUR *8G2* (1km N Rural) *42.88140, -0.01258* **Airotel Camping Pyrénées, 46 Ave du Barège, La Ferme Theil, 65120 Esquièze-Sère 05 62 92 89 18; contact@airotel-pyrenees.com; www.airotel-pyrenees.com**

★ €1.50 ♦♦♦(htd) ⬚ ⬚ ⛆ ♿ ⤢ ∅ / MSP 🦋 ♈ 🍽 ⊕ ⚲ 🅿 nr ⤢ ∥ 🖉 ⤢ (covrd)

On main rd fr Lourdes to Luz on L past Int'l Campsite. L U-turn into ent archway needs care - use full width of rd & forecourt. 5*, Med, mkd, shd, pt sl, EHU (3-10A) €3.50-6.50 (rev pol); gas; TV; 30% statics; Eng spkn; adv bkg acc; ccard acc; horseriding; sauna; site clsd Oct & Nov; fishing; CKE. *"Beautiful area; facs poss stretched high ssn; ski in winter; walking; excel walking & wildlife; lovely vill; well organised; ACSI discount."* **€37.00, 1 May-24 Sep.** 2017

LUZ ST SAUVEUR *8G2* (0.2km E Urban) *42.87342, -0.00057* **Camping Toy, 17 Place du 8 mai 1945, 65120 Luz Saint Sauveur 05 62 92 86 85; campingtoy@gmail.com; www.camping-toy.com**

12 🐾 ♦♦♦ ⬚ ⬚ ♿ ∅ / 🦋 ♈ 🍽 nr ⊕ nr 🅿 nr ⤢

Fr Lourdes D921, at Luz St Sauveur turn L onto sq after x-ing rv. Site in 100m. Med, mkd, pt shd, pt sl, EHU (1-10A); bbq; bus adj; Eng spkn. *"In cent of town; helpful, friendly owners; pool 0.5km; magnificent views; gd walking/cycling area; st foot of Col du Tourmalet; excel."* **€15.00** 2015

LUZ ST SAUVEUR *8G2* (2km NW Rural) *42.88218, -0.02270* **Camping Le Pyrénévasion, Route de Luz-Andiden 65120 Sazos 05 62 92 91 54; camping-pyrenevasion@wanadoo.fr; www.camping pyrenevasion.com**

12 🐾 €2.50 ♦♦♦(htd) ⬚ ⬚ ⛆ ♿ ⤢ ∅ / 🦋 ♈ 🍽 ⊕ ⚲ 🅿 nr ⤢ ∥ 🖉 ⤢ 🏔

Fr Lourdes S on D921 twd Gavarnie. Shortly bef Luz-St Sauveur after petrol stn & campsites sp, take R fork onto D12 sp Sazos. Cont thro vill & turn R sp Luz-Andiden, then immed R again sp Sazos (D12) & Luz-Andiden. Cont uphill, site on R just after Sazon sp. 3*, Med, mkd, hdg, pt shd, EHU (3A/6A/10A) €3.5/€7/€8; gas; bbq (charcoal, elec, gas); 60% statics; Eng spkn; fishing; games rm; site clsd 20 Oct-19 Nov. *"Fair site in mountains; no o'fits over 7.5m high ssn; long, steep trek to/fr shops."* **€28.00** 2017

LUZY *4H4* (1km NE Rural) *46.79622, 3.97685* **Camping La Bédure, Route d'Autun, 58170 Luzy 03 86 30 68 27; info@campinglabedure.com; www.campinglabedure.com**

★ €1.50 ♦♦♦ ⬚ ⬚ ∅ / 🦋 🅿 nr ⤢

Foll sps on D981 to site. 2*, Med, mkd, pt shd, pt sl, EHU (6A) €3 (poss rev pol); Eng spkn. *"Pleasant site; pool adj; gd walking & touring base; adjoins Lidl."* **€18.60, 14 Apr-30 Sep.** 2018

LYON *9B2* (8km NW Urban) *45.81948, 4.76168* **Camping Indigo Lyon, Ave de la Porte de Lyon, 69570 Dardilly 04 78 35 64 55; lyon@camping-indigo.com; www.camping-indigo.com**

12 🐾 €4 ♦♦♦(htd) ⬚ ⬚ ⛆ ♿ ⤢ ∅ / MSP 🦋 ♈ 🍽 nr ⊕ nr 🅿 nr ⤢ ⛵

Fr D306 Paris rd, take Limonest-Dardilly-Porte de Lyon exit at Auchan supmkt. Fr A6 exit junc 33 Porte de Lyon. Site on W side of A6 adj m'way & close to junc, foll sp (poss obscured by trees) for 'Complexe Touristique'. Fr E take N ring rd dir Roanne, Paris, then as above. 4*, Lge, mkd, hdg, hdstg, pt shd, serviced pitches; EHU (6-10A) €4.70-7.50; twin axles; TV; 10% statics; phone; bus/train to city nr; Eng spkn; adv bkg acc; ccard acc; games rm; CKE. *"Well-run, secure site; Lyon easy by bus & metro, tickets can be bought fr recep; bar 100m; gd touring base for interesting area; helpful recep; gd, clean san facs; gas 100m; cafes nrby."* **€30.00** 2017

"That's changed – Should I let the Club know?"

If you find something on site that's different from the site entry, fill in a report and let us know. See camc.com/europereport.

MACHECOUL *2H4* (0.5km SE Urban) *46.98987, -1.81562* **Camp Municipal La Rabine, Allée de la Rabine, 44270 Máchecoul 02 40 02 30 48 or 06 08 49 22 88; camprabine@wanadoo.fr; camping-la-rabine.com**

★ €0.90 ♦♦♦ ⬚ ⬚ ⤢ ∅ / 🦋 ♈ 🅿 nr ⤢ 🖉

Sp fr most dirs. Look out for prominent twin-spired church in cent; take sm one-way rd that leads away fr spire end; site on R in 400m. 2*, Med, pt shd, EHU (4-13A) €2-3.20; bbq (gas); adv bkg acc. *"Pleasant site with lge generous size pitches & gd facs; excel base for birdwatching & cycling over marshes; pleasant town; mkt Wed & Sat; pool adj; lovely friendly well managed site; excel facs; lovely site rv fishing."* **€15.00, 1 Apr-30 Sep.** 2017

For a guide to symbols see the fold out on the rear cover

MACON *9A2* (4km N Urban) *46.33023, 4.84491*
Camp Municipal Les Varennes, 1 Route des Grandes Varennes, Sancé, 71000 Mâcon **03 85 38 16 22 or 03 85 38 54 08; camping@ville-macon.fr; www.macon.fr/Tourisme/Camping**
€1.40 (htd)

Fr both N & S exit A6 junc 28 & cont S on N6 twd Mâcon; site on L in approx 3km, sp. (Fr S, leaving A6 at junc 28 avoids long trip thro town). 4*, Lge, mkd, pt shd, pt sl, EHU (5-10A) inc (poss rev pol); gas; red long stay; twin axles; TV; phone; bus; Eng spkn; adv bkg acc; ccard acc; golf 6km; tennis 1km; CKE. *"Well-kept, busy NH nr A6; rec arr early as poss full after 1800; friendly staff; vg, immac san facs; hypmkt 1km; excel rest; gates clsd 2200-0630; poss flooding bottom end of site; long level walk to town; excel; perfect new facs (2014)."* **€27.00, 15 Mar-31 Oct.** **2019**

MACON *9A2* (8km S Rural) *46.25167, 4.82610* **Base de loisirs du lac de Cormoranche,** Les Luizant, 01290 Cormoranche-sur-Saône **03 85 23 97 10; contact@lac-cormoranche.com; www.lac-cormoranche.com**
€2.20 (htd)

Exit A26 junc 29 sp Mâcon Sud onto N6 S to Crêches-sur-Saône. Turn L in town at traff lts onto D31 sp Cormoranche, then D51A. Cross rv, site sp on L. Alt rte: exit N6 in Mâcon & turn E onto D1079 dir St Laurent-sur-Saône then take D933 S to Pont-de-Veyle. Cont on D933 & foll sp to Cormoranche. 4*, Med, mkd, hdg, pt shd, EHU (10A) inc; sw nr; TV; 25% statics; Eng spkn; adv bkg acc; ccard acc; fishing; bike hire; CKE. *"Spacious pitches, some with narr access; vg; tight access to some pitches; gd for families."* **€21.00, 1 May-30 Sep.** **2018**

MAICHE *6G3* (1km S Rural) *47.24705, 6.79952*
Camp Municipal St Michel, 23 Rue St Michel, 25120 Maîche **03 81 64 12 56 or 03 81 64 03 01 (Mairie); contact@mairie-maiche.fr; www.mairie-maiche.fr**
12 (htd) nr

Fr S turn R off D437 onto D442. App on D464 L on o'skts of town. Sp fr both dir. 3*, Med, pt shd, sl, terr, EHU (6A) inc; 10% statics; phone; adv bkg acc; games area; site clsd 3rd week Nov & Dec; games rm. *"Beautiful, neat, well-run site with lovely views; many trees & wild flowers; lower pitches are quieter; pool adj; clean facs; phone ahead LS to check open; gd walks in woods."* **€18.00** **2017**

MAILLEZAIS *7A2* (0.4km S Rural) *46.36921, -0.74054*
Camp Municipal de l'Autize, Rue du Champ de Foire, 85420 Maillezais **02 51 00 70 79 or 06 43 19 14 90 (mob); camping.lautize@orange.fr; www.maillezais.fr**
nr

Fr Fontenay take D148 twd Niort; after 9km, turn R onto D15 to Maillezais; pass church in vill on L, site on R after 200m. Or fr A83, exit junc 9 onto D148, then D15 (do not use v minor rds, as poss directed by sat nav). 3*, Sm, hdg, mkd, pt shd, EHU (4-13A) €3-5; twin axles; TV; adv bkg acc; ccard acc; games rm; games area; CKE. *"Lovely, clean site; spacious pitches, gd views fr some; friendly, helpful warden; excel, immac san facs; warden calls am & pm; some low branches (2010); excel mkd cycle paths; conv Marais Poitevin area & Venise Verte; nrby abbey worth a visit; vg NH fr A83; excel; boat rides fr Vieux Port."* **€17.00, 1 Jun-30 Sep.** **2018**

MAILLY LE CHATEAU *4G4* (5km S Rural) *47.56267, 3.64671* **Camping Merry Sur Yonne (formerly Municipal Escale),** 5 Impasse de Sables, 89660 Merry-sur-Yonne **03 86 34 59 55; gite.merrysuryonne@wanadoo.fr; www.campingmerrysuryonne.com**
12

Fr N on D100, turn R over bdge, sp Merry Sur Yonne. At t-junc in vill turn L. At end of vill bear L at war memorial into site. 2*, Med, hdstg, mkd, pt shd, EHU; bbq; cooking facs; sw nr; twin axles; Eng spkn; adv bkg acc; games rm; games area; CCI. *"New British owners; takeaway; beautiful location nr rv and canal; canal walks adj; excel."* **€15.00** **2016**

MAINTENON *4E2* (6km NW Rural) *48.60890, 1.54760*
Camping Les Ilots de St Val, Le Haut Bourray, 28130 Villiers-le-Morhier **02 37 82 71 30; lesilots@campinglesilotsdestval.com; www.campinglesilotsdestval.com**
€2 (htd) nr

Take D983 N fr Maintenon twd Nogent-le-Roi, in 5km 2nd L onto D101 sp Néron/Vacheresses-les-Basses/Camping to site in 1km on L at top of hill. NB New by-pass around Nogent le Roi fr N. 3*, Lge, hdg, mkd, hdstg, pt shd, EHU (6-10A) €4-7; gas; bbq; red long stay; 50% statics; Eng spkn; adv bkg acc; games rm; rv fishing 1km; tennis; CKE. *"Pleasant, peaceful site in open countryside; lge private pitches; some vg, modern san facs; helpful staff; gd value site; conv Chartres, Versailles, Maintenon Château, train to Paris; dog walking fr the site is gd; improved access for lge o'fits; pool 4km; phone ahead late Dec to mid Feb as site may be clsd to tourers."*
€32.00, 1 Feb-22 Dec. **2016**

MALBUISSON 6H2 (1.4km SW Urban) 46.79176, 6.29257 **Camping Les Fuvettes,** 24 Route de la Plage et des Perrières, 25160 Malbuisson **03 81 69 31 50; les-fuvettes@wanadoo.fr; www.camping-fuvettes.com**

🐕 €1.50 ♦♦♦ (htd) ॑ 🖳 🖉 ⚕ 🦋 ⊤ ⊕ ≋ 🐾 ⚖

Site 19km S of Pontarlier on N57 & D437 to Malbuisson, thro town, R down rd to Plage.
3*, Lge, pt shd, pt sl, EHU (4-6A) €3.60-4; gas; sw; 30% statics; fishing; games rm; boating; CKE. *"Popular, lakeside, family site; mkd walks/cycle paths in adj woods; petting zoo (llamas etc) nrby."*
€28.00, 5 Apr-30 Sep.   2019

MALENE, LA 9D1 (0.2km W Rural) 44.30120, 3.31923 **FFCC Camp Municipal Le Pradet,** 48210 La Malène **04 66 48 58 55 or 04 66 48 51 16 (LS); camping. lamalene@gmail.com; www.gorgesdutarn-camping.com**

🐕 €0.30 ♦♦♦ ॑ 🖳 🖉 🌐 🦋 ⊤ nr ⊕ nr 🐾 nr ⚖

W fr La Malène on D907B dir Les Vignes. Site on L in 200m. Well sp. 2*, Sm, hdstg, mkd, pt shd, pt sl, EHU (10A) €2.50; bbq; sw; phone; adv bkg acc; ccard acc; fishing; CKE. *"Kayak hire; boat trips fr vill; helpful warden; excel; v narr pitches; rvside site; steep slope down to recep; spectacular scenery."*
€27.00, 1 Apr-30 Sep.   2017

MALESHERBES 4E3 (5km S Rural) 48.25659, 2.43574 **FFCC Camping Ile de Boulancourt,** 6 Allée des Marronniers, 77760 Boulancourt **01 64 24 13 38; info@camping-iledeboulancourt.com; www.camping-iledeboulancourt.com**

⑫ 🐕 €1 ♦♦♦ (htd) 🗤 ॑ 🖳 🖉 🦋 ⊕ 🐾 nr ⚖

Exit A6 at junc 14 Ury & Fontainebleau. SW on D152 to Malesherbes; S on D410 for 5km into Boulancourt. Site sp fr D410 & in vill. 3*, Med, pt shd, EHU (3-6A) €2.70; bbq; 90% statics; Eng spkn; waterslide 5km; fishing 3km; tennis; CKE. *"Attractive rv thro site; well-maintained facs, ltd LS; sep field for tourers; friendly, helpful staff; golf course in vill; chateau nr; excel."* **€15.70**   2016

MALESTROIT 2F3 (0.5km E Urban) 47.80865, -2.37922 **Camp Municipal de la Daufresne,** Chemin des Tanneurs, 56140 Malestroit **02 97 75 13 33 or 02 97 75 11 75 (Mairie); etat.civil@malestroit.fr; www.villede malestroit.bzh**

🐕 ♦♦♦ 🗤 ॑ ॑ ⚕ 🖉 🌐 ⍦ ⊤ nr ⊕ nr 🐾 nr ⚖

S fr Ploërmel on N166 dir Vannes for 9km. Turn L onto D764 to Malestroit; site sp just off Blvd du Pont Neuf on E bank of Rv Oust, not well sp.
2*, Sm, hdg, pt shd, EHU (10A) €2.70 (poss long lead req); adv bkg acc; ccard acc; rv fishing adj; tennis; canoeing nr; CKE. *"Pleasant site in excel location; narr site rds, some pitches poss diff to manoeuvre; no twin axles; clean san facs, basic but ok, poss stretched high ssn; canal towpath adj; gd cycle rtes; Museum of Breton Resistance in St Marcel; v nice, pretty site, highly rec."* **€10.00, 1 May-15 Sep.**   2017

MAMERS 4E1 (0.5km N Rural) 48.35778, 0.37181 **Camp Municipal du Saosnois,** Route de Contilly, 72600 Mamers **02 43 97 68 30; camping.mamers@ free.fr; www.mairie-mamers.fr**

🐕 €0.50 ♦♦♦ (htd) ॑ ॑ 🖳 🖉 🌐 🦋 ⍦ ⚕ 🐾

Fr W on D311, at rndabt at top of hill on circular rd, turn R (sp); then easy L (sp). Fr E on D311, strt thro rndabt (at Super U), ignore 1st camping sp, turn R at traff its & 2nd camping sp; at mini-rndabt turn L, sp Contilly; see lake & site. 3*, Sm, hdg, hdstg, pt shd, pt sl, terr, EHU (10A) inc (long lead poss req); TV; 30% statics; adv bkg acc; games area; CKE. *"Well-kept, secure site; admittance LS 1700-1900 only; Mamers pretty; pool 200m; lakeside; easy walk to town."*
€15.00, 15 Apr-30 Sep.   2016

> ## "There aren't many sites open at this time of year"
>
> If you're travelling outside peak season remember to call ahead to check site opening dates – even if the entry says 'open all year'.

MANDRES AUX QUATRE TOURS 5D2 (2km S Rural) 48.82739, 5.78936 **Camp Municipal Orée de la Forêt de la Reine,** Route Forêt de la Reine, 54470 Mandres-aux-Quatre-Tours **03 83 23 17 31; mandres. 54470@wandoo.fr**

🐕 ♦♦♦ 🗤 ॑ 🖉 🦋 ⊕ ⍦ ⚖

On D958 Commercy to Pont-à-Mousson, sp as Camping Mandres. Turn R at sp in Beaumont & foll sp to vill Mandres-aux-Quatre-Tours.
1*, Sm, mkd, hdg, pt shd, EHU (10A) inc (poss long lead req); red long stay; 10% statics; tennis; sailing 500m; watersports 500m; horseriding adj. *"Gd, peaceful site; basic san facs; site poss muddy when wet; gd birdwatching, walking, cycling; popular NH."*
€17.00, 1 Apr-31 Oct.   2018

MANOSQUE 10E3 (4km E Rural) 43.82352, 5.85424 **Camping Oxygene,** 04210 Valensole **04 92 72 41 77; info@camping-oxygene.com; www.camping-oxygene.com**

🐕 €2.50 ♦♦♦ 🗤 ॑ ⚕ ॑ ⚕ 🖉 🌐 🦋 ⊤ ⚕ 🏊

Exit A51 junc 18 onto D907 E dir Vinon-sur-Verdon; in 1km turn L at rndabt onto D4 N dir Oraison; site in 2.5km on L, at Les Chabrands, just bef Villedieu. Med, mkd, pt shd, EHU (6-10A) €3.50-4.50; bbq (elec, gas); gym; horseriding nr; games area. *"Peaceful, well-kept site with hill views; excel well-run site; vg pool; many places of interest nrby, inc Gorges du Verdon; canyoning, angling & rafting nr; paragliding nr; vg farm shop nr."* **€33.50, 20 Apr-17 Sep.**   2019

FRANCE

MANS, LE *4F1* (7.6km NE Rural) *48.01904, 0.27996*
Camping Le Pont Romain, Allée des Ormeaux, Lieu-dit La Châtaigneraie, 72530 Yvré-l'Evêque
02 43 82 25 39; contact@campinglepontromain.fr

🐕 €1 ♟(htd) 📶 ♨ ♿ 🚻 ⚙ / 🗺 🦋 ☂ ⑪ ♨ 🐾 🔥 /🏊 ⚓(htd) ⛵

Fr Le Mans take D314 to Yvré-l'Evêque - but do not ent town; just after rv bdge take 1st L into Allée des Ormeaux; site on L in 800m. Or exit A28 junc 23 onto D314 dir 'Le Mans Cent'; site on R just bef Yvré-l'Evêque. Avoid direct rte into vill over bridge. 4*, Med, hdstg, mkd, hdg, pt shd, EHU (16A) inc; gas; bbq; 15% statics; phone; bus; Eng spkn; adv bkg acc; games rm; CKE. *"Excel modern san facs but ltd number of toilets; sep car park; conv Le Mans & m'way; vg; uneven pitches, need TLC; pleasant rural site; easy access to city; recep open 0830-1200 & 1430-2000; gd; bus to Le Mans 1.5km; beautiful site; easy access to bus; excel pitches."* **€28.60, 16 Mar-11 Nov.** **2018**

"That's changed – Should I let the Club know?"

If you find something on site that's different from the site entry, fill in a report and let us know. See camc.com/europereport.

MANS, LE *4F1* (20km SW Urban) *47.889024, 0.033594*
Camp Municipal Le Port, Ave de la Piscine, 72210 La Suze-sur-Sarthe 02 43 77 32 74 or 02 43 77 39 48; contact@lasuzero.fr; www.lasuze.fr

12 🐕 €0.45 ♟ 📶 ♨ ♿ / 🗺 🐾 /🏊 ⚓(htd)

Fr A11 take exit 9 twrds Tours/Allonnes on A11.1, 1st exit on rndabt onto D309. Foll sp to La Suze Sur Sarthe on D233. Cross rlwy and turn L as you come into town, foll sp for MH. Turn R into Ave de la Piscine, then right into parking area. Pay at barrier to be let thro to site. 2*, Med, mkd, pt shd, EHU (10A) €2.30; bbq; red long stay; TV; boating; rv adj; own san; tennis; adv bkg; fishing. *"Narr gate to site; ample hdstg for m'vans in adj car park."* **€4.50** **2018**

MANSLE *7B2* (0.4km NE Urban) *45.87841, 0.18175*
Camp Municipal Le Champion, Rue de Watlington, 16230 Mansle 05 45 20 31 41 or 05 45 22 20 43; mairie.mansle@wanadoo.fr; www.mansle.fr

♟ 📶 ♨ ♿ / 🗺 🦋 ☂ nr ⑪ 🐾 /🏊 ♨

N on N10 fr Angoulême, foll sp Mansle Ville. Leave N10 at exit to N of town, site rd on L, well sp. Rec ent/leave fr N as rte thro town diff due to parked cars. Site beside Rv Charente. 3*, Med, hdg, pt shd, EHU (16A) €2.80 (poss long lead req); bbq; sw nr; 5% statics; phone; Eng spkn; adv bkg acc; fishing; boating adj; CKE. *"Popular, peaceful, well-kept NH nr N10; lge pitches, choose own; helpful warden; immac san facs; grnd poss boggy after heavy rain; mkt Tues, Fri am; great site in excel location, well run; vg; gd rest; easy walk to town."* **€16.40, 15 May-15 Sep.** **2017**

MANSLE *7B2* (10km SE Rural) *45.84137, 0.27319*
Camping Devezeau, 16230 St Angeau 05 45 94 63 09; ask@campingdevezeau.com; www.camping devezeau.com

12 🐕 ♟(htd) 📶 ♨ ♿ 🚻 / 🗺 🦋 ☂ ☂ ⑪ ♨ 🐾 nr 🔥

N or S on N10 exit Mansle; in cent vill at traff lts foll sp twd La Rochefoucauld (D6); past Super U supmkt; over bdge; 1st R onto D6. In approx 9km at T-junc turn R, site sp. App down narr rd. 2*, Sm, hdstg, hdg, pt shd, sl, EHU (6A-10A) €2; gas; bbq; twin axles; 25% statics; Eng spkn; adv bkg acc; cycling; canoeing; horseriding; fishing; CKE. *"Nice CL-type site; v friendly British owners; excel san facs modernised (2015); traction diff in wet (4x4 avail); blocks & steel pegs needed; gd cycling country; phone ahead in winter; lovely tranquil site; walking; vg; friendly atmosphere; bar snacks & English breakfast."* **€20.00** **2017**

MARANS *7A1* (1km N Rural) *46.31682, -0.99158*
Camp Municipal Le Bois Dinot, Route de Nantes, 17230 Marans 05 46 01 10 51; campingmarans@orange.fr; www.ville-marans.fr

🐕 €1.10 ♟ ♨ / ⑪ ☂ nr ⑪ nr 🐾 nr

Heading S, site on L of D137 bef ent Marans. Heading N, site is well sp on R 300m after supmkt on L. 3*, Lge, shd, EHU (6-10A) €3; red long stay; Eng spkn; adv bkg rec; fishing; boat hire; CKE. *"Well-kept, wooded site; v helpful, efficient staff; quieter pitches at back of site; vg pool adj; poss mosquitoes; gd cycling; mkt Tues & Sat; excel; v clean san facs; grass pitch avail subj to rainfall; woodland pitches quietest; poss diff lger o'fits."* **€16.50, 1 Apr-30 Sep.** **2019**

MARENNES *7B1* (10.5km SE Rural) *45.77324, -0.96301* **Camping Le Valerick,** La Petite Mauvinière, 17600 St Sornin 05 46 85 15 95; camplevalerick@aol.com; www.camping-le-valerick.fr

🐕 €1.40 ♟(htd) 📶 🚻 / 🦋 ☂ 🐾 /🏊

Fr Marennes take D728 sp Saintes for 10km; L to St Sornin; site sp in vill. Fr Saintes D728 W for 26km; take 2nd R turn R in vill D118, site on L sp La Gripperie. 2*, Sm, mkd, pt shd, pt sl, EHU (4-6A) €3-€3.70 (poss rev pol); bbq (charcoal, gas); adv bkg acc; ccard acc; CKE. *"Nice, friendly site; gd san facs; plenty of bird life - herons, storks etc; poss mosquito problem; excel; spotless san facs; lge pitches; v warm welcome; highly rec."* **€19.00, 1 Apr-30 Sep.** **2019**

"I like to fill in the reports as I travel from site to site"

You'll find report forms at the back of this guide, or you can fill them in online at camc.com/europereport.

FRANCE

MARENNES *7B1* (5km SE Rural) *45.81083, -1.06027*
Camping Séquoia Parc, La Josephtrie, 17320 St
Just-Luzac 05 46 85 55 55; info@sequoiaparc.com;
www.sequoiaparc.com

Fr A10/E05 m'way exit at Saintes, foll sp Royan
(N150) turning off onto D728 twd Marennes & Ile
d'Oléron; site sp to R off D728, just after leaving
St Just-Luzac. Or fr Rochefort take D733 & D123 S;
just bef Marennes turn L on D241 sp St Just-Luzac.
Best ent to site fr D728, well sp fr each dir.
5*, Lge, mkd, hdg, unshd, sl, serviced pitches; EHU
(6A) inc (poss rev pol); gas; bbq; red long stay; TV;
60% statics; adv bkg acc; ccard acc; fishing 1.5km;
bike hire; watersports 3km; games area; horseriding;
tennis; games rm; CKE. "High standard site; aqua park:
o'fits over 8m on request; max 1 dog; waterslides,
waterjets & whirlpool; barrier clsd 2230-0700; 3 pools
(2 htd); lge pitches; cash machine; clean san facs;
superb pools; excel free club for children."
€54.00, 5 May-5 Sep, A28.   2019
See advertisement

"We must tell the Club about that great site we found"

Get your site reports in by mid-August and we'll
do our best to get your updates into the next
edition.

MARENNES *7B1* (2km NW Coastal) *45.83139, -1.15092*
Camp Municipal La Giroflée, 17560 Bourcefranc-le-
Chapus 05 46 85 06 43 or 05 46 85 02 02 (Mairie);
campinglagiroflee@orange.fr; www.bourcefranc-le-
chapus.fr

Fr Saintes on D728/D26 to Boucefranc, turn
L at traff lts. Site on L after 1km (after sailing
school) opp beach. 2*, Med, pt shd, EHU (6A) €3.
€7.60, 1 May-30 Sep.   2017

MAREUIL *7B2* (4km SE Rural) *45.44481, 0.50474*
Camping L'Etang Bleu, 24340 Vieux-Mareuil 05 53 60
92 70; letangbleu@ornage.fr; www.letangbleu.com

On D939 Angoulême-Périgueux rd, after 5km turn
L cent of Vieux-Mareuil onto D93, foll camping
sp to site in 2km. Narr app thro vill, care needed.
2*, Lge, hdg, mkd, pt shd, EHU 6-10A (poss rev pol);
gas; bbq; TV; 10% statics; adv bkg acc; ccard acc;
lake fishing 500m; CKE. "Pleasant site in unspoilt
countryside; lge pitches, but narr site rds; access
diff lge o'fits without mover; friendly British owners;
gd san facs, ltd LS; gd walking/cycling area; excel."
€23.50, 1 Apr-20 Oct.   2018

"I need an on-site restaurant"

We do our best to make sure site information
is correct, but it is always best to check any
must-have facilities are still available or will
be open during your visit.

MAREUIL *7B2* (8km SE Rural) *45.42429, 0.53070*
Camping La Charrue, Les Chambarrières, 24340
Vieux-Mareuil 05 53 56 65 59; bookings@lacharrue.
biz or clive.davie@sfr.fr; www.lacharrue.biz
sand nrby

SE fr Angoulême on D939 sp Périgueux to Mareuil.
Fr Mareuil stay on D939 twds Brantôme, thro Vieux-
Mareuil then in 2km site immed on L after passing a
lge lay-by on R with white stone chippings. Awkward
turn. Sm, mkd, pt shd, EHU (4A) €3; bbq; red long
stay; adv bkg req; watersports nr; fishing 3km; bike
hire; golf nr; CKE. "CL-type site in Regional Park;
friendly, helpful British owners; no dogs high ssn; bar
500m; immac facs; gd touring base for beautiful area;
lakes nrby; B&B & gites avail; excel."
€14.50, 1 May-31 Oct.   2015

MARNAY (HAUTE SAONE) *6G2* (0.5km SE Urban) *47.28975, 5.77628* **Camping Vert Lagon,** Route de Besançon, 70150 Marnay **03 84 31 73 16 or 06 40 78 58 13; accueil@camping-vertlagon.com; www.camping-vertlagon.com**

🛠 €1 ♦♦ ⬚ ♨ ♿ ▣ ∥ ⬚ 🐾 ⊕nr 🐕 🏋nr /Ⅱ 🔥(htd)

Fr N stay on D67 Marnay by-pass; ignore old camping sp into town. Proceed to S of town on by-pass then turn L at junc. Bef bdge in 1km take gravel rd on S side, round under bdge to site (app thro town fr N v narr). 4*, Med, hdg, mkd, pt shd, EHU (10A) €4; bbq; 40% statics; adv bkg acc; ccard acc; games area; canoeing; fishing; CKE. *"Pleasant, popular, family site by Rv Ognon; gd san facs; lake adj; tree-top walks; vg."* **€21.00, 2 May-30 Sep.** **2017**

"Satellite navigation makes touring much easier"

Remember most sat navs don't know if you're towing or in a larger vehicle – always use yours alongside maps and site directions.

MARQUION *3B4* (2.7km NE Rural) *50.22280, 3.10863* **FFCC Camping de l'Epinette,** 7 Rue du Calvaire, 62860 Sauchy-Lestrée **03 21 59 50 13; lepinette62@wanadoo.fr; www.lepinette62.com**

🛠 ♦♦ ⬚ ♨ ∥ 🏋nr /Ⅱ

Fr A26 exit junc 8 onto D939 to Marquion. On ent Marquion turn R at x-rds to Sauchy-Lestrée; on ent vill turn R at 1st T-junc & site on L in 100m. Fr Cambrai take D939 twd Arras, then as above. 2*, Sm, pt shd, pt sl, EHU (10A) €3 (poss rev pol); own san rec; gas; 80% statics; adv bkg acc; games area; CKE. *"Charming, well-kept site in tranquil spot; sm CL-type area for tourers; clean, simple, dated but adequate facs, no facs LS, NH only; levelling blocks ess for m'vans; conv Calais/Dunkerque; quiet but some military aircraft noise; WW1 cemetary nr; gd value; popular excel NH."* **€15.00, 1 Apr-31 Oct.** **2019**

MARQUISE *3A3* (5km SW Rural) *50.78389, 1.66917* **FFCC Camping L'Escale,** 15 Route Nationale, 62250 Wacquinghen **03 21 32 00 69; camp-escale@wanadoo.fr; www.escale-camping.fr**

🛠 ♦♦(cont) ▣ ⬚ ♿ ∥ ⬚ 🐾 ♈ ⊕🐕 🏋 /Ⅱ 🗡

Fr A16 S fr Calais exit junc 34. Fr A16 N fr Boulogne exit junc 33. Foll sp. 3*, Lge, pt shd, EHU (4A) €3.50 (poss rev pol); gas; 90% statics; ccard acc. *"Pleasant, busy site; open 24 hrs; conv NH nr ferries, A16, Channel tunnel & WW2 coastal defences; o'fits staying 1 night pitch on meadow at front of site for ease of exit (but some noise fr m'way); m'van 'aire' open all yr; vg; site relandscaped (2017), vg; comfort pitches."* **€25.00, 1 Apr-15 Oct.** **2017**

MARSANNE *9D2* (2.5km NE Rural) *44.65769, 4.89098* **Camping Les Bastets,** Quartier Les Bastets, 26740 Marsanne **04 75 90 35 03; contact@campingles bastets.com; www.campinglesbastets.com**

🛠 €4 ♦♦(htd) ▣ ⬚ ♨ ♿ ▣ ∥ ⬚ 🐾 ♈ ♈ ♈ ⊕🐕 🏋 /Ⅱ ♪ 🗡

Exit A7 junc 17 onto N7; pass thro Les Tourettes & La Coucourde to Marsanne. In La Coucourde turn L onto D74 & in 6km L onto D105 thro Marsanne. Site sp fr D105. App fr N on D57 not rec. 4*, Med, mkd, hdg, pt shd, sl, terr, EHU (10A); bbq; TV; 10% statics; Eng spkn; adv bkg acc; games rm; archery; bike hire; games area. *"Pleasant site; gd views; beautiful area; vg; infinity pool with views over Valdaine Plaine; 30 new easy access level hdg pitches, some in woods; welcoming site; mini golf; golf 10km; highly rec."* **€24.50, 1 Apr-1 Oct.** **2016**

MARSEILLAN PLAGE *10F1* (7km SE Coastal) *43.31904, 3.55655* **Flower Camping Robinson,** Quai de Plaisance, 34340 Marseillan Plage **04 67 21 90 07; reception@camping-robinson.com; www.camping-robinson.com**

♦♦ ▣ ⬚ ♨ ♿ ▣ ∥ ⬚ 🐾 ♈ 🏋 /Ⅱ 🐾opp

Fr Agde take D612 twds Sete. In Marseillan Plage cont on D612 & cross canal bdge. In abt 300m turn R and foll sp to site. 3*, Med, mkd, pt shd, EHU (10A); twin axles; 33% statics; Eng spkn; adv bkg acc; games area; CKE. *"Gd."* **€38.00, 23 Apr-23 Sep.** **2016**

MARSEILLAN PLAGE *10F1* (1.3km SW Coastal) *43.31036, 3.54601* **Camping La Plage,** 69 Chemin du Pairollet, 34340 Marseillan-Plage **04 67 21 92 54; info@laplage-camping.net; www.laplage-camping.net**

🛠 €4 ♦♦ ▣ ⬚ ♨ ♿ ▣ ∥ ⬚ 🐾 ♈ ♈ ⊕/Ⅱ ♪ 🐾sand adj

On D612 fr Agde to Sète, turn R at rndabt dir Marseillan-Plage. Foll sp for site at 2nd rndabt. Site on L in 150m. 3*, Med, hdg, pt shd, EHU (10A) inc; gas; bbq; TV; 1% statics; phone; Eng spkn; adv bkg acc; ccard acc; games area; watersports; CKE. *"Excel, popular, family-run site; superb beach; extra for beach front pitches; sm pitches, some diff for lge o'fits; gd, friendly atmosphere."* **€42.00, 14 Mar-31 Oct.** **2015**

MARTRES TOLOSANE *8F3* (1.5km S Rural) *43.19060, 1.01840* **Camping Le Moulin,** 31220 Martres-Tolosane **05 61 98 86 40; info@domainelemoulin.com; www.domainelemoulin.com or www.campingle moulin.com/en/toulouse-campsite-france/**

🛠 €3 ♦♦ ▣ ⬚ ♨ ♿ ▣ ∥ ⬚ 🐾 ♈ ♈ 🏋nr /Ⅱ ♪ 🗡(htd) 🍽

Exit A64 junc 22 (fr N or S) & foll camping sps. Site sp adj Rv Garonne. 4*, Med, hdg, pt shd, pt sl, EHU (6-10A) €4-6; gas; bbq; red long stay; TV; 20% statics; Eng spkn; adv bkg rec; ccard acc; games area; tennis; games rm; bike hire; rv fishing adj; outdoor fitness; canoeing; massages; canoeing; CKE. *"Excel, well-maintained site; friendly welcome; gd, modern san facs; water on all pitches; gd touring base for Spain, Lourdes, etc."* **€26.90, 1 Apr-27 Sep, D28.** **2019**

MARVEJOLS 9D1 (1km NE Rural) 44.55077, 3.30440
Camping Village Le Coulagnet, Quartier de l'Empery,
48100 Marvejols 04 66 32 03 69

Exit A75 junc 38 onto D900 & N9. Foll E ring rd
onto D999, cont over rv & foll sp to site; no R turn
into site, cont 500m to Aire de Retournement, &
turn L into site. Foll sp 'VVF', camping pt of same
complex. NB U-turn bef ent impossible long o'fits;
nasty speed humps on app rd. 2*, Sm, hdg, pt shd,
EHU (5A) inc (poss rev pol); bbq (sep area); TV;
50% statics; phone; Eng spkn; adv bkg acc; ccard acc;
games rm; tennis; games area. "Well equiped site; san
facs immac; sep area for tourers; interesting walled
town; rv adj; excel; ent too tight to make u-turn."
€21.00, 5 May-15 Sep. 2019

MASEVAUX 6F3 (1km N Urban) 47.77820, 6.99090
Camping Les Rives de la Doller (formerly de Masevaux),
3 Rue du Stade, 68290 Masevaux 03 89 39 83 94 or
06 33 49 44 88 (mob); www.masevaux-camping.fr

Fr N83 Colmar-Belfort rd take N466 W to Masevaux;
site sp. NB D14 fr Thann to Masevaux narr & steep -
not suitable c'vans. 3*, Med, mkd, pt shd, EHU (3-6A)
€3.20-3.80; red long stay; TV; 40% statics; Eng spkn;
adv bkg acc; ccard acc; CKE. "Pleasant walks; htd pool
adj; interesting town - annual staging of Passion Play;
helpful, friendly owners; excel facs; sports complex adj;
gd cycle rtes; excel; gd site in nice little town; supmkt
nrby; close to Ballon d'Alsace."
€20.00, 1 Apr-19 Oct. 2019

MASSERET 7B3 (11km N Rural) 45.61142, 1.50110
Camping de Montréal, Rue du Petit Moulin, 87380 St
Germain-les-Belles 05 55 71 86 20; contact@camping
demontreal.com; www.campingdemontreal.com

S fr Limoges on A20; exit junc 42 onto D7B to
St Germain-les-Belles; turn R onto D216; site on L in
500m. Site sp in vill. NB Care needed due narr rds.
3*, Med, mkd, hdg, pt shd, terr, EHU (10A) €3; bbq; sw
nr; 12% statics; phone; Eng spkn; adv bkg acc; ccard
acc; tennis; fishing; watersports; CKE. "Peaceful, lovely,
well-run site in attractive setting o'looking lake; excel,
modern, spotless san facs; bike hire 1km; conv A20;
a gem of a site; gd rest; vg NH; shops 10 min walk."
€19.00 2018

MASSEUBE 8F3 (0.4km E Rural) 43.42914, 0.58516
Camping Berges du Gers, Route de Simorre, 32140
Masseube 05 62 66 01 75; camping.masseube@
orange.fr; www.camping-masseube-lesbergesdugers.fr

S fr Auch on D929 to Masseube; turn L onto D27 dir
Simorre; site on L in 500m. 3*, Med, shd, EHU (6A) €3;
bbq; TV; 10% statics; Eng spkn; adv bkg acc; ccard acc;
games area; tennis; bike hire; games rm; CKE. "Well-run
site in pleasant setting; security barrier; htd pool adj;
access to rv; vg." €13.00, 1 May-31 Oct. 2017

MASSEUBE 8F3 (2km E Rural) 43.42748, 0.61142
Camping Aux Mêmes, 32140 Bellegarde 05 62 66
91 45 or 06 83 62 02 22; info@gascogne-camping.fr;
www.gascogne-camping.fr

Fr Masseube take D27 E dir Simorre & Bellegarde; in
2.5km turn L (having past sports stadium & driven
up hill thro trees); site is 1st farm on R in 300m.
Site sp. 3*, Sm, unshd, pt sl, EHU (6A) €3; bbq; TV;
Eng spkn; adv bkg acc; tennis; canoeing; games rm;
sailing nr; golf nr; watersports; bike hire; windsurfing
nr; fishing. "Excel; v friendly & helpful Eng owners."
€25.00, 1 Apr-15 Sep. 2017

MATHES, LES 7B1 (1km WSW Urban) 45.71517,
-1.15520 Camping Monplaisir, 26 avenue de la
Palmyre, 17250 Les Mathes 05 46 22 50 31; camping-
monplaisir@orange.fr; www.campingmonplaisir
lesmathes.fr

beach 3.5km

Fr Saujon take D14 to the o'skirts of Tremblade,
avoid vill of Arvert & Etaule if towing c'van, rd
surface poor & narr. At rndabt take D25 for a sh dist
& take L onto D268 twrds La Palmyre. Cont along
D141 to o'skirts of Les Mathes, then L at rndabt. Site
on L within approx 450m opp cycle hire.
3*, Med, pt shd, pt sl, EHU €4.50; bbq; TV; Eng spkn;
ccard acc; games area; games rm. "Bike hire nrby;
crazy golf & childrens car track on site; friendly family
owned site, clean & tidy; gd cycle tracks in area; bar
300m; zoo 4km; vg; v clean san facs; open mkt in vill
most days." €20.00, Apr-Sep. 2016

MATHES, LES 7B1 (3.5km N Rural) 45.72980, -1.17929
Camping Sandaya L'Orée du Bois, 225 Route de la
Bouverie, La Fouasse, 17570 Les Mathes 05 46 22 42 43;
www.sandaya.fr/nos-campings/l-oree-du-bois

sand 4km

Fr A10 to Saintes, then dir Royan. Fr Royan take
D25 thro St Palais & La Palmyre twd Phare de la
Coubre. Cont 4km past Phare & turn R on D268 to
La Fouasse. Site on R in 4km. 4*, Lge, hdstg, mkd,
hdg, pt shd, EHU (6A) inc; gas; bbq; red long stay; TV;
50% statics; Eng spkn; adv bkg rec; ccard acc; games
rm; bike hire; waterslide; games area; golf 20km;
tennis; CKE. "Well-kept site in pine wood; local beaches
ideal for sw & surfing; helpful staff; excel pool area;
private san facs some pitches; zoo in La Palmyre worth
visit; excel." €40.00, 24 May-14 Sep. 2019

MATHES, LES 7B1 (1km SW Rural) 45.70256, -1.15638
Camping Palmyre Loisirs, 28 Ave des Mathes, 17570
La Palmyre 05 46 23 67 66; www.palmyreloisirs.com
🐕 €4.50 ⛺🚻♿ ✉ 🦋 ▾ Ⓨ ⑭♨🍴 🏊 ⚓ sand 3km

S fr La Tremblade on D14; at Arvert take D141 SW
thro Les Mathes; site on L of rd 1km fr Les Mathes.
Lge, pt shd, EHU (6A) inc; adv bkg acc. "Excel new
san facs; new pool complex for 2015; 1 dog per pitch;
pitches away fr bar/rest are quiet; barrier clsd 12-6am."
€51.50, Apr-Sep.   2015

"There aren't many sites open at this time of year"

If you're travelling outside peak season
remember to call ahead to check site opening
dates – even if the entry says 'open all year'.

MAUBEUGE 3B4 (10km NE Rural) 50.34525,
4.02842 **Camping Les Avallées,** 19 Rue du Faubourg,
59600 Villers-Sire-Nicole 03 27 67 92 56; loisirs-les-
avallees@wanadoo.fr; www.loisirs-les-avallees.fr
🐕 ⛺🚻♿ ▾ ✉ ▾ Ⓨ ⑭♨🍴 /🅼

N fr Maubeuge on N2; in 5km R onto D159 to
Villers-Sire-Nicole. Site well sp. Last 4km narr
country rd. 1*, Lge, pt shd, pt sl, terr, EHU (4A) €2;
bbq; 80% statics. "Friendly owners; lake fishing; no twin
axles; vg; lovely site." €11.00, 1 Apr-14 Oct.   2015

MAULEON LICHARRE 8F1 (2km S Rural) 43.20795,
-0.89695 **Camping Uhaitza Le Saison,** Route de
Libarrenx, 64130 Mauléon-Licharre 05 59 28 18 79;
camping.uhaitza@wanadoo.fr; www.camping-
uhaitza.com
🐕 €2 ⛺🚻♿ ▾ ♨🍴 / 🅼 🦋 Ⓨ ♨🅿nr /🅼

Fr Sauveterre take D936 twd Oloron. In 500m turn
R onto D23 to Mauléon, then take D918 dir Tardets,
site on R. 3*, Sm, hdg, mkd, pt shd, EHU (6A) €2.65-
4.90; bbq; 10% statics; adv bkg acc; tennis 2km; rv
fishing adj; games rm; CKE. "Lovely, quiet site beside
rv; lge pitches; friendly owners."
€25.00, 1 Apr-15 Oct.   2015

MAURS 7D4 (0.8km S Rural) 44.70522, 2.20586
Camp Municipal Le Vert, Route de Decazeville, 15600
Maurs 04 71 49 04 15 or 06 75 46 74 17; camping@
ville-maurs.fr/tourisme/camping
🚻♿ ▾ ♨🅿 / 🦋 🅿nr /🅼 ♨

Fr Maurs take D663 dir Decazeville. Site on L 400m
after level x-ing thro sports complex. Narr ent.
3*, Med, mkd, shd, EHU (15A) inc; adv bkg acc; rv
fishing; tennis. "V pleasant on side of rv; sports
complex adj; friendly helpful warden."
€11.00, 2 May-30 Sep.   2019

MAYENNE 4E1 (2km N Rural) 48.31350, -0.61296
Camp Municipal du Gué St Léonard, 818 Rue de St
Léonard, 53100 Mayenne 02 43 04 57 14 or 02 43
04 19 37; www.campingduguesaintleonard.fr
⛺🚻(htd) 🆆♿♨🅿 / ⑭nr ♨ 🅿 /🅼 ♨(htd)

Fr N, sp to E of D23 & well sp fr cent of Mayenne on
rvside. 3*, Med, hdg, mkd, pt shd, serviced pitches;
EHU (10A) €2.20; bbq; twin axles; 8% statics; phone;
adv bkg acc; rv fishing adj; CKE. "Peaceful, well-kept
site by rv; pleasant location adj parkland walks; modern
san facs with piping hot water; some pitches sm &
access poss diff; vg value."
€13.70, 15 Mar-30 Sep.   2015

MAZAMET 8F4 (1.5km E Urban) 43.49634, 2.39075
FFCC Camp Municipal de la Lauze, Chemin de la Lauze,
81200 Mazamet 05 63 61 24 69; contact@camping-
mazamet.com; www.camping-mazamet.com
🐕 ⛺🚻 ♨ ♿♨ / 🅼

Exit Mazamet dir St Pons on D612, site on R past
rugby grnd. 3*, Med, hdstg, pt shd, pt sl, EHU (15A)
€3.50; bbq; red long stay; adv bkg acc; tennis; CKE.
"Well-kept site in 2 adj parts, 1 flat & other sl; office
thro gateway - warden needed for access; htd pool
adj; san facs excel; gd touring base 'Black Mountain'
region." €12.00, 1 Jun-30 Sep.   2019

"That's changed – Should I let the Club know?"

If you find something on site that's different
from the site entry, fill in a report and let us
know. See camc.com/europereport.

MEAUX 3D3 (4km NE Rural) 49.00301, 2.94139
Camping Village Parisien, Route des Otages, 77910
Varreddes 02 51 20 41 94; direction@villageparisien.
com; http://villageparisien.camp-atlantique.nl
🐕 ⛺🚻🆆♨♿♨ / 🅼 Ⓨ 🍴 ⑭♨🅿 /🅼 ♂ ♨ ⛳

Fr Meaux foll sp on D405 dir Soissons then
Varreddes, site sp on D121 dir Congis. 4*, Med, mkd,
hdg, pt shd, EHU (6A) €2; gas; bbq; red long stay; TV;
85% statics; Eng spkn; adv bkg acc; waterslide; games
area; golf 5km; tennis; games rm; fishing; bike hire;
CKE. "Conv Paris cent (drive to metro), Parc Astérix &
Disneyland - tickets avail fr site; friendly, helpful staff;
cash only; sm pitches; narr site rds; v busy, well-used
site." €41.00, 1 Apr-5 Nov.   2017

MEAUX *3D3* (10km SW Rural) *48.91333, 2.73416* **Camping L'International de Jablines,** 77450 Jablines **01 60 26 09 37; welcome@camping-jablines.com; www.camping-jablines.com**

Fr N on A1 then A104 exit Claye-Souilly. Fr E on A4 then A104 exit Meaux. Fr S on A6, A86, A4, A104 exit Meaux. Site well sp 'Base de Loisirs de Jablines'. 3*, Lge, mkd, pt shd, pt sl, EHU (10A) inc; bbq; sw nr; bus to Eurodisney; Eng spkn; adv bkg req; ccard acc; horseriding; windsurfing; bike hire; tennis 500m; fishing; sailing; CKE. *"Clean, well-run, well-guarded site; vg pitches; pelasant staff; san facs poss tired high ssn; ideal for Disneyland (tickets for sale), Paris & Versaille."*
€28.00, 31 Mar-29 Sep. **2017**

See advertisement

MEES, LES *10E3* (11km S Rural) *43.95377, 5.93304* **Camping Les Olivettes,** Hameau-Les-Pourcelles, 04190 Les Mées **04 92 34 18 97; campingolivette@club-internet.fr; www.campinglesolivettes.com**

Exit A51 junc 20 (fr N) or 19 (fr S) & cross Rv Durance onto D4. Site bet Oraison & Les Mées. Turn onto D754 to Les Pourcelles & foll site sp. 3*, Sm, hdg, mkd, pt shd, pt sl, terr, EHU (6-10A) €4.90; 5% statics; Eng spkn; adv bkg acc. *"Views over beautiful area; friendly owners; occasional out of ssn pitches avail; unrel opening; vg."*
€33.50, 29 Apr-30 Sep. **2016**

MEGEVE *9B3* (2km SW Rural) *45.84120, 6.58887* **FFCC Camping Gai Séjour,** 332 Route de Cassioz, 74120 Megève **04 50 21 22 58**

On D1212 Flumet-Megève rd, site on R 1km after Praz-sur-Arly, well sp. 2*, Med, mkd, pt shd, sl, EHU (4A); Eng spkn; adv bkg acc; CKE. *"Pleasant site with gd views, lge pitches; gd walks; 40km fr Mont Blanc; helpful owners; no free parking in Megeve."*
€15.00, 6 Jan-15 Sep. **2019**

MEHUN SUR YEVRE *4H3* (0.5km N Urban) *47.14797, 2.21725* **Camp Municipal,** Ave Jean Châtelet, 18500 Mehun-sur-Yèvre **02 48 57 44 51 or 02 48 57 30 25 (Mairie); www.ville-mehun-sur-yevre.fr/Le-camping**

Leave A71 junc 6 onto D2076 (N76) dir Bourges. App Mehun & turn L into site at 2nd traff lts. Ave Jean Châtelet is pt of D2076. 2*, Sm, mkd, pt shd, EHU (6A) €2.80 (poss rev pol & long lead req some pitches); twin axles; tennis adj. *"Excel NH conv for m'way; clean, modern san facs; water pnts poss long walk; gates locked 2200-0700 (high ssn); facs open to elements; pool adj; town rather run down, nice park."*
€13.00, 8 May-30 Sep. **2017**

MELE SUR SARTHE, LE *4E1* (0.5km SE Rural) *48.50831, 0.36298* **Camp Intercommunal La Prairie,** La Bretèche, St Julien-Sarthe, 61170 Le Mêle-sur-Sarthe **02 33 27 18 74**

Turn off N12 onto D4; site sp in vill. 2*, Med, mkd, pt shd, EHU (6A) inc; adv bkg acc; sailing; tennis; CKE. *"Pt of excel sports complex; vg."*
€11.00, 1 May-30 Sep. **2019**

"I like to fill in the reports as I travel from site to site"

You'll find report forms at the back of this guide, or you can fill them in online at camc.com/europereport.

MELISEY *6F2* (0.5km E Rural) *47.75484, 6.58683* **Camping La Bergereine,** 17bis Route des Vosges, 70270 Mélisey **06 23 36 87 16 (mob); isabelle.schweizer0704@orange.fr**

Fr Lure (or by-pass) take D486 dir Le Thillot; site sp. 1*, Sm, pt shd, EHU inc; gas; 25% statics; adv bkg acc; rv fishing adj; CKE. *"Ok NH; simple farm site; leisure cent 500m; attractive scenery; improvd san block; pool 500m; v scruffy."* **€8.00, 1 Apr-30 Sep.** **2015**

FRANCE

MELISEY 6F2 (8km E Rural) 47.75525, 6.65273
Camping La Broche, Le Voluet, 70270 Fresse
03 84 63 31 40; www.camping-broche.com

🏕 €1 ♦♦ �🅦🅓 ♨ ᴕ 🅑 ∥ 🐶 🅩 nr /🛖

Fr Lure head NE on D486 twd Melisey. Fr Mélisey
stay on D486 twd Le Thillot, in 2.5km turn R onto
D97 dir Plancher-les-Mines. In approx 5.5km site sp
on R in Fresse. 2*, Sm, mkd, pt shd, pt sl, terr, EHU
(10A) €2.50; bbq; sw nr; 10% statics; phone; adv bkg
acc; games rm; fishing adj; ice; games area; CKE.
"Secluded, relaxing site next to lake, in attractive
setting in regional park; friendly owner; conv Rte of
1000 lakes; great site; vg."
€12.00, 15 Apr-15 Oct.   2015

"We must tell the Club about that great site we found"

Get your site reports in by mid-August and we'll
do our best to get your updates into the next
edition.

MELLE 7A2 (11km SW Rural) 46.14421, -0.21983
Camp Municipal, Rue des Merlonges, 79170 Brioux-
sur-Boutonne 05 49 07 50 46

♦♦ ♨ 🅑 ∥ 🐶 🅩 nr /🛖

On ent Brioux fr Melle on D150 turn R immed over
bdge; site on R in 100m. 1*, Sm, pt shd, EHU (6A)
€1.80. "Pleasant rural setting; tidy, well-cared for site;
ltd facs but clean; choose own pitch & pay at Mairie
on dep if no warden; conv for town; great value; vg sh
stay/NH." €8.00, 1 Apr-31 Oct.   2018

MENDE 9D1 (3km W Rural) 44.51409, 3.47363
Camping Tivoli, Route des Gorges du Tarn, 48000
Mende 04 66 65 31 10; camping.tivoli0601@orange.fr;
www.camping-tivoli.com

12 🏕 €1 ♦♦ �🅦🅓 ♨ 🅑 ∥ 🅼🅿 🐶 🅈 🅩 /🛖 ⚓

Sp fr N88, turn R 300m downhill (narr but easy rd).
Site adj Rv Lot. 3*, Med, pt shd, EHU (6A) inc; TV;
10% statics; adv bkg rec; rv fishing. "Gd site nr town at
back of cent commerciale; hypmkt 1km; v narr ent with
little rm to park." €20.00   2015

MERDRIGNAC 2E3 (2km N Rural) 48.19786, -2.41622
Camping Le Val de Landrouët, 14 rue du Gouède,
22230 Merdrignac 02 96 28 47 98; contact@
valdelandrouet.com; www.valdelandrouet.com

🏕 ♦♦ �🅦🅓 ♨ 🅑 ∥ 🐶 🅈 🅩 nr /🛖 ⚓ (htd)

Sp fr town cent, 500m fr town on D793 twd Broons,
site on L. Med, hdg, mkd, pt shd, pt sl, EHU (4A) €3;
bbq; sw nr; twin axles; 5% statics; bus adj; adv bkg
acc; ccard acc; fishing; tennis; CKE. "Superb, spacious
site; mv service pnt (emptying only); gd touring ctr;
activities adj; excel." €19.00, 30 Apr-30 Sep.   2019

MERENS LES VALS 8G4 (1km W Rural) 42.64633,
1.83083 **Camp Municipal Ville de Bau,** Ville de Bau,
09110 Mérens-les-Vals 05 61 02 85 40 or 05 61 64 33
77; camping.merens@wanadoo.fr; merenslesvals.fr

12 🏕 €0.70 ♦♦ (htd) ♨ 🅑 ∥ 🐶 🅿 🅈 🅩 /🛖

Fr Ax-les-Thermes on N20 sp Andorra past Mérens-
les-Vals turn R nr start of dual c'way sp Camp
Municipal. Site on R in 800m. 3*, Med, hdg, EHU
(6-10A) inc (poss rev pol); bbq; 20% statics; ccard acc;
CKE. "Excel site; gd clean san facs; gd walks fr site;
conv Andorra, Tunnel de Puymorens; all pitches have
water taps; pool 8km; lovely walk fr site past Eglise
Romane in vill to hot spring with natural bathing pools."
€17.00   2017

MERS LES BAINS 3B2 (1.5km NE Rural) 50.07730,
1.41540 **Flower Camping Le Rompval,** Lieudit Blengues,
154 Rue André Dumont, 80350 Mers-les-Bains
02 35 84 43 21 or 06 50 02 79 57 (mob); www.camping-
lerompval.com

🏕 €3 ♦♦ (htd) �🅦🅓 ♨ ᴕ 🅑 ∥ 🅼🅿 🐶 🅈 🅿 🅩 /🛖 ⚓
⚓ (covrd, htd) 🅔 🌳 sand 2.5km

Fr Calais on A16, exit junc 23 at Abbeville onto A28. In
5km exit junc 2 onto D925 dir Friville-Escarbotin, Le
Tréport. In approx 20km at rndabt junc with D19 foll
sp Ault & at next rndabt take D940 twd Mers-les-Bains.
In St Quentin-la-Motte turn R, site on R, sp. Fr S on
A28 exit junc 5 onto D1015 to Mers-les-Bains & foll sp
Blengues & site. 3*, Med, hdstg, mkd, hdg, unshd, EHU
(6-13A) €4-6.50; gas; bbq; red long stay; TV; 25% statics;
Eng spkn; adv bkg acc; ccard acc; tennis 3km; games
rm; bike hire; games area; CKE. "Vg site; library; gd facs."
€28.80, 5 Apr-3 Nov.   2019

MESNIL ST PERE 6F1 (2km NE Rural) 48.26329,
4.34633 **Kawan Village Camping Lac d'Orient,** Rue
du Lac, 10140 Mesnil-St Père 03 25 40 61 85 or
03 85 72 27 21 (LS); info@camping-lacdorient.com;
www.camping-lacdorient.com

🏕 €3 ♦♦ (htd) �🅦🅓 ♨ ᴕ 🅑 ∥ 🅼🅿 🐶 🅈 ⑪ nr 🅩 🅩 /🛖 🎿
⚓ (covrd, htd) 🅔

On D619 foll sps Lac de la Forêt d'Orient. Approx
10km fr Vendeuvre or 20km fr Troyes turn N on
D43A, to Mesnil-St Père; site sp. Sp at ent to site:
'Camping Lac d'Orient' (with 'Kawan Village' in v sm
lettering). 4*, Lge, hdstg, hdg, mkd, pt shd, pt sl, EHU
(10A) inc; bbq; sw nr; 10% statics; phone; Eng spkn;
adv bkg acc; ccard acc; watersports 500m; games rm;
fishing; games area; tennis; jacuzzi; CKE. "Peaceful site
with mature trees next to lake & forest; lge pitches; 1st
class san facs; no o'fits over 10m high ssn; poss muddy
when wet; conv Nigloland theme park & Champagne
area; conv A26; excel spacious site; excel cycle rte;
private san facs some pitches; fantastic rest over
looking lake; vg." €36.00, 9 Apr-23 Sep, J07.   2016

FRANCE

MESSANGES *8E1* (2km SW Coastal) *43.79790, -1.40135* **Airotel Camping Le Vieux Port,** Plage Sud, 40660 Messanges **01 76 76 70 00; contact@ levieuxport.com; www.levieuxport.com**

🐕 €5.50 ♨♨ ⚿ ♨ ☕ ♿ ☕ ⚡ 〰 ♠ ♥ ⛱ ☂ ① 🏊 ⚓ ⚠ ✗
⚓ (htd) 🏖 ⛱ sand 400m

Fr S take D652 past Vieux-Boucau; site sp. Turn W at Super U rndabt. 5*, V lge, hdstg, mkd, shd, EHU (6A) inc; gas; bbq; red long stay; TV; 10% statics; Eng spkn; adv bkg acc; ccard acc; horseriding; waterslide; tennis; bike hire; games area; CKE. *"V pleasant, clean site; dir access to sand beach; quad bikes; superb, v lge pool complex; excel touring base."*
€85.00, 24 Mar-4 Nov, A14. 2017

METZ *5D2* (1.5km NW Urban) *49.12402, 6.16917* **Camp Municipal Metz-Plage,** Allée de Metz-Plage, 57000 Metz **03 87 68 26 48; campingmetz@mairie- metz.fr; www.mairie-metz.fr**

🐕 €0.50 ♨♨ ⚿ ♨ ☕ ♿ ☕ ⚡ 〰 ♠ ♥ 🏊 ⚠

Fr W exit A31 junc 33 Metz-Nord/Pontiffroy exit; cross rv bdges Pont Canal & Pont des Morts; then immed turn L into Allée de Metz-Plage; site in 200m (or after leaving A31 at junc 33, at rndabt turn R & foll sps). Fr E foll 'Autres Directions' over A31 & Rv Moselle, then as above. 3*, Lge, hdstg, mkd, pt shd, pt sl, EHU (10A) inc (poss rev pol); twin axles; Eng spkn; adv bkg acc; ccard acc; rv fishing adj; CKE. *"Spacious, well-situated on rv with views; some gd sized pitches; helpful staff; poss long walk to san facs; rv unfenced; facs stretched if site full; early arr ess high ssn; vg; fac's need updating; wifi in designated areas; pool adj; excel."*
€21.00, 15 Apr-1 Oct. 2015

MEZE *10F1* (3km N Rural) *43.44541, 3.61595* **Camp Municipal Loupian,** Route de Mèze, 34140 Loupian **04 67 43 57 67 or 04 67 43 82 07 (LS); camping@loupian.fr; www.loupian.fr**

🐕 €1 ♨♨ ⚿ ♨ ☕ ♿ ☕ ⚡ 〰 ♥ ☂ 🏊 ⚠ ✗ ⛱ sand 3km

Fr Mèze tak D613 & turn L at 1st Loupian sp, then foll sp for site. 3*, Med, hdg, mkd, pt shd, EHU (6A); bbq; phone; Eng spkn; adv bkg acc; tennis; CKE. *"Pleasant site in popular area; plenty shd; friendly, helpful staff; vg san facs; takeaway; gd beaches; excel fisherman's rest; gd rests at Mèze & Bouzigues; superb cycling on old rlwy rte fr site to Mèze (Voie Verte); rec; cent to main attractions; vg."*
€19.00, 6 Apr-14 Oct. 2018

MILLAS *8G4* (7km SW Urban) *42.67165, 2.62907* **Camp Municipal Le Colomer,** Rue Colonel Fabien, 66130 Ile-sur-Tet **04 68 84 72 40; camping@ille-sur- tet.com; www.ille-sur-tet.com**

🐕 €1.50 ♨♨ ♨ ☕ ⚡ 〰 ♥ ⚠

Exit N116 on NE of town, R twds Ille sur Tet on D916, L at next rndabt foll sp to site. Med, hdg, pt shd, EHU (10A) €4; 30% statics; bus adj; train 0.5km; Eng spkn; adv bkg req; games area; CKE. *"Conv for Les Orgues cliffs & Prieure de Serrabone; gd rests in attractive town; pool 200m; adj rlwy not busy but conv for Perpignan; vg."* **€11.30, 1 Nov-30 Sep.** 2016

MILLAU *10E1* (7km N Rural) *44.15188, 3.09899* **Camping La Belle Etoile (formerly d'Aguessac),** Chemin des Prades, 12520 Aguessac **05 65 72 91 07 or 06 72 23 10 56 (mob); contact@camping- labelleetoile.fr; www.camping-labelleetoile.fr**

🐕 €2 ♨♨ ⚿ ♨ ☕ ♿ ☕ ⚡ 〰 ♥ ♥ ☂ 🏊 ⚠ nr ✗

Site on N907 in vill; ent on R v soon after level x-ing when app fr Millau. 2*, Med, mkd, pt shd, EHU (6A) inc; gas; canoeing; games area; rv fishing adj; CKE. *"Nice, spacious, clean rvside site; gd position with mountain views; gd sized pitches; helpful & friendly staff; public footpath thro site along rv to picturesque vill; poss youth groups high ssn; sports grnd adj; excel touring base; vg location; vg quiet site."*
€23.00, 27 Apr-30 Sep. 2019

MILLAU *10E1* (1.6km NE Rural) *44.10640, 3.08800* **Camping Les Erables,** Route de Millau-Plage, 12100 Millau **05 65 59 15 13; camping-les-erables@orange.fr; www.campingleserables.fr**

🐕 €1.20 ♨♨ (htd) ☕ ♨ ☕ ♿ ☕ ⚡ 〰 ♥ ☂ 🏊 ⚠ ✗

Exit Millau on D991 (sp Nant) over Rv Tarn bdge; take L at island sp to Millau-Plage & site on L immed after Camping du Viaduc & bef Camping Larribal. On ent Millau fr N or S foll sps 'Campings'. 3*, Med, mkd, hdg, shd, EHU (10A) €3 (rev pol); bbq; sw nr; TV; phone; Eng spkn; adv bkg acc; ccard acc; canoeing adj; CKE. *"Peaceful, well-kept, clean site on banks of Rv Tarn; lge shd pitches; friendly, helpful owners; excel modern san facs; some pitches poss diff lge o'fits; excel walking; beavers nrby; Millau Viaduct Vistor Cent a must; excel."* **€21.00, 1 Apr-30 Sep.** 2017

MILLAU *10E1* (2km NE Urban) *44.10240, 3.09100* **Camping Indigo Millau,** Ave de l'Aigoual, 12100 Millau **05 65 61 18 83; millau@camping-indigo.com; www.camping-indigo.com or www.europe.huttopia. com/site/camping-millau**

🐕 €4.60 ♨♨ ⚿ ☕ ♨ ☕ ⚡ 〰 ♥ ① 🏊 ⚓ ⚠ ✗ (htd) 🏖

Fr N exit A75 junc 45 to Millau. Turn L at 2nd traff island sp 'Camping'. Site on R over bdge in 200m. Fr S exit A75 junc 47 onto D809 & cross rv on by- pass, turn R at 1st traff island sp Nant on D991, cross bdge, site on R in 200m, sp. Site a S confluence of Rv Dourbie & Rv Tarn. 3*, Med, mkd, shd, pt sl, EHU (5A) €3.50; gas; sw nr; 10% statics; Eng spkn; adv bkg acc; fishing nr; games; CKE. *"Excel site; gd san facs, renovated 2015; hang-gliding nrby; pleasant, helpful owner; canoe hire nr; conv Tarn Gorges; lge mkt Fri."* **€28.90, 19 Apr-29 Sep, D17.** 2019

MILLAU *10E1* (1km E Rural) *44.10166, 3.09611*
Camping Les Rivages, Ave de l'Aigoual, 12100 Millau
05 65 61 01 07 or 06 10 75 65 94 (mob); info@
campinglesrivages.com; www.campinglesrivages.com

🅃€4 ♨(htd) 🆆◫ ♨ ♿ 🍴 ⬚ ⧄ ✉ 🦋 ♈ ⛾ Ⓗ♨ 🏊 ⚔ 🛝

Fr Millau take D991 dir Nant (sp Gorges de la
Dourbie & Campings). Cross Rv Tarn & cont on this
rd, site is 500m after bdge on R. 4*, Lge, pt shd,
serviced pitches; EHU (10A) inc (poss rev pol); bbq; sw
nr; red long stay; twin axles; TV; 10% statics; phone;
Eng spkn; adv bkg acc; ccard acc; canoeing nr; squash;
fishing; games area; tennis; games rm; CKE. *"Pleasant,
busy, scenic site - esp rv/side pitches; helpful & friendly
staff; immac, clean san facs; vg rest/snack bar - home
cooked & inexpensive; gd security; views of Millau
viaduct; hang-gliding; spa; easy access to town; mkt
Wed & Fri; pleasant cycle ride along rvbank; v nice site."*
€37.00, 15 Apr-30 Sep, D20. **2015**

MIMIZAN PLAGE *7D1* (0.7km E Coastal) *44.21629,
-1.28584* **Camping de la Plage,** Blvd d'Atlantique,
40200 Mimizan-Plage 05 58 09 00 32; contact@
mimizan-camping.com; www.mimizan-camping.com

🅃€1.80 ♨♨ ♨ ♿ ⬚ ⧄ ✉ 🦋 ♈ 🏊 ⧄ ♨ 🏖sand 850m

Turn off N10 at Labouheyre on D626 to Mimizan
(28km). Approx 5km after Mimizan turn R. Site
in approx 500m. 3*, V lge, shd, pt sl, EHU (10A)
inc; bbq; 20% statics; games area. *"Gd facs; town
nrby; big busy coastal site; many cycle paths; excel."*
€24.00, 7 Apr-30 Sep. **2018**

MIMIZAN PLAGE *7D1* (3km E Coastal) *44.20420,
-1.2908* **Club Marina-Landes,** Rue Marina, 40202
Mimizan-Plage-Sud 05 58 09 12 66; contact@
clubmarina.com; www.marinalandes.com

🅃€5 ♨♨ 🆆 ♨ ♿ ⬚ ⧄ ✉ 🦋 ♈ ⛾ Ⓗ♨ 🏊 ⧄ ✉
🏊(covrd, htd) 📍 🏖sand 500m

Turn R off N10 at Labouheyre onto D626 to Mimizan
(28km). Approx 5km fr Mimizan-Plage turn L at
Camping Marina sp on dual c'way. Site sp on S bank
of rv. 4*, V lge, hdg, hdstg, pt shd, EHU (10A) €7; gas;
bbq; TV; 10% statics; Eng spkn; adv bkg acc; ccard acc;
ice; golf 7km; games area; horseriding; games rm; bike
hire; waterslide; fitness rm; tennis; CKE. *"Excursions nr
Dax, Biarritz & Bordeaux areas; excel leisure facs; excel;
great location."* **€61.00, 15 May-16 Sep.** **2017**

MIRAMBEAU *7C2* (15km W Coastal) *45.38333,
-0.72250* **Camping L'Estuaire,** La Grange Godinet,
17150 St Thomas-de-Cônac 05 46 86 08 20; info@
lestuaire.com; www.lestuaire.com

🄛2 🅃€4 ♨(htd) ♨ ♿ ⬚ ⧄ ✉ 🦋 ♈ Ⓗ♨ 🏊 ⧄ ✉
🏊 📍

Exit A10 junc 37 Mirambeau onto D730 dir Royan.
At St Ciers-du-Taillon foll sp St Thomas-de-Cônac,
site sp. 4*, Lge, hdg, mkd, unshd, EHU (16A) inc; bbq;
TV; 60% statics; adv bkg acc; games area; gym; bike
hire; watersports nr; fishing; tennis. *"Interesting area nr
Gironde estuary; gd walking & cycling."* **€20.00** **2016**

MIRAMONT DE GUYENNE *7D2* (7km NW Rural)
44.62877, 0.29135 **Camp Municipal Le Dropt,** Rue du
Pont, 47800 Allemans-du-Dropt 05 53 20 25 59 or
05 53 20 23 37 (Mairie)

♨♨ 🆆 ♨ ✉ 🦋 ♈ ⛾nr Ⓗnr 🏊nr ⧄

Fr D668 site well sp in vill. Sm, shd, EHU (20A) €2;
canoeing; kayaking; CKE. *"Attractive site on opp side of
Rv Dropt to vill; friendly warden; ltd pitches for c'vans
& lge o'fits due trees & o'hanging branches; basic but
clean facs; excel."* **€7.00, 1 Apr-15 Oct.** **2019**

MIRANDE *8F2* (0.5km E Rural) *43.51432, 0.40990*
Camp Municipal L'Ile du Pont, Au Batardeau, 32300
Mirande 05 62 66 64 11; info@camping-gers.com;
www.groupevla.fr

🅃€1 ♨(htd) 🆆 ♨ ♿ ⬚ ⧄ ✉ 🦋 ♈ ⛾ Ⓗ♨ ⧄ 🏊 ⚔

On N21 Auch-Tarbes, foll sp to site on island in Rv
Grande Baise. 3*, Med, pt shd, EHU (6A) inc; bbq;
20% statics; adv bkg rec; bike hire; games rm; sailing;
canoeing; windsurfing; tennis; waterslide; fishing;
CKE. *"Excel site; helpful staff; quiet location; 5min
walk to town; gd stopover if heading to pyrenees."*
€20.00, 15 Apr-30 Sep. **2016**

MIREPOIX (ARIEGE) *8F4* (1km E Rural) *43.08871,
1.88585* **Camping Les Nysades,** Route de Limoux,
09500 Mirepoix 05 61 60 28 63; campinglesnysades@
orange.fr; www.camping-mirepoix-ariege.com

🅃€2 ♨♨ 🆆 ♨ ♿ ✉ 🦋 ♈ 🏊nr 🏊

E fr Pamiers on D119 to Mirepoix. Site well sp on
D626. 2*, Med, hdg, mkd, shd, EHU (6A) €3.50;
10% statics; fishing 1km; tennis. *"Lge pitches; san facs
ok; site a bit tired; interesting medieval town; mkt Mon
rec; gd little site, walks along rv; barrier open 0700-
2300, if warden not on site he will collect fees later."*
€15.00, 16 Apri-31 Oct. **2017**

**"Satellite navigation makes
touring much easier"**

Remember most sat navs don't know if you're
towing or in a larger vehicle – always use yours
alongside maps and site directions.

MIRMANDE *9D2* (3km SE Rural) *44.68705, 4.85444*
Camping La Poche, 26270 Mirmande 04 75 63 02 88;
camping@la-poche.com; wwwcamping-lapoche.com

♨♨ 🆆 ♨ ⬚ ⧄ ✉ 🦋 ♈ Ⓗ♨ 🏊 ⧄ 🏊 ⚔ 📍

Fr N on N7, 3km after Loriol turn L onto D57 sp
Mirmande. Site in 7km on L. Fr S on N7 turn R
onto D204 in Saulce & foll sp. 3*, Med, hdg, hdstg,
mkd, shd, terr, EHU (6A) €3; TV; 90% statics; adv bkg
acc; games area; CKE. *"Pleasant, scenic, gd site in
wooded valley; gd walking/cycling; v friendly, helpful
Dutch owners."* **€26.00, 1 Apr-1 Oct.** **2015**

MODANE 9C4 (12km ENE Rural) 45.22870, 6.78116
Camp Municipal Val d'Ambin, Plan de l'Eglise, 73500
Bramans-le-Verney 04 79 05 03 05 or 06 16 51 90 91
(mob); campingbramans@gmail.com; www.camping-
bramansvanoise.com

🐕 €1.60 ⅋ (htd) ♨ ⊛ 🖥 🕭 MP 🦋 ⓕ 𝕀 nr ⓓ nr 🏊 ⚠ ⚓

10km after Modane on D1006 twd Lanslebourg, take
2nd turning R twd vill of Bramans, & foll camping sp,
site by church. App fr Lanslebourg, after 12km turn L
at camping sp on D306 at end of vill. 2*, Med, unshd,
EHU (12-16A) €3.70-5.20; bbq; TV; games area. "Away-
fr-it-all site worth the climb; beautiful area, mountain
views; gd dog walk adj, excel, brilliant site; great for
walkers & outdoor enthusiasts; v well rec; friendly staff."
€17.00, 20 Apr-30 Oct. **2015**

MOISSAC 8E3 (2km S Rural) 44.09664, 1.08878
Camping Le Moulin du Bidounet, St Benoît, 82200
Moissac 05 63 32 52 52; info@camping-moissac.com;
www.camping-moissac.com

🐕 €1.50 ⅋ WD ♨ ⊛ 🚿 🕭 MP 🦋 ⓕ 𝕀 ⓓ nr 🏊 nr ⚠ ⚓ 🏊

Exit A62/E72 at junc 9 at Castelsarrasin onto D813
dir Moissac. Or fr N on D813 cross Rv Tarn, turn
L at 1st rndabt & foll camp sp, site on L by rv. NB
Height restriction 3.05m for tunnel at ent & tight
turn lge o'fits. 3*, Med, hdg, mkd, hdstg, shd, EHU
(6A) €3.10; bbq; red long stay; 10% statics; phone;
Eng spkn; adv bkg acc; ccard acc; canoe hire; fishing;
bike hire; watersports; boat hire; CKE. "Excel, pleasant,
rvside site in lovely area; extra for twin axles; helpful
staff; basic, clean san facs; conv lovely town & abbey;
gd fishing; walking/cycling; vg cycle track by canal; gd
NH; entry tight for lge o'fits; passport identity needed."
€24.20, 1 Apr-30 Sep. **2018**

MOLIETS ET MAA 8E1 (2km W Coastal) 43.85166,
-1.38375 Camping Les Cigales, Ave de l'Océan, 40660
Moliets-Plage 05 58 48 51 18; reception@camping-
les-cigales.fr; www.camping-les-cigales.fr

🐕 €2 ⅋ WD ♨ 🕭 MP 🦋 𝕀 ⓓ 🚿 🏊 ⚠ 🏄 sand 300m

In Moliets-et-Maa, turn W for Moliets-Plage, site on
R in vill. 3*, Lge, shd, pt sl, EHU (5A) €3.50; bbq; TV;
80% statics; adv bkg acc; ccard acc; games area; CKE.
"Site in pine wood - sandy soil; narr access tracks; excel
beach & surfing; many shops, rests 100m; gd forest
walk to N." €30.70, 1 Apr-30 Sep. **2019**

MOLIETS ET MAA 8E1 (2km W Coastal) 43.85210,
-1.38730 Camping St Martin, Ave de l'Océan 40660
Moliets-Plage 05 58 48 52 30; contact@camping-
saint-martin.fr; www.camping-saint-martin.fr

🐕 €5 ⅋ (htd) WD ♨ ⊛ 🕭 🦋 𝕀 ⓓ 🚿 🏊
⚠ ⚓ 🏊 (covrd, htd) 🏖 🏄 sand 300m

On N10 exit for Léon, Moliets-et-Maa. At Moliets foll
sp to Moliets-Plage. Camp site after Les Cigales, by
beach. 4*, V lge, mkd, hdg, pt shd, pt sl, terr; serviced
pitches; EHU (10A) €5.30; gas; TV; Eng spkn; adv
bkg rec; ccard acc; games area; jacuzzi; tennis nr;
watersports; golf nr; sauna; CKE. "Excel family site;
cycle paths; vg san facs; gd for teenagers; gd cycling,
walking." €43.00, 8 Apr-1 Nov. **2017**

MOLSHEIM 6E3 (0.9km SE Urban) 48.54124, 7.50003
Camp Municipal de Molsheim, 6 Rue des Sports, 67120
Molsheim 03 88 49 82 45 or 03 88 49 58 58 (LS);
camping-molsheim@orange.fr; www.mairie-
molsheim.fr

🐕 €1.30 ⅋ WD ♨ 🕭 🖥 MP ⓕ

On ent town fr Obernai on D1422 site sp on R
immed after x-ing sm rv bdge. 2*, Med, mkd, pt shd,
EHU (10A) €3.40; bbq; train to Strasbourg 700m; Eng
spkn; adv bkg acc; bike hire; CKE. "Pleasant site;
excel san facs; pool adj; easy walk to town cent &
shops; Bugatti museum in town; vg."
€18.00, 7 Apr-29 Oct. **2017**

MONESTIER DE CLERMONT 9C3 (0.7km SW Urban)
44.91515, 5.62809 Camping Les Portes du Trièves,
Chemin de Chambons, 38650 Monestier-de-Clermont
04 76 34 01 24 or 04 76 34 06 20 (LS); camping.les
portesdutrieves@wanadoo.fr; www.campingisere.com

🐕 ⅋ (htd) WD ♨ 🕭 🖥 MP 🦋 ⓕ 𝕀 nr ⓓ nr 🏊 ⚠

Turn W off D1075. Sp in vill. 700m up hill adj sw
pool & school. Fr Grenoble take A51 to S end
of vill & foll sps to site. 3*, Sm, hdg, hdstg, mkd,
pt shd, terr, EHU (10A) €3.40; red long stay; bus 500m;
Eng spkn; adv bkg acc; tennis adj; games rm; CKE.
"Attractive, immac, well-run site; friendly, helpful
staff; clean san facs but sm; watersports at lake;
htd pool 200m; spectacular countryside; train to
Grenoble; gd NH; off clsd 1200-1530, site self."
€15.00, 1 May-30 Sep. **2015**

MONETIER LES BAINS, LE 9C3 (1km NW Rural)
44.98059, 6.49537 Camp Municipal Les Deux
Glaciers, 05220 Le Monêtier-les-Bains 07 89 56 58 77;
camping.monetier@orange.fr; www.monetier.com

🐕 €1 ⅋ (htd) WD ♨ ⊛ 🕭 🖥 MP 🦋 𝕀 nr ⓓ nr ⚠

On D1091 12km NW of Briançon; pass thro Le
Monêtier-les-Bains, in 1km site sp on L. 2*, Med,
hdstg, mkd, shd, terr, EHU (16A) €3.50; bus 1km; adv
bkg acc; CKE. "Excel, scenic site bef x-ing Montgenèvre
pass; gd base for Ecrins National Park; easy access fr
D1091; footpath to vill; v friendly helpful staff; immac
gd facs; excel for hiking, cycling, wildlife & flowers;
fantastic loc; clean." €15.50, 1 Jun-30 Sep. **2017**

MONISTROL D'ALLIER 9C1 (4km N Rural) 44.99148,
3.67781 Camp Municipal Le Marchat, 43580 St Privat-
d'Allier 04 71 57 22 13; info@mairie-saintprivat
dallier.fr; www.mairie-saintprivatdallier.fr

⅋ WD ♨ 🚿 🦋 𝕀 nr 🏊 nr ⚠

Fr Le Puy-en-Velay W on D589. Turn R in cent of
vill at petrol stn, site on R in 200m. 2*, Sm, hdg, shd,
terr, EHU (10A) €1.10. "Beautifully-kept, superb sm
site; friendly warden; not suitable lge o'fits; bars & shop
within 200mtrs." €6.00, 1 May-1 Nov. **2018**

MONISTROL SUR LOIRE *9C1* (7km SE Rural) *45.21630, 4.21240* **Kawan Village Camping de Vaubarlet,** 43600 Ste Sigolène **04 71 66 64 95; camping@ vaubarlet.com; www.vaubarlet.com**

🐾 €1 ♂♀ 🅆🄳 🚿 ♿ 🛒 ⊘ 🄼🅂🄿 🦋 ♈ � ♒ ⑨ ♨ 🆎 ⚠ ⚓ ♒(htd) 🛶

Fr Monistrol take D44 SE twd Ste Sigolène & turn R into vill. In vill take D43 dir Grazac for 6km. Site by Rv Dunière, ent L bef bdge. Site well sp fr vill.
4*, Med, mkd, pt shd, EHU (6A) €3 (poss rev pol); bbq; sw nr; TV; 15% statics; phone; Eng spkn; adv bkg acc; ccard acc; trout fishing; games area; bike hire; CKE. *"Friendly, helpful staff; well-run site; excel, spotless san facs; interesting museums nrby; ideal for families."* **€33.00, 27 Apr-30 Sep, L23.** **2019**

MONISTROL SUR LOIRE *9C1* (8km NW Urban) *45.31087, 4.12004* **Camping Municipal La Garenne,** Route du Camping, 43210 Bas-en-Basset **04 71 66 72 37 or 04 71 66 70 01; contact@basenbasset.fr; www.basenbasset.fr**

🐾 ♂♀ 🅆🄳 🚿 ♿ 🛒 ⊘ 🄼🅂🄿 🦋 ♈ ♒ ♨ 🆎nr ⚠ ♒(htd)

Fr N88 take the S exit (D47) sp Monistrol-sur-Loire. L at 1st rndabt; downhill on D12 dir Gourdon & Bas-en-Basset. Immed after Rv Loire turn R on D46. At rndabt turn R & foll sp to site.
Med, hdg, mkd, pt shd, EHU (10A); bbq; twin axles; 95% statics; phone; games rm; games area; CKE. *"Fishing adj; bustling static site, sm quiet area next to rv for tourers; takeaway; clean modern san facs; vg value; gd NH."* **€7.00, 15 Apr-30 Sep.** **2015**

"There aren't many sites open at this time of year"

If you're travelling outside peak season remember to call ahead to check site opening dates – even if the entry says 'open all year'.

MONNERVILLE *4E3* (2km S Rural) *48.33256, 2.04702* Camping Le Bois de la Justice, Méréville, 91930 Monnerville **01 64 95 05 34; leboisdelajustice@gmail.com; www.campingleboisdelajustice.com**

🐾 €1 ♂♀(htd) 🅆🄳 🚿 ♿ 🛒 ⊘ 🦋 ♨ 🆎 ⚠ ♒(htd)

Fr N20 S of Etampes, turn onto D18 at Monnerville, site well sp. Long narr app rd. 3*, Med, hdg, mkd, pt shd, pt sl, EHU (5A) inc; bbq; cooking facs; TV; 50% statics; phone; Eng spkn; adv bkg acc; ccard acc; tennis; games area. *"Delightful woodland oasis in open countryside; beware caterpillars in spring (poisonous to dogs); friendly welcome; clean san facs; ideal for Chartres, Fontainebleau, Orléans, Paris or excel NH just off N20; excel."* **€25.00, 7 Feb-24 Nov.** **2015**

MONPAZIER *7D3* (3km SW Rural) *44.65875, 0.87925* **Camping Moulin de David,** Route de Villeréal, 24540 Gaugeac-Monpazier **05 53 22 65 25; contact@moulindedavid.com; www.moulindedavid.com**

🐾 €3 ♂♀(htd) 🅆🄳 🚿 ♿ 🛒 ⊘ 🦋 ♈ ♒ ♨ ⑨ ♨ 🆎 ⚠ ♒ 🛶 🌊

Fr Monpazier, take D2 SW twd Villeréal, site sp on L after 3km. Narr app rds. 4*, Lge, mkd, hdg, pt shd, serviced pitches; EHU (10A) inc gas; bbq; sw; TV; 80% statics; Eng spkn; adv bkg acc; ccard acc; games rm; waterslide; archery; bike hire; tennis; fishing adj; games area; CKE. *"Charming site nr lovely town; welcoming, helpful owners; excel facs, ltd LS; poss mosquitoes nr rv thro site; mkt Thur Monpazier; highly rec; v rural; superb rest."* **€31.00, 1 May-15 Sep.** **2019**

MONT DORE, LE *7B4* (4km SE Rural) *45.571474, 2.817692* **Domaine de la Grande Cascade,** Route de Besse, 63240 Le Mont-Dore **04 73 65 06 23; contact@camping-grandecascade.com; www.camping-grande cascade.com**

🐾 €1 ♂♀ 🅆🄳 🚿 ♿ 🛒 ⊘ 🄼🅂🄿 🦋 ♈ ♒ ⚠

Fr Le Mont-Dore take D36 (12% incline) via col rte twd Besse-en-Chandesse. Site on R visible fr rd after 4km. App fairly steep & winding with poor surface. 2*, Med, mkd, hdg, pt shd, pt sl, EHU (6A); cooking facs; 5% statics; Eng spkn; adv bkg acc; games area; CKE. *"Excel; simple with magnificent, stunning mountain views; walk to waterfall; modern clean san facs; helpful staff."* **€15.00, 1 Jun-30 Sep.** **2018**

MONT LOUIS *8G4* (5km W Rural) *42.50636, 2.04671* **Camping Huttopia Font-Romeu,** Route de Mont-Louis, 66120 Font-Romeu **04 68 30 09 32; font-romeu@huttopia.com; www.huttopia.com**

🐾 €3.50 ♂♀(htd) 🛒 ⊘ 🦋 ♈ ♒ ♨ ⑨ 🆎 ⚓ 🌊(htd) 🛶

W fr Mont-Louis on D618. Site on L bef Font-Romeu, opp stadium. Fr Aix-les-Thermes or Puigcerdà turn E at Ur up longish hill, thro town to site on R at o'skts. Lge, pt shd, sl, EHU (6-10A) €4.20-6.20; 10% statics; phone; adv bkg acc; tennis 500m; horseriding 1km. *"Gd cent for mountain walks; site at 1800m altitude."* **€30.50, 29 May-15 Sep, D29.** **2019**

MONT ST MICHEL, LE *2E4* (10km E Rural) *48.62822, -1.41508* **Camping St Michel,** Route du Mont-St Michel, 50220 Courtils **02 33 70 96 90; infos@campingsaint michel.com; www.campingsaintmichel.com**

🐾 €2-3 ♂♀(htd) 🅆🄳 🚿 ♿ 🛒 ⊘ 🄼🅂🄿 🦋 ♈ 🐾 ♒ 🆎 ♨ ⚠ ♒ 🌊(htd)

Fr A84 exit J33. Foll sp for Courtils on Mont St Michel rd. Site on L at far end of vill. 3*, Med, mkd, hdg, pt shd, pt sl, EHU (6A) €3.50; gas; bbq; TV; 40% statics; phone; bus adj; Eng spkn; adv bkg acc; ccard acc; bike hire; games area; games rm; CKE. *"Excel, flat site; helpful, friendly owner; excel modern san facs (unisex); cycle paths adj; gd NH for St Malo; attractive; vg."* **€29.00, 31 Mar-1 Nov.** **2017**

MONTAIGU *2H4* (10km SE Rural) *46.93769, -1.21975* **Camping L'Eden,** La Raillière, 85600 La Boissière-de-Montaigu 02 51 41 62 32; contact@ camping-domaine-eden.fr; www.domaine-eden.fr

12 🏕 €2 ♦️↑ ♨ ♨ ᠔ 🔲 / 🏊 ⑪ ♨ 🔁 ⚠ 🏊 ♨(htd)

Fr Montaigu S on D137, in 8km turn E on D62, thro Le Pont-Legé. Site sp on L off D62. 3*, Med, mkd, shd, EHU (10A) inc; gas; TV; 40% statics; adv bkg acc; tennis; CKE. *"Pleasant, quiet site in woodlands; site poss open all year; clean facs; motor mover useful; site looking a bit tired."* **€23.00** **2017**

MONTBARD *6G1* (1km N Urban) *47.6314, 4.33303* **Camp Municipal Les Treilles,** Rue Michel Servet, 21500 Montbard 03 80 92 69 50; camping.montbard@ wanadoo.fr; www.montbard.com

🏕 €2 ♦️↑ 🔲 ♨ ᠔ 🔁 / ᠔ 🏊nr ⚠

Lies off N side D980. Camping sp clearly indicated on all app including by-pass. Turn onto by-pass at traff lts at rndabt at junc of D905 & D980. Site nr **pool.** 3*, Med, hdg, pt shd, EHU (16A) €4; bbq; sw nr; phone; bike hire; CKE. *"Pleasant & well-kept site; gd pitches; lge, smart san facs; poss contract worker campers; pool complex adj inc; quiet but rd/rlwy noise at far end; interesting area; excel NH."* **€20.00, 26 Mar-30 Oct.** **2016**

MONTBARREY *6H2* (1km SW Rural) *47.01230, 5.63161* **FLOWER Camping Les Trois Ours,** 28 Rue du Pont, 39380 Montbarrey 03 84 81 50 45; h.rabbe@ orange.fr; www.camping-les3ours-jura.com or www.flowercampings.com

🏕 ♦️↑(htd) 🔲 ♨ ᠔ 🔁 / 🔲 🦋 ⑪ Ⓣ ⑪ ♨ 🏊nr ⚠ 🏊

Exit A39 junc onto D905 E; 1km after Mont-sur-Vaudrey on D472 turn L dir Montbarrey. Cross rv, site on L at rvside on edge of vill. 3*, Med, mkd, hdg, shd, EHU (10A) inc; bbq; TV; 10% statics; phone; bus; Eng spkn; adv bkg acc; ccard acc; games rm. *"Improvements planned; vg walking/cycling fr site; excel menu in rest."* **€25.00, 13 Apr-28 Sep.** **2019**

MONTBAZON *4G2* (0.8km N Rural) *47.29044, 0.71595* **Camping de la Grange Rouge,** 37250 Montbazon 02 47 26 06 43; infos@camping-montbazon.com; www.camping-montbazon.com

🏕 €2 ♦️↑ 🔲 ♨ ᠔ 🔁 / 🦋 🏊nr ⑪nr ♨ 🏊nr ⚠ 🏊(htd)

On D910 thro Montbazon fr S to N, after x-ing bdge (pt of D910) immed turn L to site. Clearly visible & clearly sp on W side of rd at N end of town. 3*, Med, mkd, pt shd, EHU (10A) €4; TV; 10% statics; Eng spkn; adv bkg acc; ccard acc; fishing; tennis; CKE. *"Lovely, spacious rvside site in pretty town (walkable); helpful, friendly owner; bar adj; basic facs dated but clean; conv Tours & a'routes; poorly maintained."* **€20.50, 1 Apr-15 Oct.** **2016**

MONTBERT *2H4* (0.5km SE Rural) *47.05133, -1.47930* **Camping Le Relais des Garennes (Gendron),** La Bauche Coiffée, 44140 Montbert 02 40 04 78 73; lerelaisdesgarennes@gmail.com; www.camping-lerelaisdesgarennes.com

🏕 ♦️↑(htd) 🔲 ♨ ᠔ 🔁 / 🦋 ⑪

Fr Nantes on N937 dir La Roche, at Geneston turn L dir Montbert & foll site sp. Or fr Nantes on N137 dir La Rochelle turn R at Aigrefeuille-sur-Maine for Montbert. Sm, mkd, pt shd, pt sl, EHU (10A) inc; Eng spkn; adv bkg acc; lake fishing adj; tennis nr; CKE. *"Peaceful, picturesque site; lge pitches; friendly owners; immac facs, but no individual wash rms; rabbits & hens on site; toys for children; many attractions nrby; pleasant walk to town; gd value; sports facs nrby; excel; highly rec; bus avail to Nantes fr vill; excel."* **€13.00, 1 Jun-30 Sep.** **2018**

"That's changed – Should I let the Club know?"

If you find something on site that's different from the site entry, fill in a report and let us know. See camc.com/europereport.

MONTBRISON *9B1* (1.5km S Urban) *45.59133, 4.07806* **Camp Municipal Le Surizet,** 31 Rue du Surizet, Moingt, 42600 Montbrison 04 77 58 08 30

🏕 €0.85 ♦️↑ 🔲 ♨ 🔁 / 🔲 🦋 🏊nr ⚠ 🏊

Fr St Etienne on D8, at rndabt junc with D204 turn L sp St Anthème & Ambert. Cross rlwy & turn R in 400m, site sp. 3*, Med, pt shd, EHU (5-10A) inc; bbq; 10% statics; bus (every hr); adv bkg acc; fishing; tennis 2km; CKE. *"Pleasant, well-kept site; no twin axles; vg value; highly rec NH or sh stay; bird reserve (20km)."* **€13.00, 15 Apr-15 Oct.** **2017**

MONTBRON *7B3* (6km SE Rural) *45.65972, 0.55805* **Camping Les Gorges du Chambon,** Le Chambon, 16220 Eymouthiers 05 45 70 71 70; info@ gorgesduchambon.fr; www.gorgesduchambon.fr

🏕 €6 ♦️↑(htd) 🔲 ♨ ᠔ 🔁 / 🔲 🦋 ⑪ Ⓣ ⑪ ♨ 🏊 ⚠ 🏊 🏊(htd)

Fr N141 turn SE onto D6 at La Rochefoucauld; cont on D6 out of Montbron; after 5km turn L at La Tricherie onto D163; foll camp sp to site in approx 1.9km. NB Fr La Tricherie narr in places & some sharp bends. 4*, Med, hdstg, mkd, pt shd, pt sl, EHU (10A) inc; gas; bbq (charcoal, gas); red long stay; twin axles; TV; 25% statics; Eng spkn; adv bkg acc; ccard acc; horseriding nr; games rm; tennis; bike hire; games area; golf nr; canoe hire; rv fishing; CKE. *"Beautiful, 'away fr it all', scenic site in grnds of old farm; welcoming, helpful & friendly staff; lge pitches but some sl; excel san facs; superb rest; gd mkd walks; birdwatching & wildlife; poss motorbike rally on site end June; excel."* **€45.00, 19 Apr-13 Sep, D11.** **2019**

MONTECH *8E3* (1km E Rural) *43.96608, 1.24003*
Camping de Montech (formerly Camping Paradis), Chemin de la Pierre, 82700 Montech **05 63 31 14 29;** contact@camping-montech.fr; www.camping-montech.fr

🐕 €2.80 ⚌ ⌨ ☂ ⚐ ⧗ ⏚ 🍽 Ⓨ ⊕ 🛝 🏊 🛒

Exit A20 junc 65 Montauban Sud onto D928 dir Auch. In Montech turn R just bef canal, site well sp. 3*, Lge, hdg, mkd, unshd, EHU (16A) €4; bbq; twin axles; 60% statics; Eng spkn; adv bkg acc; games area; lake fishing nrby; CKE. "*Gd cycle paths.*"
€24.00, 1 Mar-31 Oct.   2019

MONTENDRE *7C2* (4km NW Rural) *45.30037, -0.43495*
Camping Twin Lakes, La Faiencérie, 17130 Souméras **05 46 49 77 12** or **0114 2463800 (UK); twinlakesinfo@hotmail.co.uk; www.twinlakesfrance.com

12 🐕 €1.50 ⚌ ⌨ ☂ ♿ ⚐ ⧗ 🍽 Ⓨ ⏚nr 🛝 🏊(htd) 🛶

Exit N10/E606 at Montlieu-la-Garde onto D730 thro Montendre dir Mirambeau; go past Souméras vill on R, site sp on L. Or exit A10 junc 37; turn R onto D730; at rndabt turn R onto N137; in Mirambeau turn L onto D730; site on R in approx 14 km. Sm, hdg, pt shd, pt sl, EHU (10-16A) €3; gas; bbq; red long stay; TV; 15% statics; Eng spkn; adv bkg acc; clsd 15 Dec-5 Jan; lake fishing; games rm. "*Vg British-owned site; meals arranged; gd touring base; vg; best to pitch on field beside lake.*" €25.00   2017

MONTESQUIOU *8F2* (4km W Rural) *43.57705, 0.29111* **Camping l'Anjou,** L'Anjou 32320 Montesquiou **05 62 70 95 24; clemens.van-voorst@wanadoo.fr; www.camping-anjou.com

🐕 €2.50 ⚌ ⌨ ☂ ♿ ⚐ ⚐ ⧗ 🍽 Ⓨ ⏚ 🏊 🛶

Campsite is bet Montesquiou & Bassoues on the D943. Site is well mkd. A sm lane leads to site ent. 1*, Sm, hdg, hdstg, mkd, pt shd, pt sl, EHU (6A) €2.50; bbq; 50% statics; Eng spkn; adv bkg acc; games area; playgd; CCI. "*Excel; no twin axles; friendly welcoming owners; mini farm; ideally situated for those attending Marciac Jazz Festival.*" €19.50, 1 May-30 Sep.   2015

MONTFAUCON *7D3* (3km W Rural) *44.69197, 1.53480* **Kawan Village Domaine de la Faurie,** 46240 Sénìergues **05 65 21 14 36; contact@camping-lafaurie.com; www.camping-lafaurie.com

🐕 €3 ⧗(htd) ⌨ ☂ ♿ ⚐ ⚐ ⧗ 🦋 Ⓨ ⊕ ⏚ 🛝 🏊(htd) 🛶

Fr N20 turn E onto D2 sp Montfaucon, or fr A20 exit junc 56. In 5km site sp. Rd to site (off D2) is 500m long, single-track with passing places & steep but passable. Well sp fr A20. 4*, Med, mkd, pt shd, pt sl, terr, EHU (6-10A) €4.50-6.70; twin axles; TV; 30% statics; Eng spkn; adv bkg acc; ccard acc; games area; bike hire. "*Superb, pretty site with great views; quiet & peaceful; lge pitches; excel facs & rest; gd touring base; poss intermittent elec supply some pitches (2010); many walks; conv A20; award winning site; one of the best sites.*" €30.00, 5 Apr-31 Oct.   2015

MONTFERRAND *8F4* (4.8km N Rural) *43.39007, 1.82788* **FFCC Domaine St Laurent,** Les Touzets, 11320 Montferrand **04 68 60 15 80** or **06 76 60 58 42 (mob); info@camping-carcassonne-toulouse.com; www.camping-carcassonne-toulouse.com

🐕 €2 ⚌ ⌨ ☂ ⚐ ⚐ 🍽 Ⓨ ⊕ 🛝 ⏚ 🏊 🛶

S fr Toulouse on N113/D1113 past Villefranche-de-Lauragais. Turn L onto D43 for 4.2km; then R to St Laurent. Or turn L onto D218 bypassing Montferrand & cont directly to St Laurent; turn L at church. Site well sp. 3*, Sm, hdg, pt shd, EHU (6A) inc; TV; 10% statics; Eng spkn; adv bkg acc; tennis; bike hire; games rm; sauna; archery. "*Attractive, peaceful, well-kept site; clean san facs; friendly owners; gd views; woodland walks; vg site but narr access rds.*"
€26.00, 1 Apr-15 Oct.   2017

MONTIGNAC *7C3* (7km E Rural) *45.05375, 1.23980* **Yelloh! Village Lascaux Vacances,** Route des Malénies, 24290 St Amand-de-Coly **05 53 50 81 57; mail@campinglascauxvacances.com; www.campinglascauxvacances.com** or **www.yellohvillage.co.uk

🐕 €4 ⚌ ⌨ ☂ ♿ ⚐ ⧗ 🦋 Ⓨ ⊕ ⏚ 🛝 🏊 🛶 🛶

Exit A89 junc 17 (Peyrignac) SE onto D6089 to Le Lardin-St Lazare. Join D62 S to Coly & then foll sp to Saint Amand-de-Coly. Site well sp. 3*, Med, mkd, hdg, pt shd, EHU (10A) inc; bbq; red long stay; TV; 60% statics; phone; adv bkg acc; ccard acc; fishing nr; waterslide; games area; sauna; games rm. "*Excel, peaceful, renovated site in superb location; warm welcome; lge pitches; excel touring base.*"
€33.00, 15 Apr-11 Sep.   2017

MONTIGNAC *7C3* (8km SE Rural) *45.07211, 1.23431* **Camping La Tournerie Ferme,** La Tournerie, 24290 Aubas **05 53 51 04 16; la-tournerie@orange.fr; www.la-tournerie.com

🐕 ⚌(htd) ⌨ ☂ ♿ ⚐ ⚐ Ⓨnr ⊕nr

Fr Montignac on D704 dir Sarlat-la-Canéda; in 5.5km turn L onto C1 sp St Amand-de-Coly; in 1.6km at x-rds turn L sp Malardel & Drouille; in 400m at Y-junc foll rd to R sp Manardel & La Genèbre; cont on this rd ignoring minor rds; in 1.6km at elongated junc take rd to R of post box; immed after passing Le Treuil farm on R turn R at x-rds La Tournerie. Site opp farm. Sm, hdstg, unshd, sl, terr, EHU (6A) inc; bbq; twin axles; Eng spkn; adv bkg req. "*Lovely, tranquil site; adults only; lge pitches with beautiful views; friendly, helpful British owners (CC members); excel san facs; request detailed dirs or see website - sat nav not rec; excel touring base; excel site; fenced dog pitches.*" €23.00, 1 Mar-30 Nov.   2016

MONTIGNAC 7C3 (9km S Rural) 45.01765, 1.18811
FFCC Camping La Fage, 24290 La Chapelle-Aubareil
05 53 50 76 50 or 06 87 37 5 891 (Mob); contact@
camping-lafage.com; www.camping-lafage.com

€1.80 (htd)

Fr Montignac take D704 twd Sarlat. In about 8km
turn R onto La Chapelle-Aubareil & foll camp sp.
4*, Med, hdstg, pt shd, pt sl, EHU (10A); bbq; TV;
30% statics; adv bkg acc; games area; CKE. "Excel site;
helpful owners; vg, clean san facs; red facs LS; gd rest
at auberge in vill; conv Lascaux 2 & other pre-historic
sites; gd walking." €30.00, 11 Apr-10 Oct.   2015

> ## "I like to fill in the reports as I travel from site to site"
>
> You'll find report forms at the back of this
> guide, or you can fill them in online at
> camc.com/europereport.

MONTIGNAC 7C3 (14km SW Rural) 45.00178,
1.07155 Camping Le Paradis, La Reybeyrolle, 24290
St Léon-sur-Vézère 05 53 50 72 64; le-paradis@
perigord.com; www.le-paradis.fr

€2.50 (htd) (htd, indoor) adj

On W bank of Rv Vézère on D706 Montignac-Les
Eyzies rd, 1km fr Le Moustier. D706 poss rough rd.
5*, Med, hdg, pt shd, EHU (10A); bbq; sw; red long
stay; TV; 25% statics; phone; Eng spkn; adv bkg acc;
ccard acc; boat hire; tennis; fishing; sauna; games
area; bike hire; CKE. "Excel, high standard site in gd
location; friendly, conscientious Dutch owners; immac
san facs; gd pool, rest & takeaway; vg for families;
tropical vegetation around pitches, grnds like a garden;
excel, espec LS; ACSI acc."
€38.00, 1 Apr-20 Oct, D30.   2017

See advertisement

MONTLUCON 7A4 (12km NW Rural) 46.37795, 2.46695
Camp Municipal Le Moulin de Lyon, 03380 Huriel
06 11 75 05 63 or 04 70 28 60 08 (Mairie); mairie.
huriel@wanadoo.fr

wo nr

Exit A71 junc 10 & foll sp Domérat, then D916 to
Huriel. Site well sp. Or fr N D943 turn SW at La
Chapelaude to Huriel on D40, foll sp to site. Last km
single track (but can pass on level grass) with steep
incline to site ent. Site adj Rv Magieure.
2*, Med, hdg, pt shd, pt sl, EHU (10A) inc (poss rev pol);
gas; bbq; TV; 10% statics; Eng spkn; lake fishing; tennis.
"Peaceful, wooded site in lovely setting by lake; well-
kept; friendly; site yourself, warden calls am & pm; no
apparent security; uphill walk to vill (1km); lovely quiet
site, clean facs." €9.00, 15 Apr-15 Oct.   2016

MONTMAUR 9D3 (7km SE Rural) 44.55003, 5.95114
Camping au Blanc Manteau, Route de Céüse, 05400
Manteyer 92 57 82 56 or 92 57 85 89; pierre.wampach@
wanadoo.fr; www.campingaublancmanteau.fr

12 (htd) wo nr (htd)

Take D994 fr Veynes twd Gap, past Montmaur; site
sp fr vill of La Roche-des-Arnauds on D18 in 1km.
3*, Sm, mkd, pt shd, EHU (10A) €5.35; adv bkg rec;
tennis. "Gd sized pitches; pleasant owner; pretty,
in wooded area with beautiful views of mountains."
€24.00   2019

MONTMEDY 5C1 (0.7km NW Urban) 49.52126,
5.36090 Camp Municipal La Citadelle, Rue Vauban,
55600 Montmédy 03 29 80 10 40 (Mairie); mairie.
montmedy@wanadoo.fr; www.montmedy.fr

€2.24 wo nr

Fr D643 foll sp to Montmédy cent & foll site sp.
Steep app. 2*, Sm, hdg, pt shd, pt sl, EHU (4-10A)
€2.80-3.97; red long stay; CKE. "Warden calls am & pm;
facs clean, ltd LS; nr Montmedy Haut fortified town;
10A hook-up not avail high ssn; vg; lovely, delightful
little site; gd views." €9.60, 1 May-30 Sep.   2019

FRANCE

MONTMORILLON 7A3 (0.8km S Urban) 46.42035, 0.87554 **Camp Municipal de l'Allochon,** 31 Ave Fernand Tribot, 86500 Montmorillon 05 49 91 02 33 or 05 49 91 13 99 (Mairie); www.montmorillon.fr

🏕 👫👫(htd) ♨ ♿ 🗑 ⊿ 🅿 ♟ ⊤ nr ⊕ nr ☎ nr /◫

On D54 to Le Dorat, approx 400m SE fr main rd bdge over rv at S of town. Site on L. Fr S v sharp RH turn into site. 3*, Med, mkd, pt shd, terr, EHU (10A); bbq; TV; Eng spkn; adv bkg acc; ccard acc; games area; fishing; CKE. *"Delightful, peaceful, well-kept site; lge pitches; friendly, hard-working warden; gd touring base; vg value; v clean facs, old but working shwrs; htd covrd pool adj; relaxing; rec; security barrier; gd walking area, maps fr TO; ltd facs LS."* **€12.00, 1 Mar-31 Oct.** 2018

"We must tell the Club about that great site we found"

Get your site reports in by mid-August and we'll do our best to get your updates into the next edition.

MONTOIRE SUR LE LOIR 4F2 (0.5km S Rural) 47.74750, 0.86351 **Camp Municipal Les Reclusages,** Ave des Reclusages, 41800 Montoire-sur-le Loir 02 54 85 02 53; camping.reclusages@orange.fr; www.mairie-montoire.fr

🏕 €0.97 👫👫 wo ♨ ♿ 🗑 ⊿ 🅿 ✗ ♟ ⊤ nr /◫

Foll site sp, out of town sq, over rv bdge & 1st L on blind corner at foot of old castle. 3*, Med, mkd, pt shd, EHU (6-10A) €3.10-3.93; 5% statics; Eng spkn; adv bkg acc; ccard acc; canoeing; fishing; CKE. *"Lovely location nr Rv Loir; peaceful, well-kept, secure site; some rvside pitches; friendly, helpful warden; excel clean san facs, ltd LS; gd cycling; conv troglodyte vills; excel; pleasant sh walk into town across rv; htd pool adj; attractive town; Int'l Folk Festival mid Aug."* **€14.00, 1 Apr-30 Sep.** 2017

MONTPELLIER 10F1 (8km N Rural) 43.65135, 3.89630 **Sandaya Le Plein Air des Chênes,** 531 Avenue Georges France, 34830 Clapiers 04 67 02 02 53; pac@sandaya.fr; www.sandaya.co.uk

🏕 €s 👫👫 ♨ ♿ 🗑 ⊿ ✗ ♟ ⊤ ⊕ ♟ ☎ nr /◫ 🚲 🏊 ⛵

Exit A9 junc 28 onto N113/D65 twd Montpellier. Leave at junc with D21 sp Jacou & Teyran, site sp on L. NB Site ent/exit v narr & no place to stop when leaving. 4*, Med, mkd, pt shd, pt sl, terr, serviced pitches; EHU (10A) inc; gas; red long stay; 75% statics; horseriding; tennis; games area; waterslide. *"Vg site; site rds tight for lge o'fits; private san facs some pitches (extra charge); pitches muddy in wet."* **€25.00, 3 Apr-13 Sep.** 2019

MONTPON MENESTEROL 7C2 (1km N Rural) 45.01280, 0.15828 **Camping La Cigaline,** 1 Rue de la Paix, Route de Ribérac, 24700 Montpon-Ménestérol 05 53 80 22 16; contact@lacigaline.fr; www.lacigaline.fr

🏕 €1.50 👫👫 wo ♨ ♿ 🗑 ⊿ 🕸 ♟ ⊤ ⊕ ♨ ☎ nr /◫

Fr Montpon town cent traff lts take D730 N to Ménestérol. Site on L bef bdge beside Rv Isle. 3*, Med, hdg, mkd, shd, EHU (10A) inc; bbq; sw nr; 1% statics; train 1km; Eng spkn; adv bkg acc; ccard acc; fishing; tennis 200m; boat hire; CKE. *"Gd touring base for St Emilion region; gd walking, cycling; vg; new young owners (2014); leisure park nrby; bike hire 500m; gd food in bar/rest; terr o'looks rv; site improving."* **€19.60, 6 Apr-30 Sep.** 2019

MONTREJEAU 8F3 (7km S Rural) 43.02864, 0.57852 **Camping Es Pibous,** Chemin de St Just, 31510 St Bertrand-de-Comminges 05 61 88 31 42; contact@es-pibous.fr; www.espibous.fr

🏕 👫👫(htd) wo ♨ ♿ 🗑 ⊿ 🅿 🕸 ⊤ nr ⊕ nr ☎ /◫ 🏊

Turn S fr D817 onto D825 sp Bagnères-de-Luchon & Espagne. Foll past 'Super U' to lge rndabt & turn R sp St Bertrand-de-Comminges/Valcabrère then at 1st traff lts turn R & foll sp for St Bertrand. Turn R off N125 onto D825 to roman excavation site. Site on L. Or exit A64 junc 17 onto A645 sp Bagnères-de-Luchon to lge rndabt, then as above. 3*, Med, mkd, hdg, pt shd, EHU (10A) inc; gas; TV; 20% statics; adv bkg acc; ccard acc; fishing 3km; tennis 3km. *"Peaceful, friendly site; pitches among trees; clean dated san facs, ltd LS; lndry is owner's washing machine, not always avail (2010); gd touring area nr mountains; picturesque town in walking dist."* **€20.40, 1 Apr-31 Oct.** 2017

"I need an on-site restaurant"

We do our best to make sure site information is correct, but it is always best to check any must-have facilities are still available or will be open during your visit.

MONTREJEAU 8F3 (1km W Rural) 43.08624, 0.55414 **Camping Couleurs Garonne (formerly Camping Les Hortensias),** Route de Tarbes, 31210 Montréjeau 05 61 88 52 30; campingcouleursgaronne@orange.fr; www.campingcouleursgaronne.fr

👫👫 wo ♨ ✗ ☎ nr /◫

Fr St Gaudens on D817, R at foot of steep hill, sp 'Tarbes Poids Lourds' to avoid Montréjeau cent. Site on L in 1km. On W o'skirts of town, well sp on rd to Tarbes. Sm, pt shd, EHU (15A) inc; bbq; CKE. *"Gd NH; no twin axles; spacious grassy site; friendly."* **€15.00, 15 Apr-31 Oct.** 2015

MONTRESOR *4H2* (3km W Rural) *47.15782, 1.16026* Camping Les Coteaux du Lac, 37460 Cheillé-sur-Indrois 02 47 92 77 83; lescoteauxdulac@wanadoo.fr; www.lescoteauxdulac.com

🐕 €1.70 [icons] ⚓

Fr Loches on D764; then D10 dir Montrésor; cont to Chemillé-sur-Indrois. 4*, Med, pt sl, EHU (6A) €3.90; bbq; TV; phone; Eng spkn; fishing; games rm; boating. *"Excel setting by lake; immac, modern san facs; beautiful vill 600m; trekking in Val d'Indrois; 3km along cycle track (old rlwy)."* **€34.00, 3 Mar-15 Oct.** 2019

See advertisement

MONTREUIL *3B3* (0.5km W Rural) *50.46853, 1.76280* FFCC Camping La Fontaine des Clercs, 1 Rue de l'Eglise, 62170 Montreuil 03 21 06 07 28; desmarest.mi@wanadoo.fr; www.campinglafontaine desclercs.fr

[12] 🐕 €2 [icons] nr

Fr N or S turn SW off D901 at rndabt onto D349 to Montreuil; turn R immed after rlwy x-ing (onto Rue des Préaux); in 120m turn R; site in 100m on R; sp on Rv Canche. Or take 2nd R ALMOST immed after (20m) rlwy-xing (onto Grande Ville Basse); in 50m fork R (Rue de l'Eglise); site in 200m on R. NB Poss difff access lge o'fits. 3*, Med, mkd, hdstg, pt shd, pt sl, terr, EHU (6-10A) €3.70-€4.80; bbq; 60% statics; adv bkg rec; rv fishing adj; site clsd over New Year; games rm; CKE. *"Busy, basic site in beautiful spot; helpful, friendly owner; gd san facs; steep & narr site rd with tight turns to terr pitches, some sm; pool 1.5km; not suitable lge o'fits; some generous pitches beside rv; vet in Montreuil; attractive, historic town with amazing restaurants- uphill walk; conv NH Le Touquet, beaches & ferry; wine society outlet; excel site; some Eng spkn."* **€19.50** 2017

MONTREUIL BELLAY *4H1* (1km W Urban) *47.13191, -0.15897* Camping Les Nobis D'Anjou, Rue Georges Girouy, 49260 Montreuil-Bellay 02 41 52 33 66; camping-les-nobis@orange.fr; www.campingles nobis.com

🐕 [icons] (htd)

Fr S on D938 turn L immed on ent town boundary & foll rd for 1km to site; sp fr all dir. Fr N on D347 ignore 1st camping sp & cont on D347 to 2nd rndabt & foll sp. Fr NW on D761 turn R onto D347 sp Thouars to next rndabt, foll site sp. 4*, Lge, hdg, mkd, pt shd, EHU (10A) €3 (poss long cable req, rev pol); gas; red long stay; TV; 50% statics; phone; Eng spkn; adv bkg acc; ccard acc; bike hire; CKE. *"Spacious site bet castle & rv; gd, modern san facs; local chateaux & town worth exploring; 'aire de service' for m'vans adj; gd patissiere in town; some pitches o'look rv Thouet; extremely well managed, friendly site; nr Saumur vineyards; excel."* **€29.00, 31 Mar-30 Sep.** 2018

MONTRICHARD *4G2* (1km S Rural) *47.33384, 1.18766* Camping Couleurs du Monde, 1 Rond Point de Montparnasse, 41400 Faverolles-sur-Cher 02 54 32 06 08 or 06 74 79 56 29 (mob); touraine-vacances@ wanadoo.fr; www.camping-couleurs-du-monde.com

🐕 €2 [icons] nr ⚓

E fr Tours on D796 thro Bléré; at Montrichard turn S on D764 twd Faverolles-sur-Cher, site 200m fr junc, adj to Carrefour supmkt - on L by 2nd rndabt. 4*, Med, mkd, hdstg, pt shd, EHU (10A) €4; bbq; sw nr; TV; Eng spkn; adv bkg acc; ccard acc; tennis 500m; games rm; sauna; bike hire; games area; waterslide 500m; CKE. *"Level site in gd location nr vineyards; beauty cent; gd sports activities; vg; excel facs; gd sw pool with canopy; ideal for exploring Cher & Loire Valley."* **€30.00, 31 Mar-29 Sep.** 2017

MONTRICOUX *8E3* (0.5km W Rural) *44.07660, 1.61103*
FFCC Camping Le Clos Lalande, Route de Bioule, 82800 Montricoux **06 49 27 48 28; contact@ camping-lecloslalande.com; www.camping-leclos lalande.com**

🐕 €2.50 ♿ wc ⚡ ♨ ♿ 🚿 ∅ MSP 👙 👕 🍴 ♿ nr ⚓ ⛵

Fr A20 exit junc 59 to Caussade; fr Caussade take D964 to Montricoux, where site well sp. 3*, Med, hdg, mkd, pt shd, EHU (6A) €3.60; bbq; TV; 10% statics; phone; bus 400m; Eng spkn; adv bkg rec; games area; rv fishing 400m; canoe hire; watersports; tennis; bike hire; CKE. *"Peaceful, quiet, well-kept site by rv at mouth of Aveyron gorges; beautiful area, inc Bastide vills; great family site; friendly, helpful owners; mkt Weds; easy walk to town; highly rec."* €25.40, 30 Mar-6 Oct.   **2019**

MONTROLLET *7B3* (0.1km N Rural) *45.98316, 0.89702* **Camping Auberge La Marchadaine,** Beaulieu, 16420 Montrollet **05 45 71 09 88 or 06 63 07 82 48 (mob); aubergedelamarchadaine@gmail.com**

🐕 ♿ wc ♨ ♿ ∅ MSP 🦋 👕 🍴 ⊕ ♿ nr ⚓

N fr St Junien on D675, turn W onto D82 to Montrollet. Auberge sp in vill. Sm, pt shd, EHU (6A) inc; gas; bbq; twin axles; phone; adv bkg acc; games area; fishing; CKE. *"Delightful CL-type site nr beautiful lake; vg rest; many mkd walks; Oradour sur Glane nrby (wartime museum); Vienne rv; gd; rund down (2017)."* €12.00   **2017**

MONTSAUCHE LES SETTONS *4G4* (5.4km SE Rural) *47.19276, 4.06047* **FFCC Camping de la Plage des Settons,** Rive Gauche, Lac des Settons, 58230 Montsauche-les-Settons **03 86 84 51 99; camping@ settons-tourisme.com; www.settons-tourisme.com**

🐕 ♿ wc ♨ ♿ ∅ MSP ♿ nr ⚓

Fr Montsauche foll sp Château-Chinon. In 500m fork L to Les Settons. After 2km foll sp for Rive Gauche, after 1km L at bend for site. 3*, Med, hdg, mkd, pt shd, terr, EHU (4A) inc (long lead req); bbq; sw; Eng spkn; ccard acc; bike hire; fishing; CKE. *"In cent of Parc du Morvan; lake adj; direct access to Lac des Settons; pedalos; access rd busy pm."* €20.00, 15 Apr-15 Oct.   **2015**

MONTSAUCHE LES SETTONS *4G4* (7km SE Rural) *47.18175, 4.05293* **FFCC Camping Les Mésanges,** Rive Gauche, 58230 Montsauche-les-Settons **03 86 84 55 77; info@campinglesmesanges.fr; www.campinglesmesanges.fr**

🐕 €0.80 ♿ wc ♨ ♿ ∅ MSP 🦋 👙 ⊕ nr ⚓ ♿

Fr Montsauche take D193 twds Les Settons, just bef Les Settons fork R onto D520 dir Chevigny. After 1km turn L and foll sp to site on R on W side of lake. 3*, Med, mkd, shd, pt sl, terr, EHU (16A) inc; gas; sw; Eng spkn; adv bkg acc; games rm; fishing; games area; CKE. *"Beautiful site; well-maintained; gd for families - lge play areas; excel."* €22.00, 14 May-15 Sep.   **2015**

MONTSAUCHE LES SETTONS *4G4* (7.6km SE Rural) *47.18578, 4.07056* **Camping Plage du Midi,** Lac des Settons Les Branlasses, 58230 Montsauche-les-Settons **03 86 84 51 97; campplagedumidi@aol.com; www.settons-camping.com**

🐕 €1 ♿ (htd) wc ♨ ♿ ∅ MSP 👙 👕 🍴 ⊕ nr ⚓ ♿ ⛵
⛵ (covrd, htd) ☂ sand adj

Fr Salieu take D977 bis to Monsauche, then D193 'Rive Droite' to Les Settons for 5km. Cont a further 3km & take R fork sp 'Les Branlasses' Cent du Sport. Site on L after 500m at lakeside. 3*, Med, mkd, pt shd, terr, EHU (10A) €3.60; gas; sw; phone; Eng spkn; adv bkg acc; ccard acc; horseriding 2km; watersports; bike hire; CKE. *"Site in gd situation; muddy when wet."* €20.00, 19 Apr-15 Sep.   **2015**

MONTSOREAU *4G1* (1.3km NW Rural) *47.21805, 0.05270* **Camping L'Isle Verte,** Ave de la Loire, 49730 Montsoreau **02 41 51 76 60 or 02 41 67 37 81; isleverte@cvtloisirs.fr; www.campingisleverte.com**

🐕 €2 ♿ wc ♨ ♿ ∅ MSP 👙 👕 ⊕ ♿ nr ⚓ ♿ ⛵ ⚓

At Saumur on S side of rv turn R immed bef bdge over Rv Loire; foll sp to Chinon & site. Fr N foll sp for Fontevraud & Chinon fr Rv Loire bdge; site on D947 in vill on banks of Loire opp 'Charcuterie' shop. 4*, Med, mkd, pt shd, EHU (16A) poss long lead req; gas; TV; 20% statics; bus to Saumur; Eng spkn; adv bkg rec; ccard acc; games area; rv fishing; bike hire; watersports; golf 13km; tennis; CKE. *"Pleasant rvside site in beautiful situation; v busy high ssn; various sized/shaped pitches; car hire; adequate san facs, poss irreg cleaning LS; vg rest; barrier clsd 2200-0700; gd security; pleasant vill; gd; excel; helpful staff."* €38.50, 3 Apr-14 Oct, L34.   **2019**

MOREE *4F2* (2.5km SW Urban) *47.88932, 1.20109* **Camping La Maladrerie,** Rue du Plessis, 41160 Fréteval **06 50 23 11 88 or 06 67 31 55 52**

♿ wc ♨ ♿ ∅ MSP 🍴 ♿ nr ⚓ ⛵

E fr Le Mans on D357 to Fréteval; turn L in vill. Sp. 3*, Med, mkd, pt shd, EHU (4-6A) €1.55-2.30; gas; bbq; sw nr; 60% statics; Eng spkn; ccard acc; lake fishing; CKE. *"Delightful, well-kept, quiet site; friendly owner; unisex wc; poss ltd facs LS; site was a medieval leper colony; new owners but site still run down (2017)."* €12.00, 1 Apr-30 Oct.   **2017**

MORESTEL *9B3* (8km S Urban) *45.63521, 5.57231* **Camping Couleur Nature (formerly Les Avenières),** 6 Rue du Stade, 38630 Les Avenières **04 74 33 92 92; camping@lesavenieres.fr; www.camping-couleur-nature.fr**

🐕 ♿ (htd) wc ♨ ♿ ∅ MSP 🍴 ⊕ ♿ ⚓ ♿

S fr Morestel on D1075, turn onto D40 to Les Avenières, site well sp. 3*, Med, hdg, mkd, hdstg, pt shd, EHU (10A); bbq; sw nr; TV; 35% statics; phone; adv bkg acc; ccard acc; CKE. *"Phone ahead LS to check open; pool adj; noise fr adj stadium."* €27.00, 1 May-30 Sep.   **2019**

MORLAIX *2E2* (11km E Rural) *48.60283, -3.73833*
Camping Aire Naturelle la Ferme de Croas Men
(Cotty), Garlan, 29610 Plouigneau 02 98 79 11 50;
info@ferme-de-croasmen.com; www.ferme-de-croasmen.com

🛏 €1 ♨♨ [wc] ♨ ♿ 🖧 🥗 [MsP] 💛 🐖 /🏔

Fr D712 rndabt W of Plouigneau twd Morlaix (exit
fr N12) 2km R sp Garlan; thro Garlan site 1km on L,
well sp. Sm, hdg, pt shd, serviced pitches; EHU (6A)
€3.50; 10% statics; Eng spkn; horseriding 200m; CKE.
*"Lovely, well-kept CL-type farm site; excel facs; farm
museum; donkey/tractor rides; ideal for children;
produce avail inc cider & crêpes; vg."*
€19.00, 1 Apr-31 Oct.   **2017**

MORTAIN *2E4* (12km S Rural) *48.57039, -0.94883*
Camping Les Taupinières, La Raisnais, 50140
Notre-Dame-du-Touchet 02 33 69 49 36 or
06 33 26 78 82 (mob); belinfrance@fsmail.net;
www.lestaupinieres.com

🛏 ♨♨ [wc] ♨ 🥗 💛 ♀ 🕸 nr 🐖 nr

Fr Mortain S on D977 sp St Hilaire-du-Harcouët;
shortly after rndabt take 2nd L at auberge to Notre-
Dame-deTouchet. In vill turn L at PO, sp Le Teilleul
D184, then 2nd R sp La Raisnais. Site at end of lane
on R (haycart on front lawn). Sm, hdstg, pt shd, pt
sl, EHU (10A) inc (poss long lead req); adv bkg acc.
*"Pleasant, tranquil, spacious CL-type site adj farm;
lovely outlook; washing machine on request; adults
only; NB no wc or shwrs Dec-Feb but water & EHU all
year; DVD library; friendly, helpful British owners; htd
pool 8km; well-kept, clean san facs; adv bkg rec; highly
rec."* **€15.00, 1 Mar-31 Oct.**   **2017**

"Satellite navigation makes touring much easier"

Remember most sat navs don't know if you're
towing or in a larger vehicle – always use yours
alongside maps and site directions.

MOSNAC *7B2* (0km E Rural) *45.50557, -0.52304*
Camp Municipal Les Bords de la Seugne, 34 Rue de
la Seugne, 17240 Mosnac 05 46 70 48 45; mosnac@
mairie17.com

🛏 ♨♨(htd) ♨ 🥗 💛

Fr Pons S on N137 for 4.5km; L on D134 to Mosnac;
foll sp to site behind church. 2*, Sm, mkd, pt shd,
EHU (10A) inc; gas; red long stay; Eng spkn; adv bkg
acc; CKE. *"Charming, clean, neat site in sm hamlet;
site yourself, warden calls; helpful staff; excel,
spotless san facs; conv Saintes, Cognac & Royan."*
€13.50, 1 May-30 Sep.   **2017**

MOTHE ACHARD, LA *2H4* (5km NW Rural) *46.65285,
-1.74759* Camping La Guyonnière, 85150 St Julien-
des-Landes 02 51 46 62 59; info@laguyonniere.com;
www.laguyonniere.com

🛏 €4 ♨♨ [wc] ♨ ♿ 🖧 🥗 ♀ ♀ 💛 ① 🚿 🐖 /🏔 🛶 (covrd, htd)

Leave A83 junc 5 onto D160 W twd La Roche-sur-
Yon. Foll ring rd N & cont on D160 twd Les Sables-
d'Olonne. Leave dual c'way foll sp La Mothe-Achard,
then take D12 thro St Julien-des-Landes twd La
Chaize-Giraud. Site sp on R. 3*, Lge, hdg, pt shd, pt
sl, EHU (6A) €3.50 (long lead rec); gas; bbq; TV;
10% statics; phone; Eng spkn; adv bkg acc; ccard acc;
waterpark; lake fishing 400m; waterslide; windsurfing
400m; bike hire. *"V lge pitches; canoe hire 400m; gd
views; friendly owners; gd walking area."*
€23.50, 26 Apr-28 Sep, A12.   **2019**

MOTHE ACHARD, LA *2H4* (6km NW Rural) *46.64469,
-1.73346* FLOWER Camping La Bretonnière, 85150
St Julien-des-Landes 02 51 46 62 44 or 06 14 18 26
42 (mob); camp.la-bretonniere@wanadoo.fr; www.
la-bretonniere.com or www.flowercampings.com

🛏 €2-5 ♨♨ [wc] ♨ ♿ 🖧 🥗 /[MsP] 💛 🐖 ♀ nr /🏔 🐖 🛶 (covrd, htd)

Fr La Roche-sur-Yon take D160 to La Mothe-Achard,
then D12 dir St Gilles-Croix-de-Vie. Site on R 2km
after St Julien. 4*, Med, mkd, pt shd, pt sl, EHU
(6-12A) €2-4.50; bbq; sw nr; TV; 20% statics; Eng spkn;
adv bkg acc; ccard acc; bike hire; fishing; ice; games
area; sailing 2km; tennis; games rm; CKE. *"Excel,
friendly site adj dairy farm; v lge pitches; san facs
stretched in high ssn; 10 mins fr Bretignolles-sur-Mer
sand dunes."* **€33.00, 9 Apr-30 Sep.**   **2017**

MOULINS *9A1* (21km N Rural) *46.709544, 3.323283*
Camping Municipal des Baillys, Les Bailly, 58390
Dornes 06 74 82 04 02

[12] 🛏 ♨♨ [wc] ♨ 🖧 🥗 💛 ♀ nr ① nr 🐖 nr

On the D22 bet Dornes and Chantenay Saint Imbert.
2nd turning on the left after Dornes. Sm, pt shd,
EHU; adv bkg acc. *"O'looking fishing lake (no sw);
v welcoming warden; no fixed pitches but warden
allocates; vg."* **€11.00**   **2019**

MOURIES *10E2* (2km E Rural) *43.68207, 4.91769*
Camping à la Ferme Les Amandaies (Crouau),
Mas de Bou Malek, 13890 Mouriès 04 90 47 50 59;
www.les-amandaies.fr

[12] 🛏 ♨♨ 🥗 💛

Fr Mouriès take D17 E sp Salon-de-Provence. Site sp
on R 200m past D5 junc. Foll site sp to farm in 2km.
Sm, pt shd, EHU €2 (rec long lead) (poss rev pol); bbq.
*"Simple CL-type site; a few lge pitches; friendly owners;
dated, dimly-lit san facs; conv coast & Avignon; book
in using intercom on LH wall at ent to shwr block."*
€15.40   **2018**

FRANCE

MOURIES *10E2* (7km NW Urban) *43.72138, 4.80950* **Camp Municipal Les Romarins,** Route de St Rémy-de-Provence, 13520 Maussane-les-Alpilles **04 90 54 33 60; camping-municipal-maussane@wanadoo.fr; www.maussane.com**

⌂ €3 ♦♦ Ⓦ ♨ ♒ ⅗ ▱ ⬭ ⭹ ᴹᴾ ✿ ⵂ ♒ nr

Fr Mouriès N on D17, turn onto D5 on o'skts of vill dir St Rémy-de-Provence, turn immed L site on R adj municipal pool. 4*, Med, hdg, mkd, pt shd, EHU (10A) €3.80; red long stay; twin axles; TV; phone; bus in ssn; Eng spkn; adv bkg rec; ccard acc; bike hire; games area; games rm; tennis; CKE. "Well-kept, well-run site in lovely area; on edge of vill; excel san facs; pool adj inc; some pitches diff m'vans due low trees; gd security; in Natural Park; hiking; mountain biking; excel."
€26.00, 15 Mar-3 Nov. 2017

MOUSTIERS STE MARIE *10E3* (1km W Rural) *43.84371, 6.21475* **FFCC Camping St Jean,** Route de Riez, 04360 Moustiers-Ste Marie **04 92 74 66 85; camping-saint-jean@wanadoo.fr; www.camping-st-jean.com**

⌂ €2.10 ♦♦ (htd) Ⓦ ♨ ♒ ⅗ ▱ ⬭ ᴹᴾ ✿ ⵂ ⅊ ♒ ▱

On D952 opp Renault g'ge & petrol stn.
3*, Med, hdg, pt shd, pt sl, EHU (6-10A) €3.60-4.70; gas; bbq (elec, gas); sw nr; TV; 10% statics; Eng spkn; adv bkg acc; ccard acc; games rm; fishing; games area; CKE. "Excel site in lovely location by rv; climbing nr; dated san facs (2010); boating 4km; some pitches diff lge o'fits; easy uphill walk to beautiful vill; conv Gorges du Verdon; cycle rtes; gd value."
€23.00, 28 Mar-11 Oct. 2015

MOYAUX *3D1* (3.4km NE Rural) *49.20860, 0.39230* **Camping Château Le Colombier,** Chemin du Val Séry, 14590 Moyaux **02 31 63 63 08; mail@camping-le colombier.com; www.camping-normandie-le colombier.com**

⌂ ♦♦♦ Ⓦ ♨ ♒ ⅗ ▱ ⬭ ᴹᴾ ✿ ⵂ ⅊ Ⓣ ⓘ ▱ ⵂ ♒ ⅊ (htd)

Fr Pont de Normandie on A29, at junc with A13 branch R sp Caen. At junc with A132 branch R & foll sp Lisieux, D579. Turn L onto D51 sp Blangy-le-Château. Immed on leaving Moyaux turn L onto D143 & foll sp to site on R in 3km. 4*, Lge, mkd, pt shd, EHU (10A) inc (poss lead req); gas; bbq; red long stay; TV; 30% statics; phone; Eng spkn; adv bkg acc; ccard acc; excursions; games rm; bike hire; tennis; horseriding nr; games area; CKE. "Beautiful, peaceful, spacious site in chateau grnds; ltd san facs LS; lge pool, but no shd, seats or sunshades around; vg for children; gd shop & crêperie; some static tents/tour ops; shgl paths poss diff some wheelchairs/pushchairs; if dep bef 0800 must move to car park o'night; mkt Sun; gd site; some pitches boggy when wet; no o'fits over 7m high ssn; gd facs; excel site to explore Normandy landing beaches; easy walk to vill with shops and rest and sh drive to larger town, lovely site, v helpful owners; poss travellers on site."
€33.70, 19 Apr-29 Sep, N04. 2019

MUIDES SUR LOIRE *4G2* (1km N Rural) *47.67191, 1.52596* **Camp Municipal Belle Vue,** Ave de la Loire, 41500 Muides-sur-Loire **02 54 87 01 56 or 02 54 87 50 08 (Mairie); contact.muides@orange.fr; www.muides.fr**

⌂ €2.55 ♦♦ Ⓦ ♨ ♒ ⅗ ▱ ⬭ ᴹᴾ ✿ ⓘ nr ♒ nr ▱

Fr A10/E5/E60 exit junc 16 S onto D205. Turn R onto D2152 then D112 over rv. Site on S bank of rv on D112 W of bdge. Tight U-turn into site fr N.
2*, Med, mkd, pt shd, EHU (6A) €4.80 (poss long lead req),(poss rev pol); sw nr; rv fishing adj; cycling; CKE. "Neat, clean, basic, spacious site; ladies shwrs need upgrade (2011); vehicle barrier; gd views over rv; some pitches by fast-flowing (unfenced) rv; little shd; excel cycling; site self when off clsd (open 0800-1000 & 1700-1900)." €14.00, 1 May-15 Sep. 2018

"There aren't many sites open at this time of year"

If you're travelling outside peak season remember to call ahead to check site opening dates – even if the entry says 'open all year'.

MUIDES SUR LOIRE *4G2* (0.5km S Rural) *47.66611, 1.52916* **Sandaya Château des Marais,** 27 Rue de Chambord, 41500 Muides-sur-Loire **02 54 87 05 42; mar@sandaya.fr; www.sandaya.co.uk**

⌂ €5 ♦♦ (htd) Ⓦ ♨ ♒ ⅗ ▱ ⬭ ᴹᴾ ⅊ Ⓣ ⅊ ♒ ▱ ⵂ (covrd, htd) ⅗

Exit A10 at junc 16 sp Chambord & take D2152 sp Mer, Chambord, Blois. At Mer take D112 & cross Rv Loire; at Muides-sur-Loire x-rds cont strt on for 800m; then turn R at Camping sp; site on R in 800m. 5*, Lge, mkd, shd, pt sl, serviced pitches; EHU (6A) inc (poss rev pol); gas; bbq (charcoal); twin axles; TV; 65% statics; Eng spkn; adv bkg acc; ccard acc; watersports nr; lake fishing; games area; bike hire; waterslide; tennis; jacuzzi; games rm; sauna; CKE. "Busy lively site in wooded area in chateau grnds; gd sized pitches; excel, clean san facs; friendly staff; plenty of gd quality children's play equipment; sh walk to rv; conv Loire chateaux; plenty to do in area; mkt Sat Blois; pitches grass, can be a problem when wet." €25.00, 3 Apr-20 Sep, L10. 2019

MULHOUSE *6F3* (10km SW Rural) *47.72225, 7.22590* **FFCC Camping Parc La Chaumière,** 62 Rue de Galfinque, 68990 Heimsbrunn **03 89 81 93 43 or 03 89 81 93 21; reception@camping-lachaumiere.com; www.camping-lachaumiere.com**

12 ⌂ €1 ♦♦ (htd) Ⓦ ♨ ♒ ⅗ ▱ ⬭ ᴹᴾ ✿ ⵂ ⅊ ♒ nr ▱ ⅗

Exit A36 junc 15; turn L over m'way; at rndabt exit on D166 sp Heimsbrunn; in vill turn R at rndabt; site end of houses on R. 2*, Med, hdg, hdstg, mkd, pt shd, pt sl, EHU (10A) €3.50 (poss rev pol); bbq; twin axles; 50% statics; phone; bus 1km; Eng spkn; adv bkg acc; ccard acc; CKE. "Sm pitches not suitable long o'fits; beautiful wine vills on La Route des Vins; museum of trains & cars in Mulhouse; conv; vg san facs."
€11.00 2015

FRANCE

MULHOUSE 6F3 (2km SW Rural) 47.73405, 7.3235
Camping de l'Ill, 1 Rue de Pierre Coubertin, 68100 Mulhouse 03 89 06 20 66; campingdelill@wanadoo.fr; www.camping-de-lill.com

🏕 €1.50 ♦♦♦ wc 🚿 ⚌ ⚂ 🚮 ᵐᵖ ⑲ Ⓘ nr 🚴 🛒 nr ♒

Fr A36 take Mulhouse/Dornach exit & foll sp Brunstatt at 1st traff lts. At 2nd traff lts turn R, foll University/Brunstatt/Camping sps, site approx 2.5km on rvside. 3*, Lge, mkd, pt shd, pt sl, EHU (10A); gas; tram 500m; CKE. "Welcoming recep; cycle/walk along rv to town cent; OK NH."
€22.30, 1 Apr-30 Sep.   **2017**

MULHOUSE 6F3 (30km W Rural) 47.73554, 7.01497
Flower Camping du Lac de la Seigneurie, 3 Rue de la Seigneurie, 90110 Leval 03 84 23 00 13; contact@camping-lac-seigneurie.com; www.camping-lac-seigneurie.com

🏕 ♦♦♦ wc ⚌ ⚂ 🚮 ᵐᵖ ⑲ 🍴 Ⓘ 🚴 /🇱 ♒ (htd) 🛶

Off N83 dir Belfort-Mulhouse. D11 NW Petitefontaine twds Roughmont sp to Leval.
3*, Med, hdg, mkd, pt shd, pt sl, EHU (6-10A); bbq; 6% statics; adv bkg acc; ccard acc; games area.
€21.00, 1 Apr-31 Oct.   **2016**

MUNSTER 6F3 (13km SW Rural) 47.98250, 7.01865
Camp Municipal de Mittlach Langenwasen, 68380 Mittlach 03 89 77 63 77; mairiemittlach@wanadoo.fr; www.mittlach.fr

🏕 €0.80 ♦♦♦ wc ⚌ ⚂ 🚮 /🚴 🛒 /🇱

Fr Munster on D10 to Metzeral then R onto D10. Site at end rd in 6km. 1*, Med, mkd, hdg, pt shd, pt sl, EHU (6-10A) €2.45-6; gas; 10% statics; Eng spkn; adv bkg acc; CKE. "Peaceful, wooded site at bottom of valley; helpful staff; san facs gd & clean; gd walking base; plenty of interest locally; excel."
€14.00, 20 Apr-10 Oct.   **2015**

MUNSTER 6F3 (2km SW Rural) 48.03105, 7.11350
FFCC Camping Les Amis de la Nature, 4 Rue du Château, 68140 Luttenbach-près-Munster 03 89 77 38 60; an-munster@wanadoo.fr; www.camping-an.fr

🏕 €1.50 ♦♦♦ (htd) wc ⚌ ⚂ & 🚮 /🚴 ᵐᵖ ⚞ 🇱 🍴 ⑲ Ⓘ 🚴 🛒 /🇱 /🇱 (htd)

Fr Munster take D10 sp Luttenbach; site sp.
3*, Lge, mkd, pt shd, EHU (4-6A) €3.25-4.40/6.20; bbq; TV; 50% statics; Eng spkn; ccard acc; games rm; sauna; fishing; tennis 1km; games area. "Lovely setting by stream; dir access to rv; gd value; new san facs (2017); pleasant walk to town; excel rest; gd touring area." **€16.50, 21 Mar-11 Nov.**   **2018**

MURAT 7C4 (5km SW Rural) 45.07781, 2.83047
Aire Naturelle Municipal, 15300 Albepierre-Bredons 04 71 20 20 49

🏕 ♦♦♦ ⚌ /🚴 🇱 🍴 nr ⑲ nr 🛒 nr

SW fr Murat on D39 dir Prat-de-Bouc; site sp fr cent of Albepierre. Sm, pt shd, EHU (10A) €2; CKE. "Excel, peaceful location; basic, clean facs; warden visits am & pm; bar 300m; vg walking amidst extinct volcanoes; gd; beautiful sm friendly site." **€9.00, 15 Jun-15 Sep.**   **2016**

MUROL 7B4 (1km S Rural) 45.57400, 2.95735
FFCC Camp Le Repos du Baladin, Groire, 63790 Murol 04 73 88 61 93; reposbaladin@free.fr; www.camping-auvergne-france.com

🏕 €3 ♦♦♦ (htd) wc ⚌ ⚂ 🚮 /🚴 ⑲ 🍴 ⚂ 🛒 nr ♒ /🇱 (htd)

Fr D996 at Murol foll sp 'Groire' to E, site on R in 1.5km just after vill. 3*, Med, hdg, mkd, shd, pt sl, terr, EHU (6A); sw nr; Eng spkn; sauna; CKE. "Lovely site with immac san facs; friendly, helpful owners; easy walk into town thro fields." **€28.00, 29 Apr-16 Sep.**   **2018**

NAMPONT ST MARTIN 3B3 (3km W Rural) 50.33595, 1.71230 **La Ferme des Aulnes**, 1 Rue du Marais, Fresne-sur-Authie, 80120 Nampont-St Martin 03 22 29 22 69 or 06 22 41 86 54 (mob LS); contact@fermedesaulnes.com; www.fermedesaulnes.com

🏕 €4 ♦♦♦ (htd) wc ⚌ ⚂ 🚮 ⚃ /🚴 ᵐᵖ ⚞ 🍴 ⑲ Ⓘ 🛒 nr /🇱 ✐ 🛶 (covrd, htd)

D901 S fr Montreuil 13km thro Nampont-St Firmin to Nampont-St Martin; turn R in vill onto D485; site in 3km; sp fr D901. 4*, Med, hdg, pt shd, pt sl, EHU (6-10A) €6-12; bbq (charcoal, gas); TV; 80% statics; Eng spkn; adv bkg acc; games area; golf 1km; archery; CKE. "Attractive site nr Calais; some pitches sm, some very sl; friendly welcoming staff; clsd 2200-0800; cinema rm; old fm bldgs retain character of an old fmstead; clean san facs." **€32.50, 1 Apr-31 Oct, P13.**   **2017**

NANCAY 4G3 (0.9km NW Rural) 47.35215, 2.18522 **Camp Municipal des Pins**, Route de Salbris, La Chaux, 18330 Nançay 02 48 51 81 80 or 02 48 51 81 35 (Mairie); campingdenancay@orange.fr; www.nancay.a3w.fr

♦♦♦ (htd) wc ⚌ 🚮 /🚴 🛒 nr /🇱

Site on D944 fr Salbris twd Bourges on L immed bef ent Nançay. 2*, Med, mkd, hdstg, shd, EHU (6A) inc; gas; adv bkg acc; golf 2km; fishing; tennis; CKE. "Lovely spot in pine woods; friendly recep; clean san facs; poor site lighting; beautiful vill; gd walking; rec open am and pm." **€8.50, 1 May-30 Sep.**   **2017**

NANCY 6E2 (6.5km SW Rural) 48.65730, 6.14028 **Campéole Le Brabois**, 2301 Ave Paul Muller, 54600 Villers-lès-Nancy 03 83 27 18 28; brabois@campeole.com; www.campeole.nl/le-brabois

🏕 €2.60 ♦♦♦ (htd) wc ⚌ ⚂ & 🚮 /🚴 ᵐᵖ ⚞ 🍴 ⑲ Ⓘ 🛒 nr /🇱

Fr A33 exit junc 2b sp Brabois onto D974 dir Nancy; after 400m turn L at 2nd traff lts; at slip rd after 2nd further traff lts turn R on slip rd & site on R; site well sp. 3*, Lge, mkd, pt shd, EHU (4-15A) €4.50-5.25 (poss rev pol)(ask for pitch with 15A if req); gas; bbq; TV; 10% statics; bus adj; Eng spkn; adv bkg acc; ccard acc; games area; CKE. "Popular, well-run site; mostly lge pitches, but some sm, all grass; supmkt & petrol 2km; friendly, helpful staff; gd, clean, all new san facs; no twin axles over 5.5m (m'vans OK); interesting town; rec arr early; vg NH; excel." **€21.30, 30 Mar-14 Oct, J03.**   **2018**

NANCY 6E2 (10km NW Rural) 48.74733, 6.05700
Camping Les Boucles de la Moselle, Ave Eugène
Lerebourg, 54460 Liverdun 03 83 24 43 78 or 06 03
27 69 71 (mob); francis.iung@orange.fr
🛉 €1.20 ♔(htd) ⚓ ♨ 🗑 ⚭ ∥ ⵉ Ⓗ ♨ 🐛 /🏔 🐾 🛶

Fr A31 exit junc 22 to Frouard. In Frouard bear L
onto D90 to Liverdun; cross rv bdge (sp Liverdun);
under rlwy bdge L at traff lts, thro town, fork L &
foll sp to site by on rvside by sports area. Do not
turn L at site exit when towing. 2*, Lge, pt shd, EHU
(6A) €3.20; 10% statics; CKE. "Lovely site & area;
helpful staff; Nancy worth visit; pleasant rvside site."
€23.00, 1 May-30 Sep.   2017

NANT 10E1 (2km N Rural) 44.03578, 3.29008
Camping Le Roc Qui Parle, Les Cuns, 12230 Nant
05 65 62 22 05; contact@camping-roc-qui-parle-
aveyron.fr; www.camping-roc-qui-parle-aveyron.fr
🛉 ♔ ⵣ ⚓ ♨ ⚭ ∥ ⵉ 🦋 ⵈ 🐛 /🏔

Fr Millau take D991E to site passing Val de
Cantobre. Fr La Cavalerie take D999E to Nant & at
T-junc on o'skts of Nant turn N; Millau & Les Cuns
approx 2km; site on R. NB Steep decent into site.
3*, Med, hdg, mkd, pt shd, pt sl, serviced pitches;
EHU (10A) €3.50; bbq; sw; adv bkg acc; fishing; CKE.
"Excel, well-run site in magnificent surroundings; lge
pitches with views; warm welcome, friendly & helpful;
excel facs; rv walk; rec; same price year round."
€15.00, 13 Mar-21 Oct.   2016

NANT 10E1 (11km E Rural) 44.01117, 3.20457
Camping La Dourbie, Route de Nant, 12230 Saint-
Jean-du-Bruel, Aveyron 05 65 46 06 40; campingla
dourbie@orange.fr; www.camping-dourbie-
aveyron.com
🛉 ♔ ⵣ ⚓ ♨ ⵣ ∥ ⵉ 🦋 ⵈ 🐛 Ⓗ /🏔 🛶 (htd)

Fr A75 take exit 47, twrds La cavalerie, Nat, St-
Eulalie-de-Cernon. At rndabt take 3rd exit onto
D999, go thro next rndabt, turn R cont D999 to site.
4*, Med, hdg, pt shd, EHU (10A); bbq; 20% statics;
canoeing. "Excel site, such a lot to do & see; very
friendly; bungee jumping; paragliding; clean san facs;
spa; 1 dog per pitch; rest open Fri & Sat nights in LS."
€25.00, 14 Apr-30 Sep.   2018

NANT 10E1 (1km S Rural) 44.01698, 3.30125
Camping Les Deux Vallées, 12230 Nant 05 65 62 26 89
or 05 65 62 10 40; contact@lesdeuxcallees.com;
www.lesdeuxvallees.com
🛉 €1 ♔ ⵣ ⚓ ♨ ⵣ ∥ ⵉ 🦋 ⵉ Ⓗ ♨ 🐛 nr /🏔 🐾

Exit A75 junc 47 onto D999 for 14km to Nant; site sp.
3*, Med, mkd, pt shd, serviced pitches; EHU (6A) €2 (poss
rev pol); own san req; TV; phone; adv bkg acc; rv fishing;
CKE. "Peaceful, well-kept, scenic site; friendly; clean,
modern san facs; pool 500m; 15 mins walk fr vill cent; gd
walking; rec." €21.50, 15 Apr-17 Oct.   2016

NANT 10E1 (0.7km SW Rural) 44.02105, 3.29390
Camping Les Vernèdes, Route St Martin-Le Bourg,
12230 Nant 05 65 62 15 19; http://patocheperso.
pagesperso-orange.fr/camping/accueil.htm
🛉 ♔ ⵣ ⚓ 🗑 ∥ 🦋 /🏔

Site sp fr vill cent. 1*, Sm, shd, EHU (10A) inc (long
lead req); bbq; Eng spkn; adv bkg acc; CKE. "Orchard
site set in beautiful location; pleasant stroll to Nant
cent; gd trout rest adj; gd touring base; very helpful
owners; excel and great site to stay on; CL style, not
modern but idyilic; gd rest next door."
€13.50, 1 Mar-31 Oct.   2015

NANTES 2G4 (3km N Urban) 47.24261, -1.55703
Nantes Camping, 21 Blvd de Petit Port, 44300 Nantes
02 40 74 47 94; nantes-camping@nge-nantes.fr;
www.nantes-camping.fr
⑫ 🛉 €3.10 ♔(htd) ⚓ ⵣ ⚭ ♨ ⵣ ∥ ⵍⵙⴾ 🦋 ⵉ ⵉ Ⓗ ♨ 🐛 /🏔 🐾

Fr ring rd exit junc 39 sp Porte de la Chapelle &
foll sp Cent Ville, Camping Petit Port or University
when ent o'skts of Nantes. Site ent opp Hippodrome
& nr racecourse & university; well sp. Take care
tram lines. 5*, Lge, mkd, hdg, hdstg, pt shd, serviced
pitches; EHU (16A) €5; gas; bbq (charcoal); twin axles;
red long stay; TV; 30% statics; bus & tram to city
cent adj; Eng spkn; adv bkg req; ccard acc; bike hire;
CKE. "Well kept and maintained; htd covrd pool adj;
waterslide adj inc; excel san facs; tram stop next to site,
easy access to Nantes cent; excel site, great location;
o'night m'van area; ACSI red LS; popular; recep clsd
1230-1500." €41.00   2018

NANTES 2G4 (6km E Rural) 47.25416, -1.45361
Camping Belle Rivière, Route des Perrières, 44980
Ste Luce-sur-Loire 02 40 25 85 81; belleriviere@
wanadoo.fr; www.camping-belleriviere.com
⑫ 🛉 €1.45 ♔(htd) ⵠ ⚓ ♨ ⵣ ∥ 🦋 ⵉ ⵉ Ⓗ nr ♨ 🐛 nr /🏔

Fr 'Nantes Périphérique Est' take exit 43 (at Porte
d'Anjou) onto A811; exit A811 junc 24 dir Thouaré-
sur-Loire on D68; at double rndabt by car showroom
turn S & foll sp over rlwy bdge; site sp. Fr E via D68,
thro Thouaré dir Ste Luce; at double rndabt by car
showroom, S over rlwy bdge twd rv; site sp.
3*, Med, mkd, hdstg, hdg, pt shd, EHU (3-10A) €2.70-
3.90 (extra charge in winter); gas; bbq; 50% statics;
Eng spkn; adv bkg acc; CKE. "Beautifully-kept site;
helpful owners; gd clean san facs; rvside walks; conv
Nantes Périphérique & city cent; gd touring base;
excel." €17.00   2017

FRANCE

FRANCE

NANTUA *9A3* (1km W Urban) *46.14999, 5.60017*
Camping du Signal, 17 Ave du Camping, 01130 Nantua
04 74 75 02 09 or 06 71 76 36 17 (mob); contact@camping-nantua.fr; www.camping-nantua.fr

🛏 🏕 🛆 ⚊ 🚿 MSP 🦋 📶 ⏣ ♨ 🗲 nr 🏰

E on D1084 fr Pont d'Ain, rd passes alongside Nantua lake on R. At end of lake bef ent town turn R & foll sps. 2*, Sm, mkd, hdg, unshd, EHU (16A) €3 (rev pol); sw nr; 10% statics. *"Attractive, spacious, well-kept site in lovely setting; nice lrg pitches; friendly staff; town & shops mins away; conv for m'way; sports cent nr; Lidl store 3 mins away; gd shwrs."*
€17.60, 1 Apr-31 Oct. **2017**

NARBONNE *10F1* (6km S Rural) *43.13662, 3.02595*
Village-Camping Les Mimosas, Chaussée de Mandirac, 11100 Narbonne **04 68 49 03 72**; info@lesmimosas.com; www.lesmimosas.com

🛏 €4 🏕(htd) WD 🛆 ♨ ♿ ⚊ 🚿 MSP 🦋 📶 ⏣ ♨ 🗲 🏰 ⚓
🛶(htd) 🚲

Leave A9 junc 38 at Narbonne Sud & at rndabt foll sp La Nautique. Turn L opp ent to Camping La Nautique & foll sp Mandirac & site. 4*, Lge, mkd, hdg, hdstg, pt shd, serviced pitches; EHU (6A) inc; gas; bbq (elec, gas); red long stay; TV; 6% statics; Eng spkn; adv bkg acc; ccard acc; sauna; games rm; horseriding adj; lake fishing 300m; waterslide; bike hire; rv fishing adj; jacuzzi; watersports; games area; gym; tennis; CKE. *"Attractive site, lge pitches; gd choice of pitches; friendly, helpful staff; vg san facs, poss ltd LS; excel pool complex; vg for children; lge o'fits rec phone in adv high ssn; excel touring base in historic area; gd birdwatching; cycle path to Narbonne."*
€46.00, 17 Mar-31 Oct, C35. **2017**

See advertisement

NARBONNE *10F1* (12km SW Rural) *43.16296, 2.89186*
Camping La Figurotta, Route de Narbonne, 11200 Bizanet **04 68 45 16 26** or 06 88 16 12 30 (mob); camping.figurotta@gmail.com; www.camping-figurotta.com

12 🛏 €3 🏕(htd) WD 🛆 ♿ 🚿 MSP 📶 ⏣ ♨ 🗲 🏰 🛶

Exit A9 at Narbonne Sud onto slip rd N9/D6113 twd Lézignan-Corbières; in 3km at new rndabt head L twd D613 & then D224 sp Bizanet & site. App fr W not rec due narr D rds. 1*, Sm, mkd, hdstg, shd, pt sl, terr, EHU (4-10A) €2.50-3.50 (poss long lead req); gas; red long stay; 5% statics; phone; Eng spkn; adv bkg acc; games area; CKE. *"Pleasant, simple, well-run, scenic site; friendly & helpful owners; sm dogs only; gd pool with new snack bar o'looking; gusty & stony site - steel pegs req; excel drainage; gd NH en rte Spain; vg; new san facs (2018)."* **€25.00** **2018**

NARBONNE *10F1* (4km SW Urban) *43.14702, 3.00424*
Camping La Nautique, Chemin de la Nautique,11100 Narbonne 04 68 90 48 19; info@campinglanautique.com; www.campinglanautique.com

🛏 €6 🏕(htd) WD 🛆 ♿ ⚊ 🚿 MSP 🦋 📶 ⏣ ♨ 🗲 🏰 ⚓ 🛶(htd) 🚲

Exit junc 38 fr A9 at Narbonne Sud. After toll take last rndabt exit & foll sp La Nautique. Site on R 2.5km fr A9 exit. 4*, Lge, hdstg, mkd, hdg, pt shd, EHU (10A) inc; gas; bbq (elec); red long stay; 30% statics; Eng spkn; adv bkg acc; ccard acc; waterslide; windsurfing; canoeing; tennis; CKE. *"Helpful, friendly Dutch owners; caution - hot water very hot; individual san facs on each pitch inc; some pitches lge but narr; steel pegs req; pitches sheltered but some muddy after heavy rain; excel rest; many sports activities avail; cycle trips; gd walks nrby."* **€47.70, 1 Mar-31 Oct, C07.**
2018

NARBONNE PLAGE *10F1* (8km NE Coastal) *43.20592, 3.21056* **Camping La Grande Cosse,** St Pierre-sur-Mer, 11560 Fleury-d'Aude **04 68 33 61 87; grande-cosse@ franceloc.fr; www.camping-grandecosse.fr**

🐕 €9 ♿ WC ♨ ♿ 🚿 ⊘ MSP 🏐 🍽 ⊕ 🛍 🐟 ⚓ 🏊 (htd)

🏖 sand 300m

Exit A9 junc 37 & foll sp Narbonne-Plage. Cont thro Narbonne-Plage to St Pierre-sur-Mer, pass municipal site & turn R twd L'Oustalet, site sp. 4*, Lge, hdg, mkd, pt shd, serviced pitches; EHU (10A); gas; red long stay; TV; 20% statics; phone; Eng spkn; adv bkg acc; ccard acc; boat hire; INF card req; games rm; fishing; games area; tennis; gym. *"Excel; gd pitches; helpful, friendly staff; excel san facs; lovely walk to beach thro lagoons & dunes (poss flooded early ssn); mosquitoes poss problem Jun-Sep; ACSI; flood risk after heavy rain; gd mkt St Pierre-sur-Mer; access rds can be diff, very narr; new owners, no longer a naturist site (2017)."* **€50.00, 15 Apr-30 Oct.** **2017**

"I need an on-site restaurant"

We do our best to make sure site information is correct, but it is always best to check any must-have facilities are still available or will be open during your visit.

NASBINALS *9D1* (1km N Rural) *44.67016, 3.04036* **Camp Municipal,** Route de St Urcize, 48260 Nasbinals **02 46 32 51 87 or 04 66 32 50 17; mairie. nasbinals@laposte.net; www.mairie-nasbinals.info**

🐕 ♟️ (htd) WC ♨ ♿ ⊘ MSP ⊕ nr 🛒 nr

Fr A75 exit 36 to Aumont-Aubrac, then W on D987 to Nasbinals. Turn R onto D12, site sp. Med, pt shd, pt sl, EHU (16A) €3; bbq; CKE. *"Lovely location; gd views; no shd; facs inadequate peak ssn; excel communal rm."* **€12.00, 15 May-30 Sep.** **2016**

NAVARRENX *8F1* (0.2km S Urban) *43.31988, -0.76143* **Camping Beau Rivage,** Allée des Marronniers, 64190 Navarrenx **05 59 66 10 00; beaucamping@free.fr; www.beaucamping.com**

🐕 €1.50 ♟️ (htd) WC ♨ ♿ ⊘ MSP 🏐 🏊 nr ⊕ nr 🛒 nr 🏔 ⚓

Fr E exit A64 junc 9 at Artix onto D281 dir Mourenx, then Navarrenx. Fr N on D947 thro Orthez to Navarrenx (D947 fr Orthez much improved). Site well sp bet walled (Bastide) town & rv. 3*, Med, hdstg, hdg, mkd, pt shd, pt sl, terr, serviced pitches; EHU (6-10A) inc; bbq; 15% statics; phone; Eng spkn; adv bkg acc; ccard acc; rv fishing; games rm; rafting; tennis; CKE. *"Lovely, peaceful, well-run site; no o'fits over 9m high ssn; nr interesting walled town; helpful, friendly, British owners; bike hire in town; clean san facs; gd pool; bar 300m; gd area for walking, cycling; conv local shops & rests; mkt Wed; rec; outstanding."* **€28.70, 25 Mar-8 Oct**, D26. **2017**

NAY *8F2* (2km N Rural) *43.20027, -0.25722* **Camping Les Ô Kiri,** Ave du Lac, 64800 Baudreix **05 59 92 97 73; contact@lesokiri.com; www.lesokiri.com**

🐕 €2 ♟️ (htd) WC ♨ ♿ 🚿 ⊘ MSP 🏐 🍽 ⊕ 🛍 🏊

Exit A64 junc 10 onto Pau ring rd D317 S, then D938 dir Nay & Lourdes. Exit sp Baudreix & in 2km turn R at rndabt & foll sp to lake & site. 4*, Med, hdg, mkd, pt shd, EHU (6-10A) €4-5.50; bbq; sw; 50% statics; adv bkg acc; ccard acc; tennis; waterslide; bike hire. *"Conv Biarritz, N Spain & Pyrennees; lake sw complex booking ess; on arr use carpark for recep; excel rest; superb lake facs; picturesque; basic but OK san facs, poss stretched if site full."* **€19.50, 1 Apr-30 Sep.** **2019**

NEBOUZAT *9B1* (2km NW Rural) *45.72569, 2.89008* **Camping Les Domes,** Les Quatre Routes de Nébouzat, 63210 Nébouzat **04 73 87 14 06 or 04 73 93 21 02 (LS); camping-les-domes@wanadoo.fr; www.les-domes.com**

🐕 ♟️ WC ♨ ♿ 🚿 ⊘ 🛥 🏐 🛍 🏔 🏊 ⚓ (covrd, htd)

Exit 5 fr A75 onto D213 twd Col de la Ventouse; turn L on D2089 sp Tulle. Do not ent vill of Nébouzat but cont for 1km. Take L onto D216 sp Orcival then immed L. Site on L in 100m. 3*, Med, mkd, hdstg, pt shd, EHU (10-15A) €6 (poss long lead req); gas; TV; phone; Eng spkn; adv bkg acc; sailing; windsurfing; CKE. *"Immac site; walking; boules area; warm welcome; friendly, helpful staff; sm pitches; gd san facs; conv Vulcania; excel rest nrby; gd base for Auvergne."* **€26.50, 23 Apr-3 Oct.** **2016**

NERAC *8E2* (6km SW Rural) *44.09948, 0.31028* **Aire Naturelle Les Contes d'Albret,** 47600 Nérac **05 53 65 18 73 or 06 84 70 07 78; lescontesdalbret@ orange.fr; www.albret.com**

♟️ (htd) ♨ ♿ ⊘ 🛥 ⊕ 🛒 🏔 ⚓

Exit A62 junc 7 onto D931 to Laplume. Then turn W onto D15 & D656 to Nérac. Cont on D656 dir Mézin & foll site sp 'Les Contes d'Albert' to end of rd in 3km. Sm, pt shd, pt sl, EHU (6A) €2; Eng spkn; adv bkg acc; kayaking. *"Vg, peaceful, CL-type site; farm shop; excel views; glorious garden."* **€17.00, 1 May-30 Sep.** **2019**

NERET *4H3* (3km N Rural) *46.58885, 2.13425* **Campsite Le Bonhomme,** Mulles 36400 Neret **02 54 31 46 11; info@camping-lebonhomme.com; www.camping-lebonhomme.com**

♟️ WC ♨ ♿ ⊘ MSP 🛥 🏐 ⊕

Fr Vierzon on the A20 take exit 12 to Chateauroux, then the D943 twds Montlucon.Turn L at Neret exit and foll Aire Naturelle signs. Site is 2km beyond Neret on L. 2*, Sm, mkd, hdstg, pt shd, sl, EHU (16A); bbq; Eng spkn; adv bkg acc; games area. *"Excel; lovely rural, quiet site; food avail fr owners."* **€20.50, 1 Apr-1 Oct.** **2016**

NEUF BRISACH *6F3* (1km E Urban) *48.01638, 7.53565*
Camp Municipal Vauban, Entrée Porte de Bâle,
68600 Neuf-Brisach **03 89 72 54 25 or 03 89 72 51 68**
(Mairie); contact@camping-vauban.fr;
www.camping-vauban.fr

🐕 €1 ♦♦♦ 🏕 ⅃ 🚐 🖾 💗 🗲nr 🏧

Fr D415 (Colmar-Freiburg) at E of Neuf-Brisach turn
NE on D1 bis (sp Neuf-Brisach & Camping Vauban).
At next junc turn L & immed R into site rd.
2*, Med, pt shd, EHU (10A) €4; 5% statics; adv bkg acc;
CKE. *"Gd, well-run site; fascinating ramparts around
town; lge pitches; friendly, helpful staff; excel cycle rtes
fr site along Rhine & thro historic vill; pool 3km; site
won many awards; long elec leads req; ideal long stay;
supmkt 2km."* **€17.00, 1 Apr-31 Oct.** **2018**

NEUF BRISACH *6F3* (6km SE Rural) *47.97988,
7.59639* **FFCC Camping L'Orée du Bois,** 5 Rue du
Bouleau, 68600 Geiswasser **03 89 72 80 13;**
valerie.schappler@orange.fr; valerieschappler1.
wixsite.com/campingaloreedubois

🐕 ♦♦♦ (htd) 🚐 🖾 🕭 🖾 ⅃ 💗 🍴 🏧

Site in vill cent; rd name on bungalow; ent bet
bungalow & vegetable garden - tight turn, watch
out bungalow gutters. 1*, Sm, hdg, pt shd, EHU
(10A) €3.60; bbq; 60% statics; bus adj; Eng spkn; adv
bkg acc; CKE. *"Gd touring base; friendly owner; gd."*
€6.60, 1 Apr-30 Sep. **2017**

NEUFCHATEL EN BRAY *3C2* (1.4km NW Urban)
49.73781, 1.42803 **Camping Sainte Claire,** 19 rue
Grande Flandre, 76270 Neufchâtel-en-Bray
**02 35 93 03 93 or 06 20 12 20 98 (mob); fancelot@
wanadoo.fr; www.camping-sainte-claire.com**

🐕 ♦♦♦ 🖾 🚐 🕭 🖾 ⅃ 💗 🍴 🍽 ⑪ 🗲 🏧

Fr N & S exit A28 junc 9 onto D928 sp Neufchâtel;
in 1km at mini rndabt at bottom hill, turn L into
Rue de la Grande Flandre, foll Leclerk supmkt sp;
cont past supmkt for 400m to Rue Ste Claire. (NB
Motorvan aire immed bef site ent, do not turn in by
mistake as there are charges). 3*, Med, hdstg, mkd,
hdg, pt shd, pt sl, terr, serviced pitches; EHU (6-10A)
inc; bbq; red long stay; twin axles; 20% statics; phone;
bus 400m; Eng spkn; adv bkg acc; ccard acc; bike hire;
fishing; CKE. *"Beautiful, spacious, well-run, well-kept,
busy site by rv; lge, med & sm pitches; not all pitches
have 10A, poss 6A pitches better; friendly, helpful
owner; excel clean san facs - poss long walk LS; wet rm
for disabled; wheelchair access/easy walking; pleasant
walk along cycle rte (old rlwy line) to town & vet; Sat
mkt; conv Le Havre/Dieppe ferries & A28; sep o'night
area; some drive-thro pitches; gd value sh or long stay;
popular NH; excel; nice site as always; Aire for m'vans
now open adj (OAY, €12, all hdstg, full facs, 10A elec &
acc ccards only); busy, efficient site; gd easy access fr
a'route; ent tight for lge o'fits; best book for twin axles;
excel rest; adj 40km greenway cycle ride; ACSI acc; lge
Leclerc nrby."* **€17.00, 1 Apr-15 Oct.** **2019**

NEUNG SUR BEUVRON *4G3* (0.5km NE Rural)
47.53893, 1.81488 **FFCC Camp Municipal de la
Varenne,** 34 Rue de Veilleas, 41210 Neung-sur-Beuvron
**02 54 83 68 52 or 06 27 92 39 14 (mob); camping.
lavarenne@wanadoo.fr; www.neung-sur-beuvron.
fr/camping**

🐕 ♦♦♦ 🖾 🚐 🖾 ⅃ 💗 🍴 🍽nr ⑪nr 🗲nr 🏧

On A10 heading S take Orléans Sud exit & join N20
S. At end of La Ferté-St Aubin take D922 SW twd
Romorantin-Lanthenay. In 20km R onto D925 to
Neung. Turn R at church pedestrian x-ing in cent of
vill ('stade' sp), R at fork (white, iron cross) & site
on R in 1km. Site by rvside. Fr A71 exit junc 3 onto
D923; turn R onto D925 & as above.
2*, Sm, mkd, hdg, pt shd, pt sl, EHU (6A) €3.10; gas;
10% statics; Eng spkn; adv bkg acc; ccard acc; tennis.
*"Friendly, helpful warden; gd, immac facs; lge pitches;
barrier clsd 2200-0800; vg cent for hiking, cycling,
birdwatching; mkt Sat; excel well maintained site."*
€12.00, Easter-20 Oct. **2017**

NEUVE LYRE, LA *3D2* (0.4km W Urban) *48.90750,
0.74486* **Camp Municipal La Salle,** Rue de l'Union,
27330 La Neuve-Lyre **02 32 60 14 98 or 02 32 30
50 01 (Mairie); mairie.la-neuve-lyre@wanadoo.fr**

🐕 ♦♦♦ 🖾 🚐 🕭 ⅃ 🖾 💗 🗲nr

Fr NE on D830 into vill turn R at church (sp not
visible), fr S (Rugles) foll sp. Well sp fr vill.
1*, Med, pt shd, EHU (5A) inc (poss long lead req);
2% statics; fishing; CKE. *"Delightful, peaceful, clean
site; site yourself, warden calls; excel sh stay/NH."*
€10.00, 15 Mar-15 Oct. **2017**

"Satellite navigation makes touring much easier"

Remember most sat navs don't know if you're
towing or in a larger vehicle – always use yours
alongside maps and site directions.

NEUVIC (CORREZE) *7C4* (4km N Rural) *45.38245,
2.22901* **Camping Domaine de Mialaret,**
Route d'Egletons, 19160 Neuvic **05 55 46 02 50;**
info@lemialaret.com; www.lemialaret.com

🐕 ♦♦♦ (htd) 🖾 🚐 🕭 🖾 ⅃ 🖾 💗 🍴 🍽 ⑪ 🕭 🗲 🏧 🛶 ♒

Fr N on A89 exit 23 twds St Angel then D171 to
Neuvic or foll sp fr Neuvic on D991.
4*, Med, hdg, pt shd, pt sl, EHU (10A) €3-4; red long
stay; TV; 30% statics; phone; bus 4km; Eng spkn; adv
bkg acc; games rm; watersports nr; CKE. *"Excel site
in grnds of chateau; 2 carp fishing pools; charming
owner, friendly staff; facs ltd LS; blocks req most
pitches; mini farm; walking tours; mountain bike
trails; children's mini zoo & rare sheep breeds nrby."*
€42.60, 26 Apr-5 Oct. **2019**

NEVERS *4H4* (1km S Rural) *46.98210, 3.16110*
FFCC Camping de Nevers, Rue de la Jonction, 58000
Nevers **03 86 36 40 75; campingdenevers@orange.fr;
www.aquadis-loisirs.com/camping-de-nevers**

🛖 €1.50 👫(cont) ⓦ ♨ ⚱ ♿ ⊘ ⁄ 🔧 🦋 ♈ 🍽 ⑭ nr 🅿 🆖nr 🏕

🏊 sand 200m

Fr E exit A77 junc 37 & foll dir 'Cent Ville'. Site on R
immed bef bdge over Rv Loire. Fr W (Bourges) on
D976 foll sp 'Nevers Centre' onto D907. In approx
3km bef bdge turn R, site on L. 3*, Sm, mkd, hdg,
hdstg, shd, pt sl, terr, EHU (10A); bbq; TV; 3% statics;
phone; bus 20m; Eng spkn; adv bkg acc; ccard acc; rv
fishing; bike hire; CKE. *"Pleasant, scenic site on bank of
Rv Loire; on 3 levels - ltd EHU on lower; gd clean san
facs, poss stretched high ssn; cycle paths along Loire; no
twin axles; poss noisy when events at Nevers Magny-
Cours racing circuit; gd site; easy walk over bdge to
interesting town; nr town; excel recep staff; ltd no of
elec pitches, arr early."* **€23.00, 6 Mar-5 Nov.** **2017**

NEVERS *4H4* (7km NW Urban) *47.01222, 3.07822*
FFCC Camping La Loire, 2 Rue de la Folie, 58600
Fourchambault **03 86 60 81 59 or 06 11 05 18 69 (mob);
campingdelaloire@dbmail.com; www.camping-de-
loire.fr.st**

🛖 €0.50 👫 ⓦ ♨ ♿ ⊘ ⁄ 🔧 🍽 ⑭ nr 🅿 🆖nr

Fr Nevers on D40 thro town, site on L bef rv bdge. 2*,
Med, pt shd, EHU (6-10A) €3-4.50; bbq; red long stay; bus;
CKE. *"Friendly, helpful staff; rv adj; san facs need update &
poss unclean; NH only."* **€17.50, 9 Apr-31 Oct.** **2017**

NEXON *7B3* (6km SSW Rural) *45.63471, 1.16176*
Flower Camping L'Air Du Lac, Impasse du Lac Plaisance,
87800 St Hilaire-les-Places **05 55 58 79 18; campinglair
dulac@flowercampings.com; www.campinglair
dulac.com**

🛖 €2 👫 ⓦ ♨ ⚱ ♿ ⊘ ⁄ 🔧 🦋 ♈ 🍽 🅿 🆖 🏕 🚤 🏊 adj

S fr Nexon on D11. Soon after ent St Hilaire-les-
Places take a L sp Lac Plaisance & Camping. Site adj
to lake. 3*, Med, hdg, shd, pt sl, EHU (10A) inc; bbq;
sw; TV; 20% statics; Eng spkn; adv bkg acc; ccard acc;
games rm; games area; CKE. *"Pleasant site adj to lake
sw beach; dep req; very helpful staff; gd sized pitches;
clean facs; vg for families; interesting touring area;
excel."* **€14.50, 15 Apr-30 Sep.** **2017**

NIEDERBRONN LES BAINS *5D3* (1.5km SW Rural)
48.92958, 7.60428 **Camping Oasis Oberbronn,**
3 Rue de Frohret, 67110 Oberbronn **03 88 09 71 96;
contact@opale-dmcc.com; www.opale-dmcc.fr**

🛖 €2.65 👫 ⓦ ♨ ♿ ⊘ ⁄ 🔧 🦋 🍽 ⑭ 🅿 🆖 🏕

🚣 (covrd, htd) 🛝

Fr D1062 turn S on D28 away fr Niederbronn; thro
Oberbronn, site sp. 3*, Lge, mkd, pt shd, pt sl, EHU
(6A) €4.30; bbq; red long stay; 20% statics; adv bkg
rec; ccard acc; golf; cycling; fishing 2km; sauna; games
rm; clsd 1200-1300; tennis; CKE. *"Vg site with views;
pt of leisure complex; sl area for tourers; horseriding
rtes; some san facs tired; walking; wellness cent; fitness
rm; site gravel paths not suitable wheelchair users."*
€15.00, 1 Apr-30 Sep. **2016**

NIMES *10E2* (8km S Rural) *43.78776, 4.35196*
Camp La Bastide (formerly Municipal), route de
Générac, 30900 Nîmes **04 66 62 05 82; bastide@
capfun.com; www.camping-nimes.com**

⑫ 🛖 €2.70 👫(htd) ⓦ ♨ ⚱ ♿ ⊘ ⁄ 🔧 🦋 ♈ 🍽 ⑭ 🅿
🆖nr 🏕

Fr A9 exit junc 25 onto A54 dir Arles; in 2km exit
A54 junc 1 onto D42 sp St Gilles; in 1.5km (at 2nd
rndabt) turn R onto D135; in 2.5km at rndabt turn
R onto D13; site on L. Or N fr Montpellier on N113/
D6113 to Nimes; at Périphique Sud turn S onto D13
sp Générac; site on R 500m after rndabt junc with
D613. Site well sp fr town cent. 4*, Lge, hdg, mkd,
hdstg, shd, EHU (10A) inc; gas; TV; 50% statics; phone;
bus; Eng spkn; adv bkg acc; games area; CKE. *"Excel,
well-run site; lge pitches; friendly, helpful recep; Nîmes
20 mins by bus fr site; gd site; exciting water complex;
vg bistro on site; child's entmnt; old san facs; busy, used
by workers; gd NH."* **€27.50** **2019**

NOIRETABLE *9B1* (1km S Rural) *45.80817, 3.76844*
Camp Municipal de la Roche, Route de la Roche,
42440 Noirétable **04 77 24 72 68; www.noiretable.fr/
plan_eau_camping_Roche.aspx**

👫(htd) ♨ ⁄ 🍽 nr 🆖nr 🏕

Leave A72/E70 junc 4 sp Noirétable; thro toll & turn
SW onto D53. Ignore narr tourist rte sp to W; cont
downhill to T-junc & turn R onto D1089. Take next
L & site on R in 750m. 2*, Sm, hdstg, mkd, pt shd, pt
sl, terr, EHU (10A) €2.80; own san rec; 40% statics;
Eng spkn. *"Warden lives on site, but barrier poss locked
LS; recep open 0900-1230, 1800-1930; camperstop
100m; lake adj; €3 for water & chem disp, token fr site."*
€10.00, 1 Apr-1 Nov. **2017**

NOIRMOUTIER EN L'ILE *2H3* (2km E Coastal)
46.99697, -2.22057 **Huttopia Noirmoutier,** Bois de
la Chaize, 23 Rue des Sableaux, 85330 Noirmoutier-
en-l'Ile **02 51 39 06 24; www.europe.huttopia.com**

🛖 €4.50 👫 ⓦ ♨ ⚱ ⊘ ⁄ 🔧 🦋 ♈ 🍽 ⑭ 🏕 🏊 sand adj

Ent Noirmoutier on D948, strt on over bdge & foll sp
for Bois-de-la-Chaize, then 'campings'.
2*, Lge, pt shd, EHU (10A); 10% statics; phone; adv
bkg acc; bike hire; fishing; boat launch; CKE. *"Peaceful
site in pine forest nr salt water marshes; gd for
children."* **€32.00, 1 Apr-1 Oct, A45.** **2017**

NOIRMOUTIER EN L'ILE *2H3* (10km SE Coastal)
46.94503, -2.18542 **Sandaya Domaine le Midi,** 17 Rue
du Camping, 85630 Barbâtre **02 51 39 63 74; mid@
sandaya.fr; www.sandaya.co.uk**

🛖 €5 👫 ♨ ⚱ ♿ ⊘ ⁄ 🔧 🦋 🍽 ⑭ 🅿 🆖 🏕 🚤 🚣 (htd) 🛝 🏊 sand adj

Cross to island by Passage du Gois D948 (low tide -
2.5 hrs per day) or bdge D38. Turn L after 2.5km off
dual c'way to Barbâtre. Site sp N thro vill.
5*, Lge, pt shd, pt sl, EHU (10A) inc; gas; bbq (gas);
45% statics; ccard acc; games area; tennis. *"Gd site;
sandy but firm pitches; food, wine and pool only avail
high ssn."* **€25.00, 3 Apr-13 Sep.** **2019**

NOLAY *6H1* (1km NW Rural) *46.95084, 4.62266*
Camping La Bruyère, Rue du Moulin Larché, 21340
Nolay 03 80 21 87 59 or 06 88 16 06 18 (mob);
www.nolay.com/fr/?/Logement/Les-campings

🏕 ♦♦♦(htd) 📶 ♨ ♿ 🖾 ⁄ MP 🦋 🍴 nr ⓗ nr 🏖 nr

Fr Beaune take D973 W dir Autun. In approx 20km,
arr in vill of Nolay & cont on D973 thro vill. Site on L
in 1km after vill, opp supmkt. 3*, Sm, mkd, hdg, pt shd,
terr, EHU (10-12A) €3.60-4; bbq; 10% statics; bus adj;
Eng spkn; ccard acc; CKE. *"Lovely, peaceful, well-kept
site; friendly staff; gd, clean san facs, poss stretched if
site busy; poss grape pickers in Sep; poss school & youth
groups; attractive walk to bustling old town; gd touring
base in wine area or NH; excel."* **€19.00**   **2016**

NONANCOURT *4E2* (4km E Urban) *48.76410,
1.23686* **Camp Municipal du Pré de l'Eglise,**
Rue Pré de l'Eglise, 28380 St Rémy-sur-Avre 02 37 48
93 87 or 02 37 62 52 00 (LS); mairiesaintremy2@
wanadoo.fr; www.ville-st-remy-sur-avre.fr

🐕 ♦♦♦ 📶 ♨ ♿ 🖾 ⁄ ⓗ nr 🏔

Fr Dreux take N12 W to St Rémy; strt over 1st rndabt
& at traff lts complex in 500m turn R & then immed R
& foll site sp. Fr Evreux (W) on N12 to St Rémy; after
x-ing rv bdge at traff lts complex strt ahead to rndabt
(no L turn at traff lts), then immed R at end rv bdge
to cross N12 as above. Site clearly sp in vill cent, sp
'Oscar' is for sports cent adj. NB Speed ramps on site
app rd. 3*, Sm, mkd, hdg, pt shd, EHU (6-10A) €2.83
(poss rev pol); TV; phone; Eng spkn; adv bkg rec; tennis
adj; fishing adj; CKE. *"Pleasant, popular, well-kept NH nr
rv; welcoming warden; clean, fair facs, some modern, ltd
LS; no twin axles (but negotiable); some pitches poss diff
access; factory adj poss noisy; vill in walking dist; a gd find;
Carrefour with fuel 1km; excel site in middle of vill; site
van, warden will call."* **€14.60, 1 Apr-30 Sep.**   **2017**

NONTRON *7B3* (11km NE Rural) *45.55138, 0.79472*
Kawan Village Le Château Le Verdoyer, 24470
Champs-Romain 05 53 56 94 64; chateau@verdoyer.fr;
www.verdoyer.fr

🐕 €3 ♦♦♦ 📶 ♨ ♿ 🖾 ⁄ MP 🦋 🍴 ⓗ 🏖 🏔 🎣
🛶 (covrd, htd) 🏖

Fr Limoges on N21 twd Périgueux. At Châlus turn R sp
Nontron (D6 bis-D85). After approx 18km turn L twd
Champs Romain on D96 to site on L in 2km.
4*, Lge, hdg, pt shd, terr, EHU (5-10A) inc (poss rev pol);
gas; bbq (charcoal, gas); TV; 20% statics; phone; Eng
spkn; adv bkg acc; ccard acc; lake fishing; games rm;
waterslide; bike hire; tennis; golf 25km; boating; CKE.
*"Peaceful, Dutch-run site in grnds of chateau; B&B in
chateau; lovely location; no o'fits over 10m; gd sized
pitches, but terr; friendly staff; superb facs; poss steep
access some pitches; grnd hard, but awnings poss; excel;
highly rec."* **€30.00, 20 Apr-30 Sep, D21.**   **2019**

NONTRON *7B3* (8km NE Rural) *45.56185, 0.71979*
Camping Manzac Ferme, Manzac, 24300 Augignac
05 53 56 31 34; info@manzac-ferme.com;
www.manzac-ferme.com

🐕 ♦♦♦(htd) 📶 ♨ ♿ ⁄ 🦋 🍴 ⓗ nr 🏖 nr

Fr Nontron take D675 N dir Rochechouart & after
7km on ent Augignac turn R sp Abjat-sur-Bandiat
then immed R sp Manzac. Site on R 3.5km.
Sm, mkd, hdstg, pt shd, pt sl, EHU (6A) inc; bbq; sw
nr; Eng spkn; adv bkg acc; rv fishing; CKE. *"Superb,
peaceful, well-kept CL-type, adults only site; helpful
British owners; dogs by prior arrangement; excel san
facs; phone ahead in winter; ideal for birdwatching &
wildlife; highly rec; most pitches in dense shd; excel."*
€24.00, 15 May-15 Sep.   **2016**

NONTRON *7B3* (1km S Urban) *45.51992, 0.65876*
Camping de Nontron, St Martiel-de-Valette, 24300
Nontron 05 53 56 02 04 or 06 30 66 25 74 (mob);
camping-de-nontron@orange.fr; www.campingde
nontron.com

🏕 🐕 €1 ♦♦♦(htd) ♨ 🖾 ⁄ MP 🦋 🍴 nr ⓗ nr 🏖 nr 🏔 🎣 🛶

Thro Nontron S twd Brantôme on D675. Site on
o'skts of town on L nr stadium. Sp. Med, mkd, hdg, pt
shd, EHU (10A) €3.50; gas; TV; Eng spkn; games area;
games rm; CKE. *"Pleasant owners; site clsd mid-Dec
to early Jan; excel, modern san facs; gd touring base;
town 1km walk along footpath."* **€22.50**   **2018**

NORT SUR ERDRE *2G4* (1km S Rural) *47.42770,
-1.49877* **Camping Seasonova du Port Mulon,** Rue
des Mares Noires, 44390 Nort-sur-Erdre 02 36 81 00 01
or 02 40 72 23 57; contact@camping-portmulon.com;
www.camping-portmulon.com

🐕 €0.90 ♦♦♦ 📶 ♨ ⁄ 🦋 🏖 nr 🏔

Sp fr all ents to town; foll 'Camping' & 'Hippodrome'
sp. NB: C'vans banned fr town cent, look for diversion
sp. 3*, Med, shd, EHU (6A) €2.40; adv bkg acc; fishing;
boating; tennis; CKE. *"Delightful, spacious, under-used
site; gd walking & cycling area, espec along Nantes canal
& Rv Erdre; Barrier perm locked, access when warden on
site only; new site rd & toilet block (2014); friendly staff."*
€22.00, 1 Apr-31 Oct.   **2019**

NOUAN LE FUZELIER *4G3* (0.7km S Urban) *47.53328,
2.03508* **Camping La Grande Sologne,** Rue des
Peupliers, 41600 Nouan-le-Fuzelier 02 54 88 70 22;
info@campinggrandesologne.com; www.campinggrande
sologne.com

🐕 €1 ♦♦♦ 📶 ♨ 🖾 ⁄ 🦋 🍴 🏖 nr 🏔

On E side of D2020, at S end of Nouan opp rlwy stn.
Sp fr town cent & opp rlwy stn. NB sat nav not rec.
3*, Med, mkd, pt shd, EHU (10A) €3; red long stay;
2% statics; Eng spkn; adv bkg acc; golf 15km; tennis;
fishing; games area; CKE. *"Pretty site adj lake (no sw);
some pitches boggy when wet; facs poss stretched high
ssn; ltd facs end of ssn & poss unclean; htd pool adj;
public park at ent to site, but quiet; rec arr early; excel
NH; phone for entry LS; excel site; office open 0700-
1500; voucher for nrby sw pool; san facs dated; friendly
owners."* **€24.50, 1 Apr-15 Oct.**   **2019**

NOUVION EN THIERACHE, LE *3B4* (2km S Rural) *50.00538, 3.78292* **Camp Municipal du Lac de Condé,** Promenade Henri d'Orléans, Rue de Guise (Le Lac), 02170 Le Nouvion-en-Thiérache **03 23 98 98 58;** campinglacdeconde@gmail.com; www.camping-thierache.com

🏕 €0.80 ⁂ [wc] ⚱ ♿ 🚿 ⚊ ∥ [MSP] 🍽 ⓝr ① 🏪nr /🏧

Sp fr cent of Le Nouvion fr D1043 on D26, dir Guise opp chateau. 2*, Sm, hdstg, hdg, mkd, pt shd, pt sl, EHU (4-8A) €2.50; bbq; red long stay; 70% statics; phone; Eng spkn; adv bkg acc; ccard acc; tennis nr; horseriding nr; CKE. *"Beautiful, spacious, lakeside site; busy even LS - rec phone ahead; gd sized pitches; warm welcome, staff helpful; htd pool adj; gd san facs; gd for families; canoe hire nr; some pitches not suitable m'vans due slope; muddy when wet; walk around lake; conv NH; excel; coarse fishing in adj lake."* **€12.50, 1 Apr-30 Sep.** 2017

NOYON *3C3* (4.5km E Rural) *49.58882, 3.04370* **FFCC Camping L'Etang du Moulin,** 54 Rue du Moulin, 60400 Salency **03 44 09 99 81**

[12] 🏕 €1 ⁂(htd) [wc] ⚱ ♿ ∥ [MSP] 🦋 🍽 ① ⓝr 🏪nr /🏧

Take D1032 fr Noyon dir Chauny. On ent Salency turn L & foll site sp. Site in 1km. 2*, Sm, shd, pt sl, EHU (10A) €1.60; gas; bbq; 75% statics; fishing; tennis; CKE. *"Site adj to fishing lake; gd facs; very clean & tidy; elec french 2 pin; security barrier card; pool 3km; v quiet location."* **€13.00** 2016

NOYON *3C3* (10km S Rural) *49.50667, 3.01765* **FFCC Camping Les Araucarias,** 870 Rue du Général Leclerc, 60170 Carlepont **03 44 75 27 39;** camping-les-araucarias@wanadoo.fr; www.camping-les-araucarias.com

🏕 €1 ⁂(htd) [wc] ⚱ ♿ 🚿 ⚊ ∥ [MSP] 🦋 🍽 ⓝr ① 🏪nr /🏧

Fr S, fr A1 exit junc 9 or 10 for Compiègne. There take D130 sp Tracy-le-Val & Carlepont. Site on L 100m fr Carlepont vill sp. Or fr N on D934 Noyon-Soissons rd take D130 dir Carlepont & Tracy-le-Val. Site on R after vill on SW twd Compiegne - not well sp. 2*, Sm, mkd, pt shd, pt sl, EHU (6-10A) €3 (poss rev pol); gas; bbq; 80% statics; Eng spkn; adv bkg acc; CKE. *"Secluded site, previously an arboretum; close Parc Astérix & La Mer-de-Sable (theme park); 85km Disneyland; san facs poss scruffy LS; vg."* **€12.50, 1 Apr-31 Oct.** 2016

NUITS ST GEORGES *6G1* (5km S Urban) *47.10323, 4.94148* **Camping Le Moulin de Prissey,** 14 rue du Moulin de Prissey, 21700 Premeaux-Prissey **03 80 62 31 15;** cpg.moulin.prissey@free.fr; www.cpg-moulin-prissey.fr

🏕 €0.90 ⁂ [wc] ⚱ ♿ 🚿 ⚊ ∥ [MSP] 🍽 ⓝr ① 🏪nr /🏧

Fr A31 take D8 to Nuits St Georges then D974 twrds Beaune. After Premeaux turn L onto D115E. Thro Prissey and site on R. 3*, Sm, mkd, pt shd, pt sl, EHU (6A) inc; gas; bbq; adv bkg acc; ccard acc; CKE. *"Popular NH - arr early; sm pitches; access poss diff lge o'fits; basic facs; gd cycling; noisy rlwy adj; site well laid out & tidy (2015)."* **€20.00, 4 Apr-15 Oct.** 2019

NYONS *9D2* (1km NE Rural) *44.36523, 5.15365* **Camping Les Clos,** Route de Gap, 26110 Nyons **04 75 26 29 90;** info@campinglesclos.com; www.campinglesclos.com

🏕 €2.20 ⁂ [wc] ⚱ ♿ 🚿 ⚊ ∥ 🍽 ① ⓝr ⚊ 🏪nr /🏧 ∥ 🏊

Fr rndabt in town cent take D94 sp Gap & site on R in 1km. 4*, Med, hdg, mkd, hdstg, pt shd, EHU (10A) inc; gas; bbq (elec, gas); 20% statics; phone; Eng spkn; adv bkg acc; ccard acc; rv; fishing; CKE. *"Quiet, well-kept site in lovely area; friendly, helpful staff; excel touring base; 20 min walk to town along quiet side rd; mkt Thu & Sat; popular site."* **€22.00, 1 Apr-30 Sep.** 2019

NYONS *9D2* (12km NE Rural) *44.42569, 5.21904* **Camping de Trente Pas,** 26110 St Ferréol-Trente-Pas **04 75 27 70 69;** contact@campingtrentepas.com; www.campingtrentepas.com

🏕 €2 ⁂ ⚱ ∥ 🦋 🍽 ① ⓝr ⚊ 🏪nr /🏧 ∥ 🏊

Exit A7 junc 19 Bollène onto D994 & D94. L on D70 to St Ferréol-Trente-Pas. Site 100m fr vill on banks of stream. 2*, Med, shd, EHU (6A) €3.10; TV; 5% statics; bike hire; tennis; games rm; horseriding 4km. *"Peaceful site nr rv; scenic area, views fr site; gd, clean san facs; gd pool; on flood plain; excel value; rec."* **€22.80, 1 May-31 Aug.** 2017

NYONS *9D2* (18km E Rural) *44.34319, 5.28357* **Camp Municipal Les Cigales,** Allée des Platanes, 26110 Ste Jalle **04 75 27 34 88 or 04 75 27 32 78 (mairie);** mairie.saintejalle@orange.fr

🏕 ⁂ [wc] ⚱ ⚊ ∥ 🦋 🍽 ⓝr ① 🏪nr /🏧

Fr Nyons take D94 dir Serres; in 10 km at Curnier turn R onto D64 to Ste-Jalle. In vill turn R onto D108 dir Buis-les-Baronnies. Site in 300m. NB Dist by rd fr Nyons is 20km. 2*, Sm, hdg, pt shd, EHU (10A) €2.20; 15% statics; adv bkg acc. *"Vg site in attractive old vill; friendly warden; facs dated but clean."* **€13.00, 1 May-30 Sep.** 2016

OBERNAI *6E3* (16.5km ESE Urban) *48.41413, 7.66983* **Camping Municipal Le Wagerlott,** 1 rue de la Sucrerie, 67150 Erstein **33 88 98 09 88 or 33 88 98 14 33 (Municipal);** campingerstein@gmail.com

🏕 €2.30 ⁂(htd) ⚱ ⚊ ∥ 🚽 ① ⓝr 🏪nr ⚊

Fr Strasbourg on A35 then D1083. R onto D426. At rndabt turn L then 1st R to site. Med, mkd, hdg, unshd, EHU (16A) €3.50; 50% statics; phone; Eng spkn; adv bkg acc; ccard acc. *"Gd municipal site; cls to Strasbourg; gd cycle rts; clean facs."* **€16.00, 1 Apr-30 Sep.** 2018

"There aren't many sites open at this time of year"

If you're travelling outside peak season remember to call ahead to check site opening dates – even if the entry says 'open all year'.

FRANCE

OBERNAI *6E3* (1.5km W Urban) *48.46460, 7.46750*
Camp Municipal Le Vallon de l'Ehn, 1 Rue de Berlin,
67210 Obernai **03 88 95 38 48; camping@obernai.fr;**
www.obernai.fr

€1.10 (htd)

Fr N exit A35 junc 11 onto D426 sp Obernai. Foll
D426 W around Obernai & foll sp Mont St Odile
& Camping VVF; at final rndabt turn R & immed L
to site. Fr S on A35 exit junc 12 sp Obernai. At 3rd
rndabt turn L onto D426 Ottrott-Mont Ste Odile
(look for sp Camping VVF). Do not tow into Obernai.
3*, Lge, hdstg, mkd, pt shd, pt sl, serviced pitches; EHU
(10-16A) €4.50; bbq; twin axles; red long stay; phone;
bus to Strasbourg & Obernai adj, train; Eng spkn; adv
bkg acc; ccard acc; horseriding adj; tennis adj; CKE.
*"Attractive, well-kept, busy site on edge of picturesque
town; sm pitches; welcoming, helpful staff; superb,
excel, modern clean san facs; no entry after 1930; rec
arr early high ssn; lge pool 200m;10% red CC members
LS; c'vans, m'vans & tents all sep areas; excel bus/train
links; ideal NH; highly rec; very well run, gd site; office
clsd 1230-1400; popular."*
€21.00, 1 Jan-8 Jan & 17 Mar-31 Dec. 2017

OCTON *10F1* (2km NE Rural) *43.65948, 3.32052*
Camping Le Village du Bosc (Naturist), Chemin de
Ricazouls, 34800 Octon **04 67 96 07 37;**
r.villagedubosc@free.net; www.villagedubosc.net
€3 (htd)

Exit 54 or 55 fr N9/A75 dir Octon onto D148, foll
sp to Ricazouls/site. 2*, Med, hdg, mkd, pt shd, pt sl,
terr, EHU (10A)inc; sw; red long stay; TV; 5% statics;
Eng spkn; adv bkg acc; watersports; INF card; games
area; games rm. *"Lovely, quiet site with wooded walks;
friendly owners; clean facs; tight turns on terr access
for lge o'fits; Octon vill pretty; wheelchair facs in san
facs."* **€30.00, 21 Apr-30 Sep.** 2017

**"That's changed – Should I let
the Club know?"**

If you find something on site that's different
from the site entry, fill in a report and let us
know. See camc.com/europereport.

OLARGUES *8F4* (0.4km N Rural) *43.55798, 2.91440*
Camp Municipal Le Baoüs, 34390 Olargues
04 67 97 71 50; otsi.olargues@wanadoo.fr;
www.olargues.org
(cont)

Take D908 W fr Bédarieux, site immed bef ent
Olargues. Site sp over sm bdge on L. At end of bdge
turn R to site. Last 50m rough track & narr turn into
site. 2*, Sm, pt shd, EHU (6A); adv bkg req; canoeing;
bike hire. *"Helpful warden; hill climb to services block;
site poss flooded by Rv Jaur in spring; sh walk to
amazing hilltop vill."* **1 Jul-15 Sep.** 2019

OLLIERGUES *9B1* (4km N Rural) *45.69008, 3.63289*
Camping Les Chelles, 63880 Olliergues
04 73 95 54 34; info@camping-les-chelles.com;
www.camping-les-chelles.com
€1 nr (htd)

Fr Olliergues take D37 N up hill dir Le Brugeron;
then sharp L onto D87 dir La Chabasse; site sp.
3*, Med, hdg, mkd, shd, terr, EHU (15A) €2.80; TV;
phone; Eng spkn; adv bkg acc; ccard acc; games area;
games rm. *"Facs excel for families with young children;
enthusiastic, helpful & kind Dutch owners; gd walking;
gd touring base; excel."* **€19.00, 1 Apr-31 Oct.** 2015

OLORON STE MARIE *8F2* (3km SW Urban) *43.17886,
-0.62328* Camping Pyrenees Nature (formerly Gîtes
du Stade), Chemin de Lagravette, 64400 Oloron-Ste
Marie **05 59 39 11 26; camping.pyrenees.nature@
gmail.com; www.campingpyreneesnature.fr**
12 €1.20 nr

Fr N on ring rd foll sp to Saragosse (Spain); at
rndabt take 2nd exit onto D6 still sp Saragosse, site
sp on R just after sports field. Fr S on D55 join ring
rd & turn W at rndabt by McDonalds; sp.
3*, Med, hdg, mkd, pt shd, EHU (6-10A) €4-6 (some rev
pol); bbq; sw nr; twin axles; TV; adv bkg acc; tennis; rv
fishing 1km; bike hire; CKE. *"Well-kept site; lge pitches;
helpful staff; clean facs but ltd LS & stretched high ssn;
take care low tree; grnd poss soft & damp after rain;
barrier clsd 1200-1500; excel base for Pyrenees; pool
adj; gd walking."* **€23.60** 2019

ONESSE ET LAHARIE *8E1* (0.5km N Rural) *44.06344,
-1.07257* FFCC Camping Le Bienvenu, 259 Route de
Mimizan, 40110 Onesse-et-Laharie **05 58 07 30 49
or 06 81 32 12 56 (mob); www.camping-onesse.fr**
€1 nr nr

On N10 Bordeaux-Bayonne rd, turn W onto D38 at
Laharie. Site in 5km. 2*, Med, mkd, pt shd, EHU (10A)
€4; red long stay; TV; 10% statics; adv bkg acc; CKE.
"Well-run, nice, family site; gd facs; very helpful staff."
€18.00, 1 Mar-30 Sep. 2019

ONZAIN *4G2* (6km W Rural) *47.51030, 1.10400*
Yelloh! Village Le Parc du Val de Loire, 155 Route
de Fleuray, 41150 Mesland **02 54 70 27 18; parcdu
valdeloire@orange.fr; www.parcduvaldeloire.com
or www.yellohvillage.co.uk**
€4
(covrd, htd)

Fr Blois take D952 SW twd Amboise. Approx
16km outside Blois turn R to Onzain & foll sp to
Mesland; go thro Mesland vill & turn L dir Fleuray;
site on R after 1.5km. 4*, Lge, hdg, mkd, pt shd,
pt sl, serviced pitches; EHU (10A) inc; gas; bbq
(charcoal, gas); TV; 30% statics; Eng spkn; adv bkg
acc; ccard acc; waterslide; bike hire; tennis; games
area; games rm; CKE. *"Secluded site; wine-tasting;
excursions to vineyards; mkt Thur Onzain; excel."*
€35.00, 11 Apr-20 Sep, L02. 2016

ORANGE *10E2* (12km NE Rural) *44.16222, 4.93531*
Camping des Favards (formerly Aire Naturelle Domaine), 1335 Route d'Orange, 84150 Violès 04 90 70 90 93; campingfavards@gmail.com; www.favards.com

🐕 €1.70-€1.90 ⊞(htd) ♨ ♿ 🆘 ⅃ ⊮ ⊮ ♟ 🍴 🧺 ⅏ ⚓

Fr N exit A7 junc 19 Bollène. Foll D8 dir Carpentras & Violès. In Violès foll dir Orange & look for camp sp. Fr S exit A7 junc 22 sp Carpentras, take dir Avignon, then dir Vaison-la-Romaine to Violès. Avoid cent of Orange when towing. 3*, Sm, hdg, mkd, unshd, EHU (6-10A) €3.65 (poss rev pol); Eng spkn; adv bkg acc; ccard acc; CKE. *"Well-kept site; excel pitches - some very lge (extra charge); superb san facs, poss stretched; wine-tasting on site high ssn; gd touring base; poss dust clouds fr Mistral wind; pitches muddy when wet; gd."* **€23.60, 13 Apr-30 Sep.** **2018**

ORBEC *3D1* (1.5km N Urban) *49.02829, 0.40857*
Camp Municipal Les Capucins, Rue des Frères Bigot, 14290 Orbec 02 31 32 76 22; camping.sivom@orange.fr

🐕 ⊞ ⊡ ♨ ⅃ ⊮ 🧺 nr ⅏

Exit A28 junc 15 to Orbec; on ent town foll site sp. If app fr D519 or D819 steep drag up to site & care req down to town. 2*, Sm, pt shd, EHU (10A) €2. *"Well-kept site; site yourself if office clsd; san facs old but clean; no twin axles; access easy for lge o'fits; delightful countryside; excel."* **€12.00, 25 May-8 Sep.** **2015**

ORBEY *6F3* (7km SE Rural) *48.09198, 7.19741*
Camping des Deux Hohnack, Giragoutte 68910 Labaroche 03 89 49 83 72; camping-labaroche@orange.fr; www.camping-labaroche.fr

🐕 €1 ⊞ ⊡ ♨ ♿ 🆘 ⅃ 🍴 ⅏

Fr Colmar take D11 thro Turckheim (do not turn off on D10). Cont thro Trois Epis. At fork turn L sp Linge. In half km turn R. 2*, Med, mkd, hdg, hdstg, pt shd, pt sl, EHU (6A) €4; bbq; TV; games area; CKE. *"Gd walks; rural museum at Labaroche 1.5km; vg."* **€17.50, 1 Apr-30 Sep.** **2015**

ORLEANS *4F3* (11km E Rural) *47.88830, 2.02744*
Camp Municipal Les Pâtures, 55 Chemin du Port, 45430 Chécy 02 38 91 13 27; camping@checy.fr; www.checy.fr

🐕 €1 ⊞ ⊡ ♨ ♿ 🆘 ⅃ ⊮ 🧺 nr

Take D960 E twd Châteauneuf. In Chécy, foll site sp. Access thro town via narr rds. 2*, Sm, hdg, pt shd, EHU (16A) €3.80; bbq; twin axles; red long stay; Eng spkn; adv bkg acc; fishing; golf 5km; tennis; CKE. *"Excel, well-run site on Rv Loire; vg location; friendly, helpful warden; gd san facs; conv Orléans, park & ride tram; poss open bef & after dates given; popular NH."* **€19.00, 12 May-25 Sep.** **2018**

ORLEANS *4F3* (5km S Rural) *47.85603, 1.92555*
Camp Municipal d'Olivet, Rue du Pont-Bouchet, 45160 Olivet 02 38 63 53 94; infos@camping-olivet.org; www.camping-olivet.org

🐕 €2 ⊞(htd) ⊡ ♨ ♿ 🆘 ⅃ ⊮ ⊮ ♟ 🧺 ⅏

To avoid height restriction, best app fr A71 exit junc 2 onto N271 dir Orléans-La Source. Cont on N271 until rd crosses N20 into Rue de Bourges. Pass commercial estate & hotel on L & turn L at traff lts into Rue de Châteauroux. Pass university (Parc Technologique), cross tramway & turn L at traff lts onto D14, Rue de la Source, then in 500m turn R (watch for pharmacy on L & green site sp) into Rue du Pont-Bouchet (narr rd). Site well sp on D14. NB Beware height restrictions on junc underpasses in Orléans cent. 2*, Sm, hdg, pt shd, pt sl, EHU (16A) €3.10 (rev pol); bus 400m; Eng spkn; adv bkg rec; CKE. *"Well-run, busy site by Rv Loiret; friendly; excel clean san facs; guided tours of Orléans by site staff; gd walking; vineyards nr; vg."* **€21.70, 1 Apr-30 Sep.** **2018**

"I like to fill in the reports as I travel from site to site"

You'll find report forms at the back of this guide, or you can fill them in online at camc.com/europereport.

ORLEANS *4F3* (15km SW Urban) *47.85539, 1.75352*
Camp Municipal Fontaine de Rabelais, Chemin de la Plage, 45130 St Ay 02 38 88 44 44 (Mairie); maire@ville-saint-ay.fr; www.ville-saint-ay.fr

🐕 ⊞ ⊡ ♨ ♿ 🆘 ⅃ ⊮ ⅏ nr 🧺 nr ⅏

Exit A10/E60 at junc 15 Meung-sur-Loire onto N152 dir Orléans, sp La Chapelle-St Mesmin; site sp on app to St Ay on N bank Rv Loire. Fr A71 exit junc 1 dir Blois & Beaugency onto N152. 1*, Lge, pt shd, pt sl, EHU (6A) inc (poss rev pol); gas; bbq; red long stay; phone; bus 500m; Eng spkn; adv bkg acc; rv fishing adj; boating adj; CKE. *"Pleasant, clean, tidy, flat site on Rv Loire; excel modern facs for sm site but poss stretched high ssn; rvside cycling/walking; conv Orléans & chateaux; poss early closure or late opening - rec call in adv to check; perfect NH; lge spaces."* **€14.00, 15 Apr-31 Oct.** **2016**

ORNANS *6G2* (1km E Rural) *47.10064, 6.16036*
Camping La Roche d'Ully, Allée de la Tour de Peiltz, 25290 Ornans 03 81 57 17 79; contact@larochedully.com; www.camping-larochedully.com

🐕 €3 ⊞(htd) ⊡ ♨ ♿ 🆘 ⅃ ⊮ 🦋 ♟ 🍴 ⅏ 🧺 ⅏
🧺 (covrd, htd) 🏊

Fr Ornans foll blue sps to site nr rvside. 4*, Med, mkd, unshd, EHU (10A) €4; bbq; 20% statics; adv bkg acc; ccard acc; rv fishing; bike hire; sauna; canoeing; games area. *"Pleasant, family-run site in gd location in rv valley; popular with students; some noise in ssn."* **€36.00, 2 Apr-9 Oct.** **2016**

ORPIERRE *9D3* (0.5km E Rural) *44.31110, 5.69650*
Camping Les Princes d'Orange, Flonsaine, 05700
Orpierre **04 92 66 22 53; campingorpierre@orange.fr;
www.campingorpierre.com**

🛉 €1.60 ♦♦♦ [wc] ♨ ♣ ⓖ ⊞ ⧄ / [MsP] ⬚ ⟈ ▲ ♨ /∆ ⧄ 💧 (htd)

N75 S fr Serres for 11km to Eyguians. Turn R in
Eyguians onto D30, 8km to Orpierre, turn L in vill to
site (sp). 4*, Med, mkd, hdstg, pt shd, pt sl, terr, EHU
(10A) €4.50; gas; TV; 10% statics; adv bkg acc; fishing;
games area; waterslide; tennis. *"Rock-climbing area;
gd walking; beautiful, interesting vill."*
€46.40, 1 Apr-3 Nov. 2019

OUISTREHAM *3D1* (1km S Urban) *49.26909, -0.25498*
Camping Le Riva Bella, Rue de la Haie Breton, 14150
Ouistreham **02 31 97 12 66; camping-rivabella@
vacances-seasonova.com; www.vacances-
seasonova.com/camping-riva-bella**

🛉 €1.50 ♦♦♦ (htd) [wc] ♨ ♣ ⓖ ⊞ / [MsP] ✿ ⟈ ⬚ ▲ ♨ /∆ ⧄
💧 (htd) 🌳 sand 1.8km

Fr ferry terminal foll sp Caen on D84 (Rue de l'Yser/
Ave du Grand Large); in approx 1.5km site sp at
rndabt; take 3rd exit. 3*, Lge, hdg, pt shd, EHU (10A)
inc; gas; twin axles; 40% statics; bus; Eng spkn; adv
bkg acc; ccard acc; games area; tennis; bike hire; CKE.
*"V conv for late or early ferry (5 mins to terminal),
site stays open for late Brittany ferry; busy high ssn;
gd sized pitches; sandy soil; gates open 0630-2300
(dep out of hrs, by request); opens for late arr; no twin
axles; nice walk/cycle along canal to town; wonderful
beaches; interesting area; mkt Thur; conv & sep area
for NH without unhitching; British twin axle c'vans acc;
gd for long stay; takeaway food and bread shop on site;
new management has improved site (2017); new san
facs & pool."* **€30.00, 30 Mar-4 Nov, N10.** 2018

OUISTREHAM *3D1* (7km S Rural) *49.23838, -0.25763*
FFCC Camping des Capucines, rue de la Côte Fleurie,1
4860 Ranville **02 31 78 69 82; campingdescapucines.
14@orange.fr; www.campingdescapucines.com**

[12] 🛉 €1.80 ♦♦♦ (htd) ♨ ♣ ⓖ / [MsP] ✿ ⟈ ⬚ nr ⓗ nr ▲ /∆
🌳 sand 3km

App Caen fr E or W, take Blvd Péripherique Nord,
then exit 3a sp Ouistreham car ferry (D515). In
approx 8.5km turn R onto D514 sp Cabourg, cross
Pegasus Bdge & foll sp Ranville across 2 rndabts;
at x-rds in 500m turn L (at sm campsite sp); site
in 300m on L. Fr Ouistreham foll D514 dir Caborg
to Pegasus Bdge, then as above. 3*, Med, hdg,
mkd, pt shd, terr, EHU (10A) inc (poss rev pol); gas;
60% statics; phone; bus 500m; Eng spkn; adv bkg rec;
ccard acc. *"Well established site in pleasant position;
some pitches sm, best pitches without ehu; gd clean
san facs but dated; barrier open 0600-2400 but if clsd
LS use intercom at recep; conv ferries (if arr late fr
ferry, phone in adv for pitch number & barrier code);
take care o'hanging trees; conv vill, Pegasus Bdge,
museum & war cemetery; vg, quiet well run site;
hypmkt 4.8km; site run down in LS; reliable freq visited
stop nr port."* **€21.40** 2019

OUISTREHAM *3D1* (5km SW Urban) *49.24970,
-0.27190* **Camping Les Hautes Coutures,** avenue de
la Côte de Nacre, 14970 Bénouville **02 31 44 73 08 or
06 07 25 26 90 (mob LS); info@campinghautes
coutures.com; www.campinghautescoutures.com**

🛉 €3 ♦♦♦ (htd) [wc] ♨ ♣ ⓖ ⊞ / [MsP] ⟈ ⬚ /∆ ⧄
💧 (covrd, htd) 🚿 🌳 2km

Leave Ouistreham ferry & foll sp Caen & A13 over
2 rndabts. After 2nd rndabt join dual c'way. Leave
at 1st exit (D35) sp St Aubin d'Arquenay & ZA
de Bénouville. Turn R at end of slip rd, then L at
T-junc; site in 200m uphill on R. Or fr Caen twd
port on dual c'way, site has own exit shortly after
Pegasus Memorial Bdge exit; site clearly visible
on R of dual c'way. 4*, Lge, hdg, pt shd, pt sl, EHU
(10A) €5.50 (rev pol)(adaptors avail €18); bbq; TV;
30% statics; Eng spkn; adv bkg acc; ccard acc; jacuzzi;
golf 4km; bike hire; fishing; horseriding 1km; games
rm; windsurfing 1km; waterslide; CKE. *"Busy, poss
noisy holiday complex o'looking Caen Canal; friendly
staff; sm pitches; access tight some pitches when
busy; recep 0800-2000 high ssn, but staff will open
for late ferry if req in adv; no o'fits over 12m high
ssn; ltd EHU (2009); cycle path to Caen; daily mkt in
Ouistreham; conv NH; access to pitches diff as high
kerbs, some pitches on steep slopes; excel pool."*
€35.00, 25 Mar-25 Sep. 2016

OUNANS *6H2* (1km N Rural) *47.00290, 5.66550*
Huttopia La Plage Blanche, 3 Rue de la Plage,
39380 Ounans **03 84 37 69 63; plageblanche@
camping-indigo.com; europe.huttopia.com/en/site/
la-plage-blanche**

🛉 €2 ♦♦♦ [wc] ♨ ♣ ⓖ / [MsP] ✿ ⟈ ⓗ ⬚ nr /∆ ⧄ 💧 🚿

Exit A39 junc 6 sp Dole Cent. Foll N5 SE for 18km dir
Pontarlier. After passing Souvans, turn L on D472 sp
Mont-sous-Vaudrey. Foll sp to Ounans. Site well sp
in vill. 3*, Lge, mkd, hdstg, pt shd, EHU (6A) €4 (poss
rev pol); sw nr; TV; 1% statics; Eng spkn; adv bkg rec;
ccard acc; lake fishing; bike hire; horseriding; canoeing;
CKE. *"Superb rvside pitches; trout & carp fishing; friendly
recep; excel san facs, recently updated (2013); gd rest;
excel."* **€27.90, 19 Apr-22 Sep, J02.** 2019

OUST *8G3* (12km SE Rural) *42.81105, 1.25558*
Camping Le Montagnou, Route de Guzet, 09140 Le
Trein-d'Ustou **05 61 66 94 97 or 06 07 85 37 65;
campinglemontagnou@wanadoo.fr;
www.lemontagnou.com**

🛉 €1.50 ♦♦♦ (htd) [wc] ♨ ♣ ⓖ / ✿ ⟈ ⓗ nr ⬚ ▲ /∆ 💧

Fr St Girons S on D618 & D3 to Oust. Fr Oust SE on
D3 & D8 thro Seix & at Pont de la Taule turn L onto
D8 twd Le Trein-d'Ustou. Site on L just bef vill, sp.
3*, Med, hdg, EHU (6-10A) €3.50-5.50; bbq; sw
nr; 30% statics; phone; adv bkg acc; ccard acc; tennis;
fishing; CKE. *"Well-situated, well-run, delightful rvside
site; mountain views; skiing 9km; gd sized pitches;
friendly, helpful French owners; gd walking; highly rec."*
€22.00, 1 Jan-31 Oct & 1 Dec-31 Dec. 2015

For a guide to symbols see the fold out on the rear cover

FRANCE

OUST *8G3* (0.6km S Rural) *42.87042, 1.21947*
Camping Les Quatre Saisons, Route d'Aulus-les-Bains, 09140 Oust **05 61 96 55 55; camping.ariege@ gmail.com; www.camping4saisons.com**

🔢 ⛺ €1.50 ♿(htd) [wc] ⚍ 🚿 ⚏ ✉ 🐕 💈 ⏲ 🛒nr 🏔 ⛵

Take D618 S fr St Girons; then D3 to Oust; on N o'skts of town turn L (sp Aulus) onto D32; in 1km site on R nr Rv Garbet. 3*, Med, hdg, pt shd, EHU (10A) inc; TV; 25% statics; phone; Eng spkn; adv bkg rec; ccard acc; games area; CKE. "*In beautiful, unspoilt area; friendly site; excel boulangerie 5mins walk on footpath to vill; excel.*" **€20.00** **2016**

OYONNAX *9A3* (13km E Rural) *46.25530, 5.55705*
Camping Les Gorges de l'Oignin, Rue du Lac, 01580 Matafelon-Granges **04 74 76 80 97; camping. lesgorgesdeloignin@wanadoo.fr; www.gorges-de-loignin.com**

⛺ €2.40 ♿(htd) [wc] ⚍ 🚿 ♨ ⚏ ✉ 🐕 💈 ⏲ ⑨ ⚓ 🛒 🏔 ⛵ 🎿

Exit A404 junc 9 onto D979 dir Bourg-en-Bresse; in 700m turn R onto D18 to Matafelon-Granges; foll sp. NB Fr Oyonnax 22km by rd. 3*, Med, hdg, mkd, hdstg, pt shd, terr, EHU (10A) €3.40; bbq; sw nr; TV; 10% statics; phone; Eng spkn; adv bkg acc; games area; CKE. "*Beautiful site on lake - boat launching; friendly, helpful staff; Jura National Park; Rv Ain gorges; excel.*" **€29.00, 15 Apr-20 Sep.** **2015**

PACAUDIERE, LA *9A1* (0.2km E Rural) *46.17512, 3.87639* **Camp Municipal Beausoleil,** Route de Vivans, 42310 La Pacaudière **04 77 64 11 50 or 04 77 64 30 18 (Mairie); lapacaudiere@wanadoo.fr; www.camping-rhonealpes.com**

♿ [wc] ⚍ 🚿 ⚏ 🐕 🛒 🏔

NW on N7 Roanne to Lapalisse; turn R in La Pacaudière, D35; site well sp; fork R in 50m; site ent in 400m. 2*, Sm, hdg, hdstg, unshd, sl, EHU (10A); gas; TV. "*Pleasant NH in beautiful countryside; public pool high ssn; ltd facs LS; interesting area; Sat mkt.*" **€15.50, 1 May-30 Sep.** **2017**

PAIMPOL *1D3* (2.5km SE Coastal) *48.76966, -3.02209*
Camp Municipal Crukin, Rue de Crukin, Kérity, 22500 Paimpol **02 96 20 78 47 or 02 96 55 31 70 (Mairie); contact@camping-paimpol.com; www.camping-paimpol.com**

⛺ €2.10 ♿(htd) [wc] ⚍ 🚿 ♨ ⚏ ✉ 🐕 💈 🛒 🏔 ⛵shgl 250m

On D786 fr St Brieuc/Paimpol, site sp in vill of Kérity 80m off main rd shortly bef abbey. 2*, Med, hdg, pt shd, EHU (6A) €3.90 (poss rev pol); TV; 10% statics; bus 100m; watersports; fishing; CKE. "*Sep m'van area; Beaufort Abbey nrby; excel sh stay/NH; plenty of space; facs ltd LS; walk to town along coast rd gd views; site unkept; boggy when wet; gd; tourist train runs past site ent to/fr Paimpol, hourly svrs.*" **€23.00, 1 Apr-30 Sep.** **2018**

PALAVAS LES FLOTS *10F1* (1km NE Coastal) *43.53346, 3.94820* **Camping Montpellier Plage,** 95 Ave St Maurice, 34250 Palavas-les-Flots **04 67 68 00 91; camping.montpellier.plage@wanadoo.fr; www.camping-montpellier-plage.com**

🐕 ♿ [wc] ⚍ 🚿 ♿ ⚏ ✉ [MP] 💈 ⑨ ⚓ 🛒 🏔 ⛵ 🎿 🏊 ⛱sand adj

Site on D21ES on o'skts of vill twd Carnon. 3*, V lge, mkd, pt shd, EHU (4A) inc; gas; bbq; 50% statics; bus high ssn; Eng spkn; adv bkg rec; games area; CKE. "*Gd location;spa facs; basic san facs, but lge pitches & friendliness of site outweigh this; gd security; poss somewhat unkempt; easy walk into Palavas - interesting sm port; flamingoes on adjoining lake; gd.*" **€36.00, 16 Apr-18 Sep.** **2017**

PARAY LE MONIAL *9A1* (1km NW Urban) *46.45750, 4.10472* **Camping de Mambré,** Route du Gué-Léger, 71600 Paray-le-Monial **03 85 88 89 20; camping. plm@gmail.com; www.campingdemambre.com**

🐕 €2 ♿ [wc] ⚍ 🚿 ⚏ 🐕 💈 🛒 🏔 ⛵

Fr N79 Moulin to Mâcon; site at W end of town; just after level x-ing turn NE into Rte du Gué-Léger. Turn R into site after x-ing rv; well sp. 4*, Lge, mkd, pt shd, EHU (10A) €3.40; CKE. "*Paray-le-Monial is pilgrimage cent; ltd facs & poorly maintained LS (2011); no designated fresh water pnts (2011); 15min walk to town along rv; excel cycling cent.*" **€22.50, 2 May-30 Sep.** **2019**

PARENTIS EN BORN *7D1* (6km SW Rural) *44.34562, -1.09241* **Camping L'Arbre d'Or,** 75 Route du Lac, 40160 Landes **05 58 78 41 56; contact@arbre-dor.com; www.arbre-dor.com**

🐕 ♿ [wc] ⚍ 🚿 ♨ ⚏ ✉ [MP] 💈 ⑨ ⏲ 🛒nr 🏔 ⚓ 🏊

Leave the Bordeaux m'way A63/N10 in Liposthey and drive twds Parentis (D43). The campsite is sp in Parentis. 4*, Med, mkd, pt shd, EHU inc (10A); bbq; sw nr; twin axles; 25% statics; phone; Eng spkn; adv bkg acc; ccard acc; games area; CKE. "*Vg; lake 500m fr site, watersports in lake; v friendly mgmt; bike hire.*" **€30.00, 1 Apr-30 Oct.** **2017**

PARENTIS EN BORN *7D1* (3km NW Rural) *44.35153, -1.10959* **Camping Calède,** Quartier Lahitte, 40160 Parentis-en-Born **05 58 78 44 63; contact@ camping-calede.com; www.camping-calede.com**

🐕 €0.50 ♿ [wc] ⚍ 🚿 ♨ ⚏ ✉ 🐕 💈 🛒nr 🏔 ⛵

Exit N10 junc 17 onto D43 to Parentis-en-Born; then take D652 dir Biscarrosse; site in 3km on L. Sp adj lake. 2*, Med, hdg, pt shd, EHU (10A) €3.30; gas; bbq; sw nr; phone; Eng spkn; adv bkg acc; sailing; fishing; CKE. "*Peaceful site in remote location; well-kept pitches & san facs; friendly, helpful staff; site yourself if office clsd; rec.*" **€22.00, 6 Apr-26 Oct.** **2019**

PARIS *3D3* (11km W Urban) *48.86843, 2.23471*
Camping Indigo Paris Bois de Boulogne,
2 Allée du Bord de l'Eau, 75016 Paris 01 45 24 30 00;
paris@camping-indigo.com; www.camping-indigo.
com or www.campingparis.fr

🔟 🏠 €4.70 ♦♦ (htd) ⬜ ♨ ♣ ♿ ◨ ◿ ▣ MP ❓ 🕭 nr ⚡ nr /🏔

Site bet bdge of Puteaux & bdge of Suresnes. App
fr A1: take Blvd Périphérique W to Bois de Boulogne
exit at Porte Maillot; foll camp sp. App fr A6: Blvd
Périphérique W to Porte Dauphine exit at Porte
Maillot; foll camp sp. App fr Pont de Sèvres (A10,
A11): on bdge take R lane & take 2nd rd R mkd
Neuilly-sur-Seine; rd runs parallel to Seine; cont to
site ent. App fr A13: after St Cloud Tunnel foll sp
twd Paris; immed after x-ing Rv Seine, 1st R sp Bois
de Boulogne; foll camp sps; traff lts at site ent. NB
Sharp turn to site, poorly sp fr N - watch for lge
'Parking Borne de l'Eau 200m'. 4*, V lge, hdg, mkd,
hdstg, pt shd, pt sl, EHU (10A) €6.20; gas; twin axles;
TV; 10% statics; phone; bus to metro; Eng spkn; adv
bkg rec; ccard acc; CKE. *"Busy site in excel location;
easy access A13; conv cent Paris - Metro Porte Maillot
4km; some v sm pitches; walk over Suresne bdge for
shops, food mkt, supmkt etc; some tour ops on site; gd
security; refurbished san facs (2014); vg; food truck;
new rest (2015)."* €40.20, P18. 2019

> ## "We must tell the Club about that great site we found"
>
> Get your site reports in by mid-August and we'll do our best to get your updates into the next edition.

PARIS *3D3* (22km NW Urban) *48.94001, 2.14563*
Sandaya Paris Maisons Laffitte, 1 Rue Johnson,
78600 Maisons-Laffitte 01 39 12 21 91; pml@
sandaya.fr; www.sandaya..co.uk

🏠 €5 ♦♦ (htd) ⬜ ♨ ♿ ◿ ▣ MP 🍽 Y 🕭 ♣ /🏔

Easy access fr A13 sp Poissy; take D308 to Maisons-
Laffitte; foll site sp bef town cent. Fr A15 take N184
S fr Poissy, foll sp St Germain; approx 6km after
x-ing Rv Seine & approx 300m after x-ing lge steel
bdge, take L lane ready for L turn onto D308 to
Maison-Laffitte; foll camp sp. Or D301 to St Denis,
then A86 exit Bezons, then dir Poissy, Noailles,
Sartrouville & Maisons-Laffitte. NB Narr app rd diff
due parked cars & high kerbs.
4*, Lge, hdg, mkd, pt shd, serviced pitches; EHU
(10-16A); gas; TV; 40% statics; Eng spkn; adv bkg acc;
ccard acc; games area; CKE. *"V busy, popular site on
island in Rv Seine; ideal for visiting Paris (20 min by
RER), Disneyland & Versailles; RER stn 1km; mobilis
ticket covers rlwy, metro & bus for day in Paris; friendly,
helpful staff; poss ltd facs LS."*
€25.00, 3 Apr-1 Nov, P03. 2019

PARTHENAY *4H1* (1km SW Urban) *46.64160, -0.26740*
Camping Flower du Bois Vert, 14 Rue Boisseau, Le
Tallud, 79200 Parthenay 05 49 64 78 43; camping
boisvert@orange.fr; www.camping-boisvert.com

♦♦ (htd) ⬜ ♨ ♣ ♿ ◨ ◿ ▣ 🏠 ❓ Y 🕭 ♣ ⚡ nr /🏔 ♣ ⚓ (htd) 🛶

Site on D743 to Niort. Sp fr N & S. Fr S 1km bef town
turn L at sp La Roche-sur-Yon immed after rv bdge
turn R; site on R in 500m. 4*, Med, hdg, hdstg, mkd,
pt shd, pt sl, EHU (6 or 10A) inc; bbq; TV; 10% statics;
phone; adv bkg acc; fishing; games rm; bike hire;
tennis; boating; CKE. *"1 hr rvside walk to town; m'van
o'night area adj; noisy nr main rd & bar; Wed mkt;
gd NH to Spain; conv Futuroscope; new facs, plenty
hot water; well spaced hdg grass pitches; excel facs."*
€28.50, 4 Apr-31 Oct. 2017

PARTHENAY *4H1* (9km W Urban) *46.62214, -0.35139*
Camp Municipal Les Peupliers, 79130 Azay-sur-Thouet
05 49 95 37 13 (Mairie); mairie-azaysurthouet@
cc-parthenay.fr; www.tourisme-gatine.com

♦♦ ♣ ◿ 🦋 ⚡ nr /🏔

Fr Parthenay take D949 dir Secondigny to Azay-sur-
Thouet; turn L onto D139 dir St Pardoux; site on
L in 200m. Site adj stadium on rvside. 2*, Sm, mkd,
pt shd, EHU (10A) €3.50; bbq. *"Pleasant, peaceful
site; barrier open ltd hrs; clean dated san facs, poss
inadequate number high ssn; MH area outside of
campsite; gd."* €9.00, 15 Jun-30 Sep. 2017

PARTHENAY *4H1* (9km W Rural) *46.65738, -0.34816*
FFCC Camping La Chagnée (Baudoin), 79450
St Aubin le Cloud 05 49 95 31 44 or 06 71 10 09 66
(mob); gerard.baudoin3@wanadoo.fr;
www.lachagneevacances.fr

🔟 🏠 ♦♦ ⬜ ♨ ♿ ◿ ▣ MP 🦋 ⚡ nr

Fr Parthenay on D949BIS dir Secondigny. Turn R
in Azay-sur-Thouet onto D139 dir St Aubin, site on
R in 2km, look for 'Gîte' sp. 3*, Sm, hdg, pt shd, terr,
EHU (10A) €3.50; Eng spkn; fishing. *"Charming, CL-
type organic fm site o'looking lake; friendly, extremely
helpful & welcoming owners; v clean, modern facs; OAY
providing use own san in winter; maps loaned for walks;
excel; m'van only during period Nov-Mar; fmhse meal
avail weekly; vg lake fishing; rec."* €15.00 2017

PAU *8F2* (5km E Rural) *43.28909, -0.26985*
FFCC Camping Les Sapins, Route de Tarbes, 64320
Ousse 05 59 81 79 03 or 05 59 81 74 21 (LS);
lessapins64@orange.fr

🔟 ♦♦ ♣ ◿ MP 🕭 nr ⚡ nr

Site adj Hôtel des Sapins on S side of D817
(Pau-Tarbes rd). 3*, Sm, pt shd, EHU (4-10A) inc;
fishing. *"Popular, pleasant NH; red facs LS; helpful
owners; NH only; bus svrs infrequent."* €17.00 2019

FRANCE

PAUILLAC 7C2 (1km S Rural) 45.18515, -0.74218 **FFCC**
Camp Municipal Les Gabarreys, Route de la Rivière,
33250 Pauillac **05 56 59 10 03 or 05 56 73 30 50;**
camping.les.gabarreys@wanadoo.fr;
www.pauillac-medoc.com

€3 (htd) /MP nr

On ent Pauillac on D206, turn R at rndabt, sp site.
On app Quays, turn R bef 'Maison du Vin'. Site on L
in 1km. 4*, Med, hdg, hdstg, mkd, pt shd, EHU (5-10A)
€5-6; bbq; TV; 6% statics; Eng spkn; adv bkg acc; ccard
acc; games rm; CKE. *"Peaceful, well-kept, well-
equipped site on estuary; nice clean san facs; conv wine
chateaux; cycle rtes; mkt Sat; excel."*
€23.00, 3 Apr-8 Oct. 2017

PAYRAC 7D3 (1km N Rural) 44.80574, 1.47479
Camping Panoramic, Route de Loupiac, 46350 Payrac-
en-Quercy **05 65 37 98 45;** info@campingpanoramic.
com; www.campingpanoramic.com

12 (htd) WD nr

N fr Payrac on D820, turn L onto D147 sp Loupiac
(200m after 'end of vill' sp), site 300m on R.
2*, Sm, hdstg, pt shd, pt sl, EHU (5A) €3 (poss rev pol);
gas; bbq; sw nr; TV; 10% statics; phone; Eng spkn; adv
bkg acc; bike hire; canoe hire; CKE. *"Well-run, clean
site; OK san facs - poss inadequate if site full; poss
muddy in bad weather but hdstg avail; pool 400m;
friendly, helpful Dutch owner; gd walking; excel winter
NH."* **€15.00** 2015

PEILLAC 2F3 (2km N Rural) 47.72635, -2.21430
Camp Municipal du Pont d'Oust, 56220 Peillac **02 99
91 39 33 or 02 99 91 26 76 (Mairie);** www.peillac.fr

(htd) nr nr nr

SW fr La Gacilly on D777; in 6km turn L onto D14 sp
Les Fougerêts; cont thro Les Fougerêts, site on R in
1km opp canal. Or N fr Peillac on D14, folls sp Pont
d'Oust; site on L. 2*, Med, pt shd, EHU (10A) €3.20
(poss rev pol); bbq. *"Nice, peaceful site by Rv Oust &
canal; spacious pitches, soft when wet; helpful warden
calls, site yourself; v flat, ideal for cycling; pretty vill;
vg; mkd cycling and walking rtes fr site; pool adj; pay at
Mairie during May."* **€12.70, 1 May-30 Sep.** 2017

PELUSSIN 9B2 (1km SE Rural) 45.41375, 4.69143
Camping Bel'Epoque du Pilat, La Vialle, Route de
Malleval, 42410 Pélussin **04 74 87 66 60;** contact@
camping-belepoque.fr; www.camping-belepoque.fr

€2.50 (htd) WD /MP nr
(htd)

Exit A7 junc 10 just S of Lyon foll N86 dir Serrières;
in Chavanay turn R onto D7 to Pélussin, then at
rndabt turn L and foll D79 S & foll site sp. Rec do
not use sat nav! 3*, Sm, hdg, pt shd, pt sl, EHU (6A)
€3.50; gas; bbq; phone; train 10km; Eng spkn; adv bkg
acc; ccard acc; games area; tennis; CKE. *"In nature
reserve; vg walking; vg, peaceful
site; supmkt in Pelussin; friendly, helpful owners."*
€28.00, 1 Apr-30 Sep. 2017

PENESTIN 2G3 (3km E Rural) 47.47687, -2.45204
Camping Les Pins, Chemin du Val au Bois de la
Lande, 56760 Pénestin **02 99 90 33 13;** camping.
lespins@wanadoo.fr; www.camping-despins.com

€1.50 (htd) WD /MP nr
(covrd, htd) sand 3km

Fr Roche-Bernard take D34 dir Pénestin, 2km
bef town turn L sp Camping Les Pins. Site on
R in 250m. 2*, Med, mkd, hdg, pt shd, pt sl, EHU
(10A) €3; bbq; red long stay; twin axles; TV;
33% statics; Eng spkn; adv bkg acc; waterslide;
games area; bike hire; games rm; CKE. *"Sun
mkt; excel; fab countryside; sandy beaches
nrby; gd facs, exceptionally clean; gd welcome."*
€26.00, 1 Apr-18 Oct. 2015

See advertisement

PENESTIN *2G3* (3km S Coastal) *47.44527, -2.48416*
Camping Les Iles, La Pointe du Bile, 56760 Pénestin
02 99 90 30 24; reservation@camping-lesiles.fr;
www.camping-des-iles.fr

🏕 €3.90 👫👫 🚻 WC ♨ 🛒 ♿ ⬛ ⚲ ⊘ MSP ♍ 🍴 ⑪ 🛖 🛒 ⚠ ⚘ 🏊

(htd) 🚮 🌳 sand direct access

**Fr La Roche Bernard take D34 to Pénestin; cont
on D201 for 2.5km & foll site sp.** 4*, Lge, mkd, hdg,
pt shd, serviced pitches; EHU (10A) inc (poss rev
pol); gas; bbq (charcoal, elec); TV; 10% statics; Eng
spkn; adv bkg acc; ccard acc; bike hire; waterslide;
fishing adj; horseriding; tennis; games rm; CKE.
*"Lovely site o'looking sea; no o'fits over 7m high ssn;
direct access to shoreline; some pitches sm; max 1
dog; helpful staff; clean modern unisex san facs; mkt
Sun (also Wed in Jul/Aug); gd cycling, walking; vg."*
€45.00, 12 Apr-30 Sep, B06.   **2019**

"Satellite navigation makes touring much easier"

Remember most sat navs don't know if you're
towing or in a larger vehicle – always use yours
alongside maps and site directions.

PERIERS *1D4* (6km NE Rural) *49.21581, -1.35093*
Camping Le Clos Castel, 50500 Raids **02 33 17 23 61
or 07789 227484 (mob); lecloscastel@live.com;
www.camping-france-normandy.com**

12 🏕 👫👫 WC ♨ ⚲ 🍴 🛒

**S fr Carentan on D791 to Raids; cont past vill on
D791 for 300m; turn R to site, ent on R in 100m. Or
N fr Periers on D791; turn L 300m bef Raids & then
as bef. Site well sp.** Sm, hdstg, unshd, EHU (6A) inc;
bbq; Eng spkn; adv bkg acc. *"Site has B&B; helpful
British owners; dogs free; conv D-day beaches; excel."*
€17.50   **2016**

PERIERS *1D4* (5km SE Rural) *49.16638, -1.34916*
FFCC Aire Naturelle Municipale Le Clos Vert,
50190 St Martin-d'Aubigny **02 33 46 57 03 or 02
33 07 73 92 (Mairie); mairie-st-martin-daubigny@
wanadoo.fr; www.gites-de-france-manche.com**

👫👫 WC ♨ ♿ ⚲ ⊘ ✂ 🛒 nr ⑪ nr 🛒 nr ⚠

**E fr Périers on D900 dir St Lô; in 4km turn R sp
St Martin-d'Aubigny; site on L in 500m adj church.**
Sm, pt shd, EHU (6A) €2.50; bbq; golf 2km; fishing
2km; tennis 2km; CKE. *"Charming, sm, well-kept, useful
site; facs basic but OK; easy 70km run to Cherbourg;
no twin axles; basic quiet site in vill, bar & rest within
walking dist; conv for ports; pay at Marie if no one calls
for payment."* **€10.50, 15 Apr-15 Oct.**   **2018**

PERIGUEUX *7C3* (13km NE Rural) *45.21975, 0.86383*
Camping Le Bois du Coderc, Route des Gaunies,
24420 Antonne-et-Trigonant **05 53 05 99 83; coderc-
camping@wanadoo.fr; www.campinglecoderc.com**

12 🏕 €1 👫👫 WC ♨ ♿ ⚲ ⊘ MSP ♍ 🍴 ⑪ nr 🛒 nr ⚠

🏊 (htd) 🌳 shgl adj

**NE fr Périgueux on N21 twd Limoges, thro Antonne
approx 1km turn R at x-rds bet car park & rest. Site
in 500m.** 3*, Med, hdg, pt shd, EHU (10A) inc; bbq;
sw nr; TV; 10% statics; phone; Eng spkn; adv bkg acc;
ccard acc; games rm; ice; games area; CKE. *"Secluded,
pleasant, peaceful site; most pitches spacious; rallies
welcome; gd value, inc rest; highly rec; quiet; well
maintained; excel site; view of website a must; gd
birdwatching; v helpful owners, v eager to please; excel
htd pool; excel wifi fr some pitches; new san block
(2018); excel."* **€22.00**   **2018**

PERIGUEUX *7C3* (20km SE Rural) *45.13165, 0.92867*
Camping de la Pélonie, La Bourgie, 24330 St
Antoine-d'Auberoche **05 53 07 55 78; info@
campinglapelonie.com; www.lapelonie.com**

🏕 €2 👫👫 WC ♨ ⚲ 🍴 ⊘ ✂ 🍴 ⑪ 🛒 ⚠ 🏊 (htd) 🚮

**Fr Périgueux on A89 twd Brive; 5km past St Pierre-
de-Chignac, site sp on L; turn L at picnic area - go
under rlwy bdge; site ent on L.** 3*, Med, mkd, pt shd,
EHU (10A) €3.80 (poss req long cable); gas; TV;
20% statics; phone; Eng spkn; adv bkg acc; ccard acc;
CKE. *"Delightful site; pleasant, welcoming owners; gd,
clean, well kept facs; excel facs for children; some
pitches diff lge o'fits; gd touring base."*
€22.00, 18 Apr-10 Oct.   **2015**

PERIGUEUX *7C3* (8km SE Rural) *45.14900, 0.77880*
Camping Le Grand Dague, Route du Grand Dague,
24750 Atur **05 53 04 21 01; info@legranddague.fr;
www.legranddague.fr**

🏕 €2 👫👫 (htd) WC ♨ ♿ ⚲ ⊘ ✂ 🍴 ⑪ 🛒 ⚠ ⚘
🛒 (htd) 🚮

**Fr cent Périgueux, take N21 & A89 twd Brive. Fork
L onto D2 to Atur (main rd bears R). In Atur turn L
after bar/tabac; foll site sp for 2.5km.**
4*, Lge, shd, pt sl, EHU (6A) inc; bbq; TV; 70% statics;
phone; Eng spkn; adv bkg acc; ccard acc; games rm;
bike hire; games area; CKE. *"Gd family site; friendly
owners; site immac, even end of ssn; poss unkempt
early ssn; lots to do; ltd touring pitches; excel."*
€39.00, 22 Apr-25 Sep.   **2016**

"There aren't many sites open at this time of year"

If you're travelling outside peak season
remember to call ahead to check site opening
dates – even if the entry says 'open all year'.

PERONNE 3C3 (0.9km NE Urban) 49.93424, 2.94140
Camp Municipal du Brochet, Rue Georges
Clémenceau, 80200 Péronne **03 22 84 02 35;**
peter.v.gent@orange.fr

🐕 👫 [wc] 🛒 🚿 / [msp] 🐾 Ⓗ nr 🔥 nr 🏕

Fr N on D1017 turn R into town. L at lights & L immed
after footbdge. 1st R & site on L. Well sp fr all dirs.
Go to town cent then foll 'Intn'l Camping Site' sps.
1*, Sm, hdstg, pt shd, pt sl, terr, EHU (16A) inc; phone;
bus 500m; Eng spkn; adv bkg acc; CKE. "Pleasant, basic
site nr park & attractive town; grass pitches soft when
wet; rec arr early high ssn; conv WW1 museum; NH, vg."
€16.00, 8 Apr-30 Oct. 2015

PERONNE 3C3 (2.6km S Rural) 49.91805, 2.93227
Camping du Port de Plaisance, Route de Paris,
80200 Péronne **03 22 84 19 31;** contact@camping-
plaisance.com; www.camping-plaisance.com

🐕 €1.30 👫 (htd) [wc] 🛒 🚿 🅰 / [msp] Ⓨ Ⓗ nr 🅰 🔥 🏕 (htd)

Exit A1/E15 junc 13 dir Peronne on D1029 to D1017.
Site on L o'looking canal. Well sp fr all dirs.
3*, Med, mkd, pt shd, EHU (6-10A) €4.30-7.95 (some
rev pol & long lead poss req); red long stay; Eng
spkn; ccard acc; jacuzzi; fishing. "Popular NH; helpful,
pleasant staff & owners; gd play park & pool; gates
locked 2200-0800 - when clsd, park outside; vg rest adj;
rec visit to war museum in Péronne castle; popular with
ralliers; facs need upgrading; vg site, pleasant situation
nr a canal; gd size pitches; gd dog walk along canal;
hypmkt 3km; san facs clean but tired; site self if recep
clsd." **€27.00, 1 Mar-31 Oct.** 2017

PERONNE 3C3 (2km NW Rural) 49.94409, 2.90826
Camping La Tortille, L'Orgibet, 80200 Cléry-sur-Somme
03 22 83 17 59 or 03 22 84 10 45 (LS); jsg-bred@
wanadoo.fr

🐕 €1.30 👫 🚿 🅰 / 🐾 🔥 nr 🏕

Exit A1/E15 junc 13.1 onto D938 to Cléry, dir Péronne.
Site sp on rvside in 5km. 2*, Med, hdstg, hdg, pt shd,
EHU (10A) €3.60; bbq; red long stay; 10% statics; adv
bkg acc; rv fishing; games area; CKE. "Peaceful site; sm,
uneven pitches; clean modern san facs; conv for A1
m'way." **€21.50, 1 Apr-31 Oct.** 2017

PERPIGNAN 8G4 (6km S Rural) 42.63754, 2.89819
Camping Les Rives du Lac, Chemin de la Serre, 66180
Villeneuve-de-la-Raho **04 68 55 83 51;** camping.ville
neuveraho@wanadoo.fr

🐕 €1.60 👫 (htd) [wc] 🛒 🚿 🅰 / [msp] Ⓨ Ⓗ 🅰 🔥 🏕 (htd) 🌊1.5km

Fr A9 exit Perpignan Sud, dir Porte d'Espagne. In
3km turn R onto N9 dir Le Boulou. In 1km after
Auchan supmkt take slip rd to N91 dir Villeneuve-
de-la-Raho. In 2km rd becomes D39, turn R to
site, site on L in 1km. Beware ford on D39 in v wet
weather (usually dry). 2*, Med, hdstg, mkd, pt shd,
pt sl, EHU (6A) inc; bbq (elec, gas); sw nr; 10% statics;
phone; Eng spkn; adv bkg acc; ccard acc; tennis 2km;
watersports 1.5km; fishing 1.5km; CKE. "Lakeside site
with views; poor san facs & insufficient for site size;
busy cycling/jogging path adj; conv trips to Spain; busy
public beach nr." **€20.00, 15 Mar-15 Nov.** 2019

PERROS GUIREC 1D2 (1km SE Coastal) 48.79657,
-3.42689 **Camp Municipal Ernest Renan,** 22700
Louannec **02 96 23 11 78;** www.camping-louannec.fr

🐕 €1.35 👫 [wc] 🛒 🚿 🅰 / [msp] Ⓨ Ⓗ 🅰 🔥 🏕 (htd) 🏖 sand adj

1km W of Louannec on D6. 3*, Lge, unshd, EHU (6A)
inc; gas; TV; Eng spkn; adv bkg acc; watersports adj;
fishing adj; games rm. "Well-kept site; pitches on
seashore; clean san facs; clsd 1200-1530, little parking
space outside; highly rec." **€17.00, 1 Jun-30 Sep.** 2017

PERROS GUIREC 1D2 (3km NW Coastal) 48.82798,
-3.47623 **Sandaya Le Ranolien,** Boulevard du
Semaphore, Ploumanac'h, 22700 Perros-Guirec **02 96
91 65 65;** ranolien@sandaya.fr; www.sanrdaya.co.uk

🐕 €5 👫 (htd) 🛒 🚿 🅰 🅰 / [msp] Ⓨ 🅰 🔥 🏊 🌊 (covrd, htd) 🏖 sand

At Perros-Guirec harbour turn R at Marina foll sp
Trégastel. Up hill above coast into Perros Guirec
town. Cont strt thro traff lts & into La Clarté vill;
strt at traff lts & sharp R at Camping & Le Ranolien
sp. Ent shortly on L. Foll Trégastel sp all way.
5*, V lge, mkd, pt shd, pt sl, serviced pitches; EHU
(16A) inc; 75% statics; Eng spkn; adv bkg acc; ccard
acc; waterslide; horseriding; fishing; tennis; golf. "Excel
beaches; spa; many tour op statics; vg coastal walks
nrby." **€25.00, 10 Apr-18 Sep.** 2019

PERTUIS 10E3 (8km N Rural) 43.75860, 5.50407
Camping de La Bonde, 84240 Cabrières-d'Aigues
04 90 77 63 64; campingdelabonde@wanadoo.fr;
www.campingdelabonde.com

[12] 🐕 €1.80 👫 🚿 🅰 / 🐾 Ⓗ 🔥 🏕

NE fr Pertuis on D956, fork L onto D9 (sp Cabrières
& Etang de la Bonde). At x-rds in 8km turn R onto
D27. Site on L in 200m. 2*, Med, pt shd, EHU (6A)
(poss rev pol) €3.20; gas; sw; 80% statics; adv bkg
acc; ccard acc; tennis; fishing; watersports; games
area; CKE. "Lovely lakeside & beach; ltd facs LS; phone
ahead to check site open; pool 8km; gd cycling area."
€18.00 2017

PESMES 6G2 (0.5km S Rural) 47.27612, 5.56451
Camp Municipal La Colombière, Route de Dole, 70140
Pesmes **03 84 31 20 15;** campcolombiere@aol.com

🐕 €1.20 👫 [wc] 🛒 🅰 / 🐾 Ⓗ nr 🔥 nr

On D475 halfway bet Gray & Dole. S fr Pesmes
immed on L after x-ing rv bdge. N fr Dole, site sp on
R immed bef rest at rv bdge. 2*, Med, hdg, pt shd,
EHU (6-10A) €2.30-3.60; phone; Eng spkn; adv bkg
rec; ccard acc; bike hire. "Picturesque vill; helpful,
friendly staff; gd san facs; vg; no twin axles."
€12.60, 1 May-31 Oct. 2018

PEYRELEAU *10E1* (1.2km NW Rural) *44.19810, 3.19442*
FFCC Camping Les Bords du Tarn, 12720 Mostuéjouls
05 65 62 62 94; lesbordsdutarn@orange.fr;
www.campinglesbordsdutarn.com

🏕 🖸€2 ⚕ ⬜ ♨ ⬧ 🖤 / 🦋 ♔ ☂ ⓘ🪑 🍴 🛶 🛼 🏊 (htd)

Exit A75 junc 44.1 onto D29 to Aguessac; turn L
onto D907 dir Le Rozier & Peyreleau; site on R 1km
bef Le Rozier. NB Do not use exit 44 fr A75 (as sat
nav might instruct). 3*, Med, mkd, pt shd, pt sl, EHU
(10A) €3.50; bbq (charcoal, gas); sw nr; 10% statics;
phone; Eng spkn; adv bkg acc; ccard acc; cycling;
fishing; games rm; canoe hire; tennis; CKE. *"Site in
beautiful area by rv; some v lge pitches; climbing; gd
for rv sports; paragliding; modern san facs; gd walking;
conv Gorges du Tarn & Gorges de la Jonte; excel."*
€36.00, 16 Jun-2 Sep. 2019

"That's changed – Should I let the Club know?"

If you find something on site that's different
from the site entry, fill in a report and let us
know. See camc.com/europereport.

PEZENAS *10F1* (0.5km SW Urban) *43.45419, 3.41573*
Campotel Municipal de Castelsec, Chemin de Castelsec,
34120 Pézenas 04 67 98 04 02; contact@camping-
pezenas.com; www.camping-gites-herault.com

🏕 🖸€1.40 ⚕ ⬜ ♨ ⬧ / 🦋 ☂ nr 🅰

Fr Béziers take N9 to Pézenas; foll Cent Ville sps
fr rndabt at edge of town onto Route de Béziers;
in 600m at next rndabt (at junc with D13) go strt
over into Ave de Verdun; in 400m take 1st L after
McDonalds & pharmacy at ent to Carrefour supmkt;
foll Campotel sps; site on L in 300m. 2*, Sm, mkd,
pt shd, pt sl, terr, EHU (10A) €2.90; TV; 30% statics;
adv bkg acc; tennis adj; CKE. *"Great little site; friendly
staff; clean, dated san facs; some pitches unsuitable lge
o'fits; easy walk/cycle to interesting town; toy museum
worth visit; vg."* €16.00, 1 Apr-30 Oct. 2019

PHALSBOURG *5D3* (3km N Rural) *48.78300, 7.25020*
FFCC Camping de Bouleaux (CC de F), 5 Rue des Trois
Journeaux, 57370 Vilsberg 03 87 24 18 72; info@
campinglesbouleaux.fr; www.campinglesbouleaux.fr
or www.campingclub.asso.fr

🏕 🖸€2 ⚕ ⬜ ♨ ⬧ ⬧ / MSP 🦋 ☂ 🅰

Fr A4 exit junc 44 dir Phalsbourg. At x-rds turn L
sp D661 Sarreguemines. Site on R in 2km. NB Site
ent off steep descent on D661. Lge o'fits take care
leaving site & turning L - watch rear overhangs.
3*, Lge, pt shd, EHU (6A) inc; bbq; 15% statics; phone;
Eng spkn; adv bkg acc; CKE. *"Peaceful, well-kept site;
welcoming, helpful Dutch owners; barrier clsd 1930;
gd facs; access to some pitches poss diff, some uneven;
conv m'way & NH to/fr Germany/Austria; gd NH."*
€18.50, 1 Apr-18 Oct. 2015

PHALSBOURG *5D3* (6km SW Rural) *48.71922,
7.22643* **Camping du Plan Incliné,** Hoffmuhl, 57820
Henridorff 03 87 25 30 13 or 06 71 21 86 91 (mob);
campingplanincline@wanadoo.fr; www.camping
planincline.fr

🏕 🖸€1 ⚕ ⬜ ♨ ⬧ 🖤 / ♔ ♕ ⓘ🪑 ☂ nr 🅰 🏊

Exit A4 at junc 44. In Phalsbourg take D38 twds
Lutzelbourg; turn R onto Arzviller & foll sp
to Henridorff & site on R adj rv (narr ent).
3*, Med, hdg, hdstg, pt shd, EHU (6A) €3; gas; sw nr;
red long stay; 60% statics; phone; Eng spkn; adv bkg
acc; fishing adj; boating adj; CKE. *"In wooded valley;
friendly, helpful owner; vg rest; grnd soft when wet;
cycle path to Strasbourg; adj to unique canal; poss dif
ent for lge units; v poor, run-down site; gd for NH or
short stay."* €18.40, 1 Apr-15 Oct. 2018

PICQUIGNY *3C3* (0.3km E Urban) *49.9445, 2.1458*
Camping De L'Abime (formerly Municipal),
66 Rue du Marais, 80310 Picquigny 03 22 51 25 83
or 06 51 64 40 25; contact@campingdelabime-
picquigny.fr; www.campingdelabime-picquigny.fr

🏕 🖽 ⚕ ⬜ ♨ ⬧ / 🦋 ♔ ☂ nr 🅰

Site sp fr town cent. 2*, Med, pt shd, EHU (10A)
inc; 80% statics; adv bkg rec; rv; fishing. *"Pleasant,
well laid out site; gd, clean, modern san facs; some
shd pitches bet statics; occasional noise fr rlwy line;
WW1 war cemetery nr town; nice, small, simple
site; easy walking dist fr town; many places to visit."*
€26.00, 1 Apr-31 Oct. 2018

PIERRE BUFFIERE *7B3* (2km SE Rural) *45.68937,
1.37101* **Camp Intercommunal Chabanas,** 87260
Pierre-Buffière 05 55 00 96 43; www.pierre-buffiere.com

🏕 🖸€1.14 ⚕ ⬜ ♨ ⬧ / 🦋 ☂ nr 🅰

Approx 20km S of Limoges on A20, take exit 40 onto
D420 S bound; site on L in 500m. Foll sps for 'Stade-
Chabanas'. 3*, Med, hdg, mkd, pt shd, pt sl, EHU (10A)
inc (poss rev pol); phone; adv bkg acc; fishing; CKE.
*"Clean, quiet site; helpful staff; excel clean san facs;
some pitches diff for lge o'fits; no twin axles; warden
on site 1600-2200, but gate poss locked all day LS
(code issued, phone ahead); conv Limoges; excel NH
fr A20; conv for Oradour Sur Glane; gd size plots."*
€13.00, 15 May-30 Sep. 2018

PIERREFITTE SUR SAULDRE *4G3* (6km NE Rural)
47.54444, 2.19138 **Sandaya Les Alicourts,** Domaine
des Alicourts, 41300 Pierrefitte-sur-Sauldre 02 54 88
63 34; www.sandaya.fr/nos-campings/les-alicourts

🏕 🖸€7 ⚕ ⬜ ♨ ⬧ ⬧ / MSP 🦋 ♕ ⓘ🪑 🍴 🅰 🏊 ☂

Fr S of Lamotte-Beuvron, turn L on D923. After
14km turn R on D24E sp Pierrefitte. After 750m turn
L, foll sp to site approx 750m on R. 5*, Med, pt shd,
EHU (6A) inc; bbq; sw; 10% statics; Eng spkn; adv bkg
acc; ccard acc; waterslide; bike hire; games rm; tennis;
CKE. *"Excel, peaceful site; skating rink; kayak/pedalo
hire; extra for lakeside pitches; fitness cent; gd, clean
facs; v lge pitches."* €56.00, 4 May-1 Sep, L22. 2019

www.legrandlarge.com
info@legrandlarge.com
Tél : 00.33.(0)2.33.52.40.75

Le Grand Large ★★★★★
50340 Les Pieux

PIEUX, LES *1C4* (3km SW Coastal) *49.49444, -1.84194*
Le Grand Large, 11 Route de Grand Large; 50340
Les Pieux 02 33 52 40 75; info@legrandlarge.com;
www.legrandlarge.com

🐕 👫(htd) �🅦 ♨ ⏚ ♿ 🖫 ∥ ᴹᴾ 🦋 ♀ ⛨ ⓝnr ♨ 🏊 ⚠ ✦

🏖(htd, indoor) 🖫 🎋 sand adj

Fr ferry at 1st rndabt take 1st exit sp Cent Ville.
Closer to town cent foll old N13 sp Caen. In about
1.5km branch R onto D900 then L onto D650 sp
Carteret. Foll this rd past Les Pieux, cont on D650
to sp Super U. Turn R & foll site sp onto D517,
then D117 for 3km until reaching beach rd to site,
site on L in 2km. 4*, Lge, hdg, mkd, pt shd, EHU
(10A) €6.50; gas; bbq; red long stay; TV; 40% statics;
phone; Eng spkn; adv bkg acc; ccard acc; tennis;
horseriding 4km; games rm; outdoor games. *"Well-
run site; rec for families; 1 dog per pitch; dir access
to superb lge beach; friendly staff; clean modern san
facs; o'fits over 8m by request; barrier clsd 22.00-
08.00; conv Cherbourg ferries but arr not rec after
dark due sm country lanes; outside pitches avail for
early dep for ferries; mkt Fri."*
€38.00, 4 Apr-20 Sep, N07.   2019

See advertisement

PITHIVIERS *4F3* (8km S Rural) *48.10365, 2.24142*
Camping Le Clos des Tourterelles, Rue des Rendillons,
45300 Bouzonville-aux-Bois 02 38 33 01 00 or 06 79
48 36 18 (mob); leclosdestourterelles@sfr.fr;
www.camping-clos-tourterelles.fr

12 👫(htd) � ♨ ⏚ 🖫 ∥ 🦋 ⚠

S fr Pithiviers on D921 twds Jargeau; enter
Bouzonville; turn R immed bef cafe; site 500m on R;
sp in vill. 2*, Med, pt shd, EHU (16A) inc; 90% statics;
adv bkg acc; CKE. *"Ltd space for tourers - phone
ahead rec; friendly, helpful owners; gd NH; cash only."*
€15.00   2019

PLAISANCE *8F2* (0.5km S Urban) *43.92511, 2.54616*
Camping Municipal Le Moulin De L'Horte,
12550 Plaisance 05 65 99 72 07 or 05 65 99 75 07;
mairie.plaisance12@laposte.net

🐕 👫 ♨ ⏚ ∥ 🦋 ♀ 🏊

Fr D999 Albi-Millau, exit at D127 to Plaisance. R
onto D77. Site on R after bdge. 1*, Sm, mkd, pt shd,
EHU (6A); gas; bbq; sw nr; twin axles; TV; 10% statics;
phone; Eng spkn; adv bkg acc; games rm. *" Vg, great
quiet site with rv adj to swim in; excel rest & café nrby
0.2km; sm town but v pleasant."*
€12.00, 15 Jun-15 Sep.   2019

"I like to fill in the reports as I travel from site to site"

You'll find report forms at the back of this
guide, or you can fill them in online at
camc.com/europereport.

PLESTIN LES GREVES *2E2* (4km NE Coastal) *48.66805,
-3.60060* Camp Municipal St Efflam, Rue Lan-Carré,
22310 Plestin-les-Grèves 02 96 35 62 15; camping
municipalplestin@wanadoo.fr; www.camping-
municipal-bretagne.com

🐕 €1.30 👫 � ♨ ⏚ ♿ 🖫 ∥ ᴹᴾ ⛨ ⓐ 🏊nr ⚠ 🎋 sand 150m

Fr Morlaix on D786 thro Plestin-les-Grèves; foll
D786 sp St Efflam down hill to bay; site on R 850m
along bay; sp. 3*, Lge, mkd, pt shd, pt sl, terr, EHU
(10A) €2.50; gas; bbq; sw nr; Eng spkn; adv bkg req;
ccard acc; boating adj; fishing adj; CKE. *"Excel; helpful
recep; v well kept; modern san facs; municipal pool on
site; superb beach nrby; grass pitches liable to
waterlogging in wet weather."*
€14.00, 26 Mar-3 Oct.   2016

FRANCE

PLOERMEL *2F3* (7.6km N Rural) *47.98425, -2.38191*
FFCC Camping Parc Merlin l'Enchanteur, 8 Rue du
Pont, Vallée de l'Yvel, 56800 Loyat **02 97 93 05 52**
or 02 97 73 89 45; camelotpark@wanadoo.fr;
www.campingmerlin.com

12 🐕 €2 ♦♦♦ (htd) 🚾 🛁 ⚙ 🖥 📶 MBP 🦋 ♀ 🛉 nr ⊕ nr 🛒

🏊 (covrd, htd)

Fr Ploërmel take D766 N sp St Malo. In 5km turn L
to Loyat. Site on L on ent vill opp g'ge, adj sm lake.
2*, Med, hdg, mkd, pt shd, EHU (10-16A) €3.50-6 (poss
rev pol); gas; bbq; sw nr; red long stay; 10% statics;
adv bkg acc; ccard acc; games area; tennis; bike
hire; fishing; watersports 4km; CKE. *"Peaceful site;
spacious pitches; welcoming British owners; vg clean
facs; gd indoor pool; poss soggy in winter; new 60km
tarmac cycle trail adj; conv Château Josselin, Lizio &
Brocéliande forest with legend of King Arthur; pleasant
site; excel walking and cycling; site rather unkept."*
€20.00   **2018**

PLOERMEL *2F3* (10km S Rural) *47.86354, -2.44612*
Camping Domaine du Roc, Rue Beaurivage, 56460
Le Roc-St André **02 97 74 91 07** or 06 48 07 68 05
(mob); contact@domaine-du-roc.com;
www.domaine-du-roc.com

🐕 €3 ♦♦♦ 🛁 ⚙ 🖥 📶 🛉 nr ⊕ nr 🛒 nr 🚿 🏊 (covrd, htd)

Fr N on N166 turn R onto D764/D4 to Le Roc-St
André. Site in approx 3km at end of bdge over
Nantes & Brest Canal. 2*, Med, mkd, hdg, pt shd,
EHU (6A) €3.50; bbq; 50% statics; adv bkg acc; ccard
acc; CKE. *"Peaceful, well-situated site; gd touring
base; excel cycle rtes adj canal; v helpful staff."*
€18.00, 1 Apr-1 Nov.   **2015**

PLOERMEL *2F3* (10km NW Rural) *47.96932, -2.47010*
Camping La Vallée du Ninian, Route du Lac, Le
Rocher, 56800 Taupont **02 97 93 53 01; infos@
camping-ninian.com; www.camping-ninian.com**

🐕 €1 ♦♦♦ 🚾 🛁 ⚙ 🖥 📶 🦋 ♀ 🚿 🛒 🏊 (htd) 🚿

🏕 sand 4km

Fr Ploërmel cent foll sp to Taupont or Lac au Duc;
N on D8. Thro vill Taupont take L hand turn sp La
Vallée du Ninian; site on L 1km fr Helléan.
3*, Sm, hdg, pt shd, EHU (3-10A) €2-3.50; sw nr; adv
bkg rec; watersports 4km. *"Farm produce; helpful,
friendly owners; peaceful; gd facs for children; vg."*
€21.50, 1 Apr-30 Sep.   **2015**

PLOMBIERES LES BAINS *6F2* (10km S Rural)
47.92460, 6.47545 **Camp Municipal Val d'Ajol,**
Rue des Oeuvres, 88340 Le Val-d'Ajol **03 29 66 55 17;
camping@valdajol.fr; www.valdajol.fr**

🐕 ♦♦♦ 🚾 🛁 ⚙ 🖥 📶 🦋 ♀ 🛒 nr

Fr N on N57 after Plombières-les-Bains turn onto
D20 sp Le Val-d'Ajol. Site sps in vill.
2*, Sm, hdg, pt shd, EHU (6A) €2.50; TV; phone; adv
bkg acc; CKE. *"Excel site; excel, clean san facs; vg
touring base; lovely; htd covrd pool adj; attractive
area."* **€13.00, 15 Apr-30 Sep.**   **2017**

PLONEVEZ PORZAY *2E2* (3km W Coastal) *48.14458,
-4.26915* **Camping La Plage de Tréguer,** Plage de
Ste Anne-la-Palud, 29550 Plonévez-Porzay **02 98 92
53 52; camping-treguer-plage@wanadoo.fr;
www.camping-treguer-plage.com**

🐕 €2.20 ♦♦♦ (htd) 🚾 🛁 ⚙ 🖥 📶 🦋 ♀ 🛒 nr 🚿 🏊
🏊 (indoor) 🚿 🏕 sand adj

On D107 S fr Châteaulin. After 8km turn R to
Ste Anne-la-Palud & foll sp. 2*, Lge, mkd, hdg,
unshd, EHU (10A) €5; gas; bbq; TV; 10% statics; Eng
spkn; adv bkg acc; ccard acc; games area; games rm;
CKE. *"Well-situated touring base; vg, friendly site;
excel beach with direct access; new san facs (2019)."*
€31.90, 27 Apr-21 Sep.   **2019**

See advertisement

PLOUGASNOU *1D2* (1.5km SE Rural) *48.68548, -3.78530* **Camping Le Trégor,** 130 route du Cosquerou, 29630 Plougasnou **02 98 67 37 64; bookings@ campingdutregor.com; www.campingdutregor.com**

🐕 €1 � 🚿 wc 🛁 🚽 ♨ 📶 ⚌ nr 🔥 🏊 sand 1.2km

At junc of D46 to Plougasnou. Site is on L just bef town sp. Sm, mkd, hdg, pt shd, EHU (6-10A) inc; gas; bbq; sw nr; 40% statics; adv bkg acc; watersports 3km; CKE. *"Well-run site in beautiful area; dated but clean facs; ideal for walking, cycling & fishing; conv Roscoff ferries & Morlaix; phone if req NH after end Oct."*
€15.00, Easter-11 Nov. 2019

PLOUGASTEL DAOULAS *2E2* (5km NE Coastal) *48.40134, -4.35419* **Camping Saint Jean,** 29470 Plougastel-Daoulas **02 98 40 32 90; info@camping saintjean.com; www.campingsaintjean.com**

🐕 €2 ♀♂ (htd) wc 🚿 🛁 ♨ 🚽 ⚌ 🦋 ♈ 🍽 🍺 🔥 🏊 ⚓
🏊 (covrd, htd) 🚣

Fr Brest, take N165 E for approx 12km then leave m'way after Plougastel exit & foll sp. Site in 2km at end of rd by rv. 4*, Med, hdstg, hdg, pt shd, pt sl, terr, EHU (6A) €3 (poss rev pol); bbq; TV; 10% statics; waterslide; games area. *"Nice site by rv; steep in places; gd facs."* **€25.00, 11 Apr-26 Sep.** 2015

PLOUGUENAST *2E3* (2km NW Rural) *48.28653, -2.72145* **Pinábre Camping & Caravaning,** Lingouet 22150 **02 96 26 80 04; campgite-brittany.com**

♀♂ wc 🛁 🚽 ♨ ♈

Site is 50 miles fr St. Malo ferry port, bet Loudeac and Moncontour off the D768. Sm, pt shd, pt sl, EHU (16A) €3; bbq; Eng spkn; adv bkg acc; CKE. *"Gd for walks & cycling; sm friendly site; excel facs; close to N & S coast; open plan, grassy site; quiet; excel."*
€12.00, Apr-Sep. 2018

PLOUGUERNEAU *2E2* (3km N Coastal) *48.63048, -4.52402* **Camping La Grève Blanche,** St Michel, 29880 Plouguerneau **02 98 04 70 35 or 02 98 04 63 97 (LS); lroudaut@free.fr; www.campinggreve blanche.com**

🐕 ♀♂ (htd) wc 🛁 🚽 ♨ 📶 ⚌ 🦋 ♈ 🍽 🍺 nr 🔥 🏊 sand

Fr Lannilis D13 to Plouguerneau, D32 sp La Grève, St Michel (look out for lorry rte sp). Avoid Plouguerneau vill when towing - tight RH bend. 2*, Med, mkd, hdg, unshd, pt sl, terr, EHU (9A) €2.80 (long cable poss req, rev pol); bbq (charcoal, elec, gas); twin axles; 20% statics; bus adj; Eng spkn; adv bkg acc; games area; games rm; CCI. *"Excel location; sea views; helpful staff; facs clean & well-kept; LS recep open eves only; in fog lighthse sounds all night otherwise quiet; walking coastal rte; san facs clean but dated."*
€16.50, 23 Mar-8 Oct. 2018

PLOUGUERNEAU *2E2* (7km NE Coastal) *48.63112, -4.44972* **Camping du Vougot,** Route de Prat-Leden, 29880 Plouguerneau **02 98 25 61 51; campingdu vougot@hotmail.fr; www.campingplagedu vougot.com**

🐕 €2.60 ♀♂ wc 🛁 🚽 ♨ 📶 ⚌ ♈ 🦋 ♈ 🍽 🔥 🏊 sand 250m

Fr N12 at Landerneau exit N onto D770 to Lesneven, then D28/D32 to Plouguerneau. Fr Plouguerneau take D10 dir Guisseny then turn W onto D52 dir Grève-du-Vougot, site sp. 3*, Med, hdg, mkd, pt shd, EHU (10A) €3.30; red long stay; 30% statics; adv bkg acc; ccard acc; watersports nr; CKE. *"Gd walking (GR34); interesting area; excel touring base; excel site; v lge pitches; friendly staff."*
€20.60, 4 Apr-24 Oct. 2015

PLOUHARNEL *2F3* (7km S Coastal) *47.55458, -3.13198* **Camping Municipal De Penthievre,** Avenue Duquesne, Penthievre 56510 St Pierre, Quiberon **02 07 52 33 86; www.saintpierrequiberon.fr**

🐕 €1.04 ♀♂ wc 🛁 🚽 ♨ 📶 ⚌ 🦋 ♈ 🍽 🍺 ⓦ 🔥 🏊 ⚓ adj

Take D768 fr N165 at Auray dir Quiberon. Foll sp at Penthievre. V lge, pt shd, pt sl, EHU (10A) €1.83; gas; bbq; twin axles; phone; bus, train; Eng spkn; ccard acc; games area. *"Traditional French municipal; v friendly; ideal watersports & cycling; coastal scenery; Quiberon magnificent; rests, mkt; park & ride; ideal base for visiting southern Brittany; pool 6km; excel."*
€15.00, 1 Apr-30 Sep. 2016

POET LAVAL, LE *9D2* (2km SE Rural) *44.52889, 5.02300* **Camp Municipal Lorette,** 26160 Le Poët-Laval **04 75 91 00 62 or 04 75 46 44 12 (Mairie); camping. lorette@wanadoo.fr; www.campinglorette.fr**

🐕 €1.80 ♀♂ (htd) wc 🛁 🚽 ♨ 📶 ⚌ 🦋 ♈ 🍽 🍺 Ⓣ nr 🔥 nr 🏊 ⚓

Site 4km W of Dieulefit on D540. 2*, Sm, mkd, pt shd, pt sl, EHU (1A) €3; bus; Eng spkn; adv bkg acc; tennis; CKE. *"Well-kept site with views; lge pitches; clean, modern facs; nr lavender fields (Jun/Jul); mkt in Dieulefit Fri; excel; gd welcome."*
€12.50, 1 May-30 Sep. 2016

POITIERS *7A2* (12km N Rural) *46.65611, 0.30194* **Camping du Futur,** 9 Rue des Bois, 86170 Avanton **05 49 54 09 67; contact@camping-du-futur.com; www.camping-du-futur.com**

🐕 €1.50 ♀♂ wc 🛁 🚽 ♨ 📶 ⚌ 🦋 ♈ 🍽 Ⓣ ⓦ nr 🔥 nr 🏊 ⚓

Exit A10 junc 28. After toll take 1st exit at rndabt sp Avanton. Site well sp fr Avanton, but care needed thro Martigny & hotel complex. 3*, Med, hdg, mkd, pt shd, EHU (6-10A) €3.50-3.8; TV; adv bkg acc; games area; games rm; CKE. *"Attractive, spacious site in rural setting; well-kept & well-run; helpful French owners; vg clean san facs, ltd early ssn; c'van storage; 5 mins Futuroscope & A10; ideal NH or longer; bread, pastries and breakfast can be ordered; mv service pnt; nr Futurscope attraction; ltd shd; lovely & peaceful; quiet parkland setting; conv for Poitiers; excel."*
€19.00, 1 Apr-31 Oct. 2016

POITIERS *7A2* (4.5km S Rural) *46.54367, 0.33230* **Saint-Benoît Camping,** 2 Rue de Passe Lourdain, 86280 St Benoît **05 49 88 48 55; camping.stbenoit@orange.fr; www.ville-saint-benoit.fr**

€0.50 nr nr nr

Fr N or S turn W off D741 to St Benoît, site well sp. 2*, Med, mkd, pt shd, EHU (4A) €3; adv bkg acc; rv fishing adj; watersports adj; CKE. *"Pleasant 10 min walk into vill; gd cheap bus service fr vill to Poitiers."* **€16.00, 1 Jun-6 Sep. 2015**

POIX DE PICARDIE *3C3* (0.3km SW Rural) *49.77621, 1.97467* **Camp Municipal Le Bois des Pêcheurs,** Route de Forges-les-Eaux, 80290 Poix-de-Picardie **03 22 90 11 71 or 03 22 90 32 90 (Mairie); camping@ville-poix-de-picardie.fr; www.ville-poix-de-picardie.fr**

€1.50 WD MSP nr nr nr

Fr town cent on D901 dir Beauvais, in 100m turn R onto D919 opp Citroën agent sp Camping; site on R in 500m. Fr Beauvais, turn L at bottom of steep hill opp Citroën agent; site in 500m on R. 3*, Med, hdg, mkd, hdstg, pt shd, EHU (6A) €4 (poss long lead req); bbq; red long stay; TV; Eng spkn; adv bkg acc; rv fishing adj; tennis 800m; bike hire; games rm; CKE. *"Pleasant, peaceful, tidy site in delightful area; v clean modern san facs; htd covrd pool 800m; gd touring base; vg walking & cycling; bar 500m; train to Amiens; lovely mkt Sun; rec; every 3rd night free; gas 300m; sh walk to town and supmkt; vg."* **€18.00, 1 Apr-30 Sep. 2018**

POLIGNY *6H2* (1km SW Rural) *46.83455, 5.69840* **Camp Communautaire de la Croix du Dan,** 39800 Poligny **03 84 37 01 35; cccgrimont@wanadoo.fr; www.ville-poligny.fr**

WD nr

Fr SW on N83 turn R at rndabt sp 'Centre'; site on R immed bef town sp Poligny. Fr N & NW take D905 into & thro town cent (no L turn on N83 S of Poligny), then foll sp Lons-Le Saunier. Site on L bef sportsgrnd - look for m'van sp. Do not overshoot ent, as diff to see. N5 fr E not rec as steep & hairpins. 2*, Med, mkd, pt shd, EHU (10A) €6.40; twin axles; phone; Eng spkn; CKE. *"Excel, clean, tidy site; helpful warden; pretty town; if recep clsd ring number on board to open barrier."* **€15.00, 15 Jun-20 Sep. 2017**

PONS (CHARENTE MARITIME) *7B2* (0.5km W Urban) *45.57791, -0.55552* **Camp Municipal Le Paradis,** 1 Ave de Poitou, 17800 Pons **05 46 91 36 72; campingmunicipalpons@voila.fr; www.pons-ville.org**

€1.76 MSP nr

Well sp fr town o'skts. 3*, Med, mkd, pt shd, EHU (6-10A) inc (poss rev pol); TV; Eng spkn; rv fishing 200m. *"Excel site in attractive grnds; helpful, friendly, super wardens; interesting town; conv for Saintes, Cognac, Royan; free wifi in snack bar; gd sized pitches; pool 100m; waterslide 100m; easy walk to old city; excel; some rd noise."* **€22.00, 1 May-30 Sep. 2019**

PONT AUDEMER *3D2* (2km NW Rural) *49.36660, 0.48739* **Camp Municipal Risle-Seine Les Etangs,** 19 Route des Etangs, 27500 Toutainville **02 32 42 46 65; camping@ville-pont-audemer.fr; www.ville-pont-audemer.fr**

WD MSP nr

Fr Le Havre on A131/E05 cross rv at Pont de Normandie (toll). Take D580 & at junc 3 branch R & take 2nd exit onto D22 sp Beuzeville. At edge of Fiquefleur take D180, then D675 dir Pont-Audemer. In Toutainville foll site sp, turn L just bef A13 underpass, then immed R. Site approx 2km on R. 3*, Med, mkd, hdg, pt shd, serviced pitches; EHU (5-10A) €3.95; bbq; red long stay; TV; bus; Eng spkn; adv bkg acc; ccard acc; fishing; bike hire; watersports; games area; tennis 1.5km; games rm; canoeing. *"Lovely, well-run site; helpful warden; barrier clsd 2200-0830 but flexible for ferry; many leisure activities; htd pool 1.5km; poss school groups at w/end; vg for dogs; 1hr Le Havre ferry; Fri mkt Pont-Audemer; conv NH; excel; facs stretched LS; boggy when wet; pitches are narr which means car has to go at the front of your pitch."* **€21.00, 25 Mar-31 Oct, N13. 2016**

PONT AVEN *2F2* (13km N Rural) *47.92512, -3.68888* **Camping Les Genêts d'Or,** KermerourPont Kereon 29380 Bannalec **02 98 39 54 35; info@holidaybrittany.com; www.holidaybrittany.com**

€1.50 WD nr

Fr Pont Aven/Bannalec exit on N165 N to Bannalec on D4; after rlwy x-ing turn R sp Quimperlé. In 1km turn R, sp Le Trévoux; site on L 500m. 3*, Sm, hdg, mkd, pt shd, pt sl, EHU (6A) €3.50; bbq (gas); red long stay; 10% statics; Eng spkn; adv bkg acc; games rm; bike hire; CKE. *"Lovely, peaceful, well-kept site in orchard; ACSI acc; lge pitches; welcoming, helpful, friendly, lovely British owners; immac san facs; Bannalec in walking dist; lovely area - excel touring base; highly rec."* **€19.00, 31 May-30 Sep. 2015**

PONT AVEN *2F2* (11km SSW Coastal) *47.79640, -3.77489* **Camping Les Chaumières,** 24 Hameau de Kerascoët, 29920 Névez **02 98 06 73 06; info@camping-des-chaumieres.com; www.camping-des-chaumieres.com**

€1.50 WD MSP nr nr nr sand 800m

S fr Pont-Aven thro Névez to Kerascoët. 2*, Med, hdg, mkd, pt shd, serviced pitches; EHU (4-10A) €3.40-4.30; bbq; Eng spkn; adv bkg req; CKE. *"Excel, well-organised, peaceful, beautiful site; immac facs poss stretched high ssn; gd play & games areas; sandy bay/beaches, cliff walks; san facs refurbished and upgraded; highly rec; friendly owner; recep clsd LS, but owner avail via mob."* **€18.00, 15 May-19 Sep. 2018**

PONT AVEN *2F2* (6km SW Coastal) *47.79906, -3.79033*
Sandaya Deux Fontaines, Raguenès, 29920 Névez
02 98 06 81 91; fon@sandaya.fr; www.sandaya.co.uk
🛒 €5 ♨ ♨ ♨ ♨ 🍴 🐾 ♨ (htd) 🏊 sand 4km

Leave N165/E60 at Kérampaou foll sp D24 twds
Pont Aven. In approx 4.5km turn R (S) foll sp Névez
then Raguenès. Site 3km fr Névez. 4*, Lge, mkd,
pt shd, EHU (10A) inc; bbq (charcoal); 80% statics;
adv bkg acc; tennis. *"Busy high ssn; popular with
British families; o'night facs for m'vans; 25 meter
conn lead req'd; price inc waterpark acc & kids club."*
€33.00, 10 Apr-13 Sep. 2019

"I need an on-site restaurant"

We do our best to make sure site information
is correct, but it is always best to check any
must-have facilities are still available or will
be open during your visit.

PONT AVEN *2F2* (8km SW Coastal) *47.79597, -3.79877*
Camping du Vieux Verger, Raguenès-Plage, 29920
Névez 02 98 06 86 08; contact@campingduvieux
verger.com; www.campingduvieuxverger.com
🛒 ♨ ♨ ♨ ♨ ⊕ 🐾 🏊 sand 500m

Fr Pont-Aven take D783 dir Concarneau; in 2.5km
L onto D77 to Névez; foll sp Raguenès-Plage; 1st
site on R. Foll 'Vieux Verger' sps. 2*, Med, hdg, mkd,
pt shd, EHU (4-10A) €3.20-4.20 (poss rev pol); phone;
CKE. *"Well-run, well-kept site with pool & waterslides;
statics (sep area); highly rec LS; excel; gd for young
children; excel site; gd value; many attractive beaches
nrby."* **€23.70, 14 Apr-15 Sep.** 2018

PONT AVEN *2F2* (8km SW Coastal) *47.79330, -3.80110*
Camping Raguénès-Plage, 19 Rue des Îles à
Raguénès, 29920 Névez 02 98 06 80 69; leraguenes
plage@orange.fr; www.camping-le-raguenes-
plage.com
🛒 €3.20 ♨ (htd) ♨ ♨ ♨ ♨ 🐾 ♨ 🍴 ⊕ 🐾 ♨ ♨
🏊 (covrd, htd) 🏖 🏊 sand adj

Fr Pont-Aven take D783 dir Trégunc; in 2.5km
turn L for Névez, foll sps to Raguénès fr Névez. Or
fr N165 take D24 at Kérampaou exit; in 3km turn R
to Nizon; at church in vill turn R onto D77 to Névez;
site on L 3km after Névez.
4*, Lge, mkd, hdstg, pt shd, EHU (6-15A) €4-6.90; gas;
bbq; 20% statics; Eng spkn; adv bkg rec; ccard acc;
games rm; watersports school adj; sauna; tennis nr;
bike hire; games area; waterslide; horseriding; CKE.
*"Pretty, wooded, family-run site; trampoline; statics
sep area; private path to beach; clean facs; 1st class
site."* **€33.00, 20 Apr-30 Sep, B12.** 2017

See advertisement.

PONT D'AIN *9A2* (1.4km SE Urban) *46.04680, 5.34446*
Camping de l'Oiselon, Rue E'mile Lebreüs, 01160
Pont-d'Ain 04 74 39 05 23; campingoiselon@free.fr;
www.campingpontdain.e-monsite.com
🛒 ♨ ♨ ♨ ♨ ♨ 🐾 ♨ ⊕ ♨ ♨ ♨ 🏊

Fr A42 exit Pont-d'Ain foll D90 to vill. In vill cent
turn R on D1075. Turn L immed after x-ing Rv L'Ain.
Foll rd passing tennis club on L. Site on L, clearly sp.
3*, Lge, pt shd, EHU (6-10A) €2.40-3.10 (poss rev pol);
bbq; sw; 30% statics; Eng spkn; adv bkg acc; fishing;
canoeing; tennis adj; games area; horseriding 5km;
bike hire; CKE. *"Gd, well-run site with easy access,
v lge; helpful, friendly staff; gd clean san facs; cash
only; site needs TLC (early ssn 2010); gd NH; excel
site."* **€17.50, 17 Mar-14 Oct.** 2018

PONT DE L'ARCHE 3D2 (0.8km N Urban) 49.3060, 1.1546 **Camp Municipal Eure et Seine,** Quai Maréchal Foch, 27340 Pont-de-l'Arche 02 35 23 06 71 or 02 32 98 90 70 (Mairie); campeure@orange.fr or campeure@pontdelarche.fr; www.pontdelarche.fr

🐕 €1.20 ♟♟ ⬛ ⛆ ♿ 🍴 ⚊ / 🍵 Ⓨ ⑭ 🐛nr ⅏

Fr Rouen S on D6015 turn 1st L after x-ing rv bdge, drive downhill then L under bdge & strt on for 300m (foll Camping Car sp at traff lts, do not go into town), site on R. Restricted width on app. Or exit A13 junc 20 onto D321 to Pont-de-l'Arche; turn L at War Memorial onto Place du Souvenir; in 300m to R at rv; site on L in 200m. 2*, Med, mkd, pt shd, EHU (6-10A) €6-6.60; red long stay; 4% statics; phone; adv bkg rec; ccard acc; rv fishing adj; CKE. *"Pleasant, peaceful, clean rvside site in attractive medieval town; sm pitches; helpful warden; gd, modern san facs; recep 1000-1200 & 1600-2000; access only after 1600, Aire outside site accessible 24/7; many shops clsd Wed pm; bus fr town to Rouen; popular NH & longer; beautiful site nr Gothic church; excel; superb setting; v busy so arrive early or ring ahead; sh walk to town."* **€12.00, 1 Apr-30 Oct.** **2017**

PONT DE SALARS 7D4 (1.5km N Rural) 44.29150, 2.72571 **Parc Camping du Lac,** 12290 Pont-de-Salars 05 65 46 84 86; contact@parc-du-lac.com; www.campingpontdesalars.com

♟♟ ⬛ ⛆ ⚥ ♿ ⚊ / Ⓨ ⑭ 🐝 🐛 ⅏ ♪ 🛶 🎣

Fr Rodez on D911 La Primaube-Millau rd, turn L bef ent Pont-de-Salars. Site sp. 3*, Lge, mkd, pt shd, pt sl, terr, EHU (3-6A) €2.50-3.50; gas; bbq; sw; TV; 90% statics; phone; adv bkg acc; ccard acc; fishing; sailing. *"Beautiful situation; poor for c'vans, OK m'vans; diff lge o'fits; blocks req; site poss unclean end of ssn; ltd facs."* **€17.00, 1 Jun-30 Sep.** **2017**

> # "Satellite navigation makes touring much easier"
>
> Remember most sat navs don't know if you're towing or in a larger vehicle – always use yours alongside maps and site directions.

PONT DE SALARS 7D4 (8km S Rural) 44.21500, 2.77777 **Camping Soleil Levant,** Lac de Pareloup, 12290 Canet-de-Salars 05 65 46 03 65; contact@camping-soleil-levant.com; www.camping-soleil-levant.com

🐕 €2 ♟♟ (htd) ⬛ ⚊ ⛆ ⚥ ♿ ⚊ / 🐝 🍵 Ⓨ ♪ 🐛nr ⅏ ♪

Exit A75 junc 44.1 onto D911 to Pont-de-Salars, then S on D993 dir Salles-Curan. Site in 8km bef bdge on L. 3*, Lge, mkd, pt shd, pt sl, terr, EHU (6A) inc; gas; bbq; sw nr; TV; 50% statics; Eng spkn; adv bkg acc; ccard acc; watersports; games area; tennis; games rm; fishing; CKE. *"Lovely lakeside site; excel san facs; vg; well run by friendly couple."* **€30.00, 1 May-30 Sep.** **2017**

PONT DE VAUX 9A2 (4km NE Rural) 46.44394, 4.98313 **Camping Les Ripettes,** St Bénigne, 01190 Chavannes-sur-Reyssouze 03 85 30 66 58; info@camping-les-ripettes.com; camping-les-ripettes.pagesperso-orange.fr

🐕 €1.50 ♟♟ (htd) ⬛ ⚊ ⛆ ♿ ⚊ / MSP 🐝 🍵 ♪ 🐛 ⅏ 🛶

Take D2 fr Pont-de-Vaux sp St Trivier-des-Courtes for 3km. Immed after water tower on R turn L onto D58 sp Romenay, then immed L. Site well sp on L in 100m. 3*, Med, hdg, mkd, pt shd, pt sl, EHU (10A) €4; 1% statics; phone; Eng spkn; adv bkg rec; ccard acc; games area; CKE. *"Lovely, popular site in beautiful location; spacious pitches; friendly, helpful owner; immac facs; gd pool area; gd touring base; hard to beat; ACSI card acc; one of the best; cycle rte maps at TO in Pont de Vaux; memb of La Via Natura; promoting many eco ideas; excel."* **€23.70, 1 Apr-30 Sep.** **2018**

PONT DE VAUX 9A2 (0.5km W Urban) 46.42979, 004.93296 **Camping Champ d'Été,** Lieu-dit Champ D'Eté, 01190 Reyssouze 0033 385 23 96 10; info@camping-champ-dete.com; www.camping-champ-dete.com

🐕 €3 ♟♟ (htd) ⬛ ⚊ ⚥ ♿ ⚊ / 🐝 🍵 Ⓨ nr ⑭ nr 🐛nr ⅏ ♪

Fr A6 N J27, take D906 dir Pont-de-Vaux. In town, foll Base-de-Loisirs & camping sp. 4*, Med, hdstg, mkd, pt shd, EHU (10A) inc; bbq; TV; 20% statics; bus adj; Eng spkn; adv bkg acc; ccard acc; games rm; CKE. *"Walking dist to town; adj to pk & free sw pool; v clean san facs; friendly owners; htd pool adj; gd for touring Burgundy area; gd for long or sh stays; some pitches tight for lge o'fits; vg."* **€23.00, 25 Mar-15 Oct.** **2016**

PONT DU CHATEAU 9B1 (5km SSW Urban) 45.77546, 3.24197 **Camping Les Ombrages,** Rue Pont du Château, 63111 Dallet 04 73 83 10 97; lesombrages@hotmail.com; www.lesombrages.nl

♟♟ ⬛ ⚊ ⚥ / 🐝 🍵 Ⓨ ⑭ ♪ 🐛 ⅏ ♪ 🛶 🎣

E fr Clermont Ferrand on D769; 200m bef x-ing Rv Allier turn R onto D783/D769A; 50m after x-ring rv turn L into Rue Pont du Château; site on L in 400m. 3*, Sm, shd, EHU (6A) (rev pol) €3.50; sw nr; TV; canoeing; fishing; games rm. *"Peaceful, pretty, gd site; excel pitches by rv; gd for fishing & canoeing; mosquitoes; gd san facs."* **€25.00, 14 May-15 Sep.** **2015**

PONT FARCY 1D4 (0.5km N Rural) 47.46810, 4.35709 **Camp Municipal Pont-Farcy,** Quai de la Vire, 14380 Pont-Farcy 02 31 68 32 06 or 02 31 68 86 48; pontfarcy@free.fr; www.pont-farcy.fr

🐕 €1 ♟♟ ⬛ ⚊ ⚥ ♿ ⚊ / MSP 🐝 Ⓨ nr ⑭ nr 🐛nr ⅏

Leave A84 junc 39 onto D21 to Pont-Farcy; site on L at ent to vill. 3*, Med, hdg, mkd, pt shd, terr, EHU (10A) €2.50; 30% statics; phone; adv bkg acc; boating adj; rv fishing adj; tennis; bike hire; CKE. *"Barrier poss locked periods during day but parking avail; bar 500m; helpful, friendly warden; clean facs; mosquitoes at dusk."* **€10.00, 3 April-30 Sep.** **2018**

PONT L'ABBE *2F2* (7km S Rural) *47.81241, -4.22147*
Camping L'Océan Breton, Route Kerlut, 29740 Lesconil
02 98 82 23 89; info@yellohvillage-loceanbreton.com;
www.camping-bretagne-oceanbreton.fr or
www.yellohvillage.co.uk

🎣 €6 👪(htd) 🆆 ♨ ᵫ 🗑 ∥ ᴹˢᴾ 🦋 𝕐 ⓗ å 🖳 ⁄Δ ✦
🏊(covrd, htd, indoor) 🏖 🌳 sand 2km

Fr Pont l'Abbé S on D102 to Plobannalec & head
for Lesconil; site on L after supmkt. 4*, Lge, hdstg,
mkd, hdg, pt shd; serviced pitches; EHU (5A) inc; gas;
red long stay; 80% statics; phone; Eng spkn; adv bkg
acc; ccard acc; tennis; games area; sauna; waterslide;
bike hire; kids clubs; bowling; adventure trail; CKE.
"Excel site for families; fitness rm; spacious pitches."
€50.00, 06 Apr-15 Sep, B39. **2019**

PONT L'ABBE *2F2* (8.6km S Rural/Coastal) *47.79715,*
-4.22868 **Camping des Dunes,** 67 Rue Paul Langevin,
29740 Plobannalec-Lesconil 02 98 87 81 78;
contact@camping-desdunes.com; www.camping-
desdunes.com

🎣 €2.10 👪(wd) ♨ 🅯 ᵫ 🗑 ∥ ᴹˢᴾ 𝕐 ⓗ nr å 🖳 nr ⁄Δ 🌳 sand 100m

Fr Pont l'Abbé, S on D102 for 5km to Plobannelec;
over x-rds; in 1km turn R, 100m after sports
field; green sp to site in 1km. 3*, Med, hdg, mkd,
pt shd, EHU (8A) €3.70; bbq; adv bkg acc; ccard
acc; games area; games rm; CKE. *"Helpful owner;
nr fishing port; gd walking, cycling & birdwatching;
site gd for children; access to beach with amazing
granite rock formations; red early ssn; well cared for."*
€25.70, 30 Mar-29 Sep. **2019**

PONT L'ABBE *2F2* (10km NW Rural) *47.89462, -4.32863*
Camping Kerlaz, Route de la Mer, 29670 Tréguennec
02 98 87 76 79; contact@kerlaz.com; www.kerlaz.com

🎣 €1.30 👪(wd) ♨ 🗑 ∥ ᴹˢᴾ 🦋 🖳 nr ⁄Δ 🏊(covrd, htd)
🌳 sand 2km

Fr Plonéour-Lanvern take D156 SW to Tréguennec.
3*, Med, hdg, pt shd, EHU (10A); bbq; 30% statics; Eng
spkn; adv bkg acc; ccard acc; bike hire. *"Nice, friendly
site; pleasant owners; attractive site; gd for cycling."*
€24.00, 1 Apr-30 Sep. **2017**

PONT ST ESPRIT *9D2* (10km NW Rural) *44.29808,*
4.56535 **Camping Les Cigales,** 30760 Aiguèze
04 66 82 18 52; www.camping-cigales.fr

12 🎣 €2 👪 🅯 🗑 ∥ ᴹˢᴾ ᵠ ⓗ nr 🖳 nr 🏊(htd)

N fr Pont-St Esprit on D6086 take D901 NW twd
Barjac & D141 to St Martin-d'Ardèche. Site on L bef
rv bdge. Avoid app fr St Martin-d'Ardèche over narr
suspension bdge. Care at ent. Diff for lge units.
2*, Sm, mkd, shd, EHU (4-10A) €3.13-5.88; gas; bbq;
sw nr; 25% statics; adv bkg acc; ccard acc; CKE.
*"Helpful, friendly owner; easy walk to St Martin-
d'Ardèche."* **€21.00** **2015**

PONT ST ESPRIT *9D2* (6km NW Rural) *44.30388,*
4.58443 **Camping Le Pontet,** 07700 St Martin-d'Ardèche
04 75 04 63 07 or 04 75 98 76 24; contact@camping
lepontet.com; www.campinglepontet.com

🎣 €3 👪 🆆 🅯 ᵫ 🗑 ∥ ᴹˢᴾ 🦋 ᵠ 𝕐 ⓗ å 🖳 ⁄Δ 🏊

N86 N of Pont-St Esprit; turn L onto D290 at sp
Gorges de l'Ardèche & St Martin-d'Ardèche, site on
R after 3km, sp. 3*, Med, mkd, pt shd, EHU (6A) €3.60
(rev pol); gas; sw nr; 5% statics; phone; Eng spkn;
adv bkg acc; CKE. *"Vg; helpful owners; peaceful out
of ssn; facs stretched when busy; online bkg fee €10."*
€22.00, 8 Apr-25 Sep. **2017**

PONT ST ESPRIT *9D2* (8km NW Rural) *44.34423,*
4.60434 **FFCC Camping Les Truffières,** 201 Route
de St Ramèze, 07700 St Marcel-d'Ardèche 04 75 04
68 35 or 06 82 01 28 30 (mob); soulier.valerie@
wanadoo.fr; www.camping-les-truffieres.com

12 🎣 €1.60 👪(htd) ♨ ᵫ 🗑 ∥ ᴹˢᴾ 🦋 𝕐 ⓗ å 🖳 nr ⁄Δ ✦ 🏊

S fr Bourg-St Andéol, turn W on D201; in vill foll sp
to site located approx 3km W of vill. 2*, Med, mkd,
pt shd, terr, EHU (6A) €6.60 (poss rev pol); gas;
70% statics; adv bkg acc; CKE. *"Friendly owners;
glorious views; gd san facs; conv NH nr A7; v pleasant;
tricky without motor mover (trees)."* **€17.00** **2017**

PONTAILLER SUR SAONE *6G1* (0.8km E Rural)
47.30817, 5.42518 **Camping La Chanoie,** 46 Rue de
la Chanoie, 21270 Pontailler-sur-Saône 03 80 67 21 98;
camping.municipal1@orange.fr; www.camping-
lachanoie.com

🎣 €1.55 👪(htd) 🆆 ♨ 🌡 🗑 ∥ ᴹˢᴾ 🦋 𝕐 ⓗ å 🖳 nr ⁄Δ

E fr Pontailler-sur-Saône on D959; pass town hall
& TO on R; after bdg take 1st L sp Camping; site in
500m. Fr W on D959 turn R bef bdg & bef ent town.
3*, Med, hdg, mkd, pt shd, EHU (6-10A) €2.85-4.10;
bbq; sw nr; red long stay; 80% statics; bus; adv bkg
acc; games area; tennis; watersports adj; games rm;
fishing adj; CKE. *"Attractive sm town; polite & helpful
owner; clean san facs, poss stretched high ssn; vg; OK
NH."* **€17.30, 15 Mar-15 Oct.** **2019**

PONTARLIER *6H2* (1km SE Rural) *46.90024, 6.37425*
FFCC Camping Le Larmont, Rue du Toulombief, 25300
Pontarlier 03 81 46 23 33; lelarmont.pontarlier@
wanadoo.fr; www.camping-pontarlier.fr

🎣 €1 👪(htd) 🆆 ♨ ᵫ 🗑 ∥ ᴹˢᴾ ᵠ å 🖳 ⁄Δ

Leave N57 at Pontarlier Gare & foll site sp. Site
uphill, turning nr Nestlé factory. 3*, Med, hdstg,
unshd, terr, EHU (10A) €4; gas; 20% statics; Eng spkn;
adv bkg acc; horseriding adj; CKE. *"Friendly; easy
access; clean san facs; ltd pitches for awnings; site self
out of office hrs; skiing winter; well-behaved zebra on
site; excel; horseriding next to site; rec."*
€22.50, 1 Jan-11 Nov. **2019**

FRANCE

PONTARLIER *6H2* (12km S Rural) *46.81176, 6.30326*
Camp Municipal, 8 Rue du Port, 25160 St Point-Lac
03 81 69 61 64 or 03 81 69 62 08 (Mairie); camping-
saintpointlac@orange.fr; www.camping-saint
pointlac.fr

🏕 €1.50 ♯♯(htd) 🚾 🛉 ♿ 🖳 ∥ 🛢 🦋 ᵠ ▼ ⑭nr 🛖 🎱 ⚠
🌳 🏖adj

Exit Pontarlier S on N57 dir Lausanne, turn R on
D437 dir Malbuisson; in 6km turn R onto D129 thro
Les Grangettes to St Point-Lac. Site sp on L.
3*, Med, mkd, hdstg, pt shd, EHU (16A) €4.50; bbq;
5% statics; Eng spkn; adv bkg rec; ccard acc; games
area; CKE. *"Delightful, well-kept lakeside site in
beautiful position; sm pitches, some may be diff for
large units to get in to; friendly staff; vg, clean san facs;
m'van o'night area with facs opp; gd fishing, walking,
birdwatching; sw; gd touring; rec adv bkg wkends/high
ssn; excel."* €20.00, 1 May-30 Sep.   2017

PONTAUBAULT *2E4* (0km W Urban) *48.62983,
-1.35205* **Camping La Vallée de la Sélune,** 7 Rue
Maréchal Leclerc, 50220 Pontaubault 02 33 60 39 00;
campselune@wanadoo.fr; www.camping-manche.com

🏕 €1.30 ♯♯ 🚾 🛉 ♿ 🖳 ∥ ᵠ ▼ 🛖 🎱 ⚠

Foll sp to Pontaubault (well sp fr all dirs). In vill
head twd Avranches. Turn L immed bef bdge
over Rv Sélune. In 100m turn L, site strt in 100m,
well sp. 2*, Med, mkd, pt shd, pt sl, EHU (10A) inc;
red long stay; 10% statics; adv bkg rec; ccard acc;
horseriding nr; fishing adj; golf nr; tennis adj; CKE.
*"Relaxing, clean, tidy, pleasant site in sm vill; vg, clean
san facs; conv Mont St Michel & Cherbourg ferries; gd
NH; cycling nr; friendly Yorkshire owner; on cycle rte."*
€15.00, 1 Apr-20 Oct.   2018

PONTCHATEAU *2G3* (7km W Rural) *47.44106, -2.15981*
Le Château du Deffay, Ste Reine-de-Bretagne, 44160
Pontchâteu 02 40 88 00 57; info@camping-le-
deffay.com; www.camping-le-deffay.com

🏕 €1 ♯♯ 🚾 🛉 ♿ 🖳 ∥ 🛢 🦋 ᵠ ▼ ⑭ 🛖 🎱 ⚠ 🌳
🏖(covrd, htd) 🎣

Leave N165 at junc 13 onto D33 twd Herbignac. Site
on R approx 1.5km after Le Calvaire de la Madeleine
x-rds, 270m past Chateau ent. Site sp fr by-pass.
4*, Lge, mkd, hdg, pt shd, pt sl, terr, EHU (10A); bbq
(charcoal, gas); TV; 40% statics; Eng spkn; adv bkg
acc; ccard acc; lake fishing; bike hire; tennis; games
rm; golf 10km; CKE. *"Excel, beautiful site with trees
in grnds of chateau by lake; free pedalos; friendly,
helpful, welcoming staff; excel clean san facs; some
pitches lakeside & not fenced; mkt Mon; gd value rest."*
€38.00, 1 May-30 Sep, B25.   2019

PONTGIBAUD *7B4* (0.2km S Rural) *45.82978, 2.84517*
FFCC Camp Municipal La Palle, 3 Avenue du General
de Gaulle, 63230 Pontgibaud 04 73 88 96 99 or 04 73
88 70 42 (LS); mairie.pontgibaud@wanadoo.fr;
www.ville-pontgibaud.fr/camping-municipal

🏕 ♯♯(htd) 🚾 🛉 ♿ 🖳 ∥ 🛢 ᵠ ⑭ 🎱nr ⚠ 🌳

At W end of Pontgibaud turn S over bdge on D986 &
site in 500m on L, past site for La Palle Chalets.
3*, Med, hdg, mkd, hdstg, pt shd, EHU (10-16A) inc;
bbq; sw nr; red long stay; Eng spkn; adv bkg acc;
games area; tennis 400m; CKE. *"Pleasant, clean, tidy
site nr sm rv; helpful staff; gd touring base; pop
concerts once a week high ssn; conv Vulcania
exhibition cent; bike hire 400m; v lge hdg plots;
minimal rd & rlwy noise; well maintained; friendly;
easy flat walk to town; gd base for Puy de Dome."*
€17.00, 15 Apr-30 Sep.   2018

> ## "There aren't many sites open at this time of year"
>
> If you're travelling outside peak season
> remember to call ahead to check site opening
> dates – even if the entry says 'open all year'.

PONTORSON *2E4* (0.9km NW Rural) *48.55805,
-1.51444* **Camping Haliotis,** Chemin des Soupirs,
50170 Pontorson 02 33 68 11 59; camping.haliotis@
wanadoo.fr; www.camping-haliotis-mont-saint-
michel.com

🏕 €2 ♯♯(htd) 🚾 🛉 ♿ 🖳 ∥ 🛢 ᵠ ▼ ⑭nr 🛖 🎱 ⚠ 🏊(htd) 🎣

Exit A84 junc 33 onto N175 dir Pontorson; foll sp
Cent Ville/Mont-St-Michel. Site well sp. 3*, Lge, mkd,
hdg, pt shd, pt sl, EHU (10-16A) inc (poss rev pol); gas;
bbq; 25% statics; phone; bus 400m; Eng spkn; adv bkg
rec; ccard acc; boating; games area; tennis; rv fishing;
games rm; bike hire; sauna; CKE. *"Popular, well-kept,
busy, superb site; lge pitches; friendly, helpful owners;
immac, unisex san facs; lovely pool & bar; rvside walk
to town; cycle rte/bus to Mont St Michel; highly rec;
serviced pitches; pitches with private bthrms avail; spa;
library; avoid pitches 77-89 due to noise fr bins; excel."*
€30.00, 30 Mar-4 Nov, N17.   2018

PONTORSON *2E4* (8km NW Rural) *48.59415, -1.59855*
Camping Les Couesnons, Route de St Malo, 35610
Roz-sur-Couesnon 02 99 80 26 86; contact@les-
couesnons.com; www.lescouesnons.com

🏕 €2 ♯♯(htd) 🚾 🛉 ♿ 🖳 ∥ 🛢 ᵠ ▼ ⑭ 🛖 ⚠

Exit N175/N176 NW onto D797 dir St Malo on
coastal rd; site sp 700m past Roz-sur-Couesnon on
R. Turn R at Les Couesnons Rest. Site behind.
3*, Sm, hdg, mkd, pt shd, EHU (6A) €3; bbq
(charcoal, gas); red long stay; TV; 10% statics; Eng
spkn; adv bkg acc; ccard acc; games rm; games
area; CKE. *"Excel site; Mont St Michel 8km; ACSI
acc; vg, spotless, htd facs; gd rest & bar; highly rec."*
€23.00, 1 Apr-31 Oct.   2017

PONTRIEUX *2E3* (0.5km W Rural) *48.69493, -3.16365*
Camping de Traou Mélédern (Moisan), Traou Mélédern, 22260 Pontrieux 02 96 95 69 27; campingpontrieux@ free.fr; www.camping-pontrieux.com

🔟 🐕 €1 ♔♔ WD ♨ ⚅ 🖵 ⋌ 🔫nr 🏛

N on D787 fr Guingamp; on ent town sq turn sharp L sp Traou Mélédern, cross rv bdge & turn R alongside church. Site in 400m. Access poss diff for lge o'fits; steep exit on 1-way system. 2*, Med, mkd, hdg, pt shd, pt sl, EHU (8A) €3.50; bbq; phone; Eng spkn; adv bkg acc; CKE. *"In orchard; excel touring base; friendly owner; quiet but some daytime factory noise; steep junc nr site poss problem for lge o'fits; gd."*
€17.50 **2016**

PORGE, LE *7C1* (9km W Coastal) *44.89430, -1.20181*
Camping La Grigne, Ave de l'Océan, 33680 Le Porge 05 56 26 54 88; info@lagrigne.com; www.camping-leporge.fr

🐕 €1.90 ♔♔ WD ♨ ⚅ 🖵 ⋌ 🦋 Y ♨ 🔫 🏛 600m

Fr Bordeaux ring rd take N215 twd Lacaneau. In 22km at Ste Hélène D5 to Saumos & onto Le Porge. Site on L of rd to Porge-Océan in approx 9km. 3*, V lge, mkd, shd, pt sl, terr, EHU (10A) €5; gas; red long stay; TV; adv bkg acc; tennis; games area. *"Vg facs; great beach; excel cycle path network."*
€22.00, 1 Apr-30 Sep. **2016**

PORNIC *2G3* (4km E Rural) *47.11885, -2.07296*
Camping Le Patisseau, 29 Rue du Patisseau, 44210 Pornic 02 40 82 10 39; contact@lepatisseau.com; www.lepatisseau.com

🐕 €6 ♔♔(htd) WD ♨ ⚅ 🖵 ⋌ 🦋 🍴 Y ⊕ ♨ 🏛 ⚓
🏊(covrd, htd) 🧺 ☂ sand 2.5km

Fr N or S on D213, take slip rd D751 Nantes. At rndabt take exit sp to Le Patisseau, foll sp. 4*, Med, mkd, hdstg, hdg, pt shd, pt sl, EHU (6A) inc; bbq; TV; 35% statics; Eng spkn; adv bkg rec; ccard acc; sauna; fitness rm; waterslide; golf 2km; tennis 1km; bike hire; games area; games rm; jacuzzi. *"Excel, modern, family site; modern san facs block - lovely shwrs; 1hr walk on path fr back of site to Pornic."*
€42.00, 7 Apr-12 Sep. **2017**

PORNIC *2G3* (6km SE Rural/Coastal) *47.08450, -2.03650* **Camping Les Ecureuils,** 24 Ave Gilbert Burlot, 44760 La Bernerie-en-Retz 02 40 82 76 95; camping. les-ecureuils@wanadoo.fr; www.camping-les-ecureuils.com

🐕 €3.90 ♔♔ WD ♨ ⚅ 🖵 ⋌ 🦋 Y ♨ 🔫nr 🏛 ⚓ 🏊(htd) 🧺
☂ sand 350m

Fr Pornic take D13 S for 5km, then D66 for 1km; site sp. 4*, Lge, hdg, pt shd, pt sl, EHU (10A) inc; bbq; 30% statics; Eng spkn; adv bkg acc; ccard acc; waterslide; golf 5km; tennis; CKE. *"Excel; children's club; v clean modern san facs; hg rec."*
€48.00, 1 Apr-30 Sep, L29. **2019**

PORNIC *2G3* (10km S Coastal) *47.07500, -2.00741*
Campsite Les Brillas, Le Bois des Treans, 44760 Les Moutiers-en-Retz 02 40 82 79 78; info@camping lesbrillas.com; www.campinglesbrillas.com

♔♔ WD ☂ 🖵 ⋌ 🦋

Fr Nantes ring rd, take D723 SW. Take exit D751 twd Pornic. Turn L on D66. Foll sp. 3*, Med, mkd, hdg, EHU (6A); Eng spkn; CCI. *"Sm coastal vill; easy walk to beach; excel; lovely location & beach; basic facs."* **€31.00, 14 Apr-1 Oct.** **2017**

PORNIC *2G3* (5km W Rural) *47.14079, -2.15306*
Camping La Tabardière, 44770 La Plaine-sur-Mer 02 40 21 58 83; info@camping-la-tabardiere.com; www.camping-la-tabardiere.com

🐕 €4 ♔♔(htd) WD ♨ ☂ ⚅ 🖵 ⋌ MsP 🦋 🍴 Y ♨ 🔫 🏛 ⚓
🏊(covrd, htd) 🧺 ☂ sand 3km

Take D13 NW out of Pornic sp Préfailles & La Plaine-sur-Mer. In about 5.5km turn R (nr water tower). Foll sps to site, about 1km fr main rd. NB C'vans not allowed in Pornic town cent, use by-pass. 4*, Lge, hdstg, mkd, hdg, pt shd, terr, serviced pitches; EHU (8A) €5; gas; bbq (charcoal, gas); TV; 40% statics; Eng spkn; adv bkg acc; ccard acc; tennis; games rm; fitness 3km; waterslide; horseriding 5km; CKE. *"Excel, peaceful site; multi-sport area; no o'fits over 7.5m high ssn; vg facs for families; v clean unisex san facs; gates clsd 2230-0800; recep clsd lunchtime."*
€47.00, 12 Apr-20 Sep, B31. **2019**

"I like to fill in the reports as I travel from site to site"

You'll find report forms at the back of this guide, or you can fill them in online at camc.com/europereport.

PORNIC *2G3* (9km NW Coastal) *47.15995, -2.16813*
Camping Thar-Cor, 43 Ave du Cormier, 44730 St Michel-Chef-Chef 02 40 27 82 81; camping@ letharcor.com; www.camping-le-thar-cor.com

🐕 €3 ♔♔(htd) WD ♨ ☂ ⚅ 🖵 ⋌ MsP 🦋 🍴 Y ⊕ ♨ 🔫nr 🏛 ⚓
🏊 ☂ sand 200m

Fr Pornic take D213 twds Saint Michel Chef Chef. Turn L onto Rue de la Dalonnerie. L at rndabt onto D96. Foll sp to site. Lge, mkd, hdg, pt shd, EHU (10A) €5; bbq; twin axles; TV; 50% statics; phone; Eng spkn; adv bkg rec; ccard acc; games area. *"Vg town site, mkt at Tharon-Plage high ssn; 200m to promenade & sandy beach; friendly staff; mainly French; beach excel."*
€26.50, 10 Apr-25 Sep. **2016**

PORT EN BESSIN HUPPAIN *3D1* (1km N Coastal) *49.34693, -0.77095* **Camping Port'land,** Chemin du Sémaphore, 14520 Port-en-Bessin **02 31 51 07 06;** campingportland@wanadoo.fr; www.camping-portland.com

🏕 €3 ♟(htd) ⓦ⃞ ♨ ♿ ▣ ⊘ ⃝ MSP ⓟ Ⓣ ⑩ å ♨ ⚐ ♦
⤢(covrd, htd) ⛱ ⵟ sand 4km

Site sp fr D514 W of Port-en-Bessin.
4*, Lge, mkd, hdg, hdstg, pt shd, EHU (16A) €5; bbq; red long stay; TV; 30% statics; Eng spkn; adv bkg acc; ccard acc; waterslide; tennis 800m; games area; games rm; CKE. *"Pleasant site; friendly, helpful staff; vg san facs; extra charge lger pitches; excel touring base for landing beaches etc; well kept clean, well spaced lge hdged pitches; well positioned for Bayeaux, Arromanche and D Day museums and cemetaries."*
€37.50, 1 Apr-30 Oct, N09. 2016

PORT LESNEY *6H2* (0.2km N Rural) *47.00358, 5.82366* **Camping Les Radeliers,** 1 Rue Edgar Faure, 39600 Port-Lesney **03 84 73 81 44; camp.portlesney@ aliceadsl.fr; www.camping-les-radeliers.com**

🏕 €2 ♟ ⓦ⃞ ♨ ♿ ▣ ⊘ ⃝ ⵟ nr ⑩ nr å ♨ nr ⚐

N fr Arbois on N83, cross junc with D472 & turn L in 1.5km sp Port-Lesney. Site sp. 3*, Med, mkd, pt shd, EHU (13A) €4; sw nr; twin axles; 2% statics; bus adj; Eng spkn; adv bkg acc; canoeing; kayak hire; CKE. *"Tranquil site in delightful rvside setting; helpful staff; poss youth groups high ssn; gd walking & cycling; Salt Mine Museum in Salins-les-Bains worth visit; canyoning; bar 200m; plenty rvside pitches."*
€23.00, 1 May-30 Sep. 2016

PORT SUR SAONE *6F2* (0.8km S Rural) *47.68056, 6.03937* **Camp Municipal Parc de la Maladière,** 70170 Port-sur-Saône **03 84 78 18 00 (Mairie); service culturel@gmail.com; www.ville-port-sur-saone.fr**

♟(cont) ⓦ⃞ ♨ ♿ ▣ ⊘ ⃝ ⵟ Ⓣ nr ⑩ nr å ♨ nr ⚐

Take N19 SE fr Langres or NW fr Vesoul. Site sp in vill bet rv & canal off D6 at municipal bathing area. 2*, Med, hdg, pt shd, EHU (6A) €3 (poss rev pol); own san rec; adv bkg acc; ccard acc; fishing; tennis; CKE. *"Peaceful site on island; rvside cycle path; gd walks; gd sh stay/NH; san facs basic & tired; pool adj; 25m cable needed; vg value."* **€15.40, 15 May-15 Sep.** 2017

PORT VENDRES *10G1* (2km E Urban) *42.51775, 3.11314* **Aire Communale des Tamarins,** Route de la Jetée, 66660 Port-Vendres **04 68 82 07 54**

12⃞ ♟ ⓦ⃞ MSP Ⓣ nr ⑩ nr å ♨ nr ⚐ ⵟ shgl 100m

Fr D914 at Port-Vendres at Banyuls side of town turn N on D86B sp Port de Commerce & Aire de Camping-Cars. Foll sp to site on R in 700m. Sm, hdstg, pt shd, own san req. *"NH, m'vans only; walking dist rlwy stn; a bit run down (Jun 2009); gd; payment collected am; popular."* **€10.00** 2016

PORTIRAGNES PLAGE *10F1* (2km NE Coastal) *43.29138, 3.37333* **Camping Les Mimosas,** Port Cassafières, 34420 Portiragnes-Plage **04 67 90 92 92;** info@mimosas.fr or les.mimosas.portiragnes@ wanado.fr; www.mimosas.com

🏕 €5.50 ♟ ⓦ⃞ ♨ ♿ ▣ ⊘ ⃝ MSP ⵟ ⓟ Ⓣ ⑩ å ♨ ⚐ ♦ ⤢
⛱ ⵟ sand 1km

Exit A9 junc 35 Béziers Est & take N112 sp Vias, Agde. After 3km at rndabt foll sp Portiragnes & cont along side of Canal du Midi. Cross canal, site sp. 4*, Lge, hdstg, mkd, pt shd, EHU (6-10A) €4; gas; bbq (gas); 50% statics; Eng spkn; adv bkg acc; ccard acc; games area; jacuzzi; sauna; games rm; waterslide; bike hire; CKE. *"Excel touring base in interesting area; friendly welcome; superb waterpark; fitness rm; private san facs avail; 4 star site; gd for families."*
€51.90, 1 Jun-7 Sep, C35. 2019

> ## "We must tell the Club about that great site we found"
>
> Get your site reports in by mid-August and we'll do our best to get your updates into the next edition.

POSES *3D2* (1.6km SE Urban) *49.29552, 1.24914* **Base de Loisirs,** Rue du Souvenir French, 27740 Poses **02 32 59 13 13; lery.poses@wanadoo.fr; www.lery-poses.fr**

♟ ⓦ⃞ ♨ ⊘ ♨

Fr Poses head NE on Rue du Bac twrd Rue das Masures, take 1st R onto Rue des Masures, turn R onto Rue du Roussillon, after 350m turn L onto Rue du Souvenir Francais, site after 220m on L. Lge, pt shd, EHU (16A); table tennis; canoeing. *"Gd san facs; gravel rdway throughout site; water ski; hiking; pedalo hire; mini golf; site adj to & overlooking the Rv Seine with direct access to the rvside; plenty of pitches for tourers; beach volleyball; supmkt 5km; older san block needs updating (2018)."*
€15.00, 1 Apr-31 Oct. 2018

POUILLY EN AUXOIS *6G1* (0.8km NW Urban) *47.26534, 4.54804* **Camping Vert Auxois,** 15 Voûte du Canal de Bourgogne, 21320 Pouilly-en-Auxois **03 80 90 71 89; contact@camping-vert-auxois.com; www.camping-vert-auxois.fr**

🏕 ♟ ⓦ⃞ ♨ ♿ ▣ ⊘ ⃝ MSP ⵟ ⓟ Ⓣ ⑩ å ♨ ⚐

Exit A6 at Dijon/Pouilly-en-Auxois onto A38. Exit A38 at junc 24. Thro vill & turn L after church on R, site sp adj Burgandy canal. 3*, Sm, hdg, pt shd, EHU (6-10A) long cable req; 10% statics; bus 300m; Eng spkn; adv bkg acc; ccard acc; rv fishing adj; CKE. *"Beautiful position, relaxed & peaceful; lge pitches, unusual layout; run by delightful, friendly couple; gd cycling; interesting area; sh walk to sm town; vg; san facs poss stretched."* **€23.00, 1 Apr-7 Oct.** 2018

POUILLY SUR LOIRE *4G3* (1km N Rural) *47.28742, 2.94427* **Camp Municipal Le Malaga,** Rue des Champs-sur-Loire, Les Loges, 58150 Pouilly-sur-Loire **03 33 86 39 12 55; www.ot-pouillysurloire.fr**

🛉 €1 ♦♦ ⓌⒹ ⚓ ㅎ 🖵 ⚟ 🍴 🛏 🐾 /🏠

Fr S exit A77 junc 26 onto D28a, turn L onto D59/D4289 W, bef rv bdge turn R, site in 1km on rv. Fr N on ent vill turn R at site sp into narr rd. Turn R along rv as above. 3*, Med, pt shd, EHU (10A) inc (poss long lead req & poss rev pol); bbq; phone; Eng spkn. "*Beautifully kept site on banks of Loire; busy NH; spacious but uneven pitches; mixed reports san facs; poss youth groups; beautiful area; wine tasting nrby; no twin axles or o'fits over 5m; poss mosquitoes; excel; delightful site adj to the Loire, spacious and leafy areas, wonderful wines in Pouilly and Sancerre, excel museum closeby.*" **€16.00, 1 May-30 Sep.** **2019**

POULDU, LE *2F2* (0.3km N Coastal) *47.76850, -3.54540* **Camping Les Embruns,** 2 Rue du Philosophe Alain, Clohars-Carnoët, 29360 Le Pouldu **02 98 39 91 07; camping-les-embruns@wanadoo.fr; www.camping-les-embruns.com**

🛉 €2.70 ♦♦(htd) ⓌⒹ ⚓ ㅎ ㅎ 🖵 ⚟ ᴹˢᴾ 🦋 ᵠ 🍴 ⊕ 🗃 🛏 /🏠
🏊(covrd, htd) 📶 🏖 sand 250m

Exit N165 dir Quimperlé Cent, onto D16 to Clohars-Carnoët. Cont on D16/D24/D1214 to Le Pouldu. Site on R on ent 1-way traff system. Site sp. 4*, Lge, hdstg, mkd, hdg, pt shd, terr, serviced pitches; EHU (10A) inc; gas; bbq; TV; 40% statics; bus nrby; Eng spkn; adv bkg acc; ccard acc; watersports; games area; tennis; horseriding nr; tennis 200m; games rm; bike hire; fishing; CKE. "*Excel family-run site in great location; children's farm; luxury pitches extra charge; friendly, helpful owners; vg clean san facs; superb facs; gd walking along coastal paths; cycle rtes; great for dogs; town was home of Paul Gauguin; highly rec.*" **€31.50, 10 Apr-19 Sep.** **2019**

See advertisements

POULDU, LE *2F2* (2km N Coastal) *47.78401, -3.54463* **FFCC Camping de Croas An Ter,** Quelvez, Le Pouldu, 29360 Clohars-Carnoët **02 98 39 94 19 or 06 24 88 68 20 (mob); campingcroasanter@orange.fr; www.campingcroasanter.com**

🛉 ♦♦ ⓌⒹ ⚓ ㅎ 🖵 ⚟ ᴹˢᴾ 🦋 ᵠ 🍴 nr ⊕ nr 🛏 nr /🏠 🐾 1.5km

On D49 fr Quimperlé to Le Pouldu. Site on L 3km after junc with D224. 2*, Med, pt shd, pt sl, EHU (6A) €3.20; Eng spkn; CKE. "*Lge pitches; friendly owners; cash only; gd bathing & sailing; walks in wood & rv fr site; Tues mkt; vg.*" **€13.60, 1 May-15 Sep.** **2016**

PRADES *8G4* (10km NE Urban) *42.64269, 2.53367* **Camping Lac De Vinca (formerly Municipal Les Escoumes),** Rue des Escoumes, 66320 Vinça **04 68 05 84 78 or 06 72 32 27 07 (mob); campingles escoumes@orange.fr; www.camping-lac-de-vinca.com/EN**

🛉 €3.50 ♦♦ ⓌⒹ ⚓ ㅎ 🖵 ⚟ ᴹˢᴾ 🦋 ᵠ 🍴 nr ⊕ nr 🛏 nr

Fr Perpignan take N116 W twd Andorra. 10km E of Prades in vill of Vinça take 1st L foll camp sps to site (400m). Vinca 32km W of Perpignan. 2*, Med, mkd, pt shd, pt sl, EHU (6-10A) €3; gas; sw; 20% statics; Eng spkn; fishing; bike hire. "*Beautiful, quiet, excel site; helpful staff; gd sized pitches; gd touring base; lake not suitable for toddlers (no sand, entry via steps); rec.*" **€17.00, 1 Apr-31 Oct.** **2017**

PRALOGNAN LA VANOISE *9B4* (13.7km NW Rural) *45.44274, 6.64874* **Camping Huttopia Bozel en Vanoise (formerly Municipal),** Route de Chevelu, 73350 Bozel **04 79 41 70 83; camping.lechevelu. bozel@gmail.com; www.camping-bozel.com**

🛉 €1.50 ♦♦ ⓌⒹ ⚓ ㅎ 🖵 ⚟ ᴹˢᴾ 🦋 ⊕ 🗃 🛏 nr /🏠

Foll D915 thro Bozel dir Pralognan. Site on R immed beyond vill. 2*, Med, mkd, hdstg, shd, pt sl, terr, EHU (6-10A) €3.50-4.50; sw nr; phone; Eng spkn; adv bkg acc; lake fishing 1km; CKE. "*In wood by rv; excel walking & climbing; vg; pleasant vill; lunchtime rest v popular with locals.*" **€18.40, 1 Jun-30 Sep.** **2019**

PRAZ SUR ARLY *9B3* (0.6km W Urban) *45.83628, 6.56747* **Chantalouette,** 384 Route du Val d'arly, 74120 Praz sur Arly **04 50 21 90 25 or 06 70 06 19 71 (mob); chantalouette@prazarly.fr; www.prazarly.fr**

12 🐕 €0.40 👪(htd) 🆆 🛁 🚮 ⚊ 🏕 ❜ 🍴nr ⓗnr 🦺nr

On D1212, Ugine to Megeve. Site on L at southern end of vill. Sm, hdstg, pt shd, EHU (6-10A) €4.60-€8.50; gas; twin axles; bus adj; Eng spkn; adv bkg acc; ccard acc; games rm; CKE. *"Walking dist to ski bus; vg."* **€19.00** 2015

PREMERY *4G4* (1km NW Urban) *47.17804, 3.33692* **Camp Municipal Le Plan D'eau (Les Prés de la Ville),** 58700 Prémery **03 86 37 99 42 or 03 86 68 12 40 (Mairie); mairie-premery@wanadoo.fr; www.mairie-premery.fr**

👪🆆 🛁 🚿 🚮 🦋 🦺nr

N fr Nevers on D977 to Prémery; turn R after 2nd rndabt. Site sp on D977. Med, pt shd, EHU (8-10A) €1-1.80; sw nr; red long stay; adv bkg acc; tennis adj; boating; fishing. *"Lovely, well-run lakeside site in town park; lake adj; clean, excel, htd, unisex san facs; popular NH; nice walk to interesting town; poss mkt traders; excel value."* **€9.30, 1 May-30 Sep.** 2016

PRESSAC *7A3* (8km SW Rural) *46.09696, 0.48081* **Camping Rural des Marronniers,** La Bussière, 16490 Pleuville **05 45 71 42 19; sgbann@btinternet.com; www.campingruraldesmarronniers.com**

12 🐕 👪(htd) 🆆 🚿 🛁 🚿 🚮 🦋 🍴nr 🦺nr 🎢 🏊

S fr Poitiers on D741 to Pressac; turn R onto D34 to Pleuville then turn onto D30 dir Charroux, site on L in 1.5km - look for sp La Bussière. Sm, unshd, pt sl, EHU (10A) €2.50; bbq; twin axles; adv bkg acc; games rm; CKE. *"Friendly, British-owned, peaceful, lovely sm CL-type farm site; open field - chickens & ducks roaming; gd touring base; ideal for exploring SW France; fam/couples welcome; excel."* **€12.00** 2017

PRIVAS *9D2* (1.5km S Urban) *44.72668, 4.59730* **Kawan Village Ardèche Camping,** Blvd de Paste, Quartier Ouvèze, 07000 Privas **04 75 64 05 80; jcray@wanadoo.fr; www.ardechecamping.fr**

🐕 €3.30 👪 🆆 🚿 🛁 🚮 🍴 ❜ 🍴 ⓗ 🦺nr 🎢 🏊 🏊(htd) 🛁

Exit A7 junc 16 dir Privas. App Privas cross rv bdge & at rndabt take 2nd exit. Site ent opp supmkt, sp. 4*, Lge, mkd, pt shd, pt sl, EHU (10A) inc; bbq; red long stay; TV; 80% statics; Eng spkn; adv bkg acc; ccard acc; rv fishing; tennis adj; CKE. *"Very gd, friendly owners; gd rest and shady pitches; interesting area to visit; pleasant site; walk to town up extremely steep rd."* **€33.00, 11 Apr-27 Sep.** 2015

PUGET THENIERS *10E4* (2km NW Rural) *43.95801, 6.85980* **Camping L'Origan (Naturist),** 2160 Route de Savé, 06260 Puget-Théniers **04 93 05 06 00; origan@orange.fr; www.origan-village.com**

🐕 €2.50 👪(htd) 🚿 🛁 🚮 🚿 🍴 ❜ ⓗ 🚮 🦺 🎢 🏊 🦺(htd) 🛁

On N202 fr Entrevaux (dir Nice) at Puget-Théniers, immed turn L at rlwy x-ing (sp), site approx 1km up track. 3*, Med, hdg, mkd, hdstg, pt shd, pt sl, terr, EHU (6A) €4; bbq; TV; 50% statics; phone; train to Nice; Eng spkn; adv bkg acc; ccard acc; INF card; tennis; fishing; waterslide; sauna; archery. *"Sm pitches not suitable o'fits over 6m; hilly site but pitches level; san facs dated (2018); interesting area; great views; ent noise poss high ssn; attractive bar/rest; tourist steam train bet Puget-Theniers & Annot on certain days."* **€36.00, Easter-3 Oct.** 2018

PUIMOISSON *10E3* (6.5km NE Rural) *43.89836, 6.18011* **Camping à la Ferme Vauvenières (Sauvaire),** 04410 St Jurs **06 50 74 37 11; ferme.de.vauvenieres@gmail.com; www.ferme-de-vauvenieres.fr**

🐕 €0.75 👪 🆆 🛁 🚮 🦋 ⓗ 🦺nr

Fr Riez take D953 N to 1km beyond Puimoisson then fork R onto D108 sp St Jurs & site sp. Sm, pt shd, EHU (6A) €2.90; bbq; sw nr; Eng spkn; adv bkg acc; games area; CKE. *"Peaceful, basic site off beaten track; wonderful views; lavendar fields; friendly Dutch owner; clean san facs, poss stretched if site full; gd for mountain walking; D17 to Majastres v narr; vg mkt on Wed & Sat in Riez; sm supmkt at filling stn at ent Puimoisson; v lge mkd pitches."* **€18.00, 1 Apr-15 Oct.** 2019

PUIVERT *8G4* (0.5km S Rural) *42.91596, 2.0441* **Camping de Puivert,** Fontclaire, 11230 Puivert **04 68 20 00 58 or 06 22 45 15 74 (mob); camping-de-puivert @orange.fr; www.campings11.fr**

🐕 👪 🆆 🛁 🚮 🦋 🍴 ❜ 🍴 ⓗnr 🚮 🦺 🎣

Take D117 W fr Quillan dir Lavelanet for 16km; at Puivert turn L onto D16; site in 500m by lake; well sp. Or E fr Foix on D117 for 45km; at Puivert turn R onto D16 & as bef. 2*, Med, hdg, hdstg, pt shd, terr, EHU (16A) €3; bbq (sep area); sw nr; fishing adj. *"Attractive area; lge pitches, some lakeside, some hill views; dated san facs but adequate & clean; museum in vill; chateau nrby; vg."* **€19.00, 20 Apr-20 Sep.** 2019

PUY EN VELAY, LE *9C1* (9km N Rural) *45.12473, 3.92177* **Camp Municipal Les Longes,** Route des Rosières, 43800 Lavoûte-sur-Loire **04 71 08 18 79; campinglavoutesurloire@orange.fr; www.lavoute surloire.fr**

🐕 €1.50 👪 🛁 🚮 🚿 🦋 🚮

Fr Le Puy take N on D103 sp Lavoûte & Retournac. In Lavoûte turn R onto D7 bef rv bdge, site on L in 1km on rvside. 3*, Med, mkd, shd, EHU (6A) €2.50; sw nr; tennis; fishing 50m. *"Gd, friendly site; gd walking; lovely quiet site by Haute Loire; san facs clean; rec; mostly statics."* **€17.00, 1 May-14 Sep.** 2017

FRANCE

PUY EN VELAY, LE *9C1* (3km E Urban) *45.04431, 3.93030* **Camp Municipal d'Audinet,** Ave des Sports, 43700 Brives-Charensac **04 71 09 10 18; camping. audinet@wanadoo.fr; www.camping-audinet.fr**

🐕 ⬚ ♨ 🛒 🗑 / 🏍 🦋 ⛱ 🍽 ① 🚮 🗲 ⵜ 🏊

Fr Le Puy foll green sp E twd Valence. Fr S on N88 foll sp twd Valence & on E side of town foll white sp. 3*, Lge, pt shd, EHU (6A) €3.30; bbq; sw; red long stay; bus to town; fishing. *"Spacious site on rvside; friendly, helpful staff; gd san facs, poss stretched high ssn; poss travellers - but not a prob; no twin axles; vg; 12 min bus to town every 1/2 hr."* **€19.00, 30 Apr-17 Sep.** **2017**

PUYSSÉGUR *8E3* (0.2km N Rural) *43.75064, 1.06065* **FFCC Camping Namasté,** 31480 Puysségur **05 61 85 77 84; contact@camping-namaste.com; www.camping-namaste.com**

🐕 €1.50 🍴 ⬚ ♨ 🛒 🗑 / 🦋 🍴 ⛱ ① 🚮 🗲 ⵜ ♿ 🏊 ⛴

Fr Toulouse NW on N224/D1 sp Cadours; at Puysségur in 30km foll Camping Namasté sp. (Puysségur is 1km NE of Cadours). 4*, Sm, pt shd, EHU (4-10A) €3-5; bbq; 10% statics; sauna; bike hire; games area; games rm; fishing. **€30.00, 1 May-15 Oct.** **2019**

PYLA SUR MER *7D1* (7km S Coastal) *44.58517, -1.20868* **Camping Village Centre La Forêt,** Route de Biscarosse, 33115 Pyla-sur-Mer **05 56 22 73 28; contact@village-center.com; www.village-center.com**

🐕 €2 🍴 ⬚ ♨ 🛒 🗑 / 🏍 🍴 ① 🚮 🗲 ⵜ 🗲 🐕 sand 600m

Fr Bordeaux app Arcachon on A660 by-pass rd; at La Teste-de-Buch at rndabt foll sp for Dune du Pilat & 'campings'. At T-junc in 4km turn L; foll 'plage' & camping sp on D218. Site on R. 3*, Lge, hdg, mkd, shd, sl, EHU (6A) inc; bbq; 80% statics; adv bkg acc; ccard acc; solarium; tennis; bike hire; CKE. *"Forest setting at foot of sand dune (own steps); well-organised; many facs; hang-gliding, surfing, sailing, cycle rtes nrby."* **€20.00, 4 Apr-20 Sep.** **2018**

PYLA SUR MER *7D1* (8km S Rural/Coastal) *44.57474, -1.22217* **Yelloh! Village Panorama du Pyla,** Route de Biscarosse, 33115 Pyla-sur-Mer **05 56 22 10 44; mail@camping-panorama.com; www.camping-panorama.com @ www.yellohvillage.co.uk**

🐕 €5 🍴 ⬚ ♨ 🛒 🗑 / 🏍 🍴 ① 🚮 🗲 ⵜ 🗲 (htd) ⛴ 🐕 sand adj

App Arcachon fr Bordeaux on A63/A660, at rndabt foll sp for Dune-du-Pilat & 'campings'. Foll sp for 'plage' & 'campings' on D218. Site on R next to Camping Le Petit Nice. 4*, Lge, mkd, hdstg, shd, sl, terr, EHU (3-10A) inc; gas; bbq; TV; 20% statics; Eng spkn; games area; tennis; games rm; sauna; waterslide; CKE. *"Pleasant site on wooded dune; pitches clsd together; adv bkg not acc; some pitches poor; direct steep access to excel beach; site rds v narr; ltd pitches for v lge o'fits; some pitches sandy; gd facs; paragliding adj."* **€46.00, 9 Apr-3 Oct.** **2016**

QUETTEHOU *1C4* (2.5km E Urban/Coastal) *49.58520, -1.26858* **Camping La Gallouette,** Rue de la Gallouette, 50550 St Vaast-la-Hougue **02 33 54 20 57; contact@ camping-lagallouette.fr; www.camping-lagallouette.fr**

🐕 €1.80 🍴 ⬚ ♨ 🛒 🗑 / 🏍 🦋 🍴 ① 🚮 🗲 ⵜ 🗲 (htd) 🐕 sand 300m

E fr Quettehou on D1, site sp in St Vaast-la-Houge to S of town. 4*, Lge, hdg, mkd, pt shd, EHU (6-10A) €3.80-4.60; gas; bbq; 10% statics; phone; adv bkg acc; games area; games rm; CKE. *"Lovely friendly site; some lge pitches; gd range of facs; sh walk to interesting town; excel site."* **€31.00, 1 Apr-30 Sep.** **2017**

QUIBERON *2G3* (3.6km N Coastal) *47.49978, -3.12021* **Camping Do Mi Si La Mi,** 31 Rue de la Vierge, 56170 Quiberon **02 97 50 22 52; camping@domisilami.com; www.domisilami.com**

🐕 €2.40 🍴 ⬚ ♨ 🛒 🗑 / 🏍 🦋 🍴 ① nr 🗲 nr ⵜ 🐕 shgl 100m

Take D768 down Quiberon Peninsular, 3km after St Pierre-Quiberon & shortly after sp for rlwy level x-ing turn L into Rue de la Vierge, site on R in 400m. 3*, Lge, hdg, mkd, pt shd, pt sl, serviced pitches; EHU (3-10A) €2.80-4.30; gas; bbq; 40% statics; Eng spkn; ccard acc; bike hire; tennis nr; horseriding nr; sailing nr; games area; CKE. *"Gd touring base; vg; excel site; great location; excel rest."* **€32.00, 31 Mar-30 Sep.** **2018**

QUIBERON *2G3* (1.5km SE Rural/Coastal) *47.47641, -3.10441* **Camping Le Bois d'Amour,** Rue St Clément, 56170 Quiberon **02 97 50 13 52; camping. boisdamour@flowercampings.com; www.quiberon-camping.com**

🐕 €5 🍴 ⬚ ♨ 🛒 🗑 / 🏍 🦋 🍴 ① 🚮 🗲 ⵜ 🗲 (htd) 🐕 200m

Exit N165 at Auray onto D768. In Quiberon foll sp 'Thalassothérapie', site sp. 3*, Lge, mkd, hdg, pt shd, EHU (16A) €5; gas; bbq; Eng spkn; adv bkg acc; ccard acc; tennis; horseriding; bike hire; games area; CKE. *"Shwrs clean but hot water can be temperamental; lovely friendly clubhse with reasonable food prices."* **€20.00, 2 Apr-24 Sep.** **2016**

QUIBERON *2G3* (2km SE Coastal) *47.47424, -3.10563* **Camp Municipal Le Goviro,** Blvd du Goviro, 56170 Quiberon **02 97 50 13 54 or 02 97 30 24 00 (LS); www.ville-quiberon.fr**

🐕 €1.65 🍴 ⬚ ♨ 🛒 🗑 / 🦋 ① nr ⵜ 🐕 sand adj

Fr D768 at Quiberon foll sp Port Maria & 'Cent Thalassothérapie'. Site 1km on L nr Sofitel hotel. 2*, Lge, hdg, mkd, pt shd, terr, EHU (13A) €3; gas; fishing adj; watersports adj. *"Popular, well-run site in excel location; lovely bay, gd sea views & coastal path into town; smallish pitches; clean, adequate san facs, ltd LS."* **€16.00, 1 Apr-12 Oct.** **2015**

FRANCE

QUILLAN *8G4* (1.2km W Urban) *42.87358, 2.17565*
FFCC Camp Municipal La Sapinette, 21 Ave René Delpech, 11500 Quillan **04 68 20 13 52; camping sapinette@wanadoo.fr; www.camping-la-sapinette.com**

🐕 €1.60 � (htd) ⬜WD 🏕 ⬧ ⚫ ⃫ ⏅MP ⍦ ⍦ ⍦ nr ⛰ ⍦

Foll D118 fr Carcassonne to Quillan; turn R at 2nd traff lts in town cent; site sp in town. 3*, Med, mkd, hdstg, hdg, pt shd, sl, terr, EHU (6A) €3.10; TV; 25% statics; adv bkg acc; ccard acc; CKE. "Gd touring base; sm pitches, some level, mostly sl; early arr rec; helpful staff; san facs a little tired; excel pool; site poss tired end ssn; mkt Wed & Sat; leisure cent 500m; vet adj; highly rec; 15min walk to nice town."
€25.00, 1 Apr-30 Oct. **2016**

QUIMPER *2F2* (10km SE Rural) *47.94133, -4.02453*
Camping de Keromen, 38 Rue de Cornouaille, 29170 Saint-Evarzec **02 98 64 09 59; contact@camping dekeromen.fr; www.campingdekeromen.fr**

🐕 � ⬜WD 🏕 ⚫ ⃫ ⍦ ⍦ ⛰

Heading S fr Quimper on D783 at end of dual c'way fork R sp Evarzec. Cont over mini rndabt, site on R in 1.5km, well sp. Med, mkd, hdg, pt shd, EHU (10A); twin axles; TV; 40% statics; bus; adv bkg acc; games area; games rm. "Adj lake area; donkeys & goats in enclosure; free fishing on sm lake; gd."
€18.50, 1 Apr-30 Oct. **2017**

"I need an on-site restaurant"

We do our best to make sure site information is correct, but it is always best to check any must-have facilities are still available or will be open during your visit.

QUIMPER *2F2* (9km SE Rural) *47.93811, -3.99959*
Camping Vert de Creac'h-Lann (Hemidy), 202 Route de Concarneau, 29170 St Evarzec **02 98 56 29 88 or 06 68 46 97 25 (mob); contact@campingvert creachlann.com; www.campingvertcreachlann.com**

🐕 � ⬜WD 🏕 ⚫ ⃫ ⍦ ⍦ ⍦ nr ⛰ ⍦ (htd)

S fr Quimper on D783, 1.5km fr St Evarzec rndabt at brow of hill (easily missed). Sm, hdg, pt shd, pt sl, EHU (4-13A) €3-3.50; bbq; 60% statics; Eng spkn; adv bkg acc; games rm. "Lovely spacious site; lge pitches; friendly, helpful owner; gd playgrnd; poss to stay after end Sep by arrangement; lovely old town; gd touring base; daily mkt; excel." **€13.00, 1 Jun-30 Sep.** **2017**

QUIMPER *2F2* (3.5km S Rural) *47.97685, -4.11060*
Camping L'Orangerie de Lanniron, Château de Lanniron, 29000 Quimper **02 98 90 62 02; camping@lanniron.com; www.lanniron.com**

🐕 €5.70 � ⬜WD 🏕 ⬧ ⚫ ⃫ 🗟 ⃫ ⏅MP ⍦ ⍦ ⍦ ⛰ ⛰

⍦ (htd) ⛰ ⍦

Fr Rennes/Lorient: on N165 Rennes-Quimper, Quimper-Centre, Quimper-Sud exit, foll dir Pont l'Abbé on S bypass until exit sp Camping de Lanninon on R. At top of slip rd turn L & foll site sp, under bypass then 2nd R to site. Recep at Old Farm 500m bef site. 5*, Lge, mkd, pt shd, serviced pitches; EHU (10A) inc; gas; bbq; TV; 40% statics; phone; bus; Eng spkn; adv bkg acc; ccard acc; bike hire; tennis; golf; canoeing; rv fishing; games rm; CKE. "Excel, busy, family-run site in grnds of chateau by Rv Odet; 9-hole golf on site; aqua park; well-spaced pitches; vg san facs; vg leisure facs; easy walk to town."
€37.00, 31 Mar-5 Nov, B21. **2018**

QUIMPER *2F2* (2.6km W Urban) *47.99198, -4.12536*
Camp Municipal Bois du Séminaire, Ave des Oiseaux, 29000 Quimper **02 98 55 61 09; camping-municipal@ quimper.bzh; www.mairie-quimper.fr**

� ⬜WD 🏕 ⚫ 🗟 ⃫ ⍦ ⍦ nr ⓤ nr ⛰ nr

Fr E on D765 to Quimper, bear L on 1-way system along rv. In 1km bear R over rv into Blvd de Boulguinan - D785. In 500m turn R onto Blvd de France (lge junc). In 1km bear R into Ave des Oiseaux, site on R in front of Auberge de Jeunesse. Med, hdg, pt shd, terr, EHU (5A) €3.30; bbq; 10% statics; phone; bus adj; ccard acc; CKE. "Conv NH/sh stay." **€12.00, 1 Jun-30 Sep.** **2015**

QUIMPERLE *2F2* (7km NE Rural) *47.90468, -3.47477*
Camping Le Ty-Nadan, Route d'Arzano, 29310 Locunolé **17 46 78 51 00 or 02 98 71 75 47; info@ tynadan-vacances.fr; www.irisparc.co.uk**

🐕 €5.50 � (htd) ⬜WD 🏕 ⬧ ⚫ 🗟 ⃫ ⏅MP ⍦ ⍦ ⍦ ⛰ ⛰ ⍦

⍦ (covrd, htd) ⛰

To avoid Quimperlé cent exit N165 dir Quimperlé. As ent town turn R onto D22 dir Arzano. In 9km turn L at W end of Arzano (un-numbered rd) sp Locunolé & Camping Ty Nadan; site on L just after x-ing Ty Elle. Or fr Roscoff on D69 S join N165/E60 but take care at uneven level x-ing at Pen-ar-Hoat 11km after Sizun. 5*, Lge, mkd, hdg, pt shd, serviced pitches; EHU (10A) inc (long lead poss req); gas; bbq (charcoal, gas); TV; 40% statics; Eng spkn; adv bkg acc; ccard acc; waterslide; games area; horseriding; rv fishing adj; tennis; archery; games rm; sauna; bike hire; canoeing adj; CKE. "Excel, peaceful site by rv; pitches poss narr for lge o'fits; friendly staff; spa; no o'fits over 8.5m high ssn; barrier clsd 2300-0800; many activities; gd touring base." **€46.00, 18 Apr-31 Aug, B20.** **2019**

QUINTIN *2E3* (0.6km SE Urban) *48.40128, -2.90672*
Camp Municipal du Lac, Chemin des Côtes, 22800
Quintin **02 96 74 92 54 or 02 96 74 84 01 (Mairie);**
mairie@quintin.fr; **www.quintin.fr**
👫 ♨ ⛄ ♿ /⃝ MSP 🦋 🍽 nr ⑩ nr 🛁 nr 🏧

Fr N exit D790 at rndabt & foll sp 'Cent Ville'; at 2nd
rndabt site sp; site on L 200m after 5th ped x-ing
(narr rd, easy to miss). Fr S on D790 do not take slip
rd (D7) but cont to rndabt - narr rds in town; then as
above. Site N (100m) of town gardens & boating lake.
2*, Sm, pt shd, pt sl, EHU (6A) €2.80; bbq; fishing. *"Fair
site; helpful warden; poss insufficient of security (2011);
interesting town."* **€8.50, 15 Apr-30 Sep.**   2016

RABASTENS *8E3* (2km NW Rural) *43.83090, 1.69805*
Camp Municipal des Auzerals, Route de Grazac,
81800 Rabastens **05 63 33 70 36 or 06 23 81 85 69
(mob);** mairie.rabastens@libertysurf.fr
👫 ♨ ♨ 🛒 /⃝ 🦋 ⑩ nr 🛁 nr 🏧

Exit A68 junc 7 onto D12. In Rabastens town cent
foll sp dir Grazac, site sp. 1*, Sm, hdg, mkd, pt shd,
pt sl, terr, EHU (10A) inc; adv bkg req; CKE. *"Attractive
lakeside site; facs old but clean; office 0900-1200 &
1500-1900, otherwise height barrier in place; conv
m'way NH; pool adj high ssn; highly rec; gd hedges
around plots; call to check if site open."*
€11.00, 1 Apr-30 Sep.   2017

RAMBOUILLET *4E3* (3km SE Rural) *48.6252, 1.84495*
Camping Huttopia Rambouillet, Route du Château
d'Eau, 78120 Rambouillet **01 30 41 07 34;**
rambouillet@huttopia.com; **www.huttopia.com**
🐕 €4.20 👫 (htd) 🆆 🛒 ♨ ⛄ /⃝ MSP 🦋 🍽 ⑩ 🛁 🏧

Fr N exit D910 at 'Rambouillet Eveuses' & foll sp to
site in 2.5km. Fr S exit at 'Rambouillet Cent' & foll sp
to site back onto D910 (in opp dir), exit 'Rambouillet
Eveuses' as above. Avoid Rambouillet town cent.
3*, Lge, hdg, pt shd, EHU (10A) inc; bbq (elec, gas);
10% statics; phone; Eng spkn; adv bkg rec; ccard acc;
fishing adj; sep car park; CKE. *"Excel, busy, wooded
site; conv Paris by train - parking at stn 3km; gd cycling
rtes; interesting town."*
€41.00, 30 Mar-3 Nov, P17.   2017

RAON L'ETAPE *6E3* (2km SE Rural) *48.39474,
6.86232* **Camping Vosgina,** 1 Rue la Cheville, 88420
Moyenmoutier **03 29 41 47 63;** info@camping-
vosgina.com; **www.camping-vosgina.com**
🐕 €1.50 👫 🆆 ♨ 🛒 /⃝ 🦋 ♈ 🍽 🛁 🏧

On N59 St Dié-Lunéville rd, take exit mkd Senones,
Moyenmoutier. At rndabt take rd twd St Blaise &
foll camping sp. Site is on minor rd parallel with
N59 bet Moyenmoutier & Raon. 2*, Med, hdg, pt shd,
terr, EHU (4-10A) €3-6; gas; TV; 20% statics; Eng spkn;
adv bkg acc; ccard acc; CKE. *"Gd site for quiet holiday
in a non-touristy area of Alsace; friendly recep; lovely
countryside; many cycle/walking rtes in area; barrier
clsd 2200-0700; park like setting; beautifully
maintained; friendly Swiss owners; excel for sh stay or
NH."* **€20.00, 25 Mar-31 Oct.**   2016

RAON L'ETAPE *6E3* (9km S Rural) *48.36355, 6.83861*
Camping Beaulieu-sur-l'Eau, 41 Rue de Trieuche,
88480 Etival-Clairefontaine **03 29 41 53 51;** camping-
beaulieu-vosges@orange.fr; www.camping-beaulieu-
vosges.com
🔟12 🐕 👫 (htd) ♨ /⃝ MSP 🦋 🍽 ⑩ nr 🛁 🏧

SE fr Baccarat on N59 turn R in vill of Etival-
Clairefontaine on D424 sp Rambervillers & Epinal &
foll sp for 3km. Ent on L. 2*, Med, mkd, pt shd, terr, EHU
(4-10A) €3.05-7.90; gas; sw nr; 10% statics; adv bkg rec;
CKE. *"Lovely, peaceful, clean site; 80% statics; dedicated
touring area; gd rural views."* **€10.50**   2015

RAUZAN *7D2* (0.2km N Rural) *44.78237, -0.12712*
Camping du Vieux Château, 6 Blabot-Bas, 33420
Rauzan **05 57 84 15 38; contact@vieuxchateau.fr;**
www.camping-levieuxchateau.com
🐕 €2 👫 🆆 ♨ ⛄ /⃝ 🦋 ♈ 🍽 ⑩ ♿ 🛁 🏧 ♣ 🏊

Fr Libourne S on D670, site is on D123 about 1.5km
fr D670, sp. 3*, Sm, mkd, shd, EHU (6A) €5 (poss
rev pol); gas; TV; 10% statics; Eng spkn; adv bkg acc;
ccard acc; tennis; bike hire; horseriding; CKE. *"Lovely
site but take care tree roots on pitches; quiet wooded
area; pleasant family run site; helpful owners; basic
san facs - ltd LS & poss not well-maintained, & poss
stretched high ssn; access to some pitches diff when
wet; conv vineyards; walking dist to vill; nice sw pool;
wine-tasting; TV rm & bar open to 9pm; events avail."*
€27.00, 30 Mar-18 Oct.   2018

REALMONT *8E4* (2.5km SW Rural) *43.77092, 2.16336*
Camp Municipal La Batisse, Route Graulhet, 81120
Réalmont **05 63 55 50 41;** camping-realmont@
wanadoo.fr; **www.realmont.fr/decouvrir/**
camping-municipal-realmont
👫 ♨ /⃝ 🦋 🍽 nr ⑩ nr 🛁 nr 🏧

On D612 fr Albi heading S thro Réalmont. On exit
Réalmont turn R on D631 where site sp. Site 1.5km
on L on Rv Dadou. 2*, Sm, pt shd, EHU (3A) inc; gas;
10% statics; rv fishing adj. *"Pleasant, peaceful, well-kept
site in rv valley; friendly, pleasant warden; dated but
clean san facs; nr Albi-Castres cycle rte; excel value; mkt
Wed; gd; hg rec."* **€12.00, 1 Apr-30 Sep.**   2017

REGUINY *2F3* (1km S Urban) *47.96928, -2.74083*
Camp Municipal de l'Etang, Rue de la Piscine, 56500
Réguiny **02 97 38 66 11; mairie.requiny@wanadoo.fr;**
www.requiny.com
🐕 €2 👫 🆆 ♨ 🛒 /⃝ MSP 🦋 🍽 nr ⑩ nr 🛁 nr 🏧

On D764 fr Pontivy to Ploërmel, turn R into D11
to Réguiny then foll sp. 2*, Med, pt shd, EHU (10A)
€2.50; phone; Eng spkn; ccard acc. *"Gd facs; htd pool
500m; gd touring base; deposit for gate remote control
(€100); v pleasant site; rec rest in vill; gd acc to S
Brittany."* **€10.40, 15 Jun-15 Sep.**   2018

REIMS *3D4* (19km SE Rural) *49.16687, 4.21416*
Camping Intercommunalité Val de Vesle (formerly Municipal), 8 Rue de Routoir, Courmelois, 51360 Val-de-Vesle **03 26 03 91 79; valdevesle.camping@orange.fr; www.reims-tourism.com**

🐕 €1 🏕️ wc ♨ ⚲ & ▣ ⁄ 🛒 nr 🏧 ⚓

Fr Reims twd Châlons-en-Champagne on D944, turn L by camp sp on D326 to Val-de-Vesle, foll camp sp; look for tall grain silos by canal. NB do not turn L bef D326 due narr lane. 2*, Med, mkd, shd, EHU (6-10A) €3 (long lead poss req); bbq; adv bkg acc; ccard acc; rv fishing; CKE. *"Charming, well-kept, busy site amongst trees; popular NH, rec arrive early; informal pitching; friendly, helpful staff; new security gate, booking in req for code (2011); in sm vill (no shops); poss mosquito prob; cycle rte to Reims along canal; gd touring base; lge pitches; lovely, clean facs; well sp fr D944."* **€15.00, 1 Apr-15 Oct.** 2018

REMOULINS *10E2* (2km NW Rural) *43.94805, 4.54583* **Camping La Sousta,** Ave du Pont de Gard, 30210 Remoulins **04 66 37 12 80; info@lasousta.fr; www.lasousta.fr**

🐕 €2 🏕️ wc ♨ ⚲ & ▣ ⁄ msp 🦋 🍴 ① nr ⚓ 🛒 🏧 🏊 🛶

Fr A9 exit Remoulins, foll sp for Nîmes, then sp 'Pont du Gard par Rive Droite' thro town. Immed over rv bdge turn R sp 'Pont du Gard etc'; site on R 800m fr Pont du Gard. 4*, Lge, hdstg, mkd, shd, pt sl, EHU (6A); gas; bbq (sep area); sw nr; TV; 20% statics; Eng spkn; adv bkg acc; ccard acc; bike hire; fishing; watersports; tennis; CKE. *"Friendly, helpful staff; poss diff lge o'fits due trees; excel touring base; in walking dist Pont-du-Gard; set in lovely woodland with plenty of shd; can be dry & dusty in Jul & Aug; bar & rest open in LS; sw pool clsd until 5th May."* **€34.00, 12 Mar-1 Nov.** 2018

REMOULINS *10E2* (4km NW Rural) *43.95594, 4.51588* **Camping International Les Gorges du Gardon,** Chemin de la Barque Vieille, Route d'Uzès, 30210 Vers-Pont-du-Gard **04 66 22 81 81; camping.international@wanadoo.fr; www.le-camping-international.com**

🐕 €2 🏕️ wc ♨ ⚲ & ▣ ⁄ 🦋 🍴 🍴 ① ⚲ 🛒 🏧 🏊 🛶 (htd)

Exit A9 junc 23 Remoulins & head NW twd Uzès on D981. Pass turn for Pont-du-Gard & site on L in 1.5km. Or fr E on N100 turn N onto D6086 then D19A to Pont-du-Gard (avoiding Remoulins cent). 4*, Lge, mkd, hdg, pt shd, EHU (6A) inc; gas; sw nr; red long stay; TV; 10% statics; Eng spkn; adv bkg acc; ccard acc; tennis; games rm; boating; fishing; games area; CKE. *"Beautiful location; many sm pitches - some lge pitches to back of site; friendly, cheerful owners; excel san facs, ltd LS; no twin axles or o'fits over 5m; beavers in rv; site poss subject to flooding & evacuation; superb; conv for the Pont du Gard, thoroughly rec staying several nights, unique site."* **€29.00, 15 Mar-30 Sep, C18.** 2018

RENNES *2F4* (4km NE Urban) *48.13529, -1.64597* **Camp Municipal des Gayeulles,** Rue du Maurice Audin, 35700 Rennes **02 99 36 91 22; info@camping-rennes.com; www.camping-rennes.com**

12 🐕 €1 🏕️ wc ♨ ⚲ & ▣ ⁄ 🛒 🖥️ 🍴 ⚓ 🛒 nr 🏧

Exit Rennes ring rd N136 junc 14 dir Maurepas & Maison Blanche, foll sp 'Les Gayeules' & site. Narr app to site. 3*, Med, mkd, hdstg, pt shd, pt sl, serviced pitches; EHU (10A) inc; bbq; red long stay; phone; bus; Eng spkn; adv bkg acc; ccard acc; tennis nr; CKE. *"Lovely, well-kept, well-run site adj activity park; friendly, helpful staff; lge pitches; slight sl for m'vans; 1st class facs; office clsd 1200-1400; reg bus to Rennes, a lovely city; sm m'van Aire de Service adj; excel; mini golf nr; archery nrby; no dogs allowed in park adj; m'van o'night area; pool adj; noise fr disco & football; great location; new san facs close to ent."* **€19.00** 2018

REOLE, LA *7D2* (1.6km SE Urban) *44.57778, -0.03360* **Camp Municipal La Rouergue,** Bords de Garonne, 33190 La Réole **05 56 61 13 55; lareole@entredeuxmers.com; www.entredeuxmers.com**

🐕 €2 🏕️ wc ♨ ⚲ ⁄ 🛒 🏧

On N113 bet Bordeaux & Agen or exit A62 at junc 4. In La Réole foll sps S on D9 to site on L immed after x-ing suspension bdge. 2*, Med, pt shd, EHU (3A) inc; gas; boating; fishing. *"Resident warden; 2m barrier clsd 1200-1500; pool 500m; Sat mkt on rv bank."* **€16.00, 1 May-30 Sep.** 2015

RETHEL *5C1* (19km E Urban) *49.48234, 4.57589* **Camping Le Vallage (formerly Municipal),** 38 Chemin de l'Assaut, 08130 Attigny **03 24 71 23 06; camping.levallage@orange.f; www.camping-levallage.fr**

🐕 🏕️ wc ♨ ⚲ ⁄ 🛒 nr 🏧

E on D983 fr Rethel to Attigny; fr town cent take D987 twd Charleville; over rv bdge; 2nd turn on L; sp. 2*, Med, mkd, hdg, hdstg, pt shd, EHU (10A) inc; 50% statics; phone; fishing; tennis; CKE. *"Lovely quiet site; lge pitches; sports facs adj; helpful staff; pool adj; gd facs."* **€16.00, 1 Apr-15 Oct.** 2015

REVEL *8F4* (0.5km E Urban) *43.45454, 2.01515* Camp Municipal Le Moulin du Roy, Tuilerie de Chazottes, off Ave de Sorèze, 31250 Revel **05 61 83 32 47 or 05 62 18 71 40 (Mairie); mairie@mairie-revel.fr; www.tourisme-revel.com**

🐕 €0.90 ♨ ⁄ msp 🛒 nr 🏧

Fr Revel ring rd take D1/D85 dir Sorèze, site sp. 2*, Med, hdg, pt shd, EHU €320; sw nr; phone; bus; Eng spkn; tennis adj; CKE. *"Pleasant, immac site; htd pool adj; helpful staff; Sat mkt; vg."* **€16.00, 2 Jun-7 Sep.** 2017

REVEL *8F4* (6km E Urban) *43.45446, 2.06953*
Camping St Martin, Les Vigariés, 81540 Sorèze **05 63
50 20 19; campingsaintmartin@gmail.com;
www.campingsaintmartin.com**

🐕 €1.50 👥 📶 ♨ ⚐ ⊡ // 🅿 ❅ ♈ ⏃ ⟐ 🍴 ⚓ 🏔 ⚑ 🏊

**Fr Revel take D85 sp Sorèze; site sp on N side of vill;
turn L at traff lts; site on R in 100m.** 3*, Sm, mkd,
hdstg, hdg, pt shd, EHU (10A) €3.60; bbq; sw nr; TV;
20% statics; tennis; games rm; CKE. *"Vg, well-kept site;
friendly staff; excel san facs; fascinating medieval town;
nr Bassin de St Ferréol; excel mkt in Revel; rec; noise fr
adj sports facs & pitches nr san fac beware of being hit
by footballs."* **€24.60, 30 Mar-14 Oct.** 2017

REVIGNY SUR ORNAIN *5D1* (0.4km S Urban) *48.82663,
4.98412* **Camp Municipal du Moulin des Gravières,**
Rue du Stade, 55800 Revigny-sur-Ornain **03 29 78
73 34; contact@ot-revigny-ornain.fr; www.ot-
revigny-ornain.fr**

🐕 👥 📶 ♨ ⚐ ⊡ // 🅿 ❅ ⚓ 🅿nr 🏔

**N fr Bar-le-Duc on D994 to Revigny-sur-Ornain;
fr town cent take D995 twd Vitry-le-François.
Site on R, sp.** 2*, Sm, hdg, mkd, pt shd, EHU (6A)
€2.70; TV; 3% statics; Eng spkn; adv bkg acc; CKE.
*"Pleasant, well-kept site; lge pitches; vg, modern facs;
trout stream runs thro site; bike hire in town; tennis in
town; gd cycling along canal; mkt Wed adj; highly rec;
excel site, beautifully kept; park like setting; far better
than any other municipal site we have stayed on."*
€13.00, 1 May-30 Sep. 2016

RHINAU *6E3* (0.5km NW Rural) *48.32123, 7.69788*
Camping Ferme des Tuileries, 1 Rue des Tuileries,
67860 Rhinau **03 88 74 60 45 or 06 85 74 98 97;
camping.fermetuileries@neuf.fr; www.fermedes
tuileries.com**

👥 📶 ♨ ⚐ ⊡ // 🅿 ❅ ♈ 🍴 ⊕ ⚓ 🅿nr 🏔 ⚑ 🏊 (htd)

**Take D1083 (between Strasbourg and Selestat). Exit
at Benfield or Sand and take D5 through Boofzheim
to Rhinau. Site sp.** 3*, Med, hdstg, mkd, pt shd, EHU
(6A) €3.20; gas; bbq; sw; 20% statics; Eng spkn;
games area; games rm; bike hire; tennis. *"Spacious
site with excel facs; regimented; free ferry across
Rv Rhine adj; vg; excel for cycling; hdstdg for MH's."*
€16.50, 1 Apr-30 Sep. 2018

RIBEAUVILLE *6E3* (2km E Urban) *48.19490, 7.33648*
Camp Municipal Pierre-de-Coubertin, Rue de
Landau, 68150 Ribeauville **03 89 73 66 71; camping.
ribeauville@wanadoo.fr; www.camping-alsace.com**

🐕 €1 👥 (htd) 📶 ♨ ⚐ ⊡ // ❅ ♈ ⚓

**Exit N83 junc 20 at Ribeauville onto D106 & foll rd
to o'skts; at traff lts turn R & then immed R again.
Site on R in 500m. Camp at sports grnd nr Lycée.**
4*, Lge, mkd, pt shd, pt sl, EHU (16A) €3.50; gas; CKE.
*"Well-run site; friendly, helpful staff; park outside site
bef checking in; clean, excel san facs; resident storks;
gd size pitches; gd touring base; mkt Sat; pool adj;
highly rec; excel."* **€17.00, 15 Mar-15 Nov.** 2017

RIBEAUVILLE *6E3* (4.5km S Rural) *48.16200, 7.31691*
Camping de Riquewihr, 1 Route du Vin, 68340
Riquewihr **03 89 47 90 08; camping.riquewihr@
wanadoo.fr; www.ribeauville-riquewihr.com**

🐕 €1.20 👥 (htd) 📶 ♨ ⚐ ⊡ // 🅿 ♈ ⚓nr 🏔

**Fr Strasbourg on N83/E25, take junc 21 (fr opp dir
take junc 22) to Blebenheim/Riquewihr. D416 & D3
thro Blebenheim. At T-junc turn R onto D1B, site on
R at rndabt.** 4*, Lge, mkd, hdg, hdstg, pt shd, pt sl,
EHU (6A) €3.50 (poss rev pol); gas; ccard acc; tennis;
CKE. *"Rec arr early; friendly staff; san facs clean; gd
for sm children; lovely town; games area adj; m'van
o'night area; office clsd 1200-1400."*
€21.00, 28 Mar-31 Dec. 2015

RIBERAC *7C2* (0.5km N Rural) *45.25755, 0.34128*
Camp Municipal La Dronne, Route d'Angoulême,
24600 Ribérac **05 53 92 41 61; ot.riberac@
perigord.tm.fr**

🐕 €0.50 👥 📶 ♨ ⚐ ⊡ // ❅ ♈ ⚓nr 🏔

**Site on W of main rd D708 immed N of bdge over
Rv Dronne on o'skts of Ribérac.** 2*, Med, hdg, pt shd,
EHU (10A) €2.50. *"Vg, well-run site; pitches in cent
hdgd & shady; facs gd & clean but inadequate high ssn;
Fri mkt."* **€14.00, 1 Jun-15 Sep.** 2017

RIBES *9D2* (0.7km S Rural) *44.29545, 4.12436*
Camping Les Cruses, Ribes 07260 Joyeuse **33 04 75
39 54 69; les-cruses@wanadoo.fr; www.camping
lescruses.com**

🐕 €3 👥 (htd) 📶 ♨ ⚐ ⊡ // 🅿 ❅ ♈ 🍴 ⊕ ⚓ 🏔 ⚑ 🏊
🏕 1km

**Head NW on rue du Mas de Laffont twd Le Cheatâu
after 120m turn L onto Le Cheatâu. Turn R onto
D550, sharp R twds Laffont, L onto Laffont, sharp
R twd D450 after 40m turn L onto D450.** Sm, mkd,
shd, EHU (10A) €4.30; bbq; TV; Eng spkn; adv bkg acc;
ccard acc; games area; CCI. *"Excel on site pool and
jacuzz; v helpful and friendly owners; nr lively town and
places to see."* **€31.70, 1 Apr-30 Sep.** 2019

RIEL LES EAUX *6F1* (2km W Rural) *47.97050, 4.64990*
Camp Municipal du Plan d'Eau, 21570 Riel-les-Eaux
03 80 93 72 76; bar-camping-du-marais@wanadoo.fr

👥 📶 ♨ ⚐ // ❅ 🍴 ⚓ 🏔

**NE fr Châtillon-sur-Seine on D965 twd Chaumont:
after 6km turn N onto D13 at Brion-sur-Ource; cont
thro Belan-sur-Ource. Site almost opp junc with D22
turning to Riel-les-Eaux; site well sp.** 2*, Sm, hdg,
pt shd, EHU (6A) €3; Eng spkn; fishing; CKE. *"Conv
Champagne area; lake adj; excel; vg, simple site; lge
hdg pitches."* **€12.00, 1 Apr-31 Oct.** 2015

FRANCE

FRANCE

RIEUX *2G3* (0.5km E Urban) *47.59801, -02.10131*
Le Parc du Château, 56350 Rieux, France **02999
19785; contact@marriederriex.fr; rieux-morbihan.fr**

🐕 ♦♦♦ WD ♠ ♿ 🔲 ⚊ 🌊 MSP ⚊ 🛈 ⛟

Turn R off D114 at R angled bend E of town. Sm,
hdg, mkd, pt shd, terr, EHU (10A) €2.60; bbq; TV;
5% statics; phone; bus 200m; Eng spkn; adv bkg acc;
canoeing; fishing; sailing; tennis; CKE. *"Beside Vilaine
canal; pretty, well kept site; vg."*
€13.40, 1 Apr-31 Oct.   **2016**

RIEZ *10E3* (0.8km SE Urban) *43.81306, 6.09931*
Camping Rose de Provence, Rue Edouard Dauphin,
04500 Riez **04 92 77 75 45; info@rose-de-provence.
com; www.rose-de-provence.com**

🐕 €1.60-2.10 ♦♦♦ WD ♠ ♿ 🔲 ⚊ 🌊 nr 🛈 nr ⛟

**Exit A51 junc 18 onto D82 to Gréoux-les-Bains then
D952 to Riez.** On reaching Riez strt across rndabt,
at T-junc turn L & immed R, site sp. 3*, Med, mkd,
pt shd, EHU (6A) inc (rev pol); 5% statics; phone; adv
bkg acc; tennis adj; CKE. *"Beautiful, well-kept site;
helpful, friendly owners; gd san facs; nice vill; conv
Verdon Gorge; mkd walks around vill; trampoline &
gym equipmnt; gate clse 1230-1500 & 2100-0830."*
€21.00, 12 Apr-1 Oct.   **2015**

RILLE *4G1* (4km W Rural) *47.45750, 0.21840*
Camping Huttopia Rillé, Base de Loisirs de
Pincemaille, Lac de Rillé, 37340 Rillé **02 47 24 62 97;
rille@huttopia.com; www.huttopia.com**

🐕 €3.50 ♦♦♦ (htd) WD ♠ ♿ ⚊ 🌊 ⚊ 🛈 ♦♦ ⛟ ⛵ (htd)

**Fr N or S D749 to Rillé, foll sp to Lac de Pincemaille,
site sp on S side of lake.** 3*, Med, shd, EHU (6-10A)
€4.20-6.20; sw nr; 10% statics; adv bkg rec; sep car
park; watersports; fishing; games rm; tennis. *"Peaceful
site; vg walking; excel."* **€38.00, 13 Apr-29 Sep.**   **2019**

RIOM *9B1* (5km NW Rural) *45.91597, 3.07682*
Camping Le Ranch des Volcans (formerly Clos de
alanède), Route de la Piscine, 63140 Châtel-Guyon
**04 73 86 02 47; contact@ranchdesvolcans.com;
www.ranchdesvolcans.com**

🐕 €1.50 ♦♦♦ ♠ ♿ 🔲 ⚊ 🌊 ♦♦ 🛈 ♦ 🌊 nr ⛟ ⛵

**Fr Riom take D227 to Châtelguyon, site on R on
o'skts of town. Tight turn into ent.** 3*, Lge, pt shd, pt
sl, EHU (6-10A) €3-3.50; gas; red long stay; Eng spkn;
adv bkg acc; tennis; poss open until 31 Dec. *"Pleasant,
well-run site; san facs dated; some pitches steep & poss
uneven; sh walk to town; m'vans/campers not allowed
up to Puy-de-Dôme - must use bus provided; conv for
A71, gd NH; gd quiet site; conv for Clermont-Ferrand
and Puy de Dôme."* **€17.00, 21 Mar-1 Nov.**   **2015**

RIOM *9B1* (6km NW Rural) *45.90614, 3.06041*
Camping de la Croze, St Hippolyte, 63140 Châtel-
Guyon **04 73 86 08 27 or 06 87 14 43 62 (mob);
info@campingcroze.com; www.campingcroze.com**

🐕 €1.80 ♦♦♦ (htd) WD ♠ 🔲 ⚊ 🌊 ⚊ 🌊 nr ⛟ (htd)

**Fr A71 exit junc 13; ring rd around Riom sp
Châtel-Guyon to Mozac, then D455. Site L bef ent
St Hippolyte. Fr Volvic on D986 turn L at rndabt
after Leclerc supmkt & L again to D455. NB Not rec
to tow thro Riom.** 3*, Lge, mkd, pt shd, pt sl, EHU
(6-10A) €3.80; 10% statics; CKE. *"Gd sightseeing area;
mini-bus to Châtel-Guyon (2km) high ssn; vg; supmkt
nrby; gd rest."* **€18.50, 26 Mar-30 Oct.**   **2017**

RIOM ES MONTAGNES *7C4* (0.9km E Rural) *45.28214,
2.66707* Camp Municipal Le Sédour, 15400 Riom-ès-
Montagnes **04 71 78 05 71**

♦♦♦ WD ♠ ♿ 🔲 ⚊ 🌊 MSP 🌊 nr ⛟

**Site on W of D678 Riom N to Condat rd, 500m out
of town over bdge, sp fr all dirs, opp Clinique du
Haut Cantal.** 3*, Med, mkd, pt shd, pt sl, EHU (6A);
bbq; twin axles; TV; Eng spkn; adv bkg acc; games
area. *"Vg; takeaway."* **€16.00, 1 May-30 Sep.**   **2015**

> ## "Satellite navigation makes touring much easier"
>
> Remember most sat navs don't know if you're
> towing or in a larger vehicle – always use yours
> alongside maps and site directions.

RIOZ *6G2* (0.9km E Rural) *47.42525, 6.07524*
Camp Municipal du Lac, Rue de la Faïencerie, 70190
Rioz **03 84 91 91 59, 03 84 91 84 84 (Mairie) or 06 33
78 63 75 (mob); camping@rioz.fr; camping.rioz.fr**

🐕 €1.50 ♦♦♦ (htd) ♠ ♿ 🌊 ♦♦ 🛈 nr 🌊 nr ⛟

Site sp off D15. 3*, Med, hdstg, hdg, pt shd, EHU
(16A) €2.50; gas. *"Site yourself, warden calls; some
lge pitches; gd facs; pool adj; footpath to vill shops."*
€10.40, 1 Apr-30 Sep.   **2016**

RIVIERE SUR TARN *10E1* (0.4km SW Rural) *44.18530,
3.13060* Camping Les Peupliers, Rue de la Combe,
12640 Rivière-sur-Tarn **05 65 59 85 17; lespeupliers
12640@orange.fr; www.campinglespeupliers.fr**

🐕 €3 ♦♦♦ WD ♠ ♿ 🔲 ⚊ 🌊 ♦♦ 🌊 ⚊ 🛈 ♦ 🌊 nr ⛟ 🚣 (htd) ⚓

**Heading N on N9 turn R dir Aguessac onto D907
twd Rivière-sur-Tarn. Site on R bef vill. Or fr A75 exit
junc 44.1 sp Aguessac/Gorges du Tarn. In Aguessac,
foll sp Rivière-sur-Tarn for 5km, site clearly sp.**
4*, Med, hdstg, mkd, hdg, pt shd, EHU (6A) inc; gas;
bbq; sw nr; TV; 10% statics; Eng spkn; adv bkg acc;
ccard acc; canoeing; fishing; horseriding; waterslide;
games; tennis; watersports; CKE. *"Lovely rural
site alongside rv Tarn; friendly staff and owners;
beautiful scenery; kayaking avail; adv bkg rec; excel site
for gorges."* **€34.00, 1 Apr-30 Sep.**   **2015**

For a guide to symbols see the fold out on the rear cover

ROANNE *9A1* (5km SW Rural) *45.98830, 4.04531*
Camping L'Orée du Lac, 68 Route du Barrage, 42300 Villerest **04 77 69 60 88; loreedulac@wanadoo.fr; www.loreedulac.net**

🅃 ♨ ♦♦ wo ♨ ⩘ 🐾 ♈ ⊤ ⊕ ⩎ 🐾 nr Ⅲ 🐾 ⩘

Take D53 SW fr Roanne to Villerest; site sp in vill. 3*, Sm, mkd, pt shd, pt sl, EHU (6A) €3.50; sw; TV; phone; Eng spkn; adv bkg rec; watersports; fishing; CKE. *"Attractive, lovely site nr medieval vill; much of site diff lge/med o'fits; lower pt of site diff when wet; sandy sw beach 800m on lake; gd facs; helpful owners."* **€24.00, 14 Apr-28 Oct.** **2019**

ROCAMADOUR *7D3* (2.7km N Rural) *44.81040, 1.61615*
FFCC Camping Ferme Branche, Route de Souillac, Les Campagnes, 46500 Rocamadour **05 65 33 63 37 or 06 75 19 69 90 (mob); campingfermebranche@ yahoo.fr; www.campingfermebranche.com**

🅃 🐕 ♦♦♦ ♨ 🐾 ♈ 🐾 🐾 nr Ⅲ

Site on D247, 1km N of Rocamadour. Sm, pt shd, EHU (6A) €2; bbq; phone. *"Lovely, open, spacious site; gd, clean facs; gd for dogs (free); nr chateau; facs stretched in ssn; friendly owner; great site for price."* **€8.50, 10 Apr-15 Nov.** **2015**

ROCHE BERNARD, LA *2G3* (0.3km NW Urban) *47.51946, -2.30517* **Camp Municipal Le Patis,** Chemin du Patis, 56130 La Roche-Bernard **02 99 90 60 13 or 02 99 90 60 51 (Mairie); camping.lrb56@ gmail.com; www.camping-larochebernard.com**

🅃 €2.30 ♦♦♦ (cont) wo ♨ ⩘ 🐾 ♈ 🐾 🐾 nr Ⅲ

Leave N165 junc 17 (fr N) junc 15 (fr S) & foll marina sp. NB Arr/exit OK on mkt day (Thurs) if avoid town cent. 3*, Med, hdstg, hdg, mkd, pt shd, EHU (6A) €4; red long stay; Eng spkn; adv bkg acc; ccard acc; boating adj; games area; sailing adj. *"Excel clean site in lovely spot on rv bank; helpful staff; facs poss stretched high ssn; grass pitches poss soft - heavy o'fits phone ahead in wet weather; Thurs mkt; m'van o'night area; organic mkt Sat; ancient, pretty town up steep hill; gd walks; highly rec."* **€19.00, 1 Apr-30 Sep.** **2015**

ROCHE CHALAIS, LA *7C2* (0.5km S Rural) *45.14892, -0.00245* **Camp Municipal Les Gerbes,** Rue de la Dronne, 24490 La Roche-Chalais **05 53 91 40 65 or 06 38 82 40 08 (mob); campinggerbes@orange.fr**

♦♦ ♨ ⩘ 🐾 ♈ 🐾 nr ⩘

Fr S on D674 turn sharp L in vill at site sp. Site on R in 500m. Fr N take Coutras-Libourne rd thro vill; site sp on L beyond sm indus est. 3*, Med, mkd, pt shd, terr, EHU (5-10A) €2.60-3.60 (poss rev pol); sw nr; red long stay; adv bkg acc; canoeing adj; fishing adj; boating adj; CKE. *"Pleasant, well-kept, well-run site nr rv; gd sized pitches, some rvside; leisure pk 5km; gd clean san facs; rec pitch N side of site to avoid factory noise; mkt Sat am; rec."* **€14.00, 15 Apr-30 Sep.** **2019**

ROCHE POSAY, LA *4H2* (1.5km N Rural) *46.7989, 0.80961* **Camping La Roche-Posay,** Route de Lésigny. 86270 La Roche-Posay **05 49 86 21 23; info@ larocheposay-vacances.com; www.larocheposay-vacances.com**

🅃 €3 ♦♦♦(htd) ♨ ⩘ 🐾 ♈ ⊤ ⊕ ⩎ 🐾 nr Ⅲ 🐾 ⩘(covrd, htd)

On A10 take exit 26 Châtellerault-Nord, La Roche-Posay; foll sp La Roche-Posay; foll the D725 to La Roche-Possay; at rndabt foll sp for 'Camping-Hippodrome'. 4*, Lge, mkd, hdg, shd, serviced pitches; EHU (10A) inc; gas; bbq (elec, gas); sw nr; red long stay; 40% statics; Eng spkn; adv bkg acc; bike hire; fishing 1.5km; tennis; waterslide; CKE. *"Excel, popular, well-maintained site; aquatic park; 1st class facs; barrier locks automatically 2300; parking avail outside; walk to town on busy rd with no pavement; spa town."* **€42.00, 7 Apr-23 Sep, L21.** **2019**

ROCHE SUR YON, LA *2H4* (8.2km SW Rural) *46.62281, 1.44983* **Campilo,** L'Auroire, 85430 Aubigny **02 51 31 68 45; accueil@campilo.com; www.campilo.com**

12 🅃 €3 wo ♨ ⩘ 🐾 ♈ ⊤ Ⅲ ⩘

Take Rue du Maréchal Joffre, D248 Rue du Maréchal Lyautey and D747 to Les Gâts in Aubign, take Rue des Mésanges and Le Champt des Landes to La Guyonnière, turn R onto Les Gâts, turn L onto Route de l'Auroire, cont onto Rue des Mésanges, turn L onto Le Champt des Landes, take the 2nd R onto La Guyonnière. Med, mkd, pt shd, sl, EHU (10A); bbq; Eng spkn. *"Tow cars not allowed besides c'vans sep car park; fishing lake on site; walks and cycling rtes; lge sports area; bicycles; sm gym; friendly staff; new san facs and pool."* **€26.00** **2019**

ROCHEFORT *7B1* (1km S Urban) *45.93013, -0.95826* **Camping Municipal Le Rayonnement,** 3, Avenue de la Fosse Aux Mâts, 17300 Rochefort **05 46 82 67 70; camping.municipal@ville-rochefort.fr; www.ville-rochefort.fr/decouvrir/camping**

🅃 €1.05 ♦♦♦ wo ♨ ⩘ 🐾 ♈ 🐾 ♈ 🐾 nr Ⅲ 🐾

Exit E602 at junc 31 & take D733 dir Rochefort. At rndabt by McDonalds, take D733 dir Royan. Cont on D733. At rndabt with plane take 3rd exit onto Bd Edouard Pouzet. At rndabt take 3rd exit onto Bd de la Résistance, at next rndabt take 1st exit & then turn L onto ave de la Fosse aux Mâts. Site on L. Med, hdg, hdstg, shd, EHU (15A) inc; bbq; TV; 15% statics; phone; bus 100m; Eng spkn; adv bkg rec; games rm; bike hire. *"Bikes hire free; rv Charente & cycle path to cent 800m away; v helpful staff; no c'vans over 6m & twin axles; san facs v clean; Ecolabel campsite; vg; excel transporter bdge & access to town; excel."* **€18.00, 27 Feb-3 Dec.** **2016**

FRANCE

ROCHEFORT *7B1* (8km W Coastal) *45.94828, -1.09592*
Camp Municipal de la Garenne, Ave de l'Ile-Madame,
17730 Port-des-Barques **05 46 84 80 66 or 06 08 57
08 75 (mob); camping@ville-portdesbarques.fr;
www.camping-municipal-portdesbarques.com**

🏕 €1.26 ⁂ WD ♨ ⚲ 🚿 🔥 ∥ MSP 🦋 ⁖ 🛒 nr ⑪ nr 🍴 🏪 nr ⚠
🅿 (htd) 🌳 shgl adj

Fr Rochefort S on D773, cross Rv Charente bdge &
take 1st exit sp Soubise & Ile Madame. Cont strt thro
Port-des-Barques, site on L opp causeway to Ile-
Madame. 3*, Lge, mkd, unshd, EHU (10A) inc; red long
stay; 25% statics; phone; bus adj; adv bkg acc; ccard
acc; CKE. *"Pleasant site; lge pitches; pitches a little
scruffy, but level; facs dated but clean; refurb (2016)
nice location to sea."* **€22.00, 1 Apr-31 Oct.** **2017**

ROCHEFORT EN TERRE *2F3* (9.8km NE Urban)
47.74455, -2.25997 **Camp Municipal de La Digue,**
Route 77 Le Guélin, 56200 St Martin sur Oust
**02 99 91 55 76 or 02 99 91 49 45; st-martin-oust@
wanadoo.fr; www.tourismebretagne.com**

🏕 €0.50 ⁂ ♨ ⚲ ∥ 🦋 🛒 nr ⚠

On D873 14km N of Redon at Gacilly, turn W onto
D777 twd Rochefort-en-Terre; site sp in 10km in
St Martin. 2*, Med, pt shd, EHU (3-5A) €3.20; bbq; adv
bkg acc; rv fishing 50m. *"Towpath walks to vill & shops;
clean facs but ltd LS; well-refurbished site; site yourself,
warden calls am & eve; excel, refurbished facs (2013)."*
€10.00, 1 May-30 Sep. **2018**

ROCHEFORT EN TERRE *2F3* (0.6km S Rural)
47.695193, -2.349117 **Camping Au Gré des Vents
(formerly du Moulin Neuf),** Chemin de Bogeais,
Route de Limerzel, 56220 Rochefort-en-Terre
**02 97 43 37 52; gredesvents@orange.fr;
www.campingaugredesvents.com**

🏕 €3 ⁂ WD ♨ ⚲ 🚿 ∥ MSP 🦋 ⑪ nr 🏪 nr 🅿 (htd)

Fr Redon W on D775 twd Vannes, approx 23km
turn R onto D774 sp Rochefort-en-Terre; immed
after vill limit sp, turn sharp L up slope to ent. NB
Do not drive thro vill. 3*, Med, hdg, mkd, pt shd, pt
sl, terr, EHU ltd (10A) €4.50; bbq; sw nr; 10% statics;
adv bkg acc; ccard acc; games area; CKE. *"Peaceful
base for touring area; helpful, lovely owners; no
vehicle movement or shwrs 2200-0700 (0800 LS), but
wcs open; no twin axles; excel; bit scruffy; v nr vill."*
€26.00, 31 Mar-30 Sep. **2019**

ROCHEFORT SUR LOIRE *4G1* (0.5km N Urban)
47.36021, -0.65611 **Camping Seasonova Les Plages
de Loire,** route de Savennières, 49190 Rochefort-
sur-Loire **02 41 68 55 91; www.camping-les
plagesdeloire.com**

🏕 €2 ⁂ (htd) WD ♨ ⚲ 🚿 🔥 ∥ MSP 🍴 ⑪ 🍴 ⚠

Fr Angers: S on A87. Exit 24 onto D160 dir Beaulieu
for 1km. At rndabt 1st R onto D54 to Rochfort.
Thro town cent over rv. Site on L. Med, EHU (10A);
twin axles; 10% statics; Eng spkn; adv bkg acc;
CKE. *"New site, nice facs up steps; interesting area."*
€19.00, 3 Apr-1 Nov. **2015**

ROCHELLE, LA *7A1* (12km N Rural/Coastal) *46.25239,
-1.11972* **Camp Municipal Les Misottes,** 46 Rue
de l'Océan, 17137 Esnandes **07 68 16 70 20;
www.campinglesmisottes.fr**

🏕 €1.60 ⁂ (cont) ♨ ⚲ ∥ 🦋 🍴 nr ⑪ nr 🍴 🏪 nr ⚠ 🌳 shgl 2km

Fr N on D938 or N1327 turn W at Marans onto
D105. In 7.5km turn S onto D9 then D202 to
Esnandes. Enter vill, at x-rds strt, site on R in 200m.
Fr La Rochelle D105 N to cent Esnandes, site sp.
2*, Med, mkd, pt shd, EHU (6-10A) €2.85; 5% statics;
Eng spkn; adv bkg acc; fishing; CKE. *"Site on the
edge of marshlands; v nice & quiet; excel bus svrs;
canal fishing; liable to flood; vg; new manager (2018)
enthusiastic and determined to update site; v clean
basic san facs; vg for La Rochelle and area; rec for sh
stay."* **€15.50, 1 Apr-15 Oct.** **2018**

ROCHELLE, LA *7A1* (5km S Rural/Coastal) *46.11659,
-1.11939* **Camping Les Sables,** Chemin du Pontreau,
17440 Aytré **05 46 45 40 30; camping_les_sables@
yahoo.fr; www.camping-les-sables.com**

🏕 €1.50 ⁂ WD ♨ ⚲ 🚿 🔥 ∥ 🍴 🍴 ⑪ 🍴 🏪 ⚠ 🖊
🅿 (covrd, htd) 🏊

Fr S (Rochefort) on D137, exit sp Aytré. At 2nd traff
lts turn L & foll site sp. Lge, hdg, pt shd, EHU (6A) €3;
bbq; 50% statics; phone; Eng spkn; adv bkg acc; ccard
acc; bike hire; games area; games rm; waterslide; CKE.
"Vg." **€35.00, 1 May-15 Oct.** **2017**

ROCROI *5C1* (12km SE Rural) *49.87200, 4.60446*
Camp Départemental du Lac des Vieilles Forges,
08500 Les Mazures **03 24 40 17 31; cmpingvieilles
forges@cg08.fr**

🏕 €1 ⁂ (htd) ♨ ⚲ ∥ MSP 🦋 🍴 🍴 ⚠ 🖊

Fr Rocroi take D1 & D988 for Les Mazures/Renwez.
Turn R D40 at sp Les Vieilles Forges. Site on R nr
lakeside. 3*, Lge, mkd, hdstg, shd, pt sl, EHU (6-10A)
€2.50-4.30 (long leads req); sw; TV; 20% statics; adv
bkg acc; bike hire; boating; tennis; fishing. *"Attractive
walks; lake views fr some pitches; vg site; recep clsd
1200-1500."* **€20.00, 11 Apr-15 Sep.** **2016**

RODEZ *7D4* (1km NE Urban) *44.35323, 2.58708*
Camp Municipal Layoule, 12000 Rodez **05 65 67 09 52;
contact@mairie-rodez.fr**

🏕 ⁂ WD ♨ ⚲ 🚿 ∥ MSP 🦋 🍴 nr ⚠

Clearly sp in Rodez town cent & all app rds. Access
at bottom steep hill thro residential area.
4*, Med, hdg, hdstg, mkd, pt shd, EHU (6A) inc; phone;
bus adj; golf nr; tennis nr; CKE. *"Site by lake & rv; gd
sized pitches; helpful warden; clean facs; steep walk
to historic town; gates clsd 2000-0700; ent is down
steep twisty rds & exit is up the same hill; interesting
wild life; gd walks & cycling; excel NH; excel for town."*
€14.00, 1 May-30 Sep. **2018**

FRANCE

ROHAN *2F3* (0.2km NW Rural) *48.07078, -2.75525*
Camp Municipal du Val d'Oust, Rue de St Gouvry,
56580 Rohan 02 97 51 57 58 or 02 97 51 50 33 (Mairie);
mairie.rohan@wanadoo.fr; www.morbihan.com

🐕 €0.90 🚾 ⌁ 🚮 😀 🚿 ∥ nr ⊕ nr 🛁 nr ⚠

**Rue de St Gouvry runs NW fr Rohan parallel to D11,
but other side of canal.** 2*, Sm, mkd, pt shd, EHU
€3.10; bbq; phone; adv bkg acc; CKE. *"Pleasant site
beside Nantes/Brest canal; gd cycling; market in vill;
some rd noise."* **€12.00, 1 Jun-15 Sep.** **2018**

ROMIEU, LA *8E2* (0.3km NE Rural) *43.98299, 0.50183*
Kawan Village Le Camp de Florence, 32480 La
Romieu 05 62 28 15 58; info@lecampdeflorence.com;
www.lecampdeflorence.com

🐕 €2.30 ⚫ 🚾 ⌁ ♨ ♿ ∥ MP 🦋 ♈ 👔 ⊕ nr 🍴 🛁 nr ⚠ ✦
🛶 🖐

**Take D931 N fr Condom & turn R onto D41, where
La Romieu sp next to radio mast. Go thro La Romieu
& turn L at sp just bef leaving vill.** 4*, Lge, hdstg,
hdg, pt shd, EHU (10A) inc (poss rev pol); bbq; twin
axles; TV; 80% statics; Eng spkn; adv bkg req; ccard
acc; bike hire; games area; games rm; tennis; CKE.
*"Peaceful, Dutch-run site in pleasant location; gd sized
pitches, most with views; welcoming, helpful staff;
waterslide; jacuzzi; leisure complex 500m; gd clean
san facs; gd rest; poss muddy when wet; archery;
some noise fr disco, ask for pitch away fr bar; rest
in 16thC farmhouse; gd pool but take care sl ent;
gd cycling; historic 11thC vill; mkt Wed Condom."*
€36.60, 28 Apr-24 Sep, D19. **2017**

ROMORANTIN LANTHENAY *4G2* (1km E Urban)
47.35486, 1.75568 Camping de Tournefeuille,
Rue de Long Eaton, 41200 Romorantin-Lanthenay
02 54 76 16 60; camping.romo@wanadoo.fr

🐕 🖐 (htd) ⌁ ∥ 🦋 ♈ 🛁 nr ⚠

**Fr town cent on D724 to Salbis, foll sp thro several
traff lts over bdge turn R into Rue de Long-Eaton,
site sp.** 4*, Med, pt shd, EHU (10A) €3; gas; fishing;
bike hire. *"Rv walk to town rec; pool adj; excel modern
san facs; helpful staff."* **€16.00, 1 Apr-30 Sep.** **2016**

ROSANS *9D3* (2.5km SW Rural) *44.38273, 5.46172*
Camping des Rosieres, Quartier des Coings, 05150
Rosans 04 92 66 62 06 or 06 70 10 69 99 (mob);
contact@camping-rosieres.com; www.camping-
rosieres.com/fr

🐕 🖐 🚾 😀 🚿 ∥ ♈ 🍴 👔 ⚠ ✦ 🛶 (htd)

**On D94 Nyons to Gap on RH side just prior to ent
Rosans.** 3*, Sm, hdg, shd, EHU (6A); twin axles; Eng
spkn; adv bkg acc; games area; CKE. *"Horseriding;
canyoning; tennis; boules; steep narr rd fr recep & sw
pool to pitches; gd."* **€24.00, 1 May-30 Sep.** **2017**

ROSCOFF *1D2* (7km SW Rural/Coastal) *48.67246,
-4.05326* Camp Municipal du Bois de la Palud, 29250
Plougoulm 02 98 29 81 82 or 02 98 29 90 76 (Mairie);
contact@plougoulm.bzh; www.plougoulm.bzh

🖐 🚾 ⌁ 🚮 😀 ∥ 🦋 🛁 nr ⚠ 🏖 sand 500m

**Fr D58 turn W on D10 sp Cléder/Plouescat; after
3km on ent Plougoulm foll sp to site.** 2*, Sm, mkd,
hdg, pt shd, terr, EHU (8A) €3.50; phone; Eng spkn;
adv bkg acc; ccard acc; CKE. *"Clean, tidy site in
delightful area; lovely views to sandy inlet; conv ferry;
if arr late, site yourself; warden calls am & pm; access
all hrs with c'van; walk in first, turning diff inside; also
lower field with EHU; sh walk to vill; excel; late arr &
late dep; beautiful beaches to the west."*
€14.00, 15 Jun-4 Sep. **2016**

ROSIERS SUR LOIRE, LES *4G1* (6km NW Rural)
47.39231, -0.27381 Camping Port St Maur, 49250
La Ménitré 02 41 45 60 80; 0611417561@sfr.fr

🐕 €1 🖐 🚾 ⌁ ♿ ∥ 🍴 👔 🛁 nr ⚠ ✦

**Exit Les Rosiers on D952 sp Angers. At rndabt 3km
past St Mathhurin sur Loire take 1st exit sp Port
St Maur. Site on R in 200m.** 2*, Med, mkd, pt shd, EHU
(5A) inc; bbq; 10% statics; Eng spkn. *"Access to san
facs by steps; helpful warden; boat trips on Loire; lovely
rvside setting with view of St Maur Abbey; gd walking &
cycling; gd."* **€12.50, 1 May-15 Sep.** **2016**

ROSNAY *4H2* (0.8km N Rural) *46.70647, 1.21161*
Camp Municipal Les Millots, Route de St Michel-en-
Brenne, 36300 Rosnay 02 54 37 80 17 (Mairie);
rosnay-mairie@wanadoo.fr

🐕 🖐 (htd) 🚾 ⌁ 🚮 😀 ♿ 🚿 🦋 ⊕ nr 🛁 nr ⚠

**NE on D27 fr Le Blanc to Rosnay; site sp 500m N of
Rosnay on D44.** 2*, Sm, mkd, pt shd, EHU (6-10A) inc
(poss rev pol); bbq; phone; adv bkg acc; lake fishing;
tennis; cycling; CKE. *"Lovely, tranquil, popular site;
well-kept; excel modern san facs; warden collects fees
twice daily; lakeside walks; excel walking, cycling,
birdwatching & fishing; gd base for exploring Brenne
National Park; vg value; excel; friendly."*
€11.40, 16 Feb-15 Nov. **2018**

ROUEN *3C2.*(5km E Urban) *49.43154, 1.15387*
Camping L'Aubette, 23 Rue du Vert- Buisson, 76160
St Léger-du-Bourg-Denis 02 32 08 32 40; accueil@
rouentourisme.com; www.rouentourisme.com

12 🐕 🖐 🚾 ⌁ ♿ ∥ MP 🛁 nr

**Fr Rouen E on N31 dir Darnétal & Beauvais; in 1km
cont strt on onto D42/D138 dir St Léger-du-Bourg-
Denis; in 400m turn L onto Rue du Vert Buisson;
site on r in 800m just past stop sp. Site well sp as
'Camping' fr Rouen cent.** 2*, Med, pt shd, pt sl, terr,
EHU (3-10A) €1.50-3; 40% statics; bus 150m; CKE. *"In
attractive rv valley; conv city cent; conv bus to town; v
ltd touring pitches; cash only; v basic site, gd NH only; v
poor."* **€15.00** **2018**

FRANCE

ROUEN *3C2* (14km NW Rural) *49.50553, 0.98409*
Camping Les Nenuphars, 765 Rue des Deux Tilleuls,
Le Bout du Haut, 76480 Roumare **02 35 33 80 75;**
www.camping-les-nenuphars.com

🐕 €1.70 ⚮ WD ♨ 🗑 ⚐

**S on D6015/A150 dir Rouen, foll sp Roumare &
site. Fr Rouen take A150/D6015 N to St Jean-du-
Cardonnay; turn L to Roumare; site sp. 500m bef
Roumare.** 2*, Med, mkd, hdg, pt shd, pt sl, EHU
(5-10A); twin axles; phone; bus 1km; Eng spkn; adv
bkg acc; games area; CKE. *"Pleasant grassy site,
handy for Rouen; v ltd sports facs; lge pitches; vg."*
€18.00, 28 Mar-15 Dec. 2015

ROYAN *7B1* (9km NE Rural) *45.64796, -0.95847*
FFCC Camping Le Bois Roland, 82 Route de Royan,
17600 Médis **05 46 05 47 58;** contact@le-bois-
roland.com; www.le-bois-roland.com

🐕 €2.80 ⚮ WD ♨ & 🗑 ⚐ ▼ Ⓨ ♨ 🍴 ⚟ ✦ 🛶 🎣 sand 4km

**On N150 Saintes-Royan rd, site sp on R 100m
beyond Médis vill sp.** 3*, Med, pt shd, EHU (5-10A)
€4.20-5.20; gas; TV; phone; Eng spkn; adv bkg acc;
ccard acc; CKE. *"Attractive, wooded site; friendly,
family-run; facs poss stretched high ssn; waiting area
avail; vg; shop/rest/bar open in July when tradsmn will
call."* **€19.00, 1 May-30 Sep.** 2015

ROYAN *7B1* (1.7km SE Coastal) *45.61817, -1.00425*
Camping La Triloterie, 44 ter, Ave Aliénor d'Aquitaine,
17200 Royan **05 46 05 26 91;** info@camping
royan.com; www.campingroyan.com

12 🐕 €1.50 (htd) WD ♨ ⚟ ⚐ 🍴 ⚟ nr ⚟ 🎣 sand 900m

Fr Royan PO, foll sp Bordeaux N730, on E of rd.
2*, Med, shd, EHU (4-12A) €4-6 (poss rev pol); bbq;
10% statics; phone; waterslide. *"Excel site; conv for
Royan town cent & St George de Didonne; site a bit
tired, ok for NH."* **€23.00** 2017

ROYAN *7B1* (16km SE Coastal) *45.55713, -0.94655*
Camping Soleil Levant, Allée de la Langée, 17132
Meschers-sur-Gironde **05 46 02 76 62;** info@camping-
soleillevant.com; www.camping-soleillevant.com

🐕 €3.50 ⚮ WD ♨ 🗑 ⚐ ▼ Ⓨ ♨ 🛒 ⚟ ✦ 🛶 🎣 👣 sand 1.5km

**Take D145 coast rd fr Royan to Talmont. At
Meschers turn R foll camp sp twd port; sp.**
4*, Med, pt shd, EHU (10A) €5.10; 20% statics; adv
bkg acc; ccard acc; horseriding adj; watersports
adj; CKE. *"Gd, busy site; v clean san facs; port & rest
300m; vill shop & daily mkt 500m; visits to Cognac &
Bordeaux distilleries; v friendly, helpful family run site."*
€31.00, 1 Apr-30 Sep. 2015

"There aren't many sites open at this time of year"

If you're travelling outside peak season
remember to call ahead to check site opening
dates – even if the entry says 'open all year'.

ROYAN *7B1* (5km SE Coastal) *45.58345, -0.98720*
Camping Bois Soleil, 2 Ave de Suzac, 17110 St
Georges-de-Didonne **05 46 05 05 94;** camping.bois.
soleil@wanadoo.fr; www.bois-soleil.com

🐕 €3 (not acc end Jun-Aug inc) ⚮ (htd) WD ♨ ♿ & 🗑 ⚐ 🍴 MP 🍴 ▼
Ⓦ ♨ 🛒 ⚟ 🎣 ✦ (htd) 👣 sand adj

**Fr A10 exit junc 35 dir Saintes & Royan; on app
Royan foll St Georges-de-Didonne sp onto bypass
D25/D730/D25/D25E; go over 2 rndabts (with
underpass bet); at 3rd rndabt turn L sp Meschers-
sur-Gironde; site on R in 500m. Site well sp.**
4*, Lge, hdstg, mkd, hdg, pt shd, terr, EHU (6A) inc
(poss rev pol); gas; bbq (gas); TV; 30% statics; phone;
Eng spkn; adv bkg rec; ccard acc; bike hire; tennis;
games area; CKE. *"Superb wooded site in vg location
nr beach; popular & busy; generous pitches, some
sandy; excel, clean san facs; vg shop & rest; many sandy
beaches nrby."* **€42.00, 2 Apr-9 Oct.** 2019

See advertisement

For a guide to symbols see the fold out on the rear cover

ROYAN 7B1 (4km NW Urban/Coastal) 45.6309, -1.0498 **Campéole Camping Clairefontaine,** 6 Rue du Colonel Lachaud, Pontaillac, 17200 Royan **05 46 39 08 11; clairefontaine@campeole.com; www. camping-clairefontaine.com or www.campeole.com**

🎫 €3 💶 WC ⛲ ♿ 🔥 🖥 ✉ MP 🦋 ♈ 🍽 ⊕ ♨ 🛒 🎢 🏊

🏖 sand 300m

Foll Pontaillac sp fr Royan. Site sp in Clairefontaine (& Pontaillac). 4*, Lge, mkd, pt shd, serviced pitches; EHU (10A); gas; bbq; TV; 80% statics; phone; Eng spkn; adv bkg req; ccard acc; tennis; CKE. *"Lovely coastline; gd for family holiday; helpful owner; clean, unisex san facs; ltd touring pitches, some sm; gd security; site poss dusty; vg walking & cycling; casino 300m; coastal path Pontaillac to Royan; gd site; easy walk/bike/bus into town; nice sw; bar & shop onsite; conv for city; vg."* **€41.00, 31 Mar-1 Oct.**   **2017**

ROYBON 9C2 (1.6km S Rural) 45.24639, 5.24806 **Camping de Roybon,** Route de St Antoine, 38940 Roybon **04 76 36 23 67 or 06 86 64 55 47; camping roybon38@gmail.com; www.campingroybon.com**

🎫 €2.65 💶 WC ⛲ ♿ ✉ 🦋 🛒 🎢

Fr Roybon go S on D71 & foll sp. 2*, Med, mkd, pt shd, pt sl, EHU (10A) €3.50; sw nr; adv bkg acc; watersports adj. *"V peaceful; gd, modern facs new; vg; can be boggy when wet."* **€18.40, 1 May-30 Sep.**   **2016**

ROYERE DE VASSIVIERE 7B4 (6km SW Rural) 45.78869, 1.89855 **Camping Les Terrasses du Lac,** Vauveix, 23460 Royère-de-Vassivière **05 55 64 76 77; lesterrasses.camping@free.fr; www.campings-vassiviere.com**

🎫 €1 💶 (htd) WC ⛲ ♿ ✉ 🦋 🛒 nr ⊕ nr 🏊 adj

Fr Eymoutiers take D43 for approx 10km then take D36 to Vauveix & foll sp. 1*, Med, mkd, hdg, pt shd, terr, EHU (10A) €3.10 (poss rev pol); TV; 50% statics; cycling; horseriding; watersports adj; CKE. *"Helpful staff; walking; lovely setting."* **€22.00, 2 Apr-31 Oct.**   **2017**

RUE 3B2 (6km N Rural) 50.31367, 1.69472 **Kawan Village Le Val d'Authie,** 20 Route de Vercourt, 80120 Villers-sur-Authie **03 22 29 92 47; camping@valdauthie.fr; www.valdauthie.fr**

🎫 €1.50 💶 (htd) WC ⛲ ♿ 🔥 🖥 ✉ MP 🦋 ♈ 🍽 ⊕ ♨ 🛒 🎢 🏊 🏖 (covrd, htd) 🎱

Exit 24 on A16 twrds Vron, foll sp Camping Vercourt thro town. 5*, Lge, mkd, hdg, pt shd, pt sl, EHU (6-10A) (rev pol); gas; TV; 60% statics; phone; Eng spkn; adv bkg acc; ccard acc; games area; games rm; fitness rm; tennis; CKE. *"Set in pleasant countryside; sauna; steam rm; helpful, friendly owners; clean, unisex facs & spacious shwrs; sm sep area for tourers, but many touring pitches bet statics (2009); poss diff for lge o'fits; gd pool; v cr & noisy high ssn; excel."* **€31.00, 1 Apr-30 Sep.**   **2017**

RUE 3B2 (4km SE Rural) 50.25278, 1.71224 **Camping de la Mottelette,** Ferme de la Mottelette, 80120 Forest-Montiers **03 22 28 32 33 or 06 72 85 73 77 (mob); contact@la-mottelette.com; www.la-mottelette.com**

🎫 €1 💶 WC ⛲ ♿ ✉ 🦋 🛒 nr 🎢

Exit A16 junc 24 onto D32 dir Rue & L Crotoy; at rndabt junc with D235 cont on D32; site on L in 1.5km. Site sp on leaving A16. 2*, Sm, mkd, hdg, unshd, EHU (6A) €4; bbq; 50% statics; Eng spkn; adv bkg acc; games area; games rm; CKE. *"Basic, CL type, clean site on wkg fm; welcoming, friendly owners; mkt Sat; conv A16; gd touring base or NH; vg; pleasant atmosphere; new facs (2015)."* **€20.00, 1 Apr-31 Oct.**   **2017**

RUFFEC 7A2 (3km SE Rural) 46.01500, 0.21304 **Camping Le Réjallant,** Les Grands Champs, 16700 Condac **05 45 31 29 06; cdc-ruffec-charente@ wanadoo.fr**

12 🎫 💶 WC ⛲ 🖥 ✉ 🦋 ♈ ⊕ nr 🎢

Site sp fr N10 & fr town. App 1km fr turn-off. 3*, Med, mkd, hdg, shd, pt sl, EHU (10A) inc; sw nr; Eng spkn; fishing 100m; CKE. *"Friendly, sm nbr of touring sites; lovely vill 2km, gd Leclerc and Lidl supmkt; gd pool; clean facs; bar 100m; great for families."* **€21.00**   **2017**

RUMILLY 9B3 (3.5km S Rural) 45.84083, 5.96277 **Camping Le Madrid,** Route de St Félix, 74150 Rumilly **04 50 01 12 57; contact@camping-le-madrid.com**

🎫 €2 💶 (htd) WC ⛲ ♿ 🔥 🖥 ✉ MP 🦋 ♈ 🍽 ⊕ ♨ 🛒 nr 🎢 🏊 🎱

S fr Rumilly on D910, take D3 L dir St Marcel for approx 600m & at 2nd rndabt turn R, site sp. 3*, Med, hdstg, hdg, mkd, pt shd, EHU (6-10A) €2.80-4.30; bbq; 50% statics; adv bkg acc; games rm; fishing; bike hire; games area. *"Pleasant owners; chosen for proximity to m'way; ideal for NH."* **€28.00, 1 Apr-31 Oct.**   **2019**

RUOMS 9D2 (4km SW Urban) 44.43101, 4.32945 **Camping La Chapoulière,** 07120 Ruoms **04 75 39 64 98 or 04 75 93 90 72; camping@lachapouliere.com; www.lachapouliere.com**

🎫 €3.50 💶 ⛲ ♿ 🔥 🖥 ✉ MP 🦋 ♈ 🍽 ⊕ ♨ 🛒 🎢 🏊 🎱

Exit Ruoms S on D579. At junc 2km S, foll D111 sp St Ambroix. Site 1.5km fr junc. 3*, Med, mkd, shd, pt sl, EHU (6A) €4.60; gas; sw nr; TV; Eng spkn; adv bkg rec; games area; tennis 2km; canoeing; fishing adj. *"Beautiful pitches on rv bank; friendly; ltd facs LS; vg; excel modern san facs; lge pitches demarcated by trees."* **€37.00, Easter-30 Sep.**   **2019**

SABLE SUR SARTHE *4F1* (0.5km S Rural) *47.83101, -0.33177* **Camp Municipal de l'Hippodrome,** Allée du Québec, 72300 Sable-sur-Sarthe **02 43 95 42 61; camping@sablesursarthe.fr; camping.sablesur sarthe.fr**

Sp in town (foll sm, white sp with c'van symbols or Hippodrome). Fr N on D306; at traff lts at junc with D309, go strt over & under rlwy brdg sp Centre Ville; foll camping sps. 3*, Med, hdg, pt shd, EHU (15A) €2.40; gas; bbq; red long stay; TV; Eng spkn; ccard acc; boat hire; canoeing; rv fishing; bike hire. *"Excel site next to racecourse; gd, clean facs; helpful staff; conv for town; some pitches diff for lge fits."* **€16.40, 3 Apr-15 Oct.**   **2018**

SABLES D'OLONNE, LES *7A1* (10km ESE Coastal) *46.471521, -1.725812* **Camping Bel Air,** 6 allee de la Chevreuse, Chateau d'Olonne 85180 **02 51 22 09 67; dubelair@cybelevacances.com; www.camping dubelair.com**

Fr La Roche-sur-Yon take D160 twrds Les Sables d'Olonne. Take D949 twrds Niort then the D2949 on Avenue de Talmont. At rndabt take D32A, 3rd exit on Rue du Brandais. Turn R onto Chemin de Bel air. Med, pt shd, bbq (gas); adv bkg acc. **€46.00, 1 Apr-1 Nov.**   **2019**

SABLES D'OR LES PINS *2E3* (1km NW Rural/Coastal) *48.63230, -2.41229* **Camping Les Salines,** Rue du Lac, 22240 Plurien **02 96 72 17 40 or 06 28 22 43 36; campinglessalinesplurien@gmail.com; www.camping lessalines.fr**

Fr D786 turn N at Plurien onto D34 to Sables-d'Or. In 1km turn L & site on L after 200m. 2*, Med, pt shd, pt sl, terr, EHU (6A) €2.35; phone; Eng spkn; adv bkg acc; CKE. *"Lovely, quiet, tranquile hillside site; some sea views; vg san facs; gates clsd 2200-0700; no pitching when office clsd, but lge car park opp; excel access to nature reserve & beautiful beaches; enthusiastic, helpful new owners (2017); lge pitches; lovely estuary walks; conv St Malo; wonderful coast; highly rec."* **€16.00, 1 Apr-12 Nov.**   **2017**

SAILLANS *9D2* (1.6km W Rural) *44.69511, 5.18124* **Camping Les Chapelains,** 26340 Saillans **04 75 21 55 47; camping@chapelains.fr; www.chapelains.fr**

Fr W on D93 turn onto D493. Site well sp just bef Saillans vill boundary adj Rv Drôme. Sm, hdg, mkd, pt shd, EHU (4-10A); gas; Eng spkn; adv bkg acc; games area; CKE. *"Attractive, well-run rvside site; some v sm pitches; friendly, helpful warden; rv walk to vill; rest open LS; san facs clean & updated (2015); gd."* **€22.60, 18 Apr-15 Sep.**   **2015**

ST AIGNAN SUR CHER *4G2* (9km N Rural) *47.32361, 1.36983* **FFCC Camping Domaine du Bien Vivre,** 13-15 Route du Petit Village, 41140 St Romain-sur-Cher **02 54 71 73 74; domainedubienvivre@free.fr; www.domainedubienvivre.fr**

Fr St Aignan-sur-Cher N on D675; in 6km in St Romain-sur-Cher site sp to L; foll sps for 3km. Sm, mkd, pt shd, pt sl, EHU (6A) inc; bbq; Eng spkn; ccard acc; CKE. *"A vineyard site; helpful owner; ltd facs in winter; sale of wines; conv Blois; gd."* **€16.50**   **2016**

ST AIGNAN SUR CHER *4G2* (1.6km SE Rural) *47.26530, 1.38875* **Camping Les Cochards,** 1 Rue du Camping, Seigy, 41110 St Aignan-sur-Cher **02 54 75 15 59 or 06 72 09 45 24 (mob); camping@ lesclochards.com; www.lesclochards.com**

On D17 heading SE fr St Aignan twd Seigy on S bank of Rv Cher. 4*, Lge, mkd, pt shd, EHU (5-10A) €4.50; bbq; sw nr; TV; 20% statics; phone; Eng spkn; ccard acc; games area; horseriding 3km; rv fishing; canoeing; CKE. *"Attractive, open site; helpful owners; gd san facs; recep clsd 2000; some pitches waterlogged after rain; easy walk to attractive town; excel; discount vouchers avail for local attractions; san facs being upgraded (2015)."* **€28.00, 1 Apr-15 Oct.**   **2015**

ST AMAND EN PUISAYE *4G4* (0.5km NE Urban) *47.53294, 3.07333* **Camp Municipal La Vrille,** Route de St Sauveur, 58310 St Amand-en-Puisaye **03 86 39 72 21 or 03 86 39 63 72 (Mairie); saintam.mairie@ wanadoo.fr; www.ot-puisaye-nivernaise.fr**

Fr N7 take D957 Neuvy-sur-Loire to St Amand, at rd junc in vill take D955 sp St Sauveur-en-Puisaye, site on R in 500m; clearly sp on all app to vill. 2*, Sm, mkd, pt shd, EHU €2.30; sailing adj; fishing in adj reservoir. *"Vg simple site; gates clsd 2200-0700."* **€12.50, 1 Jun-30 Sep.**   **2015**

ST AMAND LES EAUX *3B4* (4km SE Rural) *50.43535, 3.46290* **FFCC Camping du Mont des Bruyères,** 806 Rue Basly, 59230 St Amand-les-Eaux **03 27 48 56 87; info@campingmontdesbruyeres.com; www.camping montdesbruyeres.com**

Exit A23 m'way at junc 5 or 6 onto ring rd D169, site sp. Fr N exit E42 junc 31 onto N52/N507 then D169. Avoid St Amand cent. 4*, Med, mkd, hdg, shd, pt sl, terr, EHU (6A-10A) inc; bbq; 60% statics; adv bkg acc; CKE. *"Attractive site on forest edge; most touring pitches under trees; access to some pitches diff due slopes; gd cycling; excel birdlife on site; fac gd & clean."* **€24.00, 15 Mar-30 Oct.**   **2015**

ST AMAND MONTROND *4H3* (3km SW Rural) *46.71258, 2.49000* **Camp Municipal La Roche,** Rue de la Roche, 18200 St Amand-Montrond **02 48 96 09 36;** camping-la-roche@wanadoo.fr; www.st-amand-tourisme.com

🐕 � (htd) 🗑 ♨ 🚿 ⊟ ∥ 🛒 ♚ 🏊nr 🅿 🔥 ♻

Exit A71/E11 junc 8 dir St Amand-Montrond on D300. Then foll sp to Montluçon on D2144 until rndabt on canal, turn R onto Quai Pluviôse/Rue de la Roche, site on R. Site sp on far side of town. 3*, Med, shd, pt sl, EHU (6A) €2.90 (poss rev pol); phone; rv fishing; tennis; CKE. *"Popular NH, rec arr by 1700 high ssn; helpful warden; clean facs; tight for lge o'fits; rvside walk to pleasant town; gd."* **€17.00, 1 Apr-30 Sep.** 2015

ST ANDRE DE CUBZAC *7C2* (4km NW Rural) *45.00703, -0.47724* **FFCC Camping Le Port Neuf,** 1125 Route du Port Neuf, 33240 St André-de-Cubzac 05 57 43 16 44; contact@camping-port-neuf.com; www.camping-port-neuf.com

🐕 €1 ♯♯ (htd) 🗑 ♨ 🚿 ⊟ ∥ MSP 🛒 ♚ 🍴 ⊕ ♨

Fr A10 or N10 take exit sp St André. Well sp fr St André (narr rds) on D669. 2*, Sm, mkd, hdg, hdstg, pt shd, EHU (6A) €3.50 (poss long lead req); train to Bordeaux fr vill; Eng spkn; adv bkg acc; bike hire; lake fishing 100m; boating 100m; horseriding nr; CKE. *"Lovely spot; friendly, helpful staff; san facs clean; pedalo hire; scruffy site (2015)."* **€15.00, 1 May-30 Sep.** 2016

STE ANNE D'AURAY *2F3* (1.6km SW Rural) *47.69842, -2.96226* **Camp Municipal du Motten,** Allée des Pins, 56400 Ste Anne-d'Auray **02 97 57 60 27 or 02 97 57 63 91;** contact@sainte-anne-auray.com or camping motten@orange.fr; www.sainte-anne-auray.com

🐕 ♯♯ WD ♨ 🚿 ⊟ ∥ 🛒 ♚ 🍴 🏊nr 🅿

Fr W on N165 take D17bis N to St Anne-d'Auray; then L onto D19 to town. This rte avoids Pluneret. Foll site sp. 2*, Med, mkd, pt shd, EHU (10A) inc; TV; Eng spkn; adv bkg acc; tennis; games area. *"Peaceful, well-kept site; best pitches immed R after ent; welcoming, helpful warden; gd clean san facs; excel touring base; conv Basilica Ste Anne d'Auray; excel."* **€16.00, 13 Jun-14 Sep.** 2015

ST ANTONIN NOBLE VAL *8E4* (1.5km N Rural) *44.1595, 1.7564* **FFCC Camp Municipal Le Ponget,** Route de Caylus, 82140 St Antonin-Noble-Val **05 63 68 21 13 or 05 63 30 60 23 (Mairie);** camping-leponget@wanadoo.fr

🐕 €1.20 ♯♯ (htd) 🗑 ♨ 🚿 ∥ MSP 🛒 🍴nr ⊕nr 🏊nr 🅿

Fr Caylus take D19 S to St Antonin; site on R, well sp. 2*, Sm, hdg, pt shd, EHU (3-6A) €2.50-3.70; gas; sw nr; phone; CKE. *"Well-kept site adj sports field; modern san facs; poss diff lge o'fits; gd walking; vg friendly site; excel mkt Sun; discount for 7 days; lovely medival town; gd for Aveyron Gorges & Bastide towns."* **€11.70, 2 May-30 Sep.** 2017

FRANCE

ST AUBIN DU CORMIER *2E4* (0.3km E Urban) *48.25990, -1.39609* **Camp Municipal de l'Etang,** Rue de l'Etang, 35140 St Aubin-du-Cormier **02 99 39 10 42 (Mairie); mairie@ville-staubinducormier.fr; www.saint-aubin-du-cormier.bzh/accueil**

€0.65 nr

NE fr Rennes on A84; in 20km exit junc 28 dir St Aubin-du-Cormier. Foll sp 'Centre Ville' then site sp. Poss diff for lge o'fits - narr app. 2*, Sm, mkd, pt shd, pt sl, terr, EHU (6A) inc; bbq (charcoal, elec, gas); 10% statics; adv bkg acc; lake fishing; Jeu de boules alleys; mkd walking rtes nrby; CKE. *"Pleasant, beautifully kept site adj lake; friendly; forest walks & around lake; pretty vill, with excel shops; mkt Thur; vet 1km; lovely site; san facs; vg disabled facs; recycling; dog health certs check on arr; excel for sh or long stay; suitable for v sm vans or MHs; narr angled ent thro stone pillars."* **€15.00, 27 Apr-29 Sep.** **2015**

ST AVOLD *5D2* (2km N Urban) *49.11017, 6.71059* **FFCC Camping Le Felsberg,** Centre International de Séjour, Rue en Verrerie, 57500 St Avold **03 87 92 75 05; cis.stavold@wanadoo.fr; www.mairie-saint-avold.fr**

12 €1 nr

Fr N on A4 exit junc 39 onto D633 to St Avold, stay in L hand lane at 2nd traff lts & turn L; pass under D603 for 2km & turn R. Site well sp in & around town; app up steep incline. 3*, Sm, hdstg, hdg, mkd, pt shd, pt sl, EHU (6-10A) €3-5; red long stay; 50% statics; adv bkg acc; ccard acc; CKE. *"German border 10km; sm pitches; gd facs; coal mine & archaeological park nrby worth visit; hypmkt 1.5km; awkward, heavy duty security gate at site ent; conv NH nr m'way; gd; walking dist of town facs."* **€14.00** **2015**

ST AYGULF *10F4* (0.5km N Coastal) *43.39151, 6.72648* **Camping de St Aygulf Plage,** 270 Ave Salvarelli, 83370 St Aygulf Plage **04 94 17 62 49 or 06 12 44 36 52 (mob); info@campingdesaintaygulf.fr; www.campingdesaintaygulf.fr**

€3 sand adj

Fr Roquebrunne on D7 at rndabt 100m after vill sp St Aygulf take 3rd exit leading to Rue Roger Martin du Gard. Keep turning L. Fr Fréjus on D559, rd bends R after bdge over beach access, turn R bef rd climbs to L. 2*, V lge, hdg, mkd, shd, EHU (5A) €3.50; gas; red long stay; twin axles; adv bkg acc; ccard acc; fishing; watersports nr; games area; CKE. *"Gd; shop clsd LS; sports facs nrby; pool (2017)."* **€34.00, 1 Apr-28 Oct.** **2017**

ST AYGULF *10F4* (5km NW Rural) *43.41626, 6.70598* **Camping L'Etoile d'Argens,** Chemin des Etangs, 83370 St Aygulf **04 94 81 01 41; info@etoiledargens.com; www.etoiledargens.com**

€5 (htd) sand 3km

Exit A8 at junc 37 Puget-sur-Argens onto DN7 to Fréjus & D559 to St Aygulf, or fr DN7 take D7 to St Aygulf by-passing Fréjus & turn onto D8 to site. 4*, Lge, mkd, hdg, shd, serviced pitches; EHU (10A) inc; gas; 40% statics; Eng spkn; adv bkg acc; ccard acc; tennis; rv fishing; archery; golf 1.5km; CKE. *"Friendly, helpful owners; gd facs, poss unclean LS; excel pool complex; ferry down rv to beach in ssn; vg."* **€59.00, 1 Apr-30 Sep.** **2015**

ST BENOIT SUR LOIRE *4F3* (0.5km SE Rural) *47.80711, 2.29528* **FFCC Camping Le Port,** Rue du Port, 45730 St Benoît-sur-Loire **02 38 35 12 34; contact@campingleport.fr**

(htd) nr nr sand adj

Fr Orléans take N60 & bypass Châteauneuf-sur-Loire. Take D60 twd Sully-sur-Loire to St Benoît-sur-Loire. Foll sp fr vill, site on L side of 1-way rd. 2*, Sm, pt shd, pt sl, EHU (13A) €2.50; bbq; sw nr; fishing adj; canoeing adj; CKE. *"Gd cycling, walking; pleasant town; splendid views over Loire fr some pitches, others in wooded area; excel."* **€20.00, 1 May-30 Sep.** **2019**

ST BREVIN LES PINS *2G3* (2km N Coastal) *47.26553, -2.16918* **FFCC Camping de Mindin,** 32-40 Ave du Bois, 44250 St Brévin-les-Pins **02 40 27 46 41; info@camping-de-mindin.com; www.camping-de-mindin.com**

12 €2.35 (htd) (htd) sand adj

On beach rd at N end of St Brevin. 3*, Med, shd, EHU (16A) €5.05; 80% statics; adv bkg acc; ccard acc; CKE. *"Sm, sandy pitches; 6 touring pitches, area unkept; san facs being updated."* **€16.80** **2017**

ST BREVIN LES PINS *2G3* (2.4km S Coastal) *47.23514, -2.16739* **Camping Le Fief,** 57 Chemin du Fief, 44250 St Brévin-les-Pins **02 40 27 23 86; camping@lefief.com; www.lefief.com**

€7 (covrd, htd) sand 800m

Fr Nantes dir St Nazaire. After St Nazaire bdge S on D213. Pass Leclerc & exit sp St Brévin-l'Océan/La Courance. At rndabt foll sp Le Fief. 4*, Lge, hdstg, mkd, pt shd, EHU (8A) €6; gas; bbq (charcoal, gas); red long stay; TV; 30% statics; Eng spkn; adv bkg acc; ccard acc; sauna; gym; games area; waterslide; games rm; jacuzzi; CKE. *"Excel for families; wellness cent; fitness rm; waterpark & waterslide etc adj; vg leisure facs."* **€41.00, 4 Apr-20 Sep.** **2019**

See advertisement opposite

ST BRIAC SUR MER *2E3* (1km N Urban) *48.62765, -2.13056* **FFCC Camping Emeraude,** 7 Chemin de la Souris, 35800 St Briac-sur-Mer **02 99 88 34 55; emeraude@seagreen.fr; www.seagreen-camping emeraude.com**

€2.50 (htd) 700m

SW fr Dinard to St Lunaire on N786, after passing Dinard golf course, site is sp to L. 3*, Lge, hdg, pt shd, EHU (6A) €3.80; gas; 40% statics; adv bkg acc; bike hire; games area; waterpark; games rm. *"Excel, well-run site, quiet LS."* **€26.00, 3 Apr-19 Sep. 2016**

ST BRIAC SUR MER *2E3* (0.5km S Coastal) *48.61493, -2.12779* **Camping Le Pont Laurin,** Route de la Vallée Gatorge, 35800 St Briac-sur-Mer **02 99 88 34 64; lepontlaurin@ouest-camping.com; www.ouest-camping.com**

€1.50 sand 1km

Fr St Briac, 500m S on D3. 2*, Lge, hdstg, hdg, mkd, pt shd, EHU (10A) €3 (poss rev pol); 40% statics; Eng spkn; adv bkg acc; ccard acc; games area; sailing; tennis nr; CKE. *"Peaceful site; welcoming, helpful staff; clean, modern san facs; excel beaches; canoe hire nr; sports cent adj; gd walking; walking dist to shops, rest etc; interesting town; highly rec."* **€26.00, 1 Apr-30 Sep. 2017**

ST BRIEUC *2E3* (2km S Rural) *48.50066, -2.75938* **Camping des Vallées,** Blvd Paul-Doumer, 22000 St Brieuc **02 96 94 05 05; campingdesvallees@wanadoo.fr; www.camping-desvallees.com**

€2.40 sand 3km

Fr N12 take exit sp D700 Trégueux, Pleufragan & foll sp 'Des Vallées'. Site nr Parc de Brézillet. 3*, Sm, hdstg, mkd, hdg, pt shd, EHU (10A) €4; 25% statics; Eng spkn; adv bkg acc; waterslide adj; CKE. *"High kerbs to pitches; htd pool adj; excel."* **€25.00, 2 Mar-18 Dec. 2015**

ST CALAIS *4F2* (0.5km N Urban) *47.92691, 0.74413* **Camp Municipal du Lac,** Rue du Lac, 72120 St Calais **02 43 35 04 81; campingstcalais@orange.fr**

nr nr

E fr Le Mans on D357 to St Calais; after sharp (90 degree) L/H bend away fr town cent take L/H lane for next junc in 100m; do not foll D357 bend to R but go strt ahead on D429; in 200m turn R onto sm rd sp 'Conflans/Plan d'Eau'. Site on R after football grnd. Fr N exit A11 junc 5 onto D1 to St Calais; turn R onto D357 dir Le Mans; in 200m turn R onto D429 N; in 400 turn R into sm rd sp 'Confland/Plan d'Eau to site; leave D357 at R angle bend by Champion supmkt; site in 100m. Site by lake on N edge of town, well sp fr cent. Ent easy to miss. 3*, Med, hdg, mkd, pt shd, EHU (6A) inc; bbq; sw nr; 10% statics; adv bkg acc; CKE. *"Delightful, well-kept site; friendly, helpful warden; spacious pitches, espec nr lake; easy rvside walk to town; pool adj; gd touring base; excel; immac old style san facs; gd stopover."* **€14.00, 26 Mar-15 Oct. 2019**

ST CAST LE GUILDO *2E3* (0.5km N Coastal) *48.63690, -2.26900* **Camping Le Châtelet,** Rue des Nouettes, 22380 St Cast-le-Guildo **02 96 41 96 33; info@lechatelet.com; www.lechatelet.com**

€4.20 (covrd, htd) sand 300m

Site sp fr all dir & in St Cast-le-Guildo but best rte: fr D786 at Matignon take D13 into St Cast-le-Guildo, turn L after Intermarché supmkt on R; foll sm site sp. Or app on D19 fr St Jaguel. Care needed down ramp to main site. (NB Avoid Matignon cent Wed due to mkt). 5*, Lge, mkd, hdg, pt shd, pt sl, terr, EHU (10A) inc; gas; bbq (charcoal, elec); TV; 50% statics; adv bkg acc; ccard acc; games rm; golf 2km; fishing. *"Site o'looks coast; o'fits over 7m by req; extra for sea view pitches; gd for families; helpful staff; modern unisex san facs; bike hire 500m; gates clsd 2230-0700; access to some pitches diff lge o'fits; mkt Mon; excel site."* **€50.00, 16 Apr-15 Sep, B11. 2017**

ST CAST LE GUILDO *2E3* (3.5km S Rural) *48.58441, -2.25691* **Camping Le Château de Galinée,** Rue de Galinée, 22380 St Cast-le-Guildo **02 96 41 10 56; contact@chateaudegalinee.com; www.chateaude galinee.com**

🐕€4.50 ♦♦♦(htd) 🆆 ♨ ♣ ⚕ 🗑 ⊘ 🎱 🦋 ⓣ ⓨ ① 🍴 🎣 ⚠ ⚲
🏊(covrd, htd, indoor) 🏖 🏄 sand 4km

W fr St Malo on D168 thro Ploubalay. At La Ville-es-Comte branch onto D786 & go thro Notre Dame-du-Guildo. Approx 2km after Notre Dame-du-Guildo turn 3rd L into Rue de Galinée & foll sp to site. Do not go into St Cast. 4*, Lge, mkd, hdg, pt shd, EHU (10A) inc; bbq; cooking facs; red long stay; TV; 30% statics; Eng spkn; adv bkg acc; ccard acc; sauna; games area; waterslide; horseriding 6km; games rm; tennis; golf 3km; fishing; mini golf; CKE. *"Peaceful, family site in lovely area; spacious, well laid-out pitches; helpful staff; modern, clean, excel san facs; pitches poss muddy after rain; fishing pond; excel rest; mkt Fri & Mon; identity bracelet to be worn at all times."* **€54.50, 10 May-5 Sep, B27.** **2019**

ST CAST LE GUILDO *2E3* (6km SW Rural) *48.59111, -2.29578* **Camping Le Vallon aux Merlettes,** Route de Lamballe, 22550 Matignon **02 96 80 37 99; contact@ campingdematignon.com; www.campingde matignon.com**

🐕€0.75 ♦♦♦(cont) 🆆 ♨ ♣ ⚕ 🗑 ⊘ 🎱 🦋 ⓨ 🎣 ⚠ 🏊

Fr E & W take D786 to Matignon; 500m fr town cent turn SW on D13 twds Lamballe. 3*, Med, pt shd, pt sl, EHU (8A); gas; 10% statics; adv bkg rec; tennis; CKE. *"Lovely site on playing fields outside attractive town; vg clean facs; new hard working private owners (2015); excel & popular."* **€19.00, 4 Apr-30 Sep.** **2015**

ST CHELY D'APCHER *9D1* (3km N Rural) *44.81644, 3.27074* **Cosy Camping (formerly Municipal Croix des Anglais,** 48200 St Chély-d'Apcher **06 42 10 49 04; cosycamping48@gmail.com; cosy-camping.com**

🐕€1 ♦♦♦ 🆆 ♨ ⚕ 🗑 ⊘ 🎱 🦋 ⓨ ⓣ nr ① nr 🛒 nr ⚠

Fr N on A75 J33 onto D809, 2nd exit of rndabt, site 100m on L. Fr S J34 onto D809 thro vill dir Clermont Ferand. Site 1km on R after vill. 2*, Med, hdg, pt shd, EHU (10A) inc; twin axles; TV; 5% statics; Eng spkn; adv bkg acc; games area; games rm; CKE. *"Friendly, helpful staff; gd walks; gd NH/long stay; horse riding adj; gd."* **€14.00, 1 Apr-6 Oct.** **2018**

ST CHELY D'APCHER *9D1* (10km E Rural) *44.77506, 3.37203* **Camping Le Galier,** Route de St Chély, 48120 St Alban-sur-Limagnole **04 66 31 58 80; accueil@ campinglegalier.fr; campinglozere.net/en**

🐕€1.60 ♦♦♦(htd) 🆆 ♨ ⚕ 🗑 🎱 🦋 ⓨ ⓣ 🍴 nr ⚠ 🏊 🏖

Exit A75 junc 34 onto D806, then E on D987 for 3km. Site 1.5km SW of St Alban on rvside. 2*, Sm, mkd, pt sl, EHU (6A) inc; bbq; 10% statics; Eng spkn; adv bkg acc; tennis 800m; games rm; CKE. *"Lovely, quiet setting by rv; friendly owners; clean san facs - stretched high ssn, ltd LS; gd walking, fishing; vg NH; rec; pretty site with rv running thro; grass pitches."* **€19.00, 1 Mar-30 Sep.** **2015**

ST CHINIAN *10F1* (2km W Rural) *43.42082, 2.93395* **Camp Municipal Les Terrasses,** Route de St Pons, 34360 St Chinian **04 67 38 28 28 (Mairie); mairie@ saintchinian.fr; www.campinglesterrasses.net**

♦♦♦ ♣ ⚕ 🗑 ⊘ 🦋 🛒 nr ♨

On main Béziers-St Pons rd, D612, heading W on o'skts of St Chinian. Site on L. Med, unshd, terr, EHU (10A) €4. *"Attractive site with gd views; sm pitches; diff access some pitches; terraced site; quiet until school hols; pool; friendly hosts."* **€12.00, 1 Apr-6 Nov.** **2016**

ST CHRISTOPHE *7A3* (2.5km NE Rural) *46.01467, 0.87679* **Camping En Campagne,** Essubras, 16420 St Christophe **05 45 31 67 57; info@ encampagne.com; www.encampagne.com**

🐕€2 ♦♦♦(htd) 🆆 ♨ ♣ ⚕ 🗑 ⊘ 🎱 🦋 ⓨ ⓣ ① 🎣 ⚠
🏊(covrd, htd) 🏖

Fr Bellac take D675 direction Saint-Junien. In Chene Pignier turn R on D9/D82 to Confolens. In Saint-Christophe turn R on D330 to Nouic. Site on L in 2.6km. 3*, Sm, mkd, hdg, pt shd, EHU (6-10A) inc; bbq; Eng spkn; adv bkg acc; games area; games rm; bike hire; pingpong table; petanque court; CCI. *"Vg; tourist attractions info avail; hiking/biking rtes; excel."* **€23.80, 1 Apr-1 Oct.** **2018**

ST CIRQ LAPOPIE *7D3* (2.5km S Rural) *44.44871, 1.67468* **FFCC Camping La Truffière,** Route de Concots, 46330 St Cirq-Lapopie **05 65 30 20 22; contact@ camping-truffiere.com; www.camping-truffiere.com**

🐕€1.50 ♦♦♦(htd) 🆆 ♨ ♣ ⚕ 🗑 ⊘ 🎱 🦋 ⓨ ⓣ ① 🍴 🎱 ⚠ ⚲
🏊(htd) 🏖

Take D911, Cahors to Villefranche rd; in 20km turn N onto D42 at Concots dir St Cirq for 8km - site clearly sp. NB Do not app fr St Cirq-Lapopie. 3*, Med, shd, pt sl, terr, EHU (10A) €4; TV; phone; Eng spkn; adv bkg acc; ccard acc; fishing 3km; bike hire; CKE. *"Well-kept site in gd location; friendly owners; excel but dated san facs (2014), ltd LS; most pitches in forest clearings; muddy when wet; lovely pool; gd; 2m fr fairytale vill of St Cirq Lapopie, a must see; site 11m fr nearest supmkt."* **€25.00, 1 Apr-30 Sep.** **2019**

ST CLAUDE *9A3* (2km S Rural) *46.37153, 5.87171* **Campsite Flower Camping Le Martinet,** 12 le Martinet, 39200 St Claude **03 84 45 00 40 or 03 84 41 42 62 (LS); contact@camping-saint-claude.fr; www.camping-saint-claude.fr**

♦♦♦ 🆆 ♨ ⚕ 🦋 ① 🛒 nr

On ent town foll 1-way, under bdge mkd 4.1m high, then take R turn 'Centre Ville' lane to next traff lts. Turn R then immed L sp Genève, turn R 300m after Fiat g'ge onto D290, site on R. 3*, Med, pt shd, EHU (5A) €2.30; gas; Eng spkn; adv bkg acc; ccard acc; tennis; fishing; CKE. *"Site now pt of Flower camping group (2014), completely renovated; htd pool adj; has 3 modern san blocks; excel walking; v attractive town; gd."* **€23.00, 1 Apr-30 Sep.** **2019**

ST CYPRIEN PLAGE *10G1* (3km S Coastal) *42.59939, 3.03761* **Camping Cala Gogo,** Ave Armand Lanoux, Les Capellans, 66750 St Cyprien-Plage **04 68 21 07 12;** contact@camping-le-calagogo.fr; www.camping-le-calagogo.fr

🏕 €3-4 ♨(htd) 🚿 ♨ ⚓ ⚐ ⛽ ♿ ㎳ 🍽 ⊕ 🛒 🎿 ⛰ ✏ 🏊 ⛴
🏖 sand adj

Exit A9 at Perpignan Nord onto D617 to Canet-Plage, then D81; site sp bet St Cyprien-Plage & Argelès-Plage dir Les Capellans. 5*, V lge, hdg, mkd, pt shd, EHU (6A) €2-4; TV; 30% statics; Eng spkn; adv bkg acc; ccard acc; tennis; games area; CKE. *"Excel site; gd pitches; lovely beach; v helpful staff."* **€48.00, 8 Apr-30 Sep.** 2017

ST DENIS D'OLERON *7A1* (3.7km S Coastal) *46.00480, -1.38480* **Camping Les Seulières,** 1371 Rue des Seulières, 17650 Saint-Denis-d'Oléron **33 546 479 051;** campinglesseulieres@wanadoo.fr; www.campingles seulieres.com

🏕 €2 ♨ ⚓ ♿ ⚐ ⛽ ♿ 🍽 🦋 ⚐ 🍽 🎿 nr ✏ 🏊 🏖 sand 0.3km

Fr D734 Cheray-Saint-Denis-d'Oleron. L twd La Jausiere, cont onto Grande Rue a Chaucre and foll sp to campsite. 2*, Med, mkd, pt shd, EHU (10A); gas; 45% statics; Eng spkn; adv bkg acc; ccard acc; CCI. *"Very nice beach; sep cycling rtes (plan provided)."* **€24.00, 1 Apr-30 Oct.** 2019

"That's changed – Should I let the Club know?"

If you find something on site that's different from the site entry, fill in a report and let us know. See camc.com/europereport.

ST DONAT SUR L'HERBASSE *9C2* (0.5km S Rural) *45.11916, 4.99290* **Camping Domaine Les Ulèzes,** Route de Romans, 26260 St Donat-sur-l'Herbasse **04 75 47 83 20;** contact@domaine-des-ulezes.com; www.domaine-des-ulezes.com

🏕 €2 ♨(wo) 🚿 ♿ ⚐ ⛽ ♿ 🍽 🦋 ⚐ 🍽 ⊕ 🛒 🎿 ⛰ ✏ 🏊 (htd)

Exit A7 junc 13 onto D532 dir Romans-sur-Isère. In 5km turn N onto D67 thro St Donat. Site on edge of vill off D53 dir Peyrins, well sp. 4*, Med, mkd, hdg, pt shd, EHU (6-10A) €3.50-4.50; bbq (elec, gas); TV; 10% statics; Eng spkn; adv bkg acc; ccard acc; games rm; ice; games area; CKE. *"Lovely rvside site; gd size pitches; immac; excel facs; welcoming, friendly owners; canal-side walk to town; gd touring base; vg; rec; serviced pitches."* **€32.30, 1 Apr-31 Oct.** 2019

ST EMILION *7C2* (3km N Rural) *44.91695, -0.14160* **Camping Yelloh Saint Emilion,** 2 lieu dit Les Combes, 33330 St Emilion **05 57 24 75 80;** info@camping-saint-emilion.com; www.camping-saint-emilion.com

🏕 €4 ♨ (wo) 🚿 ♿ ⚐ ⛽ ♿ 🍽 🦋 ♈ 🍽 ⊕ 🛒 🎿 ⛰ ✏
🏊 (htd) ⛴

NB Trailer c'vans not permitted in cent of St Emilion. Fr A10 exit junc 39a sp Libourne onto D670. In Libourne turn E on D243 twd St Emilion. On o'skts of St Emilion turn L onto D122 dir Lussac & Montagne; site on R by lake in 3km. Or fr S, foll site sp off D670 to Libourne, nr Les Bigaroux. NB D122 S of St Emilion unsuitable for c'vans. 4*, Lge, hdg, hdstg, mkd, shd, EHU (10A) inc; gas; bbq (gas); TV; 40% statics; phone; Eng spkn; adv bkg acc; ccard acc; horseriding 8km; games rm; waterslide; bike hire; watersports nr; tennis; canoeing; fishing; CKE. *"Lovely, peaceful, well-run lakeside site; owners friendly & helpful; gd sized & shd pitches; pedalos avail; suitable lge o'fits; no o'fits over 10m; mountain bike circuit; clean, modern san facs but inadequate; free shuttle bus service to St Emilion; gd cycle rtes; poss boggy when wet; excel."* **€40.00, 28 Apr-25 Sep, D08.** 2017

See advertisement on next page

ST EMILION *7C2* (9km SE Rural) *44.85138, -0.10683* Aire St Emilion Domaine du Château Gerbaud, 33000 St Pey-d'Armens **06 03 27 00 32 (mob);** contact@chateau-gerbaud.com; www.chateau-gerbaud.com

🅿12 ㎳

Fr Libourne SE on D670/D936 dir Castillon-la-Bataille. In St Pey-d'Armens at bar/tabac foll sp Château Gerbaud vineyard. Eng spkn. *"Parking for max 48 hrs; friendly, lovely site among the vines."* **€5.00** 2016

ST FARGEAU *4G4* (6km SE Rural) *47.60941, 3.11961* **Camp Municipal La Calangue,** 89170 St Fargeau **03 86 74 04 55;** campingmunicipallacalangue@nordnet.fr; www.camping-lacalangue.fr

🏕 ♨(htd) (wo) 🚿 ♿ ⚐ ⛽ ♿ 🦋 🍽 nr ⛰

Take D85 fr St-Fargeau, after 1km turn R on D185, after 2km turn R onto D485. Site on L (by circus) after 2 km. 3*, Lge, mkd, shd, EHU (6-10A) €3.80; bbq; sw nr; twin axles; 2% statics; adv bkg rec; canoeing; games area; horseriding nr; fishing; CKE. *"Pleasant site in woods; tight manoeuvring round trees; sm pitches; gd; shops & rest 6km; conv for Guedelon; san facs not clean."* **€10.50, 1 Apr-30 Sep.** 2015

FRANCE

ST FLORENTIN *4F4* (1km S Rural) *47.99252, 3.73450*
Camping L'Armançon, 89600 St Florentin 03 86 35 08
03 13 or 03 86 35 11 86 (mob); ot.saint-florentin@
wanadoo.fr; www.camping-saint-florentin.fr

€0.20 (cont)

N fr Auxerre on N77 site on R app rv bdge S of town.
Fr N pass traff islands, exit town up slope, x-ing
canal & rv. Site immed on S side of rv bdge - turn R
immed at end of bdg then under bdg to site. Site
well sp fr all dirs. 2*, Med, hdg, pt shd, pt sl, EHU
(10A) inc (poss long lead req); gas; fishing. *"Well-kept
site; excel, lge pitches; friendly manager; dated but
clean san facs; diff, steep exit to main rd; gd NH."*
€14.50, 2 Apr-11 Oct. 2015

ST FLOUR *9C1* (4km N Rural) *45.05120, 3.10778*
Camping International La Roche Murat, N9 15100
St Flour 04 71 60 43 63; courrier@camping-saint-
flour.com; www.camping-saint-flour.com

(htd)

Fr N or S on A75 exit junc 28; sp off rndabt on
St Flour side of m'way. Site ent visible 150m
fr rndabt. 3*, Med, hdg, mkd, terr, EHU (16A)
inc (poss rev pol); gas; Eng spkn; adv bkg acc; CKE.
*"Busy site with gd views; sunny & secluded pitches; gd,
clean facs; some pitches sm; when pitches waterlogged
use site rds; old town high on hill worth visit; excel
touring cent & conv NH fr A75; vg; v clean facs."*
€16.50, 1 Apr-1 Nov. 2016

ST FORT SUR GIRONDE *7B2* (4km SW Rural) *45.43278,
-0.75185* Camping Port Maubert, 8 Rue de Chassillac,
17240 St Fort-sur-Gironde 05 46 04 78 86; bourdieu.
jean-luc@wanadoo.fr; www.campingportmaubert.com

€2 nr

Exit A10 junc 37 onto D730 dir Royan. Foll sp Port
Maubert & site. 2*, Sm, hdg, mkd, shd, EHU (10A)
€3.50; gas; bbq; red long stay; TV; 10% statics; Eng
spkn; adv bkg acc; ccard acc; bike hire; games rm;
CKE. *"Pleasant, well-run site; LS ltd facs, OK NH."*
€12.40, 1 Apr-30 Oct. 2019

STE FOY LA GRANDE *7C2* (1km NE Rural) *44.84426,
0.22468* Camping de la Bastide, Allée du Camping,
2 Les Tuileries, Pineuilh, 33220 Ste Foy-la-Grande
05 57 46 13 84; contact@camping-bastide.com;
www.camping-bastide.com

€2 nr

Fr W go thro town & turn off at D130 to site, well sp
on Rv Dordogne. 3*, Med, mkd, pt shd, EHU (10A) €3
(poss rev pol); 10% statics; phone; Eng spkn; adv bkg
acc; ccard acc; canoeing; games rm; jacuzzi; fishing;
CKE. *"Pretty, well-cared for site; sm pitches; helpful,
lovely British owners; immac, modern san facs; high
kerb stones onto pitches - poss diff lge o'fits; mkt Sat;
excel; ACSI acc; walking dist to supmkt & town; v clean
site."* **€25.00, 1 Apr-31 Oct.** 2017

For a guide to symbols see the fold out on the rear cover

ST GALMIER 9B2 (2km E Rural) 45.59266, 4.33528
Campéole Camping Val de Coise, Route de la Thiéry, 42330 St Galmier **04 77 54 14 82**; val-de-coise@ campeole.com; **www.camping-valdecoise.com** or www.campeole.com

🐕 €2.60 🏕 ⓦ 🔥 ♿ ⓢ 🖥 ∥ 🚰 ⓦ ⓗ nr 🅿 ⚠ 🚿 🏊(htd) ⛱

Fr St Etienne take D1082 N. In 7km turn R onto D12 sp St Galmier; after x-ing rv bdge on o'skirts of vill turn R & foll Camping sp for 2km. Or fr N on D1082 look for sp to St Galmier about 1.5km S of Montrond-les-Bains & turn L onto D6 to St Galmier. On D12 in St Galmier at floral rndabt with fountain if app fr N go L & fr S go R, uphill & foll site sp. Site approx 1.5km fr rndabt. 4*, Med, hdstg, mkd, pt shd, pt sl, EHU (16A) €4.10; gas; bbq; TV; 20% statics; phone; Eng spkn; adv bkg acc; ccard acc; bike hire; tennis 2km; fishing; games area; games rm; CKE. *"Pleasant rvside site; helpful staff; facs poss stretched high ssn; highly rec; mainly statics."* **€21.50, 11 Apr-11 Oct.** **2015**

ST GAULTIER 4H2 (0.3km W Rural) 46.63470, 1.42172 **Camp Municipal L'Illon,** Rue de Limage, 36800 St Gaultier **02 54 47 11 22** or **02 54 01 66 00** (Mairie); st-gaultier.mairie@wanadoo. fr; www.mairie-saintgaultier.fr

🏕 🔥 ∥ 🚰 🐕 nr ⚠

Site well sp in town. V narr thro town - best app fr W. NB App down sh, steep hill with sharp R turn into site ent. 2*, Med, mkd, pt shd, pt sl, EHU inc; gas; rv; fishing 50m. *"Lovely, peaceful setting nr rv; site ent poss too narr for twin axles/lge o'fits; gd cycle path on old rlwy track nrby; site now has barriers, if off clse call warden; gd."* **€13.00, Easter-30 Sep.** **2016**

"I like to fill in the reports as I travel from site to site"

You'll find report forms at the back of this guide, or you can fill them in online at camc.com/europereport.

ST GENIX SUR GUIERS 9B3 (0.3km SE Urban) 45.58878, 5.64252 **Les Bords du Guiers,** Route de Pont Beauvoisin, 73240 Saint Genix sur Guiers **04 76 31 71 40**; info@lesbordsduguiers.com; www.les bordsduguiers.com

🐕 🏕 ⓦ 🔥 ∥ 🅼🆂🅿 🚰 ⓗ 🚿

On reaching vill on D1516 foll sp Le-Pont-de-Beauvoisin, site 300m on R. Med, mkd, hdg, pt shd, EHU (8-10A); bbq; twin axles; Eng spkn; games area; games rm. *"Excel, quiet site; bike hire; v helpful owners; gd base for site seeing or star watching; town cent 5 mins walk; mkt day Wed."* **€22.00, 13 Apr-21 Sep.** **2019**

ST GEORGES DU VIEVRE 3D2 (0.2km W Rural) 49.24248, 0.58040 **Camp Municipal du Vièvre,** Route de Noards, 27450 St Georges-du-Vièvre **02 32 42 76 79** or **02 32 56 34 29 (LS)**; camping. stgeorgesduvievre@wanadoo.fr; www.saintgeorges duvievre.org

🐕 🏕(htd) ⓦ 🔥 ♿ 🖥 ∥ 🚰 🐕 nr ⚠

Fr traff lts on D130 in Pont Authou turn W onto D137 to St Georges-du-Vièvre; turn L after town square uphill sp camping; site 200m on L. If app fr S on N138 at Bernay take D834 sp Le Havre to Lieurey. Turn R onto D137 to St Georges, then turn R at camping sp by sw pool. 2*, Sm, hdg, pt shd, serviced pitches; EHU (5A) inc; bbq; sw nr; Eng spkn; adv bkg rec; bike hire; tennis 50m; CKE. *"Peaceful; gd facs & pitches; pool 150m; well-run site; interesting area; gd cycling; vg; basic but attractive site on edge of v picturesque vill; gd sized pitches."* **€11.00, 1 Apr-30 Sep.** **2018**

ST GEORGES LES BAILLARGEAUX 4H1 (1km S Rural) 46.66452, 0.39477 **Camping Le Futuriste,** Rue du Château, 86130 St Georges-les-Baillargeaux **05 49 52 47 52**; camping-le-futuriste.@wanadoo.fr; www.camping-le-futuriste.fr

12 🐕 €2.50 🏕(htd) ⓦ 🔥 ♿ 🖥 ∥ 🅼🆂🅿 🚰 🐕 ⓨ 🅿 🍴 ⚠ 🚿 🏊(covrd, htd)

On A10 fr N or S, take Futuroscope exit 28; fr toll booth at 1st rndabt take 2nd exit. Thro tech park twd St Georges. At rndabt under D910 take slip rd N onto D910. After 150m exit D910 onto D20, foll sp. At 1st rndabt bear R, over rlwy, cross sm rv & up hill, site on R. 4*, Med, hdg, mkd, pt shd, serviced pitches; EHU (6A) inc (check earth & poss rev pol); gas; bbq; twin axles; TV; 10% statics; Eng spkn; adv bkg acc; ccard acc; games area; waterslide; games rm; lake fishing; CKE. *"Lovely, busy, secure site; well-kept; friendly, helpful family owners; vg clean facs, ltd LS - facs block clsd 2200-0700; vg poolwith waterslide for kids & adults; hypmkt 2km; vg for families; ideal touring base for Poitiers & Futuroscope (tickets fr recep); vg value, espec in winter; conv a'route; excel."* **€33.00** **2017**

ST GERVAIS LES BAINS 9B4 (2.6km S Rural) 45.87333, 6.72000 **Camping Les Dômes de Miage,** 197 Route des Contamines, 74170 St Gervais-les-Bains **04 50 93 45 96**; info@camping-mont-blanc.com; www.natureandlodge.fr

🐕 €2 🏕(htd) ⓦ 🔥 ♿ 🖥 ∥ 🅼🆂🅿 🚰 🐕 ⓨ 🍴 nr 🅿 🚿 ⚠

Exit A40 junc 21; fr N thro St Gervais, at sm rndabt in cent foll sp Les Contamines onto D902, site 2km on L. 4*, Med, mkd, pt shd, EHU (6A) €3.50 (poss rev pol); gas; bbq; TV; bus adj; Eng spkn; adv bkg req; ccard acc; tennis 800m; fishing 1km; games area; CKE. *"Superb, well-kept, perfect, family-owned site in beautiful location at base of Mt Blanc; welcoming, helpful & friendly; lux chalet to rent; bike hire 800m; immac san facs; conv Tramway du Mont Blanc excursions; mkt Thurs; bkg fee; htd pool 800m; excel; free bus service to delightful sm town."* **€31.00, 15 May-16 Sep.** **2017**

FRANCE

ST GILLES *10E2* (0.3km SW Urban) *43.67569, 4.42946*
Camping de la Chicanette, Rue de la Chicanette,
30800 St Gilles 04 66 87 28 32; camping@camping
lachicanette.fr; www.campinglachicanette.fr

🐕 €2 ♿ WD ⛲ 🚿 🍴 ⛱ 🏊 nr 🌳 ⚓ 🚲

Site on D6572 W fr Arles, sp in cent of town, behind
Auberge de la Chicanette. Narr app rd, tight turn to
ent. 3*, Med, hdg, pt shd, EHU (6A) €3 (rev pol);
20% statics; CKE. *"Useful site; sm pitches; facs poss
stretched high ssn; site poss unkempt LS; interesting
old town; bus to Nîmes; mkt Sun."*
€22.00, 1 Apr-30 Oct.   2015

ST GILLES CROIX DE VIE *2H3* (4km SE Coastal)
46.67095, -1.90874 **Camping Les Cyprès,** 41 Rue du
Pont du Jaunay, 85800 St Gilles-Croix-de-Vie 02 51 55
38 98; contact@camping-lescypres85.com;
www.camping-lescypres85.com/en

🐕 €3.30 ♿ WD ⛲ 🚿 🍴 🏊 MSP 🌳 🍴 ⛱ 🚲 🌳 ⚓ (covrd, htd)

🏖 sand 600m

Site on S end of St Gilles-Croix-de-Vie off D38, after
rndabt sp Le Jaunay turn sharp L - hard to spot.
3*, Lge, hdg, shd, EHU (10A) €3; gas; red long stay;
12% statics; Eng spkn; adv bkg req; ccard acc; jacuzzi;
CKE. *"Excel for family hols; family-run site; red facs LS;
footpath along rv to town cent; busy & noisy in high
ssn."* **€33.00, 9 Apr-28 Sep.**   2019

ST GIRONS PLAGE *8E1* (1km E Coastal) *43.95105,
-1.35276.* **Camping Eurosol,** Route de la Plage,
40560 St Girons-Plage 05 58 47 90 14 or 05 58 56
54 90; contact@camping-eurosol.com;
www.camping-eurosol.com

🐕 €4 ♿ WD ⛲ 🚿 🍴 🏊 🍴 ⛱ 🚲 🌳 ⚓ 🚲 🏪

🏖 sand 700m

Turn W off D652 at St Girons on D42. Site on L in
4km. 4*, Lge, pt shd, pt sl, serviced pitches; EHU
(10A) inc; gas; TV; 10% statics; tennis; games rm;
bike hire; games area; horseriding adj. *"Pitches poss
tight for long vans; excel for beach."*
€43.00, 10 May-13 Sep, A27.   2017

See advertisement

STE HERMINE *2H4* (11km NE Rural) *46.59764, -0.96947*
FFCC Camping Le Colombier (Naturist), 85210
St Martin-Lars 02 51 27 83 84; info@lecolombier-
naturisme.com; www.lecolombier-naturisme.com

🐕 €4.50 ♿ WD ⛲ 🚿 🍴 🏊 🌳 🍴 ⛱ 🚲 nr 🌳 ⚓ 🚲

Fr junc 7 of A83 take D137 N; 3km past Ste Hermine
turn R onto D52 to Le Poteau; turn L onto D10 to
St Martin-Lars; 150m past St Martin-Lars turn R sp
Le Colombier. Site ent on L in 200m. 4*, Lge, hdg,
mkd, hdstg, pt shd, pt sl, EHU (16A) €4.50; gas;
50% statics; Eng spkn; adv bkg acc; ccard acc; jacuzzi;
sauna. *"Well-run site; diff areas diff character; lge
pitches; friendly Dutch owners; san facs clean but
tired; gd walking in site grnds & local area; conv
Mervent National Park; excel; superb facs; gd loc."*
€29.00, 1 Apr-1 Oct.   2018

ST HILAIRE DE RIEZ *2H3* (6km N Rural) *46.76332,
-1.95839* **Camping La Puerta del Sol,** 7 Chemin des
Hommeaux, 85270 St Hilaire-de-Riez 02 51 49 10 10;
info@campinglapuertadelsol.com; www.camping
lapuertadelsol.com

🐕 €4 ♿ WD ⛲ 🚿 🍴 🏊 🌳 🍴 ⛱ 🚲 🌳 ⚓ 🚲

🏊 (htd) 🌳 🏖 sand 4.5km

N on D38 fr Les Sables-d'Olonne; exit onto D69 sp
Soullans, Challans, Le Pissot. At next rndabt take
3rd exit & foll lge sp to site. Site on R in 1.5km.
4*, Lge, hdg, mkd, pt shd, pt sl, serviced pitches;
EHU (10A) inc (poss rev pol); bbq (elec, gas); TV;
50% statics; Eng spkn; adv bkg acc; ccard acc; tennis;
games area; watersports 5km; horseriding; sauna;
games rm; jacuzzi; bike hire; waterslide; fishing 2km;
golf; CKE. *"Vg site; med sized pitches, some diff lge
o'fits due odd shape; clean san facs; gd for families; no
o'fits over 10m high ssn; gd touring base; lovely pools
and playgrnd."* **€33.00, 1 Apr-30 Sep.**   2016

FRANCE

ST HILAIRE DE RIEZ *2H3* (3.5km W Coastal) *46.72289, -1.97931* **Camp Municipal de La Plage de Riez,** Allée de la Plage de Riez, Ave des Mimosas, 85270 St Hilaire-de-Riez **02 51 54 36 59; www.souslespins.com**
🐕 €3.90 ♦♦↑ ▲ 🗐 ⊿ ↑ ⴲ 🍴 ⑪ 🍴 ⴲ ∕◭ ⅃ ⅃ sand adj

Fr St Hilaire take D6A sp Sion-sur-l'Océan. Turn R at traff lts into Ave des Mimosas, site 1st L.
3*, V lge, mkd, shd, pt sl, serviced pitches; EHU (10A) €3.40; gas; TV; 30% statics; Eng spkn; bike hire. "*Vg for dogs; pool 5km; exceptionally helpful manager.*"
€22.00, 30 Mar-31 Oct. **2016**

ST HILAIRE DU HARCOUET *2E4* (1km W Urban) *48.58105, -1.09771* **FFCC Camp Municipal de la Sélune,** 50600 St Hilaire-du-Harcouët **02 33 49 43 74 or 02 33 49 70 06; info@st-hilaire.fr; www.st-hilaire.fr**
🐕 €0.70 ♦♦↑ 🆆 ▲ ⊿ ↑ ⴲ nr /◭

Sp on N side of N176 twd Mont St Michel/St Malo/ Dinan, on W side of town; well sp. 3*, Med, hdg, pt shd, pt sl, EHU (16A) €1.95; red long stay; CKE. "*Peaceful, beautifully maintained site; pool 300m; easy access; helpful, pleasant warden; superb san facs; gate locked 2200-0730; excel.*"
€22.50, 23 Apr-16 Sep. **2019**

> ## "We must tell the Club about that great site we found"
>
> Get your site reports in by mid-August and we'll do our best to get your updates into the next edition.

ST HILAIRE LA PALUD *7A2* (4km NW Rural) *46.28386, -0.74344* **Flower Camping Le Lidon,** Le Lidon, 79210 St Hilaire-la-Palud **05 49 35 33 64; info@le-lidon.com; www.le-lidon.com**
🐕 €2.50 ♦♦↑ 🆆 ▲ ↑ ⅄ ⊿ ∕ 🅼🅿 ⴲ ↑ 🍴 ⑪ ⅃ ⴲ /◭ ⅃ ⅃ (htd) 🛁

Exit A10 junc 33 onto E601 then N248 & N11 S. At Epannes foll D1 N to Sansais, then D3 to St Hilaire-la-Palud. Foll sp Canal du Mignon & site. NB Access to site over narr angled bdge, extreme care needed - v diff lge o'fits. 3*, Med, mkd, hdg, pt shd, EHU (10A) inc; bbq; 5% statics; Eng spkn; adv bkg acc; ccard acc; canoe hire; ice; rv fishing; bike hire; CKE. "*Secluded site in Marais Poitevin Regional Park (marsh land); gd sized pitches; excel clean san facs; gd walking, cycling, birdwatching; vg; might not be suitable for lge o'fits due to many trees.*" **€20.00, 11 Apr-19 Sep.** **2015**

ST HONORE LES BAINS *4H4* (0.5km W Urban) *46.90413, 3.83919* **Camp Municipal Plateau du Guet,** 13 Rue Eugène Collin, 58360 St Honoré-les-Bains **03 86 30 76 00 or 03 86 30 74 87 (Mairie); mairie-de-st-honore-les-bains@wanadoo.fr; www.st-honore-les-bains.com**
♦♦↑ (htd) ▲ ⅄ 🗐 ∕ 🅼🅿 🦋 ↑ nr ⑪ nr ⴲ nr /◭

On D985 fr Luzy to St Honoré-les-Bains. In cent vill turn L on D106 twd Vandenesse. Site on L in 150m. Or N fr Château-Chinon 27km. Then D985 to St Honoré. 2*, Med, mkd, hdstg, pt shd, terr, EHU (10A) €2.90; adv bkg acc; CKE. "*Gd, modern san facs (part unisex); htd pool 300m; pleasant, conv site town, gd walking; get barrier key for early dep.*"
€8.60, 1 Apr-26 Oct. **2019**

ST HONORE LES BAINS *4H4* (1.5km W Rural) *46.90680, 3.82843* **Camping & Gîtes Les Bains,** 15 Ave Jean Mermoz, 58360 St Honoré-les-Bains **03 86 30 73 44; campinglesbains@gmail.com; www.campinglesbains.com**
🐕 ♦♦↑ 🆆 ▲ ↑ ⅄ 🗐 ∕ 🦋 ↑ 🍴 ⑪ ⅃ ⴲ nr /◭ ⅃ ♨ 🛁

Fr St Honoré-les-Bains foll site sp as 'Village des Bains' fr town cent on D106 twd Vandenesse.
3*, Med, mkd, hdg, hdstg, pt shd, pt sl, EHU (10A) €4; gas; bbq; twin axles; TV; 20% statics; phone; Eng spkn; adv bkg acc; ccard acc; bike hire; fishing; horseriding 300m; tennis; games rm; waterslide; CKE. "*Helpful staff; poor maintenance & san facs need refurb; gd walking; sm pitches & poss waterlogged after rain; mkt Thu; new British owners.*" **€20.80, 1 Apr-31 Oct.** **2015**

ST JEAN D'ANGELY *7B2* (3km WNW Rural) *45.94868, -0.53645* **Camping Val de Boutonne,** 56 Quai de Bernouet, 17400 St Jean-d'Angély **05 46 32 26 16; info@camping-charente-maritime-17.com; www.campingcharentemaritime17.com**
🐕 €2 ♦♦↑ 🆆 ▲ ↑ ⅄ 🗐 ∕ 🅼🅿 🦋 ↑ 🍴 ⑪ nr ⴲ /◭

Exit A10 at junc 34; head SE on D939; turn R at 1st rndabt into town. Site sp. 3*, Med, mkd, shd, EHU (10A) €4; red long stay; TV; 10% statics; Eng spkn; adv bkg acc; ccard acc; CKE. "*Pleasant, friendly, well-kept site by Rv Boutonne; helpful owners; aquatic cent 500m; lovely pool, strict rules, men must wear speedos; gd, clean san facs, outdated; poss open in Oct - phone ahead; vg; lake with sm boating facs; rec; gd NH just off the A10; 10min walk to historic town; lge Sat mkt; no admittance until 14:30; gd rests.*"
€19.50, 1 Apr-30 Sep. **2018**

> ## "I need an on-site restaurant"
>
> We do our best to make sure site information is correct, but it is always best to check any must-have facilities are still available or will be open during your visit.

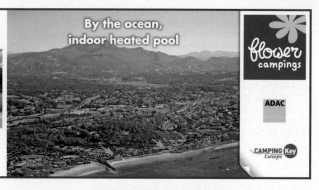
FRANCE

ST JEAN DE LUZ *8F1* (2km NE Coastal) *43.40563,*
-1.64216 **Camping de la Ferme Erromardie,**
40 Chemin d'Erromardie, 64500 St Jean-de-Luz
05 59 26 34 26; contact@camping-erromardie.com;
www.camping-erromardie.com

🐕 €3 � WD ♨ ♿ ☐ ✉ MSP ⵝ ⒶⒿ ⼜ ⵈ sand adj

Exit A63 junc 3 onto D810 sp St Jean-de-Luz.
After 1km cross rlwy and turn immed sharp R sp
Erromardie. Site ent on R in 3km just bef rest/bar.
4*, Lge, hdg, mkd, shd, EHU (6-16A) inc; gas;
80% statics; Eng spkn; adv bkg acc; CKE. *"Well-run,
popular site; cheerful, helpful staff; ltd water pnts in
2nd field; lovely, sandy beaches; coastal walk into St
Jean-de-Luz; Basque museum nrby; site in 3 sections,
lge o'fits should ask for pitch on touring field; excel
modern san facs."* **€45.00, 15 Mar-30 Sep.** 2019

See advertisement

ST JEAN DE LUZ *8F1* (3km NE Coastal) *43.40549,*
-1.64222 **Camping Bord de Mer,** 71 chemin
d'Erromardie, 64500 St Jean-de-Luz 05 59 26 24 61;
bord-de-mer64@orange.fr; www.camping-le-bord-
de-mer.fr

🐕 ♿ � WD ♨ ♿ ☐ ✉ MSP ✤ ⵝ ⒶⒿ ⵈ sand adj

Exit A63 junc 3 onto D810 dir St Jean-de-Luz. In 1km
cross rlwy & immed turn sharp R sp Erromardie. Site
on sharp turn L bef beach. Ent by plastic chain fence
bef ent to prom, but easy to miss. App poss diff lge
o'fits due hairpin turn - drive on to car park where
may be poss to turn. 3*, Med, hdg, pt sl, EHU (10A)
€3,50; bbq. *"Nice site in excel position; owner connects
EHU; cliff walk to town; NH en rte Spain; san facs
refurbished; wonderful location; site on 2 levels, sea
views on top level."* **€34.00, 10 Apr-1 Nov.** 2015

ST JEAN DE LUZ *8F1* (10km SE Rural) *43.35748,*
-1.57465 **Camping d'Ibarron,** 64310 St Pée-sur-Nivelle
05 59 54 10 43; camping.dibarron@wanadoo.fr;
www.camping-ibarron.com

🐕 €1.60 � WD ♨ ♿ ☐ ✉ MSP ✤ ⵝ ⒶⒿ ⵈ ⼜ ⵈ

Fr St Jean take D918 twd St Pée, site 2km bef
St Pée on R of rd. 3*, Lge, shd, EHU (6A) €3.95; TV;
5% statics; phone; Eng spkn; adv bkg acc; games
rm; CKE. *"Well-kept site in scenic location; spacious
pitches; welcoming, helpful owner; gd san facs; on main
rd & no footpath to vill; walk along rv into vill; mkt Sat;
excel."* **€29.00, 23 Apr-30 Sep.** 2017

ST JEAN DE LUZ *8F1* (8km SE Rural) *43.34591,*
-1.61724 **Camping Chourio,** Luberriaga, 64310 Ascain
05 59 54 06 31 or 05 59 54 04 32; www.tourisme-
aquitaine.fr

♿ � WD ♨ ✉ ✤ ⵝ ⵈ nr Ⓗ nr

Fr St Jean-de-Luz take D918 sp Ascain. In 6km turn
R at traff lts, in 250m over rv bdge & turn L at mini-
rndabt. Site sp in town. 1*, Med, pt shd, EHU (6A)
€2.80; phone; CKE. *"Friendly, family-owned, relaxed
site in lovely countryside; conv Spanish border; Tues &
Sat mkt St Jean-de-Luz; vg; v helpful owners; bar only
300mtrs."* **€12.00, 20 Mar-15 Nov.** 2018

ST JEAN DE LUZ *8F1* (3km SW Rural) *43.37064, -1.68629* **Camping Larrouleta**, 210 Route de Socoa, 64122 Urrugne **05 59 47 37 84; info@larrouleta.com; www.larrouleta.com**

12 🛒 €2 👪 (htd) 🗝 ♨ ⚡ ⚡ 🖧 🚿 ♈ ♈ Ⓣ ① 🛒 🚰 🏔 🎣

🏊 (covrd, htd) 🌳 sand 3km

Exit A63 junc 2 St Jean-de-Luz Sud. Pass under D810 & take 1st L sp Urrugne. Loop back up to N10 & turn R, site sp in 500m. Or fr S on D810, 2km beyond Urrugne vill (by-pass vill), turn L into minor rd, site 50m on R. 3*, Lge, hdstg, mkd, hdg, pt shd, EHU (10A) inc (poss rev pol); gas; sw; phone; bus 200m; Eng spkn; adv bkg req; ccard acc; games area; boating; tennis; fishing; CKE. *"Pleasant, well-run family site nr lake; satisfactory san facs (unisex LS) & pool; friendly & helpful (ask for dir on dep to avoid dangerous bend); some pitches unrel in wet but can park on site rds/hdstg; poss ltd facs LS; conv A63, Biarritz & en rte Spain; excel; conv m'way & hypmkt/ fuel 1.5km; nice walk to Urrugne & St Jean to Luz; lots of hot water shwrs."* **€33.00** 2019

See advertisement

ST JEAN DE LUZ *8F1* (9km SW Rural) *43.33277, -1.68527* **Le Camping du Col d'Ibardin**, Route d'Ascain, 64122 Urrugne **05 59 54 31 21; info@col-ibardin.com; www.col-ibardin.com**

🛒 €6 👪 wc 🗝 ♨ ⚡ 🖧 🚿 🦋 ♈ ♈ Ⓣ ① 🛒 🚰 🏔 🎣 🏊 (htd) 🛁

Exit A63 junc 2, ignore slip rd to R 50m, turn L & in 100m turn R onto D810 S. In 2km at rndabt foll sp Col d'Ibardin, Ascain; after 4km site on R immed past minor rd to Col d'Ibardin. 3*, Med, mkd, hdstg, hdg, pt shd, pt sl, terr, serviced pitches; EHU (10A) inc; gas; bbq; red long stay; TV; 50% statics; phone; Eng spkn; adv bkg acc; ccard acc; games rm; tennis; games area; CKE. *"Lovely, well-run site in woodland; fair sized pitches; helpful, friendly owner; gd san facs; pleasant bar/rest; mountain rlwy nr; gd touring base for Pyrenees & N Spain; excel."* **€50.00, 1 Apr-1 Oct, A15.** 2017

ST JEAN DE MAURIENNE *9C3* (1km SE Urban) *45.27034, 6.35023* **Camp Municipal des Grands Cols**, 422 Ave du Mont-Cenis, 73300 St Jean-de-Maurienne **09 52 17 46 55; info@campingdesgrandscols.com; www.campingdesgrandscols.com**

🛒 €1 👪 wc 🗝 ⚡ 🖧 MSP 🌊 Ⓣ 🚰 🚰 nr 🏔

Site sp fr D1006 in St Jean-de-Maurienne; site behind shops 100m fr town cent behind trees/ parking. 4*, Med, hdg, mkd, hdstg, pt shd, pt sl, serviced pitches; EHU (16A) €3; TV; Eng spkn; games rm; CKE. *"Warm welcome; helpful staff; clean san facs; pool 1.5km; interesting town; excel for serious cycling; gd NH for Fréjus tunnel; excel."* **€24.00, 10 May-22 Sep.** 2019

ST JEAN DE MONTS *2H3* (8km SE Coastal) *46.75638, -2.00749* **Camping La Yole**, Chemin des Bosses, Orouët, 85160 St Jean-de-Monts **02 51 58 67 17; contact@la-yole.com; www.vendee-camping.eu**

🛒 €7 👪 wc 🗝 ♨ ⚡ 🖧 🚿 ♈ Ⓣ ① 🛒 🚰 🏔 🎣

🏊 (covrd, htd) 🛁 🌳 sand 2km

Take D38 S fr St Jean-de-Monts dir Les Sable d'Olonne & Orouet. At Orouet turn R at L'Oasis rest dir Mouette; in 1.5km turn L at campsite sp; site on L. Situated bet D38 & coast, 1km fr Plage des Mouettes. On arr, park in carpark on R bef registering. 4*, Lge, mkd, hdg, pt shd, serviced pitches; EHU (10A) inc; bbq (gas); TV; 80% statics; Eng spkn; adv bkg req; ccard acc; tennis; watersports 6km; fishing; jacuzzi; games rm; waterslide; horseriding 3km; CKE. *"Busy, gd, well-run site; no o'fits over 8m; sm dogs only; san facs clean, not spacious; excel cycle paths; mkt Wed & Sat; vg; friendly & helpful staff."* **€46.00, 11 Apr-24 Sep, A23.** 2018

ST JEAN DE MONTS 2H3 (2.5km NW Coastal) 46.80311, -2.09300 **La Prairie,** 146 Rue du Moulin Casse, 85160 Saint-Jean-de-Monts **02 51 58 16 04; contact@campingprairie.com; campingprairie.com**

🛉 ⅋⅋ (wc) ♨ ⚓ ⅊ 🖫 ⅃ / (mp) 🖐 ♈ 🍴 ⊕ ⅊ 🛝 🐾 🏊 🚲 🎣 ♒ sand

Fr St Jean de Monts take D38 twds Notre Dame de Monts. Site abt 1.5km N of St Jean de Monts. Foll **sp.** Sm, mkd, pt shd, EHU (6A); bbq; twin axles; 40% statics; bus adj; Eng spkn; adv bkg acc; bike hire; games rm; sauna; games area. *"Gd site."* **€34.00, 1 Apr-9 Oct.** **2016**

ST JEAN DE MONTS 2H3 (4km NW Coastal) 46.80978, -2.10971 **Camping Les Places Dorées,** Route de Notre Dame de Monts, 85160 St Jean-de-Monts **02 51 59 02 93 or 02 40 73 03 70 (LS); abridespins@aol.com; www.placesdorees.com**

🛉 €2.80 ⅋⅋ (wc) ♨ ⚓ ⅊ 🖫 / 🦋 🏐 ⅊ 🎣nr 🏊 (htd) ♒ sand 800m

Fr Nantes dir Challons & St Jean-de-Monts. Then dir Notre Dame-de-Monts. 4*, Med, shd, pt sl, EHU (10A) inc; gas; Eng spkn; adv bkg acc; games area; games rm; waterslide; CKE. *"Vg; free entmnt children/adults; organised excursions; friendly family-run site; mountain views."* **€32.00, 1 Jun-10 Sep.** **2016**

ST JEAN DE MONTS 2H3 (6km NW Coastal) 46.81831, -2.13006 **Camping La Forêt,** 190 Chemin de la Rive, 85160 St Jean-de-Monts **02 51 58 84 63; camping-la-foret@wanadoo.fr; www.hpa-laforet.com**

🛉 €2.50 ⅋⅋ (wc) ♨ ⚓ ⅊ 🖫 / 🦋 🏐 ⅊ 🛝 (htd) ♒ sand 500m

Fr St Jean-de-Monts, take D38 twd Notre-Dame-de-Monts for 6km, over rndabt then turn L (last turning bef Notre-Dame-de-Monts) sp Pont d'Yeu, then immed L, site on L in 200m, on parallel rd to main rd. 4*, Med, mkd, hdg, pt shd, EHU (10A) €3.80; gas; bbq; TV; 30% statics; phone; Eng spkn; adv bkg acc; horseriding nr; CKE. *"Friendly, helpful owners; clean san facs; not suitable twin axles; some pitches diff c'vans; excel; great cycling area fr site."* **€36.00, 1 May-20 Sep.** **2015**

ST JEAN PIED DE PORT 8F1 (0.6km S Urban) 43.16126, -1.23662 **Camp Municipal de Plaza Berri,** Ave de Fronton, 64220 St Jean-Pied-de-Port **05 59 37 11 19 or 05 59 37 00 92; mairie.stjeanpieddeport@ wanadoo.fr; www.saintjeanpieddeport-paysbasquetourisme.com**

⅋⅋ (wc) ♨ ⚓ ⅊ / 🖐 🦋 ⅊nr

Fr N on D933 thro town & cross rv. In 50m bear L at sm rndabt, site in 200m, sp. Enquire at Hôtel de Ville (Town Hall) off ssn. Narr app rds. 1*, Med, mkd, pt shd, pt sl, EHU (5A) €2.50 (poss rev pol); CKE. *"Nice site; busy, rec arr early high ssn; dogs; friendly warden; if recep unmanned, site yourself & report later; san facs still need refurb (2015); gd walks & scenery; used by walkers on pilgrim rte; pelota court adj; mkt Mon; gd NH; pool 500m; lovely site."* **€13.00, 23 Apr-1 Nov.** **2016**

ST JEAN PIED DE PORT 8F1 (3km W Rural) 43.17745, -1.25970 **Camping Narbaïtz Vacances Pyrénées Basques,** Route de Bayonne, 64220 Ascarat **05 59 37 10 13 or 06 09 39 30 42 (mob); camping-narbaitz@ wanadoo.fr; www.camping-narbaitz.com**

🛉 ⅋⅋ (htd) (wc) ♨ ⚓ ⅊ 🖫 / (mp) 🦋 🖐 ♈ 🏐 ⅊ 🛝 🎣 🏊 (htd)

Site on L of D918 St Jean to Bayonne 3km fr St Jean, sp. 4*, Med, hdg, mkd, pt shd, pt sl, EHU (6-10A) €4.50-5.50 (poss rev pol); 5% statics; phone; Eng spkn; adv bkg acc; ccard acc; trout fishing; kayaking; canoeing; cycling; CKE. *"Attractive, clean, pleasant, family-run site; lovely views; helpful owners; vg facs; rec m'vans use top of site when wet; nr Spanish border (cheaper petrol); excel; gd san facs."* **€41.00, 29 Apr-24 Sep.** **2017**

ST JEAN PIED DE PORT 8F1 (2.4km NW Rural) 43.17304, -1.25416 **Europ Camping,** 64220 Ascarat **05 59 37 12 78; europcamping64@orange.fr; www.europ-camping.com**

🛉 €2.50 ⅋⅋ (wc) ♨ ⚓ ⅊ 🖫 / (mp) 🦋 ♈ ⊕ 🏐 ⅊nr 🛝 🏊 🏐

Site on D918 bet Uhart-Cize & Ascarat. Well sp. 4*, Med, hdg, mkd, pt shd, EHU (6A) €4 (poss rev pol); 30% statics; adv bkg acc; ccard acc; sauna; games area; games rm; CKE. *"Beautiful location; helpful staff; ltd facs LS; only basic food in bar/rest; grnd v soft when wet; vg."* **€33.00, 4 Apr-30 Sep.** **2016**

ST JULIEN EN GENEVOIS 9A3 (5km SE Rural) 46.12015, 6.10565 **Kawan Village La Colombière,** 166 Chemin Neuf-Chef-Lieu, 74160 Neydens **04 50 35 13 14; la.colombiere@wanadoo.fr; www.camping-la-colombiere.com**

🛉 €2.50 ⅋⅋ (htd) (wc) ♨ ⚓ ⅊ 🖫 / (mp) 🖐 ♈ ⊕ 🏐 🛝 🐾 🦋
🏊 (covrd, htd) 🚲

Exit A40 junc 13 onto D1201 dir Cruseilles; in 1.75km turn L to Neydens; turn R at church; site on R in 200m. Site sp. NB: Do not go into St Julien-en-Genevois when towing. 4*, Med, hdstg, hdg, mkd, pt shd, pt sl, EHU (6-10A) inc, extra for 15A; gas; bbq; TV; 10% statics; Eng spkn; adv bkg acc; ccard acc; bike hire; lake fishing 1km; games rm; CKE. *"Family-owned site; friendly, helpful staff; boggy after heavy rain; farm produce; conv Geneva - guided tours high ssn; no o'fits over 10m high ssn; park & ride bus; open for m'vans all year; gd NH; excel; highly rec."* **€39.70, 1 Apr-31 Oct, M08.** **2017**

ST JUNIEN 7B3 (4km E Rural) 45.88078, 0.96539 **FFCC Camp Municipal de Chambery,** 87200 St Brice-sur-Vienne **05 55 02 42 92; mairiest-brice@ wanadoo.fr; www.tourismelimousin.com**

🛖 👭(htd) ♨ ♿ 🖥 🗑 ☕ 🛒 nr 🅿

Fr St Junien take D32 E sp St Brice & St Victurnien; on leaving St Brice on D32 turn L & foll sp; site on L in 500m, on E edge of vill. Or app on D32 fr E, turn R onto C2 bef St Brice-sur-Vienne town sp, sp 'Campings & Gite Rural'. 2*, Sm, hdg, mkd, hdstg, pt shd, pt sl, serviced pitches; EHU (10A) €3.40; adv bkg acc; CKE. *"Peaceful, clean site in park; spacious pitches o'look lake & countryside; site yourself, office open 1hr am & pm; barrier clsd 2200-0700; conv Oradour-sur-Glane; excel; beautiful location; excel san facs; each pitch has own tap & drain; call to check if open."* **€10.00, 1 May-1 Sep.** 2019

ST JUST (CANTAL) 9C1 (0.5km W Urban) 44.89035, 3.21079 **FFCC Camp Municipal,** 15320 St Just 04 71 73 72 57, 04 71 73 70 48 or 06 31 47 05 15 (mob); info@saintjust.com; www.saintjust.com

🛖 👭(htd) 🆔 ♨ ♿ 🗑 ☕ 🛒 nr 🅿

Exit junc 31 fr A75, foll sp St Chély-d'Apcher D909; turn W onto D448 twds St Just (approx 6km); sp with gd access. 3*, Med, mkd, pt shd, pt sl, terr, EHU (10A) €2.30; red long stay; phone; Eng spkn; ccard acc; tennis; bike hire; fishing. *"Vg site; friendly, helpful warden; ltd facs LS; excel tennis & pool; gd touring base; area for m'vans."* **€10.20, Easter-30 Sep.** 2017

ST JUSTIN 8E2 (2.5km NW Rural) 44.00166, -0.23502 **Camping Le Pin,** Route de Roquefort, 40240 St Justin 05 58 44 88 91; camping.lepin@orange.fr; www.campinglepin.com

🛖 €2.50 👭 🆔 ♨ ♿ 🗑 ☕ 🛒 🍴 ⊕ 🛒 🅿 🏊 🛶

Fr D933 in St Justin take D626 sp Requefort, site on L in 2km (sp says 3). 3*, Sm, hdg, mkd, pt shd, EHU (6-10A) £3 (rev pol poss); bbq; TV; 10% statics; Eng spkn; adv bkg acc; rv fishing 2km; games area; bike hire; horseriding; CKE. *"Pleasant, spacious site; new facs (2016); beautiful vill; rustic wooded setting; gd welcome; helpful owner; bread avail daily; sm pond, free fishing for campers; highly rec; excel modern clean san facs; Bastide town nrby; conv to & fr Spain; excel."* **€23.00, 3 Mar-1 Dec.** 2018

ST LARY SOULAN 8G2 (4km NE Rural) 42.84482, 0.33836 **Camping Le Lustou,** 89 Chemin d'Agos, 65170 Vielle-Aure 05 62 39 40 64; contact@lustou. com; www.lustou.com

12 🛖 €1.80 👭(htd) 🆔 ♨ ♿ 🗑 ☕ 🛒 🍴 🛒 nr 🅿

Exit A64 junc 16 & head S on D929. Thro Arreau & Guchen turn R onto D19 dir Vielle-Aure. Site on R just bef Agos. 3*, Med, hdg, pt shd, pt sl, EHU (6-10A) €6.80; gas; bbq; TV; 5% statics; phone; adv bkg acc; canoeing nr; fishing nr; tennis nr; games area; CKE. *"Organised walks in mountains by owner; excel skiing; immac facs; communal meals organised weekly (high ssn); excel site."* **€19.00** 2016

ST LAURENT DE CERIS 7B3 (4.6km NE Rural) 45.95902, 0.52880 **Camp Laurent,** Le Fournet, 16450 St Laurent de Ceris Charente 06 02 22 37 15; lecamplaurent@ gmail.com

12 🛖 👭 ᴡᴰ 🆔 ♨ ♿ ☕ 🛒 🍴 nr ⊕ nr 🛒 nr 🛶

Fr St Claud on D174. Fr St Laurent de Ceris turn R at rest onto D15. Take 2nd L on D345, Le Fournet sp at junc. Site on R in about 1km. Sm, pt shd, pt sl, EHU (10A) €3; bbq; twin axles; Eng spkn; adv bkg acc. *"Adults only site; suitable for all units; Eng owners; beside sm rv; v clean facs; helpful, friendly welcome; lakes with beach nrby; new owners; ideal walking & cycling country."* **€25.00** 2015

ST LAURENT EN GRANDVAUX 6H2 (0.5km SE Rural) 46.57645, 5.96214 **Camp Municipal Le Champs de Mars,** 8 Rue du Camping, 39150 St Laurent-en-Grandvaux 03 84 60 19 30 or 06 03 61 06 61; champmars.camping@wanadoo.fr or champmars. camping@orange.fr; www.st-laurent39.fr

🛖 👭(htd) ᴡᴰ ♨ ♿ 🗑 ☕ 🛒 🛒 nr 🅿

E thro St Laurent on N5 twd Morez, site on R, sp `Caravaneige' at ent. 2*, Med, mkd, pt shd, pt sl, serviced pitches; EHU (4-10A) €5-6.4; TV; 20% statics; phone; adv bkg acc; CKE. *"Gd site; peaceful LS; gd NH; friendly staff."* **€13.80, 1 Jan-30 Sep.** 2019

ST LAURENT SUR SEVRE 2H4 (1km W Rural) 46.95790, -0.90290 **Camping Le Rouge Gorge,** Route de la Verrie, 85290 St Laurent-sur-Sèvre 02 51 67 86 39; camping lerougegorge@wanadoo.fr; www.camping-lerouge gorge-vendee.com

🛖 €2.10 👭(htd) ᴡᴰ ♨ ♿ 🗑 ☕ 🛒 🍴 🛒 🅿 🏊 📶

Fr Cholet on N160 dir La Roche-sur-Yon; at Mortagne-sur-Sèvre take N149 to St Laurent-sur-Sèvre. In St Laurent foll sp La Verrie on D111. Site on R at top of hill. Or take 762 S fr Cholet to St Laurent. Site sp in town. 3*, Med, hdg, mkd, pt shd, pt sl, EHU (4-13A) €2.95-4.10; 30% statics; adv bkg acc; lake fishing 800m; golf 15km; games area; CKE. *"Peaceful family site; woodland walks & mountain biking; attractive sm town; close to Puy du Fou Theme Park."* **€24.00, 1 Apr-30 Sep.** 2017

ST LEONARD DE NOBLAT 7B3 (15km N Rural) 45.94311, 1.51459 **Camping Pont du Dognon (formerly Municipal),** 87240 St Laurent-les-Eglises 06 75 73 25 30 or 05 55 56 57 25; www.aupontdu dognon.fr

🛖 €2 👭(htd) ᴡᴰ ♨ 🗑 ☕ 🛒 🍴 ⊕ 🛒 🅿 📶 🛶 🎣 shgl

Take D941 fr St Léonard-de-Noblat; after 1.5km turn L (N) on D19 thro Le Châtenet-en-Dognon. Site in approx 4km, bef St Laurent-les-Eglises. 3*, Med, mkd, hdg, pt shd, terr, EHU (6-16A) €3.50; gas; bbq; twin axles; adv bkg acc; tennis; bike hire; canoeing. *"Vg site."* **€13.00, 2 Apr-1 Oct.** 2016

FRANCE

ST LOUIS *6G3* (2km N Rural) *47.59428, 7.58930*
Camping au Petit Port, 10 Allée des Marronniers,
68330 Huningue **03 89 69 05 25 or 03 89 70 01 71;**
contact@campinghuningue.fr; www.camping
huningue.fr

🏕 ⛺ WC ♨ ♿ 🚿 ⊘ MP ☂ Ⓨ nr ♨ 🛒 nr ⚠

S fr Mulhouse on A35, exit onto D105 & foll sps to
Huningue; after level x-ing site sp on rvside. 2*, Med,
pt shd, EHU (6A) €3; bbq; cooking facs; TV;
50% statics; bus to Basle; Eng spkn; adv bkg acc;
games rm; bike hire; CKE. *"Excel NH on banks of Rv
Rhine; helpful staff; htd pool 2km; clean facs; poss
diff access lge o'fits; bar 500m; canoeing."*
€20.00, 15 Apr-15 Oct. 2018

ST MAIXENT L'ECOLE *7A2* (1.5km SW Urban)
46.40836, -0.21856 **Camp Municipal du Panier Fleuri,**
Rue Paul Drévin, 79400 St Maixent-l'Ecole
05 49 05 53 21

🏕 ⛺ ♨ ⊘ MP ☂ Ⓨ nr ♨ nr ⚠

Take D611 twd Niort, at 2nd set of traff lts nr top of
hill out of town turn L. Foll camping sps into ent.
3*, Med, mkd, pt shd, pt sl, EHU (10A); tennis. *"Warden
on site am & eve, if office locked go to hse nr wc
block; ltd/basic facs LS; htd pool adj; interesting town;
NH en rte Spain; immac new htd san facs (2014)."*
€10.50, 1 Apr-15 Oct. 2019

"We must tell the Club about that great site we found"

Get your site reports in by mid-August and we'll
do our best to get your updates into the next
edition.

ST MALO *2E4* (10km NE Rural) *48.67368, -1.92732*
Camping a la ferme La Vignette, 35350 St Coulomb
02 99 89 08 42; francoise.morin600@orange.fr;
www.facebook.com/campinglavignette

12 🏕 ⛺ WC ♨ ⊘ ☂ 1km

Fr St Malo foll D355 E twds St Coulomb. Just bef vill
turn L, sp 'Camping a la ferme'. Site in 400m on R.
Sm, pt shd, pt sl, EHU (10A). *"Vg site."* **€14.00** 2015

ST MALO *2E4* (11km NE Coastal) *48.69000, -1.94200*
Camping des Chevrets, La Guimorais, 35350
St Coulomb **02 99 89 01 90;** contact@campingdes
chevrets.fr; www.campingdeschevrets.fr

🏕 ⛺ ♨ ♿ 🚿 ⊘ MP ☂ Ⓨ ♨ 🛒 ⚠ ⚡ sand adj

St Malo to Cancale coast rd D201; La Guimorais on
L 3km E of Rothéneuf, strt thro vill; fairly narr app.
3*, V lge, hdg, mkd, pt shd, pt sl, EHU (6A) €3.35
(poss rev pol); gas; bbq; red long stay; 50% statics;
Eng spkn; adv bkg acc; ccard acc; games area; bike
hire; CKE. *"Vg, beautiful location with 2 bays; vg, busy,
well run site; bus fr St Malo to Cancale in the summer;
statics in sep area; vg value LS; vg facs; conv for ferry."*
€28.00, 30 Mar-16 Oct. 2017

ST MALO *2E4* (5km SE Rural) *48.60916, -1.98663*
Camping Le P'tit Bois, La Chalandouze, 35430
St Jouan-des-Guérets **02 99 21 14 30;** camping.
ptitbois@wanadoo.fr; www.ptitbois.com

🏕 €4-6 ⛺ WC ♨ ♿ 🚿 ⊘ MP ☂ Ⓨ ♨ 🛒 ⚠ ⚡

🏊 (covrd, htd) 🏖 ☂ sand 2km

Fr St Malo take D137 dir Rennes; after o'skts of
St Malo turn R twd St Jouan-des-Guérets, site sp.
4*, Lge, mkd, hdg, pt shd, serviced pitches; EHU (10A)
inc; gas; bbq (elec, gas); TV; 75% statics; adv bkg acc;
ccard acc; waterslide; games rm; tennis; bike hire;
watersports 2km; CKE. *"Well-kept, well-run site; lge
o'fits by request; busy even LS; min 3 persons high
ssn; tidal rv fishing 2km; jacuzzi; turkish bath; friendly,
helpful staff; gd clean san facs, one block unisex; some
narr site rds poss diff lge o'fits; conv Le Mont-St Michel
& ferries; excel."* **€52.00, 11 Apr-20 Sep, B03.** 2019

ST MALO *2E4* (2.7km S Coastal) *48.63558, -2.02731*
Camp Municipal Cité d'Alet, Allée Gaston Buy,
Saint-Servan 35400 St Malo **02 99 81 60 91 or 02 99
40 71 11 (LS);** camping@ville-saint-malo.fr;
www.ville-saint-malo.fr/campings

🏕 €2.95 ⛺ ♨ ♿ 🚿 ⊘ MP ☂ Ⓨ nr ♨ nr ⚠ ⚡ sand 500m

Fr ferry terminal go twd St Malo, site sp at rndabt
immed past docks. Fr all other dir foll sp for port/ferry,
then site sp. Site off Place St Pierre, St Servan-sur-Mer.
App thro old pt of city poss diff for lge o'fits. 2*, Lge,
hdstg, pt shd, pt sl, EHU (10A) inc (poss rev pol & long
elec cable poss req); bbq (charcoal, elec, gas); twin axles;
phone; bus 1km; Eng spkn; adv bkg acc; ccard acc; CKE.
*"Well-run, scenic site; staff helpful & friendly; sm pitches,
access to some diff lge o'fits; san facs basic but OK (poss v
slippery); WW2 museum adj; noise fr harbour when foggy;
mkt Fri; parts of site steep, lovely walks, cliff top views of
Dinard & St Malo, walk to St Malo worth while; site feels
cosy."* **€22.50, 26 Apr-21 May & 1 Jul-25 Sep.** 2018

ST MALO *2E4* (6km S Rural) *48.61469, -1.98663*
Camping Domaine de la Ville Huchet, Rue de la
Passagère, Quelmer, 35400 St Malo **02 99 81 11 83;**
info@lavillehuchet.com; www.lavillehuchet.com

🏕 €3.50 ⛺ WC ♨ ♿ 🚿 ⊘ MP ☂ Ⓨ ♨ 🛒 ⚠ ⚡

🏊 (covrd, htd) 🏖 ☂ sand 4km

Fr ferry port, foll sps for D137 dir Rennes; site sp
fr 'Madeleine' rndabt on leaving St Malo. Or fr S
on D137 take D301 sp St Malo cent. Take 1st exit
at next 2 rndabts (thro indus est) & cont on this rd
(sharp R-hand bend), then under bdge, site on R.
Fr S head N on D137, merge onto D301, at rndabt
take 1st exit onto Rue de la Grassinais, thro next
rndabt. At next rndabt take 1st exit. Site on the L.
4*, Lge, hdg, mkd, pt shd, pt sl, EHU (6A) inc; bbq
(charcoal, gas, sep area); TV; 40% statics; Eng
spkn; adv bkg acc; waterpark; games area; games
rm. *"Spacious site in grnds of sm chateau; helpful
team; modern san facs; no o'fits over 7.4m except by
request; lge pitches avail; some pitches v shady; conv
ferries & Mont St Michel; excel; bus to St Malo adj."*
€40.70, 4 Apr-20 Sep, B32. 2019

See advertisement

For a guide to symbols see the fold out on the rear cover

FRANCE

STE MARIE AUX MINES *6E3* (1.7km SW Urban)
48.23520, 7.16995 **FFCC Camping Les Reflets du Val
d'Argent,** 20 Rue d'Untergrombach, 68160 Ste Marie-
aux-Mines **03 89 58 64 31; reflets@calixo.net;
www.les-reflets.com**

12 ⛺ €3.50 ⁂(htd) ⬒ ⛲ ♿ 🔲 ⁄ ⟨MP⟩ 🐾 ⛱ 🍴 ⊕ 🔌 🛒 ⚠ 🏊

**Fr Sélestat N59 into Ste Marie. Go thro vill to traff
lts & turn L. 1km to site; sp.** 3*, Med, hdg, mkd, pt shd,
pt sl, EHU (5-15A) €3.30-9.90; bbq; TV; 5% statics;
phone; adv bkg acc; games rm; CKE. *"Pleasant site;
winter skiing 5km; new san facs; grnds could be
improved."* **€21.00** 2015

STES MARIES DE LA MER *10F2* (0.8km E Coastal)
43.45633, 4.43576 **Camping La Brise,** Rue Marcel
Carrière, 13460 Les Stes Maries-de-la-Mer
**04 90 97 84 67; info@camping-labrise.fr;
www.camping-labrise.fr**

⛺ €5.20 ⁂(htd) ⬒ ♿ 🔲 ⁄ ⟨MP⟩ 🐾 ⊕nr 🛒 ⚠ 🏊(htd) 🅿 ⁂adj

**Sp on o'skts on all rds. Take N570 fr Arles or D58
fr Aigues-Mortes.** 3*, V lge, unshd, EHU (16A) €4.90;
bbq; TV; 10% statics; fishing; site clsd mid-Nov to mid-
Dec. *"Gd facs; v cr Aug; poss mosquitoes; gd security;
beach improved with breakwaters; m'vans can use free
municipal car park with facs; fitness area; recep open fr
0900-1700 but clsd 1200-1400; vg winter NH; pitches
poorly mrkd, dirty & dusty."*
€17.00, 1 Jan-12 Nov & 15 Dec-31 Dec. 2016

STES MARIES DE LA MER *10F2* (2.6km W Coastal)
43.45014, 4.40163 **Camping Le Clos du Rhône,**
Route d'Aigues-Mortes, 13460 Stes Maries-de-la-Mer
**04 90 97 85 99; info@camping-leclos.fr;
www.camping-leclos.fr**

⛺ €5.50 ⁂ ⟨WD⟩ ⬒ ♿ 🔲 ⁄ ⟨MP⟩ 🐾 🍴 ⊕ 🔌 🛒 ⚠ 🚲
🏊(htd) 🅿 ⁂sand

**Fr Arles take D570 to Stes Maries; fr Aigues Mortes,
D58/D570.** 4*, Lge, mkd, pt shd, serviced pitches;
EHU (16A) €5.10; gas; bbq; cooking facs; twin axles;
TV; 30% statics; phone; Eng spkn; adv bkg acc; ccard
acc; horseriding adj; games area; games rm; bike hire;
waterslide; CKE. *"Excel pool & facs; san facs clean, poss
ltd & stretched LS; popular with families; private gate to
beach; mosquitoes; rv boat trips adj; off rd bike & foot
paths to town; vg."* **€33.00, 4 Apr-6 Nov.** 2015

ST MARTIN DES BESACES *1D4* (1.2km W Rural)
49.00889, -0.85955 **Camping Le Puits,** La Groudière,
14350 St Martin-des-Besaces Calvados **08 09 48 62;
info@sous-les-etoiles.com;www.sous-les-etoiles.camp**

⛺ ⁂(htd) ⟨WD⟩ ⬒ ♿ 🔲 ⁄ ⟨MP⟩ 🐾 🍴 ⊕ 🔌 🛒 ⚠

**Fr Caen SW on A84 dir Rennes, Villers-Bocage &
exit junc 41 to St Martin-des-Besaces. At traff lts
in vill turn R. Site on L at end of Vill after gge after
500m. Fr Cherbourg foll sp St Lô onto m'way.
After Torini-sur-Vire at junc with A84 foll sp Caen
& exit J41, then as above.** 2*, Sm, hdg, pt shd, pt sl,
serviced pitches; EHU (6A) €5 (poss rev pol); bbq;
red long stay; twin axles; TV; Eng spkn; adv bkg acc;
ccard acc; fishing; cycling; games rm; CKE. *"Pleasant
CL-type orchard site; no arr bef 1400; lge pitches with
garden; 'super' pitches extra cost; B&B in farmhouse;
equestrian trails; lake adj; suitable for rallies up to 30
vans; c'van storage; war museum in vill; conv Caen
ferries; new excel san facs (2019);excep helpful,
new English owners (2018); easy reach of D Day
beaches, Bayeaux, Falaises and Villers Bocage; excel."*
€25.00, 1 Mar-31 Oct. 2019

ST MARTIN EN CAMPAGNE *3B2* (2km N Coastal)
49.96631, 1.20469 **Camping Domaine Les Goélands,**
Rue des Grèbes, 76370 St Martin-en-Campagne
**02 35 83 82 90; domainelesgoelands@orange.fr;
www.camping-les-goelands.fr**

⛺ €2 ⁂(htd) ⟨WD⟩ ⬒ ♿ 🔲 ⁄ ⟨MP⟩ 🐾 🍴 ⊕nr 🛒nr ⚠ 🅿shgl 500m

**Fr Dieppe foll D925 twd Le Tréport & Abbeville.
Turn L at rndabt on D113 twd St Martin-en-
Campagne. Cont thro vill to St Martin-Plage (approx
3km) & foll 'Camping' sp to site on L.** 4*, Lge, hdg,
hdstg, mkd, pt shd, pt sl, terr, serviced pitches; EHU
(16A) inc (poss rev pol); gas; bbq; TV; 40% statics;
Eng spkn; adv bkg acc; ccard acc; bike hire; waterslide
1km; tennis; fishing; CKE. *"Gd touring area; ltd recep
hrs LS; no late arr area; poss resident workers LS;
mkt Dieppe Sat; golf 20km; horseriding 15km; vg
site; immac modern san facs(2017); v helpful recep."*
€23.00, 1 Apr-31 Oct. 2017

ST MARTIN SUR LA CHAMBRE 9B3 (0.5km N Rural) 45.36883, 6.31458 **Camping Le Petit Nice,** Notre Dame-de-Cruet, 73130 St Martin-sur-la-Chambre 04 79 56 37 72 or 06 76 29 19 39 (mob); camping lepetitnice@yahoo.fr; www.campinglepetitnice.com

12 ⌂ €1 ♯♯(htd) ⊡ ♨ ♿ ⊙ ✎ ➳ ❅ ♈ ▽ ⨀ ♨ ☎ ⚑ ⚐

Fr N on A43 exit junc 26 & foll sp to cent of La Chambre, thro town to rndabt & turn R into Rue Notre Dame-du-Cruet. Foll site sp & in 2km turn R thro housing, site on L in 200m. 3*, Sm, pt shd, terr, EHU (3-10A); 80% statics; Eng spkn; adv bkg acc; CKE. *"By stream with mountain views; clean, dated facs; gd location for hilly cycling; fair."* **€16.00**   2016

"I need an on-site restaurant"

We do our best to make sure site information is correct, but it is always best to check any must-have facilities are still available or will be open during your visit.

ST MARTIN SUR LA CHAMBRE 9B3 (1km SW Rural) 45.36146, 6.31300 **Camping Le Bois Joli,** 73130 St Martin-sur-la-Chambre 04 79 56 21 28; camping.le. bois.joli@wanadoo.fr; www.campingleboisjoli.com

⌂ €4 ♯♯ ⊡ ♨ ♿ ⊙ ✎ ➳ ❅ ⨀ ♈ ⚑ ⚐ ♨ ✦

Leave A43 at junc 26 onto D213 sp La Chambre & Col de la Madeleine; foll camping sp (rd narr & winding in places); site on L. 2*, Med, mkd, pt shd, pt sl, terr, EHU (6A) inc; gas; bbq; red long stay; 20% statics; phone; Eng spkn; adv bkg acc; fishing; CKE. *"Helpful staff; mountain scenery; gd walking, skiing; guided walks; ltd facs LS; conv Fréjus Tunnel."* **€13.00,** 5 Apr-6 Oct, A35.   **2017**

STE MAURE DE TOURAINE 4H2 (6km NE Rural) 47.14831, 0.65453 **Camping Le Parc de Fierbois,** 37800 Ste Catherine-de-Fierbois 02 47 65 43 35; contact@fierbois.com; www.fierbois.com or www.les-castels.com

⌂ ♯♯ ⊡ ♨ ♿ ⊙ ✎▽ ♈ ⨀ ➳ ⚑ ♨ ✦ (covrd, htd) ⊡

S on D910 fr Tours, thro Montbazon & cont twd Ste Maure & Châtellerault. About 16km outside Montbazon nr vill of Ste Catherine look for site sp. Turn L off main rd & foll sp to site. Or exit A10 junc 25 onto D760E, then D910 N sp Tours; in 6.5 km turn R to Ste Catherine-de-Fierbois; site on L 1.5km past vill. 4*, Lge, hdg, mkd, pt shd, EHU (10A) €5; bbq; twin axles; TV; Eng spkn; adv bkg acc; ccard acc; games area; waterslide; tennis; bike hire; games rm; boating; fishing; CKE. *"Excel, well-kept family site; helpful staff; gd touring base; peaceful LS; rec."* **€44.00,** 19 May-6 Sep, L20.   **2017**

STE MAURE DE TOURAINE 4H2 (1.5km SE Rural) 47.10483, 0.62574 **Camp Municipal Marans,** Rue de Toizelet, 37800 Ste Maure-de-Touraine 02 47 65 44 93 or 06 72 18 05 41; www.tourisme-saintemauredetouraine.fr

⌂ €1.42 ♯♯ ⊡ ♨ ♿ ✎ ➳ ❅ ♈ nr ⨀ nr ⚑ nr ⚐

Fr A10 take Ste Maure exit junc 25 & foll D760 twd Loches. At 4th rndabt turn L & then immed R. Site on R in 500m. Site sp fr m'way. 2*, Med, mkd, pt shd, EHU (10A) €3.20 (poss long cables req); bbq; phone; Eng spkn; adv bkg acc; fishing; tennis. *"Well-kept, basic site; cheerful staff; gd, clean facs - poss stretched when busy; pool 1.5km; if office clsd site yourself; barrier down 2200-0700; roller blade court; late arr area outside barrier; no twin axles; poss travellers in sep area; vg; wifi around office area; lovely peaceful site."* **€9.00,** 10 Apr-30 Sep.   **2017**

STE MAURE DE TOURAINE 4H2 (1.5km S Rural) 47.10861, 0.61440 **Aire de Service Camping-Cars Bois de Chaudron,** 37800 Ste Maure-de-Touraine 02 47 34 06 04

12 ♯♯ ♨ ⊡ ✎ ▽ ♈

Fr S on D910 dir Tours, as ent town, site on R adj junc at traff lts; sm sp on dual-c'way. Sm, EHU €2 (on only some pitches); Eng spkn. *"M'vans only; New Aire de Service (2009); warden calls; conv N/S journeys; easy to park; level, grass; friendly."* **€5.00**   **2017**

STE MAURE DE TOURAINE 4H2 (10km W Rural) 47.10705, 0.51016 **Camping du Château de la Rolandière,** 37220 Trogues 02 47 58 53 71; contact@larolandiere.com; www.larolandiere.com

⌂ €3 ♯♯ ⊡ ♨ ♿ ⊙ ✎ ❅ ♈ ♨ ➳ ⚑ nr ⚐ ♨(htd) ⊡

Exit A10 junc 25 onto D760 dir Chinon & L'Ile-Bouchard. Site sp on S side of rd in 5.5km. 4*, Sm, mkd, hdg, pt shd, pt sl, EHU (10A) €4.40 (poss long lead req); bbq; TV; Eng spkn; adv bkg acc; games area; games rm; CKE. *"Beautiful, well-maintained, family-run site in chateau grnds; friendly, helpful owners; gd clean san facs; excel for young families, sh or long stay; gd dog walking; conv Loire chateaux; excel pool & sports field; highly rec; Villandry gdns to N; Richlieu worth a visit; secluded and peaceful; gd size pool; football pitch & games for children; great location for Loire chateaux; gd for o'night stay."* **€24.00,** 30 Apr-18 Sep.   2016

ST MAURICE LES CHARENCEY 4E2 (0km N Rural) 48.64747, 0.75575 **Camp Municipal de la Poste,** Rue de Brest, 61190 St Maurice-lès-Charencey 02 33 25 72 98; mairie.stmaurice-charencey@wanadoo.fr

12 ♯♯ ♨ ✎ ♈ nr ⨀ nr ⚐ nr

Vill on N12 halfway bet Verneuil-sur-Avre & Mortagne-au-Perche. Site in vill cent, opp Mairie & church. 2*, Sm, hdg, mkd, pt shd, EHU; bbq; 50% statics; phone; fishing. *"Phone ahead LS to check open; helpful warden; facs basic but adequate; gd NH; lake adj; site self; gd site."* **€7.60**   2016

SAINT MAURICE SOUS LES COTES *5D2* (0.4km N Rural) *49.01796, 5.67539* **Camping Du Bois Joli,** 12 rue haute Gaston Parant, 55210 St Maurice-sous-les-Côtes **03 29 89 33 32; campingduboisjoli@voila.fr; www.forest-campingbj.com**

🛏 ⛽ ♨ 🚿 ⚕ ∥ 🦋 ⵜ nr ⊕ nr ⊿

Well sp in vill. If app on D23, turn R at t-junc & foll sp. Sm, pt shd, sl, EHU (7A) €2.20 (ltd points, long cable useful); bbq; Eng spkn. *"Conv Verdun & WW1 sites; gd view during World Air Balloon Festival."* **€14.80, 1 Apr-15 Oct.** 2019

ST MAURICE SUR MOSELLE *6F3* (4.5km NE Urban) *47.88888, 6.85758* **Sunêlia Domaine de Champé,** 14 Rue des Champs Navés, 88540 Bussang **03 29 61 61 51; info@domaine-de-champe.com; domaine-de-champe.fr**

🛏 €3 ⛽(htd) ⱳ ♨ 🚿 ⚕ ∥ ⱬ 🦋 ⵜ ⊕ ⱬ ⵜ nr ⊿ ⸙ ⸙(covrd, htd) ⻌

Fr N66/E512 in Bussang, site sp fr town sq. Opp Avia filling stn. 3*, Med, mkd, pt shd, pt sl, terr, EHU (6-10A) €5-6; bbq; TV; 50% statics; phone; bus 1km; Eng spkn; adv bkg acc; ccard acc; sauna; waterslide; games rm; bike hire; tennis; games area; CKE. *"Excel site behind hospital grnds; lovely views; welcoming, helpful owners; fitness rm; immac, state of art facs; vg rest; excel walks, cycle path; hg rec."* **€34.00, 1 Apr-15 Nov.** 2019

ST MAURICE SUR MOSELLE *6F3* (14km E Rural) *47.88170, 6.94435* **Camp Municipal Bénélux-Bâle,** Rue de la Scierie, 68121 Urbès **03 89 82 78 76 or 03 89 82 60 91 (Mairie); mairie.urbes@wanadoo.fr; camping-urbes.fr**

🛏 ⱳ(htd) ⱳ ♨ 🚿 ⚕ ∥ ⱬ 🦋 ⵜ ⊿ ⸙

Site off N66 on N side of rd at foot of hill rising W out of Urbès. At foot of Col de Bessang. Fr Bussang on N66, immed on ent Urbes turn L doubling back & foll rd, site on L. 2*, Lge, mkd, pt shd, EHU (6-10A) €6.80; bbq; sw nr; 10% statics; phone; adv bkg rec; fishing adj; games area; CKE. *"Gd sh stay/ NH; beautiful area; friendly, welcoming staff; meals avil on site; facs bit cramped & ltd with poor shwrs; horse riding; hang gliding; cycle paths fr site; walks."* **€9.00, 1 May-30 Sep.** 2017

ST MAURICE SUR MOSELLE *6F3* (1.7km W Rural) *47.8555, 6.8117* **Camping Les Deux Ballons,** 17 Rue du Stade, 88560 St Maurice-sur-Moselle **03 29 25 17 14; stan0268@orange.fr; www.camping-deux-ballons.fr**

🛏 €3.20 ⱳ ⱳ ♨ 🚿 ⚕ 🖥 ∥ ⱬ 🦋 ⵜ ⵜ nr ⸙

On N66 on E side of rd in vill, site on L bef petrol stn. Clearly sp. 3*, Lge, mkd, pt shd, pt sl, EHU (4-15A) €4.15-5.20; gas; TV; phone; Eng spkn; adv bkg acc; waterslide; tennis; games rm; CKE. *"Some pitches sm; excel site & facs; cycle path fr site."* **€32.00, 19 Apr-27 Sep.** 2015

ST MAXIMIN LA STE BAUME *10F3* (3km S Rural) *43.42848, 5.86498* **Camping Caravaning Le Provençal,** Route de Mazaugues, 83470 St Maximin-la-Ste Baume **04 94 78 16 97; camping.provencal@wanadoo.fr; www.camping-le-provencal.com**

⚕ ♨ 🚿 ∥ 🖥 ⱬ ⊕ ⱬ ⵜ ⸙

Exit St Maximin on N560 S twd Marseilles. After 1km turn L onto D64. Site on R after 2km. 3*, Lge, mkd, shd, pt sl, EHU (6-10A) €3.40-4.40; gas; TV; 40% statics; adv bkg acc; CKE. *"Gd NH; easy access fr A8."* **€29.00, 1 Apr-30 Sep.** 2019

SAINT MEEN LE GRAND *2E3* (1km S Urban) *48.183972, -2.188716* **Camping Municipal,** 35290 Saint-Meen-le-Grand **02 99 09 60 61**

🛏 ⱳ ⱳ ♨ ∥ 🦋 ⵜ nr ⊕ nr ⱬ nr

On N164 E or W leave at junc to E of town D125. Turn L at rndabt and foll rd for 1km. Site on L after gge by level x-ing. Sm, mkd, hdg, pt shd, pt sl, EHU 4A; own san rec; bbq; twin axles; bus; Eng spkn. *"Gd site for NH; facs basic, not v clean; if barrier down phone for warden, only 2 mins away."* **€6.00, 1 Jun-30Sep.** 2019

STE MENEHOULD *5D1* (1km E Rural) *49.08937, 4.90969* **Camp Municipal de la Grelette,** Chemin de l'Alleval, 51800 Ste Menéhould **03 26 60 24 76; mairie@ste-menehould.fr; www.ste-menehould.fr**

🛏 €3 ⱳ ♨ ∥ ⱬ ⵜ nr ⊕ nr ⱬ nr

Exit A4 junc 29 to Ste Menéhould; foll sp 'Centre Ville' thro town to Mairie & cent sq on D3; then foll sp 'Piscine' & 'Camping' on D3; cont uphill with rlwy on R; turn R over narr rlwy bdge, then L to site in 200m. 2*, Sm, pt shd, pt sl, EHU (10A) €4; Eng spkn; adv bkg acc; CKE. *"Delightful site; helpful warden 0830-1000 & 1700-1930, gate open at other times, access to o'fits over 2m poss restricted; confirm dep with warden; vg, clean but dated san facs(2017); interesting old town; well maintained site; new indoor pool opened nrby; conv for Reims & Verdun; ok for NH; park away fr bungalows."* **€16.00, 1 May-30 Sep.** 2019

FRANCE

STE MERE EGLISE *1C4* (9.5km NE Coastal) *49.46650, -1.23540* **Camping Le Cormoran,** 2 Rue du Cormoran, 50480 Ravenoville-Plage **02 33 41 33 94; lecormoran@wanadoo.fr; www.lecormoran.com**

🏕 €3 ♂♀ wc ♨ ☕ ♿ 🚮 ⚕ MP 🦋 ☂ 👣 ⓓ 🎿 ⚒ 🌊 (covrd, htd) ⛴ 🏖 sand adj

NE on D15 fr Ste Mère-Eglise to Ravenoville, turn L onto D14 then R back onto D15 to Ravenoville Plage. Turn R on D421, Rte d'Utah Beach, site on R in 1km. Or fr N13 sp C2 Fresville & ent Ste Mère-Eglise, then take D15. 5*, Lge, mkd, hdstg, hdg, unshd, EHU (6A) inc; gas; bbq (charcoal, gas); twin axles; TV; 60% statics; Eng spkn; adv bkg acc; ccard acc; jacuzzi; games rm; archery; tennis; bike hire; games area; horseriding; sauna; CKE. *"Popular, family-run site; lge pitches; warm welcome, helpful recep; well-kept san facs, poss tired end of ssn; poss v windy; vg children's facs; special pitches for early dep for ferry; m'van o'night area; excel."* **€33.00, 31 Mar-30 Sep, N12.** 2017

STE MERE EGLISE *1C4* (0.7km E Urban) *49.41006, -1.31078* **Camping De Sainte-Mere Eglise (formerly Municipal),** 6 Rue due 505eme Airborne, 50480 Ste Mère-Eglise **02 33 41 35 22; www.camping-sainte-mere.fr**

🏕 €1.50 ♂♀ wc ♨ ♿ 🚮 ⚕ ☂ nr ⓓ 🎿 nr 🌊

Fr Cherbourg S on N13 to cent of Ste Mère-Eglise (avoiding by-pass); at vill sq turn L on D17 to site, next adj sports grnd. 3*, Med, hdstg, pt shd, pt sl, EHU (12A) €4 (poss rev pol); bbq; 5% statics; phone; Eng spkn; adv bkg acc; games rm; bike hire; tennis; CKE. *"Nice, basic site; clean facs; friendly warden; if warden absent site yourself & pay later; conv ferries & D-Day beaches etc; gates open 6am for early dep; rec; san facs improving (2014)."* **€22.00, 15 Mar-1 Oct.** 2015

ST MICHEL EN GREVE *2E2* (1km NE Coastal) *48.69277, -3.55694* **Camping Les Capucines,** Voie Romaine, Kervourdon, 22300 Trédez-Locquémeau **02 96 35 72 28; les.capucines@wanadoo.fr; www.lescapucines.fr**

🏕 €2.10 ♂♀ wc ♨ ☕ ♿ 🚮 ⚕ MP 🦋 ☂ 👣 ⓓ 🎿 🌊 (covrd, htd) ⛴ 🏖 sand 1km

Fr Lannion on D786 SW twd St Michel-en-Grève, sp Morlaix; in approx 700m, after steep descent & 'Landebouch' sp, turn R & R again in 100m at x-rds. Fr Roscoff take D58 to join N12 at junc 17; NE of Morlaix at next junc turn onto D786 twd Lannion; site down narr app rd on L on leaving St Michel-en-Grève (slow down at town exit sp), then R at x-rds. 4*, Med, hdg, mkd, pt shd, pt sl, serviced pitches; EHU (10A) inc; gas; bbq (charcoal, gas); red long stay; TV; 15% statics; phone; Eng spkn; adv bkg acc; ccard acc; games area; watersports 1km; bike hire; games rm; CKE. *"Excel, peaceful, well-kept site; no o'fits over 9.5m high ssn; gd sized pitches; helpful owners; clean san facs; gd pool; gd touring base; mkt Lannion Thu."* **€30.00, 1 Apr-30 Sep, B13.** 2017

See advertisement

ST MICHEL EN GREVE *2E2* (1km NE Coastal) *48.69277, -3.55694* **Camping Les Capucines,** Voie Romaine, Kervourdon, 22300 Trédez-Locquémeau **02 96 35 72 28; les.capucines@wanadoo.fr; www.lescapucines.fr**

🏕 €2.10 ♂♀ wc ♨ ☕ ♿ 🚮 ⚕ MP 🦋 ☂ 👣 ⓓ 🎿 🌊 (covrd, htd) ⛴ 🏖 sand 1km

Fr Lannion on D786 SW twd St Michel-en-Grève, sp Morlaix; in approx 700m, after steep descent & 'Landebouch' sp, turn R & R again in 100m at x-rds. Fr Roscoff take D58 to join N12 at junc 17; NE of Morlaix at next junc turn onto D786 twd Lannion; site down narr app rd on L on leaving St Michel-en-Grève (slow down at town exit sp), then R at x-rds. 4*, Med, hdg, mkd, pt shd, pt sl, serviced pitches; EHU (10A) inc; gas; bbq (charcoal, gas); red long stay; TV; 15% statics; phone; Eng spkn; adv bkg acc; ccard acc; games area; watersports 1km; bike hire; games rm; CKE. *"Excel, peaceful, well-kept site; no o'fits over 9.5m high ssn; gd sized pitches; helpful owners; clean san facs; gd pool; gd touring base; mkt Lannion Thu."* **€30.00, 1 Apr-30 Sep, B13.** 2017

ST NAZAIRE LE DESERT *9D2* (0.2km E Rural) *44.56952, 5.27750* **Camp Municipal,** 26340 St Nazaire-le-Désert 04 75 26 42 99 or 04 75 27 52 31 (LS); info@camping-stnazaire.com; www.campingstnazaire.fr

🏠 ⅀₂ ♦♦ ⓦ ☂ ♫ 🏊 ⓣ ⊕ ⌷ ⅀nr 🛝 ♦ ⚓(htd)

Well sp in St Nazaire-le-Désert. 2*, Med, mkd, shd, terr, EHU €3.50; own san rec; bbq; phone; Eng spkn; adv bkg rec; games rm. *"Busy, friendly site in beautiful location; v lge o'fits poss diff to pitch; gd."* **€15.00, 1 May-30 Sep.** **2016**

> ## "There aren't many sites open at this time of year"
>
> If you're travelling outside peak season remember to call ahead to check site opening dates – even if the entry says 'open all year'.

ST NECTAIRE *9B1* (1km S Rural) *45.57541, 2.99942* **Camping La Vallée Verte,** Route des Granges, 63710 St Nectaire 04 73 88 52 68; lavalleeverte@neuf.fr; www.valleeverte.com

🏠 ⅀₃ ♦♦(htd) ⓦ ☂ ♣ ♫ 🔲 ♫ 🎣 🦋 ⓣ 🏊 ⅀ 🛝

Fr A75 exit junc 6 onto D978 & D996 to St Nectaire. On ent o'skts St Nectaire turn L immed at site sp, site in 300m. 3*, Med, pt shd, EHU (5-8A) €3-3.50; sw nr; 20% statics; phone; Eng spkn; adv bkg acc; CKE. *"Vg, friendly, well-maintained, family-run site."* **€21.00, 15 Apr-18 Sep.** **2017**

ST OMER *3A3* (15km NE Rural) *50.80152, 2.33924* **Camping La Chaumière,** 529 Langhemast Straete, 59285 Buysscheure 03 28 43 03 57; camping.lachaumiere@wanadoo.fr; www.camping lachaumiere.com

🏠 ⅀₁ ♦♦ ⓦ ☂ ♣ ♫ 🔲 ♫ 🖵 ♫ ⓣ ⊕ ⌷ ⅀nr 🛝 ♦ ⚓(htd) 🏴

Take D928 fr St Omer (see NOTE) twd Bergues & Watten & foll sp St Momelin. Stay on rd until Lederzeele & turn R onto D26 twds Cassel. After approx 2km turn R just bef rlwy bdge sp Buysscheure & site. Turn L after church, R, then site on L 500m. Single-track rd after church. NOTE on D928 fr St Omer height limit 3m; use adj level x-ing sp rte for vehicles over 3m. NB app fr Cassel diff, espec for wide or long o'fits; also rd thro Cassel cobbled & poss more diff to find. 3*, Sm, hdstg, hdg, mkd, unshd, pt sl, EHU (6A) inc; bbq; TV; Eng spkn; adv bkg acc; archery; bike hire; lake fishing; CKE. *"Lovely, well-kept site; friendly, welcoming, family-run; conv ferries - but poss no exit bef 0800; gd sized pitches - some may req o'fit manhandling due hedges; gd san facs, ltd in number, stretched when site full; no arr bef 12 noon; close to WW1/WW2 sites; local vet; excel; gd bar & food; rest open only w/end in LS."* **€23.00, 1 Apr-30 Sep.** **2015**

ST OMER *3A3* (11km E Rural) *50.73490, 2.37463* **FFCC Camping Le Bloem Straete,** 1 Rue Bloemstraete, 59173 Renescure 03 28 49 85 65 or 06 50 01 08 16 (mob); lebloemstraete@gmail.com; www.lebloem straete.fr

🏠 ♦♦(htd) ⓦ ☂ ♣ 🔲 ♫ 🖵 🦋 ♫ ⓣ ⊕nr ⅀nr 🛝

E fr St Omer on D642 thro Renescure dir Hazebrouck; turn L (site sp) onto D406 Rue André Coo on bend on leaving Renescure; over level x-ing; site on L thro gates. 3*, Sm, hdstg, hdg, mkd, pt shd, EHU (2-6A) €2.50 (poss rev pol); bbq (charcoal, gas); 20% statics; Eng spkn; adv bkg acc; tennis; games area; CKE. *"Conv Calais ferry & tourist sites; manoeuvring poss diff due high kerbs; m'van area; site clean and tidy; worth finding!; excel facs; easy access to ports; new owners, v helpful & planning on improving site (2015)."* **€27.00, 15 Apr-15 Oct.** **2016**

ST OMER *3A3* (6.5km E Urban) *50.74612, 2.30566* **Camp Municipal Beauséjour,** Rue Michelet, 62510 Arques 03 21 88 53 66; camping@ville-arques.fr; www.camping-arques.fr

🏠 ♦♦ ⓦ ☂ 🔥 ♣ 🔲 ♫ 🖵 ♫ ⓣ ⊕nr ⅀nr 🛝

Fr junc 4 of A26 foll sp Arques to town cent. Foll sp Hazebrouck. After x-ing canal site sp 'Camping *' on L. NB Drive 25m bef correct turning to site. Site signs sm and easily missed.** 4*, Med, mkd, hdg, EHU (6-10A) €3 (poss rev pol); bbq; 80% statics; phone; Eng spkn; adv bkg acc; ccard acc; lake fishing; CKE. *"Neat, tidy site; well-run; lge pitches but tight access; friendly, helpful warden; excel, clean facs; m'van o'night area adj (no EHU); gd cycling along canal; lakes & nature park nrby; conv Cristal d'Arques; canal lift & preserved rlwy in town; Calais & Dunkerque 50 mins drive; useful NH; vg."* **€17.50, 1 Apr-31 Oct.** **2019**

ST OMER *3A3* (10km NW Rural) *50.81890, 2.17870* **Kawan Village Château du Gandspette,** 133 Rue du Gandspette, 62910 Eperlecques 03 21 93 43 93; contact@chateau-gandspette.com; www.chateau-gandspette.com

🏠 ⅀₂.₅₀ ♦♦ ⓦ ☂ 🔥 ♣ 🔲 ♫ 🖵 🦋 ♫ ⓣ ⊕ ⌷ ⅀nr 🛝 ♦ ⚓(htd)

Fr Calais SE on A26/E15 exit junc 2 onto D943 foll sp Nordausques-St Omer. 1.5km after Nordausques turn L onto D221 twd Eperlecques; site 5km on L. Do not ent Eperlecques. (Larger o'fts should cont on D943 fr Nordausques to Tilques; at rndabt foll sp for Dunkerque (D300) then D221 dir Eperlecques, site on R. 4*, Med, hdstg, mkd, hdg, pt shd, pt sl, EHU (6A) €5.20 (some rev pol); gas; bbq (charcoal, gas); TV; 15% statics; phone; Eng spkn; adv bkg acc; ccard acc; tennis; bike hire; fishing 3km; golf 5km; games rm; horseriding 5km; playground; CKE. *"Beautiful, well-kept, busy site; spacious, mainly sl pitches; charming, helpful friendly owners; superb, clean san facs; excel rest; site poss muddy in wet; gd for dogs; no o'fits over 8m; rec visit WW2 'Le Blockhaus' nr site; conv A26; highly rec; conv for Calais & for ferry to Dover; spectacular location; excel ctr for visits & activities; vg; security guard with dog; excel site."* **€34.00, 1 Apr-30 Sep, P08.** **2018**

ST PALAIS SUR MER 7B1 (7km N Rural) 45.67550, -1.09670 **Camping Le Logis du Breuil,** 17570 St Augustin 05 46 23 23 45; info@logis-du-breuil.com; www.logis-du-breuil.com

⟟€4.20 ♙♙ ⓦ ♨ ♿ 🅿 ⊘ MSP ♍ ℽ ⑪ 🔥 🅿 ⚠ ⚑ ⚒ 🏖
♙sand 5km

N150 to Royan, then D25 dir St Palais-sur-Mer. Strt on at 1st rndabt & 2nd rndabt; at next rndabt take 2nd exit dir St Palais-sur-Mer. At next traff lts turn R dir St Augustin onto D145; site on L. NB sat nav can direct thro diff & narr alt rte. 3*, Lge, mkd, pt shd, pt sl, serviced pitches; EHU (6-10A) €6-8 (50m cable poss req); gas; bbq (elec, gas); TV; 10% statics; phone; Eng spkn; adv bkg acc; ccard acc; tennis; fishing 1km; golf 3km; excursions; games area; bike hire; games rm; horseriding 400m; CKE. *"Nice peaceful site; lge pitches in wooded area; gd alt to cr beach sites; friendly owner; san facs clean; no c'vans over 12m; gd for young families; excel."* €38.04, 5 May-30 Sep, A04. **2019**

ST PALAIS SUR MER 7B1 (0.5km NE Coastal) 45.64245, -1.07677 **Camping de Bernezac,** 2 Ave de Bernezac, 17420 St Palais-sur-Mer 05 46 39 00 71; acccf-bernezac@acccf.com; bernezac.acccf.com

⟟€1 ♙♙ ⓦ ♨ ♿ 🅿 ⊘ 🦋 ♍ ⑪ 🔥 🅿 nr ⚠ ⚑ ♙adj

Leave A10 at junc 35 fr N. N150 then D25, at 2nd rndabt take 3rd exit (Rue de la Roche), cross 2 rndabt then L onto Ave de Bernezac. Site on R in under 1km. 3*, Med, hdg, mkd, pt shd, pt sl, serviced pitches; EHU (6A) €4.60 (poss rev pol); bbq; twin axles; TV; 60% statics; Eng spkn; adv bkg acc; lake fishing 1km; games area. *"Helpful, friendly staff; clean, spacious pitches; new shwrs (2016); free wifi; cycle rtes nr; sm quiet site; direct access to beach; pleasant coastal walks; off rd bike rides fr beach gate; lots of activities in area; vg."* €33.00, 15 Mar-15 Oct. **2017**

ST PALAIS SUR MER 7B1 (1.5km E Rural/Coastal) 45.64656, -1.07300 **Camping Les Ormeaux,** 44 Ave de Bernezac, 17420 St Palais-sur-Mer 05 46 39 02 07; campingormeaux@aliceadsl.fr; www.camping-ormeaux.com

⟟€4 ♙♙ ♨ ♿ 🅿 ⊘ 🦋 ♍ ℽ 🅿 ⚠ ⚒ (htd) ♙sand 800m

Foll sp fr D25 Royan-St Palais rd. Rec app ent fr R. Ent & camp rds narr. 3*, Lge, pt shd, EHU (6-10A) €7.50; gas; TV; 98% statics. *"Ltd touring area & access diff for lge o'fits or m'vans - tents or sm m'vans only; one of the best campsites we have stayed in; clean spacious pitches, amazing staff, new san facs; dir access to 41km cycle rtes, mostly off-rd; no TV on pitches."* €25.00, 1 Apr-31 Oct. **2016**

ST PALAIS SUR MER 7B1 (2km E Coastal) 45.64396, -1.06325 **Camping Le Val Vert,** 108 Ave Frédéric Garnier, 17640 Vaux-sur-Mer 05 46 38 25 51; camping-val-vert@wanadoo.fr; www.val-vert.com

⟟€4.50 ♙♙ ⓦ ♨ ♿ 🅿 ⊘ MSP ♍ ⑪ 🔥 🅿 ⚠ ⚑ ⚒ (htd) 🏖

♙sand 900m

Fr Saintes on N150 dir Royan; join D25 dir St Palais-sur-Mer; turn L at rndabt sp Vaux-sur-Mer & Centre Hospitaliers; at traff lts ahead; at 2nd rndabt take 3rd exit & then turn immed R. Site on R in 500m. 3*, Med, hdg, EHU (10A) inc; gas; bbq (elec, gas); adv bkg acc; ccard acc; tennis 400m; bike hire; horseriding 5km; games rm; fishing; watersports; games area; golf 5km. *"Well-kept, family-run site; no o'fits over 6.5m high ssn; gd sized pitches; unisex san facs; a stream runs alongside site; sh walk to pleasant vill; daily mkt in Royan."* €39.72, 27 Apr-30 Sep, A25. **2019**

ST PALAIS SUR MER 7B1 (2km SE Urban/Coastal) 45.64272, -1.07183 **Camping Nauzan-Plage,** 39 Ave de Nauzan-Plage, 17640 Vaux-sur-Mer 05 46 38 29 13; info@campinglenauzanplage.com; www.camping lenauzanplage.com

⟟€5 ♙♙ ⓦ ♨ ♿ 🅿 ⊘ ♍ ℽ ⑪ 🔥 🅿 ⚠ ⚒ ♙sand 450m

Take either coast rd or inland rd fr Royan to Vaux-sur-Mer; site not well sp. 4*, Lge, mkd, pt shd, EHU (10A) €5.50; gas; red long stay; TV; 10% statics; adv bkg rec; tennis 200m; games rm; CKE. *"Gd site, busy high ssn; helpful staff; gd cycling rte; pt of Flower Camping group."* €45.00, 1 Apr-15 Oct. **2017**

"That's changed – Should I let the Club know?"

If you find something on site that's different from the site entry, fill in a report and let us know. See camc.com/europereport.

ST PALAIS SUR MER 7B1 (3km NW Coastal) 45.6500, -1.1193 **Camping La Côte de Beauté,** 157 Ave de la Grande Côte, 17420 St Palais-sur-Mer 05 46 23 20 59; campingcotedebeaute@wanadoo.fr; www.camping-cote-de-beaute.com

⟟€3 ♙♙ (htd) ♨ ♿ 🅿 ⊘ 🦋 ⑪ ⚠ ♙sand 200m

Fr St Palais-sur-Mer foll sp to La Tremblade & Ronce-les-Bains. Site on D25, 50m fr beach, look for twin flagpoles of Camping Le Puits de l'Auture & lge neon sp on R; site in 50m. 3*, Med, hdg, shd, EHU (6A) €4.20; 10% statics; adv bkg acc; tennis adj; golf 2km. *"Clean, tidy site; friendly staff; steep descent to beach opp - better beach 600m twd La Tremblade; bike hire adj; cycle track to St Palais & Pontaillac; town 3km; clean san facs; gd pitches."* €26.00, 1 May-30 Sep. **2017**

ST PALAIS SUR MER *7B1* (6.5km NW Coastal)
45.64930, -1.11785 **Camping Le Puits de l'Auture,**
La Grande Côte, 17420 St Palais-sur-Mer **05 46
23 20 31; contact@camping-puitsdelauture.
com; www.camping-puitsdelauture.com**

♦♦♦(htd) **♠ ♦ ♦ ⬚ ∥ ♥ ⚘ ☂ ⅄ ⅁ ⤢ ⽁ ⬚**(htd) ⚘ sand adj

Fr Royan take D25 onto new rd past St Palais foll
sp for La Palmyre. At 1-way section turn back L sp
La Grande Côte & site is 800m; rd runs close to sea,
flags at ent. 4*, Lge, pt shd, serviced pitches; EHU
(10A) inc; gas; 25% statics; Eng spkn; adv bkg rec;
ccard acc; fishing; games area; CKE. *"Well-maintained,
well laid-out, excel site; san facs stretched high ssn &
'tired'; poss cr but carefully controlled; friendly, helpful
staff; gd cycle paths."* **€38.00, 28 Apr-3 Oct.** **2016**

ST PANTALEON LES VIGNES *9D2* (2km E Rural)
44.39752, 5.06099 **Camping Les Cyprès,** Hameau
Font de Barral, 26770 Saint Pantaleon les Vignes
**06 81 53 78 03 or 06 82 27 19 14; contact@lescypres-
camping.com; www.lescypres-camping.com**

♦ €1.80 **♦♦♦** ⬚ ♠ ♦ ⬚ ∥ ♥ ⚘ ⅀ nr ⅃ nr ⤢

D541 fir Nyons. Fr highway A7 exit Montèlimar-Sud
Bollène or Orange Cent. 1*, Sm, pt shd, pt sl, EHU
(4,6,10A) €2.50-3.60; bbq; twin axles; games rm.
"Beautiful surroundings; friendly owners."
€11.00, 1 Apr-31 Oct. **2019**

ST PARDOUX *7A3* (1.6km S Rural) *46.04955, 1.27893*
Campsite de Fréaudour, Site de Freaudour 87250 St
Pardoux **05 55 76 57 22; camping.freaudour@
orange.fr; www.aquadis-loisirs.com**

♦ **♦♦♦** ⬚ ♠ ⬚ ∥ ♥ ⚘ ☂ ⅀ ⅃ ⤢

Fr A20 dir Limonges, take exit 25, onto D219. Cont
onto D44 thro Razes & foll sp to Lac De Saint-
Pardoux. Turn R onto D103A to Freaudour.
4*, Med, mkd, pt shd, EHU (6A); bbq; TV; 20% statics;
Eng spkn; adv bkg rec; games area. *"Fair site."*
€20.40, 1 Apr-27 Oct. **2019**

ST PAUL DE FENOUILLET *8G4* (0.4km S Rural)
42.80762, 2.50235 **Camping de l'Agly,** Ave 16 Août
1944, 66220 St Paul-de-Fenouillet **04 68 59 09 09;
contact@camping-agly.com;www.camping-agly.com**

12 **♦** **♦♦♦** ⬚ ♠ ♦ ∥ ♥ ⅀ nr

Heading W on D117; turn L at traff lts in St Paul;
site on R in 200m, well sp. 2*, Sm, mkd, hdg, pt shd,
pt sl, EHU (16A) €4.50; sw nr; site clsd Jan; CKE. *"Vg
site; friendly warden; mountain scenery; gd climbing &
cycling; conv for Château's Payrepertuse & Quéribus;
sm pitches, diff access for lge o'fits; conv NH."*
€16.00 **2017**

ST PAUL EN FORET *10E4* (3.5km N Rural) *43.58449,
6.69016* **Camping Le Parc,** Quartier Trestaure,
83440 St Paul-en-Forêt **04 94 76 15 35; contact@
campingleparc.com; www.campingleparc.com**

♦ €4.50 **♦♦♦**(htd) ⬚ ♠ ♦ ♦ ⬚ ∥ ♥ ⚘ ☂ ⅄ ⅁ ⅀ ⅃ ⤢ ⽁ ⤢
⤢(htd) ⬚

Exit A8 at junc 39, foll D37 (dir Fayence) for 8.4km
to lge rndabt on D562. Take 3rd exit at rndabt (sp
draguignan/Fayence). Foll D562 for 4.8km thro
4 more rndabts. At 5th rndabt (Intermarche Supmkt
on L) take 3rd exit D562 sp Draguignan. After 4.2km
take 3rd exit at rndabt onto D4, after 2km turn L
at bus stop. Foll rd to site. 4*, Sm, mkd, shd, sl, EHU
(10A) €5 high ssn only; twin axles; TV; 65% statics;
phone; Eng spkn; adv bkg acc; games rm; fishing;
games area; tennis; CKE. *"Conv hill vills of Provence;
gd rests in St Paul; many medieval vill; excel."*
€29.00, 2 Apr-30 Sep. **2016**

ST PAULIEN *9C1* (2.5km SW Rural) *45.12041, 3.79357*
Camping de la Rochelambert, 43350 St Paulien
**04 71 00 54 02; infos@camping-rochelambert.com;
www.camping-rochelambert.com**

♦ €1.50 **♦♦♦** ⬚ ♠ ♦ ⬚ ∥ ♥ ⚘ ☂ ⅄ ⅀ nr ⅃ ⤢ ⽁

Fr St Paulien take D13; turn L onto D25 sp La
Rochelambert; site on L in 1.5km. 4*, Med, mkd, pt
shd, terr, EHU (10A) €3.10; bbq; 15% statics; phone;
Eng spkn; adv bkg acc; tennis; CKE. *"Gd touring base;
gd walking & fishing; app poss diff lge/long o'fits; gd."*
€23.80, 1 Apr-30 Sep. **2019**

ST PHILBERT DE GRAND LIEU *2H4* (1km N Rural)
47.04202, -1.64021 **Camping La Boulogne,** 1 Ave
de Nantes, 44310 St Philbert-de-Grand-Lieu
32 40 78 88 79; accueil@camping-la-boulogne.com

♦ €1 **♦♦♦** ⬚ ♠ ♦ ♦ ⬚ ∥ ♥ ⚘ ☂ ⅀ nr ⅃ ⤢

Fr Nantes on A83 exit junc 1 or 2 onto D178 - D117
dir St Philbert; turn L onto D65 (Ave de Nantes)
to St Philbert; site on R in 500m adj rv & sp. Or
fr Machecoul take bypass to St Philbert & then D65
as narr rds thro town. 2*, Med, hdg, mkd, pt shd,
EHU (6A) inc; bbq; 10% statics; phone; bus adj; Eng
spkn; adv bkg acc; ccard acc; fishing; games area; CKE.
*"Well-kept, secure site; htd covrd pool 200m; lake adj;
new enthusiastic, helpful owners (2010); gd; ACSI acc."*
€13.50, 1 Apr-31 Oct. **2016**

ST PIERRE EN PORT *3C2* (0.5km N Coastal)
49.80943, 0.49354 **Les Falaises,** 130 rue du Camping,
76540 St Pierre-en-Port **02 35 29 51 58; lesfalaises@
cegetel.net; www.campinglesfalaises.com**

♦ **♦♦♦** ⬚ ♠ ♦ ♦ ⬚ ∥ ♥ ⚘ ☂ ⅄ ⅁ ⅀ nr ⅃ ⚘ 2km

Fr D925 turn onto D79 bet St Valery & Fecamp. Site
sp in St Pierre. 2*, Med, hdg, unshd, EHU (10A); bbq;
60% statics; bus 0.5km; Eng spkn; games area; games
rm; CKE. *"Cliff top site; path to beach steep with
steps; narr app rd; facs dated but clean; well kept site;
takeaway snacks avail high ssn only; v quiet, pleasant
site; gd."* **€19.00, 1 Apr-5 Oct.** **2017**

ST PIERRE LE MOUTIER *4H4* (8km SW Rural) *46.75722, 3.03328* **Camp Municipal de St Mayeul,** Rue de Saint-Mayeul, 03320 Le Veurdre **04 70 66 40 67** (Mairie); mairie.le.veurdre@wanadoo.fr; www.allier-tourisme.com

⛺ 🏃 ⛷ 🚿 🐶 🚌 🔒nr

Fr N7 at St Pierre-le-Moûtier SW onto D978A to Le Veurdre. Site sp on far side of Le Veurdre. 2*, Sm, hdg, mkd, pt shd, pt sl, EHU €4; bbq; adv bkg acc. *"Pleasant spot; site yourself, warden calls; friendly staff; clean, basic facs; shops in pleasant vill; rec NH; vg."* **€11.40, 1 May-15 Sep.** 2018

ST POL DE LEON *1D2* (2km E Coastal) *48.69103, -3.96730* **Camping Ar Kleguer,** Plage de Ste Anne, 29250 St Pol-de-Léon **02 98 69 18 81**; info@camping-ar-kleguer.com; www.camping-ar-kleguer.com

🐶 €2.80 ⛺ 🚐 🏊 ⛷ 🚿 🐶 ⛱ 🍽 👕 🏊 🔒nr ⛷(htd) 🏊 🌳adj

In St Pol-de-Léon foll Centre Ville sp. At cathedral sq (2 towers) with cathedral on L descend hill & in 150m, bef church with tall belfry, turn L foll Plage & camping sp. On reaching sea turn L (N); site at end, well sp. NB Narr, busy rds in town. 4*, Med, mkd, pt shd, pt sl, terr, EHU (10A) (long lead poss req); 40% statics; adv bkg acc; waterslide; games rm; tennis; CKE. *"Well-kept, attractive site; modern facs; gd views; conv Roscoff ferry."* **€31.00, 2 Apr-25 Sep.** 2015

ST POL DE LEON *1D2* (2km E Coastal) *48.69355, -3.96930* **Camping de Trologot,** Grève du Man, 29250 St Pol-de-Léon **02 98 69 06 26 or 06 62 16 39 30** (mob); camping-trologot@wanadoo.fr; www.camping-trologot.com

🐶 €2.40 ⛺ 🚐 🏊 ⛷ 🚿 🐶 ⛱ 🦋 👕 ⑪nr 🏊 🔒 🚗 🏠 ⛷
🏊(htd) 🏊 🌳 sand adj

Fr the port of Roscoff take D58 go briefly on the D769 then back on to the D58 foll the sp to Morlaix over six rndabts (approx 4miles/6.5km). Just after passing under a rlwy bdge, take the exit for the D769 (sp St Pol de Léon, Kerlaudy, Penzé) then turn L. Stay on the D769 for 1.8 km, just past the graveyard turn R at the rndabt and go strt over the next rndabt (sp Campings/Plage) at the end of the rd turn L and the turning for the site will be on L after 1km and is sp. Do not use sat nav. Fr the E on the N12 take the exit for the D19 (sp Morlaix St pol de Leon) at the rndabt take the 2nd exit cont twds St-Pol-de Leon on the D58. Take the exit to the D769 (SP St-Pol-de Leon) then foll above dirs fr the graveyard. 3*, Med, mkd, hdg, pt shd, EHU (10A) €4.50; bbq (charcoal, gas); red long stay; TV; 20% statics; adv bkg acc; ccard acc; games rm; bouncy castle; CKE. *"Lovely, well-kept site; ideal NH for Roscoff ferry; gd sized pitches; helpful owners; clean, modern san facs; no o'fits over 7m high ssn; gd for family beach holiday; peaceful area, many walks nrby; beautiful town; highly rec."* **€21.90, 31 March-27 Oct, B29.** 2019

ST POL DE LEON *1D2* (5km SE Coastal) *48.65805, -3.92805* **Les Mouettes,** La Grande Grève, 29660 Carantec **02 98 67 02 46**; camping@les-mouettes.com; www.les-mouettes.com

🐶 €6 ⛺ 🚐 🏊 ⛷ 🚿 🐶 ⛱ 👕 🍽 🔒 🚗 🏠 ⛷
🏊(covrd, htd) 🏊 🌳 shgl 1km

Fr Morlaix take D58 N sp Roscoff; at lge rndabt turn R sp Carantec on D173; turn L at 1st rndabt; strt on at 2nd & 3rd rndabt past Casino supmkt; turn L next rndabt; site on L. Or fr Roscoff take D58 sp Mortaix, then D173 to Carantec; foll sp town cent, then site. 5*, Lge, mkd, pt shd, EHU (10A) inc (poss rev pol); gas; bbq (charcoal); TV; 50% statics; Eng spkn; adv bkg acc; ccard acc; tennis; bike hire; fishing; games area; golf 1.5km; waterslide; games rm; CKE. *"Attractive site with sea views; no o'fits over 8m; clean, modern san facs; sauna; jaccuzi; impressive pool complex; plenty to do on site; mkt Thu; noise fr boatyard; conv Carnac."* **€60.00, 20 Apr-10 Sep, B14.** 2019

> ## "I like to fill in the reports as I travel from site to site"
>
> You'll find report forms at the back of this guide, or you can fill them in online at camc.com/europereport.

ST POL DE LEON *1D2* (9km SE Rural) *48.64912, -3.92126* **Camping Les Hortensias (Jacq),** Kermen, 29660 Carantec **02 98 67 08 63 or 02 98 67 96 34**; contact@leshortensias.fr; www.leshortensias.fr

🐶 €0.80 ⛺ 🚐 🏊 ⛷ 🚿 🐶 ⛱ 🦋 🔒nr 🏠 🌳2.5km

Fr Roscoff on D58 dir Morlaix. Turn L after approx 10km onto D173, then turn R at 1st rndabt, site in 200m, site sp. Sm, mkd, unshd, EHU (6A) €3; adv bkg acc; CKE. *"Conv Roscoff ferry; views of bay; friendly staff; poss unkempt LS; organic produce in shop; gd touring base; no gates allows early departure; excel NH; no o'fits over 6m."* **€12.50, 1 May-30 Sep.** 2015

ST PONS DE THOMIERES *8F4* (2km E Rural) *43.49055, 2.78527* **Camping Village Les Cerisiers du Jaur,** Les Marbrières-du-Jaur, Route de Bédarieux, 34220 St Pons-de-Thomières **04 67 95 30 33**; info@cerisierdujaur.com; www.cerisierdujaur.com

🐶 €1.50 ⛺ 🚐 🏊 ⛷ 🚿 🐶 ⛱ 🦋 👕 ⑪nr 🏊 🔒 🏠 ⛷

Fr Castres on D612 to St Pons; go thro town cent under rlwy bdge; turn L onto D908 sp Olargues. Site on R in 500m. 3*, Med, mkd, hdg, pt shd, terr, EHU (10A) €4; bbq; phone; Eng spkn; ccard acc; games area; bike hire; CKE. *"Excel site nr Rv Jaur; welcoming, friendly, helpful owner; cycle rte fr site; an oasis!; hot water not v hot; expensive in LS; san facs unkept."* **€33.00, 29 Mar-26 Oct.** 2017

ST POURCAIN SUR SIOULE *9A1* (0.7km SE Urban) *46.30643, 3.29207* **Camp Municipal de l'île de la Ronde,** Quai de la Ronde, 03500 St Pourçain-sur-Sioule **04 70 35 13 69 or 07 61 52 33 72 (mob);** camping.ronde@ville-saint-pourcain-sur-sioule.com; www.ville-saint-pourcain-sur-sioule.com

🏕 ♦♦♦ ⓦ ♨ ♿ ♿ ⚊ ∥ ▫ ✂ ❦ ⛺nr /▥

On D2009, 31km S of Moulins; in St Pourçain-sur-Sioule town cent turn R immed bef rv bdge; site ent on L in 100m. NB Sp in town easily missed. 3*, Med, hdg, pt shd, EHU (10A) inc; adv bkg acc; CKE. *"Well-run, magnificent, busy, pleasant site in pretty town; extra charge for lger pitches; barrier clsd 2000-0800; gd rest nr; mkt Sat; great value; excel; recep and barrier clsd 1200-1400; 2 supmkt in town; 2 pin adapter ess; set amongst trees; walks/rvside path adj; san facs stretched at times; gd value."*
€14.00, 31 Mar-1 Oct. **2017**

"We must tell the Club about that great site we found"

Get your site reports in by mid-August and we'll do our best to get your updates into the next edition.

ST QUAY PORTRIEUX *2E3* (3km NW Coastal) *48.66269, -2.84550* **Camping Bellevue,** 68 Blvd du Littoral, 22410 St Quay-Portrieux **02 96 70 41 84;** info@ campingbellevue.net; www.campingbellevue.net

🏕 ♦♦♦ ⓦ ♨ ♿ ♿ ⚊ ∥ ▫ ❦ ⛺ ∥ ▥ ♨(htd) ⛱ 🏖 sand adj

Foll D786 thro St Quay-Portrieux twd Paimpol; turn R at traff lts sp St Quay-Portrieux; foll site sp; site in 2.5km. 3*, Lge, hdg, hdstg, mkd, pt shd, pt sl, terr, EHU (6A) €3; gas; bbq; TV; 8% statics; Eng spkn; adv bkg acc; ccard acc; games area; golf 3km; CKE. *"Beautiful position with sea views; direct access to sm cove; friendly staff; gd, clean facs; vg; excel pool; gd exercise area for dogs."*
€23.00, 8 May-15 Sep, B05. **2015**

ST QUENTIN *3C4* (12km SW Urban) *49.78222, 3.21333* **Camping du Vivier aux Carpes,** 10 Rue Charles Voyeux, 02790 Seraucourt-le-Grand **03 23 60 50 10;** contact@camping-picardie.com; www.camping-picardie.com

🏕 €1.50 ♦♦♦ ⓦ ♨ ♿ ♿ ⚊ ∥ ▫ ❦ ⛺ ♨ ♨ /▥

Fr A26 take exit 11 St Quentin/Soissons; S 4km on D1 dir Tergnier/Soissons. Fork R onto D8 to Essigny-le-Grand & in vill foll camping sp W to Seraucourt. Fr St Quentin, S 10km on D930 to Roupy, E on D32 5km to Seraucourt-le-Grand. Site N of Seraucourt on D321. Narr ent fr rd unsuitable lge o'fits. 3*, Med, hdstg, hdg, mkd, pt shd, EHU (10A) inc (poss rev pol); gas; bbq; 30% statics; Eng spkn; adv bkg acc; tennis adj; golf adj; horseriding adj; games rm; CKE. *"Delightful, lovely, well-run site; busy, even LS - rec arr early; ltd hdstg; peaceful LS; gd, lge pitches; narr site rds; friendly, helpful staff; pitches by lake poss boggy when wet; poss flooding; mkd footpaths round lakes; vg angling; mosquito probs; Disneyland 90 mins; conv Channel ports; c'van storage; warn staff night bef if v early dep; excel; facs stretched but clean & gd; lovely cycle rte along canal to St Quentin; nice bistro in vill; new coded security barrier (2015)."*
€23.50, 20 Mar-20 Oct, P14. **2018**

ST QUENTIN EN TOURMONT *3B2* (0.5km S Rural) *50.26895, 1.60263* **Camping Le Champ Neuf,** 8 Rue du Champ Neuf, 80120 St Quentin-en-Tourmont **03 22 25 07 94;** campinglechampneuf@orange.fr; www.camping-lechampneuf.com

🏕 €1.50 ♦♦♦(htd) ⓦ ♨ ♿ ♿ ⚊ ∥ ▫ ❦ ⛺ 🍴 ♨ /▥ ✂ 🏖(covrd, htd) ⛱ ⛲2km

Exit D1001 or A16 onto D32 to Rue, take D940 around Rue & foll sp St Quentin-en-Tourmont, Parc Ornithologique & Domaine du Marquenterre to site. Site sp fr D204. 3*, Lge, mkd, hdg, pt shd, EHU (5-10A) inc; bbq; 80% statics; phone; adv bkg acc; ccard acc; horseriding 500m; bike hire; games area. *"Excel Ornithological Park nrby; well-kept, pleasant site; friendly, helpful owner; gd cycle paths."*
€30.00, 1 Apr-1 Nov. **2017**

See advertisement

ST RAPHAEL *10F4* (8.6km WSW Coastal) *43.408915, 6.708677* **Camping Sandaya Rivièra d'Azur,** 189 Les Grands Chat.de Villepey, RD7 83370, Saint Aygulf **04 11 32 90 00; www.sandaya.fr/nos-campings/ riviera-d-azur**

🛁 ⚕ 🅆🅆 ♨ ⚓ 🔥 🚻 ⊒ ✉ 👜 ⛲ ⛱ ⊞ 🎾 🚲 ∕⊞ ⚡ 🏊 (htd) 🛁

🏕 sandy 2.5km

Leave A8 exit 36 Le Muy on N555 twrds Draguignan then N7 twrds Frejus. R on d7 sp St Aygulf. Site on R in 2.5km before town. 5*, Mkd, EHU 10A; bbq (elec, gas); Eng spkn; adv bkg rec; ccard acc; bike hire; beauty ctr; fishing; tennis; security. **€74.00, 31 Mar-14 Oct.** 2019

> ## "I need an on-site restaurant"
>
> We do our best to make sure site information is correct, but it is always best to check any must-have facilities are still available or will be open during your visit.

ST RAPHAEL *10F4* (4.5km N Rural) *43.44611, 6.80610* **Sandaya Douce Quiétude,** 3435 Blvd Jacques Baudino, 83700 St Raphaël **04 94 44 30 00; dou@sandaya.fr; www.sandaya.co.uk**

🏕 €5 🚻 (htd) 🅆🅆 ♨ ⚓ 🔥 🚻 ⊒ ∕ ✉ 👜 ⛲ ⛱ 🎾 👜 ⊞ ⚡ 🏊 (htd) 🛁 🏕 sand 2km

Exit A8 at junc 38 onto D37 then D100 sp Agay. Foll sp Valescure-Boulouris, site sp. NB c'vans not permitted on St Raphaël seafront. 4*, Lge, hdstg, mkd, hdg, pt shd, pt sl, serviced pitches; EHU (10A) inc; gas; bbq (gas); TV; phone; bus; Eng spkn; adv bkg acc; ccard acc; games area; gym; waterslide; games rm; bike hire; mini golf; CKE. "*Lge pitches; excel facs; takeway; disco nightly high ssn; many tour ops statics; sm touring pitches mostly amongst statics; vg.*" **€24.00, 30 Apr-8 Oct.** 2019

ST REMY DE PROVENCE *10E2* (0.5km NE Rural) *43.79622, 4.83878* **FFCC Camping Le Mas de Nicolas,** Ave Plaisance-du-Touch, 13210 St Rémy-de-Provence **04 90 92 27 05; contact@camping-masdenicolas.com; www.camping-masdenicolas.com**

🏕 €2.15-€2.80 🚻 (htd) 🅆🅆 ♨ ⚓ 🔥 🚻 ⊒ ∕ ✉ ⛲ ⛱ 👜 ⊞ ⚡ 🏊 (htd)

Fr town ctr take D99 eastwards for abt 0.5km. Turn L at 2nd rndabt & foll sp to campsite. 4*, Lge, hdg, mkd, hdstg, pt shd, EHU (6A) €3.80; bbq; TV; TV (pitch); 20% statics; bus 1km; Eng spkn; adv bkg req; ccard acc; games area; games rm; CKE. "*Family-owned site; gd clean modern san facs; some pitches diff access long o'fits; excel; v helpful staff; interesting town.*" **€33.00, 1 Apr-14 Oct.** 2017

ST REMY DE PROVENCE *10E2* (0.9km E Urban) *43.78836, 4.84093* **Camping Pégomas,** Ave Jean Moulin, 13210 St Rémy-de-Provence **04 90 92 01 21; contact@campingpegomas.com; www.camping pegomas.com**

🏕 €1.70 🚻 (htd) 🅆🅆 ♨ ⚓ 🔥 🚻 ⊒ ∕ ✉ ⛲ ⛱ 👜 ⊞ nr ∕⊞ ⚡ 🏊 🛁

On D99 fr W dir Cavaillon, ignore R fork to St Rémy 'Centre Ville' (& sat nav!). Pass twin stone sculptures on rndabt, at 2nd rndabt turn into Ave Jean Moulin, site on R in 400m - v sharp turn into site. Fr E Exit A7 junc 25 on D99 W dir St Rémy. Ignore sp 'Centre Ville', pass under aquaduct & across rndabt. At next rndabt turn L into Ave Jean Moulin, then as above. Do not attempt to tow thro town. 3*, Med, hdg, mkd, shd, EHU (6A) €3.50 (poss rev pol & long lead req); gas; TV; phone; Eng spkn; adv bkg acc; ccard acc; games area; CKE. "*Well-run, busy site; clean san facs; lge o'fits poss diff some sm pitches; gd pool; gd touring base; recep clsd 2000 hrs, lge lay-by outside; mkt Wed am; excel for walking; lovely site.*" **€31.00, 15 Mar-24 Oct.** 2015

ST REMY DE PROVENCE *10E2* (2km NW Rural) *43.7967, 4.82378* **Camping Monplaisir,** Chemin Monplaisir, 13210 St Rémy-de-Provence **04 90 92 22 70; reception@camping-monplaisir.fr; www. camping-monplaisir.fr**

🏕 €2.50 🚻 (htd) 🅆🅆 ♨ ⚓ 🔥 🚻 ⊒ ∕ ✉ ⛲ ⛱ 👜 ⊞ ⚡ 🏊 🛁

Exit D99 at St Rémy onto D5 going NW dir Maillane, in 110m turn L & foll sp in 500m. Avoid going thro town. 4*, Med, hdstg, hdg, shd, EHU (10A) inc; gas; bbq (elec, gas); red long stay; phone; bus 1km; Eng spkn; adv bkg acc; ccard acc; bike hire; CKE. "*Immac, well-run site; mostly gd sized pitches; clean, modern san facs; gd touring base; highly rec; site clsd last Sat in Oct; excel site; lovely pool; walk to nice town; fills up quickly.*" **€41.00, 10 Mar-19 Oct.** 2017

See advertisement

ST ROME DE TARN *8E4* (0.3km N Rural) *44.05302, 2.89978* **Camping de la Cascade des Naisses,** Route du Pont, 12490 St Rome-de-Tarn **05 65 62 56 59; contact@camping-cascade-aveyron.com; www.camping-cascade-aveyron.com**

🔵12 🏕 €6 🚻 (htd) 🅆🅆 ♨ ⚓ 🔥 🚻 ⊒ ∕ ✉ ⛲ ⛱ 🎾 👜 ⊞ ⚡ 🏊 🛁

Fr Millau take D992 to St Georges-de-Luzençon, turn R onto D73 & foll sp to St Rome. In St Rome turn R along Ave du Pont-du-Tarn, site sp. Diff, steep app for sm/underpowered car+c'van o'fits. 4*, Med, hdg, hdstg, mkd, pt shd, terr, EHU (6A) inc; own san req; 40% statics; Eng spkn; adv bkg acc; boating; rv fishing; tennis; bike hire; CKE. "*Lovely rvside pitches; pleasant vill; friendly, helpful staff; each level has a wc but steep walk to shwr block; owners will site vans; conv Millau viaduct; excel tranquil, scenic site.*" **€35.00** 2016

ST SAVIN *7A3* (0.5km N Rural) *46.56892, 0.86772*
Camp Municipal Moulin de la Gassotte, 10 Rue
de la Gassotte, 86310 St Savin-sur-Gartempe
05 49 48 18 02; campingdumoulin@aol.com;
saintsavin.com/camping-moulin-de-la-gassotte
⊞†† ⲱⅅ ♨ ఉ ➲ ✦/ ⲙⲋⲣ ❦ Ⲧ nr Ⓦ nr ⲍ nr /Ⱡ

E fr Chauvigny on D951 to St Savin; fr St Savin N on
D11; well sp. Fr S on D5 cross rv; meet D951, turn
R & site on R. Fr S on D11 use 'poids lourds' (heavy
vehicles) rec rte to meet D951.
2*, Sm, pt shd, EHU (12A) inc; TV; rv fishing adj; CKE.
"Beautiful, peaceful, park like site by rv; views of Abbey;
helpful warden; san facs old but clean; sh walk to vill;
murals in Abbey restored by UNESCO; no defined
pitches." **€11.00, 8 May-30 Sep.** 2016

"Satellite navigation makes touring much easier"

Remember most sat navs don't know if you're
towing or in a larger vehicle – always use yours
alongside maps and site directions.

ST SEINE L'ABBAYE *6G1* (1.8km SE Rural) *47.44073,
4.79236* **Camp Municipal,** Rue de la Foire aux Vaches,
21440 St Seine-l'Abbaye **03 80 35 00 09 or
03 80 35 01 64 (Mairie)**
ⲏ †† (cont) ⲱⅅ ♨ ✦/ ✿ ⲍ nr

On D971 in vill of St Seine-l'Abbaye, turn N onto
D16. Turn R uphill, sp camping & turn R thro
gateway in stone wall. Narr rds in vill. Or fr N
on D974, avoiding Dijon, turn R onto D959 at
Til-Châtel, then D901 Moloy/Lamargelle. Turn L
in Lamargelle onto D16 St Seine-l'Abbaye. Turn L
uphill at edge of vill & as above (avoids narr rds).
1*, Sm, hdstg, pt sl, EHU (10A) €2.50 (rev pol); CKE.
"Pleasantly situated & peaceful site; basic but immac
san facs; fees collected fr 1900 hrs; lovely vill; conv
Dijon or as NH; pool 4km; excel; not suitable for o'fits
over 7m." **€12.00, 1 May-30 Sep.** 2015

STE SEVERE SUR INDRE *7A4* (6km SE Rural)
46.471980, 2.148024 **Camping La Grange Pérassay,**
Le Bourg, 36160 Pérassay **02 54 30 87 73 or
06 86 34 68 52 (mob); guy.timothy@orange.fr;
www.lagrangecamping.com**
ⲏ ⊞†† ⲱⅅ ♨ ఉ ➲ ✦/ ✿ ⲋ ⲋ

Fr Ste Sévère take D917 S & after approx 6km turn L
onto D71 sp Pérassay. Site on L in cent of vill.
1*, Sm, pt shd, pt sl, EHU (10A); bbq; 1% statics; Eng
spkn; adv bkg acc; bike hire. "Lovely CL-type site in
quiet location; friendly British owners; vg san facs;
vg; field for exercising dogs; gd walks direct fr site;
countryside views." **€17.00, 1 Apr-31 Oct.** 2019

ST SYMPHORIEN *7D2* (1km S Rural) *44.41831,
-0.49232* **Camping Vert Bord'Eau (formerly Camping
La Hure),** Route de Sore, 33113 St Symphorien
05 56 25 79 54 or 06 07 08 37 28 (mob); camping@
vertbordeau.com; www.vertbordeau.com**
ⲏ €1.30 ⊞†† (htd) ⲱⅅ ♨ ➲ ✦/ ⲙⲋⲣ ❦ Ⲧ Ⓦ ఉ ⲍ /Ⱡ ⲋ

S thro Langon on app. Foll sp Villandraut,
St Symphorien. Sp fr vill 1km S on D220, opp
Intermarché. 2*, Sm, shd, EHU (10A) €2.50;
80% statics; Eng spkn; adv bkg acc; games area;
tennis; rv fishing. "Helpful staff; basic facs; site in
pinewoods; gd cycling, walks, beaches; vg cycle path
run thro St Symphorien, gd level surface thro woods
and vineyard; excel." **€23.40, 2 Apr-29 Oct.** 2016

ST TROPEZ *10F4* (11km SW Rural) *43.21804, 6.57830*
Camping Moulin de Verdagne, Route du Brost, 83580
Gassin 04 91 09 10 27; www.domaine-verdagne.com**
ⲏ €3 ⊞†† ⲱⅅ ♨ ➲ ✦/ ✿ Ⲧ Ⓦ ఉ ⲍ nr /Ⱡ ⲋ ⲧ sand 5km

Foll N559 N fr Cavalaire for 6km. Take 1st R after
town traff lts in La Croix-Valmer, site sp. Site in
2km, surrounded by vineyards. Rough app rd/
track. 3*, Med, mkd, pt shd, terr, EHU (6A) €4; red
long stay; 60% statics; phone; Eng spkn; ccard acc.
"Vg, lovely site; tight bends & narr pitches poss diff
long o'fits; pool 2m deep; c'van best app fr La Croix
vill; new owners (2016); helpful; new pool (2017)."
€37.50, 1 Apr-31 Oct. 2017

ST VALERY SUR SOMME *3B2* (4.6km S Rural) *50.15333, 1.63583* **Le Domaine du Château de Drancourt,** 80230 Estréboeuf **03 22 26 93 45; chateau.drancourt@wanadoo.fr; www.chateau-drancourt.fr**

🚶 €3.80 ♦♦ wo ♨ ♁ ⚷ ⊟ ⚊ msp ⵯ 🍽 ⑨ ♨ ♨ ⚿

⚓(covrd, htd) 📷

Exit A28/E402 junc 1 at Abbeville onto D40 twd Noyelles-sur-Mer. At rndabt with D940 turn L sp St Valery-sur-Somme. At next rndabt go strt over dir Le Tréport, then at next rndabt at junc with D48 take last exit (sp Estréboeuf), turn immed L & foll sps to site. NB.1-way system at recep area. 5*, Lge, mkd, hdg, pt shd, pt sl, EHU (10A) inc (poss rev pol); gas; bbq; 80% statics; Eng spkn; adv bkg acc; ccard acc; bike hire; fishing adj; golf driving range; tennis; horseriding 12km; games rm; watersports 2km; CKE. *"Conv, busy, popular NH in grnds of chateau; friendly staff; facs poss stretched when site full; red facs LS; bird sanctuary in estuary nrby; gd."* **€40.00, 13 Apr-24 Sep, P06.** **2017**

ST VALERY SUR SOMME *3B2* (1km SW Urban/Coastal) *50.18331, 1.61786* **Camping Le Walric,** Route d'Eu, 80230 St Valery-sur-Somme **03 22 26 81 97; info@ campinglewalric.com; www.campinglewalric.com**

🚶 €3 ♦♦ wo ♨ ♁ ⚷ ⊟ ⚊ msp 🦮 ♈ 🍽 ♨ ⚿ ⚓(htd) 📷

Ringrd round St Valery D940 dir Le Tréport. Cont to 3rd rndabt (1st rndabt Carrefour supmkt on L) 3km & take 1st exit (R) sp St Valery & Cap Hornu D3. Site on R in 2km at ent to town sp. 4*, Lge, hdstg, hdg, mkd, pt shd, EHU (6A) inc; gas; bbq; red long stay; 70% statics; phone; Eng spkn; adv bkg acc; ccard acc; tennis; games area; bike hire; games rm; boat hire; fishing; CKE. *"Well-kept, well-run, busy site in excel location; clean dated san facs; cycle rtes, canal track; steam train; beach nrby; delightful medieval town; mkt Sun; excel; easy to find."* **€37.00, 1 Apr-30 Oct.** **2017**

ST VALERY SUR SOMME *3B2* (1km W Urban) *50.18447, 1.62263* **Camping de la Croix l'Abbé,** Place de la Croix l'Abbé, 80230 St Valery-sur-Somme **03 22 60 81 46; w.a.georges@wanadoo.fr**

♦♦ wo ♨ ⚊ 🦮 🍽 ♨ ⑨ ♨ ♨ 🔥 ⚓(covrd, htd) ⛺shgl 1km

Ringrd round St Valery D940 dir Le Tréport. Cont to 2nd rndabt (1st rndabt Champion supmkt on L) 3km & take exit sp St Valery & Cap Hornu D3. Site 250m beyond Camping Le Walric. Lge, mkd, hdg, unshd, pt sl, EHU (10A) inc; TV; 90% statics; bus adj; Eng spkn. *"San facs needs updating (2017); gd location for walk to town; sh stay/NH only; super town; rec steam rlwy to Le Crotoy."* **€20.00, 1 Apr-30 Nov.** **2017**

ST VALLIER *9C2* (2km N Rural) *45.18767, 4.81225* **Camp Municipal Les Iles de Silon,** 26240 St Vallier **04 75 23 22 17 or 04 73 23 07 66; camping.saint vallier@orange.fr; www.saintvallier.fr/decouvrir/ camping**

🚶 €2.30 ♦♦ wo ♨ ♁ ⚊ 🦮 ♨ ♨ 🔥

On N7 just N of town, clearly sp in both dirs on rvside. 3*, Med, hdg, pt shd, EHU (10A) €2.30 (poss long cable req); bbq; 10% statics; Eng spkn; adv bkg acc; ccard acc; watersports; tennis adj; CKE. *"Attractive, gd quality site; views over rv; lge pitches; friendly warden; gd immac san facs; rec arr bef 1600 high ssn; gd value; cycle/walking track adj, along Rhône; excel well managed site; vg facs and staff; free WiFi."* **€13.00, 15 Mar-15 Nov.** **2018**

ST VINCENT DE BARRES *9D2* (1km SW Rural) *44.65659, 4.69330* **Camping Le Rieutord,** 07210 St Vincent-de-Barrès **04 75 20 86 17; campingle rieutord@orange.fr; www.camping-le-rieutord.com**

🚶 €2 ♦♦(htd) ♨ ⊟ ⚊ 🦮 🍽 ♨ ♨ 🔥 ⚓ 📷

Fr N exit A7 junc 16 Loriol onto D104 & foll sp Le Pouzin then Chomérac (do not foll 1st sp St Vincent-de-Barrès - narr rd). At rndabt foll D2 dir Le Teil-Montélimar for 6km. When arr at St Vincent (vill on L), turn R & foll site sp for 1.5km. Fr S exit junc 18 Montélimar Sud, foll sps Montélimar then Privas. Cross Rv Rhône, go thro Rochemaure go past St Meysse turn L after bdge dir Privas. Foll D2 for 4.5km then turn L dir St Bauzile to site in 3km. 2*, Med, hdg, pt shd, pt sl, EHU (16A) €3; cooking facs; 10% statics; Eng spkn; adv bkg acc; tennis; games area; waterslide; CKE. *"Tranquil site in beautiful setting nr old walled town; pleasant owners; no c'vans over 6m or twin axles; gd touring base."* **€20.00, 4 Apr-31 Oct.** **2016**

SAINTES *7B2* (0.5km N Urban) *45.75511, -0.62871* **Camp Municipal au Fil de l'Eau,** 6 Rue de Courbiac, 17100 Saintes **05 46 93 08 00 or 06 75 24 91 96 (mob); contact@camping-saintes-17.com; www.camping-saintes-17.com**

🚶 €1.60 ♦♦ wo ♨ ♁ ⊟ 🦮 ♈ ♨ 🍽 ⑨ ♨ ♨ 🔥

Well sp as 'Camping Municipal' fr rndbts on by-pass N & S on D150 & D137 (thro indus area), adj rv. If app fr W on D128 (N side of Saintes), turn R at rndabt onto Rue de l'Abbatoir; in 800m turn L into Rue de Courbiac; site on R in 200m. NB 1st Mon in month st mkt & many rds clsd. 3*, Lge, pt shd, EHU (10A) €3.60; bbq; sw nr; red long stay; Eng spkn; adv bkg acc; ccard acc; boating adj; fishing adj; CKE. *"Excel site; vg, clean, upgraded (2019) san facs; excel rest; grnd poss boggy when wet; gd touring base; mkt Wed & Sat; easy walk to attractive Roman town; huge open site, effcient recep; friendly staff; gd NH just off A10; rest clsd on Sundays;spacious, well positioned for town."* **€21.00, 20 Apr-15 Oct.** **2019**

SALBRIS *4G3* (1km N Urban) *47.43006, 2.05427*
Camping de Sologne, 8 Allée de la Sauldre, Route de Pierrefitte, 41300 Salbris **02 54 97 06 38; camping desologne@wanadoo.fr; www.campingdesologne.fr**

🏠 €1 👫 🚿 wc ♨ ⚓ 🐕 🖥 ⚟ 🛒 ⚞ 🍴 ⓦ ⚟ 🌁nr ⚟

Fr N exit A71 J4. Take D724 bypass (2nd exit on rndabt). At next rndabt take D2020 N sp Salbris. Cont thro town. After x-ing bdge at next traff lts turn R onto D55 (Rte de Perrelefitte). Impass de la Sauldre leading to Allee de la Sauldre is 2nd turning on R in 200m (narr and easy to miss). Fr S to avoid Peage leave A71 at J5. Take D2020 N to Salbris then as abv. 3*, Med, hdg, mkd, pt shd, EHU (10A) inc (some rev pol); gas; TV; 25% statics; phone; Eng spkn; adv bkg acc; ccard acc; fishing; boat hire; CKE. "Excel, well-kept site in pleasant lakeside location; friendly, helpful owners; karting 6km; lake adj; gd san facs poss stretched if site busy & ltd LS; gd rest; gd dog walks adj; conv NH for m'way; hypmkt 1km; beautiful site; easy access to town; new shwr block (2015); ACSI accepted." **€24.00, 1 Apr-30 Sep.** **2019**

SALERS *7C4* (0.8km NE Rural) *45.14756, 2.49857*
Camp Municipal Le Mouriol, Route de Puy-Mary, 15140 Salers **04 71 40 73 09 or 04 71 40 72 33 (Mairie); www.salers.fr**

🏠 👫 wc ♨ 🅿 🐕 🖥 ⚟ 🛒 ⚟ 🍴 ⚟ nr ⓦnr ⚟

Take D922 SE fr Mauriac dir Aurillac; turn onto D680 E dir Salers; site 1km NE of Salers on D680 dir Puy Mary, opp Hôtel Le Gerfaut; sp fr all dir.
2*, Med, hdg, mkd, pt shd, sl, EHU (16A) €4.60 (long lead poss req); bbq; red long stay; phone; bus 1km; tennis; CKE. "Generous pitches; san facs gd but stretched if site full; peaceful LS; hill walking; excel cycling & walking; beautiful medieval vill; vg; well kept; footpath fr site to Salers." **€19.80, 1 Apr-30 Oct.** **2017**

"There aren't many sites open at this time of year"

If you're travelling outside peak season remember to call ahead to check site opening dates – even if the entry says 'open all year'.

SALERS *7C4* (0.8km W Rural) *45.13304, 2.48762*
Camping à la Ferme (Fruquière), Apcher, 15140 Salers **04 71 40 72 26**

🏠 👫 ♨ ⚟ 🛒 ⚟ 🌁nr

D922 S fr Mauriac for 17km; L on D680 sp Salers; in lane on R sp Apcher - immed after passing Salers town sp. Sm, pt shd, EHU (10A) €2.30; CKE. "Sm farm, CL type site; welcoming, friendly owner; excel clean san facs, plenty hot water; beautiful countryside; gd; run down end of ssn." **€10.00, 1 May-30 Sep.** **2017**

SALIES DE BEARN *8F1* (3km S Rural) *43.45277, -0.92055* **Domaine d'Esperbasque,** Chemin de Lagisquet, 64270 Salies de Béarn **05 59 38 21 04; info@esperbasque.com; www.esperbasque.com**

🏠 €1.50-€3.50 👫 wc ♨ ⚓ 🐕 🖥 ⚟ 🛒 🦋 ⚟ 🍴 ⚟ ⓦ ⚓ 🌁nr ⚟
🏇 ⛴

Site well sp on D933. E of rd bet Salies de Bearn and Sauveterre. Fr N pass the site, turn at next exit & app fr southern side. 2*, Med, hdstg, mkd, pt shd, sl, terr, EHU (6A) €3.50; bbq; twin axles; TV; Eng spkn; adv bkg acc; ccard acc; games area; games rm; CKE. "Gd touring; horse riding at site highly rec; excel; go-karts; petanque; scenic, rural, visits to wine growers & Salies de Bearn; gd." **€23.40, 1 Mar-31 Oct.** **2017**

"That's changed – Should I let the Club know?"

If you find something on site that's different from the site entry, fill in a report and let us know. See camc.com/europereport.

SALINS LES BAINS *6H2* (0.5km N Rural) *46.94650, 5.87896* **Camp Municipal,** 39110 Salins-les-Bains 03 84 37 92 70; campingsalins.kanak.fr; www.salins camping.com

👫 ♨ 🅿 🐕 🖥 ⚟ 🌁nr ⚟

SE fr Besançon on N83. At Mouchard take D472 E to Salins. Turn L at rndabt at N of Salins, well sp nr old stn. If app fr E take 2nd exit fr rndabt (blind app). 2*, Sm, pt shd, EHU (10A) €3.10; 10% statics; adv bkg acc. "Well-run site; clean, modern san facs; excel touring base N Jura; not often visited by British; far end of site quieter; htd pool adj; gd NH; barrier locked 1000-0700; chalets being built (2016)." **€13.50, 31 Mar-1 Oct.** **2017**

SALLANCHES *9A3* (4km SE Rural) *45.92388, 6.65042* **Camping Village Center Les Iles,** Lac de Passy 245 Chemin de la Cavettaz, 74190 Passy **04 30 05 15 04; www.campinglesiles.fr**

🏠 €3 👫 ♨ ⚓ 🐕 🖥 ⚟ 🦋 ⚓ 🌁 ⚟ 🏊 ⛴(htd)

E fr Geneva on A40, exit junc 21 onto D339 dir Passy; in 400m turn L onto D39 dir Sallanches; at rndabt in 1.5km turn L onto D199 dir Domancy; immed after rlwy x-ing in 500m turn R into Chemin de Mont Blanc Plage; site at end of rd in 1km. Or E fr Sallanches on D1205 dir Chamonix; in 3km turn L (1st into filter to turn L) onto D199; in 1km turn L immed bef level x-ing; site at end of rd. 3*, Lge, mkd, hdg, pt shd, EHU (8A) inc; sw nr; phone; Eng spkn; adv bkg acc; ccard acc; fishing; CKE. "Mountain views; conv Chamonix; vg site; v overgrown; nr rlwy and m'way; pitches bare of grass, some v muddy after rain, v shady; not rec." **€16.00, 1 Apr-1 Oct.** **2016**

SALLES (GIRONDE) 7D1 (4km SW Rural) 44.52039, -0.89631 **Camping Le Bilos,** 37 Route de Bilos, 33770 Salles 05 56 88 36 53; lebilos@aol.com; www.lebilos.com

🔢 🛉 ⏰(htd) ⬛ ⬛ ⬛ / 🐛 🐕 🔥

Exit A63 junc 21; foll sp Salles on D3; turn L onto D108/D108E3 sp Lugos; pass Carrefour supmkt on R; in 2km bear R & site on R in 2km. 2*, Med, pt shd, EHU (3-6A) €2.20-3.50; gas; bbq (sep area); 80% statics; adv bkg acc. *"Pleasant, peaceful site in pine forest; sm, well-drained pitches, ltd space for tourers, friendly owners, old but clean san facs, ltd LS, cycle lane thro forest, vg NH en rte Spain; friendly welcome; site cr."* **€13.00** **2016**

SALLES CURAN 8E4 (2km NW Rural) 44.18933, 2.76693 **Camping Les Genêts,** Lac de Pareloup, 12410 Salles-Curan 05 65 46 35 34; contact@camping-les-genets.fr; www.camping-les-genets.fr

🛉 ⬛€4 🛉 ⬛ ♨ ⬛ ⬛ / 🗺 🏸 🍴 ⏰ 🖐 🐕 🏊 (htd) 🏖

🌲 and lake adj. to site

Fr D911 Rodez-Millau rd take D993 S for approx 9km, then R onto D577, site sp on R by lake. 4*, Lge, shd, pt sl, EHU (10A) inc; sw; red long stay; 40% statics; adv bkg acc; fishing; sailing; bike hire; games area. *"Beautiful area; ltd facs LS; excel site."* **€36.00, 25 Apr - 22 Sep, D07.** **2019**

SALON DE PROVENCE 10E2 (5km NW Rural) 43.67820, 5.06480 **Camping Nostradamus,** Route d'Eyguières, 13300 Salon-de-Provence 04 90 56 08 36; gilles.nostra@gmail.fr; www.camping-nostradamus.com

🛉 ⬛€3 🛉 ⬛ ♨ ⬛ ⬛ / 🗺 🐛 🍴 ⏰ 🖐 🐕 nr 🔥 🏊 🏖 🖐

Exit A54/E80 junc 13 onto D569 N sp Eyguières. After approx 1.5km turn R opp airfield onto D72d, site on R in approx 4km just bef T-junc. Or fr N exit A7 junc 26 dir Salon-de-Provence. Turn R onto D17 for 5km dir Eyguières, then L onto D72, site on L. 3*, Med, mkd, hdg, pt shd, EHU (4-6A) €2.95-5.15; gas; bbq; TV; 15% statics; phone; Eng spkn; adv bkg req; ccard acc; games area; CKE. *"Pleasant site; busy high ssn; welcoming owner with vg sense of humour!; bkg fee; poss diff access lge o'fits; dusty when dry; gd walking."* **€24.00, 1 Mar-30 Oct.** **2019**

SAMOENS 9A3 (6km W Rural) 46.08944, 6.67874 **Camp Municipal Lac et Montagne,** 74440 Verchaix 06 79 57 69 59; www.verchaix.com

🔢 🛉 ⬛€1.40 ♨ ⬛ ⬛ / 🗺 🍴 nr ⏰ nr 🐕 nr 🔥

Fr Taninges take D907 sp Samoëns for 6km, site to R of main rd in Verchaix. 2*, Med, shd, EHU (10A) €4.10; 10% statics; phone; adv bkg acc; tennis. *"Gd touring base; clean facs; rv & lake adj; barrier locked 2200-0700."* **€21.00** **2016**

SANCERRE 4G3 (4km N Rural) 47.34215, 2.86571 **Flower Camping Les Portes de Sancerre,** Quai de Loire, 18300 St Satur 02 48 72 10 88; camping.sancerre@flowercampings.com; www.campingcher-sancerre.com

🛉 ⬛€2 🛉 ⬛ ⬛ ♨ ⬛ / 🗺 🖐 ⏰ nr 🐕 nr 🔥 🏊

Fr Sancerre on D955 thro cent St Satur & St Thibault. Turn L immed bef Loire bdge. Site on R in 100m. 3*, Med, hdg, shd, EHU (16A) inc (long lead poss req); sw; TV; 50% statics; Eng spkn; adv bkg acc; bike hire; games area; tennis; CKE. *"Nice site; some pitches sm, some with rv view; friendly & helpful staff; pool adj; canoe hire adj; gd clean excel san facs, rec own in peak ssn; rvside walks; gd touring cent; vg; highly rec; gd rest nrby."* **€23.00, 1 Apr-1 Oct.** **2017**

SANCERRE 4G3 (9.4km SW Rural) 47.30353, 2.74555 **Camping Crezancy en Sancerre,** 9 Route de Veagues, 18300 Crezancy en Sancerre 06 12 55 69 98; campingcrezancy@orange.fr

🛉 🛉 ⬛ ♨ ⬛ ⬛ / 🔥

Fr Sancerre take D955 dir Bourges. In 5km turn R onto D22 sp Crezancy, Henrichement. After 5km at vill turn L onto D86 sp Veagues. Site 100m on L. Sm, hdg, mkd, shd, EHU (6A); bbq; cooking facs; twin axles; phone; bus 100m; Eng spkn; adv bkg acc; CKE. *"Site in Sancerre vineyards with wine tasting & to buy; gd walks & cycling, but a bit hilly; easy acc to Sancerre and The Loire; hospitable site manager; excel; lovely sm friendly site; indiv hdg bays; rural, quiet & clean; new shwrs (2016)."* **€10.00, 1 Apr-31 Oct.** **2017**

SANGUINET 7D1 (2km SW Rural) 44.48402, -1.09098 **Camping Les Grands Pins,** Ave de Losa, Route du Lac, 40460 Sanguinet 05 58 78 61 74; info@campings grandspins.com; www.campinglesgrandspins.com

🛉 ⬛€2 🛉 ⬛ ⬛ ♨ ⬛ ⬛ / 🍴 ⏰ 🖐 🔥 🏊

Foll Le Lac sp at rndabt in Sanguinet. Turn L at lakeside. Site on L in 450m opp yacht club. 3*, Lge, hdg, shd, EHU (3-10A) inc; sw nr; TV; 50% statics; Eng spkn; adv bkg acc; canoeing; bike hire; fishing; tennis; boating; windsurfing; CKE. *"Clean site; rest & bar poss clsd LS; parking for m'vans adj."* **€37.00, 1 Apr-31 Oct.** **2016**

SANGUINET 7D1 (1.5km W Rural) 44.483045, -1.088951 **Sandaya Sanguinet Plage,** 1039 Avenue de Losa, 40460 Sanguinet 05 58 76 61 74; sap@sandaya.fr; www.sandaya.co.uk

🛉 ⬛€5 🛉 ⬛ ⬛ / 🗺 🐛 ⏰ 🍴 🖐 🐕 🔥 🏊 (htd) 🖐 🏖 sand 100mtrs

Foll Le Lac sp at rndabt in Sanguinet, turn L on lakeside, site on L in 600m. 5*, Lge, mkd, shd, EHU (10A); sw nr; twin axles; 80% statics; Eng spkn; games rm; games area; sailing nr; bike hire; watersports; CKE. *"Spacious site; cycle path around lake; watersports on lake; friendly, helpful staff."* **€36.00, 03 Apr-27 Sep.** **2019**

FRANCE

SARLAT LA CANEDA 7C3 (10km NE Rural) 44.95778,
1.27280 **Sandaya Les Péneyrals,** Le Poujol, 24590
St Crépin-et-Carlucet **05 53 28 85 71; pen@sandaya.fr;**
www.sandaya.co.uk

🏕 €5 ⛺(htd) 🆆 ⓐ♨ㅎ🔲⁄ 🅼🆂🅿 🦋 🍽 ⑪🏊🛒ﹰ🅿⚓
🏊(covrd, htd) 🛥

Fr Sarlat N on D704; D60 E dir Salignac-Eyvignes to
Le Poujol; S to St Crépin. Site sp. 5*, Lge, hdg, pt shd,
pt sl, terr, serviced pitches; EHU (5-10A); bbq (gas);
50% statics; Eng spkn; adv bkg acc; ccard acc; games
area; waterslide; fishing; tennis. "*Friendly owners;
superb family & touring site; excel aquatic ctr; some
pitches require mover.*"
€25.00, 10 Apr-13 Sep, A18.   2019

SARLAT LA CANEDA 7C3 (8km NE Rural) 44.90404,
1.28210 **Camping Les Grottes de Roffy,** 24200
Ste Nathalène **05 53 59 15 61; contact@roffy.fr;**
www.roffy.fr

🏕 €2.10 ⛺(htd) 🆆 ⓐ♨ㅎ🔲⁄ 🍽 ⑪🏊🛒ﹰ🅿⚓⁄ 🏊🛥

Fr N end of Sarlat take D47 NE for Ste Nathalène.
Site on R 1km bef vill. Or fr A20 exit junc 55 onto
ND804/D703 dir Carlux. Turn R onto D61B then
D47 to Ste Nathalène, site thro vill on L.
4*, Lge, mkd, hdg, pt shd, terr, EHU (6A) €3; gas;
bbq; 40% statics; Eng spkn; adv bkg rec; canoeing;
games rm; tennis; bike hire; games area; CKE. "*Excel
rest, bar & shop; extra for 'comfort' pitches; helpful
staff; lovely site.*" **€33.50, 25 Apr-13 Sep.**   2015

See advertisement

SARLAT LA CANEDA 7C3 (9.7km NE Rural) 44.91905,
1.27789 **Camping Domaine des Mathévies,** Les
Mathévies, 24200 Ste Nathalène **05 53 59 20 86 or**
06 14 10 95 86 (mob); info@mathevies.com;
www.mathevies.com

🏕 €5.50 ⛺⛺ ⓐ♨ㅎ⁄ 🅼🆂🅿 🦋 ⑪🍽 ⑪🏊🛒ﹰ/Λ 🏊🛥

Exit A20 junc 55 Souillac & foll sp Roufillac. At
Roufillac, foll sp to Carlux & cont to Ste Nathalène,
site sp N of Ste Nathèlene. 2*, Sm, hdg, mkd, pt
shd, EHU (10A) €4; TV (pitch); 10% statics; adv
bkg acc; tennis; games area; playground; games
rm. "*Gd, British-owned site; lge pitches, most with
views; max. 2 dogs per pitch; excel site; gd for kids.*"
€35.00, 18 May-21 Sep, D04.   2019

SARLAT LA CANEDA 7C3 (2km E Rural) 44.89328,
1.22756 **Camping Indigo Sarlat Les Périères,** Rue
Jean Gabin, 24200 Sarlat-la-Canéda **05 53 59 05 84;**
sarlat@camping-indigo.com; www.camping-
indigo.com

🏕 ⛺⛺♨ㅎ🔲⁄ 🅼🆂🅿 🦋 ⑪🍽 Ⓣ🛒/Λ 🏊(covrd, htd)

Site on R of D47 to Proissans & Ste Nathalène. NB
steep access rds. 4*, Med, mkd, shd, terr, EHU (6A);
gas; bbq (charcoal, gas); 10% statics; Eng spkn; adv
bkg acc; ccard acc; games rm; sauna; tennis. "*Lovely
site; friendly, helpful staff; san facs clean; excel pool
complex; steep site rds; access poss diff med & lge
o'fits; excel; great facs & location; v easy walk to Old
City; site extended (2015); new san facs (2016); excel
site.*" **€37.00, 24 Mar-2 Nov.**   2015

SARLAT LA CANEDA 7C3 (20km E Rural) 44.86732,
1.35796 **Camping Les Ombrages,** Rouffillac, 24370
Carlux **09 53 53 25 55; ombragesperigord@free.fr;**
www.ombrages.fr

🏕 €2 ⛺⛺ ⓐ♨⁄ 🦋 ⑪🍽 Ⓣ nr ﹰ🛒 nr /Λ

12km W thro Souillac on D703. Turn L at x-rds in
Rouffillac & immed turn L bef rv bdge into site. 2*, Med,
mkd, pt shd, EHU (6A) €2.70; bbq; sw nr; TV; 2% statics;
phone; Eng spkn; adv bkg acc; ccard acc; fishing; tennis;
bike hire; games area; canoe hire; CKE. "*Pleasant, well-
kept, rvside site; enthusiastic new owners live on site;
pitching poss diff due trees; san facs (open air) poss
stretched high ssn; cycle track; vg; lovely peaceful site;
pool adj; lots of entmnt.*" **€20.00, 19 Apr-15 Oct.**   2015

Caudon 24200 VITRAC – France
info@labouysse.com – www.labouysse.com

Site owned by French family. English spoken.

Along the river Dordogne near the well known Caudon rock, direct access to beach area where you can swim or go canoeing. Beautiful site near Montfort château, Sarlat (6km.) and many other Dordogne sights.
Green pitches, with trees and hedges giving some shade.
Lovely swimming pool. A wide range of accommodations available (country cottages, mobile homes, gîtes and pitches).
On the site: grocery's, bar and snack bar (open from 15th June until 31st August) – washing machine, dryer and iron - WiFi

---

SARLAT LA CANEDA *7C3* (11km SE Rural) *44.83274, 1.26626* **Camping Le Plein Air des Bories,** 24200 Carsac-Aillac **05 53 28 15 67; camping.lesbories@ wanadoo.fr; www.camping-desbories.com**

🐕€3 ♦♦♦ ⚓ ♨ ♿ 🛒 ⚡ Ⓦ 🦋 ⛱ ▼ ⚓ 🐚 🛶 (htd)

Take D704 SE fr Sarlat sp Gourdon; diff RH turn to site after Carsac vill. Easier access on D703 fr Vitrac. 3*, Med, shd, pt sl, EHU (16A) €4.50; gas; sw; Eng spkn; canoe hire; fishing; boating; tennis 700m; CKE. *"Clean, shady rvside site; friendly owners."*
€24.00, 1 Jun-15 Sep.　　　　　　　　　**2018**

SARLAT LA CANEDA *7C3* (10km S Rural) *44.82525, 1.25360* **Domaine de Soleil-Plage,** Caudon-par-Montfort, 24200 Vitrac **05 53 28 33 33; info@soleilplage.fr; www.soleilplage.fr**

🐕€3.50 ♦♦♦(htd) Ⓦ ⚓ ♨ ♿ 🛒 ⚡ ⓂⓈⓅ 🦋 ⛱ ▼ Ⓗ ⚓ 🐚 ⚞ ⚓ 🛶 (htd) ⚓

On D46, 6km S of Sarlat twd Vitrac, turn L onto D703 to Château Montfort, R to site dir Caudon, sp. Site beyond Camping La Bouysse on rvside, 2km E of Vitrac. If coming fr Souillac on D703, when app Montfort rd v narr with overhanging rock faces. Narr access rds on site. 5*, Lge, hdg, pt shd, serviced pitches; EHU (16A) inc (poss rev pol); gas; bbq; TV; 45% statics; phone; Eng spkn; adv bkg req; ccard acc; waterslide; bike hire; tennis; golf 1km; canoeing; rv fishing adj; horseriding 5km; games rm; CKE. *"Lovely site in beautiful location; friendly, welcoming owner; variety of pitches - extra for serviced/rvside (shady); no o'fits over 7m Jun-Aug; san facs clean; superb aquatic complex; poss muddy when wet; red groups; highly rec; first class comprehensive site; poss best site we've ever stayed at; lge private pitches; lovely cycling, but some on fairly steep rds."* **€43.70, 8 Apr-29 Sep, D15.**　　**2019**

SARLAT LA CANEDA *7C3* (12km S Rural) *44.79175, 1.16266* **Camping Bel Ombrage,** 24250 St Cybranet **05 53 28 34 14; belombrage@wanadoo.fr; www.belombrage.com**

🐕 ♦♦♦ Ⓦ ⚓ ♨ ♿ 🛒 ⚡ 🦋 ⛱ ▼ nr ⚓ nr ⚞ ⚓ 🐚 🛶

Fr Sarlat take D46 sp Bergerac, rd then conts as D57; after 8km turn L at Vézac sp Castelnaund. After 1.6km at T-junc turn L onto D703 & in 180m turn R onto D57. Cont thro Castelnaund on D57; site on L in 3km. 3*, Lge, hdg, shd, EHU (10A) inc; bbq; sw; red long stay; TV; adv bkg acc; ccard acc; tennis 800m; horseriding 2km; fishing; games area; bike hire; games rm; CKE. *"Attractive, well-run site by rv; popular with British; lge pitches; no o'fits over 8m high ssn; modern san facs; peaceful early ssn; library; ideal base for Dordogne; mkt Thur; excel."*
€25.00, 1 Jun-5 Sep, D01.　　　　　　**2017**

SARLAT LA CANEDA *7C3* (6km S Rural) *44.82375, 1.25080* **Camping La Bouysse de Caudon,** 24200 Vitrac **05 53 28 33 05; info@labouysse.com; www.labouysse.com**

🐕€2 ♦♦♦ Ⓦ ⚓ ♨ ♿ 🛒 ⚡ 🦋 ⛱ ▼ Ⓗ ⚓ 🐚 ⚞ ⚓ 🛶

S fr Sarlat on D46 dir Vitrac. At Vitrac 'port' bef bdge turn L onto D703 sp Carsac. In 2km turn R & foll site sp, site on L. Well sp. 3*, Med, hdg, mkd, pt shd, EHU (10A) €4.80; gas; bbq; sw; 8% statics; phone; Eng spkn; adv bkg req; ccard acc; canoe hire; tennis; fishing; games area; CKE. *"Beautiful family-run site on Rv Dordogne; helpful owner; plenty gd clean san facs; gd access rv beach; muddy when wet; many Bastides in area; excel."*
€21.70, 2 Apr-25 Sep.　　　　　　　　**2019**

See advertisement

SARLAT LA CANEDA *7C3* (10km SW Rural)
44.83819, 1.14846 **Camping Le Capeyrou,** 24220
Beynac-et-Cazenac **05 53 29 54 95; lecapeyrou@
wanadoo.fr; www.campinglecapeyrou.com**

🛖 €2 🕴🕴 ⓦ ♨ ⚲ ⅋ ⌁ 👜 Ⓜ🆂🅿 🍴 🍸 ⑪ nr 🍴 🛒 nr 🏔 ⛵

Fr W on D703 on R (opp sm supmkt & baker) immed
past vill of Beynac. Or fr N on D57 fr Sarlat; in vill
immed on L on rv. 3*, Med, hdg, hdstg, pt shd, EHU
(6-10A) €3.50-4.20; Eng spkn; adv bkg acc; ccard acc.
"*View of chateau most pitches; helpful, friendly owners;
clean san facs; excel lge pool; rvside walk to attractive
vill; excel NH; canoeing, hot air ballooning; v muddy
when wet.*" **€28.00, Apr-30 Sep.** **2015**

SARLAT LA CANEDA *7C3* (10km SW Rural)
44.80519, 1.15852 **Camping Maisonneuve,** Vallée
de Céou, 24250 Castelnaud-la-Chapelle **05 53 29
51 29; contact@campingmaisonneuve.com;
www.campingmaisonneuve.com**

🛖 🕴🕴(htd) ⓦ ♨ ⚲ ⅋ ⌁ 👜 Ⓜ🆂🅿 🦋 🍴 🍸 ⑪ 🍴 🛒 🏔 ⚲
🆂(htd) 🅿

Take D57 SW fr Sarlat sp Beynac. Cross Rv
Dordogne at Castelnaud; site sp 500m on L out of
Castelnaud on D57 twd Daglan. Foll narr rd across
bdge (or alt ent - cont on D57 for 2km, sp on L
for c'vans). 3*, Med, hdstg, mkd, hdg, pt shd, EHU
(6-10A) €3.10-6.40; gas; bbq; sw; TV; 10% statics;
Eng spkn; adv bkg req; ccard acc; rv; games rm;
tennis 2km; bike hire; fishing; CKE. "*Vg, spacious site;
helpful owners; excel, modern, clean facs; gd walks,
cycling; outstanding.*" **€26.70, Apr-Oct.** **2019**

See advertisement

SARLAT LA CANEDA *7C3* (10km SW Rural) *44.80519,
1.15852* **Camping Maisonneuve,** Vallée de Céou,
24250 Castelnaud-la-Chapelle **05 53 29 51 29;
contact@campingmaisonneuve.com; www.camping
maisonneuve.com**

🛖 🕴🕴(htd) ⓦ ♨ ⚲ ⅋ ⌁ 👜 Ⓜ🆂🅿 🦋 🍴 🍸 ⑪ 🍴 🛒 🏔 ⚲
🆂(htd) 🅿

Take D57 SW fr Sarlat sp Beynac. Cross Rv
Dordogne at Castelnaud; site sp 500m on L out of
Castelnaud on D57 twd Daglan. Foll narr rd across
bdge (or alt ent - cont on D57 for 2km, sp on L for
c'vans). 3*, Med, hdstg, mkd, hdg, pt shd, EHU (6-
10A) €3.10-6.40; gas; bbq; sw; TV; 10% statics; Eng
spkn; adv bkg req; ccard acc; rv; games rm; tennis
2km; bike hire; fishing; CKE. "*Vg, spacious site; helpful
owners; excel, modern, clean facs; gd walks, cycling;
outstanding.*" **€26.70, Apr-Oct.** **2019**

SARLAT LA CANEDA *7C3* (12km SW Rural) *44.82585,
1.15322* **Camping La Cabane,** 24220 Vézac
**05 53 29 52 28; contact@lacabanedordogne.com;
www.lacabanedordogne.com**

🛖 €1 🕴🕴 ♨ ⚲ ⅋ 👜 🦋 🍴 ⑪ nr 🛒 🏔 ⚲ (covrd, htd)

Fr Sarlat-La-Canéda take D57 thro Vézac. On
leaving Vézac turn L immed bef rlwy bdge, site sp
on R on bank of Rv Dordogne. 2*, Lge, hdg, mkd,
pt shd, EHU (6-10A) €2.60-3.15; gas; bbq; sw nr; TV;
10% statics; phone; Eng spkn; adv bkg acc; ccard acc;
CKE. "*Well-shd, rvside site; lge pitches; clean facs;
friendly, helpful family owners; rvside walk to Beynac
Château; gd; 2nd san facs block modernised (2015).*"
€18.00, 1 Apr-30 Sep. **2015**

SARLAT LA CANEDA 7C3 (9km W Rural) 44.90805, 1.11527 **Camping Le Moulin du Roch,** Le Roch, Route des Eyzies, 24200 Sarlat-la-Canéda **05 53 59 20 27;** moulin.du.roch@wanadoo.fr; www.moulin-du-roch.com or www.les-castels.com

🏕️(htd) ⓌⒹ 🏕️ ♨ ♿ 🔲 ⁄ 🅼🅿 🦋 ♈ 🍴 ⑪ 🎿 🔥 ⚠ ✎ 🏊(htd) 🛶

Fr A20 take exit 55 at Souillac dir Sarlat. Head for D704 twds Sarlat La Caneda. At rndabt in Sarlat (just under rlwy viaduct) take 2nd exit onto bypass. Take 2nd exit at next rndabt staying on D704. At next rndabt take 2nd exit onto D6 dir Les Eyzies (becomes D47). Site on L in approx 9 km on D47. Fr N on D704 to Sarlat, turn R at hypmkt, then as above. 5*, Lge, mkd, hdg, pt shd, terr, serviced pitches; EHU (6A) inc; gas; bbq (charcoal, gas); red long stay; twin axles; TV; 45% statics; Eng spkn; adv bkg rec; ccard acc; horseriding nr; games rm; canoeing nr; lake fishing; outdoor sports; playground; CKE. *"Well-run, family owned site; lge pitches; clean facs but poss long, steep walk; some noise fr adj rd; gd rest & pool; m'vans poss not acc after prolonged heavy rain due soft grnd; mkt Sat."* €52.00, 25 May-22 Sep, D02. 2019

SARZEAU 2G3 (8km SE Coastal) 47.50551, -2.68308 **Camping Manoir de Ker An Poul,** 1 Route de la Grée, Penvins, 56370 Sarzeau **02 57 62 04 65;** manoirdekeranpoul@wanadoo.fr; www.manoirdekeranpoul.com

🐕€4 🏕️(htd) 🏕️ ♨ ♿ 🔲 ⁄ 🦋 ♈ 🍴 ⑪nr 🎿 🔥 ⚠ ✎ 🏊(htd, indoor) 🏖️sand 1km

Fr E exit N165 1km E of Muzillac, sp Sarzeau D20 & cont approx 20km to junc of D20 & D199, S on D199 sp Penvins. Fr W, 6km E of Vannes, exit N165 onto N780 sp Sarzeau, in 9.5km S onto D199 sp Penvins. 4*, Lge, hdg, pt shd, pt sl, EHU (6-10A) €4; bbq; TV; 30% statics; Eng spkn; adv bkg acc; tennis; games area; bike hire; CKE. *"Spacious pitches; warm welcome; excel staff; no dog walk on site; san facs recently renovated (2015); noisy weekend nr pool, quieter mid week."* €41.00, 7 Apr-23 Sep. 2018

See Advertisement

SARZEAU 2G3 (2.5km S Coastal) 47.50720, -2.76083 **Camping La Ferme de Lann Hoëdic,** Rue Jean de la Fontaine, Route de Roaliguen, 56370 Sarzeau **02 97 48 01 73;** contact@camping-lannhoedic.fr; www.camping-lannhoedic.fr

🐕€2 🏕️(htd) ⓌⒹ 🏕️ ♨ ♿ 🔲 ⁄ 🅼🅿 🦋 ♈ 🍴nr ⑪nr 🎿nr ⚠ 🏖️sand 800m

Fr Vannes on N165 turn onto D780 dir Sarzeau. Do not ent Sarzeau, but at Super U rndabt foll sp Le Roaliguen. After 1.5km turn L to Lann Hoëdic. 3*, Med, mkd, pt shd, EHU (16A); gas; 10% statics; phone; Eng spkn; adv bkg acc; ccard acc; bike hire; CKE. *"Peaceful, well-managed, popular, family-run site; warm welcome; excel, clean facs; beautiful coastline - beaches & dunes; highly rec."* €24.50, 1 Apr-31 Oct. 2017

SAULIEU 6G1 (1km N Rural) 47.28936, 4.22401 **Camping de Saulieu,** Route de Paris, 21210 Saulieu **03 80 64 16 19;** camping.salieu@wanadoo.fr; www.aquadis-loisirs.com

🏕️€1.50 🏕️(htd) ⓌⒹ 🏕️ ♨ ♿ 🔲 ⁄ 🅼🅿 ♈ 🍴 ⑪ 🔥 ⚠ 🏊 🛶

On D906 on L of rd on ent fr N. Sp. 3*, Lge, hdg, mkd, pt shd, pt sl, EHU (10A) €3.90; gas; adv bkg acc; tennis; lake fishing; CKE. *"Nr town but rural feel; quiet at far end of site, away fr pool & playgrnd; no twin axles; many rests in town; gd walking area; gd."* €21.70, 8 Apr-3 Nov. 2019

SAUMUR 4G1 (2km N Urban) 47.25990, -0.06440 **Flower Camping de L'Ile d'Offard,** Rue de Verden, 49400 Saumur **02 41 40 30 00;** iledoffard@flowercampings.com; www.saumur-camping.com or www.flowercampings.com

🏕️€1.50 🏕️(htd) ⓌⒹ 🏕️ ♨ ♿ 🔲 ⁄ 🅼🅿 ♈ 🍴 ⑪ 🎿 🔥 ⚠ ✎ 🏊(htd) 🛶

Exit A85 junc 3 onto D347 and then D347E; ent town past rlwy stn & cross Rv Loire bdge; turn L immed over bdge & alongside rv. At rndabt turn L & take 1st L to site; foll sp. Site on island facing Saumur castle. 5*, Lge, mkd, hdg, hdstg, pt shd, pt sl, EHU (10A) (poss rev pol); gas; sw nr; TV; 20% statics; Eng spkn; adv bkg req; ccard acc; tennis; boating adj; fishing adj; games area; jacuzzi; bike hire; CKE. *"Pleasant, busy, well-run site; ideal for children; hdstg pitches in winter; helpful staff; clean, most pitches lge but some v sm pitches bet statics - lge o'fits check in advance; gd bar & rest; can be muddy when wet; gd cycle rtes; nice rvside and bdge walk to town; excel, but busy; great facs; easy acc to city; san facs refurb, modern & clean (2015); recep clsd 1200-1400; lovely loc; gd base for visiting Loire Valley; 35 placement municiple area adj, acc by card."* €36.00, 17 Mar-28 Oct. 2018

"That's changed – Should I let the Club know?"

If you find something on site that's different from the site entry, fill in a report and let us know. See camc.com/europereport.

SAUMUR 4G1 (7km NE Rural) 47.29937, -0.01218 **Camping Le Pô Doré,** 49650 Allonnes **02 41 38 78 80 or 06 09 26 31 28 (mob);** camping.du.po.dore@wanadoo.fr; www.camping-lepodore.com

🏕️€1.50 🏕️(htd) ⓌⒹ 🏕️ ♨ ♿ 🔲 ⁄ 🅼🅿 ♈ 🍴 ⑪ 🎿 ⚠ ✎ 🏊(htd)

NE fr Saumur on N347 & turn R onto D10. Site 3km W of Allonnes on R. 4*, Med, mkd, hdg, hdstg, pt shd, EHU (6-10A) €3-4 (poss rev pol); 25% statics; phone; Eng spkn; ccard acc; bike hire; CKE. *"Gd, clean & tidy site; helpful staff; dirty, sandy soil; conv wine rtes, caves, museums & a'route; conv NH/sh stay; excel san facs; spectacular laggon."* €29.00, 15 Mar-15 Nov. 2017

SAUMUR *4G1* (6km E Rural) *47.24755, -0.00033*
Camping Domaine de la Brèche, 5 Impasse de la
Brèche, 49730 Varennes-sur-Loire **02 41 51 22 92;**
mail@etang-breche.com; www.domainedela
breche.com

🏕️ 🍴👶 🛒 ♨️ ♿ 🚮 ♻️ MP 🛗 ♀️ 🅿️ 🚰 🐕 🎣 🏊(htd)

Exit 3 of A85, then D767 & D347 twrds Saumur, then
D952 twd Tours & site sp fr either dir. Site on N side
of rd (6km W of Varennes) app fr lge lay-by giving
easy ent. 5*, Lge, hdg, pt shd, serviced pitches; EHU
(16A); gas; TV; 50% statics; phone; Eng spkn; adv bkg
rec; ccard acc; waterslide; tennis; bike hire; games rm;
CKE. *"Spacious site & pitches; well-organised; excel
facs; auto barrier clsd 2300-0700; helpful staff; excel."*
€48.00, 14 Apr-09 Sep, A32. **2019**

"I like to fill in the reports as I travel from site to site"

You'll find report forms at the back of this
guide, or you can fill them in online at
camc.com/europereport.

SAUMUR *4G1* (7.5km NW Rural) *47.29440, -0.14120*
Camping de Chantepie, Route de Chantepie, 49400
St Hilaire-St Florent **02 41 67 95 34;** info@camping
chantepie.com; www.campingchantepie.com

🏕️ €4 🍴👶(htd) wo ♨️ 👶 ♿ 🛒 ♻️ MP 🌳 ♀️ 🅿️ 🚰 🐕 🏊
🏊(covrd, htd) 🚤

Fr Saumer take D751 on S bank of Rv Loire sp
Gennes. Turn L 3km N of St Hilaire-St-Florent just
bef lge sp for a supmkt & bef mushroom museum.
Site sp. Or fr N after x-ing rv on N347, take turn sp
St Hilaire-St-Florent & join D751 for Gennes; site is
3km N of St Hilaire-St Florent, well sp fr D751. NB
Easy to miss turning. 5*, Lge, mkd, hdg, pt shd, EHU
(10A) inc (poss rev pol); gas; bbq; TV; 10% statics;
Eng spkn; adv bkg acc; ccard acc; golf 2km; games
rm; horseriding 5km; tennis 2km; bike hire; fishing;
CKE. *"Excel well-run site nr rv; well-spaced, lge pitches,
some with excel rv views, ltd; access to some pitches
diff lge o'fits; friendly, helpful staff; no o'fits over
10m; boating 5km; excel san facs, conv Loire cycle
rte; mkt Sat Saumur; excel views, bar & rest; excel
cycle track; TV recep may be diff due to many trees."*
€39.00, 4 May-26 Sep, L06. **2016**

SAUMUR *4G1* (9km NW Rural) *47.30982, -0.14492*
Camping Terre d'Entente (formerly La Croix Rouge),
Lieu dit de la Croix Rouge, 49160 St Martin-de-la-Place
09 72 30 31 72 or 07 70 07 69 37; contact@terre-
dentente.fr; terre-dentente.fr

🏕 €1.50 ⊧⊧ WD ♨ ♿ ⬛ ∥ MSP 🦋 ℌ 🍴 nr ⑭nr ⛟nr ⏢

Exit A85 junc 3 sp Saumur. Take slip rd immed bef
bdge then L sp 'Angers Touristique'. Site on L at vill
sp. Fr Saumur take D347 N across rv then turn L
onto D952 dir Angers. At St Martin-de-la-Place foll
sp for site. 2*, Med, mkd, pt shd, EHU (6-10A) €3-4; sw
nr; bus 150m; Eng spkn; adv bkg acc; sailing adj; CKE.
"*Beautiful, tranquil site on Rv Loire; friendly, helpful
owners; 26 steps to spacious san facs; disabled facs at
grnd level; 2m high security fence by rv; barrier clsd
2200-0700; no twin axles; conv Saumur; bar 200m;
v pleasant site; poor.*" **€18.00, 8 Apr-30 Sep.** **2017**

SAVENAY *2G3* (2.5km E Rural) *47.35651, -1.92136*
Camp Municipal du Lac de Savenay, Route du Lac,
44260 Savenay 02 40 58 31 76; www.camping-lac-
savenay.fr

🏕 €1.20 ⊧⊧(htd) ♨ ♿ ⬛ ∥ 🦋 ♨ ⏢

Site well sp in Savenay. Can avoid Savenay Town by
turning off N165 SW of town on new rd, dir LAC.
2*, Med, mkd, pt shd, terr, EHU (10A) €2.07; Eng spkn;
fishing. "*Vg, clean site in attractive lakeside park; lge
pitches; gas adj; pool adj; excel modern san block; terr
pitches req long elec leads.*"
€26.00, 1 Mar-31 Oct. **2016**

SAVERNE *6E3* (2km SW Urban) *48.73329, 7.35371*
**Camping Les Portes d'Alsace (formerly Camping de
Saverne),** Rue du Père Libermann, 67700 Saverne
03 88 91 35 65; contact@camping-lesportesdalsace.
com; www.vacances-seasonova.com

🏕 €1.60 ⊧⊧(htd) WD ♨ ♿ ⬛ ∥ MSP 🦋 ♨ ⛟nr ⏢

Take Saverne exit fr A4, junc 45. Site well sp nr
town cent. 3*, Med, hdg, mkd, hdstg, pt shd, pt sl, terr,
EHU (6-10A) €3.10-5.70 (poss rev pol); 20% statics;
adv bkg acc; ccard acc; CKE. "*Pleasant, busy, well-run
site; pitches mostly terr; warm welcome, friendly staff;
long steep walk back fr town; m'van aire de service nr
ent; trains to Strasbourg fr town; poss travellers; gd.*"
€27.00, 31 Mar-4 Nov, J06. **2018**

SEES *4E1* (1km S Urban) *48.59875, 0.17103*
Camp Municipal Le Clos Normand, Ave du 8 mai
1945, 61500 Sées 02 33 28 87 37 or 02 33 28 74 79
(LS); contact@camping-sees.fr; www.ville-sees.fr

🏕 €1.25 ⊧⊧ WD ♨ ♿ ⬛ ∥ MSP ♨ 🍴 nr ⑭nr ⛟nr ⏢

C'vans & lge m'vans best app fr S - twd rndabt at S
end of by-pass (rec use this rndabt as other rtes diff
& narr). Well sp. Narr ent. 3*, Sm, hdg, pt shd, EHU
(10A) €2.50; gas; 10% statics; Eng spkn; adv bkg acc;
fishing; CKE. "*Spacious, well-cared for pitches; helpful,
friendly warden; gd san facs, poss stretched if site full;
excel mv service pnt; gates clsd 2100 (2000 LS); easy
walk to town; shop nr; vg.*"
€13.00, 16 Apr-30 Sep. **2018**

SEGRE *2F4* (7km NW Rural) *47.71003, -0.95165*
Camping Parc de St Blaise, 49520 Noyant-la-Gravoyère
02 41 26 43 48; parcsaintblaise49@gmail.com;
www.campingsaintblaise.fr

🏕 ⊧⊧ WD ♨ ♿ ∥ 🍴 ⑭ ⛟ ⏢ ∥

Fr Segré take D775 dir Pouancé to Noyant, site/park
sp in vill on R. 2*, Sm, hdg, pt shd, terr, EHU (6A) inc;
sw nr; phone; horseriding; fishing; CKE. "*Clean, well-
maintained site in leisure park; gd views; aquatic park;
slate mine worth visit.*" **€11.00, 15 Jun-30 Sep.** **2019**

SEILHAC *7C4* (4km SW Rural) *45.35018, 1.64642*
Camp Municipal du Pilard, La Barthe, 19700
Lagraulière 05 55 73 71 04; mairie.lagrauliere@
wanadoo.fr; www.lagrauliere.correze.net

🏕 €1 ⊧⊧ WD ♨ ♿ ∥ 🦋 🍴 nr ⑭nr ⛟nr ⏢

Exit A20 junc 46 onto D34 to Lagraulière, site sp.
NB Lge o'fits rec take D44 & D167E fr Seilhac.
2*, Sm, mkd, pt shd, EHU (3-6A) €3 (poss rev pol); bbq;
Eng spkn; tennis; CKE. "*Quiet, clean site nr pleasant
interesting vill; htd pool adj; warden calls; mkts on
Thurs.*" **€10.00, 15 Jun-15 Sep.** **2019**

SEISSAN *8F3* (2km WNW Rural) *43.49554, 0.57815*
Domaine Lacs de Gascogne, Route Du Lac, 32260
Seissan 05 62 66 27 94; info@domainelacsde
gascogne.eu; www.domainelacsdegascogne.eu

🏕 €3 ⊧⊧ WD ♨ ⬛ ∥ 🍴 ⑭ ♨ ⏢ ∥ 🛶

V lge, mkd, pt shd, pt sl, EHU (16A); bbq; twin axles;
TV; 25% statics; bus 2km; Eng spkn; adv bkg acc;
HCAP ltd; bike hire; games area; showrs; games rm;
pool paddling; CKE. "*Tennis, separate carpk; walks;
watersports; 1 dog per pitch; tourist attractions; table
tennis; pool; sauna; carp fishing; vg.*"
€32.00, 31 Mar-30 Sep. **2018**

SELESTAT *6E3* (7km N Rural) *48.30647, 7.50057*
Camping Rural (Weiss), 17 Rue du Buhl, 67600
Ebersheim 06 85 10 95 54; theo.sonntag@wanadoo.fr

🏕 ⊧⊧ ♨ ♿ ∥ 🦋 ⛟nr

Fr S or N on N83 in vill of Ebersheim foll green
Camping Rural sps. Sm, pt shd, EHU (16A) inc; bbq;
bus 0.5km; Eng spkn; adv bkg acc; CKE. "*Gd touring
base; friendly, helpful staff; excel Boulangerie in vill;
dogs free; site self, staff visit pm.*"
€13.00, 15 Jun-15 Sep. **2017**

SELESTAT 6E3 (1km SW Urban) 48.25470, 7.44781
Camp Municipal Les Cigognes, Rue de la 1ère
D.F.L, 67600 Sélestat **03 88 92 03 98; camping@
ville-selestat.fr; http://camping.selestat.fr**

🛏€1 🏕 �🆆ᴰ 🛁 ⟲ 🗑 🗲 🖾 🐕 🛝 Ⲑ nr ⓦ nr 🐎 ⚠ ✈

Site sp D1083 & D424. Fr S town cent turn E off
D1083 & foll sps to site adj schools & playing fields.
2*, Med, mkd, pt shd, EHU (6-16A) inc; gas; train to
Strasbourg nrby; Eng spkn; adv bkg rec; CKE. "Great,
well-run site; helpful staff; pool 300m; some noise fr
local football area; excel new san blocks; easy walk to
old town; mkt Sat; rec."
€15.50, 1 Apr-15 Oct & 15 Nov-24 Dec.   **2016**

SEMUR EN AUXOIS 6G1 (3.5km S Rural) 47.46812,
4.35589 **FFCC Camping Lac de Pont,** 16 Rue du Lac,
21140 Pont-et-Massène **03 80 97 01 26 or 03 80 97 01
26 (LS); contact@camping-lacdepont.fr or camping-
lacdepont@orange.fr; www.campinglacdepont.fr**

12 🛏€2 🏕 ⟲ Ⓦ 🛁 🗑 🗲 🖾 🦋 Ⲑ nr 🐎 🐕 ⚠

Exit A6 junc 23 twd Semur-en-Auxois on D980; after sh
dist turn R sp 'Lac de Pont' D103. 3*, Med, hdg, pt shd,
pt sl, EHU (6A) €3.50; gas; bbq; sw nr; phone; Eng spkn;
ccard acc; tennis; watersports; games rm; bike hire; CKE.
"Warm welcome, helpful owners; generous pitches, some
shady; san facs dated; vg for teenagers - games/meeting
rm; 'Petit Train' goes round site & into Semur; cycle rte/
walks adj; gd touring base; nr A6 m'way; diving platform;
walled, medieval town; muddy pitches; site neglected
(2017), NH only." **€15.00**   **2017**

SENNECEY LE GRAND 6H1 (7km E Rural) 46.65480,
4.94461 **Château de L'Epervière,** Rue du Château,
71240 Gigny-sur-Saône **03 85 94 16 90; info@
domaine-eperviere.com; www.domaine-eperviere.com**

🛏€3 🏕(htd) Ⓦ 🛁 ⟲ ⓦ 🗑 🗲 🖾 🦋 Ⲑ 🐎 🐕 ⚠ ✈
🛶(covrd, htd) 🎣

Fr N exit A6 junc 26 (Chalon Sud) onto N6 dir Mâcon
& Tournus; at Sennecey-le-Grand turn E onto D18 sp
Gigny-sur-Saône; site sp 1km S of Gigny-sur-Saône. Or
fr S exit A6 junc 27 (Tournus) onto N6 N to Sennecey-
le-Grand, then as above. NB Diff to find signs fr main
rd. 5*, Lge, hdstg, hdg, mkd, pt shd, EHU (6A) inc; gas;
bbq; TV; Eng spkn; adv bkg acc; ccard acc; sauna; bike
hire; tennis 400m; fishing; games rm; jacuzzi; CKE.
"Superb, spacious, well-run site in grnds of chateau nr
sm lake; lovely, lge pitches; warm welcome, pleasant
staff; excel san facs; gd pools & rest; vg for families;
wine tasting; tour op statics; lake nrby; interesting wild
life; no o'fits over 18m high ssn; boggy when wet; conv
NH fr a'route; fantastic site; level pitches; great facs."
€40.00, 1 Apr-30 Sep, L12.   **2016**

SENNECEY LE GRAND 6H1 (5km NW Rural) 46.67160,
4.83301 **Camping La Héronnière,** Les Lacs de Laives,
71240 Laives **03 85 44 98 85; camping.laives@
wanadoo.fr; www.camping-laheronniere.com**

🛏€1.60 🏕 Ⓦᴰ 🛁 ⟲ 🗑 🗲 Ⲑ nr 🐕 🐎 ⚠ ✈(htd)

Exit A6 junc 26 (fr N) or junc 27 (fr S) onto N6. Turn
W at Sennecey-le-Grand to Laives. Foll sp 'Lacs
de Laives'. Sp on D18. 3*, Med, hdg, mkd, hdstg, pt
shd, EHU (6A) €4.80; sw nr; Eng spkn; adv bkg acc;
fishing; windsurfing; bike hire; watersports; CKE.
"Lovely, level, lakeside site; busy NH; may fill up after
1500; popular with bikers; vg; pretty site; laid back
helpful staff; gd NH; romantic rest by lakeside 3 mins
walk (high ssn); excel facs; san facs ok but dirty."
€27.00, 3 Mar-4 Nov.   **2018**

"I need an on-site restaurant"

We do our best to make sure site information
is correct, but it is always best to check any
must-have facilities are still available or will
be open during your visit.

SENS 4F4 (1km S Urban) 48.18312, 3.28803
Camp Municipal Entre Deux Vannes, Ave de Senigallia,
89100 Sens **03 86 65 64 71 or 03 86 65 37 42 (LS);
http://ville-sens.fr**

🏕 Ⓦᴰ 🛁 ⟲ 🗑 🗲 🖾 Ⲑ nr 🐕 nr ⚠

D606/D1060 S of town. Take D606a sp sens. Site on
R in 600m. 2*, Med, mkd, pt shd, EHU (16A) inc; adv
bkg rec; ccard acc; CKE. "Excel site; opp rv & superb
park area; friendly, helpful warden; san facs old but
clean; gate locked 2200; easy walk to town; ensure
height barrier moved bef ent."
€13.50, 15 May-15 Sep.   **2019**

SERIGNAC 7D3 (5km W Rural) 44.43103, 1.06902
Camping Le Clos Barrat (Naturist), 46700 Sérignac
**06 47 50 09 78 or 04 74 24 60 82; info@leclosbarrat.fr;
www.leclosbarrat.fr**

🛏€2.50 🏕(htd) Ⓦᴰ 🛁 ⟲ 🗑 🗲 🖾 🦋 Ⲑ Ⲑ 🐎 🐕 ⚠ ✈ 🛶 🎣

Fr Fumel by-pass turn S on D139 to Montayral,
rd cont but becomes D4. Site sp bet Mauroux &
St Matré. 3*, Med, mkd, pt shd, pt sl, EHU (6A) inc;
own san rec; gas; bbq (gas); twin axles; TV; 2% statics;
phone; Eng spkn; adv bkg acc; ccard acc; games rm;
CKE. "Nr Rv Lot; INF card req - can be bought on site;
new owners (2015); helpful staff; excel & friendly site;
beautiful area." **€29.00, 1 May-25 Sep.**   **2017**

SERIGNAN PLAGE *10F1* (1km W Coastal) *43.26398, 3.3210* **Sérignan Plage,** Les Orpelières, 34410 Sérignan-Plage **04 67 32 35 33; info@leserignan plage.com; www.leserignanplage.com**

🐕 €4 ♦♦♦ 🆆 ♨ ♂ 🖥 ⚊ 🖵 ♈ 🍽 🏊 🅿 ⚓ 🝰 ⚟ ⌕

⚓ (covrd, htd) 🏖

Exit A9 junc 35. After toll turn L at traff lts onto N112 & at 1st rndabt strt on to D64. In 5km turn L onto D37E Sérignan-Plage, turn R on narr 1-way rd to site. Adj to Camping Sérignan-Plage Nature (Naturist site). 3*, V lge, mkd, hdg, pt shd, EHU (5A) inc; gas; bbq; sw; TV; 80% statics; Eng spkn; adv bkg acc; tennis; horseriding; CKE. "Busy, even LS; excel pool; Club Nautique - sw, sailing & water-ski tuition on private beach; use of naturist private beach & facs adj; some tourers amongst statics & sm sep touring area." **€78.00, 24 Apr-28 Sept.** **2019**

See advertisement

SERIGNAN PLAGE *10F1* (1.6km W Coastal) *43.26308, 3.31976* **Camping Le Sérignan-Plage Nature (Naturist),** Les Orpelière, 34410 Sérignan-Plage **04 67 32 09 61; info@leserignannature.com; www.leserignan nature.com**

🐕 €6 ♦♦♦ 🆆 ♨ ♂ 🖥 ⚊ 🖵 ♈ 🍽 🏊 🅿 ⚓ 🝰 ♒ sand

Exit A9 junc 36 Beziers Est onto D64. At Sérignan town turn L on D37E to Sérignan-Plage. After 4km turn R on dual c'way. At T-junc turn L & immed L again in 50m to site. 3*, Lge, mkd, pt shd, EHU (5A) inc (poss rev pol); gas; bbq; red long stay; TV; 75% statics; Eng spkn; adv bkg rec; golf 15km; bike hire; CKE. "Lovely, clean site & facs; max 2 dogs; helpful staff; Cmp Le Sérignan Plage (non-naturist) adj with use of same private beach & facs; pool also shared - for naturists' use 1000-1200 only; beauty cent; cycle rtes adj; excel." **€68.00, 24 Apr-28 Sept.** **2019**

"Satellite navigation makes touring much easier"

Remember most sat navs don't know if you're towing or in a larger vehicle – always use yours alongside maps and site directions.

SERRES *9D3* (1.4km S Rural) *44.41941, 5.71840* **Camping des Barillons,** Route de Nice, 05700 Serres **04 92 67 17 35 or 06 30 50 31 58; campingdes barillons@free.fr; campingdesbarillons.free.fr**

🐕 €1.60 🆆 ⚊ 🖥 ⚟ ♈ 🍽 ♂ 🝰 ♒ (covrd, htd)

D4075 dir Sistoron fr town ctr. Sm, pt shd, EHU (6A); bbq; adv bkg acc.; CKE. "Gd." **€20.00, 1 Apr-30 Sep.** **2017**

SERRIERES *9C2* (3km W Rural) *45.30872, 4.74622* **Camping Le Bas Larin,** 88 Route de Larin Le Bas, 07340 Félines **04 75 34 87 93 or 06 80 05 13 89 (mob); camping.baslarin@wanadoo.fr; www.camping-bas-larin.com**

🐕 ♦♦♦ 🆆 ⚊ ♂ ♨ 🖥 ⚟ ♈ ⊕ nr 🝰 nr 🖵 ⚓ ♒ 🏖

Exit A7 junc 12 Chanas or fr N7, exit at Serrières onto D1082; cross canal & rv; cont over rndabt up winding hill, camp on L nr hill top. Sp fr N7 & D1082, but easily missed - foll sp Safari de Peaugres. 3*, Med, shd, terr, EHU (4-10A) €2.50-3.80; 10% statics; Eng spkn; games area; games rm; CKE. "Friendly, family-run site; beautiful views; helpful staff; easy access pitches; popular with Dutch; excel; v nice site but ent to pitches may be diff." **€18.50, 1 Apr-30 Sep.** **2018**

SEVERAC LE CHATEAU *9D1* (15km SE Rural)

"There aren't many sites open at this time of year"

If you're travelling outside peak season remember to call ahead to check site opening dates – even if the entry says 'open all year'.

44.27302, 3.21538 **Camp Municipal,** 48500 St Rome-de-Dolan **04 66 44 03 81 or 04 66 48 83 59; camping-stromededolan@orange.fr; www.saint-rome-de-dolan.com**

🐕 €0.80 ♦♦♦ 🆆 ⚊ ♂ 🖥 ⚟ 🝰 ♈ ⊕ nr 🝰 nr 🖵

Exit A75 junc 42 to Sévérac, then take D995 fr Séverac-le-Château then E thro Le Massegros to St Rome-de-Dolan. Site on R at ent to vill, sp. NB Rec not to use GPS. 2*, Sm, pt shd, pt sl, terr, EHU (6A); bbq; sw nr; Eng spkn; adv bkg acc; CKE. "Simple, well-kept, well-run site in beautiful location nr Gorges du Tarn; fantastic views some pitches; friendly, helpful warden; clean san facs; some pitches sm & need mover; bird watching, inc vultures; walking; highly rec." **€13.50, 1 May-30 Sep.** **2015**

SEVERAC LE CHATEAU *9D1* (1km SW Urban) *44.31841, 3.06412* **FFCC Camping Les Calquières,** Ave Jean Moulin, 12150 Sévérac-le-Château **05 65 47 64 82; contact@camping-calquieres.com; www.camping-calquieres.com**

🐕 €1.50 (htd) ⚊ ♂ ♨ 🖥 ⚟ 🝰 ♈ 🍽 ♂ 🝰 nr 🖵

⚓ (covrd, htd)

Exit A75 junc 42 sp Sévérac & Rodez; foll 'Camping' sps to avoid narr town rds. 4*, Med, hdg, pt shd, serviced pitches; EHU (6-16A) €4.20 (poss long lead & rev pol); bbq; red long stay; 10% statics; adv bkg acc; tennis; fishing; games area; CKE. "Lovely, spacious site with gd views; lge pitches; friendly, v helpful owners; v gd touring base & NH; conv A75; busy NH, espec w/end; gd for main holiday stay; new excel san facs (2015); vg rest; chge for wifi." **€28.50, 1 Apr-30 Sep.** **2018**

FRANCE

★★★★★

Le Sérignan Plage

" PICTURE YOURSELF... ON A SANDY SHORELINE

34410 Sérignan France - Tel : +33 4 67 32 35 33
info@leserignanplage.com - www.leserignanplage.com

yelloh! VILLAGE

SEYNE *9D3* (0.8km S Rural) *44.34270, 6.35896*
Camping Les Prairies, Haute Gréyère, 04140 Seyne-les-Alpes 04 92 35 10 21; info@campinglesprairies.com; www.campinglesprairies.com

🏠 €2 ⛺ (htd) [WD] 🚿 ⚿ 🍴 / [MSP] 🦋 ⵙ ⵉ ⊕nr ⅃ ⅃nr 🏔 🏖(htd)

Fr Digne-les-Bains, take D900 N to Seyne. Turn L on ent Seyne onto D7, site sp beside Rv La Blanche. 3*, Med, mkd, pt shd, EHU (10A) €3.50; gas; bbq; phone; Eng spkn; adv bkg acc; ccard acc; tennis 300m; horseriding 500m; CKE. *"Immac, tidy, peaceful site; excel; beautifully sited and maintained; rest fr mid June; highly rec."* **€26.80, 7 May-7 Sep.** **2019**

SEZANNE *4E4* (2km NW Rural) *48.72115, 3.70247*
Camp Municipal, Route de Launat, 51120 Sézanne 03 26 80 57 00 or 03 26 80 57 00 (mob); campingdesezanne@wanadoo.fr

🏠 €1.05 ⛺ ⚿ ⅃ / ⊕nr ⅃nr 🏔

W'bound on N4 Sézanne by-pass onto D373 & foll site sp. Fr E turn R at 1st junc on Sézanne bypass & foll sps 'Camping & Piscine'. Avoid town cent. 2*, Med, pt shd, sl, serviced pitches; EHU (10A) inc; waterslide; CKE. *"Nice, well-kept site, v busy high ssn; generous pitches, some v sl; helpful manager; excel, immac san facs; levelling blocks req some pitches; request gate opening/closing at back bungalow of 2 opp site; nice vill; vg; well run site; pool adj; excel value; barrier clsd until 1500 unless adj pool open."* **€11.00, 1 Apr-30 Sep.** **2018**

SIERCK LES BAINS *5C2* (6km SW Rural) *49.426188, 6.300037* **Camp Municipal de Malling,** 2 rue du plan d'eau 57480 Malling 03 82 50 12 97; camping. malling@orange.fr; www.malling.fr/camping

🏠 €2 ⛺ [WD] ⚿ 🍴 / ⅃ ⊕nr ⅃

W of D654, well sp. Lge, mkd, pt shd, EHU 4A; bbq; sw; adv bkg acc. *"Beautifully situated between Plan d'eau and Rv Moselle; v helpful staff; v clearly sp fr D654; lovely site with wildlife on lake."* **€15.00, 1 Apr-30 Sep.** **2019**

SIERCK LES BAINS *5C2* (1.7km W Rural) *49.44544, 6.34899* **Camp Municipal les Tilleuls,** Allée des Tilleuls, 57480 Sierck-les-Bains 03 82 83 72 39; camping@siercklesbains.fr; www.siercklesbains.fr

⛺ [WD] ⚿ / [MSP] 🏔

Fr S on D654 turn L onto D64 sp Contz. Fr Schengen (Lux) turn L immed bef Moselle Bdge sp Contz. Well sp on banks of Moselle. 3*, Sm, hdg, mkd, pt shd, EHU (16A); bbq; Eng spkn; adv bkg acc; bike hire; CKE. *"Excel site."* **€14.00, 1 May-15 Oct.** **2019**

FRANCE

SIGEAN *10G1* (5km N Rural) *43.06633, 2.94100*
Camping La Grange Neuve, 17 La Grange Neuve
Nord, 11130 Sigean **04 68 48 58 70; info@camping-
sigean.com; www.campingsigean.com**

🏕️ 🐕 €3 👪 wc ♨ 🚿 🗑️ ⚡ MP 🦋 🍴 🍽️ ⊕ 🎣 🛒 ⚠️ 🏊

⛺ sand 5km

**Exit junc 39 fr A9; pass over A9 (fr N) then 1st R sp
La Réserve Africaine, then turn R just bef entering
Sigean sp La Grange Neuve.** 3*, Med, hdstg, hdg,
mkd, pt shd, pt sl, terr, EHU (6A) inc; TV; 5% statics;
adv bkg acc; waterslide; CKE. *"Easy access; gd san facs;
excel pool; ltd facs LS; phone ahead to check open LS;
gd NH."* **€30.00** 2017

SIGEAN *10G1* (10km S Rural) *42.95800, 2.99586*
Camping Le Clapotis (Naturist), 11480 La Palme
**04 68 48 15 40 or 05 56 73 73 73; info@leclapotis.com;
www.leclapotis.com**

🐕 €2 👪 (cont) ♨ 🚿 🦋 🍴 🍽️ ⊕ 🏊

**On D6009 S fr Narbonne turn L 8km S of Sigean.
After 350m turn R at camping sp. Site in 150m. Final
app rd narr but negotiable for lge vans.**
2*, Lge, mkd, pt shd, EHU (4A) €4; gas; 80% statics;
Eng spkn; adv bkg acc; ccard acc; games area;
tennis. *"Pleasant, basic, friendly site; sm pitches;
Naturists INF card req; helpful owners; san facs
dated but clean; gd pool; poss strong winds - gd
windsurfing; La Palme vill 15 mins walk; great location."*
€31.00, 11 Apr-10 Oct. 2017

SIGNY L'ABBAYE *5C1* (0.6km N Urban) *49.70123,
4.41971* **Camp Municipal de l'Abbaye,** 08460 Signy-
l'Abbaye **03 24 52 87 73; mairie-signy-l.abbaye@
wanadoo.fr; www.sud-ardennes-tourisme.com**

🐕 €0.60 👪 (htd) wc ♨ 🚿 🗑️ 🦋 ⊕ nr 🎣 nr ⚠️

**Take D985 N twd Belgium fr Rethel to Signy-
l'Abbaye. Foll sp fr town cent to Stade & Camping.
Site by sports stadium.** 2*, Sm, hdstg, hdg, pt shd,
pt sl, EHU (10A) €3.20 (poss rev pol); Eng spkn;
adv bkg acc; rv fishing adj; CKE. *"Lovely site in gd
location; friendly warden; sports cent adj; san facs
excel (shared with public); strong awning pegs req on
gravel hdg pitches, or can park on open grassed area."*
€6.40, 1 May-30 Sep. 2016

SIGOULES *7D2* (1.5km N Rural) *44.77135, 0.41076*
Camping Pomport Beach, Route de la Gardonnette,
24240 Pomport-Sigoulès **05 24 10 61 13; info@
pomport-beach.com; www.pomport-beach.com**

🐕 👪 wc ♨ 🚿 🗑️ 🦋 🍴 🍽️ 🏓 nr ⚠️ 🛒 🏊 (htd) 🛶

**S fr Bergerac take D933 S. After 6km at top of hill
turn R by La Grappe d'Or Rest onto D17 sp
Pomport/Sigoulès. Thro Pomport, site at bottom of
hill on R by lake.** 4*, Med, mkd, shd, pt sl, EHU (6A);
bbq (charcoal, gas); sw nr; TV; 25% statics; phone;
Eng spkn; adv bkg rec; ccard acc; lake; fishing; tennis;
canoeing; games area; bike hire; games rm; CKE.
*"Barrier ent; gd security; gd site; 2 san facs blocks,
clean and up to date (2019); kids loved the site; rec."*
€37.50, 4 May-8 Sep. 2019

SILLE LE GUILLAUME *4F1* (3km N Rural) *48.20352,
-0.12774* **Camping Indigo Les Mollières,** Sillé-Plage,
72140 Sillé-le-Guillaume **02 43 20 16 12; molieres@
camping-indigo.com; www.camping-indigo.com**

🐕 👪 (htd) wc ♨ 🚿 🗑️ 🦋 🍴 🍽️ 🏓 🛒 ⚠️ (htd) 🛶

Fr Sillé-le-Guillaume take D5 N, D203 to site.
3*, Med, shd, EHU (13A) inc; sw; 10% statics; ccard
acc; watersports; fishing; bike hire; games area. *"Site
in pine forest; gd dog walk around lake."*
€25.00, 30 Apr-28 Sep. 2015

SILLE LE GUILLAUME *4F1* (2km NW Rural) *48.18943,
-0.14130* **Camping Les Tournesols,** Route de Mayenne,
Le Grez, 72140 Sillé-le-Guillaume **02 43 20 12 69;
campinglestournesols@orange.fr; www.campingles
tournesols.com**

🐕 €2 👪 wc ♨ 🚿 🗑️ 🦋 🍴 🍽️ 🛒 ⚠️ 🚣

**Exit Sillé on D304/D35 sp Mayenne; in 2km at x-rds
turn R; site in 150m on L, easily visible & sp.**
3*, Med, hdg, mkd, pt shd, pt sl, EHU (6A) inc (poss
long lead req); bbq (gas); sw nr; red long stay; TV;
20% statics; Eng spkn; adv bkg acc; ccard acc; bike
hire; fishing 1km; CKE. *"Beautiful site; friendly owners;
facs dated but spotless; rabies cert req for dogs;
badminton; bouncy castle; pleasant town; canoeing
2km; mini golf; football; volleyball; jeux de boules;
conv Le Mans; gd; welcoming, helpful owner; excel
value; pretty, 'natural' site; onsite family owners."*
€18.00, 1 May-30 Sep. 2016

SILLE LE PHILIPPE *4F1* (1.4km W Rural) *48.10880,
0.33730* **Camping Le Château de Chanteloup,**
Parc de l'Epau Sarl, 72460 Sillé-le-Philippe **02 43 27
51 07 or 02 43 89 66 47; chanteloup.souffront@
wanadoo.fr; www.chateau-de-chanteloup.com**

🐕 €2 👪 (htd) wc ♨ 🚿 🗑️ 🦋 🍴 🍽️ ⊕ 🏓 ⚠️ 🛒 🛶

**Leave A11/E50 at junc 7 Sp Le Mans Z1 Nord. After
toll turn L onto N338. Foll this & turn L onto D313
sp Coulaines, Mamers & Ballon. Take D301 (at lge
supmkt) & in approx 13km site is sp just after ent to
Sillé-le-Philippe. Avoid cent Sillé-le-Philippe.**
5*, Med, mkd, pt shd, pt sl, EHU (10A) €4 (poss rev
pol); gas; bbq; twin axles; TV; Eng spkn; adv bkg acc;
ccard acc; golf 10km; games area; lake fishing; games
rm; horseriding 10km; CKE. *"Lovely, tranquil, spacious
site in chateau grnds; pleasant, helpful staff; some
pitches in wooded areas poss tight lge o'fits; gd rest;
twin axles & lge o'fits by request; gd for Le Mans; sep
o'night area with elec & water; rec; no facs to drain
waste water fr m'van; higher charge during Le Mans
events; excel san facs; clean & well maintained park."*
€46.50, 29 May-31 Aug, L13. 2019

FRANCE

SISTERON *10E3* (2.5km N Rural) *44.21467, 5.93643*
Camp Municipal Les Prés Hauts, 44 Chemin des Prés Hauts, 04200 Sisteron **04 92 61 00 37 or 04 92 61 19 69; contact@camping-sisteron.com; www.camping-sisteron.com**

🏕 €2 ♀♀ 🅆🅾 ♨ ♿ 🚻 ⊘ 🗑 🛒 ⚠ ⚕ 🏊

On W of D951. 4*, Lge, hdg, pt shd, pt sl, serviced pitches; EHU (10A) €4 (poss rev pol); Eng spkn; ccard acc; fishing; tennis; CKE. *"Lovely, well-kept, busy, excel site; excel location, gd views; lge pitches & gd for m'vans; site yourself LS; vg facs, ltd LS; interesting old town, gd mkt; conv a'route; vg; ent Barrier clsd at 2000; stunning pool; huge pitches; gd facs; friendly helpful staff; handy for m'way; 30min walk to Sisteron."*
€21.50, 1 Apr-30 Sep. **2018**

SIZUN *2E2* (1km S Rural) *48.40038, -4.07635*
Camp Municipal du Gollen, 29450 Sizun **02 98 24 11 43 or 02 98 68 80 13 (Mairie); mairie.sizun@ wanadoo.fr; www.mairie-sizun.fr**

♀♀ ♨ 🗑 ⊘ 🛒 🏪ₙᵣ ⚠

Fr Roscoff take D788 SW onto D69 to Landivisiau, D30 & D764 to Sizun. In Sizun take D18 at rndabt. At end of by-pass, at next rndabt, take 3rd exit. Site adj pool. 2*, Sm, pt shd, EHU (10A) €3 (poss rev pol); phone; CKE. *"Lovely little site; simple & restful by rv in nature park; friendly recep; htd pool adj high ssn; site yourself if warden not avail; vg."*
€13.50, 16 Apr-30 Sep. **2017**

SOISSONS *3D4* (2km N Urban) *49.39295, 3.32701*
Camp Municipal du Mail, 14 Ave du Mail, 02200 Soissons **03 23 74 52 69; campingdumail@gmail.com or camping@ville-soissons.fr; www.tourisme-soissons.fr**

🏕 €1 ♀♀(htd) 🅆🅾 ♨ ♿ 🗑 ⊘ 🛒 🏪ₙᵣ ⚀ 🏪 ⚠

Fr N on D1; foll town cent sp to 1st rndabt; turn R, cross rv & immed R into Ave du Mail. Foll sp 'Camping Piscine'. Site well sp beside sw pool. Rd humps & tight ent on last 500m of access rd. (Poss to avoid tight ent by going 150m to rndabt & returning). Or fr S on D1, turn R sp Centre Ville along Ave de Château-Thiery; at 3rd rndabt turn R into Rue du Général Leclerc to Place de la Republique; cont strt over into Blvd Gambette for 500m, then turn L into Ave de l'Aisne, leading into Ave du Petit Mail; then as above. 3*, Med, hdg, mkd, hdstg, pt shd, EHU (6A) €3.15 (poss rev pol); bbq; 5% statics; phone; ccard acc; bike hire; clsd 1 Jan & 25 Dec; CKE. *"Pleasant, excel, clean & well-run site in interesting area; gd sized pitches, some nr rv; poss muddy, park on site rds in winter; m'van pitches all hdstg; helpful, friendly staff; gd clean, modern san facs, updated (2015); rvside walks/cycling; gate clsd 2200-0700; pool adj; lge mkt Wed & Sat; vg winter NH; conv for town (15mins)."*
€16.00, 2 Jan-24 Dec & 26 Dec-31 Dec. **2019**

SOMMIERES *10E1* (2km SE Rural) *43.77550, 4.09280*
Camping Domaine de Massereau, 1990 Route d'Aubais, 30250 Sommières **04 66 53 11 20 or 06 03 31 27 21 (mob); camping@massereau.com; www.massereau.com**

🏕 €3.90 ♀♀ 🅆🅾 ♨ ♿ 🚻 ⊘ ⟋ 🛒 🍴 ♨ ⚀ 🏪 ⚠ ⚕ 🏊 🛍

Exit A9 junc 26 at Gallargues, foll sp Sommières; site sp on D12. NB Danger of grounding at ent fr D12. Use this rte 24/7 - 03/08 (due to festival in Sommières). Otherwise exit A9 junc 27 onto D34 to Sommières, foll sps to "Centre Historique" dir Aubias; cross bdge (sharp turn) & turn R onto D12; site on L in 3km. 5*, Med, mkd, hdg, pt shd, pt sl, serviced pitches; EHU (16A) inc; gas; bbq (gas); sw nr; TV; 50% statics; phone; Eng spkn; adv bkg acc; ccard acc; games rm; jacuzzi; bike hire; waterslide; canoeing nr; sauna; games area; tennis; horseriding nr; CKE. *"Lovely, tranquil, well-run site adj vineyard; lge pitches, some uneven; pleasant, cheerful staff; running track; no o'fits over 7m high ssn; trampoline; modern san facs; narr site rds, sl/uneven pitches & trees diff lge o'fits; tight ents, diff without mover; excel; pool not htd."*
€54.80, 04 Apr-30 Sep, C33. **2019**

SOMMIERES *10E1* (3km SE Rural) *43.76120, 4.11961*
Camping Les Chênes, Les Teullières Basses, 30250 Junas **04 66 80 99 07 or 06 03 29 36 32 (mob); chenes@wanadoo.fr; www.camping-les-chenes.com**

🏕 €4 ♀♀ 🅆🅾 ♨ ♿ ⊘ 🛒 🍴 ♨ 🏪 ⚠ 🏊

Fr Sommières take D12 S (sp Gallargues) 3km to junc with D140 L (N) for 1km. Site on R 300m up side rd. Sp. 2*, Med, mkd, pt shd, pt sl, EHU (10A) €5.40 (long lead poss req); gas; bbq (charcoal, gas); sw nr; 10% statics; adv bkg acc; games area; sep car park; CKE. *"Gd shd; gd san facs; friendly, helpful staff; vg; 2km fr disused rlwy cycle track; vg site."*
€23.40, 7 Apr-14 Oct. **2018**

SOMMIERES *10E1* (6km SE Urban) *43.77052, 4.12592* **Camping L'Olivier,** 112 Route de Congénies Junas, 30250 Sommieres **04 66 80 39 52; camping. lolivier@wanadoo.fr; www.campinglolivier.fr**

🏕 (€3) ♀♀ 🅆🅾 ♨ ♿ ⊘ 🛒 🍴 ♨ 🍴 🏪ₙᵣ ⚠ 🏊 🛍

Fr Nîmes, take D40 twd Sommieres. At Congenies take D140 L to Junas, site sp in vill. 3*, Sm, mkd, pt shd, pt sl, EHU (6-10A) €5, poss inc on certain pitches; cooking facs; 40% statics; phone; Eng spkn; adv bkg acc; fishing; tennis; games area; CKE. *"Excel home made pizzas; jazz festival in summer; elec BBQ for hire; excel; lovely site; ping pong; entmnt (Thur eves); trampoline; homemade jams & olive oil for sale; less than 1km fr Nimes-Sommiere Voie Verte; mini golf; new owners (2017)."* **€24.30, 30 Mar-20 Oct.** **2017**

FRANCE

SOMMIERES *10E1* (0.5km NW Urban) *43.78672, 4.08702* **Camp Municipal Le Garanel,** 110 Rue Eugène Rouché, 30250 Sommières **04 66 80 33 49; campingmunicipal.sommieres@wanadoo.fr; www.sommieres.fr**

🐕 €2 ♟♟(htd) ⬛ ⚒ ♿ ⫽ MSP 𝖳 nr ⓗnr 🛆nr ⚓

Fr S on A9 exit junc 27 N & foll D34 then take D610 twd Sommières. By-pass town on D610, over rv bdge; turn R for D40, Rue Condamine. After L turn for Nîmes pull out to make sharp R turn sp 'Camping Arena' (easy to miss this R turn). At T-junc turn R, site thro car park. Fr N on D610 turn L at 4th junc sp 'Ville Vieille' & site adj rv. Site sp fr D610 fr N. NB Narr rds nr site. 2*, Sm, hdg, mkd, pt shd, EHU (10A) inc; bbq; bus 500m; Eng spkn; adv bkg acc; tennis adj; CKE. *"Well-kept site in great location nr medieval town cent & rv; some open views; friendly, helpful warden; nice sm pool; poss some workers' statics LS; rv walks; bar 200m; Voie Verte cycle rte; interesting town & area; site subject to flooding at any time; mkt Sat; twin axle restrictions; diff in/out for lge o'fits avail in Jul/Aug; san facs updated (2018)."* **€18.50, 1 Apr-30 Sep.** **2018**

SONZAY *4G1* (0.5km W Rural) *47.52620, 0.45070* **Kawan Village L'Arada Parc,** 88 Rue de la Baratière, 37360 Sonzay **02 47 24 72 69; info@laradaparc.com; www.laradaparc.com**

🐕 €3 ♟♟ WD ⬛ ⚒ ♿ 🄰 ⫽ MSP 🦋 ♙ 𝖳 ⓗ ♨ 🛆 ⚓ ♪ ⚓(covrd, htd) 🎿

Fr N exit A28 junc 27 to Neuillé-Pont-Pierre; then D766 & D6 to Sonzay; turn R in town cent. Site on R on o'skirts immed past new houses; sp. Fr S & E use Sat Nav. 4*, Med, mkd, hdg, pt shd, pt sl, serviced pitches; EHU (10A) €4.10 (poss rev pol); gas; bbq; red long stay; TV; 15% statics; phone; bus to Tours; Eng spkn; adv bkg acc; ccard acc; bike hire; rv fishing 500m; gym; games area; CKE. *"Peaceful, well-kept site; spa; friendly, helpful owners & staff; clean, modern facs; gd views; vg rest; poss diff for lge o'fits when site full/cr; barrier clsd 2300-0800; many walks, inc in attractive orchards; 60km fr Le Mans circuit; rec."* **€36.00, 26 Mar-1 Nov.** **2019**

SORGUES *10E2* (7.4km NW Rural) *44.04163, 4.82493* **Camping L'Art de Vivre,** Islon St Luc, 84230 Châteauneuf-du-Pape **04 90 02 65 43; contact@ camping-artdevivre.com; www.camping-artdevivre.com**

🐕 €2.50 ♟♟ WD ⬛ ⚒ ⫽ MSP ♙ 𝖳 ⓗ ♨ ⚓

Exit A7 junc 22 onto D907 S dir Sorgues; in 11km (just bef Sorgues) turn R onto D17 dir Châteauneuf-du-Pape; in 4km, bef vill, turn L at site sp; site in 1km. Site well fr D17. 2*, Med, mkd, shd, EHU (10A) €4; bbq; Eng spkn; ccard acc; games area; games rm. *"Site situated in woodland nr rv; new enthusiastic owners (2011); gd walks & cycling; wine-growing area; m'van o'night area; gd; pleasant site; gd rest."* **€26.00, 4 Apr-27 Sep.** **2015**

SOSPEL *10E4* (4km NW Rural) *43.89702, 7.41685* **Camping Domaine Ste Madeleine,** Route de Moulinet, 06380 Sospel **04 93 04 10 48; camp@camping-sainte-madeleine.com; www.camping-sainte-madeleine.com**

🐕 €1.50 ♟♟ WD ⬛ ⚒ ⫽ MSP 🦋 ♒

Take D2566 fr Sospel NW to Turini & site 4km on L; sp fr town. Rd to site fr Menton steep with many hairpins. 3*, Med, mkd, shd, pt sl, terr, EHU (10A) €2.90; gas; Eng spkn; adv bkg rec; CKE. *"Friendly, busy site; gd pool but has no shallow end; stunning scenery; beautifully kept site; gd, immac facs; v well run."* **€25.40, 28 Mar-3 Oct.** **2018**

SOUILLAC *7C3* (9km N Rural) *44.95178, 1.46547* **Camping Le Lac Rouge,** 46200, Lachapelle Auzac **06 82 92 55 67 or 06 82 92 55 67 (mob); jo.camping lelacrouge@gmail.com**

🐕 ♟♟ WD ⬛ ♿ ♨ 🄰 ⫽ 𝖳 ⚙

Fr Souillac foll D15, sp Salignac, at La Forge turn R on D15 sp Gignac. Site on R by junc for Lhom, 500m past golf club. Sm, pt shd, pt sl, EHU inc; bbq; twin axles; 50% statics; adv bkg acc; games area; CKE. *"Gd site."* **€14.00, 1 Apr-31 Oct.** **2015**

SOUILLAC *7C3* (1km W Urban) *44.88895, 1.47418* **FLOWER Camping Les Ondines,** Ave de Sarlat, 46200 Souillac **05 65 37 86 44 or 06 33 54 32 00; camping. les.ondines@flowercampings.com; www.camping-lesondines.com or www.flowercampings.com**

🐕 €2 ♟♟ WD ⬛ ♿ 🄰 ⫽ 🦋 ♙ ⓗnr ♨ 🛆 🄰 ♪ ⚓(htd)

Leave A20 junc 55. D804 then D820 to Souillac. In cent of town turn W onto D804 to Sarlat. In 225m turn R into Rue des Ondines. Site on R after 200m (opp Quercyland). 3*, Lge, mkd, pt shd, EHU (6A) inc; bbq; 10% statics; phone; Eng spkn; horseriding; tennis; canoeing; fishing; CKE. *"Gd touring base nr rv; helpful staff; clean facs; conv NH Rocamadour & caves; easy access fr A20/D820; aquatic park nrby; vg; ACSI accepted."* **€27.00, 1 May-28 Sep.** **2019**

SOUILLAC *7C3* (8km NW Rural) *44.94510, 1.44140* **Domaine de la Paille Basse,** 46200 Souillac **05 65 37 85 48; info@lapaillebasse.com; www.lapaillebasse.com**

🐕 €4 ♟♟ WD ⬛ ♿ 🄰 ⫽ 🦋 ♙ 𝖳 ⓗ ♨ 🛆 🄰 ♪ ⚓ ⚙

Exit Souillac by D15 sp Salignac, turn onto D165 at Bourzolles foll sp to site in 3km. NB Narr app, few passing places. 4*, Lge, hdg, pt shd, terr, EHU (3-10A) €4-6; gas; bbq; TV; adv bkg acc; ccard acc; golf 5km; tennis; bike hire; games area; waterslide. *"Excel site in remote location; friendly, helpful staff; clean facs; organised outdoor activities; cinema rm; some shwrs unisex; restored medieval vill."* **€25.00, 15 May-14 Sep, D06.** **2016**

SOULAC SUR MER 7B1 (13km S Coastal) 45.41600, -0.12930 **Centre Naturiste Euronat (Naturist),** 33590 Grayan-l'Hôpital **05 56 09 33 33; info@euronat.fr; www.euronat.fr**

🐕 €3 ♟♟♟(htd) ⓦⅅ ♨ ♨ ♿ ▱ ∥ ⅯⅯ 🦋 ⅌ 𝖸 ⑪ ⅾ ⅀ ⅄ ∥ 🏊(covrd, htd) 📅 🧭 sand adj

Fr Soulac, take D101 twd Montalivet, turn W at camp sp onto rd leading direct to site. Fr Bordeaux, take D1215 sp Le Verdon-sur-Mer. Approx 8km after Lesparre-Médoc turn L onto D102. In Venday-Montalivet bear R onto D101. In 7.5km turn L sp Euronat. 4*, V lge, hdstg, mkd, shd, serviced pitches; EHU (10A) inc; gas; bbq; TV; 30% statics; phone; Eng spkn; adv bkg acc; bike hire; horseriding; tennis; archery; INF card req; golf driving range. *"Expensive, but well worth it; cinema; thalassotherapy & beauty treatment cent; gd lge pitches, many with elec/water; shwrs basic/dated; excel."* **€55.50, 1 Apr-29 Oct.** **2017**

SOULAC SUR MER 7B1 (5km SSW Coastal) 45.480917, -1.145109 **Sandaya Soulac Plage,** Lieu-dit l'Amelie, 33780 Soulac-sur-Mer **05 56 09 87 27; sp@sandaya.fr; www.sandaya.co.uk**

🐕 €5 ♟♟♟(htd) ⓦⅅ ♨ ♨ ♿ ▱ ∥ 🦋 ⅌ 𝖸 ⑪ ⅾ ⅀ ⅄ ∥ 🏊(covrd, htd) 🧭 sand adj

Fr S on D1215 dir Le Verdon, turn R onto D1E4 dir Soulac-sur-Mer, in 1.8km turn R onto Av de L'Europe sp Centre Ville & Plages. At rndabt go R sp plages, site sp. 4*, V lge, hdg, mkd, pt shd, EHU (10A) inc; bbq (gas); 60% statics; adv bkg acc; sauna; tennis. *"Excel site; direct access to beach."* **€25.00, 10 Apr-13 Sep.** **2019**

SOULAC SUR MER 7B1 (1.5km SW Coastal) 45.49958, -1.13899 **Camping Les Sables d'Argent,** Blvd de l'Amélie, 33780 Soulac-sur-Mer **05 56 09 82 87; sables@lelilhan.com; www.sables-d-argent.com**

🐕 €2.95 ♟♟♟ ♨ ♿ ▱ ∥ ⅌ 𝖸 ⑪ ⅾ ⅀ ⅄ ∥ 🧭 sand adj

Drive S fr Soulac twd L'Amélie-sur-Mer. Clearly sp on R. 3*, Med, mkd, pt shd, pt sl, EHU (10A) inc (poss long lead req); TV; 60% statics; tennis; fishing. *"Nice area, but major erosion of coast so no access to beach; poss diff lge o'fits; Soulac sm, lively mkt town."* **€25.00, 1 Apr-30 Sep.** **2018**

SOUSTONS 8E1 (6.5km NE Rural) 43.78430, -1.30473 **Camping Azu'Rivage,** 720 Route des Campings, 40140 Azur **05 58 48 30 72; info@campingazurivage.com; www.campingazurivage.com**

🐕 €2 ♟♟♟ ♨ ♨ ♿ ▱ ∥ ⑪ ⅾ ⅀ ⅄ ∥ 🏊 📅

Exit m'way A10 at exit Magescq & take D150 W for 8km to Azur, site sp fr church adj La Paillotte. 3*, Med, pt shd, EHU (10A) €7.40; sw; red long stay; TV; 80% statics; adv bkg acc; ccard acc; boating; tennis; watersports. *"Delightful forest setting adj lake; v busy high ssn; san facs poss stretched high ssn; rec; lovely pool; no easy access to lake; v few touring pitches; heavily commercialised."* **€29.00, 15 May-30 Sep.** **2019**

SOUSTONS 8E1 (9km W Coastal) 43.75579, -1.35384 **Camping Sandaya Souston Village,** 63 Avenue de Port d'Albret, 40140 Soustons **05 58 77 70 00; www.sandaya.fr/nos-campings/soustons-village**

♿ ⅌ 𝖸 ⑪ ⅀ ⅄ 🏊(htd, indoor) 🧭

Head S on N10. Leave at Magesq exit and head for Soustons on D116. Then follow sp. 5*, TV; adv bkg rec; Ccard acc; bike hire; fishing; watersports; spa; games area; gym; cinema. **14 Apr-1 Oct.** **2019**

STENAY 5C1 (0.3km W Urban) 49.49083, 5.18333 **Port de Plaisance - Motor Caravan Parking Area,** Rue du Port, 55700 Stenay **03 29 80 64 22 or 03 29 74 87 54; otsistenayaccueil@orange.fr**

12 ♨ ♿ ∥ ⅯⅯ 🦋 ⑪ nr ⅄ nr

Off D947 fr town cent. Foll sp to rv port. NB M'vans only. Sm, hdstg, EHU (6A) inc. *"Adj to rv; excel san facs; NH only; sh walk to Beer Museum, rest, shop."* **€8.00** **2015**

STRASBOURG 6E3 (3km W Urban) 48.57537, 7.71724 **Camping Indigo Strasbourg,** 9 rue de l'Auberge de Jeunesse, 67200 Strasbourg **03 88 30 19 96; strasbourg@camping-indigo.com; www.citykamp.com**

12 🐕 ♟♟♟ ⓦⅅ ♨ ♨ ♿ ▱ ∥ ⅯⅯ 🦋 ⅌ 𝖸 ⅾ ∥ 🏊(htd) 📅

Fr A35 exit junc 4, then foll (white) sp to Montagne Verte. Then foll D392 to site. 4*, Lge, hdg, pt shd, pt sl, EHU (10A); bbq; red long stay; twin axles; TV; 50% statics; bus; Eng spkn; adv bkg req; bike hire; games area; games rm; CKE. *"Excel site; site renovated (2015); bus/tram/cycle path to city."* **€32.90, J10.** **2018**

SULLY SUR LOIRE 4F3 (2km NW Rural) 47.77180, 2.36200 **Camping Le Jardin de Sully,** 1Route Orleans, 45600 Saint-Pere-Sur-Loire **02 38 67 10 84 or 07 81 11 47 65 (mob); lejardindesully@gmail.com; www.camping-bord-de-loire.com**

12 🐕 €2 ♟♟♟(htd) ⓦⅅ ♨ ♿ ▱ ∥ ⅯⅯ 🦋 ⅌ 𝖸 ⑪ ⅾ ⅀ ⅄ ∥ 🧭 sand adj

Fr N on D948 to Sully then turn R at rndabt immed bef x-ing bdge over Rv Loire onto D60 in St Père-sur-Loire, dir Châteauneuf-sur-Loire. Sp to site in 200m. Fr S thro Sully on D948, cross Rv Loire & turn L at rndabt onto D60. Well sp fr town. 3*, Med, hdstg, mkd, hdg, pt shd, serviced pitches; EHU (10-16A) inc (poss rev pol); gas; bbq; red long stay; TV (pitch); 18% statics; phone; bus; Eng spkn; adv bkg rec; ccard acc; tennis; bike hire; games rm; CKE. *"Pleasant, well-kept, well laid-out site on rvside adj nature reserve; pleasant walk along rv to town; long dist footpath (grande randonnée) along Loire passes site; gd dog walks; htd covrd pool 500m; gd cycling; gd winter site & NH en rte S; recep might be clsd LS, need to phone for barrier code ent; fairy-tale chateau in Sully; gd loc; helpful, friendly new owner keen to bring the standards up; excel new san fac (2018); excel."* **€25.00** **2018**

SURGERES *7A2* (0.7km S Urban) *46.10180, -0.75376* **Camping de La Gères,** 10 Rue de la Gères, 17700 Surgères **05 46 07 79 97 or 06 64 03 89 32 (mob); contact@campingdelageres.com; www.camping delageres.com**

🐕 €1.50 ♦♦(cont) 🚾 ♨ ⏚ ∥ 📶 ≍ 🍴 nr ⊕ nr ⊠ nr ⚓ (htd)

Site sp in Surgères, on banks of Rv Gères, & fr Surgères by-pass. 3*, Sm, mkd, hdg, shd, EHU (6A) €3.50; bbq; phone; ccard acc; tennis 800m; CKE. *"Adj to park; m'vans extra charge; poss travellers; excel; park with rv walks, shops and rests via traff free walk in town cent."* **€20.00, 12 Jan-11 Dec.** 2015

SURGERES *7A2* (13km SW Rural) *46.07123, -0.86742* **Aire Naturelle de Loisirs,** Le Pré Marechat, 17290 Landrais **46 27 87 29 or 46 27 73 69**

🐕 ♦♦♦ ♨ ≍ 🍴 nr ⊠ nr 🏔

Fr D911 dir Rochefort, turn R at Muron onto D112 sp Landrais. Foll camping sp (not Loisirs). Site on L at NW end of vill. Sm, mkd, hdg, shd, bbq; twin axles; adv bkg acc; games area. *"Delightful peaceful site conv for La Rochells & Rochefort; site yourself & pay at Marie or staff; vg."* **€9.50, 15 Jun-15 Sep.** 2015

SURIS *7B3* (1km N Rural) *45.85925, 0.63739* **Camping La Blanchie,** 16270 Suris **05 45 89 33 19 or 06 35 43 21 39 (mob); contact@lablanchie.co.uk; www.lablanchie.co.uk**

🐕 ♦♦♦ 🚾 ♨ ⏚ ∥ 🦋 ℗

Fr N141 halfway bet Angoulême & Limoges take D52 S at La Péruse to Suris; in 3km turn E up a narr lane to site. 2*, Sm, hdstg, pt shd, pt sl, EHU (10A) €4; bbq; sw nr; twin axles; red long stay; 10% statics; Eng spkn; adv bkg acc; golf nr; tennis nr; CKE. *"Welcoming, friendly British owners; clean site in lovely area; Futuroscope nrby; ltd facs; c'van storage; gd touring base; poor."* **€20.40, 1 Apr-30 Sep.** 2019

SURZUR *2G3* (2km NE Urban) *47.58775, -2.61913* **Camping Ty-Coët,** 38 rue du Bois, 56450 Surzur **02 97 42 09 05; contact@camping-tycoet.com; www.camping-tycoet.com**

🐕 €1 ♦♦♦ 🚾 ♨ ⏚ ⅍ ∥ 📶 🦋 ℗ 🍴 🏊 🏔

N165/E60 Vannes-Nantes. Take Exit 22. D183 twd Surzur. At rndabt bef Surzur cont onto D183, then 1st L onto Rue des Lutins. Foll sp to site. 3*, Med, hdg, mkd, pt shd, EHU (16A) €3.20; bbq; sw nr; twin axles; 30% statics; bus 0.5km; Eng spkn; adv bkg acc; games rm; CCI. *"BBQ except Jul & Aug; conv for Golfe de Morbihan; gd mkt in Vannes (Sat & Tue); lovely, quiet, well-kept site with super clean san facs; excel; gd touring area; v pleasant warden."* **€18.60, 1 Mar-15 Nov.** 2015

TAGNIERE, LA *6H1* (2km SW Rural) *46.77728, 3.56283* **Camping Le Paroy,** 71190 La Tagnière **03 85 54 59 27 or 603 56 64 82 (mob); info@campingleparoy.com; www.campingleparoy.com**

🐕 ♦♦♦ 🚾 ♨ ⏚ ∥ 📶 🦋 ℗ ⊠ 🏔

Fr Autun SW on D681, after 11km S on D994. 3km after Etang L onto D224 to La Tagniere and foll sp. Sm, hdg, pt shd, terr, EHU (10A) €4; bbq; twin axles; TV; Eng spkn; adv bkg acc; bike hire; CKE. *"Fishing at Sm adj lake; takeaway; vg."* **€23.00, 1 Apr-30 Sep.** 2015

TAIN L'HERMITAGE *9C2* (5km NE Rural) *45.10715, 4.89105* **Camping Chante-Merle,** 26600 Chantemerle-les-Blés **04 75 07 49 73; campingchantemerle@wanadoo.fr; www.campingchante-merle.fr**

12 🐕 €2 ♦♦(htd) 🚾 ♨ ⏚ ⅍ 🦽 ∥ 🦋 ℗ 🍴 ⊕ ♨ ⊠ nr 🏊 ⚓

Exit A7 at Tain-l'Hermitage. After exit toll turn L twd town, next turn R (D109) to Chantemerle; site sp. Cont for 5km, site on L. 3*, Sm, hdg, mkd, pt shd, serviced pitches; EHU (10A) €4.50; 10% statics; adv bkg req; tennis 500m; site clsd Jan; CKE. *"Helpful manager; popular site; excel facs."* **€23.00** 2017

TAIN L'HERMITAGE *9C2* (1.4km S Urban) *45.06727, 4.84880* **Camp Municipal Les Lucs,** 24 Ave du Président Roosevelt, 26600 Tain-l'Hermitage **04 75 08 32 82; camping.tainlhermitage@orange.fr; www.camping-tain.fr/en**

🐕 €1.40 ♦♦♦ 🚾 ♨ ⏚ 🦽 ∥ 📶 ⊕ nr ⊠ nr 🏔

Fr N or S exit A7 junc 13 dir Tain-l'Hermitage onto N7. Cont N twd town cent; at fuel stn on R & Netto supmkt sp prepare to turn L in 80m; ent to site in 35m. Fr N on N7 prepare to turn R after fuel stn on R. Site alongside Rv Rhône via gates (locked o/ night). Well sp adj sw pool/petrol stn. 3*, Med, mkd, hdstg, hdg, pt shd, EHU (6A) inc (poss rev pol); phone; Eng spkn; CKE. *"Pretty, well-kept, well-run site by Rhône; lovely views; secure site; friendly staff; excel, clean san facs; no twin axles, no c'vans over 5.5m & no m'vans over 6m (poss high ssn only); rvside walk to town; Valrhona chocolate factory shop nrby; mkt Sat; gd touring base; popular NH; highly rec; access gate with PIN; v sm pitches."* **€22.00, 1 Mar-31 Oct.** 2019

TALMONT SAINT HILAIRE *7A1* (8km WSW Coastal) *46.451713, -1.702118* **Camping Sandaya Le Littoral,** Le Porteau 85440, Talmont-St-Hilaire **02 51 22 04 64; www.sandaya.fr/nos-campings/le-littoral**

🐕 ♦♦♦(htd) 🚾 ♨ ⅍ ⏚ ∥ 🦋 ℗ 🍴 ⊕ ♨ ⊠ 🏔 ⚓ ⚓(htd) 🛶
🌳shgl

Fr Talmont-St-Hilaire to Les Sables d'Olonne on D949. Turn L after racecourse. Site sp. 5*, Mkd, pt shd, EHU 10A; gas; bbq (elec, gas); twin axles; Eng spkn; adv bkg rec; ccard acc; bike hire; fishing; scuba diving; games rm; security. **€56.00, 5 Apr-7 Sep.** 2019

TANINGES 9A3 (1km S Rural) 46.09899, 6.58806
Camp Municipal des Thézières, Les Vernays-sous-la-Ville, 74440 Taninges 04 50 34 25 59; camping.taninges@wanadoo.fr

12 🐕 €1.30 ♨(htd) wc ♨ & ♿ ⊿ ⊠ 🦋 ⚚ Ⴀ nr ⒽＢ nr 🝔 ⌂

Take D902 N fr Cluses; site 1km S of Taninges on L - just after 'Taninges' sp on ent town boundary; sp Camping-Caravaneige. 2*, Lge, pt shd, EHU (6-10A) €2.50-4; bbq; TV; phone; Eng spkn; ccard acc; tennis; CKE. "Splendid site with magnificent views; pool at Samoens 11km; peaceful & well-kept; lge pitches; friendly, helpful staff; excel facs; conv for N Haute Savoie & Switzerland to Lake Geneva; excel; wooded site; bit of rd noise." **€13.40**   **2017**

TARASCON 10E2 (5km SE Rural) 43.76744, 4.69331
Camping St Gabriel, Route de Fontvieille, 13150 Tarascon 04 90 91 19 83; contact@campingsaint gabriel.com; www.campingsaintgabriel.com

🐕 €2 ♨(htd) wc ♨ & ♿ ⊿ 🦋 ⚚ Ⴀ Ⓗ ⌂ Ｂ ⌂ (htd)

Take D970 fr Tarascon, at rndabt take D33 sp Fontvieille, site sp 100m on R. 3*, Med, hdg, shd, EHU (6A) €3.3; gas; TV; 30% statics; adv bkg acc; games rm; site clsd mid-Feb & Xmas/New Year; rv fishing; CKE. "Well-kept, charming site; excel base for Camargue & Arles; modern san facs; sm pitches poss not suitable lge o'fits; gd; 10 min walk into cent." **€27.00, 14 Mar-14 Nov.**   **2016**

"That's changed – Should I let the Club know?"

If you find something on site that's different from the site entry, fill in a report and let us know. See camc.com/europereport.

TARASCON SUR ARIEGE 8G3 (2km SE Rural) 42.83981, 1.61215 Kawan Village Le Pré-Lombard, Route d'Ussat, 09400 Tarascon-sur-Ariège 05 61 05 61 94; leprelombard@wanadoo.fr; www.prelombard.com

🐕 €4 ♨(htd) wc ♨ & ♿ ⊿ ⊠ ⚚ Ⓗ ⒶＢ ⌂ ⌂ 🝔 ⌂ (htd)

Travelling S twd Andorra join N20 to Tarascon. Approx 17km S of Foix after 3 rndabts & x-ing a bdge, at 4th rndabt turn L, after rlwy on D618 foll site sp. This rte avoids cent of Tarascon. 4*, Lge, hdg, mkd, pt shd, EHU (10A) inc; gas; bbq; sw nr; TV; 50% statics; Eng spkn; adv bkg rec; ccard acc; rv fishing adj; games rm; bike hire; archery; tennis; CKE. "Busy, well-run, family site in lovely location by rv; spacious pitches; helpful owner; san facs tired (2015); no o'fits over 6m; plenty for teenagers to do; canyoning & climbing nrby; gd base for exploring area; excel winter NH en rte to Spain; kayaking adj; poss rallies LS; excel; nice walk to town." **€38.60, 2 Mar-4 Oct.**   **2015**

TARASCON SUR ARIEGE 8G3 (3km SW Rural) 42.81311, 1.58908 Camping Les Grottes, Dumaines de la Hille, 09400 Alliat 05 61 05 88 21; info@campingdesgrottes.com; www.campingdes grottes.com

🐕 €2 ♨(htd) wc ♨ & ⊿ ⊠ 🦋 ⚚ Ⓗ nr Ａ Ｂ ⌂ ⌂ 🝔 ⌂ (htd) 📶

S fr Foix on N20 dir Andorra, turn R onto D8 just past Tarascon-sur-Ariège sp Niaux/Vicdessos. Site on R in 2km. 3*, Med, hdg, hdstg, mkd, pt shd, EHU (6-10A) €2; TV; 20% statics; phone; adv bkg acc; waterslide; games area. "Lovely, peaceful site in valley; ideal NH for Andorra or long stay; Miglos Castle & Niaux cave nr; excel modern san facs; excel." **€28.00, 1 Mar-15 Oct.**   **2017**

TARDETS SORHOLUS 8F1 (1km S Rural) 43.11143, -0.86362 Camping du Pont d'Abense, 64470 Tardets-Sorholus 05 59 28 58 76 or 06 78 73 53 59 (mob); camping.abense@wanadoo.fr; www.camping-pontabense.com

12 🐕 €2 ♨(htd) wc ♨ & ⊿ 🦋 ⚚ Ⴀ nr Ⓗ nr Ｂ nr

Take D918 S to Tardets, turn R to cross bdge onto D57. Site sp on R. Tardets cent narr. 2*, Med, shd, EHU (3A) €3.20; 10% statics; adv bkg acc; rv fishing nr; CKE. "Informal pitching; facs old; gd birdwatching; lovely, quaint site, a gem; nr gorges; heavenly!" **€26.00**   **2017**

TEICH, LE 7D1 (1.8km W Rural) 44.63980, -1.04272 Camping Ker Helen, Ave de la Côte d'Argent, 33470 Le Teich 05 56 66 03 79; camping.kerhelen@wanadoo.fr; www.kerhelen.com

♨(htd) wc ♨ ♨ & ⊿ ⊠ ⚚ Ⓗ Ａ 🝔 ⌂

Fr A63 take A660 dir Arcachon & exit junc 2 onto D3 then D650 thru Le Teich. Site sp on L. 3*, Med, hdg, pt shd, EHU (10A) €3.70; TV; 75% statics; adv bkg acc; canoeing; horseriding; CKE. "Less cr than coastal sites in Arcachon region; bird reserve nrby; vg; rest and snacks bar only open in July and August." **€25.30, 16 Apr-16 Oct.**   **2015**

TELGRUC SUR MER 2E2 (1km S Coastal) 48.22386, -4.37223 Camping Le Panoramic, 130 Route de la Plage, 29560 Telgruc-sur-Mer 02 98 27 78 41; info@camping-panoramic.com; www.camping-panoramic.com

🐕 €4 ♨(htd) wc ♨ ♨ & ⊿ ⊠ ⚚ Ⓗ ⒶＢ Ａ 🝔 ⌂ (htd) 📶 ⌂ sand 700m

Fr D887 Crozon-Châteaulin rd, turn W on D208 twd Trez-Bellec Plage, site sp on R in approx 1.5km. 4*, Med, hdg, mkd, pt shd, terr, EHU (6-10A) inc; bbq; TV; 10% statics; adv bkg acc; ccard acc; jacuzzi; bike hire; tennis; games rm; CKE. "Vg, well-run, welcoming site; access to pitches poss diff due trees & narr site rds; rec; some facs tired need updating; sea views; excel rest, pool & all facs; helpful owner." **€26.50, 1 May-15 Sep.**   **2019**

THANN 6F3 (9km NW Rural) 47.85071, 7.03058
FFCC Camping La Mine d'Argent, Rue des Mines,
68690 Moosch 03 89 82 30 66 or 03 89 60 34 74;
moosch@camping-la-mine-argent.com; www.camping-
la-mine-argent.com

€0.60 🏕️🚻 wc 🏊 🗑️ ✉️ 🛒 MSP 🦋 ♨️nr 🏔️

**Turn L off N66 Thann-Thillot rd in cent of Moosch
opp church; foll sps for 1.5km, ent on R, narr app.**
2*, Med, mkd, pt shd, pt sl, terr, EHU (6-10A) €3-5.60;
gas; 10% statics; phone; adv bkg acc; ccard acc; CKE.
"Well-kept site in wooded valley; busy w/end; helpful
staff; excel walking; highly rec."
€12.50, 5 Apr-15 Oct. 2015

THENON 7C3 (3km SE Rural) 45.11883, 1.09119
Camping Le Verdoyant, Route de Montignac, 24210
Thenon 05 53 05 20 78; contact@campingle
verdoyant.fr; www.campingleverdoyant.fr

€1.75 🏕️🚻 wc 🏊 ♿ 🗑️ ✉️ 🛒 MSP ♨️ 🍽️ 🍷 ♨️nr 🏔️ 🏊

**Sp fr A89, take D67 fr Thenon to Montignac. Site
on R in 4km.** 3*, Med, mkd, pt shd, sl, terr, EHU (10A)
€3.15 (rev pol) may req long lead; gas; 20% statics;
Eng spkn; adv bkg acc; lake fishing; CKE. "Beautiful
setting away fr tourist bustle; friendly owners; excel
base for area." **€16.50, 1 Apr-30 Sep.** 2017

THIEZAC 7C4 (0.5km E Rural) 45.01360, 2.67027
Camping La Bédisse, 3 Rue de la Bédisse, 15800
Thiézac 0471 47 00 41; camping.thiezac@orange.fr;
camping-thiezac.pagesperso-orange.fr

12 🏕️ ♿ 🗑️ ✉️ 🛒 MSP ♨️ 🍷 🏔️

**Fr Murat, take N122 twds Vic sur Cere & Aurillac. In
approx 24km foll sp to Thiezac. Site posted fr vill
cent.** EHU €4; bbq; sw; twin axles; 10% statics; Eng
spkn; adv bkg acc; games area; CKE. "Tennis court;
lovely rvside site; sh uphill walk to vill & shops; view of
mountains; gd walks; rec; excel." **€13.00** 2016

THILLOT, LE 6F3 (3.7km NNE Rural) 47.90694,
6.78138 **Camping l'Oree du Bois,** 51 Bis Grande Rue,
88160 Le Ménil 03 29 25 04 88; contact@loree-du-
bois.fr; www.loree-du-bois.fr

12 🏕️ €1 🚻 wc 🏊 ♿ 🗑️ ✉️ 🍷 ♨️ 🏔️

**Fr N66 bet Ramonchamp & St Maurice, in Le Thillot
turn L (N) on D486. After 3km ent Le Menil. In
middle of vill, immed opp church turn L to enter site
behind hse selling honey. Gd sp after Le Thillot.**
Sm, unshd, terr, EHU (10A) €5; 75% statics; phone;
bus; Eng spkn; adv bkg acc; games rm; games area;
CKE. "Gd walking & cycling, mkd trails fr site; htd pool
adj; access to winter sports nrby; vg."
€18.00 2015

THIONVILLE 5C2 (0.5km NE Urban) 49.36127,
6.17534 **Camp Municipal Touristique,** 6 Rue du Parc,
57100 Thionville 03 82 53 83 75; camping.municipal@
mairie-thionville.fr; www.thionville.fr/fr/content/
camping-municipal-touristique-1

€1.20 🏕️🚻 wc 🏊 ♿ ✉️ 🛒 ♨️ 🍷nr ⑪nr ♨️nr 🏔️

**Exit A31 at sp Thionville Cent; foll sp 'Centre Ville';
foll site sp dir Manom.** 2*, Sm, hdstg, mkd, pt shd,
EHU (3-10A) €2.40-4.65; red long stay; Eng spkn;
adv bkg acc; fishing; boating; CKE. "Well-kept site;
some rvside pitches which can be noisy in eve; friendly
warden; gd san facs; rec arr early high ssn; 5 min walk
thro lovely adj park to town; vg; walk alongside rv as
adj." **€16.50, 1 May-30 Sep.** 2017

THIVIERS 7C3 (7km N Rural) 45.47390, 0.93808
Camping La Petite Lande, Lieu-dite La Petite Lande,
24800 St Jory-de-Chalais 09 64 44 82 79; info@la-
petite-lande.com; www.la-petite-lande.com

12 🏕️ €1 🚻(htd) wc 🏊 ♿ 🗑️ ✉️ MSP 🦋 ⑪nr ♨️nr 🏔️ 🏊

**N fr Thiviers on D21; in 6km turn L after La Poste
onto unclassified rd sp 'La Petite Lande' campsite;
foll sps to site in 500m.** Sm, unshd, EHU (6-10A)
€3.75; bbq; Eng spkn; ccard acc. "Relaxing, CL-type
site; new site (2011); helpful Dutch owners; vg, clean
facs plans to expand." **€11.00** 2016

THIVIERS 7C3 (2km E Rural) 45.41299, 0.93209
Camping Le Repaire, Ave de Verdun, 24800 Thiviers
05 53 52 69 75; contact@camping-le-repaire.fr;
www.camping-le-repaire.fr

🏕️ €2 🚻(htd) wc 🏊 ♿ 🗑️ ✉️ MSP 🦋 🗑️ ♨️nr 🏔️ 🖊️ 🏊(covrd)

**N21 to Thiviers; at rndabt take D707 E dir
Lanouaille; site in 1.5km on R.** 3*, Med, mkd, hdg,
pt shd, pt sl, terr, EHU (12A) €3; bbq; TV; 5% statics;
phone; Eng spkn; adv bkg acc; games rm; lake fishing;
CKE. "Lovely site, one of best in area; friendly owners;
clean san facs; some pitches unrel in wet weather;
excel; v nice tree shd plots." **€20.00, 1 Apr-4 Nov.**
2017

THONNANCE LES MOULINS 6E1 (2km W Rural)
48.40630, 5.27110 **Camping La Forge de Ste Marie,**
52230 Thonnance-les-Moulins 03 25 94 42 00;
info@laforgedesaintemarie.com; www.laforgede
saintemarie.com or www.les-castels.com

🏕️ €2 🚻 wc 🏊 ♿ 🗑️ ✉️ MSP ♨️ 🍽️ ⑪ 🗑️ ♨️ 🖊️ 🏊(covrd, htd) 🛝

**Fr N67 exit sp Joinville-Est, foll D60 NE sp
Vaucouleurs. In 500m turn R onto D427 sp Poissons
& Neufchâteau. Site on R in 11km. NB Swing wide
at turn into site fr main c'way, not fr what appears
to be a run in. Site ent narr.** 5*, Lge, hdg, mkd, pt shd,
pt sl, terr, serviced pitches; EHU (6A) inc; gas; bbq; TV;
25% statics; phone; Eng spkn; adv bkg acc; ccard acc;
games rm; bike hire; boating; lake fishing; games area;
CKE. "Vg, well-kept, busy site; friendly, helpful owners;
freshwater fishing; access poss diff to some terr pitches/
sharp bends on site rds; muddy after rain; vg rest; no
o'fits over 8m; mkt Fri; lovely spacious, well run site,
beautiful area; swing wide at ent; poss no mob phone
recep; san facs fair." **€40.00, 18 Apr-4 Sep, J04.** 2015

FRANCE

THONON LES BAINS *9A3* (3km NE Rural) *46.39944, 6.50416* **Camping Le Saint Disdille,** 117 Ave de St Disdille, 74200 Thonon-Les-Bains **04 50 71 14 11;** camping@disdille.com; www.disdille.com

🐾€3 ♦♦♦ ⛺ ♨ ♿ 🚿 ∥ 🛒 ♉ ⛲ ⓘ♨ 🗜 ⚠ ✎

Exit A41/A40 junc 14 Annemasse onto D1005 & foll sp Thonon twd Evian. At Vongy rndabt foll sp St Disdille & site. Site 200m fr Lake Geneva.
3*, V lge, mkd, shd, EHU (6-10A) €4; gas; bbq; sw nr; 30% statics; adv bkg req; ccard acc; fishing; watersports; tennis; games area; bike hire; games rm; CKE. *"Well-situated; well-equipped site; gd touring base for v nice area."* **€33.50, 1 Apr-30 Sep.** 2019

See advertisement

THONON LES BAINS *9A3* (13km W Rural) *46.35638, 6.35250* **Campéole Camping La Pinède,** 74140 Excenevex **04 50 72 85 05 or 04 50 72 81 27** (Mairie); pinede@campeole.com; www.camping-lac-leman.info or www.campeole.com

🐾€3.50 ♦♦♦(htd) ⬜ ⛺ ♨ 🔲 ∥ ⬜ 🛒 ♉ ⛲ ⓘ♨ 🗜 ⚠ ✎

🏕 sand adj

On D1005 to Geneva, 10km fr Thonon, turn R at Camping sp. 3*, V lge, mkd, shd, EHU (10A) €4.10; gas; bbq; sw nr; TV; 75% statics; adv bkg acc; horseriding 1km; games area; tennis; watersports adj; fishing adj. *"Excel lakeside site; friendly & efficient staff; ltd touring emplacements."* **€30.00, 28 Apr-30 Sep.** 2016

THURY HARCOURT *3D1* (0.9km NE Rural) *48.98930, -0.46966* **FFCC Camping Vallée du Traspy,** Rue du Pont Benoît, 14220 Thury-Harcourt **02 31 29 90 86;** contact@campingdutraspy.com; www.campingdu traspy.com

🐾€2.90 ♦♦♦ ⬜ ⛺ ♨ ♿ ∥ ⬜ 🛒 ♉ ⛲ nr ⚠ ✎

App fr N on D562 fr Caen, take L fork into town after pool complex. In 100m turn L at Hôtel de la Poste, 1st L to site, clearly sp adj Rv Orne.
3*, Med, mkd, pt shd, terr, EHU (4A) inc; gas; bbq; 20% statics; phone; Eng spkn; adv bkg rec; fishing; canoeing; CKE. *"Friendly owners; well-maintained pitches; o'night m'vans area; gd walking; site under new management with some refurbishment (2014); rec."* **€25.00, 1 Apr-30 Sep.** 2019

TIL CHATEL *6G1* (2km E Rural) *47.53042, 5.18700* **Camping Les Sapins,** 21120 Til-Châtel **03 80 95 16 68;** www.restaurantlessapins.eresto.net

♦♦♦ ⛺ ∥ 🗜 nr

Leave A31 junc 5 onto D974 dir Til-Châtel. Site on R in 500m adj Rest Les Sapins.
1*, Sm, pt shd, pt sl, serviced pitches; EHU (10A) inc; Eng spkn; adv bkg acc; CKE. *"Clean, CL type site; basic san facs; no twin axles; conv NH fr a'route."* **€16.50, 1 Apr-30 Sep.** 2016

TINTENIAC *2E4* (0.5km N Rural) *48.33111, -1.83315* **Camp Municipal du Pont L'Abbesse,** Rue du 8 Mai 1945, 35190 Tinténiac **02 99 68 09 91 or 02 99 68 02 15 (Mairie)**

♦♦♦(htd) ⛺ ♿ ∥ 🛒 ♉ nr ⓘ nr 🗜 nr ⚠

Fr D137 turn E onto D20 to Tinténiac; go strt thro vill to canal; sp just bef canal bdge; turn L. Site behind Brit Hôtel La Guinguette, on Canal d'Ille et Rance. 2*, Sm, hdg, mkd, pt shd, pt sl, EHU inc; 10% statics; fishing; CKE. *"Delightful, busy site; gd san facs; lovely walks/cycling along canal; vg; unreliable end of ssn closing; clsd at night by barrier; NH."* **€10.00, 1 Mar-30 Sep.** 2017

FRANCE

TINTENIAC 2E4 (2km S Rural) 48.31058, -1.82027
Camping Les Peupliers, Manoir de la Besnelais,
35190 Tinténiac **02 99 45 49 75; contact@
domainelespeupliers.fr; www.domainelespeupliers.fr**

🐾 €1.60 👫 🅦 ⚂ ⚄ ♿ ☇ 🖪 ♈ 🍴 ⛺ 🛒 nr ⚠ ♒ (htd)

On D137 Rennes to St Malo rd; after Hédé foll rd to
Tinténiac about 2km; site on main rd on R, sp.
3*, Med, hdg, mkd, pt shd, pt sl, EHU (6A) €2.90 (poss
rev pol); TV; 30% statics; phone; adv bkg acc; games
area; tennis; lake fishing; CKE. *"Pleasant, quiet, well-
kept site; gd pool & park; on pilgrim rte to Spain; conv
for acc to canal."* **€25.50, 1 Apr-1 Oct.** 2018

"We must tell the Club about that great site we found"

Get your site reports in by mid-August and we'll
do our best to get your updates into the next
edition.

TONNERRE 4F4 (1.5km NE Urban) 47.86003, 3.98429
Camp Municipal de la Cascade, Ave Aristide Briand,
89700 Tonnerre **03 86 55 15 44 or 03 86 55 22 55**
(Mairie); **ot.tonnerre@wanadoo.fr; www.revea-
camping.fr or www.tonnerre.fr**

👫 (htd) 🅦 ⚂ ⚄ ♿ ☇ ♈ 🍴 🛒 ⚠ ♒

Best app via D905 (E by-pass); turn at rndabt twd
town cent L after x-ing 1st rv bdge. Foll site sp
to avoid low bdge (height 2.9m, width 2.4m). On
banks of Rv Armançon & nr Canal de l'Yonne, 100m
fr junc D905 & D944. 2*, Med, pt shd, EHU (6A) inc;
sw nr; TV; 10% statics; Eng spkn; adv bkg acc; ccard
acc; fishing; CKE. *"Pleasant, spacious, shady site in
arboretum; friendly warden; lge pitches; excel clean san
facs; often damp underfoot; no twin axles; interesting
town; gd cycling/walking along canal; conv site; excel."*
€15.00, 15 Apr-30 Oct. 2015

TORIGNI SUR VIRE 1D4 (1km S Rural) 49.02833,
-0.97194 **Camping Le Lac des Charmilles,** Route de
Vire, 50160 Torigni-sur-Vire **02 33 75 85 05 or 06 08
85 15 99; contact@camping-lacdescharmilles.com;
www.camping-lacdescharmilles.com**

🐾 €2 👫 (htd) 🅦 ⚂ ⚄ ♿ ☇ ♈ 🍴 🛒 ⚠ ♒ (htd)

Exit A84 junc 40 onto D974 dir Torigni-sur-Vire/
St Lô; site on R in 4km. Opp municipal stadium.
3*, Med, hdg, hdstg, mkd, pt shd, pt sl, EHU (10A)
inc (long lead poss req); gas; bbq; sw nr; twin axles;
TV; 30% statics; phone; Eng spkn; adv bkg acc; ccard
acc; games area; bike hire; games rm; CKE. *"Lovely,
well-kept, well-laid out site; clean, modern san facs,
new shwr (2016); attractive, interesting town; excel;
excel shopping in the town within walking dist; v
helpful,friendly new owner (2016); picturesque lakes;
tree-lined walks."* **€31.00, 1 Apr-30 Sep.** 2017

TORREILLES PLAGE 10G1 (0.9km N Coastal)
42.76750, 3.02972 **Camping Sunêlia Les Tropiques,**
Blvd de la Méditerranée, 66440 Torreilles-Plage **04 68
28 05 09; contact@campinglestropiques.com;
www.campinglestropiques.com**

🐾 €4 👫 🅦 ⚂ ⚄ ♿ ☇ 🖪 ♈ 🍴 🛒 ⚠ ♒ ♒ ⚑
♒ sand 400m

Exit A9 junc 41 onto D83 E dir Le Barcarès, then D81
dir Canet-Plage. At 1st rndabt turn L onto D11 sp
Torreilles-Plage, site sp. 4*, Lge, mkd, hdg, shd, EHU
(6A) inc; gas; red long stay; TV; 80% statics; Eng spkn;
ccard acc; waterslide; gym; bike hire; tennis; games
area; CKE. *"Vg family site; excel leisure & san facs."*
€48.50, 9 Apr-1 Oct. 2017

TOUCY 4F4 (0.7km S Urban) 47.73159, 3.29677
Camping des Quatre Merlettes, Rue du Pâtis, 89130
Toucy **03 86 44 13 84; 4merlettestoucy@orange.fr;
www.ville-toucy.fr/public/?code=camping-municipal**

👫 ⚂ ♿ ☇ 🛒 🛒 nr ♒ (htd)

On D3, 25km SW of Auxerre to Toucy. After rv x-ing
take 1st L sp 'Base de Loisirs'. Site on S bank of Rv
Quanne. 2*, Med, pt shd, EHU (8A) €3.50; 10% statics;
adv bkg acc; fishing. *"Pleasant vill; pleasant, helpful
warden; no twin axles; mkt Sat; rests in walking dist;
gd."* **€12.00, 1 Apr-14 Oct.** 2016

TOUL 6E2 (10km E Rural) 48.65281, 5.99260
Camping de Villey-le-Sec, 34 Rue de la Gare, 54840
Villey-le-Sec **03 83 63 64 28; info@campingvilley
lesec.com; www.campingvilleylesec.com**

🐾 €1.80 👫 ⚂ ⚄ ♿ ☇ 🖪 ♈ 🍴 🛒 ⚠

Exit Toul E on D909 or exit A31 junc 15 ondo D400
(W, in dir Hôpital Jeanne d'Arc); at rndabt turn L
onto D909 to Villey-le-Sec; in vill site S by Rv
Moselle, sp. V steep app rd. 3*, Med, hdg, mkd, hdstg,
pt shd, EHU (6-10A) €3.70-4.50; gas; bbq; red long
stay; phone; Eng spkn; ccard acc; games area.
*"Peaceful, well-kept site on rvside; lovely location;
lge pitches; friendly; vg san facs, poss stretched; gd
cycle paths; popular NH, ess arr bef 1800 high ssn."*
€22.00, 1 Apr-15 Oct. 2015

TOULOUSE 8F3 (5km N Urban) 43.65569, 1.41585
Camping Toulouse Le Rupé, 21 Chemin du Pont de
Rupé, 31200 Toulouse **05 61 70 07 35; camping
lerupe31@wanadoo.fr; www.camping-toulouse.com**

🅒 🐾 €1.50 👫 (htd) 🅦 ⚂ ⚄ ♿ ☇ ♈ 🍴 🛒 ⚠

N fr Toulouse on D820, sp. Poss tricky app fr N for
long vans, suggest cont past Pont de Rupé traff lts to
next rndabt & double back to turn. Fr S on ring rd
exit junc 33A (after junc 12), turn immed R & foll sp.
3*, Lge, hdg, hdstg, mkd, pt shd, EHU (10A) €4; TV;
50% statics; phone; bus; Eng spkn; ccard acc; games rm;
lake fishing; CKE. *"If site clsd 1200-1500, park in layby
just bef site & use speakerphone; gd clean san facs; rock
pegs poss req; ssn workers camp opp but no probs, site
security excel; conv Airbus factory tours; space theme
park 10km; well maintained; v helpful staff; ideal for
dogs, children or walkers."* **€28.00** 2017

TOUQUET PARIS PLAGE, LE *3B2* (2km S Coastal) *50.51091, 1.58867* **Camping Caravaning Municipal Stoneham,** Ave François Godin, 62520 Le Touquet-Paris-Plage **03 21 05 16 55; caravaning.stoneham@ letouquet.com; www.letouquet.com**

🏕 €2 🏕 ♨ 🛒 🖃 ⁄ 🏊nr 🏔 ⛱sand 1km

Fr Etaples on D939; stay in L-hand lane at traff lts dir airport & cont strt on (Ave du Général de Gaulle); L at traff lts sp Golf (Ave du Golf); foll rd to rndabt; turn R onto Ave François Godin (site sp); at next rndabt site on R. Or cont another 500m along Ave du Général de Gaulle to x-rds; turn L into Ave Louis Quetelart; in 500m at T-junc turn L into Ave François Godin; site on L in 200m. 2*, Lge, hdg, mkd, pt shd, EHU (16A) €5.80 (poss rev pol); 82% statics; adv bkg rec; ccard acc; CKE. *"Pleasant & well kept site; conv for town; helpful staff; excel facs; recep closes 1800 (LS 2010); htd pool 2km; m'van 'aires' nr harbour & equestrian cent; mkt Thu/Sat; walking & cycle paths to South Beach; town has many rest; gd sh stay."* **€26.40, 2 Feb-15 Nov.** 2017

TOUQUIN *4E4* (2.5km W Rural) 48.73305, 3.04697 **Camping Les Etangs Fleuris,** Route de la Couture, 77131 Touquin **01 64 04 16 36; contact@etangs-fleuris.com; www.etangs-fleuris.com**

🏕 €1.50 🏕(htd) 🆆🅳 ♨ 🛒 ⁄ 🖃 🦋 ♛ 🍽 ♨ 🏊 🏔 ♣ ⛱(htd) 🛶

On D231 fr Provins, turn R to Touquin. Turn sharp R in vill & foll sp to site on R in approx 2km. Or fr Coulommiers, take D402 SW twd Mauperthuis, after Mauperthuis L twd Touquin. Foll sp in vill. NB Beware two unmkd speed bumps on entering vill. 3*, Med, hdstg, mkd, hdg, pt shd, EHU (10A) inc; gas; bbq; TV; 20% statics; phone; adv bkg acc; ccard acc; games rm; fishing; games area; CKE. *"Peaceful site; no twin axles high ssn; conv Paris & Disneyland; helpful, supportive staff; no noise after 11pm."* **€30.00, 13 Apr-14 Sep.** 2019

TOURNON SUR RHONE *9C2* (0.4km N Rural) *45.07000, 4.83000* **FFCC Camping de Tournon HPA,** 1 Promenade Roche-de-France, 07300 Tournon-sur-Rhône **04 75 08 05 28; camping@camping-tournon.com; www.camping-tournon.fr**

12 🏕 €2 🏕(htd) 🆆🅳 ♨ 🛒 ⁄ 🖃 🍽 ♨ 🏔nr ⓑnr 🏊nr 🏔

Fr Tain l'Hermitage cross Rhône, turn R onto D86; in approx 1km R at end of car park; turn L after 50m, site on R on Rv Rhône. Or fr N on D86, sp on L by car park. 3*, Med, shd, EHU (6-10A) €4-6.50; gas; red long stay; 10% statics; phone; Eng spkn; adv bkg rec; canoeing; CKE. *"Pleasant, well-kept site in wooded location; rvside pitches; friendly owners; clean, dated san facs (unisex LS); m'van o'night area; c'van storage avail; some sm pitches & narr site rds poss diff lge o'fits; gd security; footbdge to Tain-l'Hermitage; fr mid-Jun rock concerts poss held nrby at w/end; gd; conv NH; interesting old town."* **€24.00** 2016

TOURNUS *9A2* (1km N Urban) 46.57244, 4.90854 **Camping de Tournus,** 14 Rue des Canes, 71700 Tournus **03 85 51 16 58; camping-tournus@orange.fr; www.camping-tournus.com**

🏕 €2.60 🏕 🆆🅳 ♨ 🛒 🖃 ⁄ 🍽 ♨ 🍽 ♣ 🏔

Fr N6 at N of town turn E opp rlwy stn & rest 'Le Terminus;' foll site sp. 3*, Med, hdstg, mkd, pt shd, pt sl, EHU (10A) €4.70 (long lead poss req)(poss rev pol); gas; bbq; TV; Eng spkn; rv fishing 100m; CKE. *"Peaceful, rvside site in nice position; popular NH, conv A6 - rec arr early; helpful staff; clean facs poss stretched high ssn & ltd LS; htd pools adj; poss extra charge twin axles; rv walk into town; gd cycling nrby; quiet but rd & rlwy noise some pitches; abbey worth visit; vg; well kept site; helpful staff."* **€27.00, 1 Apr-30 Sep.** 2017

TOURNUS *9A2* (9km S Rural) 46.48768, 4.91286 **Camping International d'Uchizy - Le National 6,** 71700 Uchizy **03 85 40 53 90; camping.uchizylen6@ wanadoo.fr; www.camping-lenational6.com**

🏕 €1 🏕 ♨ ⁄ ♣ 🏊 🏔 ⛱

Exit A6 junc 27 & foll N6 S; sp on L, turn L over rwly bdge on lane to site on L. Adj Rv Saône. 2*, Med, shd, EHU (6A) €3.90; gas; adv bkg acc; fishing; boat hire. *"Attractive, well-maintained site; gd, modern san facs; pitches soft & muddy in rain; cash only; arr early for rvside pitch; lovely position."* **€26.40, 1 Apr-30 Sep.** 2017

TOURS *4G2* (8km E Rural) 47.40226, 0.77845 **Camping Les Acacias,** Rue Berthe Morisot, 37700 La Ville-aux-Dames **02 47 44 08 16; contact@camping-tours.fr; www.camping-tours.fr**

12 🏕 €2 🏕(htd) 🆆🅳 ♨ 🛒 🖃 ⁄ 🍽 ♨ ⓗ 🏊nr 🏔

Fr Tours take D751 E sp Amboise; after 6km at rndabt where La Ville-aux-Dames sp to R, go strt on for 200m, then turn R, site sp. 3*, Med, hdg, mkd, hdstg, pt shd, EHU (10A) inc; bbq; red long stay; 10% statics; bus nr; Eng spkn; adv bkg acc; ccard acc; tennis 600m; fishing 100m; games area; bike hire; CKE. *"Well-kept, well-run, level site; excel san facs, ltd LS; conv town cent; fitness trail; many long-term residents; gd site; conv NH; lovely friendly helpful owners; mountain bike circuit; lge supmkt nr; bus to city nr; pool 500m; gd for long or sh stays; country park adj for dog walks; gd for Chateaux."* **€32.00, L03.** 2019

TOURS *4G2* (8km E Rural) 47.39273, 0.81085 **Camping Les Peupliers,** 37270 Montlouis-sur-Loire **02 47 50 81 90; aquadis1@wanadoo.fr; www.aquadis-loisirs.com**

🏕 €1.90 🏕(htd) 🆆🅳 ♨ 🛒 ⁄ 🍽 🏊nr 🏔

On D751, 2km W of vill of Montlouis. Fr N foll sp to Vouvray (keep on N side of Rv Loire to avoid Tours) & cross rv by bdge to Montlouis. Sp at last min. NB App fr E a 'Q-turn' to get into site. 3*, Lge, hdg, pt shd, EHU (6A) €2; 12% statics; Eng spkn; adv bkg acc; ccard acc; tennis; CKE. *"Clean, tidy site; poss clsd mid-Oct; lge pitches; mkt Sun in Amboise; vg."* **€19.60, 8 Apr-27 Oct.** 2019

FRANCE

TOURS *4G2* (8km SW Urban) *47.35530, 0.63401* **Camping La Mignardière,** 22 Ave des Aubépines, 37510 Ballan-Miré **02 47 73 31 00; info@mignardiere.com; www.mignardiere.com**

(htd) nr (covrd, htd)

Fr A10 exit junc 24 onto N585 & D37 by-pass. At exit for Joué-lès-Tours foll sp Ballan-Miré onto D751. Turn R at 1st set traff lts & foll site sp to W of lake. 4*, Lge, hdstg, mkd, hdg, pt shd, serviced pitches; EHU (6-10A) €3.50; bbq; TV; phone; Eng spkn; adv bkg acc; squash; bike hire; tennis; windsurfing 1km; fishing 1km; CKE. *"Conv Loire valley & chateaux; friendly, helpful staff; unisex facs LS; gd cycle paths; vg site; rec; bar 200m; gd san facs; v conv for bus/tram to Tours."*
€27.00, 1 Apr-25 Sep. 2018

See advertisement

TOURS *4G2* (10km W Rural) *47.35054, 0.54964* **Camp La Confluence,** Route du Bray, 37510 Savonnières **02 47 50 00 25; contact@campinglaconfluence.fr; www.onlycamp.fr**

€1.20 nr nr nr

Fr Tours take D7 on S of Rv Cher. Site on R on ent Savonnières on rvside. 3*, Med, hdstg, hdg, mkd, pt shd, EHU (10A) €4.20; bbq; phone; bus 200m; Eng spkn; adv bkg acc; tennis adj; canoe hire; CKE. *"Well-kept, clean, pleasant site; friendly, efficient staff; modern unisex san facs (a bit dated, 2018); some pitches narr & awnings diff; lovely vill with basic facs; gd touring base; gd birdwatching, cycling; bar adj; highly rec; gd touring base; on cycle rte; Vallendry Chateau 3.5km."* **€25.00, 30 Apr-30 Sep.** 2019

"I need an on-site restaurant"

We do our best to make sure site information is correct, but it is always best to check any must-have facilities are still available or will be open during your visit.

TRANCHE SUR MER, LA *7A1* (0.5km E Coastal) *46.34945, -1.43280* **Camping Bel,** Rue de Bottereau, 85360 La Tranche-sur-Mer **02 51 30 47 39; campbel@wanadoo.fr; www.campingbel.com**

nr nr

Ent La Tranche on D747, take 2nd R at rndabt, R at traff lts, ent on L. 4*, Med, hdg, mkd, pt shd, EHU (10A) inc; TV; phone; Eng spkn; adv bkg acc; table tennis; CKE. *"Ideal for families with young children; bike hire nrby; adv bkg is only for current year."*
€36.00, May- Sep, A34. 2019

TRANCHE SUR MER, LA *7A1* (3km E Coastal) *46.34810, -1.38730* **Camping du Jard,** 123 Blvd du Lattre de Tassigny, 85360 La Tranche-sur-Mer **02 51 27 43 79; info@campingdujard.fr; www.campingdujard.fr**

(covrd, htd) sand 700m

Foll D747 S fr La Roche-sur-Yon twd La Tranche; at rndabt on o'skirts of La Tranche turn L onto D46 sp La Faute-sur-Mer; cont for approx 5km. At rndabt turn R sp La Faute-sur-Mer 'par la côte'; then R at next rndabt onto D46 sp La Tranche-sur-Mer 'par la côte' & La Grière-Plage (ignore all previous La Grière sps); site on R in 1km. Rough app rd. 4*, Lge, mkd, hdg, pt shd, serviced pitches; EHU (10A) inc; bbq (charcoal, gas); red long stay; TV; 75% statics; Eng spkn; adv bkg acc; ccard acc; horseriding 10km; games area; bike hire; games rm; waterslide; tennis; golf 20km; sauna; CKE. *"Lovely, well-run, clean & tidy site; busy high ssn; gd sized pitches, some sm; gd, well-kept san facs; fitness cent; no c'vans over 8m high ssn; gd pool; superb beach across busy coastal rd; easy parking at other beaches; poss flooding in wet weather; mkt Tue & Sat."*
€36.00, 17 May-12 Sep, A03. 2018

TREBEURDEN *1D2* (3.5km NW Coastal) *48.79905, -3.58386* **Camp Municipal Le Dourlin,** L'Île Grande, 22560 Pleumeur-Bodou **02 96 91 92 41 or 02 96 23 91 17 (Mairie);** infos.tourisme@pleumeur-bodou.com; www.pleumeur-bodou.com

🏠 €0.60 ♦♦♦ ⬜ ♨ ♦ 🅰 ⬛ ⁄ ⛟ ℗ 🍴 Ⴌ nr ⋀ ⲁ shgl adj

Off D788 N fr Trébeurden. Foll minor rd thro vill to site on coast. Well sp. 2*, Med, mkd, unshd, EHU (6A) €2.35; bbq; phone; bus; Eng spkn; sailing; games area; fishing; CKE. *"Popular site in excel location - fine sea views; excel facs; gd walking, cycling; ornithological cent nr; 8km circular coast rd round peninsula; gd; lovely coastal walk; well stocked shop in vill."* **€9.00, 30 Apr-27 Sep.** **2017**

TREGASTEL *1D2* (3km NE Coastal) *48.82549, -3.49135* **Tourony Camping,** 105 Rue de Poul-Palud, 22730 Trégastel **02 96 23 86 61;** contact@camping-tourony.com; www.camping-tourony.com

🏠 €1.50 ♦♦♦ ⬜ ♨ ♦ 🅰 ⬛ ⁄ ᴹˢᴾ ⛟ 🍴 Ⴌ nr ⋀ ⲁ sand adj

On D788 fr Trébeurden dir Perros Guirec, site on R immed after exit Trégastel town sp & immed bef bdge over Traouieros inlet, opp Port de Ploumanac'h. 3*, Med, hdg, mkd, pt shd, EHU (6A) €3; gas; bbq; red long stay; TV; 15% statics; Eng spkn; adv bkg acc; ccard acc; tennis; bike hire; games area; horseriding nr; lake fishing; golf nr; CKE. *"Pleasant, lovely sm site in gd location; friendly, helpful staff; gd touring base Granit Rose coast; sm pitches dif for lge o'fits; clean but dated san facs (2015)."* **€25.00, 31 Mar-22 Sep.** **2018**

> ## "Satellite navigation makes touring much easier"
>
> Remember most sat navs don't know if you're towing or in a larger vehicle – always use yours alongside maps and site directions.

TREGASTEL *1D2* (3.8km SW Rural/Coastal) *48.80995, -3.54140* **Camping du Port,** 3 Chemin des Douaniers, 22560 Landrellec **02 96 23 87 79 or 06 73 78 32 64 (mob);** renseignements@camping-du-port-22.com; www.camping-du-port-22.com

🏠 €2.50 ♦♦♦ ⬜ ♨ ♦ 🅰 ⬛ ⁄ ᴹˢᴾ ⛟ 🍴 ℗ 🍴 Ⴌ ⋀ ⲁ sand

Turn off D788 to Landrellec & foll rd thro vill past shop for 100m, take care tight turn L. Site in 500m. 4*, Med, mkd, hdg, pt shd, pt sl, serviced pitches; EHU (10-15A) €3.20-3.50; gas; bbq; TV; 25% statics; Eng spkn; adv bkg acc; ccard acc; waterskiing; games rm; bike hire; boating; fishing; CKE. *"Immac, family-owned site; beautiful location; direct access beach; beach front pitches extra charge but narr; coastal path runs thro site; lots of lovely beaches nrby; telecoms museum worth visit; excel."* **€22.00, 21 Mar-8 Nov.** **2015**

TREGUNC *2F2* (3.5km SW Coastal) *47.83384, -3.89173* **Camping La Plage Loc'h Ven,** Plage de Pendruc, 29910 Trégunc **02 98 50 26 20;** contact@lochven.com; www.lochven.com

🏠 €1.60 ♦♦♦(htd) ⬜ ♨ ♦ 🅰 ⬛ ⁄ ⛟ ℗ nr Ⴌ nr ⋀ ⲁ shgl adj

Fr N165 exit at Kérampaou sp Trégunc. At rndbt W of Trégunc foll Loc'h Ven sp thro Lambell, site on coast. 2*, Med, hdg, mkd, pt shd, pt sl, EHU (4-10A) €3.50-4.70; gas; TV; 40% statics; Eng spkn; adv bkg acc; games area. *"Easy walk to beach, rock pools & coastal footpath; helpful owners."* **€18.50, 28 Apr-20 Sep.** **2019**

TREPORT, LE *3B2* (1km N Urban) *50.05805, 1.38860* **Camp Municipal Les Boucaniers,** Rue Pierre Mendès-France, 76470 Le Tréport **02 35 86 35 47;** camping@ ville-le-treport.fr; www.ville-le-treport.fr

🏠 €1.60 ♦♦♦(htd) ♨ ♦ 🅰 ⬛ ⁄ ⛟ 🍴 ℗ 🍴 Ⴌ ⋀ ⲁ sand 2km

Fr Eu take minor rd sp to Le Tréport under low bdge. On ent o'skts of Le Tréport, turn R at traff lts, camp ent 100m on R. Site nr stadium. 3*, Lge, hdstg, pt shd, EHU (6A) €4.60; TV; 10% statics; games rm. *"Busy, well-kept, well-run site; some lge pitches; gd, clean san facs; gd sep m'van area; lots to see in Le Tréport; m'van Aire de Service adj; gd value; excel; check elec lead is long enough bef unhitching."* **€18.00, 28 Mar-30 Sep.** **2017**

TREPT *9B2* (3km E Rural) *45.68701, 5.35190* **Camping les 3 Lacs du Soleil,** La Plaine de Serrières, 38460 Trept **04 74 92 92 06;** info@les3lacsdusoleil.com; www.camping-les3lacsdusoleil.com

🏠 €2.50 ♦♦♦ ⬜ ♨ ♦ 🅰 ⬛ ⁄ ⛟ 🍴 ℗ 🍴 Ⴌ ⋀ ⲁ ⛴ 🏊

Exit A432 at junc 3 or 3 & head twd Crémieu then Morestel. Trept bet these 2 towns on D517, site sp by lakes. 4*, Lge, pt shd, EHU (6A) inc; bbq (gas); sw nr; TV; 5% statics; phone; Eng spkn; adv bkg acc; ccard acc; waterslide; fishing; tennis; games area; archery; horseriding 2km. *"Gd family site; gd, modern san facs; fitness rm; lge & busy site with lots of activities."* **€38.00, 27 Apr-8 Sep.** **2019**

TRETS *10F3* (4km SW Rural) *43.44178, 5.62847* **Camping Le Devançon,** Chemin de Pourachon, 13790 Peynier **04 42 53 10 06;** reservation@ledevancon.fr; www.ledevancon.fr

🏠 €1 ♦♦♦(htd) ⬜ ♨ ♦ 🅰 ⬛ ⁄ ᴹˢᴾ ⛟ 🍴 ℗ 🍴 Ⴌ ⋀ ⲁ ⛴ 🏊

Leave A8 at Canet or Pas-de-Trets or leave D6 at Trets & take D908 to Peynier. In vill cont on D908 sp Marseille. Site on R at end vill after g'ge. 3*, Med, mkd, hdstg, shd, pt sl, EHU (3-10A) €3-5; gas; bbq; red long stay; TV; 50% statics; Eng spkn; adv bkg acc; ccard acc; tennis; CKE. *"Excel facs & site; helpful owner; poss diff manoeuvring onto pitches for lge o'fits; few water points; gd touring area."* **€27.00, 1 Mar-5 Nov.** **2017**

FRANCE

TREVIERES *1D4* (1.4km NE Rural) *49.31308, -0.90578*
Camp Municipal Sous Les Pommiers, Rue du Pont de
la Barre, 14710 Trévières **02 31 92 89 24 or 06 24 06
10 92; mairie@ville-trevieres.fr; http://trevieres.eu/
camping-municipal/**

🛏(cont) ⓦⓓ 🚿 ⅙ 🖵 🖉 ᴹᴾ 🦋 🕈 ⊕ 🐟 nr ⚱

Turn S off N13 onto D30 sp Trévières. Site on R on
ent to vill. 2*, Med, mkd, hdg, pt shd, EHU (10A) €3;
adv bkg rec; rv fishing adj; CKE. *"Delightful site in
apple orchard; lge pitches; vg san facs; conv D-Day
beaches; excel site; sm town in walking dist."*
€14.00, 1 Apr-30 Sep. 2019

TRIE-SUR-BAISE *8F2* (22km WNW Urban) *43.388595,
0.155504* **Camping Municipal La Galotte,** 44 Rue de
Mirande, 65140 Rabastens de Bigorre **05 62 36 57 64
or 06 10 35 34 95; camping.lagalotte@gmail.com;
www.camping-lagalotte.com**

🛏 ⓦⓓ 🚿 🖵 🖉 ᴹᴾ 🦋 🐟 nr

Turn R (fr Tarbes, S) in ctr of Rabastens-de-Bigorre
and foll N21. Site on R on outskirts of town abt 1km.
Sm, shd, EHU (10A); gas; bbq (charcoal, elec, gas, sep
area); twin axles; Eng spkn; adv bkg acc; CKE. *"Gd,
basic site on edge of vill; suitable for short stays."*
NP 19.8, 1 Apr-30 Sep. 2018

"There aren't many sites open at this time of year"

If you're travelling outside peak season
remember to call ahead to check site opening
dates – even if the entry says 'open all year'.

TROYES *4E4* (3km NE Urban) *48.31150, 4.09630*
Camp Municipal de Troyes, 7 Rue Roger Salengro,
10150 Pont-Ste Marie **03 25 81 02 64; info@troyes
camping.net; www.troyescamping.net**

🛏 €1.15 🛏(htd) ⓦⓓ 🚿 ⅙ 🖵 🖉 ᴹᴾ 🕈 ⊕ nr ♨ 🐟 ⚱ 🛶 (htd)

Fr N exit A26 junc 22 onto D677. site on R opp
stadium & adj Esso g'ge, just pass junc with D960.
Fr S exit A26 junc 23 for Pont-Ste-Marie. Pont-Ste-
Marie & site 'municipal' well sp fr all dirs & in town.
NB Queues form onto rd outside site, use Esso g'ge
to turn if queue too long. 3*, Med, hdstg, hdg, mkd,
pt shd, EHU (10A) (long lead poss req); gas; bbq; red
long stay; TV; bus opp; Eng spkn; adv bkg acc; ccard
acc; games area; bike hire; games rm; CKE. *"Busy,
popular, transit site in parkland - rec arr early; can
be noisy at w/ends; vg pool; some lge pitches; some
pitches soft when wet; diff access some pitches; twin
axles acc at recep's discretion; red facs LS; takeaway;
Troyes Cathedral, museums & old quarter worth visit;
Lac d'Orient & Lac du Temple nrby; conv NH; gd rest by
rv bdge 3 min fr site; conv for m'way; pleasant friendly
site; clean facs; excel snacks/rest; stay 7 nights pay for
6."* **€27.00, 1 Apr-16 Oct.** 2017

TROYES *4E4* (16km E Rural) *48.28998, 4.28279*
Camping La Fromentelle, Ferme Fromentelle, 10220
Dosches **03 25 41 52 67; www.tourisme-champagne-
ardenne.com**

🛏 €1.50 🛏 ⓦⓓ 🚿 ⅙ 🖉 ᴹᴾ 🦋 🐟 nr ⚱ 🌲 sand 5km

Exit A26 junc 23 onto D619 dir Bar-sur-Aube. In
8.5km turn L onto D1 sp Géraudot (take care bends).
Site on L in 5km. 2*, Sm, mkd, pt shd, pt sl, EHU
(6-10A) €3 (long lead poss req)(poss rev pol); bbq; sw
nr; adv bkg acc; games area; CKE. *"Beautiful, lovely
farm/CL-type site in old orchard; well-kept & well-run;
warm welcome, charming owner; v clean san facs; gd for
birdwatching, sailing, watersports on lakes; excel cycle
tracks; nr nature reserve, lakes & forest; conv A26; excel
spacious pitches; gd facs; some rd noise; hg rec old town
in Troyes."* **€15.00, 30 Apr-15 Oct.** 2018

TROYES *4E4* (14km SE Rural) *48.20106, 4.16620*
Le Base de Loisirs au Plan d'Eau 'Les Terres Rouges',
10390 Cléry **06 70 00 76 75; terres-rouges@
wanadoo.fr; www.les-terres-rouges.com**

🛏 🛏(htd) ⓦⓓ 🚿 ⅙ 🖉 🕈 ⅄ ⊕ 🐟 nr ⚱

Exit A5 junc 21 onto D671 S dir Bar-sur-Seine &
Dijon; site on R in 3.5km. Or SE fr Troyes on D671
dir Bar-sur-Seine, foll sp Cléry; then as bef. Site
well sp. App over gravel track thro gravel quarry
area. 2*, Sm, hdstg, pt shd, EHU (5-10A) €3.20
(poss rev pol); sw; 10% statics; phone; adv bkg acc;
tennis; waterskiing; fishing; boating; CKE. *"Gd, basic
NH; clean, v basic san facs; friendly, helpful new
owners(2017); gate opens 0600, recep clsd 1900;
conv fr a'route to Calais; commuter traff noise."*
€19.00, 2 April-30 Sep. 2017

TUCHAN *8G4* (1km S Rural) *42.88302, 2.71861*
Camping La Peiriere, route de Paziols, 11350 Tuchan
**04 68 45 46 50; lapeiriere@lapeiriere.com;
www.lapeiriere.com**

🛏 €3 🛏 ⓦⓓ 🚿 ⅙ 🖉 ᴹᴾ 🕈 ⅄ ⊕ ♨ ⚱ 🛶 🖐

Fr Tuchan dir Paziols on L, 200m fr edge of town.
Med, hdg, mkd, shd, EHU (9A); bbq; 10% statics; bus
adj; Eng spkn; adv bkg acc; CKE. *"Mini farm & free lake
fishing on site; excel base; access rds are v tight; vg."*
€26.00, 1 Apr-30 Sep. 2016

URCAY *4H3* (6km NE Rural) *46.6430, 2.6620*
Camping Champ de la Chapelle, St Bonnet-Tronçais,
03360 Braize **00 33 470 07 82 46; simon.swinn@sfr.fr;
www.champdelachapelle.com**

🛏 €1 🛏 ⓦⓓ 🚿 ⅙ 🖉 🕈 ⅄ ⊕ nr ♨ 🐟 ⚱ 🛶

Fr D2144 take D978A for Tronçais. 1.5km on L
fr rndabt(Montaloyer) x-ing D28. Site sp.
3*, Med, mkd, pt shd, pt sl, EHU (10A) inc; sw nr;
10% statics; Eng spkn; adv bkg acc; ccard acc; games
area; CKE. *"Excel walking & flora/fauna in ancient oak
forest; some lge pitches; peaceful site; new British
owner (2016)."* **€22.00, 14 Apr-17 Oct.** 2019

FRANCE

URDOS *8G2* (0.5km N Rural) *42.87705, -0.55670*
Camp Municipal Le Gave d'Aspe, 64490 Urdos
05 59 34 88 26; guittonb@hotmail.com

🏕️ wc ♨ 🖪 / mp ☕ ⓨ Ⲧ nr ⓦ nr ☕ nr 🚶 ⛷️

Turn W off N134 onto site access rd by disused
Urdos stn approx 1km bef vill, clear sp. Other
access rds in vill v diff lge o'fits. 2*, Sm, mkd,
pt shd, pt sl, EHU (10A) €2.40; bbq; phone; Eng
spkn; adv bkg acc; ccard acc; rv; CKE. *"Adj Rv Aspe;
14km fr Col du Somport/Tunnel; surrounded by
mountains; conv x-ing into Spain; vg; lovely sm site;
beautiful mountain scenery; gd facs; gd walking."*
€16.00, 1 May-15 Sep. **2017**

URT *8F1* (0.9km E Rural) *43.49353, -1.27960* Camping
Ferme Mimizan, 64240 Urt 05 59 56 21 51; contact@
lafermedemimizan.fr; www.lafermedemimizan.fr

12 🏕️ ♨ / ⓨ 🚶 ⛷️ 🖼️

E fr Bayonne on A64/E80, exit junc 4 sp Urt; in vill
turn sharp R at PO & foll sps; site on R in 1km. Fr N
on D12 cross Rv Adour by metal bdge & turn L
immed past church, site on R in 1.5km.
2*, Med, pt shd, EHU (10A) €3.50; 10% statics; adv
bkg acc; CKE. *"V peaceful out of ssn; friendly owners;
gd walking & cycling; conv coast & Pyrenees; gd NH."*
€19.50 **2017**

UZERCHE *7B3* (8km NE Rural) *45.45200, 1.65056*
Camping Aimée Porcher (Naturist), 19140
Pingrieux Eyburie 05 55 73 20 97 or 06 01 11 51 90;
aimeeporcher@hotmail.com; www.aimee-porcher.com

🐕 🏕️ wc ♨ 🖪 🖪 / ⓨ ⓨ Ⲧ 🚶

Fr Uzerche take D3 NE to Eyburie & in Eyburie
turn R at site sp (Cheyron/Pingrieux). In 1km turn
L at site sp; site at end of narr lane. 2*, Sm, mkd,
pt shd, terr, EHU (6A) (poss long lead req); bbq;
sw nr; red long stay; adv bkg acc; games area; INF
card. *"Beautiful views; wonderful location; INF not
req; excel san facs; spacious pitches; basic; site rd
steep in places; superb; v friendly Dutch owners."*
€26.50, 20 May-11 Sep. **2017**

UZES *10E2* (2km E Rural) *44.03202, 4.45557*
Camping Le Moulin Neuf, 30700 St Quentin-la-
Poterie 04 66 22 17 21; lemoulinneuf@yahoo.fr;
www.le-moulin-neuf.fr

🐕 €1.50 🏕️ wc ♨ 🖪 / mp ☕ ⓨ Ⲧ 🖪 ☕ 🚶 ⛷️ (htd)

N fr Uzès on D982; after 3km turn L onto D5; in
1.5km fork R, keeping on D5; in 200m turn R onto
D405 (Chemin du Moulin Neuf); site on L in 500m.
3*, Med, mkd, pt shd, EHU (5A) €3.50; 10% statics;
fishing; horseriding; bike hire; tennis. *"Site off beaten
track; busy high ssn, rec phone in adv; conv touring base;
o'night m'van area; barrier clsd 2230-0700; poss mosquito
problem; Uzès a lovely town; wonderful helpful staff;
excel facs."* **€24.50, 1 Apr-22 Sep.** **2017**

VAISON LA ROMAINE *9D2* (1.5km NE Urban)
44.24472, 5.07861 Camping du Théâtre Romain,
Chemin du Brusquet, 84110 Vaison-la-Romaine 04 90
28 78 66; info@camping-theatre.com;
www.camping-theatre.com

🐕 €2 🏕️ (htd) wc ♨ ♨ 🖪 / ☕ ⓨ ⓨ Ⲧ ☕ nr 🚶 ⛷️

Fr D975, cont onto Ave de Martigny to Chemin du
Brusquet. Foll sp for Théâtre Romain & site. Ent to
Chemin du Busquet on rndabt at Théâtre Romain.
Or site sp off Orange-Nyons rd thro town (do not
ent town cent). 4*, Med, hdg, mkd, pt shd, serviced
pitches; EHU (5-10A); bbq; 10% statics; Eng spkn;
adv bkg req; ccard acc; games rm; CKE. *"Excel, well-
kept, friendly site; busy LS due long stay residents,
rec book in adv; mainly gd sized pitches but some sm;
most pitches suitable m'vans; clean, unisex san facs;
attractive town; mkt Tues; highly rec; excel as usual;
old Roman town cent, 10 mins walk fr campsite; conv
for town; refurbed sw & new paddling pool (2016); long
stay red."* **€28.00, 15 Mar-5 Nov.** **2019**

VAISON LA ROMAINE *9D2* (3.7km SE Rural)
44.22357, 5.10428 Camping Le Voconce, route de
St Marcellin, 84110 St Marcellin 04 90 36 28 10;
contact@camping-voconce.com; www.camping-
voconce.com

🐕 €3-4 🏕️ wc ♨ 🖪 🖪 / ⓨ ⓨ Ⲧ ☕ nr 🚶 🖼️ ⛷️

Fr Vaison S on D977. Turn L onto D938 after 1km.
Turn R onto D151 after 0.5km to St Marcellin-les-
Vaison. Turn R at rndabt by a chapel & foll sp to
site. 3*, Med, mkd, hdg, pt shd, EHU (10A) €5; gas;
15% statics; Eng spkn; adv bkg acc; ccard acc; games
area; CKE. *"Tranquil site bet 2 vineyards; friendly, fam
run site; vg base for cycling, walking & exploring;
boules; great views; acc to rv; vg."*
€24.00, 1 Apr-15 Oct. **2016**

VAL D'ISERE *9B4* (1km E Rural) *45.44622, 6.99218*
Camping Les Richardes, Le Laisinant, 73150 Val-
d'Isère 04 79 06 26 60; campinglesrichardes@free.fr;
www.campinglesrichardes.free.fr

🐕 €0.50 🏕️ ♨ / ⓨ

Leave Val d'Isère going E twds Col de l'Iseran on
D902, site on R 1.5km bef Le Fornet vill.
1*, Med, unshd, pt sl, EHU (3-6A) €1.90-3.80; CKE.
"Peaceful site; pool 1.5km; delightful owner."
€13.00, 15 Jun-15 Sep. **2016**

VALENCAY *4H2* (1.7km W Urban) *47.15656, 1.55202*
Camp Municipal Les Chênes, Route de Loches,
36600 Valençay **02 54 00 03 92 or 02 54 00 32 32;**
www.valencay.fr

🏕 👫 ⌨ 🛁 🚿 🔥 🍴 ✈ 🦋 🏊nr 🏔

App town fr E on D960 or N/S on D956, foll sp for
D960 Luçay-le-Mâle. D960 is next L in town. Foll
sp for pool & camping. Site adj pool mkd by flags.
3*, Sm, hdg, mkd, pt shd, EHU (6A) €3.20 (poss rev
pol); bbq; red long stay; TV; adv bkg acc; fishing;
tennis adj; CKE. *"Excel, well-kept site in parkland with
lake; lge pitches; gd, clean facs; poss muddy after
heavy rain; htd pool adj (high ssn); gate clsd 2100-
0700; sh walk to impressive chateau; day's drive to
Calais or Le Havre ferries; motor museum & vill 1km."*
€15.00, 1 May-30 Sep. 2015

VALENCE *9C2* (8.5km N Rural) *44.99723, 4.89383*
Camping Le Soleil Fruité, Les Pêches, 26300
Chateauneuf-sur-Isère **04 75 84 19 70; contact@
lesoleilfruite.com; www.lesoleilfruite.com**

🏕 €2 👫 ⌨ 🛁 🚿 🔥 🍴 🗺 🦋 ♿ 🍴 🏊 🏔 ✎ 🚣 ⛵

Exit A7 junc 14 Valence Nord onto D67 sp
Chateauneuf-sur-Isère, site sp to W of vill. Alt rte
foll N7 turn onto D877 twrds Chateauneuf and
foll sp to campsite. 4*, Med, hdg, mkd, pt shd, EHU
(10A) €4; bbq; TV; 15% statics; phone; Eng spkn;
adv bkg acc; ccard acc; CKE. *"Vg, family-run site; lge
pitches; friendly owner; no dogs high ssn; excel, clean,
modern san facs; rest/takeaway open early Jun (2011);
ltd water pnts; cycle friendly; gd bar/rest; smart
site; v busy HS; gd for families with young children."*
€33.00, 26 Apr-15 Sep. 2016

VALENCE *9C2* (9km NW Rural) *45.00726, 4.84862*
Camp Municipal Les Vernes, 26600 La Roche-de-Glun
**04 75 84 54 11 or 04 75 84 60 52 (Mairie); mairie.rdg@
wanadoo.fr; www.ladrometourisme.com**

👫 ⌨ 🛁 🚿 🔥 🍴 🦋 🏊nr

Turn W off N7 at Pont-d'Isère. On ent La Roche-de-
Glun foll camping sp. 4*, Sm, mkd, hdg, shd, serviced
pitches; EHU (10A) €1.40; bbq; 50% statics; phone; adv
bkg acc; CKE. *"Pleasant site; friendly resident warden;
htd pool adj in ssn inc; sports cent adj; gd, clean san facs;
vg municipal pool adj; barrier clsd 2200-0700; vg value;
vg NH."* **€17.00, 1 May-30 Sep.** 2015

VALLOIRE *9C3* (0.5km N Rural) *45.17000, 6.42960*
Camp Caravaneige Municipal Ste Thècle, Route des
Villards, 73450 Valloire **04 79 83 30 11; camping-
caravaneige@valloire.net; www.valloire.net**

🏕 👫 (htd) ⌨ 🛁 🚿 🔥 🍴 🗺 🦋 🍴 🏊nr ♿nr 🏔
🚣 ⛷

Exit A43 junc 29 onto D306 to St Michel-de-
Maurienne, then onto D902 to Valloire. At vill mkt
turn R over rv to site. Climb fr valley 15% gradient
max. 3*, Med, hdstg, mkd, unshd, EHU (13A) €3.60;
red long stay; TV; bus; Eng spkn; adv bkg acc; ccard
acc; waterslide; tennis; fishing. *"Superb mountain
scenery for walking & cycling; fitness rm; bar 200m;
excel, well kept site."*
€20.00, 12 Dec-23 Apr & 1 Jun-30 Sep. 2015

VALLON EN SULLY *7A4* (1.2km SE Rural) *46.53019,
2.61447* Camp Municipal Les Soupirs, Allée des
Soupirs, 03190 Vallon-en-Sully **04 70 06 50 96 or 04
70 06 50 10 (LS); mairie.vallonensully@wanadoo.fr**

🏕 👫 (cont) ⌨ 🛁 ✎ 🦋 🍴nr ♿nr 🏊nr

N fr Montluçon on D2144; in 23km at traff lts where
D11 crosses D2144 turn L & foll camping sp for
Vallon-en-Sully. After bdge over Rv Cher turn L in
50m. Site in 500m. If N or S on A71 exit at junc 9
Vallon-en-Sully; turn N on D2144; in 3km at traff
lts turn L. 2*, Med, pt shd, EHU (6-20A) €2-4; TV;
bus 500m; adv bkg acc. *"Peaceful, spacious site on
banks of rv & canal; immac san facs; lge pitches; risk
of flooding in wet; gd cycling along canal; gd NH; vg."*
€10.40, 1 Jul-12 Sep. 2017

VALLON PONT D'ARC *9D2* (1km SE Rural) *44.39777,
4.39861* Camping Nature Park L'Ardéchois, Route
des Gorges de l'Ardèche, 07150 Vallon-Pont-d'Arc
**04 75 88 06 63; info@ardechois-camping.com;
www.ardechois-camping.com**

🏕 €9 👫 (htd) ⌨ 🛁 🚿 🔥 🍴 🗺 🦋 🍴 🏊 ♿ 🏊 🏔 ✎
🚣 (htd) ⛵

Fr Vallon take D290 Rte des Gorges & site on R bet
rd & rv. 5*, Lge, hdstg, mkd, hdg, shd, pt sl, serviced
pitches; EHU (6-10A) inc; gas; bbq; TV; Eng spkn; adv
bkg acc; ccard acc; tennis; bike hire; canoeing; games
area; CKE. *"Spectacular scenery; private bthrm avail
(by reservation); excel rvside site; helpful staff; price
depends on size of pitch; gd san facs; 5 star site."*
€60.00, 4 Apr-10 Sep, M14. 2019

See advertisement

VALLON PONT D'ARC *9D2* (1.5km SE Rural) *44.39467, 4.39909* **Mondial Camping,** Route des Gorges, 07150 Vallon-Pont-d'Arc **04 75 88 00 44; reserv-info@mondial-camping.com; www.mondial-camping.com**

🏕€4.50 � (htd) 🔲 ▲ 🌐 🛁 🔲 ∥ (msp) 🦋 ⚑ Ψ 🍴 ⑪ 🍴 🗲 🛝 🎣 🦺(htd) 🛶

Fr N exit A7 Montélimar Nord junc 17 onto N7 then N102 dir Le Teil, Villeneuve-de-Berg. Turn S onto D103/D579 dir Vogüé, Ruoms then Vallon-Pont-d'Arc. Take D290, Rte des Gorges de l'Ardèche to site in 1.5km. Fr S exit A7 junc 19 at Bollène, dir Bourg-St Andéol, then D4 to St Remèze & Vallon-Pont-d'Arc. App to Vallon fr E thro Gorges de l'Ardeche not rec. 4*, Lge, mkd, hdg, shd, serviced pitches; EHU (6-10A) inc; gas; TV; 10% statics; phone; Eng spkn; adv bkg acc; ccard acc; tennis adj; canoeing; games rm; CKE. *"Dir access to rv, Ardèche gorges & canoe facs; gd touring base; waterslides & aqua park; excel site."* **€42.00, 1 Apr-30 Sep.** 2017

VALLON PONT D'ARC *9D2* (4.6km S Rural) *44.39333, 4.39465* **Camping Le Clapas,** La Vernède, 07150 Salavas **04 75 37 14 76; contact@camping-le-clapas.com; www.camping-le-clapas.com**

🏕€2 ♕ 🔲 ▲ 🛁 🔲 ∥ 🦋 ⚑ Ψ 🍴 ⑪ nr 🍴 🗲 🛝 🎣

D579 S fr Vallon-Pont-d'Arc to Salavas; 250m after Salavas turn L. Well sp. Med, mkd, shd, pt sl, EHU (10A) €3; bbq (elec, gas); sw; TV; Eng spkn; adv bkg acc; ccard acc; games rm; rafting; fishing; canoeing; games area; CKE. *"Beautiful, well-kept site by Rv Ardèche with beach; friendly, helpful staff; poss diff lge o'fits; canyoning; conv Ardèche Gorges; excel; French adaptor needed, site sells or loans."* **€27.50, 17 Apr-27 Sep.** 2015

VALLON PONT D'ARC *9D2* (2km W Rural) *44.41517, 4.37796* **Domaine de L'Esquiras,** chemin du Fez, 07150 Vallon-Pont-d'Arc **04 75 88 04 16; esquiras@orange.fr; www.camping-esquiras.com**

🏕€3.50 ♕ 🔲 ▲ 🛁 🔲 ∥ (msp) Ψ 🍴 ⑪ 🍴 🗲 🎣 🛶

Fr Ruoms L at rndabt bef the Lidl nr the vill. Foll sp. Fr Vallon foll dir Ruoms. R after Lidl. 4*, Med, mkd, pt shd, pt sl, gas; twin axles; TV; phone; Eng spkn; adv bkg acc; ccard acc; games area; games rm; CKE. *"Lovely vill (10 min walk) with lots of bars & rest; caving, climbing or kayaking; excel; ACSI acc."* **€40.00, 25 Mar-30 Sep.** 2016

FRANCE

VALLON PONT D'ARC *9D2* (4km W Rural) *44.41251, 4.35018* **Camping L'Arc en Ciel,** Route de Ruoms, Les Mazes, 07150 Vallon-Pont-d'Arc **04 75 88 04 65;** camping.arcenciel@wanadoo.fr; www.arcenciel-camping.com

🐕 €3.50 ♦♦ wo ♨ ♿ 🗑 🧺 🦋 ☂ 🍴 ⊕ 🛒 ♨ ⚠ 🏊 ☂ 🛶

Fr Ruoms take D579 dir Vallon. After 4km bear R for Les Mazes. Pass thro vill & in about 1.7km bear L at camp sp. 3*, Lge, pt shd, pt sl, EHU (10A) €4; bbq (elec, gas); 10% statics; bus; adv bkg acc; ccard acc; games rm; rv; canoeing; horseriding nr; tennis nr; fishing. *"Pleasant site on rv bank; excel; some pitches diff to access."* **€41.00, 29 Apr-18 Sep.** 2016

VALLORCINE *9A4* (1km SE Rural) *46.0242, 6.92370* **Camping des Montets,** Le Buet, 74660 Vallorcine **06 79 02 18 81;** b.stam@orange.fr; http://camping-montets.com

🐕 ♦♦ wo ♨ ♿ 🗑 🦋 ⊕ 🛒 ♨ nr

N fr Chamonix on D1506 via Col de Montets; Le Buet 2km S of Vallorcine; site sp nr Le Buet stn. Fr Martigny (Switzerland) cross border via Col de la Forclaz; then D1506 to Vallorcine; cont to Le Buet in 1km. 2*, Med, hdg, mkd, pt shd, EHU (3-6A) €2-3; red long stay; train 500m; Eng spkn; tennis adj; CKE. *"Site with spectacular views; friendly owners; ltd flat pitches for o'fits (others for tents in field), rec phone ahead; clean san facs; excel walking direct fr site; free train pass to Chamonix; vg."* **€16.00, 1 Jun-15 Sep.** 2016

VALRAS PLAGE *7E3* (2.5km SW Coastal) *43.227408, 3.243536* **Camping Sandaya Blue Bayou,** Vendres Plage Ouest 34350, Valras-Plage **04 67 37 41 97** or **04 11 32 90 00;** www.sandaya.fr/nos-campings/blue-bayou

🐕 🐕 ♦♦(htd) wo ♨ ♿ 🗑 🦋 ☂ 🍴 ⊕ 🛒 ♨ ⚠ 🏊 ☂(htd) 🛶 ☂ sandy 0.5

Take exit 36 off the A9. Then onto the D64 twrds Vendres-Plage. 5*, Mkd, unshd, EHU 10A; bbq (elec, gas); TV; Eng spkn; ccard acc; bike hire; beauty ctr; fishing; watersports. **€67.00, 12 Apr-14 Sep.** 2019

VALRAS PLAGE *10F1* (3km SW Coastal) *43.23101, 3.25330* **Sandaya Les Vagues,** Chemin des Montilles, 34350 Vendres-Plage **04 67 37 03 62;** vag@sandaya.fr; www.sandaya.co.uk

🐕 €5 ♦♦ ♨ ♿ 🗑 🦋 ☂ 🍴 ⊕ 🛒 ♨ ⚠ 🏊 ☂(htd) 🛶 ☂ sand 400m

Exit A9 junc 36 onto D64 to Valras-Plage then Vendres-Plage. Site sp. 4*, Lge, pt shd, EHU (10A) inc; bbq (sep area); TV; 75% statics; Eng spkn; adv bkg acc; games area; horseriding 5km; waterslide; jacuzzi. *"Recep helpful; clean san facs; wave machine excel."* **€25.00, 20 May-13 Sep.** 2019

VALRAS PLAGE *10F1* (6km NW Rural) *43.29273, 3.26710* **Camping La Gabinelle,** 7 Rue de la Grille, 34410 Sauvian **04 67 39 50 87;** info@lagabinelle.com; www.lagabinelle.com

🐕 €3.50 ♦♦ wo ♨ ♿ 🗑 🦋 ☂ 🍴 ⊕ nr ♨ nr ⚠ 🏊 ☂ sand 5km

Exit A9 at Béziers Ouest, turn R twd beaches sp S to Sauvian on D19. Site 500m on L thro town. 3*, Med, pt shd, EHU (6A) €3; red long stay; TV; adv bkg acc; fishing 1km; tennis; games area; games rm. *"Friendly, helpful staff; suitable lge m'vans; canoeing 2km; LS ltd san facs & poss unkempt; sh walk to delightful old vill; popular; bar/pool shut LS."* **€13.80, 12 Apr-12 Sep.** 2016

VALREAS *9D2* (1km N Rural) *44.39264, 4.99245* **Camping La Coronne,** Route de Pègue, 84600 Valréas **04 88 70 00 13;** contact@lacoronne.com; www.vaucluse-camping.fr

🐕 €4 ♦♦ wo ♨ ♿ 🗑 mp 🦋 ☂ 🍴 ⊕ 🛒 ♨ ⚠ 🏊 ☂ 🛶

Fr Nyons take D538 W to Valréas. Exit town on D10 rd to Taulignan, immed after x-ing bdge over Rv Coronne turn R into D196 sp Le Pègue. Site on R in 100m on rvside. Sp app fr E but easy to miss; app fr W; well sp in Valréas. 3*, Med, hdg, mkd, pt shd, EHU (6A) inc; gas; bbq; TV; phone; Eng spkn; adv bkg acc; ccard acc; fishing; CKE. *"Sm pitches; excel pool; facs need refurb & poss unclean; site clsd 2200-0700."* **€25.70, 31 Mar-15 Oct.** 2017

For a guide to symbols see the fold out on the rear cover

VANDENESSE EN AUXOIS *6G1* (2.5km NE Rural) *47.23661, 4.62880* **Camping Le Lac de Panthier,** 21320 Vandenesse-en-Auxois **03 80 49 21 94; info@lac-de-panthier.com; www.lac-de-panthier.com**

€3 (covrd, htd)

Exit A6 junc 24 (A38) at Pouilly-en-Auxois; foll D16/D18 to Vandenesse; turn L on D977bis, cross canal bdge & cont strt for 3km to site on L. Fr SW (Autun) on D981 approx 12km after Arnay-le-Duc turn R onto D994 sp Châteauneuf. At x-rds cont onto D977bis then as above. 4*, Lge, hdg, mkd, pt shd, pt sl, terr, EHU (6A) inc (some rev pol); bbq; TV (pitch); adv bkg req; fishing; waterslide; bike hire; sauna; CKE. *"Lovely area; Oct open Fri, Sat & Sun; views fr higher pitches; well-run site operating with Les Voiliers adj; lge pitches, most sl & blocks req; facs poss stretched high ssn, adequate; gd cycling & walks round lake; popular NH; vg."* **€28.00, 1 Apr-28 Sep, L31.** **2019**

"Satellite navigation makes touring much easier"

Remember most sat navs don't know if you're towing or in a larger vehicle – always use yours alongside maps and site directions.

VANNES *2F3* (3km S Rural) *47.62754, -2.74117* **FFCC Camping Moulin de Cantizac,** 2 Rue des Orchidées, 56860 Séné **02 98 92 53 52; info@camping-vannes.com; www.camping-vannes.com**

12 €2.30 (htd) sand 4km

S fr Vannes on D199 twds Séné. Site on L at rndabt beside rv. 3*, Med, hdg, pt shd, pt sl, EHU (10A) €3.90; gas; 50% statics; ccard acc; games rm; boating; games area. *"Superb cent for birdwatching; excel new facs; buses to Vannes."* **€29.00** **2019**

VANNES *2F3* (4km SW Coastal) *47.63365, -2.78008* **Flower Camping Le Conleau (formerly Municipal),** 188 Ave Maréchal Juin, 56000 Vannes **02 97 63 13 88; camping.conleau@flowercampings.com; en.vannes-camping.com**

€3 (covrd, htd) sand 300m

Exit N165 at Vannes Ouest junc; Conleau sp on R. Site twd end of rd on R. If on N165 fr Auray take 1st exit sp Vannes & at 2nd rndabt R (sp) to avoid town cent. C'vans not allowed thro town cent. 4*, Lge, mkd, hdg, pt shd, pt sl, EHU (6A) €3.50 (some rev pol); bbq; twin axles; TV; 20% statics; phone; bus adj; Eng spkn; adv bkg acc; ccard acc; games area; bike hire; CKE. *"Most pitches sl; sep area for m'vans by rd - little shd & poss long walk to san facs; v busy/noisy in high ssn; sea water pool nr; lovely easy walk to Port Conleau; site full of atmosphere - rec; excel; great location & facs."* **€32.00, 1 Apr-1 Oct.** **2017**

VANNES *2F3* (5km SW Coastal) *47.62190, -2.80056* **Camping de Penboch,** 9 Chemin de Penboch, 56610 Arradon **02 97 44 71 29; camping.penboch@orange.fr; www.camping-penboch.fr**

€3.50 (covrd, htd, indoor) sand 200m

Exit Brest-Nantes N165 Vannes by-pass at junc with D127 sp Ploeren & Arradon. Foll sp Arradon. Site well sp. 4*, Lge, mkd, hdg, pt shd, EHU (10A) inc (poss rev pol); gas; bbq; TV; 10% statics; Eng spkn; adv bkg rec; ccard acc; games rm; waterslide; games area; playground; CKE. *"Excel site; gd clean san facs; bike hire 2km; some pitches sm; steel pegs req; o'flow area with facs; no o'fits over 7m high ssn; plenty for youngsters; 20 mins walk to Arradon; gd coast walks."* **€41.00, 12 Apr-26 Sep, B33.** **2019**

VANS, LES *9D1* (2.5km E Rural) *44.40953, 4.16768* **Camping Domaine des Chênes,** 07140 Chassagnes-Haut **04 75 37 34 35; reception@domaine-des-chenes.fr; www.domaine-des-chenes.fr**

€2.50

Fr town cent take D104A dir Aubenas. After Peugeot g'ge turn R onto D295 at garden cent twd Chassagnes. Site on L after 2km; sp adj Rv Chassezac. 3*, Med, pt shd, pt sl, terr, EHU (10A) inc; bbq; 80% statics; adv bkg acc; ccard acc; rv fishing 500m; CKE. *"Lovely shady site; ideal for birdwatchers; gd rest; rec."* **€18.00, 4 Apr-27 Sep.** **2016**

VARENNES EN ARGONNE *5D1* (0.4km N Rural) *49.22935, 5.03424* **Camp Municipal Le Pâquis,** Rue St Jean, 55270 Varennes-en-Argonne **03 29 80 71 01 (Mairie); mairievarennesenargonne@wanadoo.fr; www.varennesenargonne.fr/pages/annexe/reglement-du-camping**

€0.40 nr

On D946 Vouziers/Clermont-en-Argonne rd; sp by bdge in vill, on banks of Rv Aire, 200m N of bdge. NB Ignore sp by bdge to Camping Lac Vert (not nr). 2*, Med, pt shd, EHU (6-16A) €3.65; bbq; Eng spkn; rv fishing. *"Pleasant site with gd facs; gd (hilly) cycle ride taking in US WWI cemetary."* **€14.60, 31 Mar-6 Oct.** **2019**

VARILHES *8G3* (0.4km NE Urban) *43.04714, 1.63096* **FFCC Camp Municipal du Parc du Château,** Ave de 8 Mai 1945, 09120 Varilhes **05 61 67 42 84 or 05 61 60 55 54 (TO); campingdevarilhes@orange.fr; www.campingdevarilhes.com**

12 (htd) nr nr nr

Exit N20/E9 at sp Varilhes. Turn N in town on D624. Site 250m on L (sp) just bef leisure cent adj Rv Ariège. 2*, Med, mkd, pt shd, terr, EHU (5-10A) €5.90-6.40; 20% statics; adv bkg acc; rv fishing adj; games area. *"Shwr & sinks locked 2100-0700; hot water unreliable."* **€13.00** **2018**

VARILHES *8G3* (3km NW Rural) *43.06258, 1.62101*
FFCC Camping Les Mijeannes, Route de Ferriès,
09120 Rieux-de-Pelleport **05 61 60 82 23;**
www.vap-camping.fr

12 🐕 €1.10 ♟(htd) ⬛ ⛟ ✈ 🦋 ♈ 🍷 ⚂ 🏊

Exit N20 sp Varilhes; on app Varilhes cent join 1-way
system; 1st R at Hôtel de Ville; over rv bdge; foll
camp sps; site 2km on R. 3*, Med, hdg, pt shd, EHU
(10A) €4.60; bbq; TV; Eng spkn; adv bkg acc; fishing;
games area; CKE. *"Peaceful site by rv, on island formed
by rv; ACSI; helpful owner; kids club; badminton; gd size
pitches; excel san facs; weekly theme nights high ssn;
volley; excel; ltd facs LS."* **€27.00**   **2017**

VATAN *4H3* (9km N Rural) *47.13479, 1.85121*
Camp Municipal St Phalier, 2 Chemin Trompe-Souris,
18310 Graçay **02 48 51 24 14 or 02 48 51 42 07**
(Mairie); camping-gracay@wanadoo.fr;
www.camping.gracay.info

🐕 €1.02 ♟ ⬛ ✈ 🦋 🏔

Leave A20 at junc 9 & take D83 to Graçay. On o'skts
of vill turn L & immed turn L foll sp to Cent
Omnisport & site. 2*, Sm, pt shd, EHU (10A) €2.69;
phone; Eng spkn; fishing; CKE. *"Lovely, peaceful, well-
kept, pleasant site by sm unfenced lake & park; plenty
of space lge o'fits - site yourself; excel clean san facs;
poss travellers, but no problem; rest nr; bar nr; pool
adj; shop nr; vill in walking dist; gd NH fr A20."*
€8.70, 1 Apr-15 Sep.   **2016**

VATAN *4H3* (0.5km W Urban) *47.07131, 1.80573*
Camp Municipal de la Ruelle au Loup, Rue du Collège,
36150 Vatan **02 54 49 91 37 or 02 54 49 76 31**
(Mairie); vatan-mairie1@wanadoo.fr; www.vatan-
en-berry.com

♟ ✈ ⛟ ⬛ ✈ 🦋 ⚂nr ⚂nr 🏔

Exit A20 junc 10 onto D922 to town cent. Take D2
dir Guilly & foll site sp - 2nd on L (easily missed).
2*, Med, hdg, mkd, pt shd, EHU (10A) inc (rev pol);
adv bkg acc; CKE. *"Pleasant, well-kept, beautiful site
in park o'looking lake; spacious pitches; v clean; gd san
facs (2019); twin axles; warden onsite daytime into
early eve; easy access fr a'route; pool adj; conv Loire
chateaux."* **€17.00, 15 Apr-15 Sep.**   **2019**

VAUVERT *10E2* (6km SE Rural) *43.65440, 4.29610*
FLOWER Camping Le Mas de Mourgues, Gallician,
30600 Vauvert **04 66 73 30 88;** info@masdemourgues.
com; www.masdemourgues.com or www.flower
campings.com

🐕 €3 ♟ ⬛ ✈ ⛟ ⬛ ✈ 🦋 ♈ ⚂ 🏊

Exit A9 junc 26 onto D6313/D6572. Site on L at x-rds
with D779 sp to Gallician & Stes Marie-de-la-Mer.
2*, Med, mkd, pt shd, EHU (6A) inc; bbq; 15% statics;
phone; Eng spkn; adv bkg acc; ccard acc; games area;
CKE. *"Enthusiastic, helpful British owners; some diff,
long narr pitches; grnd stony; rd & farming noise; clean
facs but poss stretched high ssn; excel pool; excel
cycling; vg site."* **€27.00, 15 Mar-15 Oct.**   **2015**

VENAREY LES LAUMES *6G1* (0.6km W Urban)
47.54448, 4.45043 **Camp Municipal Alésia,** Rue du
Docteur Roux, 21150 Venarey-les-Laumes **03 80 96
07 76 or 03 80 96 01 59 (Mairie); camping@ville-
venareyleslaumes.fr; www.venareyleslaumes.fr

🐕 €1 ♟(htd) ✈ ⛟ ⬛ ✈ ⚂nr 🏔

SE fr Montbard on D905, site well sp fr Venarey on
D954. 3*, Med, mkd, hdg, hdstg, pt shd, EHU (16A) €3;
bbq; sw; red long stay; TV; 10% statics; phone; Eng
spkn; adv bkg acc; ccard acc; bike hire; CKE. *"Well-kept
site in scenic area; lge pitches; pleasant wardens; gd,
sm htd refurbished san facs; barrier clsd 2200-0700;
cycle tracks to Canal de Bourgogne, ltd facs in LS."*
€14.70, 1 Apr-15 Oct.   **2015**

VENCE *10E4* (3km W Rural) *43.7117, 7.0905*
Camping Domaine La Bergerie, 1330 Chemin de la
Sine, 06140 Vence **04 93 58 09 36;** info@camping-
domainedelabergerie.com; www.camping-domaine
delabergerie.com

🐕 ♟ ⬛ ✈ ⛟ ✈ ⛟ ⬛ ✈ 🦋 ♈ ⚂ 🏔 🏊

Fr A8 exit junc 47 & foll sp Vence thro Cagnes-sur-
Mer. Take detour to W around Vence foll sp Grasse/
Tourrettes-sur-Loup. At rndabt beyond viaduct take
last exit, foll site sp S thro La Sine town; long, narr
rd to site, up driveway on R. 3*, Lge, mkd, hdstg, shd,
pt sl, EHU (5A); gas; bbq (gas); red long stay; Eng spkn;
adv bkg acc; ccard acc; lake fishing; games area;
tennis; CKE. *"Shady site; helpful staff; clean san facs;
no twin axles or c'vans over 5m; gd dog walks; Vence
lovely & excel touring base."*
€33.40, 25 Mar-16 Oct.   **2019**

VENDAYS MONTALIVET *7C1* (8.6km W Coastal)
45.36325, -1.14496 **Camping CHM Montalivet
(Naturist),** 46 Ave de l'Europe, 33930 Vendays-
Montalivet **05 33 09 20 92;** infos@socnat.fr;
www.chm-montalivet.com

12 🐕 €6.90 ♟ ⬛ ✈ ⛟ ⬛ ✈ 🦋 ♈ 🍷 ⚂ 🏔 🏊
🏊 (htd) ☂ sand adj

D101 fr Soulac to Vendays-Montalivet; D102 to
Montalivet-les-Bains; site bef ent to vill; turn L at
petrol stn; site 1km on R. 3*, V lge, hdstg, mkd, pt
shd, pt sl, EHU (6A) inc; gas; red long stay; TV;
50% statics; phone; Eng spkn; adv bkg acc; ccard acc;
games rm; bike hire; INF card; games area. *"Vast,
peaceful site in pine forest; superb lge naturist beach
adj; excel facs for children of all ages; vg; excel; hdstg
with elec for MH's."* **€48.00**   **2018**

VENDOIRE *7B2* (3km W Rural) *45.40860, 0.28079*
Camping du Petit Lion, 24320 Vendoire
05 53 91 00 74; contact@camping-petit-lion.com;
www.camping-petit-lion.com

12 🐕 €3 ♟(htd) ✈ ⛟ ⬛ ✈ 🦋 ♈ 🍷 ⚂ 🏔 🏊

S fr Angoulême on D939 or D674, take D5 to Villebois-
Lavalette, then D17 to Gurat. Then take D102 to
Vendoire, site sp. 1*, Sm, hdg, hdstg, pt shd, EHU (10A)
€4; 10% statics; adv bkg acc; lake fishing; tennis; CKE.
"British owners; rally fields." **€17.00**   **2016**

FRANCE

VENDOME *4F2* (0.5km E Urban) *47.79122, 1.07586*
Camping au Coeur de Vendôme, Rue Geoffroy-Martel, 41100 Vendôme **02 54 77 00 27 or 09 70 35 83 31; aucoeurdevendome@camp-in-ouest.com; www.aucoeurdevendome.com**

🐕 €2.50 ⭑⭑ wc ♨ ⚬ ♿ 🖥 ⁄ 🦋 ⴷ ⁀ 🍴 nr ⓗnr 🛒nr 🄰

Fr N10 by-pass foll sp for town cent; in town foll sp Camping; site adj to pool 500m. 3*, Lge, mkd, pt shd, EHU (10A) inc; bbq; red long stay; 5% statics; phone; Eng spkn; rv fishing adj; tennis; CKE. *"Pleasant rvside setting; clean san facs - a trek fr outer pitches; sports cent, pool & theatre adj; statics sep area; recep 0900-2100; htd pool adj; games area adj; barrier clsd 2200-0630; vg; friendly; bar 500m; level site; narr ent/exit over bdge, poss diff for lge o'fits."*
€20.00, 15 Apr-30 Oct. **2017**

VERDUN *5D1* (2km SW Urban) *49.15428, 5.36598*
Camping Les Breuils, 8 Allée des Breuils, 55100 Verdun **03 29 86 15 31; contact@camping-lesbreuils.com; www.camping-lesbreuils.com**

🐕 €2.10 ⭑⭑ wc ♨ ⚬ ♿ 🖥 ⁄ MSP ⁀ 🄰 🛶

Fr W (Paris) on A4/E50, exit junc 30 onto D1916/D603/D330; cont over rndabt junc with D34 onto D330; at next rndabt in 100m turn R into Allée des Breuils. Or fr E (Metz) exit junc 31 onto D964/D330; cont on D330 past junc with D34A; at rndabt in 150m turn L into Allée des Breuils. Site sp nr Citadel. Avoid Verdun town cent due to 1-way rds. Allée des Breuils runs parallel to D34 on E side of rwly. Site well sp fr D603 & all other dirs. Steepish ent. 3*, Lge, hdg, mkd, hdstg, pt shd, pt sl, EHU (16A) €4.55 (poss some rev pol); gas; red long stay; phone; Eng spkn; adv bkg rec; ccard acc; fishing; bike hire; waterslide; CKE. *"Pleasant, clean, well-kept, lovely, busy site; grass pitches beside lge pond, some lge; poss long walk to water taps; some site rds tight for lge o'fits; gd pool; poss lge youth groups Sept; interesting historial town; cycle rtes around WWI battlefields; easy walk to Citadel with WWI museum; excel; gd rest; friendly staff; sports cent; bus tours fr site; san facs block refurbished (2018); facs expanding."*
€25.00, 15 Mar-15 Oct. **2018**

VERDUN SUR LE DOUBS *6H1* (0.5km W Rural) *46.90259, 5.01777* **Camp Municipal La Plage,** Quai du Doubs Prolongé, 71350 Verdun-sur-le-Doubs **03 85 91 55 50 or 03 85 91 52 52; mairie.verdunsurledoubs@wanadoo.fr; www.tourisme-verdun-en-bourgogne.com**

🐕 €1 ⭑⭑ wc ♨ ⁄ 🦋 ⁀ 🍴 nr ⓗnr 🛒nr 🄰

SE on D970 fr Beaune to Verdun-sur-le-Doubs & foll sp in town. Or on D973 or N73 twd Chalon fr Seurre, turn R onto D115 to Verdun; site on bank of Rv Saône. 2*, Lge, mkd, shd, pt sl, EHU (10A) €2.10; bbq; phone; waterslide; tennis; fishing. *"Lovely rvside location; lge pitches; helpful warden; interesting sm town; confluence of 3 rvs: La Saône, Le Doubs & La Dheune; htd pool adj; fishermen's paradise; excel."*
€16.50, 1 May-15 Sep. **2017**

VERMENTON *4G4* (0.9km S Rural) *47.65897, 3.73087*
Camp Municipal Les Coullemières, route de Coullemières, 89270 Vermenton **03 86 81 53 02; contact@camping-vermenton.com; www.camping-vermenton.com**

🐕 €1 ⭑⭑ (htd) wc ♨ ⚬ ♿ ⁄ 🦋 ⁀ ⓗnr 🛒nr 🄰

Lies W of D606 - turn off D606 into Rue Pasteur (tight turn & narr rd), strt on at x-rds into Ave de la Gare. Turn R at stn, L over level x-ing. Well sp in vill adj to rv but sps low down & easy to miss. 3*, Med, mkd, hdg, pt shd, EHU (6A) inc; TV; 5% statics; bus; adv bkg rec; ccard acc; fishing; boating; tennis; bike hire. *"Peaceful, well-run rvside site; excel san facs; absolutely immac; weight limit on access rds & pitches; no twin axles; gd walks & cycling; conv Chablis vineyards; town with 12thC church; excel site; staff helpful; delightful site in interesting area."*
€17.00, 1 Apr-30 Sep. **2019**

VERNANTES *4G1* (7km NW Rural) *47.43717, 0.00641*
Camping La Fortinerie, La Fortinerie, 49390 Mouliherne **02 41 67 59 76; north.john.a@gmail.com; www.lafortinerie.com**

🐕 ⭑⭑ wc ♨ ♿ ⁄ 🦋 ⓗnr 🛒nr

Fr Vernantes take D58 dir Mouliherne; opp Château Loroux (Plaissance) turn L; at x-rds turn R, site over 1.5km on L. Sm, pt shd, EHU (16A) €5 (poss rev pol); bbq; adv bkg acc. *"Peaceful CL-type site; only sound is crickets!;dogs by prior arrangement; lge pitches; helpful, friendly British owners; B&B avail; beautiful chateau town; conv Loire valley & vineyards; excel."*
€12.00, 1 May-30 Sep. **2016**

VERNET LES BAINS *8G4* (4km S Rural) *42.53330, 2.39847* **Domaine-St-Martin,** 6 Boulevard de la Cascade 66820 Casteil **04 68 05 52 09; info@domainestmartin.com**

🐕 ⭑⭑ wc ♨ ⚬ ♿ ⁄ 🦋 ⴷ ⁀ 🍴 ⓗ 🛒nr 🄰 🛶

Fr Prade to Villefranche on N116. Twd Vernet-les-Bains/Casteil at rndabt. Sp to campsite. 3*, Med, mkd, hdstg, shd, terr, EHU (10A); bbq; cooking facs; TV; 20% statics; phone; bus adj; Eng spkn; adv bkg acc; games rm; CCI. *"Mountain hiking/biking; Grottoes 6km; Abbey in vill; friendly, helpful staff; excel rest; vg."*
€29.70, 31 Mar-31 Oct. **2019**

VERNET LES BAINS *8G4* (8km NW Rural) *42.56255, 2.36050* **Camping Le Rotja,** Ave de la Rotja, 66820 Fuilla **04 68 96 52 75; info@camping-lerotja.com; www.camping-lerotja.com**

🐕 €2 ⭑⭑ (htd) wc ♨ ⚬ ♿ 🖥 ⁄ 🦋 ⓗnr ⴷ 🛒nr 🄰 🛶

Take N116 fr Prades dir Mont-Louis, 500m after Villefranche-de-Conflens turn L onto D6 sp Fuilla; in 3km just bef church, turn R at sp to site. D6 narr but passing places. 3*, Sm, mkd, pt shd, pt sl, terr, EHU (10A) €3.25; gas; bbq (gas); red long stay; 10% statics; phone; Eng spkn; adv bkg acc; ccard acc; CKE. *"Peaceful site; views of Mount Canigou; friendly, helpful Dutch owners; gd hiking/walks."*
€27.50, 1 Apr-17 Oct. **2015**

VERNET, LE *9D3* (0.8km N Rural) *44.28170, 6.39080*
Camping Lou Passavous, Route de Roussimat,
04140 Le Vernet **04 92 35 14 67; loupassavous@
orange.fr; www.loupassavous.com**

🐕€1.50 �(htd) ⊞ ▲ ♿ ⛽ ⬛ ⁄ ✖ 👍 ⛲ 🍴 ⊕ ☕ 🎯 ⚠ ✍ ⛷

Fr N on A51 exit junc 21 Volonne onto N85 sp
Digne. Fr Digne N on D900 to Le Vernet; site on R.
Fr S exit A51 junc 20 Les Mées onto D4, then N85 E
to Digne, then as above. 3*, Sm, pt shd, pt sl, EHU
(6A) €4; TV; 10% statics; Eng spkn; adv bkg acc;
fishing; games area; CKE. "Scenic location; gd, clean
facs; Dutch owners; gd walking, mkd walks fr site,
escorted walks by owner; excel; highly rec."
€24.00, 1 May-15 Sep.   **2016**

VERNON *3D2* (2km W Rural) *49.09625, 1.43851*
Camping Les Fosses Rouges, Chemin de Réanville,
27950 St Marcel **02 32 51 59 86 or 06 22 42 19 11 (LS);
camping@cape27.fr; www.cape27.fr**

🐕€0.50 ♫♪♩(htd) ⊞ ▲ ♿ ⬛ ✖ 📦nr ⚠

Exit A13/E5 junc 16 dir Vernon onto D181; in 2km at
rndabt turn L onto D64e dir St Marcel; in 2km at
5-exit rndabt take 1st R onto Chemin de Réanville
(D64) & foll camping sp. At 1st major bend to R,
cont strt ahead, site on L in 50m. 2*, Med, mkd, pt
shd, pt sl, EHU (6-10A) €3.20-4.20; gas; bbq;
10% statics; adv bkg acc; CKE. "Well-kept, well-run
scenic site; gd clean san facs but tired; parking for
m'vans at St Marcel - cont past site over rndabt for
900m, turn sharp L past hotel on R & parking on R;
lovely little vill; conv Giverny, but access diff lge o'fits;
pool 4km; gd size pitches; peaceful site."
€11.00, 1 Mar-31 Oct.   **2017**

> ## "There aren't many sites open at this time of year"
>
> If you're travelling outside peak season
> remember to call ahead to check site opening
> dates – even if the entry says 'open all year'.

VERSAILLES *4E3* (3km E Urban) *48.79455, 2.16038*
Camping Huttopia Versailles, 31 Rue Berthelot,
Porchefontaine, 78000 Versailles **01 39 51 23 61;
versailles@huttopia.com; www.huttopia.com**

🐕€4 ♫♪♩(htd) ⊞ ▲ ♿ ⬛ ✖ 👍 ⛲ 🍴 ⊕ ☕ 📦nr ⚠ ⛷(htd)

Foll sp to Château de Versailles; fr main ent take
Ave de Paris dir Porchefontaine & turn R immed
after twin gate lodges; sp. Narr access rd due
parked cars & sharp bends. No sp rec use sat nav.
3*, Lge, mkd, pt shd, pt sl, terr, EHU inc (6-10A)
€4.60-6.80; gas; bbq; red long stay; TV; 20% statics;
bus 500m; Eng spkn; adv bkg acc; ccard acc; bike
hire; games area; CKE. "Wooded site; sm, sl, uneven
pitches poss diff lge o'fits; friendly, helpful staff;
excel, clean san facs, stretched high ssn; conv Paris
trains & Versailles Château; bus 171 to town."
€45.50, 24 Mar-2 Nov, P19.   **2016**

VERVINS *3C4* (8.5km N Rural) *49.90676, 3.91977*
FFCC Camping du Val d'Oise, 3 Rue du Mont d'Origny,
02580 Etréaupont **03 23 97 48 04; www.campingdu
valdoisern2.com**

🐕€0.30 ♫♪♩ ⊞ ▲ ♿ ⁄ MSP 👍 ⛲ 📦nr ⚠

Site to E of Etréaupont off N2, Mons-Reims rd.
Site adj football pitch on banks of Rv Oise. Well sp
fr main rd. 2*, Sm, mkd, hdg, pt shd, EHU (10A) €4
(poss rev pol); Eng spkn; adv bkg acc; rv fishing adj;
tennis; CKE. "Pretty, tidy site; sports field adj; warm
welcome; v clean san facs; site self if recep clsd; conv
rte to Zeebrugge ferry (approx 200km); gd walking
& cycling; gd; delightful site; canoe hire adj; vg."
€16.00, 1 Apr-31 Oct.   **2017**

VESOUL *6G2* (3km W Rural) *47.63026, 6.12858*
Camping International du Lac, Ave des Rives du Lac,
70000 Vesoul **03 84 76 22 86; camping_dulac@
yahoo.fr; www.camping-vesoul.com**

12 🐕€2 ♫♪♩(htd) ⊞ ▲ ♿ ⬛ ⁄ MSP 🍴 ⊕ 📦nr ⚠

2km fr D619, sp fr W end of by-pass, pass indus est
to lge lake on W o'skts. Ent opp Peugeot/Citroën
factory on lakeside. 3*, Lge, mkd, pt shd, EHU (6A)
€3; gas; 10% statics; adv bkg acc; ccard acc; tennis;
fishing; waterslide 300m; games area; CKE. "Super
site screened fr indus est by trees; pool & paddling pool
300m; site clsd mid-Dec to early Jan; gd size pitches
but poss soft after rain; excel aqua park nr; gd cycle
rtes; vg." **€19.00**   **2016**

VEULES LES ROSES *3C2* (0.3km S Rural/Coastal)
49.87586, 0.80314 Camping Les Mouettes, 7 Ave Jean
Moulin, 76980 Veules-les-Roses **02 35 97 61 98;
camping.les.mouettes0509@orange.fr;
www.camping-lesmouettes-normandie.com**

🐕€2 ♫♪♩(htd) ⊞ ▲ ♿ ⬛ ⁄ MSP 👍 ⛲ 🍴 ⊕ 📦nr ⚠ ✍
⛷(covrd, htd) ⛵ 🏖shgl 800m

On ent vill fr Dieppe on D925, turn R onto D68, site
in 500m up hill (14%). 3*, Lge, hdg, mkd, pt shd, EHU
(6A) €4.70; gas; bbq; red long stay; TV; 10% statics;
Eng spkn; adv bkg acc; ccard acc; games area; games
rm; fitness rm; CKE. "Pleasant area; peaceful, well-
kept site; vg; site a bit scruffy start of ssn (2017)."
€29.30, 1 Apr-15 Oct.   **2017**

VEZELAY *4G4* (4.6km S Rural) *47.45675, 3.78768*
FFCC Camping de Vézelay L'Ermitage, 1 Route de
l'Étang, 89450 Vézelay **03 86 33 24 18; auberge.
jeunesse.vezelay@orange.fr; www.camping-
auberge-vezelay.com**

♫♪♩ ⊞ ▲ ⁄ MSP 📦nr

Foll sp fr cent of Vézelay to 'Camping Vézelay' &
Youth Hostel. 1*, Sm, pt shd, pt sl, serviced pitches;
EHU (4-6A) €3; Eng spkn; CKE. "Pleasant, peaceful,
scenic site; welcoming; gd, clean facs; some pitches diff
lge o'fits & blocks req; recep eve only - site self & sign
in when open; some pitches muddy after heavy rain;
Vézelay the starting point of one of the pilgrim rtes -
superb abbey; excel." **€8.50, 1 Apr-31 Oct.**   **2015**

For a guide to symbols see the fold out on the rear cover

VIAS *10F1* (3km S Coastal) *43.29055, 3.39863*
Camping Californie Plage, 34450 Vias-Plage
04 67 21 64 69; info@californie-plage.fr;
www.californie-plage.fr

🛏🏕€4.60 ♨🆚♨ ▲ ᕃ 🗗 ⁄ ⫯ 🍽 ⊕ ▨ ዿ 🏔 ✎ 🏊(covrd, htd)
🛥 🌴sand adj

W fr Agde on D612 to Vias; turn S in town & foll sps
'Mer' over canal bdge & sp to site. 4*, Lge, mkd, shd,
EHU (5-10A) €1.50-3.50; gas; TV; 10% statics; Eng
spkn; adv bkg acc; ccard acc; bike hire; waterslide; CKE.
€33.00, 1 Apr-30 Oct. **2016**

VIAS *10F1* (3km S Coastal) *43.29083, 3.41783*
Yelloh! Village Le Club Farret, Farinette-Plage,
34450 Vias-Plage 04 67 21 64 45; info@farret.com;
www.camping-farret.com

🛏🏕€6 ♨🆚♨ ▲ ᕃ 🗗 ⁄ 🍽 🦋 ⫯ ⊕ ▨ ዿ 🏔 ✎
🏊(htd) 🌴sand adj

Fr A9, exit Agde junc 34. Foll sp Vias-Plage on
D137. Sp fr cent of Vias-Plage on L, immed after
Gendarmerie. 4*, V lge, mkd, pt shd, EHU (6A) inc;
gas; TV; 10% statics; Eng spkn; adv bkg acc; ccard acc;
games rm; bike hire; fitness rm; games area; tennis;
watersports; CKE. *"Excel facs, entmnt; excursions; gd
security."* **€65.00, 12 Apr-29 Sep.** **2017**

VIAS *10F1* (3km W Rural) *43.31222, 3.36320*
Camping Sunêlia Le Domaine de la Dragonnière,
34450 Vias 04 67 01 03 10; contact@dragonniere.
com; www.dragonniere.com

🛏🏕€5 ♨🆚♨ ▲ ᕃ 🗗 ⁄ ⫯ 🍽 ⫯ 🍽 ⊕ ▨ ዿ 🏔 ✎ 🏊(htd)
🌴sand 3km

Exit A9 junc 35 onto D64 twd Valras-Plage, then
D612 dir Agde & Vias. Site on R bef Vias. Or exit junc
34 onto D612A. At Vias turn R onto D612 sp Béziers,
site on L. NB Take care high speed humps at sh
intervals. 4*, V lge, mkd, hdg, pt shd, EHU (16A) inc;
gas; bbq; TV; 80% statics; phone; Eng spkn; adv bkg
acc; ccard acc; games area; spa; bike hire; tennis; CKE.
*"Vg site; excel for children & teenagers high ssn; Canal
du Midi nrby; opp Béziers airport; free bus to beach;
site poss flooded after heavy rain; touring pitches
have individual shwr block on pitch; v busy at w/ends."*
€85.00, 5 Apr-3 Nov, C06. **2016**

VICHY *9A1* (4km S Rural) *46.11555, 3.43006*
Camping Beau Rivage, Rue Claude Decloître,
03700 Bellerive-sur-Allier 04 70 32 26 85;
camping-beaurivage@wanadoo.fr; www.camping-
beaurivage.com

🛏🏕€1 ♨🆚♨ ▲ ᕃ 🗗 ⁄ 🍽 🦋 ⫯ ▨ ዿ 🏔 ✎ 🏊(covrd, htd)

Fr Vichy cross rv bdge over Rv Allier onto D1093,
turn L at rndabt foll sp Campings, sp to Beau
Rivage. Site on L on rv bank, past Cmp Les Acacias.
4*, Med, shd, EHU (10A) €3.10; gas; bbq; TV;
50% statics; tennis 2km; games area; bike hire;
archery; waterslide; canoeing; fishing. *"Lovely rvside
site, but no rv sw allowed; lge o'fits have diff pitching;
easy cycle ride to lovely city."*
€23.60, 1 Apr-8 Oct. **2016**

VICHY *9A1* (4km S Urban) *46.10756, 3.43670*
FFCC Camping La Croix St Martin, Allée du Camping,
99 Ave des Graviers, 03200 Abrest 04 70 32 67 74 or
06 10 94 70 90 (mob); camping-vichy@orange.fr;
www.camping-vichy.com

🛏♨🆚♨ ▲ ᕃ 🗗 ⁄ 🍽 🦋 ⫯ ⫯ 🏔 🏊(htd) 🛥

Exit D906 at Abrest onto D426 N (Ave des Graviers);
in 900m turn L into Allée du Camping. Site sp
fr D906, both N & S of Abrest. 3*, Med, mkd, hdg, pt
shd, EHU (10A) €3.80; 15% statics; phone; Eng spkn;
adv bkg acc; ccard acc; games area; CKE. *"Gd cycling
along rv allier thro Vichy; san facs clean; well
maintained, well run, attractive site; friendly staff; flat
walking dist fr a v attractive town; free wifi over all site;
pool now covrd."* **€20.00, 2 Apr-2 Oct.** **2015**

VICHY *9A1* (1km SW Rural) *46.11648, 3.42560*
Camping Les Acacias, Rue Claude Decloître, 03700
Bellerive-sur-Allier 04 70 32 36 22; camping-acacias03@
orange.fr; www.camping-acacias.com

🛏🐕€1 ♨🆚♨ ▲ ᕃ ⁄ ⫯ ዿ nr 🏔 🏊

Cross bdge to Bellerive fr Vichy & foll Hauterive
sp onto D1093. Strt over at 1st rndabt & turn L at
2nd rndabt onto D131 dir Hauterive. At 3rd rndabt
turn L sp 'piscine'. Foll sm camping sps along rv
side. Or fr S leave D906 at St Yorre & cross Rv Allier,
then foll sp to Bellerive. Site sp at rndabt on app to
Bellerive adj Rv Allier. On final app, at sp showing
site in either dir, keep L & foll site sp along rv
bank to recep. NB Many other sites in area, foll sp
carefully. 4*, Med, mkd, hdg, shd, EHU (10A) €3.40;
gas; bbq; TV; 20% statics; adv bkg acc; ccard acc;
boating; fishing; CKE. *"Well-run site; helpful owner; gd
san facs; free Vichy Célestins water at spring in lovely
town."* **€19.00, 7 Apr-7 Oct.** **2015**

VIERZON *4G3* (2.5km SW Urban) *47.20937, 2.08079*
Camp O'village Vierzon (formerly Municipal), Route
de Bellon, 18100 Vierzon 02 48 53 99 89; contact@
campovillage.com; www.campovillage.com

🛏♨🆚♨ ▲ ᕃ 🗗 ⁄ 🍽 ⫯ 🍽 ⊕ ▨ ዿ nr 🏔

Fr N on A71 take A20 dir Châteauroux, leave at
junc 7 onto D2020 & then D27 dir Bourges; pass
Intermarché supmkt on L, after next traff lts turn
L into Route de Bellon; site in 1km on R, sp. NB Do
not go into town cent. 2*, Med, hdg, mkd, pt shd, pt
sl, EHU (6A) €3 (some rev pol); gas; bbq (elec, gas);
phone; Eng spkn; adv bkg acc; boat hire; fishing; CKE.
*"Attractive, well-kept site by rv; gd sized pitches but
some poss diff to negotiate; nice little rest o'looking
rv; gates clsd 2300-0700; helpful staff; poss travellers;
ideal NH; gd site; friendly recep; new facs, v clean
(2017)."* **€23.50, 15 Jun-14 Sep.** **2019**

VIEURE 7A4 (2km NE Rural) 46.50305, 2.90754
Plan d'eau de Vieure, La Borde, 03430 Vieure **04 70
02 04 46** or **09 60 36 53 41; plandeau03@orange.fr;
www.locationschaletscampingdelaborde.fr**

🐕 ♦♦ ♣ 🛁 ♿ 🏊 ☂ Ⓣ ⓓ ♨ ⚠

**Exit A71-E11 at junc 10. Take D94 NE to Cosne
d'Allier, then R onto D11. L onto D459, 1st R onto La
Bordé. Foll sp to campsite.** Med, hdg, pt shd, pt sl,
EHU (10A) €3.10; sw; twin axles; 35% statics; phone;
ccard acc; CCI. *"Large, open & shd pitches; dated san
facs; v pleasant remote site by lake; fishing & canoeing;
family friendly; gd."* **€11.50, 11 Apr-30 Sep.** **2019**

VIHIERS 4G1 (15km SE Rural) 47.07419, -0.41104
Camping Le Serpolin, St Pierre-à-Champ, 49560
Cléré-sur-Layon **02 41 52 43 08; info@loirecamping.
com; www.loirecamping.com**

12 🐕 ♦♦ (htd) ⓦ ♣ ☕ ♿ 🏊 ☂ 🖓 ⚠ ⚓

**Take D748 S fr Vihiers by-pass sp Argenton Château.
In 2km turn L at sp Cléré-sur-Layon onto D54. Cont
thro vill to 1st mkd x-rd, turn R, site last house
along this lane.** Sm, hdstg, pt shd, EHU (10A) €4;
bbq; Eng spkn; adv bkg rec; bike hire; fishing; CKE.
*"Peaceful, CL-type site; clean san facs; helpful British
owners; dogs free; rallies by arrangement; conv
chateaux; Futuroscope; vg."* **€15.00** **2015**

VILLARD DE LANS 9C3 (1.5km N Rural) 45.07750,
5.55620 **Camping Caravaneige L'Oursière,**
38250 Villard-de-Lans **04 76 95 14 77; oursiere@
franceloc.fr; www.camping-oursiere.fr**

12 🐕 €5 ♦♦ (htd) ⓦ ♣ ☕ ♿ 🏊 ☂ 🖓 ⓓ ♨ ☂ ⚠

**Site clearly visible on app to town fr D531 Gorges
d'Engins rd (13km SW Grenoble). App fr W on D531
not rec for c'vans & m'vans due o'hangs.**
3*, Lge, unshd, terr, EHU (10A) €4-6; gas; bbq;
20% statics; Eng spkn; adv bkg acc; ccard acc; CKE.
*"Excel all winter sports; friendly owners; drying rm; san
facs need upgrade (2010); pool 800m; waterpark 800m;
new htd indoor sw pool (2015)."* **€26.00** **2016**

VILLARD DE LANS 9C3 (12km N Rural) 45.12951,
5.53215 **Camping Caravaneige Les Buissonnets,**
38112 Méaudre **04 76 95 21 04; camping-les-
buissonnets@wanadoo.fr; www.camping-les-
buissonnets.com**

♦♦ (htd) ⓦ ♣ ☕ ♿ 🏊 ☂ 🖓 ⓓ nr ☂ nr ⚠

**Fr Grenoble take D1532 to Sassenage then D531 to
Lans-en-Vercors. Turn R at rndabt onto D106 twrds
Meaudre. Turn L just bef rndabt in vill off D106.
Approx 30km SW of Grenoble by rd & 18km as crow
flies.** 3*, Med, unshd, sl, EHU (6-10A) €4-6; bus to ski
slopes; games area; clsd 1 Dec-10 Nov. *"Gd skiing cent;
conv touring Vercous; levellers ess; highly rec; friendly,
v well managed site; higher price in winter; pool 300m;
lovely area; slightly sl, levelling necessary; v pleasant."*
€21.00, 1 Jan-31 Oct & 12 Dec-31 Dec. **2017**

VILLARS LES DOMBES 9A2 (0.2km S Urban) 45.99763,
5.03163 **Camping Le Nid du Parc (formerly Parc des
Oiseaux),** 164 Ave des Nations, 01330 Villars-les-
Dombes **04 74 98 00 21; camping@parcdes
oiseaux.com; www.lenidduparc.com**

🐕 €3 ♦♦ ♣ ☕ ♿ 🏊 ☂ 🖓 ⓜⓢⓟ Ⓣ ⓓ ♨ ☂ nr ⚠ 🚲 🛶

N fr Lyon on N83, site in town cent on R by sw pool.
4*, Lge, hdstg, pt shd, EHU (10A) €4.50; bbq (gas);
60% statics; games area; rv fishing adj; bike hire;
tennis. *"Excel site; lge pitches; modern, gd san facs;
htd pool adj inc; gd security; bird park 10 mins walk;
popular NH."* **€33.50, 29 Mar-11 Nov.** **2019**

"That's changed – Should I let the Club know?"

If you find something on site that's different
from the site entry, fill in a report and let us
know. See camc.com/europereport.

VILLEDIEU LES POELES 1D4 (0.6km S Urban)
48.83638, -1.21694 **Camping Les Chevaliers de Malte,**
2 Impasse Pré de la Rose, 50800 Villedieu-les-Poêles
**02 33 59 49 04; contact@camping-deschevaliers.com;
www.camping-deschevaliers.com**

🐕 €1.50 ♦♦ (htd) ⓦ ♣ ☕ ♿ 🏊 ☂ 🖓 ⓜⓢⓟ ☂ 🖓 Ⓣ ⓓ ☂ nr ⚠ 🚲
🛶 (htd)

**Exit A84 junc 38 onto D999 twd Villedieu, then R
onto D975 & R onto D924 to avoid town cent. Foll
sp fr car park on R after x-ing rv. Site behind PO &
cinema.** 3*, Med, hdstg, hdg, mkd, pt shd, EHU (6A)
inc (poss rev pol); bbq; TV; 40% statics; phone; Eng
spkn; adv bkg acc; games area; boating; games rm; rv
fishing; tennis; CKE. *"Peaceful, lovely site; lge pitches
but kerbs poss diff lger o'fits; interesting historic town;
avoid arr Tue am due mkt; conv A84 & Cherbourg
ferry; vg; gd modern facs, all new; well worth a visit to
town; excel site; rest extended 2011; staff v helpful;
bell foundry worth a visit; new owners (2016); vg."*
€28.00, 1 Apr-15 Oct. **2017**

VILLEFORT (LOZERE) 9D1 (0.6km S Rural) 44.43536,
3.93323 **Le Mas Les Sédariès,** Ave des Cévennes,
48800 Villefort **04 66 46 25 20; vacances48@gmail.
com; www.sedaries.com**

🐕 €1 ♦♦ ⓦ ♣ ♿ 🏊 ☂ 🖓 Ⓣ nr ⓓ nr ☂ nr

On D906 heading S fr Villefort twd Alès.
2*, Sm, pt shd, terr, EHU (6A) €2; bbq; sw nr; phone;
fishing 2km; CKE. *"Attractive, scenic site; bureau clsd
1000-1830; privately owned now (2014); not many
touring places."* **€15.00, 1 Jun-30 Sep.** **2019**

Make sure you check any essential information with the site before you travel

FRANCE

VILLEFRANCHE DE LAURAGAIS *8F3* (8km SW Rural) *43.35498, 1.64862* **Camping Le Lac de la Thésauque,** Nailloux, 31560 Montgeard **05 61 81 34 67; camping@thesauque.com; www.camping-thesauque.com**

[12] 🐕 ♦♦(htd) [WD] 🚿 🔥 🛒 🚽 ♦ ♀ 🍽 ⑪ 🚗 🛒 ⚠ 🏊

Fr S exit A61 at Villefrance-de-Lauragais junc 20 onto D622, foll sp Auterive then Lac after Gardouch vill, site sp. Fr N turn off A61 at 1st junc after tolls S of Toulouse onto A66 (sp Foix). Leave A66 at junc 1 & foll sp Nailloux. Turn L on ent vill onto D662 & in 2km turn R onto D25 & immed R to site, sp. 3*, Med, mkd, hdstg, pt shd, terr, EHU (10A) inc; bbq; 70% statics; ccard acc; boating; fishing; tennis; CKE. *"Scenic, peaceful location; conv NH for A61; helpful owners; ltd facs LS; gd security; steep app to sm terr pitches poss diff lge o'fits; facs basic but adequate."* **€24.00** 2019

> ## "I like to fill in the reports as I travel from site to site"
>
> You'll find report forms at the back of this guide, or you can fill them in online at camc.com/europereport.

VILLEFRANCHE DE ROUERGUE *7D4* (9km SE Rural) *44.26695, 2.11575* **Camping Le Muret,** 12200 St Salvadou **05 65 81 80 69 or 05 65 29 84 87; info@lemuret.com; www.lemuret.com**

🐕 €2 ♦♦ 🔥 🛒 🚽 ♦ 🦋 ♀ 🍽 ⑪ 🚗

Fr Villefranche on D911 twd Millau, R on D905A sp camping & foll camping sp 7km. 3*, Sm, mkd, hdg, shd, EHU (16A) €4.50; red long stay; phone; adv bkg acc; fishing; CKE. *"Lovely setting; gas & ice at farm; lake adj; gd sized pitches."* **€23.00**, 5 Apr-22 Oct. 2017

VILLEFRANCHE DU PERIGORD *7D3* (8km SW Rural) *44.59025, 1.04799* **Moulin du Périé Camping - Caravaning,** 47500 Sauveterre-la-Lémance **05 53 40 67 26; moulinduperie@wanadoo.fr; www.camping-moulin-perie.com or www.flowercampings.com**

🐕 €4.60 ♦♦ [WD] 🔥 🛒 🚽 ♦ 🦋 🍽 ⑪ 🚗 ⚠ 🛶 🏊 🚣

Fr N fr Villefranche-du-Périgord take D710 S dir Fumel. At Sauveterre-la-Lémance turn L at traff lts, cross level x-ing & in 400m turn L sp Loubejac & site; site on R in 4km. Tight ent bet tall hedges 2.6m apart for 30m. Fr E fr Cahors on D660 & turn L onto D46 sp Loubejac. Cont thro Loubejac & turn L at T-junc, foll sp Sauveterre. Site on R in 4km. 4*, Med, pt shd, pt sl, EHU (6-10A) €3 (poss rev pol); gas; bbq; TV; 25% statics; Eng spkn; adv bkg rec; ccard acc; tennis 3km; bike hire; archery; trout fishing; games rm; CKE. *"Beautiful, well-run site in grnds of old mill; welcoming, friendly family owners; clean, dated san facs; vg rest; site rds narr, not suitable v lge o'fits; gd touring base; excel; poor maintenance (2015)."* **€30.00**, 13 May-16 Sep. 2015

VILLEFRANCHE SUR CHER *4G3* (8km SE Rural) *47.26917, 1.86265* **FFCC Camp Municipal Val Rose,** Rue du Val Rose, 41320 Mennetou-sur-Cher **02 54 98 11 02 or 02 54 98 01 19 (Mairie); mairie.mennetou@wanadoo.fr; http://mennetou.fr/tourisme/se-loger-restauration/camping-municipal**

🐕 €0.20 ♦♦(htd) [WD] 🔥 🛒 🚽 ♦ ♀ ⑪ nr 🛒 nr ⚠

Site sp fr D976/D2076 fr Villefranche (sm white sp); site on R in SW side of vill of Mennetou. To avoid narr bdge in town fr N76 onto A20, just outside town, turn imm R, site sp after L turn. 2*, Sm, pt shd, EHU (4A); Eng spkn; adv bkg acc. *"Pleasant, well-kept site; friendly, helpful warden; excel, spotless san facs; excel lndry; pretty, walled town 5 mins walk along canal; mkt Thurs; htd pool adj; vg value; access for lge o'fits diff; excel NH."* **€13.00**, 13 May-18 Sep. 2018

VILLEFRANCHE SUR SAONE *9B2* (10km E Rural) *45.99104, 4.81802* **FFCC Camp Municipal le Bois de la Dame,** 521 Chemin du Bois de la Dame, 01480 Ars-sur-Formans **04 74 00 77 23 or 04 74 00 71 84 (Mairie); camping.boisdeladame@orange.fr; www.ars-village.fr**

🐕 €3 ♦♦(cont) [WD] 🔥 🛒 🚽 ♦ ⚠

Exit A6 junc 31.1 or 31.2 onto D131/D44 E dir Villars-les-Dombes. Site 500m W of Ars-sur-Formans on lake, sp. 3*, Med, mkd, pt shd, pt sl, terr, EHU (10-16A) €3-5; 60% statics; adv bkg rec; lake fishing; CKE. *"Average site, but pretty & interesting vill; ltd facs LS; no twin axles; higher pitches have unguarded precipices."* **€16.00**, 1 Apr-30 Sep. 2017

> ## "We must tell the Club about that great site we found"
>
> Get your site reports in by mid-August and we'll do our best to get your updates into the next edition.

VILLEFRANCHE SUR SAONE *9B2* (10km SE Rural) *45.93978, 4.76811* **Camping Kanopee (formerly Municipal La Petite Saône),** Rue Robert Baltié, 01600 Trévoux **04 74 08 44 83; contact@kanopee-village.com; www.kanopee-village.com**

🐕 ♦♦ 🔥 🛒 ♦ 🦋 🛒 nr ⚠ 🛶

Fr Villefranche take D306 S to Anse. Turn L onto D39/D6 for Trévoux, site sp in town, on bank of Rv Saône. 3*, Lge, pt shd, EHU (6A) inc; sw nr; 75% statics; adv bkg req; rv fishing adj; CKE. *"Spacious rvside site nr vill; helpful staff; well maintained; access poss diff lge o'fits due statics; gd cycling rtes nrby; Trévoux interesting history; m'van o'night area at ent; excel shwr blocks; Aire at ent to camp; vg."* **€28.00**, 1 Apr-30 Sep. 2018

Down to the medieval village of Pujols listed as one of the most beautiful villages of France

contact@camping-lot-et-bastides.fr
Allée de malbentre F47300 Pujols ☎33(0)5 53 36 86 79 💻 www.camping-lot-et-bastides.fr

VILLEFRANCHE SUR SAONE 9B2 (5km SE Rural) 45.97243, 4.75237 **Camp Municipal La Plage Plan d'Eau,** 2788 Route de Riottier, 69400 Villefranche-sur-Saône 04 74 65 33 48; campingvillefranche@ voila.fr; www.villefranche.net

Exit A6 junc 31.2 Villefranche. Fr N turn R at rndabt, cross over a'route & str over next rndabt; cont to site on R bef Rv Saône. Or fr S turn R at rndabt & cont to site as above. Look for sp on rndabt. 3*, Med, shd, EHU (10A); gas; sw nr; 10% statics; adv bkg acc; ccard acc; fishing; CKE. "Busy site in gd position; easy access & nr m'way but quiet; a bit run down; gd rvside walking; NH only; san facs clean (2015); card ent sys." €22.00, 1 May-30 Sep. **2015**

VILLENEUVE SUR LOT 7D3 (3km S Urban) 44.39483, 0.68680 **Camping Lot et Bastides,** Allée de Malben-tre, 47300 Pujols 05 53 36 86 79 or 06 14 13 78 93 (mob); contact@camping-lot-et-bastides.fr; www.camping-lot-et-bastides.fr

Fr Villeneuve Sur Lot on D911 take L onto D118. At rndabt take 1st exit onto D911. Turn L onto Rue du General. Site on the R. 3*, Med, hdg, pt shd, EHU (16A); bbq; twin axles; 25% statics; bus adj; adv bkg acc; ccard acc; games area; CCI. "New site 2012; neat and clean; views of Pujols, most beautiful vill in France; lots to see & do in area; v scenic; friendly staff; bike hire." €24.00, 30 Mar-2 Nov. **2019**

See advertisement

VILLEREAL 7D3 (9km SE Rural) 44.61426, 0.81889 **Camping Fontaine du Roc,** Les Moulaties, 47210 Dévillac 05 53 36 08 16; reception@fontaine duroc.com; www.fontaineduroc.com

Fr Villeréal take D255 sp Dévillac, just beyond Dévillac at x-rds turn L & L again sp Estrade; site on L in 500m. 3*, Med, mkd, hdstg, hdg, pt shd, EHU (5-10A) €3.50-4.50 gas; bbq; red long stay; TV; 2% statics; phone; Eng spkn; adv bkg acc; fishing 500m; bike hire; games rm; CKE. "Peaceful, well-cared for site; helpful owner; lge pitches; ACSI acc (LS); excel." €15.00, 1 Apr-15 Oct. **2016**

VILLEREAL 7D3 (3km NW Rural) 44.65253, 0.72375 **Camping de Bergougne,** 47210 Rives 05 53 36 01 30; info@camping-de-bergougne.com; www.camping-de-bergougne.com/camping/

Fr Villeréal, take D207 NW sp Issigeac/Bergerac. In 1km turn L onto D250 W sp Doudrac. Foll sm green sp to site. 3*, Med, mkd, hdg, pt shd, pt sl, terr, EHU (6A) inc; gas; bbq (sep area); TV; 15% statics; Eng spkn; adv bkg acc; ccard acc; games rm; fishing; games area; CKE. "Vg site; small café; bread del in Jul & Aug; friendly welcoming new owners; occasional events in bar/rest; v peaceful rustic ambience; vg." €24.00, 1 May-30 Sep. **2018**

VILLERSEXEL 6G2 (1km N Rural) 47.55763, 6.43628 **Camping Le Chapeau Chinois,** 92 Rue du Chapeau Chinois, 70110 Villersexel 03 84 63 40 60; contact@ camping-villersexel.eu; camping-villersexel.eu

Leave vill on D468 N, site on R immed after rv bdge. 3*, Med, hdg, mkd, pt shd, EHU (10A) €3.30; bbq; sw; 5% statics; Eng spkn; adv bkg acc; games area; CKE. "Vg." €19.00, 1 Apr-6 Oct. **2016**

VILLIERS SUR ORGE 4E3 (0.6km SE Urban) 48.65527, 2.30409 **Camping Le Beau Village,** 1 Voie des Prés, 91700 Villiers-sur-Orge 01 60 16 17 86; contact@ campingaparis.com; www.campingaparis.com

Fr S on N20 turn off onto D35 heading E twrds Villiers sur Orge. Cont strt on to traff lts & sm Renault g'ge, turn R alongside rv. Turn just bef St Genieve des Bois. 3*, Med, hdg, pt shd, EHU (10A) (poss rev pol); gas; bbq; phone; train 700m; games rm; kayaking; fishing. "Pleasant, well-run site; conv Paris; some statics/chalets; ltd space for lge o'fits; helpful staff." €22.00 **2017**

For a guide to symbols see the fold out on the rear cover

VIMOUTIERS *3D1* (0.6km N Urban) *48.93236, 0.19646* Camp Municipal La Campière, Ave Dr Dentu, 61120 Vimoutiers 02 33 39 18 86 (Mairie); campingmunicipal vimoutiers@wanadoo.fr; www.vimoutiers.fr

🐕 €1.50 🍴(htd) ⬛ ⛺ ♿ 🗑 ╱ ⓗ nr 📶 nr 🏔

App Vimoutiers fr N on on D579/D979/D916, site on R 300m after passing junc with D16; turn R at flag poles (200m after Avia petrol stn). Or appr fr Gacé on D979 turn L at flag poles (on D916 just bef junc with D16). Site nr stadium & not well sp. 2*, Sm, hdg, pt shd, EHU (6A) €2.85; sw nr; 10% statics; adv bkg acc; tennis; bike hire; rv fishing 2km; CKE. *"Excel, well-maintained, pretty site at cent of Camembert cheese industry; helpful, friendly warden; sports facs 2km; vg, clean san facs; noise fr nrby factory; boating 2km; unrel opening dates - phone ahead LS; attractive town; gd value."* **€13.00, 1 Apr-31 Oct.** **2018**

VIRIEU LE GRAND *9B3* (5km NE Rural) *45.87483, 5.68428* Camping Le Vaugrais, Chemin de Vaugrais, 01510 Artemare 04 79 87 37 34; contact@camping-le-vaugrais.fr; www.camping-savoie-levaugrais.com

🐕 €1 🍴 ⬛ ⛺ ♿ 🗑 ╱ MSP 🦋 ⛟ 🍽 ⓗ nr 📶 nr 🏔 ⛵

N fr Belley on D1504 then D904 to Artemare; sp in vill. Well sp fr D904 on rvside. 3*, Sm, hdg, pt shd, EHU (10A); bbq; 10% statics; Eng spkn; adv bkg acc; fishing; CKE. *"Charming site in gd location; some lge pitches with views; friendly owners; clean san facs, poss inadequate high ssn; nice pool; Artemare within walking dist; gd food at hotel in town; vg local walks; excel; app over narr bdge; gd views; highly rec."* **€25.00, 1 Mar-1 Dec, M12.** **2016**

"I need an on-site restaurant"

We do our best to make sure site information is correct, but it is always best to check any must-have facilities are still available or will be open during your visit.

VITRY LE FRANCOIS *6E1* (6km SE Rural) *48.69673, 4.63039* Aire Naturelle Camping Nature (Scherschell), 13 Rue de l'Evangile, 51300 Luxémont-et-Villotte 03 26 72 61 14 or 06 83 42 83 53 (mob); eric.scherschell@wanadoo.fr; www.camping-nature.net

🐕 €1 🍴 ⬛ ⛺ ╱ MSP 🦋 🏔

Fr N44 at rndabt take N4 sp St Dizier. Take exit sp Luxemont. At rndabt take 1st exit D396, at next rndabt take 4th exit sp Luxemont (D316). After 2.1km turn R, site on L in 100km. Sm, hdstg, shd, pt sl, EHU (6A) inc (poss rev pol & long lead req); bbq; sw nr; Eng spkn; adv bkg acc; fishing; CKE. *"Delightful, CL-type site; well-kept & immac; helpful, friendly owners; gd, clean unisex san facs; nr canal & cycle paths; interesting area to visit; excel; poss mosquitoes."* **€14.40, 1 May-15 Oct.** **2017**

VOLLORE-VILLE *9B1* (1km NE Rural) *45.79199, 3.60583* Camping Des Plaines, Le Grun de Chignore, Les Plaines, 63120 Vollore-Ville 04 73 53 73 37; jenny-loisel@orange.fr; www.campingauvergne.fr

⑫ 🍴 ⬛ ⛺ ♿ 🗑 🦋 🍽 🍽 ⓗ nr 🏔 ⛵

Leave A89/E70 at junc 29 onto D906 S to Courpiere. Fr Courpiere take D7 to Vollore-Ville. Site on the R at turning to Chabrier. 2*, Sm, hdg, mkd, pt shd, gas; bbq; twin axles; 20% statics; adv bkg acc; ccard acc; CKE. *"Excel, well-kept little site; friendly owners; pleasant vill; conv for A89/E70."* **€15.00** **2019**

VOLVIC *9B1* (0.7km E Urban) *45.87208, 3.04591* Camp Municipal Pierre et Sources, Rue de Chancelas, 63530 Volvic 04 73 33 50 16; camping@ville-volvic.fr; www.ville-volvic.fr

🐕 €1.50 🍴(htd) ⬛ ⛺ 🗑 🦋 ⛟

Exit Riom on D986: foll sp for Pontgibaud & Volvic. Site sp to R on app to town. 4*, Sm, shd, EHU (12A) €3.50; 10% statics; Eng spkn; adv bkg acc. *"Pleasant, tidy site with lovely views; welcoming & helpful; excel, cleans san facs; access some pitches poss diff, particularly for lge o'fits; conv Volvic factory tour; no access for new arrivals when off is clsd."* **€20.00, 1 May-30 Sep.** **2015**

VOREY *9C1* (0.4km SW Rural) *45.18576, 3.90679* Camping Les Moulettes, Chemin de Félines, 43800 Vorey-sur-Arzon 04 71 03 70 48 or 04 71 03 79 49; contact@camping-les-moulettes.fr; www.camping-les-moulettes.fr

🐕 €1.50 🍴 ♿ 🗑 ╱ 🦋 ⛟ 🍽 ⓗ 📶 nr 🏔 ⛵ 🚣

Fr Le Puy take D103 sp Vorey. Site sp in vill; L in main sq. 4*, Sm, hdg, pt shd, EHU (10A) €3.50; 10% statics; Eng spkn; adv bkg acc; fishing adj; waterslide; games area. *"Peaceful site by rv; gd sized pitched, many on rv bank; friendly owners; gd quality rest acc rv."* **€23.50, May-Sep.** **2015**

VOUECOURT *6E1* (0.1km E Rural) *48.26774, 5.13671* Camp Municipal Rives de Marne, Rue de Verdun 52320 Vouécourt 06 78 52 50 54 or 03 25 02 44 46 46; commune.vouecourt@bbox.fr; www.camping vouecourt.sopixi.fr

🐕 🍴 ⬛ ⛺ ♿ 🗑 ╱ ⓗ nr 📶 nr 🏔

N fr Chaumont on N67; sp to site in 17km; thro vill by Rv Marne; site on L bef main rv bdge, almost opp Mairie; well sp. 2*, Sm, mkd, pt shd, EHU (10A) €2.50 (poss rev pol); gas; adv bkg acc; ccard acc; fishing; CKE. *"Lovely, peaceful, rvside site; gd sized pitches; friendly warden calls pm; clean; rv poss floods in winter; forest walks & cycling; popular NH; new excel san facs (2015); crowded; excel."* **€15.00, 29 Apr-30 Sep.** **2017**

VOULTE SUR RHONE, LA *9D2* (5km N Rural)
44.82663, 4.76171 **Camping La Garenne,** Quartier
La Garenne, 07800 St Laurent-du-Pape **04 75 62 24 62;**
info@lagarenne.org; www.campinglagarenne-
ardeche.fr

🐕 €2.50 ⁂ 🚿 ♿ ⛽ 🖉 ⁄ 🌳 ♉ ⓨ ① ♨ 🛒 🗻 🏕 ⚓ 🏊

Well sp fr La Voulte. Fr Valence S on D86 La Voulte,
approx 15km turn W onto D120; 300m after
St Laurent-du-Pape cent, turn R bef PO. 3*, Med, pt
shd, terr, EHU (6A) inc (poss rev pol); gas; red long stay;
Eng spkn; adv bkg acc; bike hire; CKE. *"Popular site;
friendly, helpful Dutch owners; views fr terr pitches; gd
clean san facs; sh walk to vill; vg; in cycling dist of the
Dolce Via rte."* **€37.00, 1 Apr-1 Oct.**   2015

VRAIGNES EN VERMANDOIS *3C4* (0.2km N Rural)
49.88538, 3.06623 **Camping des Hortensias,** 22 Rue
Basse, 80240 Vraignes-en-Vermandois **03 22 85 64 68;**
campinghortensias@free.fr; www.camping
hortensias.com

12 🐕 €2 ⁂ (htd) 🚿 ⛽ ⁄ 🌳 ♉ ⓨ nr 🛒 nr

Fr N on A1/E15 take exit 13 onto D1029 sp
St Quentin; strt rd 16km until rndabt, take D15
(Vraignes) exit; site sp 1st on R in vill. Or fr S & A26,
take junc 10 onto D1029 sp Péronne; after 15km
at rndabt take D15 as bef. 2*, Sm, hdg, hdstg, pt
shd, EHU (4-8A) €2.50-4.50 (poss long lead req); bbq;
red long stay; 10% statics; CKE. *"Lovely farm site;
sm pitches, poss muddy when wet; helpful, friendly
owners; vg, clean san facs; conv for Somme battlefields
& m'way; excel; rec torch."* **€13.00**   2016

WASSELONNE *6E3* (1km W Urban) *48.63739, 7.43209*
FFCC Camp Municipal, Rue des Sapins, 67310
Wasselonne **03 88 87 00 08;** camping-wasselonne@
wanadoo.fr; www.suisse-alsace.com

🐕 €0.60 ⁂ 🚿 ⛽ ⁄ 🌳 ♉ ⓨ ① ♨ 🛒 🗻 ⚓ (covrd, htd)

Fr D1004 take D244 to site.
2*, Med, mkd, pt shd, terr, EHU (5-10A) €2.30-3.70;
gas; 30% statics; CKE. *"Pleasant, pretty town; facs
excel; cycle rte & bus (adj) to Strasbourg; gd NH."*
€17.00, 15 Apr-15 Oct.   2017

WATTEN *3A3* (0.6km N Urban) *50.83521, 2.21047*
Camping Le Val Joly (Le Val Joli), Rue de Aa, 59143
Watten **03 21 88 23 26 or 03 21 88 24 75;**
www.campings-nord.com

🐕 €1.55 ⁂ 🚿 ⛽ ⁄ 🛒 nr 🏕

NW fr St Omer on D943; N of Tilques turn N onto
D300; in 5km at rndabt turn R onto D207 sp Watten;
at T-junc turn L onto D213; cross rv brdg & turn L in
500m at camping sp. 2*, Med, mkd, pt shd, EHU (10A)
€3.70; 90% statics; adv bkg acc; fishing. *"Spacious,
attractive, well-kept site; conv NH for ferries;
welcoming, friendly, helpful owner; basic, clean san
facs; secure gates, locked 2200-0700, but off rd
parking; cycling along rv/canal; no site lighting (2010);
few touring pitches - arr early or phone ahead high ssn;
access to rv walk; glass works at Arques; vet nr; vg."*
€12.00, 1 Apr-31 Oct.   2019

WIMEREUX *3A2* (1.5km S Coastal) *50.75277, 1.60722*
Caravaning L'Eté Indien, Hameau de Honvault,
62930 Wimereux **03 21 30 23 50;** ete.indien@
wanadoo.fr; www.eteindien-wimereux.com

12 🐕 €3 ⁂ 🅦 🚿 ♿ ⛽ ⁄ 🖿 ♉ ⓨ 🛒 🗻 🏕 ⚓ 🏊 (htd) ⛵

🏕 sand 1.5km

Fr Calais on A16 exit junc 32 sp Wimereux Sud. Thro
Terlincthun R after x-ing rlwy, site in 700m on R (do
not enter 1st site, correct site is the 2nd one clearly
sp above gate with site name) - narr, v rough rd.
4*, Med, unshd, pt sl, terr, serviced pitches; EHU (10A)
inc; gas; bbq (gas); red long stay; 90% statics; phone;
Eng spkn; adv bkg acc; games area; games rm. *"Conv
A16, Calais ferries; rec LS phone to check site open;
ltd touring pitches & poss steep; muddy & unpleasant
in winter; rlwy runs along one side of site; NH only if
desperate!; new sw pool and MV area; gd clean facs
(2012); poor facs for waste water."* **€28.00**   2019

WINGEN SUR MODER *5D3* (1.3km S Rural) *48.91565,
7.36934* **Camp Municipal/Aire Naturelle,** Rue de
Zittersheim, 67290 Wingen-sur-Moder **03 88 89 71 27**
(Mairie); mairie@wingensurmoder.fr;
www.wingensurmoder.fr

⁂ 🅦 🚿 ⁄ 🌳 ① nr 🛒 nr

W fr Haguenau on D919 to W end Wingen-sur-
Moder. Site sp by rlwy arch. Sm, mkd, pt shd, terr,
EHU (13A); Eng spkn; adv bkg acc; CKE. *"Excel,
peaceful site but adj sports field poss used by youth
groups/motorbikers high ssn; clean facs; warden calls
am & pm; gd walking/cycling; pitch layout plan at the
gate."* **€11.50, 1 May-30 Sep.**   2015

**"Satellite navigation makes
touring much easier"**

Remember most sat navs don't know if you're
towing or in a larger vehicle – always use yours
alongside maps and site directions.

WISSANT *3A2* (7.6km NE Coastal) *50.91226,
1.72054* **Camping Les Erables,** 17 Rue du Château
d'Eau, 62179 Escalles **03 21 85 25 36;** boutroy.les-
erables@wanadoo.fr; www.camping-les-erables.fr

🐕 ⁂ (htd) 🅦 🚿 ♿ ⛽ ⁄ 🖿 ♉ ① nr 🛒 nr 🏕 sand 2km

Fr A16 take exit 40 onto D243 thro Peuplingues. Site
sp to L on ent Escalles (on sharp R bend). Steep ent.
Don't be put off by No Entry sp - 1-way system for
c'vans on app rd. 1*, Sm, hdstg, mkd, pt shd, terr, EHU
(6-10A) €3.50-€4.50; bbq; phone; Eng spkn; adv bkg
rec; CKE. *"Lovely, well-kept open site with great views;
family owned; spacious pitches but poss haphazard
pitching; immac, modern facs; gates open 0800-2200; 2
pitches for disabled visitors with san facs; coast walks; sh
walk to vill; private san facs extra; conv tunnel & ferries;
gd site with view of Channel; excel grass pitch site;
friendly, welcoming, helpful owners; popular site; ideal
NH."* **€19.00, 1 Apr-11 Nov.**   2017

YPORT *3C1* (0.9km SE Rural) *49.73221, 0.32098*
Camp Municipal La Chenaie, Rue Henri-Simon,
76111 Yport **02 35 27 33 56; www.camping-
normandie-yport.com**

🚶 ⚌ 🔭 🦋 🔭 nr 🌳 shgl 1km

Take D940 fr Fécamp SW, D211 to Yport to site.
3*, Med, pt shd, EHU (10A); 80% statics. *"Conv Le
Havre."* **€33.00, 31 Mar-30 Sep.**   **2018**

> ## "There aren't many sites open at this time of year"
>
> If you're travelling outside peak season
> remember to call ahead to check site opening
> dates – even if the entry says 'open all year'.

CORSICA

GHISONACCIA *10H2* (4km E Coastal) *41.99850,
9.44220* **Camping Arinella Bianca,**
Bruschetto, 20240 Ghisonaccia **04 95 56 04 78;
arinella@arinellabianca.com; www.arinellabianca.com**

🐕 €6 🚶 ⚌ 🔭 👶 🔭 🌳 🍽 ⛺ 🛒 ⚱ 🌳 🏊 (htd) 🛏

🌳 sand adj

**S fr Bastia on N193/N198 approx 70km to
Ghisonaccia. At Ghisonaccia foll sp opp pharmacy
to beach (plage) & Rte de la Mer. In 3km turn R
at rndabt & site well sp. NB When towing keep to
main, coastal rds.** 4*, Lge, mkd, hdg, shd, EHU (6A)
€5.50 (poss rev pol); gas; bbq; TV; 45% statics; Eng
spkn; adv bkg acc; ccard acc; games area; horseriding
adj; games rm; bike hire; fishing; watersports; tennis;
CKE. *"Clean, well-run site; attractive lake in cent; trees
make access to pitches diff; helpful owner & staff."*
€38.00, 16 Apr-30 Sep.   **2016**

PIETRACORBARA *10G2* (4km SE Coastal) *42.83908,
9.4736* **Camping La Pietra,** Marine de Pietracorbara,
20233 Pietracorbara **04 95 35 27 49; lapietra@
wanadoo.fr; www.la-pietra.com**

🐕 €3.50 🚶(htd) ⚌ 👶 🔭 🌳 🍽 ⛺ 🛒 🌳 🏊 🌳 sand 600m

**Fr Bastia on D80 N. In 20km ent vill & turn L onto
D232. Site on R in 1km at marina beach. Well sp.**
3*, Med, mkd, hdg, shd, EHU (20A) €3.60; bbq; TV;
bus nr; Eng spkn; ccard acc; lake fishing; tennis; CKE.
*"Generous pitches; helpful owners; excel facs; beautiful
pool; gd beach rest."* **€29.80, 20 Mar-4 Nov.**   **2017**

PORTO VECCHIO *10H2* (7.3km N Rural) *41.646168,
9.296385* **Camping Cupulatta,** 20170 Porto Vecchio
06 12 81 50 89; www.campingcorse-cupulatta.com

🐕 €2 🚶(cont) 🔭 ⚌ 👶 🔭 🌳 nr 🌳 🏊 ⛺ 🌳 10km shgl

**Fr Lecci on N198 (T10). Site on R after dbl bdge
direction Porto Vecchio in 4km.** 3*, Sm, mkd, pt shd,
EHU (6A) €4; bbq (elec, gas); twin axles; 90% statics;
phone; adv bkg acc; CKE. *"Driving distance fr coast
with all facs; close to scenic mountains; rest on access
rd; gd."* **€25.00, 1 Apr-31 Sep.**   **2019**

SOLENZARA *10H2* (12km W Rural) *41.83495, 9.32144*
Camping U Ponte Grossu, Route de Bavella, 20145
Sari-Solenzara **04 95 48 26 61 or 06 64 79 80 46
(mob); lucchinitoussaint[at]gmail.com;
www.upontegrossu.com**

🐕 🚶 ⚌ 🔭 👶 🔭 🍽 🎾 🌳 ⚱

Fr N198, take D268 to U Ponte Grossu.
Sm, mkd, pt shd, terr, EHU (6A); adv bkg acc; CCI. *"Site
alongside rv; rv adj; canyoning; rafting; access to fab
mountain areas; vg."* **€26.50, 1 May-20 Sep.**   **2019**

ILE DE RE

ARS EN RE *7A1* (0.4km S Coastal) *46.20395, -1.52014*
FFCC Camping du Soleil, 57 Route de la Grange, 17590
Ars-en-Ré **05 46 29 40 62; contact@campdusoleil.com;
www.campdusoleil.com**

🐕 €3.20 🚶 ⚌ 🔭 👶 🔭 🌳 🍽 🎾 🌳 ⚱ 🛒 🌳 🏊(htd) 🛏

🌳 sand 400m

**On ent Ars-en-Ré on D735, pass Citroën g'ge & in
700m take 3rd L dir Plage de la Grange. Site sp.**
3*, Med, mkd, hdg, shd, EHU (4-10A) €3.70-4.90;
bbq (elec, gas); TV; 35% statics; phone; adv bkg
acc; games area; bike hire; tennis; CKE. *"Pleasant,
pretty site with pines & bamboo; helpful, friendly
staff; gd pool; gd cycling & walking; sm pitches tight."*
€48.00, 1 Apr-1 Oct.   **2017**

ARS EN RE *7A1* (1.6km SW Coastal) *46.20282,
-1.52733* **Camping Essi,** 15 Route de la Pointe de
Grignon, 17590 Ars-en-Ré **05 46 29 44 73 or
05 46 29 46 09 (LS); camping.essi@wanadoo.fr;
www.campingessi.com**

🐕 €2.10 🚶(htd) ⚌ 🔭 👶 🔭 🌳 🦋 🍽 ⚱ 🛒 🌳 🏊

**D735 to Ars-en-Ré; do not enter town; turn L at
supmkt. Site sp.** 3*, Med, hdg, pt shd, EHU (5-10A)
€3.95-5.60; bbq; 20% statics; phone; Eng spkn; adv bkg
acc; bike hire; watersports; CKE. *"Attractive waterfront
town; excel beaches 2km; gd cycling; gd oysters; vg;
well run & clean facs."* **€28.50, 1 Apr-31 Oct.**   **2015**

FRANCE

Route de Radia 17590 ARS EN RÉ
Tel. 05 46 29 46 04
info@cormoran.com - www.cormoran.com

Le Cormoran

CAMPING ★★★★★ ILE DE RÉ

500m from the sea, at the border of a forest and 800m from the picturesque village Ars en Ré ; campsite Le Cormoran is a true paradise for young and old. Heated aquatic park (from april to September) with one pool, a children's pool and a spa, the «serenity space» with hammam, sauna and tisanerie, and high standard toilet blocks with air conditioning (renovated in 2015).

ARS EN RE *7A1* (0.3km NW Coastal) *46.21130, -1.53017* **Camping Le Cormoran,** Route de Radia, 17590 Ars-en-Ré **05 46 29 46 04; info@cormoran.com; www.cormoran.com**

€5.00 nr (htd) 500m

Fr La Rochelle take D735 onto Ile-de-Ré, site sp fr Ars-en-Ré. 4*, Med, hdstg, hdg, mkd, pt shd, EHU (10A) €6; 10% statics; Eng spkn; adv bkg acc; ccard acc; games rm; sauna; golf 10km; bike hire; tennis; games area; CKE. *"Delightful vill; vg site."* **€49.00, 1 Apr-30 Sep.** **2019**

See advertisement

COUARDE SUR MER, LA *7A1* (5km SE Coastal) *46.17405, -1.37865* **Sunêlia Parc Club Interlude,** 8 Route de Gros Jonc, 17580 Le Bois-Plage-en-Ré **05 46 09 18 22; infos@interlude.fr; www.interlude.fr**

€8 (htd) (covrd, htd) sand

Fr toll bdge at La Rochelle foll D201 to Gros-Jonc. Turn L at rndabt at site sp. Site 400m on L. 4*, Lge, hdg, hdstg, mkd, pt shd, serviced pitches; EHU (10A) inc; gas; bbq; TV; 45% statics; Eng spkn; adv bkg req; bike hire; watersports; fitness rm; boat hire; solarium; sauna; tennis nr; games area; jacuzzi. *"Excel, well-run, clean, relaxing site; busy but not noisy; vg facs; some sm, sandy pitches - extra for lger; gd rest; nrby beaches excel; o'night m'vans area; walk to great beach; gd atmosphere, entmnt and shop."* **€50.00, 11 Apr-20 Sep.** **2016**

COUARDE SUR MER, LA *7A1* (1km W Urban/Coastal) *46.19348, -1.43427* **Camp Municipal Le Remondeau,** 12 Route Petite Noue, 17670 La Couarde-sur-Mer **05 46 29 84 27; campingleremondeau@wanadoo.fr; www.leremondeau.fr**

€3 (htd) sand adj

Fr toll bdge foll D735 to rndabt on W side of La Couarde-sur-Mer & take D201. Foll sp to site. 3*, Lge, pt shd, pt sl, EHU (10A) €4.70; bbq; red long stay; 10% statics; Eng spkn; CKE. *"Vg site; great cycling base."* **€25.00, 15 Mar-7 Nov.** **2018**

COUARDE SUR MER, LA *7A1* (3.6km NW Coastal) *46.20408, -1.46740* **Camping de l'Océan,** 50 Route d'Ars, 17670 La Couarde-sur-Mer **05 46 29 87 70; info@campingocean.com; www.campingocean.com**

€5 (htd) (htd) sand adj

Fr La Rochelle take D735 over bdge to Ile de Ré. Past St Martin-de-Re & La Couarde twd Ars-en-Ré. Site on R, 2.5km after La Couarde. 3*, Lge, mkd, hdg, shd, EHU (10A) €5.50; 40% statics; phone; Eng spkn; adv bkg acc; ccard acc; bike hire; games area; golf 6km; tennis; watersports; horseriding 1.5km; CKE. *"Popular site in superb location; some sm pitches with diff access; site rds & ent to pitches narr; rd noisy; gd, clean san facs; friendly staff; twin axles not rec; recep clsd 1230-1400, if clsd, park in yard facing recep; gd walking & cycling; excel; toll fee to island €16."* **€39.00, 16 Apr-18 Sep.** **2015**

"That's changed – Should I let the Club know?"

If you find something on site that's different from the site entry, fill in a report and let us know. See camc.com/europereport.

ST CLEMENT DES BALEINES *7A1* (0.5km E Rural/Coastal) *46.24041, -1.56070* **Camping Les Baleines,** Chemin Devaude, 17590 St. Clement-des-Baleines **05 46 29 40 76; camping.lesbaleines@wanadoo.fr; www.camping-lesbaleines.com**

€2-€3 nr nr nr sand adj

Fr bdge foll sp for Phare De Baleines. Sp 500m bef lighthouse. Do not foll sat nav. Narr vill rds. 3*, Lge, hdg, mkd, pt shd, EHU (10A) €5-6; bbq; twin axles; TV; 10% statics; phone; bus 200m; Eng spkn; ccard acc; games area; games rm; CKE. *"Vg, quiet site in natural surroundings; helpful staff; clean modern shwrs; direct access to beach; bar 500m; 5mins walk to lighthouse."* **€42.00, 27 Apr-21 Sep.** **2019**

For a guide to symbols see the fold out on the rear cover

STE MARIE DE RE *7A1 (4km NW Coastal) 46.16112, -1.35428* **Camping Les Grenettes,** Route De L'Ermitage, 17740 Ste Marie De Re **05 46 30 22 47; contact@ hotel-les-grenettes.com; www.campingles grenettes.com**

🎫12 🐕 €4 ♯♯ ⓌⒹ ♨ ⚲ / ᴹˢᴾ ♈ ⑪ ▨ ⚙ ⚇ ⛵ ⚓ ⚓ 200m

Foll sp for D201 'Itinéraire Sud' after toll bdge in the dir of Le Bois-de-Plage; after approx 2km turn L. 2*, Med, mkd, pt shd, EHU (6A) €4.50; gas; bbq; TV; Eng spkn; adv bkg acc; ccard acc; tennis; fishing; waterslide; bike hire. *"Nice site close to sea; vg rest; many facs, but stretched in high ssn."* **€44.00**   2016

ST MARTIN DE RE *7A1 (4km E Urban/Coastal) 46.18194, -1.33110* **Flower Camping de Bel Air,** Route de la Noué, 17630 La Flotte-en-Ré **05 46 09 63 10; camping.bel-air@flowercampings.com; www.bel-air-camping.com**

♯♯ ⓌⒹ ♨ ⚲ & ▨ / ᴹˢᴾ 🦋 ♈ ♈ ⑪ ▨ ⚙ ⚇ 800m

Fr toll bdge take D735 to La Flotte. Turn R at rndabt to town into Route de la Noué, site sp. 3*, Lge, hdg, mkd, pt shd, EHU (6A) €3.84; phone; adv bkg acc; games rm; tennis. *"Walk to shops, harbour, beach etc; gd; friendly staff; toll bdge €8 winter ssn, €16 summer ssn."* **€29.00, 30 Mar-3 Nov.**   2015

ST MARTIN DE RE *7A1 (0.5km S Urban) 46.19913, -1.36682* **Camp Municipal Les Remparts,** Rue Les Remparts, 17410 St Martin-de-Ré **05 46 09 21 96; camping.stmartindere@wanadoo.fr; www.saint-martin-de-re.fr**

🐕 €2 ♯♯ ⓌⒹ ♨ & ▨ / ᴹˢᴾ 🦋 ⚲ ▨ ⚙ sand 1.3km

Foll D735 fr toll bdge to St Martin; sp in town fr both ends. 2*, Med, mkd, hdg, pt shd, pt sl, EHU (10A) €3.70; bbq; Eng spkn; adv bkg acc; ccard acc; CKE. *"Busy site in brilliant location; san facs dated but clean; gd basic rest; poss children's groups mid-ssn; some pitches boggy when wet; gd cycling; site poss unkempt end ssn; vg mkt; beautiful situation on o'skirts of a lovely town, gd size pitches; pool 3km; superb position."* **€25.00, 12 Mar-18 Nov.**   2017

ILE D'OLERON

BREE LES BAINS, LA *7A1 (0.8km NW Coastal) 46.01861, -1.35446* **Camp Municipal Le Planginot,** Allée du Gai Séjour, 17840 La Brée-les-Bains **05 46 47 82 18; camping.planginot@orange.fr; www.labreelesbains.com**

🐕 €2 ♯♯ (htd) ⓌⒹ ♨ & ▨ / ᴹˢᴾ 🦋 ⑪ ▨ ⚙ adj

N fr St Pierre d'Oléron on D734, turn R for La Brée on D273, site sp (if sp diff to see - foll 'plage' sp). 2*, Lge, mkd, pt shd, EHU (10A) €3.60; 15% statics; Eng spkn; adv bkg acc. *"Well-kept site in quiet location; friendly, helpful staff; gd cycling; daily mkt nrby; gd."* **€15.00, 15 Mar-15 Oct.**   2015

CHATEAU D'OLERON, LE *7B1 (2.5km NW Coastal) 45.90415, -1.21525* **Camping La Brande,** Route des Huîtres, 17480 Le Château-d'Oléron **05 46 47 62 37; info@camping-labrande.com; www.camping-labrande.com or www.campings-oleron.com**

🐕 €3 ♯♯ ♨ & ▨ / ᴹˢᴾ ♈ ♈ ⑪ ▨ ⚙ ⚇ (covrd, htd)

⛵ sand 300m

Cross bdge on D26, turn R & go thro Le Château-d'Oléron. Foll Rte des Huîtres to La Gaconnière to site. 5*, Lge, shd, EHU (6-10A) €4-6; gas; bbq; TV; 60% statics; Eng spkn; adv bkg acc; ccard acc; tennis; golf 6km; games area; sep car park; bike hire; waterslide; CKE. *"Pleasant owners; pitches at far end adj oyster farm - some noise fr pumps & poss mosquitoes; sauna; steam rm; 10 min cycle ride into town; vg."* **€44.00, 1 Apr-5 Nov.**   2017

ST GEORGES D'OLERON *7A1 (7km E Coastal) 45.96820, -1.24483* **Camp Atlantique Signol,** Ave des Albatros, Boyardville, 17190 St Georges-d'Oléron **02 51 20 41 94; contact@signol.com; signol.camp-atlantique.co.uk/en**

🐕 €4 ♯♯ ⓌⒹ ♨ ⚲ & ▨ / ᴹˢᴾ ♈ ⑪ ▨ ⚙ ⚇

⛵ (htd, indoor) ⚓ sand 800m

Cross bdge onto Ile d'Oléron & cont on main rd twd St Pierre-d'Oléron. Turn R at Dolus-d'Oléron for Boyardville & foll sp in vill. 4*, Lge, hdg, mkd, pt shd, pt sl, EHU (6A); gas; 70% statics; Eng spkn; adv bkg acc. *"Size of pitches variable; san facs stretched in high ssn; impressive pool complex; narr site rds;1 dog per pitch; gd site & facs; vg activities for kids; low overhanging branches."* **€22.00, 3 Apr-20 Sep.**   2017

ST GEORGES D'OLERON *7A1 (2km SE Rural) 45.96796, -1.31874* **Camping Le Domaine d'Oléron,** La Jousselinière, 17190 St Georges-d'Oléron **05 46 76 54 97 or 02 51 33 05 05 (LS); info@chadotel.com; www.chadotel.com**

🐕 €3.90 ♯♯ ♨ ⚲ & ▨ / ᴹˢᴾ 🦋 ♈ ♈ ⚇ ▨ ⚙ ⚇ ⛵ ⚇

⚓ sand 3km

After x-ing Viaduct (bdge) onto island foll sp dir St Pierre d'Oléron & St Georges-d'Oléron on D734; turn R on rndabt immed see Leclerc supmkt on R; at next rndabt turn L sp 'Le Bois Fleury'; pass airfield 'Bois 'Fleury' on R; take next R & then immed L. Site on L in 500m. 4*, Lge, mkd, hdg, pt shd, terr, EHU (6A) inc; gas; bbq (gas, sep area); red long stay; TV; 40% statics; Eng spkn; adv bkg rec; ccard acc; bike hire; games area; games rm; waterslide; CKE. *"Popular, well-organised, clean site; friendly, helpful staff; lovely pool; no o'fits over 8m high ssn; max 1 dog; cycle paths; fair."* **€42.14, 1 Apr-30 Sep, A41.**   2019

ST GEORGES D'OLERON *7A1* (6km SW Coastal)
45.95386, -1.37932 **Camping Les Gros Joncs,** Les
Sables Vigniers, 17190 St Georges-d'Oléron **05 46 76
52 29; info@camping-les-gros-joncs.com;
www.camping-les-gros-joncs.com**

12 🐕 €3 ⚄ ♨ ⛲ ⚒ / 🦋 ⓨ ⊕ ⚓ 🏕 ⛰ ⚓ (htd) 🏊
🌲 shgl 200m

Fr bdge D734 to St Pierre, at 2nd traff lts (police
stn) turn L to La Cotinière 4km, at x-rds turn R dir
Domino (Ave De Pins) for 5km. Site on L past Le
Suroit. 5*, V lge, pt shd, EHU (10A) €3; TV;
10% statics; adv bkg acc; games area; jacuzzi. "*Excel
pool; beach sand 1km; hydrotherapy sprays; great
location; clean facs; rec.*" **€50.00**   **2016**

ST GEORGES D'OLERON *7A1* (7km SW Coastal)
45.94756, -1.37386 **Camping Le Suroit,** L'Ileau de la
Grande Côte, 17190 St Georges-d'Oléron
**05 46 47 07 25 or 06 80 10 93 18 (mob); camping@
lesuroit.fr; www.camping-lesuroit.fr**

🐕 €5 ⚄ (htd) ♨ ⚓ ⛲ ⚒ / 🦋 ⓨ ⊕ ⚓ 🏕 ⛰ ⚓
⚓ (covrd, htd) 🌲 sand adj

Fr Domino cent foll sp for beach, turn L for L'Ileau.
Strt at x-rds. Fork L for La Cotinière, site on R in 150m.
4*, Lge, mkd, shd, EHU (10A) €4.50; gas; bbq;
TV; 10% statics; adv bkg acc; ccard acc; bike hire;
games area; tennis; CKE. "*Excel, well-organised site.*"
€35.00, 1 Apr-33 Sep.   **2015**

ST PIERRE D'OLERON *7B1* (4km SW Coastal) *45.92315,
-1.34130* **Camping Le Sous Bois,** avenue des Pins,
17310 Saint Pierre d'Oleron **05 46 47 22 46;
resa.lesousbois@orange.fr; www.camping-
lesousbois-oleron.com**

🐕 €4 ⚄ wo ♨ ⚓ ⛲ ⚒ / ⓨ ⓣ nr 🏕 nr ⚓

Fr St Pierre take D274 to La Cotiniere. In La Cotiniere
foll dir L'Ileau, turn R onto Ave des Pins. Campsite
500m out of town on R. 3*, Med, mkd, hdg, pt shd,
EHU (3A, 6A-10A) €5-7; Eng spkn; adv bkg acc; sauna;
games area; beac 200m. "*Gd cycle tracks; sailing school;
jet ski; equestrian ctr in Cotiniere; conv location; bar
20m; vg.*" **€33.50, 1 Apr-31 Oct.**   **2016**

ST PIERRE D'OLERON *7B1* (3.5km W Coastal)
45.92394, -1.34273 **FFCC Camp Municipal La Fauche
Prère,** Ave des Pins, La Cotinière, 17310 St Pierre
d'Oléron **05 46 47 10 53; camping@saintpierreoleron.
com; www.saintpierreoleron.com**

🐕 €2 ⚄ ⚒ wo ♨ ⚓ ⛲ / mp 🏕 ⛰ ⚓ 🌲 sand adj

Fr bdge foll D734 N to St Pierre-d'Oléron. Turn L
onto D274 for La Cotinière, site bef vill on L, sp.
Med, mkd, shd, pt sl, EHU (12A) €4.10; CKE. "*Direct
access to beach; most pitches sandy; gd; lovely site
amongst pine trees; new san facs (2017); quiet.*"
€22.00, 1 Apr-30 Sep.   **2017**

"I like to fill in the reports as I travel from site to site"

You'll find report forms at the back of this
guide, or you can fill them in online at
camc.com/europereport.

ST TROJAN LES BAINS *7B1* (1.5km SW Rural)
45.82947, -1.21632 **Flower Camping St-Tro'Park
(formerly Camping La Combinette),** 36 Ave des Bris,
17370 St Trojan-les-Bains **05 46 76 00 47; info@
st-tro-park.com; www.st-tro-park.com**

🐕 ⚄ ♨ ⚓ ⛲ ⚒ / 🦋 ⓣ ⊕ ⚓ 🏕 ⛰ ⚓ 🚣 🌲 2km

Fr toll bdge stay on D26 for 1km, L onto D275 &
L onto D126 to St Trojan-les-Bains. Strt ahead at
rndabt with figure sculpture, then R at next rndabt
sp Campings. In 1km turn L at rd fork, site on R in
1km. 4*, Lge, shd, EHU (5-10A) (poss rev pol); gas;
games area; bike hire. "*Gd touring base; some super
pitches; poss flooding in heavy rain; lovely site amongst
pine trees; sauna; spa; gym; new san facs (2017); vg.*"
€35.00, 15 Apr-15 Oct.   **2017**

Sites in Andorra

CANILLO (ANDORRA) *8G3* (0.3km ENE Urban) *42.56740, 1.60235.* **Camping Pla,** Ctra General s/n, AD100 Canillo **601 283; www.facebook.com/ paco.cristina**

12 🏇 👫(htd) wc ⛲ ♨ 🗑 ∥ ⊤ Ⓗnr 🏕

App Canillo fr S, pass Tarrado petrol stn on R; take 1st exit at 1st rndabt opp lge hotel, over bdge & turn L to site. Med, mkd, pt shd, EHU (5-10A) €3; gas; 75% statics; bus adj; Eng spkn; adv bkg acc. *"Excel location for skiing but poss unkempt/untidy LS; htd covrd pool in town; sports facs in town; ski lift 100m."* **€14.00** 2016

MASSANA, LA (ANDORRA) *8G3* (2km N Rural) *42.56601, 1.52448* **Camping Borda d'Ansalonga,** Ctra General del Serrat, AD300 Ordino **850 374; www.campingbordaansalonga.com**

🏇 👫(htd) wc ⛲ ♨ 🗑 ∥ 🦋 ⊤ Ⓗ 🐾 🏕 ⛷

Fr Andorra-la-Vella foll sp La Massana & Ordino. Turn L twd El Serrat, site on R, well sp. Lge, pt shd, EHU (10A) €5.60; gas; bbq; phone; Eng spkn; games rm; CKE. *"Statics moved to storage area in summer; winter statics for skiers; quieter than sites on main thro rte."* **€24.00, 17 Oct-25 Apr & 15 Jun-15 Sep.** 2016

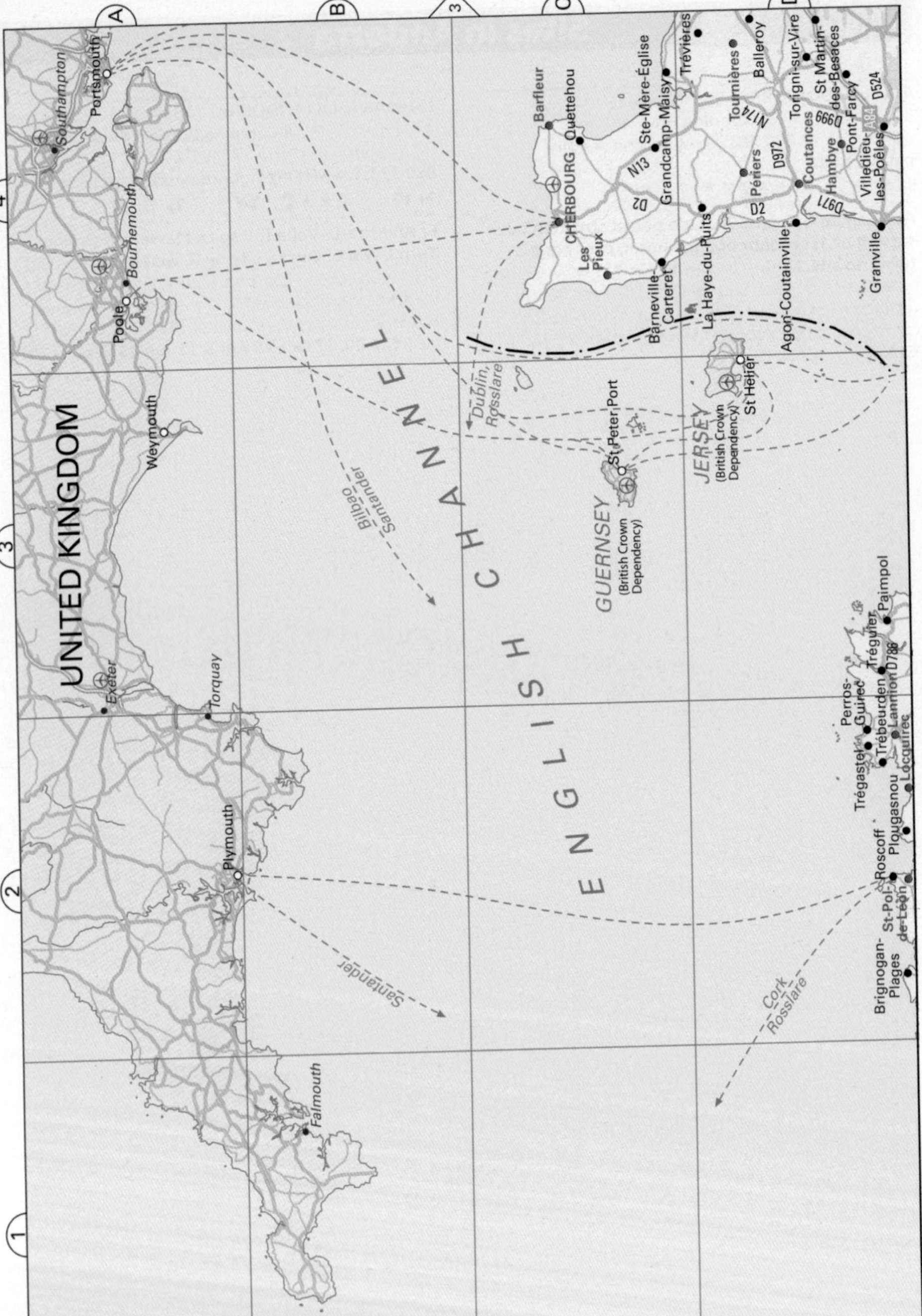
UNITED KINGDOM
ENGLISH CHANNEL
Southampton
Portsmouth
Bournemouth
Poole
Weymouth
Exeter
Torquay
Plymouth
Falmouth
Bilbao
Santander
Dublin, Rosslare
Cork
Rosslare
GUERNSEY
(British Crown Dependency)
St Peter Port
JERSEY
(British Crown Dependency)
St Helier
Barfleur
Quettehou
CHERBOURG
Les Pieux
Ste-Mère-Église
Grandcamp-Maisy
Trévières
Tournières
Balleroy
Barneville-Carteret
La Haye-du-Puits
Périers
Agon-Coutainville
Coutances
Torigni-sur-Vire
St Martin-des-Besaces
Pont-Farcy
Hambye
Villedieu-les-Poêles
Granville
N13
D2
N174
D972
D971
D999
D524
A84
Paimpol
Tréguier
D786
Perros-Guirec
Trégastel
Trébeurden
Lannion
Locquirec
Plougasnou
Roscoff
St-Pol-de-Léon
Brignogan-Plages
A
B
C
D
1
2
3
4

Map 1

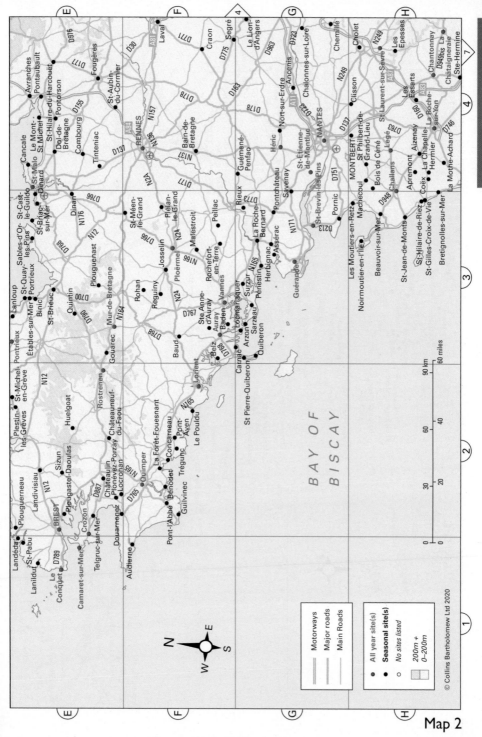

FRANCE

BAY OF BISCAY

	Motorways		
	Major roads		
	Main Roads		

- All year site(s)
- **Seasonal site(s)**
- ○ *No sites listed*

200m +
0–200m

© Collins Bartholomew Ltd 2020

Map 2

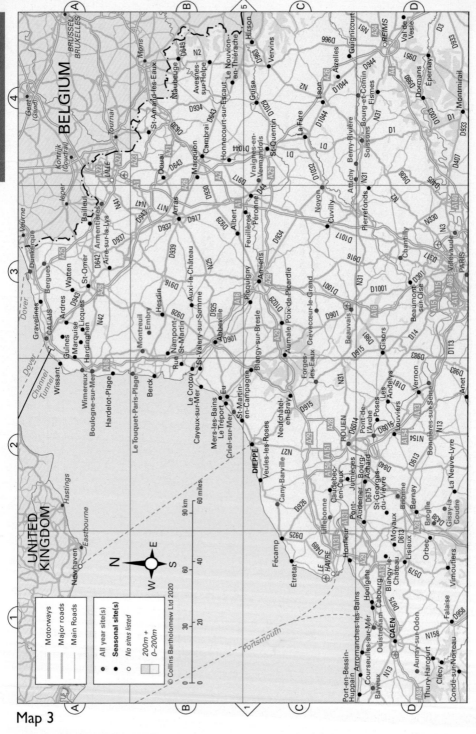

Map 3

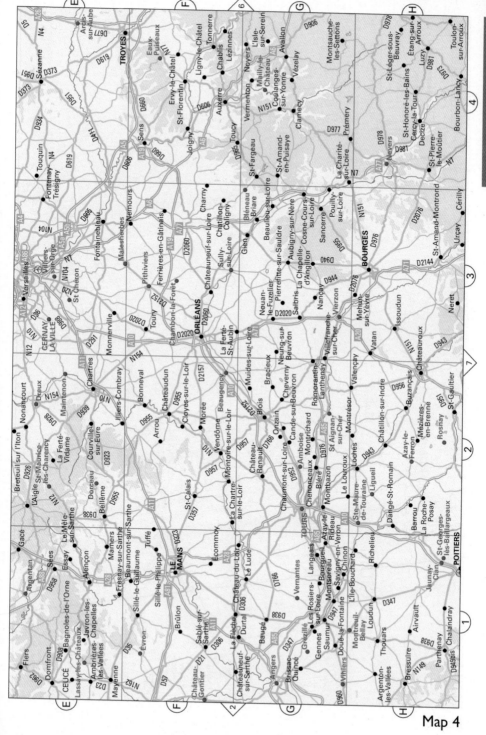

FRANCE

Map 4

355

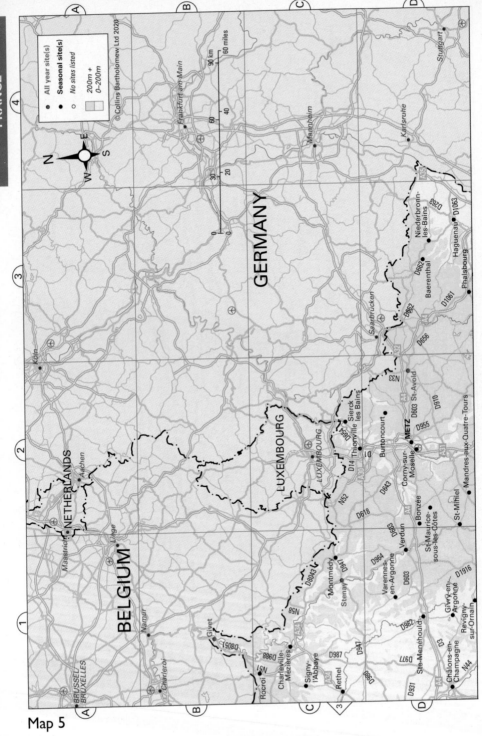

Map 5

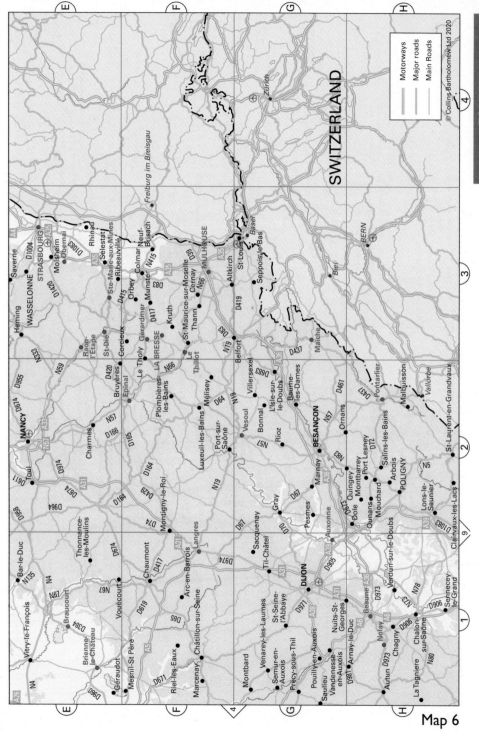

Motorways
Major roads
Main Roads

SWITZERLAND

Zürich

BERN

Basel
Biel

Map 6

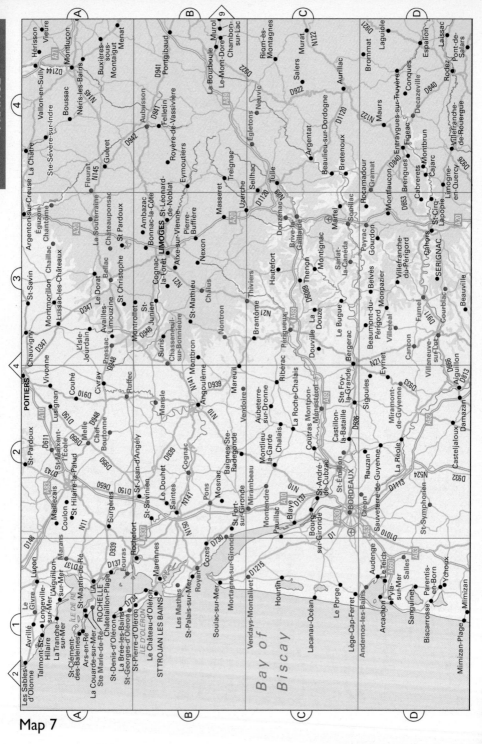

FRANCE

Map 7

358

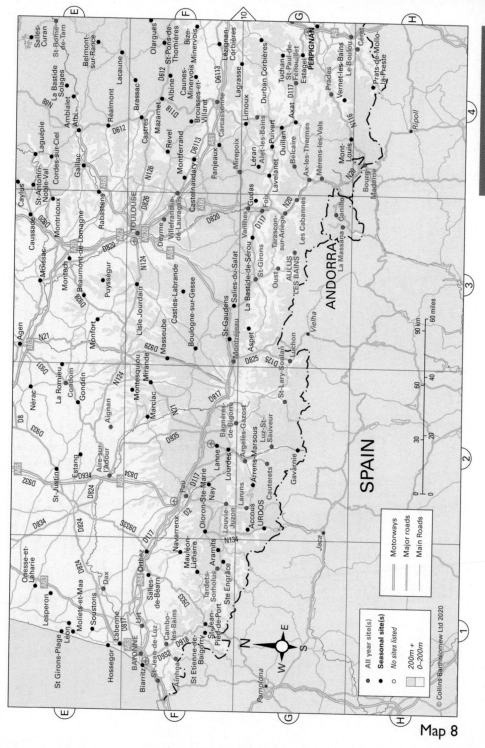

Map 8

359

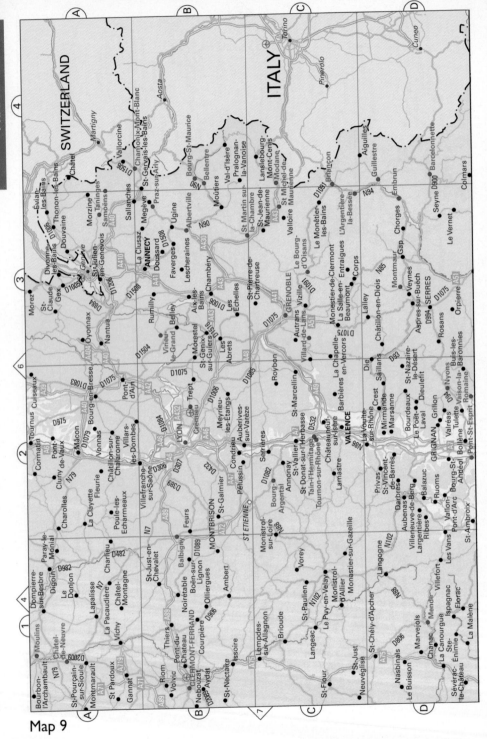

Map 9

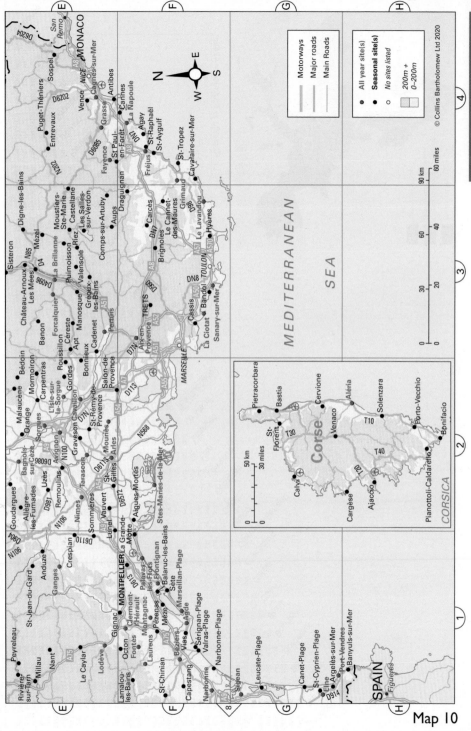

Map 10

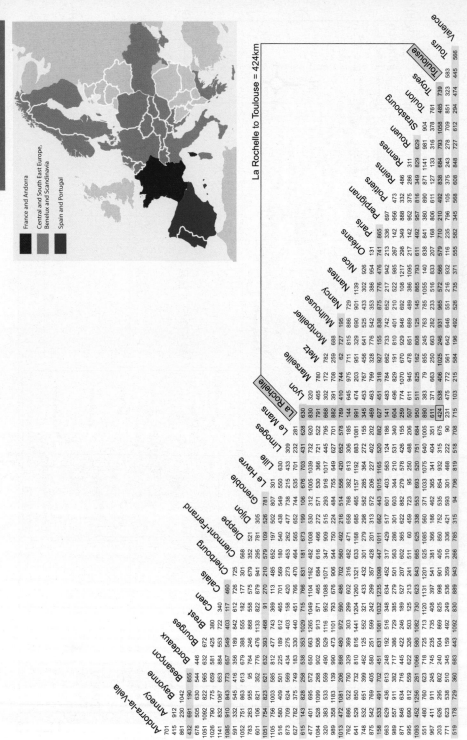

UK Campsites

We have the largest UK network with over 2700 quality sites

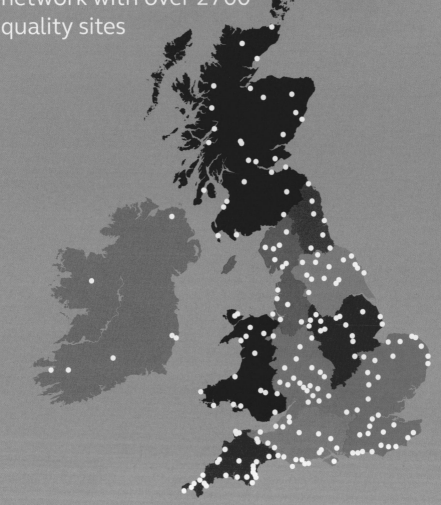

Visit camc.com/uksites

CARAVAN AND MOTORHOME CLUB
SINCE 1907

Site Report Form

If campsite is already listed, complete only those sections of the form where changes apply
or alternatively use the Abbreviated Site Report form on the following pages.

Sites not reported on for 5 years may be deleted from the guide

Year of guide used	20..........	Is site listed?	Listed on page no............	Unlisted	Date of visit	......../........./.........

A – CAMPSITE NAME AND LOCATION

Country		Name of town/village site listed under *(see Sites Location Maps)*				
Distance & direction from centre of town site is listed under *(in a straight line)*		....................km	eg N, NE, S, SW	Urban	Rural	Coastal
Site open all year?	Y / N	Period site is open *(if not all year)*	................./................. to ..../.................			
Site name					Naturist site	Y / N
Site address						
Telephone			Fax			
E-mail			Website			

B – CAMPSITE CHARGES

Charge for outfit + 2 adults in local currency	PRICE		

C – DIRECTIONS

Brief, specific directions to site (in km) *To convert miles to kilometres multiply by 8 and divide by 5 or use Conversion Table in guide*	
GPS	Latitude...(eg 12.34567) Longitude..(eg 1.23456 or -1.23456)

D – SITE INFORMATION

Dogs allowed	DOGS	Y / N	Price per night .... *(if allowed)*
Facilities for disabled			
Public Transport within 5km	BUS / TRAM / TRAIN	Adj	Nearby
Reduction long stay	RED LONG STAY	Credit Card accepted	CCARD ACC
Advance bookings accepted/recommended/required		ADV BKG ACC / REC / REQ	
Camping Key Europe or Camping Card International accepted in lieu of passport		CKE/CCI	

E – SITE DESCRIPTION

SITE size ie number of pitches	Small Max 50	SM	Medium 51-150	MED	Large 151-500	LGE	Very large 500+	V LGE	Unchanged
Pitch features if **NOT** open-plan/grassy	HDG PITCH	Hedged	HDG PITCH	Marked or numbered	MKD PITCH	Hardstanding or gravel	HDSTG	Unchanged
If site is **NOT** level, is it	PT SL	Part sloping	PT SL	Sloping	SL	Terraced	TERR	Unchanged
Is site shaded?	SHD	Shaded	SHD	Part shaded	PT SHD	Unshaded	UNSHD	Unchanged
ELECTRIC HOOK UP *if not included in price above*	EL PNTS			Price...			Amps......................	
% Static caravans / mobile homes / chalets / cottages / fixed tents on site							.................% STATICS	
Serviced Pitched		Y / N		Twin axles caravans allowed?			TWIN AXLES Y / N	

You can also complete forms online: camc.com/europereport

CUT ALONG DOTTED LINE

E – SITE DESCRIPTION CONTINUED...

Phone on site	PHONE			Wifi Internet	WIFI
Television	TV RM		TV CAB / SAT	Playground	PLAYGRND
Entertainment in high season	ENTMNT			English spoken	ENG SPKN
Motorhome Service Point	Y / N				

F – CATERING

Bar	BAR	On site	or	Within 2km	
Restaurant	REST	On site	or	Within 2km	
Shop(s)	SHOP(S)	On site	or	Within 2km	
Snack bar / take-away	SNACKS	On site	Y / N		
Cooking facilities	COOKING FACS	On site	Y / N		
Supplies of bottled gas on site	GAS	Y / N			
Barbecue allowed	BBQ	Charcoal	Gas	Elec	Sep area

G – SANITARY FACILITIES

WC		Heated	HTD WC	Continental	CONT	Own San recommended	OWN SAN REC
Chemical disposal point			CHEM DISP				
Hot shower(s)		SHWR(S)	Inc in site fee?		Y / N		
Child / baby facilities (bathroom)			FAM BTHRM		Launderette / Washing Machine		LNDRY

H – OTHER INFORMATION

Swimming pool	POOL	HEATED	COVERED	INDOOR	PADDLING POOL	
Beach	BEACH	Adj	or ....km	Sand	Shingle	
Alternative swimming (lake)	SW	Adj	or ....km	Sand	Shingle	
Games /sports area / Games room	GAMES AREA		GAMES ROOM			

I – ADDITIONAL REMARKS AND/OR ITEMS OF INTEREST

Tourist attractions, unusual features or other facilities, eg waterslide, tennis, cycle hire, watersports, horseriding, separate car park, walking distance to shops etc	YOUR OPINION OF THE SITE:	
	EXCEL	
	VERY GOOD	
	GOOD	
	FAIR	POOR
	NIGHT HALT ONLY	

Your comments & opinions may be used in future editions of the guide, if you do not wish them to be used please tick ....

J – MEMBER DETAILS

ARE YOU A:	Caravanner		Motorhomer		Trailer-tenter?	
NAME:			MEMBERSHIP NO:			
			POST CODE:			
DO YOU NEED MORE BLANK SITE REPORT FORMS?		YES			NO	

Please use a separate form for each campsite and do not send receipts. Owing to the large number of site reports received, it is not possible to enter into correspondence. Please return completed form to:

The Editor, Overseas Touring Guides, East Grinstead House
East Grinstead, West Sussex RH19 1UA

Please note that due to changes in the rules regarding freepost we are no longer able to provide a freepost address for the return of Site Report Forms. You can still supply your site reports free online by visiting camc.com/europereport. We apologise for any inconvenience this may cause.

Site Report Form

If campsite is already listed, complete only those sections of the form where changes apply
or alternatively use the Abbreviated Site Report form on the following pages.
Sites not reported on for 5 years may be deleted from the guide

Year of guide used	20.........	Is site listed?	Listed on page no............	Unlisted	Date of visit ..../........./.........

A – CAMPSITE NAME AND LOCATION

Country		Name of town/village site listed under *(see Sites Location Maps)*				
Distance & direction from centre of town site is listed under *(in a straight line)*		...................km	eg N, NE, S, SW	Urban	Rural	Coastal
Site open all year?	Y / N	Period site is open *(if not all year)*	................./................. to ..../.................			
Site name					Naturist site	Y / N
Site address						
Telephone			Fax			
E-mail			Website			

B – CAMPSITE CHARGES

Charge for outfit + 2 adults in local currency	PRICE	

C – DIRECTIONS

Brief, specific directions to site (in km) *To convert miles to kilometres multiply by 8 and divide by 5 or use Conversion Table in guide*	
GPS	Latitude..(eg 12.34567) Longitude...(eg 1.23456 or -1.23456)

D – SITE INFORMATION

Dogs allowed	DOGS	Y / N	Price per night.................................. *(if allowed)*	
Facilities for disabled				
Public Transport within 5km	BUS / TRAM / TRAIN	Adj	Nearby	
Reduction long stay	RED LONG STAY	Credit Card accepted		CCARD ACC
Advance bookings accepted/recommended/required		ADV BKG ACC / REC / REQ		
Camping Key Europe or Camping Card International accepted in lieu of passport		CKE/CCI		

E – SITE DESCRIPTION

SITE size ie number of pitches	Small Max 50	SM	Medium 51-150	MED	Large 151-500	LGE	Very large 500+	V LGE	Unchanged
Pitch features if **NOT** open-plan/grassy	HDG PITCH	Hedged	HDG PITCH	Marked or numbered	MKD PITCH	Hardstanding or gravel		HDSTG	Unchanged
If site is **NOT** level, is it	PT SL	Part sloping	PT SL	Sloping	SL	Terraced		TERR	Unchanged
Is site shaded?		SHD	Shaded	SHD	Part shaded	PT SHD	Unshaded	UNSHD	Unchanged
ELECTRIC HOOK UP *if not included in price above*	EL PNTS			Price............................		Amps......................			
% Static caravans / mobile homes / chalets / cottages / fixed tents on site					.................% STATICS				
Serviced Pitched		Y / N		Twin axles caravans allowed?			TWIN AXLES Y / N		

You can also complete forms online: camc.com/europereport

CUT ALONG DOTTED LINE

E – SITE DESCRIPTION CONTINUED...

Phone on site	PHONE			Wifi Internet		WIFI
Television	TV RM		TV CAB / SAT	Playground		PLAYGRND
Entertainment in high season	ENTMNT			English spoken		ENG SPKN
Motorhome Service Point	Y / N					

F – CATERING

Bar	BAR	On site		or		Within 2km
Restaurant	REST	On site		or		Within 2km
Shop(s)	SHOP(S)	On site		or		Within 2km
Snack bar / take-away	SNACKS	On site		Y / N		
Cooking facilities	COOKING FACS	On site		Y / N		
Supplies of bottled gas on site	GAS	Y / N				
Barbecue allowed	BBQ	Charcoal		Gas	Elec	Sep area

G – SANITARY FACILITIES

WC	Heated	HTD WC	Continental	CONT	Own San recommended	OWN SAN REC
Chemical disposal point		CHEM DISP				
Hot shower(s)	SHWR(S)	Inc in site fee?		Y / N		
Child / baby facilities (bathroom)		FAM BTHRM		Launderette / Washing Machine		LNDRY

H – OTHER INFORMATION

Swimming pool	POOL	HEATED	COVERED	INDOOR	PADDLING POOL
Beach	BEACH	Adj	or ....km	Sand	Shingle
Alternative swimming (lake)	SW	Adj	or ....km	Sand	Shingle
Games /sports area / Games room	GAMES AREA		GAMES ROOM		

I – ADDITIONAL REMARKS AND/OR ITEMS OF INTEREST

Tourist attractions, unusual features or other facilities, eg waterslide, tennis, cycle hire, watersports, horseriding, separate car park, walking distance to shops etc	YOUR OPINION OF THE SITE:	
	EXCEL	
	VERY GOOD	
	GOOD	
	FAIR	POOR
	NIGHT HALT ONLY	

Your comments & opinions may be used in future editions of the guide, if you do not wish them to be used please tick ....

J – MEMBER DETAILS

ARE YOU A:	Caravanner		Motorhomer		Trailer-tenter?	
NAME:			MEMBERSHIP NO:			
			POST CODE:			
DO YOU NEED MORE BLANK SITE REPORT FORMS?			YES		NO	

Please use a separate form for each campsite and do not send receipts. Owing to the large number of site reports received, it is not possible to enter into correspondence. Please return completed form to:

**The Editor, Overseas Touring Guides, East Grinstead House
East Grinstead, West Sussex RH19 1UA**

Please note that due to changes in the rules regarding freepost we are no longer able to provide a freepost address for the return of Site Report Forms. You can still supply your site reports free online by visiting camc.com/europereport. We apologise for any inconvenience this may cause.

Site Report Form

If campsite is already listed, complete only those sections of the form where changes apply or alternatively use the Abbreviated Site Report form on the following pages.

Sites not reported on for 5 years may be deleted from the guide

Year of guide used	20..........	Is site listed?	Listed on page no............	Unlisted	Date of visit	........./........./.........

A – CAMPSITE NAME AND LOCATION

Country		Name of town/village site listed under *(see Sites Location Maps)*					
Distance & direction from centre of town site is listed under *(in a straight line)*		....................km	eg N, NE, S, SW		Urban	Rural	Coastal
Site open all year?	Y / N	Period site is open *(if not all year)*	................./................. to ..../.................				
Site name						Naturist site	Y / N
Site address							
Telephone				Fax			
E-mail				Website			

B – CAMPSITE CHARGES

Charge for outfit + 2 adults in local currency	PRICE	

C – DIRECTIONS

Brief, specific directions to site (in km) *To convert miles to kilometres multiply by 8 and divide by 5 or use Conversion Table in guide*	
GPS	Latitude.....................................*(eg 12.34567)* Longitude...*(eg 1.23456 or -1.23456)*

D – SITE INFORMATION

Dogs allowed	DOGS	Y / N	Price per night.................................. *(if allowed)*	
Facilities for disabled				
Public Transport within 5km	BUS / TRAM / TRAIN	Adj	Nearby	
Reduction long stay	RED LONG STAY	Credit Card accepted	CCARD ACC	
Advance bookings accepted/recommended/required		ADV BKG ACC / REC / REQ		
Camping Key Europe or Camping Card International accepted in lieu of passport			CKE/CCI	

E – SITE DESCRIPTION

SITE size ie number of pitches	Small Max 50	SM	Medium 51-150	MED	Large 151-500	LGE	Very large 500+	V LGE	Unchanged
Pitch features if **NOT** open-plan/grassy		HDG PITCH	Hedged	HDG PITCH	Marked or numbered	MKD PITCH	Hardstanding or gravel	HDSTG	Unchanged
If site is **NOT** level, is it		PT SL	Part sloping	PT SL	Sloping	SL	Terraced	TERR	Unchanged
Is site shaded?		SHD	Shaded	SHD	Part shaded	PT SHD	Unshaded	UNSHD	Unchanged
ELECTRIC HOOK UP *if not included in price above*	EL PNTS			Price...........................			Amps......................		
% Static caravans / mobile homes / chalets / cottages / fixed tents on site							.................% STATICS		
Serviced Pitched		Y / N			Twin axles caravans allowed?		TWIN AXLES Y / N		

You can also complete forms online: camc.com/europereport

E – SITE DESCRIPTION CONTINUED...

Phone on site	PHONE			Wifi Internet	WIFI
Television	TV RM		TV CAB / SAT	Playground	PLAYGRND
Entertainment in high season	ENTMNT			English spoken	ENG SPKN
Motorhome Service Point	Y / N				

F – CATERING

Bar	BAR	On site	or	Within 2km	
Restaurant	REST	On site	or	Within 2km	
Shop(s)	SHOP(S)	On site	or	Within 2km	
Snack bar / take-away	SNACKS	On site	Y / N		
Cooking facilities	COOKING FACS	On site	Y / N		
Supplies of bottled gas on site	GAS	Y / N			
Barbecue allowed	BBQ	Charcoal	Gas	Elec	Sep area

G – SANITARY FACILITIES

WC		Heated	HTD WC	Continental	CONT	Own San recommended	OWN SAN REC
Chemical disposal point			CHEM DISP				
Hot shower(s)		SHWR(S)	Inc in site fee?		Y / N		
Child / baby facilities (bathroom)			FAM BTHRM		Launderette / Washing Machine		LNDRY

H – OTHER INFORMATION

Swimming pool	POOL	HEATED	COVERED	INDOOR	PADDLING POOL
Beach	BEACH	Adj	or ....km	Sand	Shingle
Alternative swimming (lake)	SW	Adj	or ....km	Sand	Shingle
Games /sports area / Games room	GAMES AREA		GAMES ROOM		

I – ADDITIONAL REMARKS AND/OR ITEMS OF INTEREST

Tourist attractions, unusual features or other facilities, eg waterslide, tennis, cycle hire, watersports, horseriding, separate car park, walking distance to shops etc	YOUR OPINION OF THE SITE:	
	EXCEL	
	VERY GOOD	
	GOOD	
	FAIR	POOR
	NIGHT HALT ONLY	

Your comments & opinions may be used in future editions of the guide, if you do not wish them to be used please tick ....

J – MEMBER DETAILS

ARE YOU A:	Caravanner		Motorhomer		Trailer-tenter?	
NAME:			MEMBERSHIP NO:			
			POST CODE:			
DO YOU NEED MORE BLANK SITE REPORT FORMS?		YES			NO	

Please use a separate form for each campsite and do not send receipts. Owing to the large number of site reports received, it is not possible to enter into correspondence. Please return completed form to:

The Editor, Overseas Touring Guides, East Grinstead House
East Grinstead, West Sussex RH19 1UA

Please note that due to changes in the rules regarding freepost we are no longer able to provide a freepost address for the return of Site Report Forms. You can still supply your site reports free online by visiting camc.com/europereport. We apologise for any inconvenience this may cause.

Abbreviated Site Report Form

Use this abbreviated Site Report Form if you have visited a number of sites and there are no changes (or only small changes) to their entries in the guide. If reporting on a new site, or reporting several changes, please use the full version of the report form. If advising prices, these should be for an outfit, and 2 adults for one night's stay. **Please indicate high or low season prices and whether electricity is included.**

Remember, if you don't tell us about sites you have visited, they may eventually be deleted from the guide.

Year of guide used	20..........	Page No.	....	Name of town/village site listed under	
Site Name					Date of visit ..../......./........
GPS	Latitude..(eg 12.34567) Longitude...(eg 1.23456 or -1.23456)				
Site is in: Andorra / Austria / Belgium / Croatia / Czech Republic / Denmark / Finland / France / Germany / Greece / Hungary / Italy / Luxembourg / Netherlands / Norway / Poland / Portugal / Slovakia / Slovenia / Spain / Sweden / Switzerland					
Comments:					

Charge for outfit + 2 adults in local currency	High Season	Low Season	Elec inc in price?	Y / N	.............amps
			Price of elec (if not inc)		.............amps

Year of guide used	20..........	Page No.	....	Name of town/village site listed under	
Site Name					Date of visit ..../......./........
GPS	Latitude..(eg 12.34567) Longitude...(eg 1.23456 or -1.23456)				
Site is in: Andorra / Austria / Belgium / Croatia / Czech Republic / Denmark / Finland / France / Germany / Greece / Hungary / Italy / Luxembourg / Netherlands / Norway / Poland / Portugal / Slovakia / Slovenia / Spain / Sweden / Switzerland					
Comments:					

Charge for outfit + 2 adults in local currency	High Season	Low Season	Elec inc in price?	Y / N	.............amps
			Price of elec (if not inc)		.............amps

Year of guide used	20..........	Page No.	....	Name of town/village site listed under	
Site Name					Date of visit ..../......./........
GPS	Latitude..(eg 12.34567) Longitude...(eg 1.23456 or -1.23456)				
Site is in: Andorra / Austria / Belgium / Croatia / Czech Republic / Denmark / Finland / France / Germany / Greece / Hungary / Italy / Luxembourg / Netherlands / Norway / Poland / Portugal / Slovakia / Slovenia / Spain / Sweden / Switzerland					
Comments:					

Charge for car, caravan & 2 adults in local currency	High Season	Low Season	Elec inc in price?	Y / N	.............amps
			Price of elec (if not inc)		.............amps

Please fill in your details and send to the address on the reverse of this form.
You can also complete forms online: camc.com/europereport

CUT ALONG DOTTED LINE

Year of guide used	20..........	Page No.	....	Name of town/village site listed under			
Site Name					Date of visit	......./......./........	
GPS	Latitude...(eg 12.34567) Longitude...(eg 1.23456 or -1.23456)						
Site is in: Andorra / Austria / Belgium / Croatia / Czech Republic / Denmark / Finland / France / Germany / Greece / Hungary / Italy / Luxembourg / Netherlands / Norway / Poland / Portugal / Slovakia / Slovenia / Spain / Sweden / Switzerland							
Comments:							
Charge for outfit + 2 adults in local currency	High Season	Low Season	Elec inc in price?		Y / N	.............amps	
			Price of elec (if not inc)			.............amps	

Year of guide used	20..........	Page No.	....	Name of town/village site listed under			
Site Name					Date of visit	......./......./........	
GPS	Latitude...(eg 12.34567) Longitude...(eg 1.23456 or -1.23456)						
Site is in: Andorra / Austria / Belgium / Croatia / Czech Republic / Denmark / Finland / France / Germany / Greece / Hungary / Italy / Luxembourg / Netherlands / Norway / Poland / Portugal / Slovakia / Slovenia / Spain / Sweden / Switzerland							
Comments:							
Charge for outfit + 2 adults in local currency	High Season	Low Season	Elec inc in price?		Y / N	.............amps	
			Price of elec (if not inc)			.............amps	

Year of guide used	20..........	Page No.	....	Name of town/village site listed under			
Site Name					Date of visit	......./......./........	
GPS	Latitude...(eg 12.34567) Longitude...(eg 1.23456 or -1.23456)						
Site is in: Andorra / Austria / Belgium / Croatia / Czech Republic / Denmark / Finland / France / Germany / Greece / Hungary / Italy / Luxembourg / Netherlands / Norway / Poland / Portugal / Slovakia / Slovenia / Spain / Sweden / Switzerland							
Comments:							
Charge for outfit + 2 adults in local currency	High Season	Low Season	Elec inc in price?		Y / N	.............amps	
			Price of elec (if not inc)			.............amps	

Your comments & opinions may be used in future editions of the guide, if you do not wish them to be used please tick ....

Name ....

Membership No. ....

Post Code ....

Are you a Caravanner / Motorhomer / Trailer-Tenter?

Do you need more blank Site Report forms?   YES / NO

Please return completed forms to:
The Editor – Overseas Touring Guides
East Grinstead House
East Grinstead
West Sussex
RH19 1FH
**Please note that due to changes in the rules regarding freepost we are no longer able to provide a freepost address for the return of Site Report Forms. You can still supply your site reports free online by visiting camc.com/europereport.
We apologise for any inconvenience this may cause.**

You can also complete forms online: camc.com/europereport

Abbreviated Site Report Form

Use this abbreviated Site Report Form if you have visited a number of sites and there are no changes (or only small changes) to their entries in the guide. If reporting on a new site, or reporting several changes, please use the full version of the report form. If advising prices, these should be for an outfit, and 2 adults for one night's stay. **Please indicate high or low season prices and whether electricity is included.**

Remember, if you don't tell us about sites you have visited, they may eventually be deleted from the guide.

Year of guide used	20..........	Page No.	....	Name of town/village site listed under		
Site Name					Date of visit	......./......./........
GPS	Latitude...(eg 12.34567) Longitude..(eg 1.23456 or -1.23456)					
Site is in: Andorra / Austria / Belgium / Croatia / Czech Republic / Denmark / Finland / France / Germany / Greece / Hungary / Italy / Luxembourg / Netherlands / Norway / Poland / Portugal / Slovakia / Slovenia / Spain / Sweden / Switzerland						
Comments:						

Charge for outfit + 2 adults in local currency	High Season	Low Season	Elec inc in price?		Y / N	............amps
			Price of elec (if not inc)			............amps

Year of guide used	20..........	Page No.	....	Name of town/village site listed under		
Site Name					Date of visit	......./......./........
GPS	Latitude...(eg 12.34567) Longitude..(eg 1.23456 or -1.23456)					
Site is in: Andorra / Austria / Belgium / Croatia / Czech Republic / Denmark / Finland / France / Germany / Greece / Hungary / Italy / Luxembourg / Netherlands / Norway / Poland / Portugal / Slovakia / Slovenia / Spain / Sweden / Switzerland						
Comments:						

Charge for outfit + 2 adults in local currency	High Season	Low Season	Elec inc in price?		Y / N	............amps
			Price of elec (if not inc)			............amps

Year of guide used	20..........	Page No.	....	Name of town/village site listed under		
Site Name					Date of visit	......./......./........
GPS	Latitude...(eg 12.34567) Longitude..(eg 1.23456 or -1.23456)					
Site is in: Andorra / Austria / Belgium / Croatia / Czech Republic / Denmark / Finland / France / Germany / Greece / Hungary / Italy / Luxembourg / Netherlands / Norway / Poland / Portugal / Slovakia / Slovenia / Spain / Sweden / Switzerland						
Comments:						

Charge for car, caravan & 2 adults in local currency	High Season	Low Season	Elec inc in price?		Y / N	............amps
			Price of elec (if not inc)			............amps

Please fill in your details and send to the address on the reverse of this form.
You can also complete forms online: camc.com/europereport

CUT ALONG DOTTED LINE

Year of guide used 20..........		Page No.		Name of town/village site listed under		
Site Name					Date of visit	......./......./........
GPS	Latitude...(eg 12.34567) Longitude..(eg 1.23456 or -1.23456)					

Site is in: Andorra / Austria / Belgium / Croatia / Czech Republic / Denmark / Finland / France / Germany / Greece / Hungary / Italy / Luxembourg / Netherlands / Norway / Poland / Portugal / Slovakia / Slovenia / Spain / Sweden / Switzerland

Comments:

Charge for outfit + 2 adults in local currency	High Season	Low Season	Elec inc in price?	Y / N	.............amps
			Price of elec (if not inc)		.............amps

Year of guide used 20..........		Page No.		Name of town/village site listed under		
Site Name					Date of visit	......./......./........
GPS	Latitude...(eg 12.34567) Longitude..(eg 1.23456 or -1.23456)					

Site is in: Andorra / Austria / Belgium / Croatia / Czech Republic / Denmark / Finland / France / Germany / Greece / Hungary / Italy / Luxembourg / Netherlands / Norway / Poland / Portugal / Slovakia / Slovenia / Spain / Sweden / Switzerland

Comments:

Charge for outfit + 2 adults in local currency	High Season	Low Season	Elec inc in price?	Y / N	.............amps
			Price of elec (if not inc)		.............amps

Year of guide used 20..........		Page No.		Name of town/village site listed under		
Site Name					Date of visit	......./......./........
GPS	Latitude...(eg 12.34567) Longitude..(eg 1.23456 or -1.23456)					

Site is in: Andorra / Austria / Belgium / Croatia / Czech Republic / Denmark / Finland / France / Germany / Greece / Hungary / Italy / Luxembourg / Netherlands / Norway / Poland / Portugal / Slovakia / Slovenia / Spain / Sweden / Switzerland

Comments:

Charge for outfit + 2 adults in local currency	High Season	Low Season	Elec inc in price?	Y / N	.............amps
			Price of elec (if not inc)		.............amps

Your comments & opinions may be used in future editions of the guide, if you do not wish them to be used please tick ....

Name ....

Membership No. ....

Post Code ....

Are you a Caravanner / Motorhomer / Trailer-Tenter?

Do you need more blank Site Report forms?   YES / NO

Please return completed forms to:
The Editor – Overseas Touring Guides
East Grinstead House
East Grinstead
West Sussex
RH19 1FH
Please note that due to changes in the rules regarding freepost we are no longer able to provide a freepost address for the return of Site Report Forms. You can still supply your site reports free online by visiting camc.com/europereport. We apologise for any inconvenience this may cause.

You can also complete forms online: camc.com/europereport

Index

Index

PEFC Certified

This product is
from sustainably
managed forests and
controlled sources

PEFC™
PEFC/16-33-254   www.pefc.org